THE DECLINE AND FALL OF THE ROMAN EMPIRE

Edward Gibbon

The Decline and Fall of the Roman Empire

Edited, Abridged, and with a Critical Foreword by
Hans-Friedrich Mueller

Introduction by Daniel J. Boorstin

Illustrations by Giovanni Battista Piranesi

THE MODERN LIBRARY

NEW YORK

2003 Modern Library Paperback Edition

Grateful acknowledgment is made to HarperCollins Publishers, Inc.,
for permission to reprint "The Intimacy of Gibbon's *Decline and Fall*,"
chapter 4 from *Hidden History* by Daniel J. Boorstin.
Copyright © 1987 by Daniel J. Boorstin.
Reprinted by permission of HarperCollins Publishers, Inc.

LIBRARY OF CONGRESS CATALOGING-IN-PUBLICATION DATA
Gibbon, Edward, 1737–1794.
[History of the decline and fall of the Roman empire]
The decline and fall of the Roman empire / Edward Gibbon; edited, abridged, and with a
critical foreword by Hans-Friedrich Mueller; introduction by Daniel J. Boorstin.
p.   cm.
Includes bibliographical references.
ISBN 0-375-75811-9
1. Rome—History—Empire, 30 B.C.–476 A.D.   2. Byzantine Empire—History.
I. Mueller, Hans-Friedrich, 1959–   II. Title.

DG311 .G5 2003

937'.06—dc21   2002032585

Modern Library website address: www.modernlibrary.com

Printed in the United States of America

6   8   9   7

PARENTIBVS · OPTIMIS
HVNC · LIBRVM · SACRVM · ESSE · VOLVIT
FILIVS

Acknowledgments

I can understand why Will Murphy, senior editor at Random House, was eager to produce a new abridgment of Edward Gibbon's *Decline and Fall of the Roman Empire* for the Modern Library Paperback Classics series. Gibbon's work has much to tell us, if only we can find the time. Why Will should have chosen me to serve as the editor who would produce this new abridgment remains obscure, but it has never been my custom to inquire too closely into the gifts of fortune. I offer rather my sincerest thanks. And my gratitude to Will goes beyond that initial choice. Will Murphy combines professionalism and congeniality in the highest degree; it has been another stroke of good fortune to work with him, and, again, I offer my heartfelt thanks. Others at Random House too deserve grateful mention: Vincent La Scala worked on the text with careful ingenuity. Evan Camfield, who served as copy editor, performed an enormous labor with grace and wit, rescuing the abridged text from numerous infelicities and corruptions. I thank my colleagues in the Department of Classics at the University of Florida for their encouragement, advice, and unstinting support. I do not know whether my wife, Terri, or my daughters, Sarah, Anna, Paula, and Laura, will forgive me for stealing away from them so often in order to spend so many hours with another man, but I do hope that they may someday find in these pages a partial compensation as well as a record of my conduct. In appreciation for all that they have done, I gratefully dedicate this edition to my parents, Hans O. and Dorothy C. Mueller.

CONTENTS

THE DECLINE AND FALL OF
THE ROMAN EMPIRE

VOLUME THE FIRST

VOLUME THE SECOND

VOLUME THE THIRD

VOLUME THE FOURTH

VOLUME THE FIFTH

VOLUME THE SIXTH

List of Maps and Illustrations

Maps

Illustrations

by Giovanni Battista Piranesi

INTRODUCTION

Daniel J. Boorstin

There are many reasons to admire Edward Gibbon's *History of the Decline and Fall of the Roman Empire.* Since it was first published in several volumes between 1776 and 1788, few books of history have been so widely or so indiscriminately praised. His twentieth-century editor, historian J. B. Bury, calls him "one of those few writers who hold as high a place in the history of literature as in the roll of great historians." Most students of history and of literature would agree.

Praise of Gibbon (1737–1794) has become especially fashionable with the rise of liberal and Marxist prejudices against religion. And as pessimism has become increasingly fashionable about the future of our Western civilization, the *Decline and Fall of the Roman Empire* has become a handy guide to the sources of decay in other empires and civilizations. I will not enter the debate over the adequacy of Gibbon's explanations of the fall of Rome. Nor will I explore the easy—or uneasy—analogies between the career of the ancient Roman empire and that of our modern Western civilization.

My interest in Gibbon's work is quite different. I will not assess it as a "great" book. Rather I will consider it as an "intimate" book. By this I mean a book that has something personal to say to us today. I am aware that it may seem odd to characterize a man of Gibbon's grandiloquence of phrase and a multivolume work on such a grandiose subject as "intimate."

For me personally Gibbon's book has an especially intimate significance. It was the first extensive work of English literature (or of history) which I read and reread. It occupied much of my thought during my university years as an undergraduate. And the engraving of Gibbon's rotund face, made by Chapman in 1807, a dozen years after his death, hangs on the wall of my study. Gibbon's face has been with me ever since I first made his acquaintance.

Gibbon's work can have an intimate, personal significance for all history readers and history writers in our age. He may help us discover some of the peculiar weaknesses and strengths of our way of looking at the past. To discover this intimacy we must try to see Gibbon not simply as a spokesman for the Enlightenment, nor his work as an effort to perfect one genre in the social sciences. Rather, let us think of him as an original, giving his own form to a large chunk of the past.

Toward this end it will help us at the outset to recognize a distinctive, if not entirely unique, feature of his place in the roll of great Western historians. Despite the wide popularity and continuity of Gibbon's audience, he seems not to have founded a "Gibbonian" school of historical interpretation. For example, the authoritative *International Encyclopedia of the Social Sciences,* which includes extensive articles on such lesser figures as Bryce, Burckhardt, Huizinga, Maitland, Ranke, Savigny, and Spengler, gives no such attention to Gibbon. Serious scholars do not doubt the originality or the significance of Gibbon's work. Still, he has not become the founder of a "school." He has not taken a place as the originator of any large new conceptual framework, or any novel way of pigeonholing the human past. I will suggest that this is a clue to the intimacy of his message about that past, and what he can tell each of us about the role of people in the grand chronicle of empires and civilizations.

The historical profession, with all its paraphernalia of learned societies and prestigious academic specialties, has grown up only since Gibbon's day. Not until the early nineteenth century did professional historians reach beyond the techniques of classical scholarship and textual criticism to draw on the new disciplines of archaeology and philology, anthropology, sociology, and economics to create new vocations of searchers for facts and movements and forces.

It is doubtful if there is another example in the social sciences of a work of similar longevity, respectability, and popularity which has had so small a dogmatic or doctrinaire ingredient. The comprehensive historical works of recent years—those which are taken seriously by students of the social sciences—are heavily laced with dogma. I am thinking of the potent works, for example, of Macaulay, Carlyle, Marx, Pareto, Tawney, and Toynbee. These seem to owe much of their fame and their influence to the special charm of some new formulas to explain or contain historical experience.

How, then, can we explain the power and longevity and appeal of Gibbon, despite his lack of substantial original conceptual content?

In the first place, we must remember that Gibbon had the advantage of being an amateur. Unlike some other great interpreters of the past, many of whom were also amateurs, he was not enticed or driven to his subject by the urgencies of his time, or by a revolutionary, a religious, or a patriotic passion. In the original sense of the word "amateur," he was simply a lover of his subject. And in a famous passage in his memoirs he recalls the precise moment when, as he sat in the Colosseum in Rome, he first felt that passion. In another, less famous passage, he recalled his mixed emotions as that exacting love affair came to an end:

> It was on the night of June 27, 1787, between the hours of eleven and twelve, that I wrote the last lines of the last page, in a Summerhouse garden. . . . I will not dissemble the first emotions of joy on the recovery of my freedom, and perhaps, the establishment of my fame. But my pride was soon humbled, and a sober melancholy was spread over my mind, by the idea that I had taken an everlasting leave of an old and agreeable companion, and that whatsoever might be the future date of my History, the life of the historian must be short and precarious.

Like other great amateurs—and other lovers—he had taken his plunge without really being ready for it. He was not equipped by formal training for his work as a historian of the Roman Empire. His fourteen "unprofitable months" at Magdalen College, in an Oxford which, according to him, was "steeped in port and prejudice," did not give him the academic tools he needed. He lamented that his desultory training in Greek left him without the "scrupulous ear of the well-flogged critic." His work as an ancient historian was never part of the perfunctory duties of an academic post.

Except for this one passion, he was not a man of passionate commitment. At the age of sixteen he did commit himself to the Roman Catholic Church, but when he was sent to Lausanne by his father, his tutor there quickly brought him back to Protestantism. Despite his skepticism of established Christianity, he found it natural to be a Tory. He had the advantage of some political experience—as a member of Parliament and a commissioner of trade and plantations. His politics were prudent and pragmatic. He was a friend and admirer of Lord North, for whom he wrote a state paper against France in the years before the Revolution. When the American colonies protested the power of Parliament and began a civil war to break away, he believed that they were wrong. But after the Battle of Saratoga made it plain that the ocean and independent enthusiasms had already separated the American colonies, he confessed that Lord North's costly efforts to subject the Americans were hopeless.

In an age that was filled with sycophants and that rewarded sycophancy, he did not dedicate his work to anyone—a fact for which he has not received the credit that is his due. He helps us understand why, and incidentally helps us share his vision of the significance of *people* in the vicissitudes of empire. He wrote these words in the preface to his fourth and final volume, published soon after Lord North had fallen from power:

> Were I ambitious of any other Patron than the Public, I would inscribe this work to a Statesman, who in a long, a stormy, and at length an unfortunate administration, had many political opponents, almost without a personal enemy: who has retained, in his fall from power, many faithful and disinterested friends; and who, under the pressure of severe infirmity, enjoys the lively vigour of his mind, and the felicity of his incomparable temper. Lord North will permit me to express the feelings of friendship in the language of truth: but even truth and friendship should be silent, if he still dispensed the favours of the crown.

Gibbon remained uncommitted to any but his own opinions. The shrewd observer Horace Walpole, as he greeted the first volume of Gibbon's history with surprise as "a truly classic work," also noted that in Parliament Gibbon had been called "a whimsical because he votes variously as his opinion leads him. I . . . never suspected the extent of his talents, he is perfectly modest."

Gibbon's amorous commitments also were dominated by prudence and propriety. As a young man of twenty in Lausanne (1757) he became infatuated by the beautiful and witty Suzanne Curchod (1739–1794), then only eighteen. But when Gibbon's father objected, he broke off the engagement. Later she married Jacques Necker, the French financier and statesman, and established one of the celebrated salons of modern Paris. (*Their* daughter, incidentally, was the saloniste and prolific author Madame de Staël!) Gibbon's broken engagement took place seven years before he conceived the *Decline and Fall*. What might Gibbon have done with his talents if, instead of listening to his father, he had shared his life with the charming Suzanne?

Gibbon once modestly declared that "diligence and accuracy are the only merits which an historical writer may ascribe to himself; if any merit indeed can be assumed from the performance of an indispensable duty." Yet the product of his twenty years' passion showed that a historical masterpiece required much more. Not least was his inexhaustible sense of wonder and his tolerant curiosity about the foibles of the human race. The cast of an eye, the excess of an appetite, the perversity of tastes, the beauty or deformity of stature—he witnessed all these with delight.

He managed with deceptive ease to translate the catastrophes of nature into parables of human nature. The earthquakes which shook the eastern Mediterranean on July 21, A.D. 365, led him to observe:

> . . . their affrighted imagination enlarged the real extent of a momentary evil. . . . And their fearful vanity was disposed to confound the symptoms of a declining empire and a sinking world. It was the fashion of the times to attribute every remarkable event to the particular will of the Deity; the alterations of nature were connected, by an invisible chain, with the moral and metaphysical opinions of the human mind; and the most sagacious divines could distinguish, according to the colour of their respective prejudices, that the establishment of heresy tended to produce an earthquake, or that a deluge was the inevitable consequence of the progress of sin and error. Without presuming to discuss the truth or propriety of these lofty speculations, the

historian may content himself with the observation, which seems to be justified by experience, that man has much more to fear from the passions of his fellow-creatures than from the convulsions of the elements.

The daily habits of remote and unfamiliar peoples help us understand their life-and-death commitments. Of the Scythians or Tartars he noted "with some reluctance" that "the pastoral manners which have been adorned with the fairest attributes of peace and innocence are much better adapted to the fierce and cruel habits of a military life." Their diet (not corn but freshly slaughtered meat) and their light and easily moved tents both help us grasp that it was easy for them to behave as they did. "The exploits of the hunters of Scythia are not confined to the destruction of timid or innoxious beasts; they boldly encounter the angry wild boar, when he turns against his pursuers, excite the sluggish courage of the bear, and provoke the fury of the tiger, as he slumbers in the thicket." And so the nuances of human nature are newly revealed to us "on the immense plains of Scythia or Tartary."

Gibbon was fortunate to be born into an age when men of letters were expected to provide "amusement and instruction." The world of science—despite our clichés of an Age of Reason—was newly liberated from the medieval demand for meaning. In the Royal Society and other "invisible colleges" scientists, virtuosi, and amateurs were expanding the world with tiny increments of knowledge. Of course there were a few dazzlers, like Sir Isaac Newton. But the most important shift in attitude toward knowledge was from the interest in the cosmos to the interest in facts. Now it seemed possible for every man to become his own scientist. The telescope, the "flea glass" (microscope), the thermometer, and scores of other measuring devices were transforming experience into experiment. This new incremental approach to the physical world—spawning a wonderful newgrown wilderness of facts and contraptions—was also Gibbon's approach to the world of human nature. The time had not yet come when scientific quest for meaning threatened to transform the social world into another cosmos of dogmatic simplicities. Gibbon gives us incremental history on a grand scale.

For Gibbon, while human nature is anything but unintelligible, it remains only partly explicable. For him the menace to understanding was not so much ignorance as the illusion of knowledge. His explanations of rise and fall, of prosperity and decline are always *lists*. What he recounts is "the triumph of barbarism *and* religion." He recounts the quirks and quibbles of theologians, the rivalries of Eastern monarchs, their wives and mistresses and sons and daughters, not simply because they are amusing, but also because they are instructive. Without such trivia we cannot understand what the Eastern empire was or what it became.

It is more accurate to insist that for Gibbon there are no trivia. Human habits, utterances, exclamations, and emotions are the very essence of his history—not mere raw material for distilling "forces" and "movements." The more vividly we see them, the better we know our subject. Inevitably, then, he must remain a skeptic about our capacity finally to grasp the whole story.

But despite—perhaps because of—this recognition, he is not a pessimist. The spectacle which he has unfolded of "the greatest, perhaps, and the most awful scene in the history of mankind" rewards us. He sees the whole planet as a stage for more grand spectacles, which will also be a stage for renewal. "If a savage conqueror should issue from the deserts of Tartary, he must repeatedly vanquish the robust peasants of Russia, the numerous armies of Germany, the gallant nobles of France, and the intrepid freemen of Britain; who, perhaps, might confederate for their common defense. Should the victorious Barbarians carry slavery and desolation as far as the Atlantic Ocean, ten thousand vessels would transport beyond their pursuit the remains of civilized society; and Europe would revive and flourish in the American world which is already filled with her colonies and institutions."

In his optimism Gibbon seems a spokesman for the Age of the Enlightenment. He seems, sometimes, to speak for a faith, burgeoning in his lifetime, that man's uninhibited critical faculties can grasp the world. I once thought of Gibbon in precisely that way. He spoke to me from and for a *period* of history. But in the years since Gibbon first spoke to me, he has come to say something more. He has become a more personal historian and hence more intimate, both in what he said and in what I hear.

Some eloquent outspoken prophets of the Age of Reason make it easy for historians to confine the epoch in that epithet. Among historians the great systematizers include such authors as Montesquieu (1689–1755) and Vico (1668–1744) and Voltaire (1694–1778). Of course these men—who are copiously treated in encyclopedias of the social sciences—still interest their fellow systematizers. Among the writers of narrative history in his epoch, Voltaire still speaks vividly to some of us. But his most popular contemporary competitors in narrative history—David Hume and William Robertson—have become historiographical antiques. Gibbon still can and does speak to all of us.

What he saw and what he accomplished was possible, he gladly acknowledged, only because of the peculiar opportunities of his place and time. "I shall ever glory in the name and character of an Englishman," he observed gratefully at the conclusion of his work, "I am proud of my birth in a free and enlightened country; and the approbation of that country is the best and most honorable reward for my labors." If he had not exploited the new opportunities and shared the new vistas of his age, he could not have given us his history. Yet his greatness, the intimate ingredient in his work, is his peculiar talent at transcending the characteristic enthusiasms of his age. Nowadays John Dryden and Alexander Pope and Jonathan Swift, and even Laurence Sterne and Henry Fielding, seem to have a certain quaintness. It is doubly remarkable that Edward Gibbon, whose style was at least as idiosyncratic as theirs, somehow manages to talk to us in our own idiom.

This is what I mean by the intimacy of Gibbon's *Decline and Fall*. Gibbon succeeds in this intimacy precisely because he does not offer us obsolescing parables of science or the social sciences. Nor is he stultified by the etiquette of a particular genre of literature. The chronological lopsidedness of his work—which gives more space to the first few centuries than to the last millennium of his thirteen-century tale—is itself a witness to his determination to shape the story not by the a priori dimensions of centuries, but by his own concerns. He has the courage to juxtapose his lists of large causes with the minutiae of persons and places. He reminds us of our ties to the cosmos without pretending to unlock its secrets. He remains a modest man, refusing to carve neat channels where the course of history must flow. He lacks the conceit of the system builder, whose naïveté is revealed only with the centuries.

No historian has seen more vividly how nettlesome is the texture of the human past. Yet few have been bolder or more successful at grasping the nettle. He helps us share his pleasure at touching the random prickliness of experience. All this he does because he does not overestimate the dogmatic capacities of his own "enlightened age," nor does he underestimate the mystery of what remains untold and untellable.

At the end of his twenty years' voyage into the Roman empire, he asks himself whether he should try another such voyage. With characteristic prudence he concludes that "in the repetition of similar attempts a successful Author has much more to lose, than he can hope to gain." Yet he insists that "the annals of ancient and modern times may afford many rich and interesting subjects. . . . To an active mind, indolence is more painful than labor." So he cheers us on, both readers and writers of history. For he, as much as any other writer in our language, reminds us that, even across the centuries and the oceans, people can talk to people about people. Just as Gibbon was not imprisoned in the jargon and special conceits of his age, so perhaps we need not be imprisoned in ours.

———

DANIEL J. BOORSTIN, Pulizer Prize–winning historian and Librarian of Congress emeritus, is the author of many books, including *The Creators* and *The Discoverers.*

This essay appeared as "The Intimacy of Gibbon's *Decline and Fall*" in *Hidden History* (New York: Harper & Row, 1987).

CRITICAL FOREWORD

Hans-Friedrich Mueller

Method, choice, and fidelity [are] the humble,
though indispensable, virtues of a compiler.

—EDWARD GIBBON

Edward Gibbon repeatedly calls "fanatics" all those whose deeply held religious convictions form the basis of their actions. But then Edward Gibbon lived during the Enlightenment, the Age of Reason, a time when confidence in the capacity of human beings to think freely (and to govern themselves with justice) abounded. We may note that his *History of the Decline and Fall of the Roman Empire* began appearing in 1776, just as most of Britain's North American colonies had declared their independence. He concluded the sixth and final volume in 1787, the year a constitution charted a republican destiny as free from religious interference as possible for a newly established United States of America. The volume appeared in 1788. The following year, the United States would acquire a Bill of Rights (and the French their revolution). After a millennium and a half of monarchy and Christianity, republican government was coming again into fashion. And the founding fathers of the United States, like Edward Gibbon, were not devout, evangelical Christians. For this reason alone, many Americans today, should they find occasion to read his book, will find Edward Gibbon offensive. (I write anno Domini 2002.) Gibbon excoriates devouts of *all* persuasions: adherents of Islam, Christianity (in all its many heretical varieties), Judaism, and polytheisms, both Greco-Roman and non-Classical. There is much in Gibbon to offend, and this abridgment makes no attempt to curb the caustic wit of a freer and more eloquent age. Let us, however, postpone for a moment the mechanics of abridgment in favor of a brief overview of Gibbon's work, its history, and his life.

GIBBON'S WORK AND LIFE

The history of religion is for Gibbon intimately connected to the decline and fall of the Roman empire, but religion is hardly his only theme. We encounter also "Barbarians" (a term loosely applied to those outside the empire, who often coveted the riches they saw), mercenary militarism (without efficiency, bravery, or patriotism), oppressive taxes (levied unfairly and exacted most mercilessly from those least able to pay), corrupt politicians, tyrannical government, and endless warfare against the enemies of the Roman order, both at home and abroad. These themes are not without resonance today.

Gibbon's canvas is large geographically and chronologically. One expects a sharp focus on the Mediterranean, but Gibbon ranges from sub-Saharan Africa to China. And although he ostensibly covers the period from the Antonines in the second century after Christ until the final collapse of Constantinople in 1453, even this broad range does not contain our author. Three chapters follow the fall of Constantinople. Gibbon traces the rise of the papacy's political power in the West, and he surveys the ruins of Rome in his own day. Earlier chapters, moreover, take their beginnings from an historical presence that is felt throughout the work, the military dictator who finally buried the Roman republic and has served as a role model for so many dictators since: the man born Gaius Octavius, Caesar Augustus, adoptive son of Julius Caesar. Gibbon, writing in an age that was fast embracing individual liberty, republican institutions, and freedom from religious constraints, chose to narrate a history that took as its starting point the *end* of the last great experiment in popular sovereignty and representative government (we except such anomalies as the Venetian republic). After ridding itself of monarchy, Rome was (like the United States today) not a democracy but a republic. Some five hundred years later, at the dawn of the Augustan age, Rome had gained an empire but irretrievably lost the republic: the Roman people were sovereign only in name. The world belonged to Caesar. The result was less liberty for individuals, but greater equality for all: a trade many were (and remain) willing to make. The history of Roman law (brilliantly traced by Gibbon in his forty-fourth chapter), for example, reveals an ever more inclusive conception of citizenship as well as a praiseworthy increase in protections and rights for women and slaves. On the other hand, personal conduct received closer scrutiny. Free speech was severely curtailed. Sexual practices were criminalized. Punishments became increasingly harsh. What the republic might have punished with a fine (and a wink) could, by the late empire, be punished with burning alive.

These short notices of Gibbon's reach still fail, however, to sketch just how inclusive his scope truly is. Beginning with the end of republican government, he traces the vicissitudes of empire. Rome did not fall in the West without a struggle or for no good reason. Gibbon's answers (like his questions) may differ from those of more recent scholars, but he assembles a compelling case. Military despotism and anarchy almost wrecked the state on more than one occasion. The blood shed and the economies wrecked by civil war were propped up again and again on an ever more oppressive basis. Internal religious conflicts between those addicted to their ancestral faiths and those who had abandoned tradition for a revolutionary and zealously exclusive monotheism tore the social fabric. In victory, the new religion triumphantly persecuted its old antagonists as well as its own heretics. Domestic conflicts only increased with increasing Christianization. All the while, wave after wave of fresh invaders hammered against defenses erected by an increasingly undisciplined, corrupt, and oppressive military. "Barbarians" were not infrequently seen by provincials as liberators from unbearable tax burdens. We witness the division of East and West, first militarily and politically, and eventually religiously. Rome falls, but the emperor Constantine's new and Christian Rome, Constantinople, perseveres for almost another thousand years, a millennium that sees the rise of another zealous monotheism, Islam, as well as empires of Arabs, various nomads (including Zingis, or Genghis, Khan), and the Ottoman Turks. The feudal West reclaims territory lost to Islam in a series of religious crusades. All this (and more) is described by Gibbon's indefatigably eloquent pen.

Throughout his work, Gibbon does more than simply tell good stories (though he does that too). He looks for explanations, and he looks for those explanations in institutions (government, military, law), ethnography (the "customs" of a people), economics (Gibbon is endlessly fascinated with trade, agriculture, the mechanical arts), geography (many a detailed disquisition is devoted to surveys of the climates and localities that serve as the scenes to history), and the heart. Gibbon looks for motivation in his human actors. He offers greed and the hunger for power as the most banal and common movers of political men and women, but he allows room also for jealousy, love, and the entire range of human emotions. Gibbon looks, in short, for causes where he can find them, and in religion he finds a cause that can motivate both individuals and societies while, in turn, serving also as a means by which historical personages, with the most varied agendas, can accomplish their own ends.

It bears repeating in our own distant era, so different from his, that Gibbon wrote in the first bloom of Europe's great surge of secular liberalism, an era of expanding freedom and promise that has with difficulty survived the bloodbaths of the twentieth century and the subsequent subordination of America's economy and society to endless war, whether hot or cold, against all enemies, both domestic and foreign. It is striking that Gibbon, in that first season of renewed republican hope and optimism, should have offered a detailed diagnosis of the imperial ambition and military despotism that had buried the world's last great experiment in freedom and republican government beneath more than a thousand years of servile religiosity.

A natural curiosity arises about the man who wrote the work. While Gibbon's words may speak for themselves, a brief recapitulation of his life's salient points is not without illumination. Born on May 8 (April 27, old style), 1737, Gibbon published the first volume of his great work at the age of thirty-nine. Gibbon died on January 16, 1794, some seven years after concluding the sixth and final volume. This does not tell us much. Edward Gibbon was an Englishman, a fact in which he always took great pride. And despite the impression our introductory remarks may have created, Edward Gibbon was no radical. Descended from (somewhat dissipated) wealth and privilege, he was a supporter of the established government. What, then, might lead anyone to consider him subversive? Gibbon had a passion for truth, and those who interpret history as best suits their interests will always consider subversive the intellects that call attention to facts corrosive of established convictions (and, by way of extension, the intellectual basis on which vested privilege rests). Gibbon, moreover, coupled a stomach for truth with a delight in irony. A simple method of assessing a person's character, for example, consists in comparing what somebody says with what that person does. When the two spheres do not correspond, a situation ripe for irony arises. The one who makes such comparisons may speak the truth, but the object of scrutiny feels maligned. Such methods may be applied to historical individuals or to groups. Gibbon's comparisons of the professions of the gospel and the early church, for example, with the actions of early Christians result in ironical juxtapositions that many have considered insulting and unfair. It is in this light that Gibbon's personal religious history becomes interesting, and perhaps relevant. At the age of fifteen, Gibbon matriculated prematurely at Oxford University. His education had been rather informal. Neglected by his mother, Gibbon had been reared, cared for, and educated throughout a sickly childhood most tenderly and assiduously by his mother's unmarried sister. He had also studied occasionally with private tutors and had experienced brief stays in schools, always soon interrupted by illness. Gibbon, however, had read widely in the family library, and so arrived at Oxford not entirely devoid of knowledge. Oxford was not to his liking. Oxford's scholars were, as Gibbon claims in his *Memoirs,* steeped in "port and prejudice." Of his own tutor, Gibbon adds that "Dr. —— well remembered that he had a salary to receive, and only forgot that he had a duty to perform." Happily, Gibbon was soon expelled from Oxford for religious treason. Raised a Protestant in a country Protestant by law, he converted at the age of sixteen to Roman Catholicism, an illegal act and one carrying with it civil penalties. Alerted by a lengthy letter in which his son justified his conversion, Gibbon's father was not idle. He sent the son to a Calvinist minister in Lausanne, Switzerland. After two years of private study, in which Gibbon mastered French, Latin, Greek, and mathematics as far as "conic sections," he also came—more importantly, from the paternal and patriotic point of view—to renounce his belief in transubstantiation (the transformation in the Eucharist of the bread and wine into the actual body and blood of Christ), and thus acquiesced, as Gibbon puts it, "with implicit belief in the tenets and mysteries which are adopted by the general consent of Catholics and Protestants." He received again the Protestant sacrament of communion on Christmas Day, 1754, in Lausanne, and abandoned forever religious "enthusiasm." If we must look for explanations of an author's work in the anecdotes of his private life, we cannot do better than this story of a young man's conversion to enthusiastic belief in Roman Catholicism and his subsequent "deprogramming" (if we may use the modern American equivalent). Those who see in Gibbon's analyses of religion merely the philosophical musings of a born skeptic in an age of shallow reason miss the passion of a broken heart, a mind converted from the sincerest vibrations of reverent faith to the rational investigation of humanly verifiable truth, wherever this decidedly more humble (and, to the unsympathetic, cynical) path might lead. We may also note that Gibbon's studies were, during his teenage deprogramming, more intense than many Ph.D. candidates could today endure. Gibbon read ten to twelve hours a day, and his readings were more often than not in the classical languages of Greek and Latin. A journal entry from January 1756 (Gibbon was eighteen): "I determined to read over the Latin authors in order, and read this year Virgil, Sallust, Livy, Velleius Paterculus, Valerius Maximus, Tacitus, Suetonius, Quintus Curtius, Justin, Florus, Plautus, Terence and Lucretius. I also read and meditated Locke's *Upon the Understanding.*" Almost exactly one year later, he writes: "I began to study algebra under M. de Traytorrens, went through the elements of algebra and geometry, and the three first books of the Marquis de l'Hôpital's *Conic Sections.* I also read Tibullus, Catullus, Propertius, Horace (with Dacier's and Torrentius' notes), Virgil, Ovid's *Epistles,* with Meziriac's commentary, the *Ars amandi* and the *Elegies;* likewise the *Augustus* and *Tiberius* of Suetonius, and a Latin translation of Dion Cassius from the death of Julius Caesar to the death of Augustus. I also continued my correspondence, begun last year, with M. Allamand of Bex, and the Professor Breitinger of Göttingen. *N.B.*—Last year and this I read St. John's Gospel, with part of Xenophon's *Cyropaedia,* the *Iliad,* and Herodotus; but, upon the whole, I rather neglected my Greek."

We find in these anecdotes illumination. Gibbon the student mastered the languages and authors essential for serious inquiry into European history. And Gibbon the reconverted convert never abandoned his investigations of Christianity. But does such illumination really explain anything? How might we read Gibbon's neglectful mother into his *Decline and Fall,* or his unhappy love affair? Gibbon fell in love at the age of twenty, he tells us, with Susan Churchod, in Lausanne. His father, who paid his allowance (Gibbon's sole means of support), did not approve. Gibbon writes, "I soon discovered that my father would not hear of this strange alliance, and that without his consent I was myself destitute and helpless. After a painful struggle I yielded to my fate; I sighed as a lover, I obeyed as a son; my wound was insensibly healed by time, by absence, and the habits of a new life." Does Gibbon's love life (or lack thereof) matter to a reader of the *Decline and Fall*? Yes and no. It matters to us because our own age delights in the sex lives of actors, politicians, and littérateurs, as if the gratification of this particular biological function (as opposed to, say, ingestion and digestion) somehow formed part and parcel of our quintessential selves rather than, in most cases, our eminently forgettable and inconsequential selves; but we digress—such details matter, one supposes, if a reader chooses them as an interpretive framework. "Aha," our psychologically and biographically inclined reader might say, "neglectful mother, virgin aunt, overbearing father, no heterosexual union on a permanent basis— surely the key to Gibbon on the monastic life!" On the other hand, readers might choose to grapple with Gibbon's arguments on their own merits. Gibbon argues that the monastic life corrodes the human intellect. He offers a cogent analysis.

In the end, Gibbon's work will stand on its own, with or without his private life. Lest I linger only in the more purely private, I should also mention that Gibbon was active politically (serving Lord North, prime minister during America's Revolutionary War) as well as militarily (leading for some time in England a soldier's life as a member of the Hampshire militia). These practical experiences of military life and politics surely shaped the mind that analyzed their ancient counterparts. And Gibbon's morbid obesity towards the end of his life, or his social and literary acquaintances, ranging from Diderot to Johnson, not to mention the many other colorful personal details that one might array? We lack space. Interested readers are referred to Gibbon's *Memoirs* and Patricia Craddock's biographies in the bibliography at the end of this foreword. We shall content ourselves in this brief sketch with a final glance at Gibbon's grand tour of Italy, undertaken in 1764. Gibbon was twenty-seven years old. He had, at the urging of his father, published a short work in French three years earlier, but, continuing to live as a dependent of his father (as he would until his father's death in 1770), he had not yet accomplished the historical work at which his ambition aimed. If we may believe Gibbon (and modern scholars quibble over the details of Gibbon's purported recollections), the trip was decisive: "My temper is not very susceptible of enthusiasm, and the enthusiasm which I do not feel I have ever scorned to affect. But at the distance of twenty-five years I can neither forget nor express the strong emotions which agitated my mind as I first approached and entered the Eternal City. After a sleepless night, I trod with a lofty step the ruins of the forum; each memorable spot, where Romulus stood, or Tully [Cicero] spoke, or Caesar fell, was at once present to my eye; and several days of intoxication were lost or enjoyed before I could descend to a cool and minute investigation." Here, Gibbon tells us, he found the topic of a history worth composing: "It was at Rome, on the 15th of October 1764, as I sat musing amidst the ruins of the Capitol, while the barefooted friars were singing vespers in the temple of Jupiter, that the idea of writing the decline and fall of the city first started into my mind." The work which Gibbon eventually delivered to the world is much larger than the one contained in the present volume. We must turn now to editions and abridgments.

EDITIONS OF *THE DECLINE AND FALL OF THE ROMAN EMPIRE*

We have already mentioned the appearance of the first edition (1776–1788). It is no longer in print. Antiquarians with money may still purchase copies. Others may peruse microfiche in research libraries. For those who prefer paper and are willing to sacrifice some authenticity for substantial savings, David Womersley has recuperated Gibbon's words and original format as closely as possible in a three-volume Penguin paperback edition. Because Gibbon changed his mind and adjusted his text from edition to edition, Womersley appends a list of variant readings. Without an original manuscript, it would be difficult to approach any more closely to our author's very words. Gibbon was an accurate and a meticulous scholar, and Womersley's edition reproduces Gibbon's footnotes in their full glory. What is more, Womersley has, in the third volume, appended complete bibliographical information for all Gibbon's now rather cryptic abbreviations. (The editions and scholars cited by Gibbon are of even more difficult access than his first edition.) An index to the material of all three volumes graces the third volume, as well as a reprint of the *Vin-*

dication (1779) that Gibbon wrote in response to attacks made on his sketch of the rise of Christianity. Womersley's volumes are both excellent and essential. One cannot praise them enough. But perfect? Alas, the Greek. Those who read ancient Greek will need only a glance to feel chagrin. As our modern fate would have it, most will have no use for the original Greek; should need arise, other editions prove superior. J. B. Bury's seven-volume edition (1909–1914) is still available from AMS Press. This edition treats Gibbon as an historian rather than a literary stylist. The Greek is good, and the edition offers once state-of-the-art (now a century out of date) supplements to Gibbon's treatment of issues and sources. Those who seek more up-to-date scholarly treatments of the history covered by Gibbon should consult recent and relevant volumes of the *Cambridge Ancient History, Cambridge Medieval History,* and other similar standards. One other complete edition requires mention here. The Rev. H. H. Milman's edition of 1845 served as the basis of the present abridgment, because it is in the public domain and because, thanks to the efforts of a man named David Reed, it is available in machine-readable format. Were it not for the work of David Reed, the present compiler could hardly have contemplated or concluded his labors.

ABRIDGMENTS

The present abridgment is hardly the first, and will likely not remain the last. Each age and each reader will find his or her own Gibbon. We must first ask then why Gibbon's words should be abridged at all. The short answer: because there are so many of them. Milman's edition weighs in at more than 1,500,000 words. The present abridgment reduces that number by more than two thirds. The result is still a very large book but, I hope, a more manageable and more efficiently readable one. I assume that most readers will be interested in the main argument, in the spectacle of the decline and fall of a civilization across a thousand years, in its vivid details and striking scenes. History, for all its instructive value, can also be most entertaining, and Gibbon was a master storyteller. I have thus aimed to preserve both the entire thread of his argument and as many good stories (or as much instructive history) as possible. Other abridgments have cut much of the scandalous religious material. This edition cannot include everything, but has included as much religious history as possible, and certainly more than enough to offend.

David Womersley's recent abridgment (Penguin, 2000) includes, in their entirety and complete with footnotes, eleven of Gibbon's original seventy-one chapters. This abridgment has pursued a very different route. Gibbon's footnotes have yielded their place to continuous narrative, with substantial excerpts from all seventy-one chapters. I confess this absence of footnotes as the grievous fault it is. Gibbon was a meticulous and accurate scholar whose statements are always grounded in thoroughly documented evidence. But in weighing Gibbon's connected prose against thousands of references to authors unknown to most modern readers and long citations in Latin, Greek, and French (languages no longer widely understood among English speakers), I opted for the former. Gibbon's prose will present challenges enough. Those who read the abridgment and wish to recover the sources may easily do so, either on-line or in one of the editions already cited and listed at the end of this introduction.

Gibbon in his entirety is superior to any abridgment. This bears repeating. Abridgments address themselves to the needs of the times in which they are produced. The most ubiquitous abridgments of recent vintage are those of Dero A. Saunders (1952) and D. M. Low (1960). These abridgments concentrate primarily on the downfall of the Western empire. The rise of Islam, the fall of the Eastern empire, the Crusades, and the rise of the Papal states are neglected. The abridgment of Moses Hadas (1962) for Random House (the rights are now held by CBS Publications and the edition is still published by Fawcett Premier) offers a very concise Gibbon indeed, and presents excerpts (or at least titles) from all seventy-one chapters. On the other hand, it eschews theological matters entirely as "remote from the interests of the ordinary reader." I venture to assert that the interests of the ordinary reader have changed over the last forty years. One merely need mention Northern Ireland, the Middle East, or the United States (e.g., abortion): sectarian violence is the order of our present day.

What the present abridgment eliminates most relentlessly (in addition to scholarly footnotes) are geographical surveys, details of battle formations, long narratives of military campaigns, extensive ethnographies, and intricate genealogies (especially of medieval aristocracies).

A lighter touch has been applied to Gibbon's studies of institutions, political history, and religious history. My hope is thereby to have provided for the patient reader the entire argument and as much of Gibbon's vivid prose as feasible within the space of a single volume.

As to the text itself, three dots or ellipsis points (. . .) indicate all cuts within sentences or paragraphs. More substantial cuts are indicated by daggers (†). Square brackets enclose alterations to Gibbon's text. Two innovations, however, I introduce here, but do not mark in the text. Gibbon hesitated between "Mahomet" and "Mohammed"; tradition, he tells us, constrained him to use the former. I rather doubt, however, that most of my English-speaking contemporaries would even know how to pronounce the now thoroughly archaic version of the prophet's name. I have eliminated this distraction. "Mussulman" has, on similar grounds, been changed uniformly to "Moslem." I am well aware that these spellings themselves are no longer preferred, but they seemed, for that very reason, less a violation of Gibbon's original, which is, after all, over two hundred years old.

We may conclude this brief foreword with a final glance at Gibbon's argument. He traces the decline and fall not just of an empire or city but of a way of life, a civilization. In some respects, the story is a depressing one. In 31 B.C. the Roman republic surrendered unconditionally (completely and forever) to the military dictator Caesar Augustus. Not until A.D. 1776 would an experiment in republican government be revived on a large scale. The way had of course been paved intellectually by the Renaissance, Reformation, and Enlightenment. Gibbon tells the story of the long intervening and tyrannical night, keeping always a sharp watch for the sparks of freedom and independence that were preserved, however dim and in places however unlikely. The work, moreover, ends on a note of hope. Upon the collapse of the Eastern empire, the West is ready to receive the knowledge of Greek learning. And Gibbon, we may recall, concluded his writing in 1787, a much more hopeful age. Our present age, although it may prolong individual lives through the application of unsurpassed technologies, appears inclined to bury our ancestral freedoms in the name of security. Of course, it need not be so. After the fact, history is, to be sure, fait accompli. Gibbon did not indulge in the composition of speculative and alternative histories, but for those interested in lessons or instruction, we might nevertheless ask: "What if, instead of vesting all powers in the hands of an incredibly corrupt and rapacious upper class, the Roman republic had developed a voting system that allowed representation of all its citizens and dependents? Would military dictatorship have been inevitable?" These are questions that cannot be answered. The Roman republic never overcame the corruption that set in after its armies achieved military supremacy over the Mediterranean world (the "entire" world to their limited geographical horizons). The answer to the crisis of Rome's corrupted imperial republic was military dictatorship. Gibbon describes in detail the outcomes of their solution. Gibbon, who wrote his history at the beginning of our present republican experiment, diagnosed the ruin of the last, a ruin that was only repaired almost two thousand years later. We who look back now on Lincoln's Civil War, on two world wars, and on Truman's national security state, and who presently behold the military supremacy of the United States of America over the entire planet, may well indeed wonder what our New World Order might hold, both at home and abroad. The story of the Roman empire offers instructive lessons: oppressive taxes for the sake of a despotic military establishment, tyrannical government, religious bigotry, endless warfare, and, finally, collapse. Let us hope (and pray) that we read not a blueprint but a salutary warning in Gibbon's immortal and pleasurably instructive pages.

SELECTED BIBLIOGRAPHY

GIBBON'S WORKS

The History of the Decline and Fall of the Roman Empire, 6 volumes (London: A. Strahan & T. Cadell in the Strand, 1776–1788).

Of the subsequent editions (described above), see especially those of
  J. B. Bury, editor, 7 volumes (London: Methuen, 1909–1914), currently reprinted by AMS Press.
  D. Womersley, editor, 3 volumes (London: Penguin Books, 1994).
The Miscellaneous Works of Edward Gibbon, Esq., with Memoirs of His Life and Writings, Composed by Himself: Illustrated from His Letters, with Occasional Notes and Narrative, by the Right Honourable John, Lord Sheffield, new ed. (London: J. Murray, 1814).
The Letters of Edward Gibbon, edited by J. E. Norton, 3 volumes (New York: Macmillan, 1956).

GIBBON'S LIFE

Various editions of Gibbon's Memoirs *or* Autobiography *are available. The two most recent include:*

> *Memoirs of My Life,* edited with an introduction by B. Radice (Harmondsworth: Penguin, 1984).

> *Memoirs of My Life and Writings; Illustrated from His Letters, with Occasional Notes and Narrative, by John, Lord Sheffield,* edited by A.O.J. Cockshut and S. Constantine (Halifax: Ryburn Publications, 1994).

The best modern biographies:

> Craddock, P. B., *Young Edward Gibbon: Gentleman of Letters* (Baltimore: Johns Hopkins University Press, 1982).

> ———. *Edward Gibbon: Luminous Historian, 1772–1794* (Baltimore: Johns Hopkins University Press, 1989).

DISCUSSIONS OF GIBBON'S *THE DECLINE AND FALL OF THE ROMAN EMPIRE*

Badian, E., ed., *Gibbon et Rome à la lumière de l'historiographie moderne* (Geneva: Droz, 1977).

Bowersock, G. W., *Gibbon's Historical Imagination* (Stanford, Calif.: Stanford University Press, 1988).

Bowersock, G. W., J. Clive, and S. R. Graubard, eds., *Edward Gibbon and the Decline and Fall of the Roman Empire* (Cambridge, Mass.: Harvard University Press, 1977).

Momigliano, A., "Gibbon's Contribution to Historical Method," in *Studies in Historiography* (New York: Harper & Row, 1966), pp. 40–55.

Pocock, J.G.A., *Barbarism and Religion,* 2 volumes (Cambridge, England: Cambridge University Press, 1999).

Womersley, D. J., *Gibbon and the 'Watchmen of the Holy City': The Historian and His Reputation 1776–1815* (Oxford: Clarendon Press, 2002).

———. *The Transformation of* The Decline and Fall of the Roman Empire (Cambridge, England: Cambridge University Press, 1988).

Womersley, D. J., J. Burrow, and J. Pocock, eds., *Edward Gibbon: Bicentenary Essays* (Oxford: Voltaire Foundation, 1997).

FURTHER BIBLIOGRAPHY

Craddock, P. B., *Edward Gibbon: A Reference Guide* (Boston: G. K. Hall, 1987).

Norton, J. E., *A Bibliography of the Works of Edward Gibbon* (London: Oxford University Press, 1940).

THE DECLINE AND
FALL OF THE
ROMAN EMPIRE

Preface of the Author

It is not my intention to detain the reader by expatiating on the variety or the importance of the subject which I have undertaken to treat, since the merit of the choice would serve to render the weakness of the execution still more apparent, and still less excusable. But as I have presumed to lay before the public a first volume only of the History of the Decline and Fall of the Roman Empire, it will, perhaps, be expected that I should explain, in a few words, the nature and limits of my general plan.

The memorable series of revolutions which in the course of about thirteen centuries gradually undermined, and at length destroyed, the solid fabric of human greatness may, with some propriety, be divided into the three following periods:

I. The first of these periods may be traced from the age of Trajan and the Antonines, when the Roman monarchy, having attained its full strength and maturity, began to verge towards its decline; and will extend to the subversion of the Western empire by the Barbarians of Germany and Scythia, the rude ancestors of the most polished nations of modern Europe. This extraordinary revolution, which subjected Rome to the power of a Gothic conqueror, was completed about the beginning of the sixth century.

II. The second period of the Decline and Fall of Rome may be supposed to commence with the reign of Justinian, who, by his laws, as well as by his victories, restored a transient splendor to the Eastern Empire. It will comprehend the invasion of Italy by the Lombards; the conquest of the Asiatic and African provinces by the Arabs, who embraced the religion of Mohammed; the revolt of the Roman people against the feeble princes of Constantinople; and the elevation of Charlemagne, who, in the year eight hundred, established the second, or German, Empire of the West.

III. The last and longest of these periods includes about six centuries and a half; from the revival of the Western Empire, till the taking of Constantinople by the Turks and the extinction of a degenerate race of princes who continued to assume the titles of Caesar and Augustus after their dominions were contracted to the limits of a single city; in which the language, as well as manners, of the ancient Romans, had been long since forgotten. The writer who should undertake to relate the events of this period would find himself obliged to enter into the general history of the Crusades, as far as they contributed to the ruin of the Greek Empire; and he would scarcely be able to restrain his curiosity from making some inquiry into the state of the city of Rome during the darkness and confusion of the middle ages.

As I have ventured, perhaps too hastily, to commit to the press a work which in every sense of the word deserves the epithet of imperfect, I consider myself as contracting an engagement to finish, most probably in a second volume, the first of these memorable periods; and to deliver to the Public the complete History of the Decline and Fall of Rome, from the age of the Antonines to the subversion of the Western Empire. With regard to the subsequent periods, though I may entertain some hopes, I dare not presume to give any assurances. The execution of the extensive plan which I have described would connect the ancient and modern history of the world; but it would require many years of health, of leisure, and of perseverance.

BENTINCK STREET, FEBRUARY 1, 1776.

P.S. The entire History, which is now published, of the Decline and Fall of the Roman Empire in the West abundantly discharges my engagements with the Public. Perhaps their favorable opinion may encourage me to prosecute a work which, however laborious it may seem, is the most agreeable occupation of my leisure hours.

BENTINCK STREET, MARCH 1, 1781.

An Author easily persuades himself that the public opinion is still favorable to his labors; and I have now embraced the serious resolution of proceeding to the last period of my original design, and of the Roman Empire, the taking of Constantinople by the Turks, in the year one thousand four hundred and fifty-three. The most patient Reader, who computes that three ponderous volumes have been already employed on the events of four centuries, may, perhaps, be alarmed at the long prospect of nine hundred years. But it is not my intention to expatiate with the same minuteness on the whole series of the Byzantine history. At our entrance into this period, the reign of Justinian and the conquests of the Mohammedans will deserve and detain our attention, and the last age of Constantinople (the Crusades and the Turks) is connected with the revolutions of modern Europe. From the seventh to the eleventh century, the obscure interval will be supplied by a concise narrative of such facts as may still appear either interesting or important.

BENTINCK STREET, MARCH 1, 1782.

VOLUME THE FIRST

[1776]

THE ROMAN EMPIRE
AT THE DEATH OF AUGUSTUS
A.D. 14

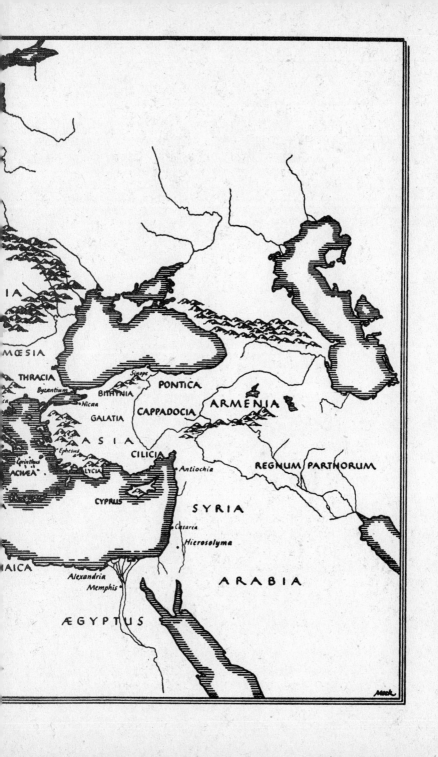

CHAPTER I

THE EXTENT OF THE EMPIRE IN THE AGE OF THE ANTONINES

Introduction. • *The extent and military force of
the empire in the age of the Antonines.*

In the second century of the Christian Era, the empire of Rome comprehended the fairest part of the earth and the most civilized portion of mankind. The frontiers of that extensive monarchy were guarded by ancient renown and disciplined valor. The gentle but powerful influence of laws and manners had gradually cemented the union of the provinces. Their peaceful inhabitants enjoyed and abused the advantages of wealth and luxury. The image of a free constitution was preserved with decent reverence: the Roman senate appeared to possess the sovereign authority, and devolved on the emperors all the executive powers of government. During a happy period of more than fourscore years [A.D. 98–180], the public administration was conducted by the virtue and abilities of Nerva, Trajan, Hadrian, and the two Antonines. It is the design of this, and of the two succeeding chapters, to describe the prosperous condition of their empire; and afterwards, from the death of Marcus Antoninus, to deduce the most important circumstances of its decline and fall, a revolution which will ever be remembered, and is still felt by the nations of the earth.

The principal conquests of the Romans were achieved under the republic; and the emperors, for the most part, were satisfied with preserving those dominions which had been acquired by the policy of the senate, the active emulation of the consuls, and the martial enthusiasm of the people. The seven first centuries were filled with a rapid succession of triumphs; but it was reserved for Augustus to relinquish the ambitious design of subduing the whole earth, and to introduce a spirit of moderation into the public councils. Inclined to peace by his temper and situation, it was easy for him to discover that Rome, in her present exalted situation, had much less to hope than to fear from the chance of arms; and that, in the prosecution of remote wars, the undertaking became every day more difficult, the event more doubtful, and the possession more precarious, and less beneficial.[†]

Happily for the repose of mankind, the moderate system recommended by the wisdom of Augustus was adopted by the fears and vices of his immediate successors. Engaged in the pursuit of pleasure, or in the exercise of tyranny, the first Caesars seldom showed themselves to the armies, or to the provinces; nor were they disposed to suffer that those triumphs which *their* indolence neglected should be usurped by the conduct and valor of their lieutenants. The military fame of a subject was considered as an insolent invasion of the Imperial prerogative; and it became the duty, as well as interest, of every Roman general to guard the frontiers entrusted to his care without aspiring to conquests which might have proved no less fatal to himself than to the vanquished Barbarians.

The only accession which the Roman empire received during the first century of the Christian Era was the province of Britain. In this single instance, the successors of Caesar and Augustus were persuaded to follow the example of the former, rather than the precept of the latter. The proximity of its situation to the coast of Gaul seemed to invite their arms; the pleasing though doubtful intelligence of a pearl fishery attracted their avarice; and as Britain was viewed in the light of a distinct and insulated world, the conquest scarcely formed any exception to the general system of continental measures. After a war of about forty years, undertaken by the most stupid, maintained by the most dissolute, and terminated by the most timid of all the emperors, the far greater part of the island submitted to the Roman yoke. The various tribes of Britain possessed valor without conduct, and the love of freedom without the spirit of union. They took up arms with savage fierceness; they laid them down, or turned them against each other, with wild inconsistency; and while they fought singly, they were successively subdued. Neither the fortitude of Caractacus, nor the despair of Boadicea, nor the fanaticism of the Druids could avert the slavery of their country, or resist the steady progress of the Imperial generals, who maintained the national glory when the throne was disgraced by the weakest, or the most vicious of mankind.[†]

Such was the state of the Roman frontiers, and such the maxims of Imperial policy, from the death of Augustus to the accession of Trajan. That virtuous and active prince had received the education of a soldier and possessed the talents of a general. The peaceful system of his predecessors was interrupted by scenes of war and conquest; and the legions, after a long interval, beheld a military emperor at their head. The first exploits of Trajan were against the Dacians, the most warlike of men, who dwelt beyond the Danube and who, during the reign of Domitian, had insulted with impunity the Majesty of Rome. To the strength and fierceness of Barbarians they added a contempt for life, which was derived from a warm persuasion of the immortality and transmigration of the soul. Decebalus, the Dacian king, approved himself a rival not unworthy of Trajan; nor did he despair of his own and the public fortune till, by the confession of his enemies, he had exhausted every resource both of valor and policy. This memorable war, with a very short suspension of hostilities, lasted five years [A.D. 101–106]; and as the emperor could exert, without control, the whole force of the state, it was terminated by an absolute submission of the Barbarians. The new province of Dacia . . . formed a second exception to the precept of Augustus.†

Trajan was ambitious of fame; and as long as mankind shall continue to bestow more liberal applause on their destroyers than on their benefactors, the thirst of military glory will ever be the vice of the most exalted characters. The praises of Alexander, transmitted by a succession of poets and historians, had kindled a dangerous emulation in the mind of Trajan. Like him, the Roman emperor undertook an expedition against the nations of the East; but he lamented with a sigh that his advanced age scarcely left him any hopes of equaling the renown of the son of Philip. Yet the success of Trajan, however transient, was rapid and specious. The degenerate Parthians, broken by intestine discord, fled before his arms. He descended the River Tigris in triumph, from the mountains of Armenia to the Persian Gulf. He enjoyed the honor of being the first, as he was the last, of the Roman generals who ever navigated that remote sea. His fleets ravaged the coast of Arabia; and Trajan vainly flattered himself that he was approaching towards the confines of India. Every day the astonished senate received the intelligence of new names and new nations that acknowledged his sway. They were informed that . . . the rich countries of Armenia, Mesopotamia, and Assyria were reduced into the state of provinces. But the death of Trajan soon clouded the splendid prospect; and it was justly to be dreaded that so many distant nations would throw off the unaccustomed yoke when they were no longer restrained by the powerful hand which had imposed it.

It was an ancient tradition that when the Capitol was founded by one of the Roman kings, the god Terminus (who presided over boundaries, and was represented, according to the fashion of that age, by a large stone) alone, among all the inferior deities, refused to yield his place to Jupiter himself. A favorable inference was drawn from his obstinacy, which was interpreted by the augurs as a sure presage that the boundaries of the Roman power would never recede. During many ages, the prediction, as it is usual, contributed to its own accomplishment. But though Terminus had resisted the majesty of Jupiter, he submitted to the authority of the emperor Hadrian. The resignation of all the eastern conquests of Trajan was the first measure of his reign . . . ; and, in compliance with the precept of Augustus, once more established the Euphrates as the frontier of the empire. Censure, which arraigns the public actions and the private motives of princes, has ascribed to envy a conduct which might be attributed to the prudence and moderation of Hadrian. The various character of that emperor, capable, by turns, of the meanest and the most generous sentiments, may afford some color to the suspicion. It was, however, scarcely in his power to place the superiority of his predecessor in a more conspicuous light than by thus confessing himself unequal to the task of defending the conquests of Trajan.[†]

Notwithstanding this difference in their personal conduct, the general system of Augustus was equally adopted and uniformly pursued by Hadrian and by the two Antonines. They persisted in the design of maintaining the dignity of the empire without attempting to enlarge its limits. By every honorable expedient they invited the friendship of the Barbarians; and endeavored to convince mankind that the Roman power, raised above the temptation of conquest, was actuated only by the love of order and justice. During a long period of forty-three years, their virtuous labors were crowned with success; and if we except a few slight hostilities that served to exercise the legions of the frontier, the reigns of Hadrian and Antoninus Pius offer the fair prospect of universal peace. The Roman name was revered among the most remote nations of the earth. The fiercest Barbarians frequently submitted their differences to the arbitration of the emperor; and we are informed by a contemporary historian that he had seen ambassadors who were refused the honor which they came to solicit of being admitted into the rank of subjects.

The terror of the Roman arms added weight and dignity to the moderation of the emperors. They preserved peace by a constant preparation for war; and while justice regulated their conduct, they announced to the nations on their confines that they were as little disposed to endure as to offer an injury. The military strength which it had been sufficient for Hadrian and the elder Antoninus to display was exerted against the Parthians and the Germans by the emperor Marcus. The hostilities of the Barbarians provoked the resentment of that philosophic monarch, and, in the prosecution of a just defense, Marcus and his generals obtained many signal victories, both on the Euphrates and on the Danube. The military establishment of the Roman empire, which thus assured either its tranquility or success, will now become the proper and important object of our attention.

In the purer ages of the commonwealth, the use of arms was reserved for those ranks of citizens who had a country to love, a property to defend, and some share in enacting those laws which it was their interest as well as duty to maintain. But in proportion as the public freedom was lost in extent of conquest, war was gradually improved into an art, and degraded into a trade. The legions themselves, even at the time when they were recruited in the most distant provinces, were supposed to consist of Roman citizens. That distinction was generally considered either as a legal qualification or as a proper recompense for the soldier; but a more serious regard was paid to the essential merit of age, strength, and military stature. . . . After every qualification of property had been laid aside, the armies of the Roman emperors were still commanded, for the most part, by officers of liberal birth and education; but the common soldiers, like the mercenary troops of modern Europe, were drawn from the meanest, and very frequently from the most profligate, of mankind.

That public virtue which among the ancients was denominated patriotism is derived from a strong sense of our own interest in the preservation and prosperity of the free government of which we are members. Such a sentiment, which had rendered the legions of the republic almost invincible, could make but a very feeble impression on the mercenary servants of a despotic prince; and it became necessary to supply that defect by other motives, of a different but not less forcible nature—honor and religion. The peasant, or mechanic, imbibed the useful prejudice that he was advanced to the more dignified profession of arms, in which his rank and reputation would depend on his own valor; and that, although the prowess of a private soldier must often escape the notice of fame, his own behavior might sometimes confer glory or disgrace on the company, the legion, or even the army, to whose honors he was associated. On his first entrance into the service, an oath was administered to him with every circumstance of solemnity. He promised never to desert his standard, to submit his own will to the commands of his leaders, and to sacrifice his life for the safety of the emperor and the empire. The attachment of the Roman troops to their standards was inspired by the united influence of religion and of honor. The golden eagle which glittered in the front of the legion was the object of their fondest devotion; nor was it esteemed less impious than it was ignominious to abandon that sacred ensign in the hour of danger. These motives, which derived their strength from the imagination, were enforced by fears and hopes of a more substantial kind. Regular pay, occasional donatives, and a stated recompense after the appointed time of service alleviated the hardships of the military life, whilst, on the other hand, it was impossible for cowardice or disobedience to escape the severest punishment. The centurions were authorized to chastise with blows, the generals had a right to punish with death; and it was an inflexible maxim of Roman discipline that a good soldier should dread his officers far more than the enemy. From such laudable arts did the valor of the Imperial troops receive a degree of firmness and docility unattainable by the impetuous and irregular passions of Barbarians.

And yet so sensible were the Romans of the imperfection of valor without skill and practice that, in their language, the name of an army [i.e., *exercitus*] was borrowed from the word which signified exercise. Military exercises were the important and unremitted object of their discipline. The recruits and young soldiers were constantly trained, both in the morning and in the evening, nor was age or knowledge allowed to excuse the veterans from the daily repetition of what they had completely learnt. Large sheds were erected in the winter-quarters of the troops, that their useful labors might not receive any interruption from the most tempestuous weather; and it was carefully observed that the arms destined to this imitation of war should be of double the weight which was required in real action. It is not the purpose of this work to enter into any minute description of the Roman exercises. We shall only remark that they comprehended whatever could add strength to the body, activity to the limbs, or grace to the motions. The soldiers were diligently instructed to march, to run, to leap, to swim, to carry heavy burdens, to handle every species of arms that was used either for offense or for defense, either in distant engagement or in a closer onset; to form a variety of evolutions; and to move to the sound of flutes in the Pyrrhic or martial dance. In the midst of peace, the Roman troops familiarized themselves with the practice of war; and it is prettily remarked by an ancient historian who had fought against them that the effusion of blood was the only circumstance which distinguished a field of battle from a field of exercise. It was the policy of the ablest generals, and even of the emperors themselves, to encourage these military studies by their presence and example; and we are informed that Hadrian, as well as Trajan, frequently condescended to instruct the unexperienced soldiers, to reward the diligent, and sometimes to dispute with them the prize of superior strength or dexterity. Under the reigns of those princes, the science of tactics was cultivated with success; and as long as the empire retained any vigor, their military instructions were respected as the most perfect model of Roman discipline.[†]

Such were the arts of war by which the Roman emperors defended their extensive conquests, and preserved a military spirit, at a time when every other virtue was oppressed by luxury and despotism.[†]

[A] long enumeration of provinces, whose broken fragments have formed so many powerful kingdoms, might almost induce us to forgive the vanity or ignorance of the ancients. Dazzled with the extensive sway, the irresistible strength, and the real or affected moderation of the emperors, they permitted themselves to despise, and sometimes to forget, the outlying countries which had been left in the enjoyment of a barbarous independence; and they gradually usurped the license of confounding the Roman monarchy with the globe of the earth. But the temper, as well as knowledge, of a modern historian require a more sober and accurate language. He may impress a juster image of the greatness of Rome by observing that the empire was above two thousand miles in breadth, from the wall of Antoninus and the northern limits of Dacia, to Mount Atlas and the tropic of Cancer; that it extended in length more than three thousand miles from the Western Ocean to the Euphrates; that it was situated in the finest part of the Temperate Zone, between the twenty-fourth and fifty-sixth degrees of northern latitude; and that it was supposed to contain above sixteen hundred thousand square miles, for the most part of fertile and well-cultivated land.

CHAPTER II

OF THE INTERNAL PROSPERITY OF THE ROMAN EMPIRE IN THE AGE OF THE ANTONINES

*Of the union and internal prosperity of the
Roman empire in the age of the Antonines.*

It is not alone by the rapidity, or extent of conquest, that we should estimate the greatness of Rome. The sovereign of the Russian deserts commands a larger portion of the globe. In the seventh summer after his passage of the Hellespont, Alexander erected the Macedonian trophies on the banks of the Hyphasis. Within less than a century, the irresistible Zingis, and the Mogul princes of his race, spread their cruel devastations and transient empire from the Sea of China to the confines of Egypt and Germany. But the firm edifice of Roman power was raised and preserved by the wisdom of ages. The obedient provinces of Trajan and the Antonines were united by laws and adorned by arts. They might occasionally suffer from the partial abuse of delegated authority; but the general principle of government was wise, simple, and beneficent. They enjoyed the religion of their ancestors, whilst in civil honors and advantages they were exalted, by just degrees, to an equality with their conquerors.

I. The policy of the emperors and the senate, as far as it concerned religion, was happily seconded by the reflections of the enlightened, and by the habits of the superstitious, part of their subjects. The various modes of worship which prevailed in the Roman world were all considered by the people as equally true; by the philosopher, as equally false; and by the magistrate, as equally useful. And thus toleration produced not only mutual indulgence, but even religious concord.

The superstition of the people was not embittered by any mixture of theological rancor; nor was it confined by the chains of any speculative system. The devout polytheist, though fondly attached to his national rites, admitted with implicit faith the different religions of the earth. Fear, gratitude, and curiosity, a dream or an omen, a singular disorder or a distant journey, perpetually disposed him to multiply the articles of his belief, and to enlarge the list of his protectors. The thin texture of the Pagan mythology was interwoven with various but not discordant materials. As soon as it was allowed that sages and heroes who had lived or who had died for the benefit of their country were exalted to a state of power and immortality, it was universally confessed that they deserved, if not the adoration, at least the reverence, of all mankind. The deities of a thousand groves and a thousand streams possessed, in peace, their local and respective influence; nor could the Romans who deprecated the wrath of the Tiber deride the Egyptian who presented his offering to the beneficent genius of the Nile. The visible powers of nature, the planets, and the elements were the same throughout the universe. The invisible governors of the moral world were inevitably cast in a similar mold of fiction and allegory. Every virtue, and even vice, acquired its divine representative; every art and profession its patron, whose attributes, in the most distant ages and countries, were uniformly derived from the character of their peculiar votaries. A republic of gods of such opposite tempers and interests required, in every system, the moderating hand of a supreme magistrate, who, by the progress of knowledge and flattery, was gradually invested with the sublime perfections of an Eternal Parent, and an Omnipotent Monarch. Such was the mild spirit of antiquity that the nations were less attentive to the difference than to the resemblance of their religious worship. The Greek, the Roman, and the Barbarian, as they met before their respective altars, easily persuaded themselves that under various names, and with various ceremonies, they adored the same deities. The elegant mythology of Homer gave a beautiful and almost a regular form to the polytheism of the ancient world.

The philosophers of Greece deduced their morals from the nature of man, rather than from that of God. They meditated, however, on the Divine Nature, as a very curious and important speculation; and in the profound inquiry, they displayed the strength and weakness of the human understanding. Of the four most celebrated schools, the Stoics and the Platonists endeavored to reconcile the jarring interests of reason and piety. They have left us the most sublime proofs of the existence and perfections of the first cause; but, as it was impossible for them to conceive the creation of matter, the workman in the Stoic philosophy was not sufficiently distinguished from the work; whilst, on the contrary, the spiritual God of Plato and his disciples resembled an idea, rather than a substance. The opinions of the Academics and Epicureans were of a less religious cast; but whilst the modest science of the former induced them to doubt, the positive ignorance of the latter urged them to deny, the providence of a Supreme Ruler. The spirit of inquiry, prompted by emulation and supported by freedom, had divided the public teachers of philosophy into a variety of contending sects; but the ingenuous youth who, from every part, resorted to Athens and the other seats of learning in the Roman empire were alike instructed in every school to reject and to despise the religion of the multitude. How, indeed, was it possible that a philosopher should accept, as divine truths, the idle tales of the poets, and the incoherent traditions of antiquity; or that he should adore as gods those imperfect beings whom he must have despised as men? Against such unworthy adversaries, Cicero condescended to employ the arms of reason and eloquence; but the satire of Lucian was a much more adequate, as well as more efficacious, weapon. We may be well assured that a writer conversant with the world would never have ventured to expose the gods of his country to public ridicule, had they not already been the objects of secret contempt among the polished and enlightened orders of society.

Notwithstanding the fashionable irreligion which prevailed in the age of the Antonines, both the interest of the priests and the credulity of the people were sufficiently respected. In their writings and conversation, the philosophers of antiquity asserted the independent dignity of reason; but they resigned their actions to the commands of law and of custom. Viewing, with a smile of pity and indulgence, the various errors of the vulgar, they diligently practiced the ceremonies of their fathers, devoutly frequented the temples of the gods; and sometimes condescending to act a part on the theater of superstition, they concealed the sentiments of an atheist under the sacerdotal robes. Reasoners of such a temper were scarcely inclined to wrangle about their respective modes of faith, or of worship. It was indifferent to them what shape the folly of the multitude might choose to assume; and they approached with the same inward contempt, and the same external reverence, the altars of the Libyan, the Olympian, or the Capitoline Jupiter.

It is not easy to conceive from what motives a spirit of persecution could introduce itself into the Roman councils. The magistrates could not be actuated by a blind, though honest, bigotry, since the magistrates were themselves philosophers; and the schools of Athens had given laws to the senate. They could not be impelled by ambition or avarice, as the temporal and ecclesiastical powers were united in the same hands. The pontiffs were chosen among the most illustrious of the senators; and the office of supreme pontiff was constantly exercised by the emperors themselves. They knew and valued the advantages of religion as it is connected with civil government. They encouraged the public festivals which humanize the manners of the people. They managed the arts of divination as a convenient instrument of policy; and they respected, as the firmest bond of society, the useful persuasion that, either in this or in a future life, the crime of perjury is most assuredly punished by the avenging gods. But whilst they acknowledged the general advantages of religion, they were convinced that the various modes of worship contributed alike to the same salutary purposes; and that, in every country, the form of superstition which had received the sanction of time and experience was the best adapted to the climate and to its inhabitants. Avarice and taste very frequently despoiled the vanquished nations of the elegant statues of their gods and the rich ornaments of their temples; but in the exercise of the religion which they derived from their ancestors, they uniformly experienced the indulgence, and even protection, of the Roman conquerors. The province of Gaul seems, and indeed only seems, an exception to this universal toleration. Under the specious pretext of abolishing human sacrifices, the emperors Tiberius and Claudius suppressed the dangerous power of the Druids: but the priests themselves, their gods and their altars, subsisted in peaceful obscurity till the final destruction of Paganism.

Rome, the capital of a great monarchy, was incessantly filled with subjects and strangers from every part of the world, who all introduced and enjoyed the favorite superstitions of their native country. Every city in the empire was justified in maintaining the purity of its ancient ceremonies; and the Roman senate, using the common privilege, sometimes interposed to check this inundation of foreign rites. The Egyptian superstition, of all the most contemptible and abject, was frequently prohibited: the temples of Serapis and Isis demolished, and their worshipers banished from Rome and Italy. But the zeal of fanaticism prevailed over the cold and feeble efforts of policy. The exiles returned, the proselytes multiplied, the temples were restored with increasing splendor, and Isis and Serapis at length assumed their place among the Roman Deities. Nor was this indulgence a departure from the old maxims of government. In the purest ages of the commonwealth, Cybele and Aesculapius had been invited by solemn embassies; and it was customary to tempt the protectors of besieged cities by the promise of more distinguished honors than they possessed in their native country. Rome gradually became the common temple of her subjects; and the freedom of the city was bestowed on all the gods of mankind.

II. The narrow policy of preserving, without any foreign mixture, the pure blood of the ancient citizens had checked the fortune, and hastened the ruin, of Athens and Sparta. The aspiring genius of Rome sacrificed vanity to ambition, and deemed it more prudent, as well as honorable, to adopt virtue and merit for her own wheresoever they were found, among slaves or strangers, enemies or Barbarians. During the most flourishing era of the Athenian commonwealth, the number of citizens gradually decreased from about thirty to twenty-one thousand. If, on the contrary, we study the growth of the Roman republic, we may discover that, notwithstanding the incessant demands of wars and colonies, the citizens, who in the first census of Servius Tullius amounted to no more than eighty-three thousand, were multiplied, before the commencement of the social war, to the number of four hundred and sixty-three thousand men able to bear arms in the service of their country. When the allies of Rome claimed an equal share of honors and privileges, the senate indeed preferred the chance of arms to an ignominious concession. The Samnites and the Lucanians paid the severe penalty of their rashness; but the rest of the Italian states, as they successively returned to their duty, were admitted into the bosom of the republic, and soon contributed to the ruin of public freedom. Under a democratical government, the citizens exercise the powers of sovereignty; and those powers will be first abused and afterwards lost if they are committed to an unwieldy multitude. But when the popular assemblies had been suppressed by the administration of the emperors, the conquerors were distinguished from the vanquished nations only as the first and most honorable order of subjects; and their increase, however rapid, was no longer exposed to the same dangers. Yet the wisest princes, who adopted the maxims of Augustus, guarded with the strictest care the dignity of the Roman name, and diffused the freedom of the city with a prudent liberality.

Till the privileges of Romans had been progressively extended to all the inhabitants of the empire, an important distinction was preserved between Italy and the provinces. The former was esteemed the center of public unity and the firm basis of the constitution. Italy claimed the birth, or at least the residence, of the emperors and the senate. The estates of the Italians were exempt from taxes, their persons from the arbitrary jurisdiction of governors. Their municipal corporations, formed after the perfect model of the capital, were entrusted, under the immediate eye of the supreme power, with the execution of the laws. From the foot of the Alps to the extremity of Calabria, all the natives of Italy were born citizens of Rome. Their partial distinctions were obliterated, and they insensibly coalesced into one great nation, united by language, manners, and civil institutions, and equal to the weight of a powerful empire. The republic gloried in her generous policy, and was frequently rewarded by the merit and services of her adopted sons. Had she always confined the distinction of Romans to the ancient families within the walls of the city, that immortal name would have been deprived of some of its noblest ornaments. . . . The patriot family of the Catos emerged from Tusculum; and the little town of Arpinum claimed the double honor of producing Marius and Cicero, the former of whom deserved, after Romulus and Camillus, to be styled the Third Founder of Rome; and the latter, after saving his country from the designs of Catiline, enabled her to contend with Athens for the palm of eloquence.

The provinces of the empire . . . were destitute of any public force or constitutional freedom. In Etruria, in Greece, and in Gaul, it was the first care of the senate to dissolve those dangerous confederacies which taught mankind that, as the Roman arms prevailed by division, they might be resisted by union. Those princes whom the ostentation of gratitude or generosity permitted for a while to hold a precarious scepter were dismissed from their thrones as soon as they had performed their appointed task of fashioning to the yoke the vanquished nations. The free states and cities which had embraced the cause of Rome were rewarded with a nominal alliance, and insensibly sunk into real servitude. The public authority was everywhere exercised by the ministers of the senate and of the emperors, and that authority was absolute and without control. But the same salutary maxims of government which had secured the peace and obedience of Italy were extended to the most distant conquests. A nation of Romans was gradually formed in the provinces, by the double expedient of introducing colonies and of admitting the most faithful and deserving of the provincials to the freedom of Rome.

"Wheresoever the Roman conquers, he inhabits," is a very just observation of Seneca, confirmed by history and experience. The natives of Italy, allured by pleasure or by interest, hastened to enjoy the advantages of victory; and we may remark that, about forty years after the reduction of Asia, eighty thousand Romans were massacred in one day by the cruel orders of Mithridates. These voluntary exiles were engaged, for the most part, in the occupations of commerce, agriculture, and the farm of the revenue. But after the legions were rendered permanent by the emperors, the provinces were peopled by a race of soldiers; and the veterans, whether they received the reward of their service in land or in money, usually settled with their families in the country where they had honorably spent their youth. Throughout the empire, but more particularly in the western parts, the most fertile districts and the most convenient situations were reserved for the establishment of colonies; some of which were of a civil and others of a military nature. In their manners and internal policy, the colonies formed a perfect representation of their great parent; and as they were soon endeared to the natives by the ties of friendship and alliance, they effectually diffused a reverence for the Roman name, and a desire, which was seldom disappointed, of sharing, in due time, its honors and advantages. The municipal cities insensibly equaled the rank and splendor of the colonies; and in the reign of Hadrian it was disputed which was the preferable condition, of those societies which had issued from or those which had been received into the bosom of Rome. The right of Latium, as it was called, conferred on the cities to which it had been granted a more partial favor. The magistrates only, at the expiration of their office, assumed the quality of Roman citizens; but as those offices were annual, in a few years they circulated round the principal families. Those of the provincials who were permitted to bear arms in the legions; those who exercised any civil employment; all, in a word, who performed any public service or displayed any personal talents were rewarded with a present whose value was continually diminished by the increasing liberality of the emperors. Yet even in the age of the Antonines, when the freedom of the city had been bestowed on the greater number of their subjects, it was still accompanied with very solid advantages. The bulk of the people acquired with that title the benefit of the Roman laws, particularly in the interesting articles of marriage, testaments, and inheritances; and the road of fortune was open to those whose pretensions were seconded by favor or merit. The grandsons of the Gauls who had besieged Julius Caesar in Alesia commanded legions, governed provinces, and were admitted into the senate of Rome. Their ambition, instead of disturbing the tranquility of the state, was intimately connected with its safety and greatness.

So sensible were the Romans of the influence of language over national manners that it was their most serious care to extend, with the progress of their arms, the use of the Latin tongue. The ancient dialects of Italy, the Sabine, the Etruscan, and the Venetian, sunk into oblivion; but in the provinces, the East was less docile than the West to the voice of its victorious preceptors. This obvious difference marked the two portions of the empire with a distinction of colors which, though it was in some degree concealed during the meridian splendor of prosperity, became gradually more visible as the shades of night descended upon the Roman world. The western countries were civilized by the same hands which subdued them. As soon as the Barbarians were reconciled to obedience, their minds were open to any new impressions of knowledge and politeness. The language of Virgil and Cicero, though with some inevitable mixture of corruption, was so universally adopted in Africa, Spain, Gaul, Britain, and Pannonia that the faint traces of the Punic or Celtic idioms were preserved only in the mountains or among the peasants. Education and study insensibly inspired the natives of those countries with the sentiments of Romans; and Italy gave fashions as well as laws to her Latin provincials. They solicited with more ardor, and obtained with more facility, the freedom and honors of the state; supported the national dignity in letters and in arms; and at length, in the person of Trajan, produced an emperor whom the Scipios would not have disowned for their countryman. The situation of the Greeks was very different from that of the Barbarians. The former had been long since civilized and corrupted. They had too much taste to relinquish their language, and too much vanity to adopt any foreign institutions. Still preserving the prejudices, after they had lost the virtues, of their ancestors, they affected to despise the unpolished manners of the Roman conquerors, whilst they were compelled to respect their superior wisdom and power. Nor was the influence of the Grecian language and sentiments confined to the narrow limits of that once celebrated country. Their empire, by the progress of colonies and conquest, had been diffused from the Adriatic to the Euphrates and the Nile. Asia was covered with Greek cities, and the long reign of the Macedonian kings had introduced a silent revolution into Syria and Egypt. In their pompous courts, those princes united the elegance of Athens with the luxury of the East, and the example of the court was imitated, at an humble distance, by the higher ranks of their subjects. Such was the general division of the Roman empire into the Latin and Greek languages. To these we may add a third distinction for the body of the natives in Syria, and especially in Egypt. The use of their ancient dialects, by secluding them from the commerce of mankind, checked the improvements of those Barbarians. The slothful effeminacy of the former exposed them to the contempt, the sullen ferociousness of the latter excited the aversion, of the conquerors. Those nations had submitted to the Roman power, but they seldom desired or deserved the freedom of the city: and it was remarked that more than two hundred and thirty years elapsed after the ruin of the Ptolemies before an Egyptian was admitted into the senate of Rome.

It is a just though trite observation that victorious Rome was herself subdued by the arts of Greece. Those immortal writers who still command the admiration of modern Europe soon became the favorite object of study and imitation in Italy and the western provinces. But the elegant amusements of the Romans were not suffered to interfere with their sound maxims of policy. Whilst they acknowledged the charms of the Greek, they asserted the dignity of the Latin tongue, and the exclusive use of the latter was inflexibly maintained in the administration of civil as well as military government. The two languages exercised at the same time their separate jurisdiction throughout the empire: the former as the natural idiom of science; the latter as the legal dialect of public transactions. Those who united letters with business were equally conversant with both; and it was almost impossible, in any province, to find a Roman subject of a liberal education who was at once a stranger to the Greek and to the Latin language.

It was by such institutions that the nations of the empire insensibly melted away into the Roman name and people. But there still remained, in the center of every province and of every family, an unhappy condition of men who endured the weight, without sharing the benefits, of society. In the free states of antiquity, the domestic slaves were exposed to the wanton rigor of despotism. The perfect settlement of the Roman empire was preceded by ages of violence and rapine. The slaves consisted, for the most part, of Barbarian captives, taken in thousands by the chance of war, purchased at a vile price, accustomed to a life of independence, and impatient to break and to revenge their fetters. Against such internal enemies, whose desperate insurrections had more than once reduced the republic to the brink of destruction, the most severe regulations and the most cruel treatment seemed almost justified by the great law of self-preservation. But when the principal nations of Europe, Asia, and Africa were united under the laws of one sovereign, the source of foreign supplies flowed with much less abundance, and the Romans were reduced to the milder but more tedious method of propagation. In their numerous families, and particularly in their country estates, they encouraged the marriage of their slaves. The sentiments of nature, the habits of education, and the possession of a dependent species of property contributed to alleviate the hardships of servitude. The existence of a slave became an object of greater value, and though his happiness still depended on the temper and circumstances of the master, the humanity of the latter, instead of being restrained by fear, was encouraged by the sense of his own interest. The progress of manners was accelerated by the virtue or policy of the emperors; and by the edicts of Hadrian and the Antonines, the protection of the laws was extended to the most abject part of mankind. The jurisdiction of life and death over the slaves, a power long exercised and often abused, was taken out of private hands and reserved to the magistrates alone. The subterraneous prisons were abolished; and upon a just complaint of intolerable treatment, the injured slave obtained either his deliverance or a less cruel master.

Hope, the best comfort of our imperfect condition, was not denied to the Roman slave; and if he had any opportunity of rendering himself either useful or agreeable, he might very naturally expect that the diligence and fidelity of a few years would be rewarded with the inestimable gift of freedom. The benevolence of the master was so frequently prompted by the meaner suggestions of vanity and avarice that the laws found it more necessary to restrain than to encourage a profuse and undistinguishing liberality, which might degenerate into a very dangerous abuse. It was a maxim of ancient jurisprudence that a slave had not any country of his own; he acquired with his liberty an admission into the political society of which his patron was a member. The consequences of this maxim would have prostituted the privileges of the Roman city to a mean and promiscuous multitude. Some seasonable exceptions were therefore provided; and the honorable distinction was confined to such slaves only as, for just causes and with the approbation of the magistrate, should receive a solemn and legal manumission. Even these chosen freedmen obtained no more than the private rights of citizens, and were rigorously excluded from civil or military honors. Whatever might be the merit or fortune of their sons, *they* likewise were esteemed unworthy of a seat in the senate; nor were the traces of a servile origin allowed to be completely obliterated till the third or fourth generation. Without destroying the distinction of ranks, a distant prospect of freedom and honors was presented even to those whom pride and prejudice almost disdained to number among the human species.

It was once proposed to discriminate the slaves by a peculiar habit; but it was justly apprehended that there might be some danger in acquainting them with their own numbers. Without interpreting, in their utmost strictness, the liberal appellations of legions and myriads, we may venture to pronounce that the proportion of slaves, who were valued as property, was more considerable than that of servants, who can be computed only as an expense. The youths of a promising genius were instructed in the arts and sciences, and their price was ascertained by the degree of their skill and talents. Almost every profession, either liberal or mechanical, might be found in the household of an opulent senator. The ministers of pomp and sensuality were multiplied beyond the conception of modern luxury. It was more for the interest of the merchant or manufacturer to purchase than to hire his workmen; and in the country, slaves were employed as the cheapest and most laborious instruments of agriculture. To confirm the general observation, and to display the multitude of slaves, we might allege a variety of particular instances. It was discovered, on a very melancholy occasion, that four hundred slaves were maintained in a single palace of Rome. The same number of four hundred belonged to an estate which an African widow, of a very private condition, resigned to her son, whilst she reserved for herself a much larger share of her property. A freedman under the reign of Augustus, though his fortune had suffered great losses in the civil wars, left behind him three thousand six hundred yoke of oxen, two hundred and fifty thousand head of smaller cattle, and what was almost included in the description of cattle, four thousand one hundred and sixteen slaves.

The number of subjects who acknowledged the laws of Rome, of citizens, of provincials, and of slaves, cannot now be fixed with such a degree of accuracy as the importance of the object would deserve. We are informed that when the emperor Claudius exercised the office of censor, he took an account of six millions nine hundred and forty-five thousand Roman citizens, who, with the proportion of women and children, must have amounted to about twenty millions of souls. The multitude of subjects of an inferior rank was uncertain and fluctuating. But, after weighing with attention every circumstance which could influence the balance, it seems probable that there existed, in the time of Claudius, about twice as many provincials as there were citizens, of either sex and of every age; and that the slaves were at least equal in number to the free inhabitants of the Roman world. The total amount of this imperfect calculation would rise to about one hundred and twenty millions of persons; a degree of population which possibly exceeds that of modern Europe, and forms the most numerous society that has ever been united under the same system of government.

Domestic peace and union were the natural consequences of the moderate and comprehensive policy embraced by the Romans. If we turn our eyes towards the monarchies of Asia, we shall behold despotism in the center and weakness in the extremities; the collection of the revenue, or the administration of justice, enforced by the presence of an army; hostile Barbarians established in the heart of the country, hereditary satraps usurping the dominion of the provinces, and subjects inclined to rebellion, though incapable of freedom. But the obedience of the Roman world was uniform, voluntary, and permanent. The vanquished nations, blended into one great people, resigned the hope, nay, even the wish, of resuming their independence, and scarcely considered their own existence as distinct from the existence of Rome. The established authority of the emperors pervaded without an effort the wide extent of their dominions, and was exercised with the same facility on the banks of the Thames or of the Nile as on those of the Tiber. The legions were destined to serve against the public enemy, and the civil magistrate seldom required the aid of a military force. In this state of general security, the leisure, as well as opulence, both of the prince and people, were devoted to improve and to adorn the Roman empire.

Among the innumerable monuments of architecture constructed by the Romans, how many have escaped the notice of history, how few have resisted the ravages of time and barbarism! And yet, even the majestic ruins that are still scattered over Italy and the provinces would be sufficient to prove that those countries were once the seat of a polite and powerful empire. Their greatness alone, or their beauty, might deserve our attention: but they are rendered more interesting by two important circumstances, which connect the agreeable history of the arts with the more useful history of human manners. Many of those works were erected at private expense, and almost all were intended for public benefit.[†]

In the commonwealths of Athens and Rome, the modest simplicity of private houses announced the equal condition of freedom; whilst the sovereignty of the people was represented in the majestic edifices designed to the public use; nor was this republican spirit totally extinguished by the introduction of wealth and monarchy. It was in works of national honor and benefit that the most virtuous of the emperors affected to display their magnificence. The golden palace of Nero excited a just indignation, but the vast extent of ground which had been usurped by his selfish luxury was more nobly filled under the succeeding reigns by the Colosseum, the baths of Titus, the Claudian portico, and the temples dedicated to the goddess of Peace, and to the genius of Rome. These monuments of architecture, the property of the

Roman people, were adorned with the most beautiful productions of Grecian painting and sculpture; and in the temple of Peace, a very curious library was open to the curiosity of the learned. At a small distance from thence was situated the Forum of Trajan. It was surrounded by a lofty portico in the form of a quadrangle, into which four triumphal arches opened a noble and spacious entrance: in the center arose a column of marble whose height, of one hundred and ten feet, denoted the elevation of the hill that had been cut away. This column, which still subsists in its ancient beauty, exhibited an exact representation of the Dacian victories of its founder. The veteran soldier contemplated the story of his own campaigns, and by an easy illusion of national vanity, the peaceful citizen associated himself to the honors of the triumph. All the other quarters of the capital, and all the provinces of the empire, were embellished by the same liberal spirit of public magnificence, and were filled with amphitheaters, theaters, temples, porticoes, triumphal arches, baths and aqueducts, all variously conducive to the health, the devotion, and the pleasures of the meanest citizen. The last mentioned of those edifices deserve our peculiar attention. The boldness of the enterprise, the solidity of the execution, and the uses to which they were subservient rank the aqueducts among the noblest monuments of Roman genius and power. The aqueducts of the capital claim a just preeminence; but the curious traveler who, without the light of history, should examine those of Spoleto, of Metz, or of Segovia, would very naturally conclude that those provincial towns had formerly been the residence of some potent monarch. The solitudes of Asia and Africa were once covered with flourishing cities whose populousness, and even whose existence, was derived from such artificial supplies of a perennial stream of fresh water.†

All these cities were connected with each other and with the capital by the public highways, which, issuing from the Forum of Rome, traversed Italy, pervaded the provinces, and were terminated only by the frontiers of the empire. If we carefully trace the distance from the wall of Antoninus to Rome, and from thence to Jerusalem, it will be found that the great chain of communication, from the north-west to the south-east point of the empire, was drawn out to the length of four thousand and eighty Roman miles. The public roads were accurately divided by mile-stones, and ran in a direct line from one city to another, with very little respect for the obstacles either of nature or private property. Mountains were perforated, and bold arches thrown over the broadest and most rapid streams. The middle part of the road was raised into a terrace which commanded the adjacent country, consisted of several strata of sand, gravel, and cement, and was paved with large stones, or, in some places near the capital, with granite. Such was the solid construction of the Roman highways, whose firmness has not entirely yielded to the effort of fifteen centuries. They united the subjects of the most distant provinces by an easy and familiar intercourse; but their primary object had been to facilitate the marches of the legions; nor was any country considered as completely subdued till it had been rendered, in all its parts, pervious to the arms and authority of the conqueror. The advantage of receiving the earliest intelligence, and of conveying their orders with celerity, induced the emperors to establish, throughout their extensive dominions, the regular institution of posts. Houses were everywhere erected at the distance only of five or six miles; each of them was constantly provided with forty horses, and by the help of these relays it was easy to travel a hundred miles in a day along the Roman roads. The use of posts was allowed to those who claimed it by an Imperial mandate; but though originally intended for the public service, it was sometimes indulged to the business or conveniency of private citizens. Nor was the communication of the Roman empire less free and open by sea than it was by land. The provinces surrounded and enclosed the Mediterranean: and Italy, in the shape of an immense promontory, advanced into the midst of that great lake. The coasts of Italy are, in general, destitute of safe harbors; but human industry had corrected the deficiencies of nature; and the artificial port of Ostia, in particular, situated at the mouth of the Tiber and formed by the emperor Claudius, was a useful monument of Roman greatness. From this port, which was only sixteen miles from the capital, a favorable breeze frequently carried vessels in seven days to the columns of Hercules, and in nine or ten to Alexandria in Egypt.

Whatever evils either reason or declamation have imputed to extensive empire, the power of Rome was attended with some beneficial consequences to mankind; and the same freedom of intercourse which extended the vices diffused likewise the improvements of social life. In the more remote ages of antiquity, the world was unequally divided. The East was in the immemorial possession of arts and luxury; whilst the West was inhabited by rude and warlike Barbarians who either disdained agriculture or to whom it was totally unknown. Under the protection of an established government, the productions of happier climates and the industry of more civilized nations were gradually introduced into the western countries of Europe; and the natives were encouraged, by an open and profitable commerce, to multiply the former, as well as to improve the latter. It would be almost impossible to enumerate all the articles, either of the animal or the vegetable reign, which were successively imported into Europe from Asia and Egypt. . . . To all these [agricultural] improvements may be added an assiduous attention to mines and fisheries, which, by employing a multitude of laborious hands, serve to increase the pleasures of the rich and the subsistence of the poor. The elegant treatise of Columella describes the advanced state of the Spanish husbandry under the reign of Tiberius; and it may be observed that those famines, which so frequently afflicted the infant republic were seldom or never experienced by the extensive empire of Rome. The accidental scarcity in any single province was immediately relieved by the plenty of its more fortunate neighbors.

Agriculture is the foundation of manufactures; since the productions of nature are the materials of art. Under the Roman empire, the labor of an industrious and ingenious people was variously, but incessantly, employed in the service of the rich. In their dress, their table, their houses, and their furniture, the favorites of fortune united every refinement of conveniency, of elegance, and of splendor, whatever could soothe their pride or gratify their sensuality. Such refinements, under the odious name of luxury, have been severely arraigned by the moralists of every age; and it might perhaps be more conducive to the virtue, as well as happiness, of mankind, if all possessed the necessaries, and none the superfluities, of life. But in the present imperfect condition of society, luxury, though it may proceed from vice or folly, seems to be the only means that can correct the unequal distribution of property. The diligent mechanic and the skillful artist who have obtained no share in the division of the earth receive a voluntary tax from the possessors of land; and the latter are prompted, by a sense of interest, to improve those estates with whose produce they may purchase additional pleasures. This operation, the particular effects of which are felt in every society, acted with much more diffusive energy in the Roman world. The provinces would soon have been exhausted of their wealth if the manufactures and commerce of luxury had not insensibly restored to the industrious subjects the sums which were exacted from them by the arms and authority of Rome. As long as the circulation was confined within the bounds of the empire, it impressed the political machine with a new degree of activity, and its consequences, sometimes beneficial, could never become pernicious.

But it is no easy task to confine luxury within the limits of an empire. The most remote countries of the ancient world were ransacked to supply the pomp and delicacy of Rome. The forests of Scythia afforded some valuable furs. Amber was brought over land from the shores of the Baltic to the Danube; and the Barbarians were astonished at the price which they received in exchange for so useless a commodity. There was a considerable demand for Babylonian carpets and other manufactures of the East; but the most important and unpopular branch of foreign trade was carried on with Arabia and India. . . . As the natives of Arabia and India were contented with the productions and manufactures of their own country, silver, on the side of the Romans, was the principal, if not the only, instrument of commerce. It was a complaint worthy of the gravity of the senate that, in the purchase of female ornaments, the wealth of the state was irrecoverably given away to foreign and hostile nations. The annual loss is computed, by a writer of an inquisitive but censorious temper, at upwards of eight hundred thousand pounds sterling. Such was the style of discontent, brooding over the dark prospect of approaching poverty. And yet, if we compare the proportion between gold and silver as it stood in the time of Pliny and as it was fixed in the reign of Constantine, we shall discover within that period a very considerable increase. There is not the least reason to suppose that gold was become more scarce; it is therefore evident that silver was grown more common; that whatever might be the amount of the Indian and Arabian exports, they were far from exhausting the wealth of the Roman world; and that the produce of the mines abundantly supplied the demands of commerce.

Notwithstanding the propensity of mankind to exalt the past and to depreciate the present, the tranquil and prosperous state of the empire was warmly felt, and honestly confessed, by the provincials as well as Romans. "They acknowledged that the true principles of social life, laws, agriculture, and science, which had been first invented by the wisdom of Athens, were now firmly established by the power of Rome, under whose auspicious influence the fiercest Barbarians were united by an equal government and common language. They affirm that with the improvement of arts, the human species were visibly multiplied. They celebrate the increasing splendor of the cities, the beautiful face of the country, cultivated and adorned like an immense garden; and the long festival of peace which was enjoyed by so many nations, forgetful of the ancient animosities, and delivered from the apprehension of future danger." Whatever suspicions may be suggested by the air of rhetoric and declamation which seems to prevail in these passages, the substance of them is perfectly agreeable to historic truth.

It was scarcely possible that the eyes of contemporaries should discover in the public felicity the latent causes of decay and corruption. This long peace, and the uniform government of the Romans, introduced a slow and secret poison into the vitals of the empire. The minds of men were gradually reduced to the same level, the fire of genius was extinguished, and even the military spirit evaporated. The natives of Europe were brave and robust. Spain, Gaul, Britain, and Illyricum supplied the legions with excellent soldiers, and constituted the real strength of the monarchy. Their personal valor remained, but they no longer possessed that public courage which is nourished by the love of independence, the sense of national honor, the presence of danger, and the habit of command. They received laws and governors from the will of their sovereign, and trusted for their defense to a mercenary army. The posterity of their boldest leaders was contented with the rank of citizens and subjects. The most aspiring spirits resorted to the court or standard of the emperors; and the deserted provinces, deprived of political strength or union, insensibly sunk into the languid indifference of private life.

The love of letters, almost inseparable from peace and refinement, was fashionable among the subjects of Hadrian and the Antonines, who were themselves men of learning and curiosity. It was diffused over the whole extent of their empire; the most northern tribes of Britons had acquired a taste for rhetoric; Homer as well as Virgil were transcribed and studied on the banks of the Rhine and Danube; and the most liberal rewards sought out the faintest glimmerings of literary merit. The sciences of physic and astronomy were successfully cultivated by the Greeks; the observations of Ptolemy and the writings of Galen are studied by those who have improved their discoveries and corrected their errors; but if we except the inimitable Lucian, this age of indolence passed away without having produced a single writer of original genius, or who excelled in the arts of elegant composition. The authority of Plato and Aristotle, of Zeno and Epicurus, still reigned in the schools; and their systems, transmitted with blind deference from one generation of disciples to another, precluded every generous attempt to exercise the powers or enlarge the limits of the human mind. The beauties of the poets and orators, instead of kindling a fire like their own, inspired only cold and servile imitations: or if any ventured to deviate from those models, they deviated at the same time from good sense and propriety. On the revival of letters, the youthful vigor of the imagination after a long repose, national emulation, a new religion, new languages, and a new world, called forth the genius of Europe. But the provincials of Rome, trained by a uniform artificial foreign education, were engaged in a very unequal competition with those bold ancients who, by expressing their genuine feelings in their native tongue, had already occupied every place of honor. The name of Poet was almost forgotten; that of Orator was usurped by the sophists. A cloud of critics, of compilers, of commentators, darkened the face of learning, and the decline of genius was soon followed by the corruption of taste.

The sublime Longinus, who, in somewhat a later period and in the court of a Syrian queen preserved the spirit of ancient Athens, observes and laments this degeneracy of his contemporaries, which debased their sentiments, enervated their courage, and depressed their talents. "In the same manner," says he, "as some children always remain pygmies, whose infant limbs have been too closely confined, thus our tender minds, fettered by the prejudices and habits of a just servitude, are unable to expand themselves, or to attain that well-proportioned greatness which we admire in the ancients; who, living under a popular government, wrote with the same freedom as they acted." This diminutive stature of mankind, if we pursue the metaphor, was daily sinking below the old standard, and the Roman world was indeed peopled by a race of pygmies; when the fierce giants of the North broke in, and mended the puny breed. They restored a manly spirit of freedom; and after the revolution of ten centuries, freedom became the happy parent of taste and science.

CHAPTER III

THE CONSTITUTION IN THE AGE OF THE ANTONINES

Of the constitution of the Roman empire, in the age of the Antonines.

The obvious definition of a monarchy seems to be that of a state in which a single person, by whatsoever name he may be distinguished, is entrusted with the execution of the laws, the management of the revenue, and the command of the army. But unless public liberty is protected by intrepid and vigilant guardians, the authority of so formidable a magistrate will soon degenerate into despotism. The influence of the clergy, in an age of superstition, might be usefully employed to assert the rights of mankind; but so intimate is the connection between the throne and the altar that the banner of the church has very seldom been seen on the side of the people. A martial nobility and stubborn commons, possessed of arms, tenacious of property, and collected into constitutional assemblies, form the only balance capable of preserving a free constitution against enterprises of an aspiring prince.

Every barrier of the Roman constitution had been leveled by the vast ambition of the dictator; every fence had been extirpated by the cruel hand of the triumvir. After the victory of Actium, the fate of the Roman world depended on the will of Octavianus, surnamed Caesar by his uncle's adoption, and afterwards Augustus [i.e., "the divinely blessed" or "the holy one"] by the flattery of the senate. The conqueror was at the head of forty-four veteran legions, conscious of their own strength and of the weakness of the constitution, habituated, during twenty years' civil war, to every act of blood and violence, and passionately devoted to the house of Caesar, from whence alone they had received and expected the most lavish rewards. The provinces, long oppressed by the ministers of the republic, sighed for the government of a single person who would be the master, not the accomplice, of those petty tyrants. The people of Rome, viewing, with a secret pleasure, the humiliation of the aristocracy, demanded only bread and public shows; and were supplied with both by the liberal hand of Augustus. The rich and polite Italians, who had almost universally embraced the philosophy of Epicurus, enjoyed the present blessings of ease and tranquility, and suffered not the pleasing dream to be interrupted by the memory of their old tumultuous freedom. With its power, the senate had lost its dignity; many of the most noble families were extinct. The republicans of spirit and ability had perished in the field of battle, or in the proscription [extrajudicial executions of political opponents]. The door of the assembly had been designedly left open for a mixed multitude of more than a thousand persons, who reflected disgrace upon their rank instead of deriving honor from it.

The reformation of the senate was one of the first steps in which Augustus laid aside the tyrant and professed himself the father of his country. He was elected censor; and, in concert with his faithful Agrippa, he examined the list of the senators, expelled a few members whose vices or whose obstinacy required a public example, persuaded near two hundred to prevent the shame of an expulsion by a voluntary retreat, raised the [financial] qualification of a senator . . . , created a sufficient number of patrician families, and accepted for himself the honorable title of Prince of the Senate, which had always been bestowed by the censors on the citizen the most eminent for his honors and services. But whilst he thus restored the dignity he destroyed the independence of the senate. The principles of a free constitution are irrecoverably lost when the legislative power is nominated by the executive.

Before an assembly thus modeled and prepared, Augustus pronounced a studied oration which displayed his patriotism and disguised his ambition. "He lamented, yet excused, his past conduct. Filial piety had required at his hands the revenge of his father's murder; the humanity of his own nature had sometimes given way to the stern laws of necessity, and to a forced connection with two unworthy colleagues: as long as Antony lived, the republic forbade him to abandon her to a degenerate Roman, and a Barbarian queen. He was now at liberty to satisfy his duty and his inclination. He solemnly restored the senate and people to all their ancient rights; and wished only to mingle with the crowd of his fellow-citizens, and to share the blessings which he had obtained for his country."

It would require the pen of [Rome's greatest historian] Tacitus (if Tacitus had assisted at this assembly) to describe the various emotions of the senate, those that were suppressed and those that were affected. It was dangerous to trust the sincerity of Augustus; to seem to distrust it was still more dangerous. The respective advantages of monarchy and a republic have often divided speculative inquirers; the present greatness of the Roman state, the corruption of manners, and the license of the soldiers supplied new arguments to the advocates of monarchy; and these general views of government were again warped by the hopes and fears of each individual. Amidst this confusion of sentiments, the answer of the senate was unanimous and decisive. They refused to accept the resignation of Augustus; they conjured him not to desert the republic which he had saved. After a decent resistance, the crafty tyrant submitted to the orders of the senate; and consented to receive the government of the provinces, and the general command of the Roman armies, under the well-known names of PROCONSUL and IMPERATOR. But he would receive them only for ten years. Even before the expiration of that period, he hoped that the wounds of civil discord would be completely healed and that the republic, restored to its pristine health and vigor, would no longer require the dangerous interposition of so extraordinary a magistrate. The memory of this comedy, repeated several times during the life of Augustus, was preserved to the last ages of the empire by the peculiar pomp with which the perpetual monarchs of Rome always solemnized the tenth years of their reign.

Without any violation of the principles of the constitution, the general of the Roman armies might receive and exercise an authority almost despotic over the soldiers, the enemies, and the subjects of the republic. With regard to the soldiers, the jealousy of freedom had, even from the earliest ages of Rome, given way to the hopes of conquest and a just sense of military discipline. The dictator, or consul, had a right to command the service of the Roman youth, and to punish an obstinate or cowardly disobedience by the most severe and ignominious penalties, by striking the offender out of the list of citizens, by confiscating his property, and by selling his person into slavery. The most sacred rights of freedom, confirmed by the Porcian and Sempronian laws, were suspended by the military engagement. In his camp the general exercised an absolute power of life and death; his jurisdiction was not confined by any forms of trial or rules of proceeding, and the execution of the sentence was immediate and without appeal. The choice of the enemies of Rome was regularly decided by the legislative authority. The most important resolutions of peace and war were seriously debated in the senate and solemnly ratified by the people. But when the arms of the legions were carried to a great distance from Italy, the generals assumed the liberty of directing them against whatever people, and in whatever manner, they judged most advantageous for the public service. It was from the success, not from the justice, of their enterprises that they expected the honors of a triumph. In the use of victory, especially after they were no longer controlled by the commissioners of the senate, they exercised the most unbounded despotism. When Pompey commanded in the East, he rewarded his soldiers and allies, dethroned princes, divided kingdoms, founded colonies, and distributed the treasures of Mithridates. On his return to Rome, he obtained, by a single act of the senate and people, the universal ratification of all his proceedings. Such was the power over the soldiers, and over the enemies of Rome, which was either granted to or assumed by the generals of the republic. They were, at the same time, the governors, or rather monarchs, of the conquered provinces, united the civil with the military character, administered justice as well as the finances, and exercised both the executive and legislative power of the state.

From what has already been observed in the first chapter of this work, some notion may be formed of the armies and provinces thus entrusted to the ruling hand of Augustus. But as it was impossible that he could personally command the regions of so many distant frontiers, he was indulged by the senate, as Pompey had already been, in the permission of devolving the execution of his great office on a sufficient number of lieutenants. In rank and authority these officers seemed not inferior to the ancient proconsuls; but their station was dependent and precarious. They received and held their commissions at the will of a superior, to whose *auspicious* influence the merit of their action was legally attributed. They were the representatives of the emperor. The emperor alone was the general of the republic, and his jurisdiction, civil as well as military, extended over all the conquests of Rome. It was some satisfaction, however, to the senate that he always delegated his power to the members of their body. The imperial lieutenants were of consular or praetorian dignity; the legions were commanded by senators, and the praefecture of Egypt was the only important trust committed to a Roman knight.

Within six days after Augustus had been compelled to accept so very liberal a grant, he resolved to gratify the pride of the senate by an easy sacrifice. He represented to them that they had enlarged his powers even beyond that degree which might be required by the melancholy condition of the times. They had not permitted him to refuse the laborious command of the armies and the frontiers; but he must insist on being allowed to restore the more peaceful and secure provinces to the mild administration of the civil magistrate. In the division of the provinces, Augustus provided for his own power and for the dignity of the republic. The proconsuls of the senate, particularly those of Asia, Greece, and Africa, enjoyed a more honorable character than the lieutenants of the emperor, who commanded in Gaul or Syria. The former were attended by lictors, the latter by soldiers. A law was passed that wherever the emperor was present, his extraordinary commission should supersede the ordinary jurisdiction of the governor; a custom was introduced that the new conquests belonged to the Imperial portion; and it was soon discovered that the authority of the *Prince,* the favorite epithet of Augustus, was the same in every part of the empire.

In return for this imaginary concession, Augustus obtained an important privilege which rendered him master of Rome and Italy. By a dangerous exception to the ancient maxims, he was authorized to preserve his military command, supported by a numerous body of guards, even in time of peace and in the heart of the capital. His command, indeed, was confined to those citizens who were engaged in the service by the military oath; but such was the propensity of the Romans to servitude that the oath was voluntarily taken by the magistrates, the senators, and the equestrian order, till the homage of flattery was insensibly converted into an annual and solemn protestation of fidelity.

Although Augustus considered a military force as the firmest foundation, he wisely rejected it as a very odious instrument of government. It was more agreeable to his temper, as well as to his policy, to reign under the venerable names of ancient magistracy, and artfully to collect in his own person all the scattered rays of civil jurisdiction. With this view, he permitted the senate to confer upon him, for his life, the powers of the consular and tribunician offices, which were, in the

same manner, continued to all his successors. The consuls had succeeded to the kings of Rome, and represented the dignity of the state.
They superintended the ceremonies of religion, levied and commanded
the legions, gave audience to foreign ambassadors, and presided in the
assemblies both of the senate and people. The general control of the
finances was entrusted to their care; and though they seldom had leisure
to administer justice in person, they were considered as the supreme
guardians of law, equity, and the public peace. Such was their ordinary
jurisdiction; but whenever the senate empowered the first magistrate
to consult the safety of the commonwealth, he was raised by that decree above the laws, and exercised, in the defense of liberty, a temporary despotism. The character of the tribunes was in every respect
different from that of the consuls. The appearance of the former was
modest and humble; but their persons were sacred and inviolable.
Their force was suited rather for opposition than for action. They were
instituted to defend the oppressed, to pardon offenses, to arraign the
enemies of the people, and, when they judged it necessary, to stop, by
a single word, the whole machine of government. As long as the republic subsisted, the dangerous influence which either the consul or
the tribune might derive from their respective jurisdiction was diminished by several important restrictions. Their authority expired with
the year in which they were elected; the former office was divided between two, the latter among ten persons; and, as both in their private
and public interest they were averse to each other, their mutual conflicts contributed, for the most part, to strengthen rather than to destroy the balance of the constitution. But when the consular and
tribunician powers were united, when they were vested for life in a
single person, when the general of the army was, at the same time, the
minister of the senate and the representative of the Roman people, it
was impossible to resist the exercise, nor was it easy to define the limits, of his Imperial prerogative.

To these accumulated honors, the policy of Augustus soon added
the splendid as well as important dignities of supreme pontiff and of
censor. By the former he acquired the management of the religion, and
by the latter a legal inspection over the manners and fortunes of the
Roman people. If so many distinct and independent powers did not
exactly unite with each other, the complaisance of the senate was prepared to supply every deficiency by the most ample and extraordinary

concessions. The emperors, as the first ministers of the republic, were exempted from the obligation and penalty of many inconvenient laws: they were authorized to convoke the senate, to make several motions in the same day, to recommend candidates for the honors of the state, to enlarge the bounds of the city, to employ the revenue at their discretion, to declare peace and war, to ratify treaties; and by a most comprehensive clause, they were empowered to execute whatsoever they should judge advantageous to the empire and agreeable to the majesty of things private or public, human or divine.

When all the various powers of executive government were committed to the *Imperial magistrate*, the ordinary magistrates of the commonwealth languished in obscurity, without vigor and almost without business. The names and forms of the ancient administration were preserved by Augustus with the most anxious care. The usual number of consuls, praetors, and tribunes were annually invested with their respective ensigns of office, and continued to discharge some of their least important functions. Those honors still attracted the vain ambition of the Romans; and the emperors themselves, though invested for life with the powers of the consulship, frequently aspired to the title of that annual dignity which they condescended to share with the most illustrious of their fellow-citizens. In the election of these magistrates, the people during the reign of Augustus were permitted to expose all the inconveniences of a wild democracy. That artful prince, instead of discovering the least symptom of impatience, humbly solicited their suffrages for himself or his friends, and scrupulously practiced all the duties of an ordinary candidate. But we may venture to ascribe to his councils the first measure of the succeeding reign, by which the elections were transferred to the senate. The assemblies of the people were forever abolished, and the emperors were delivered from a dangerous multitude who, without restoring liberty, might have disturbed and perhaps endangered the established government.

By declaring themselves the protectors of the people, Marius and Caesar had subverted the constitution of their country. But as soon as the senate had been humbled and disarmed, such an assembly, consisting of five or six hundred persons, was found a much more tractable and useful instrument of dominion. It was on the dignity of the senate that Augustus and his successors founded their new empire; and they affected, on every occasion, to adopt the language and principles of patricians. In the administration of their own powers, they frequently consulted the great national council, and *seemed* to refer to its decision the most important concerns of peace and war. Rome, Italy, and the internal provinces were subject to the immediate jurisdiction of the senate. With regard to civil objects, it was the supreme court of appeal; with regard to criminal matters, a tribunal constituted for the trial of all offenses that were committed by men in any public station, or that affected the peace and majesty of the Roman people. The exercise of the judicial power became the most frequent and serious occupation of the senate; and the important causes that were pleaded before them afforded a last refuge to the spirit of ancient eloquence. As a council of state, and as a court of justice, the senate possessed very considerable prerogatives; but in its legislative capacity, in which it was supposed virtually to represent the people, the rights of sovereignty were acknowledged to reside in that assembly. Every power was derived from their authority, every law was ratified by their sanction. Their regular meetings were held on three stated days in every month, the Calends, the Nones, and the Ides. The debates were conducted with decent freedom; and the emperors themselves, who gloried in the name of senators, sat, voted, and divided with their equals.

To resume, in a few words, the system of the Imperial government, as it was instituted by Augustus and maintained by those princes who understood their own interest and that of the people, it may be defined an absolute monarchy disguised by the forms of a commonwealth. The masters of the Roman world surrounded their throne with darkness, concealed their irresistible strength, and humbly professed themselves the accountable ministers of the senate, whose supreme decrees they dictated and obeyed.

The face of the court corresponded with the forms of the administration. The emperors, if we except those tyrants whose capricious folly violated every law of nature and decency, disdained that pomp and ceremony which might offend their countrymen but could add nothing to their real power. In all the offices of life, they affected to confound themselves with their subjects, and maintained with them an equal intercourse of visits and entertainments. Their habit, their palace, their table, were suited only to the rank of an opulent senator. Their family, however numerous or splendid, was composed entirely of their domestic slaves and freedmen. Augustus or Trajan would have blushed at employing the meanest of the Romans in those menial offices, which, in the household and bedchamber of a limited monarch, are so eagerly solicited by the proudest nobles of Britain.

The deification of the emperors is the only instance in which they departed from their accustomed prudence and modesty. The Asiatic Greeks were the first inventors, the successors of Alexander the first objects, of this servile and impious mode of adulation. It was easily transferred from the kings to the governors of Asia; and the Roman magistrates very frequently were adored as provincial deities, with the pomp of altars and temples, of festivals and sacrifices. It was natural that the emperors should not refuse what the proconsuls had accepted; and the divine honors which both the one and the other received from the provinces attested rather the despotism than the servitude of Rome. But the conquerors soon imitated the vanquished nations in the arts of flattery; and the imperious spirit of the first Caesar too easily consented to assume, during his lifetime, a place among the tutelar deities of Rome. The milder temper of his successor declined so dangerous an ambition, which was never afterwards revived, except by the madness of Caligula and Domitian. Augustus permitted indeed some of the provincial cities to erect temples to his honor, on condition that they should associate the worship of Rome with that of the sovereign; he tolerated private superstition of which he might be the object; but he contented himself with being revered by the senate and the people in his human character, and wisely left to his successor the care of his public deification. A regular custom was introduced that on the decease of every emperor who had neither lived nor died like a tyrant, the senate by a solemn decree should place him in the number of the gods: and the ceremonies of his apotheosis were blended with those of his funeral. This legal and, as it should seem, injudicious profanation, so abhorrent to our stricter principles, was received with a very faint murmur by the easy nature of Polytheism; but it was received as an institution not of religion but of policy. We should disgrace the virtues of the Antonines by comparing them with the vices of Hercules or Jupiter. Even the characters of Caesar or Augustus were far superior to those of the popular deities. But it was the misfortune of the former to live in an enlightened age, and their actions were too faithfully recorded to admit of such a mixture of fable and mystery as the devotion of the vulgar requires. As soon as their divinity was established by law, it sunk into oblivion, without contributing either to their own fame or to the dignity of succeeding princes.

In the consideration of the Imperial government, we have frequently mentioned the artful founder under his well-known title of Augustus, which was not, however, conferred upon him till the edifice was almost completed. The obscure name of Octavianus he derived from a mean family in the little town of Aricia. It was stained with the blood of the proscription; and he was desirous, had it been possible, to erase all memory of his former life. The illustrious surname of Caesar he had assumed as the adopted son of the dictator: but he had too much good sense either to hope to be confounded, or to wish to be compared with, that extraordinary man. It was proposed in the senate to dignify their minister with a new appellation [January 16, 27 B.C.]; and after a serious discussion, that of Augustus was chosen, among several others, as being the most expressive of the character of peace and sanctity which he uniformly affected. *Augustus* was therefore a personal, *Caesar* a family distinction. The former should naturally have expired with the prince on whom it was bestowed; and, however the latter was diffused by adoption and female alliance, Nero was the last prince who could allege any hereditary claim to the honors of the Julian line. But at the time of his death, the practice of a century had inseparably connected those appellations with the Imperial dignity, and they have been preserved by a long succession of emperors, Romans, Greeks, Franks, and Germans, from the fall of the republic to the present time. A distinction was, however, soon introduced. The sacred title of Augustus was always reserved for the monarch, whilst the name of Caesar was more freely communicated to his relations; and from the reign of Hadrian at least, was appropriated to the second person in the state, who was considered as the presumptive heir of the empire.

The tender respect of Augustus for a free constitution which he had destroyed can only be explained by an attentive consideration of the character of that subtle tyrant. A cool head, an unfeeling heart, and a cowardly disposition prompted him at the age of nineteen to assume the mask of hypocrisy, which he never afterwards laid aside. With the same hand, and probably with the same temper, he signed the proscription of Cicero and the pardon of Cinna. His virtues, and even his vices, were artificial; and according to the various dictates of his interest, he was at first the enemy and at last the father of the Roman world.

When he framed the artful system of the Imperial authority, his moderation was inspired by his fears. He wished to deceive the people by an image of civil liberty, and the armies by an image of civil government.

I. The death of Caesar was ever before his eyes. He had lavished wealth and honors on his adherents; but the most favored friends of his uncle were in the number of the conspirators. The fidelity of the legions might defend his authority against open rebellion; but their vigilance could not secure his person from the dagger of a determined republican; and the Romans, who revered the memory of Brutus, would applaud the imitation of his virtue. Caesar had provoked his fate as much as by the ostentation of his power as by his power itself. The consul or the tribune might have reigned in peace. The title of king had armed the Romans against his life. Augustus was sensible that mankind is governed by names; nor was he deceived in his expectation that the senate and people would submit to slavery, provided they were respectfully assured that they still enjoyed their ancient freedom. A feeble senate and enervated people cheerfully acquiesced in the pleasing illusion, as long as it was supported by the virtue, or even by the prudence, of the successors of Augustus. It was a motive of self-preservation, not a principle of liberty, that animated the conspirators against Caligula, Nero, and Domitian. They attacked the person of the tyrant without aiming their blow at the authority of the emperor.

There appears, indeed, *one* memorable occasion in which the senate, after seventy years of patience, made an ineffectual attempt to reassume its long-forgotten rights. When the throne was vacant by the murder of Caligula, the consuls convoked that assembly in the Capitol, condemned the memory of the Caesars, gave the watchword *liberty* to the few cohorts who faintly adhered to their standard, and during eight-and-forty hours acted as the independent chiefs of a free commonwealth. But while they deliberated, the Praetorian guards had resolved. The stupid Claudius, brother of Germanicus, was already in their camp, invested with the Imperial purple and prepared to support his election by arms. The dream of liberty was at an end; and the senate awoke to all the horrors of inevitable servitude. Deserted by the people and threatened by a military force, that feeble assembly was compelled to ratify the choice of the Praetorians and to embrace the benefit of an amnesty, which Claudius had the prudence to offer and the generosity to observe.

II. The insolence of the armies inspired Augustus with fears of a still more alarming nature. The despair of the citizens could only attempt what the power of the soldiers was, at any time, able to execute. How precarious was his own authority over men whom he had taught to violate every social duty! He had heard their seditious clamors; he dreaded their calmer moments of reflection. One revolution had been purchased by immense rewards; but a second revolution might double those rewards. The troops professed the fondest attachment to the house of Caesar; but the attachments of the multitude are capricious and inconstant. Augustus summoned to his aid whatever remained in those fierce minds of Roman prejudices; enforced the rigor of discipline by the sanction of law; and, interposing the majesty of the senate between the emperor and the army, boldly claimed their allegiance as the first magistrate of the republic.

During a long period of two hundred and twenty years from the establishment of this artful system to the death of Commodus, the dangers inherent to a military government were, in a great measure, suspended. The soldiers were seldom roused to that fatal sense of their own strength, and of the weakness of the civil authority, which was, before and afterwards, productive of such dreadful calamities. Caligula and Domitian were assassinated in their palace by their own domestics: the convulsions which agitated Rome on the death of the former were confined to the walls of the city. But Nero involved the whole empire in his ruin. In the space of eighteen months, four princes perished by the sword; and the Roman world was shaken by the fury of the contending armies. Excepting only this short though violent eruption of military license, the two centuries from Augustus to Commodus passed away unstained with civil blood, and undisturbed by revolutions. The emperor was elected by *the authority of the senate,* and *the consent of the soldiers.* The legions respected their oath of fidelity; and it requires a minute inspection of the Roman annals to discover three inconsiderable rebellions, which were all suppressed in a few months, and without even the hazard of a battle.

In elective monarchies, the vacancy of the throne is a moment big with danger and mischief. The Roman emperors, desirous to spare the legions that interval of suspense and the temptation of an irregular choice, invested their designed successor with so large a share of present power as should enable him, after their decease, to assume the remainder without suffering the empire to perceive the change of masters. Thus Augustus, after all his fairer prospects had been snatched from him by untimely deaths, rested his last hopes on Tiberius, obtained for his adopted son the censorial and tribunician powers, and dictated a law by which the future prince was invested with an authority equal to his own over the provinces and the armies. Thus Vespasian subdued the generous mind of his eldest son. Titus was adored by the Eastern legions, which, under his command, had recently achieved the conquest of Judaea. His power was dreaded, and, as his virtues were clouded by the intemperance of youth, his designs were suspected. Instead of listening to such unworthy suspicions, the prudent monarch associated Titus to the full powers of the Imperial dignity; and the grateful son ever approved himself the humble and faithful minister of so indulgent a father.

The good sense of Vespasian engaged him indeed to embrace every measure that might confirm his recent and precarious elevation. The military oath, and the fidelity of the troops, had been consecrated, by the habits of a hundred years, to the name and family of the Caesars; and although that family had been continued only by the fictitious rite of adoption, the Romans still revered, in the person of Nero, the grandson of Germanicus and the lineal successor of Augustus. It was not without reluctance and remorse that the Praetorian guards had been persuaded to abandon the cause of the tyrant. The rapid downfall of Galba, Otho, and Vitellius taught the armies to consider the emperors as the creatures of *their* will and the instruments of *their* license. The birth of Vespasian was mean: his grandfather had been a private soldier, his father a petty officer of the revenue; his own merit had raised him, in an advanced age, to the empire; but his merit was rather useful than shining, and his virtues were disgraced by a strict and even sordid parsimony. Such a prince consulted his true interest by the association of a son whose more splendid and amiable character might turn the public attention from the obscure origin to the future glories of the Flavian house. Under the mild administration of Titus, the Roman world enjoyed a transient felicity, and his beloved memory served to protect, above fifteen years, the vices of his brother Domitian.

Nerva had scarcely accepted the purple from the assassins of Domitian [A.D. 96] before he discovered that his feeble age was unable to stem the torrent of public disorders which had multiplied under the long tyranny of his predecessor. His mild disposition was respected by the good; but the degenerate Romans required a more vigorous character, whose justice should strike terror into the guilty. Though he had several relations, he fixed his choice on a stranger. He adopted Trajan, then about forty years of age, and who commanded a powerful army in the Lower Germany; and immediately, by a decree of the senate, declared him his colleague and successor in the empire [A.D. 98]. It is sincerely to be lamented that whilst we are fatigued with the disgustful relation of Nero's crimes and follies, we are reduced to collect the actions of Trajan from the glimmerings of an abridgment, or the doubtful light of a panegyric. There remains, however, one panegyric far removed beyond the suspicion of flattery. Above two hundred and fifty years after the death of Trajan, the senate, in pouring out the customary acclamations on the accession of a new emperor, wished that he might surpass the felicity of Augustus and the virtue of Trajan.

We may readily believe that the father of his country hesitated whether he ought to entrust the various and doubtful character of his kinsman Hadrian with sovereign power [A.D. 117]. In his last moments, the arts of the empress Plotina either fixed the irresolution of Trajan or boldly supposed a fictitious adoption, the truth of which could not be safely disputed, and Hadrian was peaceably acknowledged as his lawful successor. Under his reign, as has been already mentioned, the empire flourished in peace and prosperity. He encouraged the arts, reformed the laws, asserted military discipline, and visited all his provinces in person. His vast and active genius was equally suited to the most enlarged views and the minute details of civil policy. But the ruling passions of his soul were curiosity and vanity. As they prevailed, and as they were attracted by different objects, Hadrian was, by turns, an excellent prince, a ridiculous sophist, and a jealous tyrant. The general tenor of his conduct deserved praise for its equity and moderation. Yet in the first days of his reign, he put to death four consular senators, his personal enemies and men who had been judged worthy of empire; and the tediousness of a painful illness rendered him at last peevish and cruel. The senate doubted whether they should pronounce him a god or a tyrant; and the honors decreed to his memory were granted to the prayers of the pious Antoninus.

The caprice of Hadrian influenced his choice of a successor. After revolving in his mind several men of distinguished merit whom he es-

teemed and hated, he adopted Aelius Verus, a gay and voluptuous nobleman, recommended by uncommon beauty to the lover of Antinous.
But whilst Hadrian was delighting himself with his own applause and
the acclamations of the soldiers, whose consent had been secured by
an immense donative, the new Caesar was ravished from his embraces
by an untimely death. He left only one son. Hadrian commended the
boy to the gratitude of the Antonines. He was adopted by Pius; and, on
the accession of Marcus, was invested with an equal share of sovereign
power. Among the many vices of this younger Verus, he possessed one
virtue: a dutiful reverence for his wiser colleague, to whom he willingly abandoned the ruder cares of empire. The philosophic emperor
dissembled his follies, lamented his early death, and cast a decent veil
over his memory.

As soon as Hadrian's passion was either gratified or disappointed,
he resolved to deserve the thanks of posterity by placing the most exalted merit on the Roman throne. His discerning eye easily discovered
a senator about fifty years of age, blameless in all the offices of life; and
a youth of about seventeen, whose riper years opened a fair prospect
of every virtue: the elder of these was declared the son and successor
of Hadrian, on condition, however, that he himself should immediately adopt the younger. The two Antonines (for it is of them that we
are now speaking) governed the Roman world forty-two years, with
the same invariable spirit of wisdom and virtue [A.D. 138–180]. Although Pius had two sons, he preferred the welfare of Rome to the interest of his family, gave his daughter Faustina in marriage to young
Marcus, obtained from the senate the tribunician and proconsular
powers, and, with a noble disdain, or rather ignorance, of jealousy, associated him to all the labors of government. Marcus, on the other
hand, revered the character of his benefactor, loved him as a parent,
obeyed him as his sovereign, and, after he was no more, regulated his
own administration by the example and maxims of his predecessor.
Their united reigns are possibly the only period of history in which
the happiness of a great people was the sole object of government.

Titus Antoninus Pius has been justly denominated a second Numa
[the legendary second king of Rome]. The same love of religion, justice, and peace was the distinguishing characteristic of both princes.
But the situation of the latter opened a much larger field for the exercise of those virtues. Numa could only prevent a few neighboring vil-

lages from plundering each other's harvests. Antoninus diffused order and tranquility over the greatest part of the earth. His reign is marked by the rare advantage of furnishing very few materials for history; which is, indeed, little more than the register of the crimes, follies, and misfortunes of mankind. In private life, he was an amiable as well as a good man. The native simplicity of his virtue was a stranger to vanity or affectation. He enjoyed with moderation the conveniences of his fortune and the innocent pleasures of society; and the benevolence of his soul displayed itself in a cheerful serenity of temper.

The virtue of Marcus Aurelius Antoninus was of severer and more laborious kind. It was the well-earned harvest of many a learned conference, of many a patient lecture, and many a midnight lucubration. At the age of twelve years he embraced the rigid system of the Stoics, which taught him to submit his body to his mind, his passions to his reason; to consider virtue as the only good, vice as the only evil, all things external as things indifferent. His meditations, composed in the tumult of the camp, are still extant; and he even condescended to give lessons of philosophy, in a more public manner than was perhaps consistent with the modesty of a sage or the dignity of an emperor. But his life was the noblest commentary on the precepts of Zeno. He was severe to himself, indulgent to the imperfections of others, just and beneficent to all mankind. He regretted that Avidius Cassius, who excited a rebellion in Syria, had disappointed him, by a voluntary death, of the pleasure of converting an enemy into a friend; and he justified the sincerity of that sentiment by moderating the zeal of the senate against the adherents of the traitor. War he detested as the disgrace and calamity of human nature; but when the necessity of a just defense called upon him to take up arms, he readily exposed his person to eight winter campaigns on the frozen banks of the Danube, the severity of which was at last fatal to the weakness of his constitution. His memory was revered by a grateful posterity, and above a century after his death, many persons preserved the image of Marcus Antoninus among those of their household gods.

If a man were called to fix the period in the history of the world during which the condition of the human race was most happy and prosperous, he would, without hesitation, name that which elapsed from the death of Domitian to the accession of Commodus. The vast extent of the Roman empire was governed by absolute power, under the guidance of virtue and wisdom. The armies were restrained by the firm but gentle hand of four successive emperors whose characters and authority commanded involuntary respect. The forms of the civil administration were carefully preserved by Nerva, Trajan, Hadrian, and the Antonines, who delighted in the image of liberty, and were pleased with considering themselves as the accountable ministers of the laws. Such princes deserved the honor of restoring the republic, had the Romans of their days been capable of enjoying a rational freedom.

The labors of these monarchs were overpaid by the immense reward that inseparably waited on their success; by the honest pride of virtue, and by the exquisite delight of beholding the general happiness of which they were the authors. A just but melancholy reflection embittered, however, the noblest of human enjoyments. They must often have recollected the instability of a happiness which depended on the character of a single man. The fatal moment was perhaps approaching when some licentious youth, or some jealous tyrant, would abuse, to the destruction, that absolute power which they had exerted for the benefit of their people. The ideal restraints of the senate and the laws might serve to display the virtues, but could never correct the vices, of the emperor. The military force was a blind and irresistible instrument of oppression; and the corruption of Roman manners would always supply flatterers eager to applaud, and ministers prepared to serve, the fear or the avarice, the lust or the cruelty, of their master.

These gloomy apprehensions had been already justified by the experience of the Romans. The annals of the emperors exhibit a strong and various picture of human nature which we should vainly seek among the mixed and doubtful characters of modern history. In the conduct of those monarchs we may trace the utmost lines of vice and virtue; the most exalted perfection and the meanest degeneracy of our own species. The golden age of Trajan and the Antonines had been preceded by an age of iron. It is almost superfluous to enumerate the unworthy successors of Augustus. Their unparalleled vices, and the splendid theater on which they were acted, have saved them from oblivion. The dark, unrelenting Tiberius, the furious Caligula, the feeble Claudius, the profligate and cruel Nero, the beastly Vitellius, and the timid, inhuman Domitian are condemned to everlasting infamy. During fourscore years (excepting only the short and doubtful respite of Vespasian's reign) Rome groaned beneath an unremitting tyranny, which exterminated the ancient families of the republic and was fatal to almost every virtue and every talent that arose in that unhappy period.

Under the reign of these monsters, the slavery of the Romans was accompanied with two peculiar circumstances, the one occasioned by their former liberty, the other by their extensive conquests, which rendered their condition more completely wretched than that of the victims of tyranny in any other age or country. From these causes were derived, 1. The exquisite sensibility of the sufferers; and, 2. The impossibility of escaping from the hand of the oppressor.

I. When Persia was governed by the descendants of Sefi, a race of princes whose wanton cruelty often stained their divan, their table, and their bed with the blood of their favorites, there is a saying recorded of a young nobleman that he never departed from the sultan's presence without satisfying himself whether his head was still on his shoulders. The experience of every day might almost justify the skepticism of Rustan. Yet the fatal sword, suspended above him by a single thread, seems not to have disturbed the slumbers or interrupted the tranquility of the Persian. The monarch's frown, he well knew, could level him with the dust; but the stroke of lightning or apoplexy might be equally fatal; and it was the part of a wise man to forget the inevitable calamities of human life in the enjoyment of the fleeting hour. He was dignified with the appellation of the king's slave; had, perhaps, been purchased from obscure parents, in a country which he had never known; and was trained up from his infancy in the severe discipline of the seraglio. His name, his wealth, his honors were the gift of a master who might, without injustice, resume what he had bestowed. Rustan's knowledge, if he possessed any, could only serve to confirm his habits by prejudices. His language afforded not words for any form of government except absolute monarchy. The history of the East informed him that such had ever been the condition of mankind. The Koran, and the interpreters of that divine book, inculcated to him that the sultan was the descendant of the prophet, and the vicegerent of heaven; that patience was the first virtue of a Moslem, and unlimited obedience the great duty of a subject.

The minds of the Romans were very differently prepared for slavery. Oppressed beneath the weight of their own corruption and of military violence, they for a long while preserved the sentiments, or at least the ideas, of their free-born ancestors. [Their] education ... was the same as that of Cato and Cicero. From Grecian philosophy, they had imbibed the justest and most liberal notions of the dignity of human nature and the origin of civil society. The history of their own country had taught them to revere a free, a virtuous, and a victorious commonwealth; to abhor the successful crimes of Caesar and Augustus; and inwardly to despise those tyrants whom they adored with the most abject flattery. As magistrates and senators they were admitted into the great council which had once dictated laws to the earth, whose authority was so often prostituted to the vilest purposes of tyranny. Tiberius, and those emperors who adopted his maxims, attempted to disguise their murders by the formalities of justice, and perhaps enjoyed a secret pleasure in rendering the senate their accomplice as well as their victim. By this assembly, the last of the Romans were condemned for imaginary crimes and real virtues. Their infamous accusers assumed the language of independent patriots who arraigned a dangerous citizen before the tribunal of his country; and the public service was rewarded by riches and honors. The servile judges professed to assert the majesty of the commonwealth, violated in the person of its first magistrate, whose clemency they most applauded when they trembled the most at his inexorable and impending cruelty. The tyrant beheld their baseness with just contempt, and encountered their secret sentiments of detestation with sincere and avowed hatred for the whole body of the senate.

II. The division of Europe into a number of independent states, connected, however, with each other by the general resemblance of religion, language, and manners, is productive of the most beneficial consequences to the liberty of mankind. A modern tyrant who should find no resistance either in his own breast or in his people would soon experience a gentle restraint from the example of his equals, the dread of present censure, the advice of his allies, and the apprehension of his enemies. The object of his displeasure, escaping from the narrow limits of his dominions, would easily obtain, in a happier climate, a secure refuge, a new fortune adequate to his merit, the freedom of complaint, and perhaps the means of revenge. But the empire of the Romans filled the world, and when the empire fell into the hands of a single person, the world became a safe and dreary prison for his enemies. The slave of Imperial despotism, whether he was condemned to drag his gilded chain in Rome and the senate or to wear out a life of exile on the barren rock of Seriphus or the frozen bank of the Danube, expected his fate in silent despair. To resist was fatal, and it was impossible to fly. On every side he was encompassed with a vast extent of sea and land which he could never hope to traverse without being discovered, seized, and restored to his irritated master. Beyond the frontiers, his anxious view could discover nothing except the ocean, inhospitable deserts, hostile tribes of Barbarians of fierce manners and unknown language, or dependent kings, who would gladly purchase the emperor's protection by the sacrifice of an obnoxious fugitive. "Wherever you are," said Cicero to the exiled Marcellus, "remember that you are equally within the power of the conqueror."

CHAPTER IV

The Cruelty, Follies, and Murder of Commodus

*The cruelty, follies, and murder of Commodus. • Election of
Pertinax. • His attempts to reform the state. • His assassination by
the Praetorian guards.*

The mildness of Marcus, which the rigid discipline of the Stoics was
unable to eradicate, formed, at the same time, the most amiable and
the only defective part of his character. His excellent understanding
was often deceived by the unsuspecting goodness of his heart. Artful
men who study the passions of princes and conceal their own approached his person in the disguise of philosophic sanctity, and acquired riches and honors by affecting to despise them. His excessive
indulgence to his brother, his wife, and his son exceeded the bounds of
private virtue and became a public injury by the example and consequences of their vices.

Faustina, the daughter of Pius and the wife of Marcus, has been as
much celebrated for her gallantries as for her beauty. The grave simplicity of the philosopher was ill calculated to engage her wanton levity, or to fix that unbounded passion for variety which often discovered
personal merit in the meanest of mankind. The Cupid of the ancients
was, in general, a very sensual deity; and the amours of an empress, as
they exact on her side the plainest advances, are seldom susceptible of
much sentimental delicacy. Marcus was the only man in the empire
who seemed ignorant or insensible of the irregularities of Faustina;
which, according to the prejudices of every age, reflected some disgrace on the injured husband. He promoted several of her lovers to
posts of honor and profit, and, during a connection of thirty years, invariably gave her proofs of the most tender confidence, and of a respect which ended not with her life. In his Meditations, he thanks the
gods who had bestowed on him a wife so faithful, so gentle, and of such
a wonderful simplicity of manners. The obsequious senate, at his
earnest request, declared her a goddess. She was represented in her

temples with the attributes of Juno, Venus, and Ceres; and it was decreed that, on the day of their nuptials, the youth of either sex should pay their vows before the altar of their chaste patroness.

The monstrous vices of the son have cast a shade on the purity of the father's virtues. It has been objected to Marcus that he sacrificed the happiness of millions to a fond partiality for a worthless boy; and that he chose a successor in his own family, rather than in the republic. Nothing, however, was neglected by the anxious father, and by the men of virtue and learning whom he summoned to his assistance, to expand the narrow mind of young Commodus, to correct his growing vices, and to render him worthy of the throne for which he was designed. But the power of instruction is seldom of much efficacy, except in those happy dispositions where it is almost superfluous. The distasteful lesson of a grave philosopher was, in a moment, obliterated by the whisper of a profligate favorite; and Marcus himself blasted the fruits of this labored education by admitting his son, at the age of fourteen or fifteen, to a full participation of the Imperial power. He lived but four years afterwards: but he lived long enough to repent a rash measure which raised the impetuous youth above the restraint of reason and authority.

Most of the crimes which disturb the internal peace of society are produced by the restraints which the necessary but unequal laws of property have imposed on the appetites of mankind, by confining to a few the possession of those objects that are coveted by many. Of all our passions and appetites, the love of power is of the most imperious and unsociable nature, since the pride of one man requires the submission of the multitude. In the tumult of civil discord, the laws of society lose their force, and their place is seldom supplied by those of humanity. The ardor of contention, the pride of victory, the despair of success, the memory of past injuries, and the fear of future dangers, all contribute to inflame the mind, and to silence the voice of pity. From such motives almost every page of history has been stained with civil blood; but these motives will not account for the unprovoked cruelties of Commodus, who had nothing to wish and everything to enjoy. The beloved son of Marcus succeeded to his father amidst the acclamations of the senate and armies [A.D. 180]; and when he ascended the throne, the happy youth saw round him neither competitor to remove nor enemies to punish. In this calm, elevated station, it was surely natural that he should prefer the love of mankind to their detestation, the mild glories of his five predecessors to the ignominious fate of Nero and Domitian.

Yet Commodus was not, as he has been represented, a tiger born with an insatiate thirst of human blood, and capable, from his infancy, of the most inhuman actions. Nature had formed him of a weak rather than a wicked disposition. His simplicity and timidity rendered him the slave of his attendants, who gradually corrupted his mind. His cruelty, which at first obeyed the dictates of others, degenerated into habit, and at length became the ruling passion of his soul.

Upon the death of his father, Commodus found himself embarrassed with the command of a great army and the conduct of a difficult war against the Quadi and Marcomanni. The servile and profligate youths whom Marcus had banished soon regained their station and influence about the new emperor. They exaggerated the hardships and dangers of a campaign in the wild countries beyond the Danube; and they assured the indolent prince that the terror of his name and the arms of his lieutenants would be sufficient to complete the conquest of the dismayed Barbarians, or to impose such conditions as were more advantageous than any conquest. By a dexterous application to his sensual appetites, they compared the tranquility, the splendor, the refined pleasures of Rome with the tumult of a Pannonian camp, which afforded neither leisure nor materials for luxury. Commodus listened to the pleasing advice; but whilst he hesitated between his own inclination and the awe which he still retained for his father's counselors, the summer insensibly elapsed, and his triumphal entry into the capital was deferred till the autumn. His graceful person, popular address, and imagined virtues attracted the public favor; the honorable peace which he had recently granted to the Barbarians diffused a universal joy; his impatience to revisit Rome was fondly ascribed to the love of his country; and his dissolute course of amusements was faintly condemned in a prince of nineteen years of age.

During the three first years of his reign, the forms and even the spirit of the old administration were maintained by those faithful counselors to whom Marcus had recommended his son, and for whose wisdom and integrity Commodus still entertained a reluctant esteem. The young prince and his profligate favorites reveled in all the license of sovereign power; but his hands were yet unstained with blood; and he had even displayed a generosity of sentiment which might perhaps have ripened into solid virtue. A fatal incident decided his fluctuating character.

One evening, as the emperor was returning to the palace through a dark and narrow portico in the amphitheater, an assassin, who waited his passage, rushed upon him with a drawn sword, loudly exclaiming, *"The senate sends you this"* [A.D. 183]. The menace prevented the deed; the assassin was seized by the guards and immediately revealed the authors of the conspiracy. It had been formed not in the state, but within the walls of the palace. Lucilla, the emperor's sister and widow of Lucius Verus, impatient of the second rank and jealous of the reigning empress, had armed the murderer against her brother's life. She had not ventured to communicate the black design to her second husband, Claudius Pompeianus, a senator of distinguished merit and unshaken loyalty; but among the crowd of her lovers (for she imitated the manners of Faustina) she found men of desperate fortunes and wild ambition who were prepared to serve her more violent as well as her tender passions. The conspirators experienced the rigor of justice, and the abandoned princess was punished, first with exile and afterwards with death.

But the words of the assassin sunk deep into the mind of Commodus, and left an indelible impression of fear and hatred against the whole body of the senate. Those whom he had dreaded as importunate ministers, he now suspected as secret enemies. The Delators [informers], a race of men discouraged and almost extinguished under the former reigns, again became formidable as soon as they discovered that the emperor was desirous of finding disaffection and treason in the senate. That assembly, whom Marcus had ever considered as the great council of the nation, was composed of the most distinguished of the Romans; and distinction of every kind soon became criminal. The possession of wealth stimulated the diligence of the informers; rigid virtue implied a tacit censure of the irregularities of Commodus; important services implied a dangerous superiority of merit; and the friendship of the father always insured the aversion of the son. Suspicion was equivalent to proof; trial to condemnation. The execution of a considerable senator was attended with the death of all who might lament or revenge his fate; and when Commodus had once tasted human blood, he became incapable of pity or remorse.†

The tyrant's rage, after having shed the noblest blood of the senate, at length recoiled on the principal instrument of his cruelty. Whilst Commodus was immersed in blood and luxury, he devolved the detail of the public business on Perennis, a servile and ambitious minister who had obtained his post by the murder of his predecessor, but who possessed a considerable share of vigor and ability. By acts of extortion, and the forfeited estates of the nobles sacrificed to his avarice, he had accumulated an immense treasure. The Praetorian guards were under his immediate command; and his son, who was already discovered a military genius, was at the head of the Illyrian legions. Perennis aspired to the empire; or what, in the eyes of Commodus, amounted to the same crime, he was capable of aspiring to it, had he not been prevented, surprised, and put to death [A.D. 185]. The fall of a minister is a very trifling incident in the general history of the empire; but it was hastened by an extraordinary circumstance which proved how much the nerves of discipline were already relaxed. The legions of Britain, discontented with the administration of Perennis, formed a deputation of fifteen hundred select men with instructions to march to Rome and lay their complaints before the emperor. These military petitioners, by their own determined behavior, by inflaming the divisions of the guards, by exaggerating the strength of the British army, and by alarming the fears of Commodus, exacted and obtained the minister's death as the only redress of their grievances. This presumption of a distant army, and their discovery of the weakness of government, was a sure presage of the most dreadful convulsions.†

After the fall of Perennis, the terrors of Commodus had, for a short time, assumed the appearance of a return to virtue. He repealed the most odious of his acts, loaded his memory with the public execration, and ascribed to the pernicious counsels of that wicked minister all the errors of his inexperienced youth. But his repentance lasted only thirty days; and, under [Perennis' successor] Cleander's tyranny, the administration of Perennis was often regretted.

Pestilence and famine contributed to fill up the measure of the calamities of Rome. The first could be only imputed to the just indignation of the gods; but a monopoly of corn [grain], supported by the riches and power of the minister, was considered as the immediate cause of the second. The popular discontent, after it had long circulated in whispers, broke out in the assembled circus. The people quit-

ted their favorite amusements for the more delicious pleasure of revenge, rushed in crowds towards a palace in the suburbs, one of the
emperor's retirements, and demanded, with angry clamors, the head of
the public enemy [A.D. 189]. Cleander, who commanded the Praetorian guards, ordered a body of cavalry to sally forth and disperse the
seditious multitude. The multitude fled with precipitation towards the
city; several were slain, and many more were trampled to death; but
when the cavalry entered the streets, their pursuit was checked by a
shower of stones and darts from the roofs and windows of the houses.
The foot guards, who had been long jealous of the prerogatives and insolence of the Praetorian cavalry, embraced the party of the people.
The tumult became a regular engagement, and threatened a general
massacre. The Praetorians at length gave way, oppressed with numbers; and the tide of popular fury returned with redoubled violence
against the gates of the palace, where Commodus lay, dissolved in
luxury and alone unconscious of the civil war. It was death to approach
his person with the unwelcome news. He would have perished in this
supine security had not two women, his eldest sister, Fadilla, and Marcia, the most favored of his concubines, ventured to break into his
presence. Bathed in tears, and with disheveled hair, they threw themselves at his feet; and with all the pressing eloquence of fear, discovered to the affrighted emperor the crimes of the minister, the rage of
the people, and the impending ruin which, in a few minutes, would
burst over his palace and person. Commodus started from his dream of
pleasure and commanded that the head of Cleander should be thrown
out to the people. The desired spectacle instantly appeased the tumult; and the son of Marcus might even yet have regained the affection and confidence of his subjects.

But every sentiment of virtue and humanity was extinct in the
mind of Commodus. Whilst he thus abandoned the reins of empire to
these unworthy favorites, he valued nothing in sovereign power, except the unbounded license of indulging his sensual appetites. His
hours were spent in a seraglio of three hundred beautiful women and
as many boys, of every rank and of every province; and wherever the
arts of seduction proved ineffectual, the brutal lover had recourse to
violence. The ancient historians have expatiated on these abandoned
scenes of prostitution, which scorned every restraint of nature or
modesty; but it would not be easy to translate their too faithful de-

scriptions into the decency of modern language. The intervals of lust were filled up with the basest amusements. The influence of a polite age and the labor of an attentive education had never been able to infuse into his rude and brutish mind the least tincture of learning; and he was the first of the Roman emperors totally devoid of taste for the pleasures of the understanding. Nero himself excelled, or affected to excel, in the elegant arts of music and poetry: nor should we despise his pursuits, had he not converted the pleasing relaxation of a leisure hour into the serious business and ambition of his life. But Commodus, from his earliest infancy, discovered an aversion to whatever was rational or liberal and a fond attachment to the amusements of the populace; the sports of the circus and amphitheater, the combats of gladiators, and the hunting of wild beasts. The masters in every branch of learning whom Marcus provided for his son were heard with inattention and disgust; whilst the Moors and Parthians who taught him to dart the javelin and to shoot with the bow found a disciple who delighted in his application and soon equaled the most skillful of his instructors in the steadiness of the eye and the dexterity of the hand.

The servile crowd whose fortune depended on their master's vices applauded these ignoble pursuits. The perfidious voice of flattery reminded him that by exploits of the same nature, by the defeat of the Nemean lion and the slaughter of the wild boar of Erymanthus, the Grecian Hercules had acquired a place among the gods and an immortal memory among men. They only forgot to observe that, in the first ages of society, when the fiercer animals often dispute with man the possession of an unsettled country, a successful war against those savages is one of the most innocent and beneficial labors of heroism. In the civilized state of the Roman empire, the wild beasts had long since retired from the face of man and the neighborhood of populous cities. To surprise them in their solitary haunts and to transport them to Rome that they might be slain in pomp by the hand of an emperor was an enterprise equally ridiculous for the prince and oppressive for the people. Ignorant of these distinctions, Commodus eagerly embraced the glorious resemblance, and styled himself (as we still read on his medals) the *Roman Hercules*. The club and the lion's hide were placed by the side of the throne, amongst the ensigns of sovereignty; and statues were erected in which Commodus was represented in the character and with the attributes of the god whose valor and dexterity he endeavored to emulate in the daily course of his ferocious amusements.†

But the meanest of the populace were affected with shame and indignation when they beheld their sovereign enter the lists as a gladiator, and glory in a profession which the laws and manners of the Romans had branded with the justest note of infamy. He chose the habit and arms of the *Secutor,* whose combat with the *Retiarius* formed one of the most lively scenes in the bloody sports of the amphitheater. The *Secutor* was armed with a helmet, sword, and buckler; his naked antagonist had only a large net and a trident; with the one he endeavored to entangle, with the other to despatch his enemy. If he missed the first throw, he was obliged to fly from the pursuit of the *Secutor* till he had prepared his net for a second cast. The emperor fought in this character seven hundred and thirty-five several times. These glorious achievements were carefully recorded in the public acts of the empire; and that he might omit no circumstance of infamy, he received from the common fund of gladiators a stipend so exorbitant that it became a new and most ignominious tax upon the Roman people. It may be easily supposed that in these engagements the master of the world was always successful; in the amphitheater, his victories were not often sanguinary; but when he exercised his skill in the school of gladiators or his own palace, his wretched antagonists were frequently honored with a mortal wound from the hand of Commodus and obliged to seal their flattery with their blood. He now disdained the appellation of Hercules. The name of Paulus, a celebrated *Secutor,* was the only one which delighted his ear. It was inscribed on his colossal statues and repeated in the redoubled acclamations of the mournful and applauding senate. Claudius Pompeianus, the virtuous husband of Lucilla, was the only senator who asserted the honor of his rank. As a father, he permitted his sons to consult their safety by attending the amphitheater. As a Roman, he declared that his own life was in the emperor's hands, but that he would never behold the son of Marcus prostituting his person and dignity. Notwithstanding his manly resolution, Pompeianus escaped the resentment of the tyrant, and, with his honor, had the good fortune to preserve his life.

Commodus had now attained the summit of vice and infamy. Amidst the acclamations of a flattering court, he was unable to disguise from himself that he had deserved the contempt and hatred of every man of sense and virtue in his empire. His ferocious spirit was irritated by the consciousness of that hatred, by the envy of every kind of merit, by the just apprehension of danger, and by the habit of slaughter, which he contracted in his daily amusements. History has preserved a long list of consular senators sacrificed to his wanton suspicion, which sought out, with peculiar anxiety, those unfortunate persons connected, however remotely, with the family of the Antonines, without sparing even the ministers of his crimes or pleasures. His cruelty proved at last fatal to himself. He had shed with impunity the noblest blood of Rome: he perished as soon as he was dreaded by his own domestics. Marcia, his favorite concubine, Eclectus, his chamberlain, and Laetus, his Praetorian praefect, alarmed by the fate of their companions and predecessors, resolved to prevent the destruction which every hour hung over their heads, either from the mad caprice of the tyrant or the sudden indignation of the people. Marcia seized the occasion of presenting a draught of wine to her lover after he had fatigued himself with hunting some wild beasts. Commodus retired to sleep; but whilst he was laboring with the effects of poison and drunkenness, a robust youth, by profession a wrestler, entered his chamber and strangled him without resistance [December 31, A.D. 192]. The body was secretly conveyed out of the palace before the least suspicion was entertained in the city, or even in the court, of the emperor's death. Such was the fate of the son of Marcus, and so easy was it to destroy a hated tyrant who, by the artificial powers of government, had oppressed, during thirteen years, so many millions of subjects, each of whom was equal to their master in personal strength and personal abilities.

The measures of the conspirators were conducted with the deliberate coolness and celerity which the greatness of the occasion required. They resolved instantly to fill the vacant throne with an emperor whose character would justify and maintain the action that had been committed. They fixed on Pertinax, praefect of the city, an ancient senator of consular rank whose conspicuous merit had broken through the obscurity of his birth and raised him to the first honors of the state. He had successively governed most of the provinces of the empire; and in all his great employments, military as well as civil, he had uniformly distinguished himself by the firmness, the prudence, and the integrity of his conduct. He now remained almost alone of the friends and ministers of Marcus; and when, at a late hour of the night, he was awakened with the news that the chamberlain and the praefect were at his door, he received them with intrepid resignation, and desired they would execute their master's orders. Instead of death, they offered him the throne of the Roman world. During some moments he distrusted their intentions and assurances. Convinced at length of the death of Commodus, he accepted the purple with a sincere reluctance, the natural effect of his knowledge both of the duties and of the dangers of the supreme rank.

Laetus conducted without delay his new emperor to the camp of the Praetorians, diffusing at the same time through the city a seasonable report that Commodus died suddenly of an apoplexy; and that the virtuous Pertinax had *already* succeeded to the throne. The guards were rather surprised than pleased with the suspicious death of a prince whose indulgence and liberality they alone had experienced; but the emergency of the occasion, the authority of their praefect, the reputation of Pertinax, and the clamors of the people obliged them to stifle their secret discontents, to accept the donative promised by the new emperor, to swear allegiance to him, and with joyful acclamations and laurels in their hands to conduct him to the senate house, that the military consent might be ratified by the civil authority.

This important night was now far spent; with the dawn of day and the commencement of the new year, the senators expected a summons to attend an ignominious ceremony [January 1, A.D. 193]. In spite of all remonstrances, even of those of his creatures who yet preserved any regard for prudence or decency, Commodus had resolved to pass the night in the gladiators' school, and from thence to take possession of the consulship in the habit and with the attendance of that infamous crew. On a sudden, before the break of day, the senate was called together in the temple of Concord to meet the guards and to ratify the election of a new emperor. For a few minutes they sat in silent suspense, doubtful of their unexpected deliverance and suspicious of the cruel artifices of Commodus: but when at length they were assured that the tyrant was no more, they resigned themselves to all the transports of joy and indignation. Pertinax, who modestly represented the meanness of his extraction and pointed out several noble senators more deserving than himself of the empire, was constrained by their dutiful violence to ascend the throne and received all the titles of Imperial power, confirmed by the most sincere vows of fidelity. The memory of Commodus was branded with eternal infamy. The names of tyrant, of gladiator, of public enemy resounded in every corner of the house. They decreed in tumultuous votes that his honors should be reversed, his titles erased from the public monuments, his statues thrown down, his body dragged with a hook into the stripping room of the gladiators to satiate the public fury; and they expressed some indignation against those officious servants who had already presumed to screen his remains from the justice of the senate. But Pertinax could not refuse those last rites to the memory of Marcus and the tears of his first protector Claudius Pompeianus, who lamented the cruel fate of his brother-in-law, and lamented still more that he had deserved it.

These effusions of impotent rage against a dead emperor whom the senate had flattered when alive with the most abject servility betrayed a just but ungenerous spirit of revenge. The legality of these decrees was, however, supported by the principles of the Imperial constitution. To censure, to depose, or to punish with death the first magistrate of the republic who had abused his delegated trust was the ancient and undoubted prerogative of the Roman senate; but the feeble assembly was obliged to content itself with inflicting on a fallen tyrant that public justice from which, during his life and reign, he had been shielded by the strong arm of military despotism.†

To heal, as far as it was possible, the wounds inflicted by the hand of tyranny was the pleasing but melancholy task of Pertinax. The innocent victims who yet survived were recalled from exile, released from prison, and restored to the full possession of their honors and fortunes. The unburied bodies of murdered senators (for the cruelty of Commodus endeavored to extend itself beyond death) were deposited in the sepulchres of their ancestors; their memory was justified and every consolation was bestowed on their ruined and afflicted families. Among these consolations, one of the most grateful was the punishment of the Delators; the common enemies of their master, of virtue, and of their country. Yet even in the inquisition of these legal assassins, Pertinax proceeded with a steady temper which gave everything to justice and nothing to popular prejudice and resentment.

The finances of the state demanded the most vigilant care of the emperor. Though every measure of injustice and extortion had been adopted which could collect the property of the subject into the coffers of the prince, the rapaciousness of Commodus had been so very inadequate to his extravagance that, upon his death, no more than eight thousand pounds were found in the exhausted treasury to defray the current expenses of government and to discharge the pressing demand of a liberal donative which the new emperor had been obliged to promise to the Praetorian guards. Yet under these distressed circumstances, Pertinax had the generous firmness to remit all the oppressive taxes invented by Commodus and to cancel all the unjust claims of the treasury; declaring, in a decree of the senate, "that he was better satisfied to administer a poor republic with innocence than to acquire riches by the ways of tyranny and dishonor."†

Amidst the general joy, the sullen and angry countenance of the Praetorian guards betrayed their inward dissatisfaction. They had reluctantly submitted to Pertinax; they dreaded the strictness of the ancient discipline which he was preparing to restore; and they regretted the license of the former reign.†

On the twenty-eighth of March [A.D. 193], eighty-six days only after the death of Commodus, a general sedition broke out in the camp which the officers wanted either power or inclination to suppress. Two or three hundred of the most desperate soldiers marched at noonday, with arms in their hands and fury in their looks, towards the Imperial palace. The gates were thrown open by their companions upon guard and by the domestics of the old court, who had already formed a secret conspiracy against the life of the too virtuous emperor. On the news of their approach, Pertinax, disdaining either flight or concealment, advanced to meet his assassins; and recalled to their minds his own innocence and the sanctity of their recent oath. For a few moments they stood in silent suspense, ashamed of their atrocious design, and awed by the venerable aspect and majestic firmness of their sovereign, till at length, the despair of pardon reviving their fury, a Barbarian of the country of Tongress leveled the first blow against Pertinax, who was instantly despatched with a multitude of wounds. His head, separated from his body and placed on a lance, was carried in triumph to the Praetorian camp in the sight of a mournful and indignant people, who lamented the unworthy fate of that excellent prince and the transient blessings of a reign, the memory of which could serve only to aggravate their approaching misfortunes.

CHAPTER V

SALE OF THE EMPIRE TO DIDIUS JULIANUS

Public sale of the empire to Didius Julianus by the Praetorian guards. • Clodius Albinus in Britain, Pescennius Niger in Syria, and Septimius Severus in Pannonia declare against the murderers of Pertinax. • Civil wars and victory of Severus over his three rivals. • Relaxation of discipline. • New maxims of government.

The power of the sword is more sensibly felt in an extensive monarchy than in a small community. It has been calculated by the ablest politicians that no state, without being soon exhausted, can maintain above the hundredth part of its members in arms and idleness. But although this relative proportion may be uniform, the influence of the army over the rest of the society will vary according to the degree of its positive strength. The advantages of military science and discipline cannot be exerted unless a proper number of soldiers are united into one body and actuated by one soul. With a handful of men, such a union would be ineffectual; with an unwieldy host, it would be impracticable; and the powers of the machine would be alike destroyed by the extreme minuteness or the excessive weight of its springs. To illustrate this observation, we need only reflect that there is no superiority of natural strength, artificial weapons, or acquired skill which could enable one man to keep in constant subjection one hundred of his fellow-creatures: the tyrant of a single town, or a small district, would soon discover that a hundred armed followers were a weak defense against ten thousand peasants or citizens; but a hundred thousand well-disciplined soldiers will command, with despotic sway, ten millions of subjects; and a body of ten or fifteen thousand guards will strike terror into the most numerous populace that ever crowded the streets of an immense capital.

The Praetorian bands, whose licentious fury was the first symptom and cause of the decline of the Roman empire, scarcely amounted to the last-mentioned number. They derived their institution from Augustus. That crafty tyrant, sensible that laws might color but that arms alone could maintain his usurped dominion, had gradually formed this powerful body of guards in constant readiness to protect his person, to awe the senate, and either to prevent or to crush the first motions of rebellion. He distinguished these favored troops by a double pay and superior privileges; but, as their formidable aspect would at once have alarmed and irritated the Roman people, three cohorts only were stationed in the capital, whilst the remainder was dispersed in the adjacent towns of Italy. But after fifty years of peace and servitude, Tiberius ventured on a decisive measure which forever riveted the fetters of his country. Under the fair pretenses of relieving Italy from the heavy burden of military quarters and of introducing a stricter discipline among the guards, he assembled them at Rome in a permanent camp, which was fortified with skillful care and placed on a commanding situation.

Such formidable servants are always necessary but often fatal to the throne of despotism. By thus introducing the Praetorian guards as it were into the palace and the senate, the emperors taught them to perceive their own strength, and the weakness of the civil government; to view the vices of their masters with familiar contempt, and to lay aside that reverential awe which distance only, and mystery, can preserve towards an imaginary power. In the luxurious idleness of an opulent city, their pride was nourished by the sense of their irresistible weight; nor was it possible to conceal from them that the person of the sovereign, the authority of the senate, the public treasure, and the seat of empire were all in their hands. To divert the Praetorian bands from these dangerous reflections, the firmest and best established princes were obliged to mix blandishments with commands, rewards with punishments, to flatter their pride, indulge their pleasures, connive at their irregularities, and to purchase their precarious faith by a liberal donative; which, since the elevation of Claudius, was enacted as a legal claim on the accession of every new emperor.

The advocates of the guards endeavored to justify by arguments the power which they asserted by arms; and to maintain that, according to the purest principles of the constitution, *their* consent was essentially necessary in the appointment of an emperor. The election of consuls, of generals, and of magistrates, however it had been recently usurped by the senate, was the ancient and undoubted right of the Roman people. But where was the Roman people to be found? Not surely amongst the mixed multitude of slaves and strangers that filled the streets of Rome; a servile populace, as devoid of spirit as destitute of property. The defenders of the state, selected from the flower of the Italian youth and trained in the exercise of arms and virtue, were the genuine representatives of the people, and the best entitled to elect the military chief of the republic. These assertions, however defective in reason, became unanswerable when the fierce Praetorians increased their weight by throwing, like the Barbarian conqueror of Rome, their swords into the scale.

The Praetorians had violated the sanctity of the throne by the atrocious murder of Pertinax; they dishonored the majesty of it by their subsequent conduct. The camp was without a leader, for even the praefect Laetus, who had excited the tempest, prudently declined the public indignation. Amidst the wild disorder, Sulpicianus, the emperor's father-in-law and governor of the city, who had been sent to the camp on the first alarm of mutiny, was endeavoring to calm the fury of the multitude when he was silenced by the clamorous return of the murderers, bearing on a lance the head of Pertinax. Though history has accustomed us to observe every principle and every passion yielding to the imperious dictates of ambition, it is scarcely credible that, in these moments of horror, Sulpicianus should have aspired to ascend a throne polluted with the recent blood of so near a relation and so excellent a prince. He had already begun to use the only effectual argument, and to treat for the Imperial dignity; but the more prudent of the Praetorians, apprehensive that, in this private contract, they should not obtain a just price for so valuable a commodity, ran out upon the ramparts; and, with a loud voice, proclaimed that the Roman world was to be disposed of to the best bidder by public auction [March 28, A.D. 193].

This infamous offer, the most insolent excess of military license, diffused a universal grief, shame, and indignation throughout the city. It reached at length the ears of Didius Julianus, a wealthy senator who, regardless of the public calamities, was indulging himself in the luxury of the table. His wife and his daughter, his freedmen and his parasites, easily convinced him that he deserved the throne, and earnestly conjured him to embrace so fortunate an opportunity. The vain old man hastened to the Praetorian camp, where Sulpicianus was still in treaty with the guards, and began to bid against him from the foot of the rampart. The unworthy negotiation was transacted by faithful emissaries who passed alternately from one candidate to the other and acquainted each of them with the offers of his rival. Sulpicianus had already promised a donative of five thousand drachmas (above one hundred and sixty pounds) to each soldier; when Julian, eager for the prize, rose at once to the sum of six thousand two hundred and fifty drachmas, or upwards of two hundred pounds sterling. The gates of the camp were instantly thrown open to the purchaser; he was declared emperor and received an oath of allegiance from the soldiers, who retained humanity enough to stipulate that he should pardon and forget the competition of Sulpicianus.

It was now incumbent on the Praetorians to fulfill the conditions of the sale. They placed their new sovereign, whom they served and despised, in the center of their ranks, surrounded him on every side with their shields, and conducted him in close order of battle through the deserted streets of the city. The senate was commanded to assemble; and those who had been the distinguished friends of Pertinax, or the personal enemies of Julian, found it necessary to affect a more than common share of satisfaction at this happy revolution. After Julian had filled the senate house with armed soldiers, he expatiated on the freedom of his election, his own eminent virtues, and his full assurance of the affections of the senate. The obsequious assembly congratulated their own and the public felicity; engaged their allegiance, and conferred on him all the several branches of the Imperial power. From the senate Julian was conducted, by the same military procession, to take possession of the palace. The first objects that struck his eyes were the abandoned trunk of Pertinax and the frugal entertainment prepared for his supper. The one he viewed with indifference, the other with contempt. A magnificent feast was prepared by his order, and he amused himself, till a very late hour, with dice and the performances of Pylades, a celebrated dancer. Yet it was observed that after the crowd of flatterers dispersed and left him to darkness, solitude, and terrible reflection, he passed a sleepless night; revolving most probably in his mind his own rash folly, the fate of his virtuous predecessor, and the doubtful and dangerous tenure of an empire which had not been acquired by merit but purchased by money.

He had reason to tremble. On the throne of the world he found himself without a friend, and even without an adherent. The guards themselves were ashamed of the prince whom their avarice had persuaded them to accept; nor was there a citizen who did not consider his elevation with horror, as the last insult on the Roman name. The nobility, whose conspicuous station and ample possessions exacted the strictest caution, dissembled their sentiments, and met the affected civility of the emperor with smiles of complacency and professions of duty. But the people, secure in their numbers and obscurity, gave a free vent to their passions. The streets and public places of Rome resounded with clamors and imprecations. The enraged multitude affronted the person of Julian, rejected his liberality, and, conscious of the impotence of their own resentment, they called aloud on the legions of the frontiers to assert the violated majesty of the Roman empire.

The public discontent was soon diffused from the center to the frontiers of the empire. The armies of Britain, of Syria, and of Illyricum lamented the death of Pertinax, in whose company, or under whose command, they had so often fought and conquered. They received with surprise, with indignation, and perhaps with envy the extraordinary intelligence that the Praetorians had disposed of the empire by public auction; and they sternly refused to ratify the ignominious bargain. Their immediate and unanimous revolt was fatal to Julian, but it was fatal at the same time to the public peace, as the generals of the respective armies, Clodius Albinus [in Britain], Pescennius Niger [in Syria], and Septimius Severus [in Pannonia], were still more anxious to succeed than to revenge the murdered Pertinax. Their forces were exactly balanced. Each of them was at the head of three legions, with a numerous train of auxiliaries; and however different in their characters, they were all soldiers of experience and capacity.[†]

The Pannonian army was at this time commanded by Septimius Severus, a native of Africa who, in the gradual ascent of private honors, had concealed his daring ambition, which was never diverted from its steady course by the allurements of pleasure, the apprehension of danger, or the feelings of humanity. On the first news of the murder of Pertinax, he assembled his troops, painted in the most lively colors the crime, the insolence, and the weakness of the Praetorian guards, and animated the legions to arms and to revenge. He concluded (and the peroration was thought extremely eloquent) with promising every soldier about four hundred pounds; an honorable donative, double in value to the infamous bribe with which Julian had purchased the empire. The acclamations of the army immediately saluted Severus with the names of Augustus, Pertinax, and Emperor; and he thus attained the lofty station to which he was invited by conscious merit and a long train of dreams and omens, the fruitful offsprings either of his superstition or policy [April 13, A.D. 193].

The new candidate for empire saw and improved the peculiar advantage of his situation. His province extended to the Julian Alps, which gave an easy access into Italy; and he remembered the saying of Augustus that a Pannonian army might in ten days appear in sight of Rome. By a celerity proportioned to the greatness of the occasion, he might reasonably hope to revenge Pertinax, punish Julian, and receive the homage of the senate and people as their lawful emperor before his competitors, separated from Italy by an immense tract of sea and land, were apprised of his success, or even of his election. During the whole expedition, he scarcely allowed himself any moments for sleep or food; marching on foot and in complete armor at the head of his columns, he insinuated himself into the confidence and affection of his troops, pressed their diligence, revived their spirits, animated their hopes, and was well satisfied to share the hardships of the meanest soldier, whilst he kept in view the infinite superiority of his reward.

The wretched Julian had expected, and thought himself prepared, to dispute the empire with the governor of Syria; but in the invincible and rapid approach of the Pannonian legions, he saw his inevitable ruin. The hasty arrival of every messenger increased his just apprehensions. He was successively informed that Severus had passed the Alps; that the Italian cities, unwilling or unable to oppose his progress, had received him with the warmest professions of joy and duty; that the important place of Ravenna had surrendered without resistance, and that the Hadriatic fleet was in the hands of the conqueror. The enemy was now within two hundred and fifty miles of Rome; and every moment diminished the narrow span of life and empire allotted to Julian.

He attempted, however, to prevent, or at least to protract, his ruin. He implored the venal faith of the Praetorians, filled the city with unavailing preparations for war, drew lines round the suburbs, and even strengthened the fortifications of the palace; as if those last entrenchments could be defended, without hope of relief, against a victorious invader. Fear and shame prevented the guards from deserting his standard; but they trembled at the name of the Pannonian legions, commanded by an experienced general and accustomed to vanquish the Barbarians on the frozen Danube. They quitted, with a sigh, the pleasures of the baths and theaters to put on arms whose use they had almost forgotten, and beneath the weight of which they were oppressed. The unpracticed elephants, whose uncouth appearance, it was hoped, would strike terror into the army of the North, threw their unskillful riders; and the awkward evolutions of the marines, drawn from the fleet of Misenum, were an object of ridicule to the populace; whilst the senate enjoyed, with secret pleasure, the distress and weakness of the usurper.

Every motion of Julian betrayed his trembling perplexity. He insisted that Severus should be declared a public enemy by the senate. He entreated that the Pannonian general might be associated to the empire. He sent public ambassadors of consular rank to negotiate with his rival; he despatched private assassins to take away his life. He designed that the Vestal virgins and all the colleges of priests, in their sacerdotal habits and bearing before them the sacred pledges of the Roman religion, should advance in solemn procession to meet the Pannonian legions; and, at the same time, he vainly tried to interrogate or to appease the fates by magic ceremonies and unlawful sacrifices.

Severus, who dreaded neither his arms nor his enchantments, guarded himself from the only danger of secret conspiracy by the faithful attendance of six hundred chosen men, who never quitted his person or their cuirasses, either by night or by day, during the whole march. Advancing with a steady and rapid course, he passed without difficulty the defiles of the Apennine, received into his party the troops and ambassadors sent to retard his progress, and made a short halt at Interamnia, about seventy miles from Rome. His victory was already secure, but the despair of the Praetorians might have rendered it bloody; and Severus had the laudable ambition of ascending the throne without drawing the sword. His emissaries, dispersed in the capital, assured the guards that, provided they would abandon their worthless prince and the perpetrators of the murder of Pertinax to the justice of the conqueror, he would no longer consider that melancholy event as the act of the whole body. The faithless Praetorians, whose resistance was supported only by sullen obstinacy, gladly complied with the easy conditions, seized the greatest part of the assassins, and signified to the senate that they no longer defended the cause of Julian. That assembly, convoked by the consul, unanimously acknowledged Severus as lawful emperor, decreed divine honors to Pertinax, and pronounced a sentence of deposition and death against his unfortunate successor [June 2, A.D. 193]. Julian was conducted into a private apartment of the baths of the palace and beheaded as a common criminal, after having purchased, with an immense treasure, an anxious and precarious reign of only sixty-six days. The almost incredible expedition of Severus, who in so short a space of time conducted a numerous army from the banks of the Danube to those of the Tiber, proves at once the plenty of provisions produced by agriculture and commerce, the goodness of the roads, the discipline of the legions, and the indolent, subdued temper of the provinces.

The first cares of Severus were bestowed on two measures, the one dictated by policy, the other by decency; the revenge, and the honors, due to the memory of Pertinax. Before the new emperor entered Rome, he issued his commands to the Praetorian guards, directing them to wait his arrival on a large plain near the city, without arms but in the habits of ceremony in which they were accustomed to attend their sovereign. He was obeyed by those haughty troops, whose contrition was the effect of their just terrors. A chosen part of the Illyrian army encompassed them with leveled spears. Incapable of flight or resistance, they expected their fate in silent consternation. Severus mounted the tribunal, sternly reproached them with perfidy and cowardice, dismissed them with ignominy from the trust which they had betrayed, despoiled them of their splendid ornaments, and banished them, on pain of death, to the distance of a hundred miles from the capital. During the transaction, another detachment had been sent to seize their arms, occupy their camp, and prevent the hasty consequences of their despair.

The funeral and consecration of Pertinax was next solemnized with every circumstance of sad magnificence. The senate, with a melancholy pleasure, performed the last rites to that excellent prince, whom they had loved and still regretted. The concern of his successor was probably less sincere; he esteemed the virtues of Pertinax, but those virtues would forever have confined his ambition to a private station.

Severus pronounced his funeral oration with studied eloquence, inward satisfaction, and well-acted sorrow; and by this pious regard to his memory convinced the credulous multitude that he alone was worthy to supply his place. Sensible, however, that arms, not ceremonies, must assert his claim to the empire, he left Rome at the end of thirty days, and without suffering himself to be elated by this easy victory prepared to encounter his more formidable rivals.

The uncommon abilities and fortune of Severus have induced an elegant historian to compare him with the first and greatest of the Caesars. The parallel is, at least, imperfect. Where shall we find, in the character of Severus, the commanding superiority of soul, the generous clemency, and the various genius which could reconcile and unite the love of pleasure, the thirst of knowledge, and the fire of ambition? In one instance only they may be compared with some degree of propriety, in the celerity of their motions and their civil victories. In less than four years, Severus subdued the riches of the East and the valor of the West. He vanquished two competitors of reputation and ability, and defeated numerous armies provided with weapons and discipline equal to his own. In that age, the art of fortification and the principles of tactics were well understood by all the Roman generals; and the constant superiority of Severus was that of an artist who uses the same instruments with more skill and industry than his rivals. I shall not, however, enter into a minute narrative of these military operations.

[*Septimius Severus defeats first Niger in the East (A.D. 194) and then Albinus in the West (A.D. 197).*]

Till the final decision of the war, the cruelty of Severus was, in some measure, restrained by the uncertainty of the event and his pretended reverence for the senate. The head of Albinus, accompanied with a menacing letter, announced to the Romans that he was resolved to spare none of the adherents of his unfortunate competitors. He was irritated by the just suspicion that he had never possessed the affections of the senate, and he concealed his old malevolence under the recent discovery of some treasonable correspondences. Thirty-five senators, however, accused of having favored the party of Albinus, he freely pardoned and, by his subsequent behavior, endeavored to convince them that he had forgotten as well as forgiven their supposed offenses.

But, at the same time, he condemned forty-one other senators whose names history has recorded; their wives, children, and clients attended them in death, and the noblest provincials of Spain and Gaul were involved in the same ruin. Such rigid justice—for so he termed it—was, in the opinion of Severus, the only conduct capable of insuring peace to the people or stability to the prince; and he condescended slightly to lament that, to be mild, it was necessary that he should first be cruel.

The true interest of an absolute monarch generally coincides with that of his people. Their numbers, their wealth, their order, and their security are the best and only foundations of his real greatness; and were he totally devoid of virtue, prudence might supply its place, and would dictate the same rule of conduct. Severus considered the Roman empire as his property, and had no sooner secured the possession than he bestowed his care on the cultivation and improvement of so valuable an acquisition. Salutary laws, executed with inflexible firmness, soon corrected most of the abuses with which, since the death of Marcus, every part of the government had been infected. In the administration of justice, the judgments of the emperor were characterized by attention, discernment, and impartiality; and whenever he deviated from the strict line of equity, it was generally in favor of the poor and oppressed; not so much indeed from any sense of humanity as from the natural propensity of a despot to humble the pride of greatness, and to sink all his subjects to the same common level of absolute dependence. His expensive taste for building, magnificent shows, and above all a constant and liberal distribution of corn and provisions were the surest means of captivating the affection of the Roman people. The misfortunes of civil discord were obliterated. The claim of peace and prosperity was once more experienced in the provinces; and many cities, restored by the munificence of Severus, assumed the title of his colonies and attested by public monuments their gratitude and felicity. The fame of the Roman arms was revived by that warlike and successful emperor, and he boasted, with a just pride, that, having received the empire oppressed with foreign and domestic wars, he left it established in profound, universal, and honorable peace.

Although the wounds of civil war appeared completely healed, its mortal poison still lurked in the vitals of the constitution. Severus possessed a considerable share of vigor and ability; but the daring soul of the first Caesar, or the deep policy of Augustus, were scarcely equal to

the task of curbing the insolence of the victorious legions. By gratitude, by misguided policy, by seeming necessity, Severus was induced
to relax the nerves of discipline. The vanity of his soldiers was flattered with the honor of wearing gold rings [a privilege originally confined to wealthy citizens]; their ease was indulged in the permission of
living with their wives in the idleness of quarters. He increased their
pay beyond the example of former times and taught them to expect,
and soon to claim, extraordinary donatives on every public occasion of
danger or festivity. Elated by success, enervated by luxury, and raised
above the level of subjects by their dangerous privileges, they soon became incapable of military fatigue, oppressive to the country, and impatient of a just subordination. Their officers asserted the superiority
of rank by a more profuse and elegant luxury. There is still extant a
letter of Severus lamenting the licentious state of the army and exhorting one of his generals to begin the necessary reformation from
the tribunes themselves; since, as he justly observes, the officer who
has forfeited the esteem will never command the obedience of his soldiers. Had the emperor pursued the train of reflection, he would have
discovered that the primary cause of this general corruption might be
ascribed not indeed to the example but to the pernicious indulgence,
however, of the commander-in-chief.†

The command of the most favored and formidable troops [the
Praetorian guards] soon became the first office of the empire. As the
government degenerated into military despotism, the Praetorian praefect, who in his origin had been a simple captain of the guards, was
placed not only at the head of the army but of the finances, and even
of the law. In every department of administration, he represented the
person and exercised the authority of the emperor. The first praefect
who enjoyed and abused this immense power was Plautianus, the favorite minister of Severus. His reign lasted above ten years, till the
marriage of his daughter with the eldest son of the emperor, which
seemed to assure his fortune, proved the occasion of his ruin. The animosities of the palace, by irritating the ambition and alarming the fears
of Plautianus, threatened to produce a revolution and obliged the emperor, who still loved him, to consent with reluctance to his death. After
the fall of Plautianus, an eminent lawyer, the celebrated Papinian, was
appointed to execute the motley office of Praetorian praefect.

Till the reign of Severus, the virtue and even the good sense of the emperors had been distinguished by their zeal or affected reverence for the senate, and by a tender regard to the nice frame of civil policy instituted by Augustus. But the youth of Severus had been trained in the implicit obedience of camps, and his riper years spent in the despotism of military command. His haughty and inflexible spirit could not discover, or would not acknowledge, the advantage of preserving an intermediate power, however imaginary, between the emperor and the army. He disdained to profess himself the servant of an assembly that detested his person and trembled at his frown; he issued his commands where his requests would have proved as effectual, assumed the conduct and style of a sovereign and a conqueror, and exercised, without disguise, the whole legislative as well as the executive power.

The victory over the senate was easy and inglorious. Every eye and every passion were directed to the supreme magistrate, who possessed the arms and treasure of the state; whilst the senate, neither elected by the people nor guarded by military force nor animated by public spirit, rested its declining authority on the frail and crumbling basis of ancient opinion. The fine theory of a republic insensibly vanished, and made way for the more natural and substantial feelings of monarchy. As the freedom and honors of Rome were successively communicated to the provinces, in which the old government had been either unknown or was remembered with abhorrence, the tradition of republican maxims was gradually obliterated. The Greek historians of the age of the Antonines observe with a malicious pleasure that although the sovereign of Rome, in compliance with an obsolete prejudice, abstained from the name of king, he possessed the full measure of regal power. In the reign of Severus, the senate was filled with polished and eloquent slaves from the Eastern provinces who justified personal flattery by speculative principles of servitude. These new advocates of prerogative were heard with pleasure by the court, and with patience by the people, when they inculcated the duty of passive obedience and descanted on the inevitable mischiefs of freedom. The lawyers and historians concurred in teaching that the Imperial authority was held not by the delegated commission but by the irrevocable resignation of the senate; that the emperor was freed from the restraint of civil laws, could command by his arbitrary will the lives and fortunes of his subjects, and might dispose of the empire as of his private patrimony. The most eminent of the civil lawyers, and particularly Papinian, Paulus, and Ulpian, flourished under the house of Severus; and the Roman jurisprudence, having closely united itself with the system of monarchy, was supposed to have attained its full majority and perfection.

The contemporaries of Severus in the enjoyment of the peace and glory of his reign forgave the cruelties by which it had been introduced. Posterity, who experienced the fatal effects of his maxims and example, justly considered him as the principal author of the decline of the Roman empire.

CHAPTER VI

DEATH OF SEVERUS, TYRANNY OF CARACALLA, USURPATION OF MACRINUS

The death of Severus. • Tyranny of Caracalla. • Usurpation of Macrinus. • Follies of Elagabalus. • Virtues of Alexander Severus. • Licentiousness of the army. • General state of the Roman finances.

The ascent to greatness, however steep and dangerous, may entertain an active spirit with the consciousness and exercise of its own powers: but the possession of a throne could never yet afford a lasting satisfaction to an ambitious mind. This melancholy truth was felt and acknowledged by Severus. Fortune and merit had, from an humble station, elevated him to the first place among mankind. "He had been all things," as he said himself, "and all was of little value." Distracted with the care not of acquiring but of preserving an empire, oppressed with age and infirmities, careless of fame, and satiated with power, all his prospects of life were closed. The desire of perpetuating the greatness of his family was the only remaining wish of his ambition and paternal tenderness.

Like most of the Africans, Severus was passionately addicted to the vain studies of magic and divination, deeply versed in the interpretation of dreams and omens, and perfectly acquainted with the science of judicial astrology; which, in almost every age except the present, has maintained its dominion over the mind of man. He had lost his first wife while he was governor of the Lyonnese Gaul. In the choice of a second, he sought only to connect himself with some favorite of fortune; and as soon as he had discovered that the young lady of Emesa in Syria had a *royal nativity,* he solicited and obtained her hand. Julia Domna (for that was her name) deserved all that the stars could promise her. She possessed, even in advanced age, the attractions of beauty, and united to a lively imagination a firmness of mind and strength of judgment seldom bestowed on her sex. Her amiable qualities never made any deep impression on the dark and jealous temper of her husband; but in her son's reign, she administered the principal affairs of the empire with a prudence that supported his authority, and with a moderation that sometimes corrected his wild extravagancies. Julia applied herself to letters and philosophy, with some success and with the most splendid reputation. She was the patroness of every art and the friend of every man of genius. The grateful flattery of the learned has celebrated her virtues; but, if we may credit the scandal of ancient history, chastity was very far from being the most conspicuous virtue of the empress Julia.

Two sons, Caracalla and Geta, were the fruit of this marriage, and the destined heirs of the empire. The fond hopes of the father and of the Roman world were soon disappointed by these vain youths, who displayed the indolent security of hereditary princes, and a presumption that fortune would supply the place of merit and application. Without any emulation of virtue or talents, they discovered, almost from their infancy, a fixed and implacable antipathy for each other.

Their aversion, confirmed by years and fomented by the arts of their interested favorites, broke out in childish, and gradually in more serious, competitions; and at length divided the theater, the circus, and the court into two factions, actuated by the hopes and fears of their respective leaders. The prudent emperor endeavored, by every expedient of advice and authority, to allay this growing animosity. The unhappy discord of his sons clouded all his prospects, and threatened to overturn a throne raised with so much labor, cemented with so much blood, and guarded with every defense of arms and treasure. With an impartial hand he maintained between them an exact balance of favor, conferred on both the rank of Augustus, with the revered name of Antoninus; and for the first time the Roman world beheld three emperors. Yet even this equal conduct served only to inflame the contest, whilst the fierce Caracalla asserted the right of primogeniture and the milder Geta courted the affections of the people and the soldiers. In the anguish of a disappointed father, Severus foretold that the weaker of his sons would fall a sacrifice to the stronger; who, in his turn, would be ruined by his own vices.[†]

The declining health and last illness of Severus inflamed the wild ambition and black passions of Caracalla's soul. Impatient of any delay or division of empire, he attempted more than once to shorten the small remainder of his father's days, and endeavored, but without success, to excite a mutiny among the troops. The old emperor had often censured the misguided lenity of Marcus, who by a single act of justice might have saved the Romans from the tyranny of his worthless son. Placed in the same situation, he experienced how easily the rigor of a judge dissolves away in the tenderness of a parent. He deliberated, he threatened, but he could not punish; and this last and only instance of mercy was more fatal to the empire than a long series of cruelty. The disorder of his mind irritated the pains of his body; he wished impatiently for death, and hastened the instant of it by his impatience. He expired at York in the sixty-fifth year of his life, and in the eighteenth of a glorious and successful reign [February 4, A.D. 211]. In his last moments he recommended concord to his sons, and his sons to the army. The salutary advice never reached the heart, or even the understanding, of the impetuous youths; but the more obedient troops, mindful of their oath of allegiance and of the authority of their deceased master, resisted the solicitations of Caracalla and proclaimed both brothers emperors of Rome. The new princes soon left the Caledonians in peace, returned to the capital, celebrated their father's funeral with divine honors, and were cheerfully acknowledged as lawful sovereigns by the senate, the people, and the provinces. Some preeminence of rank seems to have been allowed to the elder brother; but they both administered the empire with equal and independent power.

Such a divided form of government would have proved a source of discord between the most affectionate brothers. It was impossible that it could long subsist between two implacable enemies who neither desired nor could trust a reconciliation. It was visible that one only could reign, and that the other must fall; and each of them, judging of his rival's designs by his own, guarded his life with the most jealous vigilance from the repeated attacks of poison or the sword. Their rapid journey through Gaul and Italy, during which they never ate at the same table or slept in the same house, displayed to the provinces the odious spectacle of fraternal discord. On their arrival at Rome, they immediately divided the vast extent of the Imperial palace. No communication was allowed between their apartments; the doors and passages were diligently fortified, and guards posted and relieved with the same strictness as in a besieged place. The emperors met only in public, in the presence of their afflicted mother, and each surrounded by a numerous train of armed followers. Even on these occasions of ceremony, the dissimulation of courts could ill disguise the rancor of their hearts.

This latent civil war already distracted the whole government, when a scheme was suggested that seemed of mutual benefit to the hostile brothers. It was proposed that since it was impossible to reconcile their minds, they should separate their interest, and divide the empire between them. . . .

Had the treaty been carried into execution, the sovereign of Europe might soon have been the conqueror of Asia; but Caracalla obtained an easier, though a more guilty, victory [February 27, A.D. 212]. He artfully listened to his mother's entreaties and consented to meet his brother in her apartment on terms of peace and reconciliation. In the midst of their conversation, some centurions, who had contrived to conceal themselves, rushed with drawn swords upon the unfortunate Geta. His distracted mother strove to protect him in her arms; but in the unavailing struggle, she was wounded in the hand and covered with the blood of her younger son while she saw the elder animating and assisting the fury of the assassins. As soon as the deed was perpetrated, Caracalla, with hasty steps and horror in his countenance, ran towards the Praetorian camp, as his only refuge, and threw himself on the ground before the statues of the tutelar deities. The soldiers attempted to raise and comfort him. In broken and disordered words he informed them of his imminent danger and fortunate escape, insinuating that he had prevented the designs of his enemy, and declared his resolution to live and die with his faithful troops. Geta had been the favorite of the soldiers; but complaint was useless, revenge was dangerous, and they still reverenced the son of Severus. Their discontent died away in idle murmurs, and Caracalla soon convinced them of the justice of his cause by distributing in one lavish donative the accumulated treasures of his father's reign. The real *sentiments* of the soldiers alone were of importance to his power or safety. Their declaration in his favor commanded the dutiful *professions* of the senate. The obsequious assembly was always prepared to ratify the decision of fortune; but as Caracalla wished to assuage the first emotions of public indignation, the name of Geta was mentioned with decency, and he received the funeral honors of a Roman emperor. Posterity, in pity to his misfortune, has cast a veil over his vices. We consider that young prince as the innocent victim of his brother's ambition, without recollecting that he himself wanted power, rather than inclination, to consummate the same attempts of revenge and murder.

The crime went not unpunished. Neither business, nor pleasure, nor flattery could defend Caracalla from the stings of a guilty conscience; and he confessed, in the anguish of a tortured mind, that his disordered fancy often beheld the angry forms of his father and his brother rising into life to threaten and upbraid him. The consciousness of his crime should have induced him to convince mankind, by the virtues of his reign, that the bloody deed had been the involuntary effect of fatal necessity. But the repentance of Caracalla only prompted him to remove from the world whatever could remind him of his guilt, or recall the memory of his murdered brother. . . . It was computed that, under the vague appellation of the friends of Geta, above twenty thousand persons of both sexes suffered death.†

It had hitherto been the peculiar felicity of the Romans, and in the worst of times the consolation, that the virtue of the emperors was active and their vice indolent. Augustus, Trajan, Hadrian, and Marcus visited their extensive dominions in person, and their progress was marked by acts of wisdom and beneficence. The tyranny of Tiberius, Nero, and Domitian, who resided almost constantly at Rome or in the adjacent villas, was confined to the senatorial and equestrian orders. But Caracalla was the common enemy of mankind. He left the capital (and he never returned to it) about a year after the murder of Geta [A.D. 213]. The rest of his reign was spent in the several provinces of the empire, particularly those of the East, and every province was by turns the scene of his rapine and cruelty. The senators, compelled by fear to attend his capricious motions,were obliged to provide daily entertainments at an immense expense, which he abandoned with contempt to his guards; and to erect, in every city, magnificent palaces and theaters, which he either disdained to visit or ordered immediately thrown down. The most wealthy families were ruined by partial fines and confiscations, and the great body of his subjects oppressed by ingenious and aggravated taxes. In the midst of peace, and upon the slightest provocation, he issued his commands, at Alexandria in Egypt, for a general massacre. From a secure post in the temple of Serapis, he viewed and directed the slaughter of many thousand citizens, as well as strangers, without distinguishing the number or the crime of the sufferers, since, as he coolly informed the senate, *all* the Alexandrians, those who perished and those who had escaped, were alike guilty.

The wise instructions of Severus never made any lasting impression on the mind of his son, who, although not destitute of imagination and eloquence, was equally devoid of judgment and humanity. One dangerous maxim, worthy of a tyrant, was remembered and abused by Caracalla: "To secure the affections of the army, and to esteem the rest of his subjects as of little moment." But the liberality of the father had been restrained by prudence, and his indulgence to the troops was tempered by firmness and authority. The careless profusion of the son was the policy of one reign, and the inevitable ruin both of the army and of the empire. The vigor of the soldiers, instead of being confirmed by the severe discipline of camps, melted away in the luxury of cities. The excessive increase of their pay and donatives exhausted the state to enrich the military order, whose modesty in peace and service in war is best secured by an honorable poverty. The demeanor of Caracalla was haughty and full of pride; but with the troops he forgot even the proper dignity of his rank, encouraged their insolent familiarity, and, neglecting the essential duties of a general, affected to imitate the dress and manners of a common soldier.

It was impossible that such a character, and such conduct as that of Caracalla, could inspire either love or esteem; but as long as his vices were beneficial to the armies, he was secure from the danger of rebellion. A secret conspiracy, provoked by his own jealousy, was fatal to the tyrant [March 8, A.D. 217]. The Praetorian praefecture was divided between two ministers. The military department was entrusted to Adventus, an experienced rather than able soldier; and the civil affairs were transacted by Opilius Macrinus, who, by his dexterity in business, had raised himself, with a fair character, to that high office. But his favor varied with the caprice of the emperor, and his life might depend on the slightest suspicion or the most casual circumstance. Malice or fanaticism had suggested to an African deeply skilled in the knowledge of futurity a very dangerous prediction, that Macrinus and his son were destined to reign over the empire. The report was soon diffused through the province; and when the man was sent in chains to Rome, he still asserted, in the presence of the praefect of the city, the faith of his prophecy. That magistrate, who had received the most pressing instructions to inform himself of the successors of Caracalla, immediately communicated the examination of the African to the Imperial court, which at that time resided in Syria. But notwithstanding the diligence of the public messengers, a friend of Macrinus found means to apprise him of the approaching danger. The emperor received the letters from Rome; and as he was then engaged in the conduct of a chariot race, he delivered them unopened to the Praetorian praefect, directing him to despatch the ordinary affairs and to report the more important business that might be contained in them. Macrinus read his fate, and resolved to prevent it. He inflamed the discontents of some inferior officers and employed the hand of Martialis, a desperate soldier who had been refused the rank of centurion. The devotion of Caracalla prompted him to make a pilgrimage from Edessa to the celebrated temple of the Moon at Carrhae. He was attended by a body of cavalry: but having stopped on the road for some necessary occasion, his guards preserved a respectful distance, and Martialis, approaching his person under a presence of duty, stabbed him with a dagger. The bold assassin was instantly killed by a Scythian archer of the Imperial guard. Such was the end of a monster whose life disgraced human nature, and whose reign accused the patience of the Romans. The grateful soldiers forgot his vices, remembered only his partial liberality, and obliged the senate to prostitute their own dignity and that of religion by granting him a place among the gods. Whilst he was upon earth, Alexander the Great was the only hero whom this god deemed worthy of his admiration. He assumed the name and ensigns of Alexander, formed a Macedonian phalanx of guards, persecuted the disciples of Aristotle, and displayed, with a puerile enthusiasm, the only sentiment by which he discovered any regard for virtue or glory . . . ; but in no one action of his life did Caracalla express the faintest resemblance of the Macedonian hero, except in the murder of a great number of his own and of his father's friends.

After the extinction of the house of Severus, the Roman world remained three days without a master. The choice of the army (for the authority of a distant and feeble senate was little regarded) hung in anxious suspense, as no candidate presented himself whose distinguished birth and merit could engage their attachment and unite their suffrages. The decisive weight of the Praetorian guards elevated the hopes of their praefects, and these powerful ministers began to assert their legal claim to fill the vacancy of the Imperial throne. Adventus, however, the senior praefect, conscious of his age and infirmities, of his small reputation and his smaller abilities, resigned the dangerous honor to the crafty ambition of his colleague Macrinus, whose well-dissembled grief removed all suspicion of his being accessory to his master's death. The troops neither loved nor esteemed his character. They cast their eyes around in search of a competitor, and at last yielded with reluctance to his promises of unbounded liberality and indulgence [March 11, A.D. 217].[†]

[In the management of a necessary reformation of the army,] Macrinus proceeded with a cautious prudence which would have restored health and vigor to the Roman army in an easy and almost imperceptible manner. To the soldiers already engaged in the service, he was constrained to leave the dangerous privileges and extravagant pay given by Caracalla; but the new recruits were received on the more moderate though liberal establishment of Severus, and gradually formed to modesty and obedience. One fatal error destroyed the salutary effects of this judicious plan. The numerous army assembled in the East by the late emperor, instead of being immediately dispersed by Macrinus through the several provinces, was suffered to remain united in Syria during the winter that followed his elevation. In the luxurious idleness of their quarters, the troops viewed their strength and numbers, communicated their complaints, and revolved in their minds the advantages of another revolution. The veterans, instead of being flattered by the advantageous distinction, were alarmed by the first steps of the emperor, which they considered as the presage of his future intentions. The recruits, with sullen reluctance, entered on a service whose labors were increased while its rewards were diminished by a covetous and unwarlike sovereign. The murmurs of the army swelled with impunity into seditious clamors; and the partial mutinies betrayed a spirit of discontent and disaffection that waited only for the slightest occasion to break out on every side into a general rebellion. To minds thus disposed, the occasion soon presented itself.

The empress Julia had experienced all the vicissitudes of fortune. From an humble station she had been raised to greatness, only to taste the superior bitterness of an exalted rank. She was doomed to weep over the death of one of her sons, and over the life of the other. The cruel fate of Caracalla, though her good sense must have long taught her to expect it, awakened the feelings of a mother and of an empress. Notwithstanding the respectful civility expressed by the usurper towards the widow of Severus, she descended with a painful struggle into the condition of a subject and soon withdrew herself, by a voluntary death, from the anxious and humiliating dependence. Julia Maesa, her sister, was ordered to leave the court and Antioch. She retired to Emesa with an immense fortune, the fruit of twenty years' favor, accompanied by her two daughters, Soaemias and Mamaea, each of whom was a widow, and each had an only son. Bassianus, for that was the name of the son of Soaemias, was consecrated to the honorable ministry of high priest of the Sun; and this holy vocation, embraced either from prudence or superstition, contributed to raise the Syrian youth to the empire of Rome. A numerous body of troops was stationed at Emesa; and as the severe discipline of Macrinus had constrained them to pass the winter encamped, they were eager to revenge the cruelty of such unaccustomed hardships. The soldiers, who resorted in crowds to the temple of the Sun, beheld with veneration and delight the elegant dress and figure of the young pontiff; they recognized, or they thought that they recognized, the features of Caracalla, whose memory they now adored. The artful Maesa saw and cherished their rising partiality, and readily sacrificing her daughter's reputation to the fortune of her grandson, she insinuated that Bassianus was the natural son of their murdered sovereign. The sums distributed by her emissaries with a lavish hand silenced every objection, and the profusion sufficiently proved the affinity, or at least the resemblance, of Bassianus with the great original. The young Antoninus (for he had assumed and polluted that respectable name) was declared emperor by the troops of Emesa, asserted his hereditary right, and called aloud on the armies to follow the standard of a young and liberal prince who had taken up arms to revenge his father's death and the oppression of the military order [May 16, A.D. 218].

Whilst a conspiracy of women and eunuchs was concerted with prudence and conducted with rapid vigor, Macrinus, who by a decisive motion might have crushed his infant enemy, floated between the opposite extremes of terror and security, which alike fixed him inactive at Antioch. A spirit of rebellion diffused itself through all the camps and garrisons of Syria; successive detachments murdered their officers and joined the party of the rebels; and the tardy restitution of military pay and privileges was imputed to the acknowledged weakness of Macrinus. At length he marched out of Antioch to meet the increasing and zealous army of the young pretender [June 7, A.D. 218]. His own troops seemed to take the field with faintness and reluctance; but in the heat of the battle, the Praetorian guards, almost by an involuntary impulse, asserted the superiority of their valor and discipline. The rebel ranks were broken when the mother and grandmother of the Syrian prince, who according to their Eastern custom had attended the army, threw themselves from their covered chariots and, by exciting the compassion of the soldiers, endeavored to animate their drooping courage. Antoninus himself, who in the rest of his life never acted like a man, in this important crisis of his fate approved himself a hero, mounted his horse, and, at the head of his rallied troops charged sword in hand among the thickest of the enemy; whilst the eunuch Gannys, whose occupations had been confined to female cares and the soft luxury of Asia, displayed the talents of an able and experienced general. The battle still raged with doubtful violence, and Macrinus might have obtained the victory had he not betrayed his own cause by a shameful and precipitate flight. His cowardice served only to protract his life a few days, and to stamp deserved ignominy on his misfortunes. . . . As soon as the stubborn Praetorians could be convinced that they fought for a prince who had basely deserted them, they surrendered to the conqueror: the contending parties of the Roman army, mingling tears of joy and tenderness, united under the banners of the imagined son of Caracalla, and the East acknowledged with pleasure the first emperor of Asiatic extraction.†

The specious letters in which the young conqueror announced his victory to the obedient senate were filled with professions of virtue and moderation; the shining examples of Marcus and Augustus, he should ever consider as the great rule of his administration; and he affected to dwell with pride on the striking resemblance of his own age and fortunes with those of Augustus, who in the earliest youth had revenged, by a successful war, the murder of his father. By adopting the style of Marcus Aurelius Antoninus, son of Antoninus and grandson of Severus, he tacitly asserted his hereditary claim to the empire; but by assuming the tribunician and proconsular powers before they had been conferred on him by a decree of the senate, he offended the delicacy of Roman prejudice. This new and injudicious violation of the constitution was probably dictated either by the ignorance of his Syrian courtiers or the fierce disdain of his military followers.

As the attention of the new emperor was diverted by the most trifling amusements, he wasted many months in his luxurious progress from Syria to Italy, passed at Nicomedia his first winter after his victory, and deferred till the ensuing summer his triumphal entry into the capital [A.D. 219]. A faithful picture, however, which preceded his arrival and was placed by his immediate order over the altar of Victory in the senate house, conveyed to the Romans the just but unworthy resemblance of his person and manners. He was drawn in his sacerdotal robes of silk and gold after the loose flowing fashion of the Medes and Phoenicians; his head was covered with a lofty tiara, his numerous collars and bracelets were adorned with gems of an inestimable value. His eyebrows were tinged with black, and his cheeks painted with an artificial red and white. The grave senators confessed with a sigh that, after having long experienced the stern tyranny of their own countrymen, Rome was at length humbled beneath the effeminate luxury of Oriental despotism.

The Sun was worshiped at Emesa under the name of Elagabalus, and under the form of a black conical stone which, as it was universally believed, had fallen from heaven on that sacred place. To this protecting deity, Antoninus, not without some reason, ascribed his elevation to the throne. The display of superstitious gratitude was the only serious business of his reign. The triumph of the god of Emesa over all the religions of the earth was the great object of his zeal and vanity; and the appellation of Elagabalus (for he presumed as pontiff and favorite to adopt that sacred name) was dearer to him than all the titles of Imperial greatness. In a solemn procession through the streets of Rome, the way was strewed with gold dust; the black stone, set in precious gems, was placed on a chariot drawn by six milk-white horses richly caparisoned. The pious emperor held the reins and, supported by his ministers, moved slowly backwards, that he might perpetually enjoy the felicity of the divine presence. In a magnificent temple raised on the Palatine Mount, the sacrifices of the god Elagabalus were celebrated with every circumstance of cost and solemnity. The richest wines, the most extraordinary victims, and the rarest aromatics were profusely consumed on his altar. Around the altar, a chorus of Syrian damsels performed their lascivious dances to the sound of Barbarian music, whilst the gravest personages of the state and army, clothed in long Phoenician tunics, officiated in the meanest functions with affected zeal and secret indignation.

To this temple, as to the common center of religious worship, the Imperial fanatic attempted to remove the *Ancilia* [shields], the *Palladium* [statue of Minerva], and all the sacred pledges of the faith of Numa. A crowd of inferior deities attended in various stations the majesty of the god of Emesa; but his court was still imperfect till a female of distinguished rank was admitted to his bed. Pallas had been first chosen for his consort; but as it was dreaded lest her warlike terrors might affright the soft delicacy of a Syrian deity, the Moon, adored by the Africans under the name of Astarte, was deemed a more suitable companion for the Sun. Her image, with the rich offerings of her temple as a marriage portion, was transported with solemn pomp from Carthage to Rome, and the day of these mystic nuptials was a general festival in the capital and throughout the empire.

A rational voluptuary adheres with invariable respect to the temperate dictates of nature, and improves the gratifications of sense by social intercourse, endearing connections, and the soft coloring of taste and the imagination. But Elagabalus (I speak of the emperor of that name), corrupted by his youth, his country, and his fortune, abandoned himself to the grossest pleasures with ungoverned fury, and soon found disgust and satiety in the midst of his enjoyments. The inflammatory powers of art were summoned to his aid: the confused multitude of women, of wines, and of dishes, and the studied variety of attitude and sauces, served to revive his languid appetites. New terms and new inventions in these sciences, the only ones cultivated and patronized by the monarch, signalized his reign, and transmitted his infamy to succeeding times. A capricious prodigality supplied the want of taste and elegance; and whilst Elagabalus lavished away the treasures of his people in the wildest extravagance, his own voice and that of his flatterers applauded a spirit of magnificence unknown to the tameness of his predecessors. To confound the order of seasons and climates, to sport with the passions and prejudices of his subjects, and to subvert every law of nature and decency were in the number of his most delicious amusements. A long train of concubines and a rapid succession of wives, among whom was a vestal virgin, ravished by force from her sacred asylum, were insufficient to satisfy the impotence of his passions. The master of the Roman world affected to copy the dress and manners of the female sex, preferred the distaff to the scepter, and dishonored the principal dignities of the empire by distributing them among his numerous lovers; one of whom was publicly invested with the title and authority of the emperor's, or, as he more properly styled himself, of the empress's, husband.[†]

The most worthless of mankind are not afraid to condemn in others the same disorders which they allow in themselves; and can readily discover some nice difference of age, character, or station to justify the partial distinction. The licentious soldiers who had raised to the throne the dissolute son of Caracalla blushed at their ignominious choice, and turned with disgust from that monster to contemplate with pleasure the opening virtues of his cousin Alexander, the son of Mamaea. The crafty Maesa, sensible that her grandson Elagabalus must inevitably destroy himself by his own vices, had provided another and surer support of her family. Embracing a favorable moment of fondness and devotion, she had persuaded the young emperor to adopt Alexander and to invest him with the title of Caesar, that his own divine occupations might be no longer interrupted by the care of the earth. In the second rank that amiable prince soon acquired the affections of the public and excited the tyrant's jealousy, who resolved to terminate the dangerous competition, either by corrupting the manners or by taking away the life of his rival.[†]

He soon attempted, by a dangerous experiment, to try the temper of the soldiers. The report of the death of Alexander, and the natural suspicion that he had been murdered, inflamed their passions into fury, and the tempest of the camp could only be appeased by the presence and authority of the popular youth. Provoked at this new instance of their affection for his cousin and their contempt for his person, the emperor ventured to punish some of the leaders of the mutiny. His unseasonable severity proved instantly fatal to his minions, his mother, and himself. Elagabalus was massacred by the indignant Praetorians, his mutilated corpse dragged through the streets of the city and thrown into the Tiber [March 10, A.D. 222]. His memory was branded with eternal infamy by the senate; the justice of whose decree has been ratified by posterity.

In every age and country, the wiser, or at least the stronger, of the two sexes has usurped the powers of the state, and confined the other to the cares and pleasures of domestic life. In hereditary monarchies, however, and especially in those of modern Europe, the gallant spirit of chivalry and the law of succession have accustomed us to allow a singular exception; and a woman is often acknowledged the absolute sovereign of a great kingdom in which she would be deemed incapable of exercising the smallest employment, civil or military. But as the Roman emperors were still considered as the generals and magistrates of the republic, their wives and mothers, although distinguished by the name of Augusta, were never associated to their personal honors; and a female reign would have appeared an inexpiable prodigy in the eyes of those primitive Romans, who married without love, or loved without delicacy and respect. The haughty Agrippina aspired, indeed, to share the honors of the empire which she had conferred on her son; but her mad ambition, detested by every citizen who felt for the dignity of Rome, was disappointed by the artful firmness of Seneca and Burrhus. The good sense, or the indifference, of succeeding princes restrained them from offending the prejudices of their subjects; and it was reserved for the profligate Elagabalus to discharge the acts of the senate with the name of his mother Soaemias, who was placed by the side of the consuls and subscribed, as a regular member, the decrees of the legislative assembly. Her more prudent sister, Mamaea, declined the useless and odious prerogative, and a solemn law was enacted excluding women forever from the senate, and devoting to the infernal gods the head of the wretch by whom this sanction should be violated. The substance, not the pageantry, of power was the object of Mamaea's manly ambition. She maintained an absolute and lasting empire over the mind of her son, and in his affection the mother could not brook a rival. Alexander, with her consent, married the daughter of a Patrician; but his respect for his father-in-law, and love for the empress, were inconsistent with the tenderness of interest of Mamaea. The patrician was executed on the ready accusation of treason, and the wife of Alexander driven with ignominy from the palace and banished into Africa.

Notwithstanding this act of jealous cruelty, as well as some instances of avarice with which Mamaea is charged, the general tenor of her administration was equally for the benefit of her son and of the empire. With the approbation of the senate, she chose sixteen of the wisest and most virtuous senators as a perpetual council of state, before whom every public business of moment was debated and determined. The celebrated Ulpian, equally distinguished by his knowledge of and his respect for the laws of Rome, was at their head; and the prudent firmness of this aristocracy restored order and authority to the government. As soon as they had purged the city from foreign superstition and luxury, the remains of the capricious tyranny of Elagabalus, they applied themselves to remove his worthless creatures from every department of the public administration and to supply their places with men of virtue and ability. Learning, and the love of justice, became the only recommendations for civil offices; valor, and the love of discipline, the only qualifications for military employments.

But the most important care of Mamaea and her wise counselors was to form the character of the young emperor on whose personal qualities the happiness or misery of the Roman world must ultimately depend. The fortunate soil assisted, and even prevented, the hand of cultivation. An excellent understanding soon convinced Alexander of the advantages of virtue, the pleasure of knowledge, and the necessity of labor. A natural mildness and moderation of temper preserved him from the assaults of passion and the allurements of vice. His unalterable regard for his mother, and his esteem for the wise Ulpian, guarded his unexperienced youth from the poison of flattery.[†]

Since the accession of Commodus, the Roman world had experienced, during the term of forty years, the successive and various vices of four tyrants. From the death of Elagabalus, it enjoyed an auspicious calm of thirteen years [A.D. 223–235]. The provinces, relieved from the oppressive taxes invented by Caracalla and his pretended son, flourished in peace and prosperity under the administration of magistrates, who were convinced by experience that to deserve the love of the subjects was their best and only method of obtaining the favor of their sovereign. While some gentle restraints were imposed on the innocent luxury of the Roman people, the price of provisions and the interest of money were reduced by the paternal care of Alexander, whose prudent liberality, without distressing the industrious, supplied the wants and amusements of the populace. The dignity, the freedom, the authority of the senate was restored; and every virtuous senator might approach the person of the emperor without a fear and without a blush.[†]

In the civil administration of Alexander, wisdom was enforced by power, and the people, sensible of the public felicity, repaid their bene-factor with their love and gratitude. There still remained a greater, a more necessary, but a more difficult enterprise: the reformation of the military order, whose interest and temper, confirmed by long impunity, rendered them impatient of the restraints of discipline, and careless of the blessings of public tranquility. In the execution of his design, the emperor affected to display his love and to conceal his fear of the army. The most rigid economy in every other branch of the adminis-tration supplied a fund of gold and silver for the ordinary pay and the extraordinary rewards of the troops. In their marches he relaxed the severe obligation of carrying seventeen days' provision on their shoul-ders. Ample magazines were formed along the public roads, and as soon as they entered the enemy's country, a numerous train of mules and camels waited on their haughty laziness. As Alexander despaired of correcting the luxury of his soldiers, he attempted at least to direct it to objects of martial pomp and ornament, fine horses, splendid armor, and shields enriched with silver and gold. He shared whatever fatigues he was obliged to impose, visited in person the sick and wounded, pre-served an exact register of their services and his own gratitude, and expressed on every occasion the warmest regard for a body of men whose welfare, as he affected to declare, was so closely connected with that of the state. By the most gentle arts he labored to inspire the fierce multitude with a sense of duty, and to restore at least a faint image of that discipline to which the Romans owed their empire over so many other nations as warlike and more powerful than themselves. But his prudence was vain, his courage fatal, and the attempt towards a refor-mation served only to inflame the ills it was meant to cure.

The Praetorian guards were attached to the youth of Alexander. They loved him as a tender pupil whom they had saved from a tyrant's fury and placed on the Imperial throne. That amiable prince was sen-sible of the obligation; but as his gratitude was restrained within the limits of reason and justice, they soon were more dissatisfied with the virtues of Alexander than they had ever been with the vices of Elaga-balus. Their praefect, the wise Ulpian, was the friend of the laws and of the people; he was considered as the enemy of the soldiers, and to his pernicious counsels every scheme of reformation was imputed. Some trifling accident blew up their discontent into a furious mutiny; and the civil war raged during three days in Rome, whilst the life of that excellent minister was defended by the grateful people. Terrified, at length, by the sight of some houses in flames and by the threats of a general conflagration, the people yielded with a sigh and left the virtuous but unfortunate Ulpian to his fate. He was pursued into the Imperial palace and massacred at the feet of his master, who vainly strove to cover him with the purple and to obtain his pardon from the inexorable soldiers. Such was the deplorable weakness of government that the emperor was unable to revenge his murdered friend and his insulted dignity without stooping to the arts of patience and dissimulation.[†]

The lenity of the emperor confirmed the insolence of the troops; the legions imitated the example of the guards, and defended their prerogative of licentiousness with the same furious obstinacy. The administration of Alexander was an unavailing struggle against the corruption of his age. In Illyricum, in Mauritania, in Armenia, in Mesopotamia, in Germany, fresh mutinies perpetually broke out; his officers were murdered, his authority was insulted, and his life at last sacrificed to the fierce discontents of the army. . . . The fatigues of the Persian war irritated the military discontent; the unsuccessful event degraded the reputation of the emperor as a general, and even as a soldier. Every cause prepared and every circumstance hastened a revolution, which distracted the Roman empire with a long series of intestine calamities.

The dissolute tyranny of Commodus, the civil wars occasioned by his death, and the new maxims of policy introduced by the house of Severus had all contributed to increase the dangerous power of the army and to obliterate the faint image of laws and liberty that was still impressed on the minds of the Romans. The internal change which undermined the foundations of the empire, we have endeavored to explain with some degree of order and perspicuity. The personal characters of the emperors, their victories, laws, follies, and fortunes, can interest us no farther than as they are connected with the general history of the Decline and Fall of the monarchy. Our constant attention to that great object will not suffer us to overlook a most important edict of Antoninus Caracalla, which communicated to all the free inhabitants of the empire the name and privileges of Roman citizens. His unbounded liberality flowed not, however, from the sentiments of a generous mind; it was the sordid result of avarice, and will naturally be illustrated by some observations on the finances of that state, from the victorious ages of the commonwealth to the reign of Alexander Severus.

The siege of Veii in Tuscany, the first considerable enterprise of the Romans, was protracted to the tenth year, much less by the strength of the place than by the unskillfulness of the besiegers [396 B.C.]. The unaccustomed hardships of so many winter campaigns, at the distance of near twenty miles from home, required more than common encouragements; and the senate wisely prevented the clamors of the people by the institution of a regular pay for the soldiers, which was levied by a general tribute assessed according to an equitable proportion on the property of the citizens. During more than two hundred years after the conquest of Veii, the victories of the republic added less to the wealth than to the power of Rome. The states of Italy paid their tribute in military service only, and the vast force, both by sea and land, which was exerted in the Punic wars was maintained at the expense of the Romans themselves. That high-spirited people (such is often the generous enthusiasm of freedom) cheerfully submitted to the most excessive but voluntary burdens, in the just confidence that they should speedily enjoy the rich harvest of their labors. Their expectations were not disappointed. In the course of a few years, the riches of Syracuse, of Carthage, of Macedonia, and of Asia were brought in triumph to Rome. The treasures of Perseus alone amounted to near two millions sterling, and the Roman people, the sovereign of so many nations, was forever delivered from the weight of taxes. The increasing revenue of the provinces was found sufficient to defray the ordinary establishment of war and government, and the superfluous mass of gold and silver was deposited in the temple of Saturn and reserved for any unforeseen emergency of the state.[†]

It is not easy to determine whether [Augustus] acted as the common father of the Roman world or as the oppressor of liberty; whether he wished to relieve the provinces or to impoverish the senate and the equestrian order. But no sooner had he assumed the reins of government than he frequently intimated the insufficiency of the tributes, and the necessity of throwing an equitable proportion of the public burden upon Rome and Italy. In the prosecution of this unpopular design he advanced, however, by cautious and well-weighed steps. The introduction of customs was followed by the establishment of an excise, and the scheme of taxation was completed by an artful assessment on the real and personal property of the Roman citizens, who had been exempted from any kind of contribution above a century and a half.

I. . . . In the reign of Augustus and his successors, duties were imposed on every kind of merchandise, which through a thousand channels flowed to the great center of opulence and luxury; and in whatsoever manner the law was expressed, it was the Roman purchaser, and not the provincial merchant, who paid the tax.†

II. The excise introduced by Augustus after the civil wars was extremely moderate, but it was general. It seldom exceeded one percent; but it comprehended whatever was sold in the markets or by public auction, from the most considerable purchases of lands and houses to those minute objects which can only derive a value from their infinite multitude and daily consumption. Such a tax, as it affects the body of the people, has ever been the occasion of clamor and discontent. An emperor well acquainted with the wants and resources of the state was obliged to declare by a public edict that the support of the army depended in a great measure on the produce of the excise.

III. When Augustus resolved to establish a permanent military force for the defense of his government against foreign and domestic enemies, he instituted a peculiar treasury for the pay of the soldiers, the rewards of the veterans, and the extraordinary expenses of war. The ample revenue of the excise, though peculiarly appropriated to those uses, was found inadequate. To supply the deficiency, the emperor suggested a new tax of five percent on all legacies and inheritances. But the nobles of Rome were more tenacious of property than of freedom. Their indignant murmurs were received by Augustus with his usual temper. He candidly referred the whole business to the senate and exhorted them to provide for the public service by some other expedient of a less odious nature. They were divided and perplexed. He insinuated to them that their obstinacy would oblige him to *propose* a general land tax and capitation. They acquiesced in silence. The new imposition on legacies and inheritances was, however, mitigated by some restrictions. It did not take place unless the object was of a certain value . . . ; nor could it be exacted from the nearest of kin on the father's side. When the rights of nature and poverty were thus secured, it seemed reasonable that a stranger or a distant relation who acquired an unexpected accession of fortune should cheerfully resign a twentieth part of it for the benefit of the state.†

In the first and golden years of the reign of Nero, that prince, from a desire of popularity, and perhaps from a blind impulse of benevolence, conceived a wish of abolishing the oppression of the customs and excise. The wisest senators applauded his magnanimity: but they diverted him from the execution of a design which would have dissolved the strength and resources of the republic. Had it indeed been possible to realize this dream of fancy, such princes as Trajan and the Antonines would surely have embraced with ardor the glorious opportunity of conferring so signal an obligation on mankind.†

The sentiments, and indeed the situation, of Caracalla were very different from those of the Antonines. Inattentive, or rather averse, to the welfare of his people, he found himself under the necessity of gratifying the insatiate avarice which he had excited in the army. Of the several impositions introduced by Augustus, the twentieth on inheritances and legacies was the most fruitful, as well as the most comprehensive. As its influence was not confined to Rome or Italy, the produce continually increased with the gradual extension of the Roman City. The new citizens, though charged on equal terms with the payment of new taxes which had not affected them as subjects, derived an ample compensation from the rank they obtained, the privileges they acquired, and the fair prospect of honors and fortune that was thrown open to their ambition. But the favor which implied a distinction was lost in the prodigality of Caracalla, and the reluctant provincials were compelled to assume the vain title, and the real obligations, of Roman citizens. Nor was the rapacious son of Severus contented with such a measure of taxation as had appeared sufficient to his moderate predecessors. Instead of a twentieth, he exacted a tenth of all legacies and inheritances; and during his reign (for the ancient proportion was restored after his death) he crushed alike every part of the empire under the weight of his iron scepter.

When all the provincials became liable to the peculiar impositions of Roman citizens, they seemed to acquire a legal exemption from the tributes which they had paid in their former condition of subjects. Such were not the maxims of government adopted by Caracalla and his pretended son. The old as well as the new taxes were, at the same time, levied in the provinces. It was reserved for the virtue of Alexander to relieve them in a great measure from this intolerable grievance by reducing the tributes to a thirteenth part of the sum exacted at the time of his accession. It is impossible to conjecture the motive that engaged him to spare so trifling a remnant of the public evil; but the noxious weed, which had not been totally eradicated, again sprang up with the most luxuriant growth, and in the succeeding age darkened the Roman world with its deadly shade. In the course of this history, we shall be too often summoned to explain the land tax, the capitation, and the heavy contributions of corn, wine, oil, and meat, which were exacted from the provinces for the use of the court, the army, and the capital.

As long as Rome and Italy were respected as the center of government, a national spirit was preserved by the ancient, and insensibly imbibed by the adopted, citizens. The principal commands of the army were filled by men who had received a liberal education, were well instructed in the advantages of laws and letters, and who had risen, by equal steps, through the regular succession of civil and military honors. To their influence and example we may partly ascribe the modest obedience of the legions during the two first centuries of the Imperial history.

But when the last enclosure of the Roman constitution was trampled down by Caracalla, the separation of professions gradually succeeded to the distinction of ranks. The more polished citizens of the internal provinces were alone qualified to act as lawyers and magistrates. The rougher trade of arms was abandoned to the peasants and Barbarians of the frontiers, who knew no country but their camp, no science but that of war, no civil laws, and scarcely those of military discipline. With bloody hands, savage manners, and desperate resolutions, they sometimes guarded, but much oftener subverted, the throne of the emperors.

CHAPTER VII

Tyranny of Maximin, Rebellion, Civil Wars, Death of Maximin

The elevation and tyranny of Maximin. • Rebellion in Africa and Italy, under the authority of the senate. • Civil wars and seditions. • Violent deaths of Maximin and his son, of Maximus and Balbinus, and of the three Gordians. • Usurpation and secular games of Philip.

Of the various forms of government which have prevailed in the world, an hereditary monarchy seems to present the fairest scope for ridicule. Is it possible to relate, without an indignant smile, that on the father's decease the property of a nation, like that of a drove of oxen, descends to his infant son, as yet unknown to mankind and to himself; and that the bravest warriors and the wisest statesmen, relinquishing their natural right to empire, approach the royal cradle with bended knees and protestations of inviolable fidelity? Satire and declamation may paint these obvious topics in the most dazzling colors, but our more serious thoughts will respect a useful prejudice that establishes a rule of succession independent of the passions of mankind; and we shall cheerfully acquiesce in any expedient which deprives the multitude of the dangerous, and indeed the ideal, power of giving themselves a master.

In the cool shade of retirement, we may easily devise imaginary forms of government in which the scepter shall be constantly bestowed on the most worthy by the free and incorrupt suffrage of the whole community. Experience overturns these airy fabrics and teaches us that in a large society, the election of a monarch can never devolve to the wisest or to the most numerous part of the people. The army is the only order of men sufficiently united to concur in the same sentiments and powerful enough to impose them on the rest of their fellow-citizens; but the temper of soldiers, habituated at once to violence and to slavery, renders them very unfit guardians of a legal, or even a civil, constitution. Justice, humanity, or political wisdom are qualities they are too little acquainted with in themselves to appreciate them in others. Valor will acquire their esteem, and liberality will purchase their suffrage; but the first of these merits is often lodged in the most savage breasts; the latter can only exert itself at the expense of the public; and both may be turned against the possessor of the throne by the ambition of a daring rival.

The superior prerogative of birth, when it has obtained the sanction of time and popular opinion, is the plainest and least invidious of all distinctions among mankind. The acknowledged right extinguishes the hopes of faction, and the conscious security disarms the cruelty of the monarch. To the firm establishment of this idea we owe the peaceful succession and mild administration of European monarchies. . . . But the Roman empire, after the authority of the senate had sunk into contempt, was a vast scene of confusion. The royal, and even noble, families of the provinces had long since been led in triumph before the car of the haughty republicans. The ancient families of Rome had successively fallen beneath the tyranny of the Caesars; and whilst those princes were shackled by the forms of a commonwealth and disappointed by the repeated failure of their posterity, it was impossible that any idea of hereditary succession should have taken root in the minds of their subjects. The right to the throne, which none could claim from birth, everyone assumed from merit. The daring hopes of ambition were set loose from the salutary restraints of law and prejudice; and the meanest of mankind might, without folly, entertain a hope of being raised by valor and fortune to a rank in the army in which a single crime would enable him to wrest the scepter of the world from his feeble and unpopular master. After the murder of Alexander Severus and the elevation of Maximin, no emperor could think himself safe upon the throne, and every Barbarian peasant of the frontier might aspire to that august but dangerous station.

About thirty-two years before that event, the emperor Severus, returning from an Eastern expedition, halted in Thrace to celebrate, with military games, the birthday of his younger son, Geta. The country flocked in crowds to behold their sovereign, and a young Barbarian of gigantic stature earnestly solicited, in his rude dialect, that he might be allowed to contend for the prize of wrestling. As the pride of discipline would have been disgraced in the overthrow of a Roman soldier by a Thracian peasant, he was matched with the stoutest followers of the camp, sixteen of whom he successively laid on the ground. His victory was rewarded by some trifling gifts and a permission to enlist in the troops. The next day, the happy Barbarian was distinguished above a crowd of recruits, dancing and exulting after the fashion of his country. As soon as he perceived that he had attracted the emperor's notice, he instantly ran up to his horse and followed him on foot, without the least appearance of fatigue, in a long and rapid career. "Thracian," said Severus with astonishment, "art thou disposed to wrestle after thy race?" "Most willingly, sir," replied the unwearied youth; and, almost in a breath, overthrew seven of the strongest soldiers in the army. A gold collar was the prize of his matchless vigor and activity, and he was immediately appointed to serve in the horse-guards who always attended on the person of the sovereign.

Maximin, for that was his name, though born on the territories of the empire, descended from a mixed race of Barbarians. His father was a Goth, and his mother of the nation of the Alani. He displayed on every occasion a valor equal to his strength; and his native fierceness was soon tempered or disguised by the knowledge of the world. Under the reign of Severus and his son, he obtained the rank of centurion, with the favor and esteem of both those princes, the former of whom was an excellent judge of merit. Gratitude forbade Maximin to serve under the assassin of Caracalla. Honor taught him to decline the effeminate insults of Elagabalus. On the accession of Alexander he returned to court and was placed by that prince in a station useful to the service and honorable to himself. The fourth legion, to which he was appointed tribune, soon became, under his care, the best disciplined of the whole army. With the general applause of the soldiers, who bestowed on their favorite hero the names of Ajax and Hercules, he was successively promoted to the first military command; and had not he still retained too much of his savage origin, the emperor might perhaps have given his own sister in marriage to the son of Maximin.

Instead of securing his fidelity, these favors served only to inflame the ambition of the Thracian peasant, who deemed his fortune inadequate to his merit as long as he was constrained to acknowledge a superior. Though a stranger to real wisdom, he was not devoid of a selfish cunning, which showed him that the emperor had lost the affection of the army and taught him to improve their discontent to his own advantage. . . . One day, as he entered the field of exercise, the troops, either from a sudden impulse or a formed conspiracy, saluted him emperor, silenced by their loud acclamations his obstinate refusal, and hastened to consummate their rebellion by the murder of Alexander Severus [March 19, A.D. 235].[†]

The son of Mamaea, betrayed and deserted, withdrew into his tent, desirous at least to conceal his approaching fate from the insults of the multitude. He was soon followed by a tribune and some centurions, the ministers of death; but instead of receiving with manly resolution the inevitable stroke, his unavailing cries and entreaties disgraced the last moments of his life and converted into contempt some portion of the just pity which his innocence and misfortunes must inspire. His mother, Mamaea, whose pride and avarice he loudly accused as the causes of his ruin, perished with her son. The most faithful of his friends were sacrificed to the first fury of the soldiers. Others were reserved for the more deliberate cruelty of the usurper; and those who experienced the mildest treatment were stripped of their employments and ignominiously driven from the court and army.

The former tyrants Caligula and Nero, Commodus, and Caracalla were all dissolute and unexperienced youths, educated in the purple and corrupted by the pride of empire, the luxury of Rome, and the perfidious voice of flattery. The cruelty of Maximin was derived from a different source, the fear of contempt. Though he depended on the attachment of the soldiers, who loved him for virtues like their own, he was conscious that his mean and Barbarian origin, his savage appearance, and his total ignorance of the arts and institutions of civil life formed a very unfavorable contrast with the amiable manners of the unhappy Alexander. He remembered that, in his humbler fortune, he had often waited before the door of the haughty nobles of Rome, and had been denied admittance by the insolence of their slaves. He recollected too the friendship of a few who had relieved his poverty and assisted his rising hopes. But those who had spurned and those who had protected the Thracian were guilty of the same crime, the knowledge of his original obscurity. For this crime many were put to death; and by the execution of several of his benefactors Maximin published, in characters of blood, the indelible history of his baseness and ingratitude.

The dark and sanguinary soul of the tyrant was open to every suspicion against those among his subjects who were the most distinguished by their birth or merit. Whenever he was alarmed with the sound of treason, his cruelty was unbounded and unrelenting. A conspiracy against his life was either discovered or imagined, and Magnus, a consular senator, was named as the principal author of it. Without a witness, without a trial, and without an opportunity of defense, Magnus, with four thousand of his supposed accomplices, was put to death. Italy and the whole empire were infested with innumerable spies and informers. On the slightest accusation, the first of the Roman nobles, who had governed provinces, commanded armies, and been adorned with the consular and triumphal ornaments, were chained on the public carriages and hurried away to the emperor's presence. Confiscation, exile, or simple death were esteemed uncommon instances of his lenity. Some of the unfortunate sufferers he ordered to be sewed up in the hides of slaughtered animals, others to be exposed to wild beasts, others again to be beaten to death with clubs. During the three years of his reign, he disdained to visit either Rome or Italy. His camp, occasionally removed from the banks of the Rhine to those of the Danube, was the seat of his stern despotism, which trampled on every principle of law and justice and was supported by the avowed power of the sword. No man of noble birth, elegant accomplishments, or knowledge of civil business was suffered near his person; and the court of a Roman emperor revived the idea of those ancient chiefs of slaves and gladiators, whose savage power had left a deep impression of terror and detestation.

As long as the cruelty of Maximin was confined to the illustrious senators, or even to the bold adventurers who in the court or army exposed themselves to the caprice of fortune, the body of the people viewed their sufferings with indifference, or perhaps with pleasure. But the tyrant's avarice, stimulated by the insatiate desires of the soldiers, at length attacked the public property. Every city of the empire was possessed of an independent revenue, destined to purchase corn for the multitude and to supply the expenses of the games and entertainments. By a single act of authority, the whole mass of wealth was at once confiscated for the use of the Imperial treasury. The temples were stripped of their most valuable offerings of gold and silver, and the statues of gods, heroes, and emperors were melted down and coined into money. These impious orders could not be executed without tumults and massacres, as in many places the people chose rather to die in the defense of their altars than to behold in the midst of peace their cities exposed to the rapine and cruelty of war. The soldiers themselves, among whom this sacrilegious plunder was distributed, received it with a blush; and hardened as they were in acts of violence, they dreaded the just reproaches of their friends and relations. Throughout the Roman world a general cry of indignation was heard, imploring vengeance on the common enemy of humankind; and at length, by an act of private oppression, a peaceful and unarmed province was driven into rebellion against him.

The procurator of Africa was a servant worthy of such a master who considered the fines and confiscations of the rich as one of the most fruitful branches of the Imperial revenue. An iniquitous sentence had been pronounced against some opulent youths of that country, the execution of which would have stripped them of far the greater part of their patrimony. In this extremity, a resolution that must either complete or prevent their ruin was dictated by despair. A respite of three days, obtained with difficulty from the rapacious treasurer, was employed in collecting from their estates a great number of slaves and peasants blindly devoted to the commands of their lords and armed with the rustic weapons of clubs and axes. The leaders of the conspiracy, as they were admitted to the audience of the procurator, stabbed him with the daggers concealed under their garments and, by the assistance of their tumultuary train, seized on the little town of Thysdrus and erected the standard of rebellion against the sovereign of the Roman empire [April A.D. 237]. They rested their hopes on the hatred of mankind against Maximin, and they judiciously resolved to oppose to that detested tyrant an emperor whose mild virtues had already acquired the love and esteem of the Romans, and whose authority over the province would give weight and stability to the enterprise. Gordianus, their proconsul and the object of their choice, refused, with unfeigned reluctance, the dangerous honor, and begged with tears that they would suffer him to terminate in peace a long and innocent life without staining his feeble age with civil blood. Their menaces compelled him to accept the Imperial purple, his only refuge, indeed, against the jealous cruelty of Maximin; since, according to the reasoning of tyrants, those who have been esteemed worthy of the throne deserve death, and those who deliberate have already rebelled.

The family of Gordianus was one of the most illustrious of the Roman senate. On the father's side he was descended from the Gracchi; on his mother's, from the emperor Trajan. A great estate enabled him to support the dignity of his birth, and in the enjoyment of it he displayed an elegant taste and beneficent disposition. The palace in Rome formerly inhabited by the great Pompey had been, during several generations, in the possession of Gordian's family. It was distinguished by ancient trophies of naval victories, and decorated with the works of modern painting. . . . He was twice elevated to the [consulship], by Caracalla and by Alexander; for he possessed the uncommon talent of acquiring the esteem of virtuous princes without alarming the jealousy of tyrants. His long life was innocently spent in the study of letters and the peaceful honors of Rome; and, till he was named proconsul of Africa by the voice of the senate and the approbation of Alexander, he appears prudently to have declined the command of armies and the government of provinces. As long as that emperor lived, Africa was happy under the administration of his worthy representative: after the barbarous Maximin had usurped the throne, Gordianus alleviated the miseries which he was unable to prevent. When he reluctantly accepted the purple, he was above fourscore years old; a last and valuable remains of the happy age of the Antonines, whose virtues he revived in his own conduct and celebrated in an elegant poem of thirty books. With the venerable proconsul, his son, who had accompanied him into Africa as his lieutenant, was likewise declared emperor. His manners were less pure, but his character was equally amiable with that of his father. Twenty-two acknowledged concubines and a library of sixty-two thousand volumes attested the variety of his inclinations; and from the productions which he left behind him, it appears that the former as well as the latter were designed for use rather than for ostentation. The Roman people acknowledged in the features of the younger Gordian the resemblance of Scipio Africanus, recollected with pleasure that his mother was the granddaughter of Antoninus Pius, and rested the public hope on those latent virtues which had hitherto, as they fondly imagined, lain concealed in the luxurious indolence of private life.

As soon as the Gordians had appeased the first tumult of a popular election, they removed their court to Carthage. They were received with the acclamations of the Africans, who honored their virtues and who, since the visit of Hadrian, had never beheld the majesty of a Roman emperor. But these vain acclamations neither strengthened nor confirmed the title of the Gordians. They were induced by principle, as well as interest, to solicit the approbation of the senate; and a deputation of the noblest provincials was sent without delay to Rome to relate and justify the conduct of their countrymen, who, having long suffered with patience, were at length resolved to act with vigor. The letters of the new princes were modest and respectful, excusing the necessity which had obliged them to accept the Imperial title; but submitting their election and their fate to the supreme judgment of the senate.

The inclinations of the senate were neither doubtful nor divided. The birth and noble alliances of the Gordians had intimately connected them with the most illustrious houses of Rome. Their fortune had created many dependents in that assembly, their merit had acquired many friends. Their mild administration opened the flattering prospect of the restoration not only of the civil but even of the republican government. The terror of military violence, which had first obliged the senate to forget the murder of Alexander and to ratify the election of a Barbarian peasant, now produced a contrary effect, and provoked them to assert the injured rights of freedom and humanity. The hatred of Maximin towards the senate was declared and implacable; the tamest submission had not appeased his fury, the most cautious innocence would not remove his suspicions; and even the care of their own safety urged them to share the fortune of an enterprise of which (if unsuccessful) they were sure to be the first victims. These considerations, and perhaps others of a more private nature, were debated in a previous conference of the consuls and the magistrates. As soon as their resolution was decided, they convoked in the temple of Castor the whole body of the senate, according to an ancient form of secrecy calculated to awaken their attention and to conceal their decrees. "Conscript fathers," said the consul Syllanus, "the two Gordians, both of consular dignity, the one your proconsul, the other your lieutenant, have been declared emperors by the general consent of Africa. Let us return thanks," he boldly continued, "to the youth of Thysdrus; let us return thanks to the faithful people of Carthage, our generous deliverers from a horrid monster—Why do you hear me thus coolly, thus timidly? Why do you cast those anxious looks on each other? Why hesitate? Maximin is a public enemy! May his enmity soon expire with him, and may we long enjoy the prudence and felicity of Gordian the father, the valor and constancy of Gordian the son!" The noble ardor of the consul revived the languid spirit of the senate. By a unanimous decree, the election of the Gordians was ratified, Maximin, his son, and his adherents were pronounced enemies of their country, and liberal rewards were offered to whosoever had the courage and good fortune to destroy them.

During the emperor's absence, a detachment of the Praetorian guards remained at Rome to protect, or rather to command, the capital. The praefect Vitalianus had signalized his fidelity to Maximin by the alacrity with which he had obeyed and even prevented the cruel mandates of the tyrant. His death alone could rescue the authority of the senate and the lives of the senators from a state of danger and suspense. Before their resolves had transpired, a quaestor and some tribunes were commissioned to take his devoted life. They executed the order with equal boldness and success; and with their bloody daggers in their hands ran through the streets, proclaiming to the people and the soldiers the news of the happy revolution. The enthusiasm of liberty was seconded by the promise of a large donative, in lands and money; the statues of Maximin were thrown down; the capital of the empire acknowledged, with transport, the authority of the two Gordians and the senate; and the example of Rome was followed by the rest of Italy.

A new spirit had arisen in that assembly, whose long patience had been insulted by wanton despotism and military license. The senate assumed the reins of government and, with a calm intrepidity, prepared to vindicate by arms the cause of freedom. Among the consular senators recommended by their merit and services to the favor of the emperor Alexander, it was easy to select twenty not unequal to the command of an army and the conduct of a war. To these was the defense of Italy entrusted. Each was appointed to act in his respective department, authorized to enroll and discipline the Italian youth, and instructed to fortify the ports and highways against the impending invasion of Maximin. A number of deputies, chosen from the most illustrious of the senatorian and equestrian orders, were despatched at the same time to the governors of the several provinces, earnestly conjuring them to fly to the assistance of their country, and to remind the nations of their ancient ties of friendship with the Roman senate and people. The general respect with which these deputies were received, and the zeal of Italy and the provinces in favor of the senate, suffi-ciently prove that the subjects of Maximin were reduced to that un-common distress in which the body of the people has more to fear from oppression than from resistance. The consciousness of that mel-ancholy truth inspires a degree of persevering fury seldom to be found in those civil wars which are artificially supported for the benefit of a few factious and designing leaders.

For, while the cause of the Gordians was embraced with such diffu-sive ardor, the Gordians themselves were no more. The feeble court of Carthage was alarmed by the rapid approach of Capelianus, governor of Mauritania, who, with a small band of veterans and a fierce host of Barbarians, attacked a faithful but unwarlike province. The younger Gordian sallied out to meet the enemy at the head of a few guards and a numerous undisciplined multitude educated in the peaceful luxury of Carthage. His useless valor served only to procure him an honor-able death on the field of battle [July 3, A.D. 237]. His aged father, whose reign had not exceeded thirty-six days, put an end to his life on the first news of the defeat. Carthage, destitute of defense, opened her gates to the conqueror, and Africa was exposed to the rapacious cru-elty of a slave obliged to satisfy his unrelenting master with a large account of blood and treasure.

The fate of the Gordians filled Rome with just but unexpected ter-ror. The senate, convoked in the temple of Concord, affected to trans-act the common business of the day; and seemed to decline, with trembling anxiety, the consideration of their own and the public dan-ger. A silent consternation prevailed in the assembly till a senator of the name and family of Trajan awakened his brethren from their fatal lethargy. He represented to them that the choice of cautious, dilatory measures had been long since out of their power; that Maximin, im-placable by nature and exasperated by injuries, was advancing towards Italy at the head of the military force of the empire; and that their only remaining alternative was either to meet him bravely in the field or tamely to expect the tortures and ignominious death reserved for unsuccessful rebellion. "We have lost," continued he, "two excellent princes; but unless we desert ourselves, the hopes of the republic have not perished with the Gordians. Many are the senators whose virtues have deserved, and whose abilities would sustain, the Imperial dignity. Let us elect two emperors, one of whom may conduct the war against the public enemy, whilst his colleague remains at Rome to direct the civil administration. I cheerfully expose myself to the danger and envy of the nomination, and give my vote in favor of Maximus and Balbinus. Ratify my choice, conscript fathers, or appoint in their place others more worthy of the empire." The general apprehension silenced the whispers of jealousy; the merit of the candidates was universally acknowledged; and the house resounded with the sincere acclamations of "Long life and victory to the emperors Maximus and Balbinus. You are happy in the judgment of the senate; may the republic be happy under your administration!"

The virtues and the reputation of the new emperors justified the most sanguine hopes of the Romans. The various nature of their talents seemed to appropriate to each his peculiar department of peace and war without leaving room for jealous emulation. Balbinus was an admired orator, a poet of distinguished fame, and a wise magistrate who had exercised with innocence and applause the civil jurisdiction in almost all the interior provinces of the empire. His birth was noble, his fortune affluent, his manners liberal and affable. In him the love of pleasure was corrected by a sense of dignity, nor had the habits of ease deprived him of a capacity for business. The mind of Maximus was formed in a rougher mold. By his valor and abilities he had raised himself from the meanest origin to the first employments of the state and army. His victories over the Sarmatians and the Germans, the austerity of his life, and the rigid impartiality of his justice while he was a praefect of the city, commanded the esteem of a people whose affections were engaged in favor of the more amiable Balbinus. The two colleagues had both been consuls (Balbinus had twice enjoyed that honorable office), both had been named among the twenty lieutenants of the senate; and since the one was sixty and the other seventy-four years old, they had both attained the full maturity of age and experience.

After the senate had conferred on Maximus and Balbinus an equal portion of the consular and tribunician powers, the title of Fathers of their country, and the joint office of supreme pontiff, they ascended to the Capitol to return thanks to the gods, protectors of Rome. The solemn rites of sacrifice were disturbed by a sedition of the people. The licentious multitude neither loved the rigid Maximus, nor did they sufficiently fear the mild and humane Balbinus. Their increasing numbers surrounded the temple of Jupiter; with obstinate clamors they asserted their inherent right of consenting to the election of their sovereign; and demanded with an apparent moderation that, besides the two emperors chosen by the senate, a third should be added of the family of the Gordians, as a just return of gratitude to those princes who had sacrificed their lives for the republic. At the head of the city-guards and the youth of the equestrian order, Maximus and Balbinus attempted to cut their way through the seditious multitude. The multitude, armed with sticks and stones, drove them back into the Capitol. It is prudent to yield when the contest, whatever may be the issue of it, must be fatal to both parties. A boy, only thirteen years of age, the grandson of the elder and nephew of the younger Gordian, was produced to the people, invested with the ornaments and title of Caesar. The tumult was appeased by this easy condescension; and the two emperors, as soon as they had been peaceably acknowledged in Rome, prepared to defend Italy against the common enemy.

Whilst in Rome and Africa, revolutions succeeded each other with such amazing rapidity that the mind of Maximin was agitated by the most furious passions. He is said to have received the news of the rebellion of the Gordians and of the decree of the senate against him not with the temper of a man but the rage of a wild beast; which, as it could not discharge itself on the distant senate, threatened the life of his son, of his friends, and of all who ventured to approach his person. The grateful intelligence of the death of the Gordians was quickly followed by the assurance that the senate, laying aside all hopes of pardon or accommodation, had substituted in their room two emperors with whose merit he could not be unacquainted. Revenge was the only consolation left to Maximin, and revenge could only be obtained by arms.†

When the troops of Maximin, advancing in excellent order, arrived at the foot of the Julian Alps, they were terrified by the silence and desolation that reigned on the frontiers of Italy [February A.D. 238]. The villages and open towns had been abandoned on their approach by the inhabitants, the cattle was driven away, the provisions removed or destroyed, the bridges broken down, nor was anything left which could afford either shelter or subsistence to an invader. Such had been the wise orders of the generals of the senate: whose design was to protract the war, to ruin the army of Maximin by the slow operation of famine, and to consume his strength in the sieges of the principal cities of Italy, which they had plentifully stored with men and provisions from the deserted country. Aquileia received and withstood the first shock of the invasion. . . . The army of Maximin was repulsed in repeated attacks, his machines destroyed by showers of artificial fire; and the generous enthusiasm of the Aquileians was exalted into a confidence of success by the opinion that Belenus, their tutelar deity, combated in person in the defense of his distressed worshipers.

The emperor Maximus, who had advanced as far as Ravenna, to secure that important place and to hasten the military preparations, beheld the event of the war in the more faithful mirror of reason and policy. He was too sensible that a single town could not resist the persevering efforts of a great army; and he dreaded lest the enemy, tired with the obstinate resistance of Aquileia, should on a sudden relinquish the fruitless siege and march directly towards Rome. The fate of the empire and the cause of freedom must then be committed to the chance of a battle; and what arms could he oppose to the veteran legions of the Rhine and Danube? Some troops newly levied among the generous but enervated youth of Italy; and a body of German auxiliaries on whose firmness, in the hour of trial, it was dangerous to depend. In the midst of these just alarms, the stroke of domestic conspiracy punished the crimes of Maximin, and delivered Rome and the senate from the calamities that would surely have attended the victory of an enraged Barbarian.

The people of Aquileia had scarcely experienced any of the common miseries of a siege; their magazines were plentifully supplied, and several fountains within the walls assured them of an inexhaustible resource of fresh water. The soldiers of Maximin were, on the contrary, exposed to the inclemency of the season, the contagion of disease, and the horrors of famine. The open country was ruined, the rivers filled with the slain and polluted with blood. A spirit of despair and disaffection began to diffuse itself among the troops; and as they were cut off from all intelligence, they easily believed that the whole empire had embraced the cause of the senate, and that they were left as devoted victims to perish under the impregnable walls of Aquileia. The fierce temper of the tyrant was exasperated by disappointments, which he imputed to the cowardice of his army; and his wanton and ill-timed cruelty, instead of striking terror, inspired hatred and a just desire of revenge. A party of Praetorian guards, who trembled for their wives and children in the camp of Alba, near Rome, executed the sentence of the senate. Maximin, abandoned by his guards, was slain in his tent with his son (whom he had associated to the honors of the purple), Anulinus the praefect, and the principal ministers of his tyranny [April A.D. 238]. The sight of their heads borne on the point of spears convinced the citizens of Aquileia that the siege was at an end; the gates of the city were thrown open, a liberal market was provided for the hungry troops of Maximin, and the whole army joined in solemn protestations of fidelity to the senate and the people of Rome, and to their lawful emperors Maximus and Balbinus. Such was the deserved fate of a brutal savage, destitute, as he has generally been represented, of every sentiment that distinguishes a civilized or even a human being. The body was suited to the soul. The stature of Maximin exceeded the measure of eight feet, and circumstances almost incredible are related of his matchless strength and appetite. Had he lived in a less enlightened age, tradition and poetry might well have described him as one of those monstrous giants whose supernatural power was constantly exerted for the destruction of mankind.

It is easier to conceive than to describe the universal joy of the Roman world on the fall of the tyrant, the news of which is said to have been carried in four days from Aquileia to Rome. The return of Maximus was a triumphal procession; his colleague and young Gordian went out to meet him, and the three princes made their entry into the capital attended by the ambassadors of almost all the cities of Italy, saluted with the splendid offerings of gratitude and superstition, and received with the unfeigned acclamations of the senate and people, who persuaded themselves that a golden age would succeed to an age of iron. The conduct of the two emperors corresponded with these expectations. They administered justice in person; and the rigor of the one was tempered by the other's clemency. The oppressive taxes with which Maximin had loaded the rights of inheritance and succession were repealed, or at least moderated. Discipline was revived, and with the advice of the senate many wise laws were enacted by their Imperial ministers, who endeavored to restore a civil constitution on the ruins of military tyranny. "What reward may we expect for delivering Rome from a monster?" was the question asked by Maximus, in a moment of freedom and confidence. Balbinus answered it without hesitation—"The love of the senate, of the people, and of all mankind." "Alas!" replied his more penetrating colleague—"alas! I dread the hatred of the soldiers, and the fatal effects of their resentment." His apprehensions were but too well justified by the event.[†]

When the senate elected two princes, it is probable that, besides the declared reason of providing for the various emergencies of peace and war, they were actuated by the secret desire of weakening by division the despotism of the supreme magistrate. Their policy was effectual, but it proved fatal both to their emperors and to themselves. The jealousy of power was soon exasperated by the difference of character. Maximus despised Balbinus as a luxurious noble, and was in his turn disdained by his colleague as an obscure soldier. Their silent discord was understood rather than seen; but the mutual consciousness prevented them from uniting in any vigorous measures of defense against their common enemies of the Praetorian camp. The whole city was employed in the Capitoline games, and the emperors were left almost alone in the palace. On a sudden, they were alarmed by the approach of a troop of desperate assassins. Ignorant of each other's situation or designs (for they already occupied very distant apartments), afraid to give or to receive assistance, they wasted the important moments in idle debates and fruitless recriminations. The arrival of the guards put an end to the vain strife. They seized on these emperors of the senate, for such they called them with malicious contempt, stripped them of their garments, and dragged them in insolent triumph through the streets of Rome with the design of inflicting a slow and cruel death on these unfortunate princes [July 15, A.D. 238]. The fear of a rescue from the faithful Germans of the Imperial guards shortened their tortures; and their bodies, mangled with a thousand wounds, were left exposed to the insults or to the pity of the populace.

In the space of a few months, six princes had been cut off by the sword. Gordian, who had already received the title of Caesar, was the only person that occurred to the soldiers as proper to fill the vacant throne. They carried him to the camp, and unanimously saluted him Augustus and Emperor. His name was dear to the senate and people; his tender age promised a long impunity of military license; and the submission of Rome and the provinces to the choice of the Praetorian guards saved the republic, at the expense indeed of its freedom and dignity, from the horrors of a new civil war in the heart of the capital.

As the third Gordian was only nineteen years of age at the time of his death, the history of his life, were it known to us with greater accuracy than it really is, would contain little more than the account of his education and the conduct of the ministers, who by turns abused or guided the simplicity of his unexperienced youth. Immediately after his accession, he fell into the hands of his mother's eunuchs, that pernicious vermin of the East who, since the days of Elagabalus, had infested the Roman palace. By the artful conspiracy of these wretches, an impenetrable veil was drawn between an innocent prince and his oppressed subjects, the virtuous disposition of Gordian was deceived, and the honors of the empire sold without his knowledge, though in a very public manner, to the most worthless of mankind. We are ignorant by what fortunate accident the emperor escaped from this ignominious slavery and devolved his confidence on a minister whose wise counsels had no object except the glory of his sovereign and the happiness of the people. It should seem that love and learning introduced Misitheus to the favor of Gordian [A.D. 240]. The young prince married the daughter of his master of rhetoric, and promoted his father-in-law to the first offices of the empire.†

The life of Misitheus had been spent in the profession of letters, not of arms; yet such was the versatile genius of that great man that, when he was appointed Praetorian praefect, he discharged the military duties of his place with vigor and ability. The Persians had invaded Mesopotamia and threatened Antioch. By the persuasion of his father-in-law, the young emperor quitted the luxury of Rome, opened, for the last time recorded in history, the temple of Janus, and marched in person into the East [A.D. 242]. On his approach with a great army, the Persians withdrew their garrisons from the cities which they had already taken and retired from the Euphrates to the Tigris. Gordian enjoyed the pleasure of announcing to the senate the first success of his arms, which he ascribed, with a becoming modesty and gratitude, to the wisdom of his father and praefect. During the whole expedition, Misitheus watched over the safety and discipline of the army; whilst he prevented their dangerous murmurs by maintaining a regular plenty in the camp and by establishing ample magazines of vinegar, bacon, straw, barley, and wheat in all the cities of the frontier. But the prosperity of Gordian expired with Misitheus, who died of a flux, not without very strong suspicions of poison [A.D. 243]. Philip, his successor in the praefecture, was an Arab by birth, and consequently, in the earlier part of his life, a robber by profession. His rise from so obscure a station to the first dignities of the empire seems to prove that he was a bold and able leader. But his boldness prompted him to aspire to the throne, and his abilities were employed to supplant, not to serve, his indulgent master. The minds of the soldiers were irritated by an artificial scarcity created by his contrivance in the camp; and the distress of the army was attributed to the youth and incapacity of the prince. It is not in our power to trace the successive steps of the secret conspiracy and open sedition which were at length fatal to Gordian. A sepulchral monument was erected to his memory on the spot where he was killed, near the conflux of the Euphrates with the little river Aboras [March A.D. 244]. The fortunate Philip, raised to the empire by the votes of the soldiers, found a ready obedience from the senate and the provinces.

We cannot forbear transcribing the ingenious though somewhat fanciful description which a celebrated writer of our own times has traced of the military government of the Roman empire. "What in that age was called the Roman empire was only an irregular republic, not unlike the aristocracy of Algiers, where the militia, possessed of the sovereignty, creates and deposes a magistrate, who is styled a Dey. Perhaps, indeed, it may be laid down as a general rule, that a military government is, in some respects, more republican than monarchical. Nor can it be said that the soldiers only partook of the government by their disobedience and rebellions. The speeches made to them by the emperors, were they not at length of the same nature as those formerly pronounced to the people by the consuls and the tribunes? And although the armies had no regular place or forms of assembly; though their debates were short, their action sudden, and their resolves seldom the result of cool reflection, did they not dispose, with absolute sway, of the public fortune? What was the emperor except the minister of a violent government, elected for the private benefit of the soldiers?"†

On his return from the East to Rome, Philip, desirous of obliterating the memory of his crimes and of captivating the affections of the people, solemnized the secular games with infinite pomp and magnificence [April 21, A.D. 248]. Since their institution or revival by Augustus, they had been celebrated by Claudius, by Domitian, and by

Severus, and were now renewed the fifth time, on the accomplishment of the full period of a thousand years from the foundation of Rome. Every circumstance of the secular games was skillfully adapted to inspire the superstitious mind with deep and solemn reverence. The long interval between them exceeded the term of human life; and as none of the spectators had already seen them, none could flatter themselves with the expectation of beholding them a second time. The mystic sacrifices were performed, during three nights, on the banks of the Tiber; and the Campus Martius resounded with music and dances, and was illuminated with innumerable lamps and torches. Slaves and strangers were excluded from any participation in these national ceremonies. A chorus of twenty-seven youths and as many virgins, of noble families and whose parents were both alive, implored the propitious gods in favor of the present and for the hope of the rising generation; requesting, in religious hymns, that according to the faith of their ancient oracles, they would still maintain the virtue, the felicity, and the empire of the Roman people. The magnificence of Philip's shows and entertainments dazzled the eyes of the multitude. The devout were employed in the rites of superstition, whilst the reflecting few revolved in their anxious minds the past history and the future fate of the empire.

Since Romulus, with a small band of shepherds and outlaws, fortified himself on the hills near the Tiber, ten centuries had already elapsed. During the four first ages, the Romans, in the laborious school of poverty, had acquired the virtues of war and government: by the vigorous exertion of those virtues, and by the assistance of fortune, they had obtained, in the course of the three succeeding centuries, an absolute empire over many countries of Europe, Asia, and Africa. The last three hundred years had been consumed in apparent prosperity and internal decline. The nation of soldiers, magistrates, and legislators who composed the thirty-five tribes of the Roman people were dissolved into the common mass of mankind, and confounded with the millions of servile provincials who had received the name, without adopting the spirit, of Romans. A mercenary army, levied among the subjects and Barbarians of the frontier, was the only order of men who preserved and abused their independence. By their tumultuary election, a Syrian, a Goth, or an Arab was exalted to the throne of Rome,

A View of the Roman Forum

and invested with despotic power over the conquests and over the country of the Scipios.

The limits of the Roman empire still extended from the Western Ocean to the Tigris, and from Mount Atlas to the Rhine and the Danube. To the undiscerning eye of the vulgar, Philip appeared a monarch no less powerful than Hadrian or Augustus had formerly been. The form was still the same, but the animating health and vigor were fled. The industry of the people was discouraged and exhausted by a long series of oppression. The discipline of the legions, which alone, after the extinction of every other virtue, had propped the greatness of the state, was corrupted by the ambition or relaxed by the weakness of the emperors. The strength of the frontiers, which had always consisted in arms rather than in fortifications, was insensibly undermined; and the fairest provinces were left exposed to the rapaciousness or ambition of the Barbarians, who soon discovered the decline of the Roman empire.

CHAPTER VIII

STATE OF PERSIA AND RESTORATION OF THE MONARCHY

Of the state of Persia after the restoration of the monarchy by Artaxerxes.[†]

From the reign of Augustus to the time of Alexander Severus, the enemies of Rome were in her bosom—the tyrants and the soldiers; and her prosperity had a very distant and feeble interest in the revolutions that might happen beyond the Rhine and the Euphrates. But when the military order had leveled, in wild anarchy, the power of the prince, the laws of the senate, and even the discipline of the camp, the Barbarians of the North and of the East, who had long hovered on the frontier, boldly attacked the provinces of a declining monarchy. Their vexatious inroads were changed into formidable irruptions, and after a long vicissitude of mutual calamities, many tribes of the victorious invaders established themselves in the provinces of the Roman empire. To obtain a clearer knowledge of these great events, we shall endeavor to form a previous idea of the character, forces, and designs of those nations who avenged the cause of Hannibal and Mithridates.

In the more early ages of the world, whilst the forest that covered Europe afforded a retreat to a few wandering savages, the inhabitants of Asia were already collected into populous cities, and reduced under extensive empires, the seat of the arts, of luxury, and of despotism.[†]

[Artaxerxes, A.D. 211–241, founder of the New Persian Empire of the Sassanids,] assumed the double diadem, and the title of King of Kings, which had been enjoyed by his predecessor. But these pompous titles, instead of gratifying the vanity of the Persian, served only to admonish him of his duty, and to inflame in his soul the ambition of restoring in their full splendor the religion and empire of Cyrus [sixth century B.C.].

I. During the long servitude of Persia under the Macedonian and the Parthian yoke, the nations of Europe and Asia had mutually adopted and corrupted each other's superstitions. The Arsacides, indeed, practiced the worship of the Magi; but they disgraced and polluted it with a various mixture of foreign idolatry. The memory of Zoroaster, the ancient prophet and philosopher of the Persians, was still revered in the East; but the obsolete and mysterious language in which the Zendavesta was composed opened a field of dispute to seventy sects, who variously explained the fundamental doctrines of their religion and were all indifferently divided by a crowd of infidels, who rejected the divine mission and miracles of the prophet. To suppress the idolaters, reunite the schismatics, and confute the unbelievers, by the infallible decision of a general council, the pious Artaxerxes summoned the Magi from all parts of his dominions. . . . A short delineation of that celebrated system will be found useful, not only to display the character of the Persian nation but to illustrate many of their most important transactions, both in peace and war, with the Roman empire.

The great and fundamental article of the system was the celebrated doctrine of the two principles; a bold and injudicious attempt of Eastern philosophy to reconcile the existence of moral and physical evil with the attributes of a beneficent Creator and Governor of the world. The first and original Being, in whom or by whom the universe exists, is denominated in the writings of Zoroaster, *Time without bounds;* but it must be confessed that this infinite substance seems rather a metaphysical abstraction of the mind than a real object endowed with self-consciousness or possessed of moral perfections. From either the blind or the intelligent operation of this infinite Time, which bears but too near an affinity with the chaos of the Greeks, the two secondary but active principles of the universe were from all eternity produced, Ormusd and Ahriman, each of them possessed of the powers of creation but each disposed, by his invariable nature, to exercise them with different designs. The principle of good is eternally absorbed in light; the principle of evil eternally buried in darkness. The wise benevolence of Ormusd formed man capable of virtue and abundantly provided his fair habitation with the materials of happiness. By his vigilant providence, the motion of the planets, the order of the seasons, and the temperate mixture of the elements are preserved. But the malice of Ahriman has long since pierced *Ormusd's egg;* or, in other words, has violated the harmony of his works. Since that fatal eruption, the most minute articles of good and evil are intimately intermingled and agitated together; the rankest poisons spring up amidst the most salutary plants; deluges, earthquakes, and conflagrations attest the conflict of Nature, and the little world of man is perpetually shaken by vice and misfortune. Whilst the rest of humankind are led away captives in the chains of their infernal enemy, the faithful Persian alone reserves his religious adoration for his friend and protector Ormusd and fights under his banner of light, in the full confidence that he shall, in the last day, share the glory of his triumph. At that decisive period, the enlightened wisdom of goodness will render the power of Ormusd superior to the furious malice of his rival. Ahriman and his followers, disarmed and subdued, will sink into their native darkness; and virtue will maintain the eternal peace and harmony of the universe.

The theology of Zoroaster was darkly comprehended by foreigners, and even by the far greater number of his disciples; but the most careless observers were struck with the philosophic simplicity of the Persian worship. "That people," said Herodotus, "rejects the use of temples, of altars, and of statues, and smiles at the folly of those nations who imagine that the gods are sprung from, or bear any affinity with, the human nature. The tops of the highest mountains are the places chosen for sacrifices. Hymns and prayers are the principal worship; the Supreme God, who fills the wide circle of heaven, is the object to whom they are addressed." Yet at the same time, in the true spirit of a polytheist, he accuses them of adoring Earth, Water, Fire, the Winds, and the Sun and Moon. But the Persians of every age have denied the charge, and explained the equivocal conduct which might appear to give a color to it. The elements, and more particularly Fire, Light, and the Sun, whom they called Mithra, were the objects of their religious reverence, because they considered them as the purest symbols, the noblest productions, and the most powerful agents of the Divine Power and Nature.

Every mode of religion, to make a deep and lasting impression on the human mind, must exercise our obedience by enjoining practices of devotion for which we can assign no reason; and must acquire our esteem by inculcating moral duties analogous to the dictates of our own hearts. The religion of Zoroaster was abundantly provided with the former and possessed a sufficient portion of the latter. At the age of puberty, the faithful Persian was invested with a mysterious girdle, the badge of the divine protection; and from that moment all the actions of his life, even the most indifferent or the most necessary, were sanctified by their peculiar prayers, ejaculations, or genuflections; the omission of which, under any circumstances, was a grievous sin, not inferior in guilt to the violation of the moral duties. The moral duties, however, of justice, mercy, liberality, etc., were in their turn required of the disciple of Zoroaster, who wished to escape the persecution of Ahriman and to live with Ormusd in a blissful eternity, where the degree of felicity will be exactly proportioned to the degree of virtue and piety.

But there are some remarkable instances in which Zoroaster lays aside the prophet, assumes the legislator, and discovers a liberal concern for private and public happiness seldom to be found among the groveling or visionary schemes of superstition. Fasting and celibacy, the common means of purchasing the divine favor, he condemns with abhorrence as a criminal rejection of the best gifts of Providence. The saint, in the Magian religion, is obliged to beget children, to plant useful trees, to destroy noxious animals, to convey water to the dry lands of Persia, and to work out his salvation by pursuing all the labors of agriculture. We may quote from the Zendavesta a wise and benevolent maxim which compensates for many an absurdity. "He who sows the ground with care and diligence acquires a greater stock of religious merit than he could gain by the repetition of ten thousand prayers." In the spring of every year a festival was celebrated, destined to represent the primitive equality and the present connection of mankind. The stately kings of Persia, exchanging their vain pomp for more genuine greatness, freely mingled with the humblest but most useful of their subjects. On that day the husbandmen were admitted without distinction to the table of the king and his satraps. The monarch accepted their petitions, inquired into their grievances, and conversed with them on the most equal terms. "From your labors," was he accustomed to say (and to say with truth, if not with sincerity), "from your labors we receive our subsistence; you derive your tranquility from our vigilance: since, therefore, we are mutually necessary to each other, let us live together like brothers in concord and love." Such a festival must indeed have degenerated, in a wealthy and despotic empire, into a theatrical representation; but it was at least a comedy well worthy of a royal audience, and which might sometimes imprint a salutary lesson on the mind of a young prince.

Had Zoroaster, in all his institutions, invariably supported this exalted character, his name would deserve a place with those of Numa and Confucius, and his system would be justly entitled to all the applause which it has pleased some of our divines, and even some of our philosophers, to bestow on it. But in that motley composition dictated by reason and passion, by enthusiasm and by selfish motives, some useful and sublime truths were disgraced by a mixture of the most abject and dangerous superstition. The Magi, or sacerdotal order, were extremely numerous. . . . Their forces were multiplied by discipline. A regular hierarchy was diffused through all the provinces of Persia; and the Archimagus, who resided at Balch, was respected as the visible head of the church and the lawful successor of Zoroaster. The property of the Magi was very considerable. Besides the less invidious possession of a large tract of the most fertile lands of Media, they levied a general tax on the fortunes and the industry of the Persians. "Though your good works," says the interested prophet, "exceed in number the leaves of the trees, the drops of rain, the stars in the heaven, or the sands on the seashore, they will all be unprofitable to you unless they are accepted by the *destour,* or priest. To obtain the acceptation of this guide to salvation, you must faithfully pay him *tithes* of all you possess, of your goods, of your lands, and of your money. If the destour be satisfied, your soul will escape hell tortures; you will secure praise in this world and happiness in the next. For the destours are the teachers of religion; they know all things, and they deliver all men."

These convenient maxims of reverence and implicit faith were doubtless imprinted with care on the tender minds of youth; since the Magi were the masters of education in Persia, and to their hands the children even of the royal family were entrusted. The Persian priests, who were of a speculative genius, preserved and investigated the secrets of Oriental philosophy; and acquired, either by superior knowledge or superior art, the reputation of being well versed in some occult sciences which have derived their appellation from the Magi. Those of more active dispositions mixed with the world in courts and cities; and it is observed that the administration of Artaxerxes was in a great measure directed by the counsels of the sacerdotal order, whose dignity, either from policy or devotion, that prince restored to its ancient splendor.

The first counsel of the Magi was agreeable to the unsociable genius of their faith, to the practice of ancient kings, and even to the example of their legislator, who had fallen a victim to a religious war, excited by his own intolerant zeal. By an edict of Artaxerxes, the exercise of every worship except that of Zoroaster was severely prohibited. The temples of the Parthians and the statues of their deified monarchs were thrown down with ignominy. The sword of Aristotle (such was the name given by the Orientals to the polytheism and philosophy of the Greeks) was easily broken; the flames of persecution soon reached the more stubborn Jews and Christians; nor did they spare the heretics of their own nation and religion. The majesty of Ormusd, who was jealous of a rival, was seconded by the despotism of Artaxerxes, who could not suffer a rebel; and the schismatics within his vast empire were soon reduced to the inconsiderable number of eighty thousand. This spirit of persecution reflects dishonor on the religion of Zoroaster; but as it was not productive of any civil commotion, it served to strengthen the new monarchy by uniting all the various inhabitants of Persia in the bands of religious zeal.

II. Artaxerxes, by his valor and conduct, had wrested the scepter of the East from the ancient royal family of Parthia. There still remained the more difficult task of establishing, throughout the vast extent of Persia, a uniform and vigorous administration.... But the active victor, at the head of a numerous and disciplined army, visited in person every province of Persia. The defeat of the boldest rebels and the reduction of the strongest fortifications diffused the terror of his arms and prepared the way for the peaceful reception of his authority. An obstinate resistance was fatal to the chiefs; but their followers were treated with lenity. A cheerful submission was rewarded with honors and riches, but the prudent Artaxerxes, suffering no person except himself to assume the title of king, abolished every intermediate power between the throne and the people.[†]

As soon as the ambitious mind of Artaxerxes had triumphed over the resistance of his vassals, he began to threaten the neighboring states, who, during the long slumber of his predecessors, had insulted Persia with impunity. He obtained some easy victories over the wild Scythians and the effeminate Indians; but the Romans were an enemy who, by their past injuries and present power, deserved the utmost efforts of his arms.[†]

Prudence as well as glory might have justified a war on the side of Artaxerxes, had his views been confined to the defense or acquisition of a useful frontier, but the ambitious Persian openly avowed a far more extensive design of conquest; and he thought himself able to support his lofty pretensions by the arms of reason as well as by those of power. Cyrus, he alleged, had first subdued, and his successors had for a long time possessed, the whole extent of Asia, as far as the Propontis and the Aegean Sea; the provinces of Caria and Ionia under their empire had been governed by Persian satraps, and all Egypt, to the confines of Aethiopia, had acknowledged their sovereignty. Their rights had been suspended but not destroyed by a long usurpation; and as soon as he received the Persian diadem, which birth and successful valor had placed upon his head, the first great duty of his station called upon him to restore the ancient limits and splendor of the monarchy. The Great King, therefore (such was the haughty style of his embassies to the emperor Alexander), commanded the Romans instantly to depart from all the provinces of his ancestors and, yielding to the Persians the empire of Asia, to content themselves with the undisturbed possession of Europe. This haughty mandate was delivered by four hundred of the tallest and most beautiful of the Persians; who, by their fine horses, splendid arms, and rich apparel, displayed the pride and greatness of their master. Such an embassy was much less an offer of negotiation than a declaration of war. Both Alexander Severus and Artaxerxes, collecting the military force of the Roman and Persian monarchies, resolved in this important contest to lead their armies in person.

If we credit what should seem the most authentic of all records, an oration still extant and delivered by the emperor himself to the senate, we must allow that the victory of Alexander Severus [A.D. 233] was not inferior to any of those formerly obtained over the Persians by the son of Philip [Alexander the Great (334–330 B.C.)]. . . . [But] the circumstances of this ostentatious and improbable relation, dictated, as it too plainly appears, by the vanity of the monarch, adorned by the unblushing servility of his flatterers, and received without contradiction by a distant and obsequious senate, [induces us] to suspect that all this blaze of imaginary glory was designed to conceal some real disgrace.†

The reign of Artaxerxes, which from the last defeat of the Parthians lasted only fourteen years, forms a memorable era in the history of the East, and even in that of Rome. His character seems to have been marked by those bold and commanding features that generally distinguish the princes who conquer from those who inherit an empire. Till the last period of the Persian monarchy, his code of laws was respected as the groundwork of their civil and religious policy. Several of his sayings are preserved. One of them in particular discovers a deep insight into the constitution of government. "The authority of the prince," said Artaxerxes, "must be defended by a military force; that force can only be maintained by taxes; all taxes must, at last, fall upon agriculture; and agriculture can never flourish except under the protection of justice and moderation." Artaxerxes bequeathed his new empire, and his ambitious designs against the Romans, to Sapor, a son not unworthy of his great father [A.D. 241]; but those designs were too extensive for the power of Persia, and served only to involve both nations in a long series of destructive wars and reciprocal calamities.[†]

CHAPTER IX

STATE OF GERMANY
UNTIL THE BARBARIANS

*The state of Germany till the invasion of the Barbarians in the
time of the emperor Decius.*

The government and religion of Persia have deserved some notice
from their connection with the decline and fall of the Roman empire. We shall occasionally mention the Scythian or Sarmatian tribes,
which, with their arms and horses, their flocks and herds, their wives
and families, wandered over the immense plains which spread themselves from the Caspian Sea to the Vistula, from the confines of Persia
to those of Germany. But the warlike Germans, who first resisted, then
invaded, and at length overturned the Western monarchy of Rome,
will occupy a much more important place in this history, and possess a
stronger and, if we may use the expression, a more domestic claim to
our attention and regard. The most civilized nations of modern Europe issued from the woods of Germany; and in the rude institutions
of those Barbarians we may still distinguish the original principles of
our present laws and manners.†

[T]he use of letters is the principal circumstance that distinguishes
a civilized people from a herd of savages incapable of knowledge or
reflection. Without that artificial help, the human memory soon dissi-
pates or corrupts the ideas entrusted to her charge; and the nobler
faculties of the mind, no longer supplied with models or with materials, gradually forget their powers; the judgment becomes feeble and
lethargic, the imagination languid or irregular. Fully to apprehend this
important truth, let us attempt, in an improved society, to calculate the
immense distance between the man of learning and the illiterate peasant. The former, by reading and reflection, multiplies his own experience and lives in distant ages and remote countries; whilst the latter,
rooted to a single spot and confined to a few years of existence, surpasses but very little his fellow-laborer, the ox, in the exercise of his
mental faculties. The same, and even a greater, difference will be

found between nations than between individuals; and we may safely pronounce that without some species of writing, no people has ever preserved the faithful annals of their history, ever made any considerable progress in the abstract sciences, or ever possessed, in any tolerable degree of perfection, the useful and agreeable arts of life.

Of these arts, the ancient Germans were wretchedly destitute. They passed their lives in a state of ignorance and poverty, which it has pleased some declaimers to dignify with the appellation of virtuous simplicity.[†]

The climate of ancient Germany has been modified, and the soil fertilized, by the labor of ten centuries from the time of Charlemagne. The same extent of ground which at present maintains, in ease and plenty, a million of husbandmen and artificers was unable to supply a hundred thousand lazy warriors with the simple necessaries of life. The Germans abandoned their immense forests to the exercise of hunting, employed in pasturage the most considerable part of their lands, bestowed on the small remainder a rude and careless cultivation, and then accused the scantiness and sterility of a country that refused to maintain the multitude of its inhabitants. When the return of famine severely admonished them of the importance of the arts, the national distress was sometimes alleviated by the emigration of a third, perhaps, or a fourth part of their youth. The possession and the enjoyment of property are the pledges which bind a civilized people to an improved country. But the Germans, who carried with them what they most valued, their arms, their cattle, and their women, cheerfully abandoned the vast silence of their woods for the unbounded hopes of plunder and conquest. The innumerable swarms that issued, or seemed to issue, from the great storehouse of nations were multiplied by the fears of the vanquished and by the credulity of succeeding ages. And from facts thus exaggerated, an opinion was gradually established, and has been supported by writers of distinguished reputation, that in the age of Caesar and Tacitus the inhabitants of the North were far more numerous than they are in our days. A more serious inquiry into the causes of population seems to have convinced modern philosophers of the falsehood, and indeed the impossibility, of the supposition.[†]

A warlike nation like the Germans, without either cities, letters, arts, or money, found some compensation for this savage state in the enjoyment of liberty. Their poverty secured their freedom, since our desires and our possessions are the strongest fetters of despotism. "Among the Suiones (says Tacitus) riches are held in honor. They are *therefore* subject to an absolute monarch who, instead of entrusting his people with the free use of arms, as is practiced in the rest of Germany, commits them to the safe custody not of a citizen, or even of a freedman, but of a slave. The neighbors of the Suiones, the Sitones, are sunk even below servitude; they obey a woman." In the mention of these exceptions, the great historian sufficiently acknowledges the general theory of government. We are only at a loss to conceive by what means riches and despotism could penetrate into a remote corner of the North and extinguish the generous flame that blazed with such fierceness on the frontier of the Roman provinces, or how the ancestors of those Danes and Norwegians, so distinguished in latter ages by their unconquered spirit, could thus tamely resign the great character of German liberty. Some tribes, however, on the coast of the Baltic, acknowledged the authority of kings, though without relinquishing the rights of men, but in the far greater part of Germany, the form of government was a democracy, tempered, indeed, and controlled, not so much by general and positive laws as by the occasional ascendant of birth or valor, of eloquence or superstition.

Civil governments, in their first institution, are voluntary associations for mutual defense. To obtain the desired end, it is absolutely necessary that each individual should conceive himself obliged to submit his private opinions and actions to the judgment of the greater number of his associates. The German tribes were contented with this rude but liberal outline of political society. As soon as a youth born of free parents had attained the age of manhood, he was introduced into the general council of his countrymen, solemnly invested with a shield and spear, and adopted as an equal and worthy member of the military commonwealth. The assembly of the warriors of the tribe was convened at stated seasons, or on sudden emergencies. The trial of public offenses, the election of magistrates, and the great business of peace and war were determined by its independent voice. Sometimes, indeed, these important questions were previously considered and prepared in a more select council of the principal chieftains. The magistrates might deliberate and persuade, the people only could resolve and execute; and the resolutions of the Germans were for the most part hasty and violent. Barbarians accustomed to place their freedom in gratifying the present passion, and their courage in overlooking all future consequences, turned away with indignant contempt from the remonstrances of justice and policy, and it was the practice to signify by a hollow murmur their dislike of such timid counsels. But whenever a more popular orator proposed to vindicate the meanest citizen from either foreign or domestic injury, whenever he called upon his fellow-countrymen to assert the national honor or to pursue some enterprise full of danger and glory, a loud clashing of shields and spears expressed the eager applause of the assembly. For the Germans always met in arms, and it was constantly to be dreaded lest an irregular multitude, inflamed with faction and strong liquors, should use those arms to enforce as well as to declare their furious resolves. We may recollect how often the diets of Poland have been polluted with blood, and the more numerous party has been compelled to yield to the more violent and seditious.

A general of the tribe was elected on occasions of danger; and if the danger was pressing and extensive, several tribes concurred in the choice of the same general. The bravest warrior was named to lead his countrymen into the field, by his example rather than by his commands. But this power, however limited, was still invidious. It expired with the war, and in time of peace the German tribes acknowledged not any supreme chief. *Princes* were, however, appointed in the general assembly to administer justice, or rather to compose differences, in their respective districts. In the choice of these magistrates, as much regard was shown to birth as to merit. To each was assigned by the public a guard and a council of a hundred persons, and the first of the princes appears to have enjoyed a preeminence of rank and honor which sometimes tempted the Romans to compliment him with the regal title.

The comparative view of the powers of the magistrates, in two remarkable instances, is alone sufficient to represent the whole system of German manners. The disposal of the landed property within their district was absolutely vested in their hands, and they distributed it every year according to a new division. At the same time they were not authorized to punish with death, to imprison, or even to strike a private citizen. A people thus jealous of their persons and careless of their possessions must have been totally destitute of industry and the arts, but animated with a high sense of honor and independence.

The Germans respected only those duties which they imposed on themselves. The most obscure soldier resisted with disdain the authority of the magistrates. "The noblest youths blushed not to be numbered among the faithful companions of some renowned chief to whom they devoted their arms and service. A noble emulation prevailed among the companions to obtain the first place in the esteem of their chief; amongst the chiefs, to acquire the greatest number of valiant companions. To be ever surrounded by a band of select youths was the pride and strength of the chiefs, their ornament in peace, their defense in war. The glory of such distinguished heroes diffused itself beyond the narrow limits of their own tribe. Presents and embassies solicited their friendship, and the fame of their arms often insured victory to the party which they espoused. In the hour of danger it was shameful for the chief to be surpassed in valor by his companions; shameful for the companions not to equal the valor of their chief. To survive his fall in battle was indelible infamy. To protect his person, and to adorn his glory with the trophies of their own exploits, were the most sacred of their duties. The chiefs combated for victory, the companions for the chief. The noblest warriors, whenever their native country was sunk into the laziness of peace, maintained their numerous bands in some distant scene of action, to exercise their restless spirit and to acquire renown by voluntary dangers. Gifts worthy of soldiers—the warlike steed, the bloody and even victorious lance—were the rewards which the companions claimed from the liberality of their chief. The rude plenty of his hospitable board was the only pay that *he* could bestow, or *they* would accept. War, rapine, and the free-will offerings of his friends supplied the materials of this munificence." This institution, however it might accidentally weaken the several republics, invigorated the general character of the Germans, and even ripened amongst them all the virtues of which Barbarians are susceptible; the faith and valor, the hospitality and the courtesy, so conspicuous long afterwards in the ages of chivalry. The honorable gifts bestowed by the chief on his brave companions have been supposed by an ingenious writer to contain the first rudiments of the fiefs distributed after the conquest of the Roman provinces by the Barbarian lords among their vassals, with a similar duty of homage and military service. These conditions are, however, very repugnant to the maxims of the ancient Germans, who delighted in mutual presents; but without either imposing or accepting the weight of obligations.

"In the days of chivalry, or more properly of romance, all the men were brave, and all the women were chaste"; and, notwithstanding the latter of these virtues is acquired and preserved with much more difficulty than the former, it is ascribed, almost without exception, to the wives of the ancient Germans. Polygamy was not in use except among the princes, and among them only for the sake of multiplying their alliances. Divorces were prohibited by manners rather than by laws. Adulteries were punished as rare and inexpiable crimes; nor was seduction justified by example and fashion. We may easily discover that Tacitus indulges an honest pleasure in the contrast of Barbarian virtue with the dissolute conduct of the Roman ladies; yet there are some striking circumstances that give an air of truth, or at least probability, to the conjugal faith and chastity of the Germans.

Although the progress of civilization has undoubtedly contributed to assuage the fiercer passions of human nature, it seems to have been less favorable to the virtue of chastity, whose most dangerous enemy is the softness of the mind. The refinements of life corrupt while they polish the intercourse of the sexes. The gross appetite of love becomes most dangerous when it is elevated, or rather, indeed, disguised by sentimental passion. The elegance of dress, of motion, and of manners gives a luster to beauty and inflames the senses through the imagination. Luxurious entertainments, midnight dances, and licentious spectacles present at once temptation and opportunity to female frailty. From such dangers the unpolished wives of the Barbarians were secured by poverty, solitude, and the painful cares of a domestic life. The German huts, open on every side to the eye of indiscretion or jealousy, were a better safeguard of conjugal fidelity than the walls, the bolts, and the eunuchs of a Persian harem. To this reason another may be added, of a more honorable nature. The Germans treated their women with esteem and confidence, consulted them on every occasion of importance, and fondly believed that in their breasts resided a sanctity and wisdom more than human. Some of these interpreters of fate, such as Velleda, in the Batavian war, governed, in the name of the deity, the fiercest nations of Germany. The rest of the sex, without being adored as goddesses, were respected as the free and equal companions of soldiers; associated even by the marriage ceremony to a life of toil, of danger, and of glory. In their great invasions, the camps of the Barbarians were filled with a multitude of women, who remained firm and undaunted amidst the sound of arms, the various forms of destruction, and the honorable wounds of their sons and husbands. Fainting armies of Germans have, more than once, been driven back upon the enemy by the generous despair of the women, who dreaded death much less than servitude. If the day was irrecoverably lost, they well knew how to deliver themselves and their children, with their own hands, from an insulting victor. Heroines of such a cast may claim our admiration; but they were most assuredly neither lovely nor very susceptible of love. Whilst they affected to emulate the stern virtues of *man,* they must have resigned that attractive softness in which principally consist the charm and weakness of *woman.* Conscious pride taught the German females to suppress every tender emotion that stood in competition with honor, and the first honor of the sex has ever been that of chastity. The sentiments and conduct of these high-spirited matrons may at once be considered as a cause, as an effect, and as a proof of the general character of the nation. Female courage, however it may be raised by fanaticism or confirmed by habit, can be only a faint and imperfect imitation of the manly valor that distinguishes the age or country in which it may be found.

The religious system of the Germans (if the wild opinions of savages can deserve that name) was dictated by their wants, their fears, and their ignorance. They adored the great visible objects and agents of nature, the Sun and the Moon, the Fire and the Earth; together with those imaginary deities who were supposed to preside over the most important occupations of human life. They were persuaded that, by some ridiculous arts of divination, they could discover the will of the superior beings, and that human sacrifices were the most precious and acceptable offering to their altars. Some applause has been hastily bestowed on the sublime notion, entertained by that people, of the Deity, whom they neither confined within the walls of the temple, nor represented by any human figure; but when we recollect that the Germans were unskilled in architecture and totally unacquainted with the art of sculpture, we shall readily assign the true reason of a scruple, which arose not so much from a superiority of reason as from a want of ingenuity. The only temples in Germany were dark and ancient groves consecrated by the reverence of succeeding generations. Their secret gloom, the imagined residence of an invisible power, by presenting no distinct object of fear or worship impressed the mind with a still deeper sense of religious horror; and the priests, rude and illiterate as they were, had been taught by experience the use of every artifice that could preserve and fortify impressions so well suited to their own interest.

The same ignorance which renders Barbarians incapable of conceiving or embracing the useful restraints of laws exposes them naked and unarmed to the blind terrors of superstition. The German priests, improving this favorable temper of their countrymen, had assumed a jurisdiction even in temporal concerns, which the magistrate could not venture to exercise; and the haughty warrior patiently submitted to the lash of correction when it was inflicted not by any human power but by the immediate order of the god of war. The defects of civil policy were sometimes supplied by the interposition of ecclesiastical authority. The latter was constantly exerted to maintain silence and decency in the popular assemblies; and was sometimes extended to a more enlarged concern for the national welfare. A solemn procession was occasionally celebrated in the present countries of Mecklenburgh and Pomerania. The unknown symbol of the *Earth,* covered with a thick veil, was placed on a carriage drawn by cows; and in this manner the goddess, whose common residence was in the Isles of Rugen, visited several adjacent tribes of her worshipers. During her progress the sound of war was hushed, quarrels were suspended, arms laid aside, and the restless Germans had an opportunity of tasting the blessings of peace and harmony. The *truce of God,* so often and so ineffectually proclaimed by the clergy of the eleventh century, was an obvious imitation of this ancient custom.

But the influence of religion was far more powerful to inflame than to moderate the fierce passions of the Germans. Interest and fanaticism often prompted its ministers to sanctify the most daring and the most unjust enterprises by the approbation of Heaven, and full assurances of success. The consecrated standards, long revered in the groves of superstition, were placed in the front of the battle; and the hostile army was devoted with dire execrations to the gods of war and of thunder. In the faith of soldiers (and such were the Germans) cowardice is the most unpardonable of sins. A brave man was the worthy favorite of their martial deities; the wretch who had lost his shield was alike banished from the religious and civil assemblies of his countrymen. Some tribes of the North seem to have embraced the doctrine of transmigration, others imagined a gross paradise of immortal drunkenness. All agreed that a life spent in arms and a glorious death in battle were the best preparations for a happy futurity, either in this or in another world.

The immortality so vainly promised by the priests was in some degree conferred by the bards. That singular order of men has most deservedly attracted the notice of all who have attempted to investigate the antiquities of the Celts, the Scandinavians, and the Germans. Their genius and character, as well as the reverence paid to that important office, have been sufficiently illustrated. But we cannot so easily express, or even conceive, the enthusiasm of arms and glory which they kindled in the breast of their audience. Among a polished people, a taste for poetry is rather an amusement of the fancy than a passion of the soul. And yet when in calm retirement we peruse the combats described by Homer or Tasso, we are insensibly seduced by the fiction and feel a momentary glow of martial ardor. But how faint, how cold is the sensation which a peaceful mind can receive from solitary study! It was in the hour of battle, or in the feast of victory, that the bards celebrated the glory of the heroes of ancient days, the ancestors of those warlike chieftains who listened with transport to their artless but animated strains. The view of arms and of danger heightened the effect of the military song; and the passions which it tended to excite, the desire of fame and the contempt of death, were the habitual sentiments of a German mind.

Such was the situation, and such were the manners of the ancient Germans. Their climate, their want of learning, of arts, and of laws, their notions of honor, of gallantry, and of religion, their sense of freedom, impatience of peace, and thirst of enterprise, all contributed to form a people of military heroes. And yet we find that during more than two hundred and fifty years that elapsed from the defeat of Varus [A.D. 9] to the reign of Decius [A.D. 249–251], these formidable Barbarians made few considerable attempts, and not any material impression on the luxurious and enslaved provinces of the empire. Their progress was checked by their want of arms and discipline, and their fury was diverted by the intestine divisions of ancient Germany.

It has been observed, with ingenuity and not without truth, that the command of iron soon gives a nation the command of gold. But the rude tribes of Germany, alike destitute of both those valuable metals, were reduced slowly to acquire by their unassisted strength the possession of the one as well as the other. The face of a German army displayed their poverty of iron. . . . When we recollect the complete armor of the Roman soldiers, their discipline, exercises, evolutions, fortified camps, and military engines, it appears a just matter of surprise how the naked and unassisted valor of the Barbarians could dare to encounter in the field the strength of the legions and the various troops of the auxiliaries which seconded their operations. The contest was too unequal, till the introduction of luxury had enervated the vigor, and a spirit of disobedience and sedition had relaxed the discipline, of the Roman armies.[†]

CHAPTER X

EMPERORS DECIUS, GALLUS, AEMILIANUS, VALERIAN, AND GALLIENUS

The emperors Decius, Gallus, Aemilianus, Valerian, and Gallienus. •
The general irruption of the Barbarians. • The thirty tyrants.

From the great secular games celebrated by Philip to the death of the
emperor Gallienus, there elapsed twenty years of shame and misfortune [A.D. 248–268]. During that calamitous period, every instant of
time was marked, every province of the Roman world was afflicted,
by barbarous invaders and military tyrants, and the ruined empire
seemed to approach the last and fatal moment of its dissolution. The
confusion of the times, and the scarcity of authentic memorials, oppose equal difficulties to the historian who attempts to preserve a clear
and unbroken thread of narration. Surrounded with imperfect fragments, always concise, often obscure, and sometimes contradictory, he
is reduced to collect, to compare, and to conjecture: and though he
ought never to place his conjectures in the rank of facts, yet the knowledge of human nature, and of the sure operation of its fierce and
unrestrained passions, might on some occasions supply the want of
historical materials.

There is not, for instance, any difficulty in conceiving that the successive murders of so many emperors had loosened all the ties of allegiance between the prince and people; that all the generals of Philip
were disposed to imitate the example of their master; and that the
caprice of armies, long since habituated to frequent and violent revolutions, might every day raise to the throne the most obscure of their
fellow-soldiers. History can only add that the rebellion against the
emperor Philip broke out in the summer of the year two hundred and
forty-nine, among the legions of Moesia; and that a subaltern officer
named Marinus was the object of their seditious choice. Philip was
alarmed. He dreaded lest the treason of the Moesian army should

prove the first spark of a general conflagration. Distracted with the consciousness of his guilt and of his danger, he communicated the intelligence to the senate. A gloomy silence prevailed, the effect of fear and perhaps of disaffection; till at length Decius, one of the assembly, assuming a spirit worthy of his noble extraction, ventured to discover more intrepidity than the emperor seemed to possess. He treated the whole business with contempt, as a hasty and inconsiderate tumult, and Philip's rival as a phantom of royalty, who in a very few days would be destroyed by the same inconstancy that had created him. The speedy completion of the prophecy inspired Philip with a just esteem for so able a counselor; and Decius appeared to him the only person capable of restoring peace and discipline to an army whose tumultuous spirit did not immediately subside after the murder of Marinus. Decius, who long resisted his own nomination, seems to have insinuated the danger of presenting a leader of merit to the angry and apprehensive minds of the soldiers; and his prediction was again confirmed by the event. The legions of Moesia forced their judge to become their accomplice. They left him only the alternative of death or the purple. His subsequent conduct after that decisive measure was unavoidable. He conducted, or followed, his army to the confines of Italy, whither Philip, collecting all his force to repel the formidable competitor whom he had raised up, advanced to meet him. The Imperial troops were superior in number; but the rebels formed an army of veterans, commanded by an able and experienced leader. Philip was either killed in the battle or put to death a few days afterwards at Verona. His son and associate in the empire was massacred at Rome by the Praetorian guards; and the victorious Decius, with more favorable circumstances than the ambition of that age can usually plead, was universally acknowledged by the senate and provinces. It is reported that, immediately after his reluctant acceptance of the title of Augustus, he had assured Philip, by a private message, of his innocence and loyalty, solemnly protesting that on his arrival on Italy he would resign the Imperial ornaments and return to the condition of an obedient subject. His professions might be sincere; but in the situation where fortune had placed him, it was scarcely possible that he could either forgive or be forgiven.

The emperor Decius had employed a few months in the works of peace and the administration of justice when he was summoned to the banks of the Danube by the invasion of the GOTHS [A.D. 250]. This is the first considerable occasion in which history mentions that great people who afterwards broke the Roman power, sacked the Capitol, and reigned in Gaul, Spain, and Italy. So memorable was the part which they acted in the subversion of the Western empire that the name of GOTHS is frequently but improperly used as a general appellation of rude and warlike barbarism.

[*We may state that the Goths were of Scandinavian origin, but we lack reliable records of their earliest history.*]

Till the end of the eleventh century, a celebrated temple subsisted at Upsal, the most considerable town of the Swedes and Goths. It was enriched with the gold which the Scandinavians had acquired in their piratical adventures, and sanctified by the uncouth representations of the three principal deities, the god of war, the goddess of generation, and the god of thunder. In the general festival that was solemnized every ninth year, nine animals of every species (without excepting the human) were sacrificed and their bleeding bodies suspended in the sacred grove adjacent to the temple. The only traces that now subsist of this Barbaric superstition are contained in the Edda, a system of mythology compiled in Iceland about the thirteenth century and studied by the learned of Denmark and Sweden as the most valuable remains of their ancient traditions.

Notwithstanding the mysterious obscurity of the Edda, we can easily distinguish two persons confounded under the name of Odin; the god of war, and the great legislator of Scandinavia. The latter, the Mohammed of the North, instituted a religion adapted to the climate and to the people. Numerous tribes on either side of the Baltic were subdued by the invincible valor of Odin, by his persuasive eloquence, and by the fame which he acquired of a most skillful magician. The faith that he had propagated during a long and prosperous life, he confirmed by a voluntary death. Apprehensive of the ignominious approach of disease and infirmity, he resolved to expire as became a warrior. In a solemn assembly of the Swedes and Goths, he wounded himself in nine mortal places, hastening away (as he asserted with his dying voice) to prepare the feast of heroes in the palace of the god of war.

The native and proper habitation of Odin is distinguished by the appellation of As-gard. The happy resemblance of that name with As-burg, or As-of, words of a similar signification, has given rise to an historical system of so pleasing a contexture that we could almost wish to persuade ourselves of its truth. It is supposed that Odin was the chief of a tribe of Barbarians which dwelt on the banks of the Lake Maeotis, till the fall of Mithridates and the arms of Pompey menaced the North with servitude. That Odin, yielding with indignant fury to a power which he was unable to resist, conducted his tribe from the frontiers of the Asiatic Sarmatia into Sweden, with the great design of forming, in that inaccessible retreat of freedom, a religion and a people which, in some remote age, might be subservient to his immortal revenge; when his invincible Goths, armed with martial fanaticism, should issue in numerous swarms from the neighborhood of the Polar circle to chastise the oppressors of mankind.

[*The Goths threaten the Illyrian provinces (A.D. 250).*]

Decius found the Goths engaged before Nicopolis, one of the many monuments of Trajan's victories. On his approach they raised the siege, but with a design only of marching away to a conquest of greater importance, the siege of Philippopolis, a city of Thrace founded by the father of Alexander, near the foot of Mount Haemus. Decius followed them through a difficult country and by forced marches; but when he imagined himself at a considerable distance from the rear of the Goths, Cniva [king of the Goths] turned with rapid fury on his pursuers. The camp of the Romans was surprised and pillaged, and for the first time their emperor fled in disorder before a troop of half-armed Barbarians. After a long resistance, Philippopolis, destitute of succor, was taken by storm. A hundred thousand persons are reported to have been massacred in the sack of that great city. Many prisoners of consequence became a valuable accession to the spoil; and Priscus, a brother of the late emperor Philip, blushed not to assume the purple under the protection of the barbarous enemies of Rome. The time, however, consumed in that tedious siege enabled Decius to revive the courage, restore the discipline, and recruit the numbers of his troops. He intercepted several parties of Carpi and other Germans who were hastening to share the victory of their countrymen, entrusted the passes of the mountains to officers of approved valor and fidelity, repaired and strengthened the fortifications of the Danube, and exerted his utmost vigilance to oppose either the progress or the retreat of the Goths. Encouraged by the return of fortune, he anxiously waited for an opportunity to retrieve, by a great and decisive blow, his own glory and that of the Roman arms.

At the same time when Decius was struggling with the violence of the tempest, his mind, calm and deliberate amidst the tumult of war, investigated the more general causes that, since the age of the Antonines, had so impetuously urged the decline of the Roman greatness. He soon discovered that it was impossible to replace that greatness on a permanent basis without restoring public virtue, ancient principles and manners, and the oppressed majesty of the laws. To execute this noble but arduous design, he first resolved to revive the obsolete office of censor; an office which, as long as it had subsisted in its pristine integrity, had so much contributed to the perpetuity of the state, till it was usurped and gradually neglected by the Caesars. Conscious that the favor of the sovereign may confer power but that the esteem of the people can alone bestow authority, he submitted the choice of the censor to the unbiased voice of the senate. By their unanimous votes, or rather acclamations, Valerian, who was afterwards emperor and who then served with distinction in the army of Decius, was declared the most worthy of that exalted honor [October 27, A.D. 251]. As soon as the decree of the senate was transmitted to the emperor, he assembled a great council in his camp, and before the investiture of the censor elect, he apprised him of the difficulty and importance of his great office. "Happy Valerian," said the prince to his distinguished subject, "happy in the general approbation of the senate and of the Roman republic! Accept the censorship of mankind; and judge of our manners. You will select those who deserve to continue members of the senate; you will restore the equestrian order to its ancient splendor; you will improve the revenue, yet moderate the public burdens. You will distinguish into regular classes the various and infinite multitude of citizens, and accurately view the military strength, the wealth, the virtue, and the resources of Rome. Your decisions shall obtain the force of laws. The army, the palace, the ministers of justice, and the great officers of the empire are all subject to your tribunal. None are exempted, excepting only the ordinary consuls, the praefect of the city, the king of the sacrifices, and (as long as she preserves her chastity inviolate) the eldest of the Vestal virgins. Even these few who may not dread the severity will anxiously solicit the esteem of the Roman censor."

A magistrate invested with such extensive powers would have appeared not so much the minister as the colleague of his sovereign. Valerian justly dreaded an elevation so full of envy and of suspicion. He modestly argued the alarming greatness of the trust, his own insufficiency, and the incurable corruption of the times. He artfully insinuated that the office of censor was inseparable from the Imperial dignity, and that the feeble hands of a subject were unequal to the support of such an immense weight of cares and of power. The approaching event of war soon put an end to the prosecution of a project so specious but so impracticable; and whilst it preserved Valerian from the danger, it saved the emperor Decius from the disappointment which would most probably have attended it. A censor may maintain, he can never restore, the morals of a state. It is impossible for such a magistrate to exert his authority with benefit, or even with effect, unless he is supported by a quick sense of honor and virtue in the minds of the people, by a decent reverence for the public opinion, and by a train of useful prejudices combating on the side of national manners. In a period when these principles are annihilated, the censorial jurisdiction must either sink into empty pageantry or be converted into a partial instrument of vexatious oppression. It was easier to vanquish the Goths than to eradicate the public vices; yet even in the first of these enterprises, Decius lost his army and his life.

The Goths were now on every side surrounded and pursued by the Roman arms. The flower of their troops had perished in the long siege of Philippopolis, and the exhausted country could no longer afford subsistence for the remaining multitude of licentious Barbarians. Reduced to this extremity, the Goths would gladly have purchased, by the surrender of all their booty and prisoners, the permission of an undisturbed retreat. But the emperor, confident of victory, and resolving by the chastisement of these invaders to strike a salutary terror into the nations of the North, refused to listen to any terms of accommodation. The high-spirited Barbarians preferred death to slavery. An obscure town of Moesia called Forum Terebronii was the scene of the battle. The Gothic army was drawn up in three lines, and either from choice or accident, the front of the third line was covered by a morass.

In the beginning of the action, the son of Decius, a youth of the fairest hopes, and already associated to the honors of the purple, was slain by an arrow in the sight of his afflicted father; who, summoning all his fortitude, admonished the dismayed troops that the loss of a single soldier was of little importance to the republic. The conflict was terrible; it was the combat of despair against grief and rage. The first line of the Goths at length gave way in disorder; the second, advancing to sustain it, shared its fate; and the third only remained entire, prepared to dispute the passage of the morass, which was imprudently attempted by the presumption of the enemy. "Here the fortune of the day turned, and all things became adverse to the Romans; the place deep with ooze, sinking under those who stood, slippery to such as advanced; their armor heavy, the waters deep; nor could they wield, in that uneasy situation, their weighty javelins. The Barbarians, on the contrary, were inured to encounter in the bogs, their persons tall, their spears long, such as could wound at a distance." In this morass the Roman army, after an ineffectual struggle, was irrecoverably lost; nor could the body of the emperor ever be found. Such was the fate of Decius, in the fiftieth year of his age; an accomplished prince, active in war and affable in peace; who, together with his son, has deserved to be compared, both in life and death, with the brightest examples of ancient virtue.

This fatal blow humbled, for a very little time, the insolence of the legions. They appeared to have patiently expected, and submissively obeyed, the decree of the senate which regulated the succession to the throne. From a just regard for the memory of Decius, the Imperial title was conferred on Hostilianus, his only surviving son; but an equal rank, with more effectual power, was granted to Gallus, whose experience and ability seemed equal to the great trust of guardian to the young prince and the distressed empire [December A.D. 251]. The first care of the new emperor was to deliver the Illyrian provinces from the intolerable weight of the victorious Goths [A.D. 252]. He consented to leave in their hands the rich fruits of their invasion, an immense booty, and what was still more disgraceful, a great number of prisoners of the highest merit and quality. He plentifully supplied their camp with every conveniency that could assuage their angry spirits or facilitate their so much wished-for departure; and he even promised to pay them annually a large sum of gold, on condition they should never afterwards infest the Roman territories by their incursions.

In the age of the Scipios, the most opulent kings of the earth, who courted the protection of the victorious commonwealth, were gratified with such trifling presents as could only derive a value from the hand that bestowed them; an ivory chair, a coarse garment of purple, an inconsiderable piece of plate, or a quantity of copper coin. After the wealth of nations had centered in Rome, the emperors displayed their greatness, and even their policy, by the regular exercise of a steady and moderate liberality towards the allies of the state. They relieved the poverty of the Barbarians, honored their merit, and recompensed their fidelity. These voluntary marks of bounty were understood to flow not from the fears but merely from the generosity or the gratitude of the Romans; and whilst presents and subsidies were liberally distributed among friends and suppliants, they were sternly refused to such as claimed them as a debt. But this stipulation of an annual payment to a victorious enemy appeared without disguise in the light of an ignominious tribute; the minds of the Romans were not yet accustomed to accept such unequal laws from a tribe of Barbarians; and the prince, who by a necessary concession had probably saved his country, became the object of the general contempt and aversion. The death of Hostilianus, though it happened in the midst of a raging pestilence, was interpreted as the personal crime of Gallus; and even the defeat of the late emperor was ascribed by the voice of suspicion to the perfidious counsels of his hated successor. The tranquility which the empire enjoyed during the first year of his administration served rather to inflame than to appease the public discontent; and as soon as the apprehensions of war were removed, the infamy of the peace was more deeply and more sensibly felt.

But the Romans were irritated to a still higher degree when they discovered that they had not even secured their repose, though at the expense of their honor. The dangerous secret of the wealth and weakness of the empire had been revealed to the world. New swarms of Barbarians, encouraged by the success and not conceiving themselves bound by the obligation of their brethren, spread devastation through the Illyrian provinces and terror as far as the gates of Rome. The defense of the monarchy, which seemed abandoned by the pusillanimous emperor, was assumed by Aemilianus, governor of Pannonia and Moesia; who rallied the scattered forces and revived the fainting spirits of the troops [A.D. 253]. The Barbarians were unexpectedly attacked, routed, chased, and pursued beyond the Danube. The victorious leader distributed as a donative the money collected for the tribute, and the acclamations of the soldiers proclaimed him emperor on the field of battle. Gallus, who, careless of the general welfare, indulged himself in the pleasures of Italy, was almost in the same instant informed of the success of the revolt and of the rapid approach of his aspiring lieutenant. He advanced to meet him as far as the plains of Spoleto. When the armies came in sight of each other, the soldiers of Gallus compared the ignominious conduct of their sovereign with the glory of his rival. They admired the valor of Aemilianus; they were attracted by his liberality, for he offered a considerable increase of pay to all deserters. The murder of Gallus, and of his son Volusianus, put an end to the civil war; and the senate gave a legal sanction to the rights of conquest [May A.D. 253]. The letters of Aemilianus to that assembly displayed a mixture of moderation and vanity. He assured them that he should resign to their wisdom the civil administration; and, contenting himself with the quality of their general, would in a short time assert the glory of Rome, and deliver the empire from all the Barbarians both of the North and of the East. His pride was flattered by the applause of the senate; and medals are still extant, representing him with the name and attributes of Hercules the Victor and Mars the Avenger.

If the new monarch possessed the abilities, he wanted the time necessary to fulfill these splendid promises. Less than four months intervened between his victory and his fall. He had vanquished Gallus: he sunk under the weight of a competitor more formidable than Gallus. That unfortunate prince had sent Valerian, already distinguished by the honorable title of censor, to bring the legions of Gaul and Germany to his aid. Valerian executed that commission with zeal and fidelity; and as he arrived too late to save his sovereign, he resolved to revenge him. The troops of Aemilianus, who still lay encamped in the plains of Spoleto, were awed by the sanctity of his character, but much more by the superior strength of his army; and as they were now become as incapable of personal attachment as they had always been of constitutional principle, they readily imbrued their hands in the blood of a prince who so lately had been the object of their partial choice [August A.D. 253]. The guilt was theirs, but the advantage of it was Valerian's; who obtained the possession of the throne by the means indeed of a civil war, but with a degree of innocence singular in that age of revolutions; since he owed neither gratitude nor allegiance to his predecessor whom he dethroned.

Valerian was about sixty years of age when he was invested with the purple, not by the caprice of the populace or the clamors of the army, but by the unanimous voice of the Roman world. In his gradual ascent through the honors of the state, he had deserved the favor of virtuous princes, and had declared himself the enemy of tyrants. His noble birth, his mild but unblemished manners, his learning, prudence, and experience were revered by the senate and people; and if mankind (according to the observation of an ancient writer) had been left at liberty to choose a master, their choice would most assuredly have fallen on Valerian. Perhaps the merit of this emperor was inadequate to his reputation; perhaps his abilities, or at least his spirit, were affected by the languor and coldness of old age. The consciousness of his decline engaged him to share the throne with a younger and more active associate; the emergency of the times demanded a general no less than a prince; and the experience of the Roman censor might have directed him where to bestow the Imperial purple, as the reward of military merit. But instead of making a judicious choice which would have confirmed his reign and endeared his memory, Valerian, consulting only the dictates of affection or vanity, immediately invested with the supreme honors his son Gallienus, a youth whose effeminate vices had been hitherto concealed by the obscurity of a private station. The joint government of the father and the son subsisted about seven, and the sole administration of Gallienus continued about eight, years [A.D. 253–268]. But the whole period was one uninterrupted series of confusion and calamity. As the Roman empire was at the same time and on every side attacked by the blind fury of foreign invaders and the wild ambition of domestic usurpers, we shall consult order and perspicuity by pursuing not so much the doubtful arrangement of dates as the more natural distribution of subjects. The most dangerous enemies of Rome, during the reigns of Valerian and Gallienus, were, 1. The Franks; 2. The Alemanni; 3. The Goths; and 4. The Persians. Under these general appellations, we may comprehend the adventures of less considerable tribes, whose obscure and uncouth names would only serve to oppress the memory and perplex the attention of the reader.

I. †The Rhine, though dignified with the title of Safeguard of the provinces, was an imperfect barrier against the daring spirit of enterprise with which the Franks were actuated. Their rapid devastations stretched from the river to the foot of the Pyrenees; nor were they stopped by those mountains. Spain, which had never dreaded, was unable to resist the inroads of the Germans. During twelve years, the greatest part of the reign of Gallienus, that opulent country was the theater of unequal and destructive hostilities.... When the exhausted country no longer supplied a variety of plunder, the Franks seized on some vessels in the ports of Spain, and transported themselves into Mauritania. The distant province was astonished with the fury of these Barbarians, who seemed to fall from a new world, as their name, manners, and complexion were equally unknown on the coast of Africa.

II. In that part of Upper Saxony, beyond the Elbe, which is at present called the Marquisate of Lusace, there existed in ancient times a sacred wood, the awful seat of the superstition of the Suevi. None were permitted to enter the holy precincts without confessing, by their servile bonds and suppliant posture, the immediate presence of the sovereign Deity. Patriotism contributed, as well as devotion, to consecrate the Sonnenwald, or wood of the Semnones. It was universally believed that the nation had received its first existence on that sacred spot. At stated periods, the numerous tribes who gloried in the Suevic blood resorted thither by their ambassadors; and the memory of their common extraction was perpetrated by Barbaric rites and human sacrifices. The wide-extended name of Suevi filled the interior countries of Germany, from the banks of the Oder to those of the Danube. They were distinguished from the other Germans by their peculiar mode of dressing their long hair, which they gathered into a rude knot on the crown of the head; and they delighted in an ornament that showed their ranks more lofty and terrible in the eyes of the enemy. Jealous as the Germans were of military renown, they all confessed the superior valor of the Suevi; and the tribes of the Usipetes and Tencteri, who, with a vast army, encountered the dictator Caesar, declared that they esteemed it not a disgrace to have fled before a people to whose arms the immortal gods themselves were unequal.

In the reign of the emperor Caracalla, an innumerable swarm of Suevi appeared on the banks of the Main, and in the neighborhood of the Roman provinces, in quest either of food, of plunder, or of glory.

The hasty army of volunteers gradually coalesced into a great and permanent nation and, as it was composed from so many different tribes, assumed the name of Alemanni, or Allmen; to denote at once their various lineage and their common bravery. The latter was soon felt by the Romans in many a hostile inroad. The Alemanni fought chiefly on horseback; but their cavalry was rendered still more formidable by a mixture of light infantry, selected from the bravest and most active of the youth, whom frequent exercise had inured to accompany the horsemen in the longest march, the most rapid charge, or the most precipitate retreat.

This warlike people of Germans had been astonished by the immense preparations of Alexander Severus; they were dismayed by the arms of his successor, a Barbarian equal in valor and fierceness to themselves. But still hovering on the frontiers of the empire, they increased the general disorder that ensued after the death of Decius. They inflicted severe wounds on the rich provinces of Gaul; they were the first who removed the veil that covered the feeble majesty of Italy. A numerous body of the Alemanni penetrated across the Danube and through the Rhaetian Alps into the plains of Lombardy, advanced as far as Ravenna, and displayed the victorious banners of Barbarians almost in sight of Rome.

The insult and the danger rekindled in the senate some sparks of their ancient virtue. Both the emperors were engaged in far distant wars, Valerian in the East and Gallienus on the Rhine. All the hopes and resources of the Romans were in themselves. In this emergency, the senators resumed the defense of the republic, drew out the Praetorian guards who had been left to garrison the capital, and filled up their numbers by enlisting into the public service the stoutest and most willing of the Plebeians. The Alemanni, astonished with the sudden appearance of an army more numerous than their own, retired into Germany, laden with spoil; and their retreat was esteemed as a victory by the unwarlike Romans.

When Gallienus received the intelligence that his capital was delivered from the Barbarians, he was much less delighted than alarmed with the courage of the senate, since it might one day prompt them to rescue the public from domestic tyranny as well as from foreign invasion. His timid ingratitude was published to his subjects in an edict which prohibited the senators from exercising any military employment, and even from approaching the camps of the legions. But his fears were groundless. The rich and luxurious nobles, sinking into their natural character, accepted as a favor this disgraceful exemption from military service; and as long as they were indulged in the enjoyment of their baths, their theaters, and their villas, they cheerfully resigned the more dangerous cares of empire to the rough hands of peasants and soldiers.[†]

III. Under the reigns of Valerian and Gallienus, the frontier of the [Danube] river was perpetually infested by the inroads of Germans and Sarmatians; but it was defended by the Romans with more than usual firmness and success. The provinces that were the seat of war recruited the armies of Rome with an inexhaustible supply of hardy soldiers; and more than one of these Illyrian peasants attained the station and displayed the abilities of a general. Though flying parties of the Barbarians who incessantly hovered on the banks of the Danube penetrated sometimes to the confines of Italy and Macedonia, their progress was commonly checked, or their return intercepted, by the Imperial lieutenants. But the great stream of the Gothic hostilities was diverted into a very different channel. The Goths, in their new settlement of the Ukraine, soon became masters of the northern coast of the Euxine: to the south of that inland sea were situated the soft and wealthy provinces of Asia Minor, which possessed all that could attract and nothing that could resist a Barbarian conqueror.

[*In various expeditions, the Goths plunder the cities of Asia Minor, ravage Greece, and threaten Italy.*]

The Goths had already advanced within sight of Italy when the approach of such imminent danger awakened the indolent Gallienus from his dream of pleasure. The emperor appeared in arms; and his presence seems to have checked the ardor and to have divided the strength of the enemy. Naulobatus, a chief of the Heruli, accepted an honorable capitulation, entered with a large body of his countrymen into the service of Rome, and was invested with the ornaments of the consular dignity, which had never before been profaned by the hands of a Barbarian. Great numbers of the Goths, disgusted with the perils and hardships of a tedious voyage, broke into Moesia, with a design of forcing their way over the Danube to their settlements in the Ukraine.

The wild attempt would have proved inevitable destruction if the discord of the Roman generals had not opened to the Barbarians the means of an escape. The small remainder of this destroying host returned on board their vessels; and, measuring back their way through the Hellespont and the Bosphorus, ravaged in their passage the shores of Troy, whose fame, immortalized by Homer, will probably survive the memory of the Gothic conquests.[†]

In the general calamities of mankind, the death of an individual, however exalted, the ruin of an edifice, however famous, are passed over with careless inattention. Yet we cannot forget that the temple of Diana at Ephesus, after having risen with increasing splendor from seven repeated misfortunes, was finally burnt by the Goths in their third naval invasion. The arts of Greece and the wealth of Asia had conspired to erect that sacred and magnificent structure. . . . The temple of Diana was . . . admired as one of the wonders of the world. Successive empires, the Persian, the Macedonian, and the Roman, had revered its sanctity and enriched its splendor. But the rude savages of the Baltic were destitute of a taste for the elegant arts, and they despised the ideal terrors of a foreign superstition.

Another circumstance is related of these invasions, which might deserve our notice were it not justly to be suspected as the fanciful conceit of a recent sophist. We are told that in the sack of Athens the Goths had collected all the libraries and were on the point of setting fire to this funeral pile of Grecian learning, had not one of their chiefs, of more refined policy than his brethren, dissuaded them from the design; by the profound observation, that as long as the Greeks were addicted to the study of books, they would never apply themselves to the exercise of arms. The sagacious counselor (should the truth of the fact be admitted) reasoned like an ignorant Barbarian. In the most polite and powerful nations, genius of every kind has displayed itself about the same period; and the age of science has generally been the age of military virtue and success.

IV. The new sovereign of Persia, Artaxerxes and his son Sapor, had triumphed . . . over the house of Arsaces. Of the many princes of that ancient race, Chosroes, king of Armenia, had alone preserved both his life and his independence. He defended himself by the natural strength of his country; by the perpetual resort of fugitives and malcontents; by the alliance of the Romans, and above all, by his own courage. Invincible in arms, during a thirty years' war, he was at length assassinated by the emissaries of Sapor, king of Persia. The patriotic satraps of Armenia, who asserted the freedom and dignity of the crown, implored the protection of Rome in favor of Tiridates, the lawful heir. But the son of Chosroes was an infant, the allies were at a distance, and the Persian monarch advanced towards the frontier at the head of an irresistible force. Young Tiridates, the future hope of his country, was saved by the fidelity of a servant, and Armenia continued above twenty-seven years a reluctant province of the great monarchy of Persia. Elated with this easy conquest, and presuming on the distresses or the degeneracy of the Romans, Sapor obliged the strong garrisons of Carrhae and Nisibis to surrender, and spread devastation and terror on either side of the Euphrates.

The loss of an important frontier, the ruin of a faithful and natural ally, and the rapid success of Sapor's ambition affected Rome with a deep sense of the insult as well as of the danger. Valerian flattered himself that the vigilance of his lieutenants would sufficiently provide for the safety of the Rhine and of the Danube; but he resolved, notwithstanding his advanced age, to march in person to the defense of the Euphrates. During his progress through Asia Minor, the naval enterprises of the Goths were suspended, and the afflicted province enjoyed a transient and fallacious calm. He passed the Euphrates, encountered the Persian monarch near the walls of Edessa, was vanquished, and taken prisoner by Sapor. The particulars of this great event are darkly and imperfectly represented; yet, by the glimmering light which is afforded us, we may discover a long series of imprudence, of error, and of deserved misfortunes on the side of the Roman emperor. He reposed an implicit confidence in Macrianus, his Praetorian praefect. That worthless minister rendered his master formidable only to the oppressed subjects, and contemptible to the enemies of Rome. By his weak or wicked counsels, the Imperial army was betrayed into a situation where valor and military skill were equally unavailing. The vigorous attempt of the Romans to cut their way through the Persian host was repulsed with great slaughter; and Sapor, who encompassed the camp with superior numbers, patiently waited till the increasing rage of famine and pestilence had insured his victory. The licentious murmurs of the legions soon accused Valerian as the cause of their calamities; their seditious clamors demanded an instant capitulation. An immense sum of gold was offered to purchase the permission of a disgraceful retreat. But the Persian, conscious of his superiority, refused the money with disdain; and, detaining the deputies, advanced in order of battle to the foot of the Roman rampart and insisted on a personal conference with the emperor. Valerian was reduced to the necessity of entrusting his life and dignity to the faith of an enemy. The interview ended as it was natural to expect. The emperor was made a prisoner, and his astonished troops laid down their arms [A.D. 260]. In such a moment of triumph, the pride and policy of Sapor prompted him to fill the vacant throne with a successor entirely dependent on his pleasure. Cyriades, an obscure fugitive of Antioch, stained with every vice, was chosen to dishonor the Roman purple; and the will of the Persian victor could not fail of being ratified by the acclamations, however reluctant, of the captive army.

The Imperial slave was eager to secure the favor of his master by an act of treason to his native country. He conducted Sapor over the Euphrates and, by the way of Chalcis, to the metropolis of the East. So rapid were the motions of the Persian cavalry that, if we may credit a very judicious historian, the city of Antioch was surprised when the idle multitude was fondly gazing on the amusements of the theater. The splendid buildings of Antioch, private as well as public, were either pillaged or destroyed; and the numerous inhabitants were put to the sword or led away into captivity. The tide of devastation was stopped for a moment by the resolution of the high priest of Emesa. Arrayed in his sacerdotal robes, he appeared at the head of a great body of fanatic peasants armed only with slings, and defended his god and his property from the sacrilegious hands of the followers of Zoroaster. But the ruin of Tarsus, and of many other cities, furnishes a melancholy proof that, except in this singular instance, the conquest of Syria and Cilicia scarcely interrupted the progress of the Persian arms. The advantages of the narrow passes of Mount Taurus were abandoned, in which an invader whose principal force consisted in his cavalry would have been engaged in a very unequal combat: and Sapor was permitted to form the siege of Caesarea, the capital of Cappadocia; a city, though of the second rank, which was supposed to contain four hundred thousand inhabitants. Demosthenes commanded in the place, not so much by the commission of the emperor as in the voluntary defense of his country. For a long time he deferred its fate; and when at last Caesarea was betrayed by the perfidy of a physician, he cut his way through the Persians, who had been ordered to exert their utmost diligence to take him alive. This heroic chief escaped the power of a foe who might either have honored or punished his obstinate valor; but many thousands of his fellow-citizens were involved in a general massacre, and Sapor is accused of treating his prisoners with wanton and unrelenting cruelty. Much should undoubtedly be allowed for national animosity, much for humbled pride and impotent revenge; yet, upon the whole, it is certain that the same prince who in Armenia had displayed the mild aspect of a legislator, showed himself to the Romans under the stern features of a conqueror. He despaired of making any permanent establishment in the empire and sought only to leave behind him a wasted desert, whilst he transported into Persia the people and the treasures of the provinces.

At the time when the East trembled at the name of Sapor, he received a present not unworthy of the greatest kings; a long train of camels laden with the most rare and valuable merchandises. The rich offering was accompanied with an epistle, respectful but not servile, from Odenathus, one of the noblest and most opulent senators of Palmyra. "Who is this Odenathus" (said the haughty victor, and he commanded that the present should be cast into the Euphrates) "that he thus insolently presumes to write to his lord? If he entertains a hope of mitigating his punishment, let him fall prostrate before the foot of our throne, with his hands bound behind his back. Should he hesitate, swift destruction shall be poured on his head, on his whole race, and on his country." The desperate extremity to which the Palmyrenian was reduced called into action all the latent powers of his soul. He met Sapor; but he met him in arms. Infusing his own spirit into a little army collected from the villages of Syria and the tents of the desert, he hovered round the Persian host, harassed their retreat, carried off part of the treasure, and, what was dearer than any treasure, several of the women of the great king; who was at last obliged to repass the Euphrates with some marks of haste and confusion. By this exploit, Odenathus laid the foundations of his future fame and fortunes. The majesty of Rome, oppressed by a Persian, was protected by a Syrian or Arab of Palmyra.

The voice of history, which is often little more than the organ of hatred or flattery, reproaches Sapor with a proud abuse of the rights of conquest. We are told that Valerian, in chains but invested with the Imperial purple, was exposed to the multitude, a constant spectacle of fallen greatness; and that whenever the Persian monarch mounted on horseback, he placed his foot on the neck of a Roman emperor. Notwithstanding all the remonstrances of his allies, who repeatedly advised him to remember the vicissitudes of fortune, to dread the returning power of Rome, and to make his illustrious captive the pledge of peace, not the object of insult, Sapor still remained inflexible. When Valerian sunk under the weight of shame and grief, his skin, stuffed with straw and formed into the likeness of a human figure, was preserved for ages in the most celebrated temple of Persia; a more real monument of triumph than the fancied trophies of brass and marble so often erected by Roman vanity. The tale is moral and pathetic, but the truth of it may very fairly be called in question. The letters still extant from the princes of the East to Sapor are manifest forgeries; nor is it natural to suppose that a jealous monarch should, even in the person of a rival, thus publicly degrade the majesty of kings. Whatever treatment the unfortunate Valerian might experience in Persia, it is at least certain that the only emperor of Rome who had ever fallen into the hands of the enemy languished away his life in hopeless captivity.

The emperor Gallienus, who had long supported with impatience the censorial severity of his father and colleague, received the intelligence of his misfortunes with secret pleasure and avowed indifference. "I knew that my father was a mortal," said he; "and since he has acted as it becomes a brave man, I am satisfied." Whilst Rome lamented the fate of her sovereign, the savage coldness of his son was extolled by the servile courtiers as the perfect firmness of a hero and a stoic. It is difficult to paint the light, the various, the inconstant character of Gallienus, which he displayed without constraint as soon as he became sole possessor of the empire. In every art that he attempted, his lively genius enabled him to succeed; and as his genius was destitute of judgment, he attempted every art except the important ones of war and government. He was a master of several curious but useless sciences, a ready orator, an elegant poet, a skillful gardener, an excellent cook, and most contemptible prince. When the great emergencies of the state required his presence and attention, he was engaged in conversation with the philosopher Plotinus, wasting his time in trifling or licentious pleasures, preparing his initiation to the Grecian mysteries, or soliciting a place in the Arcopagus of Athens. His profuse magnificence insulted the general poverty; the solemn ridicule of his triumphs impressed a deeper sense of the public disgrace. The repeated intelligence of invasions, defeats, and rebellions he received with a careless smile; and singling out with affected contempt some particular production of the lost province, he carelessly asked whether Rome must be ruined unless it was supplied with linen from Egypt and arras cloth from Gaul. There were, however, a few short moments in the life of Gallienus when, exasperated by some recent injury, he suddenly appeared the intrepid soldier and the cruel tyrant; till, satiated with blood or fatigued by resistance, he insensibly sunk into the natural mildness and indolence of his character.

At the time when the reins of government were held with so loose a hand, it is not surprising that a crowd of usurpers should start up in every province of the empire against the son of Valerian. It was probably some ingenious fancy of comparing the thirty tyrants of Rome with the thirty tyrants of Athens that induced the writers of the Augustan History to select that celebrated number, which has been gradually received into a popular appellation. But in every light the parallel is idle and defective. What resemblance can we discover between a council of thirty persons, the united oppressors of a single city, and an uncertain list of independent rivals who rose and fell in irregular succession through the extent of a vast empire? Nor can the number of thirty be completed unless we include in the account the women and children who were honored with the Imperial title. The reign of Gallienus, distracted as it was, produced only nineteen pretenders to the throne.†

The rapid and perpetual transitions from the cottage to the throne, and from the throne to the grave, might have amused an indifferent philosopher; were it possible for a philosopher to remain indifferent amidst the general calamities of humankind. The election of these precarious emperors, their power and their death, were equally destructive to their subjects and adherents. The price of their fatal elevation was instantly discharged to the troops by an immense donative, drawn from the bowels of the exhausted people. However virtuous was their character, however pure their intentions, they found themselves reduced to the hard necessity of supporting their usurpation by frequent acts of rapine and cruelty. When they fell, they involved armies and provinces in their fall. There is still extant a most savage mandate

from Gallienus to one of his ministers after the suppression of Ingenuus, who had assumed the purple in Illyricum. "It is not enough,"
says that soft but inhuman prince, "that you exterminate such as have
appeared in arms; the chance of battle might have served me as effectually. The male sex of every age must be extirpated; provided that,
in the execution of the children and old men, you can contrive means
to save our reputation. Let every one die who has dropped an expression, who has entertained a thought against me, against *me,* the son of
Valerian, the father and brother of so many princes. Remember that
Ingenuus was made emperor: tear, kill, hew in pieces. I write to you
with my own hand, and would inspire you with my own feelings."
Whilst the public forces of the state were dissipated in private quarrels, the defenseless provinces lay exposed to every invader. The bravest
usurpers were compelled by the perplexity of their situation to conclude ignominious treaties with the common enemy, to purchase with
oppressive tributes the neutrality or services of the Barbarians, and
to introduce hostile and independent nations into the heart of the
Roman monarchy.†

Our habits of thinking so fondly connect the order of the universe
with the fate of man that this gloomy period of history has been decorated with inundations, earthquakes, uncommon meteors, preternatural darkness, and a crowd of prodigies fictitious or exaggerated. But
a long and general famine was a calamity of a more serious kind. It
was the inevitable consequence of rapine and oppression, which extirpated the produce of the present and the hope of future harvests.
Famine is almost always followed by epidemical diseases, the effect of
scanty and unwholesome food. Other causes must, however, have contributed to the furious plague which, from the year two hundred and
fifty to the year two hundred and sixty-five, raged without interruption in every province, every city, and almost every family of the
Roman empire. During some time five thousand persons died daily in
Rome; and many towns that had escaped the hands of the Barbarians
were entirely depopulated.

We have the knowledge of a very curious circumstance, of some
use perhaps in the melancholy calculation of human calamities. An
exact register was kept at Alexandria of all the citizens entitled to receive the distribution of corn. It was found that the ancient number of
those comprised between the ages of forty and seventy had been equal

to the whole sum of claimants, from fourteen to fourscore years of age, who remained alive after the reign of Gallienus. Applying this authentic fact to the most correct tables of mortality, it evidently proves that above half the people of Alexandria had perished; and could we venture to extend the analogy to the other provinces, we might suspect that war, pestilence, and famine had consumed, in a few years, the moiety of the human species.

CHAPTER XI

REIGN OF CLAUDIUS, DEFEAT OF THE GOTHS

*Reign of Claudius. • Defeat of the Goths. • Victories, triumph,
and death of Aurelian.*

Under the deplorable reigns of Valerian and Gallienus, the empire was
oppressed and almost destroyed by the soldiers, the tyrants, and the
Barbarians. It was saved by a series of great princes who derived their
obscure origin from the martial provinces of Illyricum. Within a period of about thirty years, Claudius, Aurelian, Probus, Diocletian and
his colleagues triumphed over the foreign and domestic enemies of
the state, reestablished, with the military discipline, the strength of the
frontiers, and deserved the glorious title of Restorers of the Roman
world.

The removal of an effeminate tyrant made way for a succession of
heroes. The indignation of the people imputed all their calamities to
Gallienus, and the far greater part were indeed the consequence of his
dissolute manners and careless administration. He was even destitute
of a sense of honor, which so frequently supplies the absence of public virtue; and as long as he was permitted to enjoy the possession of
Italy, a victory of the Barbarians, the loss of a province, or the rebellion
of a general seldom disturbed the tranquil course of his pleasures.[†]

A conspiracy was formed by Heraclianus, the Praetorian praefect,
by Marcian, a general of rank and reputation, and by Cecrops, who
commanded a numerous body of Dalmatian guards. The death of
Gallienus was resolved. . . . At a late hour of the night, but while the
emperor still protracted the pleasures of the table, an alarm was suddenly given . . . ; Gallienus, who was never deficient in personal bravery, started from his silken couch, and without allowing himself time
either to put on his armor or to assemble his guards, he mounted on
horseback and rode full speed towards the supposed place of the attack. Encompassed by his declared or concealed enemies, he soon,
amidst the nocturnal tumult, received a mortal dart from an uncertain

hand [March 20, A.D. 268]. Before he expired, a patriotic sentiment rising in the mind of Gallienus induced him to name a deserving successor; and it was his last request that the Imperial ornaments should be delivered to Claudius, who then commanded a detached army in the neighborhood of Pavia. The report at least was diligently propagated and the order cheerfully obeyed by the conspirators, who had already agreed to place Claudius on the throne. On the first news of the emperor's death, the troops expressed some suspicion and resentment, till the one was removed and the other assuaged by a donative of twenty pieces of gold to each soldier. They then ratified the election and acknowledged the merit of their new sovereign.

The obscurity which covered the origin of Claudius, though it was afterwards embellished by some flattering fictions, sufficiently betrays the meanness of his birth. We can only discover that he was a native of one of the provinces bordering on the Danube; that his youth was spent in arms, and that his modest valor attracted the favor and confidence of Decius. The senate and people already considered him as an excellent officer, equal to the most important trusts; and censured the inattention of Valerian, who suffered him to remain in the subordinate station of a tribune. But it was not long before that emperor distinguished the merit of Claudius by declaring him general and chief of the Illyrian frontier, with the command of all the troops in Thrace, Moesia, Dacia, Pannonia, and Dalmatia, the appointments of the praefect of Egypt, the establishment of the proconsul of Africa, and the sure prospect of the consulship. By his victories over the Goths, he deserved from the senate the honor of a statue, and excited the jealous apprehensions of Gallienus. It was impossible that a soldier could esteem so dissolute a sovereign, nor is it easy to conceal a just contempt.... At last, indeed, [Claudius] received from [military] conspirators the bloody purple of Gallienus: but he had been absent from their camp and counsels; and however he might applaud the deed, we may candidly presume that he was innocent of the knowledge of it. When Claudius ascended the throne, he was about fifty-four years of age.[†]

In the arduous task which Claudius had undertaken of restoring the empire to its ancient splendor, it was first necessary to revive among his troops a sense of order and obedience. With the authority of a veteran commander, he represented to them that the relaxation of discipline had introduced a long train of disorders, the effects of which were at length experienced by the soldiers themselves; that a people ruined by oppression and indolent from despair could no longer supply a numerous army with the means of luxury, or even of subsistence; that the danger of each individual had increased with the despotism of the military order, since princes who tremble on the throne will guard their safety by the instant sacrifice of every obnoxious subject. The emperor expatiated on the mischiefs of a lawless caprice which the soldiers could only gratify at the expense of their own blood; as their seditious elections had so frequently been followed by civil wars which consumed the flower of the legions either in the field of battle or in the cruel abuse of victory. He painted in the most lively colors the exhausted state of the treasury, the desolation of the provinces, the disgrace of the Roman name, and the insolent triumph of rapacious Barbarians. It was against those Barbarians, he declared, that he intended to point the first effort of their arms.[†]

The event surpassed his own expectations and those of the world [A.D. 269]. By the most signal victories he delivered the empire from this host of Barbarians, and was distinguished by posterity under the glorious appellation of the Gothic Claudius. The imperfect historians of an irregular war do not enable us to describe the order and circumstances of his exploits; but . . . [a] vast circle of Roman posts, distributed with skill, supported with firmness, and gradually closing towards a common center forced the Barbarians into the most inaccessible parts of Mount Haemus, where they found a safe refuge but a very scanty subsistence. During the course of a rigorous winter, in which they were besieged by the emperor's troops, famine and pestilence, desertion and the sword, continually diminished the imprisoned multitude. On the return of spring, nothing appeared in arms except a hardy and desperate band.[†]

The pestilence which swept away such numbers of the Barbarians at length proved fatal to their conqueror. After a short but glorious reign of two years, Claudius expired at Sirmium, amidst the tears and acclamations of his subjects [March A.D. 270]. In his last illness, he convened the principal officers of the state and army, and in their presence recommended Aurelian, one of his generals, as the most deserving of the throne, and the best qualified to execute the great design which he himself had been permitted only to undertake. The virtues of Claudius, his valor, affability, justice, and temperance, his love of fame and of his country, place him in that short list of emperors who added luster to the Roman purple. Those virtues, however, were celebrated with peculiar zeal and complacency by the courtly writers of the age of Constantine, who was the great grandson of Crispus, the elder brother of Claudius. The voice of flattery was soon taught to repeat that gods, who so hastily had snatched Claudius from the earth, rewarded his merit and piety by the perpetual establishment of the empire in his family.[†]

The reign of Aurelian lasted only four years and about nine months [A.D. 270–275]; but every instant of that short period was filled by some memorable achievement. He put an end to the Gothic war, chastised the Germans who invaded Italy, recovered Gaul, Spain, and Britain out of the hands of [the usurper] Tetricus, and destroyed the proud monarchy which Zenobia had erected in the East on the ruins of the afflicted empire.

It was the rigid attention of Aurelian even to the minutest articles of discipline which bestowed such uninterrupted success on his arms. His military regulations are contained in a very concise epistle to one of his inferior officers, who is commanded to enforce them as he wishes to become a tribune, or as he is desirous to live. Gaming, drinking, and the arts of divination were severely prohibited. Aurelian expected that his soldiers should be modest, frugal, and laborious; that their armor should be constantly kept bright, their weapons sharp, their clothing and horses ready for immediate service; that they should live in their quarters with chastity and sobriety, without damaging the cornfields, without stealing even a sheep, a fowl, or a bunch of grapes, without exacting from their landlords either salt, or oil, or wood. "The public allowance," continues the emperor, "is sufficient for their support; their wealth should be collected from the spoils of the enemy, not from the tears of the provincials." A single instance will serve to display the rigor, and even cruelty, of Aurelian. One of the soldiers had seduced the wife of his host. The guilty wretch was fastened to two trees forcibly drawn towards each other, and his limbs were torn asunder by their sudden separation. A few such examples impressed a salutary consternation. The punishments of Aurelian were terrible; but he had seldom occasion to punish more than once the same offense. His own conduct gave a sanction to his laws, and the seditious legions dreaded a chief who had learned to obey, and who was worthy to command.†

[After] a twenty years' war, the Goths and the Romans consented to a lasting and beneficial treaty. It was earnestly solicited by the Barbarians and cheerfully ratified by the legions, to whose suffrage the prudence of Aurelian referred the decision of that important question. The Gothic nation engaged to supply the armies of Rome with a body of two thousand auxiliaries, consisting entirely of cavalry, and stipulated in return an undisturbed retreat, with a regular market as far as the Danube, provided by the emperor's care but at their own expense. . . . But the most important condition of peace was understood rather than expressed in the treaty. Aurelian withdrew the Roman forces from Dacia, and tacitly relinquished that great province to the Goths and Vandals [circa A.D. 275]. His manly judgment convinced him of the solid advantages, and taught him to despise the seeming disgrace, of thus contracting the frontiers of the monarchy.†

While the vigorous and moderate conduct of Aurelian restored the Illyrian frontier, the nation of the Alemanni violated the conditions of peace which either Gallienus had purchased or Claudius had imposed, and, inflamed by their impatient youth, suddenly flew to arms. Forty thousand horse appeared in the field, and the numbers of the infantry doubled those of the cavalry. The first objects of their avarice were a few cities of the Rhaetian frontier; but their hopes soon rising with success, the rapid march of the Alemanni traced a line of devastation from the Danube to the Po.†

Three considerable battles are mentioned in which the principal force of both armies was obstinately engaged. The success was various. In the first, fought near Placentia, the Romans received so severe a blow that, according to the expression of a writer extremely partial to Aurelian, the immediate dissolution of the empire was apprehended. The crafty Barbarians, who had lined the woods, suddenly attacked the legions in the dusk of the evening and, it is most probable, after the fatigue and disorder of a long march. The fury of their charge was irresistible; but at length, after a dreadful slaughter, the patient firmness of the emperor rallied his troops and restored, in some degree, the honor of his arms. The second battle was fought near Fano in Umbria, on the spot which, five hundred years before, had been fatal to the brother of Hannibal. Thus far the successful Germans had advanced along the

Aemilian and Flaminian way, with a design of sacking the defenseless mistress of the world. But Aurelian, who, watchful for the safety of Rome, still hung on their rear, found in this place the decisive moment of giving them a total and irretrievable defeat. The flying remnant of their host was exterminated in a third and last battle near Pavia; and Italy was delivered from the inroads of the Alemanni.

Fear has been the original parent of superstition, and every new calamity urges trembling mortals to deprecate the wrath of their invisible enemies. Though the best hope of the republic was in the valor and conduct of Aurelian, yet such was the public consternation when the Barbarians were hourly expected at the gates of Rome that, by a decree of the senate, the Sibylline books were consulted. Even the emperor himself, from a motive either of religion or of policy, recommended this salutary measure, chided the tardiness of the senate, and offered to supply whatever expense, whatever animals, whatever captives of any nation the gods should require. Notwithstanding this liberal offer, it does not appear that any human victims expiated with their blood the sins of the Roman people [January 11, A.D. 271]. The Sibylline books enjoined ceremonies of a more harmless nature, processions of priests in white robes attended by a chorus of youths and virgins; lustrations of the city and adjacent country; and sacrifices whose powerful influence disabled the Barbarians from passing the mystic ground on which they had been celebrated. However puerile in themselves, these superstitious arts were subservient to the success of the war; and if, in the decisive battle of Fano, the Alemanni fancied they saw an army of specters combating on the side of Aurelian, he received a real and effectual aid from this imaginary reinforcement.

But whatever confidence might be placed in ideal ramparts, the experience of the past and the dread of the future induced the Romans to construct fortifications of a grosser and more substantial kind. The seven hills of Rome had been surrounded by the successors of Romulus with an ancient wall of more than thirteen miles. The vast enclosure may seem disproportioned to the strength and numbers of the infant state. But it was necessary to secure an ample extent of pasture and arable land against the frequent and sudden incursions of the tribes of Latium, the perpetual enemies of the republic. With the progress of Roman greatness, the city and its inhabitants gradually increased, filled up the vacant space, pierced through the useless walls, covered the field of Mars, and, on every side, followed the public highways in long and beautiful suburbs. The extent of the new walls, erected by Aurelian and finished in the reign of Probus, was magnified by popular estimation to near fifty, but is reduced by accurate measurement to about twenty-one miles. It was a great but a melancholy labor, since the defense of the capital betrayed the decline of the monarchy. The Romans of a more prosperous age, who trusted to the arms of the legions the safety of the frontier camps, were very far from entertaining a suspicion that it would ever become necessary to fortify the seat of empire against the inroads of the Barbarians.

The victory of Claudius over the Goths, and the success of Aurelian against the Alemanni, had already restored to the arms of Rome their ancient superiority over the barbarous nations of the North. To chastise domestic tyrants and to reunite the dismembered parts of the empire was a task reserved for the second of those warlike emperors. Though he was acknowledged by the senate and people, the frontiers of Italy, Africa, Illyricum, and Thrace confined the limits of his reign. Gaul, Spain, and Britain, Egypt, Syria, and Asia Minor, were still possessed by two rebels who alone, out of so numerous a list, had hitherto escaped the dangers of their situation; and to complete the ignominy of Rome, these rival thrones had been usurped by women.

A rapid succession of monarchs had arisen and fallen in the provinces of Gaul. . . . After the murder of so many valiant princes, it is somewhat remarkable that a female for a long time controlled the fierce legions of Gaul, and still more singular that she was the mother of the unfortunate Victorinus. The arts and treasures of Victoria enabled her successively to place Marius and Tetricus on the throne, and to reign with a manly vigor under the name of those dependent emperors. Money of copper, of silver, and of gold was coined in her name; she assumed the titles of Augusta and Mother of the Camps: her power ended only with her life.[†]

Aurelian had no sooner secured the person and provinces of Tetricus than he turned his arms against Zenobia, the celebrated queen of Palmyra and the East [A.D. 272]. Modern Europe has produced several illustrious women who have sustained with glory the weight of empire; nor is our own age destitute of such distinguished characters. But if we except the doubtful achievements of Semiramis, Zenobia is perhaps the only female whose superior genius broke through the servile indolence imposed on her sex by the climate and manners of Asia. She claimed her descent from the Macedonian kings of Egypt, equaled in beauty her ancestor Cleopatra, and far surpassed that princess in chastity and valor. Zenobia was esteemed the most lovely as well as the most heroic of her sex. She was of a dark complexion (for in speaking of a lady these trifles become important). Her teeth were of a pearly whiteness, and her large black eyes sparkled with uncommon fire, tempered by the most attractive sweetness. Her voice was strong and harmonious. Her manly understanding was strengthened and adorned by study. She was not ignorant of the Latin tongue, but possessed in equal perfection the Greek, the Syriac, and the Egyptian languages. She had drawn up for her own use an epitome of Oriental history, and familiarly compared the beauties of Homer and Plato under the tuition of the sublime Longinus.

This accomplished woman gave her hand to Odenathus, who, from a private station, raised himself to the dominion of the East. She soon became the friend and companion of a hero. In the intervals of war, Odenathus passionately delighted in the exercise of hunting; he pursued with ardor the wild beasts of the desert, lions, panthers, and bears; and the ardor of Zenobia in that dangerous amusement was not inferior to his own. She had inured her constitution to fatigue, disdained the use of a covered carriage, generally appeared on horseback in a military habit, and sometimes marched several miles on foot at the head of the troops. The success of Odenathus was in a great measure ascribed to her incomparable prudence and fortitude. Their splendid victories over the Great King, whom they twice pursued as far as the gates of Ctesiphon, laid the foundations of their united fame and power. The armies which they commanded, and the provinces which they had saved, acknowledged not any other sovereigns than their invincible chiefs. The senate and people of Rome revered a stranger who had avenged their captive emperor, and even the insensible son of Valerian accepted Odenathus for his legitimate colleague.

After a successful expedition against the Gothic plunderers of Asia, the Palmyrenian prince returned to the city of Emesa in Syria. Invincible in war, he was there cut off by domestic treason, and his favorite amusement of hunting was the cause, or at least the occasion, of his death. His nephew Maeonius presumed to dart his javelin before that of his uncle; and though admonished of his error, repeated the same insolence. As a monarch and as a sportsman, Odenathus was provoked, took away his horse, a mark of ignominy among the Barbarians, and chastised the rash youth by a short confinement. The offense was soon forgot, but the punishment was remembered; and Maeonius, with a few daring associates, assassinated his uncle in the midst of a great entertainment [A.D. 267]. Herod, the son of Odenathus, though not of Zenobia, a young man of a soft and effeminate temper, was killed with his father. But Maeonius obtained only the pleasure of revenge by this bloody deed. He had scarcely time to assume the title of Augustus before he was sacrificed by Zenobia to the memory of her husband.

With the assistance of his most faithful friends, she immediately filled the vacant throne, and governed with manly counsels Palmyra, Syria, and the East above five years. By the death of Odenathus, that authority was at an end which the senate had granted him only as a personal distinction; but his martial widow, disdaining both the senate and Gallienus, obliged one of the Roman generals who was sent against her to retreat into Europe with the loss of his army and his reputation. Instead of the little passions which so frequently perplex a female reign, the steady administration of Zenobia was guided by the most judicious maxims of policy. If it was expedient to pardon, she could calm her resentment; if it was necessary to punish, she could impose silence on the voice of pity. Her strict economy was accused of avarice; yet on every proper occasion she appeared magnificent and liberal. The neighboring states of Arabia, Armenia, and Persia dreaded her enmity and solicited her alliance. To the dominions of Odenathus, which extended from the Euphrates to the frontiers of Bithynia, his widow added the inheritance of her ancestors, the populous and fertile kingdom of Egypt. The emperor Claudius acknowledged her merit and was content that, while *he* pursued the Gothic war, *she* should assert the dignity of the empire in the East. The conduct, however, of Zenobia was attended with some ambiguity; nor is it unlikely that she had conceived the design of erecting an independent and hostile monarchy. She blended with the popular manners of Roman princes the stately pomp of the courts of Asia, and exacted from her subjects the same adoration that was paid to the successor of Cyrus. She bestowed on her three sons a Latin education, and often showed them to the troops adorned with the Imperial purple. For herself she reserved the diadem, with the splendid but doubtful title of Queen of the East.

When Aurelian passed over into Asia, against an adversary whose sex alone could render her an object of contempt, his presence restored obedience to the province of Bithynia, already shaken by the arms and intrigues of Zenobia [A.D. 272]. Advancing at the head of his legions, he accepted the submission of Ancyra, and was admitted into Tyana after an obstinate siege. . . . Antioch was deserted on his approach, till the emperor, by his salutary edicts, recalled the fugitives and granted a general pardon to all who, from necessity rather than choice, had been engaged in the service of the Palmyrenian queen. The unexpected mildness of such a conduct reconciled the minds of the Syrians, and as far as the gates of Emesa, the wishes of the people seconded the terror of his arms.

Zenobia would have ill deserved her reputation had she indolently permitted the emperor of the West to approach within a hundred miles of her capital. The fate of the East was decided in two great battles; so similar in almost every circumstance that we can scarcely distinguish them from each other, except by observing that the first was fought near Antioch and the second near Emesa. In both the queen of Palmyra animated the armies by her presence. . . . After the defeat of Emesa, Zenobia found it impossible to collect a third army. As far as the frontier of Egypt, the nations subject to her empire had joined the standard of the conqueror, who detached Probus, the bravest of his generals, to possess himself of the Egyptian provinces. Palmyra was the last resource of the widow of Odenathus. She retired within the walls of her capital, made every preparation for a vigorous resistance, and declared, with the intrepidity of a heroine, that the last moment of her reign and of her life should be the same.†

In his march over the sandy desert between Emesa and Palmyra, the emperor Aurelian was perpetually harassed by the Arabs; nor could he always defend his army, and especially his baggage, from those flying troops of active and daring robbers who watched for the moment of surprise and eluded the slow pursuit of the legions. The siege of Palmyra was an object far more difficult and important, and the emperor, who, with incessant vigor, pressed the attacks in person, was himself wounded with a dart. "The Roman people," says Aurelian, in an original letter, "speak with contempt of the war which I am waging against a woman. They are ignorant both of the character and of the power of Zenobia. It is impossible to enumerate her warlike preparations, of stones, of arrows, and of every species of missile weapons. Every part of the walls is provided with two or three *ballistae* [catapults], and artificial fires are thrown from her military engines. The fear of punishment has armed her with a desperate courage. Yet still I trust in the protecting deities of Rome, who have hitherto been favorable to all my undertakings." Doubtful, however, of the protection of the gods and of the event of the siege, Aurelian judged it more prudent to offer terms of an advantageous capitulation; to the queen, a splendid retreat; to the citizens, their ancient privileges. His proposals were obstinately rejected, and the refusal was accompanied with insult.

The firmness of Zenobia was supported by the hope that in a very short time famine would compel the Roman army to repass the desert; and by the reasonable expectation that the kings of the East, and particularly the Persian monarch, would arm in the defense of their most natural ally. But fortune, and the perseverance of Aurelian, overcame every obstacle. The death of Sapor, which happened about this time, distracted the councils of Persia, and the inconsiderable succors that attempted to relieve Palmyra were easily intercepted either by the arms or the liberality of the emperor [A.D. 273]. From every part of Syria, a regular succession of convoys safely arrived in the camp, which was increased by the return of Probus with his victorious troops from the conquest of Egypt. It was then that Zenobia resolved to fly. She mounted the fleetest of her dromedaries and had already reached the banks of the Euphrates, about sixty miles from Palmyra, when she was overtaken by the pursuit of Aurelian's light horse, seized, and brought back a captive to the feet of the emperor. Her capital soon afterwards surrendered and was treated with unexpected lenity. The arms, horses, and camels, with an immense treasure of gold, silver, silk, and precious stones, were all delivered to the conqueror, who, leaving only a garrison of six hundred archers, returned to Emesa and employed some time in the distribution of rewards and punishments at the end of so memorable a war, which restored to the obedience of Rome those provinces that had renounced their allegiance since the captivity of Valerian.

When the Syrian queen was brought into the presence of Aurelian, he sternly asked her, How she had presumed to rise in arms against the emperors of Rome! The answer of Zenobia was a prudent mixture of respect and firmness. "Because I disdained to consider as Roman emperors an Aureolus or a Gallienus. You alone I acknowledge as my conqueror and my sovereign." But as female fortitude is commonly artificial, so it is seldom steady or consistent. The courage of Zenobia deserted her in the hour of trial; she trembled at the angry clamors of the soldiers who called aloud for her immediate execution, forgot the generous despair of Cleopatra, which she had proposed as her model, and ignominiously purchased life by the sacrifice of her fame and her friends. It was to their counsels, which governed the weakness of her sex, that she imputed the guilt of her obstinate resistance; it was on their heads that she directed the vengeance of the cruel Aurelian. The fame of Longinus, who was included among the numerous and perhaps innocent victims of her fear, will survive that of the queen who betrayed or the tyrant who condemned him. Genius and learning were incapable of moving a fierce unlettered soldier, but they had served to elevate and harmonize the soul of Longinus. Without uttering a complaint, he calmly followed the executioner, pitying his unhappy mistress and bestowing comfort on his afflicted friends.

Returning from the conquest of the East, Aurelian had already crossed the Straits which divided Europe from Asia when he was provoked by the intelligence that the Palmyrenians had massacred the governor and garrison which he had left among them and again erected the standard of revolt. Without a moment's deliberation, he once more turned his face towards Syria. Antioch was alarmed by his rapid approach, and the helpless city of Palmyra felt the irresistible weight of his resentment. We have a letter of Aurelian himself in which he acknowledges that old men, women, children, and peasants had been involved in that dreadful execution, which should have been confined to armed rebellion; and although his principal concern seems directed to the reestablishment of a temple of the Sun, he discovers some pity for the remnant of the Palmyrenians, to whom he grants the permission of rebuilding and inhabiting their city. But it is easier to destroy than to restore. The seat of commerce, of arts, and of Zenobia gradually sunk into an obscure town, a trifling fortress, and at length a miserable village.[†]

Since the foundation of Rome, no general had more nobly deserved a triumph than Aurelian; nor was a triumph ever celebrated with superior pride and magnificence [A.D. 274]. The pomp was opened by twenty elephants, four royal tigers, and above two hundred of the most curious animals from every climate of the North, the East, and the South. They were followed by sixteen hundred gladiators, devoted to the cruel amusement of the amphitheater. The wealth of Asia, the arms and ensigns of so many conquered nations, and the magnificent plate and wardrobe of the Syrian queen were disposed in exact symmetry or artful disorder. The ambassadors of the most remote parts of the earth, of Aethiopia, Arabia, Persia, Bactriana, India, and China, all remarkable by their rich or singular dresses, displayed the fame and power of the Roman emperor, who exposed likewise to the public view the presents that he had received, and particularly a great number of crowns of gold, the offerings of grateful cities. The victories of Aurelian were attested by the long train of captives who reluctantly attended his triumph, Goths, Vandals, Sarmatians, Alemanni, Franks, Gauls, Syrians, and Egyptians. Each people was distinguished by its peculiar inscription, and the title of Amazons was bestowed on ten martial heroines of the Gothic nation who had been taken in arms. But every eye, disregarding the crowd of captives, was fixed on the emperor Tetricus and the queen of the East. The former, as well as his son, whom he had created Augustus, was dressed in Gallic trousers, a saffron tunic, and a robe of purple. The beauteous figure of Zenobia was confined by fetters of gold; a slave supported the gold chain which encircled her neck, and she almost fainted under the intolerable weight of jewels. She preceded on foot the magnificent chariot in which she once hoped to enter the gates of Rome. It was followed by two other chariots, still more sumptuous, of Odenathus and of the Persian monarch. The triumphal car of Aurelian (it had formerly been used by a Gothic king) was drawn, on this memorable occasion, either by four stags or by four elephants. The most illustrious of the senate, the people, and the army closed the solemn procession. Unfeigned joy, wonder, and gratitude swelled the acclamations of the multitude; but the satisfaction of the senate was clouded by the appearance of Tetricus; nor could they suppress a rising murmur, that the haughty emperor should thus expose to public ignominy the person of a Roman and a magistrate.

But however in the treatment of his unfortunate rivals Aurelian might indulge his pride, he behaved towards them with a generous clemency which was seldom exercised by the ancient conquerors. Princes who, without success, had defended their throne or freedom were frequently strangled in prison as soon as the triumphal pomp ascended the Capitol. These usurpers, whom their defeat had convicted of the crime of treason, were permitted to spend their lives in affluence and honorable repose. The emperor presented Zenobia with an elegant villa at Tibur, or Tivoli, about twenty miles from the capital; the Syrian queen insensibly sunk into a Roman matron, her daughters married into noble families, and her race was not yet extinct in the fifth century. Tetricus and his son were reinstated in their rank and fortunes.†

So long and so various was the pomp of Aurelian's triumph that although it opened with the dawn of day, the slow majesty of the procession ascended not the Capitol before the ninth hour; and it was already dark when the emperor returned to the palace. The festival was protracted by theatrical representations, the games of the circus, the hunting of wild beasts, combats of gladiators, and naval engagements. Liberal donatives were distributed to the army and people, and several institutions, agreeable or beneficial to the city, contributed to perpetuate the glory of Aurelian. A considerable portion of his Oriental spoils was consecrated to the gods of Rome; the Capitol, and every other temple, glittered with the offerings of his ostentatious piety; and the temple of the Sun alone received above fifteen thousand pounds of gold. This last was a magnificent structure, erected by the emperor on the side of the Quirinal hill and dedicated, soon after the triumph, to that deity whom Aurelian adored as the parent of his life and fortunes. His mother had been an inferior priestess in a chapel of the Sun; a peculiar devotion to the god of Light was a sentiment which the fortunate peasant imbibed in his infancy; and every step of his elevation, every victory of his reign, fortified superstition by gratitude.†

Aurelian used his victory with unrelenting rigor. He was naturally of a severe disposition. A peasant and a soldier, his nerves yielded not easily to the impressions of sympathy, and he could sustain without emotion the sight of tortures and death. Trained from his earliest youth in the exercise of arms, he set too small a value on the life of a citizen, chastised by military execution the slightest offenses, and transferred the stern discipline of the camp into the civil administration of the laws. His love of justice often became a blind and furious passion, and whenever he deemed his own or the public safety endangered, he disregarded the rules of evidence and the proportion of punishments. The unprovoked rebellion with which the Romans rewarded his services exasperated his haughty spirit. The noblest families of the capital were involved in the guilt or suspicion of this dark conspiracy. A nasty spirit of revenge urged the bloody prosecution, and it proved fatal to one of the nephews of the emperor. The executioners (if we may use the expression of a contemporary poet) were fatigued, the prisons were crowded, and the unhappy senate lamented the death or absence of its most illustrious members. Nor was the pride of Aurelian less offensive to that assembly than his cruelty. Ignorant or impatient of the restraints of civil institutions, he disdained to hold his power by any other title than that of the sword, and governed by right of conquest an empire which he had saved and subdued.

It was observed by one of the most sagacious of the Roman princes that the talents of his predecessor Aurelian were better suited to the command of an army than to the government of an empire. Conscious of the character in which nature and experience had enabled him to excel, he again took the field a few months after his triumph [October A.D. 274]. It was expedient to exercise the restless temper of the legions in some foreign war, and the Persian monarch, exulting in the shame of Valerian, still braved with impunity the offended majesty of Rome. At the head of an army less formidable by its numbers than by its discipline and valor, the emperor advanced as far as the Straits which divide Europe from Asia. He there experienced that the most absolute power is a weak defense against the effects of despair. He had threatened one of his secretaries who was accused of extortion; and it was known that he seldom threatened in vain. The last hope which remained for the criminal was to involve some of the principal officers of the army in his danger, or at least in his fears. Artfully counterfeiting his master's hand, he showed them, in a long and bloody list, their own names devoted to death. Without suspecting or examining the fraud, they resolved to secure their lives by the murder of the emperor. On his march between Byzantium and Heraclea, Aurelian was suddenly attacked by the conspirators, whose stations gave them a right to surround his person, and after a short resistance fell by the hand of Mucapor, a general whom he had always loved and trusted [January A.D. 275]. He died regretted by the army, detested by the senate, but universally acknowledged as a warlike and fortunate prince, the useful though severe reformer of a degenerate state.

CHAPTER XII

REIGNS OF TACITUS, PROBUS, CARUS, AND HIS SONS

Conduct of the army and senate after the death of Aurelian. •
Reigns of Tacitus, Probus, Carus, and his sons.

Such was the unhappy condition of the Roman emperors that, whatever might be their conduct, their fate was commonly the same. A life of pleasure or virtue, of severity or mildness, of indolence or glory, alike led to an untimely grave; and almost every reign is closed by the same disgusting repetition of treason and murder. The death of Aurelian, however, is remarkable by its extraordinary consequences. The legions admired, lamented, and revenged their victorious chief. The artifice of his perfidious secretary was discovered and punished. The deluded conspirators attended the funeral of their injured sovereign with sincere or well-feigned contrition, and submitted to the unanimous resolution of the military order which was signified by the following epistle: "The brave and fortunate armies to the senate and people of Rome.—The crime of one man, and the error of many, have deprived us of the late emperor Aurelian. May it please you, venerable lords and fathers! to place him in the number of the gods, and to appoint a successor whom your judgment shall declare worthy of the Imperial purple! None of those whose guilt or misfortune have contributed to our loss shall ever reign over us." The Roman senators heard without surprise that another emperor had been assassinated in his camp; they secretly rejoiced in the fall of Aurelian; but the modest and dutiful address of the legions, when it was communicated in full assembly by the consul, diffused the most pleasing astonishment. Such honors as fear and perhaps esteem could extort, they liberally poured forth on the memory of their deceased sovereign. Such acknowledgments as gratitude could inspire, they returned to the faithful armies of the republic, who entertained so just a sense of the legal authority of the senate in the choice of an emperor [A.D. 275]. Yet, notwithstanding this flattering appeal, the most prudent of the assembly declined exposing their safety and dignity to the caprice of an armed multitude. The strength of the legions was indeed a pledge of their sincerity, since those who may command are seldom reduced to the necessity of dissembling; but could it naturally be expected that a hasty repentance would correct the inveterate habits of fourscore years? Should the soldiers relapse into their accustomed seditions, their insolence might disgrace the majesty of the senate and prove fatal to the object of its choice. Motives like these dictated a decree by which the election of a new emperor was referred to the suffrage of the military order.

The contention that ensued is one of the best attested but most improbable events in the history of mankind. The troops, as if satiated with the exercise of power, again conjured the senate to invest one of its own body with the Imperial purple. The senate still persisted in its refusal; the army in its request. The reciprocal offer was pressed and rejected at least three times, and, whilst the obstinate modesty of either party was resolved to receive a master from the hands of the other, eight months insensibly elapsed; an amazing period of tranquil anarchy during which the Roman world remained without a sovereign, without a usurper, and without a sedition. The generals and magistrates appointed by Aurelian continued to execute their ordinary functions; and it is observed that a proconsul of Asia was the only considerable person removed from his office in the whole course of the interregnum.†

On the twenty-fifth of September [A.D. 275], near eight months after the murder of Aurelian, the consul convoked an assembly of the senate and reported the doubtful and dangerous situation of the empire. He slightly insinuated that the precarious loyalty of the soldiers depended on the chance of every hour and of every accident; but he represented with the most convincing eloquence the various dangers that might attend any further delay in the choice of an emperor. Intelligence, he said, was already received that the Germans had passed the Rhine and occupied some of the strongest and most opulent cities of Gaul. The ambition of the Persian king kept the East in perpetual alarms; Egypt, Africa, and Illyricum were exposed to foreign and domestic arms; and the levity of Syria would prefer even a female scepter to the sanctity of the Roman laws. The consul, then addressing himself to Tacitus, the first of the senators, required his opinion on the important subject of a proper candidate for the vacant throne.†

The senator Tacitus was then seventy-five years of age. The long period of his innocent life was adorned with wealth and honors. He had twice been invested with the consular dignity, and enjoyed with elegance and sobriety his ample patrimony.†

He arose to speak, when from every quarter of the house he was saluted with the names of Augustus and emperor. "Tacitus Augustus, the gods preserve thee! we choose thee for our sovereign; to thy care we entrust the republic and the world. Accept the empire from the authority of the senate. It is due to thy rank, to thy conduct, to thy manners." As soon as the tumult of acclamations subsided, Tacitus attempted to decline the dangerous honor, and to express his wonder, that they should elect his age and infirmities to succeed the martial vigor of Aurelian.†

The reluctance of Tacitus (and it might possibly be sincere) was encountered by the affectionate obstinacy of the senate. Five hundred voices repeated at once, in eloquent confusion, that the greatest of the Roman princes, Numa, Trajan, Hadrian, and the Antonines, had ascended the throne in a very advanced season of life; that the mind not the body, a sovereign not a soldier, was the object of their choice; and that they expected from him no more than to guide by his wisdom the valor of the legions. . . . The emperor elect submitted to the authority of his country and received the voluntary homage of his equals. The judgment of the senate was confirmed by the consent of the Roman people and of the Praetorian guards.

The administration of Tacitus was not unworthy of his life and principles. A grateful servant of the senate, he considered that national council as the author and himself as the subject of the laws. He studied to heal the wounds which Imperial pride, civil discord, and military violence had inflicted on the constitution, and to restore at least the image of the ancient republic as it had been preserved by the policy of Augustus and the virtues of Trajan and the Antonines. It may not be useless to recapitulate some of the most important prerogatives which the senate appeared to have regained by the election of Tacitus. 1. To invest one of their body, under the title of emperor, with the general command of the armies, and the government of the frontier provinces. 2. To determine the list or, as it was then styled, the College of Consuls. They were twelve in number, who, in successive pairs, each during the space of two months, filled the year and represented the dignity of that ancient office. The authority of the senate in the nomination of the consuls was exercised with such independent freedom that no regard was paid to an irregular request of the emperor in favor of his brother Florianus. "The senate," exclaimed Tacitus, with the honest transport of a patriot, "understand the character of a prince whom they have chosen." 3. To appoint the proconsuls and presidents of the provinces, and to confer on all the magistrates their civil jurisdiction. 4. To receive appeals through the intermediate office of the praefect of the city from all the tribunals of the empire. 5. To give force and validity, by their decrees, to such as they should approve of the emperor's edicts. 6. To these several branches of authority we may add some inspection over the finances, since, even in the stern reign of Aurelian, it was in their power to divert a part of the revenue from the public service.

Circular epistles were sent without delay to all the principal cities of the empire, Treves, Milan, Aquileia, Thessalonica, Corinth, Athens, Antioch, Alexandria, and Carthage, to claim their obedience, and to inform them of the happy revolution which had restored the Roman senate to its ancient dignity.... [Their] lofty expectations were, however, soon disappointed; nor, indeed, was it possible that the armies and the provinces should long obey the luxurious and unwarlike nobles of Rome. On the slightest touch, the unsupported fabric of their pride and power fell to the ground. The expiring senate displayed a sudden luster, blazed for a moment and was extinguished forever.

All that had yet passed at Rome was no more than a theatrical representation unless it was ratified by the more substantial power of the legions [A.D. 276]. Leaving the senators to enjoy their dream of freedom and ambition, Tacitus proceeded to the Thracian camp and was there, by the Praetorian praefect, presented to the assembled troops as the prince whom they themselves had demanded and whom the senate had bestowed. As soon as the praefect was silent, the emperor addressed himself to the soldiers with eloquence and propriety. He gratified their avarice by a liberal distribution of treasure, under the names of pay and donative. He engaged their esteem by a spirited declaration that although his age might disable him from the performance of military exploits, his counsels should never be unworthy of a Roman general, the successor of the brave Aurelian.[†]

But the glory and life of Tacitus were of short duration. Transported in the depth of winter from the soft retirement of Campania to the foot of Mount Caucasus, he sunk under the unaccustomed hardships of a military life. The fatigues of the body were aggravated by the cares of the mind. For a while, the angry and selfish passions of the soldiers had been suspended by the enthusiasm of public virtue. They soon broke out with redoubled violence and raged in the camp, and even in the tent of the aged emperor. His mild and amiable character served only to inspire contempt, and he was incessantly tormented with factions which he could not assuage and by demands which it was impossible to satisfy. Whatever flattering expectations he had conceived of reconciling the public disorders, Tacitus soon was convinced that the licentiousness of the army disdained the feeble restraint of laws, and his last hour was hastened by anguish and disappointment. It may be doubtful whether the soldiers imbrued their hands in the blood of this innocent prince. It is certain that their insolence was the cause of his death. He expired at Tyana in Cappadocia, after a reign of only six months and about twenty days [April 12, A.D. 276].

The eyes of Tacitus were scarcely closed before his brother Florianus showed himself unworthy to reign by the hasty usurpation of the purple without expecting the approbation of the senate. The reverence for the Roman constitution which yet influenced the camp and the provinces was sufficiently strong to dispose them to censure, but not to provoke them to oppose, the precipitate ambition of Florianus. The discontent would have evaporated in idle murmurs had not the general of the East, the heroic Probus, boldly declared himself the avenger of the senate. The contest, however, was still unequal; nor could the most able leader, at the head of the effeminate troops of Egypt and Syria, encounter, with any hopes of victory, the legions of Europe, whose irresistible strength appeared to support the brother of Tacitus. But the fortune and activity of Probus triumphed over every obstacle. The hardy veterans of his rival, accustomed to cold climates, sickened and consumed away in the sultry heats of Cilicia, where the summer proved remarkably unwholesome. Their numbers were diminished by frequent desertion; the passes of the mountains were feebly defended; Tarsus opened its gates; and the soldiers of Florianus, when they had permitted him to enjoy the Imperial title about three months, delivered the empire from civil war by the easy sacrifice of a prince whom they despised.[†]

The peasants of Illyricum, who had already given Claudius and Aurelian to the sinking empire, had an equal right to glory in the elevation of Probus. Above twenty years before, the emperor Valerian, with his usual penetration, had discovered the rising merit of the young soldier . . . , who, in every step of his promotion, showed himself superior to the station which he filled. . . . Aurelian was indebted to him for the conquest of Egypt, and still more for the honest courage with which he often checked the cruelty of his master. Tacitus, who desired by the abilities of his generals to supply his own deficiency of military talents, named him commander-in-chief of all the Eastern provinces, with five times the usual salary, the promise of the consulship, and the hope of a triumph. When Probus ascended the Imperial throne, he was about forty-four years of age, in the full possession of his fame, of the love of the army, and of a mature vigor of mind and body.

His acknowledged merit, and the success of his arms against Florianus, left him without an enemy or a competitor. Yet if we may credit his own professions, very far from being desirous of the empire, he had accepted it with the most sincere reluctance. "But it is no longer in my power," says Probus, in a private letter, "to lay down a title so full of envy and of danger. I must continue to personate the character which the soldiers have imposed upon me. . . . To me they have offered the title of Augustus. But I submit to your clemency my pretensions and my merits." When this respectful epistle was read by the consul, the senators were unable to disguise their satisfaction, that Probus should condescend thus humbly to solicit a scepter which he already possessed [August 3, A.D. 276]. They celebrated with the warmest gratitude his virtues, his exploits, and above all his moderation. A decree immediately passed, without a dissenting voice, to ratify the election of the Eastern armies, and to confer on their chief all the several branches of the Imperial dignity: the names of Caesar and Augustus, the title of Father of his country, the right of making in the same day three motions in the senate, the office of Pontifex Maximus, the tribunician power, and the proconsular command; a mode of investiture which, though it seemed to multiply the authority of the emperor, expressed the constitution of the ancient republic. The reign of Probus corresponded with this fair beginning. The senate was permitted to direct the civil administration of the empire. Their faithful general asserted the honor of the Roman arms, and often laid at their feet crowns of gold and Barbaric trophies, the fruits of his numerous victories. Yet whilst he gratified their vanity, he must secretly have despised their indolence and weakness. Though it was every moment in their power to repeal the disgraceful edict of Gallienus, the proud successors of the Scipios patiently acquiesced in their exclusion from all military employments. They soon experienced that those who refuse the sword must renounce the scepter.

The strength of Aurelian had crushed on every side the enemies of Rome. After his death they seemed to revive with an increase of fury and of numbers. They were again vanquished by the active vigor of Probus, who, in a short reign of about six years [A.D. 276–282], equaled the fame of ancient heroes and restored peace and order to every province of the Roman world.[†]

But the most important service which Probus rendered to the republic was the deliverance of Gaul and the recovery of seventy flourishing cities oppressed by the Barbarians of Germany, who, since the death of Aurelian, had ravaged that great province with impunity [A.D. 277]. . . . The deliverance of Gaul is reported to have cost the lives of four hundred thousand of the invaders; a work of labor to the Romans, and of expense to the emperor, who gave a piece of gold for the head of every Barbarian. But as the fame of warriors is built on the destruction of humankind, we may naturally suspect that the sanguinary account was multiplied by the avarice of the soldiers and accepted without any very severe examination by the liberal vanity of Probus.[†]

Among the useful conditions of peace imposed by Probus on the vanquished nations of Germany was the obligation of supplying the Roman army with sixteen thousand recruits, the bravest and most robust of their youth. The emperor dispersed them through all the provinces and distributed this dangerous reinforcement, in small bands of fifty or sixty each, among the national troops; judiciously observing that the aid which the republic derived from the Barbarians should be felt but not seen. Their aid was now become necessary. The feeble elegance of Italy and the internal provinces could no longer support the weight of arms. The hardy frontiers of the Rhine and Danube still produced minds and bodies equal to the labors of the camp; but a perpetual series of wars had gradually diminished their numbers. The infrequency of marriage and the ruin of agriculture affected the principles of population, and not only destroyed the strength of the present but intercepted the hope of future generations. The wisdom of Probus embraced a great and beneficial plan of replenishing the exhausted frontiers by new colonies of captive or fugitive Barbarians, on whom he bestowed lands, cattle, instruments of husbandry, and every encouragement that might engage them to educate a race of soldiers for the service of the republic.... But the expectations of Probus were too often disappointed. The impatience and idleness of the Barbarians could ill brook the slow labors of agriculture. Their unconquerable love of freedom, rising against despotism, provoked them into hasty rebellions, alike fatal to themselves and to the provinces; nor could these artificial supplies, however repeated by succeeding emperors, restore the important limit of Gaul and Illyricum to its ancient and native vigor.[†]

The arms of Probus had now suppressed all the foreign and domestic enemies of the state [A.D. 281]. His mild but steady administration confirmed the reestablishment of the public tranquility; nor was there left in the provinces a hostile Barbarian, a tyrant, or even a robber to revive the memory of past disorders. It was time that the emperor should revisit Rome, and celebrate his own glory and the general happiness. The triumph due to the valor of Probus was conducted with a magnificence suitable to his fortune, and the people who had so lately admired the trophies of Aurelian gazed with equal pleasure on those of his heroic successor. We cannot on this occasion forget the desperate courage of about fourscore gladiators, reserved, with near six hundred others, for the inhuman sports of the amphitheater. Disdaining to shed their blood for the amusement of the populace, they killed their keepers, broke from the place of their confinement, and filled the streets of Rome with blood and confusion. After an obstinate resistance, they were overpowered and cut in pieces by the regular forces; but they obtained at least an honorable death and the satisfaction of a just revenge.

The military discipline which reigned in the camps of Probus was less cruel than that of Aurelian, but it was equally rigid and exact. The latter had punished the irregularities of the soldiers with unrelenting severity, the former prevented them by employing the legions in constant and useful labors. When Probus commanded in Egypt, he executed many considerable works for the splendor and benefit of that rich country. The navigation of the Nile, so important to Rome itself, was improved; and temples, buildings, porticos, and palaces were constructed by the hands of the soldiers, who acted by turns as architects, as engineers, and as husbandmen. . . . [I]n order to preserve his troops from the dangerous temptations of idleness, . . . Probus exercised his legions in covering with rich vineyards the hills of Gaul and Pannonia. . . . An army thus employed constituted perhaps the most useful as well as the bravest portion of Roman subjects.

But in the prosecution of a favorite scheme, the best of men, satisfied with the rectitude of their intentions, are subject to forget the bounds of moderation; nor did Probus himself sufficiently consult the patience and disposition of his fierce legionaries. The dangers of the military profession seem only to be compensated by a life of pleasure and idleness; but if the duties of the soldier are incessantly aggravated by the labors of the peasant, he will at last sink under the intolerable burden or shake it off with indignation. The imprudence of Probus is said to have inflamed the discontent of his troops. More attentive to the interests of mankind than to those of the army, he expressed the vain hope that, by the establishment of universal peace, he should soon abolish the necessity of a standing and mercenary force. The unguarded expression proved fatal to him. In one of the hottest days of summer, as he severely urged the unwholesome labor of draining the marshes of Sirmium, the soldiers, impatient of fatigue, on a sudden threw down their tools, grasped their arms, and broke out into a furious mutiny. The emperor, conscious of his danger, took refuge in a lofty tower constructed for the purpose of surveying the progress of the work. The tower was instantly forced, and a thousand swords were plunged at once into the bosom of the unfortunate Probus [August A.D. 282]. The rage of the troops subsided as soon as it had been gratified. They then lamented their fatal rashness, forgot the severity of the emperor whom they had massacred, and hastened to perpetuate, by an honorable monument, the memory of his virtues and victories.

When the legions had indulged their grief and repentance for the death of Probus, their unanimous consent declared Carus, his Praetorian praefect, the most deserving of the Imperial throne. Every circumstance that relates to this prince appears of a mixed and doubtful nature. He gloried in the title of Roman Citizen; and affected to compare the purity of *his* blood with the foreign and even barbarous origin of the preceding emperors; yet the most inquisitive of his contemporaries, very far from admitting his claim, have variously deduced his own birth, or that of his parents, from Illyricum, from Gaul, or from Africa. Though a soldier, he had received a learned education; though a senator, he was invested with the first dignity of the army; and in an age when the civil and military professions began to be irrecoverably separated from each other, they were united in the person of Carus. Notwithstanding the severe justice which he exercised against the assassins of Probus, to whose favor and esteem he was highly indebted, he could not escape the suspicion of being accessory to a deed from whence he derived the principal advantage. He enjoyed, at least before his elevation, an acknowledged character of virtue and abilities; but his austere temper insensibly degenerated into moroseness and cruelty; and the imperfect writers of his life almost hesitate whether they shall not rank him in the number of Roman tyrants. When Carus assumed the purple, he was about sixty years of age, and his two sons, Carinus and Numerian, had already attained the season of manhood.

The authority of the senate expired with Probus; nor was the repentance of the soldiers displayed by the same dutiful regard for the civil power which they had testified after the unfortunate death of Aurelian. The election of Carus was decided without expecting the approbation of the senate, and the new emperor contented himself with announcing, in a cold and stately epistle, that he had ascended the vacant throne. A behavior so very opposite to that of his amiable predecessor afforded no favorable presage of the new reign: and the Romans, deprived of power and freedom, asserted their privilege of licentious murmurs. The voice of congratulation and flattery was not, however, silent; and we may still peruse, with pleasure and contempt, an eclogue which was composed on the accession of the emperor Carus. Two shepherds, avoiding the noontide heat, retire into the cave of Faunus. On a spreading beech they discover some recent characters. The rural deity had described, in prophetic verses, the felicity promised to the empire under the reign of so great a prince. Faunus hails the approach of that hero, who, receiving on his shoulders the sinking weight of the Roman world, shall extinguish war and faction, and once again restore the innocence and security of the golden age.

It is more than probable that these elegant trifles never reached the ears of a veteran general, who, with the consent of the legions, was preparing to execute the long-suspended design of the Persian war. Before his departure for this distant expedition, Carus conferred on his two sons, Carinus and Numerian, the title of Caesar, and investing the former with almost an equal share of the Imperial power directed the young prince first to suppress some troubles which had arisen in Gaul, and afterwards to fix the seat of his residence at Rome, and to assume the government of the Western provinces. The safety of Illyricum was confirmed by a memorable defeat of the Sarmatians; sixteen thousand of those Barbarians remained on the field of battle, and the number of captives amounted to twenty thousand. The old emperor, animated with the fame and prospect of victory, pursued his march in the midst of winter through the countries of Thrace and Asia Minor, and at length, with his younger son, Numerian, arrived on the confines of the Persian monarchy. There, encamping on the summit of a lofty mountain, he pointed out to his troops the opulence and luxury of the enemy whom they were about to invade.

The successor of Artaxerxes, Varanes, or Bahram, though he had subdued the Segestans, one of the most warlike nations of Upper Asia, was alarmed at the approach of the Romans, and endeavored to retard their progress by a negotiation of peace [A.D. 283]. His ambassadors entered the camp about sunset, at the time when the troops were satisfying their hunger with a frugal repast. The Persians expressed their desire of being introduced to the presence of the Roman emperor. They were at length conducted to a soldier who was seated on the grass. A piece of stale bacon and a few hard peas composed his supper. A coarse woollen garment of purple was the only circumstance that announced his dignity. The conference was conducted with the same disregard of courtly elegance. Carus, taking off a cap which he wore to conceal his baldness, assured the ambassadors that, unless their master acknowledged the superiority of Rome, he would speedily render Persia as naked of trees as his own head was destitute of hair. Notwithstanding some traces of art and preparation, we may discover in this scene the manners of Carus, and the severe simplicity which the martial princes who succeeded Gallienus had already restored in the Roman camps. The ministers of the Great King trembled and retired.

The threats of Carus were not without effect. He ravaged Mesopotamia, cut in pieces whatever opposed his passage, made himself master of the great cities of Seleucia and Ctesiphon (which seemed to have surrendered without resistance), and carried his victorious arms beyond the Tigris. He had seized the favorable moment for an invasion. The Persian councils were distracted by domestic factions, and the greater part of their forces were detained on the frontiers of India. Rome and the East received with transports the news of such important advantages. Flattery and hope painted, in the most lively colors, the fall of Persia, the conquest of Arabia, the submission of Egypt, and a lasting deliverance from the inroads of the Scythian nations. But the reign of Carus was destined to expose the vanity of predictions. They were scarcely uttered before they were contradicted by his death; an event attended with such ambiguous circumstances that it may be related in a letter from his own secretary to the praefect of the city [December 25, A.D. 283]. "Carus," says he, "our dearest emperor, was confined by sickness to his bed, when a furious tempest arose in the camp. The darkness which overspread the sky was so thick that we could no longer distinguish each other; and the incessant flashes of lightning took from us the knowledge of all that passed in the general confusion. Immediately after the most violent clap of thunder, we heard a sudden cry that the emperor was dead; and it soon appeared that his chamberlains, in a rage of grief, had set fire to the royal pavilion; a circumstance which gave rise to the report that Carus was killed by lightning. But, as far as we have been able to investigate the truth, his death was the natural effect of his disorder."

The vacancy of the throne was not productive of any disturbance. The ambition of the aspiring generals was checked by their natural fears, and young Numerian, with his absent brother Carinus, were unanimously acknowledged as Roman emperors. The public expected that the successor of Carus would pursue his father's footsteps and, without allowing the Persians to recover from their consternation, would advance sword in hand to the palaces of Susa and Ecbatana. But the legions, however strong in numbers and discipline, were dismayed by the most abject superstition. Notwithstanding all the arts that were practiced to disguise the manner of the late emperor's death, it was found impossible to remove the opinion of the multitude, and the power of opinion is irresistible. Places or persons struck with lightning were considered by the ancients with pious horror as singularly devoted to the wrath of Heaven. An oracle was remembered which marked the River Tigris as the fatal boundary of the Roman arms. The troops, terrified with the fate of Carus and with their own danger, called aloud on young Numerian to obey the will of the gods and to lead them away from this inauspicious scene of war. The feeble emperor was unable to subdue their obstinate prejudice, and the Persians wondered at the unexpected retreat of a victorious enemy.

The intelligence of the mysterious fate of the late emperor was soon carried from the frontiers of Persia to Rome; and the senate as well as the provinces congratulated the accession of the sons of Carus [A.D. 284]. These fortunate youths were strangers, however, to that conscious superiority, either of birth or of merit, which can alone render the possession of a throne easy, and as it were natural. Born and educated in a private station, the election of their father raised them at once to the rank of princes; and his death, which happened about sixteen months afterwards, left them the unexpected legacy of a vast empire. To sustain with temper this rapid elevation, an uncommon share of virtue and prudence was requisite; and Carinus, the elder of the brothers, was more than commonly deficient in those qualities. In the Gallic war he discovered some degree of personal courage; but from the moment of his arrival at Rome, he abandoned himself to the luxury of the capital and to the abuse of his fortune. He was soft, yet cruel; devoted to pleasure, but destitute of taste; and though exquisitely susceptible of vanity, indifferent to the public esteem. In the course of a few months, he successively married and divorced nine wives, most of whom he left pregnant; and, notwithstanding this legal inconstancy, found time to indulge such a variety of irregular appetites as brought dishonor on himself and on the noblest houses of Rome. He beheld with inveterate hatred all those who might remember his former obscurity or censure his present conduct. He banished or put to death the friends and counselors whom his father had placed about him to guide his inexperienced youth; and he persecuted with the meanest revenge his school-fellows and companions who had not sufficiently respected the latent majesty of the emperor. With the senators, Carinus affected a lofty and regal demeanor, frequently declaring that he designed to distribute their estates among the populace of Rome. From the dregs of that populace he selected his favorites, and even his ministers. The palace, and even the Imperial table, were filled with singers, dancers, prostitutes, and all the various retinue of vice and folly. One of his doorkeepers he entrusted with the government of the city. In the room of the Praetorian praefect, whom he put to death, Carinus substituted one of the ministers of his looser pleasures. Another, who possessed the same or even a more infamous title to favor, was invested with the consulship. A confidential secretary who had acquired uncommon skill in the art of forgery delivered the indolent emperor, with his own consent, from the irksome duty of signing his name.[†]

The only merit of the administration of Carinus that history could record, or poetry celebrate, was the uncommon splendor with which, in his own and his brother's name, he exhibited the Roman games of the theater, the circus, and the amphitheater.[†]

In the midst of this glittering pageantry, the emperor Carinus, secure of his fortune, enjoyed the acclamations of the people, the flattery of his courtiers, and the songs of the poets, who, for want of a more essential merit, were reduced to celebrate the divine graces of his person. In the same hour, but at the distance of nine hundred miles from Rome, his brother expired; and a sudden revolution transferred into the hands of a stranger the scepter of the house of Carus [September 12, A.D. 284].

The sons of Carus never saw each other after their father's death. The arrangements which their new situation required were probably deferred till the return of the younger brother to Rome, where a triumph was decreed to the young emperors for the glorious success of the Persian war. It is uncertain whether they intended to divide between them the administration or the provinces of the empire; but it is very unlikely that their union would have proved of any long duration. The jealousy of power must have been inflamed by the opposition of characters. In the most corrupt of times, Carinus was unworthy to live: Numerian deserved to reign in a happier period. . . . But the talents of Numerian were rather of the contemplative than of the active kind. When his father's elevation reluctantly forced him from the shade of retirement, neither his temper nor his pursuits had qualified him for the command of armies. His constitution was destroyed by the hardships of the Persian war; and he had contracted from the heat of the climate such a weakness in his eyes as obliged him, in the course of a long retreat, to confine himself to the solitude and darkness of a tent or litter. The administration of all affairs, civil as well as military, was devolved on Arrius Aper, the Praetorian praefect, who to the power of his important office added the honor of being father-in-law to Numerian. The Imperial pavilion was strictly guarded by his most trusty adherents; and during many days, Aper delivered to the army the supposed mandates of their invisible sovereign.

It was not till eight months after the death of Carus that the Roman army, returning by slow marches from the banks of the Tigris, arrived on those of the Thracian Bosphorus. . . . But a report soon circulated through the camp, at first in secret whispers and at length in loud clamors, of the emperor's death and of the presumption of his ambitious minister, who still exercised the sovereign power in the name of a prince who was no more. The impatience of the soldiers could not long support a state of suspense. With rude curiosity they broke into the Imperial tent and discovered only the corpse of Numerian. The gradual decline of his health might have induced them to believe that his death was natural; but the concealment was interpreted as an evidence of guilt, and the measures which Aper had taken to secure his election became the immediate occasion of his ruin. Yet, even in the transport of their rage and grief, the troops observed a regular proceeding, which proves how firmly discipline had been reestablished by the martial successors of Gallienus. A general assembly of the army was appointed to be held at Chalcedon, whither Aper was transported in chains as a prisoner and a criminal. A vacant tribunal was erected in the midst of the camp, and the generals and tribunes formed a great military council. They soon announced to the multitude that their choice had fallen on Diocletian, commander of the domestics or bodyguards, as the person the most capable of revenging and succeeding their beloved emperor [A.D. 284]. The future fortunes of the candidate depended on the chance or conduct of the present hour. Conscious that the station which he had filled exposed him to some suspicions, Diocletian ascended the tribunal and, raising his eyes towards the Sun, made a solemn profession of his own innocence in the presence of that all-seeing Deity. Then, assuming the tone of a sovereign and a judge, he commanded that Aper should be brought in chains to the foot of the tribunal. "This man," said he, "is the murderer of Numerian"; and without giving him time to enter on a dangerous justification, drew his sword and buried it in the breast of the unfortunate praefect. A charge supported by such decisive proof was admitted without contradiction, and the legions, with repeated acclamations, acknowledged the justice and authority of the emperor Diocletian.

Before we enter upon the memorable reign of that prince, it will be proper to punish and dismiss the unworthy brother of Numerian. Carinus possessed arms and treasures sufficient to support his legal title to the empire. But his personal vices overbalanced every advantage of birth and situation. The most faithful servants of the father despised the incapacity and dreaded the cruel arrogance of the son. The hearts of the people were engaged in favor of his rival, and even the senate was inclined to prefer a usurper to a tyrant. The arts of Diocletian inflamed the general discontent; and the winter was employed in secret intrigues and open preparations for a civil war. In the spring, the forces of the East and of the West encountered each other in the plains of Margus, a small city of Moesia, in the neighborhood of the Danube [A.D. 285]. The troops, so lately returned from the Persian war, had acquired their glory at the expense of health and numbers; nor were they in a condition to contend with the unexhausted strength of the legions of Europe. Their ranks were broken, and for a moment Diocletian despaired of the purple and of life. But the advantage which Carinus had obtained by the valor of his soldiers, he quickly lost by the infidelity of his officers. A tribune whose wife he had seduced seized the opportunity of revenge, and by a single blow extinguished civil discord in the blood of the adulterer.

CHAPTER XIII

REIGN OF DIOCLETIAN AND
HIS THREE ASSOCIATES

*The reign of Diocletian and his three associates, Maximian,
Galerius, and Constantius. • General reestablishment of order and
tranquility. • The Persian war, victory, and triumph. •
The new form of administration. • Abdication and retirement of
Diocletian and Maximian.*

As the reign of Diocletian was more illustrious than that of any of his
predecessors [A.D. 284–305], so was his birth more abject and obscure.
The strong claims of merit and of violence had frequently superseded
the ideal prerogatives of nobility; but a distinct line of separation was
hitherto preserved between the free and the servile part of mankind.
The parents of Diocletian had been slaves in the house of Anulinus, a
Roman senator; nor was he himself distinguished by any other name
than that which he derived from a small town in Dalmatia from whence
his mother deduced her origin. It is, however, probable that his father
obtained the freedom of the family, and that he soon acquired an office of scribe, which was commonly exercised by persons of his condition. Favorable oracles, or rather the consciousness of superior merit,
prompted his aspiring son to pursue the profession of arms and the
hopes of fortune; and it would be extremely curious to observe the
gradation of arts and accidents which enabled him in the end to fulfill
those oracles and to display that merit to the world. Diocletian was
successively promoted to the government of Moesia, the honors of the
consulship, and the important command of the guards of the palace.
He distinguished his abilities in the Persian war; and after the death of
Numerian, the slave, by the confession and judgment of his rivals, was
declared the most worthy of the Imperial throne. The malice of religious zeal, whilst it arraigns the savage fierceness of his colleague
Maximian, has affected to cast suspicions on the personal courage of
the emperor Diocletian. It would not be easy to persuade us of the
cowardice of a soldier of fortune who acquired and preserved the es-

teem of the legions as well as the favor of so many warlike princes. Yet even calumny is sagacious enough to discover and to attack the most vulnerable part. The valor of Diocletian was never found inadequate to his duty, or to the occasion; but he appears not to have possessed the daring and generous spirit of a hero who courts danger and fame, disdains artifice, and boldly challenges the allegiance of his equals. His abilities were useful rather than splendid: a vigorous mind, improved by the experience and study of mankind; dexterity and application in business; a judicious mixture of liberality and economy, of mildness and rigor; profound dissimulation under the disguise of military frankness; steadiness to pursue his ends; flexibility to vary his means; and above all, the great art of submitting his own passions, as well as those of others, to the interest of his ambition, and of coloring his ambition with the most specious pretenses of justice and public utility. Like Augustus, Diocletian may be considered as the founder of a new empire. Like the adopted son of Caesar, he was distinguished as a statesman rather than as a warrior; nor did either of those princes employ force whenever their purpose could be effected by policy.

The victory of Diocletian [over Carinus] was remarkable for its singular mildness [A.D. 285]. A people accustomed to applaud the clemency of the conqueror if the usual punishments of death, exile, and confiscation were inflicted with any degree of temper and equity, beheld, with the most pleasing astonishment, a civil war the flames of which were extinguished in the field of battle. . . . Such a conduct, however, displayed to the Roman world the fairest prospect of the new reign, and the emperor affected to confirm this favorable prepossession by declaring that, among all the virtues of his predecessors, he was the most ambitious of imitating the humane philosophy of Marcus Antoninus.

The first considerable action of his reign seemed to evince his sincerity as well as his moderation. After the example of Marcus, he gave himself a colleague in the person of Maximian, on whom he bestowed at first the title of Caesar [A.D. 285], and afterwards that of Augustus [A.D. 286]. But the motives of his conduct, as well as the object of his choice, were of a very different nature from those of his admired predecessor. By investing a luxurious youth with the honors of the purple, Marcus had discharged a debt of private gratitude, at the expense, indeed, of the happiness of the state. By associating a friend and a fellow-soldier to the labors of government, Diocletian, in a time of public danger, provided for the defense both of the East and of the West. Maximian was born a peasant and, like Aurelian, in the territory of Sirmium. Ignorant of letters, careless of laws, the rusticity of his appearance and manners still betrayed in the most elevated fortune the meanness of his extraction. War was the only art which he professed. In a long course of service, he had distinguished himself on every frontier of the empire; and though his military talents were formed to obey rather than to command, though, perhaps, he never attained the skill of a consummate general, he was capable, by his valor, constancy, and experience, of executing the most arduous undertakings. Nor were the vices of Maximian less useful to his benefactor. Insensible to pity and fearless of consequences, he was the ready instrument of every act of cruelty which the policy of that artful prince might at once suggest and disclaim. As soon as a bloody sacrifice had been offered to prudence or to revenge, Diocletian, by his seasonable intercession, saved the remaining few whom he had never designed to punish, gently censured the severity of his stern colleague, and enjoyed the comparison of a golden and an iron age, which was universally applied to their opposite maxims of government. Notwithstanding the difference of their characters, the two emperors maintained on the throne that friendship which they had contracted in a private station. The haughty, turbulent spirit of Maximian, so fatal afterwards to himself and to the public peace, was accustomed to respect the genius of Diocletian, and confessed the ascendant of reason over brutal violence. From a motive either of pride or superstition, the two emperors assumed the titles, the one of Jovius, the other of Herculius. Whilst the motion of the world (such was the language of their venal orators) was maintained by the all-seeing wisdom of Jupiter, the invincible arm of Hercules purged the earth from monsters and tyrants.

But even the omnipotence of Jovius and Herculius was insufficient to sustain the weight of the public administration. The prudence of Diocletian discovered that the empire, assailed on every side by the Barbarians, required on every side the presence of a great army, and of an emperor. With this view, he resolved once more to divide his unwieldy power, and with the inferior title of *Caesars* to confer on two generals of approved merit an unequal share of the sovereign authority. Galerius, surnamed Armentarius, from his original profession of a herdsman, and Constantius, who from his pale complexion had acquired the denomination of Chlorus, were the two persons invested with the second honors of the Imperial purple [A.D. 293]. In describing the country, extraction, and manners of Herculius, we have already delineated those of Galerius, who was often, and not improperly, styled the younger Maximian, though in many instances, both of virtue and ability, he appears to have possessed a manifest superiority over the elder. The birth of Constantius was less obscure than that of his colleagues. Eutropius, his father, was one of the most considerable nobles of Dardania, and his mother was the niece of the emperor Claudius. Although the youth of Constantius had been spent in arms, he was endowed with a mild and amiable disposition, and the popular voice had long since acknowledged him worthy of the rank which he at last attained. To strengthen the bonds of political, by those of domestic, union, each of the emperors assumed the character of a father to one of the Caesars, Diocletian to Galerius and Maximian to Constantius; and each, obliging them to repudiate their former wives, bestowed his daughter in marriage on his adopted son. These four princes distributed among themselves the wide extent of the Roman empire. The defense of Gaul, Spain, and Britain was entrusted to Constantius: Galerius was stationed on the banks of the Danube as the safeguard of the Illyrian provinces. Italy and Africa were considered as the department of Maximian; and for his peculiar portion, Diocletian reserved Thrace, Egypt, and the rich countries of Asia. Every one was sovereign with his own jurisdiction; but their united authority extended over the whole monarchy, and each of them was prepared to assist his colleagues with his counsels or presence. The Caesars, in their exalted rank, revered the majesty of the emperors, and the three younger princes invariably acknowledged, by their gratitude and obedience, the common parent of their fortunes. The suspicious jealousy of power found not any place among them; and the singular happiness of their union has been compared to a chorus of music whose harmony was regulated and maintained by the skillful hand of the first artist.

This important measure was not carried into execution till about six years after the association of Maximian, and that interval of time had not been destitute of memorable incidents. But we have preferred, for the sake of perspicuity, first to describe the more perfect form of Diocletian's government, and afterwards to relate the actions of his reign, following rather the natural order of the events than the dates of a very doubtful chronology.

The first exploit of Maximian, though it is mentioned in a few words by our imperfect writers, deserves, from its singularity, to be recorded in a history of human manners. He suppressed the peasants of Gaul, who, under the appellation of Bagaudae, had risen in a general insurrection [A.D. 287]; very similar to those which in the fourteenth century successively afflicted both France and England. It should seem that very many of those institutions referred by an easy solution to the feudal system are derived from the Celtic Barbarians. When Caesar subdued the Gauls, that great nation was already divided into three orders of men; the clergy, the nobility, and the common people. The first governed by superstition, the second by arms, but the third and last was not of any weight or account in their public councils. It was very natural for the plebeians, oppressed by debt or apprehensive of injuries, to implore the protection of some powerful chief, who acquired over their persons and property the same absolute right as, among the Greeks and Romans, a master exercised over his slaves. The greatest part of the nation was gradually reduced into a state of servitude, compelled to perpetual labor on the estates of the Gallic nobles, and confined to the soil, either by the real weight of fetters or by the no less cruel and forcible restraints of the laws. During the long series of troubles which agitated Gaul from the reign of Gallienus to that of Diocletian, the condition of these servile peasants was peculiarly miserable; and they experienced at once the complicated tyranny of their masters, of the Barbarians, of the soldiers, and of the officers of the revenue.

Their patience was at last provoked into despair. On every side they rose in multitudes, armed with rustic weapons and with irresistible fury. The ploughman became a foot soldier, the shepherd mounted on horseback, the deserted villages and open towns were abandoned to the flames, and the ravages of the peasants equaled those of the fiercest Barbarians. They asserted the natural rights of men, but they asserted those rights with the most savage cruelty. The Gallic nobles, justly dreading their revenge, either took refuge in the fortified cities or fled from the wild scene of anarchy. The peasants reigned without control; and two of their most daring leaders had the folly and rashness to assume the Imperial ornaments. Their power soon expired at the approach of the legions. The strength of union and discipline obtained an easy victory over a licentious and divided multitude. A severe retaliation was inflicted on the peasants who were found in arms; the affrighted remnant returned to their respective habitations, and their unsuccessful effort for freedom served only to confirm their slavery.[†]

Maximian had no sooner recovered Gaul from the hands of the peasants than he lost Britain by the usurpation of Carausius.

[*Constantius subsequently recovers Britain (A.D. 296).*]

Notwithstanding the policy of Diocletian, it was impossible to maintain an equal and undisturbed tranquility during a reign of twenty years and along a frontier of many hundred miles. Sometimes the Barbarians suspended their domestic animosities, and the relaxed vigilance of the garrisons sometimes gave a passage to their strength or dexterity. Whenever the provinces were invaded, Diocletian conducted himself with that calm dignity which he always affected or possessed; reserved his presence for such occasions as were worthy of his interposition, never exposed his person or reputation to any unnecessary danger, insured his success by every means that prudence could suggest, and displayed with ostentation the consequences of his victory. In wars of a more difficult nature and more doubtful event, he employed the rough valor of Maximian; and that faithful soldier was content to ascribe his own victories to the wise counsels and auspicious influence of his benefactor. But after the adoption of the two Caesars, the emperors themselves, retiring to a less laborious scene of action, devolved on their adopted sons the defense of the Danube and of the Rhine. The vigilant Galerius was never reduced to the necessity of vanquishing an army of Barbarians on the Roman territory. The brave and active Constantius delivered Gaul from a very furious inroad of the Alemanni.[†]

The conduct which the emperor Probus had adopted in the disposal of the vanquished was imitated by Diocletian and his associates. The captive Barbarians, exchanging death for slavery, were distributed among the provincials and assigned to those districts (in Gaul, the territories of Amiens, Beauvais, Cambray, Treves, Langres, and Troyes are particularly specified) which had been depopulated by the calamities of war. They were usefully employed as shepherds and husband-men but were denied the exercise of arms, except when it was found expedient to enroll them in the military service. Nor did the emperors refuse the property of lands, with a less servile tenure, to such of the Barbarians as solicited the protection of Rome. They granted a settle-ment to several colonies of the Carpi, the Bastarnae, and the Sarma-tians; and, by a dangerous indulgence, permitted them in some measure to retain their national manners and independence. Among the pro-vincials, it was a subject of flattering exultation that the Barbarian, so lately an object of terror, now cultivated their lands, drove their cattle to the neighboring fair, and contributed by his labor to the public plenty. They congratulated their masters on the powerful accession of subjects and soldiers; but they forgot to observe that multitudes of se-cret enemies, insolent from favor or desperate from oppression, were introduced into the heart of the empire.

While the Caesars exercised their valor on the banks of the Rhine and Danube, the presence of the emperors was required on the south-ern confines of the Roman world. From the Nile to Mount Atlas, Africa was in arms.[†]

[*Diocletian restores Roman rule in Africa and Egypt (A.D. 296–297).*]

The reduction of Egypt was immediately followed by the Persian war. It was reserved for the reign of Diocletian to vanquish that powerful nation, and to extort a confession from the successors of Artaxerxes of the superior majesty of the Roman empire.[†]

[A] solemn peace was concluded and ratified between the two na-tions [A.D. 297]. The conditions of a treaty so glorious to the empire, and so necessary to Persia, may deserve a more peculiar attention, as the history of Rome presents very few transactions of a similar nature; most of her wars having either been terminated by absolute conquest or waged against Barbarians ignorant of the use of letters. I. The Abo-ras, or, as it is called by Xenophon, the Araxes, was fixed as the boundary between the two monarchies. . . . Mesopotamia, the object of so many wars, was ceded to the empire; and the Persians, by this treaty, re-nounced all pretensions to that great province. II. They relinquished to the Romans five provinces beyond the Tigris. Their situation formed a very useful barrier, and their natural strength was soon improved by art and military skill. . . . III. . . . Tiridates, the faithful ally of Rome, was restored to the throne of [Armenia], and . . . the rights of the Imperial supremacy were fully asserted and secured. The limits of Armenia were extended. . . . IV. . . . The nomination of the kings of Iberia, which was resigned by the Persian monarch to the emperors, contributed to the strength and security of the Roman power in Asia. The East enjoyed a profound tranquility during forty years; and the treaty between the rival monarchies was strictly observed till the death of Tiridates; when a new generation, animated with different views and different passions, succeeded to the government of the world; and the grandson of Narses undertook a long and memorable war against the princes of the house of Constantine.

The arduous work of rescuing the distressed empire from tyrants and Barbarians had now been completely achieved by a succession of Illyrian peasants. As soon as Diocletian entered into the twentieth year of his reign [A.D. 303], he celebrated that memorable era, as well as the success of his arms, by the pomp of a Roman triumph. Maximian, the equal partner of his power, was his only companion in the glory of that day. The two Caesars had fought and conquered, but the merit of their exploits was ascribed, according to the rigor of ancient maxims, to the auspicious influence of their fathers and emperors. The triumph of Diocletian and Maximian was less magnificent, perhaps, than those of Aurelian and Probus, but it was dignified by several circumstances of superior fame and good fortune. Africa and Britain, the Rhine, the Danube, and the Nile furnished their respective trophies; but the most distinguished ornament was of a more singular nature, a Persian victory followed by an important conquest. The representations of rivers, mountains, and provinces were carried before the Imperial car. The images of the captive wives, the sisters, and the children of the Great King afforded a new and grateful spectacle to the vanity of the people. In the eyes of posterity, this triumph is remarkable by a distinction of a less honorable kind. It was the last that Rome ever beheld. Soon after this period, the emperors ceased to vanquish, and Rome ceased to be the capital of the empire.

The spot on which Rome was founded had been consecrated by ancient ceremonies and imaginary miracles. The presence of some god or the memory of some hero seemed to animate every part of the city, and the empire of the world had been promised to the Capitol. The native Romans felt and confessed the power of this agreeable illusion. It was derived from their ancestors, had grown up with their earliest habits of life, and was protected, in some measure, by the opinion of political utility. The form and the seat of government were intimately blended together, nor was it esteemed possible to transport the one without destroying the other. But the sovereignty of the capital was gradually annihilated in the extent of conquest; the provinces rose to the same level, and the vanquished nations acquired the name and privileges without imbibing the partial affections of Romans. During a long period, however, the remains of the ancient constitution and the influence of custom preserved the dignity of Rome. The emperors, though perhaps of African or Illyrian extraction, respected their adopted country as the seat of their power and the center of their extensive dominions. The emergencies of war very frequently required their presence on the frontiers; but Diocletian and Maximian were the first Roman princes who fixed, in time of peace, their ordinary residence in the provinces; and their conduct, however it might be suggested by private motives, was justified by very specious considerations of policy. The court of the emperor of the West was, for the most part, established at Milan, whose situation, at the foot of the Alps, appeared far more convenient than that of Rome for the important purpose of watching the motions of the Barbarians of Germany. Milan soon assumed the splendor of an Imperial city. The houses are described as numerous and well built; the manners of the people as polished and liberal. A circus, a theater, a mint, a palace, baths, which bore the name of their founder Maximian; porticos adorned with statues and a double circumference of walls contributed to the beauty of the new capital; nor did it seem oppressed even by the proximity of Rome. To rival the majesty of Rome was the ambition likewise of Diocletian, who employed his leisure, and the wealth of the East, in the embellishment of Nicomedia, a city placed on the verge of Europe and Asia, almost at an equal distance between the Danube and the Euphrates. By the taste of the monarch and at the expense of the people, Nicomedia acquired, in the space of a few years, a degree of magnificence which might appear to have required the labor of ages, and became inferior only to Rome, Alexandria, and Antioch in extent of populousness. The life of Diocletian and Maximian was a life of action, and a considerable portion of it was spent in camps or in the long and frequent marches; but whenever the public business allowed them any relaxation, they seemed to have retired with pleasure to their favorite residences of Nicomedia and Milan. Till Diocletian, in the twentieth year of his reign, celebrated his Roman triumph, it is extremely doubtful whether he ever visited the ancient capital of the empire. Even on that memorable occasion his stay did not exceed two months. Disgusted with the licentious familiarity of the people, he quitted Rome with precipitation thirteen days before it was expected that he should have appeared in the senate, invested with the ensigns of the consular dignity.

The dislike expressed by Diocletian towards Rome and Roman freedom was not the effect of momentary caprice, but the result of the most artful policy. That crafty prince had framed a new system of Imperial government, which was afterwards completed by the family of Constantine; and as the image of the old constitution was religiously preserved in the senate, he resolved to deprive that order of its small remains of power and consideration. We may recollect, about eight years before the elevation of Diocletian, the transient greatness and the ambitious hopes of the Roman senate. As long as that enthusiasm prevailed, many of the nobles imprudently displayed their zeal in the cause of freedom; and after the successes of Probus had withdrawn their countenance from the republican party, the senators were unable to disguise their impotent resentment. As the sovereign of Italy, Maximian was entrusted with the care of extinguishing this troublesome rather than dangerous spirit, and the task was perfectly suited to his cruel temper. The most illustrious members of the senate, whom Diocletian always affected to esteem, were involved by his colleague in the accusation of imaginary plots; and the possession of an elegant villa or a well-cultivated estate was interpreted as a convincing evidence of guilt. The camp of the Praetorians, which had so long oppressed, began to protect, the majesty of Rome; and as those haughty troops were conscious of the decline of their power, they were naturally disposed to unite their strength with the authority of the senate. By the prudent measures of Diocletian, the numbers of the Praetorians were insensibly reduced, their privileges abolished, and their place supplied by two faithful legions of Illyricum, who, under the new titles of Jovians and Herculians, were appointed to perform the service of the Imperial guards. But the most fatal though secret wound, which the senate received from the hands of Diocletian and Maximian, was inflicted by the inevitable operation of their absence. As long as the emperors resided at Rome, that assembly might be oppressed, but it could scarcely be neglected. The successors of Augustus exercised the power of dictating whatever laws their wisdom or caprice might suggest; but those laws were ratified by the sanction of the senate. The model of ancient freedom was preserved in its deliberations and decrees; and wise princes who respected the prejudices of the Roman people were in some measure obliged to assume the language and behavior suitable to the general and first magistrate of the republic. In the armies and in the provinces, they displayed the dignity of monarchs; and when they fixed their residence at a distance from the capital, they forever laid aside the dissimulation which Augustus had recommended to his successors. In the exercise of the legislative as well as the executive power, the sovereign advised with his ministers instead of consulting the great council of the nation. The name of the senate was mentioned with honor till the last period of the empire; the vanity of its members was still flattered with honorary distinctions; but the assembly which had so long been the source and so long the instrument of power was respectfully suffered to sink into oblivion. The senate of Rome, losing all connection with the Imperial court and the actual constitution, was left a venerable but useless monument of antiquity on the Capitoline hill.

When the Roman princes had lost sight of the senate and of their ancient capital, they easily forgot the origin and nature of their legal power. The civil offices of consul, of proconsul, of censor, and of tribune, by the union of which it had been formed, betrayed to the people its republican extraction. Those modest titles were laid aside; and if they still distinguished their high station by the appellation of Emperor, or IMPERATOR, that word was understood in a new and more dignified sense, and no longer denoted the general of the Roman armies but the sovereign of the Roman world. The name of Emperor, which was at first of a military nature, was associated with another of a more servile kind. The epithet of DOMINUS, or Lord, in its primitive signification was expressive not of the authority of a prince over his subjects or of a commander over his soldiers, but of the despotic power of a master over his domestic slaves. Viewing it in that odious light, it had been rejected with abhorrence by the first Caesars. Their resistance insensibly became more feeble, and the name less odious; till at length the style of *our Lord and Emperor* was not only bestowed by flattery but was regularly admitted into the laws and public monuments. Such lofty epithets were sufficient to elate and satisfy the most excessive vanity; and if the successors of Diocletian still declined the title of King, it seems to have been the effect not so much of their moderation as of their delicacy. Wherever the Latin tongue was in use (and it was the language of government throughout the empire), the Imperial title, as it was peculiar to themselves, conveyed a more respectable idea than the name of king, which they must have shared with a hundred Barbarian chieftains; or which, at the best, they could derive only from Romulus or from Tarquin. But the sentiments of the East were very different from those of the West. From the earliest period of history, the sovereigns of Asia had been celebrated in the Greek language by the title of BASILEUS, or King; and since it was considered as the first distinction among men, it was soon employed by the servile provincials of the East in their humble addresses to the Roman throne. Even the attributes, or at least the titles, of the DIVINITY were usurped by Diocletian and Maximian, who transmitted them to a succession of Christian emperors. Such extravagant compliments, however, soon lose their impiety by losing their meaning; and when the ear is once accustomed to the sound, they are heard with indifference, as vague though excessive professions of respect.

From the time of Augustus to that of Diocletian, the Roman princes, conversing in a familiar manner among their fellow-citizens, were saluted only with the same respect that was usually paid to senators and magistrates. Their principal distinction was the Imperial or military robe of purple; whilst the senatorial garment was marked by a broad, and the equestrian by a narrow, band or stripe of the same honorable color. The pride, or rather the policy, of Diocletian engaged that artful prince to introduce the stately magnificence of the court of Persia. He ventured to assume the diadem, an ornament detested by the Romans as the odious ensign of royalty, and the use of which had been considered as the most desperate act of the madness of Caligula. It was no more than a broad white fillet set with pearls which encircled the emperor's head. The sumptuous robes of Diocletian and his successors were of silk and gold; and it is remarked with indignation that even their shoes were studded with the most precious gems. The access to their sacred person was every day rendered more difficult by the institution of new forms and ceremonies. The avenues of the palace were strictly guarded by the various *schools,* as they began to be called, of domestic officers. The interior apartments were entrusted to the jealous vigilance of the eunuchs, the increase of whose numbers and influence was the most infallible symptom of the progress of despotism. When a subject was at length admitted to the Imperial presence, he was obliged, whatever might be his rank, to fall prostrate on the ground and to adore, according to the Eastern fashion, the divinity of his lord and master. Diocletian was a man of sense who, in the course of private as well as public life, had formed a just estimate both of himself and of mankind: nor is it easy to conceive that in substituting the manners of Persia to those of Rome, he was seriously actuated by so mean a principle as that of vanity. He flattered himself that an ostentation of splendor and luxury would subdue the imagination of the multitude; that the monarch would be less exposed to the rude license of the people and the soldiers as his person was secluded from the public view; and that habits of submission would insensibly be productive of sentiments of veneration. Like the modesty affected by Augustus, the state maintained by Diocletian was a theatrical representation; but it must be confessed that of the two comedies, the former was of a much more liberal and manly character than the latter. It was the aim of the one to disguise, and the object of the other to display, the unbounded power which the emperors possessed over the Roman world.

Ostentation was the first principle of the new system instituted by Diocletian. The second was division. He divided the empire, the provinces, and every branch of the civil as well as military administration. He multiplied the wheels of the machine of government and rendered its operations less rapid but more secure. Whatever advantages and whatever defects might attend these innovations, they must be ascribed in a very great degree to the first inventor; but as the new frame of policy was gradually improved and completed by succeeding princes, it will be more satisfactory to delay the consideration of it till the season of its full maturity and perfection. Reserving, therefore, for the reign of Constantine a more exact picture of the new empire, we shall content ourselves with describing the principal and decisive outline as it was traced by the hand of Diocletian. He had associated three colleagues in the exercise of the supreme power; and as he was convinced that the abilities of a single man were inadequate to the public defense, he considered the joint administration of four princes not as a temporary expedient but as a fundamental law of the constitution. It was his intention that the two elder princes should be distinguished by the use of the diadem and the title of *Augusti;* that, as affection or esteem might direct their choice, they should regularly call to their assistance two subordinate colleagues; and that the *Caesars,* rising in their turn to the first rank, should supply an uninterrupted succession of emperors. The empire was divided into four parts. The East and Italy were the most honorable, the Danube and the Rhine the most laborious stations. The former claimed the presence of the *Augusti,* the latter were entrusted to the administration of the *Caesars.* The strength of the legions was in the hands of the four partners of sovereignty, and the despair of successively vanquishing four formidable rivals might intimidate the ambition of an aspiring general. In their civil government, the emperors were supposed to exercise the undivided power of the monarch, and their edicts, inscribed with their joint names, were received in all the provinces as promulgated by their mutual councils and authority. Notwithstanding these precautions, the political union of the Roman world was gradually dissolved, and a principle of division was introduced which, in the course of a few years, occasioned the perpetual separation of the Eastern and Western empires.

The system of Diocletian was accompanied with another very material disadvantage which cannot even at present be totally overlooked; a more expensive establishment, and consequently an increase of taxes, and the oppression of the people. Instead of a modest family of slaves and freedmen, such as had contented the simple greatness of Augustus and Trajan, three or four magnificent courts were established in the various parts of the empire, and as many Roman *kings* contended with each other and with the Persian monarch for the vain superiority of pomp and luxury. The number of ministers, of magistrates, of officers, and of servants who filled the different departments of the state was multiplied beyond the example of former times; and (if we may borrow the warm expression of a contemporary) "when the proportion of those who received exceeded the proportion of those who contributed, the provinces were oppressed by the weight of tributes." From this period to the extinction of the empire, it would be easy to deduce an uninterrupted series of clamors and complaints. According to his religion and situation, each writer chooses either Diocletian, or Constantine, or Valens, or Theodosius, for the object of his invectives; but they unanimously agree in representing the burden of the public impositions, and particularly the land tax and capitation, as the intolerable and increasing grievance of their own times. From such a concurrence, an impartial historian, who is obliged to extract truth from satire as well as from panegyric, will be inclined to divide the blame among the princes whom they accuse, and to ascribe their exactions much less to their personal vices than to the uniform system of their administration. The emperor Diocletian was indeed the author of that system; but during his reign, the growing evil was confined within the bounds of modesty and discretion, and he deserves the reproach of establishing pernicious precedents rather than of exercising actual oppression. It may be added that his revenues were managed with prudent economy; and that after all the current expenses were discharged, there still remained in the Imperial treasury an ample provision either for judicious liberality or for any emergency of the state.

It was in the twenty-first year of his reign that Diocletian executed his memorable resolution of abdicating the empire; an action more naturally to have been expected from the elder or the younger Antoninus than from a prince who had never practiced the lessons of philosophy either in the attainment or in the use of supreme power. Diocletian acquired the glory of giving to the world the first example of a resignation, which has not been very frequently imitated by succeeding monarchs.[†]

The ceremony of his abdication was performed in a spacious plain about three miles from Nicomedia [May 1, A.D. 305]. The emperor ascended a lofty throne, and in a speech full of reason and dignity declared his intention both to the people and to the soldiers who were assembled on this extraordinary occasion. As soon as he had divested himself of his purple, he withdrew from the gazing multitude; and traversing the city in a covered chariot proceeded without delay to the favorite retirement which he had chosen in his native country of Dalmatia. On the same day, which was the first of May, Maximian, as it had been previously concerted, made his resignation of the Imperial dignity at Milan. Even in the splendor of the Roman triumph, Diocletian had meditated his design of abdicating the government. As he wished to secure the obedience of Maximian, he exacted from him either a general assurance that he would submit his actions to the authority of his benefactor, or a particular promise that he would descend from the throne whenever he should receive the advice and the example. This engagement, though it was confirmed by the solemnity of an oath before the altar of the Capitoline Jupiter, would have proved a feeble restraint on the fierce temper of Maximian, whose passion was the love of power and who neither desired present tranquility nor future reputation. But he yielded, however reluctantly, to the ascendant which his wiser colleague had acquired over him, and retired immediately after his abdication to a villa in Lucania, where it was almost impossible that such an impatient spirit could find any lasting tranquility.

Diocletian, who from a servile origin had raised himself to the throne, passed the nine last years of his life in a private condition. Reason had dictated, and content seems to have accompanied, his retreat, in which he enjoyed for a long time the respect of those princes to whom he had resigned the possession of the world. It is seldom that minds long exercised in business have formed the habits of conversing with themselves, and in the loss of power they principally regret the want of occupation. The amusements of letters and of devotion, which afford so many resources in solitude, were incapable of fixing the attention of Diocletian; but he had preserved, or at least he soon recovered, a taste for the most innocent as well as natural pleasures, and his leisure hours were sufficiently employed in building, planting, and gardening. His answer to Maximian is deservedly celebrated. He was solicited by that restless old man to reassume the reins of government and the Imperial purple. He rejected the temptation with a smile of pity, calmly observing that if he could show Maximian the cabbages which he had planted with his own hands at Salona, he should no longer be urged to relinquish the enjoyment of happiness for the pursuit of power. In his conversations with his friends, he frequently acknowledged that of all arts, the most difficult was the art of reigning; and he expressed himself on that favorite topic with a degree of warmth which could be the result only of experience. "How often," was he accustomed to say, "is it the interest of four or five ministers to combine together to deceive their sovereign! Secluded from mankind by his exalted dignity, the truth is concealed from his knowledge; he can see only with their eyes, he hears nothing but their misrepresentations. He confers the most important offices upon vice and weakness, and disgraces the most virtuous and deserving among his subjects. By such infamous arts," added Diocletian, "the best and wisest princes are sold to the venal corruption of their courtiers." A just estimate of greatness, and the assurance of immortal fame, improve our relish for the pleasures of retirement; but the Roman emperor had filled too important a character in the world to enjoy without alloy the comforts and security of a private condition. It was impossible that he could remain ignorant of the troubles which afflicted the empire after his abdication. It was impossible that he could be indifferent to their consequences. Fear, sorrow, and discontent sometimes pursued him into the solitude of Salona. His tenderness, or at least his pride, was deeply wounded by the misfortunes of his wife and daughter; and the last moments of Diocletian were embittered by some affronts which Licinius and Constantine might have spared the father of so many emperors, and the first author of their own fortune. A report, though of a very doubtful nature, has reached our times that he prudently withdrew himself from their power by a voluntary death [A.D. 313].†

It is almost unnecessary to remark that the civil distractions of the empire, the license of the soldiers, the inroads of the Barbarians, and the progress of despotism had proved very unfavorable to genius, and even to learning. The succession of Illyrian princes restored the empire without restoring the sciences. Their military education was not calculated to inspire them with the love of letters; and even the mind of Diocletian, however active and capacious in business, was totally uninformed by study or speculation. The professions of law and physic are of such common use and certain profit that they will always secure a sufficient number of practitioners endowed with a reasonable degree of abilities and knowledge; but it does not appear that the students in those two faculties appeal to any celebrated masters who have flourished within that period. The voice of poetry was silent. History was reduced to dry and confused abridgments, alike destitute of amusement and instruction. A languid and affected eloquence was still retained in the pay and service of the emperors, who encouraged not any arts except those which contributed to the gratification of their pride or the defense of their power.

The declining age of learning and of mankind is marked, however, by the rise and rapid progress of the new Platonists. The school of Alexandria silenced those of Athens; and the ancient sects enrolled themselves under the banners of the more fashionable teachers, who recommended their system by the novelty of their method and the austerity of their manners. Several of these masters, Ammonius, Plotinus, Amelius, and Porphyry, were men of profound thought and intense application; but by mistaking the true object of philosophy, their labors contributed much less to improve than to corrupt the human understanding. The knowledge that is suited to our situation and powers, the whole compass of moral, natural, and mathematical science, was neglected by the new Platonists; whilst they exhausted their strength in the verbal disputes of metaphysics, attempted to explore the secrets of the invisible world, and studied to reconcile Aristotle with Plato on subjects of which both these philosophers were as ignorant as the rest of mankind. Consuming their reason in these deep but unsubstantial meditations, their minds were exposed to illusions of fancy. They flattered themselves that they possessed the secret of disengaging the soul from its corporal prison; claimed a familiar intercourse with demons and spirits; and, by a very singular revolution, converted the study of philosophy into that of magic. The ancient sages had derided the popular superstition; after disguising its extravagance by the thin pretense of allegory, the disciples of Plotinus and Porphyry became its most zealous defenders. As they agreed with the Christians in a few mysterious points of faith, they attacked the remainder of their theological system with all the fury of civil war. The new Platonists would scarcely deserve a place in the history of science, but in that of the church the mention of them will very frequently occur.

CHAPTER XIV

Six Emperors at the Same Time, Reunion of the Empire

Troubles after the abdication of Diocletian. • Death of Constantius. • Elevation of Constantine and Maxentius. • Six emperors at the same time. • Death of Maximian and Galerius. • Victories of Constantine over Maxentius and Licinius. • Reunion of the empire under the authority of Constantine.

The balance of power established by Diocletian subsisted no longer than while it was sustained by the firm and dexterous hand of the founder. It required such a fortunate mixture of different tempers and abilities as could scarcely be found or even expected a second time; two emperors without jealousy, two Caesars without ambition, and the same general interest invariably pursued by four independent princes. The abdication of Diocletian and Maximian was succeeded by eighteen years of discord and confusion [A.D. 305–323]. The empire was afflicted by five civil wars; and the remainder of the time was not so much a state of tranquility as a suspension of arms between several hostile monarchs, who, viewing each other with an eye of fear and hatred, strove to increase their respective forces at the expense of their subjects.

As soon as Diocletian and Maximian had resigned the purple, their station, according to the rules of the new constitution, was filled by the two Caesars, Constantius and Galerius, who immediately assumed the title of Augustus. The honors of seniority and precedence were allowed to the former of those princes, and he continued under a new appellation to administer his ancient department of Gaul, Spain, and Britain. The government of those ample provinces was sufficient to exercise his talents and to satisfy his ambition. Clemency, temperance, and moderation distinguished the amiable character of Constantius, and his fortunate subjects had frequently occasion to compare the virtues of their sovereign with the passions of Maximian, and even with the arts of Diocletian. Instead of imitating their Eastern pride and magnificence, Constantius preserved the modesty of a Roman prince. . . . The provincials of Gaul, Spain, and Britain, sensible of his worth and of their own happiness, reflected with anxiety on the declining health of the emperor Constantius and the tender age of his numerous family, the issue of his second marriage with the daughter of Maximian.

The stern temper of Galerius was cast in a very different mold; and while he commanded the esteem of his subjects, he seldom condescended to solicit their affections. His fame in arms and, above all, the success of the Persian war had elated his haughty mind, which was naturally impatient of a superior, or even of an equal.[†]

After the elevation of Constantius and Galerius to the rank of *Augusti,* two new *Caesars* were required to supply their place, and to complete the system of the Imperial government. Diocletian was sincerely desirous of withdrawing himself from the world; he considered Galerius, who had married his daughter, as the firmest support of his family and of the empire; and he consented without reluctance that his successor should assume the merit as well as the envy of the important nomination. It was fixed without consulting the interest or inclination of the princes of the West. Each of them had a son who was arrived at the age of manhood and who might have been deemed the most natural candidates for the vacant honor. But the impotent resentment of Maximian was no longer to be dreaded; and the moderate Constantius, though he might despise the dangers, was humanely apprehensive of the calamities of civil war. The two persons whom Galerius promoted to the rank of Caesar were much better suited to serve the views of his ambition; and their principal recommendation seems to have consisted in the want of merit or personal consequence. The first of these was Daza, or, as he was afterwards called, Maximin, whose mother was the sister of Galerius. The unexperienced youth still betrayed, by his manners and language, his rustic education, when, to his own astonishment as well as that of the world, he was invested by Diocletian with the purple, exalted to the dignity of Caesar, and entrusted with the sovereign command of Egypt and Syria. At the same time, Severus, a faithful servant, addicted to pleasure but not incapable of business, was sent to Milan to receive from the reluctant hands of Maximian the Caesarian ornaments and the possession of Italy and Africa. According to the forms of the constitution, Severus acknowledged the supremacy of the Western emperor; but he was absolutely devoted to the commands of his benefactor Galerius, who, reserving to himself the intermediate countries from the confines of Italy to those of Syria, firmly established his power over three fourths of the monarchy. In the full confidence that the approaching death of Constantius would leave him sole master of the Roman world, we are assured that he had arranged in his mind a long succession of future princes, and that he meditated his own retreat from public life after he should have accomplished a glorious reign of about twenty years.

But within less than eighteen months, two unexpected revolutions overturned the ambitious schemes of Galerius. The hopes of uniting the Western provinces to his empire were disappointed by the elevation of Constantine, whilst Italy and Africa were lost by the successful revolt of Maxentius.

I. The fame of Constantine has rendered posterity attentive to the most minute circumstances of his life and actions. The place of his birth, as well as the condition of his mother, Helena, have been the subject not only of literary but of national disputes. Notwithstanding the recent tradition which assigns for her father a British king, we are obliged to confess that Helena was the daughter of an innkeeper; but at the same time, we may defend the legality of her marriage against those who have represented her as the concubine of Constantius. The great Constantine was most probably born at Naissus, in Dacia [A.D. 274]; and it is not surprising that in a family and province distinguished only by the profession of arms, the youth should discover very little inclination to improve his mind by the acquisition of knowledge. He was about eighteen years of age when his father was promoted to the rank of Caesar [A.D. 293]; but that fortunate event was attended with his mother's divorce; and the splendor of an Imperial alliance reduced the son of Helena to a state of disgrace and humiliation. Instead of following Constantius in the West, he remained in the service of Diocletian, signalized his valor in the wars of Egypt and Persia, and gradually rose to the honorable station of a tribune of the first order. The figure of Constantine was tall and majestic; he was dexterous in all his exercises, intrepid in war, affable in peace; in his whole conduct, the active spirit of youth was tempered by habitual prudence; and while his mind was engrossed by ambition, he appeared cold and insensible to the allurements of pleasure. The favor of the people and soldiers, who had named him as a worthy candidate for the rank of Caesar, served only to exasperate the jealousy of Galerius; and though prudence might restrain him from exercising any open violence, an absolute monarch is seldom at a loss how to execute a sure and secret revenge. Every hour increased the danger of Constantine and the anxiety of his father, who, by repeated letters, expressed the warmest desire of embracing his son. For some time the policy of Galerius supplied him with delays and excuses; but it was impossible long to refuse so natural a request of his associate without maintaining his refusal by arms. The permission of the journey was reluctantly granted, and whatever precautions the emperor might have taken to intercept a return, the consequences of which he with so much reason apprehended, they were effectually disappointed by the incredible diligence of Constantine. Leaving the palace of Nicomedia in the night, he traveled post through Bithynia, Thrace, Dacia, Pannonia, Italy, and Gaul, and, amidst the joyful acclamations of the people, reached the port of Boulogne in the very moment when his father was preparing to embark for Britain.

The British expedition, and an easy victory over the Barbarians of Caledonia, were the last exploits of the reign of Constantius. He ended his life in the Imperial palace of York [July 25, A.D. 306], fifteen months after he had received the title of Augustus and almost fourteen years and a half after he had been promoted to the rank of Caesar. His death was immediately succeeded by the elevation of Constantine. The ideas of inheritance and succession are so very familiar that the generality of mankind consider them as founded not only in reason, but in nature itself. Our imagination readily transfers the same principles from private property to public dominion: and whenever a virtuous father leaves behind him a son whose merit seems to justify the esteem or even the hopes of the people, the joint influence of prejudice and of affection operates with irresistible weight.... The soldiers were ... prepared to salute him with the names of Augustus and Emperor. The throne was the object of his desires; and had he been less actuated by ambition, it was his only means of safety. He was well acquainted with the character and sentiments of Galerius, and sufficiently apprised that if he wished to live he must determine to reign. The decent and even obstinate resistance which he chose to affect was contrived to justify his usurpation; nor did he yield to the acclamations of the army till he had provided the proper materials for a letter, which he immediately despatched to the emperor of the East. Constantine informed him of the melancholy event of his father's death, modestly asserted his natural claim to the succession, and respectfully lamented that the affectionate violence of his troops had not permitted him to solicit the Imperial purple in the regular and constitutional manner. The first emotions of Galerius were those of surprise, disappointment, and rage; and as he could seldom restrain his passions, he loudly threatened that he would commit to the flames both the letter and the messenger. But his resentment insensibly subsided; and when he recollected the doubtful chance of war, when he had weighed the character and strength of his adversary, he consented to embrace the honorable accommodation which the prudence of Constantine had left open to him. Without either condemning or ratifying the choice of the British army, Galerius accepted the son of his deceased colleague as the sovereign of the provinces beyond the Alps; but he gave him only the title of Caesar and the fourth rank among the Roman princes, whilst he conferred the vacant place of Augustus on his favorite, Severus. The apparent harmony of the empire was still preserved, and Constantine, who already possessed the substance, expected without impatience an opportunity of obtaining the honors of supreme power.[†]

II. The ambitious spirit of Galerius was scarcely reconciled to the disappointment of his views upon the Gallic provinces before the unexpected loss of Italy wounded his pride as well as power in a still more sensible part. The long absence of the emperors had filled Rome with discontent and indignation; and the people gradually discovered that the preference given to Nicomedia and Milan was not to be ascribed to the particular inclination of Diocletian but to the permanent form of government which he had instituted. It was in vain that, a few months after his abdication, his successors dedicated under his name those magnificent baths whose ruins still supply the ground as well as the materials for so many churches and convents. The tranquility of those elegant recesses of ease and luxury was disturbed by the impatient murmurs of the Romans, and a report was insensibly circulated that the sums expended in erecting those buildings would soon be required at their hands. About that time the avarice of Galerius, or perhaps the exigencies of the state, had induced him to make a very strict and rigorous inquisition into the property of his subjects for the purpose of a general taxation, both on their lands and on their persons. A very minute survey appears to have been taken of their real estates;

and wherever there was the slightest suspicion of concealment, torture was very freely employed to obtain a sincere declaration of their personal wealth. The privileges which had exalted Italy above the rank of the provinces were no longer regarded: and the officers of the revenue already began to number the Roman people and to settle the proportion of the new taxes. Even when the spirit of freedom had been utterly extinguished, the tamest subjects have sometimes ventured to resist an unprecedented invasion of their property; but on this occasion the injury was aggravated by the insult, and the sense of private interest was quickened by that of national honor. The conquest of Macedonia, as we have already observed, had delivered the Roman people from the weight of personal taxes. Though they had experienced every form of despotism, they had now enjoyed that exemption near five hundred years; nor could they patiently brook the insolence of an Illyrian peasant who, from his distant residence in Asia, presumed to number Rome among the tributary cities of his empire. The rising fury of the people was encouraged by the authority, or at least the connivance, of the senate; and the feeble remains of the Praetorian guards, who had reason to apprehend their own dissolution, embraced so honorable a pretense and declared their readiness to draw their swords in the service of their oppressed country. It was the wish, and it soon became the hope, of every citizen that after expelling from Italy their foreign tyrants they should elect a prince who, by the place of his residence and by his maxims of government, might once more deserve the title of Roman emperor. The name as well as the situation of Maxentius determined in his favor the popular enthusiasm.

Maxentius was the son of the emperor Maximian, and he had married the daughter of Galerius. His birth and alliance seemed to offer him the fairest promise of succeeding to the empire; but his vices and incapacity procured him the same exclusion from the dignity of Caesar which Constantine had deserved by a dangerous superiority of merit. The policy of Galerius preferred such associates as would never disgrace the choice nor dispute the commands of their benefactor. An obscure stranger was therefore raised to the throne of Italy, and the son of the late emperor of the West was left to enjoy the luxury of a private fortune in a villa a few miles distant from the capital. The gloomy passions of his soul, shame, vexation, and rage, were inflamed by envy on the news of Constantine's success; but the hopes of Maxentius revived with the public discontent, and he was easily persuaded to unite his personal injury and pretensions with the cause of the Roman people. Two Praetorian tribunes and a commissary of provisions undertook the management of the conspiracy; and as every order of men was actuated by the same spirit, the immediate event was neither doubtful nor difficult. The praefect of the city, and a few magistrates who maintained their fidelity to Severus, were massacred by the guards; and Maxentius, invested with the Imperial ornaments, was acknowledged by the applauding senate and people as the protector of the Roman freedom and dignity [October 28, A.D. 306]. It is uncertain whether Maximian was previously acquainted with the conspiracy; but as soon as the standard of rebellion was erected at Rome, the old emperor broke from the retirement where the authority of Diocletian had condemned him to pass a life of melancholy and solitude, and concealed his returning ambition under the disguise of paternal tenderness. At the request of his son and of the senate, he condescended to reassume the purple. His ancient dignity, his experience, and his fame in arms added strength as well as reputation to the party of Maxentius.

According to the advice, or rather the orders, of his colleague, the emperor Severus immediately hastened to Rome, in the full confidence that, by his unexpected celerity, he should easily suppress the tumult of an unwarlike populace commanded by a licentious youth. But he found on his arrival the gates of the city shut against him, the walls filled with men and arms, an experienced general at the head of the rebels, and his own troops without spirit or affection. A large body of Moors deserted to the enemy, allured by the promise of a large donative and, if it be true that they had been levied by Maximian in his African war, preferring the natural feelings of gratitude to the artificial ties of allegiance. Anulinus, the Praetorian praefect, declared himself in favor of Maxentius, and drew after him the most considerable part of the troops accustomed to obey his commands. Rome, according to the expression of an orator, recalled her armies; and the unfortunate Severus, destitute of force and of counsel, retired, or rather fled, with precipitation to Ravenna. Here he might for some time have been safe. The fortifications of Ravenna were able to resist the attempts, and the morasses that surrounded the town were sufficient to prevent the approach, of the Italian army. The sea, which Severus commanded with a powerful fleet, secured him an inexhaustible supply of provisions and gave a free entrance to the legions which, on the return of spring, would advance to his assistance from Illyricum and the East. Maximian, who conducted the siege in person, was soon convinced that he might waste his time and his army in the fruitless enterprise, and that he had nothing to hope either from force or famine. With an art more suitable to the character of Diocletian than to his own, he directed his attack not so much against the walls of Ravenna, as against the mind of Severus. The treachery which he had experienced disposed that unhappy prince to distrust the most sincere of his friends and adherents. The emissaries of Maximian easily persuaded his credulity that a conspiracy was formed to betray the town, and prevailed upon his fears not to expose himself to the discretion of an irritated conqueror but to accept the faith of an honorable capitulation [February A.D. 307]. He was at first received with humanity and treated with respect. Maximian conducted the captive emperor to Rome and gave him the most solemn assurances that he had secured his life by the resignation of the purple. But Severus could obtain only an easy death and an Imperial funeral. When the sentence was signified to him, the manner of executing it was left to his own choice; he preferred the favorite mode of the ancients, that of opening his veins; and as soon as he expired, his body was carried to the sepulchre which had been constructed for the family of Gallienus.

Though the characters of Constantine and Maxentius had very little affinity with each other, their situation and interest were the same; and prudence seemed to require that they should unite their forces against the common enemy. Notwithstanding the superiority of his age and dignity, the indefatigable Maximian passed the Alps and, courting a personal interview with the sovereign of Gaul, carried with him his daughter Fausta as the pledge of the new alliance. The marriage was celebrated at Arles with every circumstance of magnificence; and the ancient colleague of Diocletian, who again asserted his claim to the Western empire, conferred on his son-in-law and ally the title of Augustus. By consenting to receive that honor from Maximian, Constantine seemed to embrace the cause of Rome and of the senate; but his professions were ambiguous and his assistance slow and ineffectual. He considered with attention the approaching contest between the masters of Italy and the emperor of the East, and was prepared to consult his own safety or ambition in the event of the war.

The importance of the occasion called for the presence and abilities of Galerius. At the head of a powerful army collected from Illyricum and the East, he entered Italy, resolved to revenge the death of Severus and to chastise the rebellious Romans; or, as he expressed his intentions in the furious language of a Barbarian, to extirpate the senate and to destroy the people by the sword. But the skill of Maximian had concerted a prudent system of defense. The invader found every place hostile, fortified, and inaccessible; and though he forced his way as far as Narni, within sixty miles of Rome, his dominion in Italy was confined to the narrow limits of his camp. Sensible of the increasing difficulties of his enterprise, the haughty Galerius made the first advances towards a reconciliation and despatched two of his most considerable officers to tempt the Roman princes by the offer of a conference and the declaration of his paternal regard for Maxentius, who might obtain much more from his liberality than he could hope from the doubtful chance of war. The offers of Galerius were rejected with firmness, his perfidious friendship refused with contempt, and it was not long before he discovered that, unless he provided for his safety by a timely retreat, he had some reason to apprehend the fate of Severus. The wealth which the Romans defended against his rapacious tyranny, they freely contributed for his destruction. The name of Maximian, the popular arts of his son, the secret distribution of large sums, and the promise of still more liberal rewards checked the ardor and corrupted the fidelity of the Illyrian legions; and when Galerius at length gave the signal of the retreat, it was with some difficulty that he could prevail on his veterans not to desert a banner which had so often conducted them to victory and honor.[†]

The legions of Galerius exhibited a very melancholy proof of their disposition by the ravages which they committed in their retreat. They murdered, they ravished, they plundered, they drove away the flocks and herds of the Italians; they burnt the villages through which they passed, and they endeavored to destroy the country which it had not been in their power to subdue. During the whole march Maxentius hung on their rear, but he very prudently declined a general engagement with those brave and desperate veterans. His father had undertaken a second journey into Gaul with the hope of persuading Constantine, who had assembled an army on the frontier, to join in the pursuit and to complete the victory. But the actions of Constantine were guided by reason and not by resentment. He persisted in the wise resolution of maintaining a balance of power in the divided empire, and he no longer hated Galerius when that aspiring prince had ceased to be an object of terror.

The mind of Galerius was the most susceptible of the sterner passions, but it was not, however, incapable of a sincere and lasting friendship. Licinius, whose manners as well as character were not unlike his own, seems to have engaged both his affection and esteem. Their intimacy had commenced in the happier period, perhaps, of their youth and obscurity. It had been cemented by the freedom and dangers of a military life; they had advanced almost by equal steps through the successive honors of the service; and as soon as Galerius was invested with the Imperial dignity, he seems to have conceived the design of raising his companion to the same rank with himself. During the short period of his prosperity, he considered the rank of Caesar as unworthy of the age and merit of Licinius, and rather chose to reserve for him the place of Constantius and the empire of the West. While the emperor was employed in the Italian war, he entrusted his friend with the defense of the Danube; and immediately after his return from that unfortunate expedition, he invested Licinius with the vacant purple of Severus, resigning to his immediate command the provinces of Illyricum. The news of his promotion was no sooner carried into the East than Maximin, who governed, or rather oppressed, the countries of Egypt and Syria, betrayed his envy and discontent, disdained the inferior name of Caesar, and, notwithstanding the prayers as well as arguments of Galerius, exacted, almost by violence, the equal title of Augustus. For the first and indeed for the last time, the Roman world was administered by six emperors [A.D. 308]. In the West, Constantine and Maxentius affected to reverence their father Maximian. In the East, Licinius and Maximin honored with more real consideration their benefactor Galerius. The opposition of interest and the memory of a recent war divided the empire into two great hostile powers; but their mutual fears produced an apparent tranquility and even a feigned reconciliation, till the death of the elder princes, of Maximian and more particularly of Galerius, gave a new direction to the views and passions of their surviving associates.[†]

[I]t was impossible that minds like those of Maximian and his son could long possess in harmony an undivided power. Maxentius considered himself as the legal sovereign of Italy, elected by the Roman senate and people; nor would he endure the control of his father, who arrogantly declared that by *his* name and abilities the rash youth had been established on the throne. The cause was solemnly pleaded before the Praetorian guards; and those troops, who dreaded the severity of the old emperor, espoused the party of Maxentius. The life and freedom of Maximian were, however, respected, and he retired from Italy into Illyricum, affecting to lament his past conduct and secretly contriving new mischiefs. But Galerius, who was well acquainted with his character, soon obliged him to leave his dominions, and the last refuge of the disappointed Maximian was the court of his son-in-law Constantine. He was received with respect by that artful prince, and with the appearance of filial tenderness by the empress Fausta. That he might remove every suspicion, he resigned the Imperial purple a second time, professing himself at length convinced of the vanity of greatness and ambition. Had he persevered in this resolution, he might have ended his life with less dignity, indeed, than in his first retirement, yet, however, with comfort and reputation. But the near prospect of a throne brought back to his remembrance the state from whence he was fallen, and he resolved by a desperate effort either to reign or to perish. An incursion of the Franks had summoned Constantine, with a part of his army, to the banks of the Rhine; the remainder of the troops were stationed in the southern provinces of Gaul, which lay exposed to the enterprises of the Italian emperor, and a considerable treasure was deposited in the city of Arles. Maximian either craftily invented or easily credited a vain report of the death of Constantine. Without hesitation he ascended the throne, seized the treasure, and scattering it with his accustomed profusion among the soldiers, endeavored to awake in their minds the memory of his ancient dignity and exploits. Before he could establish his authority or finish the negotiation which he appears to have entered into with his son Maxentius, the celerity of Constantine defeated all his hopes. On the first news of his perfidy and ingratitude, that prince returned by rapid marches. . . . A secret but irrevocable sentence of death was pronounced against the usurper; he obtained only the same favor which he had indulged to Severus, and it was published to the world that, oppressed by the remorse of his repeated crimes, he strangled himself with his own hands [February A.D. 310]. After he had lost the assistance and disdained the moderate counsels of Diocletian, the second period of his active life was a series of public calamities and personal mortifications, which were terminated, in about three years, by an ignominious death. He deserved his fate; but we should find more reason to applaud the humanity of Constantine if he had spared an old man, the benefactor of his father, and the father of his wife. During the whole of this melancholy transaction, it appears that Fausta sacrificed the sentiments of nature to her conjugal duties.

The last years of Galerius were less shameful and unfortunate; and though he had filled with more glory the subordinate station of Caesar than the superior rank of Augustus, he preserved till the moment of his death the first place among the princes of the Roman world. He survived his retreat from Italy about four years; and wisely relinquishing his views of universal empire, he devoted the remainder of his life to the enjoyment of pleasure and to the execution of some works of public utility, among which we may distinguish the discharging into the Danube the superfluous waters of the Lake Pelso and the cutting down the immense forests that encompassed it; an operation worthy of a monarch, since it gave an extensive country to the agriculture of his Pannonian subjects. His death was occasioned by a very painful and lingering disorder [May A.D. 311]. His body, swelled by an intemperate course of life to an unwieldy corpulence, was covered with ulcers and devoured by innumerable swarms of those insects which have given their name to a most loathsome disease; but as Galerius had offended a very zealous and powerful party among his subjects, his sufferings, instead of exciting their compassion, have been celebrated as the visible effects of divine justice. He had no sooner expired in his palace of Nicomedia than the two emperors who were indebted for their purple to his favors began to collect their forces, with the intention either of disputing or of dividing the dominions which he had left without a master. They were persuaded, however, to desist from the former design and to agree in the latter. The provinces of Asia fell to the share of Maximin, and those of Europe augmented the portion of

Licinius. . . . The deaths of Maximian and of Galerius reduced the number of emperors to four. The sense of their true interest soon connected Licinius and Constantine; a secret alliance was concluded between Maximin and Maxentius, and their unhappy subjects expected with terror the bloody consequences of their inevitable dissensions, which were no longer restrained by the fear or the respect which they had entertained for Galerius.

Among so many crimes and misfortunes occasioned by the passions of the Roman princes, there is some pleasure in discovering a single action which may be ascribed to their virtue. In the sixth year of his reign, Constantine visited the city of Autun and generously remitted the arrears of tribute, reducing at the same time the proportion of their assessment from twenty-five to eighteen thousand heads, subject to the real and personal capitation. Yet even this indulgence affords the most unquestionable proof of the public misery. This tax was so extremely oppressive, either in itself or in the mode of collecting it, that whilst the revenue was increased by extortion, it was diminished by despair: a considerable part of the territory of Autun was left uncultivated; and great numbers of the provincials rather chose to live as exiles and outlaws than to support the weight of civil society. It is but too probable that the bountiful emperor relieved, by a partial act of liberality, one among the many evils which he had caused by his general maxims of administration. But even those maxims were less the effect of choice than of necessity. And if we except the death of Maximian, the reign of Constantine in Gaul seems to have been the most innocent and even virtuous period of his life. The provinces were protected by his presence from the inroads of the Barbarians, who either dreaded or experienced his active valor. After a signal victory over the Franks and Alemanni, several of their princes were exposed by his order to the wild beasts in the amphitheater of Treves, and the people seem to have enjoyed the spectacle without discovering, in such a treatment of royal captives, anything that was repugnant to the laws of nations or of humanity.

The virtues of Constantine were rendered more illustrious by the vices of Maxentius. Whilst the Gallic provinces enjoyed as much happiness as the condition of the times was capable of receiving, Italy and Africa groaned under the dominion of a tyrant, as contemptible as he was odious. The zeal of flattery and faction has indeed too frequently sacrificed the reputation of the vanquished to the glory of their successful rivals; but even those writers who have revealed with the most freedom and pleasure the faults of Constantine unanimously confess that Maxentius was cruel, rapacious, and profligate.... The wealth of Rome supplied an inexhaustible fund for his vain and prodigal expenses, and the ministers of his revenue were skilled in the arts of rapine. It was under his reign that the method of exacting a *free gift* from the senators was first invented; and as the sum was insensibly increased, the pretenses of levying it, a victory, a birth, a marriage, or an imperial consulship, were proportionably multiplied. Maxentius had imbibed the same implacable aversion to the senate which had characterized most of the former tyrants of Rome; nor was it possible for his ungrateful temper to forgive the generous fidelity which had raised him to the throne and supported him against all his enemies. The lives of the senators were exposed to his jealous suspicions; the dishonor of their wives and daughters heightened the gratification of his sensual passions. It may be presumed that an Imperial lover was seldom reduced to sigh in vain; but whenever persuasion proved ineffectual, he had recourse to violence; and there remains *one* memorable example of a noble matron who preserved her chastity by a voluntary death. The soldiers were the only order of men whom he appeared to respect, or studied to please. He filled Rome and Italy with armed troops, connived at their tumults, suffered them with impunity to plunder and even to massacre the defenseless people; and indulging them in the same licentiousness which their emperor enjoyed, Maxentius often bestowed on his military favorites the splendid villa or the beautiful wife of a senator. A prince of such a character, alike incapable of governing either in peace or in war, might purchase the support, but he could never obtain the esteem, of the army. Yet his pride was equal to his other vices. Whilst he passed his indolent life either within the walls of his palace or in the neighboring gardens of Sallust, he was repeatedly heard to declare that he alone was emperor, and that the other princes were no more than his lieutenants, on whom he had devolved the defense of the frontier provinces that he might enjoy without interruption the elegant luxury of the capital. Rome, which had so long regretted the absence, lamented, during the six years of his reign, the presence of her sovereign.

Though Constantine might view the conduct of Maxentius with

abhorrence and the situation of the Romans with compassion, we have no reason to presume that he would have taken up arms to punish the one or to relieve the other. But the tyrant of Italy rashly ventured to provoke a formidable enemy whose ambition had been hitherto restrained by considerations of prudence rather than by principles of justice. After the death of Maximian, his titles, according to the established custom, had been erased and his statues thrown down with ignominy. His son, who had persecuted and deserted him when alive, affected to display the most pious regard for his memory, and gave orders that a similar treatment should be immediately inflicted on all the statues that had been erected in Italy and Africa to the honor of Constantine [A.D. 312]. That wise prince, who sincerely wished to decline a war, with the difficulty and importance of which he was sufficiently acquainted, at first dissembled the insult and sought for redress by the milder expedient of negotiation, till he was convinced that the hostile and ambitious designs of the Italian emperor made it necessary for him to arm in his own defense. Maxentius, who openly avowed his pretensions to the whole monarchy of the West, had already prepared a very considerable force to invade the Gallic provinces on the side of Rhaetia; and though he could not expect any assistance from Licinius, he was flattered with the hope that the legions of Illyricum, allured by his presents and promises, would desert the standard of that prince, and unanimously declare themselves his soldiers and subjects. Constantine no longer hesitated. He had deliberated with caution; he acted with vigor.

[*Constantine invades Italy and captures Turin, then Verona.*]

The celerity of Constantine's march has been compared to the rapid conquest of Italy by the first of the Caesars; nor is the flattering parallel repugnant to the truth of history, since no more than fifty-eight days elapsed between the surrender of Verona and the final decision of the war. Constantine had always apprehended that the tyrant would consult the dictates of fear, and perhaps of prudence; and that, instead of risking his last hopes in a general engagement, he would shut himself up within the walls of Rome. His ample magazines secured him against the danger of famine; and as the situation of Constantine admitted not of delay, he might have been reduced to the sad necessity of destroying with fire and sword the Imperial city, the noblest reward of his victory and the deliverance of which had been the motive, or rather indeed the pretense, of the civil war. It was with equal surprise and pleasure that on his arrival at a place called Saxa Rubra, about nine miles from Rome, he discovered the army of Maxentius prepared to give him battle. Their long front filled a very spacious plain, and their deep array reached to the banks of the Tiber, which covered their rear and forbade their retreat. We are informed, and we may believe, that Constantine disposed his troops with consummate skill, and that he chose for himself the post of honor and danger. Distinguished by the splendor of his arms, he charged in person the cavalry of his rival; and his irresistible attack determined the fortune of the day [October 28, A.D. 312]. . . . [T]he undisciplined Italians fled without reluctance from the standard of a tyrant whom they had always hated and whom they no longer feared. The Praetorians, conscious that their offenses were beyond the reach of mercy, were animated by revenge and despair. Notwithstanding their repeated efforts, those brave veterans were unable to recover the victory: they obtained, however, an honorable death; and it was observed that their bodies covered the same ground which had been occupied by their ranks. The confusion then became general, and the dismayed troops of Maxentius, pursued by an implacable enemy, rushed by thousands into the deep and rapid stream of the Tiber. The emperor himself attempted to escape back into the city over the Milvian bridge; but the crowds which pressed together through that narrow passage forced him into the river, where he was immediately drowned by the weight of his armor. His body, which had sunk very deep into the mud, was found with some difficulty the next day. The sight of his head, when it was exposed to the eyes of the people, convinced them of their deliverance, and admonished them to receive with acclamations of loyalty and gratitude the fortunate Constantine, who thus achieved by his valor and ability the most splendid enterprise of his life.

In the use of victory, Constantine neither deserved the praise of clemency nor incurred the censure of immoderate rigor. He inflicted the same treatment to which a defeat would have exposed his own person and family, put to death the two sons of the tyrant, and carefully extirpated his whole race. The most distinguished adherents of Maxentius must have expected to share his fate, as they had shared his prosperity and his crimes; but when the Roman people loudly demanded a greater number of victims, the conqueror resisted with firmness and humanity those servile clamors, which were dictated by flattery as well as by resentment. Informers were punished and discouraged; the innocent, who had suffered under the late tyranny, were recalled from exile and restored to their estates. A general act of oblivion quieted the minds and settled the property of the people, both in Italy and in Africa. The first time that Constantine honored the senate with his presence, he recapitulated his own services and exploits in a modest oration, assured that illustrious order of his sincere regard, and promised to reestablish its ancient dignity and privileges. The grateful senate repaid these unmeaning professions by the empty titles of honor which it was yet in their power to bestow; and without presuming to ratify the authority of Constantine, they passed a decree to assign him the first rank among the three *Augusti* who governed the Roman world. Games and festivals were instituted to preserve the fame of his victory, and several edifices raised at the expense of Maxentius were dedicated to the honor of his successful rival. The triumphal arch of Constantine still remains a melancholy proof of the decline of the arts, and a singular testimony of the meanest vanity. As it was not possible to find in the capital of the empire a sculptor who was capable of adorning that public monument, the arch of Trajan, without any respect either for his memory or for the rules of propriety, was stripped of its most elegant figures. The difference of times and persons, of actions and characters, was totally disregarded. The Parthian captives appear prostrate at the feet of a prince who never carried his arms beyond the Euphrates; and curious antiquarians can still discover the head of Trajan on the trophies of Constantine. The new ornaments which it was necessary to introduce between the vacancies of ancient sculpture are executed in the rudest and most unskillful manner.

The final abolition of the Praetorian guards was a measure of prudence as well as of revenge. Those haughty troops, whose numbers and privileges had been restored and even augmented by Maxentius, were forever suppressed by Constantine. Their fortified camp was destroyed, and the few Praetorians who had escaped the fury of the sword were dispersed among the legions and banished to the frontiers of the empire, where they might be serviceable without again becoming dangerous. By suppressing the troops which were usually stationed in Rome, Constantine gave the fatal blow to the dignity of the senate and people, and the disarmed capital was exposed without protection to the insults or neglect of its distant master. We may observe that in this last effort to preserve their expiring freedom, the Romans, from the apprehension of a tribute, had raised Maxentius to the throne. He exacted that tribute from the senate under the name of a free gift. They implored the assistance of Constantine. He vanquished the tyrant, and converted the free gift into a perpetual tax. The senators, according to the declaration which was required of their property, were divided into several classes. The most opulent paid annually eight pounds of gold, the next class paid four, the last two, and those whose poverty might have claimed an exemption were assessed, however, at seven pieces of gold. Besides the regular members of the senate, their sons, their descendants, and even their relations enjoyed the vain privileges and supported the heavy burdens of the senatorial order; nor will it any longer excite our surprise that Constantine should be attentive to increase the number of persons who were included under so useful a description. After the defeat of Maxentius, the victorious emperor passed no more than two or three months in Rome, which he visited twice during the remainder of his life, to celebrate the solemn festivals of the tenth and of the twentieth years of his reign. Constantine was almost perpetually in motion, to exercise the legions or to inspect the state of the provinces. Treves, Milan, Aquileia, Sirmium, Naissus, and Thessalonica were the occasional places of his residence, till he founded a NEW ROME on the confines of Europe and Asia.

Before Constantine marched into Italy, he had secured the friendship, or at least the neutrality, of Licinius, the Illyrian emperor. He had promised his sister Constantia in marriage to that prince; but the celebration of the nuptials was deferred till after the conclusion of the war, and the interview of the two emperors at Milan which was appointed for that purpose appeared to cement the union of their families and interests [March A.D. 313]. In the midst of the public festivity they were suddenly obliged to take leave of each other. An inroad of the Franks summoned Constantine to the Rhine, and the hostile approach of the sovereign of Asia demanded the immediate presence of Licinius. Maximin had been the secret ally of Maxentius, and without being discouraged by his fate, he resolved to try the fortune of a civil war. He moved out of Syria towards the frontiers of Bithynia in the depth of winter. . . . After a fruitless negotiation in which the two princes attempted to seduce the fidelity of each other's adherents, they had recourse to arms [April 30, A.D. 313]. . . . [Maximin] survived his misfortune only three or four months. His death, which happened at Tarsus, was variously ascribed to despair, to poison, and to the divine justice. As Maximin was alike destitute of abilities and of virtue, he was lamented neither by the people nor by the soldiers. The provinces of the East, delivered from the terrors of civil war, cheerfully acknowledged the authority of Licinius.†

The Roman world was now divided between Constantine and Licinius, the former of whom was master of the West and the latter of the East. It might perhaps have been expected that the conquerors, fatigued with civil war and connected by a private as well as public alliance, would have renounced, or at least would have suspended, any further designs of ambition. And yet a year had scarcely elapsed after the death of Maximin before the victorious emperors turned their arms against each other [A.D. 314]. The genius, the success, and the aspiring temper of Constantine may seem to mark him out as the aggressor; but the perfidious character of Licinius justifies the most unfavorable suspicions.†

The first battle was fought near Cibalis, a city of Pannonia situated on the river Save, about fifty miles above Sirmium [October 8, A.D. 315]. . . . The judicious retreat of Licinius saved the remainder of his troops from a total defeat. . . . In his flight [Licinius] bestowed the precarious title of Caesar on Valens, his general on the Illyrian frontier.

The plain of Mardia in Thrace was the theater of a second battle no less obstinate and bloody than the former. The troops on both sides displayed the same valor and discipline; and the victory was once more decided by the superior abilities of Constantine. . . . The loss of two battles and of his bravest veterans reduced the fierce spirit of Licinius to sue for peace. His ambassador Mistrianus was admitted to the audience of Constantine: he expatiated on the common topics of moderation and humanity which are so familiar to the eloquence of the vanquished; represented in the most insinuating language that the event of the war was still doubtful, whilst its inevitable calamities were alike pernicious to both the contending parties; and declared that he was authorized to propose a lasting and honorable peace in the name of the *two* emperors his masters. Constantine received the mention of Valens with indignation and contempt. "It was not for such a purpose," he sternly replied, "that we have advanced from the shores of the Western ocean in an uninterrupted course of combats and victories that, after rejecting an ungrateful kinsman, we should accept for our colleague a contemptible slave. The abdication of Valens is the first article of the treaty." It was necessary to accept this humiliating condition; and the unhappy Valens, after a reign of a few days, was deprived of the purple and of his life. As soon as this obstacle was removed, the tranquility of the Roman world was easily restored. The successive defeats of Licinius had ruined his forces, but they had displayed his courage and abilities. His situation was almost desperate, but the efforts of despair are sometimes formidable, and the good sense of Constantine preferred a great and certain advantage to a third trial of the chance of arms. He consented to leave his rival, or, as he again styled Licinius, his friend and brother, in the possession of Thrace, Asia Minor, Syria, and Egypt; but the provinces of Pannonia, Dalmatia, Dacia, Macedonia, and Greece were yielded to the Western empire, and the dominions of Constantine now extended from the confines of Caledonia to the extremity of Peloponnesus. It was stipulated by the same treaty that three royal youths, the sons of emperors, should be called to the hopes of the succession. Crispus and the young Constantine were soon afterwards declared Caesars in the West, while the younger Licinius was invested with the same dignity in the East. In this double proportion of honors, the conqueror asserted the superiority of his arms and power.

The reconciliation of Constantine and Licinius, though it was embittered by resentment and jealousy, by the remembrance of recent injuries, and by the apprehension of future dangers, maintained, however, above eight years, the tranquility of the Roman world [A.D. 315–323]. As a very regular series of the Imperial laws commences about this period, it would not be difficult to transcribe the civil regulations which employed the leisure of Constantine. But the most important of his institutions are intimately connected with the new system of policy and religion, which was not perfectly established till the last and peaceful years of his reign. There are many of his laws which, as far as they concern the rights and property of individuals and the practice of the bar, are more properly referred to the private than to the public jurisprudence of the empire; and he published many edicts of so local and temporary a nature that they would ill deserve the notice of a general history. Two laws, however, may be selected from the crowd; the one for its importance, the other for its singularity; the former for its remarkable benevolence, the latter for its excessive severity. 1. The horrid practice, so familiar to the ancients, of exposing or murdering their new-born infants was become every day more frequent in the provinces, and especially in Italy. It was the effect of distress; and the distress was principally occasioned by the intolerant burden of taxes and by the vexatious as well as cruel prosecutions of the officers of the revenue against their insolvent debtors. The less opulent or less industrious part of mankind, instead of rejoicing in an increase of family, deemed it an act of paternal tenderness to release their children from the impending miseries of a life which they themselves were unable to support. The humanity of Constantine, moved, perhaps, by some recent and extraordinary instances of despair, engaged him to address an edict to all the cities of Italy, and afterwards of Africa, directing immediate and sufficient relief to be given to those parents who should produce before the magistrates the children whom their own poverty would not allow them to educate. But the promise was too liberal, and the provision too vague, to effect any general or permanent benefit. The law, though it may merit some praise, served rather to display than to alleviate the public distress. It still remains an authentic monument to contradict and confound those venal orators who were too well satisfied with their own situation to discover either vice or misery under the government of a generous sovereign. 2. The laws of Constantine against rapes were dictated with very little indulgence for the most amiable weaknesses of human nature; since the description of that crime was applied not only to the brutal violence which compelled but even to the gentle seduction which might persuade an unmarried woman under the age of twenty-five to leave the house of her parents. "The successful ravisher was punished with death; and as if simple death was inadequate to the enormity of his guilt, he was either burnt alive or torn in pieces by wild beasts in the amphitheater. The virgin's declaration that she had been carried away with her own consent instead of saving her lover exposed her to share his fate. The duty of a public prosecution was entrusted to the parents of the guilty or unfortunate maid; and if the sentiments of nature prevailed on them to dissemble the injury and to repair by a subsequent marriage the honor of their family, they were themselves punished by exile and confiscation. The slaves, whether male or female, who were convicted of having been accessory to rape or seduction were burnt alive, or put to death by the ingenious torture of pouring down their throats a quantity of melted lead. As the crime was of a public kind [i.e., a criminal offense against the state], the accusation was permitted even to strangers. The commencement of the action was not limited to any term of years, and the consequences of the sentence were extended to the innocent offspring of such an irregular union." But whenever the offense inspires less horror than the punishment, the rigor of penal law is obliged to give way to the common feelings of mankind. The most odious parts of this edict were softened or repealed in the subsequent reigns; and even Constantine himself very frequently alleviated, by partial acts of mercy, the stern temper of his general institutions. Such, indeed, was the singular humor of that emperor, who showed himself as indulgent and even remiss in the execution of his laws as he was severe and even cruel in the enacting of them. It is scarcely possible to observe a more decisive symptom of weakness, either in the character of the prince, or in the constitution of the government.

The civil administration was sometimes interrupted by the military defense of the empire. Crispus, a youth of the most amiable character, who had received with the title of Caesar the command of the Rhine, distinguished his conduct, as well as valor, in several victories over the Franks and Alemanni, and taught the Barbarians of that frontier to dread the eldest son of Constantine and the grandson of Constantius. The emperor himself had assumed the more difficult and important province of the Danube. . . . At the head of his legions he passed the Danube after repairing the bridge which had been constructed by Trajan, penetrated into the strongest recesses of Dacia, and when he had inflicted a severe revenge condescended to give peace to the suppliant Goths, on condition that, as often as they were required, they should supply his armies with a body of forty thousand soldiers. Exploits like these were no doubt honorable to Constantine and beneficial to the state; but it may surely be questioned whether they can justify the exaggerated assertion of Eusebius that ALL SCYTHIA, as far as the extremity of the North, divided as it was into so many names and nations of the most various and savage manners, had been added by his victorious arms to the Roman empire.

In this exalted state of glory, it was impossible that Constantine should any longer endure a partner in the empire. Confiding in the superiority of his genius and military power, he determined, without any previous injury, to exert them for the destruction of Licinius, whose advanced age and unpopular vices seemed to offer a very easy conquest. But the old emperor, awakened by the approaching danger, deceived the expectations of his friends as well as of his enemies. Calling forth that spirit and those abilities by which he had deserved the friendship of Galerius and the Imperial purple, he prepared himself for the contest.

[*Constantine vanquishes the forces of Licinius at Hadrianople, Byzantium, and Chrysopolis. Crispus, the son of Constantine, achieves signal successes on his father's behalf as a naval commander, but excites paternal jealousy (A.D. 323).*]

[Licinius] retired to Nicomedia, rather with the view of gaining some time for negotiation than with the hope of any effectual defense. Constantia, his wife and the sister of Constantine, interceded with her brother in favor of her husband and obtained from his policy, rather than from his compassion, a solemn promise, confirmed by an oath, that after . . . the resignation of the purple, Licinius himself should be permitted to pass the remainder of his life in peace and affluence. The behavior of Constantia, and her relation to the contending parties, naturally recalls the remembrance of that virtuous matron who was the sister of Augustus and the wife of Antony. But the temper of mankind was altered, and it was no longer esteemed infamous for a Roman to survive his honor and independence. Licinius solicited and accepted the pardon of his offenses, laid himself and his purple at the feet of his *lord* and *master,* was raised from the ground with insulting pity, was admitted the same day to the Imperial banquet, and soon afterwards was sent away to Thessalonica, which had been chosen for the place of his confinement. His confinement was soon terminated by death, and it is doubtful whether a tumult of the soldiers or a decree of the senate was suggested as the motive for his execution. According to the rules of tyranny, he was accused of forming a conspiracy and of holding a treasonable correspondence with the Barbarians; but as he was never convicted, either by his own conduct or by any legal evidence, we may perhaps be allowed, from his weakness, to presume his innocence. The memory of Licinius was branded with infamy, his statues were thrown down, and by a hasty edict of such mischievous tendency that it was almost immediately corrected, all his laws and all the judicial proceedings of his reign were at once abolished. By this victory of Constantine, the Roman world was again united under the authority of one emperor [A.D. 324], thirty-seven years after Diocletian had divided his power and provinces with his associate Maximian.

The successive steps of the elevation of Constantine, from his first assuming the purple at York to the resignation of Licinius at Nicomedia, have been related with some minuteness and precision, not only as the events are in themselves both interesting and important, but still more as they contributed to the decline of the empire by the expense of blood and treasure, and by the perpetual increase, as well of the taxes, as of the military establishment. The foundation of Constantinople, and the establishment of the Christian religion, were the immediate and memorable consequences of this revolution.

CHAPTER XV

PROGRESS OF THE CHRISTIAN RELIGION

The progress of the Christian religion, and the sentiments,
manners, numbers, and condition of the primitive Christians.

A candid but rational inquiry into the progress and establishment of Christianity may be considered as a very essential part of the history of the Roman empire. While that great body was invaded by open violence or undermined by slow decay, a pure and humble religion gently insinuated itself into the minds of men, grew up in silence and obscurity, derived new vigor from opposition, and finally erected the triumphant banner of the Cross on the ruins of the Capitol. Nor was the influence of Christianity confined to the period or to the limits of the Roman empire. After a revolution of thirteen or fourteen centuries, that religion is still professed by the nations of Europe, the most distinguished portion of humankind in arts and learning as well as in arms. By the industry and zeal of the Europeans, it has been widely diffused to the most distant shores of Asia and Africa; and by the means of their colonies has been firmly established from Canada to Chile, in a world unknown to the ancients.

But this inquiry, however useful or entertaining, is attended with two peculiar difficulties. The scanty and suspicious materials of ecclesiastical history seldom enable us to dispel the dark cloud that hangs over the first age of the church. The great law of impartiality too often obliges us to reveal the imperfections of the uninspired teachers and believers of the gospel; and, to a careless observer, *their* faults may seem to cast a shade on the faith which they professed. But the scandal of the pious Christian, and the fallacious triumph of the Infidel, should cease as soon as they recollect not only *by whom*, but likewise *to whom*, the Divine Revelation was given. The theologian may indulge the pleasing task of describing Religion as she descended from Heaven, arrayed in her native purity. A more melancholy duty is imposed on the historian. He must discover the inevitable mixture of error and corruption which she contracted in a long residence upon earth, among a weak and degenerate race of beings.

Our curiosity is naturally prompted to inquire by what means the Christian faith obtained so remarkable a victory over the established religions of the earth. To this inquiry, an obvious but satisfactory answer may be returned; that it was owing to the convincing evidence of the doctrine itself, and to the ruling providence of its great Author. But as truth and reason seldom find so favorable a reception in the world, and as the wisdom of Providence frequently condescends to use the passions of the human heart and the general circumstances of mankind as instruments to execute its purpose, we may still be permitted, though with becoming submission, to ask not indeed what were the first but what were the secondary causes of the rapid growth of the Christian church. It will, perhaps, appear that it was most effectually favored and assisted by the five following causes: I. The inflexible, and if we may use the expression, the intolerant zeal of the Christians, derived, it is true, from the Jewish religion, but purified from the narrow and unsocial spirit which, instead of inviting, had deterred the Gentiles from embracing the law of Moses. II. The doctrine of a future life, improved by every additional circumstance which could give weight and efficacy to that important truth. III. The miraculous powers ascribed to the primitive church. IV. The pure and austere morals of the Christians. V. The union and discipline of the Christian republic, which gradually formed an independent and increasing state in the heart of the Roman empire.

I. We have already described the religious harmony of the ancient world and the facility with which the most different and even hostile nations embraced, or at least respected, each other's superstitions. A single people refused to join in the common intercourse of mankind. The Jews, who, under the Assyrian and Persian monarchies had languished for many ages the most despised portion of their slaves, emerged from obscurity under the successors of Alexander; and as they multiplied to a surprising degree in the East, and afterwards in the West, they soon excited the curiosity and wonder of other nations. The sullen obstinacy with which they maintained their peculiar rites and unsocial manners seemed to mark them out as a distinct species of men, who boldly professed or who faintly disguised their implacable habits to the rest of humankind. Neither the violence of Antiochus, nor the arts of Herod, nor the example of the circumjacent nations could ever persuade the Jews to associate with the institutions of Moses the elegant mythology of the Greeks. According to the maxims of universal toleration, the Romans protected a superstition which they despised. The polite Augustus condescended to give orders that sacrifices should be offered for his prosperity in the temple of Jerusalem; whilst the meanest of the posterity of Abraham who should have paid the same homage to the Jupiter of the Capitol would have been an object of abhorrence to himself and to his brethren. But the moderation of the conquerors was insufficient to appease the jealous prejudices of their subjects, who were alarmed and scandalized at the ensigns of Paganism which necessarily introduced themselves into a Roman province. The mad attempt of Caligula to place his own statue in the temple of Jerusalem was defeated by the unanimous resolution of a people who dreaded death much less than such an idolatrous profanation. Their attachment to the law of Moses was equal to their detestation of foreign religions. The current of zeal and devotion, as it was contracted into a narrow channel, ran with the strength, and sometimes with the fury, of a torrent.

This inflexible perseverance, which appeared so odious or so ridiculous to the ancient world, assumes a more awful character, since Providence has deigned to reveal to us the mysterious history of the chosen people. But the devout and even scrupulous attachment to the Mosaic religion, so conspicuous among the Jews who lived under the second temple, becomes still more surprising if it is compared with the stubborn incredulity of their forefathers. When the law was given in thunder from Mount Sinai, when the tides of the ocean and the course of the planets were suspended for the convenience of the Israelites, and when temporal rewards and punishments were the immediate consequences of their piety or disobedience, they perpetually relapsed into rebellion against the visible majesty of their Divine King, placed the idols of the nations in the sanctuary of Jehovah, and imitated every fantastic ceremony that was practiced in the tents of the Arabs or in the cities of Phoenicia. As the protection of Heaven was deservedly withdrawn from the ungrateful race, their faith acquired a proportionable degree of vigor and purity. The contemporaries of Moses and Joshua had beheld with careless indifference the most amazing miracles. Under the pressure of every calamity, the belief of those miracles has preserved the Jews of a later period from the universal contagion of idolatry; and in contradiction to every known principle of the human mind, that singular people seems to have yielded a stronger and more ready assent to the traditions of their remote ancestors than to the evidence of their own senses.

The Jewish religion was admirably fitted for defense, but it was never designed for conquest; and it seems probable that the number of proselytes was never much superior to that of apostates. The divine promises were originally made, and the distinguishing rite of circumcision was enjoined, to a single family. When the posterity of Abraham had multiplied like the sands of the sea, the Deity, from whose mouth they received a system of laws and ceremonies, declared himself the proper and as it were the national God of Israel, and with the most jealous care separated his favorite people from the rest of mankind. The conquest of the land of Canaan was accompanied with so many wonderful and with so many bloody circumstances that the victorious Jews were left in a state of irreconcilable hostility with all their neighbors. They had been commanded to extirpate some of the most idolatrous tribes, and the execution of the divine will had seldom been retarded by the weakness of humanity. With the other nations they were forbidden to contract any marriages or alliances; and the prohibition of receiving them into the congregation, which in some cases was perpetual, almost always extended to the third, to the seventh, or even to the tenth generation. The obligation of preaching to the Gentiles the faith of Moses had never been inculcated as a precept of the law, nor were the Jews inclined to impose it on themselves as a voluntary duty.

In the admission of new citizens, that unsocial people was actuated by the selfish vanity of the Greeks rather than by the generous policy of Rome. The descendants of Abraham were flattered by the opinion that they alone were the heirs of the covenant, and they were apprehensive of diminishing the value of their inheritance by sharing it too easily with the strangers of the earth. A larger acquaintance with mankind extended their knowledge without correcting their prejudices; and whenever the God of Israel acquired any new votaries, he was much more indebted to the inconstant humor of Polytheism than to the active zeal of his own missionaries. The religion of Moses seems to be instituted for a particular country as well as for a single nation; and if a strict obedience had been paid to the order that every male, three times in the year, should present himself before the Lord Jehovah, it would have been impossible that the Jews could ever have spread themselves beyond the narrow limits of the promised land. That obstacle was indeed removed by the destruction of the temple of Jerusalem; but the most considerable part of the Jewish religion was involved in its destruction; and the Pagans, who had long wondered at the strange report of an empty sanctuary, were at a loss to discover what could be the object or what could be the instruments of a worship which was destitute of temples and of altars, of priests and of sacrifices. Yet even in their fallen state, the Jews, still asserting their lofty and exclusive privileges, shunned instead of courting the society of strangers. They still insisted with inflexible rigor on those parts of the law which it was in their power to practice. Their peculiar distinctions of days, of meats, and a variety of trivial though burdensome observances were so many objects of disgust and aversion for the other nations, to whose habits and prejudices they were diametrically opposite. The painful and even dangerous rite of circumcision was alone capable of repelling a willing proselyte from the door of the synagogue.

Under these circumstances, Christianity offered itself to the world armed with the strength of the Mosaic law and delivered from the weight of its fetters. An exclusive zeal for the truth of religion and the unity of God was as carefully inculcated in the new as in the ancient system: and whatever was now revealed to mankind concerning the nature and designs of the Supreme Being was fitted to increase their reverence for that mysterious doctrine. The divine authority of Moses and the prophets was admitted, and even established, as the firmest basis of Christianity. From the beginning of the world, an uninterrupted series of predictions had announced and prepared the long-expected coming of the Messiah, who, in compliance with the gross apprehensions of the Jews, had been more frequently represented under the character of a King and Conqueror than under that of a Prophet, a Martyr, and the Son of God. By his expiatory sacrifice, the imperfect sacrifices of the temple were at once consummated and abolished. The ceremonial law, which consisted only of types and figures, was succeeded by a pure and spiritual worship, equally adapted to all climates as well as to every condition of mankind; and to the initiation of blood was substituted a more harmless initiation of water.

The promise of divine favor, instead of being partially confined to the posterity of Abraham, was universally proposed to the freeman and the slave, to the Greek and to the Barbarian, to the Jew and to the Gentile. Every privilege that could raise the proselyte from earth to Heaven, that could exalt his devotion, secure his happiness, or even gratify that secret pride which, under the semblance of devotion, insinuates itself into the human heart, was still reserved for the members of the Christian church; but at the same time all mankind was permitted, and even solicited, to accept the glorious distinction, which was not only proffered as a favor but imposed as an obligation. It became the most sacred duty of a new convert to diffuse among his friends and relations the inestimable blessing which he had received, and to warn them against a refusal that would be severely punished as a criminal disobedience to the will of a benevolent but all-powerful Deity.

The enfranchisement of the church from the bonds of the synagogue was a work, however, of some time and of some difficulty. The Jewish converts, who acknowledged Jesus in the character of the Messiah foretold by their ancient oracles, respected him as a prophetic teacher of virtue and religion; but they obstinately adhered to the ceremonies of their ancestors and were desirous of imposing them on the Gentiles, who continually augmented the number of believers. These Judaizing Christians seem to have argued with some degree of plausibility from the divine origin of the Mosaic law, and from the immutable perfections of its great Author. They affirmed that if the Being, who is the same through all eternity, had designed to abolish those sacred rites which had served to distinguish his chosen people, the repeal of them would have been no less clear and solemn than their first promulgation: *that,* instead of those frequent declarations which either suppose or assert the perpetuity of the Mosaic religion, it would have been represented as a provisionary scheme intended to last only to the coming of the Messiah, who should instruct mankind in a more perfect mode of faith and of worship: *that* the Messiah himself, and his disciples who conversed with him on earth, instead of authorizing by their example the most minute observances of the Mosaic law, would have published to the world the abolition of those useless and obsolete ceremonies, without suffering Christianity to remain during so many years obscurely confounded among the sects of the Jewish church. Arguments like these appear to have been used in the defense of the expiring cause of the Mosaic law; but the industry of our learned divines has abundantly explained the ambiguous language of the Old Testament and the ambiguous conduct of the apostolic teachers. It was proper gradually to unfold the system of the gospel, and to pronounce, with the utmost caution and tenderness, a sentence of condemnation so repugnant to the inclination and prejudices of the believing Jews.

The history of the church of Jerusalem affords a lively proof of the necessity of those precautions, and of the deep impression which the Jewish religion had made on the minds of its sectaries. The first fifteen bishops of Jerusalem were all circumcised Jews; and the congregation over which they presided united the law of Moses with the doctrine of Christ. It was natural that the primitive tradition of a church which was founded only forty days after the death of Christ, and was governed almost as many years under the immediate inspection of his apostle, should be received as the standard of orthodoxy. The distant churches very frequently appealed to the authority of their venerable Parent, and relieved her distresses by a liberal contribution of alms. But when numerous and opulent societies were established in the great cities of the empire, in Antioch, Alexandria, Ephesus, Corinth, and Rome, the reverence which Jerusalem had inspired to all the Christian colonies insensibly diminished. The Jewish converts, or, as they were afterwards called, the Nazarenes, who had laid the foundations of the church, soon found themselves overwhelmed by the increasing multitudes that from all the various religions of Polytheism enlisted under the banner of Christ: and the Gentiles, who, with the approbation of their peculiar apostle, had rejected the intolerable weight of the Mosaic ceremonies, at length refused to their more scrupulous brethren the same toleration which at first they had humbly solicited for their own practice.[†]

The name of Nazarenes was deemed too honorable for those Christian Jews, and they soon received, from the supposed poverty of their understanding as well as of their condition, the contemptuous epithet of Ebionites. [It] became a matter of doubt and controversy whether a man who sincerely acknowledged Jesus as the Messiah, but who still continued to observe the law of Moses, could possibly hope for salvation. The humane temper of Justin Martyr inclined him to answer this question in the affirmative; and though he expressed himself with the most guarded diffidence, he ventured to determine in favor of such an imperfect Christian if he were content to practice the Mosaic ceremonies without pretending to assert their general use or necessity. But when Justin was pressed to declare the sentiment of the church, he confessed that there were very many among the orthodox Christians who not only excluded their Judaizing brethren from the hope of salvation, but who declined any intercourse with them in the common offices of friendship, hospitality, and social life. The more rigorous opinion prevailed, as it was natural to expect, over the milder; and an eternal bar of separation was fixed between the disciples of Moses and those of Christ. The unfortunate Ebionites, rejected from one religion as apostates and from the other as heretics, found themselves compelled to assume a more decided character; and although some traces of that obsolete sect may be discovered as late as the fourth century, they insensibly melted away, either into the church or the synagogue.

While the orthodox church preserved a just medium between excessive veneration and improper contempt for the law of Moses, the various heretics deviated into equal but opposite extremes of error and extravagance. From the acknowledged truth of the Jewish religion, the Ebionites had concluded that it could never be abolished. From its supposed imperfections, the Gnostics as hastily inferred that it never was instituted by the wisdom of the Deity. There are some objections against the authority of Moses and the prophets which too readily present themselves to the skeptical mind; though they can only be derived from our ignorance of remote antiquity, and from our incapacity to form an adequate judgment of the divine economy. These objections were eagerly embraced and as petulantly urged by the vain science of the Gnostics. As those heretics were, for the most part, averse to the pleasures of sense, they morosely arraigned the polygamy of the patriarchs, the gallantries of David, and the seraglio of Solomon. The conquest of the land of Canaan, and the extirpation of the unsuspecting natives, they were at a loss how to reconcile with the common notions of humanity and justice. But when they recollected the sanguinary list of murders, of executions, and of massacres which stain almost every page of the Jewish annals, they acknowledged that the Barbarians of Palestine had exercised as much compassion towards their idolatrous enemies as they had ever shown to their friends or countrymen. Passing from the sectaries of the law to the law itself, they asserted that it was impossible that a religion which consisted only of bloody sacrifices and trifling ceremonies, and whose rewards as well as punishments were all of a carnal and temporal nature, could inspire the love of virtue or restrain the impetuosity of passion. The Mosaic account of the creation and fall of man was treated with profane derision by the Gnostics, who would not listen with patience to the repose of the Deity after six days' labor, to the rib of Adam, the garden of Eden, the trees of life and of knowledge, the speaking serpent, the forbidden fruit, and the condemnation pronounced against humankind for the venial offense of their first progenitors. The God of Israel was impiously represented by the Gnostics as a being liable to passion and to error, capricious in his favor, implacable in his resentment, meanly jealous of his superstitious worship, and confining his partial providence to a single people and to this transitory life. In such a character they could discover none of the features of the wise and omnipotent Father of the universe. They allowed that the religion of the Jews was somewhat less criminal than the idolatry of the Gentiles; but it was their fundamental doctrine that the Christ whom they adored as the first and brightest emanation of the Deity appeared upon earth to rescue mankind from their various errors and to reveal a new system of truth and perfection. The most learned of the fathers, by a very singular condescension, have imprudently admitted the sophistry of the Gnostics. Acknowledging that the literal sense is repugnant to every principle of faith as well as reason, they deem themselves secure and invulnerable behind the ample veil of allegory, which they carefully spread over every tender part of the Mosaic dispensation.

It has been remarked with more ingenuity than truth that the virgin purity of the church was never violated by schism or heresy before the reign of Trajan or Hadrian, about one hundred years after the death of Christ. We may observe with much more propriety that during that period the disciples of the Messiah were indulged in a freer latitude, both of faith and practice, than has ever been allowed in succeeding ages. As the terms of communion were insensibly narrowed, and the spiritual authority of the prevailing party was exercised with increasing severity, many of its most respectable adherents who were called upon to renounce were provoked to assert their private opinions, to pursue the consequences of their mistaken principles, and openly to erect the standard of rebellion against the unity of the church. The Gnostics were distinguished as the most polite, the most learned, and the most wealthy of the Christian name; and that general appellation, which expressed a superiority of knowledge, was either assumed by their own pride or ironically bestowed by the envy of their adversaries. They were almost without exception of the race of the Gentiles, and their principal founders seem to have been natives of Syria or Egypt, where the warmth of the climate disposes both the mind and the body to indolent and contemplative devotion. The Gnostics blended with the faith of Christ many sublime but obscure tenets which they derived from Oriental philosophy, and even from the religion of Zoroaster, concerning the eternity of matter, the existence of two principles, and the mysterious hierarchy of the invisible world. As soon as they launched out into that vast abyss, they delivered themselves to the guidance of a disordered imagination; and as the paths of error are various and infinite, the Gnostics were imperceptibly divided into more than fifty particular sects, of whom the most celebrated appear to have been the Basilidians, the Valentinians, the Marcionites, and, in a still later period, the Manichaeans. Each of these sects could boast of its bishops and congregations, of its doctors and martyrs; and instead of the Four Gospels adopted by the church, the heretics produced a multitude of histories, in which the actions and discourses of Christ and of his apostles were adapted to their respective tenets. The success of the Gnostics was rapid and extensive. They covered Asia and Egypt, established themselves in Rome, and sometimes penetrated into the provinces of the West. For the most part they arose in the second century, flourished during the third, and were suppressed in the fourth or fifth, by the prevalence of more fashionable controversies and by the superior ascendant of the reigning power. Though they constantly disturbed the peace, and frequently disgraced the name, of religion, they contributed to assist rather than to retard the progress of Christianity. The Gentile converts, whose strongest objections and prejudices were directed against the law of Moses, could find admission into many Christian societies, which required not from their untutored mind any belief of an antecedent revelation. Their faith was insensibly fortified and enlarged, and the church was ultimately benefited by the conquests of its most inveterate enemies.

But whatever difference of opinion might subsist between the Orthodox, the Ebionites, and the Gnostics concerning the divinity or the obligation of the Mosaic law, they were all equally animated by the same exclusive zeal, and by the same abhorrence for idolatry, which had distinguished the Jews from the other nations of the ancient world. The philosopher who considered the system of Polytheism as a composition of human fraud and error could disguise a smile of contempt under the mask of devotion without apprehending that either the mockery or the compliance would expose him to the resentment of any invisible or, as he conceived them, imaginary powers. But the established religions of Paganism were seen by the primitive Christians in a much more odious and formidable light. It was the universal sentiment both of the church and of heretics that the demons were the authors, the patrons, and the objects of idolatry. Those rebellious spirits who had been degraded from the rank of angels and cast down into the infernal pit were still permitted to roam upon earth, to torment the bodies and to seduce the minds of sinful men. The demons soon discovered and abused the natural propensity of the human heart towards devotion, and, artfully withdrawing the adoration of mankind from their Creator, they usurped the place and honors of the Supreme Deity. By the success of their malicious contrivances, they at once gratified their own vanity and revenge and obtained the only comfort of which they were yet susceptible, the hope of involving the human species in the participation of their guilt and misery. It was confessed, or at least it was imagined, that they had distributed among themselves the most important characters of Polytheism, one demon assuming the name and attributes of Jupiter, another of Aesculapius, a third of Venus, and a fourth perhaps of Apollo; and that, by the advantage of their long experience and aerial nature, they were enabled to execute with sufficient skill and dignity the parts which they had undertaken. They lurked in the temples, instituted festivals and sacrifices, invented fables, pronounced oracles, and were frequently allowed to perform miracles. The Christians, who by the interposition of evil spirits could so readily explain every preternatural appearance, were disposed and even desirous to admit the most extravagant fictions of the Pagan mythology. But the belief of the Christian was accompanied with horror. The most trifling mark of respect to the national worship he considered as a direct homage yielded to the demon, and as an act of rebellion against the majesty of God.

In consequence of this opinion, it was the first but arduous duty of a Christian to preserve himself pure and undefiled by the practice of idolatry. The religion of the nations was not merely a speculative doctrine professed in the schools or preached in the temples. The innumerable deities and rites of Polytheism were closely interwoven with every circumstance of business or pleasure, of public or of private life; and it seemed impossible to escape the observance of them without at the same time renouncing the commerce of mankind and all the offices and amusements of society. The important transactions of peace and war were prepared or concluded by solemn sacrifices in which the magistrate, the senator, and the soldier were obliged to preside or to participate. The public spectacles were an essential part of the cheerful devotion of the Pagans, and the gods were supposed to accept, as the most grateful offering, the games that the prince and people celebrated in honor of their peculiar festivals. The Christian, who with pious horror avoided the abomination of the circus or the theater, found himself encompassed with infernal snares in every convivial entertainment, as often as his friends, invoking the hospitable deities, poured out libations to each other's happiness. When the bride, struggling with well-affected reluctance, was forced into hymeneal pomp over the threshold of her new habitation, or when the sad procession of the dead slowly moved towards the funeral pile; the Christian, on these interesting occasions, was compelled to desert the persons who were the dearest to him rather than contract the guilt inherent to those impious ceremonies. Every art and every trade that was in the least concerned in the framing or adorning of idols was polluted by the stain of idolatry; a severe sentence, since it devoted to eternal misery the far greater part of the community which is employed in the exercise of liberal or mechanic professions. If we cast our eyes over the numerous remains of antiquity, we shall perceive that besides the immediate representations of the gods and the holy instruments of their worship, the elegant forms and agreeable fictions consecrated by the imagination of the Greeks were introduced as the richest ornaments of the houses, the dress, and the furniture of the Pagan. Even the arts of music and painting, of eloquence and poetry, flowed from the same impure origin. In the style of the fathers, Apollo and the Muses were the organs of the infernal spirit; Homer and Virgil were the most eminent of his servants; and the beautiful mythology which pervades and animates the compositions of their genius is destined to celebrate the glory of the demons. Even the common language of Greece and Rome abounded with familiar but impious expressions which the imprudent Christian might too carelessly utter, or too patiently hear.

The dangerous temptations which on every side lurked in ambush to surprise the unguarded believer assailed him with redoubled violence on the days of solemn festivals. So artfully were they framed and disposed throughout the year that superstition always wore the appearance of pleasure, and often of virtue. Some of the most sacred festivals in the Roman ritual were destined to salute the new calends of January with vows of public and private felicity; to indulge the pious remembrance of the dead and living; to ascertain the inviolable bounds of property; to hail, on the return of spring, the genial powers of fecundity; to perpetuate the two memorable eras of Rome, the foundation of the city and that of the republic; and to restore, during the humane license of the Saturnalia, the primitive equality of mankind. Some idea may be conceived of the abhorrence of the Christians for such impious ceremonies by the scrupulous delicacy which they displayed on a much less alarming occasion. On days of general festivity, it was the custom of the ancients to adorn their doors with lamps and with branches of laurel, and to crown their heads with a garland of flowers. This innocent and elegant practice might perhaps have been tolerated as a mere civil institution. But it most unluckily happened that the doors were under the protection of the household gods, that the laurel was sacred to the lover of Daphne, and that garlands of flowers, though frequently worn as a symbol of joy or mourning, had been dedicated in their first origin to the service of superstition. The trembling Christians who were persuaded in this instance to comply with the fashion of their country and the commands of the magistrate, labored under the most gloomy apprehensions, from the reproaches of their own conscience, the censures of the church, and the denunciations of divine vengeance.

Such was the anxious diligence which was required to guard the chastity of the gospel from the infectious breath of idolatry. The superstitious observances of public or private rites were carelessly practiced, from education and habit, by the followers of the established religion. But as often as they occurred, they afforded the Christians an opportunity of declaring and confirming their zealous opposition. By these frequent protestations their attachment to the faith was continually fortified; and in proportion to the increase of zeal, they combated with the more ardor and success in the holy war which they had undertaken against the empire of the demons.

II. . . . [Since] the most sublime efforts of philosophy can extend no further than feebly to point out the desire, the hope, or, at most, the probability of a future state, there is nothing, except a divine revelation, that can ascertain the existence and describe the condition of the invisible country which is destined to receive the souls of men after their separation from the body. But we may perceive several defects inherent to the popular religions of Greece and Rome which rendered them very unequal to so arduous a task. 1. The general system of their mythology was unsupported by any solid proofs; and the wisest among the Pagans had already disclaimed its usurped authority. 2. The description of the infernal regions had been abandoned to the fancy of painters and of poets, who peopled them with so many phantoms and monsters, who dispensed their rewards and punishments with so little equity, that a solemn truth, the most congenial to the human heart, was opposed and disgraced by the absurd mixture of the wildest fictions. 3. The doctrine of a future state was scarcely considered among the devout Polytheists of Greece and Rome as a fundamental article of faith. The providence of the gods, as it related to public communities rather than to private individuals, was principally displayed on the visible theater of the present world. The petitions which were offered on the altars of Jupiter or Apollo expressed the anxiety of their worshipers for temporal happiness, and their ignorance or indifference concerning a future life. The important truth of the immortality of the soul was inculcated with more diligence, as well as success, in India, in Assyria, in Egypt, and in Gaul; and since we cannot attribute such a difference to the superior knowledge of the Barbarians, we must ascribe it to the influence of an established priesthood, which employed the motives of virtue as the instrument of ambition.

We might naturally expect that a principle so essential to religion would have been revealed in the clearest terms to the chosen people of Palestine, and that it might safely have been entrusted to the hereditary priesthood of Aaron. It is incumbent on us to adore the mysterious dispensations of Providence when we discover that the doctrine of the immortality of the soul is omitted in the law of Moses; it is darkly insinuated by the prophets, and during the long period which elapsed between the Egyptian and the Babylonian servitudes, the hopes as well as fears of the Jews appear to have been confined within the narrow compass of the present life. After Cyrus had permitted the exiled nation to return into the promised land, and after Ezra had restored the ancient records of their religion, two celebrated sects, the Sadducees and the Pharisees, insensibly arose at Jerusalem. The former, selected from the more opulent and distinguished ranks of society, were strictly attached to the literal sense of the Mosaic law, and they piously rejected the immortality of the soul as an opinion that received no countenance from the divine book which they revered as the only rule of their faith. To the authority of Scripture the Pharisees added that of tradition, and they accepted, under the name of traditions, several speculative tenets from the philosophy or religion of the eastern nations. The doctrines of fate or predestination, of angels and spirits, and of a future state of rewards and punishments were in the number of these new articles of belief; and as the Pharisees, by the austerity of their manners, had drawn into their party the body of the Jewish people, the immortality of the soul became the prevailing sentiment of the synagogue under the reign of the Asmonaean princes and pontiffs. The temper of the Jews was incapable of contenting itself with such a cold and languid assent as might satisfy the mind of a Polytheist; and as soon as they admitted the idea of a future state, they embraced it with the zeal which has always formed the characteristic of the nation. Their zeal, however, added nothing to its evidence, or even probability: and it was still necessary that the doctrine of life and immortality, which had been dictated by nature, approved by reason, and received by superstition, should obtain the sanction of divine truth from the authority and example of Christ.

When the promise of eternal happiness was proposed to mankind on condition of adopting the faith and of observing the precepts of the gospel, it is no wonder that so advantageous an offer should have been accepted by great numbers of every religion, of every rank, and of every province in the Roman empire. The ancient Christians were animated by a contempt for their present existence, and by a just confidence of immortality, of which the doubtful and imperfect faith of modern ages cannot give us any adequate notion. In the primitive church, the influence of truth was very powerfully strengthened by an opinion which, however it may deserve respect for its usefulness and antiquity, has not been found agreeable to experience. It was universally believed that the end of the world and the kingdom of Heaven were at hand. The near approach of this wonderful event had been predicted by the apostles; the tradition of it was preserved by their earliest disciples, and those who understood in their literal senses the discourse of Christ himself were obliged to expect the second and glorious coming of the Son of Man in the clouds before that generation was totally extinguished which had beheld his humble condition upon earth, and which might still be witness of the calamities of the Jews under Vespasian or Hadrian. The revolution of seventeen centuries has instructed us not to press too closely the mysterious language of prophecy and revelation; but as long as, for wise purposes, this error was permitted to subsist in the church, it was productive of the most salutary effects on the faith and practice of Christians, who lived in the awful expectation of that moment when the globe itself, and all the various races of mankind, should tremble at the appearance of their divine Judge.[†]

The condemnation of the wisest and most virtuous of the Pagans on account of their ignorance or disbelief of the divine truth seems to offend the reason and the humanity of the present age. But the primitive church, whose faith was of a much firmer consistence, delivered over without hesitation to eternal torture the far greater part of the human species. A charitable hope might perhaps be indulged in favor of Socrates or some other sages of antiquity who had consulted the light of reason before that of the gospel had arisen. But it was unanimously affirmed that those who, since the birth or the death of Christ, had obstinately persisted in the worship of the demons neither deserved nor could expect a pardon from the irritated justice of the Deity. These rigid sentiments, which had been unknown to the ancient world, appear to have infused a spirit of bitterness into a system of love and harmony. The ties of blood and friendship were frequently torn asunder by the difference of religious faith; and the Christians, who, in this world, found themselves oppressed by the power of the Pagans, were sometimes seduced by resentment and spiritual pride to delight in the prospect of their future triumph. "You are fond of spectacles," exclaims the stern Tertullian; "expect the greatest of all spectacles, the last and eternal judgment of the universe. How shall I admire, how laugh, how rejoice, how exult, when I behold so many proud monarchs, so many fancied gods, groaning in the lowest abyss of darkness; so many magistrates who persecuted the name of the Lord liquefying in fiercer fires than they ever kindled against the Christians; so many sage philosophers blushing in red-hot flames with their deluded scholars; so many celebrated poets trembling before the tribunal not of Minos but of Christ; so many tragedians, more tuneful in the expression of their own sufferings; so many dancers—!" But the humanity of the reader will permit me to draw a veil over the rest of this infernal description, which the zealous African pursues in a long variety of affected and unfeeling witticisms.

Doubtless there were many among the primitive Christians of a temper more suitable to the meekness and charity of their profession. There were many who felt a sincere compassion for the danger of their friends and countrymen, and who exerted the most benevolent zeal to save them from the impending destruction. The careless Polytheist, assailed by new and unexpected terrors against which neither his priests nor his philosophers could afford him any certain protection, was very frequently terrified and subdued by the menace of eternal tortures. His fears might assist the progress of his faith and reason; and if he could once persuade himself to suspect that the Christian religion might possibly be true, it became an easy task to convince him that it was the safest and most prudent party that he could possibly embrace.

III. The supernatural gifts which even in this life were ascribed to the Christians above the rest of mankind must have conduced to their own comfort, and very frequently to the conviction of infidels. Besides the occasional prodigies, which might sometimes be effected by the immediate interposition of the Deity when he suspended the laws of nature for the service of religion, the Christian church, from the time of the apostles and their first disciples, has claimed an uninterrupted succession of miraculous powers, the gift of tongues, of vision, and of prophecy, the power of expelling demons, of healing the sick, and of raising the dead. The knowledge of foreign languages was frequently communicated to the contemporaries of Irenaeus, though Irenaeus himself was left to struggle with the difficulties of a barbarous dialect whilst he preached the gospel to the natives of Gaul. The divine inspiration, whether it was conveyed in the form of a waking or of a sleeping vision, is described as a favor very liberally bestowed on all ranks of the faithful, on women as on elders, on boys as well as upon bishops.

When their devout minds were sufficiently prepared by a course of prayer, of fasting, and of vigils to receive the extraordinary impulse, they were transported out of their senses and delivered in ecstasy what was inspired, being mere organs of the Holy Spirit, just as a pipe or flute is of him who blows into it. We may add that the design of these visions was for the most part either to disclose the future history, or to guide the present administration, of the church. The expulsion of the demons from the bodies of those unhappy persons whom they had been permitted to torment was considered as a signal though ordinary triumph of religion, and is repeatedly alleged by the ancient apologists as the most convincing evidence of the truth of Christianity. The awful ceremony was usually performed in a public manner and in the presence of a great number of spectators; the patient was relieved by the power or skill of the exorcist, and the vanquished demon was heard to confess that he was one of the fabled gods of antiquity who had impiously usurped the adoration of mankind. But the miraculous cure of diseases of the most inveterate or even preternatural kind can no longer occasion any surprise when we recollect that in the days of Iranaeus, about the end of the second century, the resurrection of the dead was very far from being esteemed an uncommon event; that the miracle was frequently performed on necessary occasions, by great fasting and the joint supplication of the church of the place, and that the persons thus restored to their prayers had lived afterwards among them many years. At such a period, when faith could boast of so many wonderful victories over death, it seems difficult to account for the skepticism of those philosophers who still rejected and derided the doctrine of the resurrection. A noble Grecian had rested on this important ground the whole controversy, and promised Theophilus, Bishop of Antioch, that if he could be gratified with the sight of a single person who had been actually raised from the dead, he would immediately embrace the Christian religion. It is somewhat remarkable that the prelate of the first Eastern church, however anxious for the conversion of his friend, thought proper to decline this fair and reasonable challenge.†

Whatever opinion may be entertained of the miracles of the primitive church since the time of the apostles, this unresisting softness of temper, so conspicuous among the believers of the second and third centuries, proved of some accidental benefit to the cause of truth and religion. In modern times, a latent and even involuntary skepticism adheres to the most pious dispositions. Their admission of supernatural truths is much less an active consent than a cold and passive acquiescence. Accustomed long since to observe and to respect the variable order of nature, our reason, or at least our imagination, is not sufficiently prepared to sustain the visible action of the Deity. But in the first ages of Christianity, the situation of mankind was extremely different. The most curious, or the most credulous, among the Pagans were often persuaded to enter into a society which asserted an actual claim of miraculous powers. The primitive Christians perpetually trod on mystic ground, and their minds were exercised by the habits of believing the most extraordinary events. They felt, or they fancied, that on every side they were incessantly assaulted by demons, comforted by visions, instructed by prophecy, and surprisingly delivered from danger, sickness, and from death itself by the supplications of the church. The real or imaginary prodigies of which they so frequently conceived themselves to be the objects, the instruments, or the spectators very happily disposed them to adopt with the same ease, but with far greater justice, the authentic wonders of the evangelic history; and thus miracles that exceeded not the measure of their own experience inspired them with the most lively assurance of mysteries which were acknowledged to surpass the limits of their understanding. It is this deep impression of supernatural truths which has been so much celebrated under the name of faith; a state of mind described as the surest pledge of the divine favor and of future felicity, and recommended as the first or perhaps the only merit of a Christian. According to the more rigid doctors, the moral virtues, which may be equally practiced by infidels, are destitute of any value or efficacy in the work of our justification.

IV. But the primitive Christian demonstrated his faith by his virtues; and it was very justly supposed that the divine persuasion which enlightened or subdued the understanding must, at the same time, purify the heart and direct the actions of the believer. The first apologists of Christianity who justify the innocence of their brethren, and the writers of a later period who celebrate the sanctity of their ancestors, display, in the most lively colors, the reformation of manners which was introduced into the world by the preaching of the gospel. As it is my intention to remark only such human causes as were permitted to second the influence of revelation, I shall slightly mention two motives which might naturally render the lives of the primitive Christians much purer and more austere than those of their Pagan contemporaries or their degenerate successors; repentance for their past sins, and the laudable desire of supporting the reputation of the society in which they were engaged.

It is a very ancient reproach, suggested by the ignorance or the malice of infidelity, that the Christians allured into their party the most atrocious criminals, who, as soon as they were touched by a sense of remorse, were easily persuaded to wash away in the water of baptism the guilt of their past conduct, for which the temples of the gods refused to grant them any expiation. But this reproach, when it is cleared from misrepresentation, contributes as much to the honor as it did to the increase of the church. The friends of Christianity may acknowledge without a blush that many of the most eminent saints had been before their baptism the most abandoned sinners. Those persons who in the world had followed, though in an imperfect manner, the dictates of benevolence and propriety derived such a calm satisfaction from the opinion of their own rectitude as rendered them much less susceptible of the sudden emotions of shame, of grief, and of terror which have given birth to so many wonderful conversions. After the example of their divine Master, the missionaries of the gospel disdained not the society of men, and especially of women, oppressed by the consciousness and very often by the effects of their vices. As they emerged from sin and superstition to the glorious hope of immortality, they resolved to devote themselves to a life not only of virtue but of penitence. The desire of perfection became the ruling passion of their soul; and it is well known that while reason embraces a cold mediocrity, our passions hurry us with rapid violence over the space which lies between the most opposite extremes.

When the new converts had been enrolled in the number of the faithful and were admitted to the sacraments of the church, they found themselves restrained from relapsing into their past disorders by another consideration of a less spiritual but of a very innocent and respectable nature. Any particular society that has departed from the great body of the nation, or the religion to which it belonged, immediately becomes the object of universal as well as invidious observation. In proportion to the smallness of its numbers, the character of the society may be affected by the virtues and vices of the persons who compose it; and every member is engaged to watch with the most vigilant attention over his own behavior and over that of his brethren, since, as he must expect to incur a part of the common disgrace, he may hope to enjoy a share of the common reputation.†

The acquisition of knowledge, the exercise of our reason or fancy, and the cheerful flow of unguarded conversation may employ the leisure of a liberal mind. Such amusements, however, were rejected with abhorrence, or admitted with the utmost caution, by the severity of the fathers, who despised all knowledge that was not useful to salvation, and who considered all levity of discourse as a criminal abuse of the gift of speech. In our present state of existence the body is so inseparably connected with the soul that it seems to be our interest to taste, with innocence and moderation, the enjoyments of which that faithful companion is susceptible. Very different was the reasoning of our devout predecessors; vainly aspiring to imitate the perfection of angels, they disdained, or they affected to disdain, every earthly and corporeal delight. Some of our senses indeed are necessary for our preservation, others for our subsistence, and others again for our information; and thus far it was impossible to reject the use of them. The first sensation of pleasure was marked as the first moment of their abuse. The unfeeling candidate for Heaven was instructed not only to resist the grosser allurements of the taste or smell, but even to shut his ears against the profane harmony of sounds, and to view with indifference the most finished productions of human art. Gay apparel, magnificent houses, and elegant furniture were supposed to unite the double guilt of pride and of sensuality; a simple and mortified appearance was more suitable to the Christian who was certain of his sins and doubtful of his salvation. In their censures of luxury, the fathers are extremely minute and circumstantial; and among the various articles which excite their pious indignation, we may enumerate false hair, garments of any color except white, instruments of music, vases of gold or silver, downy pillows (as Jacob reposed his head on a stone), white bread, foreign wines, public salutations, the use of warm baths, and the practice of shaving the beard, which, according to the expression of Tertullian, is a lie against our own faces, and an impious attempt to improve the works of the Creator. When Christianity was introduced among the rich and the polite, the observation of these singular laws was left, as it would be at present, to the few who were ambitious of superior sanctity. But it is always easy, as well as agreeable, for the inferior ranks of mankind to claim a merit from the contempt of that pomp and pleasure which fortune has placed beyond their reach. The virtue of the primitive Christians, like that of the first Romans, was very frequently guarded by poverty and ignorance.

The chaste severity of the fathers in whatever related to the commerce of the two sexes flowed from the same principle; their abhorrence of every enjoyment which might gratify the sensual and degrade the spiritual nature of man. It was their favorite opinion that if Adam had preserved his obedience to the Creator, he would have lived forever in a state of virgin purity, and that some harmless mode of vegetation might have peopled paradise with a race of innocent and immortal beings. The use of marriage was permitted only to his fallen posterity, as a necessary expedient to continue the human species, and as a restraint, however imperfect, on the natural licentiousness of desire. The hesitation of the orthodox casuists on this interesting subject betrays the perplexity of men unwilling to approve an institution which they were compelled to tolerate. The enumeration of the very whimsical laws which they most circumstantially imposed on the marriage-bed would force a smile from the young and a blush from the fair. It was their unanimous sentiment that a first marriage was adequate to all the purposes of nature and of society. The sensual connection was refined into a resemblance of the mystic union of Christ with his church, and was pronounced to be indissoluble either by divorce or by death. The practice of second nuptials was branded with the name of a legal adultery; and the persons who were guilty of so scandalous an offense against Christian purity were soon excluded from the honors, and even from the alms, of the church. Since desire was imputed as a crime and marriage was tolerated as a defect, it was consistent with the same principles to consider a state of celibacy as the nearest approach to the divine perfection. It was with the utmost difficulty that ancient Rome could support the institution of six Vestals; but the primitive church was filled with a great number of persons of either sex who had devoted themselves to the profession of perpetual chastity. A few of these, among whom we may reckon the learned Origen, judged it the most prudent to disarm the tempter. Some were insensible and some were invincible against the assaults of the flesh. Disdaining an ignominious flight, the virgins of the warm climate of Africa encountered the enemy in the closest engagement; they permitted priests and deacons to share their bed, and gloried amidst the flames in their unsullied purity. But insulted Nature sometimes vindicated her rights, and this new species of martyrdom served only to introduce a new scandal into the church. Among the Christian ascetics, however (a name which they soon acquired from their painful exercise), many, as they were less presumptuous, were probably more successful. The loss of sensual pleasure was supplied and compensated by spiritual pride. Even the multitude of Pagans were inclined to estimate the merit of the sacrifice by its apparent difficulty; and it was in the praise of these chaste spouses of Christ that the fathers have poured forth the troubled stream of their eloquence. Such are the early traces of monastic principles and institutions which, in a subsequent age, have counterbalanced all the temporal advantages of Christianity.

The Christians were not less averse to the business than to the pleasures of this world. The defense of our persons and property they knew not how to reconcile with the patient doctrine which enjoined an unlimited forgiveness of past injuries and commanded them to invite the repetition of fresh insults. Their simplicity was offended by the use of oaths, by the pomp of magistracy, and by the active contention of public life; nor could their humane ignorance be convinced that it was lawful on any occasion to shed the blood of our fellow-creatures, either by the sword of justice, or by that of war; even though their criminal or hostile attempts should threaten the peace and safety of the whole community. It was acknowledged that, under a less perfect law, the powers of the Jewish constitution had been exercised, with the approbation of Heaven, by inspired prophets and by anointed kings. The Christians felt and confessed that such institutions might be necessary for the present system of the world, and they cheerfully submitted to the authority of their Pagan governors. But while they inculcated the maxims of passive obedience, they refused to take any active part in the civil administration or the military defense of the empire. Some indulgence might, perhaps, be allowed to those persons who, before their conversion, were already engaged in such violent and sanguinary occupations; but it was impossible that the Christians, without renouncing a more sacred duty, could assume the character of soldiers, of magistrates, or of princes. This indolent or even criminal disregard to the public welfare exposed them to the contempt and reproaches of the Pagans, who very frequently asked what must be the fate of the empire, attacked on every side by the Barbarians, if all mankind should adopt the pusillanimous sentiments of the new sect. To this insulting question the Christian apologists returned obscure and ambiguous answers, as they were unwilling to reveal the secret cause of their security; the expectation that, before the conversion of mankind was accomplished, war, government, the Roman empire, and the world itself would be no more. It may be observed that, in this instance likewise, the situation of the first Christians coincided very happily with their religious scruples, and that their aversion to an active life contributed rather to excuse them from the service than to exclude them from the honors of the state and army.

V. But the human character, however it may be exalted or depressed by a temporary enthusiasm, will return by degrees to its proper and natural level, and will resume those passions that seem the most adapted to its present condition. The primitive Christians were dead to the business and pleasures of the world; but their love of action, which could never be entirely extinguished, soon revived and found a new occupation in the government of the church. A separate society which attacked the established religion of the empire was obliged to adopt some form of internal policy and to appoint a sufficient number of ministers, entrusted not only with the spiritual functions but even with the temporal direction of the Christian commonwealth. The safety of that society, its honor, its aggrandizement, were productive, even in the most pious minds, of a spirit of patriotism such as the first of the Romans had felt for the republic, and sometimes of a similar indifference in the use of whatever means might probably conduce to so desirable an end.†

The government of the church has often been the subject as well as the prize of religious contention. . . . The scheme of policy which, under their approbation, was adopted for the use of the first century may be discovered from the practice of Jerusalem, of Ephesus, or of Corinth. The societies which were instituted in the cities of the Roman empire were united only by the ties of faith and charity. Independence and equality formed the basis of their internal constitution. The want of discipline and human learning was supplied by the occasional assistance of the *prophets*, who were called to that function without distinction of age, of sex, or of natural abilities, and who, as often as they felt the divine impulse, poured forth the effusions of the Spirit in the assembly of the faithful. But these extraordinary gifts were frequently abused or misapplied by the prophetic teachers. They displayed them at an improper season, presumptuously disturbed the service of the assembly, and by their pride or mistaken zeal they introduced, particularly into the apostolic church of Corinth, a long and melancholy train of disorders. As the institution of prophets became useless, and even pernicious, their powers were withdrawn and their office abolished. The public functions of religion were solely entrusted to the established ministers of the church, the *bishops* and the *presbyters;* two appellations which, in their first origin, appear to have distinguished the same office and the same order of persons. The name of Presbyter was expressive of their age, or rather of their gravity and wisdom. The title of Bishop denoted their inspection over the faith and manners of the Christians who were committed to their pastoral care. In proportion to the respective numbers of the faithful, a larger or smaller number of these *episcopal presbyters* guided each infant congregation with equal authority and with united counsels.

But the most perfect equality of freedom requires the directing hand of a superior magistrate: and the order of public deliberations soon introduces the office of a president, invested at least with the authority of collecting the sentiments and of executing the resolutions of the assembly. A regard for the public tranquility, which would so frequently have been interrupted by annual or by occasional elections, induced the primitive Christians to constitute an honorable and perpetual magistracy, and to choose one of the wisest and most holy among their presbyterians to execute, during his life, the duties of their ecclesiastical governor. It was under these circumstances that the lofty title of Bishop began to raise itself above the humble appellation of Presbyter; and while the latter remained the most natural distinction for the members of every Christian senate, the former was appropriated to the dignity of its new president. The advantages of this episcopal form of government, which appears to have been introduced before the end of the first century, were so obvious, and so important for the future greatness as well as the present peace of Christianity, that it was adopted without delay by all the societies which were already scattered over the empire, had acquired in a very early period the sanction of antiquity, and is still revered by the most powerful churches, both of the East and of the West, as a primitive and even as a divine establishment.†

Such was the mild and equal constitution by which the Christians were governed more than a hundred years after the death of the apostles. Every society formed within itself a separate and independent republic; and although the most distant of these little states maintained a mutual as well as friendly intercourse of letters and deputations, the Christian world was not yet connected by any supreme authority or legislative assembly. As the numbers of the faithful were gradually multiplied, they discovered the advantages that might result from a closer union of their interest and designs. Towards the end of the second century, the churches of Greece and Asia adopted the useful institutions of provincial synods, and they may justly be supposed to have borrowed the model of a representative council from the celebrated examples of their own country, the Amphictyons, the Achaean league, or the assemblies of the Ionian cities. It was soon established as a custom and as a law that the bishops of the independent churches should meet in the capital of the province at the stated periods of spring and autumn. Their deliberations were assisted by the advice of a few distinguished presbyters, and moderated by the presence of a listening multitude. Their decrees, which were styled Canons, regulated every important controversy of faith and discipline; and it was natural to believe that a liberal effusion of the Holy Spirit would be poured on the united assembly of the delegates of the Christian people. The institution of synods was so well suited to private ambition and to public interest that in the space of a few years it was received throughout the whole empire. A regular correspondence was established between the provincial councils which mutually communicated and approved their respective proceedings; and the catholic church soon assumed the form, and acquired the strength, of a great federative republic.

As the legislative authority of the particular churches was insensibly superseded by the use of councils, the bishops obtained by their alliance a much larger share of executive and arbitrary power; and as soon as they were connected by a sense of their common interest, they were enabled to attack with united vigor the original rights of their clergy and people. The prelates of the third century imperceptibly changed the language of exhortation into that of command, scattered the seeds of future usurpations, and supplied, by Scripture, allegories and declamatory rhetoric, their deficiency of force and of reason. They exalted the unity and power of the church as it was represented in the EPISCOPAL OFFICE, of which every bishop enjoyed an equal and undivided portion. Princes and magistrates, it was often repeated, might boast an earthly claim to a transitory dominion; it was the episcopal authority alone which was derived from the Deity and extended itself over this and over another world. The bishops were the viceregents of Christ, the successors of the apostles, and the mystic substitutes of the high priest of the Mosaic law. Their exclusive privilege of conferring the sacerdotal character invaded the freedom both of clerical and of popular elections; and if in the administration of the church they still consulted the judgment of the presbyters or the inclination of the people, they most carefully inculcated the merit of such a voluntary condescension. The bishops acknowledged the supreme authority which resided in the assembly of their brethren; but in the government of his peculiar diocese, each of them exacted from his flock the same implicit obedience as if that favorite metaphor had been literally just, and as if the shepherd had been of a more exalted nature than that of his sheep. This obedience, however, was not imposed without some efforts on one side and some resistance on the other. The democratical part of the constitution was, in many places, very warmly supported by the zealous or interested opposition of the inferior clergy. But their patriotism received the ignominious epithets of faction and schism; and the episcopal cause was indebted for its rapid progress to the labors of many active prelates who, like Cyprian of Carthage, could reconcile the arts of the most ambitious statesman with the Christian virtues which seem adapted to the character of a saint and martyr.[†]

From every cause, either of a civil or of an ecclesiastical nature, it was easy to foresee that Rome must enjoy the respect and would soon claim the obedience of the provinces. The society of the faithful bore a just proportion to the capital of the empire; and the Roman church was the greatest, the most numerous, and, in regard to the West, the most ancient of all the Christian establishments, many of which had received their religion from the pious labors of her missionaries. Instead of one apostolic founder, the utmost boast of Antioch, of Ephesus, or of Corinth, the banks of the Tiber were supposed to have been honored with the preaching and martyrdom of the two most eminent among the apostles; and the bishops of Rome very prudently claimed the inheritance of whatsoever prerogatives were attributed either to the person or to the office of St. Peter. The bishops of Italy and of the provinces were disposed to allow them a primacy of order and association (such was their very accurate expression) in the Christian aristocracy. But the power of a monarch was rejected with abhorrence, and the aspiring genius of Rome experienced from the nations of Asia and Africa a more vigorous resistance to her spiritual, than she had formerly done to her temporal, dominion. The patriotic Cyprian, who ruled with the most absolute sway the church of Carthage and the provincial synods, opposed with resolution and success the ambition of the Roman pontiff, artfully connected his own cause with that of the Eastern bishops, and, like Hannibal, sought out new allies in the heart of Asia. If this Punic war was carried on without any effusion of blood, it was owing much less to the moderation than to the weakness of the contending prelates. Invectives and excommunications were *their* only weapons; and these, during the progress of the whole controversy, they hurled against each other with equal fury and devotion. The hard necessity of censuring either a pope or a saint and martyr distresses the modern Catholics whenever they are obliged to relate the particulars of a dispute in which the champions of religion indulged such passions as seem much more adapted to the senate or to the camp.

The progress of the ecclesiastical authority gave birth to the memorable distinction of the laity and of the clergy, which had been unknown to the Greeks and Romans. The former of these appellations comprehended the body of the Christian people; the latter, according to the signification of the word, was appropriated to the chosen portion that had been set apart for the service of religion; a celebrated order of men which has furnished the most important, though not always the most edifying, subjects for modern history. Their mutual hostilities sometimes disturbed the peace of the infant church, but their zeal and activity were united in the common cause, and the love of power which (under the most artful disguises) could insinuate itself into the breasts of bishops and martyrs animated them to increase the number of their subjects and to enlarge the limits of the Christian empire. They were destitute of any temporal force, and they were for a long time discouraged and oppressed, rather than assisted, by the civil magistrate; but they had acquired, and they employed within their own society, the two most efficacious instruments of government, rewards and punishments; the former derived from the pious liberality, the latter from the devout apprehensions, of the faithful.

I. The community of goods, which had so agreeably amused the imagination of Plato and which subsisted in some degree among the austere sect of the Essenians, was adopted for a short time in the primitive church. The fervor of the first proselytes prompted them to sell those worldly possessions which they despised, to lay the price of them at the feet of the apostles, and to content themselves with receiving an equal share out of the general distribution. The progress of the Christian religion relaxed and gradually abolished this generous institution, which, in hands less pure than those of the apostles, would too soon have been corrupted and abused by the returning selfishness of human nature; and the converts who embraced the new religion were permitted to retain the possession of their patrimony, to receive legacies and inheritances, and to increase their separate property by all the lawful means of trade and industry. Instead of an absolute sacrifice, a moderate proportion was accepted by the ministers of the gospel; and in their weekly or monthly assemblies, every believer, according to the exigency of the occasion and the measure of his wealth and piety, presented his voluntary offering for the use of the common fund. Nothing, however inconsiderable, was refused; but it was diligently inculcated that, in the article of Tithes, the Mosaic law was still of divine obligation; and that since the Jews, under a less perfect discipline, had been commanded to pay a tenth part of all that they possessed, it would become the disciples of Christ to distinguish themselves by a superior degree of liberality and to acquire some merit by resigning a superfluous treasure, which must so soon be annihilated with the world itself.†

The bishop was the natural steward of the church; the public stock was entrusted to his care without account or control; the presbyters were confined to their spiritual functions, and the more dependent order of the deacons was solely employed in the management and distribution of the ecclesiastical revenue. If we may give credit to the vehement declamations of Cyprian, there were too many among his African brethren who, in the execution of their charge, violated every precept not only of evangelical perfection but even of moral virtue. By some of these unfaithful stewards the riches of the church were lavished in sensual pleasures; by others they were perverted to the purposes of private gain, of fraudulent purchases, and of rapacious usury. But as long as the contributions of the Christian people were free and unconstrained, the abuse of their confidence could not be very frequent, and the general uses to which their liberality was applied reflected honor on the religious society. A decent portion was reserved for the maintenance of the bishop and his clergy; a sufficient sum was allotted for the expenses of the public worship, of which the feasts of love, the *agapae*, as they were called, constituted a very pleasing part. The whole remainder was the sacred patrimony of the poor. According to the discretion of the bishop, it was distributed to support widows and orphans, the lame, the sick, and the aged of the community; to comfort strangers and pilgrims, and to alleviate the misfortunes of prisoners and captives, more especially when their sufferings had been occasioned by their firm attachment to the cause of religion. A generous intercourse of charity united the most distant provinces, and the smaller congregations were cheerfully assisted by the alms of their more opulent brethren. Such an institution, which paid less regard to the merit than to the distress of the object, very materially conduced to the progress of Christianity. The Pagans who were actuated by a sense of humanity, while they derided the doctrines, acknowledged the benevolence, of the new sect. The prospect of immediate relief and of future protection allured into its hospitable bosom many of those unhappy persons whom the neglect of the world would have abandoned to the miseries of want, of sickness, and of old age. There is some reason likewise to believe that great numbers of infants who, according to the inhuman practice of the times, had been exposed by their parents were frequently rescued from death, baptized, educated, and maintained by the piety of the Christians, and at the expense of the public treasure.

II. It is the undoubted right of every society to exclude from its communion and benefits such among its members as reject or violate those regulations which have been established by general consent. In the exercise of this power, the censures of the Christian church were chiefly directed against scandalous sinners, and particularly those who were guilty of murder, of fraud, or of incontinence; against the authors or the followers of any heretical opinions which had been condemned by the judgment of the episcopal order; and against those unhappy persons who, whether from choice or compulsion, had polluted themselves after their baptism by any act of idolatrous worship. The consequences of excommunication were of a temporal as well as a spiritual nature. The Christian against whom it was pronounced was deprived of any part in the oblations of the faithful. The ties both of religious and of private friendship were dissolved: he found himself a profane object of abhorrence to the persons whom he the most esteemed, or by whom he had been the most tenderly beloved; and as far as an expulsion from a respectable society could imprint on his character a mark of disgrace, he was shunned or suspected by the generality of mankind. The situation of these unfortunate exiles was in itself very painful and melancholy; but, as it usually happens, their apprehensions far exceeded their sufferings. The benefits of the Christian communion were those of eternal life; nor could they erase from their minds the awful opinion that to those ecclesiastical governors by whom they were condemned, the Deity had committed the keys of Hell and of Paradise. The heretics, indeed, who might be supported by the consciousness of their intentions, and by the flattering hope that they alone had discovered the true path of salvation, endeavored to regain in their separate assemblies those comforts, temporal as well as spiritual, which they no longer derived from the great society of Christians. But almost all those who had reluctantly yielded to the power of vice or idolatry were sensible of their fallen condition, and anxiously desirous of being restored to the benefits of the Christian communion.†

The well-tempered mixture of liberality and rigor, the judicious dispensation of rewards and punishments according to the maxims of policy as well as justice, constituted the *human* strength of the church. The bishops, whose paternal care extended itself to the government of both worlds, were sensible of the importance of these prerogatives; and covering their ambition with the fair pretense of the love of order, they were jealous of any rival in the exercise of a discipline so necessary to prevent the desertion of those troops which had enlisted themselves under the banner of the cross, and whose numbers every day became more considerable. From the imperious declamations of Cyprian, we should naturally conclude that the doctrines of excommunication and penance formed the most essential part of religion; and that it was much less dangerous for the disciples of Christ to neglect the observance of the moral duties than to despise the censures and authority of their bishops. Sometimes we might imagine that we were listening to the voice of Moses when he commanded the earth to open and to swallow up, in consuming flames, the rebellious race which refused obedience to the priesthood of Aaron; and we should sometimes suppose that we hear a Roman consul asserting the majesty of the republic, and declaring his inflexible resolution to enforce the rigor of the laws. "If such irregularities are suffered with impunity" (it is thus that the bishop of Carthage chides the lenity of his colleague), "if such irregularities are suffered, there is an end of EPISCOPAL VIGOR; an end of the sublime and divine power of governing the church, an end of Christianity itself." Cyprian had renounced those temporal honors which it is probable he would never have obtained; but the acquisition of such absolute command over the consciences and understanding of a congregation, however obscure or despised by the world, is more truly grateful to the pride of the human heart than the possession of the most despotic power imposed by arms and conquest on a reluctant people.

In the course of this important though perhaps tedious inquiry, I have attempted to display the secondary causes which so efficaciously assisted the truth of the Christian religion. . . . It was by the aid of these causes, exclusive zeal, the immediate expectation of another world, the claim of miracles, the practice of rigid virtue, and the constitution of the primitive church, that Christianity spread itself with so much success in the Roman empire. To the first of these the Christians were indebted for their invincible valor, which disdained to capitulate with the enemy whom they were resolved to vanquish. The three succeeding causes supplied their valor with the most formidable arms. The last of these causes united their courage, directed their arms, and gave their efforts that irresistible weight which even a small band of well-trained and intrepid volunteers has so often possessed over an undisciplined multitude ignorant of the subject and careless of the event of the war. . . . The ministers of Polytheism, both in Rome and in the provinces, were for the most part men of a noble birth and of an affluent fortune, who received as an honorable distinction the care of a celebrated temple or of a public sacrifice, exhibited, very frequently at their own expense, the sacred games, and with cold indifference performed the ancient rites according to the laws and fashion of their country. As they were engaged in the ordinary occupations of life, their zeal and devotion were seldom animated by a sense of interest, or by the habits of an ecclesiastical character. Confined to their respective temples and cities, they remained without any connection of discipline or government; and whilst they acknowledged the supreme jurisdiction of the senate, of the college of pontiffs, and of the emperor, those civil magistrates contented themselves with the easy task of maintaining in peace and dignity the general worship of mankind. We have already seen how various, how loose, and how uncertain were the religious sentiments of Polytheists. They were abandoned, almost without control, to the natural workings of a superstitious fancy. The accidental circumstances of their life and situation determined the object as well as the degree of their devotion; and as long as their adoration was successively prostituted to a thousand deities, it was scarcely possible that their hearts could be susceptible of a very sincere or lively passion for any of them.

When Christianity appeared in the world, even these faint and imperfect impressions had lost much of their original power. Human reason, which by its unassisted strength is incapable of perceiving the mysteries of faith, had already obtained an easy triumph over the folly of Paganism; and when Tertullian or Lactantius employ their labors in exposing its falsehood and extravagance, they are obliged to transcribe the eloquence of Cicero or the wit of Lucian. The contagion of these skeptical writings had been diffused far beyond the number of their readers. The fashion of incredulity was communicated from the philosopher to the man of pleasure or business, from the noble to the plebeian, and from the master to the menial slave who waited at his table and who eagerly listened to the freedom of his conversation. On public occasions the philosophic part of mankind affected to treat with respect and decency the religious institutions of their country; but their secret contempt penetrated through the thin and awkward disguise; and even the people, when they discovered that their deities were rejected and derided by those whose rank or understanding they were accustomed to reverence, were filled with doubts and apprehensions concerning the truth of those doctrines to which they had yielded the most implicit belief. The decline of ancient prejudice exposed a very numerous portion of humankind to the danger of a painful and comfortless situation. A state of skepticism and suspense may amuse a few inquisitive minds. But the practice of superstition is so congenial to the multitude that if they are forcibly awakened, they still regret the loss of their pleasing vision. Their love of the marvelous and supernatural, their curiosity with regard to future events, and their strong propensity to extend their hopes and fears beyond the limits of the visible world were the principal causes which favored the establishment of Polytheism. So urgent on the vulgar is the necessity of believing that the fall of any system of mythology will most probably be succeeded by the introduction of some other mode of superstition. Some deities of a more recent and fashionable cast might soon have occupied the deserted temples of Jupiter and Apollo if, in the decisive moment, the wisdom of Providence had not interposed a genuine revelation fitted to inspire the most rational esteem and conviction, whilst at the same time it was adorned with all that could attract the curiosity, the wonder, and the veneration of the people. In their actual disposition, as many were almost disengaged from their artificial prejudices but equally susceptible and desirous of a devout attachment; an object much less deserving would have been sufficient to fill the vacant place in their hearts and to gratify the uncertain eagerness of their passions. Those who are inclined to pursue this reflection, instead of viewing with astonishment the rapid progress of Christianity, will perhaps be surprised that its success was not still more rapid and still more universal.

It has been observed, with truth as well as propriety, that the conquests of Rome prepared and facilitated those of Christianity. . . . The public highways, which had been constructed for the use of the legions, opened an easy passage for the Christian missionaries from Damascus to Corinth, and from Italy to the extremity of Spain or Britain; nor did those spiritual conquerors encounter any of the obstacles which usually retard or prevent the introduction of a foreign religion into a distant country. There is the strongest reason to believe that before the reigns of Diocletian and Constantine, the faith of Christ had been preached in every province and in all the great cities of the empire; but the foundation of the several congregations, the numbers of the faithful who composed them, and their proportion to the unbelieving multitude are now buried in obscurity, or disguised by fiction and declamation.[†]

The progress of Christianity was not confined to the Roman empire; and according to the primitive fathers, who interpret facts by prophecy, the new religion, within a century after the death of its divine Author, had already visited every part of the globe. "There exists not," says Justin Martyr, "a people, whether Greek or Barbarian or any other race of men, by whatsoever appellation or manners they may be distinguished, however ignorant of arts or agriculture, whether they dwell under tents or wander about in covered wagons, among whom prayers are not offered up in the name of a crucified Jesus to the Father and Creator of all things." But this splendid exaggeration, which even at present it would be extremely difficult to reconcile with the real state of mankind, can be considered only as the rash sally of a devout but careless writer, the measure of whose belief was regulated by that of his wishes. But neither the belief nor the wishes of the fathers can alter the truth of history. It will still remain an undoubted fact that the Barbarians of Scythia and Germany, who afterwards subverted the Roman monarchy, were involved in the darkness of Paganism; and that even the conversion of Iberia, of Armenia, or of Aethiopia was not attempted with any degree of success till the scepter was in the hands of an orthodox emperor. . . . [T]he principles of Christianity were easily introduced into the Greek and Syrian cities which obeyed the successors of Artaxerxes; but they do not appear to have made any deep impression on the minds of the Persians, whose religious system, by the labors of a well disciplined order of priests, had been constructed with much more art and solidity than the uncertain mythology of Greece and Rome.

From this impartial though imperfect survey of the progress of Christianity, it may perhaps seem probable that the number of its proselytes has been excessively magnified by fear on the one side and by devotion on the other. According to the irreproachable testimony of Origen, the proportion of the faithful was very inconsiderable when compared with the multitude of an unbelieving world; but, as we are left without any distinct information, it is impossible to determine, and it is difficult even to conjecture, the real numbers of the primitive Christians. The most favorable calculation, however, that can be deduced from the examples of Antioch and of Rome will not permit us to imagine that more than a twentieth part of the subjects of the empire had enlisted themselves under the banner of the cross before the important conversion of Constantine. But their habits of faith, of zeal, and of union seemed to multiply their numbers; and the same causes which contributed to their future increase served to render their actual strength more apparent and more formidable.

Such is the constitution of civil society that whilst a few persons are distinguished by riches, by honors, and by knowledge, the body of the people is condemned to obscurity, ignorance, and poverty. The Christian religion, which addressed itself to the whole human race, must consequently collect a far greater number of proselytes from the lower than from the superior ranks of life. This innocent and natural circumstance has been improved into a very odious imputation, which seems to be less strenuously denied by the apologists than it is urged by the adversaries of the faith; that the new sect of Christians was almost entirely composed of the dregs of the populace, of peasants and mechanics, of boys and women, of beggars and slaves, the last of whom might sometimes introduce the missionaries into the rich and noble families to which they belonged. These obscure teachers (such was the charge of malice and infidelity) are as mute in public as they are loquacious and dogmatical in private. Whilst they cautiously avoid the dangerous encounter of philosophers, they mingle with the rude and illiterate crowd and insinuate themselves into those minds whom their age, their sex, or their education has the best disposed to receive the impression of superstitious terrors.

This unfavorable picture, though not devoid of a faint resemblance, betrays, by its dark coloring and distorted features, the pencil of an enemy. As the humble faith of Christ diffused itself through the world, it was embraced by several persons who derived some consequence from the advantages of nature or fortune. Aristides, who presented an eloquent apology to the emperor Hadrian, was an Athenian philosopher. Justin Martyr had sought divine knowledge in the schools of Zeno, of Aristotle, of Pythagoras, and of Plato before he fortunately was accosted by the old man, or rather the angel, who turned his attention to the study of the Jewish prophets. Clemens of Alexandria had acquired much various reading in the Greek, and Tertullian in the Latin, language. Julius Africanus and Origen possessed a very considerable share of the learning of their times; and although the style of Cyprian is very different from that of Lactantius, we might almost discover that both those writers had been public teachers of rhetoric. Even the study of philosophy was at length introduced among the

Christians, but it was not always productive of the most salutary effects; knowledge was as often the parent of heresy as of devotion.[†]

Nor can it be affirmed with truth that the advantages of birth and fortune were always separated from the profession of Christianity. Several Roman citizens were brought before the tribunal of Pliny, and he soon discovered that a great number of persons of *every order* of men in Bithynia had deserted the religion of their ancestors. His unsuspected testimony may, in this instance, obtain more credit than the bold challenge of Tertullian when he addresses himself to the fears as well as the humanity of the proconsul of Africa by assuring him that if he persists in his cruel intentions he must decimate Carthage, and that he will find among the guilty many persons of his own rank, senators and matrons of noblest extraction, and the friends or relations of his most intimate friends. It appears, however, that about forty years afterwards the emperor Valerian was persuaded of the truth of this assertion, since in one of his rescripts he evidently supposes that senators, Roman knights, and ladies of quality were engaged in the Christian sect. The church still continued to increase its outward splendor as it lost its internal purity; and in the reign of Diocletian, the palace, the courts of justice, and even the army concealed a multitude of Christians, who endeavored to reconcile the interests of the present with those of a future life.

And yet these exceptions are either too few in number or too recent in time entirely to remove the imputation of ignorance and obscurity which has been so arrogantly cast on the first proselytes of Christianity. Instead of employing in our defense the fictions of later ages, it will be more prudent to convert the occasion of scandal into a subject of edification. Our serious thoughts will suggest to us that the apostles themselves were chosen by Providence among the fishermen of Galilee, and that the lower we depress the temporal condition of the first Christians, the more reason we shall find to admire their merit and success. It is incumbent on us diligently to remember that the kingdom of Heaven was promised to the poor in spirit, and that minds afflicted by calamity and the contempt of mankind cheerfully listen to the divine promise of future happiness; while, on the contrary, the fortunate are satisfied with the possession of this world; and the wise abuse in doubt and dispute their vain superiority of reason and knowledge.

We stand in need of such reflections to comfort us for the loss of some illustrious characters, which in our eyes might have seemed the most worthy of the heavenly present. The names of Seneca, of the elder and the younger Pliny, of Tacitus, of Plutarch, of Galen, of the slave Epictetus, and of the emperor Marcus Antoninus adorn the age in which they flourished and exalt the dignity of human nature. They filled with glory their respective stations, either in active or contemplative life; their excellent understandings were improved by study; Philosophy had purified their minds from the prejudices of the popular superstition; and their days were spent in the pursuit of truth and the practice of virtue. Yet all these sages (it is no less an object of surprise than of concern) overlooked or rejected the perfection of the Christian system. Their language or their silence equally discover their contempt for the growing sect, which in their time had diffused itself over the Roman empire. Those among them who condescended to mention the Christians consider them only as obstinate and perverse enthusiasts who exacted an implicit submission to their mysterious doctrines without being able to produce a single argument that could engage the attention of men of sense and learning.

It is at least doubtful whether any of these philosophers perused the apologies which the primitive Christians repeatedly published in behalf of themselves and of their religion; but it is much to be lamented that such a cause was not defended by abler advocates. They expose with superfluous wit and eloquence the extravagance of Polytheism. They interest our compassion by displaying the innocence and sufferings of their injured brethren. But when they would demonstrate the divine origin of Christianity, they insist much more strongly on the predictions which announced than on the miracles which accompanied the appearance of the Messiah. Their favorite argument might serve to edify a Christian or to convert a Jew, since both the one and the other acknowledge the authority of those prophecies, and both are obliged, with devout reverence, to search for their sense and their accomplishment. But this mode of persuasion loses much of its weight and influence when it is addressed to those who neither understand nor respect the Mosaic dispensation and the prophetic style.†

But how shall we excuse the supine inattention of the Pagan and philosophic world to those evidences which were represented by the hand of Omnipotence, not to their reason but to their senses? During the age of Christ, of his apostles, and of their first disciples, the doctrine which they preached was confirmed by innumerable prodigies. The lame walked, the blind saw, the sick were healed, the dead were raised, demons were expelled, and the laws of nature were frequently suspended for the benefit of the church. But the sages of Greece and Rome turned aside from the awful spectacle, and, pursuing the ordinary occupations of life and study, appeared unconscious of any alterations in the moral or physical government of the world. Under the reign of Tiberius, the whole earth, or at least a celebrated province of the Roman empire, was involved in a preternatural darkness of three hours. Even this miraculous event, which ought to have excited the wonder, the curiosity, and the devotion of mankind, passed without notice in an age of science and history. It happened during the lifetime of Seneca and the elder Pliny, who must have experienced the immediate effects, or received the earliest intelligence, of the prodigy. Each of these philosophers, in a laborious work, has recorded all the great phenomena of nature, earthquakes, meteors, comets, and eclipses, which his indefatigable curiosity could collect. Both the one and the other have omitted to mention the greatest phenomenon to which the mortal eye has been witness since the creation of the globe. A distinct chapter of Pliny is designed for eclipses of an extraordinary nature and unusual duration; but he contents himself with describing the singular defect of light which followed the murder of Caesar, when, during the greatest part of a year, the orb of the sun appeared pale and without splendor. The season of obscurity, which cannot surely be compared with the preternatural darkness of the Passion, had been already celebrated by most of the poets and historians of that memorable age.

CHAPTER XVI

CONDUCT TOWARDS THE CHRISTIANS, FROM NERO TO CONSTANTINE

The conduct of the Roman government towards the Christians, from the reign of Nero to that of Constantine.

If we seriously consider the purity of the Christian religion, the sanctity of its moral precepts, and the innocent as well as austere lives of the greater number of those who during the first ages embraced the faith of the gospel, we should naturally suppose that so benevolent a doctrine would have been received with due reverence, even by the unbelieving world; that the learned and the polite, however they may deride the miracles, would have esteemed the virtues of the new sect; and that the magistrates, instead of persecuting, would have protected an order of men who yielded the most passive obedience to the laws, though they declined the active cares of war and government. If, on the other hand, we recollect the universal toleration of Polytheism, as it was invariably maintained by the faith of the people, the incredulity of philosophers, and the policy of the Roman senate and emperors, we are at a loss to discover what new offense the Christians had committed, what new provocation could exasperate the mild indifference of antiquity, and what new motives could urge the Roman princes, who beheld without concern a thousand forms of religion subsisting in peace under their gentle sway, to inflict a severe punishment on any part of their subjects who had chosen for themselves a singular but an inoffensive mode of faith and worship.

The religious policy of the ancient world seems to have assumed a more stern and intolerant character to oppose the progress of Christianity. About fourscore years after the death of Christ, his innocent disciples were punished with death by the sentence of a proconsul of the most amiable and philosophic character, and according to the laws of an emperor distinguished by the wisdom and justice of his general administration. The apologies which were repeatedly addressed to the successors of Trajan are filled with the most pathetic complaints that the Christians, who obeyed the dictates and solicited the liberty of conscience, were alone, among all the subjects of the Roman empire, excluded from the common benefits of their auspicious government. The deaths of a few eminent martyrs have been recorded with care; and from the time that Christianity was invested with the supreme power, the governors of the church have been no less diligently employed in displaying the cruelty than in imitating the conduct of their Pagan adversaries. To separate (if it be possible) a few authentic as well as interesting facts from an undigested mass of fiction and error, and to relate in a clear and rational manner the causes, the extent, the duration, and the most important circumstances of the persecutions to which the first Christians were exposed, is the design of the present chapter.

The sectaries of a persecuted religion, depressed by fear, animated with resentment, and perhaps heated by enthusiasm, are seldom in a proper temper of mind calmly to investigate, or candidly to appreciate, the motives of their enemies, which often escape the impartial and discerning view even of those who are placed at a secure distance from the flames of persecution. A reason has been assigned for the conduct of the emperors towards the primitive Christians, which may appear the more specious and probable as it is drawn from the acknowledged genius of Polytheism. It has already been observed that the religious concord of the world was principally supported by the implicit assent and reverence which the nations of antiquity expressed for their respective traditions and ceremonies. It might therefore be expected that they would unite with indignation against any sect or people which should separate itself from the communion of mankind and, claiming the exclusive possession of divine knowledge, should disdain every form of worship except its own as impious and idolatrous. The rights of toleration were held by mutual indulgence: they were justly forfeited by a refusal of the accustomed tribute. As the payment of this tribute was inflexibly refused by the Jews and by them alone, the consideration of the treatment which they experienced from the Roman magistrates will serve to explain how far these speculations are justified by facts, and will lead us to discover the true causes of the persecution of Christianity.

Without repeating what has already been mentioned of the reverence of the Roman princes and governors for the temple of Jerusalem, we shall only observe that the destruction of the temple and city was accompanied and followed by every circumstance that could exasperate the minds of the conquerors and authorize religious persecution by the most specious arguments of political justice and the public safety. From the reign of Nero to that of Antoninus Pius, the Jews discovered a fierce impatience of the dominion of Rome, which repeatedly broke out in the most furious massacres and insurrections. Humanity is shocked at the recital of the horrid cruelties which they committed in the cities of Egypt, of Cyprus, and of Cyrene, where they dwelt in treacherous friendship with the unsuspecting natives; and we are tempted to applaud the severe retaliation which was exercised by the arms of the legions against a race of fanatics whose dire and credulous superstition seemed to render them the implacable enemies not only of the Roman government but of humankind. The enthusiasm of the Jews was supported by the opinion that it was unlawful for them to pay taxes to an idolatrous master; and by the flattering promise which they derived from their ancient oracles that a conquering Messiah would soon arise, destined to break their fetters and to invest the favorites of Heaven with the empire of the earth. It was by announcing himself as their long-expected deliverer, and by calling on all the descendants of Abraham to assert the hope of Israel, that the famous Barchochebas collected a formidable army, with which he resisted during two years the power of the emperor Hadrian.

Notwithstanding these repeated provocations, the resentment of the Roman princes expired after the victory; nor were their apprehensions continued beyond the period of war and danger. By the general indulgence of Polytheism and by the mild temper of Antoninus Pius, the Jews were restored to their ancient privileges, and once more obtained the permission of circumcising their children, with the easy restraint that they should never confer on any foreign proselyte that distinguishing mark of the Hebrew race. The numerous remains of that people, though they were still excluded from the precincts of Jerusalem, were permitted to form and to maintain considerable establishments both in Italy and in the provinces, to acquire the freedom of Rome, to enjoy municipal honors, and to obtain at the same time an exemption from the burdensome and expensive offices of society. The moderation or the contempt of the Romans gave a legal sanction to the form of ecclesiastical police which was instituted by the vanquished sect. The patriarch, who had fixed his residence at Tiberias, was empowered to appoint his subordinate ministers and apostles, to exercise a domestic jurisdiction, and to receive from his dispersed brethren an annual contribution. New synagogues were frequently erected in the principal cities of the empire; and the sabbaths, the fasts, and the festivals which were either commanded by the Mosaic law or enjoined by the traditions of the Rabbis were celebrated in the most solemn and public manner. Such gentle treatment insensibly assuaged the stern temper of the Jews. Awakened from their dream of prophecy and conquest, they assumed the behavior of peaceable and industrious subjects. Their irreconcilable hatred of mankind, instead of flaming out in acts of blood and violence, evaporated in less dangerous gratifications. They embraced every opportunity of overreaching the idolaters in trade; and they pronounced secret and ambiguous imprecations against the haughty kingdom of Edom (the name applied by the Jews to the Roman empire).

Since the Jews, who rejected with abhorrence the deities adored by their sovereign and by their fellow-subjects, enjoyed, however, the free exercise of their unsocial religion, there must have existed some other cause which exposed the disciples of Christ to those severities from which the posterity of Abraham was exempt. The difference between them is simple and obvious; but, according to the sentiments of antiquity, it was of the highest importance. The Jews were a *nation;* the Christians were a *sect:* and if it was natural for every community to respect the sacred institutions of their neighbors, it was incumbent on them to persevere in those of their ancestors. The voice of oracles, the precepts of philosophers, and the authority of the laws unanimously enforced this national obligation. By their lofty claim of superior sanctity the Jews might provoke the Polytheists to consider them as an odious and impure race. By disdaining the intercourse of other nations, they might deserve their contempt. The laws of Moses might be for the most part frivolous or absurd; yet, since they had been received during many ages by a large society, his followers were justified by the example of mankind; and it was universally acknowledged that they had a right to practice what it would have been criminal in them to neglect. But this principle, which protected the Jewish synagogue, afforded not any favor or security to the primitive church. By embracing the faith of the gospel, the Christians incurred the supposed guilt of an unnatural and unpardonable offense. They dissolved the sacred ties of custom and education, violated the religious institutions of their country, and presumptuously despised whatever their fathers had believed as true or had reverenced as sacred. Nor was this apostasy (if we may use the expression) merely of a partial or local kind; since the pious deserter who withdrew himself from the temples of Egypt or Syria would equally disdain to seek an asylum in those of Athens or Carthage. Every Christian rejected with contempt the superstitions of his family, his city, and his province. The whole body of Christians unanimously refused to hold any communion with the gods of Rome, of the empire, and of mankind. It was in vain that the oppressed believer asserted the inalienable rights of conscience and private judgment. Though his situation might excite the pity, his arguments could never reach the understanding, either of the philosophic or of the believing part of the Pagan world. To their apprehensions, it was no less a matter of surprise that any individuals should entertain scruples against complying with the established mode of worship than if they had conceived a sudden abhorrence to the manners, the dress, or the language of their native country.

The surprise of the Pagans was soon succeeded by resentment; and the most pious of men were exposed to the unjust but dangerous imputation of impiety. Malice and prejudice concurred in representing the Christians as a society of atheists who, by the most daring attack on the religious constitution of the empire, had merited the severest animadversion of the civil magistrate. They had separated themselves (they gloried in the confession) from every mode of superstition which was received in any part of the globe by the various temper of Polytheism: but it was not altogether so evident what deity, or what form of worship, they had substituted to the gods and temples of antiquity. The pure and sublime idea which they entertained of the Supreme Being escaped the gross conception of the Pagan multitude, who were at a loss to discover a spiritual and solitary God that was neither represented under any corporeal figure or visible symbol, nor was adored with the accustomed pomp of libations and festivals, of altars and sacrifices. The sages of Greece and Rome, who had elevated their minds to the contemplation of the existence and attributes of the First Cause, were induced by reason or by vanity to reserve for themselves and their chosen disciples the privilege of this philosophical devotion.

They were far from admitting the prejudices of mankind as the standard of truth, but they considered them as flowing from the original disposition of human nature; and they supposed that any popular mode of faith and worship which presumed to disclaim the assistance of the senses would, in proportion as it receded from superstition, find itself incapable of restraining the wanderings of the fancy and the visions of fanaticism. The careless glance which men of wit and learning condescended to cast on the Christian revelation served only to confirm their hasty opinion and to persuade them that the principle, which they might have revered, of the Divine Unity was defaced by the wild enthusiasm and annihilated by the airy speculations of the new sectaries. The author of a celebrated dialogue which has been attributed to Lucian, whilst he affects to treat the mysterious subject of the Trinity in a style of ridicule and contempt, betrays his own ignorance of the weakness of human reason, and of the inscrutable nature of the Divine perfections.

It might appear less surprising that the founder of Christianity should not only be revered by his disciples as a sage and a prophet, but that he should be adored as a God. The Polytheists were disposed to adopt every article of faith which seemed to offer any resemblance, however distant or imperfect, with the popular mythology; and the legends of Bacchus, of Hercules, and of Aesculapius had, in some measure, prepared their imagination for the appearance of the Son of God under a human form. But they were astonished that the Christians should abandon the temples of those ancient heroes who, in the infancy of the world, had invented arts, instituted laws, and vanquished the tyrants or monsters who infested the earth, in order to choose for the exclusive object of their religious worship an obscure teacher who, in a recent age and among a barbarous people, had fallen a sacrifice either to the malice of his own countrymen or to the jealousy of the Roman government. The Pagan multitude, reserving their gratitude for temporal benefits alone, rejected the inestimable present of life and immortality which was offered to mankind by Jesus of Nazareth. His mild constancy in the midst of cruel and voluntary sufferings, his universal benevolence, and the sublime simplicity of his actions and character were insufficient, in the opinion of those carnal men, to compensate for the want of fame, of empire, and of success; and whilst they refused to acknowledge his stupendous triumph over the powers of darkness and of the grave, they misrepresented or they insulted the equivocal birth, wandering life, and ignominious death of the divine Author of Christianity.

The personal guilt which every Christian had contracted in thus preferring his private sentiment to the national religion was aggravated in a very high degree by the number and union of the criminals. It is well known, and has been already observed, that Roman policy viewed with the utmost jealousy and distrust any association among its subjects; and that the privileges of private corporations, though formed for the most harmless or beneficial purposes, were bestowed with a very sparing hand. The religious assemblies of the Christians who had separated themselves from the public worship appeared of a much less innocent nature; they were illegal in their principle, and in their consequences might become dangerous; nor were the emperors conscious that they violated the laws of justice when, for the peace of society, they prohibited those secret and sometimes nocturnal meetings. The pious disobedience of the Christians made their conduct, or perhaps their designs, appear in a much more serious and criminal light; and the Roman princes, who might perhaps have suffered themselves to be disarmed by a ready submission, deeming their honor concerned in the execution of their commands, sometimes attempted, by rigorous punishments, to subdue this independent spirit, which boldly acknowledged an authority superior to that of the magistrate. The extent and duration of this spiritual conspiracy seemed to render it every day more deserving of his animadversion. We have already seen that the active and successful zeal of the Christians had insensibly diffused them through every province and almost every city of the empire. The new converts seemed to renounce their family and country that they might connect themselves in an indissoluble band of union with a peculiar society which everywhere assumed a different character from the rest of mankind. Their gloomy and austere aspect, their abhorrence of the common business and pleasures of life, and their frequent predictions of impending calamities inspired the Pagans with the apprehension of some danger which would arise from the new sect, the more alarming as it was the more obscure. "Whatever," says Pliny, "may be the principle of their conduct, their inflexible obstinacy appeared deserving of punishment."

The precautions with which the disciples of Christ performed the offices of religion were at first dictated by fear and necessity; but they were continued from choice. By imitating the awful secrecy which reigned in the Eleusinian mysteries, the Christians had flattered themselves that they should render their sacred institutions more respectable in the eyes of the Pagan world. But the event, as it often happens to the operations of subtle policy, deceived their wishes and their expectations. It was concluded that they only concealed what they would have blushed to disclose. Their mistaken prudence afforded an opportunity for malice to invent, and for suspicious credulity to believe, the horrid tales which described the Christians as the most wicked of humankind, who practiced in their dark recesses every abomination that a depraved fancy could suggest and who solicited the favor of their unknown God by the sacrifice of every moral virtue. There were many who pretended to confess or to relate the ceremonies of this abhorred society. It was asserted "that a new-born infant, entirely covered over with flour, was presented, like some mystic symbol of initiation, to the knife of the proselyte, who unknowingly inflicted many a secret and mortal wound on the innocent victim of his error; that as soon as the cruel deed was perpetrated, the sectaries drank up the blood, greedily tore asunder the quivering members, and pledged themselves to eternal secrecy by a mutual consciousness of guilt. It was as confidently affirmed that this inhuman sacrifice was succeeded by a suitable entertainment, in which intemperance served as a provocative to brutal lust; till, at the appointed moment, the lights were suddenly extinguished, shame was banished, nature was forgotten; and, as accident might direct, the darkness of the night was polluted by the incestuous commerce of sisters and brothers, of sons and of mothers."

But the perusal of the ancient apologies was sufficient to remove even the slightest suspicion from the mind of a candid adversary. The Christians, with the intrepid security of innocence, appeal from the voice of rumor to the equity of the magistrates. They acknowledge that if any proof can be produced of the crimes which calumny has imputed to them, they are worthy of the most severe punishment. They provoke the punishment, and they challenge the proof. At the same time they urge, with equal truth and propriety, that the charge is not less devoid of probability than it is destitute of evidence; they ask whether anyone can seriously believe that the pure and holy precepts of the gospel, which so frequently restrain the use of the most lawful enjoyments, should inculcate the practice of the most abominable crimes; that a large society should resolve to dishonor itself in the eyes of its own members; and that a great number of persons of either sex, and every age and character, insensible to the fear of death or infamy, should consent to violate those principles which nature and education had imprinted most deeply in their minds. Nothing, it should seem, could weaken the force or destroy the effect of so unanswerable a justification, unless it were the injudicious conduct of the apologists themselves, who betrayed the common cause of religion to gratify their devout hatred to the domestic enemies of the church. It was sometimes faintly insinuated, and sometimes boldly asserted, that the same bloody sacrifices and the same incestuous festivals which were so falsely ascribed to the orthodox believers were in reality celebrated by the Marcionites, by the Carpocratians, and by several other sects of the Gnostics, who, notwithstanding they might deviate into the paths of heresy, were still actuated by the sentiments of men, and still governed by the precepts of Christianity. Accusations of a similar kind were retorted upon the church by the schismatics who had departed from its communion, and it was confessed on all sides that the most scandalous licentiousness of manners prevailed among great numbers of those who affected the name of Christians. A Pagan magistrate, who possessed neither leisure nor abilities to discern the almost imperceptible line which divides the orthodox faith from heretical pravity, might easily have imagined that their mutual animosity had extorted the discovery of their common guilt. It was fortunate for the repose, or at least for the reputation, of the first Christians that the magistrates sometimes proceeded with more temper and moderation than is usually consistent with religious zeal, and that they reported, as the impartial result of their judicial inquiry, that the sectaries who had deserted the established worship appeared to them sincere in their professions and blameless in their manners, however they might incur, by their absurd and excessive superstition, the censure of the laws.

History, which undertakes to record the transactions of the past for the instruction of future ages, would ill deserve that honorable office if she condescended to plead the cause of tyrants or to justify the maxims of persecution. It must, however, be acknowledged that the conduct of the emperors who appeared the least favorable to the primitive church is by no means so criminal as that of modern sovereigns, who have employed the arm of violence and terror against the religious opinions of any part of their subjects. From their reflections, or even from their own feelings, a Charles V or a Lewis XIV might have acquired a just knowledge of the rights of conscience, of the obligation of faith, and of the innocence of error. But the princes and magistrates of ancient Rome were strangers to those principles which inspired and authorized the inflexible obstinacy of the Christians in the cause of truth, nor could they themselves discover in their own breasts any motive which would have prompted them to refuse a legal, and as it were a natural, submission to the sacred institutions of their country. The same reason which contributes to alleviate the guilt must have tended to abate the vigor of their persecutions. As they were actuated not by the furious zeal of bigots but by the temperate policy of legislators, contempt must often have relaxed, and humanity must frequently have suspended, the execution of those laws which they enacted against the humble and obscure followers of Christ. From the general view of their character and motives we might naturally conclude: I. That a considerable time elapsed before they considered the new sectaries as an object deserving of the attention of government. II. That in the conviction of any of their subjects who were accused of so very singular a crime, they proceeded with caution and reluctance. III. That they were moderate in the use of punishments; and, IV. That the afflicted church enjoyed many intervals of peace and tranquility. Notwithstanding the careless indifference which the most copious and the most minute of the Pagan writers have shown to the affairs of the Christians, it may still be in our power to confirm each of these probable suppositions by the evidence of authentic facts.

I. By the wise dispensation of Providence, a mysterious veil was cast over the infancy of the church, which, till the faith of the Christians was matured and their numbers were multiplied, served to protect them not only from the malice but even from the knowledge of the Pagan world. The slow and gradual abolition of the Mosaic ceremonies afforded a safe and innocent disguise to the more early proselytes of the gospel. As they were, for the greater part, of the race of Abraham, they were distinguished by the peculiar mark of circumcision, offered up their devotions in the Temple of Jerusalem till its final destruction, and received both the Law and the Prophets as the genuine inspirations of the Deity. The Gentile converts, who by a spiritual adoption had been associated to the hope of Israel, were likewise confounded under the garb and appearance of Jews, and as the Polytheists paid less regard to articles of faith than to the external worship, the new sect, which carefully concealed or faintly announced its future greatness and ambition, was permitted to shelter itself under the general toleration which was granted to an ancient and celebrated people in the Roman empire. It was not long, perhaps, before the Jews themselves, animated with a fiercer zeal and a more jealous faith, perceived the gradual separation of their Nazarene brethren from the doctrine of the synagogue; and they would gladly have extinguished the dangerous heresy in the blood of its adherents. But the decrees of Heaven had already disarmed their malice; and though they might sometimes exert the licentious privilege of sedition, they no longer possessed the administration of criminal justice; nor did they find it easy to infuse into the calm breast of a Roman magistrate the rancor of their own zeal and prejudice. The provincial governors declared themselves ready to listen to any accusation that might affect the public safety; but as soon as they were informed that it was a question not of facts but of words, a dispute relating only to the interpretation of the Jewish laws and prophecies, they deemed it unworthy of the majesty of Rome seriously to discuss the obscure differences which might arise among a barbarous and superstitious people. The innocence of the first Christians was protected by ignorance and contempt; and the tribunal of the Pagan magistrate often proved their most assured refuge against the fury of the synagogue. If indeed we were disposed to adopt the traditions of a too credulous antiquity, we might relate the distant peregrinations, the wonderful achievements, and the various deaths of the twelve apostles: but a more accurate inquiry will induce us to doubt whether any of those persons who had been witnesses to the miracles of Christ were permitted, beyond the limits of Palestine, to seal with their blood the truth of their testimony. From the ordinary term of human life, it may very naturally be presumed that most of them were deceased before the discontent of the Jews broke out into that furious war which was terminated only by the ruin of Jerusalem [A.D. 70]. During a long period from the death of Christ to that memorable rebellion, we cannot discover any traces of Roman intolerance, unless they are to be found in the sudden, the transient, but the cruel persecution which was exercised by Nero against the Christians of the capital, thirty-five years after the former and only two years before the latter of those great events. The character of the philosophic historian [Tacitus] to whom we are principally indebted for the knowledge of this singular transaction would alone be sufficient to recommend it to our most attentive consideration.

In the tenth year of the reign of Nero, the capital of the empire was afflicted by a fire which raged beyond the memory or example of former ages [A.D. 64]. The monuments of Grecian art and of Roman virtue, the trophies of the Punic and Gallic wars, the most holy temples and the most splendid palaces, were involved in one common destruction. Of the fourteen regions or quarters into which Rome was divided, four only subsisted entire, three were leveled with the ground, and the remaining seven, which had experienced the fury of the flames, displayed a melancholy prospect of ruin and desolation. The vigilance of government appears not to have neglected any of the precautions which might alleviate the sense of so dreadful a calamity. The Imperial gardens were thrown open to the distressed multitude, temporary buildings were erected for their accommodation, and a plentiful supply of corn and provisions was distributed at a very moderate price. The most generous policy seemed to have dictated the edicts which regulated the disposition of the streets and the construction of private houses; and as it usually happens in an age of prosperity, the conflagration of Rome in the course of a few years produced a new city, more regular and more beautiful than the former. But all the prudence and humanity affected by Nero on this occasion were insufficient to preserve him from the popular suspicion. Every crime might be imputed to the assassin of his wife and mother; nor could the prince who prostituted his person and dignity on the theater be deemed incapable of the most extravagant folly. The voice of rumor accused the emperor as the incendiary of his own capital; and as the most incredible stories are the best adapted to the genius of an enraged people, it was gravely reported and firmly believed that Nero, enjoying the calamity which he had occasioned, amused himself with singing to his lyre the destruction of ancient Troy. To divert a suspicion which the power of despotism was unable to suppress, the emperor resolved to substitute in his own place some fictitious criminals. "With this view," continues Tacitus, "he inflicted the most exquisite tortures on those men, who, under the vulgar appellation of Christians, were already branded with deserved infamy. They derived their name and origin from Christ, who in the reign of Tiberius had suffered death by the sentence of the procurator Pontius Pilate. For a while this dire superstition was checked; but it again burst forth; and not only spread itself over Judaea, the first seat of this mischievous sect, but was even introduced into Rome, the common asylum which receives and protects whatever is impure, whatever is atrocious. The confessions of those who were seized discovered a great multitude of their accomplices, and they were all convicted, not so much for the crime of setting fire to the city as for their hatred of humankind. They died in torments, and their torments were embittered by insult and derision. Some were nailed on crosses; others sewn up in the skins of wild beasts and exposed to the fury of dogs; others again, smeared over with combustible materials, were used as torches to illuminate the darkness of the night. The gardens of Nero were destined for the melancholy spectacle, which was accompanied with a horse-race and honored with the presence of the emperor, who mingled with the populace in the dress and attitude of a charioteer. The guilt of the Christians deserved indeed the most exemplary punishment, but the public abhorrence was changed into commiseration from the opinion that those unhappy wretches were sacrificed not so much to the public welfare as to the cruelty of a jealous tyrant." Those who survey with a curious eye the revolutions of mankind may observe that the gardens and circus of Nero on the Vatican, which were polluted with the blood of the first Christians, have been rendered still more famous by the triumph and by the abuse of the persecuted religion. On the same spot, a temple, which far surpasses the ancient glories of the Capitol, has been since erected by the Christian Pontiffs, who, deriving their claim of universal dominion from an humble fisherman of Galilee, have succeeded to the throne of the Caesars, given laws to the Barbarian conquerors of Rome, and extended their spiritual jurisdiction from the coast of the Baltic to the shores of the Pacific Ocean.[†]

[I]t is evident that the effect, as well as the cause, of Nero's persecution was confined to the walls of Rome, that the religious tenets of the Galilaeans or Christians were never made a subject of punishment, or even of inquiry; and that, as the idea of their sufferings was for a long time connected with the idea of cruelty and injustice, the moderation of succeeding princes inclined them to spare a sect oppressed by a tyrant whose rage had been usually directed against virtue and innocence.

It is somewhat remarkable that the flames of war consumed, almost at the same time, the temple of Jerusalem and the Capitol of Rome; and it appears no less singular that the tribute which devotion had destined to the former, should have been converted by the power of an assaulting victor to restore and adorn the splendor of the latter. The emperors levied a general capitation tax on the Jewish people; and although the sum assessed on the head of each individual was inconsiderable, the use for which it was designed, and the severity with which it was exacted, were considered as an intolerable grievance. Since the officers of the revenue extended their unjust claim to many persons who were strangers to the blood or religion of the Jews, it was impossible that the Christians, who had so often sheltered themselves under the shade of the synagogue, should now escape this rapacious persecution. Anxious as they were to avoid the slightest infection of idolatry, their conscience forbade them to contribute to the honor of that demon who had assumed the character of the Capitoline Jupiter. As a very numerous though declining party among the Christians still adhered to the law of Moses, their efforts to dissemble their Jewish origin were detected by the decisive test of circumcision; nor were the Roman magistrates at leisure to inquire into the difference of their religious tenets. Among the Christians who were brought before the tribunal of the emperor or, as it seems more probable, before that of the procurator of Judaea, two persons are said to have appeared, distinguished by their extraction, which was more truly noble than that of the greatest monarchs. These were the grandsons of St. Jude the apostle, who himself was the brother of Jesus Christ. Their natural pretensions to the throne of David might perhaps attract the respect of the people and excite the jealousy of the governor; but the meanness of their garb and the simplicity of their answers soon convinced him that they were neither desirous nor capable of disturbing the peace of the Roman empire. They frankly confessed their royal origin and their near relation to the Messiah; but they disclaimed any temporal views, and professed that his kingdom, which they devoutly expected, was purely of a spiritual and angelic nature. When they were examined concerning their fortune and occupation, they showed their hands, hardened with daily labor, and declared that they derived their whole subsistence from the cultivation of a farm near the village of Cocaba, of the extent of about twenty-four English acres.... The grandsons of St. Jude were dismissed with compassion and contempt.

But although the obscurity of the house of David might protect them from the suspicions of a tyrant, the present greatness of his own family alarmed the pusillanimous temper of Domitian, which could only be appeased by the blood of those Romans whom he either feared or hated or esteemed. Of the two sons of his uncle Flavius Sabinus, the elder was soon convicted of treasonable intentions, and the younger, who bore the name of Flavius Clemens, was indebted for his safety to his want of courage and ability [A.D. 95]. The emperor for a long time distinguished so harmless a kinsman by his favor and protection, bestowed on him his own niece Domitilla, adopted the children of that marriage to the hope of the succession, and invested their father with the honors of the consulship. But he had scarcely finished the term of his annual magistracy when, on a slight pretense, he was condemned and executed; Domitilla was banished to a desolate island on the coast of Campania; and sentences either of death or of confiscation were pronounced against a great number of persons who were involved in the same accusation. The guilt imputed to their charge was that of *Atheism* and *Jewish manners;* a singular association of ideas which cannot with any propriety be applied except to the Christians, as they were obscurely and imperfectly viewed by the magistrates and by the writers of that period. On the strength of so probable an interpretation, and too eagerly admitting the suspicions of a tyrant as an evidence of their honorable crime, the church has placed both Clemens and Domitilla among its first martyrs, and has branded the cruelty of Domitian with the name of the second persecution. But this persecution (if it deserves that epithet) was of no long duration. A few months after the death of Clemens and the banishment of Domitilla, Stephen, a freedman belonging to the latter who had enjoyed the favor, but who had not surely embraced the faith, of his mistress, assassinated the emperor in his palace. The memory of Domitian was condemned by the senate; his acts were rescinded; his exiles recalled; and under the gentle administration of Nerva, while the innocent were restored to their rank and fortunes, even the most guilty either obtained pardon or escaped punishment [A.D. 96].

II. About ten years afterwards, under the reign of Trajan, the younger Pliny was entrusted by his friend and master with the government of Bithynia and Pontus. He soon found himself at a loss to determine by what rule of justice or of law he should direct his conduct in the execution of an office the most repugnant to his humanity. Pliny had never assisted at any judicial proceedings against the Christians, with whose name alone he seems to be acquainted; and he was totally uninformed with regard to the nature of their guilt, the method of their conviction, and the degree of their punishment. In this perplexity he had recourse to his usual expedient, of submitting to the wisdom of Trajan an impartial and, in some respects, a favorable account of the new superstition, requesting the emperor that he would condescend to resolve his doubts, and to instruct *his* ignorance [A.D. 112]. The life of Pliny had been employed in the acquisition of learning and in the business of the world. Since the age of nineteen he had pleaded with distinction in the tribunals of Rome, filled a place in the senate, had been invested with the honors of the consulship, and had formed very numerous connections with every order of men, both in Italy and in the provinces. From his ignorance therefore we may derive some useful information. We may assure ourselves that when he accepted the government of Bithynia, there were no general laws or decrees of the senate in force against the Christians; that neither Trajan nor any of his virtuous predecessors whose edicts were received into the civil and criminal jurisprudence had publicly declared their intentions concerning the new sect; and that whatever proceedings had been carried on against the Christians, there were none of sufficient weight and authority to establish a precedent for the conduct of a Roman magistrate.

The answer of Trajan, to which the Christians of the succeeding age have frequently appealed, discovers as much regard for justice and humanity as could be reconciled with his mistaken notions of religious policy. Instead of displaying the implacable zeal of an inquisitor, anxious to discover the most minute particles of heresy and exulting in the number of his victims, the emperor expresses much more solicitude to protect the security of the innocent than to prevent the escape of the guilty. He acknowledged the difficulty of fixing any general plan; but he lays down two salutary rules, which often afforded relief and support to the distressed Christians. Though he directs the magistrates to punish such persons as are legally convicted, he prohibits them, with a very humane inconsistency, from making any inquiries concerning the supposed criminals. Nor was the magistrate allowed to proceed on every kind of information. Anonymous charges the emperor rejects as too repugnant to the equity of his government; and he strictly requires, for the conviction of those to whom the guilt of Christianity is imputed, the positive evidence of a fair and open accuser. It is likewise probable that the persons who assumed so invidious an office were obliged to declare the grounds of their suspicions, to specify (both in respect to time and place) the secret assemblies which their Christian adversary had frequented, and to disclose a great number of circumstances which were concealed with the most vigilant jealousy from the eye of the profane. If they succeeded in their prosecution, they were exposed to the resentment of a considerable and active party, to the censure of the more liberal portion of mankind, and to the ignominy which, in every age and country, has attended the character of an informer. If, on the contrary, they failed in their proofs, they incurred the severe and perhaps capital penalty which, according to a law published by the emperor Hadrian, was inflicted on those who falsely attributed to their fellow-citizens the crime of Christianity. The violence of personal or superstitious animosity might sometimes prevail over the most natural apprehensions of disgrace and danger, but it cannot surely be imagined that accusations of so unpromising an appearance were either lightly or frequently undertaken by the Pagan subjects of the Roman empire.

The expedient which was employed to elude the prudence of the laws affords a sufficient proof how effectually they disappointed the mischievous designs of private malice or superstitious zeal. In a large and tumultuous assembly, the restraints of fear and shame, so forcible on the minds of individuals, are deprived of the greatest part of their influence. The pious Christian, as he was desirous to obtain or to escape the glory of martyrdom, expected, either with impatience or with terror, the stated returns of the public games and festivals. On those occasions the inhabitants of the great cities of the empire were collected in the circus or the theater, where every circumstance of the place, as well as of the ceremony, contributed to kindle their devotion, and to extinguish their humanity. Whilst the numerous spectators, crowned with garlands, perfumed with incense, purified with the blood of victims, and surrounded with the altars and statues of their tutelar deities, resigned themselves to the enjoyment of pleasures which they considered as an essential part of their religious worship, they recollected that the Christians alone abhorred the gods of mankind, and by their absence and melancholy on these solemn festivals seemed to insult or to lament the public felicity. If the empire had been afflicted by any recent calamity, by a plague, a famine, or an unsuccessful war; if the Tiber had, or if the Nile had not, risen beyond its banks; if the earth had shaken, or if the temperate order of the seasons had been interrupted, the superstitious Pagans were convinced that the crimes and the impiety of the Christians, who were spared by the excessive lenity of the government, had at length provoked the divine justice. It was not among a licentious and exasperated populace that the forms of legal proceedings could be observed; it was not in an amphitheater stained with the blood of wild beasts and gladiators that the voice of compassion could be heard. The impatient clamors of the multitude denounced the Christians as the enemies of gods and men, doomed them to the severest tortures, and, venturing to accuse by name some of the most distinguished of the new sectaries, required with irresistible vehemence that they should be instantly apprehended and cast to the lions. The provincial governors and magistrates who presided in the public spectacles were usually inclined to gratify the inclinations and to appease the rage of the people by the sacrifice of a few obnoxious victims. But the wisdom of the emperors protected the church from the danger of these tumultuous clamors and irregular accusations, which they justly censured as repugnant both to the firmness and to the equity of their administration. The edicts of Hadrian and of Antoninus Pius expressly declared that the voice of the multitude should never be admitted as legal evidence to convict or to punish those unfortunate persons who had embraced the enthusiasm of the Christians.

III. Punishment was not the inevitable consequence of conviction, and the Christians, whose guilt was the most clearly proved by the testimony of witnesses, or even by their voluntary confession, still retained in their own power the alternative of life or death. It was not so much the past offense as the actual resistance which excited the indignation of the magistrate. He was persuaded that he offered them an easy pardon, since, if they consented to cast a few grains of incense upon the altar, they were dismissed from the tribunal in safety and with applause. It was esteemed the duty of a humane judge to endeavor to reclaim rather than to punish those deluded enthusiasts. Varying his tone according to the age, the sex, or the situation of the prisoners, he frequently condescended to set before their eyes every circumstance which could render life more pleasing or death more terrible; and to solicit, nay, to entreat them that they would show some compassion to themselves, to their families, and to their friends. If threats and persuasions proved ineffectual, he had often recourse to violence; the scourge and the rack were called in to supply the deficiency of argument, and every art of cruelty was employed to subdue such inflexible and, as it appeared to the Pagans, such criminal obstinacy. The ancient apologists of Christianity have censured, with equal truth and severity, the irregular conduct of their persecutors, who, contrary to every principle of judicial proceeding, admitted the use of torture in order to obtain not a confession but a denial of the crime which was the object of their inquiry. The monks of succeeding ages, who, in their peaceful solitudes, entertained themselves with diversifying the deaths and sufferings of the primitive martyrs, have frequently invented torments of a much more refined and ingenious nature. In particular, it has pleased them to suppose that the zeal of the Roman magistrates, disdaining every consideration of moral virtue or public decency, endeavored to seduce those whom they were unable to vanquish, and that by their orders the most brutal violence was offered to those whom they found it impossible to seduce. It is related that females who were prepared to despise death were sometimes condemned to a more severe trial, and called upon to determine whether they set a higher value on their religion or on their chastity. The youths to whose licentious embraces they were abandoned received a solemn exhortation from the judge to exert their most strenuous efforts to maintain the honor of Venus against the impious virgin who refused to burn incense on her altars. Their violence, however, was commonly disappointed, and the seasonable interposition of some miraculous power preserved the chaste spouses of Christ from the dishonor even of an involuntary defeat. We should not indeed neglect to remark that the more ancient as well as authentic memorials of the church are seldom polluted with these extravagant and indecent fictions.

The total disregard of truth and probability in the representation of these primitive martyrdoms was occasioned by a very natural mistake. The ecclesiastical writers of the fourth or fifth centuries ascribed to the magistrates of Rome the same degree of implacable and unrelenting zeal which filled their own breasts against the heretics or the idolaters of their own times. It is not improbable that some of those persons who were raised to the dignities of the empire might have imbibed the prejudices of the populace, and that the cruel disposition of others might occasionally be stimulated by motives of avarice or of personal resentment. But it is certain, and we may appeal to the grateful confessions of the first Christians, that the greatest part of those magistrates who exercised in the provinces the authority of the emperor or of the senate, and to whose hands alone the jurisdiction of life and death was entrusted, behaved like men of polished manners and liberal education who respected the rules of justice and who were conversant with the precepts of philosophy. They frequently declined the odious task of persecution, dismissed the charge with contempt, or suggested to the accused Christian some legal evasion by which he might elude the severity of the laws. Whenever they were invested with a discretionary power, they used it much less for the oppression than for the relief and benefit of the afflicted church. They were far from condemning all the Christians who were accused before their tribunal, and very far from punishing with death all those who were convicted of an obstinate adherence to the new superstition. Contenting themselves for the most part with the milder chastisements of imprisonment, exile, or slavery in the mines, they left the unhappy victims of their justice some reason to hope that a prosperous event, the accession, the marriage, or the triumph of an emperor, might speedily restore them, by a general pardon, to their former state. The martyrs devoted to immediate execution by the Roman magistrates appear to have been selected from the most opposite extremes. They were either bishops and presbyters, the persons the most distinguished among the Christians by their rank and influence, and whose example might strike terror into the whole sect; or else they were the meanest and most abject among them, particularly those of the servile condition, whose lives were esteemed of little value and whose sufferings were viewed by the ancients with too careless an indifference. The learned Origen, who, from his experience as well as reading, was intimately acquainted with the history of the Christians, declares in the most express terms that the number of martyrs was very inconsiderable. His authority would alone be sufficient to annihilate that formidable army of martyrs whose relics, drawn for the most part from the catacombs of Rome, have replenished so many churches, and whose marvelous achievements have been the subject of so many volumes of Holy Romance. But the general assertion of Origen may be explained and confirmed by the particular testimony of his friend Dionysius, who, in the immense city of Alexandria and under the rigorous persecution of Decius, reckons only ten men and seven women who suffered for the profession of the Christian name.

During the same period of persecution, the zealous, the eloquent, the ambitious Cyprian governed the church not only of Carthage, but even of Africa. He possessed every quality which could engage the reverence of the faithful, or provoke the suspicions and resentment of the Pagan magistrates. His character as well as his station seemed to mark out that holy prelate as the most distinguished object of envy and danger. The experience, however, of the life of Cyprian is sufficient to prove that our fancy has exaggerated the perilous situation of a Christian bishop [consecrated A.D. 248–249]; and the dangers to which he was exposed were less imminent than those which temporal ambition is always prepared to encounter in the pursuit of honors. Four Roman emperors, with their families, their favorites, and their adherents, perished by the sword in the space of ten years during which the bishop of Carthage guided by his authority and eloquence the councils of the African church. It was only in the third year of his administration that he had reason, during a few months, to apprehend the severe edicts of Decius, the vigilance of the magistrate and the clamors of the multitude, who loudly demanded that Cyprian, the leader of the Christians, should be thrown to the lions. Prudence suggested the necessity of a temporary retreat, and the voice of prudence was obeyed. He withdrew himself into an obscure solitude, from whence he could maintain a constant correspondence with the clergy and people of Carthage; and, concealing himself till the tempest was past, he preserved his life without relinquishing either his power or his reputation. His extreme caution did not, however, escape the censure of the more rigid Christians, who lamented, or the reproaches of his personal enemies, who insulted, a conduct which they considered as a pusillanimous and criminal desertion of the most sacred duty. The propriety of reserving himself for the future exigencies of the church, the example of several holy bishops, and the divine admonitions which, as he declares himself, he frequently received in visions and ecstacies were the reasons alleged in his justification. But his best apology may be found in the cheerful resolution, with which, about eight years afterwards, he suffered death in the cause of religion. The authentic history of his martyrdom has been recorded with unusual candor and impartiality. A short abstract, therefore, of its most important circumstances will convey the clearest information of the spirit and of the forms of the Roman persecutions.

When Valerian was consul for the third and Gallienus for the fourth time, Paternus, proconsul of Africa, summoned Cyprian to appear in his private council-chamber [A.D. 257]. He there acquainted him with the Imperial mandate, which he had just received, that those who had abandoned the Roman religion should immediately return to the practice of the ceremonies of their ancestors. Cyprian replied without hesitation that he was a Christian and a bishop, devoted to the worship of the true and only Deity, to whom he offered up his daily supplications for the safety and prosperity of the two emperors, his lawful sovereigns. With modest confidence he pleaded the privilege of a citizen in refusing to give any answer to some invidious and indeed illegal questions which the proconsul had proposed. A sentence of banishment was pronounced as the penalty of Cyprian's disobedience; and he was conducted without delay to Curubis, a free and maritime city of Zeugitana, in a pleasant situation, a fertile territory, and at the distance of about forty miles from Carthage. The exiled bishop enjoyed the conveniences of life and the consciousness of virtue. His reputation was diffused over Africa and Italy; an account of his behavior was published for the edification of the Christian world; and his solitude was frequently interrupted by the letters, the visits, and the congratulations of the faithful. On the arrival of a new proconsul in the province the fortune of Cyprian appeared for some time to wear a still more favorable aspect. He was recalled from banishment; and though not yet permitted to return to Carthage, his own gardens in the neighborhood of the capital were assigned for the place of his residence.

At length, exactly one year after Cyprian was first apprehended, Galerius Maximus, proconsul of Africa, received the Imperial warrant for the execution of the Christian teachers [A.D. 258]. The bishop of Carthage was sensible that he should be singled out for one of the first victims; and the frailty of nature tempted him to withdraw himself, by a secret flight, from the danger and the honor of martyrdom; but soon recovering that fortitude which his character required, he returned to his gardens and patiently expected the ministers of death. Two officers of rank who were entrusted with that commission placed Cyprian between them in a chariot, and as the proconsul was not then at leisure, they conducted him not to a prison but to a private house in Carthage which belonged to one of them. An elegant supper was provided for the entertainment of the bishop, and his Christian friends were permitted for the last time to enjoy his society, whilst the streets were filled with a multitude of the faithful, anxious and alarmed at the approaching fate of their spiritual father. In the morning he appeared before the tribunal of the proconsul, who, after informing himself of the name and situation of Cyprian, commanded him to offer sacrifice and pressed him to reflect on the consequences of his disobedience. The refusal of Cyprian was firm and decisive; and the magistrate, when he had taken the opinion of his council, pronounced with some reluctance the sentence of death. It was conceived in the following terms: "That Thascius Cyprianus should be immediately beheaded as the enemy of the gods of Rome, and as the chief and ringleader of a criminal association which he had seduced into an impious resistance against the laws of the most holy emperors, Valerian and Gallienus." The manner of his execution was the mildest and least painful that could be inflicted on a person convicted of any capital offense; nor was the use of torture admitted to obtain from the bishop of Carthage either the recantation of his principles or the discovery of his accomplices.

As soon as the sentence was proclaimed, a general cry of "We will die with him" arose at once among the listening multitude of Christians who waited before the palace gates. The generous effusions of their zeal and their affection were neither serviceable to Cyprian nor dangerous to themselves. He was led away under a guard of tribunes and centurions, without resistance and without insult, to the place of his execution, a spacious and level plain near the city, which was already filled with great numbers of spectators [September 14, A.D. 258]. His faithful presbyters and deacons were permitted to accompany their holy bishop. They assisted him in laying aside his upper garment, spread linen on the ground to catch the precious relics of his blood, and received his orders to bestow five-and-twenty pieces of gold on the executioner. The martyr then covered his face with his hands, and at one blow his head was separated from his body. His corpse remained during some hours exposed to the curiosity of the Gentiles: but in the night it was removed and transported in a triumphal procession, and with a splendid illumination, to the burial-place of the Christians. The funeral of Cyprian was publicly celebrated without receiving any interruption from the Roman magistrates; and those among the faithful who had performed the last offices to his person and his memory were secure from the danger of inquiry or of punishment. It is remarkable that of so great a multitude of bishops in the province of Africa, Cyprian was the first who was esteemed worthy to obtain the crown of martyrdom.

It was in the choice of Cyprian either to die a martyr or to live an apostate; but on the choice depended the alternative of honor or infamy. Could we suppose that the bishop of Carthage had employed the profession of the Christian faith only as the instrument of his avarice or ambition, it was still incumbent on him to support the character he had assumed and, if he possessed the smallest degree of manly fortitude, rather to expose himself to the most cruel tortures than by a single act to exchange the reputation of a whole life for the abhorrence of his Christian brethren and the contempt of the Gentile world. But if the zeal of Cyprian was supported by the sincere conviction of the truth of those doctrines which he preached, the crown of martyrdom must have appeared to him as an object of desire rather than of terror. It is not easy to extract any distinct ideas from the vague though eloquent declamations of the Fathers, or to ascertain the degree of immortal glory and happiness which they confidently promised to those who were so fortunate as to shed their blood in the cause of religion. They inculcated with becoming diligence that the fire of martyrdom supplied every defect and expiated every sin; that while the souls of ordinary Christians were obliged to pass through a slow and painful purification, the triumphant sufferers entered into the immediate fruition of eternal bliss, where, in the society of the patriarchs, the apostles, and the prophets, they reigned with Christ and acted as his assessors in the universal judgment of mankind. The assurance of a lasting reputation upon earth, a motive so congenial to the vanity of human nature, often served to animate the courage of the martyrs. The honors which Rome or Athens bestowed on those citizens who had fallen in the cause of their country were cold and unmeaning demonstrations of respect when compared with the ardent gratitude and devotion which the primitive church expressed towards the victorious champions of the faith. The annual commemoration of their virtues and sufferings was observed as a sacred ceremony, and at length terminated in religious worship. Among the Christians who had publicly confessed their religious principles, those who (as it very frequently happened) had been dismissed from the tribunal or the prisons of the Pagan magistrates obtained such honors as were justly due to their imperfect martyrdom and their generous resolution. The most pious females courted the permission of imprinting kisses on the fetters which they had worn and on the wounds which they had received. Their persons were esteemed holy, their decisions were admitted with deference, and they too often abused, by their spiritual pride and licentious manners, the preeminence which their zeal and intrepidity had acquired. Distinctions like these, whilst they display the exalted merit, betray the inconsiderable number of those who suffered, and of those who died, for the profession of Christianity.

The sober discretion of the present age will more readily censure than admire, but can more easily admire than imitate, the fervor of the first Christians, who, according to the lively expressions of Sulpicius Severus, desired martyrdom with more eagerness than his own contemporaries solicited a bishopric. The epistles which Ignatius composed as he was carried in chains through the cities of Asia breathe sentiments the most repugnant to the ordinary feelings of human nature. He earnestly beseeches the Romans that when he should be exposed in the amphitheater they would not, by their kind but unseasonable intercession, deprive him of the crown of glory; and he declares his resolution to provoke and irritate the wild beasts which might be employed as the instruments of his death. Some stories are related of the courage of martyrs who actually performed what Ignatius had intended; who exasperated the fury of the lions, pressed the executioner to hasten his office, cheerfully leaped into the fires which were kindled to consume them, and discovered a sensation of joy and pleasure in the midst of the most exquisite tortures. Several examples have been preserved of a zeal impatient of those restraints which the emperors had provided for the security of the church. The Christians sometimes supplied by their voluntary declaration the want of an accuser, rudely disturbed the public service of Paganism, and, rushing in crowds round the tribunal of the magistrates, called upon them to pronounce and to inflict the sentence of the law. The behavior of the Christians was too remarkable to escape the notice of the ancient philosophers; but they seem to have considered it with much less admiration than astonishment. Incapable of conceiving the motives which sometimes transported the fortitude of believers beyond the bounds of prudence or reason, they treated such an eagerness to die as the strange result of obstinate despair, of stupid insensibility, or of superstitious frenzy. "Unhappy men!" exclaimed the proconsul Antoninus to the Christians of Asia; "unhappy men! if you are thus weary of your lives, is it so difficult for you to find ropes and precipices?" He was extremely cautious (as it is observed by a learned and pious historian) of punishing men who had found no accusers but themselves, the Imperial laws not having made any provision for so unexpected a case: condemning therefore a few as a warning to their brethren, he dismissed the multitude with indignation and contempt. Notwithstanding this real or affected disdain, the intrepid constancy of the faithful was productive of more salutary effects on those minds which nature or grace had disposed for the easy reception of religious truth. On these melancholy occasions, there were many among the Gentiles who pitied, who admired, and who were converted. The generous enthusiasm was communicated from the sufferer to the spectators; and the blood of martyrs, according to a well-known observation, became the seed of the church.

But although devotion had raised, and eloquence continued to inflame, this fever of the mind, it insensibly gave way to the more natural hopes and fears of the human heart, to the love of life, the apprehension of pain, and the horror of dissolution. The more prudent rulers of the church found themselves obliged to restrain the indiscreet ardor of their followers, and to distrust a constancy which too often abandoned them in the hour of trial. As the lives of the faithful became less mortified and austere, they were every day less ambitious of the honors of martyrdom; and the soldiers of Christ, instead of distinguishing themselves by voluntary deeds of heroism, frequently deserted their post and fled in confusion before the enemy whom it was their duty to resist.

[*From the reign of Tiberius to Philip (circa* A.D. *30–249), we find no evidence for extensive or systematic persecution of Christians.*]

[T]he fall of Philip introduced, with the change of masters, a new system of government so oppressive to the Christians that their former condition, ever since the time of Domitian, was represented as a state of perfect freedom and security, if compared with the rigorous treatment which they experienced under the short reign of Decius [A.D. 249–251]. The virtues of that prince will scarcely allow us to suspect that he was actuated by a mean resentment against the favorites of his predecessor; and it is more reasonable to believe that in the prosecution of his general design to restore the purity of Roman manners, he was desirous of delivering the empire from what he condemned as a recent and criminal superstition. The bishops of the most considerable cities were removed by exile or death: the vigilance of the magistrates prevented the clergy of Rome during sixteen months from proceeding to a new election; and it was the opinion of the Christians that the emperor would more patiently endure a competitor for the purple than a bishop in the capital. Were it possible to suppose that the penetration of Decius had discovered pride under the disguise of humility, or that he could foresee the temporal dominion which might insensibly arise from the claims of spiritual authority, we might be less surprised that he should consider the successors of St. Peter as the most formidable rivals to those of Augustus.

The administration of Valerian was distinguished by a levity and inconstancy ill suited to the gravity of the *Roman Censor* [A.D. 253–260]. In the first part of his reign, he surpassed in clemency those princes who had been suspected of an attachment to the Christian faith. In the last three years and a half, listening to the insinuations of a minister addicted to the superstitions of Egypt, he adopted the maxims and imitated the severity of his predecessor Decius. The accession of Gallienus, which increased the calamities of the empire, restored peace to the church; and the Christians obtained the free exercise of their religion by an edict addressed to the bishops and conceived in such terms as seemed to acknowledge their office and public character [A.D. 261]. The ancient laws, without being formally repealed, were suffered to sink into oblivion; and (excepting only some hostile intentions which are attributed to the emperor Aurelian) the disciples of Christ passed above forty years in a state of prosperity far more dangerous to their virtue than the severest trials of persecution.†

Amidst the frequent revolutions of the empire, the Christians still flourished in peace and prosperity; and notwithstanding a celebrated era of martyrs has been deduced from the accession of Diocletian, the new system of policy, introduced and maintained by the wisdom of that prince, continued, during more than eighteen years, to breathe the mildest and most liberal spirit of religious toleration [A.D. 284–303]. The mind of Diocletian himself was less adapted indeed to speculative inquiries than to the active labors of war and government. His prudence rendered him averse to any great innovation, and though his temper was not very susceptible of zeal or enthusiasm, he always maintained an habitual regard for the ancient deities of the empire. But the leisure of the two empresses, of his wife Prisca and of Valeria, his daughter, permitted them to listen with more attention and respect to the truths of Christianity, which in every age has acknowledged its important obligations to female devotion. The principal eunuchs, Lucian and Dorotheus, Gorgonius and Andrew, who attended the person, possessed the favor, and governed the household of Diocletian, protected by their powerful influence the faith which they had embraced. Their example was imitated by many of the most considerable officers of the palace, who, in their respective stations, had the care of the Imperial ornaments, of the robes, of the furniture, of the jewels, and even of the private treasury; and though it might sometimes be incumbent on them to accompany the emperor when he sacrificed in the temple, they enjoyed, with their wives, their children, and their slaves, the free exercise of the Christian religion. Diocletian and his colleagues frequently conferred the most important offices on those persons who avowed their abhorrence for the worship of the gods but who had displayed abilities proper for the service of the state. The bishops held an honorable rank in their respective provinces and were treated with distinction and respect, not only by the people but by the magistrates themselves. Almost in every city, the ancient churches were found insufficient to contain the increasing multitude of proselytes; and in their place more stately and capacious edifices were erected for the public worship of the faithful. The corruption of manners and principles so forcibly lamented by Eusebius may be considered not only as a consequence but as a proof of the liberty which the Christians enjoyed and abused under the reign of Diocletian. Prosperity had relaxed the nerves of discipline. Fraud, envy, and malice prevailed in every congregation. The presbyters aspired to the episcopal office, which every day became an object more worthy of their ambition. The bishops, who contended with each other for ecclesiastical preeminence, appeared by their conduct to claim a secular and tyrannical power in the church; and the lively faith which still distinguished the Christians from the Gentiles was shown much less in their lives than in their controversial writings.

Notwithstanding this seeming security, an attentive observer might discern some symptoms that threatened the church with a more violent persecution than any which she had yet endured. The zeal and rapid progress of the Christians awakened the Polytheists from their supine indifference in the cause of those deities whom custom and education had taught them to revere. The mutual provocations of a religious war which had already continued above two hundred years exasperated the animosity of the contending parties. The Pagans were incensed at the rashness of a recent and obscure sect which presumed to accuse their countrymen of error and to devote their ancestors to eternal misery. The habits of justifying the popular mythology against the invectives of an implacable enemy produced in their minds some sentiments of faith and reverence for a system which they had been accustomed to consider with the most careless levity. The supernatural powers assumed by the church inspired at the same time terror and emulation. The followers of the established religion entrenched themselves behind a similar fortification of prodigies; invented new modes of sacrifice, of expiation, and of initiation; attempted to revive the credit of their expiring oracles; and listened with eager credulity to every impostor who flattered their prejudices by a tale of wonders. Both parties seemed to acknowledge the truth of those miracles which were claimed by their adversaries; and while they were contented with ascribing them to the arts of magic and to the power of demons they mutually concurred in restoring and establishing the reign of superstition. Philosophy, her most dangerous enemy, was now converted into her most useful ally. The groves of the academy, the gardens of Epicurus, and even the portico of the Stoics were almost deserted, as so many different schools of skepticism or impiety; and many among the Romans were desirous that the writings of Cicero should be condemned and suppressed by the authority of the senate. The prevailing sect of the new Platonicians judged it prudent to connect themselves with the priests, whom perhaps they despised, against the Christians, whom they had reason to fear. These fashionable philosophers prosecuted the design of extracting allegorical wisdom from the fictions of the Greek poets; instituted mysterious rites of devotion for the use of their chosen disciples; recommended the worship of the ancient gods as the emblems or ministers of the Supreme Deity; and composed against the faith of the gospel many elaborate treatises, which have since been committed to the flames by the prudence of orthodox emperors.

Although the policy of Diocletian and the humanity of Constantius inclined them to preserve inviolate the maxims of toleration, it was soon discovered that their two associates, Maximian and Galerius, entertained the most implacable aversion for the name and religion of the Christians. The minds of those princes had never been enlightened by science; education had never softened their temper. They owed their greatness to their swords, and in their most elevated fortune they still retained their superstitious prejudices of soldiers and peasants. In the general administration of the provinces they obeyed the laws which their benefactor had established; but they frequently found occasions of exercising within their camp and palaces a secret persecution, for which the imprudent zeal of the Christians sometimes offered the most specious pretenses. A sentence of death was executed upon Maximilianus, an African youth who had been produced by his own father before the magistrate as a sufficient and legal recruit, but who obstinately persisted in declaring that his conscience would not permit him to embrace the profession of a soldier. It could scarcely be expected that any government should suffer the action of Marcellus the centurion to pass with impunity. On the day of a public festival, that officer threw away his belt, his arms, and the ensigns of his office and exclaimed with a loud voice that he would obey none but Jesus Christ the eternal King, and that he renounced forever the use of carnal weapons and the service of an idolatrous master. The soldiers, as soon as they recovered from their astonishment, secured the person of Marcellus. He was examined in the city of Tingi by the president of that part of Mauritania; and as he was convicted by his own confession, he was condemned and beheaded for the crime of desertion. Examples of such a nature savor much less of religious persecution than of martial or even civil law; but they served to alienate the mind of the emperors, to justify the severity of Galerius, who dismissed a great number of Christian officers from their employments, and to authorize the opinion that a sect of enthusiastics which avowed principles so repugnant to the public safety must either remain useless, or would soon become dangerous, subjects of the empire.

After the success of the Persian war had raised the hopes and the reputation of Galerius, he passed a winter with Diocletian in the palace of Nicomedia; and the fate of Christianity became the object of their secret consultations. The experienced emperor was still inclined to pursue measures of lenity; and though he readily consented to exclude the Christians from holding any employments in the household or the army, he urged in the strongest terms the danger as well as cruelty of shedding the blood of those deluded fanatics. Galerius at length extorted from him the permission of summoning a council composed of a few persons, the most distinguished in the civil and military departments of the state. The important question was agitated in their presence, and those ambitious courtiers easily discerned that it was incumbent on them to second, by their eloquence, the important violence of the Caesar. The Christians (it might specially be alleged), renouncing the gods and the institutions of Rome, had constituted a distinct republic, which might yet be suppressed before it had acquired any military force; but which was already governed by its own laws and magistrates, was possessed of a public treasure, and was intimately connected in all its parts by the frequent assemblies of the bishops, to whose decrees their numerous and opulent congregations yielded an implicit obedience. Arguments like these may seem to have determined the reluctant mind of Diocletian to embrace a new system of persecution; but though we may suspect, it is not in our power to relate the secret intrigues of the palace, the private views and resentments, the jealousy of women or eunuchs, and all those trifling but decisive causes which so often influence the fate of empires and the councils of the wisest monarchs.[†]

[A] general edict of persecution was published [February 24, A.D. 303]; and though Diocletian, still averse to the effusion of blood, had moderated the fury of Galerius, who proposed that everyone refusing to offer sacrifice should immediately be burnt alive, the penalties inflicted on the obstinacy of the Christians might be deemed sufficiently rigorous and effectual. It was enacted that their churches, in all the provinces of the empire, should be demolished to their foundations; and the punishment of death was denounced against all who should presume to hold any secret assemblies for the purpose of religious worship. The philosophers who now assumed the unworthy office of directing the blind zeal of persecution had diligently studied the nature and genius of the Christian religion; and as they were not ignorant that the speculative doctrines of the faith were supposed to be contained in the writings of the prophets, of the evangelists, and of the apostles, they most probably suggested the order that the bishops and presbyters should deliver all their sacred books into the hands of the magistrates; who were commanded, under the severest penalties, to burn them in a public and solemn manner. By the same edict, the property of the church was at once confiscated; and the several parts of which it might consist were either sold to the highest bidder, united to the Imperial domain, bestowed on the cities and corporations, or granted to the solicitations of rapacious courtiers. After taking such effectual measures to abolish the worship and to dissolve the government of the Christians, it was thought necessary to subject to the most intolerable hardships the condition of those perverse individuals who should still reject the religion of nature, of Rome, and of their ancestors. Persons of a liberal birth were declared incapable of holding any honors or employments; slaves were forever deprived of the hopes of freedom, and the whole body of the people were put out of the protection of the law. The judges were authorized to hear and to determine every action that was brought against a Christian. But the Christians were not permitted to complain of any injury which they themselves had suffered; and thus those unfortunate sectaries were exposed to the severity, while they were excluded from the benefits, of public justice. This new species of martyrdom, so painful and lingering, so obscure and ignominious, was, perhaps, the most proper to weary the constancy of the faithful: nor can it be doubted that the passions and interest of mankind were disposed on this occasion to second the designs of the emperors. But the policy of a well-ordered government must sometimes have interposed in behalf of the oppressed Christians; nor was it possible for the Roman princes entirely to remove the apprehension of punishment, or to connive at every act of fraud and violence, without exposing their own authority and the rest of their subjects to the most alarming dangers.[†]

The copies as well as the versions of Scripture were already so multiplied in the empire that the most severe inquisition could no longer be attended with any fatal consequences; and even the sacrifice of those volumes which, in every congregation, were preserved for public use required the consent of some treacherous and unworthy Christians. But the ruin of the churches was easily effected by the authority of the government and by the labor of the Pagans. In some provinces, however, the magistrates contented themselves with shutting up the places of religious worship. In others, they more literally complied with the terms of the edict; and after taking away the doors, the benches, and the pulpit, which they burnt as it were in a funeral pile, they completely demolished the remainder of the edifice.[†]

Some slight disturbances, though they were suppressed almost as soon as excited, in Syria and the frontiers of Armenia afforded the enemies of the church a very plausible occasion to insinuate that those troubles had been secretly fomented by the intrigues of the bishops, who had already forgotten their ostentatious professions of passive and unlimited obedience. The resentment, or the fears, of Diocletian at length transported him beyond the bounds of moderation which he had hitherto preserved, and he declared, in a series of cruel edicts, his intention of abolishing the Christian name. By the first of these edicts, the governors of the provinces were directed to apprehend all persons of the ecclesiastical order; and the prisons destined for the vilest criminals were soon filled with a multitude of bishops, presbyters, deacons, readers, and exorcists. By a second edict, the magistrates were commanded to employ every method of severity which might reclaim them from their odious superstition and oblige them to return to the established worship of the gods. This rigorous order was extended, by a subsequent edict, to the whole body of Christians, who were exposed to a violent and general persecution. Instead of those salutary restraints which had required the direct and solemn testimony of an accuser, it became the duty as well as the interest of the Imperial officers to discover, to pursue, and to torment the most obnoxious among the faithful. Heavy penalties were denounced against all who should presume to save a prescribed sectary from the just indignation of the gods and of the emperors. Yet, notwithstanding the severity of this law, the virtuous courage of many of the Pagans in concealing their friends or relations affords an honorable proof that the rage of superstition had not extinguished in their minds the sentiments of nature and humanity.

Diocletian had no sooner published his edicts against the Christians than, as if he had been desirous of committing to other hands the work of persecution, he divested himself of the Imperial purple. The character and situation of his colleagues and successors sometimes urged them to enforce and sometimes inclined them to suspend the execution of these rigorous laws; nor can we acquire a just and distinct idea of this important period of ecclesiastical history unless we separately consider the state of Christianity in the different parts of the empire during the space of ten years which elapsed between the first edicts of Diocletian and the final peace of the church.

The mild and humane temper of Constantius was averse to the oppression of any part of his subjects. The principal offices of his palace were exercised by Christians. He loved their persons, esteemed their fidelity, and entertained not any dislike to their religious principles. But as long as Constantius remained in the subordinate station of Caesar, it was not in his power openly to reject the edicts of Diocletian or to disobey the commands of Maximian. His authority contributed, however, to alleviate the sufferings which he pitied and abhorred. He consented with reluctance to the ruin of the churches; but he ventured to protect the Christians themselves from the fury of the populace and from the rigor of the laws. The provinces of Gaul (under which we may probably include those of Britain) were indebted for the singular tranquility which they enjoyed to the gentle interposition of their sovereign.... The elevation of Constantius to the supreme and independent dignity of Augustus gave a free scope to the exercise of his virtues, and the shortness of his reign did not prevent him from establishing a system of toleration, of which he left the precept and the example to his son Constantine. His fortunate son, from the first moment of his accession declaring himself the protector of the church, at length deserved the appellation of the first emperor who publicly professed and established the Christian religion. The motives of his conversion, as they may variously be deduced from benevolence, from policy, from conviction, or from remorse, and the progress of the revolution which, under his powerful influence and that of his sons, rendered Christianity the reigning religion of the Roman empire, will form a very interesting and important chapter in the present volume of this history. At present it may be sufficient to observe that every victory of Constantine was productive of some relief or benefit to the church.

[*Violent, but short, persecutions occur in Italy and Africa under Maximin and Severus; Maxentius offers relief and toleration.*]

The sanguinary temper of Galerius, the first and principal author of the persecution, was formidable to those Christians whom their misfortunes had placed within the limits of his dominions; and it may fairly be presumed that many persons of a middle rank, who were not confined by the chains either of wealth or of poverty, very frequently deserted their native country and sought a refuge in the milder climate of the West. As long as he commanded only the armies and provinces of Illyricum, he could with difficulty either find or make a considerable number of martyrs in a warlike country which had entertained the missionaries of the gospel with more coldness and reluctance than any other part of the empire. But when Galerius had obtained the supreme power and the government of the East, he indulged in their fullest extent his zeal and cruelty, not only in the provinces of Thrace and Asia, which acknowledged his immediate jurisdiction, but in those of Syria, Palestine, and Egypt, where Maximin gratified his own inclination by yielding a rigorous obedience to the stern commands of his benefactor. The frequent disappointments of his ambitious views, the experience of six years of persecution, and the salutary reflections which a lingering and painful distemper suggested to the mind of Galerius, at length convinced him that the most violent efforts of despotism are insufficient to extirpate a whole people, or to subdue their religious prejudices. Desirous of repairing the mischief that he had occasioned, he published in his own name, and in those of Licinius and Constantine, a general edict which, after a pompous recital of the Imperial titles, proceeded in the following manner [April 30, A.D. 311]:

"Among the important cares which have occupied our mind for the utility and preservation of the empire, it was our intention to correct and reestablish all things according to the ancient laws and public discipline of the Romans. We were particularly desirous of reclaiming into the way of reason and nature the deluded Christians who had renounced the religion and ceremonies instituted by their fathers; and, presumptuously despising the practice of antiquity, had invented extravagant laws and opinions according to the dictates of their fancy, and had collected a various society from the different provinces of our empire. The edicts which we have published to enforce the worship of the gods, having exposed many of the Christians to danger and distress, many having suffered death and many more, who still persist in their impious folly, being left destitute of *any* public exercise of religion, we are disposed to extend to those unhappy men the effects of our wonted clemency. We permit them therefore freely to profess their private opinions, and to assemble in their conventicles without fear or molestation, provided always that they preserve a due respect to the established laws and government. By another rescript we shall signify our intentions to the judges and magistrates; and we hope that our indulgence will engage the Christians to offer up their prayers to the Deity whom they adore for our safety and prosperity for their own, and for that of the republic." It is not usually in the language of edicts and manifestos that we should search for the real character or the secret motives of princes; but as these were the words of a dying emperor, his situation, perhaps, may be admitted as a pledge of his sincerity.†

In this general view of the persecution, which was first authorized by the edicts of Diocletian, I have purposely refrained from describing the particular sufferings and deaths of the Christian martyrs. It would have been an easy task, from the history of Eusebius, from the declamations of Lactantius, and from the most ancient acts, to collect a long series of horrid and disgustful pictures, and to fill many pages with racks and scourges, with iron hooks and red-hot beds, and with all the variety of tortures which fire and steel, savage beasts, and more savage executioners could inflict upon the human body. These melancholy scenes might be enlivened by a crowd of visions and miracles destined either to delay the death, to celebrate the triumph, or to discover the relics of those canonized saints who suffered for the name of Christ. But I cannot determine what I ought to transcribe till I am satisfied

how much I ought to believe. The gravest of the ecclesiastical historians, Eusebius himself, indirectly confesses that he has related whatever might redound to the glory, and that he has suppressed all that
could tend to the disgrace, of religion. Such an acknowledgment will
naturally excite a suspicion that a writer who has so openly violated
one of the fundamental laws of history has not paid a very strict regard
to the observance of the other; and the suspicion will derive additional
credit from the character of Eusebius, which was less tinctured with
credulity, and more practiced in the arts of courts, than that of almost
any of his contemporaries.[†]

The vague descriptions of exile and imprisonment, of pain and torture, are so easily exaggerated or softened by the pencil of an artful orator that we are naturally induced to inquire into a fact of a more
distinct and stubborn kind; the number of persons who suffered death
in consequence of the edicts published by Diocletian, his associates,
and his successors. The recent legendaries record whole armies and
cities which were at once swept away by the undistinguishing rage of
persecution. The more ancient writers content themselves with pouring out a liberal effusion of loose and tragical invectives, without condescending to ascertain the precise number of those persons who were
permitted to seal with their blood their belief of the gospel. From the
history of Eusebius, it may, however, be collected that only nine bishops were punished with death; and we are assured, by his particular
enumeration of the martyrs of Palestine, that no more than ninety-
two Christians were entitled to that honorable appellation. As we are
unacquainted with the degree of episcopal zeal and courage which
prevailed at that time, it is not in our power to draw any useful infer-
ences from the former of these facts: but the latter may serve to justify
a very important and probable conclusion. According to the distribution of Roman provinces, Palestine may be considered as the sixteenth
part of the Eastern empire: and since there were some governors who
from a real or affected clemency had preserved their hands unstained
with the blood of the faithful, it is reasonable to believe that the country which had given birth to Christianity produced at least the sixteenth part of the martyrs who suffered death within the dominions
of Galerius and Maximin; the whole might consequently amount to
about fifteen hundred, a number which, if it is equally divided between the ten years of the persecution, will allow an annual consump-

tion of one hundred and fifty martyrs. Allotting the same proportion to the provinces of Italy, Africa, and perhaps Spain, where, at the end of two or three years, the rigor of the penal laws was either suspended or abolished, the multitude of Christians in the Roman empire on whom a capital punishment was inflicted by a judicial sentence will be reduced to somewhat less than two thousand persons. Since it cannot be doubted that the Christians were more numerous, and their enemies more exasperated, in the time of Diocletian, than they had ever been in any former persecution, this probable and moderate computation may teach us to estimate the number of primitive saints and martyrs who sacrificed their lives for the important purpose of introducing Christianity into the world.

We shall conclude this chapter by a melancholy truth which obtrudes itself on the reluctant mind; that even admitting, without hesitation or inquiry, all that history has recorded or devotion has feigned on the subject of martyrdoms, it must still be acknowledged that the Christians, in the course of their intestine dissensions, have inflicted far greater severities on each other than they had experienced from the zeal of infidels. During the ages of ignorance which followed the subversion of the Roman empire in the West, the bishops of the Imperial city extended their dominion over the laity as well as clergy of the Latin church. The fabric of superstition which they had erected, and which might long have defied the feeble efforts of reason, was at length assaulted by a crowd of daring fanatics who from the twelfth to the sixteenth century assumed the popular character of reformers. The church of Rome defended by violence the empire which she had acquired by fraud; a system of peace and benevolence was soon disgraced by proscriptions, war, massacres, and the institution of the holy office. And as the reformers were animated by the love of civil as well as of religious freedom, the Catholic princes connected their own interest with that of the clergy, and enforced by fire and the sword the terrors of spiritual censures. In the Netherlands alone, more than one hundred thousand of the subjects of Charles V are said to have suffered by the hand of the executioner; and this extraordinary number is attested by Grotius, a man of genius and learning who preserved his moderation amidst the fury of contending sects, and who composed the annals of his own age and country at a time when the invention of printing had facilitated the means of intelligence and increased the danger of detection. If we are obliged to submit our belief to the authority of Grotius, it must be allowed that the number of Protestants who were executed in a single province and a single reign far exceeded that of the primitive martyrs in the space of three centuries, and of the Roman empire. But if the improbability of the fact itself should prevail over the weight of evidence; if Grotius should be convicted of exaggerating the merit and sufferings of the Reformers; we shall be naturally led to inquire what confidence can be placed in the doubtful and imperfect monuments of ancient credulity; what degree of credit can be assigned to a courtly bishop and a passionate declaimer who, under the protection of Constantine, enjoyed the exclusive privilege of recording the persecutions inflicted on the Christians by the vanquished rivals or disregarded predecessors of their gracious sovereign.

END OF THE FIRST VOLUME [1776].

VOLUME THE SECOND

[1781]

CHAPTER XVII

FOUNDATION OF CONSTANTINOPLE

Foundation of Constantinople. • Political system of Constantine,
and his successors. • Military discipline. • The palace. •
The finances.

The unfortunate Licinius was the last rival who opposed the greatness, and the last captive who adorned the triumph, of Constantine. After a tranquil and prosperous reign, the conquerer bequeathed to his family the inheritance of the Roman empire; a new capital, a new policy, and a new religion; and the innovations which he established have been embraced and consecrated by succeeding generations. The age of the great Constantine and his sons is filled with important events; but the historian must be oppressed by their number and variety, unless he diligently separates from each other the scenes which are connected only by the order of time. He will describe the political institutions that gave strength and stability to the empire before he proceeds to relate the wars and revolutions which hastened its decline. He will adopt the division, unknown to the ancients, of civil and ecclesiastical affairs: the victory of the Christians, and their intestine discord, will supply copious and distinct materials both for edification and for scandal.

After the defeat and abdication of Licinius, his victorious rival proceeded to lay the foundations of a city destined to reign in future times the mistress of the East and to survive the empire and religion of Constantine [A.D. 324]. The motives, whether of pride or of policy, which first induced Diocletian to withdraw himself from the ancient seat of government had acquired additional weight by the example of his successors and the habits of forty years. Rome was insensibly confounded with the dependent kingdoms which had once acknowledged her supremacy; and the country of the Caesars was viewed with cold indifference by a martial prince born in the neighborhood of the Danube, educated in the courts and armies of Asia, and invested with the purple by the legions of Britain. The Italians, who had received Constantine as their deliverer, submissively obeyed the edicts which he sometimes condescended to address to the senate and people of

Rome; but they were seldom honored with the presence of their new sovereign. During the vigor of his age, Constantine, according to the various exigencies of peace and war, moved with slow dignity or with active diligence along the frontiers of his extensive dominions; and was always prepared to take the field either against a foreign or a domestic enemy. But as he gradually reached the summit of prosperity and the decline of life, he began to meditate the design of fixing in a more permanent station the strength as well as majesty of the throne. In the choice of an advantageous situation, he preferred the confines of Europe and Asia; to curb with a powerful arm the Barbarians who dwelt between the Danube and the Tanais; to watch with an eye of jealousy the conduct of the Persian monarch, who indignantly supported the yoke of an ignominious treaty. With these views, Diocletian had selected and embellished the residence of Nicomedia: but the memory of Diocletian was justly abhorred by the protector of the church: and Constantine was not insensible to the ambition of founding a city which might perpetuate the glory of his own name. During the late operations of the war against Licinius, he had sufficient opportunity to contemplate, both as a soldier and as a statesman, the incomparable position of Byzantium; and to observe how strongly it was guarded by nature against a hostile attack, whilst it was accessible on every side to the benefits of commercial intercourse.[†]

The prospect of beauty, of safety, and of wealth, united in a single spot, was sufficient to justify the choice of Constantine. But as some decent mixture of prodigy and fable has, in every age, been supposed to reflect a becoming majesty on the origin of great cities, the emperor was desirous of ascribing his resolution not so much to the uncertain counsels of human policy as to the infallible and eternal decrees of divine wisdom. In one of his laws he has been careful to instruct posterity that in obedience to the commands of God, he laid the everlasting foundations of Constantinople: and though he has not condescended to relate in what manner the celestial inspiration was communicated to his mind, the defect of his modest silence has been liberally supplied by the ingenuity of succeeding writers, who describe the nocturnal vision which appeared to the fancy of Constantine as he slept within the walls of Byzantium. The tutelar genius of the city, a venerable matron sinking under the weight of years and infirmities, was suddenly transformed into a blooming maid, whom his own hands adorned with all the symbols of Imperial greatness. The monarch awoke, interpreted the auspicious omen, and obeyed, without hesitation, the will of Heaven. The day which gave birth to a city or colony was celebrated by the Romans with such ceremonies as had been ordained by a generous superstition; and though Constantine might omit some rites which savored too strongly of their Pagan origin, yet he was anxious to leave a deep impression of hope and respect on the minds of the spectators. On foot, with a lance in his hand, the emperor himself led the solemn procession; and directed the line which was traced as the boundary of the destined capital: till the growing circumference was observed with astonishment by the assistants, who at length ventured to observe that he had already exceeded the most ample measure of a great city. "I shall still advance," replied Constantine, "till HE, the invisible guide who marches before me, thinks proper to stop."†

The master of the Roman world who aspired to erect an eternal monument of the glories of his reign could employ in the prosecution of that great work the wealth, the labor, and all that yet remained of the genius of obedient millions. Some estimate may be formed of the expense bestowed with Imperial liberality on the foundation of Constantinople by the allowance of about two millions five hundred thousand pounds for the construction of the walls, the porticos, and the aqueducts. The forests that overshadowed the shores of the Euxine, and the celebrated quarries of white marble in the little island of Proconnesus, supplied an inexhaustible stock of materials, ready to be conveyed, by the convenience of a short water carriage, to the harbor of Byzantium. A multitude of laborers and artificers urged the conclusion of the work with incessant toil: but the impatience of Constantine soon discovered that, in the decline of the arts, the skill as well as numbers of his architects bore a very unequal proportion to the greatness of his designs. The magistrates of the most distant provinces were therefore directed to institute schools, to appoint professors, and, by the hopes of rewards and privileges, to engage in the study and practice of architecture a sufficient number of ingenious youths who had received a liberal education. The buildings of the new city were executed by such artificers as the reign of Constantine could afford; but they were decorated by the hands of the most celebrated masters of the age of Pericles and Alexander. To revive the genius of Phidias

THE ARCH OF CONSTANTINE AND THE COLOSSEUM

and Lysippus surpassed indeed the power of a Roman emperor; but the immortal productions which they had bequeathed to posterity were exposed without defense to the rapacious vanity of a despot. By his commands the cities of Greece and Asia were despoiled of their most valuable ornaments. The trophies of memorable wars, the objects of religious veneration, the most finished statues of the gods and heroes, of the sages and poets, of ancient times contributed to the splendid triumph of Constantinople; and gave occasion to the remark of the historian Cedrenus, who observes with some enthusiasm that nothing seemed wanting except the souls of the illustrious men whom these admirable monuments were intended to represent. But it is not in the city of Constantine, nor in the declining period of an empire, when the human mind was depressed by civil and religious slavery, that we should seek for the souls of Homer and of Demosthenes.†

But we should deviate from the design of this history if we attempted minutely to describe the different buildings or quarters of the city. It may be sufficient to observe that whatever could adorn the dignity of a great capital, or contribute to the benefit or pleasure of its numerous inhabitants, was contained within the walls of Constantinople. A particular description, composed about a century after its foundation, enumerates a capitol or school of learning, a circus, two theaters, eight public, and one hundred and fifty-three private baths, fifty-two porticos, five granaries, eight aqueducts or reservoirs of water, four spacious halls for the meetings of the senate or courts of justice, fourteen churches, fourteen palaces, and four thousand three hundred and eighty-eight houses, which, for their size or beauty, deserved to be distinguished from the multitude of plebeian inhabitants.†

The populousness of his favored city was the next and most serious object of the attention of its founder. In the dark ages which succeeded the translation of the empire, the remote and the immediate consequences of that memorable event were strangely confounded by the vanity of the Greeks and the credulity of the Latins. It was asserted, and believed, that all the noble families of Rome, the senate, and the equestrian order, with their innumerable attendants, had followed their emperor to the banks of the Propontis; that a spurious race of strangers and plebeians was left to possess the solitude of the ancient capital; and that the lands of Italy, long since converted into gardens, were at once deprived of cultivation and inhabitants. In the course of this history, such exaggerations will be reduced to their just value: yet, since the growth of Constantinople cannot be ascribed to the general increase of mankind and of industry, it must be admitted that this artificial colony was raised at the expense of the ancient cities of the empire. Many opulent senators of Rome and of the Eastern provinces were probably invited by Constantine to adopt for their country the fortunate spot which he had chosen for his own residence. The invitations of a master are scarcely to be distinguished from commands; and the liberality of the emperor obtained a ready and cheerful obedience. He bestowed on his favorites the palaces which he had built in the several quarters of the city, assigned them lands and pensions for the support of their dignity, and alienated the demesnes of Pontus and Asia to grant hereditary estates by the easy tenure of maintaining a house in the capital. But these encouragements and obligations soon became superfluous and were gradually abolished. Wherever the seat of government is fixed, a considerable part of the public revenue will be expended by the prince himself, by his ministers, by the officers of justice, and by the domestics of the palace. The most wealthy of the provincials will be attracted by the powerful motives of interest and duty, of amusement and curiosity. A third and more numerous class of inhabitants will insensibly be formed of servants, of artificers, and of merchants, who derive their subsistence from their own labor and from the wants or luxury of the superior ranks. In less than a century, Constantinople disputed with Rome itself the preeminence of riches and numbers. New piles of buildings, crowded together with too little regard to health or convenience, scarcely allowed the intervals of narrow streets for the perpetual throng of men, of horses, and of carriages. The allotted space of ground was insufficient to contain the increasing people; and the additional foundations which, on either side, were advanced into the sea might alone have composed a very considerable city.

The frequent and regular distributions of wine and oil, of corn or bread, of money or provisions, had almost exempted the poorest citizens of Rome from the necessity of labor. The magnificence of the first Caesars was in some measure imitated by the founder of Constantinople: but his liberality, however it might excite the applause of the people, has incurred the censure of posterity. A nation of legislators and conquerors might assert their claim to the harvests of Africa, which had been purchased with their blood; and it was artfully contrived by Augustus that, in the enjoyment of plenty, the Romans should lose the memory of freedom. But the prodigality of Constantine could not be excused by any consideration either of public or private interest; and the annual tribute of corn imposed upon Egypt for the benefit of his new capital was applied to feed a lazy and insolent populace at the expense of the husbandmen of an industrious province. Some other regulations of this emperor are less liable to blame, but they are less deserving of notice. He divided Constantinople into fourteen regions or quarters, dignified the public council with the appellation of senate, communicated to the citizens the privileges of Italy, and bestowed on the rising city the title of Colony, the first and most favored daughter of ancient Rome. The venerable parent still maintained the legal and acknowledged supremacy, which was due to her age, her dignity, and to the remembrance of her former greatness.†

The foundation of a new capital is naturally connected with the establishment of a new form of civil and military administration. The distinct view of the complicated system of policy introduced by Diocletian, improved by Constantine, and completed by his immediate successors may not only amuse the fancy by the singular picture of a great empire, but will tend to illustrate the secret and internal causes of its rapid decay. In the pursuit of any remarkable institution, we may be frequently led into the more early or the more recent times of the Roman history; but the proper limits of this inquiry will be included within a period of about one hundred and thirty years, from the accession of Constantine to the publication of the Theodosian code; from which, as well as from the *Notitia* of the East and West [a late antique treatise outlining the duties of Imperial officeholders], we derive the most copious and authentic information of the state of the empire. This variety of objects will suspend, for some time, the course of the narrative; but the interruption will be censured only by those readers who are insensible to the importance of laws and manners while they peruse with eager curiosity the transient intrigues of a court or the accidental event of a battle.

The manly pride of the Romans, content with substantial power, had left to the vanity of the East the forms and ceremonies of ostentatious greatness. But when they lost even the semblance of those virtues which were derived from their ancient freedom, the simplicity of Roman manners was insensibly corrupted by the stately affectation of the courts of Asia. The distinctions of personal merit and influence, so conspicuous in a republic, so feeble and obscure under a monarchy, were abolished by the despotism of the emperors; who substituted in their room a severe subordination of rank and office, from the titled slaves who were seated on the steps of the throne to the meanest instruments of arbitrary power. This multitude of abject dependents was interested in the support of the actual government from the dread of a revolution, which might at once confound their hopes and intercept the reward of their services. In this divine hierarchy (for such it is frequently styled) every rank was marked with the most scrupulous exactness, and its dignity was displayed in a variety of trifling and solemn ceremonies, which it was a study to learn and a sacrilege to neglect. The purity of the Latin language was debased by adopting, in the intercourse of pride and flattery, a profusion of epithets, which Tully [Cicero] would scarcely have understood, and which Augustus would have rejected with indignation. The principal officers of the empire were saluted, even by the sovereign himself, with the deceitful titles of your *Sincerity*, your *Gravity*, your *Excellency*, your *Eminence*, your *sublime and wonderful Magnitude*, your *illustrious and magnificent Highness*. The codicils or patents of their office were curiously emblazoned with such emblems as were best adapted to explain its nature and high dignity; the image or portrait of the reigning emperors; a triumphal car; the book of mandates placed on a table, covered with a rich carpet and illuminated by four tapers; the allegorical figures of the provinces which they governed; or the appellations and standards of the troops whom they commanded. Some of these official ensigns were really exhibited in their hall of audience; others preceded their pompous march whenever they appeared in public; and every circumstance of their demeanor, their dress, their ornaments, and their train was calculated to inspire a deep reverence for the representatives of supreme majesty. By a philosophic observer, the system of the Roman government might have been mistaken for a splendid theater, filled with players of every character and degree, who repeated the language and imitated the passions of their original model.

All the magistrates of sufficient importance to find a place in the general state of the empire were accurately divided into three classes. 1. The *Illustrious.* 2. The *Spectabiles,* or *Respectable.* And, 3. The *Clarissimi;*

whom we may translate by the word *Honorable*. In the times of Roman simplicity, the last-mentioned epithet was used only as a vague expression of deference, till it became at length the peculiar and appropriated title of all who were members of the senate, and consequently of all who, from that venerable body, were selected to govern the provinces. The vanity of those who from their rank and office might claim a superior distinction above the rest of the senatorial order was long afterwards indulged with the new appellation of *Respectable*; but the title of *Illustrious* was always reserved to some eminent personages who were obeyed or reverenced by the two subordinate classes. It was communicated only, I. To the consuls and patricians; II. To the Praetorian praefects, with the praefects of Rome and Constantinople; III. To the masters-general of the cavalry and the infantry; and IV. To the seven ministers of the palace, who exercised their *sacred* functions about the person of the emperor. Among those illustrious magistrates who were esteemed coordinate with each other, the seniority of appointment gave place to the union of dignities. By the expedient of honorary codicils, the emperors, who were fond of multiplying their favors, might sometimes gratify the vanity, though not the ambition, of impatient courtiers.

I. As long as the Roman consuls were the first magistrates of a free state, they derived their right to power from the choice of the people. As long as the emperors condescended to disguise the servitude which they imposed, the consuls were still elected by the real or apparent suffrage of the senate. From the reign of Diocletian, even these vestiges of liberty were abolished, and the successful candidates who were invested with the annual honors of the consulship affected to deplore the humiliating condition of their predecessors. The Scipios and the Catos had been reduced to solicit the votes of plebeians, to pass through the tedious and expensive forms of a popular election, and to expose their dignity to the shame of a public refusal; while their own happier fate had reserved them for an age and government in which the rewards of virtue were assigned by the unerring wisdom of a gracious sovereign. In the epistles which the emperor addressed to the two consuls elect, it was declared that they were created by his sole authority. Their names and portraits, engraved on gilt tables of ivory, were dispersed over the empire as presents to the provinces, the cities, the magistrates, the senate, and the people. Their solemn inauguration was performed at the place of the Imperial residence; and during a period of one hundred and twenty years, Rome was constantly deprived of the presence of her ancient magistrates.

On the morning of the first of January, the consuls assumed the ensigns of their dignity. Their dress was a robe of purple, embroidered in silk and gold and sometimes ornamented with costly gems. On this solemn occasion they were attended by the most eminent officers of the state and army, in the habit of senators; and the useless fasces, armed with the once formidable axes, were borne before them by the lictors. The procession moved from the palace to the Forum or principal square of the city; where the consuls ascended their tribunal and seated themselves in the curule chairs, which were framed after the fashion of ancient times. They immediately exercised an act of jurisdiction by the manumission of a slave who was brought before them for that purpose; and the ceremony was intended to represent the celebrated action of the elder Brutus, the author of liberty and of the consulship, when he admitted among his fellow-citizens the faithful Vindex, who had revealed the conspiracy of the Tarquins [509 B.C.]. The public festival was continued during several days in all the principal cities: in Rome, from custom; in Constantinople, from imitation; in Carthage, Antioch, and Alexandria, from the love of pleasure and the superfluity of wealth. . . . As soon as the consuls had discharged these customary duties, they were at liberty to retire into the shade of private life and to enjoy, during the remainder of the year, the undisturbed contemplation of their own greatness. They no longer presided in the national councils; they no longer executed the resolutions of peace or war. Their abilities (unless they were employed in more effective offices) were of little moment; and their names served only as the legal date of the year in which they had filled the chair of Marius and of Cicero. Yet it was still felt and acknowledged, in the last period of Roman servitude, that this empty name might be compared, and even preferred, to the possession of substantial power. The title of consul was still the most splendid object of ambition, the noblest reward of virtue and loyalty. The emperors themselves, who disdained the faint shadow of the republic, were conscious that they acquired an additional splendor and majesty as often as they assumed the annual honors of the consular dignity.

The proudest and most perfect separation which can be found in any age or country between the nobles and the people is perhaps that of the Patricians and the Plebeians, as it was established in the first age of the Roman republic. Wealth and honors, the offices of the state, and the ceremonies of religion were almost exclusively possessed by the former, who, preserving the purity of their blood with the most insulting jealousy, held their clients in a condition of specious vassalage. But these distinctions, so incompatible with the spirit of a free people, were removed, after a long struggle, by the persevering efforts of the Tribunes. The most active and successful of the Plebeians accumulated wealth, aspired to honors, deserved triumphs, contracted alliances, and, after some generations, assumed the pride of ancient nobility. The Patrician families, on the other hand, whose original number was never recruited till the end of the commonwealth, either failed in the ordinary course of nature, or were extinguished in so many foreign and domestic wars, or, through a want of merit or fortune, insensibly mingled with the mass of the people. Very few remained who could derive their pure and genuine origin from the infancy of the city, or even from that of the republic, when Caesar and Augustus, Claudius and Vespasian, created from the body of the senate a competent number of new Patrician families in the hope of perpetuating an order which was still considered as honorable and sacred. But these artificial supplies (in which the reigning house was always included) were rapidly swept away by the rage of tyrants, by frequent revolutions, by the change of manners, and by the intermixture of nations. Little more was left when Constantine ascended the throne than a vague and imperfect tradition that the Patricians had once been the first of the Romans. To form a body of nobles whose influence may restrain, while it secures the authority, of the monarch would have been very inconsistent with the character and policy of Constantine; but had he seriously entertained such a design, it might have exceeded the measure of his power to ratify, by an arbitrary edict, an institution which must expect the sanction of time and of opinion. He revived, indeed, the title of PATRICIANS, but he revived it as a personal, not as an hereditary distinction. They yielded only to the transient superiority of the annual consuls; but they enjoyed the preeminence over all the great officers of state, with the most familiar access to the person of the prince. This honorable rank was bestowed on them for life; and as they were usually favorites, and ministers who had grown old in the Imperial court, the true etymology of the word was perverted by ignorance and flattery; and the Patricians of Constantine were reverenced as the adopted *Fathers* of the emperor and the republic.

II. The fortunes of the Praetorian praefects were essentially different from those of the consuls and Patricians. The latter saw their ancient greatness evaporate in a vain title. The former, rising by degrees from the most humble condition, were invested with the civil and military administration of the Roman world. From the reign of Severus to that of Diocletian, the guards and the palace, the laws and the finances, the armies and the provinces were entrusted to their superintending care; and, like the Viziers of the East, they held with one hand the seal and with the other the standard of the empire. The ambition of the praefects, always formidable and sometimes fatal to the masters whom they served, was supported by the strength of the Praetorian bands; but after those haughty troops had been weakened by Diocletian and finally suppressed by Constantine, the praefects who survived their fall were reduced without difficulty to the station of useful and obedient ministers. When they were no longer responsible for the safety of the emperor's person, they resigned the jurisdiction which they had hitherto claimed and exercised over all the departments of the palace. They were deprived by Constantine of all military command as soon as they had ceased to lead into the field, under their immediate orders, the flower of the Roman troops; and at length, by a singular revolution, the captains of the guards were transformed into the civil magistrates of the provinces. According to the plan of government instituted by Diocletian, the four princes had each their Praetorian praefect; and after the monarchy was once more united in the person of Constantine, he still continued to create the same number of FOUR PRAEFECTS, and entrusted to their care the same provinces which they already administered.[†]

After the Praetorian praefects had been dismissed from all military command, the civil functions which they were ordained to exercise over so many subject nations were adequate to the ambition and abilities of the most consummate ministers. To their wisdom was committed the supreme administration of justice and of the finances, the two objects which, in a state of peace, comprehend almost all the respective duties of the sovereign and of the people; of the former, to protect the citizens who are obedient to the laws; of the latter, to contribute the share of their property which is required for the expenses of the state. The coin, the highways, the posts, the granaries, the manufactures, whatever could interest the public prosperity was moderated by the authority of the Praetorian praefects. As the immediate representatives of the Imperial majesty, they were empowered to explain, to enforce, and on some occasions to modify the general edicts by their discretionary proclamations. They watched over the conduct of the provincial governors, removed the negligent, and inflicted punishments on the guilty. From all the inferior jurisdictions, an appeal in every matter of importance, either civil or criminal, might be brought before the tribunal of the praefect; but his sentence was final and absolute; and the emperors themselves refused to admit any complaints against the judgment or the integrity of a magistrate whom they honored with such unbounded confidence. His appointments were suitable to his dignity; and if avarice was his ruling passion, he enjoyed frequent opportunities of collecting a rich harvest of fees, of presents, and of perquisites. Though the emperors no longer dreaded the ambition of their praefects, they were attentive to counterbalance the power of this great office by the uncertainty and shortness of its duration.

From their superior importance and dignity, Rome and Constantinople were alone excepted from the jurisdiction of the Praetorian praefects. The immense size of the city, and the experience of the tardy, ineffectual operation of the laws, had furnished the policy of Augustus with a specious pretense for introducing a new magistrate who alone could restrain a servile and turbulent populace by the strong arm of arbitrary power. Valerius Messalla was appointed the first praefect of Rome, that his reputation might countenance so invidious a measure; but, at the end of a few days, that accomplished citizen resigned his office, declaring, with a spirit worthy of the friend of Brutus, that he found himself incapable of exercising a power incompatible with public freedom. As the sense of liberty became less exquisite, the advantages of order were more clearly understood; and the praefect, who seemed to have been designed as a terror only to slaves and vagrants, was permitted to extend his civil and criminal jurisdiction over the equestrian and noble families of Rome. The praetors, annually created as the judges of law and equity, could not long dispute the possession of the forum with a vigorous and permanent magistrate who was usually admitted into the confidence of the prince. Their courts were deserted, their number, which had once fluctuated between twelve and eighteen, was gradually reduced to two or three, and their important functions were confined to the expensive obligation of exhibiting games for the amusement of the people. After the office of the Roman consuls had been changed into a vain pageant which was rarely displayed in the capital, the praefects assumed their vacant place in the senate and were soon acknowledged as the ordinary presidents of that venerable assembly. They received appeals from the distance of one hundred miles; and it was allowed as a principle of jurisprudence that all municipal authority was derived from them alone. In the discharge of his laborious employment, the governor of Rome was assisted by fifteen officers, some of whom had been originally his equals, or even his superiors. The principal departments were relative to the command of a numerous watch, established as a safeguard against fires, robberies, and nocturnal disorders; the custody and distribution of the public allowance of corn and provisions; the care of the port, of the aqueducts, of the common sewers, and of the navigation and bed of the Tiber; the inspection of the markets, the theaters, and of the private as well as the public works. Their vigilance insured the three principal objects of a regular police, safety, plenty, and cleanliness; and as a proof of the attention of government to preserve the splendor and ornaments of the capital, a particular inspector was appointed for the statues; the guardian, as it were, of that inanimate people which, according to the extravagant computation of an old writer, was scarcely inferior in number to the living inhabitants of Rome. About thirty years after the foundation of Constantinople, a similar magistrate was created in that rising metropolis, for the same uses and with the same powers. A perfect equality was established between the dignity of the *two* municipal and that of the *four* Praetorian praefects.

Those who, in the imperial hierarchy, were distinguished by the title of *Respectable* formed an intermediate class between the *illustrious* praefects and the *honorable* magistrates of the provinces. In this class the proconsuls of Asia, Achaia, and Africa claimed a preeminence, which was yielded to the remembrance of their ancient dignity; and the appeal from their tribunal to that of the praefects was almost the only mark of their dependence. But the civil government of the empire was distributed into thirteen great DIOCESES, each of which equaled the just measure of a powerful kingdom. The first of these dioceses was subject to the jurisdiction of the *count* of the East; and we may convey some idea of the importance and variety of his functions by observing that six hundred apparitors, who would be styled at present either secretaries, or clerks, or ushers, or messengers, were employed in his immediate office. The place of *Augustal praefect* of Egypt was no longer filled by a Roman knight; but the name was retained; and the extraordinary powers which the situation of the country and the temper of the inhabitants had once made indispensable were still continued to the governor. The eleven remaining dioceses . . . were governed by twelve *vicars* or *vice-praefects,* whose name sufficiently explains the nature and dependence of their office. It may be added that the lieutenant-generals of the Roman armies, the military counts and dukes, who will be hereafter mentioned, were allowed the rank and title of *Respectable.*

As the spirit of jealousy and ostentation prevailed in the councils of the emperors, they proceeded with anxious diligence to divide the substance and to multiply the titles of power. The vast countries which the Roman conquerors had united under the same simple form of administration were imperceptibly crumbled into minute fragments; till at length the whole empire was distributed into one hundred and sixteen provinces, each of which supported an expensive and splendid establishment. Of these, three were governed by *proconsuls,* thirty-seven by *consulars,* five by *correctors,* and seventy-one by *presidents.* The appellations of these magistrates were different; they ranked in successive order, the ensigns of their dignity were curiously varied; and their situation, from accidental circumstances, might be more or less agreeable or advantageous. But they were all (excepting only the proconsuls) alike included in the class of *honorable* persons; and they were alike entrusted, during the pleasure of the prince and under the authority of the praefects or their deputies, with the administration of justice and the finances in their respective districts.[†]

All the civil magistrates were drawn from the profession of the law. The celebrated *Institutes* of Justinian are addressed to the youth of his dominions who had devoted themselves to the study of Roman jurisprudence; and the sovereign condescends to animate their diligence by the assurance that their skill and ability would in time be rewarded by an adequate share in the government of the republic. The rudiments of this lucrative science were taught in all the considerable cities of the East and West; but the most famous school was that of Beirut, on the coast of Phoenicia; which flourished above three centuries from the time of Alexander Severus, the author perhaps of an institution so advantageous to his native country. After a regular course of education which lasted five years, the students dispersed themselves through the provinces in search of fortune and honors; nor could they want an inexhaustible supply of business in a great empire already corrupted by the multiplicity of laws, of arts, and of vices. The court of the Praetorian praefect of the East could alone furnish employment for one hundred and fifty advocates, sixty-four of whom were distinguished by peculiar privileges, and two were annually chosen, with a salary of sixty pounds of gold, to defend the causes of the treasury. The first experiment was made of their judicial talents by appointing them to act occasionally as assessors to the magistrates; from thence they were often raised to preside in the tribunals before which they had pleaded. They obtained the government of a province; and by the aid of merit, of reputation, or of favor they ascended, by successive steps, to the illustrious dignities of the state. In the practice of the bar, these men had considered reason as the instrument of dispute; they interpreted the laws according to the dictates of private interest, and the same pernicious habits might still adhere to their characters in the public administration of the state. The honor of a liberal profession has indeed been vindicated by ancient and modern advocates who have filled the most important stations with pure integrity and consummate wisdom: but in the decline of Roman jurisprudence, the ordinary promotion of lawyers was pregnant with mischief and disgrace. The noble art, which had once been preserved as the sacred inheritance of the patricians, was fallen into the hands of freedmen and plebeians, who, with cunning rather than with skill, exercised a sordid and pernicious trade.[†]

III. In the system of policy introduced by Augustus, the governors, those at least of the Imperial provinces, were invested with the full powers of the sovereign himself. Ministers of peace and war, the distribution of rewards and punishments depended on them alone, and they successively appeared on their tribunal in the robes of civil magistracy, and in complete armor at the head of the Roman legions. The influence of the revenue, the authority of law, and the command of a military force concurred to render their power supreme and absolute; and whenever they were tempted to violate their allegiance, the loyal province which they involved in their rebellion was scarcely sensible of any change in its political state. From the time of Commodus to the reign of Constantine, near one hundred governors might be enumerated who, with various success, erected the standard of revolt; and though the innocent were too often sacrificed, the guilty might be sometimes prevented, by the suspicious cruelty of their master. To secure his throne and the public tranquility from these formidable servants, Constantine resolved to divide the military from the civil administration and to establish, as a permanent and professional distinction, a practice which had been adopted only as an occasional expedient. The supreme jurisdiction exercised by the Praetorian praefects over the armies of the empire was transferred to the two *masters-general* whom he instituted, the one for the *cavalry,* the other for the *infantry;* and though each of these *illustrious* officers was more peculiarly responsible for the discipline of those troops which were under his immediate inspection, they both indifferently commanded in the field the several bodies, whether of horse or foot, which were united in the same army. Their number was soon doubled by the division of the East and West; and as separate generals of the same rank and title were appointed on the four important frontiers of the Rhine, of the Upper and the Lower Danube, and of the Euphrates, the defense of the Roman empire was at length committed to eight masters-general of the cavalry and infantry. Under their orders, thirty-five military commanders were stationed in the provinces.[†]

The memory of Constantine has been deservedly censured for another innovation, which corrupted military discipline and prepared the ruin of the empire. The nineteen years which preceded his final victory over Licinius had been a period of license and intestine war. The rivals who contended for the possession of the Roman world had withdrawn the greatest part of their forces from the guard of the general frontier; and the principal cities which formed the boundary of their respective dominions were filled with soldiers who considered their countrymen as their most implacable enemies. After the use of these internal garrisons had ceased with the civil war, the conqueror wanted either wisdom or firmness to revive the severe discipline of Diocletian and to suppress a fatal indulgence which habit had endeared and almost confirmed to the military order. From the reign of Constantine, a popular and even legal distinction was admitted between the *Palatines* and the *Borderers;* the troops of the court, as they were improperly styled, and the troops of the frontier. The former, elevated by the superiority of their pay and privileges, were permitted, except in the extraordinary emergencies of war, to occupy their tranquil stations in the heart of the provinces. The most flourishing cities were oppressed by the intolerable weight of quarters. The soldiers insensibly forgot the virtues of their profession, and contracted only the vices of civil life. They were either degraded by the industry of mechanic trades or enervated by the luxury of baths and theaters. They soon became careless of their martial exercises, curious in their diet and apparel; and while they inspired terror to the subjects of the empire, they trembled at the hostile approach of the Barbarians. The chain of fortifications which Diocletian and his colleagues had extended along the banks of the great rivers was no longer maintained with the same care, or defended with the same vigilance. The numbers which still remained under the name of the troops of the frontier might be sufficient for the ordinary defense; but their spirit was degraded by the humiliating reflection that *they,* who were exposed to the hardships and dangers of a perpetual warfare, were rewarded only with about two thirds of the pay and emoluments which were lavished on the troops of the court. Even the bands or legions that were raised the nearest to the level of those unworthy favorites were in some measure disgraced by the title of honor which they were allowed to assume. It was in vain that Constantine repeated the most dreadful menaces of fire and sword against the Borderers who should dare desert their colors, to connive at the inroads of the Barbarians, or to participate in the spoil. The mischiefs which flow from injudicious counsels are seldom removed by the application of partial severities; and though succeeding princes labored to restore the strength and numbers of the frontier garrisons, the empire, till the last moment of its dissolution, continued to languish under the mortal wound which had been so rashly or so weakly inflicted by the hand of Constantine.

The same timid policy, of dividing whatever is united, of reducing whatever is eminent, of dreading every active power and of expecting that the most feeble will prove the most obedient, seems to pervade the institutions of several princes, and particularly those of Constantine. The martial pride of the legions, whose victorious camps had so often been the scene of rebellion, was nourished by the memory of their past exploits and the consciousness of their actual strength. As long as they maintained their ancient establishment of six thousand men, they subsisted, under the reign of Diocletian, each of them singly, a visible and important object in the military history of the Roman empire. A few years afterwards, these gigantic bodies were shrunk to a very diminutive size; and when *seven* legions, with some auxiliaries, defended the city of Amida against the Persians, the total garrison, with the inhabitants of both sexes and the peasants of the deserted country, did not exceed the number of twenty thousand persons. From this fact and from similar examples, there is reason to believe that the constitution of the legionary troops, to which they partly owed their valor and discipline, was dissolved by Constantine; and that the bands of Roman infantry, which still assumed the same names and the same honors, consisted only of one thousand or fifteen hundred men. The conspiracy of so many separate detachments, each of which was awed by the sense of its own weakness, could easily be checked; and the successors of Constantine might indulge their love of ostentation by issuing their orders to one hundred and thirty-two legions, inscribed on the muster-roll of their numerous armies. The remainder of their troops was distributed into several hundred cohorts of infantry and squadrons of cavalry. Their arms, and titles, and ensigns were calculated to inspire terror, and to display the variety of nations who marched under the Imperial standard. And not a vestige was left of that severe simplicity which, in the ages of freedom and victory, had distinguished the line of battle of a Roman army from the confused host of an Asiatic monarch.[†]

In the various states of society, armies are recruited from very different motives. Barbarians are urged by the love of war; the citizens of a free republic may be prompted by a principle of duty; the subjects, or at least the nobles, of a monarchy are animated by a sentiment of honor; but the timid and luxurious inhabitants of a declining empire must be allured into the service by the hopes of profit, or compelled by the dread of punishment. The resources of the Roman treasury were exhausted by the increase of pay, by the repetition of donatives, and by the invention of new emolument and indulgences which, in the opinion of the provincial youth, might compensate the hardships and dangers of a military life. Yet, although the stature was lowered, although slaves, at least by a tacit connivance, were indiscriminately received into the ranks, the insurmountable difficulty of procuring a regular and adequate supply of volunteers obliged the emperors to adopt more effectual and coercive methods. The lands bestowed on the veterans as the free reward of their valor were henceforward granted under a condition which contains the first rudiments of the feudal tenures; that their sons who succeeded to the inheritance should devote themselves to the profession of arms as soon as they attained the age of manhood; and their cowardly refusal was punished by the loss of honor, of fortune, or even of life. But as the annual growth of the sons of the veterans bore a very small proportion to the demands of the service, levies of men were frequently required from the provinces, and every proprietor was obliged either to take up arms, or to procure a substitute, or to purchase his exemption by the payment of a heavy fine. The sum of forty-two pieces of gold, to which it was *reduced,* ascertains the exorbitant price of volunteers, and the reluctance with which the government admitted of this alternative. Such was the horror for the profession of a soldier which had affected the minds of the degenerate Romans that many of the youth of Italy and the provinces chose to cut off the fingers of their right hand to escape from being pressed into the service.[†]

The introduction of Barbarians into the Roman armies became every day more universal, more necessary, and more fatal. The most daring of the Scythians, of the Goths, and of the Germans, who delighted in war and who found it more profitable to defend than to ravage the provinces, were enrolled not only in the auxiliaries of their respective nations but in the legions themselves, and among the most distinguished of the Palatine troops. As they freely mingled with the subjects of the empire, they gradually learned to despise their manners and to imitate their arts. They abjured the implicit reverence which the pride of Rome had exacted from their ignorance, while they acquired the knowledge and possession of those advantages by which alone she supported her declining greatness. The Barbarian soldiers who displayed any military talents were advanced, without exception, to the most important commands; and the names of the tribunes, of the *counts* and *dukes* and of the generals themselves, betray a foreign origin which they no longer condescended to disguise. They were often entrusted with the conduct of a war against their countrymen; and though most of them preferred the ties of allegiance to those of blood, they did not always avoid the guilt, or at least the suspicion, of holding a treasonable correspondence with the enemy, of inviting his invasion, or of sparing his retreat. . . . Constantine showed his successors the example of bestowing the honors of the consulship on the Barbarians, who, by their merit and services, had deserved to be ranked among the first of the Romans. But as these hardy veterans, who had been educated in the ignorance or contempt of the laws, were incapable of exercising any civil offices, the powers of the human mind were contracted by the irreconcilable separation of talents as well as of professions. The accomplished citizens of the Greek and Roman republics whose characters could adapt themselves to the bar, the senate, the camp, or the schools had learned to write, to speak, and to act with the same spirit and with equal abilities.

IV. Besides the magistrates and generals, who at a distance from the court diffused their delegated authority over the provinces and armies, the emperor conferred the rank of *Illustrious* on seven of his more immediate servants, to whose fidelity he entrusted his safety, or his counsels, or his treasures. 1. The private apartments of the palace were governed by a favorite eunuch, who, in the language of that age, was styled the *praepositus,* or praefect of the sacred bed-chamber. His duty was to attend the emperor in his hours of state, or in those of amusement, and to perform about his person all those menial services which can only derive their splendor from the influence of royalty. . . . 2. The principal administration of public affairs was committed to the diligence and abilities of the *master of the offices.* He was the supreme magistrate of the palace, inspected the discipline of the civil and military *schools,* and received appeals from all parts of the empire in the causes which related to that numerous army of privileged persons who, as the servants of the court, had obtained for themselves and families a right to decline the authority of the ordinary judges. . . . 3. In the course of nine centuries, the office of *quaestor* had experienced a very singular revolution. In the infancy of Rome, two inferior magistrates were annually elected by the people to relieve the consuls from the invidious management of the public treasure; a similar assistant was granted to every proconsul and to every praetor who exercised a military or provincial command; with the extent of conquest, the two quaestors were gradually multiplied to the number of four, of eight, of twenty, and, for a short time, perhaps, of forty; and the noblest citizens ambitiously solicited an office which gave them a seat in the senate, and a just hope of obtaining the honors of the republic. Whilst Augustus affected to maintain the freedom of election, he consented to accept the annual privilege of recommending, or rather indeed of nominating, a certain proportion of candidates; and it was his custom to select one of these distinguished youths to read his orations or epistles in the assemblies of the senate. The practice of Augustus was imitated by succeeding princes; the occasional commission was established as a permanent office; and the favored quaestor, assuming a new and more illustrious character, alone survived the suppression of his ancient and useless colleagues. As the orations which he composed in the name of the emperor acquired the force and, at length, the form of absolute edicts, he was considered as the representative of the legislative power, the oracle of the council, and the original source of the civil jurisprudence. . . . 4. The extraordinary title of *count of the sacred largesses* was bestowed on the treasurer-general of the revenue, with the intention perhaps of inculcating that every payment flowed from the voluntary bounty of the monarch. To conceive the almost infinite detail of the annual and daily expense of the civil and military administration in every part of a great empire would exceed the powers of the most vigorous imagination. The actual account employed several hundred persons, distributed into eleven different offices, which were artfully contrived to examine and control their respective operations. The multitude of these agents had a natural tendency to increase; and it was more than once thought expedient to dismiss to their native homes the useless supernumeraries who, deserting their honest labors, had pressed with too much eagerness into the lucrative profession of the finances. . . . 5. Besides the public revenue, which an absolute monarch might levy and expend according to his pleasure, the emperors, in the capacity of opulent citizens, possessed a very extensive property, which was administered by the *count or treasurer* of the private estate. . . . 6, 7. The chosen bands of cavalry and infantry which guarded the person of the emperor were under the immediate command of the *two counts of the domestics.* ... The counts of the domestics had succeeded to the office of the Praetorian praefects; like the praefects, they aspired from the service of the palace to the command of armies.

The perpetual intercourse between the court and the provinces was facilitated by the construction of roads and the institution of posts. But these beneficial establishments were accidentally connected with a pernicious and intolerable abuse. Two or three hundred *agents* or messengers were employed, under the jurisdiction of the master of the offices, to announce the names of the annual consuls and the edicts or victories of the emperors. They insensibly assumed the license of reporting whatever they could observe of the conduct either of magistrates or of private citizens; and were soon considered as the eyes of the monarch and the scourge of the people. Under the warm influence of a feeble reign, they multiplied to the incredible number of ten thousand, disdained the mild though frequent admonitions of the laws, and exercised in the profitable management of the posts a rapacious and insolent oppression. These official spies, who regularly corresponded with the palace, were encouraged by favor and reward anxiously to watch the progress of every treasonable design, from the faint and latent symptoms of disaffection to the actual preparation of an open revolt. Their careless or criminal violation of truth and justice was covered by the consecrated mask of zeal; and they might securely aim their poisoned arrows at the breast either of the guilty or the innocent who had provoked their resentment or refused to purchase their silence ...; and the defects of evidence were diligently supplied by the use of torture.

The deceitful and dangerous experiment of the criminal *quaestion,* as it is emphatically styled, was admitted rather than approved in the jurisprudence of the Romans. They applied this sanguinary mode of examination only to servile bodies, whose sufferings were seldom weighed by those haughty republicans in the scale of justice or humanity; but they would never consent to violate the sacred person of a citizen till they possessed the clearest evidence of his guilt. The annals of tyranny, from the reign of Tiberius to that of Domitian, circumstantially relate the executions of many innocent victims; but as long as the faintest remembrance was kept alive of the national freedom and honor, the last hours of a Roman were secured from the danger of ignominious torture. The conduct of the provincial magistrates was not, however, regulated by the practice of the city or the strict maxims of the civilians. They found the use of torture established not only among the slaves of Oriental despotism but among the Macedonians, who obeyed a limited monarch; among the Rhodians, who flourished by the liberty of commerce; and even among the sage Athenians, who had asserted and adorned the dignity of humankind. The acquiescence of the provincials encouraged their governors to acquire, or perhaps to usurp, a discretionary power of employing the rack to extort from vagrants or plebeian criminals the confession of their guilt, till they insensibly proceeded to confound the distinction of rank and to disregard the privileges of Roman citizens. The apprehensions of the subjects urged them to solicit, and the interest of the sovereign engaged him to grant, a variety of special exemptions which tacitly allowed, and even authorized, the general use of torture. They protected all persons of illustrious or honorable rank, bishops and their presbyters, professors of the liberal arts, soldiers and their families, municipal officers, and their posterity to the third generation, and all children under the age of puberty. But a fatal maxim was introduced into the new jurisprudence of the empire that in the case of treason, which included every offense that the subtlety of lawyers could derive from a *hostile intention* towards the prince or republic, all privileges were suspended and all conditions were reduced to the same ignominious level. As the safety of the emperor was avowedly preferred to every consideration of justice or humanity, the dignity of age and the tenderness of youth were alike exposed to the most cruel tortures; and the terrors of a malicious information which might select them as the accomplices, or even as the witnesses, perhaps, of an imaginary crime perpetually hung over the heads of the principal citizens of the Roman world.

These evils, however terrible they may appear, were confined to the smaller number of Roman subjects, whose dangerous situation was in some degree compensated by the enjoyment of those advantages, either of nature or of fortune, which exposed them to the jealousy of the monarch. The obscure millions of a great empire have much less to dread from the cruelty than from the avarice of their masters, and *their* humble happiness is principally affected by the grievance of excessive taxes, which, gently pressing on the wealthy, descend with accelerated weight on the meaner and more indigent classes of society. An ingenious philosopher has calculated the universal measure of the public impositions by the degrees of freedom and servitude; and ventures to assert that, according to an invariable law of nature, it must always increase with the former and diminish in a just proportion to the latter. But this reflection, which would tend to alleviate the miseries of despotism, is contradicted at least by the history of the Roman empire; which accuses the same princes of despoiling the senate of its authority and the provinces of their wealth. Without abolishing all the various customs and duties on merchandises which are imperceptibly discharged by the apparent choice of the purchaser, the policy of Constantine and his successors preferred a simple and direct mode of taxation, more congenial to the spirit of an arbitrary government.

[*Increasingly burdensome and ruinous taxes were levied, including those on cities* (indictions), *on land, on individuals* (capitation), *and on trade and industry, among others. Forms of payment included coins, in-kind contributions, and, in the case of personal "gifts" to the emperor, precious metals (e.g., gold crowns that could subsequently be melted down and minted).*]

A people elated by pride or soured by discontent are seldom qualified to form a just estimate of their actual situation. The subjects of Constantine were incapable of discerning the decline of genius and manly virtue which so far degraded them below the dignity of their ancestors; but they could feel and lament the rage of tyranny, the relaxation of discipline, and the increase of taxes. The impartial historian who acknowledges the justice of their complaints will observe some favorable circumstances which tended to alleviate the misery of their condition. The threatening tempest of Barbarians which so soon subverted the foundations of Roman greatness was still repelled, or suspended, on the frontiers. The arts of luxury and literature were cultivated, and the elegant pleasures of society were enjoyed, by the inhabitants of a considerable portion of the globe. The forms, the pomp, and the expense of the civil administration contributed to restrain the irregular license of the soldiers; and although the laws were violated by power or perverted by subtlety, the sage principles of the Roman jurisprudence preserved a sense of order and equity unknown to the despotic governments of the East. The rights of mankind might derive some protection from religion and philosophy; and the name of freedom, which could no longer alarm, might sometimes admonish, the successors of Augustus that they did not reign over a nation of Slaves or Barbarians.

CHAPTER XVIII

CHARACTER OF CONSTANTINE
AND HIS SONS

*Character of Constantine. • Gothic war. • Death of Constantine. •
Division of the empire among his three sons. • Persian war. •
Tragic deaths of Constantine the Younger and Constans. •
Usurpation of Magnentius. • Civil war. • Victory of Constantius.*

†In the life of Augustus, we behold the tyrant of the republic, converted, almost by imperceptible degrees, into the father of his country and of humankind. In that of Constantine, we may contemplate a hero, who had so long inspired his subjects with love and his enemies with terror, degenerating into a cruel and dissolute monarch, corrupted by his fortune or raised by conquest above the necessity of dissimulation [A.D. 323–337]. The general peace which he maintained during the last fourteen years of his reign was a period of apparent splendor rather than of real prosperity; and the old age of Constantine was disgraced by the opposite yet reconcilable vices of rapaciousness and prodigality. The accumulated treasures found in the palaces of Maxentius and Licinius were lavishly consumed; the various innovations introduced by the conqueror were attended with an increasing expense; the cost of his buildings, his court, and his festivals required an immediate and plentiful supply; and the oppression of the people was the only fund which could support the magnificence of the sovereign. His unworthy favorites, enriched by the boundless liberality of their master, usurped with impunity the privilege of rapine and corruption. A secret but universal decay was felt in every part of the public administration, and the emperor himself, though he still retained the obedience, gradually lost the esteem of his subjects. The dress and manners which, towards the decline of life, he chose to affect served only to degrade him in the eyes of mankind. The Asiatic pomp which had been adopted by the pride of Diocletian, assumed an air of softness and effeminacy in the person of Constantine. He is represented with false hair of various

colors, laboriously arranged by the skillful artists to the times; a diadem of a new and more expensive fashion; a profusion of gems and pearls, of collars and bracelets, and a variegated flowing robe of silk, most curiously embroidered with flowers of gold. In such apparel, scarcely to be excused by the youth and folly of Elagabalus, we are at a loss to discover the wisdom of an aged monarch and the simplicity of a Roman veteran. A mind thus relaxed by prosperity and indulgence was incapable of rising to that magnanimity which disdains suspicion and dares to forgive. The deaths of Maximian and Licinius may perhaps be justified by the maxims of policy as they are taught in the schools of tyrants; but an impartial narrative of the executions, or rather murders, which sullied the declining age of Constantine will suggest to our most candid thoughts the idea of a prince who could sacrifice without reluctance the laws of justice, and the feelings of nature, to the dictates either of his passions or of his interest.

The same fortune which so invariably followed the standard of Constantine seemed to secure the hopes and comforts of his domestic life. Those among his predecessors who had enjoyed the longest and most prosperous reigns, Augustus, Trajan, and Diocletian, had been disappointed of posterity; and the frequent revolutions had never allowed sufficient time for any Imperial family to grow up and multiply under the shade of the purple. But the royalty of the Flavian line, which had been first ennobled by the Gothic Claudius, descended through several generations; and Constantine himself derived from his royal father the hereditary honors which he transmitted to his children. The emperor had been twice married. Minervina, the obscure but lawful object of his youthful attachment, had left him only one son, who was called Crispus. By Fausta, the daughter of Maximian, he had three daughters, and three sons known by the kindred names of Constantine, Constantius, and Constans. The unambitious brothers of the great Constantine, Julius Constantius, Dalmatius, and Hannibalianus, were permitted to enjoy the most honorable rank and the most affluent fortune that could be consistent with a private station. The youngest of the three lived without a name, and died without posterity. His two elder brothers obtained in marriage the daughters of wealthy senators and propagated new branches of the Imperial race. Gallus and Julian afterwards became the most illustrious of the children of Julius

Constantius, the *Patrician*. The two sons of Dalmatius, who had been decorated with the vain title of *Censor,* were named Dalmatius and Hannibalianus. The two sisters of the great Constantine, Anastasia and Eutropia, were bestowed on Optatus and Nepotianus, two senators of noble birth and of consular dignity. His third sister, Constantia, was distinguished by her preeminence of greatness and of misery. She remained the widow of the vanquished Licinius; and it was by her entreaties that an innocent boy, the offspring of their marriage, preserved for some time his life, the title of Caesar, and a precarious hope of the succession. Besides the females and the allies of the Flavian house, ten or twelve males, to whom the language of modern courts would apply the title of princes of the blood, seemed, according to the order of their birth, to be destined either to inherit or to support the throne of Constantine. But in less than thirty years, this numerous and increasing family was reduced to the persons of Constantius and Julian, who alone had survived a series of crimes and calamities such as the tragic poets have deplored in the devoted lines of Pelops and of Cadmus.

Crispus, the eldest son of Constantine and the presumptive heir of the empire, is represented by impartial historians as an amiable and accomplished youth. The care of his education, or at least of his studies, was entrusted to Lactantius, the most eloquent of the Christians; a preceptor admirably qualified to form the taste and to excite the virtues of his illustrious disciple. At the age of seventeen, Crispus was invested with the title of Caesar [March 1, A.D. 317] and the administration of the Gallic provinces, where the inroads of the Germans gave him an early occasion of signalizing his military prowess. In the civil war which broke out soon afterwards, the father and son divided their powers; and this history has already celebrated the valor as well as conduct displayed by the latter in forcing the straits of the Hellespont, so obstinately defended by the superior fleet of Licinius. This naval victory contributed to determine the event of the war; and the names of Constantine and of Crispus were united in the joyful acclamations of their Eastern subjects; who loudly proclaimed that the world had been subdued, and was now governed, by an emperor endowed with every virtue; and by his illustrious son, a prince beloved of Heaven, and the lively image of his father's perfections.[†]

This dangerous popularity soon excited the attention of Constantine, who, both as a father and as a king, was impatient of an equal. Instead of attempting to secure the allegiance of his son by the generous ties of confidence and gratitude, he resolved to prevent the mischiefs which might be apprehended from dissatisfied ambition. Crispus soon had reason to complain that while his infant brother Constantius was sent, with the title of Caesar, to reign over his peculiar department of the Gallic provinces [October 10, A.D. 324], *he,* a prince of mature years, who had performed such recent and signal services, instead of being raised to the superior rank of Augustus was confined almost a prisoner to his father's court; and exposed, without power or defense, to every calumny which the malice of his enemies could suggest. Under such painful circumstances, the royal youth might not always be able to compose his behavior or suppress his discontent; and we may be assured that he was encompassed by a train of indiscreet or perfidious followers who assiduously studied to inflame, and who were perhaps instructed to betray, the unguarded warmth of his resentment. An edict of Constantine published about this time [October 1, A.D. 325] manifestly indicates his real or affected suspicions that a secret conspiracy had been formed against his person and government. By all the allurements of honors and rewards, he invites informers of every degree to accuse without exception his magistrates or ministers, his friends or his most intimate favorites, protesting with a solemn asseveration that he himself will listen to the charge, that he himself will revenge his injuries; and concluding with a prayer, which discovers some apprehension of danger, that the providence of the Supreme Being may still continue to protect the safety of the emperor and of the empire.

The informers who complied with so liberal an invitation were sufficiently versed in the arts of courts to select the friends and adherents of Crispus as the guilty persons; nor is there any reason to distrust the veracity of the emperor, who had promised an ample measure of revenge and punishment. The policy of Constantine maintained, however, the same appearances of regard and confidence towards a son whom he began to consider as his most irreconcilable enemy. Medals were struck with the customary vows for the long and auspicious reign of the young Caesar; and as the people, who were not admitted into the secrets of the palace, still loved his virtues and respected his dignity, a poet who solicits his recall from exile adores with equal devotion the majesty of the father and that of the son. The time was now arrived for celebrating the august ceremony of the twentieth year of the reign of Constantine; and the emperor, for that purpose, removed his court from Nicomedia to Rome, where the most splendid preparations had been made for his reception. Every eye and every tongue affected to express their sense of the general happiness, and the veil of ceremony and dissimulation was drawn for a while over the darkest designs of revenge and murder. In the midst of the festival, the unfortunate Crispus was apprehended by order of the emperor, who laid aside the tenderness of a father without assuming the equity of a judge. The examination was short and private; and as it was thought decent to conceal the fate of the young prince from the eyes of the Roman people, he was sent under a strong guard to Pola, in Istria, where, soon afterwards, he was put to death, either by the hand of the executioner or by the more gentle operations of poison [July A.D. 326]. The Caesar Licinius, a youth of amiable manners, was involved in the ruin of Crispus: and the stern jealousy of Constantine was unmoved by the prayers and tears of his favorite sister, pleading for the life of a son whose rank was his only crime, and whose loss she did not long survive. The story of these unhappy princes, the nature and evidence of their guilt, the forms of their trial, and the circumstances of their death, were buried in mysterious obscurity; and the courtly bishop [Eusebius] who has celebrated in an elaborate work [his *Life of Constantine*] the virtues and piety of his hero observes a prudent silence on the subject of these tragic events.[†]

The innocence of Crispus was so universally acknowledged that the modern Greeks, who adore the memory of their founder, are reduced to palliate the guilt of a parricide which the common feelings of human nature forbade them to justify. They pretend that as soon as the afflicted father discovered the falsehood of the accusation by which his credulity had been so fatally misled, he published to the world his repentance and remorse; that he mourned forty days, during which he abstained from the use of the bath and all the ordinary comforts of life; and that, for the lasting instruction of posterity, he erected a golden statue of Crispus, with this memorable inscription: TO MY SON, WHOM I UNJUSTLY CONDEMNED. A tale so moral and so interesting would deserve to be supported by less exceptionable authority; but if we consult the more ancient and authentic writers, they will inform us that the repentance of Constantine was manifested only in acts of blood and revenge; and that he atoned for the murder of an innocent son by the execution, perhaps, of a guilty wife. They ascribe the misfortunes of Crispus to the arts of his stepmother Fausta, whose implacable hatred, or whose disappointed love, renewed in the palace of Constantine the ancient tragedy of Hippolytus and of Phaedra. Like the daughter of Minos, the daughter of Maximian accused her son-in-law of an incestuous attempt on the chastity of his father's wife; and easily obtained, from the jealousy of the emperor, a sentence of death against a young prince whom she considered with reason as the most formidable rival of her own children. But Helena, the aged mother of Constantine, lamented and revenged the untimely fate of her grandson Crispus; nor was it long before a real or pretended discovery was made that Fausta herself entertained a criminal connection with a slave belonging to the Imperial stables. Her condemnation and punishment were the instant consequences of the charge; and the adulteress was suffocated by the steam of a bath which, for that purpose, had been heated to an extraordinary degree. By some it will perhaps be thought that the remembrance of a conjugal union of twenty years and the honor of their common offspring, the destined heirs of the throne, might have softened the obdurate heart of Constantine and persuaded him to suffer his wife, however guilty she might appear, to expiate her offenses in a solitary prison. But it seems a superfluous labor to weigh the propriety, unless we could ascertain the truth, of this singular event, which is attended with some circumstances of doubt and perplexity.[†]

By the death of Crispus, the inheritance of the empire seemed to devolve on the three sons of Fausta, who have been already mentioned under the names of Constantine, of Constantius, and of Constans. These young princes were successively invested with the title of Caesar; and the dates of their promotion may be referred to the tenth, the twentieth, and the thirtieth years of the reign of their father. This conduct, though it tended to multiply the future masters of the Roman world, might be excused by the partiality of paternal affection; but it is not so easy to understand the motives of the emperor when he endangered the safety both of his family and of his people by the unnecessary elevation of his two nephews, Dalmatius and Hannibalianus.[†]

[Constantine's] destined successors had the misfortune of being born and educated in the Imperial purple. Incessantly surrounded with a train of flatterers, they passed their youth in the enjoyment of luxury and the expectation of a throne; nor would the dignity of their rank permit them to descend from that elevated station from whence the various characters of human nature appear to wear a smooth and uniform aspect. The indulgence of Constantine admitted them at a very tender age to share the administration of the empire; and they studied the art of reigning at the expense of the people entrusted to their care. The younger Constantine was appointed to hold his court in Gaul; and his brother Constantius exchanged that department, the ancient patrimony of their father, for the more opulent but less martial countries of the East. Italy, the Western Illyricum, and Africa were accustomed to revere Constans, the third of his sons, as the representative of the great Constantine. He fixed Dalmatius on the Gothic frontier, to which he annexed the government of Thrace, Macedonia, and Greece. The city of Caesarea was chosen for the residence of Hannibalianus; and the provinces of Pontus, Cappadocia, and the Lesser Armenia were destined to form the extent of his new kingdom. For each of these princes a suitable establishment was provided. A just proportion of guards, of legions, and of auxiliaries was allotted for their respective dignity and defense. The ministers and generals who were placed about their persons were such as Constantine could trust to assist, and even to control, these youthful sovereigns in the exercise of their delegated power. As they advanced in years and experience, the limits of their authority were insensibly enlarged: but the emperor always reserved for himself the title of Augustus; and while he showed the *Caesars* to the armies and provinces, he maintained every part of the empire in equal obedience to its supreme head. The tranquility of the last fourteen years of his reign was scarcely interrupted by the contemptible insurrection of a camel-driver in the island of Cyprus, or by the active part which the policy of Constantine engaged him to assume in the wars of the Goths and Sarmatians.[†]

By chastising the pride of the Goths, and by accepting the homage of a suppliant nation, Constantine asserted the majesty of the Roman empire; and the ambassadors of Aethiopia, Persia, and the most remote countries of India congratulated the peace and prosperity of his government [A.D. 335]. If he reckoned, among the favors of fortune, the death of his eldest son, of his nephew, and perhaps of his wife, he enjoyed an uninterrupted flow of private as well as public felicity till the thirtieth year of his reign; a period which none of his predecessors since Augustus had been permitted to celebrate. Constantine survived that solemn festival about ten months; and at the mature age of sixty-four, after a short illness, he ended his memorable life at the palace of Aquyrion in the suburbs of Nicomedia, whither he had retired for the benefit of the air, and with the hope of recruiting his exhausted strength by the use of the warm baths [May 22, A.D. 337]. The excessive demonstrations of grief, or at least of mourning, surpassed whatever had been practiced on any former occasion. Notwithstanding the claims of the senate and people of ancient Rome, the corpse of the deceased emperor, according to his last request, was transported to the city which was destined to preserve the name and memory of its founder. The body of Constantine, adorned with the vain symbols of greatness, the purple and diadem, was deposited on a golden bed in one of the apartments of the palace, which for that purpose had been splendidly furnished and illuminated. The forms of the court were strictly maintained. Every day, at the appointed hours, the principal officers of the state, the army, and the household, approaching the person of their sovereign with bended knees and a composed countenance, offered their respectful homage as seriously as if he had been still alive. From motives of policy, this theatrical representation was for some time continued; nor could flattery neglect the opportunity of remarking that Constantine alone, by the peculiar indulgence of Heaven, had reigned after his death.

But this reign could subsist only in empty pageantry; and it was soon discovered that the will of the most absolute monarch is seldom obeyed when his subjects have no longer anything to hope from his favor or to dread from his resentment. The same ministers and generals who bowed with such reverential awe before the inanimate corpse of their deceased sovereign were engaged in secret consultations to exclude his two nephews, Dalmatius and Hannibalianus, from the share which he had assigned them in the succession of the empire.... The arguments by which they solicited the concurrence of the soldiers and people are of a more obvious nature; and they might with decency, as well as truth, insist on the superior rank of the children of Constantine, the danger of multiplying the number of sovereigns, and the impending mischiefs which threatened the republic from the discord of so many rival princes who were not connected by the tender sympathy of fraternal affection. The intrigue was conducted with zeal and secrecy, till a loud and unanimous declaration was procured from the troops that they would suffer none except the sons of their lamented monarch to reign over the Roman empire.[†]

The voice of the dying emperor had recommended the care of his funeral to the piety of Constantius; and that prince, by the vicinity of his Eastern station, could easily prevent the diligence of his brothers, who resided in their distant government of Italy and Gaul. As soon as he had taken possession of the palace of Constantinople, his first care was to remove the apprehensions of his kinsmen by a solemn oath which he pledged for their security. His next employment was to find some specious pretense which might release his conscience from the obligation of an imprudent promise. The arts of fraud were made subservient to the designs of cruelty; and a manifest forgery was attested by a person of the most sacred character. From the hands of the bishop of Nicomedia, Constantius received a fatal scroll, affirmed to be the genuine testament of his father, in which the emperor expressed his suspicions that he had been poisoned by his brothers, and conjured his sons to revenge his death, and to consult their own safety, by the punishment of the guilty. Whatever reasons might have been alleged by these unfortunate princes to defend their life and honor against so incredible an accusation, they were silenced by the furious clamors of the soldiers, who declared themselves at once their enemies, their judges, and their executioners. The spirit and even the forms of legal proceedings were repeatedly violated in a promiscuous massacre; which involved the two uncles of Constantius, seven of his cousins, of whom Dalmatius and Hannibalianus were the most illustrious, the Patrician Optatus, who had married a sister of the late emperor, and the Praefect Ablavius, whose power and riches had inspired him with some hopes of obtaining the purple. If it were necessary to aggravate the horrors of this bloody scene, we might add that Constantius himself had espoused the daughter of his uncle Julius, and that he had bestowed his sister in marriage on his cousin Hannibalianus. These alliances which the policy of Constantine, regardless of the public prejudice, had formed between the several branches of the Imperial house served only to convince mankind that these princes were as cold to the endearments of conjugal affection as they were insensible to the ties of consanguinity and the moving entreaties of youth and innocence. Of so numerous a family, Gallus and Julian alone, the two youngest children of Julius Constantius, were saved from the hands of the assassins till their rage, satiated with slaughter, had in some measure subsided. The emperor Constantius, who, in the absence of his brothers, was the most obnoxious to guilt and reproach, discovered on some future occasions a faint and transient remorse for those cruelties which the perfidious counsels of his ministers and the irresistible violence of the troops had extorted from his unexperienced youth.

The massacre of the Flavian race was succeeded by a new division of the provinces; which was ratified in a personal interview of the three brothers [September 11, A.D. 337]. Constantine, the eldest of the Caesars, obtained, with a certain preeminence of rank, the possession of the new capital, which bore his own name and that of his father. Thrace and the countries of the East were allotted for the patrimony of Constantius; and Constans was acknowledged as the lawful sovereign of Italy, Africa, and the Western Illyricum. The armies submitted to their hereditary right; and they condescended, after some delay, to accept from the Roman senate the title of *Augustus*. When they first assumed the reins of government, the eldest of these princes was twenty-one, the second twenty, and the third only seventeen years of age.[†]

The death of Constantine was [in the East] the signal of war, and the actual condition of the Syrian and Armenian frontier seemed to encourage the Persians by the prospect of a rich spoil and an easy conquest. The example of the massacres of the palace diffused a spirit of licentiousness and sedition among the troops of the East, who were no longer restrained by their habits of obedience to a veteran commander. By the prudence of Constantius, who, from the interview with his brothers in Pannonia, immediately hastened to the banks of the Euphrates, the legions were gradually restored to a sense of duty and discipline; but the season of anarchy had permitted Sapor to form the siege of Nisibis, and to occupy several of the most important fortresses of Mesopotamia.[†]

During the long period of the reign of Constantius, the provinces of the East were afflicted by the calamities of the Persian war [A.D. 337–360]. The irregular incursions of the light troops alternately spread terror and devastation beyond the Tigris and beyond the Euphrates, from the gates of Ctesiphon to those of Antioch; and this active service was performed by the Arabs of the desert, who were divided in their interest and affections; some of their independent chiefs being enlisted in the party of Sapor, whilst others had engaged their doubtful fidelity to the emperor. The more grave and important operations of the war were conducted with equal vigor; and the armies of Rome and Persia encountered each other in nine bloody fields, in two of which Constantius himself commanded in person. The event of the day was most commonly adverse to the Romans.†

After the partition of the empire, three years had scarcely elapsed before the sons of Constantine seemed impatient to convince mankind that they were incapable of contenting themselves with the dominions which they were unqualified to govern [March A.D. 340]. The eldest of those princes soon complained that he was defrauded of his just proportion of the spoils of their murdered kinsmen; and though he might yield to the superior guilt and merit of Constantius, he exacted from Constans the cession of the African provinces as an equivalent for the rich countries of Macedonia and Greece, which his brother had acquired by the death of Dalmatius. The want of sincerity which Constantine experienced in a tedious and fruitless negotiation exasperated the fierceness of his temper; and he eagerly listened to those favorites who suggested to him that his honor as well as his interest was concerned in the prosecution of the quarrel. At the head of a tumultuary band suited for rapine rather than for conquest, he suddenly broke onto the dominions of Constans by the way of the Julian Alps, and the country round Aquileia felt the first effects of his resentment. The measures of Constans, who then resided in Dacia, were directed with more prudence and ability. On the news of his brother's invasion, he detached a select and disciplined body of his Illyrian troops, proposing to follow them in person with the remainder of his forces. But the conduct of his lieutenants soon terminated the unnatural contest. By the artful appearances of flight, Constantine was betrayed into an ambuscade which had been concealed in a wood, where the rash youth, with a few attendants, was surprised, surrounded, and slain. His body, after it had been found in the obscure stream of the Alsa, obtained the honors of an Imperial sepulchre; but his provinces transferred their allegiance to the conqueror, who, refusing to admit his elder brother Constantius to any share in these new acquisitions, maintained the undisputed possession of more than two thirds of the Roman empire.

The fate of Constans himself was delayed about ten years longer, and the revenge of his brother's death was reserved for the more ignoble hand of a domestic traitor [February A.D. 350]. The pernicious tendency of the system introduced by Constantine was displayed in the feeble administration of his sons; who, by their vices and weakness, soon lost the esteem and affections of their people. The pride assumed by Constans from the unmerited success of his arms was rendered more contemptible by his want of abilities and application. His fond partiality towards some German captives distinguished only by the charms of youth was an object of scandal to the people; and Magnentius, an ambitious soldier who was himself of Barbarian extraction, was encouraged by the public discontent to assert the honor of the Roman name. The chosen bands of Jovians and Herculians, who acknowledged Magnentius as their leader, maintained the most respectable and important station in the Imperial camp. The friendship of Marcellinus, count of the sacred largesses, supplied with a liberal hand the means of seduction. The soldiers were convinced by the most specious arguments that the republic summoned them to break the bonds of hereditary servitude; and, by the choice of an active and vigilant prince, to reward the same virtues which had raised the ancestors of the degenerate Constans from a private condition to the throne of the world. As soon as the conspiracy was ripe for execution, Marcellinus, under the pretense of celebrating his son's birthday, gave a splendid entertainment to the illustrious and honorable persons of the court of Gaul, which then resided in the city of Autun. The intemperance of the feast was artfully protracted till a very late hour of the night; and the unsuspecting guests were tempted to indulge themselves in a dangerous and guilty freedom of conversation. On a sudden the doors were thrown open, and Magnentius, who had retired for a few moments, returned into the apartment, invested with the diadem and purple. The conspirators instantly saluted him with the titles of Augustus and Emperor. The surprise, the terror, the intoxication, the ambitious hopes, and the mutual ignorance of the rest of the assembly prompted them to join their voices to the general acclamation. The guards hastened to take the oath of fidelity; the gates of the town were shut; and before the dawn of day, Magnentius became master of the troops and treasure of the palace and city of Autun. By his secrecy and diligence he entertained some hopes of surprising the person of Constans, who was pursuing in the adjacent forest his favorite amusement of hunting, or perhaps some pleasures of a more private and criminal nature. The rapid progress of fame allowed him, however, an instant for flight, though the desertion of his soldiers and subjects deprived him of the power of resistance. Before he could reach a seaport in Spain where he intended to embark, he was overtaken near Helena, at the foot of the Pyrenees, by a party of light cavalry, whose chief, regardless of the sanctity of a temple, executed his commission by the murder of the son of Constantine.

As soon as the death of Constans had decided this easy but important revolution, the example of the court of Autun was imitated by the provinces of the West. The authority of Magnentius was acknowledged through the whole extent of the two great praefectures of Gaul and Italy; and the usurper prepared, by every act of oppression, to collect a treasure which might discharge the obligation of an immense donative and supply the expenses of a civil war. The martial countries of Illyricum, from the Danube to the extremity of Greece, had long obeyed the government of Vetranio, an aged general beloved for the simplicity of his manners, and who had acquired some reputation by his experience and services in war. Attached by habit, by duty, and by gratitude to the house of Constantine, he immediately gave the strongest assurances to the only surviving son of his late master that he would expose, with unshaken fidelity, his person and his troops to inflict a just revenge on the traitors of Gaul. But the legions of Vetranio were seduced, rather than provoked, by the example of rebellion; their leader soon betrayed a want of firmness, or a want of sincerity; and his ambition derived a specious pretense from the approbation of the princess Constantina. That cruel and aspiring woman, who had obtained from the great Constantine, her father, the rank of *Augusta*, placed the diadem with her own hands on the head of the Illyrian general; and seemed to expect from his victory the accomplishment of those unbounded hopes of which she had been disappointed by the death of her husband Hannibalianus. Perhaps it was without the consent of Constantina that the new emperor formed a necessary, though dishonorable, alliance with the usurper of the West, whose purple was so recently stained with her brother's blood.

[*Constantius persuades Vetranio to step down on December 25, A.D. 350. Vetranio retires. Constantius subsequently wages costly (especially in the battle of Mursa) war against Magnentius (A.D. 351–353).*]

The pride of Magnentius was reduced, by repeated misfortunes, to sue, and to sue in vain, for peace. He first despatched a senator in whose abilities he confided, and afterwards several bishops, whose holy character might obtain a more favorable audience, with the offer of resigning the purple and the promise of devoting the remainder of his life to the service of the emperor. But Constantius, though he granted fair terms of pardon and reconciliation to all who abandoned the standard of rebellion, avowed his inflexible resolution to inflict a just punishment on the crimes of an assassin, whom he prepared to overwhelm on every side by the effort of his victorious arms.†

[After a series of defeats, Magnentius] was unable to bring another army into the field; the fidelity of his guards was corrupted; and when he appeared in public to animate them by his exhortations, he was saluted with a unanimous shout of "Long live the emperor Constantius!" The tyrant, who perceived that they were preparing to deserve pardon and rewards by the sacrifice of the most obnoxious criminal, prevented their design by falling on his sword [August 10, A.D. 353]; a death more easy and more honorable than he could hope to obtain from the hands of an enemy whose revenge would have been colored with the specious pretense of justice and fraternal piety. The example of suicide was imitated by Decentius, who strangled himself on the news of his brother's death. The author of the conspiracy, Marcellinus, had long since disappeared in the battle of Mursa, and the public tranquility was confirmed by the execution of the surviving leaders of a guilty and unsuccessful faction. A severe inquisition was extended over all who, either from choice or from compulsion, had been involved in the cause of rebellion. Paul, surnamed Catena ["The Chain"] from his superior skill in the judicial exercise of tyranny, was sent to explore the latent remains of the conspiracy in the remote province of Britain.

The honest indignation expressed by Martin, vice-praefect of the island, was interpreted as an evidence of his own guilt; and the governor was urged to the necessity of turning against his breast the sword with which he had been provoked to wound the Imperial minister. The most innocent subjects of the West were exposed to exile and confiscation, to death and torture; and as the timid are always cruel, the mind of Constantius was inaccessible to mercy.

CHAPTER XIX

CONSTANTIUS SOLE EMPEROR

Constantius sole emperor. • Elevation and death of Gallus. •
Danger and elevation of Julian. • Sarmatian and Persian wars. •
Victories of Julian in Gaul.

The divided provinces of the empire were again united by the victory
of Constantius; but as that feeble prince was destitute of personal
merit, either in peace or war; as he feared his generals and distrusted
his ministers; the triumph of his arms served only to establish the
reign of the eunuchs over the Roman world. Those unhappy beings,
the ancient production of Oriental jealousy and despotism, were introduced into Greece and Rome by the contagion of Asiatic luxury.
Their progress was rapid; and the eunuchs, who, in the time of Augustus, had been abhorred as the monstrous retinue of an Egyptian queen
were gradually admitted into the families of matrons, of senators, and
of the emperors themselves. Restrained by the severe edicts of Domitian and Nerva, cherished by the pride of Diocletian, reduced to an
humble station by the prudence of Constantine, they multiplied in the
palaces of his degenerate sons, and insensibly acquired the knowledge,
and at length the direction, of the secret councils of Constantius. The
aversion and contempt which mankind had so uniformly entertained
for that imperfect species appears to have degraded their character,
and to have rendered them almost as incapable as they were supposed
to be of conceiving any generous sentiment or of performing any worthy action. But the eunuchs were skilled in the arts of flattery and intrigue; and they alternately governed the mind of Constantius by his
fears, his indolence, and his vanity. Whilst he viewed in a deceitful
mirror the fair appearance of public prosperity, he supinely permitted
them to intercept the complaints of the injured provinces, to accumulate immense treasures by the sale of justice and of honors, to disgrace
the most important dignities by the promotion of those who had purchased at their hands the powers of oppression, and to gratify their resentment against the few independent spirits who arrogantly refused
to solicit the protection of slaves. Of these slaves the most distin-

guished was the chamberlain Eusebius, who ruled the monarch and the palace with such absolute sway that Constantius, according to the sarcasm of an impartial historian, possessed some credit with this haughty favorite. By his artful suggestions, the emperor was persuaded to subscribe the condemnation of the unfortunate Gallus, and to add a new crime to the long list of unnatural murders which pollute the honor of the house of Constantine.

When the two nephews of Constantine, Gallus and Julian, were saved from the fury of the soldiers, the former was about twelve and the latter about six years of age; and, as the eldest was thought to be of a sickly constitution, they obtained with the less difficulty a precarious and dependent life from the affected pity of Constantius, who was sensible that the execution of these helpless orphans would have been esteemed by all mankind an act of the most deliberate cruelty. Different cities of Ionia and Bithynia were assigned for the places of their exile and education; but as soon as their growing years excited the jealousy of the emperor, he judged it more prudent to secure those unhappy youths in the strong castle of Macellum, near Caesarea [circa A.D. 344]. The treatment which they experienced during a six years' confinement was partly such as they could hope from a careful guardian and partly such as they might dread from a suspicious tyrant. Their prison was an ancient palace, the residence of the kings of Cappadocia; the situation was pleasant, the buildings stately, the enclosure spacious. They pursued their studies and practiced their exercises under the tuition of the most skillful masters; and the numerous household appointed to attend, or rather to guard, the nephews of Constantine was not unworthy of the dignity of their birth. But they could not disguise to themselves that they were deprived of fortune, of freedom, and of safety; secluded from the society of all whom they could trust or esteem, and condemned to pass their melancholy hours in the company of slaves devoted to the commands of a tyrant who had already injured them beyond the hope of reconciliation. At length, however, the emergencies of the state compelled the emperor, or rather his eunuchs, to invest Gallus, in the twenty-fifth year of his age, with the title of Caesar, and to cement this political connection by his marriage with the princess Constantina [March 5, A.D. 351]. After a formal interview in which the two princes mutually engaged their faith never to undertake anything to the prejudice of each other, they repaired without delay to their respective stations. Constantius continued his march towards the West, and Gallus fixed his residence at Antioch; from whence, with a delegated authority, he administered the five great dioceses of the Eastern praefecture. In this fortunate change, the new Caesar was not unmindful of his brother Julian, who obtained the honors of his rank, the appearances of liberty, and the restitution of an ample patrimony.

The writers the most indulgent to the memory of Gallus, and even Julian himself, though he wished to cast a veil over the frailties of his brother, are obliged to confess that the Caesar was incapable of reigning. Transported from a prison to a throne, he possessed neither genius nor application, nor docility to compensate for the want of knowledge and experience. A temper naturally morose and violent instead of being corrected was soured by solitude and adversity; the remembrance of what he had endured disposed him to retaliation rather than to sympathy; and the ungoverned sallies of his rage were often fatal to those who approached his person or were subject to his power. Constantina, his wife, is described not as a woman but as one of the infernal furies tormented with an insatiate thirst of human blood. Instead of employing her influence to insinuate the mild counsels of prudence and humanity, she exasperated the fierce passions of her husband; and as she retained the vanity, though she had renounced the gentleness, of her sex, a pearl necklace was esteemed an equivalent price for the murder of an innocent and virtuous nobleman. The cruelty of Gallus was sometimes displayed in the undissembled violence of popular or military executions; and was sometimes disguised by the abuse of law and the forms of judicial proceedings. The private houses of Antioch and the places of public resort were besieged by spies and informers; and the Caesar himself, concealed in a plebeian habit, very frequently condescended to assume that odious character. Every apartment of the palace was adorned with the instruments of death and torture, and a general consternation was diffused through the capital of Syria. The prince of the East, as if he had been conscious how much he had to fear and how little he deserved to reign, selected for the objects of his resentment the provincials accused of some imaginary treason and his own courtiers, whom with more reason he suspected of incensing, by their secret correspondence, the timid and suspicious mind of Constantius. But he forgot that he was depriving himself of his only support, the affection of the people; whilst he furnished the malice of his enemies with the arms of truth and afforded the emperor the fairest pretense of exacting the forfeit of his purple, and of his life.

As long as the civil war suspended the fate of the Roman world, Constantius dissembled his knowledge of the weak and cruel administration to which his choice had subjected the East; and the discovery of some assassins secretly despatched to Antioch by the tyrant of Gaul was employed to convince the public that the emperor and the Caesar were united by the same interest and pursued by the same enemies. But when the victory was decided in favor of Constantius, his dependent colleague became less useful and less formidable. Every circumstance of his conduct was severely and suspiciously examined, and it was privately resolved either to deprive Gallus of the purple or at least to remove him from the indolent luxury of Asia to the hardships and dangers of a German war.

[*Constantius sends ministers to summon Gallus. Gallus, with the encouragement of his wife Constantina, causes (or at least appears to allow) the ministers to be killed by the people of Antioch (A.D. 354).*]

After such a deed, whatever might have been the designs of Gallus, it was only in a field of battle that he could assert his innocence with any hope of success. But the mind of that prince was formed of an equal mixture of violence and weakness. Instead of assuming the title of Augustus, instead of employing in his defense the troops and treasures of the East, he suffered himself to be deceived by the affected tranquility of Constantius, who, leaving him the vain pageantry of a court, imperceptibly recalled the veteran legions from the provinces of Asia. But as it still appeared dangerous to arrest Gallus in his capital, the slow and safer arts of dissimulation were practiced with success. The frequent and pressing epistles of Constantius were filled with professions of confidence and friendship; exhorting the Caesar to discharge the duties of his high station, to relieve his colleague from a part of the public cares, and to assist the West by his presence, his counsels, and his arms. After so many reciprocal injuries, Gallus had reason to fear and to distrust. But he had neglected the opportunities of flight and of resistance; he was seduced by the flattering assurances of the tribune Scudilo, who, under the semblance of a rough soldier, disguised the most artful insinuation; and he depended on the credit of his wife

Constantina, till the unseasonable death of that princess completed the ruin in which he had been involved by her impetuous passions.

After a long delay, the reluctant Caesar set forwards on his journey to the Imperial court. From Antioch to Hadrianople, he traversed the wide extent of his dominions with a numerous and stately train; and as he labored to conceal his apprehensions from the world, and perhaps from himself, he entertained the people of Constantinople with an exhibition of the games of the circus. The progress of the journey might, however, have warned him of the impending danger. In all the principal cities he was met by ministers of confidence, commissioned to seize the offices of government, to observe his motions, and to prevent the hasty sallies of his despair. The persons despatched to secure the provinces which he left behind passed him with cold salutations or affected disdain; and the troops whose station lay along the public road were studiously removed on his approach, lest they might be tempted to offer their swords for the service of a civil war. After Gallus had been permitted to repose himself a few days at Hadrianople, he received a mandate, expressed in the most haughty and absolute style, that his splendid retinue should halt in that city while the Caesar himself, with only ten post-carriages, should hasten to the Imperial residence at Milan. In this rapid journey, the profound respect which was due to the brother and colleague of Constantius was insensibly changed into rude familiarity; and Gallus, who discovered in the countenances of the attendants that they already considered themselves as his guards, and might soon be employed as his executioners, began to accuse his fatal rashness and to recollect, with terror and remorse, the conduct by which he had provoked his fate. The dissimulation which had hitherto been preserved was laid aside at Petovio, in Pannonia. He was conducted to a palace in the suburbs where the general Barbatio, with a select band of soldiers who could neither be moved by pity nor corrupted by rewards, expected the arrival of his illustrious victim. In the close of the evening he was arrested, ignominiously stripped of the ensigns of Caesar, and hurried away to Pola, in Istria, a sequestered prison which had been so recently polluted with royal blood. The horror which he felt was soon increased by the appearance of his implacable enemy the eunuch Eusebius, who, with the assistance of a notary and a tribune, proceeded to interrogate him concerning the administration of the East. The Caesar sank under the weight of shame and guilt, confessed all the criminal actions and all the treasonable designs with which he was charged; and by imputing them to the advice of his wife exasperated the indignation of Constantius, who reviewed with partial prejudice the minutes of the examination. The emperor was easily convinced that his own safety was incompatible with the life of his cousin: the sentence of death was signed, despatched, and executed; and the nephew of Constantine, with his hands tied behind his back, was beheaded in prison like the vilest malefactor [December A.D. 354].[†]

Besides the reigning emperor, Julian alone survived of all the numerous posterity of Constantius Chlorus. The misfortune of his royal birth involved him in the disgrace of Gallus. From his retirement in the happy country of Ionia, he was conveyed under a strong guard to the court of Milan [A.D. 354]; where he languished above seven months, in the continual apprehension of suffering the same ignominious death which was daily inflicted, almost before his eyes, on the friends and adherents of his persecuted family. His looks, his gestures, his silence were scrutinized with malignant curiosity, and he was perpetually assaulted by enemies whom he had never offended, and by arts to which he was a stranger. But in the school of adversity, Julian insensibly acquired the virtues of firmness and discretion. He defended his honor, as well as his life, against the insnaring subtleties of the eunuchs, who endeavored to extort some declaration of his sentiments; and whilst he cautiously suppressed his grief and resentment, he nobly disdained to flatter the tyrant by any seeming approbation of his brother's murder. Julian most devoutly ascribes his miraculous deliverance to the protection of the gods, who had exempted his innocence from the sentence of destruction pronounced by their justice against the impious house of Constantine. As the most effectual instrument of their providence, he gratefully acknowledges the steady and generous friendship of the empress Eusebia, a woman of beauty and merit who, by the ascendant which she had gained over the mind of her husband, counterbalanced in some measure the powerful conspiracy of the eunuchs. By the intercession of his patroness, Julian was admitted into the Imperial presence: he pleaded his cause with a decent freedom, he was heard with favor; and, notwithstanding the efforts of his enemies, who urged the danger of sparing an avenger of the blood of Gallus, the milder sentiment of Eusebia prevailed in the council. But the effects of a second interview were dreaded by the eunuchs; and Julian was advised to withdraw for a while into the neighborhood of Milan, till the emperor thought proper to assign the city of Athens for the place of his honorable exile [May A.D. 355]. As he had discovered from his earliest youth a propensity, or rather passion, for the language, the manners, the learning, and the religion of the Greeks, he obeyed with pleasure an order so agreeable to his wishes. Far from the tumult of arms and the treachery of courts, he spent six months under the groves of the academy, in a free intercourse with the philosophers of the age, who studied to cultivate the genius, to encourage the vanity, and to inflame the devotion of their royal pupil. Their labors were not unsuccessful; and Julian inviolably preserved for Athens that tender regard which seldom fails to arise in a liberal mind from the recollection of the place where it has discovered and exercised its growing powers. The gentleness and affability of manners which his temper suggested and his situation imposed insensibly engaged the affections of the strangers, as well as citizens, with whom he conversed. Some of his fellow-students might perhaps examine his behavior with an eye of prejudice and aversion; but Julian established, in the schools of Athens, a general prepossession in favor of his virtues and talents which was soon diffused over the Roman world.

Whilst his hours were passed in studious retirement, the empress, resolute to achieve the generous design which she had undertaken, was not unmindful of the care of his fortune. The death of the late Caesar had left Constantius invested with the sole command, and oppressed by the accumulated weight, of a mighty empire. Before the wounds of civil discord could be healed, the provinces of Gaul were overwhelmed by a deluge of Barbarians. The Sarmatians no longer respected the barrier of the Danube. The impunity of rapine had increased the boldness and numbers of the wild Isaurians: those robbers descended from their craggy mountains to ravage the adjacent country, and had even presumed, though without success, to besiege the important city of Seleucia, which was defended by a garrison of three Roman legions. Above all, the Persian monarch, elated by victory, again threatened the peace of Asia, and the presence of the emperor was indispensably required, both in the West and in the East. For the first time, Constantius sincerely acknowledged that his single strength was unequal to such an extent of care and of dominion. Insensible to the voice of flattery, which assured him that his all-powerful virtue and celestial fortune would still continue to triumph over every obstacle, he listened with complacency to the advice of Eusebia, which gratified his indolence without offending his suspicious pride. As she perceived that the remembrance of Gallus dwelt on the emperor's mind, she artfully turned his attention to the opposite characters of the two brothers, which from their infancy had been compared to those of Domitian and of Titus. She accustomed her husband to consider Julian as a youth of a mild, unambitious disposition, whose allegiance and gratitude might be secured by the gift of the purple, and who was qualified to fill with honor a subordinate station without aspiring to dispute the commands or to shade the glories of his sovereign and benefactor. After an obstinate though secret struggle, the opposition of the favorite eunuchs submitted to the ascendency of the empress; and it was resolved that Julian, after celebrating his nuptials with Helena, sister of Constantius, should be appointed, with the title of Caesar, to reign over the countries beyond the Alps.

Although the order which recalled him to court was probably accompanied by some intimation of his approaching greatness, he appealed to the people of Athens to witness his tears of undissembled sorrow when he was reluctantly torn away from his beloved retirement. He trembled for his life, for his fame, and even for his virtue; and his sole confidence was derived from the persuasion that Minerva inspired all his actions and that he was protected by an invisible guard of angels, whom for that purpose she had borrowed from the Sun and Moon. He approached with horror the palace of Milan; nor could the ingenuous youth conceal his indignation when he found himself accosted with false and servile respect by the assassins of his family. Eusebia, rejoicing in the success of her benevolent schemes, embraced him with the tenderness of a sister; and endeavored, by the most soothing caresses, to dispel his terrors and reconcile him to his fortune. But the ceremony of shaving his beard, and his awkward demeanor when he first exchanged the cloak of a Greek philosopher for the military habit of a Roman prince, amused, during a few days, the levity of the Imperial court.

The emperors of the age of Constantine no longer deigned to consult with the senate in the choice of a colleague; but they were anxious that their nomination should be ratified by the consent of the army. On this solemn occasion, the guards, with the other troops whose stations were in the neighborhood of Milan, appeared under arms; and Constantius ascended his lofty tribunal holding by the hand his cousin Julian, who entered the same day into the twenty-fifth year of his age [November 6, A.D. 355]. In a studied speech, conceived and delivered with dignity, the emperor represented the various dangers which threatened the prosperity of the republic, the necessity of naming a Caesar for the administration of the West, and his own intention, if it was agreeable to their wishes, of rewarding with the honors of the purple the promising virtues of the nephew of Constantine. The approbation of the soldiers was testified by a respectful murmur; they gazed on the manly countenance of Julian and observed with pleasure that the fire which sparkled in his eyes was tempered by a modest blush on being thus exposed, for the first time, to the public view of mankind. As soon as the ceremony of his investiture had been performed, Constantius addressed him with the tone of authority which his superior age and station permitted him to assume; and exhorting the new Caesar to deserve, by heroic deeds, that sacred and immortal name, the emperor gave his colleague the strongest assurances of a friendship which should never be impaired by time, nor interrupted by their separation into the most distant climes. As soon as the speech was ended, the troops, as a token of applause, clashed their shields against their knees; while the officers who surrounded the tribunal expressed, with decent reserve, their sense of the merits of the representative of Constantius.[†]

The four-and-twenty days which the Caesar spent at Milan after his investiture, and the first months of his Gallic reign, were devoted to a splendid but severe captivity; nor could the acquisition of honor compensate for the loss of freedom. His steps were watched, his correspondence was intercepted; and he was obliged, by prudence, to decline the visits of his most intimate friends. Of his former domestics, four only were permitted to attend him; two pages, his physician, and his librarian; the last of whom was employed in the care of a valuable collection of books, the gift of the empress, who studied the inclinations as well as the interest of her friend. In the room of these faithful servants, a household was formed, such indeed as became the dignity of a Caesar; but it was filled with a crowd of slaves, destitute and perhaps incapable of any attachment for their new master, to whom, for the most part, they were either unknown or suspected. His want of experience might require the assistance of a wise council; but the minute instructions which regulated the service of his table and the distribution of his hours were adapted to a youth still under the discipline of his preceptors, rather than to the situation of a prince entrusted with the conduct of an important war. If he aspired to deserve the esteem of his subjects, he was checked by the fear of displeasing his sovereign; and even the fruits of his marriage-bed were blasted by the jealous artifices of Eusebia herself, who, on this occasion alone, seems to have been unmindful of the tenderness of her sex and the generosity of her character. The memory of his father and of his brothers reminded Julian of his own danger.[†]

The protection of the Rhaetian frontier, and the persecution of the Catholic church, detained Constantius in Italy above eighteen months after the departure of Julian. Before the emperor returned into the East, he indulged his pride and curiosity in a visit to the ancient capital [April 28, A.D. 357]. He proceeded from Milan to Rome along the Aemilian and Flaminian ways, and as soon as he approached within forty miles of the city, the march of a prince who had never vanquished a foreign enemy assumed the appearance of a triumphal procession. His splendid train was composed of all the ministers of luxury; but in a time of profound peace, he was encompassed by the glittering arms of the numerous squadrons of his guards and cuirassiers. Their streaming banners of silk, embossed with gold and shaped in the form of dragons, waved round the person of the emperor. Constantius sat alone in a lofty car, resplendent with gold and precious gems; and except when he bowed his head to pass under the gates of the cities, he affected a stately demeanor of inflexible, and, as it might seem, of insensible gravity. The severe discipline of the Persian youth had been introduced by the eunuchs into the Imperial palace; and such were the habits of patience which they had inculcated that during a slow and sultry march, he was never seen to move his hand towards his face, or to turn his eyes either to the right or to the left. He was received by the magistrates and senate of Rome; and the emperor surveyed, with attention, the civil honors of the republic and the consular images of the noble families. The streets were lined with an innumerable multitude. Their repeated acclamations expressed their joy at beholding, after an absence of thirty-two years, the sacred person of their sovereign, and Constantius himself expressed, with some pleasantry, his affected surprise that the human race should thus suddenly be collected on the same spot. The son of Constantine was lodged in the ancient palace of Augustus: he presided in the senate, harangued the people from the tribunal which Cicero had so often ascended, assisted with unusual courtesy at the games of the circus, and accepted the crowns of gold, as well as the panegyrics which had been prepared for the ceremony by the deputies of the principal cities. His short visit of thirty days was employed in viewing the monuments of art and power which were scattered over the seven hills and the interjacent valleys. He admired the awful majesty of the Capitol, the vast extent of the baths of Caracalla and Diocletian, the severe simplicity of the Pantheon, the massy greatness of the amphitheater of Titus, the elegant architecture of the theater of Pompey and the Temple of Peace, and, above all, the stately structure of the Forum and column of Trajan; acknowledging that the voice of fame, so prone to invent and to magnify, had made an inadequate report of the metropolis of the world. The traveler who has contemplated the ruins of ancient Rome may conceive some imperfect idea of the sentiments which they must have inspired when they reared their heads in the splendor of unsullied beauty.[†]

The departure of Constantius from Rome was hastened by the alarming intelligence of the distress and danger of the Illyrian provinces. The distractions of civil war, and the irreparable loss which the Roman legions had sustained in the battle of Mursa [against the usurper Magnentius], exposed those countries, almost without defense, to the light cavalry of the Barbarians; and particularly to the inroads of the Quadi, a fierce and powerful nation who seem to have exchanged the institutions of Germany for the arms and military arts of their Sarmatian allies. The garrisons of the frontiers were insufficient to check their progress; and the indolent monarch was at length compelled to assemble, from the extremities of his dominions, the flower of the Palatine troops, to take the field in person, and to employ a whole campaign, with the preceding autumn and the ensuing spring, in the serious prosecution of the war [A.D. 357, 358, 359].[†]

While the Roman emperor and the Persian monarch, at the distance of three thousand miles, defended their extreme limits against the Barbarians of the Danube and of the Oxus, their intermediate frontier experienced the vicissitudes of a languid war and a precarious truce. Two of the Eastern ministers of Constantius, the Praetorian praefect Musonian, whose abilities were disgraced by the want of truth and integrity, and Cassian, duke of Mesopotamia, a hardy and veteran soldier, opened a secret negotiation with the satrap Tamsapor. These overtures of peace, translated into the servile and flattering language of Asia, were transmitted to the camp of the Great King; who resolved to signify by an ambassador the terms which he was inclined to grant to the suppliant Romans [A.D. 358]. Narses, whom he invested with that character, was honorably received in his passage through Antioch and Constantinople: he reached Sirmium after a long journey and, at his first audience, respectfully unfolded the silken veil which covered the haughty epistle of his sovereign. Sapor, King of Kings, and Brother of the Sun and Moon (such were the lofty titles affected by Oriental vanity), expressed his satisfaction that his brother, Constantius Caesar, had been taught wisdom by adversity. As the lawful successor of Darius Hystaspes, Sapor asserted that the River Strymon, in Macedonia, was the true and ancient boundary of his empire; declaring, however, that as an evidence of his moderation he would content himself with the provinces of Armenia and Mesopotamia, which had been fraudulently extorted from his ancestors. He alleged that, without the restitution of these disputed countries, it was impossible to establish any treaty on a solid and permanent basis; and he arrogantly threatened that if his ambassador returned in vain, he was prepared to take the field in the spring, and to support the justice of his cause by the strength of his invincible arms. Narses, who was endowed with the most polite and amiable manners, endeavored, as far as was consistent with his duty, to soften the harshness of the message. Both the style and substance were maturely weighed in the Imperial council, and he was dismissed with the following answer: "Constantius had a right to disclaim the officiousness of his ministers, who had acted without any specific orders from the throne: he was not, however, averse to an equal and honorable treaty; but it was highly indecent, as well as absurd, to propose to the sole and victorious emperor of the Roman world the same conditions of peace which he had indignantly rejected at the time when his power was contracted within the narrow limits of the East: the chance of arms was uncertain; and Sapor should recollect that if the Romans had sometimes been vanquished in battle, they had almost always been successful in the event of the war." A few days after the departure of Narses, three ambassadors were sent to the court of Sapor, who was already returned from the Scythian expedition to his ordinary residence of Ctesiphon. A count, a notary, and a sophist had been selected for this important commission; and Constantius, who was secretly anxious for the conclusion of the peace, entertained some hopes that the dignity of the first of these ministers, the dexterity of the second, and the rhetoric of the third would persuade the Persian monarch to abate of the rigor of his demands. But the progress of their negotiation was opposed and defeated by the hostile arts of Antoninus, a Roman subject of Syria, who had fled from oppression and was admitted into the councils of Sapor, and even to the royal table, where, according to the custom of the Persians, the most important business was frequently discussed. The dexterous fugitive promoted his interest by the same conduct which gratified his revenge. He incessantly urged the ambition of his new master to embrace the favorable opportunity when the bravest of the Palatine troops were employed with the emperor in a distant war on the Danube. He pressed Sapor to invade the exhausted and defenseless provinces of the East with the numerous armies of Persia, now fortified by the alliance and accession of the fiercest Barbarians. The ambassadors of Rome retired without success, and a second embassy, of a still more honorable rank, was detained in strict confinement and threatened either with death or exile.

[*Sapor invades, and, after a costly siege, takes Amida (A.D. 359). He continues his attacks, and Constantius removes from the Danube to the East in order to conduct Roman operations (A.D. 360). In the West, Julian had, since his departure (A.D. 356), been in Gaul, facing (with success) formidable Germanic invaders.*]

In the blind fury of civil discord, Constantius had abandoned to the Barbarians of Germany the countries of Gaul, which still acknowledged the authority of his rival. A numerous swarm of Franks and Alemanni were invited to cross the Rhine by presents and promises, by the hopes of spoil, and by a perpetual grant of all the territories which they should be able to subdue. But the emperor, who for a temporary service had thus imprudently provoked the rapacious spirit of the Barbarians, soon discovered and lamented the difficulty of dismissing these formidable allies, after they had tasted the richness of the Roman soil. Regardless of the nice distinction of loyalty and rebellion, these undisciplined robbers treated as their natural enemies all the subjects of the empire who possessed any property which they were desirous of acquiring. Forty-five flourishing cities . . . , besides a far greater number of towns and villages, were pillaged, and for the most part reduced to ashes. The Barbarians of Germany, still faithful to the maxims of their ancestors, abhorred the confinement of walls, to which they applied the odious names of prisons and sepulchres. . . . From the sources to the mouth of the Rhine, the conquests of the Germans extended above forty miles to the west of that river, over a country peopled by colonies of their own name and nation: and the scene of their devastations was three times more extensive than that of their conquests. At a still greater distance the open towns of Gaul were deserted, and the inhabitants of the fortified cities, who trusted to their strength and vigilance, were obliged to content themselves with such supplies of corn as they could raise on the vacant land within the enclosure of their walls. The diminished legions, destitute of pay and provisions, of arms and discipline, trembled at the approach, and even at the name, of the Barbarians.

Under these melancholy circumstances, an unexperienced youth was appointed to save and to govern the provinces of Gaul, or rather, as he expressed it himself, to exhibit the vain image of Imperial greatness. The retired scholastic education of Julian, in which he had been more conversant with books than with arms, with the dead than with the living, left him in profound ignorance of the practical arts of war and government; and when he awkwardly repeated some military exercise which it was necessary for him to learn, he exclaimed with a sigh, "O Plato, Plato, what a task for a philosopher!" Yet even this speculative philosophy, which men of business are too apt to despise, had filled the mind of Julian with the noblest precepts and the most shining examples; had animated him with the love of virtue, the desire of fame, and the contempt of death. The habits of temperance recommended in the schools are still more essential in the severe discipline of a camp. The simple wants of nature regulated the measure of his food and sleep. Rejecting with disdain the delicacies provided for his table, he satisfied his appetite with the coarse and common fare which was allotted to the meanest soldiers. During the rigor of a Gallic winter, he never suffered a fire in his bed-chamber; and after a short and interrupted slumber, he frequently rose in the middle of the night from a carpet spread on the floor to despatch any urgent business, to visit his rounds, or to steal a few moments for the prosecution of his favorite studies. The precepts of eloquence, which he had hitherto practiced on fancied topics of declamation, were more usefully applied to excite or to assuage the passions of an armed multitude: and although Julian, from his early habits of conversation and literature, was more familiarly acquainted with the beauties of the Greek language, he had attained a competent knowledge of the Latin tongue. Since Julian was not originally designed for the character of a legislator or a judge, it is probable that the civil jurisprudence of the Romans had not engaged any considerable share of his attention: but he derived from his philosophic studies an inflexible regard for justice, tempered by a disposition to clemency; the knowledge of the general principles of equity and evidence, and the faculty of patiently investigating the most intricate and tedious questions which could be proposed for his discussion. The measures of policy, and the operations of war, must submit to the various accidents of circumstance and character, and the unpracticed student will often be perplexed in the application of the most perfect theory. But in the acquisition of this important science, Julian was assisted by the active vigor of his own genius as well as by the wisdom and experience of Sallust, an officer of rank who soon conceived a sincere attachment for a prince so worthy of his friendship; and whose incorruptible integrity was adorned by the talent of insinuating the harshest truths without wounding the delicacy of a royal ear.

[*Julian campaigns successfully* (A.D. *356, 357, 358, 359*).]

As soon as the valor and conduct of Julian had secured an interval of peace, he applied himself to a work more congenial to his humane and philosophic temper. The cities of Gaul, which had suffered from the inroads of the Barbarians, he diligently repaired; and seven important posts between Metz and the mouth of the Rhine are particularly mentioned as having been rebuilt and fortified by the order of Julian. The vanquished Germans had submitted to the just but humiliating condition of preparing and conveying the necessary materials. The active zeal of Julian urged the prosecution of the work; and such was the spirit which he had diffused among the troops that the auxiliaries themselves, waiving their exemption from any duties of fatigue, contended in the most servile labors with the diligence of the Roman soldiers. It was incumbent on the Caesar to provide for the subsistence, as well as for the safety, of the inhabitants and of the garrisons. The desertion of the former and the mutiny of the latter must have been the fatal and inevitable consequences of famine. The tillage of the provinces of Gaul had been interrupted by the calamities of war; but the scanty harvests of the continent were supplied by his paternal care from the plenty of the adjacent island. . . . The arms of Julian had restored a free and secure navigation, which Constantius had offered to purchase at the expense of his dignity, and of a tributary present of two thousand pounds of silver. The emperor parsimoniously refused to his soldiers the sums which he granted with a lavish and trembling hand to the Barbarians. The dexterity as well as the firmness of Julian was put to a severe trial when he took the field with a discontented army, which had already served two campaigns, without receiving any regular pay or any extraordinary donative.

A tender regard for the peace and happiness of his subjects was the ruling principle which directed, or seemed to direct, the administration of Julian. He devoted the leisure of his winter quarters to the offices of civil government; and affected to assume, with more pleasure, the character of a magistrate than that of a general. Before he took the field, he devolved on the provincial governors most of the public and private causes which had been referred to his tribunal; but on his return, he carefully revised their proceedings, mitigated the rigor of the law, and pronounced a second judgment on the judges themselves. Superior to the last temptation of virtuous minds, an indiscreet and intemperate zeal for justice, he restrained, with calmness and dignity, the warmth of an advocate, who prosecuted for extortion the president of the Narbonnese province. "Who will ever be found guilty," exclaimed the vehement Delphidius, "if it be enough to deny?" "And who," replied Julian, "will ever be innocent, if it be sufficient to affirm?" In the general administration of peace and war, the interest of the sovereign is commonly the same as that of his people; but Constantius would have thought himself deeply injured if the virtues of Julian had defrauded him of any part of the tribute which he extorted from an oppressed and exhausted country. The prince who was invested with the ensigns of royalty might sometimes presume to correct the rapacious insolence of his inferior agents, to expose their corrupt arts, and to introduce an equal and easier mode of collection. But the management of the finances was more safely entrusted to Florentius, Praetorian praefect of Gaul, an effeminate tyrant incapable of pity or remorse: and the haughty minister complained of the most decent and gentle opposition, while Julian himself was rather inclined to censure the weakness of his own behavior.... The precarious and dependent situation of Julian displayed his virtues and concealed his defects. The young hero who supported in Gaul the throne of Constantius was not permitted to reform the vices of the government; but he had courage to alleviate or to pity the distress of the people. Unless he had been able to revive the martial spirit of the Romans, or to introduce the arts of industry and refinement among their savage enemies, he could not entertain any rational hopes of securing the public tranquility, either by the peace or conquest of Germany. Yet the victories of Julian suspended, for a short time, the inroads of the Barbarians, and delayed the ruin of the Western empire.[†]

CHAPTER XX

CONVERSION OF CONSTANTINE

The motives, progress, and effects of the conversion of
Constantine. • Legal establishment and constitution of the
Christian or Catholic church.

The public establishment of Christianity may be considered as one of those important and domestic revolutions which excite the most lively curiosity and afford the most valuable instruction. The victories and the civil policy of Constantine no longer influence the state of Europe; but a considerable portion of the globe still retains the impression which it received from the conversion of that monarch; and the ecclesiastical institutions of his reign are still connected, by an indissoluble chain, with the opinions, the passions, and the interests of the present generation.

In the consideration of a subject which may be examined with impartiality but cannot be viewed with indifference, a difficulty immediately arises of a very unexpected nature; that of ascertaining the real and precise date of the conversion of Constantine. The eloquent Lactantius, in the midst of his court, seems impatient to proclaim to the world the glorious example of the sovereign of Gaul; who, in the first moments of his reign, acknowledged and adored the majesty of the true and only God [A.D. 306]. The learned Eusebius has ascribed the faith of Constantine to the miraculous sign which was displayed in the heavens whilst he meditated and prepared the Italian expedition [A.D. 312]. The historian Zosimus maliciously asserts that the emperor had imbrued his hands in the blood of his eldest son before he publicly renounced the gods of Rome and of his ancestors [A.D. 326]. The perplexity produced by these discordant authorities is derived from the behavior of Constantine himself. According to the strictness of ecclesiastical language, the first of the *Christian* emperors was unworthy of that name till the moment of his death; since it was only during his last illness that he received, as a catechumen, the imposition of hands, and was afterwards admitted by the initiatory rites of baptism into the number of the faithful [A.D. 337]. The Christianity of Constantine must be allowed in a much more vague and qualified sense; and the nicest accuracy is required in tracing the slow and almost imperceptible gradations by which the monarch declared himself the protector, and at length the proselyte, of the church. It was an arduous task to eradicate the habits and prejudices of his education, to acknowledge the divine power of Christ, and to understand that the truth of *his* revelation was incompatible with the worship of the gods. The obstacles which he had probably experienced in his own mind instructed him to proceed with caution in the momentous change of a national religion; and he insensibly discovered his new opinions, as far as he could enforce them with safety and with effect. During the whole course of his reign, the stream of Christianity flowed with a gentle though accelerated motion: but its general direction was sometimes checked, and sometimes diverted, by the accidental circumstances of the times, and by the prudence, or possibly by the caprice, of the monarch. His ministers were permitted to signify the intentions of their master in the various language which was best adapted to their respective principles; and he artfully balanced the hopes and fears of his subjects by publishing in the same year two edicts [A.D. 321]; the first of which enjoined the solemn observance of Sunday, and the second directed the regular consultation of the *Haruspices* [Pagan priests skilled in reading the will of the gods from the entrails of sacrificial victims]. While this important revolution yet remained in suspense, the Christians and the Pagans watched the conduct of their sovereign with the same anxiety but with very opposite sentiments. The former were prompted by every motive of zeal, as well as vanity, to exaggerate the marks of his favor and the evidences of his faith. The latter, till their just apprehensions were changed into despair and resentment, attempted to conceal from the world, and from themselves, that the gods of Rome could no longer reckon the emperor in the number of their votaries. The same passions and prejudices have engaged the partial writers of the times to connect the public profession of Christianity with the most glorious or the most ignominious era of the reign of Constantine.

Whatever symptoms of Christian piety might transpire in the discourses or actions of Constantine, he persevered till he was near forty years of age in the practice of the established religion; and the same conduct which in the court of Nicomedia might be imputed to his fear could be ascribed only to the inclination or policy of the sovereign of Gaul. His liberality restored and enriched the temples of the gods; the medals which issued from his Imperial mint are impressed with the figures and attributes of Jupiter and Apollo, of Mars and Hercules; and his filial piety increased the council of Olympus by the solemn apotheosis of his father Constantius. But the devotion of Constantine was more peculiarly directed to the genius of the Sun, the Apollo of Greek and Roman mythology; and he was pleased to be represented with the symbols of the God of Light and Poetry. The unerring shafts of that deity, the brightness of his eyes, his laurel wreath, immortal beauty, and elegant accomplishments, seem to point him out as the patron of a young hero. The altars of Apollo were crowned with the votive offerings of Constantine; and the credulous multitude were taught to believe that the emperor was permitted to behold with mortal eyes the visible majesty of their tutelar deity; and that, either walking or in a vision, he was blessed with the auspicious omens of a long and victorious reign. The Sun was universally celebrated as the invincible guide and protector of Constantine; and the Pagans might reasonably expect that the insulted god would pursue with unrelenting vengeance the impiety of his ungrateful favorite.

As long as Constantine exercised a limited sovereignty over the provinces of Gaul, his Christian subjects were protected by the authority, and perhaps by the laws, of a prince who wisely left to the gods the care of vindicating their own honor [A.D. 306–312]. If we may credit the assertion of Constantine himself, he had been an indignant spectator of the savage cruelties which were inflicted by the hands of Roman soldiers on those citizens whose religion was their only crime. In the East and in the West, he had seen the different effects of severity and indulgence; and as the former was rendered still more odious by the example of Galerius, his implacable enemy, the latter was recommended to his imitation by the authority and advice of a dying father. The son of Constantius immediately suspended or repealed the edicts of persecution and granted the free exercise of their religious ceremonies to all those who had already professed themselves members of the church. They were soon encouraged to depend on the favor as well as on the justice of their sovereign, who had imbibed a secret and sincere reverence for the name of Christ, and for the God of the Christians.

About five months after the conquest of Italy, the emperor made a solemn and authentic declaration of his sentiments by the celebrated edict of Milan, which restored peace to the Catholic church [A.D. 313]. In the personal interview of the two Western princes, Constantine, by the ascendant of genius and power, obtained the ready concurrence of his colleague, Licinius; the union of their names and authority disarmed the fury of Maximin; and after the death of the tyrant of the East, the edict of Milan was received as a general and fundamental law of the Roman world.

The wisdom of the emperors provided for the restitution of all the civil and religious rights of which the Christians had been so unjustly deprived. It was enacted that the places of worship and public lands which had been confiscated should be restored to the church, without dispute, without delay, and without expense; and this severe injunction was accompanied with a gracious promise that if any of the purchasers had paid a fair and adequate price, they should be indemnified from the Imperial treasury. The salutary regulations which guard the future tranquility of the faithful are framed on the principles of enlarged and equal toleration; and such an equality must have been interpreted by a recent sect as an advantageous and honorable distinction. The two emperors proclaim to the world that they have granted a free and absolute power to the Christians, and to all others, of following the religion which each individual thinks proper to prefer, to which he has addicted his mind, and which he may deem the best adapted to his own use. They carefully explain every ambiguous word, remove every exception, and exact from the governors of the provinces a strict obedience to the true and simple meaning of an edict which was designed to establish and secure, without any limitation, the claims of religious liberty. They condescend to assign two weighty reasons which have induced them to allow this universal toleration: the humane intention of consulting the peace and happiness of their people; and the pious hope that, by such a conduct, they shall appease and propitiate *the Deity*, whose seat is in Heaven. They gratefully acknowledge the many signal proofs which they have received of the divine favor; and they trust that the same Providence will forever continue to protect the prosperity of the prince and people. From these vague and indefinite expressions of piety, three suppositions may be deduced, of a different but not of an incompatible nature. The mind of Constantine might fluctuate between the Pagan and the Christian religions. According to the loose and complying notions of Polytheism, he might acknowledge the God of the Christians as *one* of the *many* deities who compose the hierarchy of Heaven. Or perhaps he might embrace the philosophic and pleasing idea that, notwithstanding the variety of names, of rites, and of opinions, all the sects and all the nations of mankind are united in the worship of the common Father and Creator of the universe.

But the counsels of princes are more frequently influenced by views of temporal advantage than by considerations of abstract and speculative truth. The partial and increasing favor of Constantine may naturally be referred to the esteem which he entertained for the moral character of the Christians; and to a persuasion that the propagation of the gospel would inculcate the practice of private and public virtue. Whatever latitude an absolute monarch may assume in his own conduct, whatever indulgence he may claim for his own passions, it is undoubtedly his interest that all his subjects should respect the natural and civil obligations of society. But the operation of the wisest laws is imperfect and precarious. They seldom inspire virtue, they cannot always restrain vice. Their power is insufficient to prohibit all that they condemn, nor can they always punish the actions which they prohibit. The legislators of antiquity had summoned to their aid the powers of education and of opinion. But every principle which had once maintained the vigor and purity of Rome and Sparta was long since extinguished in a declining and despotic empire. Philosophy still exercised her temperate sway over the human mind, but the cause of virtue derived very feeble support from the influence of the Pagan superstition. Under these discouraging circumstances, a prudent magistrate might observe with pleasure the progress of a religion which diffused among the people a pure, benevolent, and universal system of ethics, adapted to every duty and every condition of life, recommended as the will and reason of the supreme Deity, and enforced by the sanction of eternal rewards or punishments. The experience of Greek and Roman history could not inform the world how far the system of national manners might be reformed and improved by the precepts of a divine revelation; and Constantine might listen with some confidence to the flattering, and indeed reasonable, assurances of Lactantius. The eloquent apologist seemed firmly to expect, and almost ventured to promise, *that* the establishment of Christianity would restore the innocence and felicity of the primitive age; *that* the worship of the true God would extinguish war and dissension among those who mutually considered themselves as the children of a common parent; *that* every impure desire, every angry or selfish passion, would be restrained by the knowledge of the gospel; and *that* the magistrates might sheath the sword of justice among a people who would be universally actuated by the sentiments of truth and piety, of equity and moderation, of harmony and universal love.

The passive and unresisting obedience which bows under the yoke of authority, or even of oppression, must have appeared, in the eyes of an absolute monarch, the most conspicuous and useful of the evangelic virtues. The primitive Christians derived the institution of civil government not from the consent of the people but from the decrees of Heaven. The reigning emperor, though he had usurped the scepter by treason and murder, immediately assumed the sacred character of vicegerent of the Deity. To the Deity alone he was accountable for the abuse of his power; and his subjects were indissolubly bound, by their oath of fidelity, to a tyrant who had violated every law of nature and society. The humble Christians were sent into the world as sheep among wolves; and since they were not permitted to employ force even in the defense of their religion, they should be still more criminal if they were tempted to shed the blood of their fellow-creatures in disputing the vain privileges or the sordid possessions of this transitory life. Faithful to the doctrine of the apostle, who in the reign of Nero had preached the duty of unconditional submission, the Christians of the three first centuries preserved their conscience pure and innocent of the guilt of secret conspiracy or open rebellion. While they experienced the rigor of persecution, they were never provoked either to meet their tyrants in the field or indignantly to withdraw themselves into some remote and sequestered corner of the globe. The Protestants of France, of Germany, and of Britain, who asserted with such intrepid courage their civil and religious freedom, have been insulted by the invidious comparison between the conduct of the primitive and of the reformed Christians. Perhaps, instead of censure, some applause may be due to the superior sense and spirit of our ancestors who had convinced themselves that religion cannot abolish the unalienable rights of human nature. Perhaps the patience of the primitive church may be ascribed to its weakness, as well as to its virtue. A sect of unwarlike plebeians, without leaders, without arms, without fortifications, must have encountered inevitable destruction in a rash and fruitless resistance to the master of the Roman legions. But the Christians, when they deprecated the wrath of Diocletian or solicited the favor of Constantine, could allege, with truth and confidence, that they held the principle of passive obedience, and that, in the space of three centuries, their conduct had always been conformable to their principles. They might add that the throne of the emperors would be established on a fixed and permanent basis if all their subjects, embracing the Christian doctrine, should learn to suffer and to obey.

In the general order of Providence, princes and tyrants are considered as the ministers of Heaven, appointed to rule or to chastise the nations of the earth. But sacred history affords many illustrious examples of the more immediate interposition of the Deity in the government of his chosen people. The scepter and the sword were committed to the hands of Moses, of Joshua, of Gideon, of David, of the Maccabees; the virtues of those heroes were the motive or the effect of the divine favor, the success of their arms was destined to achieve the deliverance or the triumph of the church. If the judges of Israel were occasional and temporary magistrates, the kings of Judah derived from the royal unction of their great ancestor an hereditary and indefeasible right which could not be forfeited by their own vices, nor recalled by the caprice of their subjects. The same extraordinary Providence, which was no longer confined to the Jewish people, might elect Constantine and his family as the protectors of the Christian world; and the devout Lactantius announces, in a prophetic tone, the future glories of his long and universal reign. Galerius and Maximin, Maxentius and Licinius, were the rivals who shared with the favorite of Heaven the provinces of the empire. The tragic deaths of Galerius and Maximin soon gratified the resentment, and fulfilled the sanguine expectations, of the Christians. The success of Constantine against Maxentius and Licinius removed the two formidable competitors who still opposed the triumph of the second David, and his cause might seem to claim the peculiar interposition of Providence. The character of the Roman tyrant disgraced the purple and human nature; and though the Christians might enjoy his precarious favor, they were exposed with the rest of his subjects to the effects of his wanton and capricious cruelty. The conduct of Licinius soon betrayed the reluctance with which he had consented to the wise and humane regulations of the edict of Milan. The convocation of provincial synods was prohibited in his dominions; his Christian officers were ignominiously dismissed; and if he avoided the guilt, or rather danger, of a general persecution, his partial oppressions were rendered still more odious by the violation of a solemn and voluntary engagement. While the East, according to the lively expression of Eusebius, was involved in the shades of infernal darkness, the auspicious rays of celestial light warmed and illuminated the provinces of the West. The piety of Constantine was admitted as an unexceptionable proof of the justice of his arms; and his use of victory confirmed the opinion of the Christians that their hero was inspired and conducted by the Lord of Hosts. The conquest of Italy produced a general edict of toleration; and as soon as the defeat of Licinius had invested Constantine with the sole dominion of the Roman world, he immediately, by circular letters, exhorted all his subjects to imitate without delay the example of their sovereign and to embrace the divine truth of Christianity [A.D. 324].

The assurance that the elevation of Constantine was intimately connected with the designs of Providence instilled into the minds of the Christians two opinions which, by very different means, assisted the accomplishment of the prophecy. Their warm and active loyalty exhausted in his favor every resource of human industry; and they confidently expected that their strenuous efforts would be seconded by some divine and miraculous aid. The enemies of Constantine have imputed to interested motives the alliance which he insensibly contracted with the Catholic church, and which apparently contributed to the success of his ambition. In the beginning of the fourth century, the Christians still bore a very inadequate proportion to the inhabitants of the empire; but among a degenerate people who viewed the change of masters with the indifference of slaves, the spirit and union of a religious party might assist the popular leader to whose service, from a principle of conscience, they had devoted their lives and fortunes. The example of his father had instructed Constantine to esteem and to reward the merit of the Christians; and in the distribution of public offices, he had the advantage of strengthening his government by the choice of ministers or generals in whose fidelity he could repose a just and unreserved confidence. By the influence of these dignified missionaries, the proselytes of the new faith must have multiplied in the court and army; the Barbarians of Germany who filled the ranks of the legions were of a careless temper, which acquiesced without resistance in the religion of their commander; and when they passed the Alps it may fairly be presumed that a great number of the soldiers had already consecrated their swords to the service of Christ and of Constantine. The habits of mankind and the interests of religion gradually abated the horror of war and bloodshed which had so long prevailed among the Christians; and in the councils which were assembled under the gracious protection of Constantine, the authority of the bishops was seasonably employed to ratify the obligation of the military oath, and to inflict the penalty of excommunication on those soldiers who threw away their arms during the peace of the church. While Constantine, in his own dominions, increased the number and zeal of his faithful adherents, he could depend on the support of a powerful faction in those provinces which were still possessed or usurped by his rivals. A secret disaffection was diffused among the Christian subjects of Maxentius and Licinius; and the resentment which the latter did not attempt to conceal served only to engage them still more deeply in the interest of his competitor. The regular correspondence which connected the bishops of the most distant provinces enabled them freely to communicate their wishes and their designs, and to transmit without danger any useful intelligence, or any pious contributions, which might promote the service of Constantine, who publicly declared that he had taken up arms for the deliverance of the church.

The enthusiasm which inspired the troops, and perhaps the emperor himself, had sharpened their swords while it satisfied their conscience. They marched to battle with the full assurance that the same God who had formerly opened a passage to the Israelites through the waters of Jordan and had thrown down the walls of Jericho at the sound of the trumpets of Joshua would display his visible majesty and power in the victory of Constantine. The evidence of ecclesiastical history is prepared to affirm that their expectations were justified by the conspicuous miracle to which the conversion of the first Christian emperor has been almost unanimously ascribed. The real or imaginary cause of so important an event deserves and demands the attention of posterity; and I shall endeavor to form a just estimate of the famous vision of Constantine by a distinct consideration of the *standard*, the *dream,* and the *celestial sign;* by separating the historical, the natural, and the marvelous parts of this extraordinary story, which, in the composition of a specious argument, have been artfully confounded in one splendid and brittle mass.

I. An instrument of the tortures which were inflicted only on slaves and strangers became an object of horror in the eyes of a Roman citizen; and the ideas of guilt, of pain, and of ignominy were closely united with the idea of the cross. The piety, rather than the humanity, of Constantine soon abolished in his dominions the punishment which the Savior of mankind had condescended to suffer; but the emperor had already learned to despise the prejudices of his education and of his people before he could erect in the midst of Rome his own statue, bearing a cross in its right hand, with an inscription which referred the victory of his arms, and the deliverance of Rome, to the virtue of that salutary sign, the true symbol of force and courage. The same symbol sanctified the arms of the soldiers of Constantine; the cross glittered on their helmet, was engraved on their shields, was interwoven into their banners; and the consecrated emblems which adorned the person of the emperor himself were distinguished only by richer materials and more exquisite workmanship. But the principal standard which displayed the triumph of the cross was styled the *Labarum,* an obscure though celebrated name which has been vainly derived from almost all the languages of the world. It is described as a long pike intersected by a transversal beam. The silken veil which hung down from the beam was curiously inwrought with the images of the reigning monarch and his children. The summit of the pike supported a crown of gold which enclosed the mysterious monogram, at once expressive of the figure of the cross and the initial letters of the name of Christ, ☧ or ☧ . The safety of the labarum was entrusted to fifty guards of approved valor and fidelity; their station was marked by honors and emoluments; and some fortunate accidents soon introduced an opinion that as long as the guards of the labarum were engaged in the execution of their office, they were secure and invulnerable amidst the darts of the enemy. In the second civil war, Licinius felt and dreaded the power of this consecrated banner, the sight of which, in the distress of battle, animated the soldiers of Constantine with an invincible enthusiasm, and scattered terror and dismay through the ranks of the adverse legions. The Christian emperors, who respected the example of Constantine, displayed in all their military expeditions the standard of the cross; but when the degenerate successors of Theodosius had ceased to appear in person at the head of their armies, the labarum was deposited as a venerable but useless relic in the palace of Constantinople. Its honors are still preserved on the medals of the Flavian family. Their grateful devotion has placed the monogram of Christ in the midst of the ensigns of Rome. The solemn epithets of, safety of the republic, glory of the army, restoration of public happiness, are equally applied to the religious and military trophies; and there is still extant a medal of the emperor Constantius where the standard of the labarum is accompanied with these memorable words: BY THIS SIGN THOU SHALT CONQUER.

II. In all occasions of danger and distress, it was the practice of the primitive Christians to fortify their minds and bodies by the sign of the cross, which they used in all their ecclesiastical rites, in all the daily occurrences of life, as an infallible preservative against every species of spiritual or temporal evil. The authority of the church might alone have had sufficient weight to justify the devotion of Constantine, who in the same prudent and gradual progress acknowledged the truth and assumed the symbol of Christianity. But the testimony of a contemporary writer who in a formal treatise has avenged the cause of religion bestows on the piety of the emperor a more awful and sublime character. He affirms, with the most perfect confidence, that in the night which preceded the last battle against Maxentius, Constantine was admonished in a dream to inscribe the shields of his soldiers with the *celestial sign of God,* the sacred monogram of the name of Christ; that he executed the commands of Heaven, and that his valor and obedience were rewarded by the decisive victory of the Milvian Bridge [A.D. 312]. Some considerations might perhaps incline a skeptical mind to suspect the judgment or the veracity of the rhetorician, whose pen, either from zeal or interest, was devoted to the cause of the prevailing faction, ... but if the dream of Constantine is separately considered, it may be naturally explained either by the policy or the enthusiasm of the emperor.[†]

III. The philosopher who with calm suspicion examines the dreams and omens, the miracles and prodigies, of profane or even of ecclesiastical history will probably conclude that if the eyes of the spectators have sometimes been deceived by fraud, the understanding of the readers has much more frequently been insulted by fiction. Every event, or appearance, or accident which seems to deviate from the ordinary course of nature has been rashly ascribed to the immediate action of the Deity; and the astonished fancy of the multitude has sometimes given shape and color, language and motion, to the fleeting but uncommon meteors of the air. Nazarius and Eusebius are the two most celebrated orators who, in studied panegyrics, have labored to exalt the glory of Constantine. Nine years after the Roman victory, Nazarius describes an army of divine warriors who seemed to fall from the sky [A.D. 321]: he marks their beauty, their spirit, their gigantic forms, the stream of light which beamed from their celestial armor, their patience in suffering themselves to be heard as well as seen by mortals; and their declaration that they were sent, that they flew, to the assistance of the great Constantine. For the truth of this prodigy, the Pagan orator appeals to the whole Gallic nation, in whose presence he was then speaking; and seems to hope that the ancient apparitions would now obtain credit from this recent and public event. The Christian fable of Eusebius, which, in the space of twenty-six years, might arise from the original dream, is cast in a much more correct and elegant mold [A.D. 338]. In one of the marches of Constantine, he is reported to have seen with his own eyes the luminous trophy of the cross, placed above the meridian sun and inscribed with the following words: BY THIS CONQUER. This amazing object in the sky astonished the whole army, as well as the emperor himself, who was yet undetermined in the choice of a religion: but his astonishment was converted into faith by the vision of the ensuing night. Christ appeared before his eyes; and displaying the same celestial sign of the cross, he directed Constantine to frame a similar standard and to march, with an assurance of victory, against Maxentius and all his enemies. The learned bishop of Caesarea appears to be sensible that the recent discovery of this marvelous anecdote would excite some surprise and distrust among the most pious of his readers. Yet, instead of ascertaining the precise circumstances of time and place, which always serve to detect falsehood or establish truth; instead of collecting and recording the evidence of so many living witnesses who must have been spectators of this stupendous miracle; Eusebius contents himself with alleging a very singular testimony; that of the deceased Constantine, who, many years after the event, in the freedom of conversation, had related to him this extraordinary incident of his own life and had attested the truth of it by a solemn oath. The prudence and gratitude of the learned prelate forbade him to suspect the veracity of his victorious master; but he plainly intimates that in a fact of such a nature, he should have refused his assent to any meaner authority. This motive of credibility could not survive the power of the Flavian family; and the celestial sign, which the Infidels might afterwards deride, was disregarded by the Christians of the age which immediately followed the conversion of Constantine. But the Catholic church, both of the East and of the West, has adopted a prodigy which favors, or seems to favor, the popular worship of the cross. The vision of Constantine maintained an honorable place in the legend of superstition, till the bold and sagacious spirit of criticism presumed to depreciate the triumph and to arraign the truth of the first Christian emperor.

The Protestant and philosophic readers of the present age will incline to believe that in the account of his own conversion, Constantine attested a willful falsehood by a solemn and deliberate perjury. They may not hesitate to pronounce that in the choice of a religion, his mind was determined only by a sense of interest; and that (according to the expression of a profane poet) he used the altars of the church as a convenient footstool to the throne of the empire. A conclusion so harsh and so absolute is not, however, warranted by our knowledge of human nature, of Constantine, or of Christianity. In an age of religious fervor, the most artful statesmen are observed to feel some part of the enthusiasm which they inspire, and the most orthodox saints assume the dangerous privilege of defending the cause of truth by the arms of deceit and falsehood. Personal interest is often the standard of our belief, as well as of our practice; and the same motives of temporal advantage which might influence the public conduct and professions of Constantine would insensibly dispose his mind to embrace a religion so propitious to his fame and fortunes. His vanity was gratified by the flattering assurance that *he* had been chosen by Heaven to reign over the earth; success had justified his divine title to the throne, and that title was founded on the truth of the Christian revelation. As real virtue is sometimes excited by undeserved applause, the specious piety of Constantine, if at first it was only specious, might gradually, by the influence of praise, of habit, and of example, be matured into serious faith and fervent devotion.[†]

The awful mysteries of the Christian faith and worship were concealed from the eyes of strangers, and even of catechumens, with an
affected secrecy which served to excite their wonder and curiosity. But
the severe rules of discipline which the prudence of the bishops had
instituted were relaxed by the same prudence in favor of an Imperial
proselyte whom it was so important to allure, by every gentle condescension, into the pale of the church; and Constantine was permitted,
at least by a tacit dispensation, to enjoy *most* of the privileges, before he
had contracted *any* of the obligations, of a Christian. Instead of retiring from the congregation when the voice of the deacon dismissed the
profane multitude, he prayed with the faithful, disputed with the bishops, preached on the most sublime and intricate subjects of theology,
celebrated with sacred rites the vigil of Easter, and publicly declared
himself not only a partaker but, in some measure, a priest and hiero-
phant of the Christian mysteries. The pride of Constantine might assume, and his services had deserved, some extraordinary distinction:
an ill-timed rigor might have blasted the unripened fruits of his conversion; and if the doors of the church had been strictly closed against
a prince who had deserted the altars of the gods, the master of the empire would have been left destitute of any form of religious worship. In
his last visit to Rome, he piously disclaimed and insulted the superstition of his ancestors by refusing to lead the military procession of the
equestrian order and to offer the public vows to the Jupiter of the Capitoline Hill. Many years before his baptism and death, Constantine had
proclaimed to the world that neither his person nor his image should
ever more be seen within the walls of an idolatrous temple; while he
distributed through the provinces a variety of medals and pictures
which represented the emperor in an humble and suppliant posture of
Christian devotion.

The pride of Constantine, who refused the privileges of a catechumen, cannot easily be explained or excused; but the delay of his baptism may be justified by the maxims and the practice of ecclesiastical
antiquity. The sacrament of baptism was regularly administered by the
bishop himself, with his assistant clergy, in the cathedral church of the
diocese, during the fifty days between the solemn festivals of Easter
and Pentecost; and this holy term admitted a numerous band of infants
and adult persons into the bosom of the church. The discretion of
parents often suspended the baptism of their children till they could

understand the obligations which they contracted: the severity of ancient bishops exacted from the new converts a novitiate of two or three years; and the catechumens themselves, from different motives of a temporal or a spiritual nature, were seldom impatient to assume the character of perfect and initiated Christians. The sacrament of baptism was supposed to contain a full and absolute expiation of sin; and the soul was instantly restored to its original purity and entitled to the promise of eternal salvation. Among the proselytes of Christianity, there are many who judged it imprudent to precipitate a salutary rite which could not be repeated; to throw away an inestimable privilege which could never be recovered. By the delay of their baptism, they could venture freely to indulge their passions in the enjoyments of this world while they still retained in their own hands the means of a sure and easy absolution. The sublime theory of the gospel had made a much fainter impression on the heart than on the understanding of Constantine himself. He pursued the great object of his ambition through the dark and bloody paths of war and policy; and after the victory, he abandoned himself, without moderation, to the abuse of his fortune. Instead of asserting his just superiority above the imperfect heroism and profane philosophy of Trajan and the Antonines, the mature age of Constantine forfeited the reputation which he had acquired in his youth. As he gradually advanced in the knowledge of truth, he proportionally declined in the practice of virtue; and the same year of his reign in which he convened the council of Nice was polluted by the execution, or rather murder, of his eldest son. This date is alone sufficient to refute the ignorant and malicious suggestions of Zosimus, who affirms, that, after the death of Crispus, the remorse of his father accepted from the ministers of Christianity the expiation which he had vainly solicited from the Pagan pontiffs. At the time of the death of Crispus, the emperor could no longer hesitate in the choice of a religion; he could no longer be ignorant that the church was possessed of an infallible remedy, though he chose to defer the application of it till the approach of death had removed the temptation and danger of a relapse. The bishops whom he summoned in his last illness to the palace of Nicomedia were edified by the fervor with which he requested and received the sacrament of baptism, by the solemn protestation that the remainder of his life should be worthy of a disciple of Christ, and by his humble refusal to wear the Imperial purple after he had been clothed in the white garment of a Neophyte. The example and reputation of Constantine seemed to countenance the delay of baptism. Future tyrants were encouraged to believe that the innocent blood which they might shed in a long reign would instantly be washed away in the waters of regeneration; and the abuse of religion dangerously undermined the foundations of moral virtue.

The gratitude of the church has exalted the virtues and excused the failings of a generous patron who seated Christianity on the throne of the Roman world; and the Greeks, who celebrate the festival of the Imperial saint, seldom mention the name of Constantine without adding the title of *equal to the Apostles*. Such a comparison, if it allude to the character of those divine missionaries, must be imputed to the extravagance of impious flattery. But if the parallel be confined to the extent and number of their evangelic victories, the success of Constantine might perhaps equal that of the apostles themselves. By the edicts of toleration, he removed the temporal disadvantages which had hitherto retarded the progress of Christianity; and its active and numerous ministers received a free permission, a liberal encouragement, to recommend the salutary truths of revelation by every argument which could affect the reason or piety of mankind. The exact balance of the two religions continued but a moment; and the piercing eye of ambition and avarice soon discovered that the profession of Christianity might contribute to the interest of the present as well as of a future life. The hopes of wealth and honors, the example of an emperor, his exhortations, his irresistible smiles, diffused conviction among the venal and obsequious crowds which usually fill the apartments of a palace. The cities which signalized a forward zeal by the voluntary destruction of their temples were distinguished by municipal privileges and rewarded with popular donatives; and the new capital of the East gloried in the singular advantage that Constantinople was never profaned by the worship of idols. As the lower ranks of society are governed by imitation, the conversion of those who possessed any eminence of birth, of power, or of riches was soon followed by dependent multitudes. The salvation of the common people was purchased at an easy rate, if it be true that, in one year, twelve thousand men were baptized at Rome, besides a proportionable number of women and children, and that a white garment, with twenty pieces of gold, had been promised by the emperor to every convert. The powerful influence of Constantine was not circumscribed by the narrow limits of his life, or of his dominions. The education which he bestowed on his sons and nephews secured to the empire a race of princes whose faith was still more lively and sincere, as they imbibed in their earliest infancy the spirit, or at least the doctrine, of Christianity. War and commerce had spread the knowledge of the gospel beyond the confines of the Roman provinces; and the Barbarians, who had disdained an humble and proscribed sect, soon learned to esteem a religion which had been so lately embraced by the greatest monarch and the most civilized nation of the globe. The Goths and Germans who enlisted under the standard of Rome revered the cross which glittered at the head of the legions, and their fierce countrymen received at the same time the lessons of faith and of humanity. The kings of Iberia and Armenia worshiped the god of their protector; and their subjects, who have invariably preserved the name of Christians, soon formed a sacred and perpetual connection with their Roman brethren. The Christians of Persia were suspected, in time of war, of preferring their religion to their country; but as long as peace subsisted between the two empires, the persecuting spirit of the Magi was effectually restrained by the interposition of Constantine. The rays of the gospel illuminated the coast of India. The colonies of Jews who had penetrated into Arabia and Aethiopia opposed the progress of Christianity; but the labor of the missionaries was in some measure facilitated by a previous knowledge of the Mosaic revelation; and Abyssinia still reveres the memory of Frumentius, who, in the time of Constantine, devoted his life to the conversion of those sequestered regions [circa A.D. 330]. Under the reign of his son Constantius, Theophilus, who was himself of Indian extraction, was invested with the double character of ambassador and bishop. He embarked on the Red Sea with two hundred horses of the purest breed of Cappadocia, which were sent by the emperor to the prince of the Sabaeans, or Homerites. Theophilus was entrusted with many other useful or curious presents which might raise the admiration and conciliate the friendship of the Barbarians; and he successfully employed several years in a pastoral visit to the churches of the torrid zone.

The irresistible power of the Roman emperors was displayed in the important and dangerous change of the national religion. The terrors of a military force silenced the faint and unsupported murmurs of the

Pagans, and there was reason to expect that the cheerful submission of the Christian clergy, as well as people, would be the result of conscience and gratitude. It was long since established as a fundamental maxim of the Roman constitution that every rank of citizens was alike subject to the laws, and that the care of religion was the right as well as duty of the civil magistrate. Constantine and his successors could not easily persuade themselves that they had forfeited by their conversion any branch of the Imperial prerogatives, or that they were incapable of giving laws to a religion which they had protected and embraced. The emperors still continued to exercise a supreme jurisdiction over the ecclesiastical order, and the sixteenth book of the Theodosian Code represents, under a variety of titles, the authority which they assumed in the government of the Catholic church [A.D. 312–438].

But the distinction of the spiritual and temporal powers, which had never been imposed on the free spirit of Greece and Rome, was introduced and confirmed by the legal establishment of Christianity. The office of supreme pontiff, which, from the time of Numa to that of Augustus, had always been exercised by one of the most eminent of the senators, was at length united to the Imperial dignity. The first magistrate of the state, as often as he was prompted by superstition or policy, performed with his own hands the sacerdotal functions; nor was there any order of priests, either at Rome or in the provinces, who claimed a more sacred character among men, or a more intimate communication with the gods. But in the Christian church, which instrusts the service of the altar to a perpetual succession of consecrated ministers, the monarch, whose spiritual rank is less honorable than that of the meanest deacon, was seated below the rails of the sanctuary and confounded with the rest of the faithful multitude. The emperor might be saluted as the father of his people, but he owed a filial duty and reverence to the fathers of the church; and the same marks of respect which Constantine had paid to the persons of saints and confessors were soon exacted by the pride of the episcopal order. A secret conflict between the civil and ecclesiastical jurisdictions embarrassed the operation of the Roman government; and a pious emperor was alarmed by the guilt and danger of touching with a profane hand the ark of the covenant. The separation of men into the two orders of the clergy and of the laity was, indeed, familiar to many nations of antiquity; and the priests of India, of Persia, of Assyria, of Judea, of Aethiopia, of Egypt, and of Gaul derived from a celestial origin the temporal power and possessions which they had acquired. These venerable institutions had gradually assimilated themselves to the manners and government of their respective countries; but the opposition or contempt of the civil power served to cement the discipline of the primitive church. The Christians had been obliged to elect their own magistrates, to raise and distribute a peculiar revenue, and to regulate the internal policy of their republic by a code of laws, which were ratified by the consent of the people and the practice of three hundred years. When Constantine embraced the faith of the Christians, he seemed to contract a perpetual alliance with a distinct and independent society; and the privileges granted or confirmed by that emperor or by his successors were accepted not as the precarious favors of the court, but as the just and inalienable rights of the ecclesiastical order.

The Catholic church was administered by the spiritual and legal jurisdiction of eighteen hundred bishops; of whom one thousand were seated in the Greek and eight hundred in the Latin provinces of the empire. The extent and boundaries of their respective dioceses had been variously and accidentally decided by the zeal and success of the first missionaries, by the wishes of the people, and by the propagation of the gospel. Episcopal churches were closely planted along the banks of the Nile, on the sea-coast of Africa, in the proconsular Asia, and through the southern provinces of Italy. The bishops of Gaul and Spain, of Thrace and Pontus, reigned over an ample territory and delegated their rural suffragans to execute the subordinate duties of the pastoral office. A Christian diocese might be spread over a province or reduced to a village; but all the bishops possessed an equal and indelible character: they all derived the same powers and privileges from the apostles, from the people, and from the laws. While the *civil* and *military* professions were separated by the policy of Constantine, a new and perpetual order of *ecclesiastical* ministers, always respectable, sometimes dangerous, was established in the church and state. The important review of their station and attributes may be distributed under the following heads: I. Popular election. II. Ordination of the clergy. III. Property. IV. Civil jurisdiction. V. Spiritual censures. VI. Exercise of public oratory. VII. Privilege of legislative assemblies.

I. The freedom of election subsisted long after the legal establishment of Christianity; and the subjects of Rome enjoyed in the church the privilege which they had lost in the republic, of choosing the magistrates whom they were bound to obey. As soon as a bishop had closed his eyes, the metropolitan issued a commission to one of his suffragans to administer the vacant see and prepare, within a limited time, the future election. The right of voting was vested in the inferior clergy, who were best qualified to judge of the merit of the candidates; in the senators or nobles of the city, all those who were distinguished by their rank or property; and finally in the whole body of the people, who, on the appointed day, flocked in multitudes from the most remote parts of the diocese, and sometimes silenced by their tumultuous acclamations the voice of reason and the laws of discipline.... The civil as well as ecclesiastical laws attempted to exclude the populace from this solemn and important transaction. The canons of ancient discipline, by requiring several episcopal qualifications, of age, station, etc., restrained in some measure the indiscriminate caprice of the electors. The authority of the provincial bishops who were assembled in the vacant church to consecrate the choice of the people was interposed to moderate their passions and to correct their mistakes. The bishops could refuse to ordain an unworthy candidate, and the rage of contending factions sometimes accepted their impartial mediation.†

II. The bishops alone possessed the faculty of *spiritual* generation: and this extraordinary privilege might compensate in some degree for the painful celibacy which was imposed as a virtue, as a duty, and at length as a positive obligation. The religions of antiquity which established a separate order of priests dedicated a holy race, a tribe or family, to the perpetual service of the gods. Such institutions were founded for possession, rather than conquest. The children of the priests enjoyed, with proud and indolent security, their sacred inheritance; and the fiery spirit of enthusiasm was abated by the cares, the pleasures, and the endearments of domestic life. But the Christian sanctuary was open to every ambitious candidate who aspired to its heavenly promises or temporal possessions. This office of priests, like that of soldiers or magistrates, was strenuously exercised by those men whose temper and abilities had prompted them to embrace the ecclesiastical profession, or who had been selected by a discerning bishop as the best qualified to promote the glory and interest of the church. The bishops (till the abuse was restrained by the prudence of the laws) might constrain the reluctant and protect the distressed; and the imposition of hands forever bestowed some of the most valuable privileges of civil society. The whole body of the Catholic clergy, more numerous perhaps than the legions, was exempted by the emperors from all service, private or public, all municipal offices, and all personal taxes and contributions which pressed on their fellow-citizens with intolerable weight; and the duties of their holy profession were accepted as a full discharge of their obligations to the republic. Each bishop acquired an absolute and indefeasible right to the perpetual obedience of the clerk whom he ordained: the clergy of each episcopal church, with its dependent parishes, formed a regular and permanent society; and the cathedrals of Constantinople and Carthage maintained their peculiar establishment of five hundred ecclesiastical ministers. Their ranks and numbers were insensibly multiplied by the superstition of the times, which introduced into the church the splendid ceremonies of a Jewish or Pagan temple; and a long train of priests, deacons, sub-deacons, acolytes, exorcists, readers, singers, and doorkeepers contributed, in their respective stations, to swell the pomp and harmony of religious worship. The clerical name and privileges were extended to many pious fraternities . . . ; and the swarms of monks who arose from the Nile overspread and darkened the face of the Christian world.

III. The edict of Milan secured the revenue as well as the peace of the church [A.D. 313]. The Christians not only recovered the lands and houses of which they had been stripped by the persecuting laws of Diocletian, but they acquired a perfect title to all the possessions which they had hitherto enjoyed by the connivance of the magistrate. As soon as Christianity became the religion of the emperor and the empire, the national clergy might claim a decent and honorable maintenance; and the payment of an annual tax might have delivered the people from the more oppressive tribute which superstition imposes on her votaries. But as the wants and expenses of the church increased with her prosperity, the ecclesiastical order was still supported and enriched by the voluntary oblations of the faithful. Eight years after the edict of Milan, Constantine granted to all his subjects the free and universal permission of bequeathing their fortunes to the holy Catholic church; and their devout liberality, which during their lives was checked by luxury or avarice, flowed with a profuse stream at the hour of their death. The wealthy Christians were encouraged by the example of their sovereign. An absolute monarch who is rich without patrimony may be charitable without merit; and Constantine too easily believed that he should purchase the favor of Heaven if he maintained the idle at the expense of the industrious, and distributed among the saints the wealth of the republic.[†]

IV. The Latin clergy, who erected their tribunal on the ruins of the civil and common law, have modestly accepted, as the gift of Constantine, the independent jurisdiction which was the fruit of time, of accident, and of their own industry. But the liberality of the Christian emperors had actually endowed them with some legal prerogatives which secured and dignified the sacerdotal character. 1. Under a despotic government, the bishops alone enjoyed and asserted the inestimable privilege of being tried only by their *peers;* and even in a capital accusation, a synod of their brethren were the sole judges of their guilt or innocence. Such a tribunal, unless it was inflamed by personal resentment or religious discord, might be favorable, or even partial, to the sacerdotal order: but Constantine was satisfied that secret impunity would be less pernicious than public scandal: and the Nicene council was edified by his public declaration that if he surprised a bishop in the act of adultery, he should cast his Imperial mantle over the episcopal sinner. 2. The domestic jurisdiction of the bishops was at once a privilege and a restraint of the ecclesiastical order, whose civil causes were decently withdrawn from the cognizance of a secular judge. Their venial offenses were not exposed to the shame of a public trial or punishment; and the gentle correction which the tenderness of youth may endure from its parents or instructors was inflicted by the temperate severity of the bishops. But if the clergy were guilty of any crime which could not be sufficiently expiated by their degradation from an honorable and beneficial profession, the Roman magistrate drew the sword of justice without any regard to ecclesiastical immunities. 3. The arbitration of the bishops was ratified by a positive law; and the judges were instructed to execute, without appeal or delay, the episcopal decrees, whose validity had hitherto depended on the consent of the parties. . . . 4. The ancient privilege of sanctuary was transferred to the Christian temples and extended, by the liberal piety of the younger Theodosius, to the precincts of consecrated ground. The fugitive and even guilty suppliants were permitted to implore either the justice or the mercy of the Deity and his ministers. The rash violence of despotism was suspended by the mild interposition of the church; and the lives or fortunes of the most eminent subjects might be protected by the mediation of the bishop.

V. The bishop was the perpetual censor of the morals of his people. The discipline of penance was digested into a system of canonical jurisprudence which accurately defined the duty of private or public confession, the rules of evidence, the degrees of guilt, and the measure of punishment. It was impossible to execute this spiritual censure if the Christian pontiff, who punished the obscure sins of the multitude, respected the conspicuous vices and destructive crimes of the magistrate: but it was impossible to arraign the conduct of the magistrate without controlling the administration of civil government. Some considerations of religion, or loyalty, or fear protected the sacred persons of the emperors from the zeal or resentment of the bishops; but they boldly censured and excommunicated the subordinate tyrants who were not invested with the majesty of the purple. St. Athanasius excommunicated one of the ministers of Egypt; and the interdict which he pronounced, of fire and water, was solemnly transmitted to the churches of Cappadocia.... Such principles and such examples insensibly prepared the triumph of the Roman pontiffs, who have trampled on the necks of kings.

VI. Every popular government has experienced the effects of rude or artificial eloquence. The coldest nature is animated, the firmest reason is moved, by the rapid communication of the prevailing impulse; and each hearer is affected by his own passions and by those of the surrounding multitude. The ruin of civil liberty had silenced the demagogues of Athens and the tribunes of Rome; the custom of preaching, which seems to constitute a considerable part of Christian devotion, had not been introduced into the temples of antiquity; and the ears of monarchs were never invaded by the harsh sound of popular eloquence till the pulpits of the empire were filled with sacred orators, who possessed some advantages unknown to their profane predecessors. The arguments and rhetoric of the tribune were instantly opposed with equal arms by skillful and resolute antagonists; and the cause of truth and reason might derive an accidental support from the conflict of hostile passions. The bishop, or some distinguished presbyter to whom he cautiously delegated the powers of preaching, harangued, without the danger of interruption or reply, a submissive multitude whose minds had been prepared and subdued by the awful ceremonies of religion. Such was the strict subordination of the Catholic church that the same concerted sounds might issue at once from a hundred pulpits of Italy or Egypt if they were *tuned* by the master hand of the Roman or Alexandrian primate. The design of this institution was laudable, but the fruits were not always salutary. The preachers recommended the practice of the social duties; but they exalted the perfection of monastic virtue, which is painful to the individual and useless to mankind. Their charitable exhortations betrayed a secret wish that the clergy might be permitted to manage the wealth of the faithful for the benefit of the poor. The most sublime representations of the attributes and laws of the Deity were sullied by an idle mixture of metaphysical subleties, puerile rites, and fictitious miracles: and they expatiated, with the most fervent zeal, on the religious merit of hating the adversaries and obeying the ministers of the church. When the public peace was distracted by heresy and schism, the sacred orators sounded the trumpet of discord, and, perhaps, of sedition.[†]

VII. The representatives of the Christian republic were regularly assembled in the spring and autumn of each year; and these synods diffused the spirit of ecclesiastical discipline and legislation through the hundred and twenty provinces of the Roman world. The archbishop or metropolitan was empowered, by the laws, to summon the suffragan bishops of his province; to revise their conduct, to vindicate their rights, to declare their faith, and to examine the merits of the candidates who were elected by the clergy and people to supply the vacancies of the episcopal college. The primates of Rome, Alexandria, Antioch, Carthage, and afterwards Constantinople, who exercised a more ample jurisdiction, convened the numerous assembly of their dependent bishops. But the convocation of great and extraordinary synods was the prerogative of the emperor alone. Whenever the emergencies of the church required this decisive measure, he despatched a peremptory summons to the bishops, or the deputies of each province, with an order for the use of post-horses, and a competent allowance for the expenses of their journey.... [In A.D. 325] a numerous and celebrated assembly was convened at Nice in Bithynia to extinguish, by their final sentence, the subtle disputes which had arisen in Egypt on the subject of the Trinity. Three hundred and eighteen bishops obeyed the summons of their indulgent master; the ecclesiastics of every rank, and sect, and denomination have been computed at two thousand and forty-eight persons; the Greeks appeared in person; and the consent of the Latins was expressed by the legates of the Roman pontiff. The session, which lasted about two months, was frequently honored by the presence of the emperor. Leaving his guards at the door, he seated himself (with the permission of the council) on a low stool in the midst of the hall. Constantine listened with patience and spoke with modesty: and while he influenced the debates, he humbly professed that he was the minister, not the judge, of the successors of the apostles, who had been established as priests and as gods upon earth. Such profound reverence of an absolute monarch towards a feeble and unarmed assembly of his own subjects can only be compared to the respect with which the senate had been treated by the Roman princes who adopted the policy of Augustus. Within the space of fifty years, a philosophic spectator of the vicissitudes of human affairs might have contemplated Tacitus in the senate of Rome, and Constantine in the council of Nice. The fathers of the Capitol and those of the church had alike degenerated from the virtues of their founders; but as the bishops were more deeply rooted in the public opinion, they sustained their dignity with more decent pride, and sometimes opposed with a manly spirit the wishes of their sovereign. The progress of time and superstition erased the memory of the weakness, the passion, the ignorance, which disgraced these ecclesiastical synods; and the Catholic world has unanimously submitted to the *infallible* decrees of the general councils.

CHAPTER XXI

Persecution of Heresy, State of the Church

Persecution of heresy. • The schism of the Donatists. • The Arian controversy. • Athanasius. • Distracted state of the church and empire under Constantine and his sons. • Toleration of Paganism.

The grateful applause of the clergy has consecrated the memory of a prince who indulged their passions and promoted their interest. Constantine gave them security, wealth, honors, and revenge; and the support of the orthodox faith was considered as the most sacred and important duty of the civil magistrate. The edict of Milan, the great charter of toleration, had confirmed to each individual of the Roman world the privilege of choosing and professing his own religion. But this inestimable privilege was soon violated; with the knowledge of truth, the emperor imbibed the maxims of persecution; and the sects which dissented from the Catholic church were afflicted and oppressed by the triumph of Christianity. Constantine easily believed that the heretics who presumed to dispute his opinions or to oppose his commands were guilty of the most absurd and criminal obstinacy; and that a seasonable application of moderate severities might save those unhappy men from the danger of an everlasting condemnation. Not a moment was lost in excluding the ministers and teachers of the separated congregations from any share of the rewards and immunities which the emperor had so liberally bestowed on the orthodox clergy. But as the sectaries might still exist under the cloud of royal disgrace, the conquest of the East was immediately followed by an edict which announced their total destruction. After a preamble filled with passion and reproach, Constantine absolutely prohibits the assemblies of the heretics, and confiscates their public property to the use either of the revenue or of the Catholic church. The sects against whom the Imperial severity was directed appear to have been the adherents of Paul of Samosata; the Montanists of Phrygia, who maintained an enthusiastic succession of prophecy; the Novatians, who sternly rejected the temporal efficacy of repentance; the Marcionites and Valentinians, under whose leading banners the various Gnostics of Asia and Egypt had insensibly rallied; and perhaps the Manichaeans, who had recently imported from Persia a more artful composition of Oriental and Christian theology. The design of extirpating the name, or at least of restraining the progress, of these odious heretics was prosecuted with vigor and effect. Some of the penal regulations were copied from the edicts of Diocletian; and this method of conversion was applauded by the same bishops who had felt the hand of oppression and pleaded for the rights of humanity.

[*Doctrinal and political struggles of early Christians often converged in battles over bishoprics, as, for example, in the struggle of Caecilian and Donatus over the episcopal throne in Carthage (A.D. 312–315).*]

But this incident, so inconsiderable that it scarcely deserves a place in history, was productive of a memorable schism which afflicted the provinces of Africa above three hundred years and was extinguished only with Christianity itself. The inflexible zeal of freedom and fanaticism animated the Donatists to refuse obedience to the usurpers whose election they disputed and whose spiritual powers they denied. Excluded from the civil and religious communion of mankind, they boldly excommunicated the rest of mankind, who had embraced the impious party of Caecilian and of the Traditors, from which he derived his pretended ordination. They asserted with confidence, and almost with exultation, that the apostolical succession was interrupted; that *all* the bishops of Europe and Asia were infected by the contagion of guilt and schism; and that the prerogatives of the Catholic church were confined to the chosen portion of the African believers, who alone had preserved inviolate the integrity of their faith and discipline. This rigid theory was supported by the most uncharitable conduct. Whenever they acquired a proselyte, even from the distant provinces of the East, they carefully repeated the sacred rites of baptism and ordination; as they rejected the validity of those which he had already received from the hands of heretics or schismatics. Bishops, virgins, and even spotless infants were subjected to the disgrace of a public penance before they could be admitted to the communion of the Donatists. If they obtained possession of a church which had been used by their

Catholic adversaries, they purified the unhallowed building with the same zealous care which a temple of idols might have required. They washed the pavement, scraped the walls, burnt the altar, which was commonly of wood, melted the consecrated plate, and cast the Holy Eucharist to the dogs, with every circumstance of ignominy which could provoke and perpetuate the animosity of religious factions. Notwithstanding this irreconcilable aversion, the two parties, who were mixed and separated in all the cities of Africa, had the same language and manners, the same zeal and learning, the same faith and worship. Proscribed by the civil and ecclesiastical powers of the empire, the Donatists still maintained in some provinces, particularly in Numidia, their superior numbers; and four hundred bishops acknowledged the jurisdiction of their primate.[†]

The schism of the Donatists was confined to Africa: the more diffusive mischief of the Trinitarian controversy successively penetrated into every part of the Christian world. The former was an accidental quarrel occasioned by the abuse of freedom; the latter was a high and mysterious argument derived from the abuse of philosophy. From the age of Constantine to that of Clovis and Theodoric, the temporal interests both of the Romans and Barbarians were deeply involved in the theological disputes of Arianism. The historian may therefore be permitted respectfully to withdraw the veil of the sanctuary; and to deduce the progress of reason and faith, of error and passion from the school of Plato to the decline and fall of the empire.

The genius of Plato, informed by his own meditation or by the traditional knowledge of the priests of Egypt, had ventured to explore the mysterious nature of the Deity [360 B.C.]. When he had elevated his mind to the sublime contemplation of the first self-existent, necessary cause of the universe, the Athenian sage was incapable of conceiving *how* the simple unity of his essence could admit the infinite variety of distinct and successive ideas which compose the model of the intellectual world; *how* a Being purely incorporeal could execute that perfect model, and mold with a plastic hand the rude and independent chaos. The vain hope of extricating himself from these difficulties, which must ever oppress the feeble powers of the human mind, might induce Plato to consider the Divine Nature under the threefold modification—of the first cause, the reason, or *Logos,* and the soul or spirit of the universe. His poetical imagination sometimes fixed and animated these metaphysical abstractions; the three *archical* or original principles were represented in the Platonic system as three Gods, united with each other by a mysterious and ineffable generation; and the *Logos* was particularly considered under the more accessible character of the Son of an Eternal Father, and the Creator and Governor of the world. Such appear to have been the secret doctrines which were cautiously whispered in the gardens of the academy; and which, according to the more recent disciples of Plato, could not be perfectly understood till after an assiduous study of thirty years.

The arms of the Macedonians diffused over Asia and Egypt the language and learning of Greece; and the theological system of Plato was taught, with less reserve and perhaps with some improvements, in the celebrated school of Alexandria [300 B.C.]. A numerous colony of Jews had been invited, by the favor of the Ptolemies, to settle in their new capital. While the bulk of the nation practiced the legal ceremonies and pursued the lucrative occupations of commerce, a few Hebrews of a more liberal spirit devoted their lives to religious and philosophical contemplation. They cultivated with diligence and embraced with ardor the theological system of the Athenian sage. But their national pride would have been mortified by a fair confession of their former poverty: and they boldly marked as the sacred inheritance of their ancestors the gold and jewels which they had so lately stolen from their Egyptian masters. One hundred years before the birth of Christ, a philosophical treatise which manifestly betrays the style and sentiments of the school of Plato was produced by the Alexandrian Jews, and unanimously received as a genuine and valuable relic of the inspired Wisdom of Solomon. A similar union of the Mosaic faith and the Grecian philosophy distinguishes the works of Philo, which were composed, for the most part, under the reign of Augustus. The material soul of the universe might offend the piety of the Hebrews: but they applied the character of the *Logos* to the Jehovah of Moses and the patriarchs; and the Son of God was introduced upon earth under a visible and even human appearance to perform those familiar offices which seem incompatible with the nature and attributes of the Universal Cause.

The eloquence of Plato, the name of Solomon, the authority of the school of Alexandria, and the consent of the Jews and Greeks were insufficient to establish the truth of a mysterious doctrine which might please, but could not satisfy, a rational mind. A prophet, or apostle, inspired by the Deity can alone exercise a lawful dominion over the faith of mankind: and the theology of Plato might have been forever confounded with the philosophical visions of the Academy, the Porch, and the Lycaeum if the name and divine attributes of the *Logos* had not been confirmed by the celestial pen of the last and most sublime of the Evangelists [A.D. 97]. The Christian Revelation, which was consummated under the reign of Nerva, disclosed to the world the amazing secret that the LOGOS, who was with God from the beginning, and was God, who had made all things and for whom all things had been made, was incarnate in the person of Jesus of Nazareth; who had been born of a virgin, and suffered death on the cross.†

The divine sanction which the apostle had bestowed on the fundamental principle of the theology of Plato encouraged the learned proselytes of the second and third centuries to admire and study the writings of the Athenian sage, who had thus marvelously anticipated one of the most surprising discoveries of the Christian revelation. The respectable name of Plato was used by the orthodox, and abused by the heretics, as the common support of truth and error: the authority of his skillful commentators, and the science of dialectics, were employed to justify the remote consequences of his opinions and to supply the discreet silence of the inspired writers. The same subtle and profound questions concerning the nature, the generation, the distinction, and the equality of the three divine persons of the mysterious *Triad,* or Trinity, were agitated in the philosophical and in the Christian schools of Alexandria.†

We may observe two essential and peculiar circumstances which discriminated the doctrines of the Catholic church from the opinions of the Platonic school.

I. A chosen society of philosophers, men of a liberal education and curious disposition, might silently meditate, and temperately discuss in the gardens of Athens or the library of Alexandria, the abstruse questions of metaphysical science. . . . But after the *Logos* had been revealed as the sacred object of the faith, the hope, and the religious worship of the Christians, the mysterious system was embraced by a numerous and increasing multitude in every province of the Roman world. Those persons who, from their age, or sex, or occupations, were the least qualified to judge, who were the least exercised in the habits of abstract reasoning, aspired to contemplate the economy of the Divine Nature: and it is the boast of Tertullian that a Christian mechanic could readily answer such questions as had perplexed the wisest of the Grecian sages. . . . A theology which it was incumbent to believe, which it was impious to doubt, and which it might be dangerous and even fatal to mistake became the familiar topic of private meditation and popular discourse. The cold indifference of philosophy was inflamed by the fervent spirit of devotion.

II. The devotion of individuals was the first circumstance which distinguished the Christians from the Platonists: the second was the authority of the church. The disciples of philosophy asserted the rights of intellectual freedom, and their respect for the sentiments of their teachers was a liberal and voluntary tribute which they offered to superior reason. But the Christians formed a numerous and disciplined society; and the jurisdiction of their laws and magistrates was strictly exercised over the minds of the faithful. The loose wanderings of the imagination were gradually confined by creeds and confessions; the freedom of private judgment submitted to the public wisdom of synods; the authority of a theologian was determined by his ecclesiastical rank; and the episcopal successors of the apostles inflicted the censures of the church on those who deviated from the orthodox belief. But in an age of religious controversy, every act of oppression adds new force to the elastic vigor of the mind; and the zeal or obstinacy of a spiritual rebel was sometimes stimulated by secret motives of ambition or avarice. A metaphysical argument became the cause or pretense of political contests; the subtleties of the Platonic school were used as the badges of popular factions, and the distance which separated their respective tenets were enlarged or magnified by the acrimony of dispute. . . . After the edict of toleration had restored peace and leisure to the Christians, the Trinitarian controversy was revived in the ancient seat of Platonism, the learned, the opulent, the tumultuous city of Alexandria; and the flame of religious discord was rapidly communicated from the schools to the clergy, the people, the province, and the East. The abstruse question of the eternity of the *Logos* was agitated in ecclesiastic conferences and popular sermons; and the heterodox opinions of Arius were soon made public by his own zeal and by that of his adversaries. His most implacable adversaries have acknowledged the learning and blameless life of that eminent presbyter, who in a former election had declared, and perhaps generously declined, his pretensions to the episcopal throne. His competitor Alexander assumed the office of his judge. The important cause was argued before him; and if at first he seemed to hesitate, he at length pronounced his final sentence as an absolute rule of faith. The undaunted presbyter, who presumed to resist the authority of his angry bishop, was separated from the community of the church. But the pride of Arius was supported by the applause of a numerous party. He reckoned among his immediate followers two bishops of Egypt, seven presbyters, twelve deacons, and (what may appear almost incredible) seven hundred virgins. A large majority of the bishops of Asia appeared to support or favor his cause; and their measures were conducted by Eusebius of Caesarea, the most learned of the Christian prelates; and by Eusebius of Nicomedia, who had acquired the reputation of a statesman without forfeiting that of a saint. Synods in Palestine and Bithynia were opposed to the synods of Egypt. The attention of the prince and people was attracted by this theological dispute; and the decision, at the end of six years, was referred to the supreme authority of the general council of Nice [A.D. 318–325].

When the mysteries of the Christian faith were dangerously exposed to public debate, it might be observed that the human understanding was capable of forming three distinct though imperfect systems concerning the nature of the Divine Trinity; and it was pronounced that none of these systems, in a pure and absolute sense, were exempt from heresy and error.

I. [Arianism.] According to the first hypothesis, which was maintained by Arius and his disciples, the *Logos* was a dependent and spontaneous production, created from nothing by the will of the father. The Son, by whom all things were made, had been begotten before all worlds, and the longest of the astronomical periods could be compared only as a fleeting moment to the extent of his duration; yet this duration was not infinite, and there *had* been a time which preceded the ineffable generation of the *Logos*. On this only-begotten Son, the Almighty Father had transfused his ample spirit, and impressed the effulgence of his glory. Visible image of invisible perfection, he saw, at an immeasurable distance beneath his feet, the thrones of the brightest archangels; yet he shone only with a reflected light, and, like the sons of the Romans emperors who were invested with the titles of

Caesar or Augustus, he governed the universe in obedience to the will of his Father and Monarch.

II. [Tritheism.] In the second hypothesis, the *Logos* possessed all the inherent, incommunicable perfections which religion and philosophy appropriate to the Supreme God. Three distinct and infinite minds or substances, three coequal and coeternal beings, composed the Divine Essence; and it would have implied contradiction that any of them should not have existed, or that they should ever cease to exist. The advocates of a system which seemed to establish three independent Deities attempted to preserve the unity of the First Cause, so conspicuous in the design and order of the world, by the perpetual concord of their administration and the essential agreement of their will.[†]

III. [Sabellianism.] Three beings who, by the self-derived necessity of their existence, possess all the divine attributes in the most perfect degree; who are eternal in duration, infinite in space, and intimately present to each other, and to the whole universe; irresistibly force themselves on the astonished mind as one and the same being, who, in the economy of grace as well as in that of nature, may manifest himself under different forms and be considered under different aspects. By this hypothesis, a real substantial trinity is refined into a trinity of names and abstract modifications that subsist only in the mind which conceives them. The *Logos* is no longer a person but an attribute; and it is only in a figurative sense that the epithet of Son can be applied to the eternal reason which was with God from the beginning, and by *which*, not by *whom*, all things were made. The incarnation of the *Logos* is reduced to a mere inspiration of the Divine Wisdom, which filled the soul, and directed all the actions, of the man Jesus.[†]

If the bishops of the council of Nice [A.D. 325] had been permitted to follow the unbiased dictates of their conscience, Arius and his associates could scarcely have flattered themselves with the hopes of obtaining a majority of votes in favor of an hypothesis so directly adverse to the two most popular opinions of the Catholic world. The Arians soon perceived the danger of their situation, and prudently assumed those modest virtues which, in the fury of civil and religious dissensions, are seldom practiced or even praised, except by the weaker party. They recommended the exercise of Christian charity and moderation; urged the incomprehensible nature of the controversy; disclaimed the use of any terms or definitions which could not be found in the Scriptures; and offered, by very liberal concessions, to satisfy their adversaries without renouncing the integrity of their own principles. The victorious faction received all their proposals with haughty suspicion; and anxiously sought for some irreconcilable mark of distinction, the rejection of which might involve the Arians in the guilt and consequences of heresy. A letter was publicly read, and ignominiously torn, in which their patron, Eusebius of Nicomedia, ingenuously confessed that the admission of the HOMOOUSION, or Consubstantial, a word already familiar to the Platonists, was incompatible with the principles of their theological system. The fortunate opportunity was eagerly embraced by the bishops who governed the resolutions of the synod; and, according to the lively expression of Ambrose, they used the sword which heresy itself had drawn from the scabbard to cut off the head of the hated monster. The consubstantiality of the Father and the Son was established by the council of Nice, and has been unanimously received as a fundamental article of the Christian faith by the consent of the Greek, the Latin, the Oriental, and the Protestant churches. But if the same word had not served to stigmatize the heretics and to unite the Catholics, it would have been inadequate to the purpose of the majority by whom it was introduced into the orthodox creed. This majority was divided into two parties, distinguished by a contrary tendency to the sentiments of the Tritheists and of the Sabellians. . . . The interest of the common cause inclined them to join their numbers and to conceal their differences; their animosity was softened by the healing counsels of toleration, and their disputes were suspended by the use of the mysterious *Homoousion,* which either party was free to interpret according to their peculiar tenets. . . . Within these limits, the almost invisible and tremulous ball of orthodoxy was allowed securely to vibrate. On either side, beyond this consecrated ground, the heretics and the demons lurked in ambush to surprise and devour the unhappy wanderer. But as the degrees of theological hatred depend on the spirit of the war rather than on the importance of the controversy, the heretics who degraded were treated with more severity than those who annihilated the person of the Son. The life of Athanasius was consumed in irreconcilable opposition to the impious *madness* of the Arians; but he defended above twenty years the Sabellianism of Marcellus of Ancyra; and when at last he was compelled to withdraw himself from his communion, he continued to mention, with an ambiguous smile, the venial errors of his respectable friend.[†]

It will not be expected, it would not perhaps be endured, that I should swell this theological digression by a minute examination of the eighteen creeds, the authors of which, for the most part, disclaimed the odious name of their parent Arius. It is amusing enough to delineate the form and to trace the vegetation of a singular plant; but the tedious detail of leaves without flowers and of branches without fruit would soon exhaust the patience and disappoint the curiosity of the laborious student. One question which gradually arose from the Arian controversy may, however, be noticed, as it served to produce and discriminate the three sects, who were united only by their common aversion to the *Homoousion* of the Nicene synod. 1. If they were asked whether the Son was *like* unto the Father, the question was resolutely answered in the negative by the heretics who adhered to the principles of Arius, or indeed to those of philosophy; which seem to establish an infinite difference between the Creator and the most excellent of his creatures. . . . 2. [But] the omnipotence of the Creator suggested a specious and respectful solution of the *likeness* of the Father and the Son; and faith might humbly receive what reason could not presume to deny, that the Supreme God might communicate his infinite perfections and create a being similar only to himself. These Arians were powerfully supported by the weight and abilities of their leaders, who had succeeded to the management of the Eusebian interest and who occupied the principal thrones of the East. . . . 3. The Greek word which was chosen to express this mysterious resemblance bears so close an affinity to the orthodox symbol that the profane of every age have derided the furious contests which the difference of a single diphthong excited between the HOMOOUSIANS ["same substance"] and the HOMOIOUSIANS ["similar substance"]. As it frequently happens that the sounds and characters which approach the nearest to each other accidentally represent the most opposite ideas, the observation would be itself ridiculous if it were possible to mark any real and sensible distinction between the doctrine of the Semi-Arians, as they were improperly styled, and that of the Catholics themselves.[†]

The provinces of Egypt and Asia, which cultivated the language and manners of the Greeks, had deeply imbibed the venom of the

Arian controversy. . . . The inhabitants of the West were of a less inquisitive spirit; their passions were not so forcibly moved by invisible
objects, their minds were less frequently exercised by the habits of dispute; and such was the happy ignorance of the Gallican church that
Hilary himself, above thirty years after the first general council, was
still a stranger to the Nicene creed. The Latins had received the rays
of divine knowledge through the dark and doubtful medium of a
translation. The poverty and stubbornness of their native tongue was
not always capable of affording just equivalents for the Greek terms,
for the technical words of the Platonic philosophy, which had been
consecrated, by the gospel or by the church, to express the mysteries of
the Christian faith; and a verbal defect might introduce into the Latin
theology a long train of error or perplexity. But as the Western provincials had the good fortune of deriving their religion from an orthodox
source, they preserved with steadiness the doctrine which they had accepted with docility; and when the Arian pestilence approached their
frontiers, they were supplied with the seasonable preservative of the
Homoousion by the paternal care of the Roman pontiff.†

Such was the rise and progress, and such were the natural revolutions of those theological disputes, which disturbed the peace of
Christianity under the reigns of Constantine and of his sons. But as
those princes presumed to extend their despotism over the faith, as
well as over the lives and fortunes, of their subjects, the weight of their
suffrage sometimes inclined the ecclesiastical balance: and the prerogatives of the King of Heaven were settled, or changed, or modified in
the cabinet of an earthly monarch.

The unhappy spirit of discord which pervaded the provinces of the
East interrupted the triumph of Constantine; but the emperor continued for some time to view, with cool and careless indifference, the object of the dispute [A.D. 324]. As he was yet ignorant of the difficulty of
appeasing the quarrels of theologians, he addressed to the contending
parties, to Alexander and to Arius, a moderating epistle; which may be
ascribed with far greater reason to the untutored sense of a soldier and
statesman than to the dictates of any of his episcopal counselors. He
attributes the origin of the whole controversy to a trifling and subtle
question concerning an incomprehensible point of law which was
foolishly asked by the bishop and imprudently resolved by the presbyter. He laments that the Christian people, who had the same God,

the same religion, and the same worship, should be divided by such inconsiderable distinctions; and he seriously recommends to the clergy of Alexandria the example of the Greek philosophers; who could maintain their arguments without losing their temper, and assert their freedom without violating their friendship. The indifference and contempt of the sovereign would have been, perhaps, the most effectual method of silencing the dispute if the popular current had been less rapid and impetuous, and if Constantine himself, in the midst of faction and fanaticism, could have preserved the calm possession of his own mind. But his ecclesiastical ministers soon contrived to seduce the impartiality of the magistrate, and to awaken the zeal of the proselyte [A.D. 325]. He was provoked by the insults which had been offered to his statues; he was alarmed by the real as well as the imaginary magnitude of the spreading mischief; and he extinguished the hope of peace and toleration from the moment that he assembled three hundred bishops within the walls of the same palace. The presence of the monarch swelled the importance of the debate; his attention multiplied the arguments; and he exposed his person with a patient intrepidity which animated the valor of the combatants. Notwithstanding the applause which has been bestowed on the eloquence and sagacity of Constantine, a Roman general whose religion might be still a subject of doubt and whose mind had not been enlightened either by study or by inspiration was indifferently qualified to discuss, in the Greek language, a metaphysical question, or an article of faith. . . . The Nicene creed was ratified by Constantine; and his firm declaration that those who resisted the divine judgment of the synod must prepare themselves for an immediate exile annihilated the murmurs of a feeble opposition; which, from seventeen, was almost instantly reduced to two protesting bishops. . . . The impious Arius was banished into one of the remote provinces of Illyricum; his person and disciples were branded by law with the odious name of Porphyrians; his writings were condemned to the flames, and a capital punishment was denounced against those in whose possession they should be found. The emperor had now imbibed the spirit of controversy, and the angry, sarcastic style of his edicts was designed to inspire his subjects with the hatred which he had conceived against the enemies of Christ.

But, as if the conduct of the emperor had been guided by passion instead of principle, three years from the council of Nice [A.D. 325] were scarcely elapsed before he discovered some symptoms of mercy, and even of indulgence, towards the proscribed sect, which was secretly protected by his favorite sister [circa A.D. 328–337]. The exiles were recalled. . . . . Arius himself was treated by the whole court with the respect which would have been due to an innocent and oppressed man. His faith was approved by the synod of Jerusalem; and the emperor seemed impatient to repair his injustice by issuing an absolute command that he should be solemnly admitted to the communion in the cathedral of Constantinople. On the same day which had been fixed for the triumph of Arius, he expired; and the strange and horrid circumstances of his death [his bowels suddenly burst out in a privy] might excite a suspicion that the orthodox saints had contributed more efficaciously than by their prayers to deliver the church from the most formidable of her enemies. (Those who press the literal narrative of the death of Arius must make their option between *poison* and *miracle.*) The three principal leaders of the Catholics, Athanasius of Alexandria, Eustathius of Antioch, and Paul of Constantinople, were deposed on various accusations by the sentence of numerous councils; and were afterwards banished into distant provinces by the first of the Christian emperors, who, in the last moments of his life, received the rites of baptism from the Arian bishop of Nicomedia. The ecclesiastical government of Constantine cannot be justified from the reproach of levity and weakness. But the credulous monarch, unskilled in the stratagems of theological warfare, might be deceived by the modest and specious professions of the heretics, whose sentiments he never perfectly understood; and while he protected Arius and persecuted Athanasius, he still considered the council of Nice as the bulwark of the Christian faith and the peculiar glory of his own reign.

The sons of Constantine must have been admitted from their childhood into the rank of catechumens; but they imitated, in the delay of their baptism, the example of their father. Like him they presumed to pronounce their judgment on mysteries into which they had never been regularly initiated; and the fate of the Trinitarian controversy depended, in a great measure, on the sentiments of Constantius; who inherited the provinces of the East and acquired the possession of the whole empire.

[*Constantius favors the Arians (A.D. 337–361).*]

The sentiments of a judicious stranger who has impartially considered the progress of civil or ecclesiastical discord are always entitled to our notice; and a short passage of Ammianus, who served in the armies and studied the character of Constantius, is perhaps of more value than many pages of theological invectives. "The Christian religion, which, in itself," says that moderate historian, "is plain and simple, *he* confounded by the dotage of superstition. Instead of reconciling the parties by the weight of his authority, he cherished and promulgated, by verbal disputes, the differences which his vain curiosity had excited. The highways were covered with troops of bishops galloping from every side to the assemblies which they call synods; and while they labored to reduce the whole sect to their own particular opinions, the public establishment of the posts was almost ruined by their hasty and repeated journeys." Our more intimate knowledge of the ecclesiastical transactions of the reign of Constantius would furnish an ample commentary on this remarkable passage, which justifies the rational apprehensions of Athanasius that the restless activity of the clergy, who wandered round the empire in search of the true faith, would excite the contempt and laughter of the unbelieving world. As soon as the emperor was relieved from the terrors of the civil war, he devoted the leisure of his winter quarters at Arles, Milan, Sirmium, and Constantinople to the amusement or toils of controversy: the sword of the magistrate, and even of the tyrant, was unsheathed, to enforce the reasons of the theologian; and as he opposed the orthodox faith of Nice, it is readily confessed that his incapacity and ignorance were equal to his presumption. The eunuchs, the women, and the bishops who governed the vain and feeble mind of the emperor had inspired him with an insuperable dislike to the *Homoousion*. . . . The mind of Constantius, which could neither be moderated by reason nor fixed by faith, was blindly impelled to either side of the dark and empty abyss by his horror of the opposite extreme; he alternately embraced and condemned the sentiments, he successively banished and recalled the leaders, of the Arian and Semi-Arian factions. During the season of public business or festivity, he employed whole days and even nights in selecting the words and weighing the syllables which composed his fluctuating creeds. The subject of his meditations still pursued and occupied his slumbers: the incoherent dreams of the emperor were received as celestial visions, and he accepted with complacency the lofty title of bishop of bishops from those ecclesiastics who forgot the interest of their order for the gratification of their passions. The design of establishing a uniformity of doctrine, which had engaged him to convene so many synods in Gaul, Italy, Illyricum, and Asia, was repeatedly baffled by his own levity, by the divisions of the Arians, and by the resistance of the Catholics; and he resolved, as the last and decisive effort, imperiously to dictate the decrees of a general council. . . . The deputies of the East and of the West attended the emperor in the palace of Constantinople, and he enjoyed the satisfaction of imposing on the world a profession of faith which established the *likeness*, without expressing the *consubstantiality*, of the Son of God. But the triumph of Arianism had been preceded by the removal of the orthodox clergy whom it was impossible either to intimidate or to corrupt; and the reign of Constantius was disgraced by the unjust and ineffectual persecution of the great Athanasius [A.D. 326–373].†

The persecution of Athanasius, and of so many respectable bishops who suffered for the truth of their opinions, or at least for the integrity of their conscience, was a just subject of indignation and discontent to all Christians, except those who were blindly devoted to the Arian faction. The people regretted the loss of their faithful pastors, whose banishment was usually followed by the intrusion of a stranger into the episcopal chair; and loudly complained that the right of election was violated, and that they were condemned to obey a mercenary usurper whose person was unknown and whose principles were suspected. The Catholics might prove to the world that they were not involved in the guilt and heresy of their ecclesiastical governor by publicly testifying their dissent, or by totally separating themselves from his communion. The first of these methods was invented at Antioch, and practiced with such success that it was soon diffused over the Christian world. The doxology, or sacred hymn, which celebrates the *glory* of the Trinity is susceptible of very nice, but material, inflections; and the substance of an orthodox or an heretical creed may be expressed by the difference of a disjunctive or a copulative particle. Alternate responses and a more regular psalmody were introduced into the public service by Flavianus and Diodorus, two devout and active laymen who were attached to the Nicene faith. Under their conduct a swarm of monks issued from the adjacent desert, bands of well-disciplined singers were stationed in the cathedral of Antioch, the Glory to the Father, AND the Son, AND the Holy Ghost was triumphantly chanted by a full chorus of voices; and the Catholics insulted, by the purity of their doctrine, the Arian prelate. . . . The same zeal which inspired their songs prompted the more scrupulous members of the orthodox party to form separate assemblies, which were governed by the presbyters till the death of their exiled bishop allowed the election and consecration of a new episcopal pastor. . . . The abuse of Christianity introduced into the Roman government new causes of tyranny and sedition; the bands of civil society were torn asunder by the fury of religious factions; and the obscure citizen who might calmly have surveyed the elevation and fall of successive emperors imagined and experienced that his own life and fortune were connected with the interests of a popular ecclesiastic. The example of the two capitals, Rome and Constantinople, may serve to represent the state of the empire, and the temper of mankind, under the reign of the sons of Constantine.

I. The Roman pontiff, as long as he maintained his station and his principles, was guarded by the warm attachment of a great people; and could reject with scorn the prayers, the menaces, and the oblations of an heretical prince. When the eunuchs had secretly pronounced the exile of Liberius, the well-grounded apprehension of a tumult engaged them to use the utmost precautions in the execution of the sentence [A.D. 355]. The capital was invested on every side, and the praefect was commanded to seize the person of the bishop, either by stratagem or by open force. The order was obeyed, and Liberius, with the greatest difficulty, at the hour of midnight, was swiftly conveyed beyond the reach of the Roman people before their consternation was turned into rage. As soon as they were informed of his banishment into Thrace, a general assembly was convened, and the clergy of Rome bound themselves, by a public and solemn oath, never to desert their bishop, never to acknowledge the usurper Felix; who, by the influence of the eunuchs, had been irregularly chosen and consecrated within the walls of a profane palace. At the end of two years, their pious obstinacy subsisted entire and unshaken [A.D. 356]; and when Constantius visited Rome, he was assailed by the importunate solicitations of a people who had preserved, as the last remnant of their ancient freedom, the right of treating their sovereign with familiar insolence. The wives of many of the senators and most honorable citizens, after pressing their husbands to intercede in favor of Liberius, were advised to undertake a commission which in their hands would be less dangerous, and might prove more successful. The emperor received with politeness these female deputies [A.D. 357], whose wealth and dignity were displayed in the magnificence of their dress and ornaments: he admired their inflexible resolution of following their beloved pastor to the most distant regions of the earth; and consented that the two bishops, Liberius and Felix, should govern in peace their respective congregations. But the ideas of toleration were so repugnant to the practice, and even to the sentiments, of those times, that when the answer of Constantius was publicly read in the circus of Rome, so reasonable a project of accommodation was rejected with contempt and ridicule. The eager vehemence which animated the spectators in the decisive moment of a horse-race was now directed towards a different object; and the circus resounded with the shout of thousands, who repeatedly exclaimed, "One God, One Christ, One Bishop!" The zeal of the Roman people in the cause of Liberius was not confined to words alone; and the dangerous and bloody sedition which they excited soon after the departure of Constantius determined that prince to accept the submission of the exiled prelate and to restore him to the undivided dominion of the capital. After some ineffectual resistance, his rival was expelled from the city by the permission of the emperor and the power of the opposite faction; the adherents of Felix were inhumanly murdered in the streets, in the public places, in the baths, and even in the churches; and the face of Rome, upon the return of a Christian bishop, renewed the horrid image of the massacres of Marius and the proscriptions of Sulla.

II. Notwithstanding the rapid increase of Christians under the reign of the Flavian family, Rome, Alexandria, and the other great cities of the empire still contained a strong and powerful faction of Infidels, who envied the prosperity and who ridiculed, even in their theaters, the theological disputes of the church. Constantinople alone enjoyed the advantage of being born and educated in the bosom of the faith. The capital of the East had never been polluted by the worship of idols; and the whole body of the people had deeply imbibed the opinions, the virtues, and the passions which distinguished the Christians of that age from the rest of mankind [A.D. 336]. After the death of

Alexander, the episcopal throne was disputed by Paul and Macedonius [A.D. 342]. By their zeal and abilities they both deserved the eminent station to which they aspired; and if the moral character of Macedonius was less exceptionable, his competitor had the advantage of a prior election and a more orthodox doctrine. His firm attachment to the Nicene creed, which has given Paul a place in the calendar among saints and martyrs, exposed him to the resentment of the Arians. In the space of fourteen years he was five times driven from his throne; to which he was more frequently restored by the violence of the people than by the permission of the prince; and the power of Macedonius could be secured only by the death of his rival. The unfortunate Paul was dragged in chains from the sandy deserts of Mesopotamia to the most desolate places of Mount Taurus, confined in a dark and narrow dungeon, left six days without food, and at length strangled by the order of Philip, one of the principal ministers of the emperor Constantius [A.D. 350]. The first blood which stained the new capital was spilt in this ecclesiastical contest; and many persons were slain on both sides in the furious and obstinate seditions of the people. The commission of enforcing a sentence of banishment against Paul had been entrusted to Hermogenes, the master-general of the cavalry; but the execution of it was fatal to himself. The Catholics rose in the defense of their bishop . . . ; the first military officer of the empire was dragged by the heels through the streets of Constantinople, and, after he expired, his lifeless corpse was exposed to their wanton insults. The fate of Hermogenes instructed Philip, the Praetorian praefect, to act with more precaution on a similar occasion. In the most gentle and honorable terms, he required the attendance of Paul in the baths of Xeuxippus, which had a private communication with the palace and the sea. A vessel which lay ready at the garden stairs immediately hoisted sail; and while the people were still ignorant of the meditated sacrilege, their bishop was already embarked on his voyage to Thessalonica. They soon beheld, with surprise and indignation, the gates of the palace thrown open, and the usurper Macedonius seated by the side of the praefect on a lofty chariot, which was surrounded by troops of guards with drawn swords. The military procession advanced towards the cathedral; the Arians and the Catholics eagerly rushed to occupy that important post; and three thousand one hundred and fifty persons lost their lives in the confusion of the tumult. Macedonius, who was supported by a regular force, obtained a decisive victory; but his reign was disturbed by clamor and sedition; and the causes which appeared the least connected with the subject of dispute were sufficient to nourish and to kindle the flame of civil discord. As the chapel in which the body of the great Constantine had been deposited was in a ruinous condition, the bishop transported those venerable remains into the church of St. Acacius. This prudent and even pious measure was represented as a wicked profanation by the whole party which adhered to the *Homoousian* doctrine. The factions immediately flew to arms, the consecrated ground was used as their field of battle; and one of the ecclesiastical historians has observed as a real fact, not as a figure of rhetoric, that the well before the church overflowed with a stream of blood, which filled the porticos and the adjacent courts. The writer who should impute these tumults solely to a religious principle would betray a very imperfect knowledge of human nature; yet it must be confessed that the motive which misled the sincerity of zeal, and the pretense which disguised the licentiousness of passion, suppressed the remorse which, in another cause, would have succeeded to the rage of the Christians at Constantinople.

The cruel and arbitrary disposition of Constantius, which did not always require the provocations of guilt and resistance, was justly exasperated by the tumults of his capital, and the criminal behavior of a faction which opposed the authority and religion of their sovereign. The ordinary punishments of death, exile, and confiscation were inflicted with partial vigor; and the Greeks still revere the holy memory of two clerks, a reader and a sub-deacon, who were accused of the murder of Hermogenes and beheaded at the gates of Constantinople. By an edict of Constantius against the Catholics which has not been judged worthy of a place in the Theodosian code, those who refused to communicate with the Arian bishops, and particularly with Macedonius, were deprived of the immunities of ecclesiastics and of the rights of Christians; they were compelled to relinquish the possession of the churches; and were strictly prohibited from holding their assemblies within the walls of the city. The execution of this unjust law in the provinces of Thrace and Asia Minor was committed to the zeal of Macedonius; the civil and military powers were directed to obey his commands; and the cruelties exercised by this Semi-Arian tyrant in the support of the *Homoiousion* exceeded the commission, and disgraced the reign, of Constantius. The sacraments of the church were administered to the reluctant victims who denied the vocation, and abhorred the principles, of Macedonius. The rites of baptism were conferred on women and children who, for that purpose, had been torn from the arms of their friends and parents; the mouths of the communicants were held open by a wooden engine while the consecrated bread was forced down their throat; the breasts of tender virgins were either burnt with red-hot egg-shells, or inhumanly compressed between sharp and heavy boards.[†]

While the flames of the Arian controversy consumed the vitals of the empire, the African provinces were infested by their peculiar enemies, the savage fanatics who, under the name of *Circumcellions,* formed the strength and scandal of the Donatist party [A.D. 345 ff.]. The severe execution of the laws of Constantine had excited a spirit of discontent and resistance; the strenuous efforts of his son Constans to restore the unity of the church exasperated the sentiments of mutual hatred which had first occasioned the separation; and the methods of force and corruption employed by the two Imperial commissioners, Paul and Macarius, furnished the schismatics with a specious contrast between the maxims of the apostles and the conduct of their pretended successors. The peasants who inhabited the villages of Numidia and Mauritania were a ferocious race who had been imperfectly reduced under the authority of the Roman laws; who were imperfectly converted to the Christian faith; but who were actuated by a blind and furious enthusiasm in the cause of their Donatist teachers. They indignantly supported the exile of their bishops, the demolition of their churches, and the interruption of their secret assemblies. The violence of the officers of justice, who were usually sustained by a military guard, was sometimes repelled with equal violence; and the blood of some popular ecclesiastics, which had been shed in the quarrel, inflamed their rude followers with an eager desire of revenging the death of these holy martyrs. By their own cruelty and rashness, the ministers of persecution sometimes provoked their fate; and the guilt of an accidental tumult precipitated the criminals into despair and rebellion. Driven from their native villages, the Donatist peasants assembled in formidable gangs on the edge of the Getulian desert; and readily exchanged the habits of labor for a life of idleness and rapine which was consecrated by the name of religion and faintly condemned by the doctors of the sect. The leaders of the Circumcellions assumed the title of captains of the saints; their principal weapon, as they were indifferently provided with swords and spears, was a huge and weighty club which they termed an *Israelite*; and the well-known sound of "Praise be to God," which they used as their cry of war, diffused consternation over the unarmed provinces of Africa. At first their depredations were colored by the plea of necessity; but they soon exceeded the measure of subsistence, indulged without control their intemperance and avarice, burnt the villages which they had pillaged, and reigned the licentious tyrants of the open country. The occupations of husbandry and the administration of justice were interrupted; and as the Circumcellions pretended to restore the primitive equality of mankind and to reform the abuses of civil society, they opened a secure asylum for the slaves and debtors who flocked in crowds to their holy standard. When they were not resisted, they usually contented themselves with plunder, but the slightest opposition provoked them to acts of violence and murder; and some Catholic priests who had imprudently signalized their zeal were tortured by the fanatics with the most refined and wanton barbarity. . . . The Donatists who were taken in arms received, and they soon deserved, the same treatment which might have been shown to the wild beasts of the desert. The captives died without a murmur, either by the sword, the axe, or the fire; and the measures of retaliation were multiplied in a rapid proportion, which aggravated the horrors of rebellion and excluded the hope of mutual forgiveness.[†]

Such disorders are the natural effects of religious tyranny, but the rage of the Donatists was inflamed by a frenzy of a very extraordinary kind; and which, if it really prevailed among them in so extravagant a degree, cannot surely be paralleled in any country or in any age. Many of these fanatics were possessed with the horror of life and the desire of martyrdom; and they deemed it of little moment by what means or by what hands they perished, if their conduct was sanctified by the intention of devoting themselves to the glory of the true faith and the hope of eternal happiness. Sometimes they rudely disturbed the festivals and profaned the temples of Paganism, with the design of exciting the most zealous of the idolaters to revenge the insulted honor of their gods. They sometimes forced their way into the courts of justice and compelled the affrighted judge to give orders for their immediate execution. They frequently stopped travelers on the public highways and obliged them to inflict the stroke of martyrdom by the promise of a reward, if they consented, and by the threat of instant death, if they refused to grant so very singular a favor. When they were disappointed of every other resource, they announced the day on which, in the presence of their friends and brethren, they should cast themselves headlong from some lofty rock; and many precipices were shown which had acquired fame by the number of religious suicides. In the actions of these desperate enthusiasts, who were admired by one party as the martyrs of God and abhorred by the other as the victims of Satan, an impartial philosopher may discover the influence and the last abuse of that inflexible spirit which was originally derived from the character and principles of the Jewish nation.

The simple narrative of the intestine divisions which distracted the peace and dishonored the triumph of the church [A.D. 312–361] will confirm the remark of a Pagan historian, and justify the complaint of a venerable bishop. The experience of Ammianus had convinced him that the enmity of the Christians towards each other surpassed the fury of savage beasts against man; and Gregory Nazianzen most pathetically laments that the kingdom of Heaven was converted by discord into the image of chaos, of a nocturnal tempest, and of Hell itself. The fierce and partial writers of the times, ascribing *all* virtue to themselves and imputing *all* guilt to their adversaries, have painted the battle of the angels and demons. Our calmer reason will reject such pure and perfect monsters of vice or sanctity, and will impute an equal, or at least an indiscriminate, measure of good and evil to the hostile sectaries who assumed and bestowed the appellations of orthodox and heretics. They had been educated in the same religion and the same civil society. Their hopes and fears in the present or in a future life were balanced in the same proportion. On either side, the error might be innocent, the faith sincere, the practice meritorious or corrupt. Their passions were excited by similar objects; and they might alternately abuse the favor of the court or of the people. The metaphysical opinions of the Athanasians and the Arians could not influence their moral character; and they were alike actuated by the intolerant spirit which has been extracted from the pure and simple maxims of the gospel.[†]

A report that the ceremonies of Paganism were suppressed [by

Constantine] is formally contradicted by the emperor himself, who wisely assigns, as the principle of his moderation, the invincible force of habit, of prejudice, and of superstition. Without violating the sanctity of his promise, without alarming the fears of the Pagans, the artful monarch advanced by slow and cautious steps to undermine the irregular and decayed fabric of Polytheism. The partial acts of severity which he occasionally exercised, though they were secretly promoted by a Christian zeal, were colored by the fairest pretenses of justice and the public good; and while Constantine designed to ruin the foundations, he seemed to reform the abuses of the ancient religion. After the example of the wisest of his predecessors, he condemned, under the most rigorous penalties, the occult and impious arts of divination; which excited the vain hopes, and sometimes the criminal attempts, of those who were discontented with their present condition. An ignominious silence was imposed on the oracles, which had been publicly convicted of fraud and falsehood; the effeminate priests of the Nile were abolished; and Constantine discharged the duties of a Roman censor when he gave orders for the demolition of several temples of Phoenicia; in which every mode of prostitution was devoutly practiced in the face of day, and to the honor of Venus.†

The sons of Constantine trod in the footsteps of their father, with more zeal and with less discretion. The pretenses of rapine and oppression were insensibly multiplied; every indulgence was shown to the illegal behavior of the Christians; every doubt was explained to the disadvantage of Paganism; and the demolition of the temples was celebrated as one of the auspicious events of the reign of Constans and Constantius. . . . [But t]he evidence of facts, and the monuments which are still extant of brass and marble, continue to prove the public exercise of the Pagan worship during the whole reign of the sons of Constantine. In the East as well as in the West, in cities as well as in the country, a great number of temples were respected, or at least were spared; and the devout multitude still enjoyed the luxury of sacrifices, of festivals, and of processions by the permission or by the connivance of the civil government. . . . The senate still presumed to consecrate, by solemn decrees, the divine memory of their sovereigns; and Constantine himself was associated after his death to those gods whom he had renounced and insulted during his life. The title, the ensigns, the prerogatives, of SOVEREIGN PONTIFF, which had been instituted by Numa and assumed by Augustus, were accepted, without hesitation, by seven Christian emperors; who were invested with a more absolute authority over the religion which they had deserted than over that which they professed.

The divisions of Christianity suspended the ruin of Paganism; and the holy war against the Infidels was less vigorously prosecuted by princes and bishops who were more immediately alarmed by the guilt and danger of domestic rebellion. The extirpation of *Idolatry* might have been justified by the established principles of intolerance: but the hostile sects which alternately reigned in the Imperial court were mutually apprehensive of alienating, and perhaps exasperating, the minds of a powerful though declining faction. Every motive of authority and fashion, of interest and reason, now militated on the side of Christianity; but two or three generations elapsed before their victorious influence was universally felt. The religion which had so long and so lately been established in the Roman empire was still revered by a numerous people, less attached indeed to speculative opinion than to ancient custom. The honors of the state and army were indifferently bestowed on all the subjects of Constantine and Constantius; and a considerable portion of knowledge and wealth and valor was still engaged in the service of Polytheism. The superstition of the senator and of the peasant, of the poet and the philosopher, was derived from very different causes, but they met with equal devotion in the temples of the gods. Their zeal was insensibly provoked by the insulting triumph of a proscribed sect; and their hopes were revived by the well-grounded confidence that the presumptive heir of the empire, a young and valiant hero who had delivered Gaul from the arms of the Barbarians, had secretly embraced the religion of his ancestors.

CHAPTER XXII

JULIAN DECLARED EMPEROR

Julian is declared emperor by the legions of Gaul. •
His march and success. • The death of Constantius. •
Civil administration of Julian.

While the Romans languished under the ignominious tyranny of eunuchs and bishops, the praises of Julian were repeated with transport in every part of the empire, except in the palace of Constantius. The Barbarians of Germany had felt, and still dreaded, the arms of the young Caesar; his soldiers were the companions of his victory; the grateful provincials enjoyed the blessings of his reign; but the favorites, who had opposed his elevation, were offended by his virtues; and they justly considered the friend of the people as the enemy of the court. As long as the fame of Julian was doubtful, the buffoons of the palace, who were skilled in the language of satire, tried the efficacy of those arts which they had so often practiced with success. They easily discovered that his simplicity was not exempt from affectation: the ridiculous epithets of a hairy savage, of an ape invested with the purple, were applied to the dress and person of the philosophic warrior; and his modest despatches were stigmatized as the vain and elaborate fictions of a loquacious Greek, a speculative soldier who had studied the art of war amidst the groves of the academy. The voice of malicious folly was at length silenced by the shouts of victory; the conqueror of the Franks and Alemanni could no longer be painted as an object of contempt; and the monarch himself was meanly ambitious of stealing from his lieutenant the honorable reward of his labors. In the letters crowned with laurel which, according to ancient custom, were addressed to the provinces, the name of Julian was omitted. "Constantius had made his dispositions in person; *he* had signalized his valor in the foremost ranks; *his* military conduct had secured the victory; and the captive king of the Barbarians was presented to *him* on the field of battle," from which he was at that time distant about forty days' journey. So extravagant a fable was incapable, however, of deceiving the public credulity, or even of satisfying the pride of the emperor himself. Se-

cretly conscious that the applause and favor of the Romans accompanied the rising fortunes of Julian, his discontented mind was prepared
to receive the subtle poison of those artful sycophants who colored
their mischievous designs with the fairest appearances of truth and
candor. Instead of depreciating the merits of Julian, they acknowledged and even exaggerated his popular fame, superior talents, and
important services. But they darkly insinuated that the virtues of the
Caesar might instantly be converted into the most dangerous crimes if
the inconstant multitude should prefer their inclinations to their duty;
or if the general of a victorious army should be tempted from his allegiance by the hopes of revenge and independent greatness. The personal fears of Constantius were interpreted by his council as a laudable
anxiety for the public safety; whilst in private, and perhaps in his own
breast, he disguised, under the less odious appellation of fear, the sentiments of hatred and envy which he had secretly conceived for the inimitable virtues of Julian.

The apparent tranquility of Gaul, and the imminent danger of the
Eastern provinces, offered a specious pretense for the design which
was artfully concerted by the Imperial ministers. They resolved to disarm the Caesar; to recall those faithful troops who guarded his person and dignity; and to employ, in a distant war against the Persian
monarch, the hardy veterans who had vanquished, on the banks of the
Rhine, the fiercest nations of Germany [April A.D. 360]. While Julian
used the laborious hours of his winter quarters at Paris in the administration of power, which in his hands was the exercise of virtue, he was
surprised by the hasty arrival of a tribune and a notary with positive
orders from the emperor, which *they* were directed to execute, and *he*
was commanded not to oppose.... The Caesar foresaw and lamented
the consequences of this fatal mandate.... If Julian complied with the
orders which he had received, he subscribed his own destruction, and
that of a people who deserved his affection. But a positive refusal was
an act of rebellion and a declaration of war. The inexorable jealousy of
the emperor, the peremptory and perhaps insidious nature of his commands, left not any room for a fair apology or candid interpretation;
and the dependent station of the Caesar scarcely allowed him to pause
or to deliberate. Solitude increased the perplexity of Julian; he could
no longer apply to the faithful counsels of Sallust, who had been removed from his office by the judicious malice of the eunuchs: he could

not even enforce his representations by the concurrence of the ministers, who would have been afraid or ashamed to approve the ruin of Gaul. . . . Unable to resist, unwilling to comply, Julian expressed in the most serious terms his wish, and even his intention, of resigning the purple, which he could not preserve with honor, but which he could not abdicate with safety.

After a painful conflict, Julian was compelled to acknowledge that obedience was the virtue of the most eminent subject, and that the sovereign alone was entitled to judge of the public welfare. He issued the necessary orders for carrying into execution the commands of Constantius; a part of the troops began their march for the Alps; and the detachments from the several garrisons moved towards their respective places of assembly. They advanced with difficulty through the trembling and affrighted crowds of provincials, who attempted to excite their pity by silent despair or loud lamentations, while the wives of the soldiers, holding their infants in their arms, accused the desertion of their husbands in the mixed language of grief, of tenderness, and of indignation. This scene of general distress afflicted the humanity of the Caesar; he granted a sufficient number of post-wagons to transport the wives and families of the soldiers, endeavored to alleviate the hardships which he was constrained to inflict, and increased, by the most laudable arts, his own popularity, and the discontent of the exiled troops. The grief of an armed multitude is soon converted into rage; their licentious murmurs, which every hour were communicated from tent to tent with more boldness and effect, prepared their minds for the most daring acts of sedition; and by the connivance of their tribunes, a seasonable libel was secretly dispersed which painted in lively colors the disgrace of the Caesar, the oppression of the Gallic army, and the feeble vices of the tyrant of Asia. The servants of Constantius were astonished and alarmed by the progress of this dangerous spirit. They pressed the Caesar to hasten the departure of the troops; but they imprudently rejected the honest and judicious advice of Julian; who proposed that they should not march through Paris, and suggested the danger and temptation of a last interview.

As soon as the approach of the troops was announced, the Caesar went out to meet them and ascended his tribunal, which had been erected in a plain before the gates of the city. After distinguishing the officers and soldiers who by their rank or merit deserved a peculiar

attention, Julian addressed himself in a studied oration to the surrounding multitude: he celebrated their exploits with grateful applause;
encouraged them to accept, with alacrity, the honor of serving under
the eye of a powerful and liberal monarch; and admonished them that
the commands of Augustus required an instant and cheerful obedience. The soldiers, who were apprehensive of offending their general
by an indecent clamor, or of belying their sentiments by false and
venal acclamations, maintained an obstinate silence; and after a short
pause were dismissed to their quarters. The principal officers were entertained by the Caesar, who professed, in the warmest language of
friendship, his desire and his inability to reward according to their
deserts the brave companions of his victories. They retired from the
feast, full of grief and perplexity; and lamented the hardship of their
fate, which tore them from their beloved general and their native country. The only expedient which could prevent their separation was boldly
agitated and approved; the popular resentment was insensibly molded
into a regular conspiracy; their just reasons of complaint were heightened by passion, and their passions were inflamed by wine; as, on the
eve of their departure, the troops were indulged in licentious festivity.
At the hour of midnight, the impetuous multitude, with swords, and
bows, and torches in their hands, rushed into the suburbs; encompassed the palace; and, careless of future dangers, pronounced the
fatal and irrevocable words, JULIAN AUGUSTUS! . . . The inflexible Caesar sustained till the third hour of the day their prayers, their reproaches,
and their menaces; nor did he yield till he had been repeatedly assured
that if he wished to live, he must consent to reign. He was exalted on a
shield in the presence, and amidst the unanimous acclamations, of the
troops; a rich military collar, which was offered by chance, supplied
the want of a diadem; the ceremony was concluded by the promise of
a moderate donative; and the new emperor, overwhelmed with real or
affected grief, retired into the most secret recesses of his apartment.

The grief of Julian could proceed only from his innocence; but his
innocence must appear extremely doubtful in the eyes of those who
have learned to suspect the motives and the professions of princes. His
lively and active mind was susceptible of the various impressions of
hope and fear, of gratitude and revenge, of duty and of ambition, of
the love of fame, and of the fear of reproach. But it is impossible for us
to calculate the respective weight and operation of these sentiments;

or to ascertain the principles of action which might escape the observation, while they guided, or rather impelled, the steps, of Julian himself. The discontent of the troops was produced by the malice of his enemies; their tumult was the natural effect of interest and of passion; and if Julian had tried to conceal a deep design under the appearances of chance, he must have employed the most consummate artifice without necessity, and probably without success. He solemnly declares, in the presence of Jupiter, of the Sun, of Mars, of Minerva, and of all the other deities, that till the close of the evening which preceded his elevation, he was utterly ignorant of the designs of the soldiers; and it may seem ungenerous to distrust the honor of a hero and the truth of a philosopher. Yet the superstitious confidence that Constantius was the enemy and that he himself was the favorite of the gods might prompt him to desire, to solicit, and even to hasten the auspicious moment of his reign, which was predestined to restore the ancient religion of mankind. When Julian had received the intelligence of the conspiracy, he resigned himself to a short slumber; and afterwards related to his friends that he had seen the genius of the empire waiting with some impatience at his door, pressing for admittance, and reproaching his want of spirit and ambition. Astonished and perplexed, he addressed his prayers to the great Jupiter, who immediately signified, by a clear and manifest omen, that he should submit to the will of Heaven and of the army. The conduct which disclaims the ordinary maxims of reason excites our suspicion and eludes our inquiry. Whenever the spirit of fanaticism, at once so credulous and so crafty, has insinuated itself into a noble mind, it insensibly corrodes the vital principles of virtue and veracity.[†]

The negotiations of peace were accompanied and supported by the most vigorous preparations for war. The army, which Julian held in readiness for immediate action, was recruited and augmented by the disorders of the times. The cruel persecutions of the faction of Magnentius had filled Gaul with numerous bands of outlaws and robbers. They cheerfully accepted the offer of a general pardon from a prince whom they could trust, submitted to the restraints of military discipline, and retained only their implacable hatred to the person and government of Constantius.[†]

The ambassadors of Julian had been instructed to execute with the utmost diligence their important commission. But in their passage through Italy and Illyricum, they were detained by the tedious and affected delays of the provincial governors; they were conducted by slow journeys from Constantinople to Caesarea in Cappadocia; and when at length they were admitted to the presence of Constantius [summer A.D. 360], they found that he had already conceived, from the despatches of his own officers, the most unfavorable opinion of the conduct of Julian and of the Gallic army. The letters were heard with impatience; the trembling messengers were dismissed with indignation and contempt; and the looks, gestures, the furious language of the monarch expressed the disorder of his soul. The domestic connection, which might have reconciled the brother and the husband of Helena, was recently dissolved by the death of that princess, whose pregnancy had been several times fruitless and was at last fatal to herself. The empress Eusebia had preserved, to the last moment of her life, the warm and even jealous affection which she had conceived for Julian; and her mild influence might have moderated the resentment of a prince who, since her death, was abandoned to his own passions, and to the arts of his eunuchs. But the terror of a foreign invasion obliged him to suspend the punishment of a private enemy: he continued his march towards the confines of Persia, and thought it sufficient to signify the conditions which might entitle Julian and his guilty followers to the clemency of their offended sovereign. He required that the presumptuous Caesar should expressly renounce the appellation and rank of Augustus which he had accepted from the rebels; that he should descend to his former station of a limited and dependent minister; that he should vest the powers of the state and army in the hands of those officers who were appointed by the Imperial court; and that he should trust his safety to the assurances of pardon which were announced by Epictetus, a Gallic bishop, and one of the Arian favorites of Constantius. Several months were ineffectually consumed in a treaty which was negotiated at the distance of three thousand miles between Paris and Antioch; and as soon as Julian perceived that his modest and respectful behavior served only to irritate the pride of an implacable adversary, he boldly resolved to commit his life and fortune to the chance of a civil war. He gave a public and military audience to the quaestor Leonas..., who... was sent back to his master with an epistle in which Julian expressed, in a strain of the most vehement eloquence, the sentiments of contempt, of hatred, and of resentment which had been suppressed and embittered by the dissimulation of twenty years. After this message, which might be considered as a signal of irreconcilable war, Julian, who, some weeks before, had celebrated the Christian festival of the Epiphany, made a public declaration that he committed the care of his safety to the IMMORTAL GODS; and thus publicly renounced the religion as well as the friendship of Constantius.†

The hopes of Julian depended much less on the number of his troops than on the celerity of his motions. In the execution of a daring enterprise, he availed himself of every precaution, as far as prudence could suggest; and where prudence could no longer accompany his steps, he trusted the event to valor and to fortune.†

But the humanity of Julian was preserved from the cruel alternative which he pathetically laments, of destroying or of being himself destroyed: and the seasonable death of Constantius delivered the Roman empire from the calamities of civil war [November 3, A.D. 361]. The approach of winter could not detain the monarch at Antioch; and his favorites durst not oppose his impatient desire of revenge. A slight fever, which was perhaps occasioned by the agitation of his spirits, was increased by the fatigues of the journey; and Constantius was obliged to halt at the little town of Mopsucrene, twelve miles beyond Tarsus, where he expired, after a short illness, in the forty-fifth year of his age, and the twenty-fourth of his reign. His genuine character, which was composed of pride and weakness, of superstition and cruelty, has been fully displayed in the preceding narrative of civil and ecclesiastical events. The long abuse of power rendered him a considerable object in the eyes of his contemporaries; but as personal merit can alone deserve the notice of posterity, the last of the sons of Constantine may be dismissed from the world with the remark that he inherited the defects, without the abilities, of his father. Before Constantius expired, he is said to have named Julian for his successor; nor does it seem improbable that his anxious concern for the fate of a young and tender wife whom he left with child may have prevailed, in his last moments, over the harsher passions of hatred and revenge. Eusebius and his guilty associates made a faint attempt to prolong the reign of the eunuchs by the election of another emperor; but their intrigues were rejected with disdain by an army which now abhorred the thought of civil discord; and two officers of rank were instantly despatched to assure Julian that every sword in the empire would be drawn for his service. The military designs of that prince, who had formed three different attacks against Thrace, were prevented by this fortunate event. Without shedding the blood of his fellow-citizens, he escaped the dangers of a doubtful conflict, and acquired the advantages of a complete victory.... [I]n the thirty-second year of his age, [Julian] acquired the undisputed possession of the Roman empire.

Philosophy had instructed Julian to compare the advantages of action and retirement; but the elevation of his birth and the accidents of his life never allowed him the freedom of choice. He might perhaps sincerely have preferred the groves of the academy and the society of Athens; but he was constrained at first by the will, and afterwards by the injustice, of Constantius to expose his person and fame to the dangers of Imperial greatness; and to make himself accountable to the world, and to posterity, for the happiness of millions. Julian recollected with terror the observation of his master Plato that the government of our flocks and herds is always committed to beings of a superior species; and that the conduct of nations requires and deserves the celestial powers of the gods or of the *genii*. From this principle he justly concluded that the man who presumes to reign should aspire to the perfection of the Divine Nature; that he should purify his soul from her mortal and terrestrial part; that he should extinguish his appetites, enlighten his understanding, regulate his passions, and subdue the wild beast which, according to the lively metaphor of Aristotle, seldom fails to ascend the throne of a despot. The throne of Julian, which the death of Constantius fixed on an independent basis, was the seat of reason, of virtue, and perhaps of vanity. He despised the honors, renounced the pleasures, and discharged with incessant diligence the duties of his exalted station; and there were few among his subjects who would have consented to relieve him from the weight of the diadem, had they been obliged to submit their time and their actions to the rigorous laws which that philosophic emperor imposed on himself. One of his most intimate friends, who had often shared the frugal simplicity of his table, has remarked that his light and sparing diet (which was usually of the vegetable kind) left his mind and body always free and active for the various and important business of an author, a pontiff, a magistrate, a general, and a prince. In one and the same day, he gave audience to several ambassadors and wrote, or dictated, a great number of letters to his generals, his civil magistrates, his private friends, and the different cities of his dominions. He listened to the memorials which had been received, considered the subject of the petitions, and signified his intentions more rapidly than they could be taken in short-hand by the diligence of his secretaries. He possessed such flexibility of thought and such firmness of attention that he could employ his hand to write, his ear to listen, and his voice to dictate; and pursue at once several trains of ideas without hesitation and without error. While his ministers reposed, the prince flew with agility from one labor to another, and, after a hasty dinner, retired into his library, till the public business which he had appointed for the evening summoned him to interrupt the prosecution of his studies. The supper of the emperor was still less substantial than the former meal; his sleep was never clouded by the fumes of indigestion; and except in the short interval of a marriage which was the effect of policy rather than love, the chaste Julian never shared his bed with a female companion. He was soon awakened by the entrance of fresh secretaries, who had slept the preceding day; and his servants were obliged to wait alternately while their indefatigable master allowed himself scarcely any other refreshment than the change of occupation. The predecessors of Julian, his uncle, his brother, and his cousin, indulged their puerile taste for the games of the circus under the specious pretense of complying with the inclinations of the people; and they frequently remained the greatest part of the day as idle spectators, and as a part of the splendid spectacle, till the ordinary round of twenty-four races was completely finished. On solemn festivals, Julian, who felt and professed an unfashionable dislike to these frivolous amusements, condescended to appear in the circus; and after bestowing a careless glance at five or six of the races, he hastily withdrew with the impatience of a philosopher who considered every moment as lost that was not devoted to the advantage of the public or the improvement of his own mind. By this avarice of time, he seemed to protract the short duration of his reign; and if the dates were less securely ascertained, we should refuse to believe that only sixteen months elapsed between the death of Constantius [December A.D. 361] and the departure of his successor for the Persian war [March A.D. 363]. The actions of Julian can only be preserved by the care of the historian; but the portion of his voluminous writings which is still extant remains as a monument of the application, as well as of the genius, of the emperor. The *Misopogon,* the *Caesars,* several of his orations, and his elaborate work against the Christian religion were composed in the long nights of the two winters, the former of which he passed at Constantinople and the latter at Antioch.

The reformation of the Imperial court was one of the first and most necessary acts of the government of Julian. . . . The luxury of the palace excited the contempt and indignation of Julian, who usually slept on the ground, who yielded with reluctance to the indispensable calls of nature, and who placed his vanity not in emulating but in despising the pomp of royalty. By the total extirpation of a mischief which was magnified even beyond its real extent, he was impatient to relieve the distress and to appease the murmurs of the people; who support with less uneasiness the weight of taxes if they are convinced that the fruits of their industry are appropriated to the service of the state. But in the execution of this salutary work, Julian is accused of proceeding with too much haste and inconsiderate severity. By a single edict, he reduced the palace of Constantinople to an immense desert and dismissed with ignominy the whole train of slaves and dependents, without providing any just, or at least benevolent, exceptions for the age, the services, or the poverty of the faithful domestics of the Imperial family. Such indeed was the temper of Julian, who seldom recollected the fundamental maxim of Aristotle that true virtue is placed at an equal distance between the opposite vices.†

The numerous army of spies, of agents, and informers enlisted by Constantius to secure the repose of one man and to interrupt that of millions was immediately disbanded by his generous successor. Julian was slow in his suspicions and gentle in his punishments; and his contempt of treason was the result of judgment, of vanity, and of courage.†

Julian was not insensible of the advantages of freedom. From his studies he had imbibed the spirit of ancient sages and heroes; his life and fortunes had depended on the caprice of a tyrant; and when he ascended the throne, his pride was sometimes mortified by the reflection that the slaves who would not dare to censure his defects were not worthy to applaud his virtues. He sincerely abhorred the system of Oriental despotism which Diocletian, Constantine, and the patient habits of fourscore years had established in the empire. A motive of superstition prevented the execution of the design, which Julian had frequently meditated, of relieving his head from the weight of a costly diadem; but he absolutely refused the title of *Dominus,* or *Lord,* a word which was grown so familiar to the ears of the Romans that they no longer remembered its servile and humiliating origin. The office, or rather the name, of consul, was cherished by a prince who contemplated with reverence the ruins of the republic; and the same behavior which had been assumed by the prudence of Augustus was adopted by Julian from choice and inclination.†

The generality of princes, if they were stripped of their purple and cast naked into the world, would immediately sink to the lowest rank of society without a hope of emerging from their obscurity. But the personal merit of Julian was in some measure independent of his fortune. Whatever had been his choice of life, by the force of intrepid courage, lively wit, and intense application he would have obtained, or at least he would have deserved, the highest honors of his profession; and Julian might have raised himself to the rank of minister or general of the state in which he was born a private citizen. If the jealous caprice of power had disappointed his expectations, if he had prudently declined the paths of greatness, the employment of the same talents in studious solitude would have placed beyond the reach of kings his present happiness and his immortal fame. When we inspect, with minute or perhaps malevolent attention, the portrait of Julian, something seems wanting to the grace and perfection of the whole figure. His genius was less powerful and sublime than that of Caesar; nor did he possess the consummate prudence of Augustus. The virtues of Trajan appear more steady and natural, and the philosophy of Marcus is more simple and consistent. Yet Julian sustained adversity with firmness, and prosperity with moderation. After an interval of one hundred and twenty years from the death of Alexander Severus, the Romans beheld an emperor who made no distinction between his duties and his pleasures; who labored to relieve the distress and to revive the spirit of his subjects; and who endeavored always to connect authority with merit, and happiness with virtue. Even faction, and religious faction, was constrained to acknowledge the superiority of his genius, in peace as well as in war, and to confess with a sigh that the apostate Julian was a lover of his country, and that he deserved the empire of the world.

CHAPTER XXIII

REIGN OF JULIAN

The religion of Julian. • Universal toleration. • He attempts to restore and reform the Pagan worship, and to rebuild the temple of Jerusalem. • His artful persecution of the Christians. • Mutual zeal and injustice.

The character of Apostate has injured the reputation of Julian; and the enthusiasm which clouded his virtues has exaggerated the real and apparent magnitude of his faults. Our partial ignorance may represent him as a philosophic monarch who studied to protect, with an equal hand, the religious factions of the empire, and to allay the theological fever which had inflamed the minds of the people, from the edicts of Diocletian to the exile of Athanasius. A more accurate view of the character and conduct of Julian will remove this favorable prepossession for a prince who did not escape the general contagion of the times. We enjoy the singular advantage of comparing the pictures which have been delineated by his fondest admirers and his implacable enemies. The actions of Julian are faithfully related by a judicious and candid historian [Ammianus Marcellinus], the impartial spectator of his life and death. The unanimous evidence of his contemporaries is confirmed by the public and private declarations of the emperor himself; and his various writings express the uniform tenor of his religious sentiments, which policy would have prompted him to dissemble rather than to affect. A devout and sincere attachment for the gods of Athens and Rome constituted the ruling passion of Julian; the powers of an enlightened understanding were betrayed and corrupted by the influence of superstitious prejudice; and the phantoms which existed only in the mind of the emperor had a real and pernicious effect on the government of the empire. The vehement zeal of the Christians, who despised the worship and overturned the altars of those fabulous deities, engaged their votary in a state of irreconcilable hostility with a very numerous party of his subjects; and he was sometimes tempted by the desire of victory, or the shame of a repulse, to violate the laws of prudence, and even of justice. The triumph of the party which he deserted and opposed has fixed a stain of infamy on the name of Julian; and the unsuccessful apostate has been overwhelmed with a torrent of pious invectives, of which the signal was given by the sonorous trumpet of Gregory Nazianzen. The interesting nature of the events which were crowded into the short reign of this active emperor deserve a just and circumstantial narrative. His motives, his counsels, and his actions, as far as they are connected with the history of religion, will be the subject of the present chapter.

The cause of his strange and fatal apostasy may be derived from the early period of his life, when he was left an orphan in the hands of the murderers of his family. The names of Christ and of Constantius, the ideas of slavery and of religion, were soon associated in a youthful imagination which was susceptible of the most lively impressions. The care of his infancy was entrusted to Eusebius, bishop of Nicomedia, who was related to him on the side of his mother; and till Julian reached the twentieth year of his age, he received from his Christian preceptors the education not of a hero, but of a saint. The emperor, less jealous of a heavenly than of an earthly crown, contented himself with the imperfect character of a catechumen, while he bestowed the advantages of baptism on the nephews of Constantine. They were even admitted to the inferior offices of the ecclesiastical order; and Julian publicly read the Holy Scriptures in the church of Nicomedia. The study of religion, which they assiduously cultivated, appeared to produce the fairest fruits of faith and devotion. They prayed, they fasted, they distributed alms to the poor, gifts to the clergy, and oblations to the tombs of the martyrs. . . . As the two princes advanced towards the years of manhood, they discovered in their religious sentiments the difference of their characters. The dull and obstinate understanding of Gallus embraced, with implicit zeal, the doctrines of Christianity; which never influenced his conduct or moderated his passions. . . . But the independent spirit of Julian refused to yield the passive and unresisting obedience which was required, in the name of religion, by the haughty ministers of the church. Their speculative opinions were imposed as positive laws, and guarded by the terrors of eternal punishments; but while they prescribed the rigid formulary of the thoughts, the words, and the actions of the young prince; whilst they silenced his objections, and severely checked the freedom of his inquiries, they secretly provoked his impatient genius to disclaim the authority of his ecclesiastical guides. He was educated in the Lesser Asia, amidst the scandals of the Arian controversy. The fierce contests of the Eastern bishops, the incessant alterations of their creeds, and the profane motives which appeared to actuate their conduct insensibly strengthened the prejudice of Julian that they neither understood nor believed the religion for which they so fiercely contended. Instead of listening to the proofs of Christianity with that favorable attention which adds weight to the most respectable evidence, he heard with suspicion, and disputed with obstinacy and acuteness, the doctrines for which he already entertained an invincible aversion. Whenever the young princes were directed to compose declamations on the subject of the prevailing controversies, Julian always declared himself the advocate of Paganism; under the specious excuse that, in the defense of the weaker cause, his learning and ingenuity might be more advantageously exercised and displayed.

As soon as Gallus was invested with the honors of the purple, Julian was permitted to breathe the air of freedom, of literature, and of Paganism. The crowd of sophists who were attracted by the taste and liberality of their royal pupil had formed a strict alliance between the learning and the religion of Greece; and the poems of Homer, instead of being admired as the original productions of human genius, were seriously ascribed to the heavenly inspiration of Apollo and the muses. The deities of Olympus, as they are painted by the immortal bard, imprint themselves on the minds which are the least addicted to superstitious credulity. Our familiar knowledge of their names and characters, their forms and attributes, *seems* to bestow on those airy beings a real and substantial existence; and the pleasing enchantment produces an imperfect and momentary assent of the imagination to those fables, which are the most repugnant to our reason and experience. In the age of Julian, every circumstance contributed to prolong and fortify the illusion; the magnificent temples of Greece and Asia; the works of those artists who had expressed, in painting or in sculpture, the divine conceptions of the poet; the pomp of festivals and sacrifices; the successful arts of divination; the popular traditions of oracles and prodigies; and the ancient practice of two thousand years. The weakness of Polytheism was in some measure excused by the moderation of its claims; and the devotion of the Pagans was not incompatible with the most licentious skepticism. Instead of an indivisible and regular system, which occupies the whole extent of the believing mind, the mythology of the Greeks was composed of a thousand loose and flexible parts, and the servant of the gods was at liberty to define the degree and measure of his religious faith. The creed which Julian adopted for his own use was of the largest dimensions; and, by strange contradiction, he disdained the salutary yoke of the gospel, whilst he made a voluntary offering of his reason on the altars of Jupiter and Apollo.[†]

The theological system of Julian appears to have contained the sublime and important principles of natural religion. But as the faith which is not founded on revelation must remain destitute of any firm assurance, the disciple of Plato imprudently relapsed into the habits of vulgar superstition; and the popular and philosophic notion of the Deity seems to have been confounded in the practice, the writings, and even in the mind of Julian. The pious emperor acknowledged and adored the Eternal Cause of the universe, to whom he ascribed all the perfections of an infinite nature, invisible to the eyes and inaccessible to the understanding of feeble mortals. The Supreme God had created, or rather, in the Platonic language, had generated, the gradual succession of dependent spirits, of gods, of demons, of heroes, and of men; and every being which derived its existence immediately from the First Cause received the inherent gift of immortality. . . . To the conduct of these divine ministers he delegated the temporal government of this lower world; but their imperfect administration is not exempt from discord or error. The earth and its inhabitants are divided among them, and the characters of Mars or Minerva, of Mercury or Venus, may be distinctly traced in the laws and manners of their peculiar votaries. As long as our immortal souls are confined in a mortal prison, it is our interest as well as our duty to solicit the favor and to deprecate the wrath of the powers of Heaven; whose pride is gratified by the devotion of mankind; and whose grosser parts may be supposed to derive some nourishment from the fumes of sacrifice. The inferior gods might sometimes condescend to animate the statues and to inhabit the temples which were dedicated to their honor. They might occasionally visit the earth, but the heavens were the proper throne and symbol of their glory. The invariable order of the sun, moon, and stars was hastily admitted by Julian as a proof of their eternal duration; and their eternity was a sufficient evidence that they were the workmanship not of an inferior deity, but of the Omnipotent King. In the system of Platonists, the visible was a type of the invisible world. The celestial bodies, as they were informed by a divine spirit, might be considered as the objects the most worthy of religious worship. The SUN, whose genial influence pervades and sustains the universe, justly claimed the adoration of mankind as the bright representative of the LOGOS, the lively, the rational, the beneficent image of the intellectual Father.

In every age, the absence of genuine inspiration is supplied by the strong illusions of enthusiasm and the mimic arts of imposture. If in the time of Julian these arts had been practiced only by the Pagan priests for the support of an expiring cause, some indulgence might perhaps be allowed to the interest and habits of the sacerdotal character. But it may appear a subject of surprise and scandal that the philosophers themselves should have contributed to abuse the superstitious credulity of mankind, and that the Grecian mysteries should have been supported by the magic or theurgy of the modern Platonists. They arrogantly pretended to control the order of nature, to explore the secrets of futurity, to command the service of the inferior demons, to enjoy the view and conversation of the superior gods, and by disengaging the soul from her material bands, to reunite that immortal particle with the Infinite and Divine Spirit.

The devout and fearless curiosity of Julian tempted the philosophers with the hopes of an easy conquest; which, from the situation of their young proselyte, might be productive of the most important consequences. . . . These philosophers seem to have . . . artfully contrived, by dark hints and affected disputes, to excite the impatient hopes of the *aspirant*, till they delivered him into the hands of their associate, Maximus, the boldest and most skillful master of the Theurgic science. By his hands, Julian was secretly initiated at Ephesus, in the twentieth year of his age. His residence at Athens confirmed this unnatural alliance of philosophy and superstition. He obtained the privilege of a solemn initiation into the mysteries of Eleusis, which, amidst the general decay of the Grecian worship, still retained some vestiges of their primeval sanctity; and such was the zeal of Julian that he afterwards invited the Eleusinian pontiff to the court of Gaul for the sole purpose of consummating, by mystic rites and sacrifices, the great work of his sanctification. As these ceremonies were performed in the depth of caverns and in the silence of the night, and as the inviolable secret of the mysteries was preserved by the discretion of the initiated, I shall not presume to describe the horrid sounds and fiery apparitions which were presented to the senses, or the imagination, of the credulous aspirant, till the visions of comfort and knowledge broke upon him in a blaze of celestial light. In the caverns of Ephesus and Eleusis, the mind of Julian was penetrated with sincere, deep, and unalterable enthusiasm; though he might sometimes exhibit the vicissitudes of pious fraud and hypocrisy, which may be observed, or at least suspected, in the characters of the most conscientious fanatics. From that moment he consecrated his life to the service of the gods; and while the occupations of war, of government, and of study seemed to claim the whole measure of his time, a stated portion of the hours of the night was invariably reserved for the exercise of private devotion. The temperance which adorned the severe manners of the soldier and the philosopher was connected with some strict and frivolous rules of religious abstinence; and it was in honor of Pan or Mercury, of Hecate or Isis, that Julian, on particular days, denied himself the use of some particular food which might have been offensive to his tutelar deities. By these voluntary fasts, he prepared his senses and his understanding for the frequent and familiar visits with which he was honored by the celestial powers. Notwithstanding the modest silence of Julian himself, we may learn from his faithful friend, the orator Libanius, that he lived in a perpetual intercourse with the gods and goddesses; that they descended upon earth to enjoy the conversation of their favorite hero; that they gently interrupted his slumbers by touching his hand or his hair; that they warned him of every impending danger and conducted him, by their infallible wisdom, in every action of his life; and that he had acquired such an intimate knowledge of his heavenly guests as readily to distinguish the voice of Jupiter from that of Minerva, and the form of Apollo from the figure of Hercules. These sleeping or waking visions, the ordinary effects of abstinence and fanaticism, would almost degrade the emperor to the level of an Egyptian monk. But the useless lives of Antony or Pachomius were consumed in these vain occupations. Julian could break from the dream of superstition to arm himself for battle; and after vanquishing in the field the enemies of Rome, he calmly retired into his tent to dictate the wise and salutary laws of an empire, or to indulge his genius in the elegant pursuits of literature and philosophy.

The important secret of the apostasy of Julian was entrusted to the fidelity of the *initiated,* with whom he was united by the sacred ties of friendship and religion. The pleasing rumor was cautiously circulated among the adherents of the ancient worship; and his future greatness became the object of the hopes, the prayers, and the predictions of the Pagans in every province of the empire. From the zeal and virtues of their royal proselyte, they fondly expected the cure of every evil and the restoration of every blessing; and instead of disapproving of the ardor of their pious wishes, Julian ingenuously confessed that he was ambitious to attain a situation in which he might be useful to his country and to his religion. But this religion was viewed with a hostile eye by the successor of Constantine, whose capricious passions alternately saved and threatened the life of Julian. The arts of magic and divination were strictly prohibited under a despotic government which condescended to fear them; and if the Pagans were reluctantly indulged in the exercise of their superstition, the rank of Julian would have excepted him from the general toleration. The apostate soon became the presumptive heir of the monarchy, and his death could alone have appeased the just apprehensions of the Christians. But the young prince, who aspired to the glory of a hero rather than of a martyr, consulted his safety by dissembling his religion; and the easy temper of Polytheism permitted him to join in the public worship of a sect which he inwardly despised.... The dissimulation of Julian lasted about ten years, from his secret initiation at Ephesus to the beginning of the civil war, when he declared himself at once the implacable enemy of Christ and of Constantius. This state of constraint might contribute to strengthen his devotion; and as soon as he had satisfied the obligation of assisting, on solemn festivals, at the assemblies of the Christians, Julian returned, with the impatience of a lover, to burn his free and voluntary incense on the domestic chapels of Jupiter and Mercury. But as every act of dissimulation must be painful to an ingenuous spirit, the profession of Christianity increased the aversion of Julian for a religion which oppressed the freedom of his mind, and compelled him to hold a conduct repugnant to the noblest attributes of human nature, sincerity and courage.[†]

The Christians, who beheld with horror and indignation the apostasy of Julian, had much more to fear from his power than from his arguments. The Pagans, who were conscious of his fervent zeal, expected, perhaps with impatience, that the flames of persecution should be immediately kindled against the enemies of the gods; and that the ingenious malice of Julian would invent some cruel refinements of death and torture which had been unknown to the rude and inexperienced fury of his predecessors. But the hopes as well as the fears of the religious factions were apparently disappointed by the prudent humanity of a prince who was careful of his own fame, of the public peace, and of the rights of mankind. Instructed by history and reflection, Julian was persuaded that if the diseases of the body may sometimes be cured by salutary violence, neither steel nor fire can eradicate the erroneous opinions of the mind. The reluctant victim may be dragged to the foot of the altar; but the heart still abhors and disclaims the sacrilegious act of the hand. Religious obstinacy is hardened and exasperated by oppression; and as soon as the persecution subsides, those who have yielded are restored as penitents, and those who have resisted are honored as saints and martyrs. If Julian adopted the unsuccessful cruelty of Diocletian and his colleagues, he was sensible that he should stain his memory with the name of a tyrant and add new glories to the Catholic church, which had derived strength and increase from the severity of the Pagan magistrates. Actuated by these motives, and apprehensive of disturbing the repose of an unsettled reign, Julian surprised the world by an edict which was not unworthy of a statesman or a philosopher. He extended to all the inhabitants of the Roman world the benefits of a free and equal toleration; and the only hardship which he inflicted on the Christians was to deprive them of the power of tormenting their fellow-subjects, whom they stigmatized with the odious titles of idolaters and heretics. . . . At the same time the bishops and clergy who had been banished by the Arian monarch were recalled from exile and restored to their respective churches. . . . Julian, who understood and derided their theological disputes, invited to the palace the leaders of the hostile sects, that he might enjoy the agreeable spectacle of their furious encounters . . . ; and though he exerted the powers of oratory to persuade them to live in concord, or at least in peace, he was perfectly satisfied, before he dismissed them from his presence, that he had nothing to dread from the union of the Christians.[†]

As soon as he ascended the throne, he assumed, according to the custom of his predecessors, the character of supreme pontiff; not only as the most honorable title of Imperial greatness, but as a sacred and important office; the duties of which he was resolved to execute with pious diligence. As the business of the state prevented the emperor from joining every day in the public devotion of his subjects, he dedicated a domestic chapel to his tutelar deity the Sun; his gardens were filled with statues and altars of the gods; and each apartment of the palace displaced the appearance of a magnificent temple. Every morning he saluted the parent of light with a sacrifice; the blood of another victim was shed at the moment when the Sun sunk below the horizon; and the Moon, the Stars, and the Genii of the night received their respective and seasonable honors from the indefatigable devotion of Julian. On solemn festivals, he regularly visited the temple of the god or goddess to whom the day was peculiarly consecrated, and endeavored to excite the religion of the magistrates and people by the example of his own zeal. Instead of maintaining the lofty state of a monarch, distinguished by the splendor of his purple and encompassed by the golden shields of his guards, Julian solicited with respectful eagerness the meanest offices which contributed to the worship of the gods. Amidst the sacred but licentious crowd of priests, of inferior ministers, and of female dancers who were dedicated to the service of the temple, it was the business of the emperor to bring the wood, to blow the fire, to handle the knife, to slaughter the victim, and, thrusting his bloody hands into the bowels of the expiring animal, to draw forth the heart or liver, and to read, with the consummate skill of an haruspex, imaginary signs of future events. The wisest of the Pagans censured this extravagant superstition, which affected to despise the restraints of prudence and decency. Under the reign of a prince who practiced the rigid maxims of economy, the expense of religious worship consumed a very large portion of the revenue: a constant supply of the scarcest and most beautiful birds was transported from distant climates to bleed on the altars of the gods; a hundred oxen were frequently sacrificed by Julian on one and the same day; and it soon became a popular jest that if he should return with conquest from the Persian war, the breed of horned cattle must infallibly be extinguished. Yet this expense may appear inconsiderable when it is compared with the splendid presents which were offered either by the hand or by order of the emperor to all the celebrated places of devotion in the Roman world; and with the sums allotted to repair and decorate the ancient temples, which had suffered the silent decay of time or the recent injuries of Christian rapine. Encouraged by the example, the exhortations, the liberality of their pious sovereign, the cities and families resumed the practice of their neglected ceremonies. "Every part of the world," exclaims Libanius, with devout transport, "displayed the triumph of religion; and the grateful prospect of flaming altars, bleeding victims, the smoke of incense, and a solemn train of priests and prophets, without fear and without danger. The sound of prayer and of music was heard on the tops of the highest mountains; and the same ox afforded a sacrifice for the gods and a supper for their joyous votaries."

But the genius and power of Julian were unequal to the enterprise of restoring a religion which was destitute of theological principles, of moral precepts, and of ecclesiastical discipline; which rapidly hastened to decay and dissolution, and was not susceptible of any solid or consistent reformation. The jurisdiction of the supreme pontiff, more especially after that office had been united with the Imperial dignity, comprehended the whole extent of the Roman empire. Julian named for his vicars in the several provinces the priests and philosophers whom he esteemed the best qualified to cooperate in the execution of his great design; and his pastoral letters, if we may use that name, still represent a very curious sketch of his wishes and intentions. . . . Julian beheld with envy the wise and humane regulations of the church; and he very frankly confesses his intention to deprive the Christians of the applause, as well as advantage, which they had acquired by the exclusive practice of charity and beneficence. The same spirit of imitation might dispose the emperor to adopt several ecclesiastical institutions, the use and importance of which were approved by the success of his enemies. But if these imaginary plans of reformation had been realized, the forced and imperfect copy would have been less beneficial to Paganism than honorable to Christianity. The Gentiles, who peaceably followed the customs of their ancestors, were rather surprised than pleased with the introduction of foreign manners; and in the short period of his reign, Julian had frequent occasions to complain of the want of fervor of his own party.[†]

The favor of Julian was almost equally divided between the Pagans, who had firmly adhered to the worship of their ancestors, and the Christians, who prudently embraced the religion of their sovereign. The acquisition of new proselytes gratified the ruling passions of his soul, superstition, and vanity; and he was heard to declare, with the enthusiasm of a missionary, that if he could render each individual richer than Midas and every city greater than Babylon, he should not esteem himself the benefactor of mankind unless, at the same time, he could reclaim his subjects from their impious revolt against the immortal gods. A prince who had studied human nature, and who possessed the treasures of the Roman empire, could adapt his arguments, his promises, and his rewards to every order of Christians; and the merit of a seasonable conversion was allowed to supply the defects of a candidate, or even to expiate the guilt of a criminal. As the army is the most forcible engine of absolute power, Julian applied himself with peculiar diligence to corrupt the religion of his troops, without whose hearty concurrence every measure must be dangerous and unsuccessful; and the natural temper of soldiers made this conquest as easy as it was important. The legions of Gaul devoted themselves to the faith as well as to the fortunes of their victorious leader; and even before the death of Constantius, he had the satisfaction of announcing to his friends that they assisted with fervent devotion and voracious appetite at the sacrifices, which were repeatedly offered in his camp, of whole hecatombs of fat oxen. The armies of the East, which had been trained under the standard of the cross and of Constantius, required a more artful and expensive mode of persuasion. On the days of solemn and public festivals, the emperor received the homage and rewarded the merit of the troops. His throne of state was encircled with the military ensigns of Rome and the republic; the holy name of Christ was erased from the labarum; and the symbols of war, of majesty, and of Pagan superstition were so dexterously blended, that the faithful subject incurred the guilt of idolatry when he respectfully saluted the person or image of his sovereign. The soldiers passed successively in review; and each of them, before he received from the hand of Julian a liberal donative proportioned to his rank and services, was required to cast a few grains of incense into the flame which burnt upon the altar. Some Christian confessors might resist, and others might repent; but the far greater number, allured by the prospect of gold and awed by the presence of the emperor, contracted the criminal engagement; and their future perseverance in the worship of the gods was enforced by every consideration of duty and of interest. By the frequent repetition of these arts, and at the expense of sums which would have purchased the service of half the nations of Scythia, Julian gradually acquired for his troops the imaginary protection of the gods, and for himself the firm and effectual support of the Roman legions. It is indeed more than probable that the restoration and encouragement of Paganism revealed a multitude of pretended Christians, who, from motives of temporal advantage, had acquiesced in the religion of the former reign; and who afterwards returned, with the same flexibility of conscience, to the faith which was professed by the successors of Julian.

While the devout monarch incessantly labored to restore and propagate the religion of his ancestors, he embraced the extraordinary design of rebuilding the temple of Jerusalem. In a public epistle to the nation or community of the Jews dispersed through the provinces, he pities their misfortunes, condemns their oppressors, praises their constancy, declares himself their gracious protector, and expresses a pious hope that after his return from the Persian war, he may be permitted to pay his grateful vows to the Almighty in his holy city of Jerusalem. The blind superstition and abject slavery of those unfortunate exiles must excite the contempt of a philosophic emperor; but they deserved the friendship of Julian by their implacable hatred of the Christian name. The barren synagogue abhorred and envied the fecundity of the rebellious church; the power of the Jews was not equal to their malice; but their gravest rabbis approved the private murder of an apostate; and their seditious clamors had often awakened the indolence of the Pagan magistrates. Under the reign of Constantine, the Jews became the subjects of their revolted children, nor was it long before they experienced the bitterness of domestic tyranny. The civil immunities which had been granted or confirmed by Severus were gradually repealed by the Christian princes; and a rash tumult, excited by the Jews of Palestine, seemed to justify the lucrative modes of oppression which were invented by the bishops and eunuchs of the court of Constantius. The Jewish patriarch, who was still permitted to exercise a precarious jurisdiction, held his residence at Tiberias; and the neighboring cities of Palestine were filled with the remains of a people who fondly adhered to the promised land. But the edict of Hadrian was renewed and enforced; and they viewed from afar the walls of the holy city, which were profaned in their eyes by the triumph of the cross and the devotion of the Christians.[†]

The vain and ambitious mind of Julian might aspire to restore the ancient glory of the temple of Jerusalem. As the Christians were firmly persuaded that a sentence of everlasting destruction had been pronounced against the whole fabric of the Mosaic law, the Imperial sophist would have converted the success of his undertaking into a specious argument against the faith of prophecy and the truth of revelation. He was displeased with the spiritual worship of the synagogue; but he approved the institutions of Moses, who had not disdained to adopt many of the rites and ceremonies of Egypt. The local and national deity of the Jews was sincerely adored by a Polytheist, who desired only to multiply the number of the gods; and such was the appetite of Julian for bloody sacrifice that his emulation might be excited by the piety of Solomon, who had offered at the feast of the dedication twenty-two thousand oxen and one hundred and twenty thousand sheep. These considerations might influence his designs; but the prospect of an immediate and important advantage would not suffer the impatient monarch to expect the remote and uncertain event of the Persian war. He resolved to erect without delay, on the commanding eminence of Moriah, a stately temple which might eclipse the splendor of the church of the Resurrection on the adjacent hill of Calvary; to establish an order of priests whose interested zeal would detect the arts and resist the ambition of their Christian rivals; and to invite a numerous colony of Jews, whose stern fanaticism would be always prepared to second, and even to anticipate, the hostile measures of the Pagan government. . . . At the call of their great deliverer, the Jews, from all the provinces of the empire, assembled on the holy mountain of their fathers; and their insolent triumph alarmed and exasperated the Christian inhabitants of Jerusalem. The desire of rebuilding the temple has in every age been the ruling passion of the children of Israel. In this propitious moment the men forgot their avarice and the women their delicacy; spades and pickaxes of silver were provided by the vanity of the rich, and the rubbish was transported in mantles of silk and purple. Every purse was opened in liberal contributions, every hand claimed a share in the pious labor, and the commands of a great monarch were executed by the enthusiasm of a whole people.

Yet, on this occasion, the joint efforts of power and enthusiasm were unsuccessful; and the ground of the Jewish temple, which is now covered by a Mohammedan mosque, still continued to exhibit the same edifying spectacle of ruin and desolation. Perhaps the absence and death of the emperor and the new maxims of a Christian reign might explain the interruption of an arduous work which was attempted only in the last six months of the life of Julian. But the Christians entertained a natural and pious expectation that, in this memorable contest, the honor of religion would be vindicated by some signal miracle. An earthquake, a whirlwind, and a fiery eruption which overturned and scattered the new foundations of the temple are attested, with some variations, by contemporary and respectable evidence. . . . Such authority should satisfy a believing, and must astonish an incredulous, mind. Yet a philosopher may still require the original evidence of impartial and intelligent spectators. At this important crisis, any singular accident of nature would assume the appearance and produce the effects of a real prodigy. This glorious deliverance would be speedily improved and magnified by the pious art of the clergy of Jerusalem and the active credulity of the Christian world, and, at the distance of twenty years, a Roman historian, careless of theological disputes, might adorn his work with the specious and splendid miracle.

The restoration of the Jewish temple was secretly connected with the ruin of the Christian church. Julian still continued to maintain the freedom of religious worship, without distinguishing whether this universal toleration proceeded from his justice or his clemency. He affected to pity the unhappy Christians, who were mistaken in the most important object of their lives; but his pity was degraded by contempt, his contempt was embittered by hatred; and the sentiments of Julian were expressed in a style of sarcastic wit, which inflicts a deep and deadly wound whenever it issues from the mouth of a sovereign. As he was sensible that the Christians gloried in the name of their Redeemer, he countenanced, and perhaps enjoined, the use of the less honorable appellation of GALILAEANS. He declared that by the folly of the Galilaeans, whom he describes as a sect of fanatics, contemptible to men and odious to the gods, the empire had been reduced to the brink of destruction; and he insinuates in a public edict that a frantic patient might sometimes be cured by salutary violence. An ungenerous distinction was admitted into the mind and counsels of Julian that, according to the difference of their religious sentiments, one part of his subjects deserved his favor and friendship, while the other was entitled only to the common benefits that his justice could not refuse to an obedient people. According to a principle pregnant with mischief and oppression, the emperor transferred to the pontiffs of his own religion the management of the liberal allowances for the public revenue which had been granted to the church by the piety of Constantine and his sons. The proud system of clerical honors and immunities, which had been constructed with so much art and labor, was leveled to the ground; the hopes of testamentary donations were intercepted by the rigor of the laws; and the priests of the Christian sect were confounded with the last and most ignominious class of the people. Such of these regulations as appeared necessary to check the ambition and avarice of the ecclesiastics were soon afterwards imitated by the wisdom of an orthodox prince. The peculiar distinctions which policy has bestowed, or superstition has lavished, on the sacerdotal order *must* be confined to those priests who profess the religion of the state. But the will of the legislator was not exempt from prejudice and passion; and it was the object of the insidious policy of Julian to deprive the Christians of all the temporal honors and advantages which rendered them respectable in the eyes of the world.

A just and severe censure has been inflicted on the law which prohibited the Christians from teaching the arts of grammar and rhetoric [June 17, A.D. 362]. . . . [Julian] vainly contends that if they refuse to adore the gods of Homer and Demosthenes, they ought to content themselves with expounding Luke and Matthew in the church of the Galilaeans. . . . As soon as the resignation of the more obstinate teachers had established the unrivaled dominion of the Pagan sophists, Julian invited the rising generation to resort with freedom to the public schools, in a just confidence that their tender minds would receive the impressions of literature and idolatry. If the greatest part of the Christian youth should be deterred by their own scruples, or by those of their parents, from accepting this dangerous mode of instruction, they must at the same time relinquish the benefits of a liberal education. Julian had reason to expect that, in the space of a few years, the church would relapse into its primeval simplicity, and that the theologians, who possessed an adequate share of the learning and eloquence of the age, would be succeeded by a generation of blind and ignorant fanatics, incapable of defending the truth of their own principles or of exposing the various follies of Polytheism.

It was undoubtedly the wish and design of Julian to deprive the

Christians of the advantages of wealth, of knowledge, and of power; but the injustice of excluding them from all offices of trust and profit seems to have been the result of his general policy, rather than the immediate consequence of any positive law.... The temper of Julian was averse to cruelty; and the care of his reputation, which was exposed to the eyes of the universe, restrained the philosophic monarch from violating the laws of justice and toleration which he himself had so recently established. But the provincial ministers of his authority were placed in a less conspicuous station. In the exercise of arbitrary power, they consulted the wishes rather than the commands of their sovereign; and ventured to exercise a secret and vexatious tyranny against the sectaries on whom they were not permitted to confer the honors of martyrdom. The emperor, who dissembled as long as possible his knowledge of the injustice that was exercised in his name, expressed his real sense of the conduct of his officers by gentle reproofs and substantial rewards.

The most effectual instrument of oppression with which they were armed was the law that obliged the Christians to make full and ample satisfaction for the temples which they had destroyed under the preceding reign. The zeal of the triumphant church had not always expected the sanction of the public authority; and the bishops, who were secure of impunity, had often marched at the head of their congregation, to attack and demolish the fortresses of the prince of darkness. The consecrated lands, which had increased the patrimony of the sovereign or of the clergy, were clearly defined and easily restored. But on these lands, and on the ruins of Pagan superstition, the Christians had frequently erected their own religious edifices: and as it was necessary to remove the church before the temple could be rebuilt, the justice and piety of the emperor were applauded by one party, while the other deplored and execrated his sacrilegious violence. After the ground was cleared, the restitution of those stately structures which had been leveled with the dust, and of the precious ornaments which had been converted to Christian uses, swelled into a very large account of damages and debt. The authors of the injury had neither the ability nor the inclination to discharge this accumulated demand: and the impartial wisdom of a legislator would have been displayed in balancing the adverse claims and complaints by an equitable and temperate arbitration. But the whole empire, and particularly the East, was thrown into confusion by the rash edicts of Julian; and the Pagan magistrates, inflamed by zeal and revenge, abused the rigorous privilege of the Roman law which substitutes, in the place of his inadequate property, the person of the insolvent debtor.[†]

I have endeavored faithfully to represent the artful system by which Julian proposed to obtain the effects, without incurring the guilt or reproach, of persecution. But if the deadly spirit of fanaticism perverted the heart and understanding of a virtuous prince, it must at the same time be confessed that the *real* sufferings of the Christians were inflamed and magnified by human passions and religious enthusiasm. The meekness and resignation which had distinguished the primitive disciples of the gospel was the object of the applause, rather than of the imitation, of their successors. The Christians, who had now possessed above forty years the civil and ecclesiastical government of the empire, had contracted the insolent vices of prosperity, and the habit of believing that the saints alone were entitled to reign over the earth. As soon as the enmity of Julian deprived the clergy of the privileges which had been conferred by the favor of Constantine, they complained of the most cruel oppression; and the free toleration of idolaters and heretics was a subject of grief and scandal to the orthodox party. The acts of violence, which were no longer countenanced by the magistrates, were still committed by the zeal of the people. At Pessinus, the altar of Cybele was overturned almost in the presence of the emperor; and in the city of Caesarea in Cappadocia, the temple of Fortune, the sole place of worship which had been left to the Pagans, was destroyed by the rage of a popular tumult. On these occasions, a prince who felt for the honor of the gods was not disposed to interrupt the course of justice; and his mind was still more deeply exasperated when he found that the fanatics, who had deserved and suffered the punishment of incendiaries, were rewarded with the honors of martyrdom. The Christian subjects of Julian were assured of the hostile designs of their sovereign; and, to their jealous apprehension, every circumstance of his government might afford some grounds of discontent and suspicion. In the ordinary administration of the laws, the Christians, who formed so large a part of the people, must frequently be condemned: but their indulgent brethren, without examining the merits of the cause, presumed their innocence, allowed their claims, and imputed the severity of their judge to the partial malice of religious persecution. These present hardships, intolerable as they might appear, were represented as a slight prelude of the impending calamities. The Christians considered Julian as a cruel and crafty tyrant who suspended the execution of his revenge till he should return victorious from the Persian war.... It is impossible to determine how far the zeal of Julian would have prevailed over his good sense and humanity; but if we seriously reflect on the strength and spirit of the church, we shall be convinced that before the emperor could have extinguished the religion of Christ, he must have involved his country in the horrors of a civil war.

CHAPTER XXIV

THE RETREAT AND DEATH OF JULIAN

*Residence of Julian at Antioch. • His successful expedition against
the Persians. • Passage of the Tigris. • The retreat and death of
Julian. • Election of Jovian. • He saves the Roman army by a
disgraceful treaty.*

†In the cool moments of reflection, Julian preferred the useful and benevolent virtues of Antoninus; but his ambitious spirit was inflamed by
the glory of Alexander; and he solicited with equal ardor the esteem of
the wise and the applause of the multitude [A.D. 362]. In the season of
life when the powers of the mind and body enjoy the most active vigor,
the emperor, who was instructed by the experience and animated by
the success of the German war, resolved to signalize his reign by some
more splendid and memorable achievement. . . . As soon as the Persian
monarch was informed that the throne of Constantius was filled by a
prince of a very different character, he condescended to make some
artful, or perhaps sincere, overtures towards a negotiation of peace.
But the pride of Sapor was astonished by the firmness of Julian; who
sternly declared that he would never consent to hold a peaceful conference among the flames and ruins of the cities of Mesopotamia; and
who added, with a smile of contempt, that it was needless to treat by
ambassadors, as he himself had determined to visit speedily the court
of Persia.

[*Julian makes his preparations, winters at Antioch (where he becomes
embroiled in conflicts with local Christians), and on April 7, A.D. 363,
enters Persian territory.*]

Julian was an object of hatred and terror to the Persians: and the
painters of that nation represented the invader of their country under
the emblem of a furious lion who vomited from his mouth a consuming fire. To his friends and soldiers the philosophic hero appeared in a
more amiable light; and his virtues were never more conspicuously
displayed than in the last and most active period of his life. He prac-

ticed, without effort and almost without merit, the habitual qualities of temperance and sobriety. According to the dictates of that artificial wisdom which assumes an absolute dominion over the mind and body, he sternly refused himself the indulgence of the most natural appetites. In the warm climate of Assyria, which solicited a luxurious people to the gratification of every sensual desire, a youthful conqueror preserved his chastity pure and inviolate; nor was Julian ever tempted, even by a motive of curiosity, to visit his female captives of exquisite beauty, who instead of resisting his power would have disputed with each other the honor of his embraces. With the same firmness that he resisted the allurements of love, he sustained the hardships of war. When the Romans marched through the flat and flooded country, their sovereign, on foot at the head of his legions, shared their fatigues and animated their diligence. In every useful labor, the hand of Julian was prompt and strenuous; and the Imperial purple was as wet and dirty as the coarse garment of the meanest soldier. The two sieges allowed him some remarkable opportunities of signalizing his personal valor, which, in the improved state of the military art, can seldom be exerted by a prudent general. The emperor stood before the citadel of Perisabor, insensible of his extreme danger, and encouraged his troops to burst open the gates of iron till he was almost overwhelmed under a cloud of missile weapons and huge stones that were directed against his person. As he examined the exterior fortifications of Maogamalcha, two Persians, devoting themselves for their country, suddenly rushed upon him with drawn cimeters: the emperor dexterously received their blows on his uplifted shield and, with a steady and well-aimed thrust, laid one of his adversaries dead at his feet. The esteem of a prince who possesses the virtues which he approves is the noblest recompense of a deserving subject; and the authority which Julian derived from his personal merit enabled him to revive and enforce the rigor of ancient discipline. He punished with death or ignominy the misbehavior of three troops of horse who, in a skirmish with the Surenas, had lost their honor and one of their standards: and he distinguished with . . . crowns the valor of the foremost soldiers who had ascended into the city of Maogamalcha. After the siege of Perisabor, the firmness of the emperor was exercised by the insolent avarice of the army, who loudly complained that their services were rewarded by a trifling donative of one hundred pieces of silver.

His just indignation was expressed in the grave and manly language of a Roman. "Riches are the object of your desires; those riches are in the hands of the Persians; and the spoils of this fruitful country are proposed as the prize of your valor and discipline. Believe me," added Julian, "the Roman republic, which formerly possessed such immense treasures, is now reduced to want and wretchedness since our princes have been persuaded, by weak and interested ministers, to purchase with gold the tranquility of the Barbarians. The revenue is exhausted; the cities are ruined; the provinces are dispeopled. For myself, the only inheritance that I have received from my royal ancestors is a soul incapable of fear; and as long as I am convinced that every real advantage is seated in the mind, I shall not blush to acknowledge an honorable poverty which, in the days of ancient virtue, was considered as the glory of Fabricius. That glory, and that virtue, may be your own, if you will listen to the voice of Heaven and of your leader. But if you will rashly persist, if you are determined to renew the shameful and mischievous examples of old seditions, proceed. As it becomes an emperor who has filled the first rank among men, I am prepared to die standing; and to despise a precarious life, which, every hour, may depend on an accidental fever. If I have been found unworthy of the command, there are now among you (I speak it with pride and pleasure), there are many chiefs whose merit and experience are equal to the conduct of the most important war. Such has been the temper of my reign that I can retire, without regret and without apprehension, to the obscurity of a private station." The modest resolution of Julian was answered by the unanimous applause and cheerful obedience of the Romans, who declared their confidence of victory while they fought under the banners of their heroic prince. Their courage was kindled by his frequent and familiar asseverations (for such wishes were the oaths of Julian), "So may I reduce the Persians under the yoke!" "Thus may I restore the strength and splendor of the republic!" The love of fame was the ardent passion of his soul: but it was not before he trampled on the ruins of Maogamalcha that he allowed himself to say, "We have now provided some materials for the sophist of Antioch."

The successful valor of Julian had triumphed over all the obstacles that opposed his march to the gates of Ctesiphon. But the reduction, or even the siege, of the capital of Persia was still at a distance.

[*The attack on Ctesiphon fails; Julian orders a retreat.*]

As long as the Romans seemed to advance into the country, their march was observed and insulted from a distance by several bodies of Persian cavalry; who, showing themselves sometimes in loose and sometimes in close order, faintly skirmished with the advanced guards. These detachments were, however, supported by a much greater force; and the heads of the columns were no sooner pointed towards the Tigris than a cloud of dust arose on the plain. The Romans, who now aspired only to the permission of a safe and speedy retreat, endeavored to persuade themselves that this formidable appearance was occasioned by a troop of wild asses, or perhaps by the approach of some friendly Arabs. They halted, pitched their tents, fortified their camp, passed the whole night in continual alarms; and discovered at the dawn of day that they were surrounded by an army of Persians. . . . As the Romans continued their march, their long array, which was forced to bend or divide according to the varieties of the ground, afforded frequent and favorable opportunities to their vigilant enemies. The Persians repeatedly charged with fury; they were repeatedly repulsed with firmness; and the action at Maronga, which almost deserved the name of a battle, was marked by a considerable loss of satraps and elephants, perhaps of equal value in the eyes of their monarch. These splendid advantages were not obtained without an adequate slaughter on the side of the Romans: several officers of distinction were either killed or wounded; and the emperor himself, who on all occasions of danger inspired and guided the valor of his troops, was obliged to expose his person and exert his abilities. The weight of offensive and defensive arms, which still constituted the strength and safety of the Romans, disabled them from making any long or effectual pursuit; and as the horsemen of the East were trained to dart their javelins and shoot their arrows at full speed and in every possible direction, the cavalry of Persia was never more formidable than in the moment of a rapid and disorderly flight. But the most certain and irreparable loss of the Romans was that of time. The hardy veterans, accustomed to the cold climate of Gaul and Germany, fainted under the sultry heat of an Assyrian summer; their vigor was exhausted by the incessant repetition of march and combat; and the progress of the army was suspended by the precautions of a slow and dangerous retreat in the presence of an active enemy. Every day, every hour, as the supply diminished, the value and price of subsistence increased in the Roman camp. Julian, who always contented himself with such food as a hungry soldier would have disdained, distributed for the use of the troops the provisions of the Imperial household, and whatever could be spared from the sumpter-horses of the tribunes and generals. But this feeble relief served only to aggravate the sense of the public distress; and the Romans began to entertain the most gloomy apprehensions that, before they could reach the frontiers of the empire, they should all perish, either by famine or by the sword of the Barbarians.

While Julian struggled with the almost insuperable difficulties of his situation, the silent hours of the night were still devoted to study and contemplation. Whenever he closed his eyes in short and interrupted slumbers, his mind was agitated with painful anxiety; nor can it be thought surprising that the Genius of the empire should once more appear before him, covering with a funeral veil his head and his horn of abundance, and slowly retiring from the Imperial tent. The monarch started from his couch, and stepping forth to refresh his wearied spirits with the coolness of the midnight air, he beheld a fiery meteor, which shot athwart the sky and suddenly vanished. Julian was convinced that he had seen the menacing countenance of the god of war; the council which he summoned, of Tuscan Haruspices [specialists in reading omens, particularly from the entrails of sacrificial victims], unanimously pronounced that he should abstain from action; but on this occasion, necessity and reason were more prevalent than superstition; and the trumpets sounded at the break of day. The army marched through a hilly country; and the hills had been secretly occupied by the Persians. Julian led the van with the skill and attention of a consummate general; he was alarmed by the intelligence that his rear was suddenly attacked. The heat of the weather had tempted him to lay aside his cuirass; but he snatched a shield from one of his attendants and hastened, with a sufficient reinforcement, to the relief of the rearguard. A similar danger recalled the intrepid prince to the defense of the front; and as he galloped through the columns, the center of the left was attacked and almost overpowered by the furious charge of the Persian cavalry and elephants. This huge body was soon defeated by the well-timed evolution of the light infantry, who aimed their weapons with dexterity and effect against the backs of the horsemen and the legs of the elephants. The Barbarians fled; and Julian, who was foremost in every danger, animated the pursuit with his voice and gestures. His trembling guards, scattered and oppressed by the disorderly throng of friends and enemies, reminded their fearless sovereign that he was without armor; and conjured him to decline the fall of the impending ruin. As they exclaimed, a cloud of darts and arrows was discharged from the flying squadrons; and a javelin, after razing the skin of his arm, transpierced the ribs and fixed in the inferior part of the liver. Julian attempted to draw the deadly weapon from his side; but his fingers were cut by the sharpness of the steel, and he fell senseless from his horse. His guards flew to his relief; and the wounded emperor was gently raised from the ground and conveyed out of the tumult of the battle into an adjacent tent. The report of the melancholy event passed from rank to rank; but the grief of the Romans inspired them with invincible valor and the desire of revenge. The bloody and obstinate conflict was maintained by the two armies till they were separated by the total darkness of the night.†

The first words that Julian uttered after his recovery from the fainting fit into which he had been thrown by loss of blood were expressive of his martial spirit. He called for his horse and arms, and was impatient to rush into the battle. His remaining strength was exhausted by the painful effort; and the surgeons who examined his wound discovered the symptoms of approaching death. He employed the awful moments with the firm temper of a hero and a sage; the philosophers who had accompanied him in this fatal expedition compared the tent of Julian with the prison of Socrates; and the spectators whom duty, or friendship, or curiosity had assembled round his couch listened with respectful grief to the funeral oration of their dying emperor. "Friends and fellow-soldiers, the seasonable period of my departure is now arrived, and I discharge, with the cheerfulness of a ready debtor, the demands of nature. I have learned from philosophy how much the soul is more excellent than the body; and that the separation of the nobler substance should be the subject of joy, rather than of affliction. I have learned from religion that an early death has often been the reward of piety; and I accept, as a favor of the gods, the mortal stroke that secures me from the danger of disgracing a character which has hitherto been supported by virtue and fortitude. I die without remorse, as I have lived without guilt. I am pleased to reflect on the innocence of my private life; and I can affirm with confidence, that the supreme authority, that emanation of the Divine Power, has been preserved in my hands pure and immaculate. Detesting the corrupt and destructive maxims of despotism, I have considered the happiness of the people as the end of government. Submitting my actions to the laws of prudence, of justice, and of moderation, I have trusted the event to the care of Providence. Peace was the object of my counsels, as long as peace was consistent with the public welfare; but when the imperious voice of my country summoned me to arms, I exposed my person to the dangers of war, with the clear foreknowledge (which I had acquired from the art of divination) that I was destined to fall by the sword. I now offer my tribute of gratitude to the Eternal Being, who has not suffered me to perish by the cruelty of a tyrant, by the secret dagger of conspiracy, or by the slow tortures of lingering disease. He has given me, in the midst of an honorable career, a splendid and glorious departure from this world; and I hold it equally absurd, equally base, to solicit or to decline the stroke of fate. This much I have attempted to say; but my strength fails me, and I feel the approach of death. I shall cautiously refrain from any word that may tend to influence your suffrages in the election of an emperor. My choice might be imprudent or injudicious; and if it should not be ratified by the consent of the army, it might be fatal to the person whom I should recommend. I shall only, as a good citizen, express my hopes that the Romans may be blessed with the government of a virtuous sovereign." After this discourse, which Julian pronounced in a firm and gentle tone of voice, he distributed, by a military testament, the remains of his private fortune; and making some inquiry why Anatolius was not present, he understood from the answer of Sallust that Anatolius was killed; and bewailed, with amiable inconsistency, the loss of his friend. At the same time he reproved the immoderate grief of the spectators; and conjured them not to disgrace by unmanly tears the fate of a prince who in a few moments would be united with Heaven and with the stars. The spectators were silent; and Julian entered into a metaphysical argument with the philosophers Priscus and Maximus on the nature of the soul. The efforts which he made, of mind as well as body, most probably hastened his death. His wound began to bleed with fresh violence; his respiration was embarrassed by the swelling of the veins; he called for a draught of cold water and, as soon as he had drunk it, expired without pain, about the hour of midnight [June 26, A.D. 263]. Such was the end of that extraordinary man, in the thirty-second year of his age, after a reign of one year and about eight months from the death of Constantius. In his last moments he displayed, perhaps with some ostentation, the love of virtue and of fame which had been the ruling passions of his life.

The triumph of Christianity and the calamities of the empire may in some measure be ascribed to Julian himself, who had neglected to secure the future execution of his designs by the timely and judicious nomination of an associate and successor. But the royal race of Constantius Chlorus was reduced to his own person; and if he entertained any serious thoughts of investing with the purple the most worthy among the Romans, he was diverted from his resolution by the difficulty of the choice, the jealousy of power, the fear of ingratitude, and the natural presumption of health, of youth, and of prosperity. His unexpected death left the empire without a master and without an heir, in a state of perplexity and danger which, in the space of fourscore years, had never been experienced since the election of Diocletian. In a government which had almost forgotten the distinction of pure and noble blood, the superiority of birth was of little moment; the claims of official rank were accidental and precarious; and the candidates who might aspire to ascend the vacant throne could be supported only by the consciousness of personal merit or by the hopes of popular favor. But the situation of a famished army, encompassed on all sides by a host of Barbarians, shortened the moments of grief and deliberation. In this scene of terror and distress, the body of the deceased prince, according to his own directions, was decently embalmed; and at the dawn of day, the generals convened a military senate, at which the commanders of the legions and the officers both of cavalry and infantry were invited to assist. Three or four hours of the night had not passed away without some secret cabals; and when the election of an emperor was proposed, the spirit of faction began to agitate the assembly. . . . While they debated, a few voices saluted Jovian, who was no more than *first* of the domestics, with the names of Emperor and Augustus. The tumultuary acclamation was instantly repeated by the guards who surrounded the tent, and passed in a few minutes to the extremities of the line. The new prince, astonished with his own fortune, was hastily invested with the Imperial ornaments, and received an oath of fidelity from the generals whose favor and protection he so lately solicited [June 27, A.D. 363]. The strongest recommendation of Jovian was the merit of his father, Count Varronian, who enjoyed in honorable retirement the fruit of his long services. In the obscure freedom of a private station, the son indulged his taste for wine and women; yet he supported with credit the character of a Christian and a soldier. Without being conspicuous for any of the ambitious qualifications which excite the admiration and envy of mankind, the comely person of Jovian, his cheerful temper and familiar wit, had gained the affection of his fellow-soldiers; and the generals of both parties acquiesced in a popular election which had not been conducted by the arts of their enemies. The pride of this unexpected elevation was moderated by the just apprehension that the same day might terminate the life and reign of the new emperor. The pressing voice of necessity was obeyed without delay; and the first orders issued by Jovian, a few hours after his predecessor had expired, were to prosecute a march which could alone extricate the Romans from their actual distress.

[*Progress is delayed first by (successful) battle with the Persians and then by the ensuing negotiations with Sapor.*]

Had Jovian been capable of executing a bold and prudent measure, he would have continued his march with unremitting diligence; the progress of the treaty would have suspended the attacks of the Barbarians; and before the expiration of the fourth day, he might have safely reached the fruitful province of Corduene, at the distance only of one hundred miles. The irresolute emperor, instead of breaking through the toils of the enemy, expected his fate with patient resignation; and accepted the humiliating conditions of peace which it was no longer in his power to refuse. The five provinces beyond the Tigris which had been ceded by the grandfather of Sapor were restored to the Persian monarchy. He acquired, by a single article, the impregnable city of Nisibis; which had sustained, in three successive sieges, the effort of his arms. Singara and the castle of the Moors, one of the strongest places of Mesopotamia, were likewise dismembered from the empire. It was considered as an indulgence that the inhabitants of those fortresses were permitted to retire with their effects; but the conqueror rigorously insisted that the Romans should forever abandon the king and kingdom of Armenia. A peace, or rather a long truce, of thirty years was stipulated between the hostile nations; the faith of the treaty was ratified by solemn oaths and religious ceremonies; and hostages of distinguished rank were reciprocally delivered to secure the performance of the conditions.

The sophist of Antioch [Libanius], who saw with indignation the scepter of his hero in the feeble hand of a Christian successor, professes to admire the moderation of Sapor, in contenting himself with so small a portion of the Roman empire.†

The friends of Julian had confidently announced the success of his expedition. They entertained a fond persuasion that the temples of the gods would be enriched with the spoils of the East; that Persia would be reduced to the humble state of a tributary province, governed by the laws and magistrates of Rome; that the Barbarians would adopt the dress, and manners, and language of their conquerors; and that the youth of Ecbatana and Susa would study the art of rhetoric under Grecian masters. The progress of the arms of Julian interrupted his communication with the empire; and, from the moment that he passed the Tigris, his affectionate subjects were ignorant of the fate and fortunes of their prince. Their contemplation of fancied triumphs was disturbed by the melancholy rumor of his death; and they persisted to doubt, after they could no longer deny, the truth of that fatal event. The messengers of Jovian promulgated the specious tale of a prudent and necessary peace; the voice of fame, louder and more sincere, revealed the disgrace of the emperor and the conditions of the ignominious treaty. The minds of the people were filled with astonishment and grief, with indignation and terror, when they were informed that the unworthy successor of Julian relinquished the five provinces which had been acquired by the victory of Galerius; and that he shamefully surrendered to the Barbarians the important city of Nisibis, the firmest bulwark of the provinces of the East. The deep and dangerous question, how far the public faith should be observed when it becomes incompatible with the public safety, was freely agitated in popular conversation; and some hopes were entertained that the emperor would redeem his pusillanimous behavior by a splendid act of patriotic perfidy. The inflexible spirit of the Roman senate had always disclaimed the unequal conditions which were extorted from the distress of their captive armies; and if it were necessary to satisfy the national honor by delivering the guilty general into the hands of the Barbarians, the greatest part of the subjects of Jovian would have cheerfully acquiesced in the precedent of ancient times.

But the emperor, whatever might be the limits of his constitutional authority, was the absolute master of the laws and arms of the state; and the same motives which had forced him to subscribe now pressed him to execute the treaty of peace. He was impatient to secure an empire at the expense of a few provinces; and the respectable names of religion and honor concealed the personal fears and ambition of Jovian. Notwithstanding the dutiful solicitations of the inhabitants, decency as well as prudence forbade the emperor to lodge in the palace of Nisibis; but the next morning after his arrival, Bineses, the ambassador of Persia, entered the place, displayed from the citadel the standard of the Great King, and proclaimed in his name the cruel alternative of exile or servitude. The principal citizens of Nisibis, who till that fatal moment had confided in the protection of their sovereign, threw themselves at his feet. They conjured him not to abandon, or at least not to deliver, a faithful colony to the rage of a Barbarian tyrant exasperated by the three successive defeats which he had experienced under the walls of Nisibis. They still possessed arms and courage to repel the invaders of their country: they requested only the permission of using them in their own defense; and, as soon as they had asserted their independence, they should implore the favor of being again admitted into the ranks of his subjects. Their arguments, their eloquence, their tears, were ineffectual. Jovian alleged, with some confusion, the sanctity of oaths; and . . . he published an edict, under pain of death, that they should leave the city within the term of three days. Ammianus has delineated in lively colors the scene of universal despair, which he seems to have viewed with an eye of compassion. The martial youth deserted, with indignant grief, the walls which they had so gloriously defended: the disconsolate mourner dropped a last tear over the tomb of a son or husband, which must soon be profaned by the rude hand of a Barbarian master; and the aged citizen kissed the threshold and clung to the doors of the house where he had passed the cheerful and careless hours of infancy. The highways were crowded with a trembling multitude: the distinctions of rank and sex and age were lost in the general calamity. . . . The savage insensibility of Jovian appears to have aggravated the hardships of these unhappy fugitives. . . .

Similar orders were despatched by the emperor for the evacuation of Singara and the castle of the Moors; and for the restitution of the five provinces beyond the Tigris. Sapor enjoyed the glory and the fruits of his victory; and this ignominious peace has justly been considered as a memorable era in the decline and fall of the Roman empire. The predecessors of Jovian had sometimes relinquished the dominion of distant and unprofitable provinces; but since the foundation of the city, the genius of Rome, the god Terminus, who guarded the boundaries of the republic, had never retired before the sword of a victorious enemy.

After Jovian had performed those engagements which the voice of his people might have tempted him to violate, he hastened away from the scene of his disgrace, and proceeded with his whole court to enjoy the luxury of Antioch. Without consulting the dictates of religious zeal, he was prompted by humanity and gratitude to bestow the last honors on the remains of his deceased sovereign: and Procopius, who sincerely bewailed the loss of his kinsman, was removed from the command of the army under the decent pretense of conducting the funeral. The corpse of Julian was transported from Nisibis to Tarsus, in a slow march of fifteen days and, as it passed through the cities of the East, was saluted by the hostile factions with mournful lamentations and clamorous insults. The Pagans already placed their beloved hero in the rank of those gods whose worship he had restored; while the invectives of the Christians pursued the soul of the apostate to hell, and his body to the grave. One party lamented the approaching ruin of their altars; the other celebrated the marvelous deliverance of their church. The Christians applauded, in lofty and ambiguous strains, the stroke of divine vengeance, which had been so long suspended over the guilty head of Julian.[†]

The remains of Julian were interred at Tarsus in Cilicia; but his stately tomb, which arose in that city on the banks of the cold and limpid Cydnus, was displeasing to the faithful friends who loved and revered the memory of that extraordinary man. The philosopher expressed a very reasonable wish that the disciple of Plato might have reposed amidst the groves of the academy; while the soldier exclaimed, in bolder accents, that the ashes of Julian should have been mingled with those of Caesar, in the field of Mars, and among the ancient monuments of Roman virtue. The history of princes does not very frequently renew the examples of a similar competition.

CHAPTER XXV

REIGNS OF JOVIAN AND VALENTINIAN, DIVISION OF THE EMPIRE

The government and death of Jovian. • Election of Valentinian, who associates his brother Valens and makes the final division of the Eastern and Western empires. • Revolt of Procopius. • Civil and ecclesiastical administration. • Germany. • Britain. • Africa. • The East. • The Danube. • Death of Valentinian. • His two sons, Gratian and Valentinian II, succeed to the Western empire.

The death of Julian had left the public affairs of the empire in a very doubtful and dangerous situation [A.D. 363]. The Roman army was saved by an inglorious, perhaps a necessary, treaty; and the first moments of peace were consecrated by the pious Jovian to restore the domestic tranquility of the church and state. The indiscretion of his predecessor, instead of reconciling, had artfully fomented the religious war: and the balance which he affected to preserve between the hostile factions served only to perpetuate the contest, by the vicissitudes of hope and fear, by the rival claims of ancient possession and actual favor. The Christians had forgotten the spirit of the gospel; and the Pagans had imbibed the spirit of the church. In private families, the sentiments of nature were extinguished by the blind fury of zeal and revenge: the majesty of the laws was violated or abused; the cities of the East were stained with blood; and the most implacable enemies of the Romans were in the bosom of their country. Jovian was educated in the profession of Christianity; and as he marched from Nisibis to Antioch, the banner of the Cross, the LABARUM of Constantine, which was again displayed at the head of the legions, announced to the people the faith of their new emperor. As soon as he ascended the throne, he transmitted a circular epistle to all the governors of provinces; in which he confessed the divine truth and secured the legal establishment of the Christian religion. The insidious edicts of Julian

were abolished; the ecclesiastical immunities were restored and enlarged; and Jovian condescended to lament that the distress of the times
obliged him to diminish the measure of charitable distributions. The
Christians were unanimous in the loud and sincere applause which
they bestowed on the pious successor of Julian. But they were still ignorant what creed, or what synod, he would choose for the standard of
orthodoxy; and the peace of the church immediately revived those
eager disputes which had been suspended during the season of persecution. The episcopal leaders of the contending sects, convinced from
experience how much their fate would depend on the earliest impressions that were made on the mind of an untutored soldier, hastened
to the court of Edessa or Antioch. The highways of the East were
crowded with *Homoousian* and Arian and Semi-Arian and Eunomian
bishops, who struggled to outstrip each other in the holy race: the
apartments of the palace resounded with their clamors; and the ears
of the prince were assaulted, and perhaps astonished, by the singular mixture of metaphysical argument and passionate invective. The
moderation of Jovian, who recommended concord and charity and referred the disputants to the sentence of a future council, was interpreted as a symptom of indifference: but his attachment to the Nicene
creed was at length discovered and declared by the reverence which he
expressed for the *celestial* virtues of the great Athanasius. The intrepid
veteran of the faith, at the age of seventy, had issued from his retreat
on the first intelligence of the tyrant's death. The acclamations of the
people seated him once more on the archiepiscopal throne; and he
wisely accepted, or anticipated, the invitation of Jovian.... As soon as
he had gained the confidence and secured the faith of the Christian
emperor, he returned in triumph to his diocese and continued, with
mature counsels and undiminished vigor, to direct, ten years longer,
the ecclesiastical government of Alexandria, Egypt, and the Catholic
church [till A.D. 373].†

The slightest force, when it is applied to assist and guide the natural descent of its object, operates with irresistible weight; and Jovian
had the good fortune to embrace the religious opinions which were
supported by the spirit of the times, and the zeal and numbers of the
most powerful sect. Under his reign, Christianity obtained an easy and
lasting victory; and as soon as the smile of royal patronage was withdrawn, the genius of Paganism, which had been fondly raised and

cherished by the arts of Julian, sunk irrecoverably in the dust. In many cities, the temples were shut or deserted: the philosophers who had abused their transient favor thought it prudent to shave their beards and disguise their profession; and the Christians rejoiced that they were now in a condition to forgive, or to revenge, the injuries which they had suffered under the preceding reign. The consternation of the Pagan world was dispelled by a wise and gracious edict of toleration in which Jovian explicitly declared that although he should severely punish the sacrilegious rites of magic, his subjects might exercise, with freedom and safety, the ceremonies of the ancient worship.†

In the space of seven months, the Roman troops, who were now returned to Antioch, had performed a march of fifteen hundred miles in which they had endured all the hardships of war, of famine, and of climate. Notwithstanding their services, their fatigues, and the approach of winter, the timid and impatient Jovian allowed only, to the men and horses, a respite of six weeks [October A.D. 363]. The emperor could not sustain the indiscreet and malicious raillery of the people of Antioch. He was impatient to possess the palace of Constantinople; and to prevent the ambition of some competitor who might occupy the vacant allegiance of Europe. But he soon received the grateful intelligence that his authority was acknowledged from the Thracian Bosphorus to the Atlantic Ocean. . . . The oath of fidelity was administered and taken, with loyal acclamations; and the deputies of the Western armies saluted their new sovereign as he descended from Mount Taurus to the city of Tyana in Cappadocia. From Tyana he continued his hasty march to Ancyra, capital of the province of Galatia; where Jovian assumed, with his infant son, the name and ensigns of the consulship. Dadastana, an obscure town, almost at an equal distance between Ancyra and Nice, was marked for the fatal term of his journey and life. After indulging himself with a plentiful, perhaps an intemperate, supper, he retired to rest; and the next morning the emperor Jovian was found dead in his bed [February 17, A.D. 364]. The cause of this sudden death was variously understood. . . . But the want of a regular inquiry into the death of a prince whose reign and person were soon forgotten appears to have been the only circumstance which countenanced the malicious whispers of poison and domestic guilt. The body of Jovian was sent to Constantinople to be interred with his predecessors, and the sad procession was met on the road by his wife

Charito. . . . Her disappointment and grief were embittered by the anxiety of maternal tenderness. Six weeks before the death of Jovian, his infant son had been placed in the curule chair, adorned with the title of *Nobilissimus* and the vain ensigns of the consulship. Unconscious of his fortune, the royal youth, who from his grandfather assumed the name of Varronian, was reminded only by the jealousy of the government that he was the son of an emperor. Sixteen years afterwards he was still alive, but he had already been deprived of an eye; and his afflicted mother expected every hour that the innocent victim would be torn from her arms to appease with his blood the suspicions of the reigning prince.

After the death of Jovian, the throne of the Roman world remained ten days without a master [February 17–26, A.D. 364]. The ministers and generals still continued to meet in council; to exercise their respective functions; to maintain the public order; and peaceably to conduct the army to the city of Nice in Bithynia, which was chosen for the place of the election. . . . Several candidates were proposed; and after weighing the objections of character or situation, they were successively rejected; but as soon as the name of Valentinian was pronounced, the merit of that officer united the suffrages of the whole. . . . Valentinian was the son of Count Gratian, a native of Cibalis, in Pannonia, who from an obscure condition had raised himself, by matchless strength and dexterity, to the military commands of Africa and Britain; from which he retired with an ample fortune and suspicious integrity. The rank and services of Gratian contributed, however, to smooth the first steps of the promotion of his son; and afforded him an early opportunity of displaying those solid and useful qualifications which raised his character above the ordinary level of his fellow-soldiers. The person of Valentinian was tall, graceful, and majestic. His manly countenance, deeply marked with the impression of sense and spirit, inspired his friends with awe and his enemies with fear; and to second the efforts of his undaunted courage, the son of Gratian had inherited the advantages of a strong and healthy constitution. By the habits of chastity and temperance, which restrain the appetites and invigorate the faculties, Valentinian preserved his own and the public esteem. The avocations of a military life had diverted his youth from the elegant pursuits of literature; he was ignorant of the Greek language and the arts of rhetoric; but as the mind of the orator was never disconcerted by timid perplexity, he was able, as often as the occasion prompted him, to deliver his decided sentiments with bold and ready elocution. The laws of martial discipline were the only laws that he had studied; and he was soon distinguished by the laborious diligence and inflexible severity with which he discharged and enforced the duties of the camp. In the time of Julian he provoked the danger of disgrace by the contempt which he publicly expressed for the reigning religion; and it should seem, from his subsequent conduct, that the indiscreet and unseasonable freedom of Valentinian was the effect of military spirit rather than of Christian zeal. He was pardoned, however, and still employed by a prince who esteemed his merit; and in the various events of the Persian war, he improved the reputation which he had already acquired on the banks of the Rhine. The celerity and success with which he executed an important commission recommended him to the favor of Jovian, and to the honorable command of the second *school*, or company, of Targetters, of the domestic guards. In the march from Antioch, he had reached his quarters at Ancyra when he was unexpectedly summoned, without guilt and without intrigue, to assume, in the forty-third year of his age, the absolute government of the Roman empire.

The invitation of the ministers and generals at Nice was of little moment, unless it were confirmed by the voice of the army. The aged Sallust, who had long observed the irregular fluctuations of popular assemblies, proposed under pain of death that none of those persons whose rank in the service might excite a party in their favor should appear in public on the day of the inauguration. Yet such was the prevalence of ancient superstition that a whole day was voluntarily added to this dangerous interval, because it happened to be the intercalation of the Bissextile [a word derived from the repetition of the sixth day before the Kalends of March (i.e., February 24), for leap year]. At length, when the hour was supposed to be propitious, Valentinian showed himself from a lofty tribunal; the judicious choice was applauded; and the new prince was solemnly invested with the diadem and the purple amidst the acclamation of the troops, who were disposed in martial order round the tribunal [February 26, A.D. 364]. But when he stretched forth his hand to address the armed multitude, a busy whisper was accidentally started in the ranks, and insensibly swelled into a loud and imperious clamor, that he should name without delay a colleague in the empire. The intrepid calmness of Valentinian obtained silence and commanded respect; and he thus addressed the assembly: "A few minutes since it was in *your* power, fellow-soldiers, to have left me in the obscurity of a private station. Judging from the testimony of my past life that I deserved to reign, you have placed me on the throne. It is now *my* duty to consult the safety and interest of the republic. The weight of the universe is undoubtedly too great for the hands of a feeble mortal. I am conscious of the limits of my abilities and the uncertainty of my life; and far from declining, I am anxious to solicit the assistance of a worthy colleague. But where discord may be fatal, the choice of a faithful friend requires mature and serious deliberation. That deliberation shall be *my* care. Let *your* conduct be dutiful and consistent. Retire to your quarters; refresh your minds and bodies; and expect the accustomed donative on the accession of a new emperor." The astonished troops, with a mixture of pride, of satisfaction, and of terror, confessed the voice of their master. Their angry clamors subsided into silent reverence; and Valentinian, encompassed with the eagles of the legions and the various banners of the cavalry and infantry, was conducted in warlike pomp to the palace of Nice. As he was sensible, however, of the importance of preventing some rash declaration of the soldiers, he consulted the assembly of the chiefs; and their real sentiments were concisely expressed by the generous freedom of Dagalaiphus. "Most excellent prince," said that officer, "if you consider only your family, you have a brother; if you love the republic, look round for the most deserving of the Romans." The emperor, who suppressed his displeasure without altering his intention, slowly proceeded from Nice to Nicomedia and Constantinople. In one of the suburbs of that capital, thirty days after his own elevation, he bestowed the title of Augustus on his brother Valens [March 28, A.D. 364]; and as the boldest patriots were convinced that their opposition, without being serviceable to their country, would be fatal to themselves, the declaration of his absolute will was received with silent submission. Valens was now in the thirty-sixth year of his age; but his abilities had never been exercised in any employment, military or civil; and his character had not inspired the world with any sanguine expectations. He possessed, however, one quality which recommended him to Valentinian, and preserved the domestic peace of the empire; devout and grateful attachment to his benefactor, whose superiority of genius, as well as of authority, Valens humbly and cheerfully acknowledged in every action of his life.[†]

The festivity of a new reign received a short and suspicious interruption from the sudden illness of the two princes; but as soon as their health was restored, they left Constantinople in the beginning of the spring. In the castle, or palace, of Mediana, only three miles from Naissus, they executed the solemn and final division of the Roman empire [June A.D. 364]. Valentinian bestowed on his brother the rich praefecture of the East, from the Lower Danube to the confines of Persia; whilst he reserved for his immediate government the warlike praefectures of Illyricum, Italy, and Gaul, from the extremity of Greece to the Caledonian rampart, and from the rampart of Caledonia to the foot of Mount Atlas. The provincial administration remained on its former basis; but a double supply of generals and magistrates was required for two councils and two courts: the division was made with a just regard to their peculiar merit and situation, and seven master-generals were soon created, either of the cavalry or infantry. When this important business had been amicably transacted, Valentinian and Valens embraced for the last time. The emperor of the West established his temporary residence at Milan; and the emperor of the East returned to Constantinople to assume the dominion of fifty provinces of whose language he was totally ignorant.

The tranquility of the East was soon disturbed by rebellion; and the throne of Valens was threatened by the daring attempts of a rival whose affinity to the emperor Julian was his sole merit and had been his only crime [September 28, A.D. 365]. Procopius had been hastily promoted from the obscure station of a tribune and a notary to the joint command of the army of Mesopotamia; the public opinion already named him as the successor of a prince who was destitute of natural heirs; and a vain rumor was propagated by his friends, or his enemies, that Julian, before the altar of the Moon at Carrhae, had privately invested Procopius with the Imperial purple. He endeavored, by his dutiful and submissive behavior, to disarm the jealousy of Jovian; resigned, without a contest, his military command; and retired, with his wife and family, to cultivate the ample patrimony which he possessed in the province of Cappadocia. These useful and innocent occupations were interrupted by the appearance of an officer with a band of soldiers who, in the name of his new sovereigns, Valentinian

and Valens, was despatched to conduct the unfortunate Procopius either to a perpetual prison or an ignominious death. His presence of
mind procured him a longer respite and a more splendid fate. Without
presuming to dispute the royal mandate, he requested the indulgence
of a few moments to embrace his weeping family; and while the vigilance of his guards was relaxed by a plentiful entertainment, he dexterously escaped to the sea-coast of the Euxine, from whence he passed
over to the country of Bosphorus. In that sequestered region he remained many months, exposed to the hardships of exile, of solitude,
and of want, his melancholy temper brooding over his misfortunes and
his mind agitated by the just apprehension that, if any accident should
discover his name, the faithless Barbarians would violate, without much
scruple, the laws of hospitality. In a moment of impatience and despair, Procopius embarked in a merchant vessel which made sail for
Constantinople; and boldly aspired to the rank of a sovereign because
he was not allowed to enjoy the security of a subject.

[*After some initial success, he fails; Procopius is beheaded*
(May 28, A.D. 366).]

Such indeed are the common and natural fruits of despotism and rebellion. But the inquisition into the crime of magic, which, under the
reign of the two brothers, was so rigorously prosecuted both at Rome
and Antioch, was interpreted as the fatal symptom either of the displeasure of Heaven or of the depravity of mankind [A.D. 373 ff.]. Let
us not hesitate to indulge a liberal pride that, in the present age, the
enlightened part of Europe has abolished a cruel and odious prejudice
which reigned in every climate of the globe and adhered to every system of religious opinions. The nations and the sects of the Roman
world admitted with equal credulity, and similar abhorrence, the reality
of that infernal art which was able to control the eternal order of the
planets and the voluntary operations of the human mind. They dreaded
the mysterious power of spells and incantations, of potent herbs and
execrable rites, which could extinguish or recall life, inflame the passions of the soul, blast the works of creation, and extort from the reluctant demons the secrets of futurity. They believed, with the wildest
inconsistency, that this preternatural dominion of the air, of earth, and
of Hell was exercised, from the vilest motives of malice or gain, by

some wrinkled hags and itinerant sorcerers, who passed their obscure lives in penury and contempt. The arts of magic were equally condemned by the public opinion and by the laws of Rome; but as they tended to gratify the most imperious passions of the heart of man, they were continually proscribed, and continually practiced. An imaginary cause was capable of producing the most serious and mischievous effects. The dark predictions of the death of an emperor, or the success of a conspiracy, were calculated only to stimulate the hopes of ambition and to dissolve the ties of fidelity; and the intentional guilt of magic was aggravated by the actual crimes of treason and sacrilege. Such vain terrors disturbed the peace of society and the happiness of individuals; and the harmless flame which insensibly melted a waxen image might derive a powerful and pernicious energy from the affrighted fancy of the person whom it was maliciously designed to represent. From the infusion of those herbs which were supposed to possess a supernatural influence, it was an easy step to the use of more substantial poison; and the folly of mankind sometimes became the instrument, and the mask, of the most atrocious crimes. As soon as the zeal of informers was encouraged by the ministers of Valens and Valentinian, they could not refuse to listen to another charge, too frequently mingled in the scenes of domestic guilt; a charge of a softer and less malignant nature, for which the pious though excessive rigor of Constantine had recently decreed the punishment of death. This deadly and incoherent mixture of treason and magic, of poison and adultery, afforded infinite gradations of guilt and innocence, of excuse and aggravation, which in these proceedings appear to have been confounded by the angry or corrupt passions of the judges. They easily discovered that the degree of their industry and discernment was estimated by the Imperial court according to the number of executions that were furnished from the respective tribunals. It was not without extreme reluctance that they pronounced a sentence of acquittal; but they eagerly admitted such evidence as was stained with perjury or procured by torture to prove the most improbable charges against the most respectable characters. The progress of the inquiry continually opened new subjects of criminal prosecution; the audacious informer whose falsehood was detected retired with impunity; but the wretched victim who discovered his real or pretended accomplices was seldom permitted to receive the price of his infamy. From the extremity of

Italy and Asia, the young and the aged were dragged in chains to the tribunals of Rome and Antioch. Senators, matrons, and philosophers expired in ignominious and cruel tortures. The soldiers who were appointed to guard the prisons declared, with a murmur of pity and indignation, that their numbers were insufficient to oppose the flight or resistance of the multitude of captives. The wealthiest families were ruined by fines and confiscations; the most innocent citizens trembled for their safety; and we may form some notion of the magnitude of the evil from the extravagant assertion of an ancient writer that, in the obnoxious provinces, the prisoners, the exiles, and the fugitives formed the greatest part of the inhabitants.†

[We] turn with horror from the frequent executions which disgraced, both at Rome and Antioch, the reign of the two brothers. Valens was of a timid and Valentinian of a choleric disposition. An anxious regard to his personal safety was the ruling principle of the administration of Valens. In the condition of a subject, he had kissed, with trembling awe, the hand of the oppressor; and when he ascended the throne, he reasonably expected that the same fears which had subdued his own mind would secure the patient submission of his people. The favorites of Valens obtained, by the privilege of rapine and confiscation, the wealth which his economy would have refused. They urged, with persuasive eloquence, *that,* in all cases of treason, suspicion is equivalent to proof; *that* the power supposes the intention of mischief; *that* the intention is not less criminal than the act; and *that* a subject no longer deserves to live if his life may threaten the safety or disturb the repose of his sovereign. The judgment of Valentinian was sometimes deceived, and his confidence abused; but he would have silenced the informers with a contemptuous smile had they presumed to alarm his fortitude by the sound of danger. They praised his inflexible love of justice; and in the pursuit of justice, the emperor was easily tempted to consider clemency as a weakness, and passion as a virtue. As long as he wrestled with his equals in the bold competition of an active and ambitious life, Valentinian was seldom injured, and never insulted, with impunity: if his prudence was arraigned, his spirit was applauded; and the proudest and most powerful generals were apprehensive of provoking the resentment of a fearless soldier. After he became master of the world, he unfortunately forgot that where no resistance can be made, no courage can be exerted; and instead of consulting the dictates of reason and magnanimity, he indulged the furious emotions of his temper, at a time when they were disgraceful to himself and fatal to the defenseless objects of his displeasure. In the government of his household or of his empire, slight or even imaginary offenses—a hasty word, a casual omission, an involuntary delay—were chastised by a sentence of immediate death. The expressions which issued the most readily from the mouth of the emperor of the West were, "Strike off his head"; "Burn him alive"; "Let him be beaten with clubs till he expires"; and his most favored ministers soon understood that by a rash attempt to dispute or suspend the execution of his sanguinary commands, they might involve themselves in the guilt and punishment of disobedience. The repeated gratification of this savage justice hardened the mind of Valentinian against pity and remorse; and the sallies of passion were confirmed by the habits of cruelty. He could behold with calm satisfaction the convulsive agonies of torture and death.[†]

But in the calmer moments of reflection, when the mind of Valens was not agitated by fear, or that of Valentinian by rage, the tyrant resumed the sentiments, or at least the conduct, of the father of his country. The dispassionate judgment of the Western emperor could clearly perceive, and accurately pursue, his own and the public interest; and the sovereign of the East, who imitated with equal docility the various examples which he received from his elder brother, was sometimes guided by the wisdom and virtue of the praefect Sallust. Both princes invariably retained in the purple the chaste and temperate simplicity which had adorned their private life; and under their reign, the pleasures of the court never cost the people a blush or a sigh. They gradually reformed many of the abuses of the times of Constantius; judiciously adopted and improved the designs of Julian and his successor; and displayed a style and spirit of legislation which might inspire posterity with the most favorable opinion of their character and government.

But the most honorable circumstance of the character of Valentinian is the firm and temperate impartiality which he uniformly preserved in an age of religious contention [A.D. 364–375]. His strong sense, unenlightened but uncorrupted by study, declined with respectful indifference the subtle questions of theological debate. The government of the Earth claimed his vigilance and satisfied his ambition;

and while he remembered that he was the disciple of the church, he never forgot that he was the sovereign of the clergy. Under the reign of an apostate, he had signalized his zeal for the honor of Christianity: he allowed to his subjects the privilege which he had assumed for himself; and they might accept with gratitude and confidence the general toleration which was granted by a prince addicted to passion but incapable of fear or of disguise. The Pagans, the Jews, and all the various sects which acknowledged the divine authority of Christ were protected by the laws from arbitrary power or popular insult; nor was any mode of worship prohibited by Valentinian except those secret and criminal practices which abused the name of religion for the dark purposes of vice and disorder. The art of magic, as it was more cruelly punished, was more strictly proscribed: but the emperor admitted a formal distinction to protect the ancient methods of divination, which were approved by the senate, and exercised by the Tuscan Haruspices.[†]

The friend of toleration was unfortunately placed at a distance from the scene of the fiercest controversies. [T]he Christians of the West had . . . happily relapsed into the slumber of orthodoxy; and the small remains of the Arian party . . . might be considered rather as objects of contempt than of resentment. But in the provinces of the East . . . the strength and numbers of the hostile factions were more equally balanced; and this equality, instead of recommending the counsels of peace, served only to perpetuate the horrors of religious war. . . . Valens, who in the first years of his reign had imitated the impartial conduct of his brother, was an important victory on the side of Arianism. The two brothers had passed their private life in the condition of catechumens; but the piety of Valens prompted him to solicit the sacrament of baptism before he exposed his person to the dangers of a Gothic war. He naturally addressed himself to Eudoxus, bishop of the Imperial city; and if the ignorant monarch was instructed by that Arian pastor in the principles of heterodox theology, his misfortune, rather than his guilt, was the inevitable consequence of his erroneous choice. Whatever had been the determination of the emperor, he must have offended a numerous party of his Christian subjects, as the leaders both of the *Homoousians* and of the Arians believed that if they were not suffered to reign, they were most cruelly injured and oppressed. After he had taken this decisive step, it was extremely difficult for him to preserve either the virtue or the reputation of impartiality.... The feeble mind of Valens was always swayed by the persons with whom he familiarly conversed; and the exile or imprisonment of a private citizen are the favors the most readily granted in a despotic court. Such punishments were frequently inflicted on the leaders of the *Homoousian* party; and the misfortune of fourscore ecclesiastics of Constantinople who, perhaps accidentally, were burned on shipboard was imputed to the cruel and premeditated malice of the emperor and his Arian ministers. In every contest, the Catholics (if we may anticipate that name) were obliged to pay the penalty of their own faults and of those of their adversaries. In every election, the claims of the Arian candidate obtained the preference; and if they were opposed by the majority of the people, he was usually supported by the authority of the civil magistrate, or even by the terrors of a military force.... The free toleration of the heathen and Jewish worship was bitterly lamented as a circumstance which aggravated the misery of the Catholics and the guilt of the impious tyrant of the East [A.D. 367–378].

The triumph of the orthodox party has left a deep stain of persecution on the memory of Valens; and the character of a prince who derived his virtues as well as his vices from a feeble understanding and a pusillanimous temper scarcely deserves the labor of an apology. Yet candor may discover some reasons to suspect that the ecclesiastical ministers of Valens often exceeded the orders, or even the intentions, of their master; and that the real measure of facts has been very liberally magnified by the vehement declamation and easy credulity of his antagonists.[†]

The strict regulations which have been framed by the wisdom of modern legislators to restrain the wealth and avarice of the clergy may be originally deduced from the example of the emperor Valentinian. His edict, addressed to Damasus, bishop of Rome, was publicly read in the churches of the city [A.D. 370]. He admonished the ecclesiastics and monks not to frequent the houses of widows and virgins; and menaced their disobedience with the animadversion of the civil judge. The director was no longer permitted to receive any gift, or legacy, or inheritance from the liberality of his spiritual daughter: every testament contrary to this edict was declared null and void; and the illegal donation was confiscated for the use of the treasury. By a subsequent regulation, it should seem that the same provisions were extended to nuns and bishops; and that all persons of the ecclesiastical order were rendered incapable of receiving any testamentary gifts and strictly confined to the natural and legal rights of inheritance. As the guardian of domestic happiness and virtue, Valentinian applied this severe remedy to the growing evil. In the capital of the empire, the females of noble and opulent houses possessed a very ample share of independent property: and many of those devout females had embraced the doctrines of Christianity, not only with the cold assent of the understanding but with the warmth of affection, and perhaps with the eagerness of fashion. They sacrificed the pleasures of dress and luxury; and renounced, for the praise of chastity, the soft endearments of conjugal society. Some ecclesiastic, of real or apparent sanctity, was chosen to direct their timorous conscience and to amuse the vacant tenderness of their heart: and the unbounded confidence which they hastily bestowed was often abused by knaves and enthusiasts; who hastened from the extremities of the East to enjoy, on a splendid theater, the privileges of the monastic profession. By their contempt of the world, they insensibly acquired its most desirable advantages; the lively attachment, perhaps, of a young and beautiful woman, the delicate plenty of an opulent household, and the respectful homage of the slaves, the freedmen, and the clients of a senatorial family. The immense fortunes of the Roman ladies were gradually consumed in lavish alms and expensive pilgrimages; and the artful monk who had assigned himself the first, or possibly the sole, place in the testament of his spiritual daughter still presumed to declare, with the smooth face of hypocrisy, that he was only the instrument of charity and the steward of the poor. The lucrative but disgraceful trade which was exercised by the clergy to defraud the expectations of the natural heirs had provoked the indignation of a superstitious age: and two of the most respectable of the Latin fathers very honestly confess that the ignominious edict of Valentinian was just and necessary; and that the Christian priests had deserved to lose a privilege which was still enjoyed by comedians, charioteers, and the ministers of idols. But the wisdom and authority of the legislator are seldom victorious in a contest with the vigilant dexterity of private interest; and Jerome, or Ambrose, might patiently acquiesce in the justice of an ineffectual or salutary law.[†]

[T]he splendid vices of the church of Rome under the reign of Valentinian . . . have been curiously observed by the historian Ammianus, who delivers his impartial sense in these expressive words: "The praefecture of Juventius was accompanied with peace and plenty, but the tranquility of his government was soon disturbed by a bloody sedition of the distracted people. The ardor of Damasus and Ursinus to seize the episcopal seat surpassed the ordinary measure of human ambition. They contended with the rage of party; the quarrel was maintained by the wounds and death of their followers; and the praefect, unable to resist or appease the tumult, was constrained by superior violence to retire into the suburbs. Damasus prevailed: the well-disputed victory remained on the side of his faction; one hundred and thirty-seven dead bodies were found in the *Basilica* of Sicininus, where the Christians hold their religious assemblies; and it was long before the angry minds of the people resumed their accustomed tranquility. When I consider the splendor of the capital, I am not astonished that so valuable a prize should inflame the desires of ambitious men, and produce the fiercest and most obstinate contests. The successful candidate is secure that he will be enriched by the offerings of matrons; that, as soon as his dress is composed with becoming care and elegance, he may proceed in his chariot through the streets of Rome; and that the sumptuousness of the Imperial table will not equal the profuse and delicate entertainments provided by the taste, and at the expense, of the Roman pontiffs. How much more rationally [continues the honest Pagan] would those pontiffs consult their true happiness if, instead of alleging the greatness of the city as an excuse for their manners, they would imitate the exemplary life of some provincial bishops, whose temperance and sobriety, whose mean apparel and downcast looks, recommend their pure and modest virtue to the Deity and his true worshipers!" The schism of Damasus and Ursinus was extinguished by the exile of the latter; and the wisdom of the praefect Praetextatus restored the tranquility of the city. Praetextatus was a philosophic Pagan, a man of learning, of taste, and politeness; who disguised a reproach in the form of a jest when he assured Damasus that if he could obtain the bishopric of Rome, he himself would immediately embrace the Christian religion. This lively picture of the wealth and luxury of the popes in the fourth century becomes the more curious as it represents the intermediate degree between the humble poverty of the apostolic fishermen and the royal state of a temporal prince whose dominions extend from the confines of Naples to the banks of the Po [i.e., the Papal territories of Gibbon's day].

When the suffrage of the generals and of the army committed the scepter of the Roman empire to the hands of Valentinian, his reputation in arms, his military skill and experience, and his rigid attachment to the forms, as well as spirit, of ancient discipline were the principal motives of their judicious choice. The eagerness of the troops who pressed him to nominate his colleague was justified by the dangerous situation of public affairs; and Valentinian himself was conscious that the abilities of the most active mind were unequal to the defense of the distant frontiers of an invaded monarchy. As soon as the death of Julian had relieved the Barbarians from the terror of his name, the most sanguine hopes of rapine and conquest excited the nations of the East, of the North, and of the South. Their inroads were often vexatious and sometimes formidable; but during the twelve years of the reign of Valentinian, his firmness and vigilance protected his own dominions; and his powerful genius seemed to inspire and direct the feeble counsels of his brother [A.D. 364–375]. Perhaps the method of annals would more forcibly express the urgent and divided cares of the two emperors; but the attention of the reader, likewise, would be distracted by a tedious and desultory narrative. A separate view of the five great theaters of war, I. Germany; II. Britain; III. Africa; IV. The East; and, V. The Danube, will impress a more distinct image of the military state of the empire under the reigns of Valentinian and Valens.

I. [Germany.] ... The wise monarch, instead of aspiring to the conquest of Germany, confined his attention to the important and laborious defense of the Gallic frontier. . . . The land was covered by the fortifications of Valentinian; but the sea-coast of Gaul and Britain was exposed to the depredations of the Saxons.†

II. [Britain.] ... Six years after the death of Constantine, the ... hostile tribes of the north, who detested the pride and power of the King of the World, suspended their domestic feuds; and the Barbarians of the land and sea, the Scots, the Picts, and the Saxons, spread themselves with rapid and irresistible fury from the wall of Antoninus to the shores of Kent. Every production of art and nature, every object of convenience and luxury, which they were incapable of creating by labor or procuring by trade was accumulated in the rich and fruitful province of Britain. A philosopher may deplore the eternal discords of the human race, but he will confess that the desire of spoil is a more rational provocation than the vanity of conquest. From the age of Constantine to the Plantagenets, this rapacious spirit continued to instigate the poor and hardy Caledonians. . . . Their southern neighbors have felt, and perhaps exaggerated, the cruel depredations of the Scots and Picts; and a valiant tribe of Caledonia, the Attacotti, the enemies and afterwards the soldiers of Valentinian, are accused, by an eyewitness, of delighting in the taste of human flesh. When they hunted the woods for prey, it is said that they attacked the shepherd rather than his flock; and that they curiously selected the most delicate and brawny parts, both of males and females, which they prepared for their horrid repasts. If in the neighborhood of the commercial and literary town of Glasgow a race of cannibals has really existed, we may contemplate, in the period of the Scottish history, the opposite extremes of savage and civilized life. Such reflections tend to enlarge the circle of our ideas; and to encourage the pleasing hope that New Zealand may produce, in some future age, the Hume of the Southern Hemisphere.

[After] a long and serious consultation, the defense, or rather the recovery, of Britain was entrusted to the abilities of the brave Theodosius [A.D. 366–370]. The exploits of that general, the father of a line of emperors, have been celebrated with peculiar complacency by the writers of the age: but his real merit deserved their applause; and his nomination was received by the army and province as a sure presage of approaching victory. . . . The scattered and desultory warfare of the Barbarians who infested the land and sea deprived him of the glory of a signal victory; but the prudent spirit and consummate art of the Roman general were displayed in the operations of two campaigns, which successively rescued every part of the province from the hands of a cruel and rapacious enemy.[†]

III. [Africa.] The prince who refuses to be the judge instructs the people to consider him as the accomplice of his ministers. The military command of Africa had been long exercised by Count Romanus, and his abilities were not inadequate to his station; but, as sordid interest was the sole motive of his conduct, he acted on most occasions as if he had been the enemy of the province, and the friend of the Barbarians of the desert.

[*The conduct of Romanus provokes rebellion (A.D. 372), which is subsequently crushed by Theodosius.*]

Africa had been lost by the vices of Romanus; it was restored by the virtues of Theodosius [A.D. 373]; and our curiosity may be usefully directed to the inquiry of the respective treatment which the two generals received from the Imperial court. The authority of Count Romanus had been suspended by the master-general of the cavalry; and he was committed to safe and honorable custody till the end of the war. His crimes were proved by the most authentic evidence; and the public expected, with some impatience, the decree of severe justice. But the partial and powerful favor of Mellobaudes encouraged him to challenge his legal judges, to obtain repeated delays for the purpose of procuring a crowd of friendly witnesses, and finally to cover his guilty conduct by the additional guilt of fraud and forgery. About the same time, the restorer of Britain and Africa, on a vague suspicion that his name and services were superior to the rank of a subject, was ignominiously beheaded at Carthage. Valentinian no longer reigned; and the death of Theodosius, as well as the impunity of Romanus, may justly be imputed to·the arts of the ministers, who abused the confidence and deceived the inexperienced youth of his sons.

If the geographical accuracy of Ammianus had been fortunately bestowed on the British exploits of Theodosius, we should have traced with eager curiosity the distinct and domestic footsteps of his march. But the tedious enumeration of the unknown and uninteresting tribes of Africa may be reduced to the general remark that they were all of the swarthy race of the Moors; that they inhabited the back settlements of the Mauritanian and Numidian province, the country, as they have since been termed by the Arabs, of dates and of locusts; and that, as the Roman power declined in Africa, the boundary of civilized manners and cultivated land was insensibly contracted. Beyond the utmost limits of the Moors, the vast and inhospitable desert of the South extends above a thousand miles to the banks of the Niger. The ancients, who had a very faint and imperfect knowledge of the great peninsula of Africa, were sometimes tempted to believe that the torrid zone must ever remain destitute of inhabitants; and they sometimes amused their fancy by filling the vacant space with headless men, or rather monsters; with horned and cloven-footed satyrs; with fabulous centaurs; and with human pygmies, who waged a bold and doubtful warfare against the cranes. Carthage would have trembled at the strange intelligence that the countries on either side of the equator were filled with innumerable nations who differed only in their color from the ordinary appearance of the human species: and the subjects of the Roman empire might have anxiously expected that the swarms of Barbarians which issued from the North would soon be encountered from the South by new swarms of Barbarians, equally fierce and equally formidable. These gloomy terrors would indeed have been dispelled by a more intimate acquaintance with the character of their African enemies. The inaction of the negroes does not seem to be the effect either of their virtue or of their pusillanimity. They indulge, like the rest of mankind, their passions and appetites; and the adjacent tribes are engaged in frequent acts of hostility. But their rude ignorance has never invented any effectual weapons of defense or of destruction; they appear incapable of forming any extensive plans of government or conquest; and the obvious inferiority of their mental faculties has been discovered and abused by the nations of the temperate zone. Sixty thousand blacks are annually embarked from the coast of Guinea, never to return to their native country; but they are embarked in chains; and this constant emigration, which, in the space of two centuries, might have furnished armies to overrun the globe, accuses the guilt of Europe, and the weakness of Africa.

IV. [The East.] The ignominious treaty which saved the army of Jovian had been faithfully executed on the side of the Romans; and as they had solemnly renounced the sovereignty and alliance of Armenia and Iberia, those tributary kingdoms were exposed without protection to the arms of the Persian monarch. Sapor entered the Armenian territories at the head of a formidable host.[†]

The Persians were surprised and repulsed under the walls of Artogerassa by a bold and well-concerted sally of the besieged. But the forces of Sapor were continually renewed and increased; the hopeless courage of the garrison was exhausted; the strength of the walls yielded to the assault; and the proud conqueror, after wasting the rebellious city with fire and sword, led away captive an unfortunate queen who, in a more auspicious hour, had been the destined bride of the son of Constantine.[†]

In the general picture of the affairs of the East under the reign of Valens, the adventures of Para form one of the most striking and singular objects. The noble youth, by the persuasion of his mother Olympias, had escaped through the Persian host that besieged Artogerassa and implored the protection of the emperor of the East. By his timid councils, Para was alternately supported, and recalled, and restored, and betrayed. The hopes of the Armenians were sometimes raised by the presence of their natural sovereign, and the ministers of Valens were satisfied that they preserved the integrity of the public faith if their vassal was not suffered to assume the diadem and title of King. But they soon repented of their own rashness. They were confounded by the reproaches and threats of the Persian monarch. They found reason to distrust the cruel and inconstant temper of Para himself; . . . and the secret sentence of his death was signed in the council of Valens. The execution of the bloody deed was committed to the subtle prudence of Count Trajan; and he had the merit of insinuating himself into the confidence of the credulous prince that he might find an opportunity of stabbing him to the heart. Para was invited to a Roman banquet, which had been prepared with all the pomp and sensuality of the East; the hall resounded with cheerful music, and the company was already heated with wine; when the count retired for an instant, drew his sword, and gave the signal of the murder. A robust and desperate Barbarian instantly rushed on the king of Armenia; and though he bravely defended his life with the first weapon that chance offered to his hand, the table of the Imperial general was stained with the royal blood of a guest and an ally [A.D. 374]. Such were the weak and wicked maxims of the Roman administration that, to attain a doubtful object of political interest, the laws of nations and the sacred rights of hospitality were inhumanly violated in the face of the world.

V. [The Danube.] During a peaceful interval of thirty years, the Romans secured their frontiers and the Goths extended their dominions. The victories of the great Hermanric, king of the Ostrogoths and the most noble of the race of the Amali, have been compared by the enthusiasm of his countrymen to the exploits of Alexander. . . . His dominions, which extended from the Danube to the Baltic, included the native seats and the recent acquisitions of the Goths; and he reigned over the greatest part of Germany and Scythia with the authority of a conqueror, and sometimes with the cruelty of a tyrant. But he reigned over a part of the globe incapable of perpetuating and adorning the glory of its heroes. The name of Hermanric is almost buried in oblivion; his exploits are imperfectly known; and the Romans themselves appeared unconscious of the progress of an aspiring power which threatened the liberty of the North and the peace of the empire.

The Goths had contracted an hereditary attachment for the Imperial house of Constantine, of whose power and liberality they had received so many signal proofs. They respected the public peace; and if a hostile band sometimes presumed to pass the Roman limit, their irregular conduct was candidly ascribed to the ungovernable spirit of the Barbarian youth. Their contempt for two new and obscure princes who had been raised to the throne by a popular election inspired the Goths with bolder hopes.

[*Hostilities ensue (A.D. 367–369).*]

The splendor and magnitude of this Gothic war are celebrated by a contemporary historian: but the events scarcely deserve the attention of posterity, except as the preliminary steps of the approaching decline and fall of the empire.[†]

After the ratification of [a] treaty and the delivery of hostages, Valens returned in triumph to Constantinople; and the Goths remained in a state of tranquility about six years; till they were violently impelled against the Roman empire by an innumerable host of Scythians, who appeared to issue from the frozen regions of the North.

The emperor of the West, who had resigned to his brother the command of the Lower Danube, reserved for his immediate care the defense of the Rhaetian and Illyrian provinces, which spread so many hundred miles along the greatest of the European rivers. The active policy of Valentinian was continually employed in adding new fortifications to the security of the frontier: but the abuse of this policy provoked the just resentment of the Barbarians. The Quadi complained that the ground for an intended fortress had been marked out on their territories [A.D. 374].[†]

[T]he haughty monarch was incapable of the magnanimity which dares to acknowledge a fault. He forgot the provocation, remembered only the injury, and advanced into the country of the Quadi with an insatiate thirst of blood and revenge. The extreme devastation and promiscuous massacre of a savage war were justified, in the eyes of the emperor and perhaps in those of the world, by the cruel equity of re-taliation. . . . While the operations of war were suspended by the se-verity of the weather, the Quadi made an humble attempt to deprecate the wrath of their conqueror. . . . [T]heir ambassadors were introduced into the Imperial council. They approached the throne with bended bodies and dejected countenances; and without daring to complain of the murder of their king [by Roman assassins], they affirmed with solemn oaths that the late invasion was the crime of some irregular robbers, which the public council of the nation condemned and ab-horred. The answer of the emperor left them but little to hope from his clemency or compassion. He reviled, in the most intemperate lan-guage, their baseness, their ingratitude, their insolence. His eyes, his voice, his color, his gestures, expressed the violence of his ungoverned fury; and while his whole frame was agitated with convulsive passion, a large blood vessel suddenly burst in his body; and Valentinian fell speechless into the arms of his attendants. Their pious care immedi-ately concealed his situation from the crowd; but in a few minutes, the emperor of the West expired in an agony of pain, retaining his senses till the last; and struggling, without success, to declare his intentions to the generals and ministers who surrounded the royal couch. Valentin-ian was about fifty-four years of age; and he wanted only one hundred days to accomplish the twelve years of his reign.

The polygamy of Valentinian is seriously attested by an ecclesiasti-cal historian. "The empress Severa [I relate the fable] admitted into her familiar society the lovely Justina, the daughter of an Italian gov-ernor: her admiration of those naked charms which she had often seen in the bath was expressed with such lavish and imprudent praise that the emperor was tempted to introduce a second wife into his bed; and his public edict extended to all the subjects of the empire the same do-mestic privilege which he had assumed for himself." But we may be as-sured, from the evidence of reason as well as history, that the two marriages of Valentinian, with Severa and with Justina, were succes-sively contracted; and that he used the ancient permission of divorce, which was still allowed by the laws, though it was condemned by the church. Severa was the mother of Gratian, who seemed to unite every claim which could entitle him to the undoubted succession of the Western empire. He was the eldest son of a monarch whose glori-ous reign had confirmed the free and honorable choice of his fellow-soldiers. Before he had attained the ninth year of his age, the royal youth received from the hands of his indulgent father the purple robe and diadem, with the title of Augustus; the election was solemnly ratified by the consent and applause of the armies of Gaul; and the name of Gratian was added to the names of Valentinian and Valens in all the legal transactions of the Roman government. By his marriage with the granddaughter of Constantine, the son of Valentinian acquired all the hereditary rights of the Flavian family; which, in a series of three Imperial generations, were sanctified by time, religion, and the reverence of the people. At the death of his father, the royal youth was in the seventeenth year of his age; and his virtues already justified the favorable opinion of the army and the people. But Gratian resided without apprehension in the palace of Treves; whilst, at the distance of many hundred miles, Valentinian suddenly expired in the camp of Bregetio. The passions which had been so long suppressed by the presence of a master immediately revived in the Imperial council; and the ambitious design of reigning in the name of an infant was artfully executed by Mellobaudes and Equitius, who commanded the attachment of the Illyrian and Italian bands. They contrived the most honorable pretenses to remove the popular leaders and the troops of Gaul, who might have asserted the claims of the lawful successor; they suggested the necessity of extinguishing the hopes of foreign and domestic enemies by a bold and decisive measure. The empress Justina, who had been left in a palace about one hundred miles from Bregetio, was respectfully invited to appear in the camp with the son of the deceased emperor. On the sixth day after the death of Valentinian, the infant prince of the same name, who was only four years old, was shown, in the arms of his mother, to the legions; and solemnly invested, by military acclamation, with the titles and ensigns of supreme power. The impending dangers of a civil war were seasonably prevented by the wise and moderate conduct of the emperor Gratian. He cheerfully accepted the choice of the army; declared that he should always consider the son of Justina as a brother, not as a rival; and advised the empress with her son Valentinian to fix their residence at Milan, in the fair and peaceful province of Italy; while he assumed the more arduous command of the countries beyond the Alps. Gratian dissembled his resentment till he could safely punish or disgrace the authors of the conspiracy; and though he uniformly behaved with tenderness and regard to his infant colleague, he gradually confounded, in the administration of the Western empire, the office of a guardian with the authority of a sovereign. The government of the Roman world was exercised in the united names of Valens and his two nephews; but the feeble emperor of the East, who succeeded to the rank of his elder brother, never obtained any weight or influence in the councils of the West.

CHAPTER XXVI

PROGRESS OF THE HUNS

*Manners of the pastoral nations. • Progress of the Huns, from
China to Europe. • Flight of the Goths. • They pass the Danube. •
Gothic war. • Defeat and death of Valens. • Gratian invests
Theodosius with the Eastern empire. • His character and success. •
Peace and settlement of the Goths.*

In the second year of the reign of Valentinian and Valens, on the
morning of the twenty-first day of July [A.D. 365], the greatest part
of the Roman world was shaken by a violent and destructive earthquake. . . . This calamity, the report of which was magnified from one
province to another, astonished and terrified the subjects of Rome; and
their affrighted imagination enlarged the real extent of a momentary
evil. They recollected the preceding earthquakes which had subverted
the cities of Palestine and Bithynia: they considered these alarming
strokes as the prelude only of still more dreadful calamities, and their
fearful vanity was disposed to confound the symptoms of a declining
empire and a sinking world. It was the fashion of the times to attribute
every remarkable event to the particular will of the Deity; the alterations of nature were connected by an invisible chain with the moral
and metaphysical opinions of the human mind; and the most sagacious divines could distinguish, according to the color of their respective prejudices, that the establishment of heresy tended to produce an
earthquake, or that a deluge was the inevitable consequence of the
progress of sin and error. Without presuming to discuss the truth or
propriety of these lofty speculations, the historian may content himself with an observation, which seems to be justified by experience, that
man has much more to fear from the passions of his fellow-creatures
than from the convulsions of the elements. The mischievous effects of
an earthquake or deluge, a hurricane or the eruption of a volcano, bear
a very inconsiderable portion to the ordinary calamities of war. . . . In
the disastrous period of the fall of the Roman empire, which may justly
be dated from the reign of Valens, the happiness and security of each
individual were personally attacked; and the arts and labors of ages

were rudely defaced by the Barbarians of Scythia and Germany. The invasion of the Huns precipitated on the provinces of the West the Gothic nation, which advanced in less than forty years from the Danube to the Atlantic, and opened a way, by the success of their arms, to the inroads of so many hostile tribes more savage than themselves. The original principle of motion was concealed in the remote countries of the North; and the curious observation of the pastoral life of the Scythians, or Tartars, will illustrate the latent cause of these destructive emigrations.[†]

In every age, the immense plains of Scythia, or Tartary, have been inhabited by vagrant tribes of hunters and shepherds whose indolence refuses to cultivate the earth, and whose restless spirit disdains the confinement of a sedentary life. In every age, the Scythians and Tartars have been renowned for their invincible courage and rapid conquests. The thrones of Asia have been repeatedly overturned by the shepherds of the North; and their arms have spread terror and devastation over the most fertile and warlike countries of Europe. On this occasion, as well as on many others, the sober historian is forcibly awakened from a pleasing vision; and is compelled with some reluctance to confess that the pastoral manners, which have been adorned with the fairest attributes of peace and innocence, are much better adapted to the fierce and cruel habits of a military life.[†]

The political society of the ancient Germans has the appearance of a voluntary alliance of independent warriors. The tribes of Scythia, distinguished by the modern appellation of *Hords,* assume the form of a numerous and increasing family; which, in the course of successive generations, has been propagated from the same original stock. The meanest and most ignorant of the Tartars preserve, with conscious pride, the inestimable treasure of their genealogy; and whatever distinctions of rank may have been introduced by the unequal distribution of pastoral wealth, they mutually respect themselves, and each other, as the descendants of the first founder of the tribe. The custom, which still prevails, of adopting the bravest and most faithful of the captives may countenance the very probable suspicion that this extensive consanguinity is, in a great measure, legal and fictitious. But the useful prejudice which has obtained the sanction of time and opinion produces the effects of truth; the haughty Barbarians yield a cheerful and voluntary obedience to the head of their blood; and their chief, or *mursa,* as the representative of their great father, exercises the authority of a judge in peace, and of a leader in war. In the original state of the pastoral world, each of the *mursas* (if we may continue to use a modern appellation) acted as the independent chief of a large and separate family; and the limits of their peculiar territories were gradually fixed by superior force or mutual consent. But the constant operation of various and permanent causes contributed to unite the vagrant Hords into national communities, under the command of a supreme head [or khan]. . . . The immediate jurisdiction of the khan is confined within the limits of his own tribe; and the exercise of his royal prerogative has been moderated by the ancient institution of a national council. The *Coroultai,* or Diet, of the Tartars was regularly held in the spring and autumn, in the midst of a plain; where the princes of the reigning family and the *mursas* of the respective tribes may conveniently assemble on horseback, with their martial and numerous trains; and the ambitious monarch who reviewed the strength must consult the inclination of an armed people. The rudiments of a feudal government may be discovered in the constitution of the Scythian or Tartar nations; but the perpetual conflict of those hostile nations has sometimes terminated in the establishment of a powerful and despotic empire. The victor, enriched by the tribute and fortified by the arms of dependent kings, has spread his conquests over Europe or Asia: the successful shepherds of the North have submitted to the confinement of arts, of laws, and of cities; and the introduction of luxury, after destroying the freedom of the people, has undermined the foundations of the throne.†

The Huns, who under the reign of Valens threatened the empire of Rome, had been formidable, in a much earlier period [circa 200 B.C.], to the empire of China. Their ancient, perhaps their original, seat was an extensive though dry and barren tract of country immediately on the north side of the great wall. Their place is at present occupied by the forty-nine Hords or Banners of the Mongous, a pastoral nation which consists of about two hundred thousand families. But the valor of the Huns had extended the narrow limits of their dominions; and their rustic chiefs, who assumed the appellation of *Tanjou,* gradually became the conquerors and the sovereigns of a formidable empire. Towards the East, their victorious arms were stopped only by the ocean. . . . The submission of so many distant nations might flatter the pride of the Tanjou; but the valor of the Huns could be rewarded only by the enjoyment of the wealth and luxury of the empire of the South. In the third century before the Christian era, a wall of fifteen hundred miles in length was constructed to defend the frontiers of China against the inroads of the Huns; but this stupendous work, which holds a conspicuous place in the map of the world, has never contributed to the safety of an unwarlike people.[†]

The conquest of China has been twice achieved by the pastoral tribes of the North: the forces of the Huns were not inferior to those of the Moguls, or of the Mantcheoux; and their ambition might entertain the most sanguine hopes of success. But their pride was humbled, and their progress was checked; ... and the power of the Tanjous, after a reign of thirteen hundred years, was utterly destroyed before the end of the first century of the Christian era.

[The fate of these vanquished Huns is diversified, and it] is impossible to fill the dark interval of time which elapsed after the Huns of the Volga were lost in the eyes of the Chinese and before they showed themselves to those of the Romans. There is some reason, however, to apprehend that the same force which had driven them from their native seats still continued to impel their march towards the frontiers of Europe; ... and the Huns ... proceeded, with an increase of numbers and confidence, to invade the limits of the Gothic empire.[†]

After Valens had terminated the Gothic war with some appearance of glory and success, he made a progress through his dominions of Asia, and at length fixed his residence in the capital of Syria [A.D. 376]. The five years which he spent at Antioch were employed to watch, from a secure distance, the hostile designs of the Persian monarch; to check the depredations of the Saracens and Isaurians; to enforce, by arguments more prevalent than those of reason and eloquence, the belief of the Arian theology; and to satisfy his anxious suspicions by the promiscuous execution of the innocent and the guilty. But the attention of the emperor was most seriously engaged by the important intelligence which he received from the civil and military officers who were entrusted with the defense of the Danube. He was informed that the North was agitated by a furious tempest; that the irruption of the Huns, an unknown and monstrous race of savages, had subverted the power of the Goths; and that the suppliant multitudes of that warlike nation, whose pride was now humbled in the dust, covered a space of many miles along the banks of the river. With outstretched arms and pathetic lamentations, they loudly deplored their past misfortunes and their present danger; acknowledged that their only hope of safety was in the clemency of the Roman government; and most solemnly protested that if the gracious liberality of the emperor would permit them to cultivate the waste lands of Thrace, they should ever hold themselves bound, by the strongest obligations of duty and gratitude, to obey the laws, and to guard the limits of the republic.... The prayers of the Goths were granted, and their service was accepted by the Imperial court: and orders were immediately despatched to the civil and military governors of the Thracian diocese to make the necessary preparations for the passage and subsistence of a great people, till a proper and sufficient territory could be allotted for their future residence.

[*After their admission, the Goths rise up in revolt (A.D. 377). In the West, however, Gratian is victorious over the Alemanni (May A.D. 378).*]

While Gratian deserved and enjoyed the applause of his subjects, the emperor Valens, who at length had removed his court and army from Antioch, was received by the people of Constantinople as the author of the public calamity. Before he had reposed himself ten days in the capital [May 30–June 11, A.D. 378], he was urged by the licentious clamors of the Hippodrome to march against the Barbarians whom he had invited into his dominions; and the citizens, who are always brave at a distance from any real danger, declared with confidence that if they were supplied with arms, they alone would undertake to deliver the province from the ravages of an insulting foe. The vain reproaches of an ignorant multitude hastened the downfall of the Roman empire; they provoked the desperate rashness of Valens; who did not find, either in his reputation or in his mind, any motives to support with firmness the public contempt. He was soon persuaded by the successful achievements of his lieutenants to despise the power of the Goths, who ... were now collected in the neighborhood of Hadrianople.[†]

On the ninth of August [A.D. 378], a day which has deserved to be marked among the most inauspicious of the Roman Calendar, the emperor Valens, leaving under a strong guard his baggage and military treasure, marched from Hadrianople to attack the Goths, who were encamped about twelve miles from the city.... The event of the battle of Hadrianople, so fatal to Valens and to the empire, may be described in a few words: the Roman cavalry fled; the infantry was abandoned, surrounded, and cut in pieces. The most skillful evolutions, the firmest courage, are scarcely sufficient to extricate a body of foot encompassed on an open plain by superior numbers of horse; but the troops of Valens, oppressed by the weight of the enemy and their own fears, were crowded into a narrow space where it was impossible for them to extend their ranks, or even to use with effect their swords and javelins. In the midst of tumult, of slaughter, and of dismay, the emperor, deserted by his guards and wounded, as it was supposed, with an arrow, sought protection among the Lancearii and the Mattiarii, who still maintained their ground with some appearance of order and firmness. His faithful generals, Trajan and Victor, who perceived his danger, loudly exclaimed that all was lost unless the person of the emperor could be saved. Some troops, animated by their exhortation, advanced to his relief: they found only a bloody spot covered with a heap of broken arms and mangled bodies, without being able to discover their unfortunate prince, either among the living or the dead. Their search could not indeed be successful, if there is any truth in the circumstances with which some historians have related the death of the emperor. By the care of his attendants, Valens was removed from the field of battle to a neighboring cottage, where they attempted to dress his wound and to provide for his future safety. But this humble retreat was instantly surrounded by the enemy: they tried to force the door, they were provoked by a discharge of arrows from the roof, till at length, impatient of delay, they set fire to a pile of dry faggots and consumed the cottage with the Roman emperor and his train. Valens perished in the flames; and a youth who dropped from the window alone escaped to attest the melancholy tale, and to inform the Goths of the inestimable prize which they had lost by their own rashness. A great number of brave and distinguished officers perished in the battle of Hadrianople, which equaled in the actual loss, and far surpassed in the fatal consequences, the misfortune which Rome had formerly sustained in the fields of Cannae [216 B.C.].†

The tide of the Gothic inundation rolled from the walls of Hadrianople to the suburbs of Constantinople. The Barbarians were surprised with the splendid appearance of the capital of the East, the

height and extent of the walls, the myriads of wealthy and affrighted
citizens who crowded the ramparts, and the various prospect of the sea
and land. While they gazed with hopeless desire on the inaccessible
beauties of Constantinople, a sally was made from one of the gates by
a party of Saracens who had been fortunately engaged in the service of
Valens. The cavalry of Scythia was forced to yield to the admirable
swiftness and spirit of the Arabian horses: their riders were skilled in
the evolutions of irregular war; and the Northern Barbarians were astonished and dismayed by the inhuman ferocity of the Barbarians of
the South. A Gothic soldier was slain by the dagger of an Arab; and the
hairy, naked savage, applying his lips to the wound, expressed a horrid
delight while he sucked the blood of his vanquished enemy. The army
of the Goths, laden with the spoils of the wealthy suburbs and the adjacent territory, slowly moved from the Bosphorus to the mountains
which form the western boundary of Thrace.†

The Romans, who so coolly and so concisely mention the acts of
justice which were exercised by the legions, reserve their compassion
and their eloquence for their own sufferings when the provinces were
invaded and desolated by the arms of the successful Barbarians. The
simple circumstantial narrative (did such a narrative exist) of the ruin
of a single town, of the misfortunes of a single family, might exhibit an
interesting and instructive picture of human manners: but the tedious
repetition of vague and declamatory complaints would fatigue the attention of the most patient reader. The same censure may be applied,
though not perhaps in an equal degree, to the profane and the ecclesiastical writers of this unhappy period; that their minds were inflamed
by popular and religious animosity; and that the true size and color
of every object is falsified by the exaggerations of their corrupt eloquence. The vehement Jerome might justly deplore the calamities inflicted by the Goths and their barbarous allies on his native country of
Pannonia and the wide extent of the provinces, from the walls of Constantinople to the foot of the Julian Alps; the rapes, the massacres, the
conflagrations; and, above all, the profanation of the churches that
were turned into stables, and the contemptuous treatment of the relics
of holy martyrs. But the Saint is surely transported beyond the limits
of nature and history when he affirms "that in those desert countries,
nothing was left except the sky and the earth; that after the destruction
of the cities and the extirpation of the human race, the land was over-

grown with thick forests and inextricable brambles; and that the universal desolation announced by the prophet Zephaniah was accomplished, in the scarcity of the beasts, the birds, and even of the fish." These complaints were pronounced about twenty years after the death of Valens; and the Illyrian provinces, which were constantly exposed to the invasion and passage of the Barbarians, still continued, after a calamitous period of ten centuries, to supply new materials for rapine and destruction. Could it even be supposed that a large tract of country had been left without cultivation and without inhabitants, the consequences might not have been so fatal to the inferior productions of animated nature. The useful and feeble animals which are nourished by the hand of man might suffer and perish if they were deprived of his protection; but the beasts of the forest, his enemies or his victims, would multiply in the free and undisturbed possession of their solitary domain. The various tribes that people the air, or the waters, are still less connected with the fate of the human species; and it is highly probable that the fish of the Danube would have felt more terror and distress from the approach of a voracious pike than from the hostile inroad of a Gothic army.

Whatever may have been the just measure of the calamities of Europe, there was reason to fear that the same calamities would soon extend to the peaceful countries of Asia. The sons of the Goths had been judiciously distributed through the cities of the East; and the arts of education were employed to polish and subdue the native fierceness of their temper. In the space of about twelve years, their numbers had continually increased; and the children who in the first emigration were sent over the Hellespont had attained, with rapid growth, the strength and spirit of perfect manhood. It was impossible to conceal from their knowledge the events of the Gothic war; and as those daring youths had not studied the language of dissimulation, they betrayed their wish, their desire, perhaps their intention to emulate the glorious example of their fathers. The danger of the times seemed to justify the jealous suspicions of the provincials; and these suspicions were admitted as unquestionable evidence that the Goths of Asia had formed a secret and dangerous conspiracy against the public safety. The death of Valens had left the East without a sovereign; and Julius, who filled the important station of master-general of the troops with a high reputation of diligence and ability, thought it his duty to consult the senate of Constantinople; which he considered, during the vacancy of the throne, as the representative council of the nation. As soon as he had obtained the discretionary power of acting as he should judge most expedient for the good of the republic, he assembled the principal officers and privately concerted effectual measures for the execution of his bloody design. An order was immediately promulgated that, on a stated day, the Gothic youth should assemble in the capital cities of their respective provinces; and as a report was industriously circulated that they were summoned to receive a liberal gift of lands and money, the pleasing hope allayed the fury of their resentment and, perhaps, suspended the motions of the conspiracy. On the appointed day, the unarmed crowd of the Gothic youth was carefully collected in the square or Forum; the streets and avenues were occupied by the Roman troops, and the roofs of the houses were covered with archers and slingers. At the same hour, in all the cities of the East, the signal was given of indiscriminate slaughter; and the provinces of Asia were delivered by the cruel prudence of Julius from a domestic enemy who, in a few months, might have carried fire and sword from the Hellespont to the Euphrates [A.D. 378]. The urgent consideration of the public safety may undoubtedly authorize the violation of every positive law. How far that, or any other, consideration may operate to dissolve the natural obligations of humanity and justice is a doctrine of which I still desire to remain ignorant.

The emperor Gratian was far advanced on his march towards the plains of Hadrianople when he was informed, at first by the confused voice of fame and afterwards by the more accurate reports of Victor and Richomer, that his impatient colleague had been slain in battle, and that two thirds of the Roman army were exterminated by the sword of the victorious Goths. Whatever resentment the rash and jealous vanity of his uncle might deserve, the resentment of a generous mind is easily subdued by the softer emotions of grief and compassion; and even the sense of pity was soon lost in the serious and alarming consideration of the state of the republic. Gratian was too late to assist, he was too weak to revenge, his unfortunate colleague; and the valiant and modest youth felt himself unequal to the support of a sinking world. A formidable tempest of the Barbarians of Germany seemed ready to burst over the provinces of Gaul; and the mind of Gratian was oppressed and distracted by the administration of the Western empire.

In this important crisis, the government of the East and the conduct of the Gothic war required the undivided attention of a hero and a statesman. A subject invested with such ample command would not long have preserved his fidelity to a distant benefactor; and the Imperial council embraced the wise and manly resolution of conferring an obligation, rather than of yielding to an insult. It was the wish of Gratian to bestow the purple as the reward of virtue; but at the age of nineteen, it is not easy for a prince, educated in the supreme rank, to understand the true characters of his ministers and generals. He attempted to weigh with an impartial hand their various merits and defects; and, whilst he checked the rash confidence of ambition, he distrusted the cautious wisdom which despaired of the republic. As each moment of delay diminished something of the power and resources of the future sovereign of the East, the situation of the times would not allow a tedious debate. The choice of Gratian was soon declared in favor of an exile whose father, only three years before, had suffered, under the sanction of *his* authority, an unjust and ignominious death. The great Theodosius, a name celebrated in history and dear to the Catholic church, was summoned to the Imperial court, which had gradually retreated from the confines of Thrace to the more secure station of Sirmium. Five months after the death of Valens, the emperor Gratian produced before the assembled troops *his* colleague and *their* master; who, after a modest, perhaps a sincere, resistance, was compelled to accept, amidst the general acclamations, the diadem, the purple, and the equal title of Augustus [January 19, A.D. 379]. The provinces of Thrace, Asia, and Egypt, over which Valens had reigned, were resigned to the administration of the new emperor; but as he was specially entrusted with the conduct of the Gothic war, the Illyrian praefecture was dismembered; and the two great dioceses of Dacia and Macedonia were added to the dominions of the Eastern empire.†

From the innocent but humble labors of his farm, Theodosius was transported, in less than four months, to the throne of the Eastern empire; and the whole period of the history of the world will not perhaps afford a similar example of an elevation at the same time so pure and so honorable. . . . What confidence must have been reposed in his integrity, since Gratian could trust that a pious son would forgive, for the sake of the republic, the murder of his father! What expectations must have been formed of his abilities to encourage the hope that a single man could save, and restore, the empire of the East! Theodosius was invested with the purple in the thirty-third year of his age. The vulgar gazed with admiration on the manly beauty of his face and the graceful majesty of his person, which they were pleased to compare with the pictures and medals of the emperor Trajan; whilst intelligent observers discovered, in the qualities of his heart and understanding, a more important resemblance to the best and greatest of the Roman princes.

It is not without the most sincere regret that I must now take leave of an accurate and faithful guide who has composed the history of his own times without indulging the prejudices and passions which usually affect the mind of a contemporary. Ammianus Marcellinus, who terminates his useful work with the defeat and death of Valens, recommends the more glorious subject of the ensuing reign to the youthful vigor and eloquence of the rising generation. The rising generation was not disposed to accept his advice or to imitate his example; and in the study of the reign of Theodosius, we are reduced to illustrate the partial narrative of Zosimus by the obscure hints of fragments and chronicles, by the figurative style of poetry or panegyric, and by the precarious assistance of the ecclesiastical writers, who, in the heat of religious faction, are apt to despise the profane virtues of sincerity and moderation. Conscious of these disadvantages, which will continue to involve a considerable portion of the decline and fall of the Roman empire, I shall proceed with doubtful and timorous steps. Yet I may boldly pronounce that the battle of Hadrianople was never revenged by any signal or decisive victory of Theodosius over the Barbarians: and the expressive silence of his venal orators may be confirmed by the observation of the condition and circumstances of the times. The fabric of a mighty state which has been reared by the labors of successive ages could not be overturned by the misfortune of a single day, if the fatal power of the imagination did not exaggerate the real measure of the calamity. The loss of forty thousand Romans who fell in the plains of Hadrianople might have been soon recruited in the populous provinces of the East, which contained so many millions of inhabitants. The courage of a soldier is found to be the cheapest and most common quality of human nature; and sufficient skill to encounter an undisciplined foe might have been speedily taught by the care of the surviving centurions. If the Barbarians were mounted on the horses

and equipped with the armor of their vanquished enemies, the numerous studs of Cappadocia and Spain would have supplied new squadrons
of cavalry; the thirty-four arsenals of the empire were plentifully stored
with magazines of offensive and defensive arms: and the wealth of Asia
might still have yielded an ample fund for the expenses of the war. But
the effects which were produced by the battle of Hadrianople on the
minds of the Barbarians and of the Romans extended the victory of
the former and the defeat of the latter far beyond the limits of a single
day. . . . The same terrors which the name of the Huns had spread
among the Gothic tribes were inspired by the formidable name of the
Goths among the subjects and soldiers of the Roman empire. If Theodosius, hastily collecting his scattered forces, had led them into the
field to encounter a victorious enemy, his army would have been vanquished by their own fears; and his rashness could not have been excused by the chance of success. But the *great* Theodosius, an epithet
which he honorably deserved on this momentous occasion, conducted
himself as the firm and faithful guardian of the republic. He fixed his
head-quarters at Thessalonica, the capital of the Macedonian diocese
[spring A.D. 379]; from whence he could watch the irregular motions of
the Barbarians and direct the operations of his lieutenants, from the
gates of Constantinople to the shores of the Hadriatic. The fortifications and garrisons of the cities were strengthened; and the troops,
among whom a sense of order and discipline was revived, were insensibly emboldened by the confidence of their own safety. From these
secure stations, they were encouraged to make frequent sallies on the
Barbarians who infested the adjacent country; and as they were seldom
allowed to engage without some decisive superiority, either of ground
or of numbers, their enterprises were for the most part successful; and
they were soon convinced, by their own experience, of the possibility
of vanquishing their *invincible* enemies.[†]

The deliverance and peace of the Roman provinces was the work of
prudence rather than of valor: the prudence of Theodosius was seconded by fortune: and the emperor never failed to seize, and to improve, every favorable circumstance [A.D. 379–382].[†]

On this occasion, as well as on many others, it is a difficult task to
reconcile the passions and prejudices of the writers of the age of Theodosius. . . . The original treaty which fixed the settlement of the Goths,
ascertained their privileges, and stipulated their obligations would il-

lustrate the history of Theodosius and his successors [A.D. 383–395]. The series of their history has imperfectly preserved the spirit and substance of this single agreement. The ravages of war and tyranny had provided many large tracts of fertile but uncultivated land for the use of those Barbarians who might not disdain the practice of agriculture. A numerous colony of the Visigoths was seated in Thrace; the remains of the Ostrogoths were planted in Phrygia and Lydia; their immediate wants were supplied by a distribution of corn and cattle; and their future industry was encouraged by an exemption from tribute during a certain term of years. The Barbarians would have deserved to feel the cruel and perfidious policy of the Imperial court if they had suffered themselves to be dispersed through the provinces. They required, and they obtained, the sole possession of the villages and districts assigned for their residence; they still cherished and propagated their native manners and language; asserted, in the bosom of despotism, the freedom of their domestic government; and acknowledged the sovereignty of the emperor without submitting to the inferior jurisdiction of the laws and magistrates of Rome. The hereditary chiefs of the tribes and families were still permitted to command their followers in peace and war; but the royal dignity was abolished; and the generals of the Goths were appointed and removed at the pleasure of the emperor. An army of forty thousand Goths was maintained for the perpetual service of the empire of the East; and those haughty troops, who assumed the title of *Foederati,* or allies, were distinguished by their gold collars, liberal pay, and licentious privileges. Their native courage was improved by the use of arms and the knowledge of discipline; and while the republic was guarded, or threatened, by the doubtful sword of the Barbarians, the last sparks of the military flame were finally extinguished in the minds of the Romans. Theodosius had the address to persuade his allies that the conditions of peace which had been extorted from him by prudence and necessity were the voluntary expressions of his sincere friendship for the Gothic nation. A different mode of vindication or apology was opposed to the complaints of the people; who loudly censured these shameful and dangerous concessions. The calamities of the war were painted in the most lively colors; and the first symptoms of the return of order, of plenty, and security were diligently exaggerated. The advocates of Theodosius could affirm, with some appearance of truth and reason, that it was impossible to extirpate so many warlike tribes who were rendered desperate by the loss of their native country; and that the exhausted provinces would be revived by a fresh supply of soldiers and husbandmen. The Barbarians still wore an angry and hostile aspect; but the experience of past times might encourage the hope that they would acquire the habits of industry and obedience; that their manners would be polished by time, education, and the influence of Christianity; and that their posterity would insensibly blend with the great body of the Roman people.

Notwithstanding these specious arguments and these sanguine expectations, it was apparent to every discerning eye that the Goths would long remain the enemies, and might soon become the conquerors, of the Roman empire. Their rude and insolent behavior expressed their contempt of the citizens and provincials whom they insulted with impunity. To the zeal and valor of the Barbarians Theodosius was indebted for the success of his arms: but their assistance was precarious; and they were sometimes seduced, by a treacherous and inconstant disposition, to abandon his standard at the moment when their service was the most essential . . . ; and, as the impatient Goths could only be restrained by the firm and temperate character of Theodosius, the public safety seemed to depend on the life and abilities of a single man.

END OF THE SECOND VOLUME [1781].

VOLUME THE THIRD

[1781]

THE ROMAN EMPIRE

UNDER THEODORIC
CIRCA A.D. 500

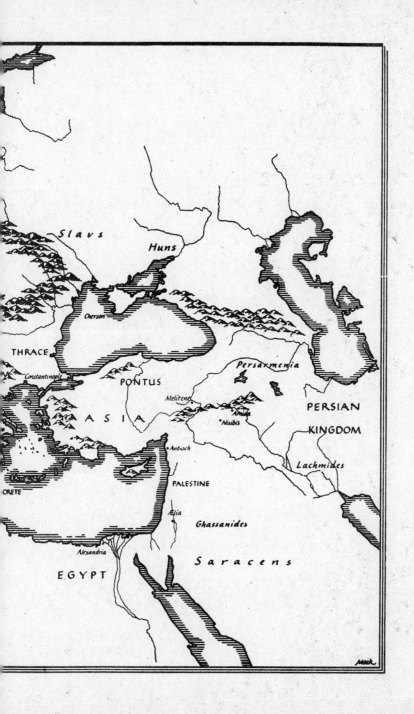

CHAPTER XXVII

CIVIL WARS, REIGN OF THEODOSIUS

*Death of Gratian. • Ruin of Arianism. • First civil war, against
Maximus. • Character and administration of Theodosius. • Death
of Valentinian II. • Second civil war, against Eugenius. •
Death of Theodosius.*

The fame of Gratian, before he had accomplished the twentieth year
of his age, was equal to that of the most celebrated princes. His gentle
and amiable disposition endeared him to his private friends, the graceful affability of his manners engaged the affection of the people: the
men of letters, who enjoyed the liberality, acknowledged the taste and
eloquence, of their sovereign; his valor and dexterity in arms were
equally applauded by the soldiers; and the clergy considered the humble piety of Gratian as the first and most useful of his virtues. The victory of Colmar had delivered the West from a formidable invasion;
and the grateful provinces of the East ascribed the merits of Theodosius to the author of *his* greatness, and of the public safety. Gratian
survived those memorable events only four or five years; but he survived his reputation; and before he fell a victim to rebellion, he had
lost, in a great measure, the respect and confidence of the Roman
world [A.D. 379–383].

The remarkable alteration of his character or conduct may not be
imputed to the arts of flattery, which had besieged the son of Valentinian from his infancy; nor to the headstrong passions which that gentle youth appears to have escaped. A more attentive view of the life of
Gratian may perhaps suggest the true cause of the disappointment of
the public hopes. His apparent virtues, instead of being the hardy productions of experience and adversity, were the premature and artificial
fruits of a royal education. The anxious tenderness of his father was
continually employed to bestow on him those advantages which he
might perhaps esteem the more highly as he himself had been deprived of them; and the most skillful masters of every science and of
every art had labored to form the mind and body of the young prince.
The knowledge which they painfully communicated was displayed

with ostentation, and celebrated with lavish praise. His soft and tractable disposition received the fair impression of their judicious precepts, and the absence of passion might easily be mistaken for the strength of reason. His preceptors gradually rose to the rank and consequence of ministers of state: and as they wisely dissembled their secret authority, he seemed to act with firmness, with propriety, and with judgment on the most important occasions of his life and reign. But the influence of this elaborate instruction did not penetrate beyond the surface; and the skillful preceptors who so accurately guided the steps of their royal pupil could not infuse into his feeble and indolent character the vigorous and independent principle of action which renders the laborious pursuit of glory essentially necessary to the happiness, and almost to the existence, of the hero. As soon as time and accident had removed those faithful counselors from the throne, the emperor of the West insensibly descended to the level of his natural genius; abandoned the reins of government to the ambitious hands which were stretched forwards to grasp them; and amused his leisure with the most frivolous gratifications. A public sale of favor and injustice was instituted, both in the court and in the provinces, by the worthless delegates of his power, whose merit it was made *sacrilege* to question [A.D. 380]. The conscience of the credulous prince was directed by saints and bishops; who procured an Imperial edict to punish, as a capital offense, the violation, the neglect, or even the ignorance of the divine law. Among the various arts which had exercised the youth of Gratian, he had applied himself with singular inclination and success to manage the horse, to draw the bow, and to dart the javelin; and these qualifications, which might be useful to a soldier, were prostituted to the viler purposes of hunting. Large parks were enclosed for the Imperial pleasures, and plentifully stocked with every species of wild beasts; and Gratian neglected the duties, and even the dignity, of his rank to consume whole days in the vain display of his dexterity and boldness in the chase. The pride and wish of the Roman emperor to excel in an art in which he might be surpassed by the meanest of his slaves reminded the numerous spectators of the examples of Nero and Commodus, but the chaste and temperate Gratian was a stranger to their monstrous vices; and his hands were stained only with the blood of animals. The behavior of Gratian, which degraded his character in the eyes of mankind, could not have disturbed the security of his reign, if the army had not been provoked to resent their peculiar injuries.

[*The soldiers of Britain revolt and declare for Maximus, who takes the offensive. Gratian is executed (A.D. 383).*]

The assassin of Gratian had usurped, but he actually possessed, the most warlike provinces of the empire: the East was exhausted by the misfortunes, and even by the success, of the Gothic war; and it was seriously to be apprehended that, after the vital strength of the republic had been wasted in a doubtful and destructive contest, the feeble conqueror would remain an easy prey to the Barbarians of the North. These weighty considerations engaged Theodosius to dissemble his resentment, and to accept the alliance of the tyrant [A.D. 383–387]. But he stipulated that Maximus should content himself with the possession of the countries beyond the Alps. The brother of Gratian was confirmed and secured in the sovereignty of Italy, Africa, and the Western Illyricum; and some honorable conditions were inserted in the treaty to protect the memory and the laws of the deceased emperor. According to the custom of the age, the images of the three Imperial colleagues were exhibited to the veneration of the people; nor should it be lightly supposed that, in the moment of a solemn reconciliation, Theodosius secretly cherished the intention of perfidy and revenge.

The contempt of Gratian for the Roman soldiers had exposed him to the fatal effects of their resentment. His profound veneration for the Christian clergy was rewarded by the applause and gratitude of a powerful order, which has claimed in every age the privilege of dispensing honors, both on earth and in Heaven. The orthodox bishops bewailed his death, and their own irreparable loss; but they were soon comforted by the discovery that Gratian had committed the scepter of the East to the hands of a prince whose humble faith and fervent zeal were supported by the spirit and abilities of a more vigorous character. Among the benefactors of the church, the fame of Constantine has been rivaled by the glory of Theodosius. If Constantine had the advantage of erecting the standard of the cross, the emulation of his successor assumed the merit of subduing the Arian heresy and of abolishing the worship of idols in the Roman world. Theodosius was the first of the emperors baptized in the true faith of the Trinity. Although he was born of a Christian family, the maxims, or at least the practice, of the age encouraged him to delay the ceremony of his initiation; till he was admonished of the danger of delay by the serious illness which threatened his life towards the end of the first year of his reign. Before he again took the field against the Goths, he received the sacrament of baptism from Acholius, the orthodox bishop of Thessalonica [February 28, A.D. 380]: and as the emperor ascended from the holy font, still glowing with the warm feelings of regeneration, he dictated a solemn edict, which proclaimed his own faith and prescribed the religion of his subjects. "It is our pleasure [such is the Imperial style] that all the nations which are governed by our clemency and moderation should steadfastly adhere to the religion which was taught by St. Peter to the Romans; which faithful tradition has preserved; and which is now professed by the pontiff Damasus and by Peter, bishop of Alexandria, a man of apostolic holiness. According to the discipline of the apostles and the doctrine of the gospel, let us believe the sole deity of the Father, the Son, and the Holy Ghost; under an equal majesty and a pious Trinity. We authorize the followers of this doctrine to assume the title of Catholic Christians; and as we judge that all others are extravagant madmen, we brand them with the infamous name of Heretics; and declare that their conventicles shall no longer usurp the respectable appellation of churches. Besides the condemnation of divine justice, they must expect to suffer the severe penalties which our authority, guided by heavenly wisdom, shall think proper to inflict upon them." The faith of a soldier is commonly the fruit of instruction, rather than of inquiry; but as the emperor always fixed his eyes on the visible landmarks of orthodoxy which he had so prudently constituted, his religious opinions were never affected by the specious texts, the subtle arguments, and the ambiguous creeds of the Arian doctors. Once indeed he expressed a faint inclination to converse with the eloquent and learned Eunomius, who lived in retirement at a small distance from Constantinople. But the dangerous interview was prevented by the prayers of the empress Flaccilla, who trembled for the salvation of her husband; and the mind of Theodosius was confirmed by a theological argument adapted to the rudest capacity. He had lately bestowed on his eldest son, Arcadius, the name and honors of Augustus, and the two princes were seated on a stately throne to receive the homage of their subjects. A bishop, Amphilochius of Iconium, approached the throne, and after saluting with due reverence the person of his sovereign, he accosted the royal youth with the same familiar tenderness which he might have used towards a plebeian child. Provoked by this insolent behavior, the monarch gave orders that the rustic priest should be instantly driven from his presence. But while the guards were forcing him to the door, the dexterous polemic had time to execute his design by exclaiming, with a loud voice, "Such is the treatment, O emperor!, which the King of Heaven has prepared for those impious men who affect to worship the Father but refuse to acknowledge the equal majesty of his divine Son." Theodosius immediately embraced the bishop of Iconium, and never forgot the important lesson, which he had received from this dramatic parable.†

The Catholics of Constantinople were animated with joyful confidence by the baptism and edict of Theodosius; and they impatiently waited the effects of his gracious promise. Their hopes were speedily accomplished; and the emperor, as soon as he had finished the operations of the campaign, made his public entry into the capital at the head of a victorious army [November 24, A.D. 380]. The next day after his arrival, he summoned Damophilus to his presence, and offered that Arian prelate the hard alternative of subscribing the Nicene creed or of instantly resigning to the orthodox believers the use and possession of the episcopal palace, the cathedral of St. Sophia, and all the churches of Constantinople. The zeal of Damophilus, which in a Catholic saint would have been justly applauded, embraced without hesitation a life of poverty and exile, and his removal was immediately followed by the purification of the Imperial city. The Arians might complain, with some appearance of justice, that an inconsiderable congregation of sectaries should usurp the hundred churches which they were insufficient to fill; whilst the far greater part of the people was cruelly excluded from every place of religious worship. Theodosius was still inexorable; but as the angels who protected the Catholic cause were only visible to the eyes of faith, he prudently reinforced those heavenly legions with the more effectual aid of temporal and carnal weapons; and the church of St. Sophia was occupied by a large body of the Imperial guards. ....The writings of the Arians, if they had been permitted to exist, would perhaps contain the lamentable story of the persecution which afflicted the church under the reign of the impious Theodosius; and the sufferings of their holy confessors might claim the pity of the disinterested reader. Yet there is reason to imagine that the violence of zeal and revenge was in some measure eluded by the want of resistance; and that in their adversity the Arians displayed much less firmness than had been exerted by the orthodox party under the reigns of Constantius and Valens. The moral character and conduct of the hostile sects appear to have been governed by the same common principles of nature and religion: but a very material circumstance may be discovered which tended to distinguish the degrees of their theological faith. Both parties, in the schools as well as in the temples, acknowledged and worshiped the divine majesty of Christ; and, as we are always prone to impute our own sentiments and passions to the Deity, it would be deemed more prudent and respectful to exaggerate than to circumscribe the adorable perfections of the Son of God. The disciple of Athanasius exulted in the proud confidence that he had entitled himself to the divine favor; while the follower of Arius must have been tormented by the secret apprehension that he was guilty, perhaps, of an unpardonable offense by the scanty praise and parsimonious honors which he bestowed on the Judge of the World. The opinions of Arianism might satisfy a cold and speculative mind: but the doctrine of the Nicene creed, most powerfully recommended by the merits of faith and devotion, was much better adapted to become popular and successful in a believing age.

The hope that truth and wisdom would be found in the assemblies of the orthodox clergy induced the emperor to convene at Constantinople a synod of one hundred and fifty bishops [A.D. 381], who proceeded, without much difficulty or delay, to complete the theological system which had been established in the council of Nice. The vehement disputes of the fourth century had been chiefly employed on the nature of the Son of God; and the various opinions which were embraced concerning the *Second* were extended and transferred, by a natural analogy, to the *Third* person of the Trinity. Yet it was found, or it was thought, necessary by the victorious adversaries of Arianism to explain the ambiguous language of some respectable doctors; to confirm the faith of the Catholics; and to condemn an unpopular and inconsistent sect of Macedonians, who freely admitted that the Son was consubstantial to the Father, while they were fearful of seeming to acknowledge the existence of *Three* Gods. A final and unanimous sentence was pronounced to ratify the equal Deity of the Holy Ghost: the mysterious doctrine has been received by all the nations and all the churches of the Christian world; and their grateful reverence has assigned to the bishops of Theodosius the second rank among the general councils. Their knowledge of religious truth may have been preserved by tradition or it may have been communicated by inspiration; but the sober evidence of history will not allow much weight to the personal authority of the Fathers of Constantinople. In an age when the ecclesiastics had scandalously degenerated from the model of apostolic purity, the most worthless and corrupt were always the most eager to frequent, and disturb, the episcopal assemblies. The conflict and fermentation of so many opposite interests and tempers inflamed the passions of the bishops: and their ruling passions were the love of gold and the love of dispute. Many of the same prelates who now applauded the orthodox piety of Theodosius had repeatedly changed, with prudent flexibility, their creeds and opinions; and in the various revolutions of the church and state, the religion of their sovereign was the rule of their obsequious faith. When the emperor suspended his prevailing influence, the turbulent synod was blindly impelled by the absurd or selfish motives of pride, hatred, or resentment. . . . Such unjust and disorderly proceedings forced the gravest members of the assembly to dissent and to secede; and the clamorous majority which remained masters of the field of battle could be compared only to wasps or magpies, to a flight of cranes or to a flock of geese.

A suspicion may possibly arise that so unfavorable a picture of ecclesiastical synods has been drawn by the partial hand of some obstinate heretic or some malicious infidel. But the name of the sincere historian who has conveyed this instructive lesson to the knowledge of posterity must silence the impotent murmurs of superstition and bigotry. He was one of the most pious and eloquent bishops of the age; a saint and a doctor of the church; the scourge of Arianism, and the pillar of the orthodox faith; a distinguished member of the council of Constantinople . . . ; in a word—Gregory Nazianzen himself. The harsh and ungenerous treatment which he experienced, instead of derogating from the truth of his evidence, affords an additional proof of the spirit which actuated the deliberations of the synod.[†]

It was not enough that Theodosius had suppressed the insolent reign of Arianism, or that he had abundantly revenged the injuries which the Catholics sustained from the zeal of Constantius and Valens. The orthodox emperor considered every heretic as a rebel against the supreme powers of Heaven and of earth; and each of those powers might exercise their peculiar jurisdiction over the soul and body of the guilty. The decrees of the council of Constantinople had ascertained the true standard of the faith; and the ecclesiastics who governed the conscience of Theodosius suggested the most effectual methods of persecution. In the space of fifteen years [A.D. 380–394], he promulgated at least fifteen severe edicts against the heretics; more especially against those who rejected the doctrine of the Trinity; and to deprive them of every hope of escape, he sternly enacted that if any laws or rescripts should be alleged in their favor, the judges should consider them as the illegal productions either of fraud or forgery. The penal statutes were directed against the ministers, the assemblies, and the persons of the heretics; and the passions of the legislator were expressed in the language of declamation and invective. I. The heretical teachers who usurped the sacred titles of bishops or presbyters were not only excluded from the privileges and emoluments so liberally granted to the orthodox clergy, but they were exposed to the heavy penalties of exile and confiscation if they presumed to preach the doctrine or to practice the rites of their *accursed* sects. A fine of ten pounds of gold was imposed on every person who should dare to confer, or receive, or promote an heretical ordination: and it was reasonably expected that if the race of pastors could be extinguished, their helpless flocks would be compelled, by ignorance and hunger, to return within the pale of the Catholic church. II. The rigorous prohibition of conventicles was carefully extended to every possible circumstance in which the heretics could assemble with the intention of worshiping God and Christ according to the dictates of their conscience. Their religious meetings, whether public or secret, by day or by night, in cities or in the country, were equally proscribed by the edicts of Theodosius; and the building or ground which had been used for that illegal purpose was forfeited to the Imperial domain. III. It was supposed that the error of the heretics could proceed only from the obstinate temper of their minds; and that such a temper was a fit object of censure and punishment. The anathemas of the church were fortified by a sort of civil excommunication, which separated them from their fellow-citizens by a peculiar brand of infamy; and this declaration of the supreme magistrate tended to justify, or at least to excuse, the insults of a fanatic populace. The sectaries were gradually disqualified from the possession of honorable or lucrative employments; and Theodosius was satisfied with his own justice when he decreed that, as the Eunomians distinguished the nature of the Son from that of the Father, they should be incapable of making their wills or of receiving any advantage from testamentary donations. The guilt of the Manichaean heresy was esteemed of such magnitude that it could be expiated only by the death of the offender; and the same capital punishment was inflicted on the Audians, or *Quartodecimans,* who should dare to perpetrate the atrocious crime of celebrating on an improper day the festival of Easter. Every Roman might exercise the right of public accusation; but the office of *Inquisitors* of the Faith, a name so deservedly abhorred, was first instituted under the reign of Theodosius. Yet we are assured that the execution of his penal edicts was seldom enforced; and that the pious emperor appeared less desirous to punish than to reclaim, or terrify, his refractory subjects.

The theory of persecution was established by Theodosius, whose justice and piety have been applauded by the saints: but the practice of it, in the fullest extent, was reserved for his rival and colleague, Maximus, the first among the Christian princes who shed the blood of his Christian subjects on account of their religious opinions. The cause of the Priscillianists, a recent sect of heretics who disturbed the provinces of Spain, was transferred, by appeal, from the synod of Bordeaux to the Imperial consistory of Treves; and by the sentence of the Praetorian praefect, seven persons were tortured, condemned, and executed. The first of these was Priscillian himself, bishop of Avila, in Spain [A.D. 385]. . . . If any credit could be allowed to confessions extorted by fear or pain, and to vague reports, the offspring of malice and credulity, the heresy of the Priscillianists would be found to include the various abominations of magic, of impiety, and of lewdness. Priscillian, who wandered about the world in the company of his spiritual sisters, was accused of praying stark naked in the midst of the congregation; and it was confidently asserted that the effects of his criminal intercourse with the daughter of Euchrocia had been suppressed by means still more odious and criminal. But an accurate, or rather a candid, inquiry will discover that if the Priscillianists violated the laws of nature, it was not by the licentiousness but by the austerity of their lives.

They absolutely condemned the use of the marriage-bed; and the peace of families was often disturbed by indiscreet separations. They enjoyed, or recommended, a total abstinence from all animal food; and their continual prayers, fasts, and vigils inculcated a rule of strict and perfect devotion. The speculative tenets of the sect concerning the person of Christ and the nature of the human soul were derived from the Gnostic and Manichaean system; and this vain philosophy, which had been transported from Egypt to Spain, was ill adapted to the grosser spirits of the West. The obscure disciples of Priscillian suffered, languished, and gradually disappeared: his tenets were rejected by the clergy and people, but his death was the subject of a long and vehement controversy. . . . The civil and ecclesiastical ministers had transgressed the limits of their respective provinces. The secular judge had presumed to receive an appeal, and to pronounce a definitive sentence, in a matter of faith and episcopal jurisdiction. The bishops had disgraced themselves by exercising the functions of accusers in a criminal prosecution. The cruelty of Ithacius, who beheld the tortures and solicited the death of the heretics, provoked the just indignation of mankind; and the vices of that profligate bishop were admitted as a proof that his zeal was instigated by the sordid motives of interest. Since the death of Priscillian, the rude attempts of persecution have been refined and methodized in the holy office, which assigns their distinct parts to the ecclesiastical and secular powers. The devoted victim is regularly delivered by the priest to the magistrate, and by the magistrate to the executioner; and the inexorable sentence of the church, which declares the spiritual guilt of the offender, is expressed in the mild language of pity and intercession.

[*Maximus invades Italy, but is defeated by Theodosius (A.D. 387). Theodosius restores Valentinian II to the throne (A.D. 388). After an attempt to dismiss the Frankish commander Arbogastes, Valentinian is assassinated, and Arbogastes elevates his secretary and rhetorician Eugenius to the throne of the West (A.D. 392). Theodosius returns to Italy and defeats the usurpers (A.D. 394).*]

[Theodosius'] victory was decisive; and the deaths of his two rivals were distinguished only by the difference of their characters. The rhetorician Eugenius, who had almost acquired the dominion of the world, was reduced to implore the mercy of the conqueror; and the unrelenting soldiers separated his head from his body as he lay prostrate at the feet of Theodosius. Arbogastes, after the loss of a battle in which he had discharged the duties of a soldier and a general, wandered several days among the mountains. But when he was convinced that his cause was desperate and his escape impracticable, the intrepid Barbarian imitated the example of the ancient Romans and turned his sword against his own breast.[†]

After the defeat of Eugenius, the merit as well as the authority of Theodosius was cheerfully acknowledged by all the inhabitants of the Roman world. The experience of his past conduct encouraged the most pleasing expectations of his future reign; and the age of the emperor, which did not exceed fifty years, seemed to extend the prospect of the public felicity. His death, only four months after his victory, was considered by the people as an unforeseen and fatal event which destroyed, in a moment, the hopes of the rising generation [January 17, A.D. 395]. But the indulgence of ease and luxury had secretly nourished the principles of disease. The strength of Theodosius was unable to support the sudden and violent transition from the palace to the camp; and the increasing symptoms of a dropsy announced the speedy dissolution of the emperor. The opinion, and perhaps the interest, of the public had confirmed the division of the Eastern and Western empires; and the two royal youths, Arcadius and Honorius, who had already obtained, from the tenderness of their father, the title of Augustus were destined to fill the thrones of Constantinople and of Rome. Those princes were not permitted to share the danger and glory of the civil war; but as soon as Theodosius had triumphed over his unworthy rivals, he called his younger son, Honorius, to enjoy the fruits of the victory, and to receive the scepter of the West from the hands of his dying father [January 16, A.D. 395]. . . . Notwithstanding the recent animosities of a civil war, his death was universally lamented. The Barbarians whom he had vanquished and the churchmen by whom he had been subdued celebrated, with loud and sincere applause, the qualities of the deceased emperor which appeared the most valuable in their eyes. The Romans were terrified by the impending dangers of a feeble and divided administration, and every disgraceful moment of the unfortunate reigns of Arcadius and Honorius revived the memory of their irreparable loss.[†]

If it can be affirmed with any degree of truth that the luxury of the Romans was more shameless and dissolute in the reign of Theodosius than in the age of Constantine, perhaps, or of Augustus, the alteration cannot be ascribed to any beneficial improvements which had gradually increased the stock of national riches. A long period of calamity or decay must have checked the industry and diminished the wealth of the people; and their profuse luxury must have been the result of that indolent despair which enjoys the present hour and declines the thoughts of futurity. The uncertain condition of their property discouraged the subjects of Theodosius from engaging in those useful and laborious undertakings which require an immediate expense and promise a slow and distant advantage. The frequent examples of ruin and desolation tempted them not to spare the remains of a patrimony which might, every hour, become the prey of the rapacious Goth. And the mad prodigality which prevails in the confusion of a shipwreck or a siege may serve to explain the progress of luxury amidst the misfortunes and terrors of a sinking nation.

The effeminate luxury that infected the manners of courts and cities had instilled a secret and destructive poison into the camps of the legions; and their degeneracy has been marked by the pen of a military writer who had accurately studied the genuine and ancient principles of Roman discipline. It is the just and important observation of Vegetius that the infantry was invariably covered with defensive armor, from the foundation of the city to the reign of the emperor Gratian. The relaxation of discipline and the disuse of exercise rendered the soldiers less able and less willing to support the fatigues of the service; they complained of the weight of the armor, which they seldom wore; and they successively obtained the permission of laying aside both their cuirasses and their helmets. The heavy weapons of their ancestors, the short sword and the formidable *pilum*, which had subdued the world, insensibly dropped from their feeble hands. As the use of the shield is incompatible with that of the bow, they reluctantly marched into the field, condemned to suffer either the pain of wounds or the ignominy of flight, and always disposed to prefer the more shameful alternative. The cavalry of the Goths, the Huns, and the Alani had felt the benefits, and adopted the use, of defensive armor; and as they excelled in the management of missile weapons, they easily overwhelmed the naked and trembling legions whose heads and breasts were exposed, without defense, to the arrows of the Barbarians. The loss of armies, the destruction of cities, and the dishonor of the Roman name ineffectually solicited the successors of Gratian to restore the helmets and the cuirasses of the infantry. The enervated soldiers abandoned their own and the public defense; and their pusillanimous indolence may be considered as the immediate cause of the downfall of the empire.

CHAPTER XXVIII

DESTRUCTION OF PAGANISM

Final destruction of Paganism. • Introduction of the worship of saints, and relics, among the Christians.

The ruin of Paganism in the age of Theodosius is perhaps the only example of the total extirpation of any ancient and popular superstition; and may therefore deserve to be considered as a singular event in the history of the human mind. The Christians, more especially the clergy, had impatiently supported the prudent delays of Constantine and the equal toleration of the elder Valentinian; nor could they deem their conquest perfect or secure as long as their adversaries were permitted to exist. The influence which Ambrose [bishop of Milan] and his brethren had acquired over the youth of Gratian and the piety of Theodosius was employed to infuse the maxims of persecution into the breasts of their Imperial proselytes. Two specious principles of religious jurisprudence were established, from whence they deduced a direct and rigorous conclusion against the subjects of the empire who still adhered to the ceremonies of their ancestors: *that* the magistrate is, in some measure, guilty of the crimes which he neglects to prohibit or to punish; and *that* the idolatrous worship of fabulous deities and real demons is the most abominable crime against the supreme majesty of the Creator. The laws of Moses and the examples of Jewish history were hastily, perhaps erroneously, applied by the clergy to the mild and universal reign of Christianity. The zeal of the emperors was excited to vindicate their own honor and that of the Deity: and the temples of the Roman world were subverted about sixty years after the conversion of Constantine.

From the age of Numa to the reign of Gratian, the Romans preserved the regular succession of the several colleges of the sacerdotal order. Fifteen PONTIFFS exercised their supreme jurisdiction over all things and persons that were consecrated to the service of the gods; and the various questions which perpetually arose in a loose and traditionary system were submitted to the judgment of their holy tribunal. Fifteen grave and learned AUGURS observed the face of the heavens and prescribed the actions of heroes according to the flight of birds. Fifteen keepers of the Sibylline books (their name of QUIN-DECEMVIRS was derived from their number) occasionally consulted the history of future and, as it should seem, of contingent events. Six VESTALS devoted their virginity to the guard of the sacred fire, and of the unknown pledges of the duration of Rome; which no mortal had been suffered to behold with impunity. Seven EPULOS prepared the table of the gods, conducted the solemn procession, and regulated the ceremonies of the annual festival. The three FLAMENS of Jupiter, of Mars, and of Quirinus were considered as the peculiar ministers of the three most powerful deities, who watched over the fate of Rome and of the universe. The KING OF THE SACRIFICES represented the person of Numa, and of his successors, in the religious functions, which could be performed only by royal hands. The confraternities of the SALIANS, the LUPERCALS, etc., practiced such rites as might extort a smile of contempt from every reasonable man, with a lively confidence of recommending themselves to the favor of the immortal gods. The authority which the Roman priests had formerly obtained in the counsels of the republic was gradually abolished by the establishment of monarchy and the removal of the seat of empire. But the dignity of their sacred character was still protected by the laws and manners of their country; and they still continued, more especially the college of pontiffs, to exercise in the capital, and sometimes in the provinces, the rights of their ecclesiastical and civil jurisdiction. Their robes of purple, chariots of state, and sumptuous entertainments attracted the admiration of the people; and they received from the consecrated lands and the public revenue an ample stipend, which liberally supported the splendor of the priesthood and all the expenses of the religious worship of the state. As the service of the altar was not incompatible with the command of armies, the Romans, after their consulships and triumphs, aspired to the place of pontiff, or of augur; the seats of Cicero and Pompey were filled in the fourth century by the most illustrious members of the senate; and the dignity of their birth reflected additional splendor on their sacerdotal character. The fifteen priests who composed the college of pontiffs enjoyed a more distinguished rank as the companions of their sovereign; and the Christian emperors condescended to accept the robe and ensigns which were appropriated to the office of supreme pontiff. But when Gratian ascended the throne,

more scrupulous or more enlightened, he sternly rejected those profane symbols; applied to the service of the state, or of the church, the
revenues of the priests and Vestals; abolished their honors and immunities; and dissolved the ancient fabric of Roman superstition which was
supported by the opinions and habits of eleven hundred years [circa
A.D. 375]. Paganism was still the constitutional religion of the senate.
The hall or temple in which they assembled was adorned by the statue
and altar of Victory; a majestic female standing on a globe, with flowing garments, expanded wings, and a crown of laurel in her outstretched hand. The senators were sworn on the altar of the goddess to
observe the laws of the emperor and of the empire: and a solemn offering of wine and incense was the ordinary prelude of their public
deliberations. The removal of this ancient monument was the only injury which Constantius had offered to the superstition of the Romans
[A.D. 357]. The altar of Victory was again restored by Julian [A.D. 360–363],
tolerated by Valentinian, and once more banished from the senate by
the zeal of Gratian [A.D. 382]. But the emperor yet spared the statues
of the gods which were exposed to the public veneration: four hundred
and twenty-four temples, or chapels, still remained to satisfy the devotion of the people; and in every quarter of Rome the delicacy of the
Christians was offended by the fumes of idolatrous sacrifice.

But the Christians formed the least numerous party in the senate of
Rome: and it was only by their absence that they could express their
dissent from the legal, though profane, acts of a Pagan majority. In that
assembly, the dying embers of freedom were for a moment revived and
inflamed by the breath of fanaticism. Four respectable deputations
were successively voted to the Imperial court to represent the grievances of the priesthood and the senate and to solicit the restoration
of the altar of Victory [A.D. 382–392]. The conduct of this important
business was entrusted to the eloquent Symmachus, a wealthy and
noble senator who united the sacred characters of pontiff and augur
with the civil dignities of proconsul of Africa and praefect of the city.
The breast of Symmachus was animated by the warmest zeal for the
cause of expiring Paganism; and his religious antagonists lamented the
abuse of his genius and the inefficacy of his moral virtues. The orator,
whose petition is extant to the emperor Valentinian, was conscious of
the difficulty and danger of the office which he had assumed. He cautiously avoids every topic which might appear to reflect on the religion

of his sovereign; humbly declares that prayers and entreaties are his only arms; and artfully draws his arguments from the schools of rhetoric, rather than from those of philosophy. Symmachus endeavors to seduce the imagination of a young prince by displaying the attributes of the goddess of Victory; he insinuates that the confiscation of the revenues which were consecrated to the service of the gods was a measure unworthy of his liberal and disinterested character; and he maintains that the Roman sacrifices would be deprived of their force and energy if they were no longer celebrated at the expense, as well as in the name, of the republic. Even skepticism is made to supply an apology for superstition. The great and incomprehensible *secret* of the universe eludes the inquiry of man. Where reason cannot instruct, custom may be permitted to guide; and every nation seems to consult the dictates of prudence by a faithful attachment to those rites and opinions which have received the sanction of ages. If those ages have been crowned with glory and prosperity, if the devout people have frequently obtained the blessings which they have solicited at the altars of the gods, it must appear still more advisable to persist in the same salutary practice; and not to risk the unknown perils that may attend any rash innovations. The test of antiquity and success was applied with singular advantage to the religion of Numa; and Rome herself, the celestial genius that presided over the fates of the city, is introduced by the orator to plead her own cause before the tribunal of the emperors. "Most excellent princes," says the venerable matron, "fathers of your country! pity and respect my age, which has hitherto flowed in an uninterrupted course of piety. Since I do not repent, permit me to continue in the practice of my ancient rites. Since I am born free, allow me to enjoy my domestic institutions. This religion has reduced the world under my laws. These rites have repelled Hannibal from the city and the Gauls from the Capitol. Were my gray hairs reserved for such intolerable disgrace? I am ignorant of the new system that I am required to adopt; but I am well assured that the correction of old age is always an ungrateful and ignominious office." The fears of the people supplied what the discretion of the orator had suppressed; and the calamities which afflicted or threatened the declining empire were unanimously imputed by the Pagans to the new religion of Christ and of Constantine.

But the hopes of Symmachus were repeatedly baffled by the firm and dexterous opposition of the archbishop of Milan, who fortified the emperors against the fallacious eloquence of the advocate of Rome [A.D. 388 ff.]. In this controversy, Ambrose condescends to speak the language of a philosopher, and to ask, with some contempt, why it should be thought necessary to introduce an imaginary and invisible power as the cause of those victories which were sufficiently explained by the valor and discipline of the legions. He justly derides the absurd reverence for antiquity which could only tend to discourage the improvements of art and to replunge the human race into their original barbarism. From thence, gradually rising to a more lofty and theological tone, he pronounces that Christianity alone is the doctrine of truth and salvation; and that every mode of Polytheism conducts its deluded votaries through the paths of error to the abyss of eternal perdition. Arguments like these, when they were suggested by a favorite bishop, had power to prevent the restoration of the altar of Victory; but the same arguments fell, with much more energy and effect, from the mouth of a conqueror; and the gods of antiquity were dragged in triumph at the chariot-wheels of Theodosius. In a full meeting of the senate, the emperor proposed, according to the forms of the republic, the important question, Whether the worship of Jupiter, or that of Christ, should be the religion of the Romans [A.D. 394]. The liberty of suffrages which he affected to allow was destroyed by the hopes and fears that his presence inspired; and the arbitrary exile of Symmachus was a recent admonition that it might be dangerous to oppose the wishes of the monarch. On a regular division of the senate, Jupiter was condemned and degraded by the sense of a very large majority; and it is rather surprising that any members should be found bold enough to declare by their speeches and votes that they were still attached to the interest of an abdicated deity. The hasty conversion of the senate must be attributed either to supernatural or to sordid motives; and many of these reluctant proselytes betrayed, on every favorable occasion, their secret disposition to throw aside the mask of odious dissimulation. But they were gradually fixed in the new religion, as the cause of the ancient became more hopeless; they yielded to the authority of the emperor, to the fashion of the times, and to the entreaties of their wives and children, who were instigated and governed by the clergy of Rome and the monks of the East. The edifying example of the Anician family was soon imitated by the rest of the nobility: the Bassi, the

Paullini, the Gracchi embraced the Christian religion; and "the luminaries of the world, the venerable assembly of Catos (such are the high-flown expressions of Prudentius) were impatient to strip themselves of their pontifical garment; to cast the skin of the old serpent; to assume the snowy robes of baptismal innocence, and to humble the pride of the consular fasces before tombs of the martyrs." The citizens who subsisted by their own industry and the populace who were supported by the public liberality filled the churches of the Lateran and Vatican with an incessant throng of devout proselytes. The decrees of the senate which proscribed the worship of idols were ratified by the general consent of the Romans; the splendor of the Capitol was defaced, and the solitary temples were abandoned to ruin and contempt. Rome submitted to the yoke of the gospel; and the vanquished provinces had not yet lost their reverence for the name and authority of Rome.

The filial piety of the emperors themselves engaged them to proceed, with some caution and tenderness, in the reformation of the eternal city. Those absolute monarchs acted with less regard to the prejudices of the provincials [A.D. 381 ff.]. The pious labor which had been suspended near twenty years since the death of Constantius was vigorously resumed, and finally accomplished, by the zeal of Theodosius. Whilst that warlike prince yet struggled with the Goths, not for the glory, but for the safety, of the republic, he ventured to offend a considerable party of his subjects by some acts which might perhaps secure the protection of Heaven, but which must seem rash and unseasonable in the eye of human prudence. The success of his first experiments against the Pagans encouraged the pious emperor to reiterate and enforce his edicts of proscription: the same laws which had been originally published in the provinces of the East were applied, after the defeat of Maximus, to the whole extent of the Western empire; and every victory of the orthodox Theodosius contributed to the triumph of the Christian and Catholic faith. He attacked superstition in her most vital part by prohibiting the use of sacrifices, which he declared to be criminal as well as infamous; and if the terms of his edicts more strictly condemned the impious curiosity which examined the entrails of the victim, every subsequent explanation tended to involve in the same guilt the general practice of *immolation,* which essentially constituted the religion of the Pagans. As the temples had been erected for the purpose of sacrifice, it was the duty of a benevolent prince to remove from his subjects the dangerous temptation of offending against the laws which he had enacted. A special commission was granted to Cynegius, the Praetorian praefect of the East, and afterwards to the counts Jovius and Gaudentius, two officers of distinguished rank in the West, by which they were directed to shut the temples, to seize or destroy the instruments of idolatry, to abolish the privileges of the priests, and to confiscate the consecrated property for the benefit of the emperor, of the church, or of the army. Here the desolation might have stopped: and the naked edifices, which were no longer employed in the service of idolatry, might have been protected from the destructive rage of fanaticism. Many of those temples were the most splendid and beautiful monuments of Grecian architecture; and the emperor himself was interested not to deface the splendor of his own cities or to diminish the value of his own possessions. Those stately edifices might be suffered to remain, as so many lasting trophies of the victory of Christ. In the decline of the arts they might be usefully converted into magazines, manufactures, or places of public assembly: and perhaps, when the walls of the temple had been sufficiently purified by holy rites, the worship of the true Deity might be allowed to expiate the ancient guilt of idolatry. But as long as they subsisted, the Pagans fondly cherished the secret hope that an auspicious revolution, a second Julian, might again restore the altars of the gods: and the earnestness with which they addressed their unavailing prayers to the throne increased the zeal of the Christian reformers to extirpate, without mercy, the root of superstition. The laws of the emperors exhibit some symptoms of a milder disposition: but their cold and languid efforts were insufficient to stem the torrent of enthusiasm and rapine which was conducted, or rather impelled, by the spiritual rulers of the church. In Gaul, the holy Martin, bishop of Tours, marched at the head of his faithful monks to destroy the idols, the temples, and the consecrated trees of his extensive diocese; and in the execution of this arduous task, the prudent reader will judge whether Martin was supported by the aid of miraculous powers or of carnal weapons. In Syria, the divine and excellent Marcellus, as he is styled by Theodoret, a bishop animated with apostolic fervor, resolved to level with the ground the stately temples within the diocese of Apamea. . . . Marcellus took the field in person against the powers of darkness; a numerous troop of soldiers and gladiators marched under the episcopal banner, and he successively attacked the villages and country temples of the diocese of Apamea. Whenever any resistance or danger was apprehended, the champion of the faith, whose lameness would not allow him either to fight or fly, placed himself at a convenient distance, beyond the reach of darts. But this prudence was the occasion of his death: he was surprised and slain by a body of exasperated rustics; and the synod of the province pronounced without hesitation that the holy Marcellus had sacrificed his life in the cause of God. In the support of this cause, the monks, who rushed with tumultuous fury from the desert, distinguished themselves by their zeal and diligence. They deserved the enmity of the Pagans; and some of them might deserve the reproaches of avarice and intemperance; of avarice, which they gratified with holy plunder, and of intemperance, which they indulged at the expense of the people, who foolishly admired their tattered garments, loud psalmody, and artificial paleness. A small number of temples was protected by the fears, the venality, the taste, or the prudence of the civil and ecclesiastical governors. The temple of the Celestial Venus at Carthage, whose sacred precincts formed a circumference of two miles, was judiciously converted into a Christian church; and a similar consecration has preserved inviolate the majestic dome of the Pantheon at Rome. But in almost every province of the Roman world, an army of fanatics, without authority and without discipline, invaded the peaceful inhabitants; and the ruin of the fairest structures of antiquity still displays the ravages of *those* Barbarians, who alone had time and inclination to execute such laborious destruction.†

The temples of the Roman empire were deserted or destroyed; but the ingenious superstition of the Pagans still attempted to elude the laws of Theodosius by which all sacrifices had been severely prohibited. The inhabitants of the country, whose conduct was less opposed to the eye of malicious curiosity, disguised their *religious,* under the appearance of *convivial,* meetings. On the days of solemn festivals, they assembled in great numbers under the spreading shade of some consecrated trees; sheep and oxen were slaughtered and roasted; and this rural entertainment was sanctified by the use of incense, and by the hymns which were sung in honor of the gods. But it was alleged that, as no part of the animal was made a burnt-offering, as no altar was provided to receive the blood, and as the previous oblation of salt cakes and the concluding ceremony of libations were carefully omitted, these festal meetings did not involve the guests in the guilt or penalty of an illegal sacrifice. Whatever might be the truth of the facts or the merit of the distinction, these vain pretenses were swept away by the last edict of Theodosius [A.D. 390], which inflicted a deadly wound on the superstition of the Pagans. This prohibitory law is expressed in the most absolute and comprehensive terms. "It is our will and pleasure," says the emperor, "that none of our subjects, whether magistrates or private citizens, however exalted or however humble may be their rank and condition, shall presume, in any city or in any place, to worship an inanimate idol by the sacrifice of a guiltless victim." The act of sacrificing, and the practice of divination by the entrails of the victim, are declared (without any regard to the object of the inquiry) a crime of high treason against the state, which can be expiated only by the death of the guilty. The rites of Pagan superstition, which might seem less bloody and atrocious, are abolished as highly injurious to the truth and honor of religion; luminaries, garlands, frankincense, and libations of wine are specially enumerated and condemned; and the harmless claims of the domestic genius, of the household gods, are included in this rigorous proscription. The use of any of these profane and illegal ceremonies subjects the offender to the forfeiture of the house or estate where they have been performed; and if he has artfully chosen the property of another for the scene of his impiety, he is compelled to discharge without delay a heavy fine of twenty-five pounds of gold. . . . A fine not less considerable is imposed on the connivance of the secret enemies of religion who shall neglect the duty of their respective stations either to reveal or to punish the guilt of idolatry. Such was the persecuting spirit of the laws of Theodosius, which were repeatedly enforced by his sons and grandsons, with the loud and unanimous applause of the Christian world.

In the cruel reigns of Decius and Diocletian, Christianity had been proscribed as a revolt from the ancient and hereditary religion of the empire; and the unjust suspicions which were entertained of a dark and dangerous faction were in some measure countenanced by the inseparable union and rapid conquests of the Catholic church. But the same excuses of fear and ignorance cannot be applied to the Christian emperors who violated the precepts of humanity and of the gospel. The experience of ages had betrayed the weakness as well as folly of

Paganism; the light of reason and of faith had already exposed to the greatest part of mankind the vanity of idols; and the declining sect which still adhered to their worship might have been permitted to enjoy, in peace and obscurity, the religious customs of their ancestors. Had the Pagans been animated by the undaunted zeal which possessed the minds of the primitive believers, the triumph of the church must have been stained with blood; and the martyrs of Jupiter and Apollo might have embraced the glorious opportunity of devoting their lives and fortunes at the foot of their altars. But such obstinate zeal was not congenial to the loose and careless temper of Polytheism. The violent and repeated strokes of the orthodox princes were broken by the soft and yielding substance against which they were directed; and the ready obedience of the Pagans protected them from the pains and penalties of the Theodosian Code. Instead of asserting that the authority of the gods was superior to that of the emperor, they desisted, with a plaintive murmur, from the use of those sacred rites which their sovereign had condemned. If they were sometimes tempted by a sally of passion, or by the hopes of concealment, to indulge their favorite superstition, their humble repentance disarmed the severity of the Christian magistrate, and they seldom refused to atone for their rashness by submitting, with some secret reluctance, to the yoke of the gospel. The churches were filled with the increasing multitude of these unworthy proselytes, who had conformed from temporal motives to the reigning religion; and whilst they devoutly imitated the postures and recited the prayers of the faithful, they satisfied their conscience by the silent and sincere invocation of the gods of antiquity. If the Pagans wanted patience to suffer they wanted spirit to resist; and the scattered myriads who deplored the ruin of the temples yielded without a contest to the fortune of their adversaries. The disorderly opposition of the peasants of Syria and the populace of Alexandria to the rage of private fanaticism was silenced by the name and authority of the emperor. The Pagans of the West, without contributing to the elevation of Eugenius, disgraced by their partial attachment the cause and character of the usurper. The clergy vehemently exclaimed that he aggravated the crime of rebellion by the guilt of apostasy; that by his permission the altar of Victory was again restored; and that the idolatrous symbols of Jupiter and Hercules were displayed in the field against the invincible standard of the cross. But the vain hopes of the Pagans were soon annihilated by the defeat of Eugenius; and they were left exposed to the resentment of the conqueror, who labored to deserve the favor of Heaven by the extirpation of idolatry.

A nation of slaves is always prepared to applaud the clemency of their master who, in the abuse of absolute power, does not proceed to the last extremes of injustice and oppression [A.D. 390–420]. Theodosius might undoubtedly have proposed to his Pagan subjects the alternative of baptism or of death; and the eloquent Libanius has praised the moderation of a prince who never enacted, by any positive law, that all his subjects should immediately embrace and practice the religion of their sovereign. The profession of Christianity was not made an essential qualification for the enjoyment of the civil rights of society, nor were any peculiar hardships imposed on the sectaries who credulously received the fables of Ovid and obstinately rejected the miracles of the gospel. The palace, the schools, the army, and the senate were filled with declared and devout Pagans; they obtained without distinction the civil and military honors of the empire. Theodosius distinguished his liberal regard for virtue and genius by the consular dignity which he bestowed on Symmachus and by the personal friendship which he expressed to Libanius; and the two eloquent apologists of Paganism were never required either to change or to dissemble their religious opinions. The Pagans were indulged in the most licentious freedom of speech and writing; the historical and philosophic remains of Eunapius, Zosimus, and the fanatic teachers of the school of Plato betray the most furious animosity, and contain the sharpest invectives, against the sentiments and conduct of their victorious adversaries. If these audacious libels were publicly known, we must applaud the good sense of the Christian princes who viewed with a smile of contempt the last struggles of superstition and despair. But the Imperial laws which prohibited the sacrifices and ceremonies of Paganism were rigidly executed; and every hour contributed to destroy the influence of a religion which was supported by custom rather than by argument. The devotion of the poet or the philosopher may be secretly nourished by prayer, meditation, and study; but the exercise of public worship appears to be the only solid foundation of the religious sentiments of the people, which derive their force from imitation and habit. The interruption of that public exercise may consummate, in the period of a few years, the important work of a national revolution. The memory of theological opinions cannot long be preserved without the artificial helps of priests, of temples, and of books. The ignorant vulgar, whose minds are still agitated by the blind hopes and terrors of superstition, will be soon persuaded by their superiors to direct their vows to the reigning deities of the age; and will insensibly imbibe an ardent zeal for the support and propagation of the new doctrine which spiritual hunger at first compelled them to accept. The generation that arose in the world after the promulgation of the Imperial laws was attracted within the pale of the Catholic church: and so rapid, yet so gentle, was the fall of Paganism that only twenty-eight years after the death of Theodosius, the faint and minute vestiges were no longer visible to the eye of the legislator.

The ruin of the Pagan religion is described by the sophists as a dreadful and amazing prodigy which covered the earth with darkness and restored the ancient dominion of chaos and of night. They relate, in solemn and pathetic strains, that the temples were converted into sepulchres, and that the holy places which had been adorned by the statues of the gods were basely polluted by the relics of Christian martyrs. "The monks" (a race of filthy animals to whom Eunapius is tempted to refuse the name of men) "are the authors of the new worship which, in the place of those deities who are conceived by the understanding, has substituted the meanest and most contemptible slaves. The heads, salted and pickled, of those infamous malefactors who for the multitude of their crimes have suffered a just and ignominious death; their bodies still marked by the impression of the lash, and the scars of those tortures which were inflicted by the sentence of the magistrate; such" (continues Eunapius) "are the gods which the earth produces in our days; such are the martyrs, the supreme arbitrators of our prayers and petitions to the Deity, whose tombs are now consecrated as the objects of the veneration of the people." Without approving the malice, it is natural enough to share the surprise of the sophist, the spectator of a revolution which raised those obscure victims of the laws of Rome to the rank of celestial and invisible protectors of the Roman empire. The grateful respect of the Christians for the martyrs of the faith was exalted, by time and victory, into religious adoration; and the most illustrious of the saints and prophets were deservedly associated to the honors of the martyrs. One hundred and fifty years after the glorious deaths of St. Peter and St. Paul, the Vatican and the Ostian road were distinguished by the tombs, or rather by the trophies, of those spiritual heroes. In the age which followed the conversion of Constantine, the emperors, the consuls, and the generals of armies devoutly visited the sepulchres of a tentmaker and a fisherman; and their venerable bones were deposited under the altars of Christ on which the bishops of the royal city continually offered the unbloody sacrifice. The new capital of the Eastern world, unable to produce any ancient and domestic trophies, was enriched by the spoils of dependent provinces. The bodies of St. Andrew, St. Luke, and St. Timothy had reposed near three hundred years in the obscure graves from whence they were transported, in solemn pomp, to the church of the Apostles which the magnificence of Constantine had founded on the banks of the Thracian Bosphorus. About fifty years afterwards, the same banks were honored by the presence of Samuel, the judge and prophet of the people of Israel. His ashes, deposited in a golden vase and covered with a silken veil, were delivered by the bishops into each other's hands. The relics of Samuel were received by the people with the same joy and reverence which they would have shown to the living prophet; the highways from Palestine to the gates of Constantinople were filled with an uninterrupted procession; and the emperor Arcadius himself, at the head of the most illustrious members of the clergy and senate, advanced to meet his extraordinary guest, who had always deserved and claimed the homage of kings. The example of Rome and Constantinople confirmed the faith and discipline of the Catholic world. The honors of the saints and martyrs, after a feeble and ineffectual murmur of profane reason, were universally established; and in the age of Ambrose and Jerome, something was still deemed wanting to the sanctity of a Christian church till it had been consecrated by some portion of holy relics which fixed and inflamed the devotion of the faithful.

In the long period of twelve hundred years which elapsed between the reign of Constantine and the reformation of Luther, the worship of saints and relics corrupted the pure and perfect simplicity of the Christian model: and some symptoms of degeneracy may be observed even in the first generations which adopted and cherished this pernicious innovation.

I. The satisfactory experience that the relics of saints were more valuable than gold or precious stones stimulated the clergy to multiply the treasures of the church. Without much regard for truth or probability, they invented names for skeletons and actions for names. The fame of the apostles, and of the holy men who had imitated their virtues, was darkened by religious fiction. To the invincible band of genuine and primitive martyrs, they added myriads of imaginary heroes who had never existed, except in the fancy of crafty or credulous legendaries; and there is reason to suspect that Tours might not be the only diocese in which the bones of a malefactor were adored, instead of those of a saint. A superstitious practice which tended to increase the temptations of fraud and credulity insensibly extinguished the light of history, and of reason, in the Christian world.

II. But the progress of superstition would have been much less rapid and victorious if the faith of the people had not been assisted by the seasonable aid of visions and miracles to ascertain the authenticity and virtue of the most suspicious relics. In the reign of the younger Theodosius, Lucian, a presbyter of Jerusalem and the ecclesiastical minister of the village of Caphargamala, about twenty miles from the city, related a very singular dream which, to remove his doubts, had been repeated on three successive Saturdays. A venerable figure stood before him in the silence of the night, with a long beard, a white robe, and a gold rod; announced himself by the name of Gamaliel, and revealed to the astonished presbyter that his own corpse, with the bodies of his son Abibas, his friend Nicodemus, and the illustrious Stephen, the first martyr of the Christian faith, were secretly buried in the adjacent field. He added with some impatience that it was time to release himself and his companions from their obscure prison; that their appearance would be salutary to a distressed world; and that they had made choice of Lucian to inform the bishop of Jerusalem of their situation and their wishes. The doubts and difficulties which still retarded this important discovery were successively removed by new visions; and the ground was opened by the bishop, in the presence of an innumerable multitude. The coffins of Gamaliel, of his son, and of his friend were found in regular order; but when the fourth coffin, which contained the remains of Stephen, was shown to the light, the earth trembled, and an odor such as that of paradise was smelt, which instantly cured the various diseases of seventy-three of the assistants.

The companions of Stephen were left in their peaceful residence of Caphargamala: but the relics of the first martyr were transported in solemn procession to a church constructed in their honor on Mount Sion; and the minute particles of those relics, a drop of blood or the scrapings of a bone, were acknowledged, in almost every province of the Roman world, to possess a divine and miraculous virtue. The grave and learned Augustine, whose understanding scarcely admits the ex-cuse of credulity, has attested the innumerable prodigies which were performed in Africa by the relics of St. Stephen; and this marvelous narrative is inserted in the elaborate work of the *City of God,* which the bishop of Hippo designed as a solid and immortal proof of the truth of Christianity. Augustine solemnly declares that he has selected those miracles only which were publicly certified by the persons who were either the objects or the spectators of the power of the martyr. Many prodigies were omitted or forgotten; and Hippo had been less favor-ably treated than the other cities of the province. And yet the bishop enumerates above seventy miracles, of which three were resurrections from the dead, in the space of two years, and within the limits of his own diocese.[†]

III. The innumerable miracles of which the tombs of the martyrs were the perpetual theater revealed to the pious believer the actual state and constitution of the invisible world; and his religious specula-tions appeared to be founded on the firm basis of fact and experience. Whatever might be the condition of vulgar souls in the long interval between the dissolution and the resurrection of their bodies, it was evident that the superior spirits of the saints and martyrs did not con-sume that portion of their existence in silent and inglorious sleep. It was evident (without presuming to determine the place of their habi-tation, or the nature of their felicity) that they enjoyed the lively and active consciousness of their happiness, their virtue, and their powers; and that they had already secured the possession of their eternal re-ward. The enlargement of their intellectual faculties surpassed the measure of the human imagination; since it was proved by experience that they were capable of hearing and understanding the various peti-tions of their numerous votaries who, in the same moment of time but in the most distant parts of the world, invoked the name and assistance of Stephen or of Martin. The confidence of their petitioners was founded on the persuasion that the saints who reigned with Christ cast an eye of pity upon earth; that they were warmly interested in the prosperity of the Catholic church; and that the individuals who imitated the example of their faith and piety were the peculiar and favorite objects of their most tender regard. Sometimes, indeed, their friendship might be influenced by considerations of a less exalted kind: they viewed with partial affection the places which had been consecrated by their birth, their residence, their death, their burial, or the possession of their relics. The meaner passions of pride, avarice, and revenge may be deemed unworthy of a celestial breast; yet the saints themselves condescended to testify their grateful approbation of the liberality of their votaries; and the sharpest bolts of punishment were hurled against those impious wretches who violated their magnificent shrines, or disbelieved their supernatural power. Atrocious, indeed, must have been the guilt, and strange would have been the skepticism, of those men if they had obstinately resisted the proofs of a divine agency which the elements, the whole range of the animal creation, and even the subtle and invisible operations of the human mind were compelled to obey. The immediate, and almost instantaneous, effects that were supposed to follow the prayer, or the offense, satisfied the Christians of the ample measure of favor and authority which the saints enjoyed in the presence of the Supreme God; and it seemed almost superfluous to inquire whether they were continually obliged to intercede before the throne of grace; or whether they might not be permitted to exercise, according to the dictates of their benevolence and justice, the delegated powers of their subordinate ministry. The imagination which had been raised by a painful effort to the contemplation and worship of the UNIVERSAL CAUSE eagerly embraced such inferior objects of adoration as were more proportioned to its gross conceptions and imperfect faculties. The sublime and simple theology of the primitive Christians was gradually corrupted; and the MONARCHY of Heaven, already clouded by metaphysical subtleties, was degraded by the introduction of a popular mythology which tended to restore the reign of Polytheism.

IV. As the objects of religion were gradually reduced to the standard of the imagination, the rites and ceremonies were introduced that seemed most powerfully to affect the senses of the vulgar. If in the beginning of the fifth century Tertullian or Lactantius had been suddenly raised from the dead to assist at the festival of some popular saint or martyr, they would have gazed with astonishment and indignation on the profane spectacle which had succeeded to the pure and spiritual worship of a Christian congregation. As soon as the doors of the church were thrown open, they must have been offended by the smoke of incense, the perfume of flowers, and the glare of lamps and tapers, which diffused at noonday a gaudy, superfluous, and, in their opinion, a sacrilegious light. If they approached the balustrade of the altar, they made their way through the prostrate crowd consisting, for the most part, of strangers and pilgrims who resorted to the city on the vigil of the feast; and who already felt the strong intoxication of fanaticism and, perhaps, of wine. Their devout kisses were imprinted on the walls and pavement of the sacred edifice; and their fervent prayers were directed, whatever might be the language of their church, to the bones, the blood, or the ashes of the saint, which were usually concealed, by a linen or silken veil, from the eyes of the vulgar. The Christians frequented the tombs of the martyrs in the hope of obtaining, from their powerful intercession, every sort of spiritual, but more especially of temporal, blessings. They implored the preservation of their health or the cure of their infirmities; the fruitfulness of their barren wives, or the safety and happiness of their children. Whenever they undertook any distant or dangerous journey, they requested that the holy martyrs would be their guides and protectors on the road; and, if they returned without having experienced any misfortune, they again hastened to the tombs of the martyrs to celebrate, with grateful thanksgivings, their obligations to the memory and relics of those heavenly patrons. The walls were hung round with symbols of the favors which they had received; eyes and hands and feet of gold and silver: and edifying pictures, which could not long escape the abuse of indiscreet or idolatrous devotion, represented the image, the attributes, and the miracles of the tutelar saint. The same uniform original spirit of superstition might suggest, in the most distant ages and countries, the same methods of deceiving the credulity and of affecting the senses of mankind: but it must ingenuously be confessed that the ministers of the Catholic church imitated the profane model which they were impatient to destroy. The most respectable bishops had persuaded themselves that the ignorant rustics would more cheerfully renounce the superstitions of Paganism if they found some resemblance, some compensation, in the bosom of Christianity. The religion of Constantine achieved, in less than a century, the final conquest of the Roman empire: but the victors themselves were insensibly subdued by the arts of their vanquished rivals.

CHAPTER XXIX

DIVISION OF ROMAN EMPIRE
BETWEEN SONS OF THEODOSIUS

*Final division of the Roman empire between the sons of
Theodosius.* • *Reign of Arcadius and Honorius.* • *Stilicho.* •
Revolt and defeat of Gildo in Africa.

The genius of Rome expired with Theodosius; the last of the successors of Augustus and Constantine, who appeared in the field at the head of their armies, and whose authority was universally acknowledged throughout the whole extent of the empire. The memory of his virtues still continued, however, to protect the feeble and inexperienced youth of his two sons. After the death of their father, Arcadius and Honorius were saluted, by the unanimous consent of mankind, as the lawful emperors of the East and of the West; and the oath of fidelity was eagerly taken by every order of the state; the senates of old and new Rome, the clergy, the magistrates, the soldiers, and the people [January 11, A.D. 395]. Arcadius, who was then about eighteen years of age, was born in Spain, in the humble habitation of a private family. But he received a princely education in the palace of Constantinople; and his inglorious life was spent in that peaceful and splendid seat of royalty, from whence he appeared to reign over the provinces of Thrace, Asia Minor, Syria, and Egypt, from the Lower Danube to the confines of Persia and Aethiopia. His younger brother Honorius assumed, in the eleventh year of his age, the nominal government of Italy, Africa, Gaul, Spain, and Britain; and the troops which guarded the frontiers of his kingdom were opposed, on one side, to the Caledonians, and on the other, to the Moors. The great and martial praefecture of Illyricum was divided between the two princes: the defense and possession of the provinces of Noricum, Pannonia, and Dalmatia still belonged to the Western empire; but the two large dioceses of Dacia and Macedonia, which Gratian had entrusted to the valor of Theodosius, were forever united to the empire of the East. The boundary in Europe was not very different from the line which now separates the

Germans and the Turks; and the respective advantages of territory, riches, populousness, and military strength were fairly balanced and compensated in this final and permanent division of the Roman empire. The hereditary scepter of the sons of Theodosius appeared to be the gift of nature, and of their father; the generals and ministers had been accustomed to adore the majesty of the royal infants; and the army and people were not admonished of their rights, and of their power, by the dangerous example of a recent election. The gradual discovery of the weakness of Arcadius and Honorius, and the repeated calamities of their reign, were not sufficient to obliterate the deep and early impressions of loyalty. The subjects of Rome, who still reverenced the persons, or rather the names, of their sovereigns, beheld with equal abhorrence the rebels who opposed and the ministers who abused the authority of the throne.[†]

[Stilicho], who so long commanded the armies of Rome [A.D. 385–408], was descended from the savage and perfidious race of the Vandals. . . . From his earliest youth he embraced the profession of arms; his prudence and valor were soon distinguished in the field; the horsemen and archers of the East admired his superior dexterity; and in each degree of his military promotions, the public judgment always prevented and approved the choice of the sovereign. He was named by Theodosius to ratify a solemn treaty with the monarch of Persia; he supported, during that important embassy, the dignity of the Roman name; and after he returned to Constantinople, his merit was rewarded by an intimate and honorable alliance with the Imperial family. Theodosius had been prompted, by a pious motive of fraternal affection, to adopt for his own the daughter of his brother Honorius; the beauty and accomplishments of Serena were universally admired by the obsequious court; and Stilicho obtained the preference over a crowd of rivals who ambitiously disputed the hand of the princess and the favor of her adopted father. The assurance that the husband of Serena would be faithful to the throne which he was permitted to approach engaged the emperor to exalt the fortunes and to employ the abilities of the sagacious and intrepid Stilicho. He rose, through the successive steps of master of the horse and count of the domestics, to the supreme rank of master-general of all the cavalry and infantry of the Roman, or at least of the Western, empire; and his enemies confessed that he invariably disdained to barter for gold the rewards of merit, or to defraud the soldiers of the pay and gratifications which they deserved or claimed from the liberality of the state. The valor and conduct which he afterwards displayed in the defense of Italy against the arms of Alaric and Radagaisus may justify the fame of his early achievements, and in an age less attentive to the laws of honor or of pride, the Roman generals might yield the preeminence of rank to the ascendant of superior genius.[†]

The impartiality which Stilicho affected, as the common guardian of the royal brothers, engaged him to regulate the equal division of the arms, the jewels, and the magnificent wardrobe and furniture of the deceased emperor. But the most important object of the inheritance consisted of the numerous legions, cohorts, and squadrons of Romans or Barbarians whom the event of the civil war had united under the standard of Theodosius. The various multitudes of Europe and Asia, exasperated by recent animosities, were overawed by the authority of a single man; and the rigid discipline of Stilicho protected the lands of the citizens from the rapine of the licentious soldier.[†]

The favorites of Arcadius fomented a secret and irreconcilable war against a formidable hero who aspired to govern, and to defend, the two empires of Rome and the two sons of Theodosius. They incessantly labored, by dark and treacherous machinations, to deprive him of the esteem of the prince, the respect of the people, and the friendship of the Barbarians. The life of Stilicho was repeatedly attempted by the dagger of hired assassins; and a decree was obtained from the senate of Constantinople to declare him an enemy of the republic, and to confiscate his ample possessions in the provinces of the East. At a time when the only hope of delaying the ruin of the Roman name depended on the firm union and reciprocal aid of all the nations to whom it had been gradually communicated, the subjects of Arcadius and Honorius were instructed by their respective masters to view each other in a foreign and even hostile light; to rejoice in their mutual calamities, and to embrace, as their faithful allies, the Barbarians, whom they excited to invade the territories of their countrymen. The natives of Italy affected to despise the servile and effeminate Greeks of Byzantium, who presumed to imitate the dress and to usurp the dignity of Roman senators; and the Greeks had not yet forgot the sentiments of hatred and contempt which their polished ancestors had so long entertained for the rude inhabitants of the West. The distinction of two governments, which soon produced the separation of two nations, will justify my design of suspending the series of the Byzantine history to prosecute without interruption the disgraceful but memorable reign of Honorius.

The prudent Stilicho, instead of persisting to force the inclinations of a prince and people who rejected his government, wisely abandoned Arcadius to his unworthy favorites; and his reluctance to involve the two empires in a civil war displayed the moderation of a minister who had so often signalized his military spirit and abilities. But if Stilicho had any longer endured the revolt of Africa, he would have betrayed the security of the capital, and the majesty of the Western emperor, to the capricious insolence of a Moorish rebel. Gildo, the brother of the tyrant Firmus, had preserved and obtained, as the reward of his apparent fidelity, the immense patrimony which was forfeited by treason: long and meritorious service in the armies of Rome raised him to the dignity of a military count; the narrow policy of the court of Theodosius had adopted the mischievous expedient of supporting a legal government by the interest of a powerful family; and the brother of Firmus was invested with the command of Africa. His ambition soon usurped the administration of justice, and of the finances, without account and without control; and he maintained, during a reign of twelve years, the possession of an office from which it was impossible to remove him without the danger of a civil war [A.D. 386–398]. During those twelve years, the provinces of Africa groaned under the dominion of a tyrant who seemed to unite the unfeeling temper of a stranger with the partial resentments of domestic faction. The forms of law were often superseded by the use of poison; and if the trembling guests who were invited to the table of Gildo presumed to express fears, the insolent suspicion served only to excite his fury, and he loudly summoned the ministers of death. Gildo alternately indulged the passions of avarice and lust; and if his *days* were terrible to the rich, his *nights* were not less dreadful to husbands and parents. The fairest of their wives and daughters were prostituted to the embraces of the tyrant, and afterwards abandoned to a ferocious troop of Barbarians and assassins, the black or swarthy natives of the desert; whom Gildo considered as the only guardians of his throne.[†]

Stilicho . . . solemnly accused the tyrant of Africa before the tribunal which had formerly judged the kings and nations of the earth;

and the image of the republic was revived, after a long interval, under the reign of Honorius [A.D. 397]. The emperor transmitted an accurate and ample detail of the complaints of the provincials and the crimes of Gildo to the Roman senate; and the members of that venerable assembly were required to pronounce the condemnation of the rebel. Their unanimous suffrage declared him the enemy of the republic; and the decree of the senate added a sacred and legitimate sanction to the Roman arms. A people who still remembered that their ancestors had been the masters of the world would have applauded, with conscious pride, the representation of ancient freedom; if they had not since been accustomed to prefer the solid assurance of bread to the unsubstantial visions of liberty and greatness. The subsistence of Rome depended on the harvests of Africa; and it was evident that a declaration of war would be the signal of famine. The praefect Symmachus, who presided in the deliberations of the senate, admonished the minister of his just apprehension that as soon as the revengeful Moor should prohibit the exportation of corn, the tranquility and perhaps the safety of the capital would be threatened by the hungry rage of a turbulent multitude. The prudence of Stilicho conceived and executed, without delay, the most effectual measure for the relief of the Roman people. A large and seasonable supply of corn, collected in the inland provinces of Gaul, was embarked on the rapid stream of the Rhone and transported by an easy navigation from the Rhone to the Tiber. During the whole term of the African war, the granaries of Rome were continually filled, her dignity was vindicated from the humiliating dependence, and the minds of an immense people were quieted by the calm confidence of peace and plenty.

[*Gildo is defeated (A.D. 398).*]

The joy of the African triumph was happily connected with the nuptials of the emperor Honorius and of his cousin Maria, the daughter of Stilicho [A.D. 398]: and this equal and honorable alliance seemed to invest the powerful minister with the authority of a parent over his submissive pupil. The muse of [the poet] Claudian was not silent on this propitious day; he sung, in various and lively strains, the happiness of the royal pair and the glory of the hero who confirmed their union and supported their throne. The ancient fables of Greece, which had almost ceased to be the object of religious faith, were saved from oblivion by the genius of poetry. The picture of the Cyprian grove, the seat of harmony and love; the triumphant progress of Venus over her native seas, and the mild influence which her presence diffused in the palace of Milan, express to every age the natural sentiments of the heart in the just and pleasing language of allegorical fiction. But the amorous impatience which Claudian attributes to the young prince must excite the smiles of the court; and his beauteous spouse (if she deserved the praise of beauty) had not much to fear or to hope from the passions of her lover. Honorius was only in the fourteenth year of his age; Serena, the mother of his bride, deferred by art of persuasion the consummation of the royal nuptials; Maria died a virgin after she had been ten years a wife; and the chastity of the emperor was secured by the coldness, perhaps the debility, of his constitution. His subjects, who attentively studied the character of their young sovereign, discovered that Honorius was without passions, and consequently without talents; and that his feeble and languid disposition was alike incapable of discharging the duties of his rank or of enjoying the pleasures of his age. In his early youth he made some progress in the exercises of riding and drawing the bow: but he soon relinquished these fatiguing occupations, and the amusement of feeding poultry became the serious and daily care of the monarch of the West, who resigned the reins of empire to the firm and skillful hand of his guardian Stilicho. The experience of history will countenance the suspicion that a prince who was born in the purple received a worse education than the meanest peasant of his dominions; and that the ambitious minister suffered him to attain the age of manhood without attempting to excite his courage or to enlighten his understanding. The predecessors of Honorius were accustomed to animate by their example, or at least by their presence, the valor of the legions; and the dates of their laws attest the perpetual activity of their motions through the provinces of the Roman world. But the son of Theodosius passed the slumber of his life a captive in his palace, a stranger in his country, and the patient, almost the indifferent, spectator of the ruin of the Western empire, which was repeatedly attacked and finally subverted by the arms of the Barbarians. In the eventful history of a reign of twenty-eight years, it will seldom be necessary to mention the name of the emperor Honorius.

CHAPTER XXX

REVOLT OF THE GOTHS

Revolt of the Goths. • They plunder Greece. • Two great invasions of Italy by Alaric and Radagaisus. • They are repulsed by Stilicho. • The Germans overrun Gaul. • Usurpation of Constantine in the West. • Disgrace and death of Stilicho.

If the subjects of Rome could be ignorant of their obligations to the great Theodosius, they were too soon convinced how painfully the spirit and abilities of their deceased emperor had supported the frail and moldering edifice of the republic. He died in the month of January; and before the end of the winter of the same year, the Gothic nation was in arms [A.D. 395]. The Barbarian auxiliaries erected their independent standard and boldly avowed the hostile designs which they had long cherished in their ferocious minds. Their countrymen who had been condemned, by the conditions of the last treaty, to a life of tranquility and labor deserted their farms at the first sound of the trumpet; and eagerly resumed the weapons which they had reluctantly laid down. The barriers of the Danube were thrown open; the savage warriors of Scythia issued from their forests; and the uncommon severity of the winter allowed the poet [Claudian] to remark "that they rolled their ponderous wagons over the broad and icy back of the indignant river." The unhappy natives of the provinces to the south of the Danube submitted to the calamities which, in the course of twenty years, were almost grown familiar to their imagination; and the various troops of Barbarians who gloried in the Gothic name were irregularly spread from the woody shores of Dalmatia, to the walls of Constantinople. The interruption, or at least the diminution, of the subsidy which the Goths had received from the prudent liberality of Theodosius was the specious pretense of their revolt: the affront was embittered by their contempt for the unwarlike sons of Theodosius. . . . The Goths, instead of being impelled by the blind and headstrong passions of their chiefs, were now directed by the bold and artful genius of Alaric. . . . [H]e had solicited the command of the Roman armies; and the Imperial court provoked him to demonstrate the folly of their refusal and the importance of their loss. Whatever hopes might be entertained of the conquest of Constantinople, the judicious general soon abandoned an impracticable enterprise. In the midst of a divided court and a discontented people, the emperor Arcadius was terrified by the aspect of the Gothic arms; but the want of wisdom and valor was supplied by the strength of the city; and the fortifications, both of the sea and land, might securely brave the impotent and random darts of the Barbarians. Alaric disdained to trample any longer on the prostrate and ruined countries of Thrace and Dacia, and he resolved to seek a plentiful harvest of fame and riches in a province which had hitherto escaped the ravages of war.[†]

[Although Greece is] a country most remarkably fortified by the hand of nature[,] Alaric . . . traversed without resistance the plains of Macedonia and Thessaly as far as the foot of Mount Oeta, a steep and woody range of hills almost impervious to his cavalry [A.D. 396]. [In the] narrow pass of Thermopylae, where Leonidas and the three hundred Spartans had gloriously devoted their lives [480 B.C.], the Goths might have been stopped or destroyed by a skillful general; and perhaps the view of that sacred spot might have kindled some sparks of military ardor in the breasts of the degenerate Greeks. The troops which had been posted to defend the Straits of Thermopylae retired, as they were directed, without attempting to disturb the secure and rapid passage of Alaric; and the fertile fields of Phocis and Boeotia were instantly covered by a deluge of Barbarians, who massacred the males of an age to bear arms, and drove away the beautiful females with the spoil and cattle of the flaming villages. The travelers who visited Greece several years afterwards could easily discover the deep and bloody traces of the march of the Goths; and Thebes was less indebted for her preservation to the strength of her seven gates than to the eager haste of Alaric, who advanced to occupy the city of Athens and the important harbor of the Piraeus. The same impatience urged him to prevent the delay and danger of a siege by the offer of a capitulation; and as soon as the Athenians heard the voice of the Gothic herald, they were easily persuaded to deliver the greatest part of their wealth as the ransom of the city of Minerva and its inhabitants. The treaty was ratified by solemn oaths and observed with mutual fidelity. The Gothic prince, with a small and select train, was admitted within the walls; he indulged himself in the refreshment of the bath, accepted a splendid banquet which was provided by the magistrate, and affected to show that he was not ignorant of the manners of civilized nations. But the whole territory of Attica, from the promontory of Sunium to the town of Megara, was blasted by his baleful presence; and if we may use the comparison of a contemporary philosopher, Athens itself resembled the bleeding and empty skin of a slaughtered victim. The distance between Megara and Corinth could not much exceed thirty miles; but the *bad road*, an expressive name which it still bears among the Greeks, was or might easily have been made impassable for the march of an enemy. The thick and gloomy woods of Mount Cithaeron covered the inland country; the Scironian rocks approached the water's edge and hung over the narrow and winding path which was confined above six miles along the sea-shore. The passage of those rocks, so infamous in every age, was terminated by the Isthmus of Corinth; and a small body of firm and intrepid soldiers might have successfully defended a temporary entrenchment of five or six miles from the Ionian to the Aegean Sea. The confidence of the cities of Peloponnesus in their natural rampart had tempted them to neglect the care of their antique walls; and the avarice of the Roman governors had exhausted and betrayed the unhappy province. Corinth, Argos, Sparta yielded without resistance to the arms of the Goths; and the most fortunate of the inhabitants were saved by death from beholding the slavery of their families and the conflagration of their cities. The vases and statues were distributed among the Barbarians, with more regard to the value of the materials than to the elegance of the workmanship; the female captives submitted to the laws of war; the enjoyment of beauty was the reward of valor; and the Greeks could not reasonably complain of an abuse which was justified by the example of the heroic times. The descendants of that extraordinary people who had considered valor and discipline as the walls of Sparta no longer remembered the generous reply of their ancestors to an invader more formidable than Alaric. "If thou art a god, thou wilt not hurt those who have never injured thee; if thou art a man, advance:—and thou wilt find men equal to thyself." From Thermopylae to Sparta, the leader of the Goths pursued his victorious march without encountering any mortal antagonists: but one of the advocates of expiring Paganism has confidently asserted that the walls of Athens were guarded by the goddess Minerva, with her formidable Aegis, and by the angry phantom of Achilles;

and that the conqueror was dismayed by the presence of the hostile deities of Greece. In an age of miracles, it would perhaps be unjust to dispute the claim of the historian Zosimus to the common benefit: yet it cannot be dissembled that the mind of Alaric was ill prepared to receive, either in sleeping or waking visions, the impressions of Greek superstition. The songs of Homer and the fame of Achilles had probably never reached the ear of the illiterate *Barbarian;* and the *Christian* faith which he had devoutly embraced taught him to despise the imaginary deities of Rome and Athens. The invasion of the Goths, instead of vindicating the honor, contributed at least accidentally to extirpate the last remains, of Paganism: and the mysteries of Ceres, which had subsisted eighteen hundred years, did not survive the destruction of Eleusis and the calamities of Greece.

The last hope of a people who could no longer depend on their arms, their gods, or their sovereign was placed in the powerful assistance of the general of the West; and Stilicho, who had not been permitted to repulse, advanced to chastise, the invaders of Greece [A.D. 397]. A numerous fleet was equipped in the ports of Italy; and the troops, after a short and prosperous navigation over the Ionian Sea, were safely disembarked on the isthmus, near the ruins of Corinth. The woody and mountainous country of Arcadia, the fabulous residence of Pan and the Dryads, became the scene of a long and doubtful conflict between the two generals not unworthy of each other. The skill and perseverance of the Roman at length prevailed; and the Goths, after sustaining a considerable loss from disease and desertion, gradually retreated to the lofty mountain of Pholoe, near the sources of the Peneus and on the frontiers of Elis; a sacred country which had formerly been exempted from the calamities of war. The camp of the Barbarians was immediately besieged; the waters of the river were diverted into another channel; and while they labored under the intolerable pressure of thirst and hunger, a strong line of circumvallation was formed to prevent their escape. After these precautions, Stilicho, too confident of victory, retired to enjoy his triumph in the theatrical games and lascivious dances of the Greeks; his soldiers, deserting their standards, spread themselves over the country of their allies, which they stripped of all that had been saved from the rapacious hands of the enemy.... This unfortunate delay allowed Alaric sufficient time to conclude the treaty which he secretly negotiated with the ministers of

Constantinople. The apprehension of a civil war compelled Stilicho to retire, at the haughty mandate of his rivals, from the dominions of Arcadius; and he respected, in the enemy of Rome, the honorable character of the ally and servant of the emperor of the East.

A Grecian philosopher who visited Constantinople soon after the death of Theodosius published his liberal opinions concerning the duties of kings and the state of the Roman republic. Synesius observes, and deplores, the fatal abuse which the imprudent bounty of the late emperor had introduced into the military service. The citizens and subjects had purchased an exemption from the indispensable duty of defending their country, which was supported by the arms of Barbarian mercenaries. The fugitives of Scythia were permitted to disgrace the illustrious dignities of the empire; their ferocious youth, who disdained the salutary restraint of laws, were more anxious to acquire the riches than to imitate the arts of a people, the object of their contempt and hatred; and the power of the Goths was the stone of Tantalus, perpetually suspended over the peace and safety of the devoted state. The measures which Synesius recommends are the dictates of a bold and generous patriot. He exhorts the emperor to revive the courage of his subjects by the example of manly virtue; to banish luxury from the court and from the camp; to substitute, in the place of the Barbarian mercenaries, an army of men interested in the defense of their laws and of their property; to force, in such a moment of public danger, the mechanic from his shop and the philosopher from his school; to rouse the indolent citizen from his dream of pleasure and to arm, for the protection of agriculture, the hands of the laborious husbandman. At the head of such troops, who might deserve the name and would display the spirit of Romans, he animates the son of Theodosius to encounter a race of Barbarians who were destitute of any real courage; and never to lay down his arms till he had chased them far away into the solitudes of Scythia; or had reduced them to the state of ignominious servitude which the Lacedaemonians formerly imposed on the captive Helots. The court of Arcadius indulged the zeal, applauded the eloquence, and neglected the advice of Synesius. Perhaps the philosopher who addresses the emperor of the East in the language of reason and virtue, which he might have used to a Spartan king, had not condescended to form a practicable scheme consistent with the temper and circumstances of a degenerate age. Perhaps the pride of the ministers, whose business was seldom interrupted by reflection, might reject as wild and visionary every proposal which exceeded the measure of their capacity and deviated from the forms and precedents of office. While the oration of Synesius and the downfall of the Barbarians were the topics of popular conversation, an edict was published at Constantinople which declared the promotion of Alaric to the rank of master-general of the Eastern Illyricum [A.D. 399]. The Roman provincials, and the allies who had respected the faith of treaties, were justly indignant that the ruin of Greece and Epirus should be so liberally rewarded. The Gothic conqueror was received as a lawful magistrate in the cities which he had so lately besieged. The fathers whose sons he had massacred, the husbands whose wives he had violated, were subject to his authority; and the success of his rebellion encouraged the ambition of every leader of the foreign mercenaries. The use to which Alaric applied his new command distinguishes the firm and judicious character of his policy. He issued his orders to the four magazines and manufactures of offensive and defensive arms, Margus, Ratiaria, Naissus, and Thessalonica, to provide his troops with an extraordinary supply of shields, helmets, swords, and spears; the unhappy provincials were compelled to forge the instruments of their own destruction; and the Barbarians removed the only defect which had sometimes disappointed the efforts of their courage. The birth of Alaric, the glory of his past exploits, and the confidence in his future designs insensibly united the body of the nation under his victorious standard; and with the unanimous consent of the Barbarian chieftains, the master-general of Illyricum was elevated, according to ancient custom, on a shield and solemnly proclaimed king of the Visigoths. Armed with this double power, seated on the verge of the two empires, he alternately sold his deceitful promises to the courts of Arcadius and Honorius; till he declared and executed his resolution of invading the dominions of the West.

[*Alaric invades Italy* (A.D. *400–403*).]

[T]he most timid, who had already embarked their valuable effects, meditated their escape to the Island of Sicily or the African coast. The public distress was aggravated by the fears and reproaches of superstition. Every hour produced some horrid tale of strange and portentous accidents; the Pagans deplored the neglect of omens and the interruption of sacrifices; but the Christians still derived some comfort from the powerful intercession of the saints and martyrs.

The emperor Honorius was distinguished above his subjects by the preeminence of fear, as well as of rank. The pride and luxury in which he was educated had not allowed him to suspect that there existed on the earth any power presumptuous enough to invade the repose of the successor of Augustus. The arts of flattery concealed the impending danger till Alaric approached the palace of Milan [A.D. 403]. But when the sound of war had awakened the young emperor, instead of flying to arms with the spirit, or even the rashness, of his age, he eagerly listened to those timid counselors who proposed to convey his sacred person and his faithful attendants to some secure and distant station in the provinces of Gaul. Stilicho alone had courage and authority to resist this disgraceful measure, which would have abandoned Rome and Italy to the Barbarians; but as the troops of the palace had been lately detached to the Rhaetian frontier, and as the resource of new levies was slow and precarious, the general of the West could only promise, that if the court of Milan would maintain their ground during his absence, he would soon return with an army equal to the encounter of the Gothic king. Without losing a moment (while each moment was so important to the public safety), Stilicho hastily embarked.

[*Stilicho defeats Alaric in the battle of Pollentia (March 29, A.D. 403). Alaric retreats first to Verona, where he is again defeated, and then to Illyricum.*]

[T]he retreat of the Gothic king was considered as the deliverance of Italy. Yet the people, and even the clergy, incapable of forming any rational judgment of the business of peace and war, presumed to arraign the policy of Stilicho, who so often vanquished, so often surrounded, and so often dismissed the implacable enemy of the republic. The first moment of the public safety is devoted to gratitude and joy; but the second is diligently occupied by envy and calumny.

The citizens of Rome had been astonished by the approach of Alaric; and the diligence with which they labored to restore the walls of the capital confessed their own fears, and the decline of the empire [A.D. 404]. After the retreat of the Barbarians, Honorius was directed to accept the dutiful invitation of the senate and to celebrate, in the Imperial city, the auspicious era of the Gothic victory and of his sixth consulship. The suburbs and the streets, from the Milvian bridge to the Palatine mount, were filled by the Roman people, who, in the space of a hundred years, had only thrice been honored with the presence of their sovereigns. While their eyes were fixed on the chariot where Stilicho was deservedly seated by the side of his royal pupil, they applauded the pomp of a triumph which was not stained, like that of Constantine or of Theodosius, with civil blood. The procession passed under a lofty arch which had been purposely erected: but in less than seven years, the Gothic conquerors of Rome might read, if they were able to read, the superb inscription of that monument which attested the total defeat and destruction of their nation. The emperor resided several months in the capital, and every part of his behavior was regulated with care to conciliate the affection of the clergy, the senate, and the people of Rome. The clergy was edified by his frequent visits and liberal gifts to the shrines of the apostles. The senate, who in the triumphal procession had been excused from the humiliating ceremony of preceding on foot the Imperial chariot, was treated with the decent reverence which Stilicho always affected for that assembly. The people was repeatedly gratified by the attention and courtesy of Honorius in the public games, which were celebrated on that occasion with a magnificence not unworthy of the spectator. As soon as the appointed number of chariot-races was concluded, the decoration of the circus was suddenly changed; the hunting of wild beasts afforded a various and splendid entertainment; and the chase was succeeded by a military dance which seems, in the lively description of Claudian, to present the image of a modern tournament.

In these games of Honorius, the inhuman combats of gladiators polluted for the last time the amphitheater of Rome. The first Christian emperor may claim the honor of the first edict which condemned the art and amusement of shedding human blood; but this benevolent law expressed the wishes of the prince without reforming an inveterate abuse which degraded a civilized nation below the condition of savage cannibals. Several hundred, perhaps several thousand, victims were annually slaughtered in the great cities of the empire; and the month of December, more peculiarly devoted to the combats of gladiators, still exhibited to the eyes of the Roman people a grateful spectacle of blood and cruelty. Amidst the general joy of the victory of Pollentia, a Christian poet exhorted the emperor to extirpate by his authority the horrid custom which had so long resisted the voice of humanity and religion. The pathetic representations of Prudentius were less effectual than the generous boldness of Telemachus, an Asiatic monk, whose death was more useful to mankind than his life. The Romans were provoked by the interruption of their pleasures; and the rash monk, who had descended into the arena to separate the gladiators, was overwhelmed under a shower of stones. But the madness of the people soon subsided; they respected the memory of Telemachus, who had deserved the honors of martyrdom; and they submitted without a murmur to the laws of Honorius, which abolished forever the human sacrifices of the amphitheater. The citizens who adhered to the manners of their ancestors might perhaps insinuate that the last remains of a martial spirit were preserved in this school of fortitude, which accustomed the Romans to the sight of blood and to the contempt of death; a vain and cruel prejudice, so nobly confuted by the valor of ancient Greece, and of modern Europe!

The recent danger to which the person of the emperor had been exposed in the defenseless palace of Milan urged him to seek a retreat in some inaccessible fortress of Italy, where he might securely remain while the open country was covered by a deluge of Barbarians. On the coast of the Adriatic, about ten or twelve miles from the most southern of the seven mouths of the Po, the Thessalians had founded the ancient colony of RAVENNA, which they afterwards resigned to the natives of Umbria. Augustus, who had observed the opportunity of the place, prepared, at the distance of three miles from the old town, a capacious harbor for the reception of two hundred and fifty ships of war. . . . This advantageous situation was fortified by art and labor; and in the twentieth year of his age, the emperor of the West, anxious only for his personal safety, retired to the perpetual confinement of the walls and morasses of Ravenna [A.D. 404]. The example of Honorius was imitated by his feeble successors, the Gothic kings and afterwards the Exarchs, who occupied the throne and palace of the emperors; and till the middle of the eighth century, Ravenna was considered as the seat of government and the capital of Italy.

The fears of Honorius were not without foundation, nor were his precautions without effect. While Italy rejoiced in her deliverance from the Goths, a furious tempest was excited among the nations of Germany, who yielded to the irresistible impulse that appears to have been gradually communicated from the Eastern extremity of the continent of Asia. The Chinese annals, as they have been interpreted by the learned industry of the present age, may be usefully applied to reveal the secret and remote causes of the fall of the Roman empire. The extensive territory to the north of the great wall was possessed, after the flight of the Huns, by the victorious Sienpi, who were sometimes broken into independent tribes and sometimes reunited under a supreme chief; till at length, styling themselves *Topa*, or masters of the earth, they acquired a more solid consistence and a more formidable power.[†]

The North must again have been alarmed and agitated by the invasion of the Huns; and the nations who retreated before them must have pressed with incumbent weight on the confines of Germany [A.D. 405]. The inhabitants of those regions which the ancients have assigned to the Suevi, the Vandals, and the Burgundians might embrace the resolution of abandoning to the fugitives of Sarmatia their woods and morasses; or at least of discharging their superfluous numbers on the provinces of the Roman empire. About four years after the victorious Toulun had assumed the title of Khan of the Geougen, another Barbarian, the haughty Rhodogast, or Radagaisus, marched from the northern extremities of Germany almost to the gates of Rome, and left the remains of his army to achieve the destruction of the West. The Vandals, the Suevi, and the Burgundians formed the strength of this mighty host; but the Alani, who had found a hospitable reception in their new seats, added their active cavalry to the heavy infantry of the Germans; and the Gothic adventurers crowded so eagerly to the standard of Radagaisus that by some historians he has been styled the King of the Goths. Twelve thousand warriors, distinguished above the vulgar by their noble birth or their valiant deeds, glittered in the van; and the whole multitude, which was not less than two hundred thousand fighting men, might be increased by the accession of women, of children, and of slaves to the amount of four hundred thousand persons.[†]

The correspondence of nations was in that age so imperfect and precarious that the revolutions of the North might escape the knowledge of the court of Ravenna till the dark cloud which was collected along the coast of the Baltic burst in thunder upon the banks of the

Upper Danube. The emperor of the West, if his ministers disturbed his amusements by the news of the impending danger, was satisfied with being the occasion, and the spectator, of the war [A.D. 405]. The safety of Rome was entrusted to the counsels and the sword of Stilicho; but such was the feeble and exhausted state of the empire that it was impossible to restore the fortifications of the Danube or to prevent by a vigorous effort the invasion of the Germans. The hopes of the vigilant minister of Honorius were confined to the defense of Italy. He once more abandoned the provinces, recalled the troops, pressed the new levies, which were rigorously exacted and pusillanimously eluded; employed the most efficacious means to arrest or allure the deserters; and offered the gift of freedom and of two pieces of gold to all the slaves who would enlist. By these efforts he painfully collected, from the subjects of a great empire, an army of thirty or forty thousand men, which, in the days of Scipio or Camillus, would have been instantly furnished by the free citizens of the territory of Rome. The thirty legions of Stilicho were reinforced by a large body of Barbarian auxiliaries. . . . The senate and people trembled at their approach within a hundred and eighty miles of Rome; and anxiously compared the danger which they had escaped with the new perils to which they were exposed. Alaric was a Christian and a soldier, the leader of a disciplined army, who understood the laws of war, who respected the sanctity of treaties, and who had familiarly conversed with the subjects of the empire in the same camps and the same churches. The savage Radagaisus was a stranger to the manners, the religion, and even the language of the civilized nations of the South. The fierceness of his temper was exasperated by cruel superstition; and it was universally believed that he had bound himself, by a solemn vow, to reduce the city into a heap of stones and ashes, and to sacrifice the most illustrious of the Roman senators on the altars of those gods who were appeased by human blood. The public danger, which should have reconciled all domestic animosities, displayed the incurable madness of religious faction. The oppressed votaries of Jupiter and Mercury respected, in the implacable enemy of Rome, the character of a devout Pagan; loudly declared that they were more apprehensive of the sacrifices, than of the arms, of Radagaisus; and secretly rejoiced in the calamities of their country, which condemned the faith of their Christian adversaries.

Florence was reduced to the last extremity. . . . Conscious that he commanded the last army of the republic, [Stilicho's] prudence would not expose it in the open field to the headstrong fury of the Germans. The method of surrounding the enemy with strong lines of circumvallation, which he had twice employed against the Gothic king, was repeated on a larger scale, and with more considerable effect. The examples of [Julius] Caesar [in his Gallic campaigns] must have been familiar to the most illiterate of the Roman warriors. . . . The imprisoned multitude of horses and men was gradually destroyed, by famine rather than by the sword. . . . The proud monarch of so many warlike nations, after the loss of his bravest warriors, was reduced to confide either in the faith of a capitulation or in the clemency of Stilicho. But the death of the royal captive, who was ignominiously beheaded, disgraced the triumph of Rome and of Christianity; and the short delay of his execution was sufficient to brand the conqueror with the guilt of cool and deliberate cruelty. The famished Germans who escaped the fury of the auxiliaries were sold as slaves, at the contemptible price of as many single pieces of gold; but the difference of food and climate swept away great numbers of those unhappy strangers; and it was observed that the inhuman purchasers, instead of reaping the fruits of their labor, were soon obliged to provide the expense of their interment. Stilicho informed the emperor and the senate of his success; and deserved, a second time, the glorious title of Deliverer of Italy [A.D. 406].[†]

[Throughout these turmoils (A.D. 404–408), Stilicho negotiated with Alaric, king of the Goths, who] had deserved the esteem, and . . . soon accepted the friendship, of Stilicho himself. Renouncing the service of the emperor of the East, Alaric concluded with the court of Ravenna a treaty of peace and alliance by which he was declared master-general of the Roman armies throughout the praefecture of Illyricum; as it was claimed, according to the true and ancient limits, by the minister of Honorius. The execution of the ambitious design which was either stipulated or implied in the articles of the treaty appears to have been suspended by the formidable irruption of Radagaisus; and the neutrality of the Gothic king may perhaps be compared to the indifference of Caesar, who, in the conspiracy of Catiline [63 B.C.], refused either to assist or to oppose the enemy of the republic.[†]

The political and secret transactions of two statesmen who labored to deceive each other and the world must forever have been concealed in the impenetrable darkness of the cabinet, if the debates of a popular assembly had not thrown some rays of light on the correspondence of Alaric and Stilicho [A.D. 408]. The necessity of finding some artificial support for a government which, from a principle not of moderation but of weakness, was reduced to negotiate with its own subjects had insensibly revived the authority of the Roman senate; and the minister of Honorius respectfully consulted the legislative council of the republic. Stilicho assembled the senate in the palace of the Caesars; represented, in a studied oration, the actual state of affairs; proposed the demands of the Gothic king, and submitted to their consideration the choice of peace or war. The senators, as if they had been suddenly awakened from a dream of four hundred years, appeared on this important occasion to be inspired by the courage rather than by the wisdom of their predecessors. They loudly declared, in regular speeches or in tumultuary acclamations, that it was unworthy of the majesty of Rome to purchase a precarious and disgraceful truce from a Barbarian king; and that, in the judgment of a magnanimous people, the chance of ruin was always preferable to the certainty of dishonor. The minister whose pacific intentions were seconded only by the voice of a few servile and venal followers attempted to allay the general ferment by an apology for his own conduct, and even for the demands of the Gothic prince. "The payment of a subsidy, which had excited the indignation of the Romans, ought not (such was the language of Stilicho) to be considered in the odious light either of a tribute or of a ransom extorted by the menaces of a Barbarian enemy. Alaric had faithfully asserted the just pretensions of the republic to the provinces which were usurped by the Greeks of Constantinople: he modestly required the fair and stipulated recompense of his services; and if he had desisted from the prosecution of his enterprise, he had obeyed in his retreat the peremptory, though private, letters of the emperor himself. These contradictory orders (he would not dissemble the errors of his own family) had been procured by the intercession of Serena. The tender piety of his wife had been too deeply affected by the discord of the royal brothers, the sons of her adopted father; and the sentiments of nature had too easily prevailed over the stern dictates of the public welfare." These ostensible reasons, which faintly disguise the obscure intrigues of the palace of Ravenna, were supported by the authority of Stilicho; and obtained, after a warm debate, the reluctant approbation of the senate. The tumult of virtue and freedom subsided; and the sum of four thousand pounds of gold was granted, under the name of a subsidy, to secure the peace of Italy and to conciliate the friendship of the king of the Goths. Lampadius alone, one of the most illustrious members of the assembly, still persisted in his dissent; exclaimed with a loud voice, "This is not a treaty of peace, but of servitude"; and escaped the danger of such bold opposition by immediately retiring to the sanctuary of a Christian church.

But the reign of Stilicho drew towards its end; and the proud minister might perceive the symptoms of his approaching disgrace [A.D. 408]. The generous boldness of Lampadius had been applauded; and the senate, so patiently resigned to a long servitude, rejected with disdain the offer of invidious and imaginary freedom. The troops who still assumed the name and prerogatives of the Roman legions were exasperated by the partial affection of Stilicho for the Barbarians: and the people imputed to the mischievous policy of the minister the public misfortunes which were the natural consequence of their own degeneracy. Yet Stilicho might have continued to brave the clamors of the people, and even of the soldiers, if he could have maintained his dominion over the feeble mind of his pupil. But the respectful attachment of Honorius was converted into fear, suspicion, and hatred. The crafty Olympius, who concealed his vices under the mask of Christian piety, had secretly undermined the benefactor by whose favor he was promoted to the honorable offices of the Imperial palace. Olympius revealed to the unsuspecting emperor, who had attained the twenty-fifth year of his age, that he was without weight or authority in his own government; and artfully alarmed his timid and indolent disposition by a lively picture of the designs of Stilicho, who already meditated the death of his sovereign, with the ambitious hope of placing the diadem on the head of his son Eucherius. The emperor was instigated by his new favorite to assume the tone of independent dignity; and the minister was astonished to find that secret resolutions were formed in the court and council which were repugnant to his interest or to his intentions. Instead of residing in the palace of Rome, Honorius declared that it was his pleasure to return to the secure fortress of Ravenna.†

In the passage of the emperor through Bologna, a mutiny of the guards was excited and appeased by the secret policy of Stilicho; who announced his instructions to decimate the guilty, and ascribed to his own intercession the merit of their pardon. After this tumult, Honorius embraced for the last time the minister whom he now considered as a tyrant, and proceeded on his way to the camp of Pavia; where he was received by the loyal acclamations of the troops who were assembled for the service of the Gallic war. On the morning of the fourth day, he pronounced, as he had been taught, a military oration in the presence of the soldiers, whom the charitable visits and artful discourses of Olympius had prepared to execute a dark and bloody conspiracy. At the first signal, they massacred the friends of Stilicho, the most illustrious officers of the empire.... The intelligence of the massacre of Pavia filled the mind of Stilicho with just and gloomy apprehensions; and he instantly summoned, in the camp of Bologna, a council of the confederate leaders who were attached to his service and would be involved in his ruin. The impetuous voice of the assembly called aloud for arms and for revenge; to march, without a moment's delay, under the banners of a hero whom they had so often followed to victory; to surprise, to oppress, to extirpate the guilty Olympius and his degenerate Romans; and perhaps to fix the diadem on the head of their injured general. Instead of executing a resolution which might have been justified by success, Stilicho hesitated till he was irrecoverably lost. He was still ignorant of the fate of the emperor; he distrusted the fidelity of his own party; and he viewed with horror the fatal consequences of arming a crowd of licentious Barbarians against the soldiers and people of Italy. The confederates, impatient of his timorous and doubtful delay, hastily retired, with fear and indignation. At the hour of midnight, Sarus, a Gothic warrior, renowned among the Barbarians themselves for his strength and valor, suddenly invaded the camp of his benefactor, plundered the baggage, cut in pieces the faithful Huns who guarded his person, and penetrated to the tent where the minister, pensive and sleepless, meditated on the dangers of his situation. Stilicho escaped with difficulty from the sword of the Goths, and, after issuing a last and generous admonition to the cities of Italy to shut their gates against the Barbarians, his confidence or his despair urged him to throw himself into Ravenna, which was already in the absolute possession of his enemies. Olympius, who had assumed the dominion of Honorius, was speedily informed that his rival had embraced as a suppliant the altar of the Christian church. The base and cruel disposition of the hypocrite was incapable of pity or remorse; but he piously affected to elude rather than to violate the privilege of the sanctuary. Count Heraclian, with a troop of soldiers, appeared at the dawn of day before the gates of the church of Ravenna. The bishop was satisfied by a solemn oath that the Imperial mandate only directed them to secure the person of Stilicho: but as soon as the unfortunate minister had been tempted beyond the holy threshold, he produced the warrant for his instant execution. Stilicho supported with calm resignation the injurious names of traitor and parricide; repressed the unseasonable zeal of his followers, who were ready to attempt an ineffectual rescue; and with a firmness not unworthy of the last of the Roman generals, submitted his neck to the sword of Heraclian [August 23, A.D. 408].[†]

The services of Stilicho are great and manifest; his crimes, as they are vaguely stated in the language of flattery and hatred, are obscure at least, and improbable. About four months after his death, an edict was published in the name of Honorius to restore the free communication of the two empires, which had been so long interrupted by the *public enemy*. The minister whose fame and fortune depended on the prosperity of the state was accused of betraying Italy to the Barbarians; whom he repeatedly vanquished at Pollentia, at Verona, and before the walls of Florence. His pretended design of placing the diadem on the head of his son Eucherius could not have been conducted without preparations or accomplices; and the ambitious father would not surely have left the future emperor till the twentieth year of his age in the humble station of tribune of the notaries. Even the religion of Stilicho was arraigned by the malice of his rival. The seasonable and almost miraculous deliverance was devoutly celebrated by the applause of the clergy; who asserted that the restoration of idols and the persecution of the church would have been the first measure of the reign of Eucherius. The son of Stilicho, however, was educated in the bosom of Christianity, which his father had uniformly professed and zealously supported. Serena had borrowed her magnificent necklace from the statue of Vesta; and the Pagans execrated the memory of the sacrilegious minister by whose order the Sibylline books, the oracles of Rome, had been committed to the flames. The pride and power of Stilicho constituted his real guilt. An honorable reluctance to shed the blood of his countrymen appears to have contributed to the success of his unworthy rival; and it is the last humiliation of the character of Honorius that posterity has not condescended to reproach him with his base ingratitude to the guardian of his youth, and the support of his empire.

CHAPTER XXXI

Invasion of Italy, Occupation of Territories by Barbarians

Invasion of Italy by Alaric. • Manners of the Roman senate and people. • Rome is thrice besieged, and at length pillaged, by the Goths. • Death of Alaric. • The Goths evacuate Italy. • Fall of Constantine. • Gaul and Spain are occupied by the Barbarians. • Independence of Britain.

The incapacity of a weak and distracted government may often assume the appearance and produce the effects of a treasonable correspondence with the public enemy [September A.D. 408]. If Alaric himself had been introduced into the council of Ravenna, he would probably have advised the same measures which were actually pursued by the ministers of Honorius. The king of the Goths would have conspired, perhaps with some reluctance, to destroy the formidable adversary by whose arms, in Italy as well as in Greece, he had been twice overthrown. *Their* active and interested hatred laboriously accomplished the disgrace and ruin of the great Stilicho. The valor of Sarus, his fame in arms, and his personal or hereditary influence over the confederate Barbarians could recommend him only to the friends of their country, who despised or detested the worthless characters of Turpilio, Varanes, and Vigilantius. By the pressing instances of the new favorites, these generals, unworthy as they had shown themselves of the names of soldiers, were promoted to the command of the cavalry, of the infantry, and of the domestic troops. The Gothic prince would have subscribed with pleasure the edict which the fanaticism of Olympius dictated to the simple and devout emperor. Honorius excluded all persons who were adverse to the Catholic church from holding any office in the state; obstinately rejected the service of all those who dissented from his religion; and rashly disqualified many of his bravest and most skillful officers who adhered to the Pagan worship, or who had imbibed the opinions of Arianism. These measures, so advantageous to an enemy, Alaric would have approved, and might perhaps have suggested; but it may seem doubtful whether the Barbarian would have promoted his interest at the expense of the inhuman and absurd cruelty which was perpetrated by the direction, or at least with the connivance, of the Imperial ministers. The foreign auxiliaries who had been attached to the person of Stilicho lamented his death; but the desire of revenge was checked by a natural apprehension for the safety of their wives and children, who were detained as hostages in the strong cities of Italy, where they had likewise deposited their most valuable effects. At the same hour, and as if by a common signal, the cities of Italy were polluted by the same horrid scenes of universal massacre and pillage, which involved, in promiscuous destruction, the families and fortunes of the Barbarians. Exasperated by such an injury, which might have awakened the tamest and most servile spirit, they cast a look of indignation and hope towards the camp of Alaric, and unanimously swore to pursue, with just and implacable war, the perfidious nation who had so basely violated the laws of hospitality. By the imprudent conduct of the ministers of Honorius, the republic lost the assistance and deserved the enmity of thirty thousand of her bravest soldiers; and the weight of that formidable army, which alone might have determined the event of the war, was transferred from the scale of the Romans into that of the Goths.

In the arts of negotiation, as well as in those of war, the Gothic king maintained his superior ascendant over an enemy whose seeming changes proceeded from the total want of counsel and design [October A.D. 408 ff.]. From his camp on the confines of Italy, Alaric attentively observed the revolutions of the palace, watched the progress of faction and discontent, disguised the hostile aspect of a Barbarian invader, and assumed the more popular appearance of the friend and ally of the great Stilicho: to whose virtues, when they were no longer formidable, he could pay a just tribute of sincere praise and regret. The pressing invitation of the malcontents who urged the king of the Goths to invade Italy was enforced by a lively sense of his personal injuries; and he might especially complain that the Imperial ministers still delayed and eluded the payment of the four thousand pounds of gold which had been granted by the Roman senate, either to reward his services or to appease his fury. His decent firmness was supported by an artful moderation, which contributed to the success of his designs. He required a fair and reasonable satisfaction; but he gave the strongest assurances that, as soon as he had obtained it, he would immediately retire. . . . The modesty of Alaric was interpreted by the ministers of Ravenna as a sure evidence of his weakness and fear. They disdained either to negotiate a treaty, or to assemble an army; and with a rash confidence derived only from their ignorance of the extreme danger, irretrievably wasted the decisive moments of peace and war. While they expected, in sullen silence, that the Barbarians would evacuate the confines of Italy, Alaric, with bold and rapid marches, passed the Alps and the Po.†

During a period of six hundred and nineteen years, the seat of empire had never been violated by the presence of a foreign enemy. The unsuccessful expedition of Hannibal served only to display the character of the senate and people; of a senate degraded, rather than ennobled, by the comparison of an assembly of kings; and of a people to whom the ambassador of Pyrrhus ascribed the inexhaustible resources of the Hydra. Each of the senators, in the time of the Punic war, had accomplished his term of the military service, either in a subordinate or a superior station; and the decree which invested with temporary command all those who had been consuls, or censors, or dictators gave the republic the immediate assistance of many brave and experienced generals. In the beginning of the war, the Roman people consisted of two hundred and fifty thousand citizens of an age to bear arms. Fifty thousand had already died in the defense of their country; and the twenty-three legions which were employed in the different camps of Italy, Greece, Sardinia, Sicily, and Spain required about one hundred thousand men. But there still remained an equal number in Rome and the adjacent territory who were animated by the same intrepid courage; and every citizen was trained, from his earliest youth, in the discipline and exercises of a soldier. Hannibal was astonished by the constancy of the senate, who, without raising the siege of Capua or recalling their scattered forces, expected his approach. He encamped on the banks of the Anio, at the distance of three miles from the city; and he was soon informed that the ground on which he had pitched his tent was sold for an adequate price at a public auction; and that a body of troops was dismissed by an opposite road to reinforce the legions of Spain. He led his Africans to the gates of Rome, where he found three armies in order of battle prepared to receive him; but Hannibal dreaded the event of a combat from which he could not hope to escape unless he destroyed the last of his enemies; and his speedy retreat confessed the invincible courage of the Romans [211 B.C.].

From the time of the Punic war, the uninterrupted succession of senators had preserved the name and image of the republic; and the degenerate subjects of Honorius ambitiously derived their descent from the heroes who had repulsed the arms of Hannibal and subdued the nations of the earth.†

By a skillful disposition of his numerous forces, who impatiently watched the moment of an assault, Alaric encompassed the walls, commanded the twelve principal gates, intercepted all communication with the adjacent country, and vigilantly guarded the navigation of the Tiber, from which the Romans derived the surest and most plentiful supply of provisions [A.D. 408]. The first emotions of the nobles and of the people were those of surprise and indignation that a vile Barbarian should dare to insult the capital of the world: but their arrogance was soon humbled by misfortune; and their unmanly rage, instead of being directed against an enemy in arms, was meanly exercised on a defenseless and innocent victim. Perhaps in the person of Serena, the Romans might have respected the niece of Theodosius, the aunt, nay, even the adoptive mother, of the reigning emperor: but they abhorred the widow of Stilicho; and they listened with credulous passion to the tale of calumny which accused her of maintaining a secret and criminal correspondence with the Gothic invader. Actuated or overawed by the same popular frenzy, the senate, without requiring any evidence of her guilt, pronounced the sentence of her death. Serena was ignominiously strangled; and the infatuated multitude were astonished to find that this cruel act of injustice did not immediately produce the retreat of the Barbarians and the deliverance of the city. That unfortunate city gradually experienced the distress of scarcity, and at length the horrid calamities of famine. The daily allowance of three pounds of bread was reduced to one half, to one third, to nothing; and the price of corn still continued to rise in a rapid and extravagant proportion. The poorer citizens, who were unable to purchase the necessaries of life, solicited the precarious charity of the rich. . . . But these private and temporary donatives were insufficient to appease the hunger of a numerous people; and the progress of famine invaded the marble palaces of the senators themselves. The persons of both sexes who had been educated in the enjoyment of ease and luxury discovered how little is requisite to supply the demands of nature; and lavished their unavailing treasures of gold and silver to obtain the coarse and scanty sustenance which they would formerly have rejected with disdain. The food the most repugnant to sense or imagination, the aliments the most unwholesome and pernicious to the constitution, were eagerly devoured and fiercely disputed by the rage of hunger. A dark suspicion was entertained that some desperate wretches fed on the bodies of their fellow-creatures, whom they had secretly murdered; and even mothers (such was the horrid conflict of the two most powerful instincts implanted by nature in the human breast), even mothers are said to have tasted the flesh of their slaughtered infants! Many thousands of the inhabitants of Rome expired in their houses or in the streets for want of sustenance; and as the public sepulchres without the walls were in the power of the enemy, the stench which arose from so many putrid and unburied carcasses infected the air; and the miseries of famine were succeeded and aggravated by the contagion of a pestilential disease. The assurances of speedy and effectual relief which were repeatedly transmitted from the court of Ravenna supported for some time the fainting resolution of the Romans, till at length the despair of any human aid tempted them to accept the offers of a preternatural deliverance. Pompeianus, praefect of the city, had been persuaded by the art or fanaticism of some Tuscan diviners that by the mysterious force of spells and sacrifices, they could extract the lightning from the clouds and point those celestial fires against the camp of the Barbarians. The important secret was communicated to Innocent, the bishop of Rome; and the successor of St. Peter is accused, perhaps without foundation, of preferring the safety of the republic to the rigid severity of the Christian worship. But when the question was agitated in the senate; when it was proposed, as an essential condition, that those sacrifices should be performed in the Capitol by the authority and in the presence of the magistrates, the majority of that respectable assembly, apprehensive either of the Divine or of the Imperial displeasure, refused to join in an act which appeared almost equivalent to the public restoration of Paganism.

[*Two sieges and a series of failed negotiations bring Alaric to a third siege, and then, on August 24, A.D. 410, to the sack of Rome.*]

A victorious leader, who united the daring spirit of a Barbarian with the art and discipline of a Roman general, was at the head of a hundred thousand fighting men; and Italy pronounced with terror and respect the formidable name of Alaric. . . . But the court and councils of Honorius still remained a scene of weakness and distraction, of corruption and anarchy. . . . While the emperor and his court enjoyed with sullen pride the security of the marshes and fortifications of Ravenna, they abandoned Rome, almost without defense, to the resentment of Alaric.[†]

The crime and folly of the court of Ravenna was expiated a third time by the calamities of Rome. The king of the Goths, who no longer dissembled his appetite for plunder and revenge, appeared in arms under the walls of the capital; and the trembling senate, without any hopes of relief, prepared by a desperate resistance to defray the ruin of their country. But they were unable to guard against the secret conspiracy of their slaves and domestics who, either from birth or interest, were attached to the cause of the enemy. At the hour of midnight, the Salarian gate was silently opened, and the inhabitants were awakened by the tremendous sound of the Gothic trumpet. Eleven hundred and sixty-three years after the foundation of Rome, the Imperial city, which had subdued and civilized so considerable a part of mankind, was delivered to the licentious fury of the tribes of Germany and Scythia.

The proclamation of Alaric when he forced his entrance into a vanquished city discovered, however, some regard for the laws of humanity and religion. He encouraged his troops boldly to seize the rewards of valor, and to enrich themselves with the spoils of a wealthy and effeminate people: but he exhorted them, at the same time, to spare the lives of the unresisting citizens, and to respect the churches of the apostles, St. Peter and St. Paul, as holy and inviolable sanctuaries. Amidst the horrors of a nocturnal tumult, several of the Christian Goths displayed the fervor of a recent conversion; and some instances of their uncommon piety and moderation are related, and perhaps adorned, by the zeal of ecclesiastical writers. . . . The learned work concerning the *City of God* was professedly composed by St. Augustine to justify the ways of Providence in the destruction of the Roman greatness. He celebrates with peculiar satisfaction this memorable triumph of Christ; and insults his adversaries by challenging them to produce some similar example of a town taken by storm in which the fabulous gods of antiquity had been able to protect either themselves or their deluded votaries.

In the sack of Rome, some rare and extraordinary examples of Barbarian virtue have been deservedly applauded. But the holy precincts of the Vatican and the apostolic churches could receive a very small proportion of the Roman people; many thousand warriors, more especially of the Huns, who served under the standard of Alaric, were strangers to the name, or at least to the faith, of Christ; and we may suspect, without any breach of charity or candor, that in the hour of savage license, when every passion was inflamed and every restraint was removed, the precepts of the Gospel seldom influenced the behavior of the Gothic Christians. The writers, the best disposed to exaggerate their clemency, have freely confessed that a cruel slaughter was made of the Romans; and that the streets of the city were filled with dead bodies, which remained without burial during the general consternation. The despair of the citizens was sometimes converted into fury: and whenever the Barbarians were provoked by opposition, they extended the promiscuous massacre to the feeble, the innocent, and the helpless. The private revenge of forty thousand slaves was exercised without pity or remorse; and the ignominious lashes which they had formerly received were washed away in the blood of the guilty or obnoxious families. The matrons and virgins of Rome were exposed to injuries more dreadful, in the apprehension of chastity, than death itself; and the ecclesiastical historian has selected an example of female virtue for the admiration of future ages. A Roman lady of singular beauty and orthodox faith had excited the impatient desires of a young Goth, who, according to the sagacious remark of Sozomen, was attached to the Arian heresy. Exasperated by her obstinate resistance, he drew his sword and, with the anger of a lover, slightly wounded her neck. The bleeding heroine still continued to brave his resentment and to repel his love, till the ravisher desisted from his unavailing efforts, respectfully conducted her to the sanctuary of the Vatican, and gave six pieces of gold to the guards of the church on condition that they should restore her inviolate to the arms of her husband. Such instances of courage and generosity were not extremely common. The brutal soldiers satisfied their sensual appetites without consulting either the inclination or the duties of their female captives: and a nice question of casuistry was seriously agitated, Whether those tender victims who had inflexibly refused their consent to the violation which they sustained had lost, by their misfortune, the glorious crown of virginity. There were other losses indeed of a more substantial kind, and more general concern. It cannot be presumed that all the Barbarians were at all times capable of perpetrating such amorous outrages; and the want of youth, or beauty, or chastity protected the greatest part of the Roman women from the danger of a rape. But avarice is an insatiate and universal passion; since the enjoyment of almost every object that can afford pleasure to the different tastes and tempers of mankind may be procured by the possession of wealth. In the pillage of Rome, a just preference was given to gold and jewels, which contain the greatest value in the smallest compass and weight: but after these portable riches had been removed by the more diligent robbers, the palaces of Rome were rudely stripped of their splendid and costly furniture. The sideboards of massy plate and the variegated wardrobes of silk and purple were irregularly piled in the wagons that always followed the march of a Gothic army. The most exquisite works of art were roughly handled or wantonly destroyed; many a statue was melted for the sake of the precious materials; and many a vase, in the division of the spoil, was shivered into fragments by the stroke of a battle-axe. The acquisition of riches served only to stimulate the avarice of the rapacious Barbarians, who proceeded, by threats, by blows, and by tortures, to force from their prisoners the confession of hidden treasure. Visible splendor and expense were alleged as the proof of a plentiful fortune; the appearance of poverty was imputed to a parsimonious disposition; and the obstinacy of some misers, who endured the most cruel torments before they would discover the secret object of their affection, was fatal to many unhappy wretches who expired under the lash for refusing to reveal their imaginary treasures.[†]

Whatever might be the numbers of equestrian or plebeian rank who perished in the massacre of Rome, it is confidently affirmed that only one senator lost his life by the sword of the enemy. But it was not easy to compute the multitudes who, from an honorable station and a prosperous fortune, were suddenly reduced to the miserable condition of captives and exiles. . . . The calamities of Rome and Italy dispersed the inhabitants to the most lonely, the most secure, the most distant places of refuge. . . . The ample patrimonies which many senatorian families possessed in Africa invited them, if they had time and prudence, to escape from the ruin of their country, to embrace the shelter of that hospitable province. . . . [Many other] Italian fugitives were dispersed through the provinces, along the coast of Egypt and Asia as far as Constantinople and Jerusalem; and the village of Bethlehem, the solitary residence of St. Jerome and his female converts, was crowded with illustrious beggars of either sex and every age, who excited the public compassion by the remembrance of their past fortune. This awful catastrophe of Rome filled the astonished empire with grief and terror. So interesting a contrast of greatness and ruin disposed the fond credulity of the people to deplore, and even to exaggerate, the afflictions of the queen of cities. The clergy, who applied to recent events the lofty metaphors of Oriental prophecy, were sometimes tempted to confound the destruction of the capital and the dissolution of the globe.

There exists in human nature a strong propensity to depreciate the advantages and to magnify the evils of the present times. Yet when the first emotions had subsided and a fair estimate was made of the real damage, the more learned and judicious contemporaries were forced to confess that infant Rome had formerly received more essential injury from the Gauls [390 B.C.], than she had now sustained from the Goths in her declining age. The experience of eleven centuries has enabled posterity to produce a much more singular parallel; and to affirm with confidence that the ravages of the Barbarians whom Alaric had led from the banks of the Danube were less destructive than the hostilities exercised by the troops of Charles the Fifth, a Catholic prince, who styled himself Emperor of the Romans. The Goths evacuated the city at the end of six days, but Rome remained above nine months in the possession of the Imperialists; and every hour was stained by some atrocious act of cruelty, lust, and rapine. The authority of Alaric preserved some order and moderation among the ferocious multitude which acknowledged him for their leader and king; but the constable of Bourbon had gloriously fallen in the attack of the walls; and the death of the general removed every restraint of discipline from an army which consisted of three independent nations, the Italians, the Spaniards, and the Germans. In the beginning of the sixteenth century, the manners of Italy exhibited a remarkable scene of the depravity of mankind. They united the sanguinary crimes that prevail in an unsettled state of society with the polished vices which spring from the abuse of art and luxury; and the loose adventurers who had violated every prejudice of patriotism and superstition to assault the palace of the Roman pontiff must deserve to be considered as the most profligate of the *Italians.* At the same era, the *Spaniards* were the terror both of the Old and New World: but their high-spirited valor was disgraced by gloomy pride, rapacious avarice, and unrelenting cruelty. Indefatigable in the pursuit of fame and riches, they had improved, by repeated practice, the most exquisite and effectual methods of torturing their prisoners: many of the Castilians who pillaged Rome were familiars of the holy inquisition; and some volunteers, perhaps, were lately returned from the conquest of Mexico. The *Germans* were less corrupt than the Italians, less cruel than the Spaniards; and the rustic or even savage aspect of those *Tramontane* warriors often disguised a simple and merciful disposition. But they had imbibed in the first fervor of the reformation the spirit as well as the principles of Luther. It was their favorite amusement to insult or destroy the consecrated objects of Catholic superstition; they indulged, without pity or remorse, a devout hatred against the clergy of every denomination and degree, who form so considerable a part of the inhabitants of modern Rome; and their fanatic zeal might aspire to subvert the throne of Anti-christ, to purify, with blood and fire, the abominations of the spiritual Babylon.†

Whether fame, or conquest, or riches were the object of Alaric, he pursued that object with an indefatigable ardor which could neither be quelled by adversity nor satiated by success. No sooner had he reached the extreme land of Italy than he was attracted by the neighboring prospect of a fertile and peaceful island. Yet even the possession of Sicily he considered only as an intermediate step to the important expedition which he already meditated against the continent of Africa. The Straits of Rhegium and Messina are twelve miles in length and, in the narrowest passage, about one mile and a half broad; and the fabulous monsters of the deep, the rocks of Scylla and the whirlpool of Charybdis, could terrify none but the most timid and unskillful mariners. Yet as soon as the first division of the Goths had embarked, a sudden tempest arose which sunk or scattered many of the transports; their courage was daunted by the terrors of a new element; and the whole design was defeated by the premature death of Alaric, which fixed, after a short illness, the fatal term of his conquests [A.D. 410]. The ferocious character of the Barbarians was displayed in the funeral of a hero whose valor and fortune they celebrated with mournful applause. By the labor of a captive multitude, they forcibly diverted the course of the Busentinus, a small river that washes the walls of Consentia. The royal sepulchre, adorned with the splendid spoils and trophies of Rome, was constructed in the vacant bed; the waters were then restored to their natural channel; and the secret spot where the remains of Alaric had been deposited was forever concealed by the inhuman massacre of the prisoners who had been employed to execute the work.

The personal animosities and hereditary feuds of the Barbarians were suspended by the strong necessity of their affairs; and the brave Adolphus, the brother-in-law of the deceased monarch, was unanimously elected to succeed to his throne. The character and political system of the new king of the Goths may be best understood from his own conversation with an illustrious citizen of Narbonne; who afterwards, in a pilgrimage to the Holy Land, related it to St. Jerome, in the presence of the historian Orosius. "In the full confidence of valor and victory, I once aspired (said Adolphus) to change the face of the universe; to obliterate the name of Rome; to erect on its ruins the dominion of the Goths; and to acquire, like Augustus, the immortal fame of the founder of a new empire. By repeated experiments, I was gradually convinced that laws are essentially necessary to maintain and regulate a well-constituted state; and that the fierce, untractable humor of the Goths was incapable of bearing the salutary yoke of laws and civil government. From that moment I proposed to myself a different object of glory and ambition; and it is now my sincere wish that the gratitude of future ages should acknowledge the merit of a stranger who employed the sword of the Goths not to subvert but to restore and maintain the prosperity of the Roman empire." With these pacific views, the successor of Alaric suspended the operations of war, and seriously negotiated with the Imperial court a treaty of friendship and alliance. It was the interest of the ministers of Honorius . . . to deliver Italy from the intolerable weight of the Gothic powers; and they readily accepted their service against the tyrants and Barbarians who infested the provinces beyond the Alps. Adolphus, assuming the character of a Roman general, directed his march from the extremity of Campania to the southern provinces of Gaul [A.D. 412]. His troops, either by force or agreement, immediately occupied the cities of Narbonne, Toulouse, and Bordeaux; and though they were repulsed by Count Boniface from the walls of Marseilles, they soon extended their quarters from the Mediterranean to the Ocean. The oppressed provincials might exclaim that the miserable remnant which the enemy had spared was cruelly ravished by their pretended allies; yet some specious colors were not wanting to palliate or justify the violence of the Goths. The cities of Gaul, which they attacked, might perhaps be considered as in a state of rebellion against the government of Honorius.†

[The Goths enter into the allied service of Honorius; indeed, they conquer Spain and restore the province to his nominal rule (A.D. 415–418), but the] ruin of the opulent provinces of Gaul may be dated from the establishment of these Barbarians, whose alliance was dangerous and oppressive and who were capriciously impelled, by interest or passion, to violate the public peace [A.D. 420 ff.]. A heavy and partial ransom was imposed on the surviving provincials who had escaped the calamities of war; the fairest and most fertile lands were assigned to the rapacious strangers for the use of their families, their slaves, and their cattle; and the trembling natives relinquished with a sigh the inheritance of their fathers. Yet these domestic misfortunes, which are seldom the lot of a vanquished people, had been felt and inflicted by the Romans themselves, not only in the insolence of foreign conquest but in the madness of civil discord. The Triumvirs proscribed eighteen of the most flourishing colonies of Italy; and distributed their lands and houses to the veterans who revenged the death of Caesar and oppressed the liberty of their country. Two poets of unequal fame have deplored, in similar circumstances, the loss of their patrimony; but the legionaries of Augustus appear to have surpassed in violence and injustice the Barbarians who invaded Gaul under the reign of Honorius. It was not without the utmost difficulty that Virgil escaped from the sword of the centurion who had usurped his farm in the neighborhood of Mantua; but Paulinus of Bordeaux received a sum of money from his Gothic purchaser, which he accepted with pleasure and surprise; and though it was much inferior to the real value of his estate, this act of rapine was disguised by some colors of moderation and equity. The odious name of conquerors was softened into the mild and friendly appellation of the *guests* of the Romans; and the Barbarians of Gaul, more especially the Goths, repeatedly declared that they were bound to the people by the ties of hospitality, and to the emperor by the duty of allegiance and military service. The title of Honorius and his successors, their laws, and their civil magistrates were still respected in the provinces of Gaul, of which they had resigned the possession to the Barbarian allies; and the kings, who exercised a supreme and independent authority over their native subjects, ambitiously solicited the more honorable rank of master-generals of the Imperial armies. Such was the involuntary reverence which the Roman name still impressed on the minds of those warriors who had borne away in triumph the spoils of the Capitol.

Whilst Italy was ravaged by the Goths and a succession of feeble tyrants oppressed the provinces beyond the Alps, the British island separated itself from the body of the Roman empire [A.D. 409]. The regular forces which guarded that remote province had been gradually withdrawn; and Britain was abandoned without defense to the Saxon pirates and the savages of Ireland and Caledonia. The Britons, reduced to this extremity, no longer relied on the tardy and doubtful aid of a declining monarchy. They assembled in arms, repelled the invaders, and rejoiced in the important discovery of their own strength. Afflicted by similar calamities and actuated by the same spirit, the Armorican provinces (a name which comprehended the maritime countries of Gaul between the Seine and the Loire) resolved to imitate the example of the neighboring island. They expelled the Roman magistrates who acted under the authority of the usurper Constantine; and a free government was established among a people who had so long been subject to the arbitrary will of a master. The independence of Britain and Armorica was soon confirmed by Honorius himself, the lawful emperor of the West; and the letters by which he committed to the new states the care of their own safety might be interpreted as an absolute and perpetual abdication of the exercise and rights of sovereignty. This interpretation was in some measure justified by the event. After the usurpers of Gaul had successively fallen, the maritime provinces were restored to the empire. Yet their obedience was imperfect and precarious: the vain, inconstant, rebellious disposition of the people was incompatible either with freedom or servitude; and Armorica, though it could not long maintain the form of a republic, was agitated by frequent and destructive revolts. Britain was irrecoverably lost. But as the emperors wisely acquiesced in the independence of a remote province, the separation was not embittered by the reproach of tyranny or rebellion; and the claims of allegiance and protection were succeeded by the mutual and voluntary offices of national friendship.[†]

It is somewhat remarkable, or rather it is extremely natural, that the revolt of Britain and Armorica should have introduced an appearance of liberty into the obedient provinces of Gaul. In a solemn edict filled with the strongest assurances of that paternal affection which princes so often express and so seldom feel, the emperor Honorius promulgated his intention of convening an annual assembly of the *seven provinces* [A.D. 418]: a name peculiarly appropriated to Aquitain and the ancient Narbonnese, which had long since exchanged their Celtic rudeness for the useful and elegant arts of Italy. Arles, the seat of government and commerce, was appointed for the place of the assembly; which regularly continued twenty-eight days, from the fifteenth of August to the thirteenth of September of every year. It consisted of the Praetorian praefect of the Gauls; of seven provincial governors, one consular, and six presidents; of the magistrates, and perhaps the bishops, of about sixty cities; and of a competent though indefinite number of the most honorable and opulent *possessors* of land, who might justly be considered as the representatives of their country. They were empowered to interpret and communicate the laws of their sovereign; to expose the grievances and wishes of their constituents; to moderate the excessive or unequal weight of taxes; and to deliberate on every subject of local or national importance that could tend to the restoration of the peace and prosperity of the seven provinces. If such an institution, which gave the people an interest in their own government, had been universally established by Trajan or the Antonines, the seeds of public wisdom and virtue might have been cherished and propagated in the empire of Rome. The privileges of the subject would have secured the throne of the monarch; the abuses of an arbitrary administration might have been prevented in some degree, or corrected, by the interposition of these representative assemblies; and the country would have been defended against a foreign enemy by the arms of natives and freemen. Under the mild and generous influence of liberty, the Roman empire might have remained invincible and immortal; or if its excessive magnitude and the instability of human affairs had opposed such perpetual continuance, its vital and constituent members might have separately preserved their vigor and independence. But in the decline of the empire, when every principle of health and life had been exhausted, the tardy application of this partial remedy was incapable of producing any important or salutary effects. The emperor Honorius expresses his surprise that he must compel the reluctant provinces to accept a privilege which they should ardently have solicited. A fine of three or even five pounds of gold was imposed on the absent representatives; who seem to have declined this imaginary gift of a free constitution as the last and most cruel insult of their oppressors.

CHAPTER XXXII

EMPERORS ARCADIUS, EUTROPIUS, THEODOSIUS II

Arcadius, emperor of the East. • Administration and disgrace of Eutropius. • Persecution of St. John Chrysostom. • Theodosius II, emperor of the East. • His sister Pulcheria. • His wife Eudocia. • The Persian war, and division of Armenia.[†]

The division of the Roman world between the sons of Theodosius marks the final establishment of the empire of the East, which, from the reign of Arcadius to the taking of Constantinople by the Turks, subsisted one thousand and fifty-eight years in a state of premature and perpetual decay [A.D. 395–1453]. The sovereign of that empire assumed, and obstinately retained, the vain and at length fictitious title of Emperor of the ROMANS; and the hereditary appellation of CAESAR and AUGUSTUS continued to declare that he was the legitimate successor of the first of men, who had reigned over the first of nations. The palace of Constantinople rivaled, and perhaps excelled, the magnificence of Persia; and the eloquent sermons of St. Chrysostom celebrate, while they condemn, the pompous luxury of the reign of Arcadius [A.D. 395–408]. "The emperor," says he, "wears on his head either a diadem or a crown of gold, decorated with precious stones of inestimable value. These ornaments, and his purple garments, are reserved for his sacred person alone; and his robes of silk are embroidered with the figures of golden dragons. His throne is of massy gold. Whenever he appears in public, he is surrounded by his courtiers, his guards, and his attendants. Their spears, their shields, their cuirasses, the bridles and trappings of their horses, have either the substance or the appearance of gold; and the large splendid boss in the midst of their shield is encircled with smaller bosses, which represent the shape of the human eye. The two mules that drew the chariot of the monarch are perfectly white, and shining all over with gold. The chariot itself, of pure and solid gold, attracts the admiration of the spectators, who contemplate the purple curtains, the snowy carpet, the size of the precious stones, and the resplendent plates of gold that glitter as they are agitated by the motion of the carriage. The Imperial pictures are white, on a blue ground; the emperor appears seated on his throne with his arms, his horses, and his guards beside him; and his vanquished enemies in chains at his feet." The successors of Constantine established their perpetual residence in the royal city which he had erected on the verge of Europe and Asia. Inaccessible to the menaces of their enemies, and perhaps to the complaints of their people, they received with each wind the tributary productions of every climate; while the impregnable strength of their capital continued for ages to defy the hostile attempts of the Barbarians. Their dominions were bounded by the Adriatic and the Tigris; and the whole interval of twenty-five days' navigation, which separated the extreme cold of Scythia from the torrid zone of Aethiopia, was comprehended within the limits of the empire of the East. The populous countries of that empire were the seat of art and learning, of luxury and wealth; and the inhabitants, who had assumed the language and manners of Greeks, styled themselves, with some appearance of truth, the most enlightened and civilized portion of the human species. The form of government was a pure and simple monarchy; the name of the ROMAN REPUBLIC, which so long preserved a faint tradition of freedom, was confined to the Latin provinces; and the princes of Constantinople measured their greatness by the servile obedience of their people. They were ignorant how much this passive disposition enervates and degrades every faculty of the mind. The subjects, who had resigned their will to the absolute commands of a master, were equally incapable of guarding their lives and fortunes against the assaults of the Barbarians or of defending their reason from the terrors of superstition.†

Under the weakest of the predecessors of Arcadius, the reign of the eunuchs had been secret and almost invisible. They insinuated themselves into the confidence of the prince; but their ostensible functions were confined to the menial service of the wardrobe and Imperial bedchamber. They might direct, in a whisper, the public counsels and blast, by their malicious suggestions, the fame and fortunes of the most illustrious citizens; but they never presumed to stand forward in the front of empire, or to profane the public honors of the state. Eutropius was the first of his artificial sex who dared to assume the character of a Roman magistrate and general [A.D. 395–399]. Sometimes, in the presence of the blushing senate, he ascended the tribunal to pronounce judgment, or to repeat elaborate harangues; and sometimes appeared on horseback at the head of his troops, in the dress and armor of a hero. The disregard of custom and decency always betrays a weak and ill-regulated mind; nor does Eutropius seem to have compensated for the folly of the design by any superior merit or ability in the execution. His former habits of life had not introduced him to the study of the laws or the exercises of the field; his awkward and unsuccessful attempts provoked the secret contempt of the spectators; the Goths expressed their wish that *such* a general might always command the armies of Rome; and the name of the minister was branded with ridicule, more pernicious, perhaps, than hatred to a public character. The subjects of Arcadius were exasperated by the recollection that this deformed and decrepit eunuch, who so perversely mimicked the actions of a man, was born in the most abject condition of servitude; that before he entered the Imperial palace he had been successively sold and purchased by a hundred masters, who had exhausted his youthful strength in every mean and infamous office and at length dismissed him, in his old age, to freedom and poverty. While these disgraceful stories were circulated, and perhaps exaggerated, in private conversation, the vanity of the favorite was flattered with the most extraordinary honors. In the senate, in the capital, in the provinces, the statues of Eutropius were erected, in brass or marble, decorated with the symbols of his civil and military virtues, and inscribed with the pompous title of the third founder of Constantinople. He was promoted to the rank of *patrician,* which began to signify in a popular, and even legal, acceptation the father of the emperor; and the last year of the fourth century was polluted by the *consulship* of a eunuch and a slave. This strange and inexpiable prodigy awakened, however, the prejudices of the Romans. The effeminate consul was rejected by the West as an indelible stain to the annals of the republic.†

The public hatred and the despair of individuals continually threatened, or seemed to threaten, the personal safety of Eutropius; as well as of the numerous adherents who were attached to his fortune and had been promoted by his venal favor. For their mutual defense, he contrived the safeguard of a law which violated every principle of humanity and justice [September 4, A.D. 397]. I. It is enacted, in the name and by the authority of Arcadius, that all those who should conspire, either with subjects or with strangers, against the lives of any of the persons whom the emperor considers as the members of his own body shall be punished with death and confiscation. This species of fictitious and metaphorical treason is extended to protect not only the illustrious officers of the state and army who were admitted into the sacred consistory, but likewise the principal domestics of the palace, the senators of Constantinople, the military commanders, and the civil magistrates of the provinces; a vague and indefinite list, which, under the successors of Constantine, included an obscure and numerous train of subordinate ministers. II. This extreme severity might perhaps be justified had it been only directed to secure the representatives of the sovereign from any actual violence in the execution of their office. But the whole body of Imperial dependents claimed a privilege, or rather impunity, which screened them, in the loosest moments of their lives, from the hasty, perhaps the justifiable, resentment of their fellow-citizens; and by a strange perversion of the laws, the same degree of guilt and punishment was applied to a private quarrel and to a deliberate conspiracy against the emperor and the empire. The edict of Arcadius most positively and most absurdly declares that in such cases of treason, *thoughts* and *actions* ought to be punished with equal severity; that the knowledge of a mischievous intention, unless it be instantly revealed, becomes equally criminal with the intention itself; and that those rash men who shall presume to solicit the pardon of traitors shall themselves be branded with public and perpetual infamy. III. "With regard to the sons of the traitors" (continues the emperor), "although they ought to share the punishment, since they will probably imitate the guilt, of their parents, yet, by the special effect of our Imperial lenity, we grant them their lives; but at the same time, we declare them incapable of inheriting, either on the father's or on the mother's side, or of receiving any gift or legacy, from the testament either of kinsmen or of strangers. Stigmatized with hereditary infamy, excluded from the hopes of honors or fortune, let them endure the pangs of poverty and contempt, till they shall consider life as a calamity, and death as a comfort and relief." In such words, so well adapted to insult the feelings of mankind, did the emperor, or rather his favorite eunuch, applaud the moderation of a law which transferred the same unjust and inhuman penalties to the children of all those who had seconded, or who had not disclosed, their fictitious conspiracies. Some of the noblest regulations of Roman jurisprudence have been suffered to expire; but this edict, a convenient and forcible engine of ministerial tyranny, was carefully inserted in the codes of Theodosius and Justinian; and the same maxims have been revived in modern ages to protect the electors of Germany and the cardinals of the church of Rome.†

Two passions, however, fear and conjugal affection, awakened the languid soul of Arcadius: he was terrified by the threats of a victorious Barbarian; and he yielded to the tender eloquence of his wife Eudoxia, who, with a flood of artificial tears, presenting her infant children to their father, implored his justice for some real or imaginary insult which she imputed to the audacious eunuch [A.D. 399]. The emperor's hand was directed to sign the condemnation of Eutropius; the magic spell which during four years had bound the prince and the people was instantly dissolved; and the acclamations that so lately hailed the merit and fortune of the favorite were converted into the clamors of the soldiers and people who reproached his crimes and pressed his immediate execution. In this hour of distress and despair, his only refuge was in the sanctuary of the church, whose privileges he had wisely or profanely attempted to circumscribe; and the most eloquent of the saints, John Chrysostom, enjoyed the triumph of protecting a prostrate minister whose choice had raised him to the ecclesiastical throne of Constantinople. The archbishop, ascending the pulpit of the cathedral that he might be distinctly seen and heard by an innumerable crowd of either sex and of every age, pronounced a seasonable and pathetic discourse on the forgiveness of injuries and the instability of human greatness. The agonies of the pale and affrighted wretch, who lay groveling under the table of the altar, exhibited a solemn and instructive spectacle; and the orator, who was afterwards accused of insulting the misfortunes of Eutropius, labored to excite the contempt, that he might assuage the fury, of the people. The powers of humanity, of superstition, and of eloquence prevailed. The empress Eudoxia was restrained by her own prejudices, or by those of her subjects, from violating the sanctuary of the church; and Eutropius was tempted to capitulate by the milder arts of persuasion and by an oath that his life should be spared. Careless of the dignity of their sovereign, the new ministers of the palace immediately published an edict to declare that his late favorite had disgraced the names of consul and patrician, to abolish his statues, to confiscate his wealth, and to inflict a perpetual exile in the Island of Cyprus. A despicable and decrepit eunuch could no longer alarm the fears of his enemies; nor was he capable of enjoying what yet remained, the comforts of peace, of solitude, and of a happy climate. But their implacable revenge still envied him the last moments of a miserable life, and Eutropius had no sooner touched the shores of Cyprus than he was hastily recalled. The vain hope of eluding, by a change of place, the obligation of an oath engaged the empress to transfer the scene of his trial and execution from Constantinople to the adjacent suburb of Chalcedon. The consul Aurelian pronounced the sentence; and the motives of that sentence expose the jurisprudence of a despotic government. The crimes which Eutropius had committed against the people might have justified his death; but he was found guilty of harnessing to his chariot the *sacred* animals, who, from their breed or color, were reserved for the use of the emperor alone.

[*The allied Goths in Lydia revolt* (A.D. 400), *and are crushed* (A.D. 401).]

The triumphs of Arcadius became the subject of epic poems; and the monarch, no longer oppressed by any hostile terrors, resigned himself to the mild and absolute dominion of his wife, the fair and artful Eudoxia, who has sullied her fame by the persecution of St. John Chrysostom.†

The pastoral labors of the archbishop of Constantinople provoked, and gradually united against him, two sorts of enemies [A.D. 398–403]; the aspiring clergy, who envied his success, and the obstinate sinners, who were offended by his reproofs. When Chrysostom thundered from the pulpit of St. Sophia against the degeneracy of the Christians, his shafts were spent among the crowd without wounding or even marking the character of any individual. When he declaimed against the peculiar vices of the rich, poverty might obtain a transient consolation from his invectives; but the guilty were still sheltered by their numbers; and the reproach itself was dignified by some ideas of superiority and enjoyment. But as the pyramid rose towards the summit, it insensibly diminished to a point; and the magistrates, the ministers, the favorite eunuchs, the ladies of the court, the empress Eudoxia herself had a much larger share of guilt to divide among a smaller proportion of criminals. The personal applications of the audience were anticipated or confirmed by the testimony of their own conscience; and the intrepid preacher assumed the dangerous right of exposing both the offense and the offender to the public abhorrence. The secret resentment of the court encouraged the discontent of the clergy and monks of Constantinople, who were too hastily reformed by the fervent zeal of their archbishop. He had condemned from the pulpit the domestic females of the clergy of Constantinople, who, under the name of servants or sisters afforded a perpetual occasion either of sin or of scandal. The silent and solitary ascetics who had secluded themselves from the world were entitled to the warmest approbation of Chrysostom; but he despised and stigmatized, as the disgrace of their holy profession, the crowd of degenerate monks who, from some unworthy motives of pleasure or profit, so frequently infested the streets of the capital. To the voice of persuasion, the archbishop was obliged to add the terrors of authority; and his ardor in the exercise of ecclesiastical jurisdiction was not always exempt from passion; nor was it always guided by prudence. Chrysostom was naturally of a choleric disposition. Although he struggled, according to the precepts of the gospel, to love his private enemies, he indulged himself in the privilege of hating the enemies of God and of the church; and his sentiments were sometimes delivered with too much energy of countenance and expression.[†]

Ignorant or careless of the impending danger, Chrysostom indulged his zeal, or perhaps his resentment; declaimed with peculiar asperity against *female* vices; and condemned the profane honors which were addressed, almost in the precincts of St. Sophia, to the statue of the empress. His imprudence tempted his enemies to inflame the haughty spirit of Eudoxia by reporting, or perhaps inventing, the famous exordium of a sermon, "Herodias is again furious; Herodias again dances; she once more requires the head of John"; an insolent allusion which, as a woman and a sovereign, it was impossible for her to forgive. The short interval of a perfidious truce was employed to concert more effectual measures for the disgrace and ruin of the archbishop. A numerous council of the Eastern prelates, who were guided from a distance by the advice of Theophilus, confirmed the validity without examining the justice of the former sentence; and a detachment of Barbarian troops was introduced into the city to suppress the emotions of the people. On the vigil of Easter, the solemn administration of baptism was rudely interrupted by the soldiers, who alarmed the modesty of the naked catechumens and violated by their presence the awful mysteries of the Christian worship. Arsacius occupied the church of St. Sophia and the archiepiscopal throne. The Catholics retreated to the baths of Constantine, and afterwards to the fields; where they were still pursued and insulted by the guards, the bishops, and the magistrates. The fatal day of [Chrysostom's] final exile was marked by the conflagration of the cathedral, of the senate-house, and of the adjacent buildings; and this calamity was imputed, without proof but not without probability, to the despair of a persecuted faction.

Cicero might claim some merit, if his voluntary banishment preserved the peace of the republic; but the submission of Chrysostom was the indispensable duty of a Christian and a subject [June 20, A.D. 404]. Instead of listening to his humble prayer that he might be permitted to reside at Cyzicus, or Nicomedia, the inflexible empress assigned for his exile the remote and desolate town of Cucusus, among the ridges of Mount Taurus in the Lesser Armenia. . . . From that solitude the archbishop, whose active mind was invigorated by misfortunes, maintained a strict and frequent correspondence with the most distant provinces; exhorted the separate congregation of his faithful adherents to persevere in their allegiance; urged the destruction of the temples of Phoenicia and the extirpation of heresy in the Isle of Cyprus; extended his pastoral care to the missions of Persia and Scythia; negotiated by his ambassadors with the Roman pontiff and the emperor Honorius; and boldly appealed, from a partial synod, to the supreme tribunal of a free and general council. The mind of the illustrious exile was still independent; but his captive body was exposed to the revenge of the oppressors, who continued to abuse the name and authority of Arcadius. An order was despatched for the instant removal of Chrysostom to the extreme desert of Pityus: and his guards so faithfully obeyed their cruel instructions that, before he reached the sea-coast of the Euxine, he expired at Comana, in Pontus, in the sixtieth year of his age [September 14, A.D. 407]. The succeeding generation acknowledged his innocence and merit. The archbishops of the East, who might blush that their predecessors had been the enemies of Chrysostom, were gradually disposed by the firmness of the Roman pontiff to restore the honors of that venerable name. At the pious solicitation of the clergy and people of Constantinople, his relics, thirty years after his death, were transported from their obscure sepulchre to the royal city. The emperor Theodosius advanced to receive them as far as Chalcedon; and, falling prostrate on the coffin, implored in the name of his guilty parents, Arcadius and Eudoxia, the forgiveness of the injured saint [January 27, A.D. 438].

Yet a reasonable doubt may be entertained whether any stain of hereditary guilt could be derived from Arcadius to his successor. Eudoxia was a young and beautiful woman who indulged her passions and despised her husband; Count John enjoyed, at least, the familiar confidence of the empress; and the public named him as the real father of Theodosius the younger. The birth of a son was accepted, however, by the pious husband as an event the most fortunate and honorable to himself, to his family, and to the Eastern world: and the royal infant, by an unprecedented favor, was invested with the titles of Caesar and Augustus. In less than four years afterwards, Eudoxia, in the bloom of youth, was destroyed by the consequences of a miscarriage; and this untimely death confounded the prophecy of a holy bishop who, amidst the universal joy, had ventured to foretell that she should behold the long and auspicious reign of her glorious son. The Catholics applauded the justice of Heaven, which avenged the persecution of St. Chrysostom; and perhaps the emperor was the only person who sincerely bewailed the loss of the haughty and rapacious Eudoxia. Such a domestic misfortune afflicted *him* more deeply than the public calamities of the East; the licentious excursions, from Pontus to Palestine, of the Isaurian robbers, whose impunity accused the weakness of the government; and the earthquakes, the conflagrations, the famine, and the flights of locusts which the popular discontent was equally disposed to attribute to the incapacity of the monarch. At length, in the thirty-first year of his age, after a reign (if we may abuse that word) of thirteen years, three months, and fifteen days, Arcadius expired in the palace of Constantinople [May 1, A.D. 408]. It is impossible to delineate his character; since, in a period very copiously furnished with historical materials, it has not been possible to remark one action that properly belongs to the son of the great Theodosius.[†]

The maxims of Roman jurisprudence, if they could fairly be transferred from private property to public dominion, would have adjudged to the emperor Honorius the guardianship of his nephew till he had attained at least the fourteenth year of his age. But the weakness of

Honorius and the calamities of his reign disqualified him from prosecuting this natural claim; and such was the absolute separation of the two monarchies, both in interest and affection, that Constantinople would have obeyed with less reluctance the orders of the Persian than those of the Italian court. Under a prince whose weakness is disguised by the external signs of manhood and discretion, the most worthless favorites may secretly dispute the empire of the palace and dictate to submissive provinces the commands of a master whom they direct and despise. But the ministers of a child, who is incapable of arming them with the sanction of the royal name, must acquire and exercise an independent authority. The great officers of the state and army who had been appointed before the death of Arcadius formed an aristocracy, which might have inspired them with the idea of a free republic; and the government of the Eastern empire was fortunately assumed by the praefect Anthemius, who obtained by his superior abilities a lasting ascendant over the minds of his equals. The safety of the young emperor proved the merit and integrity of Anthemius; and his prudent firmness sustained the force and reputation of an infant reign [A.D. 408–415].†

But the Romans had so long been accustomed to the authority of a monarch that the first, even among the females, of the Imperial family who displayed any courage or capacity was permitted to ascend the vacant throne of Theodosius. His sister Pulcheria, who was only two years older than himself, received at the age of sixteen the title of *Augusta;* and though her favor might be sometimes clouded by caprice or intrigue, she continued to govern the Eastern empire near forty years; during the long minority of her brother, and after his death, in her own name and in the name of Marcian, her nominal husband [A.D. 414–453]. From a motive either of prudence or religion, she embraced a life of celibacy; and notwithstanding some aspersions on the chastity of Pulcheria, this resolution, which she communicated to her sisters Arcadia and Marina, was celebrated by the Christian world as the sublime effort of heroic piety. In the presence of the clergy and people, the three daughters of Arcadius dedicated their virginity to God; and the obligation of their solemn vow was inscribed on a tablet of gold and gems; which they publicly offered in the great church of Constantinople. Their palace was converted into a monastery; and all males, except the guides of their conscience, the saints who had forgotten the distinction of sexes, were scrupulously excluded from the holy threshold. Pulcheria, her two sisters, and a chosen train of favorite damsels formed a religious community: they denounced the vanity of dress; interrupted by frequent fasts their simple and frugal diet; allotted a portion of their time to works of embroidery; and devoted several hours of the day and night to the exercises of prayer and psalmody. The piety of a Christian virgin was adorned by the zeal and liberality of an empress. Ecclesiastical history describes the splendid churches which were built at the expense of Pulcheria in all the provinces of the East; her charitable foundations for the benefit of strangers and the poor; the ample donations which she assigned for the perpetual maintenance of monastic societies; and the active severity with which she labored to suppress the opposite heresies of Nestorius and Eutyches. Such virtues were supposed to deserve the peculiar favor of the Deity: and the relics of martyrs, as well as the knowledge of future events, were communicated in visions and revelations to the Imperial saint. Yet the devotion of Pulcheria never diverted her indefatigable attention from temporal affairs; and she alone, among all the descendants of the great Theodosius, appears to have inherited any share of his manly spirit and abilities. The elegant and familiar use which she had acquired both of the Greek and Latin languages was readily applied to the various occasions of speaking or writing on public business: her deliberations were maturely weighed; her actions were prompt and decisive; and while she moved without noise or ostentation the wheel of government, she discreetly attributed to the genius of the emperor the long tranquility of his reign. In the last years of his peaceful life, Europe was indeed afflicted by the arms of war; but the more extensive provinces of Asia still continued to enjoy a profound and permanent repose. Theodosius the younger was never reduced to the disgraceful necessity of encountering and punishing a rebellious subject: and since we cannot applaud the vigor, some praise may be due to the mildness and prosperity, of the administration of Pulcheria.

The Roman world was deeply interested in the education of its master. A regular course of study and exercise was judiciously instituted; of the military exercises of riding, and shooting with the bow; of the liberal studies of grammar, rhetoric, and philosophy: the most skillful masters of the East ambitiously solicited the attention of their royal pupil. . . . Pulcheria alone discharged the important task of instructing her brother in the arts of government; but her precepts may countenance some suspicions of the extent of her capacity or of the purity of her intentions. She taught him to maintain a grave and majestic deportment; to walk, to hold his robes, to seat himself on his throne, in a manner worthy of a great prince; to abstain from laughter; to listen with condescension; to return suitable answers; to assume by turns a serious or a placid countenance: in a word, to represent with grace and dignity the external figure of a Roman emperor. But Theodosius was never excited to support the weight and glory of an illustrious name: and instead of aspiring to support his ancestors, he degenerated (if we may presume to measure the degrees of incapacity) below the weakness of his father and his uncle. Arcadius and Honorius had been assisted by the guardian care of a parent whose lessons were enforced by his authority and example. But the unfortunate prince who is born in the purple must remain a stranger to the voice of truth; and the son of Arcadius was condemned to pass his perpetual infancy encompassed only by a servile train of women and eunuchs. The ample leisure which he acquired by neglecting the essential duties of his high office was filled by idle amusements and unprofitable studies. Hunting was the only active pursuit that could tempt him beyond the limits of the palace; but he most assiduously labored, sometimes by the light of a midnight lamp, in the mechanic occupations of painting and carving; and the elegance with which he transcribed religious books entitled the Roman emperor to the singular epithet of *Calligraphes,* or a fair writer. Separated from the world by an impenetrable veil, Theodosius trusted the persons whom he loved; he loved those who were accustomed to amuse and flatter his indolence; and as he never perused the papers that were presented for the royal signature, the acts of injustice the most repugnant to his character were frequently perpetrated in his name. The emperor himself was chaste, temperate, liberal, and merciful; but these qualities, which can only deserve the name of virtues when they are supported by courage and regulated by discretion, were seldom beneficial, and they sometimes proved mischievous, to mankind. His mind, enervated by a royal education, was oppressed and degraded by abject superstition: he fasted, he sung psalms, he blindly accepted the miracles and doctrines with which his faith was continually nourished. Theodosius devoutly worshiped the dead and living saints of the Catholic church; and he once refused to eat till an insolent monk, who had cast an excommunication on his sovereign, condescended to heal the spiritual wound which he had inflicted.

The story of a fair and virtuous maiden exalted from a private condition to the Imperial throne might be deemed an incredible romance, if such a romance had not been verified in the marriage of Theodosius. The celebrated Athenais was educated by her father Leontius in the religion and sciences of the Greeks; and so advantageous was the opinion which the Athenian philosopher entertained of his contemporaries that he divided his patrimony between his two sons, bequeathing to his daughter a small legacy of one hundred pieces of gold, in the lively confidence that her beauty and merit would be a sufficient portion. The jealousy and avarice of her brothers soon compelled Athenais to seek a refuge at Constantinople and with some hopes, either of justice or favor, to throw herself at the feet of Pulcheria. That sagacious princess listened to her eloquent complaint; and secretly destined the daughter of the philosopher Leontius for the future wife of the emperor of the East, who had now attained the twentieth year of his age. She easily excited the curiosity of her brother by an interesting picture of the charms of Athenais; large eyes, a well-proportioned nose, a fair complexion, golden locks, a slender person, a graceful demeanor, an understanding improved by study, and a virtue tried by distress. Theodosius, concealed behind a curtain in the apartment of his sister, was permitted to behold the Athenian virgin: the modest youth immediately declared his pure and honorable love; and the royal nuptials were celebrated amidst the acclamations of the capital and the provinces [A.D. 421]. Athenais, who was easily persuaded to renounce the errors of Paganism, received at her baptism the Christian name of Eudocia; but the cautious Pulcheria withheld the title of Augusta till the wife of Theodosius had approved her fruitfulness by the birth of a daughter, who espoused, fifteen years afterwards, the emperor of the West. . . . The fondness of the emperor was not abated by time and possession; and Eudocia, after the marriage of her daughter, was permitted to discharge her grateful vows by a solemn pilgrimage to Jerusalem. . . . But this pilgrimage was the fatal term of the glories of Eudocia [A.D. 438–439]. Satiated with empty pomp and unmindful, perhaps, of her obligations to Pulcheria, she ambitiously aspired to the government of the Eastern empire; the palace was distracted by female discord; but the victory was at last decided by the superior ascendant of the sister of Theodosius. The execution of Paulinus, master of the offices [A.D. 440], and the disgrace of Cyrus, Praetorian praefect of the East, convinced the public that the favor of Eudocia was insufficient to protect her most faithful friends; and the uncommon beauty of Paulinus encouraged the secret rumor that his guilt was that of a successful lover. As soon as the empress perceived that the affection of Theodosius was irretrievably lost, she requested the permission of retiring to the distant solitude of Jerusalem. She obtained her request; but the jealousy of Theodosius, or the vindictive spirit of Pulcheria, pursued her in her last retreat; and Saturninus, count of the domestics, was directed to punish with death two ecclesiastics, her most favored servants. Eudocia instantly revenged them by the assassination of the count; the furious passions which she indulged on this suspicious occasion seemed to justify the severity of Theodosius; and the empress, ignominiously stripped of the honors of her rank, was disgraced, perhaps unjustly, in the eyes of the world. The remainder of the life of Eudocia, about sixteen years, was spent in exile and devotion; and the approach of age, the death of Theodosius, the misfortunes of her only daughter, who was led a captive from Rome to Carthage, and the society of the Holy Monks of Palestine insensibly confirmed the religious temper of her mind. After a full experience of the vicissitudes of human life, the daughter of the philosopher Leontius expired at Jerusalem in the sixty-seventh year of her age; protesting, with her dying breath, that she had never transgressed the bounds of innocence and friendship [A.D. 460].

The gentle mind of Theodosius was never inflamed by the ambition of conquest or military renown; and the slight alarm of a Persian war [A.D. 421–422] scarcely interrupted the tranquility of the East. . . . [The] rising disputes were soon terminated by an amicable, though unequal, partition of the ancient kingdom of Armenia: and a territorial acquisition, which Augustus might have despised, reflected some luster on the declining empire of the younger Theodosius [A.D. 428].

A,B. PALACE OF THE CAESARS ON
       THE PALATINE HILL;
  C. HOUSE OF AUGUSTUS;
  D. HOUSE OF TIBERIUS;
  E. HOUSE OF NERO;

F. CIRCUS MAXIMUS;
G. FOUNDATIONS OF CIRCUS
    SEATS;
H. AQUEDUCT DITCH

Megalopolis constructed in 370; as that Phaleron predecessor, in 2
years' time, constructed admittedly insufficient, Spartes? Lysander
however, monarch in manner proper, with the query which
??? ??? were ?????? ????? in the ????? S. ??? of that
inscription describes sight of Getterns of the Kypselos have
action much interdependent state. Number, the accept again
immediand ??????? force of the ??? of ??? ??? their ?? ???
??? if ???? ??? ??????? the text ?? ?????? and ?? ??????
??? ??? ?? ?? ??? ??????? ???? ?? ????? ? ??? ??? ??? ?? ???

CHAPTER XXXIII

CONQUEST OF AFRICA
BY THE VANDALS

*Death of Honorius. • Valentinian III, emperor of the East. •
Administration of his mother Placidia. • Aetius and Boniface. •
Conquest of Africa by the Vandals.*

During a long and disgraceful reign of twenty-eight years, Honorius, emperor of the West, was separated from the friendship of his brother, and afterwards of his nephew, who reigned over the East; and Constantinople beheld, with apparent indifference and secret joy, the calamities of Rome.

[*After the death of Honorius (August 27, A.D. 423), Valentinian III, the infant son of Placidia (Honorius' sister), is invested.*]

Valentinian, when he received the title of Augustus, was no more than six years of age; and his long minority was entrusted to the guardian care of a mother who might assert a female claim to the succession of the Western empire. Placidia envied, but she could not equal, the reputation and virtues of the wife and sister of Theodosius, the elegant genius of Eudocia, the wise and successful policy of Pulcheria. The mother of Valentinian was jealous of the power which she was incapable of exercising; she reigned twenty-five years in the name of her son [A.D. 425–450]; and the character of that unworthy emperor gradually countenanced the suspicion that Placidia had enervated his youth by a dissolute education and studiously diverted his attention from every manly and honorable pursuit. Amidst the decay of military spirit, her armies were commanded by two generals, Aetius and Boniface, who may be deservedly named as the last of the Romans. Their union might have supported a sinking empire; their discord was the fatal and immediate cause of the loss of Africa. The invasion and defeat of Attila have immortalized the fame of Aetius; and though time has thrown a shade over the exploits of his rival, the defense of Marseilles and the deliverance of Africa attest the military talents of Count Boniface. In the field of battle, in partial encounters, in single combats, he was still the terror of the Barbarians: the clergy, and particularly his friend Augustine, were edified by the Christian piety which had once tempted him to retire from the world; the people applauded his spotless integrity; the army dreaded his equal and inexorable justice, which may be displayed in a very singular example. A peasant who complained of the criminal intimacy between his wife and a Gothic soldier was directed to attend his tribunal the following day: in the evening the count, who had diligently informed himself of the time and place of the assignation, mounted his horse, rode ten miles into the country, surprised the guilty couple, punished the soldier with instant death, and silenced the complaints of the husband by presenting him, the next morning, with the head of the adulterer. The abilities of Aetius and Boniface might have been usefully employed against the public enemies, in separate and important commands. . . . But Aetius possessed an advantage of singular moment in a female reign; he was present; he besieged, with artful and assiduous flattery, the palace of Ravenna; disguised his dark designs with the mask of loyalty and friendship; and at length deceived both his mistress and his absent rival by a subtle conspiracy which a weak woman and a brave man could not easily suspect. He had secretly persuaded Placidia to recall Boniface from the government of Africa; he secretly advised Boniface to disobey the Imperial summons: to the one, he represented the order as a sentence of death; to the other, he stated the refusal as a signal of revolt; and when the credulous and unsuspectful count had armed the province in his defense, Aetius applauded his sagacity in foreseeing the rebellion which his own perfidy had excited [A.D. 427]. A temperate inquiry into the real motives of Boniface would have restored a faithful servant to his duty and to the republic; but the arts of Aetius still continued to betray and to inflame, and the count was urged by persecution to embrace the most desperate counsels. The success with which he eluded or repelled the first attacks could not inspire a vain confidence that at the head of some loose, disorderly Africans he should be able to withstand the regular forces of the West, commanded by a rival whose military character it was impossible for him to despise. After some hesitation, the last struggles of prudence and loyalty, Boniface despatched a trusty friend to the court, or rather to the camp, of Gonderic, king of the Vandals, with the proposal of a strict alliance and the offer of an advantageous and perpetual settlement.

After the retreat of the Goths, the authority of Honorius had obtained a precarious establishment in Spain; except only in the province of Gallicia, where the Suevi and the Vandals had fortified their camps, in mutual discord and hostile independence. The Vandals prevailed [A.D. 428]. . . . The experience of navigation, and perhaps the prospect of Africa, encouraged the Vandals to accept the invitation which they received from Count Boniface; and the death of Gonderic served only to forward and animate the bold enterprise. In the room of a prince not conspicuous for any superior powers of the mind or body, they acquired his bastard brother, the terrible Genseric; a name which, in the destruction of the Roman empire, has deserved an equal rank with the names of Alaric and Attila. . . . The vessels which transported the Vandals over the modern Straits of Gibraltar, a channel only twelve miles in breadth, were furnished by the Spaniards, who anxiously wished their departure; and by the African general who had implored their formidable assistance [May A.D. 429].

Our fancy, so long accustomed to exaggerate and multiply the martial swarms of Barbarians that seemed to issue from the North, will perhaps be surprised by the account of the army which Genseric mustered on the coast of Mauritania. The Vandals, who in twenty years had penetrated from the Elbe to Mount Atlas, were united under the command of their warlike king; and he reigned with equal authority over the Alani, who had passed within the term of human life from the cold of Scythia to the excessive heat of an African climate. The hopes of the bold enterprise had excited many brave adventurers of the Gothic nation; and many desperate provincials were tempted to repair their fortunes by the same means which had occasioned their ruin. Yet this various multitude amounted only to fifty thousand effective men. . . . But his own dexterity, and the discontents of Africa, soon fortified the Vandal powers by the accession of numerous and active allies. The parts of Mauritania which border on the Great Desert and the Atlantic Ocean were filled with a fierce and untractable race of men whose savage temper had been exasperated rather than reclaimed by their dread of the Roman arms. The wandering Moors, as they gradually ventured to approach the sea-shore and the camp of the Vandals, must have viewed with terror and astonishment the dress, the armor, the martial pride and discipline of the unknown strangers who had landed on their coast; and the fair complexions of the blue-eyed warriors of Germany formed a very singular contrast with the swarthy or olive hue which is derived from the neighborhood of the torrid zone. After the first difficulties had in some measure been removed, which arose from the mutual ignorance of their respective language, the Moors, regardless of any future consequence, embraced the alliance of the enemies of Rome; and a crowd of naked savages rushed from the woods and valleys of Mount Atlas to satiate their revenge on the polished tyrants who had injuriously expelled them from the native sovereignty of the land.

The persecution of the Donatists was an event not less favorable to the designs of Genseric. Seventeen years before he landed in Africa, a public conference was held at Carthage by the order of the magistrate. The Catholics were satisfied that, after the invincible reasons which they had alleged, the obstinacy of the schismatics must be inexcusable and voluntary; and the emperor Honorius was persuaded to inflict the most rigorous penalties on a faction which had so long abused his patience and clemency. Three hundred bishops, with many thousands of the inferior clergy, were torn from their churches, stripped of their ecclesiastical possessions, banished to the islands, and proscribed by the laws if they presumed to conceal themselves in the provinces of Africa. Their numerous congregations, both in cities and in the country, were deprived of the rights of citizens and of the exercise of religious worship. . . . By these severities, which obtained the warmest approbation of St. Augustine, great numbers of Donatists were reconciled to the Catholic church; but the fanatics who still persevered in their opposition were provoked to madness and despair; the distracted country was filled with tumult and bloodshed; the armed troops of *Circumcellions* alternately pointed their rage against themselves or against their adversaries; and the calendar of martyrs received on both sides a considerable augmentation. Under these circumstances, Genseric, a Christian but an enemy of the orthodox communion, showed himself to the Donatists as a powerful deliverer, from whom they might reasonably expect the repeal of the odious and oppressive edicts of the Roman emperors. The conquest of Africa was facilitated by the active zeal, or the secret favor, of a domestic faction; the wanton outrages against the churches and the clergy of which the Vandals are accused may be fairly imputed to the fanaticism of their allies; and the intolerant spirit which disgraced the triumph of Christianity contributed to the loss of the most important province of the West.

The court and the people were astonished by the strange intelligence that a virtuous hero, after so many favors and so many services, had renounced his allegiance and invited the Barbarians to destroy the province entrusted to his command. The friends of Boniface, who still believed that his criminal behavior might be excused by some honorable motive, solicited, during the absence of Aetius, a free conference with the Count of Africa; and Darius, an officer of high distinction, was named for the important embassy [A.D. 430]. In their first interview at Carthage, the imaginary provocations were mutually explained; the opposite letters of Aetius were produced and compared; and the fraud was easily detected. Placidia and Boniface lamented their fatal error; and the count had sufficient magnanimity to confide in the forgiveness of his sovereign, or to expose his head to her future resentment. His repentance was fervent and sincere; but he soon discovered that it was no longer in his power to restore the edifice which he had shaken to its foundations. Carthage and the Roman garrisons returned with their general to the allegiance of Valentinian; but the rest of Africa was still distracted with war and faction; and the inexorable king of the Vandals, disdaining all terms of accommodation, sternly refused to relinquish the possession of his prey. The band of veterans who marched under the standard of Boniface, and his hasty levies of provincial troops, were defeated with considerable loss; the victorious Barbarians insulted the open country; and Carthage, Cirta, and Hippo Regius were the only cities that appeared to rise above the general inundation.

The long and narrow tract of the African coast was filled with frequent monuments of Roman art and magnificence; and the respective degrees of improvement might be accurately measured by the distance from Carthage and the Mediterranean. A simple reflection will impress every thinking mind with the clearest idea of fertility and cultivation: the country was extremely populous; the inhabitants reserved a liberal subsistence for their own use; and the annual exportation, particularly of wheat, was so regular and plentiful that Africa deserved the name of the common granary of Rome and of mankind. On a sudden the seven fruitful provinces from Tangier to Tripoli were overwhelmed by the invasion of the Vandals, whose destructive rage has perhaps been exaggerated by popular animosity, religious zeal, and extravagant declamation. War in its fairest form implies a perpetual violation of humanity and justice; and the hostilities of Barbarians are inflamed by the fierce and lawless spirit which incessantly disturbs their peaceful and domestic society. The Vandals, where they found resistance, seldom gave quarter . . . ; and the calamities of war were aggravated by the licentiousness of the Moors and the fanaticism of the Donatists. Yet I shall not easily be persuaded that it was the common practice of the Vandals to extirpate the olives and other fruit trees of a country where they intended to settle: nor can I believe that it was a usual stratagem to slaughter great numbers of their prisoners before the walls of a besieged city for the sole purpose of infecting the air and producing a pestilence of which they themselves must have been the first victims.

The generous mind of Count Boniface was tortured by the exquisite distress of beholding the ruin which he had occasioned and whose rapid progress he was unable to check. After the loss of a battle he retired into Hippo Regius [May A.D. 430]; where he was immediately besieged by an enemy, who considered him as the real bulwark of Africa. . . . The military labors and anxious reflections of Count Boniface were alleviated by the edifying conversation of his friend St. Augustine; till that bishop, the light and pillar of the Catholic church, was gently released, in the third month of the siege and in the seventy-sixth year of his age, from the actual and the impending calamities of his country [August 28, A.D. 430]. The youth of Augustine had been stained by the vices and errors which he so ingenuously confesses; but from the moment of his conversion to that of his death, the manners of the bishop of Hippo were pure and austere: and the most conspicuous of his virtues was an ardent zeal against heretics of every denomination; the Manichaeans, the Donatists, and the Pelagians, against whom he waged a perpetual controversy. When the city, some months after his death, was burnt by the Vandals, the library was fortunately saved which contained his voluminous writings; two hundred and thirty-two separate books or treatises on theological subjects, besides a complete exposition of the psalter and the Gospel, and a copious magazine of epistles and homilies. According to the judgment of the most impartial critics, the superficial learning of Augustine was confined to the Latin language; and his style, though sometimes animated by the eloquence of passion, is usually clouded by false and affected rhetoric. But he possessed a strong, capacious, argumentative mind; he boldly sounded the dark abyss of grace, predestination, free will, and original sin; and the rigid system of Christianity which he framed or restored has been entertained, with public applause and secret reluctance, by the Latin church.

By the skill of Boniface, and perhaps by the ignorance of the Vandals, the siege of Hippo was protracted above fourteen months: the sea was continually open; and when the adjacent country had been exhausted by irregular rapine, the besiegers themselves were compelled by famine to relinquish their enterprise. The importance and danger of Africa were deeply felt by the regent of the West. Placidia implored the assistance of her Eastern ally; and the Italian fleet and army were reinforced by Asper, who sailed from Constantinople with a powerful armament. As soon as the force of the two empires was united under the command of Boniface, he boldly marched against the Vandals; and the loss of a second battle irretrievably decided the fate of Africa [A.D. 431]. He embarked with the precipitation of despair; and the people of Hippo were permitted, with their families and effects, to occupy the vacant place of the soldiers, the greatest part of whom were either slain or made prisoners by the Vandals. The count, whose fatal credulity had wounded the vitals of the republic, might enter the palace of Ravenna with some anxiety, which was soon removed by the smiles of Placidia. Boniface accepted with gratitude the rank of patrician and the dignity of master-general of the Roman armies; but he must have blushed at the sight of those medals in which he was represented with the name and attributes of victory. The discovery of his fraud, the displeasure of the empress, and the distinguished favor of his rival exasperated the haughty and perfidious soul of Aetius. He hastily returned from Gaul to Italy with a retinue, or rather with an army, of Barbarian followers; and such was the weakness of the government that the two generals decided their private quarrel in a bloody battle. Boniface was successful; but he received in the conflict a mortal wound from the spear of his adversary, of which he expired within a few days, in such Christian and charitable sentiments that he exhorted his wife, a rich heiress of Spain, to accept Aetius for her second husband [A.D. 432]. But Aetius could not derive any immediate advantage from the generosity of his dying enemy: he was proclaimed a rebel by the justice of Placidia; and though he attempted to defend some strong fortresses erected on his patrimonial estate, the Imperial power soon compelled him to retire into Pannonia, to the tents of his faithful Huns. The republic was deprived, by their mutual discord, of the service of her two most illustrious champions.

It might naturally be expected, after the retreat of Boniface, that the Vandals would achieve without resistance or delay the conquest of Africa. Eight years, however, elapsed, from the evacuation of Hippo to the reduction of Carthage [A.D. 431–439]. In the midst of that interval, the ambitious Genseric, in the full tide of apparent prosperity, negotiated a treaty of peace.... He subscribed a solemn treaty with the hope of deriving some advantage from the term of its continuance and the moment of its violation. The vigilance of his enemies was relaxed by the protestations of friendship which concealed his hostile approach; and Carthage was at length surprised by the Vandals, five hundred and eighty-five years after the destruction of the city and republic by the younger Scipio.[†]

Among the insipid legends of ecclesiastical history, I am tempted to distinguish the memorable fable of the SEVEN SLEEPERS; whose imaginary date corresponds with the reign of the younger Theodosius, and the conquest of Africa by the Vandals. When the emperor Decius persecuted the Christians, seven noble youths of Ephesus concealed themselves in a spacious cavern in the side of an adjacent mountain; where they were doomed to perish by the tyrant, who gave orders that the entrance should be firmly secured by a pile of huge stones. They immediately fell into a deep slumber, which was miraculously prolonged without injuring the powers of life, during a period of one hundred and eighty-seven years. At the end of that time, the slaves of Adolius, to whom the inheritance of the mountain had descended, removed the stones to supply materials for some rustic edifice: the light of the sun darted into the cavern, and the Seven Sleepers were permitted to awake. After a slumber, as they thought, of a few hours, they were pressed by the calls of hunger; and resolved that Jamblichus, one of their number, should secretly return to the city to purchase bread for the use of his companions. The youth (if we may still employ that appellation) could no longer recognize the once familiar aspect of his native country; and his surprise was increased by the appearance of a large cross triumphantly erected over the principal gate of Ephesus. His singular dress and obsolete language confounded the baker to whom he offered an ancient medal of Decius as the current coin of the empire; and Jamblichus, on the suspicion of a secret treasure, was dragged before the judge. Their mutual inquiries produced the amazing discovery that two centuries were almost elapsed since Jamblichus and his friends had escaped from the rage of a Pagan tyrant. The bishop of Ephesus, the clergy, the magistrates, the people, and, as it is said, the emperor Theodosius himself hastened to visit the cavern of the Seven Sleepers; who bestowed their benediction, related their story, and at the same instant peaceably expired. . . . James of Sarug, a Syrian bishop who was born only two years after the death of the younger Theodosius, has devoted one of his two hundred and thirty homilies to the praise of the young men of Ephesus. Their legend, before the end of the sixth century, was translated from the Syriac into the Latin language, by the care of Gregory of Tours. The hostile communions of the East preserve their memory with equal reverence; and their names are honorably inscribed in the Roman, the Abyssinian, and the Russian calendar. Nor has their reputation been confined to the Christian world. This popular tale, which Mohammed might learn when he drove his camels to the fairs of Syria, is introduced as a divine revelation into the Koran. The story of the Seven Sleepers has been adopted and adorned by the nations, from Bengal to Africa, who profess the Mohammedan religion; and some vestiges of a similar tradition have been discovered in the remote extremities of Scandinavia. . . . But if the interval between two memorable eras could be instantly annihilated; if it were possible, after a momentary slumber of two hundred years, to display the *new* world to the eyes of a spectator who still retained a lively and recent impression of the *old*, . . . [t]he scene could not be more advantageously placed than in the two centuries which elapsed between the reigns of Decius and of Theodosius the Younger. During this period, the seat of government had been transported from Rome to a new city on the banks of the Thracian Bosphorus; and the abuse of military spirit had been suppressed by an artificial system of tame and ceremonious servitude. The throne of the persecuting Decius was filled by a succession of Christian and orthodox princes, who had extirpated the fabulous gods of antiquity: and the public devotion of the age was impatient to exalt the saints and martyrs of the Catholic church on the altars of Diana and Hercules. The union of the Roman empire was dissolved; its genius was humbled in the dust; and armies of unknown Barbarians, issuing from the frozen regions of the North, had established their victorious reign over the fairest provinces of Europe and Africa.

CHAPTER XXXIV

ATTILA

The character, conquests, and court of Attila, king of the Huns. •
Death of Theodosius the Younger. • Elevation of Marcian to the
empire of the East.

The Western world was oppressed by the Goths and Vandals, who fled
before the Huns; but the achievements of the Huns themselves were
not adequate to their power and prosperity [A.D. 376–433]. Their victorious hordes had spread from the Volga to the Danube; but the public force was exhausted by the discord of independent chieftains; their
valor was idly consumed in obscure and predatory excursions; and
they often degraded their national dignity by condescending, for the
hopes of spoil, to enlist under the banners of their fugitive enemies. In
the reign of ATTILA, the Huns again became the terror of the world;
and I shall now describe the character and actions of that formidable
Barbarian; who alternately insulted and invaded the East and the West,
and urged the rapid downfall of the Roman empire.†

Attila, the son of Mundzuk, deduced his noble, perhaps his regal,
descent from the ancient Huns who had formerly contended with the
monarchs of China. His features, according to the observation of a
Gothic historian, bore the stamp of his national origin; and the portrait
of Attila exhibits the genuine deformity of a modern Calmuk; a large
head, a swarthy complexion, small, deep-seated eyes, a flat nose, a few
hairs in the place of a beard, broad shoulders, and a short square body,
of nervous strength, though of a disproportioned form. The haughty
step and demeanor of the king of the Huns expressed the consciousness of his superiority above the rest of mankind; and he had a custom
of fiercely rolling his eyes, as if he wished to enjoy the terror which he
inspired. Yet this savage hero was not inaccessible to pity; his suppliant
enemies might confide in the assurance of peace or pardon; and Attila
was considered by his subjects as a just and indulgent master. He delighted in war; but after he had ascended the throne in a mature age,
his head rather than his hand achieved the conquest of the North; and
the fame of an adventurous soldier was usefully exchanged for that of

a prudent and successful general. The effects of personal valor are so inconsiderable, except in poetry or romance, that victory, even among Barbarians, must depend on the degree of skill with which the passions of the multitude are combined and guided for the service of a single man. The Scythian conquerors, Attila and Zingis, surpassed their rude countrymen in art rather than in courage; and it may be observed that the monarchies both of the Huns and of the Moguls were erected by their founders on the basis of popular superstition. The miraculous conception which fraud and credulity ascribed to the virgin-mother of Zingis raised him above the level of human nature; and the naked prophet who in the name of the Deity invested him with the empire of the earth pointed the valor of the Moguls with irresistible enthusiasm. The religious arts of Attila were not less skillfully adapted to the character of his age and country. It was natural enough that the Scythians should adore with peculiar devotion the god of war; but as they were incapable of forming either an abstract idea or a corporeal representation, they worshiped their tutelar deity under the symbol of an iron cimeter. One of the shepherds of the Huns perceived that a heifer who was grazing had wounded herself in the foot, and curiously followed the track of the blood till he discovered, among the long grass, the point of an ancient sword, which he dug out of the ground and presented to Attila. That magnanimous, or rather that artful, prince accepted, with pious gratitude, this celestial favor; and as the rightful possessor of the *sword of Mars* asserted his divine and indefeasible claim to the dominion of the earth. If the rites of Scythia were practiced on this solemn occasion, a lofty altar, or rather pile of faggots, three hundred yards in length and in breadth, was raised in a spacious plain; and the sword of Mars was placed erect on the summit of this rustic altar, which was annually consecrated by the blood of sheep, horses, and of the hundredth captive. Whether human sacrifices formed any part of the worship of Attila, or whether he propitiated the god of war with the victims which he continually offered in the field of battle, the favorite of Mars soon acquired a sacred character which rendered his conquests more easy and more permanent; and the Barbarian princes confessed, in the language of devotion or flattery, that they could not presume to gaze with a steady eye on the divine majesty of the king of the Huns. His brother Bleda, who reigned over a considerable part of the nation, was compelled to resign his scepter and his life [A.D. 445].

Yet even this cruel act was attributed to a supernatural impulse; and the vigor with which Attila wielded the sword of Mars convinced the world that it had been reserved alone for his invincible arm. But the extent of his empire affords the only remaining evidence of the number and importance of his victories; and the Scythian monarch, however ignorant of the value of science and philosophy, might perhaps lament that his illiterate subjects were destitute of the art which could perpetuate the memory of his exploits.

If a line of separation were drawn between the civilized and the savage climates of the globe; between the inhabitants of cities, who cultivated the earth, and the hunters and shepherds, who dwelt in tents, Attila might aspire to the title of supreme and sole monarch of the Barbarians. He alone, among the conquerors of ancient and modern times, united the two mighty kingdoms of Germany and Scythia; and those vague appellations, when they are applied to his reign, may be understood with an ample latitude.... In time of peace, the dependent princes, with their national troops, attended the royal camp in regular succession; but when Attila collected his military force, he was able to bring into the field an army of five or, according to another account, of seven hundred thousand Barbarians.[†]

While the powers of Europe and Asia were solicitous to avert the impending danger, the alliance of Attila maintained the Vandals in the possession of Africa [A.D. 441 ff.]. An enterprise had been concerted between the courts of Ravenna and Constantinople for the recovery of that valuable province; and the ports of Sicily were already filled with the military and naval forces of Theodosius. But the subtle Genseric, who spread his negotiations round the world, prevented their designs by exciting the king of the Huns to invade the Eastern empire.... The armies of the Eastern empire were vanquished in three successive engagements.[†]

In all their invasions of the civilized empires of the South, the Scythian shepherds have been uniformly actuated by a savage and destructive spirit. The laws of war that restrain the exercise of national rapine and murder are founded on two principles of substantial interest: the knowledge of the permanent benefits which may be obtained by a moderate use of conquest; and a just apprehension lest the desolation which we inflict on the enemy's country may be retaliated on our own. But these considerations of hope and fear are almost unknown in the pastoral state of nations.[†]

It may be affirmed with [some] assurance that the Huns depopulated the provinces of the empire, by the number of Roman subjects whom they led away into captivity. In the hands of a wise legislator, such an industrious colony might have contributed to diffuse through the deserts of Scythia the rudiments of the useful and ornamental arts; but these captives who had been taken in war were accidentally dispersed among the hordes that obeyed the empire of Attila. The estimate of their respective value was formed by the simple judgment of unenlightened and unprejudiced Barbarians. Perhaps they might not understand the merit of a theologian profoundly skilled in the controversies of the Trinity and the Incarnation; yet they respected the ministers of every religion, and the active zeal of the Christian missionaries, without approaching the person or the palace of the monarch, successfully labored in the propagation of the gospel. The pastoral tribes, who were ignorant of the distinction of landed property, must have disregarded the use as well as the abuse of civil jurisprudence; and the skill of an eloquent lawyer could excite only their contempt or their abhorrence. The perpetual intercourse of the Huns and the Goths had communicated the familiar knowledge of the two national dialects; and the Barbarians were ambitious of conversing in Latin, the military idiom even of the Eastern empire. But they disdained the language and the sciences of the Greeks; and the vain sophist or grave philosopher who had enjoyed the flattering applause of the schools was mortified to find that his robust servant was a captive of more value and importance than himself. The mechanic arts were encouraged and esteemed, as they tended to satisfy the wants of the Huns. . . . The Huns might be provoked to insult the misery of their slaves, over whom they exercised a despotic command; but their manners were not susceptible of a refined system of oppression; and the efforts of courage and diligence were often recompensed by the gift of freedom. The historian Priscus, whose embassy is a source of curious instruction, was accosted in the camp of Attila by a stranger who saluted him in the Greek language, but whose dress and figure displayed the appearance of a wealthy Scythian. In the siege of Viminiacum, he had lost, according to his own account, his fortune and liberty; he became the slave of

Onegesius; but his faithful services against the Romans and the Acatzires had gradually raised him to the rank of the native Huns; to whom he was attached by the domestic pledges of a new wife and several children. The spoils of war had restored and improved his private property; he was admitted to the table of his former lord; and the apostate Greek blessed the hour of his captivity, since it had been the introduction to a happy and independent state; which he held by the honorable tenure of military service. This reflection naturally produced a dispute on the advantages and defects of the Roman government, which was severely arraigned by the apostate, and defended by Priscus in a prolix and feeble declamation. The freedman of Onegesius exposed, in true and lively colors, the vices of a declining empire, of which he had so long been the victim; the cruel absurdity of the Roman princes, unable to protect their subjects against the public enemy, unwilling to trust them with arms for their own defense; the intolerable weight of taxes, rendered still more oppressive by the intricate or arbitrary modes of collection; the obscurity of numerous and contradictory laws; the tedious and expensive forms of judicial proceedings; the partial administration of justice; and the universal corruption which increased the influence of the rich and aggravated the misfortunes of the poor. A sentiment of patriotic sympathy was at length revived in the breast of the fortunate exile; and he lamented, with a flood of tears, the guilt or weakness of those magistrates who had perverted the wisest and most salutary institutions.

The timid or selfish policy of the Western Romans had abandoned the Eastern empire to the Huns. The loss of armies, and the want of discipline or virtue, were not supplied by the personal character of the monarch. Theodosius might still affect the style, as well as the title, of *Invincible Augustus*; but he was reduced to solicit the clemency of Attila, who imperiously dictated ... harsh and humiliating conditions of peace [A.D. 446].[†]

The emperor Theodosius did not long survive the most humiliating circumstance of an inglorious life. As he was riding or hunting in the neighborhood of Constantinople, he was thrown from his horse into the River Lycus: the spine of the back was injured by the fall; and he expired some days afterwards, in the fiftieth year of his age, and the forty-third of his reign [July 28, A.D. 450]. His sister Pulcheria, whose authority had been controlled both in civil and ecclesiastical affairs by the pernicious influence of the eunuchs, was unanimously proclaimed Empress of the East; and the Romans, for the first time, submitted to a female reign. No sooner had Pulcheria ascended the throne than she indulged her own and the public resentment by an act of popular justice. Without any legal trial, the eunuch Chrysaphius was executed before the gates of the city; and the immense riches which had been accumulated by the rapacious favorite served only to hasten and to justify his punishment. Amidst the general acclamations of the clergy and people, the empress did not forget the prejudice and disadvantage to which her sex was exposed; and she wisely resolved to prevent their murmurs by the choice of a colleague who would always respect the superior rank and virgin chastity of his wife. She gave her hand to Marcian, a senator about sixty years of age; and the nominal husband of Pulcheria was solemnly invested with the Imperial purple [August 25, A.D. 450]. The zeal which he displayed for the orthodox creed, as it was established by the council of Chalcedon, would alone have inspired the grateful eloquence of the Catholics. But the behavior of Marcian in a private life, and afterwards on the throne, may support a more rational belief that he was qualified to restore and invigorate an empire which had been almost dissolved by the successive weakness of two hereditary monarchs. He was born in Thrace, and educated to the profession of arms; but Marcian's youth had been severely exercised by poverty and misfortune, since his only resource, when he first arrived at Constantinople, consisted in two hundred pieces of gold, which he had borrowed of a friend. He passed nineteen years in the domestic and military service of Aspar and his son Ardaburius; followed those powerful generals to the Persian and African wars; and obtained, by their influence, the honorable rank of tribune and senator. His mild disposition and useful talents, without alarming the jealousy, recommended Marcian to the esteem and favor of his patrons; he had seen, perhaps he had felt, the abuses of a venal and oppressive administration; and his own example gave weight and energy to the laws, which he promulgated for the reformation of manners.

CHAPTER XXXV

INVASION BY ATTILA

Invasion of Gaul by Attila. • He is repulsed by Aetius and the Visigoths. • Attila invades and evacuates Italy. • The deaths of Attila, Aetius, and Valentinian the Third.

It was the opinion of Marcian that war should be avoided as long as it is possible to preserve a secure and honorable peace; but it was likewise his opinion that peace cannot be honorable or secure if the sovereign betrays a pusillanimous aversion to war. This temperate courage dictated his reply to the demands of Attila, who insolently pressed the payment of the annual tribute [A.D. 450]. The emperor signified to the Barbarians that they must no longer insult the majesty of Rome by the mention of a tribute; that he was disposed to reward, with becoming liberality, the faithful friendship of his allies; but that if they presumed to violate the public peace, they should feel that he possessed troops, and arms, and resolution to repel their attacks. The same language, even in the camp of the Huns, was used by his ambassador Apollonius, whose bold refusal to deliver the presents till he had been admitted to a personal interview displayed a sense of dignity and a contempt of danger which Attila was not prepared to expect from the degenerate Romans. He threatened to chastise the rash successor of Theodosius; but he hesitated whether he should first direct his invincible arms against the Eastern or the Western empire. While mankind awaited his decision with awful suspense, he sent an equal defiance to the courts of Ravenna and Constantinople; and his ministers saluted the two emperors with the same haughty declaration [A.D. 450]. "Attila, *my* lord and *thy* lord, commands thee to provide a palace for his immediate reception." But as the Barbarian despised, or affected to despise, the Romans of the East, whom he had so often vanquished, he soon declared his resolution of suspending the easy conquest till he had achieved a more glorious and important enterprise. In the memorable invasions of Gaul and Italy, the Huns were naturally attracted by the wealth and fertility of those provinces; but the particular motives and provocations of Attila can only be explained by the state of the Western empire under the reign of Valentinian, or, to speak more correctly, under the administration of Aetius [A.D. 433–454].

After the death of his rival Boniface, Aetius had prudently retired to the tents of the Huns; and he was indebted to their alliance for his safety and his restoration. Instead of the suppliant language of a guilty exile, he solicited his pardon at the head of sixty thousand Barbarians; and the empress Placidia confessed by a feeble resistance that the condescension which might have been ascribed to clemency was the effect of weakness or fear. She delivered herself, her son Valentinian, and the Western empire into the hands of an insolent subject; nor could Placidia protect the son-in-law of Boniface, the virtuous and faithful Sebastian, from the implacable persecution which urged him from one kingdom to another, till he miserably perished in the service of the Vandals. The fortunate Aetius, who was immediately promoted to the rank of patrician and thrice invested with the honors of the consulship, assumed, with the title of master of the cavalry and infantry, the whole military power of the state; and he is sometimes styled by contemporary writers the duke, or general, of the Romans of the West. His prudence rather than his virtue engaged him to leave the grandson of Theodosius in the possession of the purple; and Valentinian was permitted to enjoy the peace and luxury of Italy, while the patrician appeared in the glorious light of a hero and a patriot who supported near twenty years the ruins of the Western empire. The Gothic historian [Jornandes] ingenuously confesses that Aetius was born for the salvation of the Roman republic; and the following portrait, though it is drawn in the fairest colors, must be allowed to contain a much larger proportion of truth than of flattery. "His mother was a wealthy and noble Italian, and his father Gaudentius, who held a distinguished rank in the province of Scythia, gradually rose from the station of a military *domestic* to the dignity of master of the cavalry. Their son, who was enrolled almost in his infancy in the guards, was given as a hostage, first to Alaric, and afterwards to the Huns; and he successively obtained the civil and military honors of the palace, for which he was equally qualified by superior merit." . . . The Barbarians who had seated themselves in the Western provinces were insensibly taught to respect the faith and valor of the patrician Aetius. He soothed their passions, consulted their prejudices, balanced their interests, and checked their ambition. A seasonable treaty which he concluded with Genseric protected Italy from the depredations of the Vandals; the independent Britons implored and acknowledged his salutary aid; the Imperial authority was restored and maintained in Gaul and Spain; and he compelled the Franks and the Suevi, whom he had vanquished in the field, to become the useful confederates of the republic.

[*Indeed, despite some restitution of imperial rule within Gaul and Spain, the West remains dismembered. The kingdoms of the Suevi (in Spain), the Visigoths (under Theodoric in southwestern Gaul, with their capital at Toulouse), the Franks (under Merovingian kings in northeastern Gaul, along the lower Rhine), and the Vandals (in North Africa) constitute independent forces that must be reckoned with both by Aetius and by Attila. Dynastic troubles in the kingdom of the Franks provide Attila with a pretext for invasion (A.D. 451). Allied forces of Visigoths and Romans beat Attila's army in the battle of Châlons. Aetius, however, fearing that the allied Goths may enjoy a dangerous increase in power, allows Attila to retreat.*]

After the departure of the Goths and the separation of the allied army, Attila was surprised at the vast silence that reigned over the plains of Châlons: the suspicion of some hostile stratagem detained him several days within the circle of his wagons, and his retreat beyond the Rhine confessed the last victory which was achieved in the name of the Western empire. Meroveus and his Franks, observing a prudent distance and magnifying the opinion of their strength by the numerous fires which they kindled every night, continued to follow the rear of the Huns till they reached the confines of Thuringia. The Thuringians served in the army of Attila: they traversed, both in their march and in their return, the territories of the Franks; and it was perhaps in this war that they exercised the cruelties which, about fourscore years afterwards, were revenged by the son of Clovis. They massacred their hostages as well as their captives: two hundred young maidens were tortured with exquisite and unrelenting rage; their bodies were torn asunder by wild horses, or their bones were crushed under the weight of rolling wagons; and their unburied limbs were abandoned on the public roads as a prey to dogs and vultures. Such were those savage ancestors whose imaginary virtues have sometimes excited the praise and envy of civilized ages.

Neither the spirit, nor the forces, nor the reputation of Attila were impaired by the failure of the Gallic expedition. In the ensuing spring he ... immediately took the field, passed the Alps, [and] invaded Italy [A.D. 452].... The Italians, who had long since renounced the exercise of arms, were surprised, after forty years' peace, by the approach of a formidable Barbarian whom they abhorred as the enemy of their religion as well as of their republic. Amidst the general consternation, Aetius alone was incapable of fear; but it was impossible that he should achieve, alone and unassisted, any military exploits worthy of his former renown. The Barbarians who had defended Gaul refused to march to the relief of Italy; and the succors promised by the Eastern emperor were distant and doubtful. Since Aetius, at the head of his domestic troops, still maintained the field and harassed or retarded the march of Attila, he never showed himself more truly great than at the time when his conduct was blamed by an ignorant and ungrateful people. If the mind of Valentinian had been susceptible of any generous sentiments, he would have chosen such a general for his example and his guide. But the timid grandson of Theodosius, instead of sharing the dangers, escaped from the sound of war; and his hasty retreat from Ravenna to Rome, from an impregnable fortress to an open capital, betrayed his secret intention of abandoning Italy as soon as the danger should approach his Imperial person. This shameful abdication was suspended, however, by the spirit of doubt and delay which commonly adheres to pusillanimous counsels, and sometimes corrects their pernicious tendency. The Western emperor, with the senate and people of Rome, embraced the more salutary resolution of deprecating, by a solemn and suppliant embassy, the wrath of Attila. This important commission was accepted by Avienus, who, from his birth and riches, his consular dignity, the numerous train of his clients, and his personal abilities, held the first rank in the Roman senate. The specious and artful character of Avienus was admirably qualified to conduct a negotiation either of public or private interest: his colleague Trigetius had exercised the Praetorian praefecture of Italy; and Leo, bishop of Rome, consented to expose his life for the safety of his flock. The genius of Leo was exercised and displayed in the public misfortunes; and he has deserved the appellation of *Great* by the successful zeal with which he labored to establish his opinions and his authority under the venerable names of orthodox faith and ecclesiastical discipline. The Roman ambassadors were introduced to the tent of Attila as he lay encamped at the place where the slow-winding Mincius is lost in the foaming waves of the Lake Benacus and, trampled, with his Scythian cavalry, the farms of Catullus and Virgil. The Barbarian monarch listened with favorable and even respectful attention; and the deliverance of Italy was purchased by the immense ransom, or dowry, of the princess Honoria. The state of his army might facilitate the treaty and hasten his retreat. Their martial spirit was relaxed by the wealth and indolence of a warm climate. The shepherds of the North, whose ordinary food consisted of milk and raw flesh, indulged themselves too freely in the use of bread, of wine, and of meat prepared and seasoned by the arts of cookery; and the progress of disease revenged in some measure the injuries of the Italians. When Attila declared his resolution of carrying his victorious arms to the gates of Rome, he was admonished by his friends as well as by his enemies that Alaric had not long survived the conquest of the eternal city. His mind, superior to real danger, was assaulted by imaginary terrors; nor could he escape the influence of superstition, which had so often been subservient to his designs. The pressing eloquence of Leo, his majestic aspect and sacerdotal robes, excited the veneration of Attila for the spiritual father of the Christians. The apparition of the two apostles, St. Peter and St. Paul, who menaced the Barbarian with instant death if he rejected the prayer of their successor, is one of the noblest legends of ecclesiastical tradition. The safety of Rome might deserve the interposition of celestial beings; and some indulgence is due to a fable which has been represented by the pencil of Raphael and the chisel of Algardi.

Before the king of the Huns evacuated Italy, he threatened to return more dreadful and more implacable if his bride, the princess Honoria [the disgraced sister of Valentinian, who, in A.D. 450, had appealed directly to Attila, and who consequently had served as one of Attila's pretexts for war], were not delivered to his ambassadors within the term stipulated by the treaty. Yet, in the meanwhile, Attila relieved his tender anxiety by adding a beautiful maid, whose name was Ildico, to the list of his innumerable wives. Their marriage was celebrated with Barbaric pomp and festivity at his wooden palace beyond the Danube; and the monarch, oppressed with wine and sleep, retired at a late hour from the banquet to the nuptial bed. His attendants continued to respect his pleasures, or his repose, the greatest part of the ensuing day, till the unusual silence alarmed their fears and suspicions;

and after attempting to awaken Attila by loud and repeated cries, they at length broke into the royal apartment. They found the trembling bride sitting by the bedside, hiding her face with her veil and lamenting her own danger as well as the death of the king, who had expired during the night [A.D. 453]. An artery had suddenly burst: and as Attila lay in a supine posture, he was suffocated by a torrent of blood which, instead of finding a passage through the nostrils, regurgitated into the lungs and stomach. His body was solemnly exposed in the midst of the plain, under a silken pavilion; and the chosen squadrons of the Huns, wheeling round in measured evolutions, chanted a funeral song to the memory of a hero, glorious in his life, invincible in his death, the father of his people, the scourge of his enemies, and the terror of the world. According to their national custom, the Barbarians cut off a part of their hair, gashed their faces with unseemly wounds, and bewailed their valiant leader as he deserved, not with the tears of women but with the blood of warriors. The remains of Attila were enclosed within three coffins, of gold, of silver, and of iron, and privately buried in the night: the spoils of nations were thrown into his grave; the captives who had opened the ground were inhumanly massacred; and the same Huns who had indulged such excessive grief feasted, with dissolute and intemperate mirth, about the recent sepulchre of their king. It was reported at Constantinople that on the fortunate night on which he expired, Marcian beheld in a dream the bow of Attila broken asunder: and the report may be allowed to prove how seldom the image of that formidable Barbarian was absent from the mind of a Roman emperor.

The revolution which subverted the empire of the Huns established the fame of Attila, whose genius alone had sustained the huge and disjointed fabric. After his death, the boldest chieftains aspired to the rank of kings; the most powerful kings refused to acknowledge a superior; and the numerous sons whom so many various mothers bore to the deceased monarch divided and disputed, like a private inheritance, the sovereign command of the nations of Germany and Scythia. . . . They were soon overwhelmed by a torrent of new Barbarians, who followed the same road which their own ancestors had formerly discovered. The *Geougen,* or Avares, whose residence is assigned by the Greek writers to the shores of the ocean, impelled the adjacent tribes; till at length the Igours of the North, issuing from the cold Si-

berian regions which produce the most valuable furs, spread themselves over the desert as far as the Borysthenes and the Caspian gates;
and finally extinguished the empire of the Huns.

Such an event might contribute to the safety of the Eastern empire,
under the reign of a prince who conciliated the friendship without forfeiting the esteem of the Barbarians. But the emperor of the West, the
feeble and dissolute Valentinian, who had reached his thirty-fifth year
without attaining the age of reason or courage, abused this apparent
security to undermine the foundations of his own throne by the murder of the patrician Aetius [A.D. 454]. From the instinct of a base and
jealous mind, he hated the man who was universally celebrated as the
terror of the Barbarians and the support of the republic; and his new
favorite, the eunuch Heraclius, awakened the emperor from the supine
lethargy which might be disguised, during the life of Placidia, by the
excuse of filial piety. The fame of Aetius, his wealth and dignity, the
numerous and martial train of Barbarian followers, his powerful dependents who filled the civil offices of the state, and the hopes of his
son Gaudentius, who was already contracted to Eudoxia, the emperor's
daughter, had raised him above the rank of a subject. The ambitious
designs of which he was secretly accused excited the fears as well as
the resentment of Valentinian. Aetius himself, supported by the consciousness of his merit, his services, and perhaps his innocence, seems
to have maintained a haughty and indiscreet behavior. The patrician
offended his sovereign by a hostile declaration; he aggravated the offense by compelling him to ratify with a solemn oath a treaty of reconciliation and alliance; he proclaimed his suspicions, he neglected his
safety; and from a vain confidence that the enemy, whom he despised,
was incapable even of a manly crime, he rashly ventured his person in
the palace of Rome. Whilst he urged, perhaps with intemperate vehemence, the marriage of his son, Valentinian, drawing his sword, the
first sword he had ever drawn, plunged it in the breast of a general who
had saved his empire: his courtiers and eunuchs ambitiously struggled
to imitate their master; and Aetius, pierced with a hundred wounds,
fell dead in the royal presence. Boethius, the Praetorian praefect, was
killed at the same moment, and before the event could be divulged, the
principal friends of the patrician were summoned to the palace and
separately murdered. The horrid deed, palliated by the specious names
of justice and necessity, was immediately communicated by the em-

peror to his soldiers, his subjects, and his allies. The nations who were strangers or enemies to Aetius generously deplored the unworthy fate of a hero: the Barbarians who had been attached to his service dissembled their grief and resentment: and the public contempt, which had been so long entertained for Valentinian, was at once converted into deep and universal abhorrence. Such sentiments seldom pervade the walls of a palace; yet the emperor was confounded by the honest reply of a Roman whose approbation he had not disdained to solicit. "I am ignorant, sir, of your motives or provocations; I only know that you have acted like a man who cuts off his right hand with his left."

The luxury of Rome seems to have attracted the long and frequent visits of Valentinian; who was consequently more despised at Rome than in any other part of his dominions. A republican spirit was insensibly revived in the senate, as their authority and even their supplies became necessary for the support of his feeble government. The stately demeanor of an hereditary monarch offended their pride; and the pleasures of Valentinian were injurious to the peace and honor of noble families. The birth of the empress Eudoxia was equal to his own, and her charms and tender affection deserved those testimonies of love which her inconstant husband dissipated in vague and unlawful amours. Petronius Maximus, a wealthy senator of the Anician family, who had been twice consul, was possessed of a chaste and beautiful wife: her obstinate resistance served only to irritate the desires of Valentinian; and he resolved to accomplish them, either by stratagem or force. Deep gaming was one of the vices of the court: the emperor, who by chance or contrivance had gained from Maximus a considerable sum, uncourteously exacted his ring as a security for the debt; and sent it by a trusty messenger to his wife, with an order, in her husband's name, that she should immediately attend the empress Eudoxia. The unsuspecting wife of Maximus was conveyed in her litter to the Imperial palace; the emissaries of her impatient lover conducted her to a remote and silent bed-chamber; and Valentinian violated without remorse the laws of hospitality. Her tears when she returned home, her deep affliction, and her bitter reproaches against a husband whom she considered as the accomplice of his own shame excited Maximus to a just revenge; the desire of revenge was stimulated by ambition; and he might reasonably aspire by the free suffrage of the Roman senate to the throne of a detested and despicable rival. Valentinian, who supposed that every human breast was devoid, like his own, of friendship and gratitude, had imprudently admitted among his guards several domestics and followers of Aetius. Two of these, of Barbarian race, were persuaded to execute a sacred and honorable duty by punishing with death the assassin of their patron; and their intrepid courage did not long expect a favorable moment. Whilst Valentinian amused himself in the field of Mars with the spectacle of some military sports, they suddenly rushed upon him with drawn weapons, despatched the guilty Heraclius, and stabbed the emperor to the heart, without the least opposition from his numerous train, who seemed to rejoice in the tyrant's death [March 16, A.D. 455]. Such was the fate of Valentinian the Third, the last Roman emperor of the family of Theodosius. He faithfully imitated the hereditary weakness of his cousin and his two uncles, without inheriting the gentleness, the purity, the innocence which alleviate in their characters the want of spirit and ability. Valentinian was less excusable, since he had passions without virtues: even his religion was questionable; and though he never deviated into the paths of heresy, he scandalized the pious Christians by his attachment to the profane arts of magic and divination.

As early as the time of Cicero and Varro, it was the opinion of the Roman augurs that the *twelve vultures* which Romulus had seen represented the *twelve centuries* assigned for the fatal period of his city. This prophecy, disregarded perhaps in the season of health and prosperity, inspired the people with gloomy apprehensions when the twelfth century, clouded with disgrace and misfortune, was almost elapsed; and even posterity must acknowledge, with some surprise, that the arbitrary interpretation of an accidental or fabulous circumstance has been seriously verified in the downfall of the Western empire. But its fall was announced by a clearer omen than the flight of vultures: the Roman government appeared every day less formidable to its enemies, more odious and oppressive to its subjects. The taxes were multiplied with the public distress; economy was neglected in proportion as it became necessary; and the injustice of the rich shifted the unequal burden from themselves to the people, whom they defrauded of the indulgences that might sometimes have alleviated their misery. The severe inquisition which confiscated their goods and tortured their persons compelled the subjects of Valentinian to prefer the more simple tyranny of the Barbarians, to fly to the woods and mountains, or to embrace the vile and abject condition of mercenary servants. They abjured and abhorred the name of Roman citizens, which had formerly excited the ambition of mankind. The Armorican provinces of Gaul and the greatest part of Spain were thrown into a state of disorderly independence by the confederations of the Bagaudae; and the Imperial ministers pursued with proscriptive laws and ineffectual arms the rebels whom they had made. If all the Barbarian conquerors had been annihilated in the same hour, their total destruction would not have restored the empire of the West: and if Rome still survived, she survived the loss of freedom, of virtue, and of honor.

CHAPTER XXXVI

TOTAL EXTINCTION OF THE WESTERN EMPIRE

Sack of Rome by Genseric, king of the Vandals. • His naval depredations. • Succession of the last emperors of the West, Maximus, Avitus, Majorian, Severus, Anthemius, Olybrius, Glycerius, Nepos, Augustulus. • Total extinction of the Western empire. • Reign of Odoacer, the first Barbarian king of Italy.

The loss or desolation of the provinces from the ocean to the Alps impaired the glory and greatness of Rome: her internal prosperity was irretrievably destroyed by the separation of Africa. The rapacious Vandals confiscated the patrimonial estates of the senators and intercepted the regular subsidies which relieved the poverty and encouraged the idleness of the plebeians. The distress of the Romans was soon aggravated by an unexpected attack; and the province, so long cultivated for their use by industrious and obedient subjects, was armed against them by an ambitious Barbarian. The Vandals and Alani who followed the successful standard of Genseric had acquired a rich and fertile territory, which stretched along the coast above ninety days' journey from Tangier to Tripoli; but their narrow limits were pressed and confined on either side by the sandy desert and the Mediterranean. The discovery and conquest of the Black nations that might dwell beneath the torrid zone could not tempt the rational ambition of Genseric; but he cast his eyes towards the sea; he resolved to create a naval power, and his bold resolution was executed with steady and active perseverance. The woods of Mount Atlas afforded an inexhaustible nursery of timber: his new subjects were skilled in the arts of navigation and ship-building; he animated his daring Vandals to embrace a mode of warfare which would render every maritime country accessible to their arms; the Moors and Africans were allured by the hopes of plunder; and after an interval of six centuries, the fleets that issued from the port of Carthage again claimed the empire of the Mediterranean [A.D. 440 ff.]. . . . The revolutions of the palace, which left the Western empire without a defender and without a lawful prince, dispelled the apprehensions and stimulated the avarice of Genseric. He immediately equipped a numerous fleet of Vandals and Moors and cast anchor at the mouth of the Tiber, about three months after the death of Valentinian and the elevation of Maximus to the Imperial throne.[†]

The injury which [the senator Petronius Maximus] received from the emperor Valentinian appears to excuse the most bloody revenge. Yet a philosopher might have reflected that if the resistance of his wife had been sincere, her chastity was still inviolate, and that it could never be restored if she had consented to the will of the adulterer. A patriot would have hesitated before he plunged himself and his country into those inevitable calamities which must follow the extinction of the royal house of Theodosius. The imprudent Maximus disregarded these salutary considerations; he gratified his resentment and ambition; he saw the bleeding corpse of Valentinian at his feet; and he heard himself saluted Emperor by the unanimous voice of the senate and people. But the day of his inauguration was the last day of his happiness [March 17, A.D. 455]. He was imprisoned (such is the lively expression of Sidonius) in the palace; and after passing a sleepless night, he sighed that he had attained the summit of his wishes and aspired only to descend from the dangerous elevation.[†]

The reign of Maximus continued about three months. His hours, of which he had lost the command, were disturbed by remorse, or guilt, or terror, and his throne was shaken by the seditions of the soldiers, the people, and the confederate Barbarians. The marriage of his son Paladius with the eldest daughter of the late emperor might tend to establish the hereditary succession of his family; but the violence which he offered to the empress Eudoxia could proceed only from the blind impulse of lust or revenge. His own wife, the cause of these tragic events, had been seasonably removed by death; and the widow of Valentinian was compelled to violate her decent mourning, perhaps her real grief, and to submit to the embraces of a presumptuous usurper whom she suspected as the assassin of her deceased husband. These suspicions were soon justified by the indiscreet confession of Maximus himself; and he wantonly provoked the hatred of his reluctant bride, who was still conscious that she was descended from a line of emperors. From the East, however, Eudoxia could not hope to obtain any effectual assistance; her father and her aunt Pulcheria were dead; her mother languished at Jerusalem in disgrace and exile; and the scepter of Constantinople was in the hands of a stranger. She directed her eyes towards Carthage; secretly implored the aid of the king of the Vandals; and persuaded Genseric to improve the fair opportunity of disguising his rapacious designs by the specious names of honor, justice, and compassion. Whatever abilities Maximus might have shown in a subordinate station, he was found incapable of administering an empire; and though he might easily have been informed of the naval preparations which were made on the opposite shores of Africa, he expected with supine indifference the approach of the enemy, without adopting any measures of defense, of negotiation, or of a timely retreat. When the Vandals disembarked at the mouth of the Tiber, the emperor was suddenly roused from his lethargy by the clamors of a trembling and exasperated multitude. The only hope which presented itself to his astonished mind was that of a precipitate flight, and he exhorted the senators to imitate the example of their prince. But no sooner did Maximus appear in the streets than he was assaulted by a shower of stones; a Roman or a Burgundian soldier claimed the honor of the first wound; his mangled body was ignominiously cast into the Tiber; the Roman people rejoiced in the punishment which they had inflicted on the author of the public calamities; and the domestics of Eudoxia signalized their zeal in the service of their mistress.

On the third day after the tumult, Genseric boldly advanced from the port of Ostia to the gates of the defenseless city. Instead of a sally of the Roman youth, there issued from the gates an unarmed and venerable procession of the bishop at the head of his clergy. The fearless spirit of Leo, his authority and eloquence, *again* mitigated the fierceness of a Barbarian conqueror; the king of the Vandals promised to spare the unresisting multitude, to protect the buildings from fire, and to exempt the captives from torture; and although such orders were neither seriously given nor strictly obeyed, the mediation of Leo was glorious to himself, and in some degree beneficial to his country. But Rome and its inhabitants were delivered to the licentiousness of the Vandals and Moors, whose blind passions revenged the injuries of Carthage. The pillage lasted fourteen days and nights [June 15–29, A.D. 455]; and all that yet remained of public or private wealth, of sa-

cred or profane treasure, was diligently transported to the vessels of
Genseric. Among the spoils, the splendid relics of two temples, or
rather of two religions, exhibited a memorable example of the vicissitudes of human and divine things. Since the abolition of Paganism, the
Capitol had been violated and abandoned; yet the statues of the gods
and heroes were still respected, and the curious roof of gilt bronze was
reserved for the rapacious hands of Genseric. The holy instruments of
the Jewish worship, the gold table and the gold candlestick with seven
branches, originally framed according to the particular instructions of
God himself, and which were placed in the sanctuary of his temple,
had been ostentatiously displayed to the Roman people in the triumph
of Titus. They were afterwards deposited in the temple of Peace; and
at the end of four hundred years, the spoils of Jerusalem were transferred from Rome to Carthage by a Barbarian who derived his origin
from the shores of the Baltic. These ancient monuments might attract
the notice of curiosity, as well as of avarice. But the Christian churches,
enriched and adorned by the prevailing superstition of the times, afforded more plentiful materials for sacrilege; and the pious liberality
of Pope Leo, who melted six silver vases, the gift of Constantine, each
of a hundred pounds weight, is an evidence of the damage which he
attempted to repair. In the forty-five years that had elapsed since the
Gothic invasion, the pomp and luxury of Rome were in some measure
restored; and it was difficult either to escape or to satisfy the avarice of
a conqueror who possessed leisure to collect and ships to transport the
wealth of the capital. The Imperial ornaments of the palace, the magnificent furniture and wardrobe, the sideboards of massy plate, were
accumulated with disorderly rapine; the gold and silver amounted to
several thousand talents; yet even the brass and copper were laboriously removed. Eudoxia herself, who advanced to meet her friend and
deliverer, soon bewailed the imprudence of her own conduct. She was
rudely stripped of her jewels; and the unfortunate empress, with her
two daughters, the only surviving remains of the great Theodosius,
was compelled, as a captive, to follow the haughty Vandal; who immediately hoisted sail and returned with a prosperous navigation to the
port of Carthage. Many thousand Romans of both sexes, chosen for
some useful or agreeable qualifications, reluctantly embarked on board
the fleet of Genseric; and their distress was aggravated by the unfeeling Barbarians who, in the division of the booty, separated the wives

from their husbands, and the children from their parents. The charity of Deogratias, bishop of Carthage, was their only consolation and support. He generously sold the gold and silver plate of the church to purchase the freedom of some, to alleviate the slavery of others, and to assist the wants and infirmities of a captive multitude whose health was impaired by the hardships which they had suffered in their passage from Italy to Africa. By his order, two spacious churches were converted into hospitals; the sick were distributed into convenient beds, and liberally supplied with food and medicines; and the aged prelate repeated his visits both in the day and night, with an assiduity that surpassed his strength and a tender sympathy which enhanced the value of his services. Compare this scene with the field of Cannae; and judge between Hannibal and the successor of St. Cyprian.

The deaths of Aetius and Valentinian had relaxed the ties which held the Barbarians of Gaul in peace and subordination. The sea-coast was infested by the Saxons; the Alemanni and the Franks advanced from the Rhine to the Seine; and the ambition of the Goths seemed to meditate more extensive and permanent conquests. The emperor Maximus relieved himself, by a judicious choice, from the weight of these distant cares; he silenced the solicitations of his friends, listened to the voice of fame, and promoted a stranger to the general command of the forces of Gaul. Avitus, the stranger whose merit was so nobly rewarded, descended from a wealthy and honorable family in the diocese of Auvergne. The convulsions of the times urged him to embrace with the same ardor the civil and military professions: and the indefatigable youth blended the studies of literature and jurisprudence with the exercise of arms and hunting. Thirty years of his life were laudably spent in the public service; he alternately displayed his talents in war and negotiation; and the soldier of Aetius, after executing the most important embassies, was raised to the station of Praetorian praefect of Gaul. Either the merit of Avitus excited envy or his moderation was desirous of repose, since he calmly retired to an estate which he possessed in the neighborhood of Clermont. A copious stream, issuing from the mountain and falling headlong in many a loud and foaming cascade, discharged its waters into a lake about two miles in length, and the villa was pleasantly seated on the margin of the lake. The baths, the porticos, the summer and winter apartments were adapted to the purposes of luxury and use; and the adjacent country afforded the various prospects of woods, pastures, and meadows. In this retreat, where Avitus amused his leisure with books, rural sports, the practice of husbandry, and the society of his friends, he received the Imperial diploma which constituted him master-general of the cavalry and infantry of Gaul. He assumed the military command; the Barbarians suspended their fury; and whatever means he might employ, whatever concessions he might be forced to make, the people enjoyed the benefits of actual tranquility. But the fate of Gaul depended on the Visigoths; and the Roman general, less attentive to his dignity than to the public interest, did not disdain to visit Toulouse in the character of an ambassador. He was received with courteous hospitality by Theodoric, the king of the Goths; but while Avitus laid the foundations of a solid alliance with that powerful nation, he was astonished by the intelligence that the emperor Maximus was slain and that Rome had been pillaged by the Vandals. A vacant throne, which he might ascend without guilt or danger, tempted his ambition; and the Visigoths were easily persuaded to support his claim by their irresistible suffrage [August 15, A.D. 455]. They loved the person of Avitus; they respected his virtues; and they were not insensible of the advantage as well as honor of giving an emperor to the West. The season was now approaching in which the annual assembly of the seven provinces was held at Arles; their deliberations might perhaps be influenced by the presence of Theodoric and his martial brothers; but their choice would naturally incline to the most illustrious of their countrymen. Avitus, after a decent resistance, accepted the Imperial diadem from the representatives of Gaul; and his election was ratified by the acclamations of the Barbarians and provincials. The formal consent of Marcian, emperor of the East, was solicited and obtained; but the senate, Rome, and Italy, though humbled by their recent calamities, submitted with a secret murmur to the presumption of the Gallic usurper.

[*Nominally the "dutiful servant of Avitus," Theodoric leads the Gothic nation of Gaul against the nation of the Suevi in Spain.*]

[But Theodoric] was stopped in the full career of success, and recalled from Spain before he could provide for the security of his conquests [A.D. 456]. . . . Whilst the king of the Visigoths fought and vanquished in the name of Avitus, the reign of Avitus had expired; and both the honor and the interest of Theodoric were deeply wounded by the disgrace of a friend whom he had seated on the throne of the Western empire.

The pressing solicitations of the senate and people persuaded the emperor Avitus to fix his residence at Rome, and to accept the consulship for the ensuing year. . . . Avitus, at a time when the Imperial dignity was reduced to a preeminence of toil and danger, indulged himself in the pleasures of Italian luxury: age had not extinguished his amorous inclinations; and he is accused of insulting, with indiscreet and ungenerous raillery, the husbands whose wives he had seduced or violated. But the Romans were not inclined either to excuse his faults or to acknowledge his virtues. The several parts of the empire became every day more alienated from each other; and the stranger of Gaul was the object of popular hatred and contempt. The senate asserted their legitimate claim in the election of an emperor; and their authority, which had been originally derived from the old constitution, was again fortified by the actual weakness of a declining monarchy. Yet even such a monarchy might have resisted the votes of an unarmed senate if their discontent had not been supported, or perhaps inflamed, by the Count Ricimer, one of the principal commanders of the Barbarian troops who formed the military defense of Italy. The daughter of Wallia, king of the Visigoths, was the mother of Ricimer; but he was descended on the father's side from the nation of the Suevi; his pride or patriotism might be exasperated by the misfortunes of his countrymen; and he obeyed with reluctance an emperor in whose elevation he had not been consulted. His faithful and important services against the common enemy rendered him still more formidable; and after destroying on the coast of Corsica a fleet of Vandals which consisted of sixty galleys, Ricimer returned in triumph with the appellation of the Deliverer of Italy. He chose that moment to signify to Avitus that his reign was at an end; and the feeble emperor, at a distance from his Gothic allies, was compelled, after a short and unavailing struggle, to abdicate the purple [October 16, A.D. 456].†

The successor of Avitus presents the welcome discovery of a great and heroic character such as sometimes arise in a degenerate age to vindicate the honor of the human species. The emperor Majorian has deserved the praises of his contemporaries, and of posterity; and these praises may be strongly expressed in the words of [Procopius,] a judicious and disinterested historian: "That he was gentle to his subjects; that he was terrible to his enemies; and that he excelled, in *every* virtue, *all* his predecessors who had reigned over the Romans." Such a testimony may justify at least the panegyric of Sidonius; and we may acquiesce in the assurance that, although the obsequious orator would have flattered with equal zeal the most worthless of princes, the extraordinary merit of his object confined him, on this occasion, within the bounds of truth. . . . [Majorian's] intimate connection with Count Ricimer was the immediate step by which he ascended the throne of the Western empire. During the vacancy that succeeded the abdication of Avitus, the ambitious Barbarian, whose birth excluded him from the Imperial dignity, governed Italy with the title of patrician; resigned to his friend the conspicuous station of master-general of the cavalry and infantry; and, after an interval of some months, consented to the unanimous wish of the Romans, whose favor Majorian had solicited by a recent victory over the Alemanni. He was invested with the purple at Ravenna [A.D. 457].[†]

The private and public actions of Majorian are very imperfectly known: but his laws, remarkable for an original cast of thought and expression, faithfully represent the character of a sovereign who loved his people, who sympathized in their distress, who had studied the causes of the decline of the empire, and who was capable of applying (as far as such reformation was practicable) judicious and effectual remedies to the public disorders [A.D. 457–461]. His regulations concerning the finances manifestly tended to remove, or at least to mitigate, the most intolerable grievances. From the first hour of his reign, he was solicitous (I translate his own words) to relieve the weary fortunes of the provincials oppressed by the accumulated weight of indictions and superindictions. With this view he granted a universal amnesty, a final and absolute discharge of all arrears of tribute, of all debts which, under any pretense, the fiscal officers might demand from the people. This wise dereliction of obsolete, vexatious, and unprofitable claims improved and purified the sources of the public revenue; and the subject who could now look back without despair might labor with hope and gratitude for himself and for his country.[†]

The spectator who casts a mournful view over the ruins of ancient Rome is tempted to accuse the memory of the Goths and Vandals for the mischief which they had neither leisure, nor power, nor perhaps

inclination to perpetrate. The tempest of war might strike some lofty turrets to the ground; but the destruction which undermined the foundations of those massy fabrics was prosecuted, slowly and silently, during
a period of ten centuries; and the motives of interest that afterwards
operated without shame or control were severely checked by the taste
and spirit of the emperor Majorian. The decay of the city had gradually impaired the value of the public works. The circus and theaters
might still excite, but they seldom gratified, the desires of the people:
the temples which had escaped the zeal of the Christians were no
longer inhabited, either by gods or men; the diminished crowds of the
Romans were lost in the immense space of their baths and porticos;
and the stately libraries and halls of justice became useless to an indolent generation whose repose was seldom disturbed either by study or
business. The monuments of consular, or Imperial, greatness were no
longer revered as the immortal glory of the capital: they were only esteemed as an inexhaustible mine of materials, cheaper and more convenient than the distant quarry. Specious petitions were continually
addressed to the easy magistrates of Rome, which stated the want of
stones or bricks for some necessary service: the fairest forms of architecture were rudely defaced for the sake of some paltry or pretended
repairs; and the degenerate Romans, who converted the spoil to their
own emolument, demolished, with sacrilegious hands, the labors of
their ancestors. Majorian, who had often sighed over the desolation
of the city, applied a severe remedy to the growing evil. He reserved to
the prince and senate the sole cognizance of the extreme cases which
might justify the destruction of an ancient edifice; imposed a fine of
fifty pounds of gold (two thousand pounds sterling) on every magistrate who should presume to grant such illegal and scandalous license,
and threatened to chastise the criminal obedience of their subordinate
officers by a severe whipping and the amputation of both their hands.
In the last instance, the legislator might seem to forget the proportion
of guilt and punishment; but his zeal arose from a generous principle,
and Majorian was anxious to protect the monuments of those ages in
which he would have desired and deserved to live. The emperor conceived that it was his interest to increase the number of his subjects;
and that it was his duty to guard the purity of the marriage-bed: but
the means which he employed to accomplish these salutary purposes
are of an ambiguous, and perhaps exceptionable, kind. The pious

maids who consecrated their virginity to Christ were restrained from taking the veil till they had reached their fortieth year. Widows under that age were compelled to form a second alliance within the term of five years, by the forfeiture of half their wealth to their nearest relations or to the state. Unequal marriages were condemned or annulled. The punishment of confiscation and exile was deemed so inadequate to the guilt of adultery that if the criminal returned to Italy, he might, by the express declaration of Majorian, be slain with impunity.

While the emperor Majorian assiduously labored to restore the happiness and virtue of the Romans, he encountered the arms of Genseric, from his character and situation their most formidable enemy [circa A.D. 457]. . . . Rome expected from [Majorian] alone the restitution of Africa; and the design which he formed of attacking the Vandals in their new settlements was the result of bold and judicious policy. If the intrepid emperor could have infused his own spirit into the youth of Italy; if he could have revived in the field of Mars the manly exercises in which he had always surpassed his equals; he might have marched against Genseric at the head of a *Roman* army. Such a reformation of national manners might be embraced by the rising generation; but it is the misfortune of those princes who laboriously sustain a declining monarchy that to obtain some immediate advantage or to avert some impending danger they are forced to countenance, and even to multiply, the most pernicious abuses. Majorian, like the weakest of his predecessors, was reduced to the disgraceful expedient of substituting Barbarian auxiliaries in the place of his unwarlike subjects: and his superior abilities could only be displayed in the vigor and dexterity with which he wielded a dangerous instrument, so apt to recoil on the hand that used it.[†]

The virtues of Majorian could not protect him from the impetuous sedition which broke out in the camp near Tortona, at the foot of the Alps. He was compelled to abdicate the Imperial purple: five days after his abdication, it was reported that he died of a dysentery [August 7, A.D. 461]; and the humble tomb which covered his remains was consecrated by the respect and gratitude of succeeding generations.[†]

It was not, perhaps, without some regret that Ricimer sacrificed his friend to the interest of his ambition: but he resolved, in a second choice, to avoid the imprudent preference of superior virtue and merit. At his command, the obsequious senate of Rome bestowed the

Imperial title on Libius Severus [A.D. 461–467], who ascended the throne of the West without emerging from the obscurity of a private condition. History has scarcely deigned to notice his birth, his elevation, his character, or his death. Severus expired as soon as his life became inconvenient to his patron; and it would be useless to discriminate his nominal reign in the vacant interval of six years between the death of Majorian and the elevation of Anthemius. During that period, the government was in the hands of Ricimer alone; and although the modest Barbarian disclaimed the name of king, he accumulated treasures, formed a separate army, negotiated private alliances, and ruled Italy with the same independent and despotic authority which was afterwards exercised by Odoacer and Theodoric.[†]

The kingdom of Italy, a name to which the Western empire was gradually reduced, was afflicted under the reign of Ricimer by the incessant depredations of the Vandal pirates. In the spring of each year, they equipped a formidable navy in the port of Carthage; and Genseric himself, though in a very advanced age, still commanded in person the most important expeditions. His designs were concealed with impenetrable secrecy till the moment that he hoisted sail. When he was asked by his pilot what course he should steer, "Leave the determination to the winds (replied the Barbarian, with pious arrogance); *they* will transport us to the guilty coast whose inhabitants have provoked the divine justice"; but if Genseric himself deigned to issue more precise orders, he judged the most wealthy to be the most criminal ...; and their arms spread desolation or terror from the columns of Hercules to the mouth of the Nile.[†]

Such crimes could not be excused by any provocations; but the war which the king of the Vandals prosecuted against the Roman empire was justified by a specious and reasonable motive. The widow of Valentinian, Eudoxia, whom he had led captive from Rome to Carthage, was the sole heiress of the Theodosian house; her elder daughter, Eudocia, became the reluctant wife of Hunneric, his eldest son; and the stern father, asserting a legal claim which could not easily be refuted or satisfied, demanded a just proportion of the Imperial patrimony. An adequate, or at least a valuable, compensation, was offered by the Eastern emperor to purchase a necessary peace [A.D. 462 ff.]. Eudoxia and her younger daughter, Placidia, were honorably restored, and the fury of the Vandals was confined to the limits of the Western empire. The

Italians, destitute of a naval force which alone was capable of protecting their coasts, implored the aid of the more fortunate nations of the East who had formerly acknowledged, in peace and war, the supremacy of Rome. But the perpetual divisions of the two empires had alienated their interest and their inclinations; the faith of a recent treaty was alleged; and the Western Romans, instead of arms and ships, could only obtain the assistance of a cold and ineffectual mediation. The haughty Ricimer, who had long struggled with the difficulties of his situation, was at length reduced to address the throne of Constantinople in the humble language of a subject; and Italy submitted, as the price and security, to accept a master from the choice of the emperor of the East.[†]

Leo [emperor of the East, A.D. 457–474] listened to the complaints of the Italians; resolved to extirpate the tyranny of the Vandals; and declared his alliance with his colleague Anthemius, whom he solemnly invested with the diadem and purple of the West [A.D. 467–472].

The emperor of the West marched from Constantinople, attended by several counts of high distinction and a body of guards almost equal to the strength and numbers of a regular army: he entered Rome in triumph, and the choice of Leo was confirmed by the senate, the people, and the Barbarian confederates of Italy. The solemn inauguration of Anthemius was followed by the nuptials of his daughter and the patrician Ricimer; a fortunate event which was considered as the firmest security of the union and happiness of the state. The wealth of two empires was ostentatiously displayed; and many senators completed their ruin, by an expensive effort to disguise their poverty. All serious business was suspended during this festival; the courts of justice were shut; the streets of Rome, the theaters, the places of public and private resort, resounded with hymeneal songs and dances: and the royal bride, clothed in silken robes with a crown on her head, was conducted to the palace of Ricimer, who had changed his military dress for the habit of a consul and a senator.[†]

The Greeks ambitiously commend the piety and Catholic faith of the emperor whom they gave to the West. . . . Yet some suspicious appearances are found to sully the theological fame of Anthemius. . . . [He] had imbibed the spirit of religious toleration; and the heretics of Rome would have assembled with impunity if the bold and vehement censure which Pope Hilary pronounced in the church of St. Peter had not obliged him to abjure the unpopular indulgence. Even the Pagans, a feeble and obscure remnant, conceived some vain hopes from the indifference or partiality of Anthemius; and his singular friendship for the philosopher Severus, whom he promoted to the consulship, was ascribed to a secret project of reviving the ancient worship of the gods. These idols were crumbled into dust: and the mythology which had once been the creed of nations was so universally disbelieved that it might be employed without scandal, or at least without suspicion, by Christian poets. Yet the vestiges of superstition were not absolutely obliterated, and the festival of the Lupercalia, whose origin had preceded the foundation of Rome, was still celebrated under the reign of Anthemius. The savage and simple rites were expressive of an early state of society before the invention of arts and agriculture. The rustic deities who presided over the toils and pleasures of the pastoral life, Pan, Faunus, and their train of satyrs, were such as the fancy of shepherds might create, sportive, petulant, and lascivious; whose power was limited and whose malice was inoffensive. A goat was the offering the best adapted to their character and attributes; the flesh of the victim was roasted on willow spits; and the riotous youths who crowded to the feast ran naked about the fields with leather thongs in their hands, communicating, as it was supposed, the blessing of fecundity to the women whom they touched. The altar of Pan was erected, perhaps by Evander the Arcadian, in a dark recess in the side of the Palatine hill, watered by a perpetual fountain, and shaded by a hanging grove. A tradition that, in the same place, Romulus and Remus were suckled by the wolf rendered it still more sacred and venerable in the eyes of the Romans; and this sylvan spot was gradually surrounded by the stately edifices of the Forum. After the conversion of the Imperial city, the Christians still continued, in the month of February, the annual celebration of the Lupercalia; to which they ascribed a secret and mysterious influence on the genial powers of the animal and vegetable world. The bishops of Rome were solicitous to abolish a profane custom so repugnant to the spirit of Christianity; but their zeal was not supported by the authority of the civil magistrate: the inveterate abuse subsisted till the end of the fifth century, and Pope Gelasius, who purified the capital from the last stain of idolatry, appeased by a formal apology the murmurs of the senate and people [A.D. 496].

In all his public declarations, the emperor Leo assumes the authority, and professes the affection, of a father for his son Anthemius, with whom he had divided the administration of the universe. The situation, and perhaps the character, of Leo dissuaded him from exposing his person to the toils and dangers of an African war. But the powers of the Eastern empire were strenuously exerted to deliver Italy and the Mediterranean from the Vandals; and Genseric, who had so long oppressed both the land and sea, was threatened from every side with a formidable invasion.

[*The invasion fails (A.D. 468).*]

After the failure of this great expedition, Genseric again became the tyrant of the sea: the coasts of Italy, Greece, and Asia were again exposed to his revenge and avarice; Tripoli and Sardinia returned to his obedience; he added Sicily to the number of his provinces; and before he died [in A.D. 477], in the fullness of years and of glory, he beheld the final extinction of the empire of the West.†

The peaceful and prosperous reign which Anthemius had promised to the West was soon clouded by misfortune and discord [A.D. 471]. Ricimer, apprehensive or impatient of a superior, retired from Rome and fixed his residence at Milan; an advantageous situation either to invite or to repel the warlike tribes that were seated between the Alps and the Danube. Italy was gradually divided into two independent and hostile kingdoms; and the nobles of Liguria, who trembled at the near approach of a civil war, fell prostrate at the feet of the patrician and conjured him to spare their unhappy country. "For my own part," replied Ricimer, in a tone of insolent moderation, "I am still inclined to embrace the friendship of the Galatian; but who will undertake to appease his anger, or to mitigate the pride which always rises in proportion to our submission?" They informed him that Epiphanius, bishop of Pavia, united the wisdom of the serpent with the innocence of the dove; and appeared confident that the eloquence of such an ambassador must prevail against the strongest opposition, either of interest or passion. Their recommendation was approved; and Epiphanius, assuming the benevolent office of mediation, proceeded without delay to Rome, where he was received with the honors due to his merit and reputation. The oration of a bishop in favor of peace may be easily supposed; he argued that in all possible circumstances the forgiveness of injuries must be an act of mercy, or magnanimity, or prudence; and he seriously admonished the emperor to avoid a contest with a fierce Barbarian, which might be fatal to himself, and must be ruinous to his dominions. Anthemius acknowledged the truth of his maxims; but he deeply felt, with grief and indignation, the behavior of Ricimer, and his passion gave eloquence and energy to his discourse. "What favors," he warmly exclaimed, "have we refused to this ungrateful man? What provocations have we not endured! Regardless of the majesty of the purple, I gave my daughter to a Goth; I sacrificed my own blood to the safety of the republic. The liberality which ought to have secured the eternal attachment of Ricimer has exasperated him against his bene-factor. What wars has he not excited against the empire! How often has he instigated and assisted the fury of hostile nations! Shall I now ac-cept his perfidious friendship? Can I hope that *he* will respect the en-gagements of a treaty, who has already violated the duties of a son?" But the anger of Anthemius evaporated in these passionate exclama-tions: he insensibly yielded to the proposals of Epiphanius; and the bishop returned to his diocese with the satisfaction of restoring the peace of Italy, by a reconciliation of which the sincerity and continu-ance might be reasonably suspected. The clemency of the emperor was extorted from his weakness; and Ricimer suspended his ambitious designs till he had secretly prepared the engines with which he re-solved to subvert the throne of Anthemius. The mask of peace and moderation was then thrown aside. The army of Ricimer was fortified by a numerous reinforcement of Burgundians and Oriental Suevi: he disclaimed all allegiance to the Greek emperor, marched from Milan to the gates of Rome, and fixing his camp on the banks of the Anio, im-patiently expected the arrival of Olybrius, his Imperial candidate.

The senator Olybrius, of the Anician family, might esteem himself the lawful heir of the Western empire. He had married Placidia, the younger daughter of Valentinian, after she was restored by Genseric; who still detained her sister Eudoxia as the wife, or rather as the cap-tive, of his son. The king of the Vandals supported, by threats and so-licitations, the fair pretensions of his Roman ally; and assigned, as one of the motives of the war, the refusal of the senate and people to ac-knowledge their lawful prince, and the unworthy preference which they had given to a stranger. The friendship of the public enemy might render Olybrius still more unpopular to the Italians; but when Ricimer meditated the ruin of the emperor Anthemius, he tempted with the offer of a diadem the candidate who could justify his rebellion by an illustrious name and a royal alliance. The husband of Placidia, who, like most of his ancestors, had been invested with the consular dignity, might have continued to enjoy a secure and splendid fortune in the peaceful residence of Constantinople; nor does he appear to have been tormented by such a genius as cannot be amused or occupied unless by the administration of an empire. Yet Olybrius yielded to the importunities of his friends, perhaps of his wife; rashly plunged into the dangers and calamities of a civil war; and, with the secret connivance of the emperor Leo, accepted the Italian purple, which was bestowed, and resumed, at the capricious will of a Barbarian [March 23, A.D. 472]. He landed without obstacle (for Genseric was master of the sea), either at Ravenna or the port of Ostia, and immediately proceeded to the camp of Ricimer, where he was received as the sovereign of the Western world.

The patrician, who had extended his posts from the Anio to the Milvian bridge, already possessed two quarters of Rome, the Vatican and the Janiculum, which are separated by the Tiber from the rest of the city; and it may be conjectured that an assembly of seceding senators imitated, in the choice of Olybrius, the forms of a legal election. But the body of the senate and people firmly adhered to the cause of Anthemius; and the more effectual support of a Gothic army enabled him to prolong his reign, and the public distress, by a resistance of three months, which produced the concomitant evils of famine and pestilence. At length Ricimer made a furious assault on the bridge of Hadrian, or St. Angelo; and the narrow pass was defended with equal valor by the Goths till the death of Gilimer, their leader. The victorious troops, breaking down every barrier, rushed with irresistible violence into the heart of the city, and Rome (if we may use the language of a contemporary pope) was subverted by the civil fury of Anthemius and Ricimer [July 11, A.D. 472]. The unfortunate Anthemius was dragged from his concealment and inhumanly massacred by the command of his son-in-law; who thus added a third, or perhaps a fourth, emperor to the number of his victims. The soldiers, who united the rage of factious citizens with the savage manners of Barbarians, were indulged without control in the license of rapine and murder: the crowd of slaves and plebeians, who were unconcerned in the event, could only gain by the indiscriminate pillage; and the face of the city exhibited the strange contrast of stern cruelty and dissolute intemperance. Forty days after this calamitous event, the subject not of glory but of guilt, Italy was delivered, by a painful disease, from the tyrant Ricimer, who bequeathed the command of his army to his nephew Gundobald, one of the princes of the Burgundians [August 20, A.D. 472]. In the same year all the principal actors in this great revolution were removed from the stage; and the whole reign of Olybrius, whose death does not betray any symptoms of violence, is included within the term of seven months [October 23, A.D. 472]. He left one daughter, the offspring of his marriage with Placidia; and the family of the great Theodosius, transplanted from Spain to Constantinople, was propagated in the female line as far as the eighth generation.

Whilst the vacant throne of Italy was abandoned to lawless Barbarians, the election of a new colleague was seriously agitated in the council of Leo. The empress Verina, studious to promote the greatness of her own family, had married one of her nieces to Julius Nepos, who succeeded his uncle Marcellinus in the sovereignty of Dalmatia, a more solid possession than the title which he was persuaded to accept, of emperor of the West [A.D. 472–475]. But the measures of the Byzantine court were so languid and irresolute that many months elapsed after the death of Anthemius, and even of Olybrius, before their destined successor could show himself, with a respectable force, to his Italian subjects. During that interval, Glycerius, an obscure soldier, was invested with the purple by his patron Gundobald [March 5, A.D. 473]; but the Burgundian prince was unable or unwilling to support his nomination by a civil war: the pursuits of domestic ambition recalled him beyond the Alps, and his client was permitted to exchange the Roman scepter for the bishopric of Salona. After extinguishing such a competitor, the emperor Nepos was acknowledged by the senate, by the Italians, and by the provincials of Gaul; his moral virtues, and military talents, were loudly celebrated; and those who derived any private benefit from his government announced, in prophetic strains, the restoration of the public felicity. Their hopes (if such hopes had been entertained) were confounded within the term of a single year, and the treaty of peace which ceded Auvergne to the Visigoths is the only event of his short and inglorious reign. The most faithful subjects of Gaul were sacrificed by the Italian emperor to the hope of domestic security; but his repose was soon invaded by a furious sedition of the Barbarian confederates who, under the command of Orestes, their general, were in full march from Rome to Ravenna. Nepos trembled at their approach; and instead of placing a just confidence in the strength of Ravenna, he hastily escaped to his ships and retired to his Dalmatian principality, on the opposite coast of the Adriatic [August 28, A.D. 475]. By this shameful abdication, he protracted his life about five years in a very ambiguous state, between an emperor and an exile, till he was assassinated at Salona by the ungrateful Glycerius, who was translated, perhaps as the reward of his crime, to the archbishopric of Milan.

The nations who had asserted their independence after the death of Attila were established, by the right of possession or conquest, in the boundless countries to the north of the Danube; or in the Roman provinces between the river and the Alps. But the bravest of their youth enlisted in the army of *confederates* who formed the defense and the terror of Italy; and in this promiscuous multitude, the names of the Heruli, the Scyrri, the Alani, the Turcilingi, and the Rugians appear to have predominated. The example of these warriors was imitated by Orestes, the son of Tatullus and the father of the last Roman emperor of the West. Orestes, who has been already mentioned in this History, had never deserted his country. His birth and fortunes rendered him one of the most illustrious subjects of Pannonia. When that province was ceded to the Huns, he entered into the service of Attila, his lawful sovereign, obtained the office of his secretary, and was repeatedly sent as ambassador to Constantinople to represent the person and signify the commands of the imperious monarch. The death of that conqueror restored him to his freedom; and Orestes might honorably refuse either to follow the sons of Attila into the Scythian desert or to obey the Ostrogoths, who had usurped the dominion of Pannonia. He preferred the service of the Italian princes, the successors of Valentinian; and as he possessed the qualifications of courage, industry, and experience, he advanced with rapid steps in the military profession, till he was elevated, by the favor of Nepos himself, to the dignities of patrician and master-general of the troops. These troops had been long accustomed to reverence the character and authority of Orestes, who affected their manners, conversed with them in their own language, and was intimately connected with their national chieftains by long habits of familiarity and friendship. At his solicitation they rose in arms against the obscure Greek who presumed to claim their obedience; and when Orestes, from some secret motive, declined the purple, they consented with the same facility to acknowledge his son Augustulus as the emperor of the West [A.D. 476]. By the abdication of Nepos, Orestes had now attained the summit of his ambitious hopes; but he soon discovered, before the end of the first year, that the lessons of perjury and ingratitude which a rebel must inculcate will be resorted to against himself; and that the precarious sovereign of Italy was only permitted to choose whether he would be the slave or the victim of his Barbarian mercenaries. The dangerous alliance of these strangers had oppressed and insulted the last remains of Roman freedom and dignity. At each revolution, their pay and privileges were augmented; but their insolence increased in a still more extravagant degree; they envied the fortune of their brethren in Gaul, Spain, and Africa, whose victorious arms had acquired an independent and perpetual inheritance; and they insisted on their peremptory demand that a *third* part of the lands of Italy should be immediately divided among them. Orestes, with a spirit which, in another situation, might be entitled to our esteem, chose rather to encounter the rage of an armed multitude than to subscribe the ruin of an innocent people. He rejected the audacious demand; and his refusal was favorable to the ambition of Odoacer, a bold Barbarian who assured his fellow-soldiers that, if they dared to associate under his command, they might soon extort the justice which had been denied to their dutiful petitions. From all the camps and garrisons of Italy, the confederates, actuated by the same resentment and the same hopes, impatiently flocked to the standard of this popular leader; and the unfortunate patrician, overwhelmed by the torrent, hastily retreated to the strong city of Pavia, the episcopal seat of the holy Epiphanius. Pavia was immediately besieged, the fortifications were stormed, the town was pillaged; and although the bishop might labor, with much zeal and some success, to save the property of the church, and the chastity of female captives, the tumult could only be appeased by the execution of Orestes. His brother Paul was slain in an action near Ravenna; and the helpless Augustulus, who could no longer command the respect, was reduced to implore the clemency, of Odoacer.†

Royalty was familiar to the Barbarians, and the submissive people of

Italy were prepared to obey without a murmur the authority which he should condescend to exercise as the vicegerent of the emperor of the West. But Odoacer [king of Italy, A.D. 476–490] had resolved to abolish that useless and expensive office; and such is the weight of antique prejudice that it required some boldness and penetration to discover the extreme facility of the enterprise. The unfortunate Augustulus was made the instrument of his own disgrace: he signified his resignation to the senate; and that assembly, in their last act of obedience to a Roman prince, still affected the spirit of freedom and the forms of the constitution. An epistle was addressed, by their unanimous decree, to the emperor Zeno, the son-in-law and successor of Leo; who had lately been restored, after a short rebellion, to the Byzantine throne. They solemnly "disclaim the necessity, or even the wish, of continuing any longer the Imperial succession in Italy; since, in their opinion, the majesty of a sole monarch is sufficient to pervade and protect, at the same time, both the East and the West. In their own name, and in the name of the people, they consent that the seat of universal empire shall be transferred from Rome to Constantinople; and they basely renounce the right of choosing their master, the only vestige that yet remained of the authority which had given laws to the world. The republic (they repeat that name without a blush) might safely confide in the civil and military virtues of Odoacer; and they humbly request that the emperor would invest him with the title of Patrician, and the administration of the *diocese* of Italy." The deputies of the senate were received at Constantinople with some marks of displeasure and indignation: and when they were admitted to the audience of Zeno, he sternly reproached them with their treatment of the two emperors, Anthemius and Nepos, whom the East had successively granted to the prayers of Italy. "The first" (continued he) "you have murdered; the second you have expelled; but the second is still alive, and whilst he lives he is your lawful sovereign." But the prudent Zeno soon deserted the hopeless cause of his abdicated colleague. His vanity was gratified by the title of sole emperor, and by the statues erected to his honor in the several quarters of Rome; he entertained a friendly though ambiguous correspondence with the *patrician* Odoacer; and he gratefully accepted the Imperial ensigns, the sacred ornaments of the throne and palace, which the Barbarian was not unwilling to remove from the sight of the people.

In the space of twenty years since the death of Valentinian, nine emperors had successively disappeared; and the son of Orestes, a youth recommended only by his beauty, would be the least entitled to the notice of posterity if his reign, which was marked by the extinction of the Roman empire in the West, did not leave a memorable era in the history of mankind. The patrician Orestes had married the daughter of Count *Romulus,* of Petovio in Noricum: the name of *Augustus,* notwithstanding the jealousy of power, was known at Aquileia as a familiar surname; and the appellations of the two great founders, of the city and of the monarchy, were thus strangely united in the last of their successors. The son of Orestes assumed and disgraced the names of Romulus Augustus; but the first was corrupted into Momyllus by the Greeks, and the second has been changed by the Latins into the contemptible diminutive Augustulus. The life of this inoffensive youth was spared by the generous clemency of Odoacer; who dismissed him, with his whole family, from the Imperial palace, fixed his annual allowance at six thousand pieces of gold, and assigned the castle of Lucullus, in Campania, for the place of his exile or retirement.[†]

Odoacer was the first Barbarian who reigned in Italy over a people who had once asserted their just superiority above the rest of mankind. The disgrace of the Romans still excites our respectful compassion, and we fondly sympathize with the imaginary grief and indignation of their degenerate posterity. But the calamities of Italy had gradually subdued the proud consciousness of freedom and glory. In the age of Roman virtue the provinces were subject to the arms, and the citizens to the laws, of the republic; till those laws were subverted by civil discord, and both the city and the province became the servile property of a tyrant. The forms of the constitution, which alleviated or disguised their abject slavery, were abolished by time and violence; the Italians alternately lamented the presence or the absence of the sovereign whom they detested or despised; and the succession of five centuries inflicted the various evils of military license, capricious despotism, and elaborate oppression. During the same period, the Barbarians had emerged from obscurity and contempt, and the warriors of Germany and Scythia were introduced into the provinces as the servants, the allies, and at length the masters of the Romans whom they insulted or protected. The hatred of the people was suppressed by fear; they respected the spirit and splendor of the martial chiefs who were invested with the honors of the empire; and the fate of Rome had long depended on the sword of those formidable strangers. The stern Ricimer, who trampled on the ruins of Italy, had exercised the power, without assuming the title, of a king; and the patient Romans were insensibly prepared to acknowledge the royalty of Odoacer and his Barbaric successors.

The king of Italy was not unworthy of the high station to which his valor and fortune had exalted him: his savage manners were polished by the habits of conversation; and he respected, though a conqueror and a Barbarian, the institutions, and even the prejudices, of his subjects. After an interval of seven years, Odoacer restored the consulship of the West. For himself, he modestly, or proudly, declined an honor which was still accepted by the emperors of the East. . . . The laws of the emperors were strictly enforced, and the civil administration of Italy was still exercised by the Praetorian praefect and his subordinate officers. . . . Like the rest of the Barbarians, he had been instructed in the Arian heresy; but he revered the monastic and episcopal characters; and the silence of the Catholics attest the toleration which they enjoyed. . . . Italy was protected by the arms of its conqueror; and its frontiers were respected by the Barbarians of Gaul and Germany, who had so long insulted the feeble race of Theodosius . . . ; and Rome, after a long period of defeat and disgrace, might claim the triumph of her Barbarian master.

Notwithstanding the prudence and success of Odoacer, his kingdom exhibited the sad prospect of misery and desolation. Since the age of Tiberius, the decay of agriculture had been felt in Italy; and it was a just subject of complaint that the life of the Roman people depended on the accidents of the winds and waves. In the division and the decline of the empire, the tributary harvests of Egypt and Africa were withdrawn; the numbers of the inhabitants continually diminished with the means of subsistence; and the country was exhausted by the irretrievable losses of war, famine, and pestilence. . . . The distress of Italy was mitigated by the prudence and humanity of Odoacer, who had bound himself, as the price of his elevation, to satisfy the demands of a licentious and turbulent multitude. The kings of the Barbarians were frequently resisted, deposed, or murdered by their native subjects, and the various bands of Italian mercenaries who associated under the standard of an elective general claimed a larger privilege of freedom and rapine. A monarchy destitute of national union and hereditary right hastened to its dissolution. After a reign of fourteen years, Odoacer was oppressed by the superior genius of Theodoric, king of the Ostrogoths; a hero alike excellent in the arts of war and of government, who restored an age of peace and prosperity, and whose name still excites and deserves the attention of mankind.

CHAPTER XXXVII

CONVERSION OF THE BARBARIANS
TO CHRISTIANITY

Origin, progress, and effects of the monastic life. •
Conversion of the Barbarians to Christianity and Arianism. •
Persecution of the Vandals in Africa. • *Extinction of*
Arianism among the Barbarians.

The indissoluble connection of civil and ecclesiastical affairs has compelled and encouraged me to relate the progress, the persecutions, the
establishment, the divisions, the final triumph, and the gradual corruption, of Christianity. I have purposely delayed the consideration of
two religious events interesting in the study of human nature and important in the decline and fall of the Roman empire. I. The institution
of the monastic life; and, II. The conversion of the Northern Barbarians.

I. Prosperity and peace introduced the distinction of the *vulgar* and
the *Ascetic Christians.* The loose and imperfect practice of religion satisfied the conscience of the multitude. The prince or magistrate, the
soldier or merchant, reconciled their fervent zeal and implicit faith
with the exercise of their profession, the pursuit of their interest, and
the indulgence of their passions: but the Ascetics, who obeyed and
abused the rigid precepts of the gospel, were inspired by the savage
enthusiasm which represents man as a criminal and God as a tyrant.
They seriously renounced the business, and the pleasures, of the age; abjured the use of wine, of flesh, and of marriage; chastised their body,
mortified their affections, and embraced a life of misery as the price of
eternal happiness. In the reign of Constantine, the Ascetics fled from a
profane and degenerate world to perpetual solitude or religious society. Like the first Christians of Jerusalem, they resigned the use or the
property of their temporal possessions; established regular communities of the same sex, and a similar disposition; and assumed the names
of *Hermits, Monks,* and *Anachorets,* expressive of their lonely retreat in
a natural or artificial desert. They soon acquired the respect of the

world, which they despised; and the loudest applause was bestowed on this DIVINE PHILOSOPHY which surpassed, without the aid of science or reason, the laborious virtues of the Grecian schools. The monks might indeed contend with the Stoics in the contempt of fortune, of pain, and of death: the Pythagorean silence and submission were revived in their servile discipline; and they disdained, as firmly as the Cynics themselves, all the forms and decencies of civil society. But the votaries of this Divine Philosophy aspired to imitate a purer and more perfect model. They trod in the footsteps of the prophets, who had retired to the desert.†

Egypt, the fruitful parent of superstition, afforded the first example of the monastic life. Antony, an illiterate youth of the lower parts of Thebais, distributed his patrimony, deserted his family and native home, and executed his monastic penance with original and intrepid fanaticism [A.D. 305]. After a long and painful novitiate among the tombs and in a ruined tower, he boldly advanced into the desert three days' journey to the eastward of the Nile; discovered a lonely spot which possessed the advantages of shade and water, and fixed his last residence on Mount Colzim, near the Red Sea; where an ancient monastery still preserves the name and memory of the saint. The curious devotion of the Christians pursued him to the desert; and when he was obliged to appear at Alexandria, in the face of mankind, he supported his fame with discretion and dignity. He enjoyed the friendship of Athanasius, whose doctrine he approved; and the Egyptian peasant respectfully declined a respectful invitation from the emperor Constantine. The venerable patriarch (for Antony attained the age of one hundred and five years) beheld the numerous progeny which had been formed by his example and his lessons [A.D. 251–356]. The prolific colonies of monks multiplied with rapid increase on the sands of Libya, upon the rocks of Thebais, and in the cities of the Nile.... The Egyptians, who gloried in this marvelous revolution, were disposed to hope and to believe that the number of the monks was equal to the remainder of the people; and posterity might repeat the saying, which had formerly been applied to the sacred animals of the same country, that in Egypt it was less difficult to find a god than a man.

Athanasius introduced into Rome the knowledge and practice of the monastic life; and a school of this new philosophy was opened by the disciples of Antony, who accompanied their primate to the holy threshold of the Vatican [A.D. 341]. The strange and savage appearance of these Egyptians excited, at first, horror and contempt, and at length applause and zealous imitation. The senators, and more especially the matrons, transformed their palaces and villas into religious houses; and the narrow institution of six Vestals was eclipsed by the frequent monasteries which were seated on the ruins of ancient temples and in the midst of the Roman forum. Inflamed by the example of Antony, a Syrian youth whose name was Hilarion fixed his dreary abode on a sandy beach between the sea and a morass, about seven miles from Gaza [A.D. 328]. The austere penance, in which he persisted forty-eight years, diffused a similar enthusiasm; and the holy man was followed by a train of two or three thousand anachorets whenever he visited the innumerable monasteries of Palestine. The fame of Basil is immortal in the monastic history of the East. With a mind that had tasted the learning and eloquence of Athens, with an ambition scarcely to be satisfied with the archbishopric of Caesarea, Basil retired to a savage solitude in Pontus; and deigned for a while to give laws to the spiritual colonies which he profusely scattered along the coast of the Black Sea [A.D. 360]. In the West, Martin of Tours, a soldier, a hermit, a bishop, and a saint, established the monasteries of Gaul [A.D. 370]; two thousand of his disciples followed him to the grave; and his eloquent historian challenges the deserts of Thebais to produce, in a more favorable climate, a champion of equal virtue. The progress of the monks was not less rapid or universal than that of Christianity itself. Every province, and at last every city, of the empire was filled with their increasing multitudes.†

These unhappy exiles from social life were impelled by the dark and implacable genius of superstition. Their mutual resolution was supported by the example of millions, of either sex, of every age, and of every rank; and each proselyte who entered the gates of a monastery was persuaded that he trod the steep and thorny path of eternal happiness. But the operation of these religious motives was variously determined by the temper and situation of mankind. Reason might subdue, or passion might suspend, their influence: but they acted most forcibly on the infirm minds of children and females; they were strengthened by secret remorse or accidental misfortune; and they might derive some aid from the temporal considerations of vanity or interest. It was naturally supposed that the pious and humble monks, who had renounced the world to accomplish the work of their salvation, were the best qualified for the spiritual government of the Christians. The reluctant hermit was torn from his cell and seated, amidst the acclamations of the people, on the episcopal throne: the monasteries of Egypt, of Gaul, and of the East supplied a regular succession of saints and bishops; and ambition soon discovered the secret road which led to the possession of wealth and honors. The popular monks, whose reputation was connected with the fame and success of the order, assiduously labored to multiply the number of their fellow-captives. They insinuated themselves into noble and opulent families; and the specious arts of flattery and seduction were employed to secure those proselytes who might bestow wealth or dignity on the monastic profession. The indignant father bewailed the loss, perhaps, of an only son; the credulous maid was betrayed by vanity to violate the laws of nature; and the matron aspired to imaginary perfection by renouncing the virtues of domestic life. Paula yielded to the persuasive eloquence of Jerome; and the profane title of mother-in-law of God tempted that illustrious widow to consecrate the virginity of her daughter Eustochium. By the advice and in the company of her spiritual guide, Paula abandoned Rome and her infant son; retired to the holy village of Bethlehem; founded a hospital and four monasteries; and acquired, by her alms and penance, an eminent and conspicuous station in the Catholic church. Such rare and illustrious penitents were celebrated as the glory and example of their age; but the monasteries were filled by a crowd of obscure and abject plebeians who gained in the cloister much more than they had sacrificed in the world. Peasants, slaves, and mechanics might escape from poverty and contempt to a safe and honorable profession whose apparent hardships are mitigated by custom, by popular applause, and by the secret relaxation of discipline. The subjects of Rome, whose persons and fortunes were made responsible for unequal and exorbitant tributes, retired from the oppression of the Imperial government; and the pusillanimous youth preferred the penance of a monastic to the dangers of a military life. The affrighted provincials of every rank who fled before the Barbarians found shelter and subsistence: whole legions were buried in these religious sanctuaries; and the same cause which relieved the distress of individuals impaired the strength and fortitude of the empire.

The monastic profession of the ancients was an act of voluntary devotion. The inconstant fanatic was threatened with the eternal vengeance of the God whom he deserted; but the doors of the monastery were still open for repentance. Those monks whose conscience was fortified by reason or passion were at liberty to resume the character of men and citizens; and even the spouses of Christ might accept the legal embraces of an earthly lover. The examples of scandal and the progress of superstition suggested the propriety of more forcible restraints. After a sufficient trial, the fidelity of the novice was secured by a solemn and perpetual vow; and his irrevocable engagement was ratified by the laws of the church and state. A guilty fugitive was pursued, arrested, and restored to his perpetual prison; and the interposition of the magistrate oppressed the freedom and the merit which had alleviated in some degree the abject slavery of the monastic discipline. The actions of a monk, his words, and even his thoughts were determined by an inflexible rule or a capricious superior: the slightest offenses were corrected by disgrace or confinement, extraordinary fasts, or bloody flagellation; and disobedience, murmur, or delay were ranked in the catalogue of the most heinous sins. A blind submission to the commands of the abbot, however absurd or even criminal they might seem, was the ruling principle, the first virtue of the Egyptian monks; and their patience was frequently exercised by the most extravagant trials. They were directed to remove an enormous rock; assiduously to water a barren staff that was planted in the ground till, at the end of three years, it should vegetate and blossom like a tree; to walk into a fiery furnace; or to cast their infant into a deep pond: and several saints, or madmen, have been immortalized in monastic story by their thoughtless and fearless obedience. The freedom of the mind, the source of every generous and rational sentiment, was destroyed by the habits of credulity and submission; and the monk, contracting the vices of a slave, devoutly followed the faith and passions of his ecclesiastical tyrant. The peace of the Eastern church was invaded by a swarm of fanatics, incapable of fear, or reason, or humanity; and the Imperial troops acknowledged without shame that they were much less apprehensive of an encounter with the fiercest Barbarians.[†]

The lives of the primitive monks were consumed in penance and solitude; undisturbed by the various occupations which fill the time and exercise the faculties of reasonable, active, and social beings. Whenever they were permitted to step beyond the precincts of the monastery, two jealous companions were the mutual guards and spies of each other's actions; and after their return, they were condemned to forget, or at least to suppress, whatever they had seen or heard in the world. Strangers who professed the orthodox faith were hospitably entertained in a separate apartment; but their dangerous conversation was restricted to some chosen elders of approved discretion and fidelity. Except in their presence, the monastic slave might not receive the visits of his friends or kindred; and it was deemed highly meritorious if he afflicted a tender sister or an aged parent by the obstinate refusal of a word or look. The monks themselves passed their lives without personal attachments, among a crowd which had been formed by accident and was detained in the same prison by force or prejudice. Recluse fanatics have few ideas or sentiments to communicate: a special license of the abbot regulated the time and duration of their familiar visits; and at their silent meals they were enveloped in their cowls, inaccessible and almost invisible to each other. Study is the resource of solitude: but education had not prepared and qualified for any liberal studies the mechanics and peasants who filled the monastic communities. They might work: but the vanity of spiritual perfection was tempted to disdain the exercise of manual labor; and the industry must be faint and languid which is not excited by the sense of personal interest.

According to their faith and zeal, they might employ the day, which they passed in their cells, either in vocal or mental prayer: they assembled in the evening, and they were awakened in the night, for the public worship of the monastery. The precise moment was determined by the stars, which are seldom clouded in the serene sky of Egypt; and a rustic horn or trumpet the signal of devotion, twice interrupted the vast silence of the desert. Even sleep, the last refuge of the unhappy, was rigorously measured: the vacant hours of the monk heavily rolled along, without business or pleasure; and before the close of each day, he had repeatedly accused the tedious progress of the sun. In this comfortless state, superstition still pursued and tormented her wretched votaries. The repose which they had sought in the cloister was disturbed by a tardy repentance, profane doubts, and guilty desires; and while they considered each natural impulse as an unpardonable sin, they perpetually trembled on the edge of a flaming and bottomless abyss. From the painful struggles of disease and despair, these unhappy victims were sometimes relieved by madness or death; and in the sixth century a hospital was founded at Jerusalem for a small portion of the austere penitents who were deprived of their senses. Their visions, before they attained this extreme and acknowledged term of frenzy, have afforded ample materials of supernatural history. It was their firm persuasion that the air which they breathed was peopled with invisible enemies; with innumerable demons, who watched every occasion and assumed every form to terrify, and above all to tempt, their unguarded virtue. The imagination, and even the senses, were deceived by the illusions of distempered fanaticism; and the hermit whose midnight prayer was oppressed by involuntary slumber might easily confound the phantoms of horror or delight which had occupied his sleeping and his waking dreams.

The monks were divided into two classes: the *Coenobites*, who lived under a common and regular discipline; and the *Anachorets*, who indulged their unsocial, independent fanaticism. The most devout, or the most ambitious, of the spiritual brethren renounced the convent as they had renounced the world. The fervent monasteries of Egypt, Palestine, and Syria were surrounded by a *Laura*, a distant circle of solitary cells; and the extravagant penance of Hermits was stimulated by applause and emulation. They sunk under the painful weight of crosses and chains; and their emaciated limbs were confined by collars, bracelets, gauntlets, and greaves of massy and rigid iron. All superfluous encumbrance of dress they contemptuously cast away; and some savage saints of both sexes have been admired whose naked bodies were only covered by their long hair. They aspired to reduce themselves to the rude and miserable state in which the human brute is scarcely distinguishable above his kindred animals; and the numerous sect of Anachorets derived their name from their humble practice of grazing in the fields of Mesopotamia with the common herd. They often usurped the den of some wild beast whom they affected to resemble; they buried themselves in some gloomy cavern which art or nature had scooped out of the rock.... The most perfect Hermits are supposed to have passed many days without food, many nights without sleep, and many years without speaking; and glorious was the *man* (I abuse that name) who contrived any cell or seat of a peculiar construction which might expose him, in the most inconvenient posture, to the inclemency of the seasons.

Among these heroes of the monastic life, the name and genius of Simeon Stylites have been immortalized by the singular invention of an aerial penance [A.D. 395–451]. At the age of thirteen, the young Syrian deserted the profession of a shepherd and threw himself into an austere monastery. After a long and painful novitiate in which Simeon was repeatedly saved from pious suicide, he established his residence on a mountain about thirty or forty miles to the east of Antioch. Within the space of a *mandra,* or circle of stones, to which he had attached himself by a ponderous chain, he ascended a column which was successively raised from the height of nine, to that of sixty, feet from the ground. In this last and lofty station, the Syrian Anachoret resisted the heat of thirty summers, and the cold of as many winters. Habit and exercise instructed him to maintain his dangerous situation without fear or giddiness, and successively to assume the different postures of devotion. He sometimes prayed in an erect attitude, with his outstretched arms in the figure of a cross, but his most familiar practice was that of bending his meager skeleton from the forehead to the feet; and a curious spectator, after numbering twelve hundred and forty-four repetitions, at length desisted from the endless account. The progress of an ulcer in his thigh might shorten, but it could not disturb, this *celestial* life; and the patient Hermit expired without descending from his column. A prince who should capriciously inflict such tortures would be deemed a tyrant; but it would surpass the power of a tyrant to impose a long and miserable existence on the reluctant victims of his cruelty. This voluntary martyrdom must have gradually destroyed the sensibility both of the mind and body; nor can it be presumed that the fanatics who torment themselves are susceptible of any lively affection for the rest of mankind. A cruel, unfeeling temper has distinguished the monks of every age and country: their stern indifference, which is seldom mollified by personal friendship, is inflamed by religious hatred; and their merciless zeal has strenuously administered the holy office of the Inquisition.

The monastic saints, who excite only the contempt and pity of a philosopher, were respected and almost adored by the prince and people. . . . The fame of the apostles and martyrs was gradually eclipsed by these recent and popular Anachorets; the Christian world fell prostrate before their shrines; and the miracles ascribed to their relics exceeded, at least in number and duration, the spiritual exploits of their

lives. But the golden legend of their lives was embellished by the artful credulity of their interested brethren; and a believing age was
easily persuaded that the slightest caprice of an Egyptian or a Syrian
monk had been sufficient to interrupt the eternal laws of the universe.
The favorites of Heaven were accustomed to cure inveterate diseases
with a touch, a word, or a distant message; and to expel the most obstinate demons from the souls or bodies which they possessed. They familiarly accosted, or imperiously commanded, the lions and serpents
of the desert; infused vegetation into a sapless trunk; suspended iron
on the surface of the water; passed the Nile on the back of a crocodile;
and refreshed themselves in a fiery furnace. These extravagant tales,
which display the fiction, without the genius, of poetry, have seriously
affected the reason, the faith, and the morals of the Christians. Their
credulity debased and vitiated the faculties of the mind: they corrupted the evidence of history; and superstition gradually extinguished
the hostile light of philosophy and science. Every mode of religious
worship which had been practiced by the saints, every mysterious doctrine which they believed, was fortified by the sanction of divine revelation, and all the manly virtues were oppressed by the servile and
pusillanimous reign of the monks. If it be possible to measure the interval between the philosophic writings of Cicero and the sacred legend of Theodoret, between the character of Cato and that of Simeon,
we may appreciate the memorable revolution which was accomplished
in the Roman empire within a period of five hundred years.

II. The progress of Christianity has been marked by two glorious
and decisive victories: over the learned and luxurious citizens of the
Roman empire; and over the warlike Barbarians of Scythia and Germany, who subverted the empire and embraced the religion of the Romans. The Goths were the foremost of these savage proselytes; and the
nation was indebted for its conversion to a countryman, or at least to a
subject, worthy to be ranked among the inventors of useful arts who
have deserved the remembrance and gratitude of posterity. A great
number of Roman provincials had been led away into captivity by the
Gothic bands who ravaged Asia in the time of Gallienus; and of these
captives, many were Christians, and several belonged to the ecclesiastical order. Those involuntary missionaries, dispersed as slaves in the
villages of Dacia, successively labored for the salvation of their masters. The seeds which they planted of the evangelic doctrine were

gradually propagated; and before the end of a century, the pious work was achieved by the labors of Ulphilas, whose ancestors had been transported beyond the Danube from a small town of Cappadocia.

Ulphilas, the bishop and apostle of the Goths, acquired their love and reverence by his blameless life and indefatigable zeal; and they received with implicit confidence the doctrines of truth and virtue which he preached and practiced [A.D. 360 ff.]. He executed the arduous task of translating the Scriptures into their native tongue, a dialect of the German or Teutonic language; but he prudently suppressed the four books of Kings, as they might tend to irritate the fierce and sanguinary spirit of the Barbarians. The rude, imperfect idiom of soldiers and shepherds, so ill qualified to communicate any spiritual ideas, was improved and modulated by his genius: and Ulphilas, before he could frame his version, was obliged to compose a new alphabet of twenty-four letters; four of which he invented to express the peculiar sounds that were unknown to the Greek and Latin pronunciation. But the prosperous state of the Gothic church was soon afflicted by war and intestine discord, and the chieftains were divided by religion as well as by interest. Fritigern, the friend of the Romans, became the proselyte of Ulphilas; while the haughty soul of Athanaric disdained the yoke of the empire and of the gospel. The faith of the new converts was tried by the persecution which he excited. A wagon bearing aloft the shapeless image of Thor, perhaps, or of Woden, was conducted in solemn procession through the streets of the camp; and the rebels who refused to worship the god of their fathers were immediately burnt, with their tents and families. The character of Ulphilas recommended him to the esteem of the Eastern court, where he twice appeared as the minister of peace; he pleaded the cause of the distressed Goths who implored the protection of Valens; and the name of *Moses* was applied to this spiritual guide who conducted his people through the deep waters of the Danube to the Land of Promise. The devout shepherds who were attached to his person and tractable to his voice acquiesced in their settlement, at the foot of the Moesian mountains, in a country of woodlands and pastures, which supported their flocks and herds and enabled them to purchase the corn and wine of the more plentiful provinces. These harmless Barbarians multiplied in obscure peace and the profession of Christianity.[†]

During the same period, Christianity was embraced by almost all the Barbarians who established their kingdoms on the ruins of the Western empire [A.D. 400 ff.]: the Burgundians in Gaul, the Suevi in Spain, the Vandals in Africa, the Ostrogoths in Pannonia, and the various bands of mercenaries that raised Odoacer to the throne of Italy. The Franks and the Saxons still persevered in the errors of Paganism; but the Franks obtained the monarchy of Gaul by their submission to the example of Clovis; and the Saxon conquerors of Britain were reclaimed from their savage superstition by the missionaries of Rome. These Barbarian proselytes displayed an ardent and successful zeal in the propagation of the faith. The Merovingian kings and their successors, Charlemagne and the Othos, extended, by their laws and victories, the dominion of the cross. England produced the apostle of Germany; and the evangelic light was gradually diffused from the neighborhood of the Rhine to the nations of the Elbe, the Vistula, and the Baltic.

The different motives which influenced the reason or the passions of the Barbarian converts cannot easily be ascertained. They were often capricious and accidental; a dream, an omen, the report of a miracle, the example of some priest or hero, the charms of a believing wife, and, above all, the fortunate event of a prayer or vow which, in a moment of danger, they had addressed to the God of the Christians. The early prejudices of education were insensibly erased by the habits of frequent and familiar society; the moral precepts of the gospel were protected by the extravagant virtues of the monks; and a spiritual theology was supported by the visible power of relics and the pomp of religious worship. . . . The advantage of temporal prosperity had deserted the Pagan cause and passed over to the service of Christianity. The Romans themselves, the most powerful and enlightened nation of the globe, had renounced their ancient superstition; and if the ruin of their empire seemed to accuse the efficacy of the new faith, the disgrace was already retrieved by the conversion of the victorious Goths. The valiant and fortunate Barbarians who subdued the provinces of the West successively received and reflected the same edifying example. Before the age of Charlemagne, the Christian nations of Europe might exult in the exclusive possession of the temperate climates, of the fertile lands which produced corn, wine, and oil; while the savage idolaters and their helpless idols were confined to the extremities of the earth, the dark and frozen regions of the North.

Christianity, which opened the gates of Heaven to the Barbarians, introduced an important change in their moral and political condition. They received at the same time the use of letters, so essential to a religion whose doctrines are contained in a sacred book; and while they studied the divine truth, their minds were insensibly enlarged by the distant view of history, of nature, of the arts, and of society. The version of the Scriptures into their native tongue, which had facilitated their conversion, must excite among their clergy some curiosity to read the original text, to understand the sacred liturgy of the church, and to examine, in the writings of the fathers, the chain of ecclesiastical tradition. These spiritual gifts were preserved in the Greek and Latin languages, which concealed the inestimable monuments of ancient learning. The immortal productions of Virgil, Cicero, and Livy, which were accessible to the Christian Barbarians, maintained a silent intercourse between the reign of Augustus and the times of Clovis and Charlemagne. The emulation of mankind was encouraged by the remembrance of a more perfect state; and the flame of science was secretly kept alive, to warm and enlighten the mature age of the Western world. In the most corrupt state of Christianity, the Barbarians might learn justice from the *law* and mercy from the *gospel;* and if the knowledge of their duty was insufficient to guide their actions or to regulate their passions, they were sometimes restrained by conscience, and frequently punished by remorse. But the direct authority of religion was less effectual than the holy communion, which united them with their Christian brethren in spiritual friendship. The influence of these sentiments contributed to secure their fidelity in the service or the alliance of the Romans, to alleviate the horrors of war, to moderate the insolence of conquest, and to preserve in the downfall of the empire a permanent respect for the name and institutions of Rome. In the days of Paganism, the priests of Gaul and Germany reigned over the people and controlled the jurisdiction of the magistrates; and the zealous proselytes transferred an equal or more ample measure of devout obedience to the pontiffs of the Christian faith. The sacred character of the bishops was supported by their temporal possessions; they obtained an honorable seat in the legislative assemblies of soldiers and freemen; and it was their interest as well as their duty to mollify by peaceful counsels the fierce spirit of the Barbarians. The perpetual correspondence of the Latin clergy, the frequent pilgrimages to Rome and Jerusalem, and the growing authority of the popes cemented the union of the Christian republic, and gradually produced the similar manners and common jurisprudence which have distinguished from the rest of mankind the independent and even hostile nations of modern Europe.

But the operation of these causes was checked and retarded by the unfortunate accident which infused a deadly poison into the cup of Salvation. Whatever might be the early sentiments of Ulphilas, his connections with the empire and the church were formed during the reign of Arianism. The apostle of the Goths ... professed with freedom, and perhaps with sincerity, that the SON was not equal, or consubstantial, to the FATHER; communicated these errors to the clergy and people; and infected the Barbaric world with a heresy which the great Theodosius proscribed and extinguished among the Romans. The temper and understanding of the new proselytes were not adapted to metaphysical subtleties; but they strenuously maintained what they had piously received as the pure and genuine doctrines of Christianity.... This irreconcilable difference of religion was a perpetual source of jealousy and hatred; and the reproach of *Barbarian* was embittered by the more odious epithet of *Heretic*. The heroes of the North, who had submitted with some reluctance to believe that all their ancestors were in hell, were astonished and exasperated to learn that they themselves had only changed the mode of their eternal condemnation. Instead of the smooth applause which Christian kings are accustomed to expect from their royal prelates, the orthodox bishops and their clergy were in a state of opposition to the Arian courts; and their indiscreet opposition frequently became criminal, and might sometimes be dangerous. The pulpit, that safe and sacred organ of sedition, resounded with the names of Pharaoh and Holofernes; the public discontent was inflamed by the hope or promise of a glorious deliverance; and the seditious saints were tempted to promote the accomplishment of their own predictions. Notwithstanding these provocations, the Catholics of Gaul, Spain, and Italy enjoyed under the reign of the Arians the free and peaceful exercise of their religion. Their haughty masters respected the zeal of a numerous people resolved to die at the foot of their altars; and the example of their devout constancy was admired and imitated by the Barbarians themselves. The conquerors evaded, however, the disgraceful reproach, or confession, of fear by attributing their toleration to the liberal motives of reason and humanity; and while they affected the language, they imperceptibly imbibed the spirit, of genuine Christianity.

The peace of the church was sometimes interrupted.

[*The Catholics are persecuted by the Arians under Genseric (A.D. 429–477); Hunneric (A.D. 477); Gundamund (A.D. 484); Thrasimund (A.D. 496); Hilderic (A.D. 523); and Gelimer (A.D. 530).*]

It is incumbent on the authors of persecution previously to reflect whether they are determined to support it in the last extreme. They excite the flame which they strive to extinguish; and it soon becomes necessary to chastise the contumacy as well as the crime of the offender. The fine which he is unable or unwilling to discharge exposes his person to the severity of the law; and his contempt of lighter penalties suggests the use and propriety of capital punishment. Through the veil of fiction and declamation we may clearly perceive that the Catholics, more especially under the reign of Hunneric, endured the most cruel and ignominious treatment. Respectable citizens, noble matrons, and consecrated virgins were stripped naked and raised in the air by pulleys with a weight suspended at their feet. In this painful attitude their naked bodies were torn with scourges, or burnt in the most tender parts with red-hot plates of iron. The amputation of the ears, the nose, the tongue, and the right hand was inflicted by the Arians; and although the precise number cannot be defined, it is evident that many persons, among whom a bishop and a proconsul may be named, were entitled to the crown of martyrdom. The same honor has been ascribed to the memory of Count Sebastian, who professed the Nicene creed with unshaken constancy; and Genseric might detest as a heretic the brave and ambitious fugitive whom he dreaded as a rival.[†]

The Catholics, oppressed by royal and military force, were far superior to their adversaries in numbers and learning. With the same weapons which the Greek and Latin fathers had already provided for the Arian controversy, they repeatedly silenced or vanquished the fierce and illiterate successors of Ulphilas. The consciousness of their own superiority might have raised them above the arts and passions of religious warfare. Yet instead of assuming such honorable pride, the orthodox theologians were tempted, by the assurance of impunity, to compose fictions which must be stigmatized with the epithets of fraud and forgery. They ascribed their own polemical works to the most venerable names of Christian antiquity; the characters of Athanasius and Augustine were awkwardly personated by Vigilius and his disciples; and the famous creed which so clearly expounds the mysteries of the Trinity and the Incarnation is deduced, with strong probability, from this African school. Even the Scriptures themselves were profaned by their rash and sacrilegious hands. The memorable text which asserts the unity of the THREE who bear witness in Heaven [1 John 5:7] is condemned by the universal silence of the orthodox fathers, ancient versions, and authentic manuscripts. It was first alleged by the Catholic bishops whom Hunneric summoned to the conference of Carthage. An allegorical interpretation in the form, perhaps, of a marginal note invaded the text of the Latin Bibles, which were renewed and corrected in a dark period of ten centuries. After the invention of printing, the editors of the Greek Testament yielded to their own prejudices, or those of the times; and the pious fraud, which was embraced with equal zeal at Rome and at Geneva, has been infinitely multiplied in every country and every language of modern Europe.

The example of fraud must excite suspicion: and the specious miracles by which the African Catholics have defended the truth and justice of their cause may be ascribed with more reason to their own industry than to the visible protection of Heaven.[†]

The Vandals and the Ostrogoths persevered in the profession of Arianism till the final ruin of the kingdoms which they had founded in Africa and Italy [A.D. 500–700]. The Barbarians of Gaul submitted to the orthodox dominion of the Franks; and Spain was restored to the Catholic church by the voluntary conversion of the Visigoths.[†]

The first missionaries who preached the gospel to the Barbarians appealed to the evidence of reason, and claimed the benefit of toleration. But no sooner had they established their spiritual dominion than they exhorted the Christian kings to extirpate without mercy the remains of Roman or Barbaric superstition. The successors of Clovis inflicted one hundred lashes on the peasants who refused to destroy their idols; the crime of sacrificing to the demons was punished by the Anglo-Saxon laws with the heavier penalties of imprisonment and confiscation; and even the wise Alfred adopted as an indispensable duty the extreme rigor of the Mosaic institutions. But the punishment and the crime were gradually abolished among a Christian people; the theological disputes of the schools were suspended by propitious ignorance; and the intolerant spirit which could find neither idolaters nor heretics was reduced to the persecution of the Jews [A.D. 612–712]. That exiled nation had founded some synagogues in the cities of Gaul; but Spain, since the time of Hadrian, was filled with their numerous colonies. The wealth which they accumulated by trade and the management of the finances invited the pious avarice of their masters; and they might be oppressed without danger, as they had lost the use, and even the remembrance, of arms. Sisebut, a Gothic king who reigned in the beginning of the seventh century, proceeded at once to the last extremes of persecution. Ninety thousand Jews were compelled to receive the sacrament of baptism; the fortunes of the obstinate infidels were confiscated, their bodies were tortured; and it seems doubtful whether they were permitted to abandon their native country. The excessive zeal of the Catholic king was moderated even by the clergy of Spain, who solemnly pronounced an inconsistent sentence: that the sacraments should not be forcibly imposed; but that the Jews who had been baptized should be constrained, for the honor of the church, to persevere in the external practice of a religion which they disbelieved and detested. Their frequent relapses provoked one of the successors of Sisebut to banish the whole nation from his dominions; and a council of Toledo published a decree that every Gothic king should swear to maintain this salutary edict. But the tyrants were unwilling to dismiss the victims whom they delighted to torture, or to deprive themselves of the industrious slaves over whom they might exercise a lucrative oppression. The Jews still continued in Spain under the weight of the civil and ecclesiastical laws which in the same country have been faithfully transcribed in the Code of the Inquisition. The Gothic kings and bishops at length discovered that injuries will produce hatred, and that hatred will find the opportunity of revenge. A nation, the secret or professed enemies of Christianity, still multiplied in servitude and distress; and the intrigues of the Jews promoted the rapid success of the Arabian conquerors.†

CHAPTER XXXVIII

REIGN OF CLOVIS

Reign and conversion of Clovis. • His victories over the Alemanni,
Burgundians, and Visigoths. • Establishment of the French
monarchy in Gaul. • Laws of the Barbarians. •
State of the Romans. • The Visigoths of Spain. •
Conquest of Britain by the Saxons.

The Gauls, who impatiently supported the Roman yoke, received a memorable lesson from one of the lieutenants of Vespasian [A.D. 70], whose weighty sense has been refined and expressed by the genius of Tacitus. "The protection of the republic has delivered Gaul from internal discord and foreign invasions. By the loss of national independence, you have acquired the name and privileges of Roman citizens. You enjoy, in common with ourselves, the permanent benefits of civil government; and your remote situation is less exposed to the accidental mischiefs of tyranny. Instead of exercising the rights of conquest, we have been contented to impose such tributes as are requisite for your own preservation. Peace cannot be secured without armies; and armies must be supported at the expense of the people. It is for your sake, not for our own, that we guard the barrier of the Rhine against the ferocious Germans, who have so often attempted, and who will always desire, to exchange the solitude of their woods and morasses for the wealth and fertility of Gaul. The fall of Rome would be fatal to the provinces; and you would be buried in the ruins of that mighty fabric which has been raised by the valor and wisdom of eight hundred years. Your imaginary freedom would be insulted and oppressed by a savage master; and the expulsion of the Romans would be succeeded by the eternal hostilities of the Barbarian conquerors." This salutary advice was accepted, and this strange prediction was accomplished. In the space of four hundred years, the hardy Gauls who had encountered the arms of Caesar were imperceptibly melted into the general mass of citizens and subjects: the Western empire was dissolved; and the Germans, who had passed the Rhine, fiercely contended for the possession of Gaul, and excited the contempt or abhorrence of its peaceful and polished inhabitants. With that conscious pride which the preeminence of knowledge and luxury seldom fails to inspire, they derided the hairy and gigantic savages of the North: their rustic manners, dissonant joy, voracious appetite, and their horrid appearance, equally disgusting to the sight and to the smell. The liberal studies were still cultivated in the schools of Autun and Bordeaux; and the language of Cicero and Virgil was familiar to the Gallic youth. Their ears were astonished by the harsh and unknown sounds of the Germanic dialect, and they ingeniously lamented that the trembling muses fled from the harmony of a Burgundian lyre. The Gauls were endowed with all the advantages of art and nature; but as they wanted courage to defend them, they were justly condemned to obey and even to flatter the victorious Barbarians by whose clemency they held their precarious fortunes and their lives.

[*Kingdoms within the ruin of the West include Euric's (king of the Visigoths in Gaul and Spain, A.D. 476–485) and Clovis' (king of the Franks in Gaul, A.D. 481–511).*]

As soon as Odoacer had extinguished the Western empire, he sought the friendship of the most powerful of the Barbarians. The new sovereign of Italy resigned to Euric, king of the Visigoths, all the Roman conquests beyond the Alps, as far as the Rhine and the Ocean: and the senate might confirm this liberal gift with some ostentation of power, and without any real loss of revenue and dominion. The lawful pretensions of Euric were justified by ambition and success; and the Gothic nation might aspire under his command to the monarchy of Spain and Gaul. . . . The fortune of nations has often depended on accidents; and France may ascribe her greatness to the premature death of the Gothic king, at a time when his son Alaric was a helpless infant and his adversary Clovis an ambitious and valiant youth.

While Childeric, the father of Clovis, lived in exile in Germany, he was hospitably entertained by the queen, as well as by the king, of the Thuringians. After his restoration, Basina escaped from her husband's bed to the arms of her lover; freely declaring that if she had known a man wiser, stronger, or more beautiful than Childeric, that man should have been the object of her preference. Clovis was the offspring of this voluntary union; and when he was no more than fifteen years of age, he succeeded by his father's death to the command of the Salian tribe. The narrow limits of his kingdom were confined to the island of the Batavians, with the ancient dioceses of Tournay and Arras; and at the baptism of Clovis the number of his warriors could not exceed five thousand. The kindred tribes of the Franks, who had seated themselves along the Belgic rivers, the Scheld, the Meuse, the Moselle, and the Rhine, were governed by their independent kings of the Merovingian race; the equals, the allies, and sometimes the enemies of the Salic prince. But the Germans, who obeyed in peace the hereditary jurisdiction of their chiefs, were free to follow the standard of a popular and victorious general; and the superior merit of Clovis attracted the respect and allegiance of the national confederacy. When he first took the field, he had neither gold and silver in his coffers nor wine and corn in his magazine; but he imitated the example of Caesar, who, in the same country, had acquired wealth by the sword and purchased soldiers with the fruits of conquest. After each successful battle or expedition, the spoils were accumulated in one common mass; every warrior received his proportionable share; and the royal prerogative submitted to the equal regulations of military law. The untamed spirit of the Barbarians was taught to acknowledge the advantages of regular discipline. At the annual review of the month of March, their arms were diligently inspected; and when they traversed a peaceful territory, they were prohibited from touching a blade of grass. The justice of Clovis was inexorable; and his careless or disobedient soldiers were punished with instant death. It would be superfluous to praise the valor of a Frank; but the valor of Clovis was directed by cool and consummate prudence. In all his transactions with mankind, he calculated the weight of interest, of passion, and of opinion; and his measures were sometimes adapted to the sanguinary manners of the Germans and sometimes moderated by the milder genius of Rome and Christianity. He was intercepted in the career of victory, since he died in the forty-fifth year of his age: but he had already accomplished, in a reign of thirty years, the establishment of the French monarchy in Gaul.[†]

Till the thirtieth year of his age, Clovis continued to worship the gods of his ancestors [circa A.D. 496]. His disbelief, or rather disregard, of Christianity might encourage him to pillage with less remorse the churches of a hostile territory: but his subjects of Gaul enjoyed the free exercise of religious worship; and the bishops entertained a more favorable hope of the idolater than of the heretics. The Merovingian prince had contracted a fortunate alliance with the fair Clotilda, the niece of the king of Burgundy, who, in the midst of an Arian court, was educated in the profession of the Catholic faith [circa A.D. 492–493]. It was her interest as well as her duty to achieve the conversion of a Pagan husband; and Clovis insensibly listened to the voice of love and religion. He consented (perhaps such terms had been previously stipulated) to the baptism of his eldest son; and though the sudden death of the infant excited some superstitious fears, he was persuaded a second time to repeat the dangerous experiment. In the distress of the battle of Tolbiac, Clovis loudly invoked the God of Clotilda and the Christians; and victory disposed him to hear with respectful gratitude the eloquent Remigius, bishop of Rheims, who forcibly displayed the temporal and spiritual advantages of his conversion. The king declared himself satisfied of the truth of the Catholic faith; and the political reasons which might have suspended his public profession were removed by the devout or loyal acclamations of the Franks, who showed themselves alike prepared to follow their heroic leader to the field of battle or to the baptismal font. The important ceremony was performed [on Christmas Day] in the cathedral of Rheims, with every circumstance of magnificence and solemnity that could impress an awful sense of religion on the minds of its rude proselytes. The new Constantine was immediately baptized, with three thousand of his warlike subjects; and their example was imitated by the remainder of the *gentle Barbarians* who, in obedience to the victorious prelate, adored the cross which they had burnt, and burnt the idols which they had formerly adored. The mind of Clovis was susceptible of transient fervor: he was exasperated by the pathetic tale of the passion and death of Christ; and, instead of weighing the salutary consequences of that mysterious sacrifice, he exclaimed with indiscreet fury, "Had I been present at the head of my valiant Franks, I would have revenged his injuries." But the savage conqueror of Gaul was incapable of examining the proofs of a religion which depends on the laborious investigation of historic evidence and speculative theology. He was still more incapable of feeling the mild influence of the gospel which persuades and purifies the heart of a genuine convert. His ambitious reign was a perpetual violation of moral and Christian duties: his hands were stained with blood in peace as well as in war; and as soon as Clovis had dismissed a synod of the Gallican church, he calmly assassinated *all* the princes of the Merovingian race. Yet the king of the Franks might sincerely worship the Christian God as a Being more excellent and powerful than his national deities; and the signal deliverance and victory of Tolbiac encouraged Clovis to confide in the future protection of the Lord of Hosts. Martin, the most popular of the saints, had filled the Western world with the fame of those miracles which were incessantly performed at his holy sepulchre of Tours. His visible or invisible aid promoted the cause of a liberal and orthodox prince; and the profane remark of Clovis himself that St. Martin was an expensive friend need not be interpreted as the symptom of any permanent or rational skepticism. But earth as well as Heaven rejoiced in the conversion of the Franks. On the memorable day when Clovis ascended from the baptismal font, he alone in the Christian world deserved the name and prerogatives of a Catholic king. The emperor Anastasius entertained some dangerous errors concerning the nature of the divine incarnation; and the Barbarians of Italy, Africa, Spain, and Gaul were involved in the Arian heresy. The eldest, or rather the only, son of the church was acknowledged by the clergy as their lawful sovereign or glorious deliverer; and the armies of Clovis were strenuously supported by the zeal and fervor of the Catholic faction.[†]

The first victory of Clovis had insulted the honor of the Goths. They viewed his rapid progress with jealousy and terror; and the youthful fame of Alaric was oppressed by the more potent genius of his rival. Some disputes inevitably arose on the edge of their contiguous dominions; and after the delays of fruitless negotiation, a personal interview of the two kings was proposed and accepted. The conference of Clovis and Alaric was held in a small island of the Loire, near Amboise. They embraced, familiarly conversed, and feasted together; and separated with the warmest professions of peace and brotherly love. But their apparent confidence concealed a dark suspicion of hostile and treacherous designs; and their mutual complaints solicited, eluded, and disclaimed a final arbitration. At Paris, which he already considered as his royal seat, Clovis declared to an assembly of the princes and warriors the pretense, and the motive, of a Gothic war. "It grieves me to see that the Arians still possess the fairest portion of Gaul. Let us march against them with the aid of God; and, having vanquished the heretics, we will possess and divide their fertile provinces." The Franks, who were inspired by hereditary valor and recent zeal, applauded the generous design of their monarch; expressed their resolution to conquer or die, since death and conquest would be equally profitable; and solemnly protested that they would never shave their beards till victory should absolve them from that inconvenient vow. The enterprise was promoted by the public or private exhortations of Clotilda. She reminded her husband how effectually some pious foundation would propitiate the Deity and his servants: and the Christian hero, darting his battle-axe with a skillful and nervous hand, "There (said he) on that spot where my *Francisca* shall fall will I erect a church in honor of the holy apostles." This ostentatious piety confirmed and justified the attachment of the Catholics, with whom he secretly corresponded; and their devout wishes were gradually ripened into a formidable conspiracy. The people of Aquitain were alarmed by the indiscreet reproaches of their Gothic tyrants, who justly accused them of preferring the dominion of the Franks: and their zealous adherent Quintianus, bishop of Rodez, preached more forcibly in his exile than in his diocese. To resist these foreign and domestic enemies, who were fortified by the alliance of the Burgundians, Alaric collected his troops, far more numerous than the military powers of Clovis. The Visigoths resumed the exercise of arms, which they had neglected in a long and luxurious peace; a select band of valiant and robust slaves attended their masters to the field; and the cities of Gaul were compelled to furnish their doubtful and reluctant aid. Theodoric, king of the Ostrogoths, who reigned in Italy, had labored to maintain the tranquility of Gaul; and he assumed or affected for that purpose the impartial character of a mediator. But the sagacious monarch dreaded the rising empire of Clovis, and he was firmly engaged to support the national and religious cause of the Goths.

The accidental or artificial prodigies which adorned the expedition of Clovis were accepted by a superstitious age as the manifest declaration of the divine favor. He marched from Paris; and as he proceeded with decent reverence through the holy diocese of Tours, his anxiety tempted him to consult the shrine of St. Martin, the sanctuary and the oracle of Gaul. His messengers were instructed to remark the words of the Psalm which should happen to be chanted at the precise moment when they entered the church. Those words most fortunately expressed the valor and victory of the champions of Heaven, and the application was easily transferred to the new Joshua, the new Gideon, who went forth to battle against the enemies of the Lord.... The counsels of the Visigoths were irresolute and distracted.... [Clovis] advanced with bold and hasty steps.... His nocturnal march was directed by a flaming meteor suspended in the air above the cathedral of Poitiers; and this signal, which might be previously concerted with the orthodox successor of St. Hilary, was compared to the column of fire that guided the Israelites in the desert. At the third hour of the day, about ten miles beyond Poitiers, Clovis overtook and instantly attacked the Gothic army; whose defeat was already prepared by terror and confusion [A.D. 507].

[*Clovis conquers Aquitain (A.D. 508).*]

After the success of the Gothic war, Clovis accepted the honors of the Roman consulship. The emperor Anastasius ambitiously bestowed on the most powerful rival of Theodoric [the Ostrogothic king of Italy] the title and ensigns of that eminent dignity; yet, from some unknown cause, the name of Clovis has not been inscribed in the *Fasti* either of the East or West. On the solemn day the monarch of Gaul, placing a diadem on his head, was invested in the church of St. Martin with a purple tunic and mantle. From thence he proceeded on horseback to the cathedral of Tours; and as he passed through the streets profusely scattered, with his own hand, a donative of gold and silver to the joyful multitude, who incessantly repeated their acclamations of *Consul* and *Augustus*. The actual or legal authority of Clovis could not receive any new accessions from the consular dignity. It was a name, a shadow, an empty pageant; and if the conqueror had been instructed to claim the ancient prerogatives of that high office, they must have expired with the period of its annual duration. But the Romans were disposed to revere, in the person of their master, that antique title which the emperors condescended to assume: the Barbarian himself seemed to contract a sacred obligation to respect the majesty of the republic; and the successors of Theodosius, by soliciting his friendship, tacitly forgave and almost ratified the usurpation of Gaul.

Twenty-five years after the death of Clovis, this important concession was more formally declared in a treaty between his sons and the emperor Justinian [A.D. 536].... Justinian, generously yielding to the

Franks the sovereignty of the countries beyond the Alps, which they already possessed, absolved the provincials from their allegiance; and established on a more lawful, though not more solid, foundation the throne of the Merovingians. From that era they enjoyed the right of celebrating at Arles the games of the circus; and by a singular privilege which was denied even to the Persian monarch, the *gold* coin impressed with their name and image obtained a legal currency in the empire. A Greek historian of that age has praised the private and public virtues of the Franks, with a partial enthusiasm which cannot be sufficiently justified by their domestic annals. He celebrates their politeness and urbanity, their regular government, and orthodox religion; and boldly asserts that these Barbarians could be distinguished only by their dress and language from the subjects of Rome.[†]

The rudest or the most servile condition of human society is regulated, however, by some fixed and general rules. When Tacitus surveyed the primitive simplicity of the Germans, he discovered some permanent maxims or customs of public and private life which were preserved by faithful tradition till the introduction of the art of writing and of the Latin tongue. Before the election of the Merovingian kings, the most powerful tribe or nation of the Franks appointed four venerable chieftains to compose the *Salic* laws; and their labors were examined and approved in three successive assemblies of the people. After the baptism of Clovis, he reformed several articles that appeared incompatible with Christianity: the Salic law was again amended by his sons; and at length, under the reign of Dagobert, the code was revised and promulgated in its actual form, one hundred years after the establishment of the French monarchy. Within the same period, the customs of the *Ripuarians* were transcribed and published; and Charlemagne himself, the legislator of his age and country, had accurately studied the two national laws, which still prevailed among the Franks....
Thus, by a singular coincidence, the Germans framed their artless institutions at a time when the elaborate system of Roman jurisprudence was finally consummated. In the Salic laws and the Pandects of Justinian we may compare the first rudiments and the full maturity of civil wisdom; and whatever prejudices may be suggested in favor of barbarism, our calmer reflections will ascribe to the Romans the superior advantages, not only of science and reason, but of humanity and justice. Yet the laws of the Barbarians were adapted to their wants and de-

sires, their occupations and their capacity; and they all contributed to preserve the peace and promote the improvement of the society for whose use they were originally established. The Merovingians, instead of imposing a uniform rule of conduct on their various subjects, permitted each people and each family of their empire freely to enjoy their domestic institutions; nor were the Romans excluded from the common benefits of this legal toleration. The children embraced the *law* of their parents, the wife that of her husband, the freedman that of his patron; and in all causes where the parties were of different nations, the plaintiff or accuser was obliged to follow the tribunal of the defendant, who may always plead a judicial presumption of right or innocence. A more ample latitude was allowed if every citizen, in the presence of the judge, might declare the law under which he desired to live and the national society to which he chose to belong. Such an indulgence would abolish the partial distinctions of victory: and the Roman provincials might patiently acquiesce in the hardships of their condition; since it depended on themselves to assume the privilege, if they dared to assert the character, of free and warlike Barbarians.

When justice inexorably requires the death of a murderer, each private citizen is fortified by the assurance that the laws, the magistrate, and the whole community are the guardians of his personal safety. But in the loose society of the Germans, revenge was always honorable, and often meritorious: the independent warrior chastised or vindicated with his own hand the injuries which he had offered or received; and he had only to dread the resentment of the sons and kinsmen of the enemy whom he had sacrificed to his selfish or angry passions. The magistrate, conscious of his weakness, interposed not to punish but to reconcile; and he was satisfied if he could persuade or compel the contending parties to pay and to accept the moderate fine which had been ascertained as the price of blood. The fierce spirit of the Franks would have opposed a more rigorous sentence; the same fierceness despised these ineffectual restraints; and when their simple manners had been corrupted by the wealth of Gaul, the public peace was continually violated by acts of hasty or deliberate guilt. In every just government the same penalty is inflicted, or at least is imposed, for the murder of a peasant or a prince. But the national inequality established by the Franks in their criminal proceedings was the last insult and abuse of conquest. In the calm moments of legislation, they solemnly pronounced that the life of a Roman was of smaller value than that of a Barbarian. The *Antrustion,* a name expressive of the most illustrious birth or dignity among the Franks, was appreciated at the sum of six hundred pieces of gold; while the noble provincial who was admitted to the king's table might be legally murdered at the expense of three hundred pieces. Two hundred were deemed sufficient for a Frank of ordinary condition; but the meaner Romans were exposed to disgrace and danger by a trifling compensation of one hundred, or even fifty, pieces of gold. Had these laws been regulated by any principle of equity or reason, the public protection should have supplied in just proportion the want of personal strength. But the legislator had weighed in the scale, not of justice but of policy, the loss of a soldier against that of a slave: the head of an insolent and rapacious Barbarian was guarded by a heavy fine; and the slightest aid was afforded to the most defenseless subjects. Time insensibly abated the pride of the conquerors and the patience of the vanquished; and the boldest citizen was taught by experience that he might suffer more injuries than he could inflict. As the manners of the Franks became less ferocious, their laws were rendered more severe; and the Merovingian kings attempted to imitate the impartial rigor of the Visigoths and Burgundians. Under the empire of Charlemagne, murder was universally punished with death; and the use of capital punishments has been liberally multiplied in the jurisprudence of modern Europe.

The civil and military professions, which had been separated by Constantine, were again united by the Barbarians. The harsh sound of the Teutonic appellations was mollified into the Latin titles of Duke, of Count, or of Praefect; and the same officer assumed within his district the command of the troops and the administration of justice. But the fierce and illiterate chieftain was seldom qualified to discharge the duties of a judge, which required all the faculties of a philosophic mind laboriously cultivated by experience and study; and his rude ignorance was compelled to embrace some simple and visible methods of ascertaining the cause of justice. In every religion, the Deity has been invoked to confirm the truth or to punish the falsehood of human testimony; but this powerful instrument was misapplied and abused by the simplicity of the German legislators. The party accused might justify his innocence by producing before their tribunal a number of friendly witnesses who solemnly declared their belief or assurance that he was not guilty. According to the weight of the charge, this legal number of compurgators was multiplied; seventy-two voices were required to absolve an incendiary or assassin: and when the chastity of a queen of France was suspected, three hundred gallant nobles swore without hesitation that the infant prince had been actually begotten by her deceased husband. The sin and scandal of manifest and frequent perjuries engaged the magistrates to remove these dangerous temptations, and to supply the defects of human testimony by the famous experiments of fire and water. These extraordinary trials were so capriciously contrived that in some cases guilt, and innocence in others, could not be proved without the interposition of a miracle. Such miracles were really provided by fraud and credulity; the most intricate causes were determined by this easy and infallible method, and the turbulent Barbarians who might have disdained the sentence of the magistrate submissively acquiesced in the judgment of God.

But the trials by single combat gradually obtained superior credit and authority among a warlike people who could not believe that a brave man deserved to suffer, or that a coward deserved to live. Both in civil and criminal proceedings, the plaintiff or accuser, the defendant, or even the witness were exposed to mortal challenge from the antagonist who was destitute of legal proofs; and it was incumbent on them either to desert their cause or publicly to maintain their honor in the lists of battle. They fought either on foot or on horseback, according to the custom of their nation; and the decision of the sword or lance was ratified by the sanction of Heaven, of the judge, and of the people. This sanguinary law was introduced into Gaul by the Burgundians; and their legislator Gundobald condescended to answer the complaints and objections of his subject Avitus. "Is it not true," said the king of Burgundy to the bishop, "that the event of national wars and private combats is directed by the judgment of God; and that his providence awards the victory to the juster cause?" By such prevailing arguments, the absurd and cruel practice of judicial duels, which had been peculiar to some tribes of Germany, was propagated and established in all the monarchies of Europe, from Sicily to the Baltic. . . . The tribunals were stained with the blood, perhaps, of innocent and respectable citizens; the law, which now favors the rich, then yielded to the strong; and the old, the feeble, and the infirm were condemned either to renounce their fairest claims and possessions, to sustain the

dangers of an unequal conflict, or to trust the doubtful aid of a mercenary champion. This oppressive jurisprudence was imposed on the
provincials of Gaul who complained of any injuries in their persons
and property. Whatever might be the strength or courage of individuals, the victorious Barbarians excelled in the love and exercise of arms;
and the vanquished Roman was unjustly summoned to repeat in his
own person the bloody contest which had been already decided against
his country.[†]

In the bloody discord and silent decay of the Merovingian line, a
new order of tyrants arose in the provinces who, under the appellation of *Seniors*, or Lords, usurped a right to govern and a license to oppress the subjects of their peculiar territory. Their ambition might be
checked by the hostile resistance of an equal: but the laws were extinguished; and the sacrilegious Barbarians who dared to provoke the
vengeance of a saint or bishop would seldom respect the landmarks of
a profane and defenseless neighbor. The common or public rights of
nature, such as they had always been deemed by the Roman jurisprudence, were severely restrained by the German conquerors, whose
amusement, or rather passion, was the exercise of hunting. The vague
dominion which MAN has assumed over the wild inhabitants of the
earth, the air, and the waters was confined to some fortunate individuals of the human species. Gaul was again overspread with woods; and
the animals, who were reserved for the use or pleasure of the lord,
might ravage with impunity the fields of his industrious vassals. The
chase was the sacred privilege of the nobles and their domestic servants. Plebeian transgressors were legally chastised with stripes and
imprisonment; but in an age which admitted a slight composition for
the life of a citizen, it was a capital crime to destroy a stag or a wild bull
within the precincts of the royal forests.

According to the maxims of ancient war, the conqueror became the
lawful master of the enemy whom he had subdued and spared: and the
fruitful cause of personal slavery, which had been almost suppressed by
the peaceful sovereignty of Rome, was again revived and multiplied by
the perpetual hostilities of the independent Barbarians. The Goth, the
Burgundian, or the Frank who returned from a successful expedition
dragged after him a long train of sheep, of oxen, and of human captives, whom he treated with the same brutal contempt. The youths of

an elegant form and an ingenuous aspect were set apart for the domestic service; a doubtful situation which alternately exposed them to the favorable or cruel impulse of passion. The useful mechanics and servants (smiths, carpenters, tailors, shoemakers, cooks, gardeners, dyers, and workmen in gold and silver, etc.) employed their skill for the use or profit of their master. But the Roman captives who were destitute of art but capable of labor were condemned, without regard to their former rank, to tend the cattle and cultivate the lands of the Barbarians. The number of the hereditary bondsmen who were attached to the Gallic estates was continually increased by new supplies; and the servile people, according to the situation and temper of their lords, was sometimes raised by precarious indulgence, and more frequently depressed by capricious despotism. An absolute power of life and death was exercised by these lords; and when they married their daughters, a train of useful servants, chained on the wagons to prevent their escape, was sent as a nuptial present into a distant country. The majesty of the Roman laws protected the liberty of each citizen against the rash effects of his own distress or despair. But the subjects of the Merovingian kings might alienate their personal freedom; and this act of legal suicide, which was familiarly practiced, is expressed in terms most disgraceful and afflicting to the dignity of human nature. The example of the poor, who purchased life by the sacrifice of all that can render life desirable, was gradually imitated by the feeble and the devout, who in times of public disorder pusillanimously crowded to shelter themselves under the battlements of a powerful chief and around the shrine of a popular saint. Their submission was accepted by these temporal or spiritual patrons; and the hasty transaction irrecoverably fixed their own condition and that of their latest posterity. From the reign of Clovis, during five successive centuries, the laws and manners of Gaul uniformly tended to promote the increase and to confirm the duration of personal servitude. Time and violence almost obliterated the intermediate ranks of society; and left an obscure and narrow interval between the noble and the slave. This arbitrary and recent division has been transformed by pride and prejudice into a *national* distinction, universally established by the arms and the laws of the Merovingians. The nobles, who claimed their genuine or fabulous descent from the independent and victorious Franks, have asserted and abused the in-

defeasible right of conquest over a prostrate crowd of slaves and plebeians to whom they imputed the imaginary disgrace of Gallic or
Roman extraction.[†]

We are now qualified to despise the opposite, and perhaps artful,
misrepresentations which have softened or exaggerated the oppression
of the Romans of Gaul under the reign of the Merovingians. The conquerors never promulgated any *universal* edict of servitude or confiscation; but a degenerate people who excused their weakness by the
specious names of politeness and peace was exposed to the arms and
laws of the ferocious Barbarians, who contemptuously insulted their
possessions, their freedom, and their safety. Their personal injuries
were partial and irregular; but the great body of the Romans survived
the revolution, and still preserved the property and privileges of citizens. A large portion of their lands was exacted for the use of the
Franks: but they enjoyed the remainder exempt from tribute; and the
same irresistible violence which swept away the arts and manufactures
of Gaul destroyed the elaborate and expensive system of Imperial
despotism. The provincials must frequently deplore the savage jurisprudence of the Salic or Ripuarian laws; but their private life, in the
important concerns of marriage, testaments, or inheritance, was still
regulated by the Theodosian Code; and a discontented Roman might
freely aspire, or descend, to the title and character of a Barbarian. The
honors of the state were accessible to his ambition: the education and
temper of the Romans more peculiarly qualified them for the offices of
civil government; and as soon as emulation had rekindled their military ardor, they were permitted to march in the ranks, or even at the
head, of the victorious Germans. I shall not attempt to enumerate
the generals and magistrates whose names attest the liberal policy of
the Merovingians. The supreme command of Burgundy, with the title
of Patrician, was successively entrusted to three Romans; and the last
and most powerful, Mummolus, who alternately saved and disturbed
the monarchy, had supplanted his father in the station of count of
Autun, and left a treasury of thirty talents of gold, and two hundred
and fifty talents of silver. The fierce and illiterate Barbarians were excluded during several generations from the dignities, and even from
the orders, of the church. The clergy of Gaul consisted almost entirely
of native provincials; the haughty Franks fell at the feet of their subjects who were dignified with the episcopal character: and the power

and riches which had been lost in war were insensibly recovered by superstition. In all temporal affairs, the Theodosian Code was the universal law of the clergy; but the Barbaric jurisprudence had liberally provided for their personal safety; a sub-deacon was equivalent to two Franks; the *antrustion* and priest were held in similar estimation: and the life of a bishop was appreciated far above the common standard, at the price of nine hundred pieces of gold. The Romans communicated to their conquerors the use of the Christian religion and Latin language; but their language and their religion had alike degenerated from the simple purity of the Augustan and Apostolic age. The progress of superstition and Barbarism was rapid and universal: the worship of the saints concealed from vulgar eyes the God of the Christians; and the rustic dialect of peasants and soldiers was corrupted by a Teutonic idiom and pronunciation. Yet such intercourse of sacred and social communion eradicated the distinctions of birth and victory; and the nations of Gaul were gradually confounded under the name and government of the Franks.[†]

The Visigoths had resigned to Clovis the greatest part of their Gallic possessions; but their loss was amply compensated by the easy conquest and secure enjoyment of the provinces of Spain. From the monarchy of the Goths, which soon involved the Suevic kingdom of Gallicia, the modern Spaniards still derive some national vanity; but the historian of the Roman empire is neither invited nor compelled to pursue the obscure and barren series of their annals. The Goths of Spain were separated from the rest of mankind by the lofty ridge of the Pyrenean mountains: their manners and institutions, as far as they were common to the Germanic tribes, have been already explained. I have anticipated in the preceding chapter the most important of their ecclesiastical events, the fall of Arianism and the persecution of the Jews.[†]

While the kingdoms of the Franks and Visigoths were established in Gaul and Spain, the Saxons achieved the conquest of Britain, the third great diocese of the praefecture of the West. Since Britain was already separated from the Roman empire, I might without reproach decline a story familiar to the most illiterate and obscure to the most learned of my readers. The Saxons, who excelled in the use of the oar or the battle-axe, were ignorant of the art which could alone perpetuate the fame of their exploits; the provincials, relapsing into barbarism, neglected to describe the ruin of their country; and the doubtful tradition was almost extinguished before the missionaries of Rome restored the light of science and Christianity. The declamations of Gildas, the fragments or fables of Nennius, the obscure hints of the Saxon laws and chronicles, and the ecclesiastical tales of the venerable Bede have been illustrated by the diligence, and sometimes embellished by the fancy, of succeeding writers, whose works I am not ambitious either to censure or to transcribe. Yet the historian of the empire may be tempted to pursue the revolutions of a Roman province till it vanishes from his sight; and an Englishman may curiously trace the establishment of the Barbarians from whom he derives his name, his laws, and perhaps his origin.[†]

Under the long dominion of the emperors, Britain had been insensibly molded into the elegant and servile form of a Roman province whose safety was entrusted to a foreign power. The subjects of Honorius contemplated their new freedom with surprise and terror; they were left destitute of any civil or military constitution; and their uncertain rulers wanted either skill, or courage, or authority to direct the public force against the common enemy. The introduction of the Saxons betrayed their internal weakness and degraded the character both of the prince and people. Their consternation magnified the danger; the want of union diminished their resources; and the madness of civil factions was more solicitous to accuse than to remedy the evils which they imputed to the misconduct of their adversaries. Yet the Britons were not ignorant, they could not be ignorant, of the manufacture or the use of arms; the successive and disorderly attacks of the Saxons allowed them to recover from their amazement and the prosperous or adverse events of the war added discipline and experience to their native valor.

While the continents of Europe and Africa yielded without resistance to the Barbarians, the British island, alone and unaided, maintained a long, a vigorous, though an unsuccessful struggle against the formidable pirates who, almost at the same instant, assaulted the northern, the eastern, and the southern coasts. The cities, which had been fortified with skill, were defended with resolution; the advantages of ground, hills, forests, and morasses were diligently improved by the inhabitants; the conquest of each district was purchased with blood; and the defeats of the Saxons are strongly attested by the discreet silence of their annalist. Hengist might hope to achieve the conquest of Britain; but his ambition, in an active reign of thirty-five years, was confined to the possession of Kent; and the numerous colony which he had planted in the north was extirpated by the sword of the Britons.[†]

After a war of a hundred years, the independent Britons still occupied the whole extent of the western coast, from the wall of Antoninus to the extreme promontory of Cornwall; and the principal cities of the inland country still opposed the arms of the Barbarians. Resistance became more languid as the number and boldness of the assailants continually increased. Winning their way by slow and painful efforts, the Saxons, the Angles, and their various confederates advanced from the north, from the east, and from the south, till their victorious banners were united in the center of the island. Beyond the Severn the Britons still asserted their national freedom, which survived the heptarchy, and even the monarchy, of the Saxons. The bravest warriors, who preferred exile to slavery, found a secure refuge in the mountains of Wales: the reluctant submission of Cornwall was delayed for some ages; and a band of fugitives acquired a settlement in Gaul, by their own valor or the liberality of the Merovingian kings.[†]

In a century of perpetual or at least implacable war, much courage and some skill must have been exerted for the defense of Britain. Yet if the memory of its champions is almost buried in oblivion, we need not repine; since every age, however destitute of science or virtue, sufficiently abounds with acts of blood and military renown.... But every British name is effaced by the illustrious name of ARTHUR, the hereditary prince of the Silures in South Wales, and the elective king or general of the nation. According to the most rational account, he defeated, in twelve successive battles, the Angles of the north and the Saxons of the west; but the declining age of the hero was embittered by popular ingratitude and domestic misfortunes. The events of his life are less interesting than the singular revolutions of his fame. During a period of five hundred years the tradition of his exploits was preserved and rudely embellished by the obscure bards of Wales and Armorica, who were odious to the Saxons and unknown to the rest of mankind. The pride and curiosity of the Norman conquerors prompted them to inquire into the ancient history of Britain: they listened with fond credulity to the tale of Arthur and eagerly applauded the merit of a prince who had triumphed over the Saxons, their common enemies.

His romance, transcribed in the Latin of Jeffrey of Monmouth and afterwards translated into the fashionable idiom of the times, was enriched with the various though incoherent ornaments which were familiar to the experience, the learning, or the fancy of the twelfth century. The progress of a Phrygian colony from the Tiber to the Thames was easily ingrafted on the fable of the Aeneid; and the royal ancestors of Arthur derived their origin from Troy and claimed their alliance with the Caesars. His trophies were decorated with captive provinces and Imperial titles; and his Danish victories avenged the recent injuries of his country. The gallantry and superstition of the British hero, his feasts and tournaments, and the memorable institution of his Knights of the *Round Table* were faithfully copied from the reigning manners of chivalry; and the fabulous exploits of Uther's son appear less incredible than the adventures which were achieved by the enterprising valor of the Normans. Pilgrimage and the holy wars introduced into Europe the specious miracles of Arabian magic. Fairies and giants, flying dragons, and enchanted palaces were blended with the more simple fictions of the West; and the fate of Britain depended on the art or the predictions of Merlin. Every nation embraced and adorned the popular romance of Arthur and the Knights of the Round Table: their names were celebrated in Greece and Italy; and the voluminous tales of Sir Lancelot and Sir Tristram were devoutly studied by the princes and nobles who disregarded the genuine heroes and historians of antiquity. At length the light of science and reason was rekindled; the talisman was broken; the visionary fabric melted into air; and by a natural though unjust reverse of the public opinion, the severity of the present age is inclined to question the *existence* of Arthur.

Resistance, if it cannot avert, must increase the miseries of conquest; and conquest has never appeared more dreadful and destructive than in the hands of the Saxons; who hated the valor of their enemies, disdained the faith of treaties, and violated without remorse the most sacred objects of the Christian worship. The fields of battle might be traced, almost in every district, by monuments of bones; the fragments of falling towers were stained with blood; the last of the Britons, without distinction of age or sex, was massacred in the ruins of Anderida; and the repetition of such calamities was frequent and familiar under the Saxon heptarchy [A.D. 455–582]. The arts and religion, the laws and language which the Romans had so carefully planted in Britain were extirpated by their barbarous successors. After the destruction of the principal churches, the bishops who had declined the crown of martyrdom retired with the holy relics into Wales and Armorica; the remains of their flocks were left destitute of any spiritual food; the practice and even the remembrance of Christianity were abolished; and the British clergy might obtain some comfort from the damnation of the idolatrous strangers. The kings of France maintained the privileges of their Roman subjects; but the ferocious Saxons trampled on the laws of Rome and of the emperors. The proceedings of civil and criminal jurisdiction, the titles of honor, the forms of office, the ranks of society, and even the domestic rights of marriage, testament, and inheritance were finally suppressed; and the indiscriminate crowd of noble and plebeian slaves was governed by the traditionary customs which had been coarsely framed for the shepherds and pirates of Germany. The language of science, of business, and of conversation, which had been introduced by the Romans, was lost in the general desolation. A sufficient number of Latin or Celtic words might be assumed by the Germans to express their new wants and ideas; but those *illiterate* Pagans preserved and established the use of their national dialect. Almost every name conspicuous either in the church or state reveals its Teutonic origin; and the geography of *England* was universally inscribed with foreign characters and appellations. The example of a revolution so rapid and so complete may not easily be found; but it will excite a probable suspicion that the arts of Rome were less deeply rooted in Britain than in Gaul or Spain; and that the native rudeness of the country and its inhabitants was covered by a thin varnish of Italian manners.

This strange alteration has persuaded historians and even philosophers that the provincials of Britain were totally exterminated; and that the vacant land was again peopled by the perpetual influx and rapid increase of the German colonies ...; but neither reason nor facts can justify the unnatural supposition that the Saxons of Britain remained alone in the desert which they had subdued. After the sanguinary Barbarians had secured their dominion and gratified their revenge, it was their interest to preserve the peasants as well as the cattle of the unresisting country. In each successive revolution, the patient herd becomes the property of its new masters; and the salutary compact of food and labor is silently ratified by their mutual necessities.... England was cultivated by a million of servants, or *villains,* who were attached to the estates of their arbitrary landlords. The indigent Barbarians were often tempted to sell their children or themselves into perpetual, and even foreign, bondage, yet the special exemptions, which were granted to *national* slaves, sufficiently declare that they were much less numerous than the strangers or captives, who had lost their liberty or changed their masters by the accidents of war. When time and religion had mitigated the fierce spirit of the Anglo-Saxons, the laws encouraged the frequent practice of manumission; and their subjects of Welsh or Cambrian extraction assumed the respectable station of inferior freemen, possessed of lands, and entitled to the rights of civil society.[†]

The independent Britons appear to have relapsed into the state of original barbarism from whence they had been imperfectly reclaimed. Separated by their enemies from the rest of mankind, they soon became an object of scandal and abhorrence to the Catholic world. Christianity was still professed in the mountains of Wales; but the rude schismatics, in the *form* of the clerical tonsure and in the *day* of the celebration of Easter, obstinately resisted the imperious mandates of the Roman pontiffs. The use of the Latin language was insensibly abolished, and the Britons were deprived of the art and learning which Italy communicated to her Saxon proselytes. In Wales and Armorica, the Celtic tongue, the native idiom of the West, was preserved and propagated; and the Bards, who had been the companions of the Druids, were still protected in the sixteenth century by the laws of Elizabeth.... The last retreats of Celtic freedom, the extreme territories of Gaul and Britain, were less adapted to agriculture than to pasturage: the wealth of the Britons consisted in their flocks and herds; milk and flesh were their ordinary food.[†]

By the revolution of Britain, the limits of science as well as of empire were contracted. The dark cloud which had been cleared by the Phoenician discoveries and finally dispelled by the arms of Caesar again settled on the shores of the Atlantic, and a Roman province was again lost among the fabulous Islands of the Ocean. One hundred and fifty years after the reign of Honorius, the gravest historian of the times describes the wonders of a remote isle whose eastern and western parts are divided by an antique wall, the boundary of life and death or, more properly, of truth and fiction. The east is a fair country inhabited by a civilized people: the air is healthy, the waters are pure and plentiful, and the earth yields her regular and fruitful increase. In the west, beyond the wall, the air is infectious and mortal; the ground is covered with serpents; and this dreary solitude is the region of departed spirits, who are transported from the opposite shores in substantial boats and by living rowers. Some families of fishermen, the subjects of the Franks, are excused from tribute in consideration of the mysterious office which is performed by these Charons of the ocean. Each in his turn is summoned at the hour of midnight to hear the voices and even the names of the ghosts: he is sensible of their weight, and he feels himself impelled by an unknown but irresistible power. After this dream of fancy, we read with astonishment that the name of this island is *Brittia;* that it lies in the ocean against the mouth of the Rhine, and less than thirty miles from the Continent; that it is possessed by three nations, the Frisians, the Angles, and the Britons; and that some Angles had appeared at Constantinople in the train of the French ambassadors.... The arts of navigation by which they acquired the empire of Britain and of the sea were soon neglected by the indolent Barbarians, who supinely renounced all the commercial advantages of their insular situation. Seven independent kingdoms were agitated by perpetual discord; and the *British world* was seldom connected, either in peace or war, with the nations of the Continent.

I have now accomplished the laborious narrative of the decline and fall of the Roman empire, from the fortunate age of Trajan and the Antonines to its total extinction in the West, about five centuries after the Christian era. At that unhappy period, the Saxons fiercely struggled with the natives for the possession of Britain: Gaul and Spain were divided between the powerful monarchies of the Franks and Visigoths and the dependent kingdoms of the Suevi and Burgundians: Africa was exposed to the cruel persecution of the Vandals and the savage insults of the Moors: Rome and Italy as far as the banks of the Danube were afflicted by an army of Barbarian mercenaries whose lawless tyranny was succeeded by the reign of Theodoric the Ostrogoth. All the subjects of the empire who, by the use of the Latin language, more particularly deserved the name and privileges of Romans were oppressed by the disgrace and calamities of foreign conquest; and the victorious nations of Germany established a new system of manners and government in the western countries of Europe. The majesty of Rome was faintly represented by the princes of Constantinople, the feeble and imaginary successors of Augustus. Yet they continued to reign over the East, from the Danube to the Nile and Tigris; the Gothic and Vandal kingdoms of Italy and Africa were subverted by the arms of Justinian; and the history of the *Greek* emperors may still afford a long series of instructive lessons and interesting revolutions.

GENERAL OBSERVATIONS ON THE FALL OF THE ROMAN EMPIRE IN THE WEST

The Greeks, after their country had been reduced into a province, imputed the triumphs of Rome, not to the merit but to the FORTUNE of the republic. The inconstant goddess who so blindly distributes and resumes her favors had *now* consented (such was the language of envious flattery) to resign her wings, to descend from her globe, and to fix her firm and immutable throne on the banks of the Tiber. A wiser Greek [the historian Polybius], who has composed with a philosophic spirit the memorable history of his own times, deprived his countrymen of this vain and delusive comfort by opening to their view the deep foundations of the greatness of Rome. The fidelity of the citizens to each other and to the state was confirmed by the habits of education and the prejudices of religion. Honor as well as virtue was the principle of the republic; the ambitious citizens labored to deserve the solemn glories of a triumph; and the ardor of the Roman youth was kindled into active emulation as often as they beheld the domestic images of their ancestors. The temperate struggles of the patricians and plebeians had finally established the firm and equal balance of the constitution; which united the freedom of popular assemblies with the authority and wisdom of a senate and the executive powers of a regal magistrate. When the consul displayed the standard of the republic, each citizen bound himself by the obligation of an oath to draw his sword in the cause of his country till he had discharged the sacred duty by a military service of ten years. This wise institution continually poured into the field the rising generations of freemen and soldiers; and their numbers were reinforced by the warlike and populous states of Italy, who, after a brave resistance, had yielded to the valor and embraced the alliance of the Romans. The sage historian who excited the virtue of the younger Scipio and beheld the ruin of Carthage has accurately described their military system; their levies, arms, exercises, subordination, marches, encampments; and the invincible legion, superior in active strength to the Macedonian phalanx of Philip and Alexander. From these institutions of peace and war Polybius has deduced the spirit and success of a people incapable of fear and impatient of repose. The ambitious design of conquest, which might have been defeated by the seasonable conspiracy of mankind, was attempted and achieved; and the perpetual violation of justice was maintained by the political virtues of prudence and courage. The arms of the republic, sometimes vanquished in battle, always victorious in war, advanced with rapid steps to the Euphrates, the Danube, the Rhine, and the Ocean; and the images of gold, or silver, or brass that might serve to represent the nations and their kings were successively broken by the *iron* monarchy of Rome.

The rise of a city which swelled into an empire may deserve, as a singular prodigy, the reflection of a philosophic mind. But the decline of Rome was the natural and inevitable effect of immoderate greatness. Prosperity ripened the principle of decay; the causes of destruction multiplied with the extent of conquest; and as soon as time or accident had removed the artificial supports the stupendous fabric yielded to the pressure of its own weight. The story of its ruin is simple and obvious; and instead of inquiring *why* the Roman empire was destroyed, we should rather be surprised that it had subsisted so long. The victorious legions who in distant wars acquired the vices of strangers and mercenaries first oppressed the freedom of the republic, and afterwards violated the majesty of the purple. The emperors, anxious for their personal safety and the public peace, were reduced to the base expedient of corrupting the discipline which rendered them alike formidable to their sovereign and to the enemy; the vigor of the military government was relaxed and finally dissolved by the partial institutions of Constantine; and the Roman world was overwhelmed by a deluge of Barbarians.

The decay of Rome has been frequently ascribed to the translation of the seat of empire; but this History has already shown that the powers of government were *divided,* rather than *removed.* The throne of Constantinople was erected in the East; while the West was still possessed by a series of emperors who held their residence in Italy and claimed their equal inheritance of the legions and provinces. This dangerous novelty impaired the strength and fomented the vices of a double reign: the instruments of an oppressive and arbitrary system were multiplied; and a vain emulation of luxury, not of merit, was introduced and supported between the degenerate successors of Theodosius. Extreme distress, which unites the virtue of a free people, embitters the factions of a declining monarchy. The hostile favorites of Arcadius and Honorius betrayed the republic to its common enemies; and the Byzantine court beheld with indifference, perhaps with pleasure, the disgrace of Rome, the misfortunes of Italy, and the loss of the West. Under the succeeding reigns, the alliance of the two empires was restored; but the aid of the Oriental Romans was tardy, doubtful, and ineffectual; and the national schism of the Greeks and Latins was enlarged by the perpetual difference of language and manners, of interests, and even of religion. Yet the salutary event approved in some measure the judgment of Constantine. During a long period of decay, his impregnable city repelled the victorious armies of Barbarians, protected the wealth of Asia, and commanded, both in peace and war, the important straits which connect the Euxine and Mediterranean Seas. The foundation of Constantinople more essentially contributed to the preservation of the East than to the ruin of the West.

As the happiness of a *future* life is the great object of religion, we may hear without surprise or scandal that the introduction, or at least the abuse, of Christianity had some influence on the decline and fall of the Roman empire. The clergy successfully preached the doctrines of patience and pusillanimity; the active virtues of society were discouraged, and the last remains of military spirit were buried in the cloister; a large portion of public and private wealth was consecrated to the specious demands of charity and devotion; and the soldiers' pay was lavished on the useless multitudes of both sexes, who could only plead the merits of abstinence and chastity. Faith, zeal, curiosity, and the more earthly passions of malice and ambition kindled the flame of theological discord; the church, and even the state, were distracted by religious factions whose conflicts were sometimes bloody and always implacable; the attention of the emperors was diverted from camps to synods; the Roman world was oppressed by a new species of tyranny; and the persecuted sects became the secret enemies of their country. Yet party spirit, however pernicious or absurd, is a principle of union as well as of dissension. The bishops, from eighteen hundred pulpits, inculcated the duty of passive obedience to a lawful and orthodox sovereign; their frequent assemblies and perpetual correspondence maintained the communion of distant churches; and the benevolent temper of the gospel was strengthened, though confined, by the spiritual alliance of the Catholics. The sacred indolence of the monks was devoutly embraced by a servile and effeminate age; but if superstition had not afforded a decent retreat, the same vices would have tempted the unworthy Romans to desert from baser motives the standard of the republic. Religious precepts are easily obeyed which indulge and sanctify the natural inclinations of their votaries; but the pure and genuine influence of Christianity may be traced in its beneficial though imperfect effects on the Barbarian proselytes of the North. If the decline of the Roman empire was hastened by the conversion of Constantine, his victorious religion broke the violence of the fall and mollified the ferocious temper of the conquerors.[†]

END OF THE THIRD VOLUME [1781].

VOLUME THE FOURTH

[1788]

Preface to the Fourth Volume of the Original Quarto Edition

I now discharge my promise and complete my design of writing the History of the Decline and Fall of the Roman Empire, both in the West and the East. The whole period extends from the age of Trajan and the Antonines to the taking of Constantinople by Mohammed the Second; and includes a review of the Crusades and the state of Rome during the middle ages. Since the publication of the first volume, twelve years have elapsed; twelve years, according to my wish, "of health, of leisure, and of perseverance." I may now congratulate my deliverance from a long and laborious service and my satisfaction will be pure and perfect if the public favor should be extended to the conclusion of my work.

It was my first intention to have collected under one view the numerous authors, of every age and language, from whom I have derived the materials of this history; and I am still convinced that the apparent ostentation would be more than compensated by real use. If I have renounced this idea, if I have declined an undertaking which had obtained the approbation of a master-artist, my excuse may be found in the extreme difficulty of assigning a proper measure to such a catalogue. A naked list of names and editions would not be satisfactory either to myself or my readers: the characters of the principal authors of the Roman and Byzantine history have been occasionally connected with the events which they describe; a more copious and critical inquiry might indeed deserve, but it would demand an elaborate volume which might swell by degrees into a general library of historical writers. For the present, I shall content myself with renewing my serious protestation that I have always endeavored to draw from the fountainhead; that my curiosity, as well as a sense of duty, has always urged me to study the originals; and that, if they have sometimes eluded my search, I have carefully marked the secondary evidence on whose faith a passage or a fact were reduced to depend.

I shall soon revisit the banks of the Lake of Lausanne, a country which I have known and loved from my early youth. Under a mild government, amidst a beauteous landscape, in a life of leisure and independence and among a people of easy and elegant manners, I have enjoyed, and may again hope to enjoy, the varied pleasures of retirement and society. But I shall ever glory in the name and character of an Englishman: I am proud of my birth in a free and enlightened country; and the approbation of that country is the best and most honorable reward of my labors. Were I ambitious of any other Patron than the Public, I would inscribe this work to a Statesman who, in a long, a stormy, and at length an unfortunate administration, had many political opponents, almost without a personal enemy; who has retained in his fall from power many faithful and disinterested friends; and who, under the pressure of severe infirmity, enjoys the lively vigor of his mind and the felicity of his incomparable temper. Lord North will permit me to express the feelings of friendship in the language of truth: but even truth and friendship should be silent if he still dispensed the favors of the crown.

In a remote solitude, vanity may still whisper in my ear that my readers perhaps may inquire whether, in the conclusion of the present work, I am now taking an everlasting farewell. They shall hear all that I know myself, and all that I could reveal to the most intimate friend. The motives of action or silence are now equally balanced; nor can I pronounce, in my most secret thoughts, on which side the scale will preponderate. I cannot dissemble that six quartos must have tried, and may have exhausted, the indulgence of the Public; that, in the repetition of similar attempts, a successful Author has much more to lose than he can hope to gain; that I am now descending into the vale of years; and that the most respectable of my countrymen, the men whom I aspire to imitate, have resigned the pen of history about the same period of their lives. Yet I consider that the annals of ancient and modern times may afford many rich and interesting subjects; that I am still possessed of health and leisure; that by the practice of writing, some skill and facility must be acquired; and that, in the ardent pursuit of truth and knowledge, I am not conscious of decay. To an active mind, indolence is more painful than labor; and the first months of my liberty will be occupied and amused in the excursions of curiosity and taste. By such temptations, I have been sometimes seduced from the rigid duty even of a pleasing and voluntary task: but my time will now be my own; and in the use or abuse of independence, I shall no longer fear my own reproaches or those of my friends. I am fairly entitled to a year of jubilee: next summer and the following winter will rapidly pass away; and experience only can determine whether I shall still prefer the freedom and variety of study to the design and composition of a regular work which animates, while it confines, the daily application of the Author. Caprice and accident may influence my choice; but the dexterity of self-love will contrive to applaud either active industry or philosophic repose.

DOWNING STREET, MAY 1, 1788.

P.S. I shall embrace this opportunity of introducing two *verbal* remarks which have not conveniently offered themselves to my notice. 1. As often as I use the definitions of *beyond* the Alps, the Rhine, the Danube, etc., I generally suppose myself at Rome, and afterwards at Constantinople; without observing whether this relative geography may agree with the local but variable situation of the reader or the historian. 2. In proper names of foreign and especially of Oriental origin, it should be always our aim to express, in our English version, a faithful copy of the original. But this rule, which is founded on a just regard to uniformity and truth, must often be relaxed; and the exceptions will be limited or enlarged by the custom of the language and the taste of the interpreter. Our alphabets may be often defective; a harsh sound, an uncouth spelling, might offend the ear or the eye of our countrymen; and some words, notoriously corrupt, are fixed and as it were naturalized in the vulgar tongue. The ... well-known cities of Aleppo, Damascus, and Cairo would almost be lost in the strange descriptions of *Haleb, Demashk,* and *Al Cahira:* the titles and offices of the Ottoman empire are fashioned by the practice of three hundred years; and we are pleased to blend the three Chinese monosyllables, *Con-fû-tzee,* in the respectable name of Confucius, or even to adopt the Portuguese corruption of Mandarin. But I would vary the use of Zoroaster and *Zerduskt* as I drew my information from Greece or Persia: since our connection with India, the genuine *Timour* is restored to the throne of Tamerlane: our most correct writers have retrenched the *Al,* the superfluous article, from the Koran. . . . In these and in a thousand examples, the shades of distinction are often minute; and I can feel, where I cannot explain, the motives of my choice.

CHAPTER XXXIX

Gothic Kingdom of Italy

*Zeno and Anastasius, emperors of the East. • Birth, education, and
first exploits of Theodoric the Ostrogoth. • His invasion and
conquest of Italy. • The Gothic kingdom of Italy. •
State of the West. • Military and civil government. •
Last acts and death of Theodoric.*[†]

After the fall of the Roman empire in the West, an interval of fifty
years till the memorable reign of Justinian is faintly marked by the obscure names and imperfect annals of Zeno, Anastasius, and Justin, who
successively ascended to the throne of Constantinople [A.D. 476–527].
During the same period, Italy revived and flourished under the government of a Gothic king who might have deserved a statue among
the best and bravest of the ancient Romans.

THEODORIC the Ostrogoth, the fourteenth in lineal descent of the
royal line of the Amali, was born in the neighborhood of Vienna two
years after the death of Attila.

[*Theodoric undertakes the conquest of Italy (A.D. 489) and defeats the
Vandal king of Italy, Odoacer, in a series of battles.
Odoacer capitulates on March 5, A.D. 493.*]

From the Alps to the extremity of Calabria, Theodoric reigned by the
right of conquest; the Vandal ambassadors surrendered the Island of
Sicily as a lawful appendage of his kingdom; and he was accepted as
the deliverer of Rome by the senate and people, who had shut their
gates against the flying usurper. Ravenna alone, secure in the fortifications of art and nature, still sustained a siege of almost three years; and
the daring sallies of Odoacer carried slaughter and dismay into the
Gothic camp. At length, destitute of provisions and hopeless of relief,
that unfortunate monarch yielded to the groans of his subjects and the
clamors of his soldiers. A treaty of peace was negotiated by the bishop
of Ravenna; the Ostrogoths were admitted into the city, and the hostile
kings consented, under the sanction of an oath, to rule with equal and

undivided authority the provinces of Italy. The event of such an agreement may be easily foreseen. After some days had been devoted to the semblance of joy and friendship, Odoacer, in the midst of a solemn banquet, was stabbed by the hand, or at least by the command, of his rival. Secret and effectual orders had been previously despatched; the faithless and rapacious mercenaries, at the same moment and without resistance, were universally massacred; and the royalty of Theodoric was proclaimed by the Goths, with the tardy, reluctant, ambiguous consent of the emperor of the East. . . . The reputation of Theodoric may repose with more confidence on the visible peace and prosperity of a reign of thirty-three years, the unanimous esteem of his own times, and the memory of his wisdom and courage, his justice and humanity, which was deeply impressed on the minds of the Goths and Italians [March 5, A.D. 493–August 30, A.D. 526].

The partition of the lands of Italy, of which Theodoric assigned the third part to his soldiers, is *honorably* arraigned as the sole injustice of his life. And even this act may be fairly justified by the example of Odoacer, the rights of conquest, the true interest of the Italians, and the sacred duty of subsisting a whole people who, on the faith of his promises, had transported themselves into a distant land. Under the reign of Theodoric and in the happy climate of Italy, the Goths soon multiplied to a formidable host of two hundred thousand men, and the whole amount of their families may be computed by the ordinary addition of women and children. Their invasion of property, a part of which must have been already vacant, was disguised by the generous but improper name of *hospitality*; these unwelcome guests were irregularly dispersed over the face of Italy, and the lot of each Barbarian was adequate to his birth and office, the number of his followers, and the rustic wealth which he possessed in slaves and cattle. The distinction of noble and plebeian were acknowledged; but the lands of every freeman were exempt from taxes, and he enjoyed the inestimable privilege of being subject only to the laws of his country. Fashion and even convenience soon persuaded the conquerors to assume the more elegant dress of the natives, but they still persisted in the use of their mothertongue; and their contempt for the Latin schools was applauded by Theodoric himself, who gratified their prejudices, or his own, by declaring that the child who had trembled at a rod would never dare to look upon a sword. Distress might sometimes provoke the indigent Roman to assume the ferocious manners which were insensibly relinquished by the rich and luxurious Barbarian; but these mutual conversions were not encouraged by the policy of a monarch who perpetuated the separation of the Italians and Goths; reserving the former for the arts of peace and the latter for the service of war. . . . A firm though gentle discipline imposed the habits of modesty, obedience, and temperance; and the Goths were instructed to spare the people, to reverence the laws, to understand the duties of civil society, and to disclaim the barbarous license of judicial combat and private revenge.

Among the Barbarians of the West, the victory of Theodoric had spread a general alarm. But as soon as it appeared that he was satisfied with conquest and desirous of peace, terror was changed into respect, and they submitted to a powerful mediation, which was uniformly employed for the best purposes of reconciling their quarrels and civilizing their manners. The ambassadors who resorted to Ravenna from the most distant countries of Europe admired his wisdom, magnificence, and courtesy; and if he sometimes accepted either slaves or arms, white horses or strange animals, the gift of a sun-dial, a water-clock, or a musician admonished even the princes of Gaul of the superior art and industry of his Italian subjects. His domestic alliances, a wife, two daughters, a sister, and a niece, united the family of Theodoric with the kings of the Franks, the Burgundians, the Visigoths, the Vandals, and the Thuringians, and contributed to maintain the harmony, or at least the balance, of the great republic of the West.[†]

The life of Theodoric represents the rare and meritorious example of a Barbarian who sheathed his sword in the pride of victory and the vigor of his age. A reign of three and thirty years was consecrated to the duties of civil government, and the hostilities in which he was sometimes involved were speedily terminated by the conduct of his lieutenants, the discipline of his troops, the arms of his allies, and even by the terror of his name. . . . He maintained with a powerful hand the balance of the West, till it was at length overthrown by the ambition of Clovis; and although unable to assist his rash and unfortunate kinsman the king of the Visigoths, he saved the remains of his family and people, and checked the Franks in the midst of their victorious career . . . ; and the Greeks themselves have acknowledged that Theodoric reigned over the fairest portion of the Western empire.

The union of the Goths and Romans might have fixed for ages the transient happiness of Italy; and the first of nations, a new people of free subjects and enlightened soldiers, might have gradually arisen from the mutual emulation of their respective virtues. But the sublime merit of guiding or seconding such a revolution was not reserved for the reign of Theodoric: he wanted either the genius or the opportunities of a legislator; and while he indulged the Goths in the enjoyment of rude liberty, he servilely copied the institutions and even the abuses of the political system which had been framed by Constantine and his successors. From a tender regard to the expiring prejudices of Rome, the Barbarian declined the name, the purple, and the diadem of the emperors; but he assumed, under the hereditary title of king, the whole substance and plenitude of Imperial prerogative. His addresses to the Eastern throne were respectful and ambiguous: he celebrated in pompous style the harmony of the two republics, applauded his own government as the perfect similitude of a sole and undivided empire, and claimed above the kings of the earth the same preeminence which he modestly allowed to the person or rank of Anastasius. The alliance of the East and West was annually declared by the unanimous choice of two consuls; but it should seem that the Italian candidate who was named by Theodoric accepted a formal confirmation from the sovereign of Constantinople. The Gothic palace of Ravenna reflected the image of the court of Theodosius or Valentinian. The Praetorian praefect, the praefect of Rome, the quaestor, the master of the offices, with the public and patrimonial treasurers whose functions are painted in gaudy colors by the rhetoric of Cassiodorus, still continued to act as the ministers of state. And the subordinate care of justice and the revenue was delegated to seven consulars, three correctors, and five presidents, who governed the fifteen regions of Italy according to the principles, and even the forms, of Roman jurisprudence. The violence of the conquerors was abated or eluded by the slow artifice of judicial proceedings; the civil administration, with its honors and emoluments, was confined to the Italians; and the people still preserved their dress and language, their laws and customs, their personal freedom, and two thirds of their landed property. It had been the object of Augustus to conceal the introduction of monarchy; it was the policy of Theodoric to disguise the reign of a Barbarian. If his subjects were sometimes awakened from this pleasing vision of a Roman government, they derived more substantial comfort from the character of a Gothic prince who had penetration to discern, and firmness to pursue, his own and the public interest. Theodoric loved the virtues which he possessed and the talents of which he was destitute. Liberius was promoted to the office of Praetorian praefect for his unshaken fidelity to the unfortunate cause of Odoacer. The ministers of Theodoric, Cassiodorus and Boethius, have reflected on his reign the luster of their genius and learning. More prudent or more fortunate than his colleague, Cassiodorus preserved his own esteem without forfeiting the royal favor; and after passing thirty years in the honors of the world, he was blessed with an equal term of repose in the devout and studious solitude of Squillace [in Calabria, where he founded his two monasteries, Vivarium and Castellum].

As the patron of the republic, it was the interest and duty of the Gothic king to cultivate the affections of the senate and people. The nobles of Rome were flattered by sonorous epithets and formal professions of respect which had been more justly applied to the merit and authority of their ancestors. The people enjoyed without fear or danger the three blessings of a capital, order, plenty, and public amusements. A visible diminution of their numbers may be found even in the measure of liberality; yet Apulia, Calabria, and Sicily poured their tribute of corn into the granaries of Rome; an allowance of bread and meat was distributed to the indigent citizens; and every office was deemed honorable which was consecrated to the care of their health and happiness. The public games such as the Greek ambassador might politely applaud exhibited a faint and feeble copy of the magnificence of the Caesars: yet the musical, the gymnastic, and the pantomime arts had not totally sunk in oblivion; the wild beasts of Africa still exercised in the amphitheater the courage and dexterity of the hunters; and the indulgent Goth either patiently tolerated or gently restrained the blue and green factions whose contests so often filled the circus with clamor and even with blood.[†]

Agriculture revived under the shadow of peace, and the number of husbandmen was multiplied by the redemption of captives.... A country possessed of so many valuable objects of exchange soon attracted the merchants of the world, whose beneficial traffic was encouraged and protected by the liberal spirit of Theodoric. The free intercourse of the provinces by land and water was restored and extended; the city gates were never shut either by day or by night; and the common saying that a purse of gold might be safely left in the fields was expressive of the conscious security of the inhabitants.

A difference of religion is always pernicious, and often fatal, to the harmony of the prince and people: the Gothic conqueror had been educated in the profession of Arianism, and Italy was devoutly attached to the Nicene faith. But the persuasion of Theodoric was not infected by zeal; and he piously adhered to the heresy of his fathers without condescending to balance the subtle arguments of theological metaphysics. Satisfied with the private toleration of his Arian sectaries, he justly conceived himself to be the guardian of the public worship, and his external reverence for a superstition which he despised may have nourished in his mind the salutary indifference of a statesman or philosopher. The Catholics of his dominions acknowledged, perhaps with reluctance, the peace of the church; their clergy, according to the degrees of rank or merit, were honorably entertained in the palace of Theodoric; he esteemed the living sanctity of Caesarius and Epiphanius, the orthodox bishops of Arles and Pavia; and presented a decent offering on the tomb of St. Peter without any scrupulous inquiry into the creed of the apostle. His favorite Goths, and even his mother, were permitted to retain or embrace the Athanasian faith, and his long reign could not afford the example of an Italian Catholic who, either from choice or compulsion, had deviated into the religion of the conqueror. The people, and the Barbarians themselves, were edified by the pomp and order of religious worship; the magistrates were instructed to defend the just immunities of ecclesiastical persons and possessions; the bishops held their synods, the metropolitans exercised their jurisdiction, and the privileges of sanctuary were maintained or moderated according to the spirit of the Roman jurisprudence. With the protection, Theodoric assumed the legal supremacy, of the church; and his firm administration restored or extended some useful prerogatives which had been neglected by the feeble emperors of the West. He was not ignorant of the dignity and importance of the Roman pontiff, to whom the venerable name of POPE was now appropriated.[†]

I have descanted with pleasure on the fortunate condition of Italy; but our fancy must not hastily conceive that the golden age of the poets, a race of men without vice or misery, was realized under the Gothic conquest. The fair prospect was sometimes overcast with clouds; the wisdom of Theodoric might be deceived, his power might be resisted, and the declining age of the monarch was sullied with popular hatred and patrician blood.... The privileges of rank, or office, or favor were too frequently abused by Italian fraud and Gothic violence, and the avarice of the king's nephew was publicly exposed, at first by the usurpation and afterwards by the restitution, of the estates which he had unjustly extorted from his Tuscan neighbors. Two hundred thousand Barbarians, formidable even to their master, were seated in the heart of Italy; they indignantly supported the restraints of peace and discipline; the disorders of their march were always felt and sometimes compensated; and where it was dangerous to punish, it might be prudent to dissemble the sallies of their native fierceness.†

Even the religious toleration which Theodoric had the glory of introducing into the Christian world was painful and offensive to the orthodox zeal of the Italians. They respected the armed heresy of the Goths; but their pious rage was safely pointed against the rich and defenseless Jews who had formed their establishments at Naples, Rome, Ravenna, Milan, and Genoa, for the benefit of trade and under the sanction of the laws. Their persons were insulted, their effects were pillaged, and their synagogues were burned by the mad populace of Ravenna and Rome, inflamed, as it should seem, by the most frivolous or extravagant pretenses. The government which could neglect, would have deserved, such an outrage. A legal inquiry was instantly directed; and as the authors of the tumult had escaped in the crowd, the whole community was condemned to repair the damage; and the obstinate bigots who refused their contributions were whipped through the streets by the hand of the executioner. This simple act of justice exasperated the discontent of the Catholics, who applauded the merit and patience of these holy confessors. Three hundred pulpits deplored the persecution of the church; and if the chapel of St. Stephen at Verona was demolished by the command of Theodoric, it is probable that some miracle hostile to his name and dignity had been performed on that sacred theater. At the close of a glorious life, the king of Italy discovered that he had excited the hatred of a people whose happiness he had so assiduously labored to promote; and his mind was soured by indignation, jealousy, and the bitterness of unrequited love.†

[A]fter a dysentery which continued three days, [Theodoric] expired in the palace of Ravenna, in the thirty-third or, if we compute from the invasion of Italy, in the thirty-seventh year of his reign. Conscious of his approaching end, he divided his treasures and provinces between his two grandsons and fixed the Rhone as their common boundary. Amalaric was restored to the throne of Spain. Italy, with all the conquests of the Ostrogoths, was bequeathed to Athalaric; whose age did not exceed ten years, but who was cherished as the last male offspring of the line of Amali, by the short-lived marriage of his mother Amalasuntha with a royal fugitive of the same blood. In the presence of the dying monarch, the Gothic chiefs and Italian magistrates mutually engaged their faith and loyalty to the young prince and to his guardian mother; and received, in the same awful moment, his last salutary advice, to maintain the laws, to love the senate and people of Rome, and to cultivate with decent reverence the friendship of the emperor. The monument of Theodoric was erected by his daughter Amalasuntha, in a conspicuous situation which commanded the city of Ravenna, the harbor, and the adjacent coast. A chapel of a circular form, thirty feet in diameter, is crowned by a dome of one entire piece of granite: from the center of the dome four columns arose which supported, in a vase of porphyry, the remains of the Gothic king, surrounded by the brazen statues of the twelve apostles. His spirit, after some previous expiation, might have been permitted to mingle with the benefactors of mankind if [according to Pope Gregory I] an Italian hermit had not been witness in a vision to the damnation of Theodoric, whose soul was plunged by the ministers of divine vengeance into the volcano of Lipari, one of the flaming mouths of the infernal world.

CHAPTER XL

REIGN OF JUSTINIAN

Elevation of Justin the Elder. • Reign of Justinian. •
I. The empress Theodora. • II. Factions of the circus, and sedition
of Constantinople. • III. Trade and manufacture of silk. •
IV. Finances and taxes. • V. Edifices of Justinian—church of
St. Sophia. • VI. Fortifications and frontiers of the
Eastern empire. • VII. Abolition of the schools of Athens and
the consulship of Rome.

The emperor Justinian was born near the ruins of Sardica (the modern Sophia) of an obscure race of Barbarians, the inhabitants of a wild and desolate country to which the names of Dardania, of Dacia, and of Bulgaria have been successively applied [circa A.D. 482]. His elevation was prepared by the adventurous spirit of his uncle Justin, who, with two other peasants of the same village, deserted for the profession of arms the more useful employment of husbandmen or shepherds. On foot, with a scanty provision of biscuit in their knapsacks, the three youths followed the high road of Constantinople, and were soon enrolled, for their strength and stature, among the guards of the emperor Leo. Under the two succeeding reigns, the fortunate peasant emerged to wealth and honors; and his escape from some dangers which threatened his life was afterwards ascribed to the guardian angel who watches over the fate of kings. His long and laudable service in the Isaurian and Persian wars would not have preserved from oblivion the name of Justin; yet they might warrant the military promotion which in the course of fifty years he gradually obtained; the rank of tribune, of count, and of general; the dignity of senator and the command of the guards, who obeyed him as their chief at the important crisis when the emperor Anastasius was removed from the world. The powerful kinsmen whom he had raised and enriched were excluded from the throne; and the eunuch Amantius, who reigned in the palace, had secretly resolved to fix the diadem on the head of the most obsequious of his creatures. A liberal donative to conciliate the suffrage of the guards was entrusted for that purpose in the hands of their commander. But these weighty arguments were treacherously employed by Justin in his own favor; and as no competitor presumed to appear, the Dacian peasant was invested with the purple by the unanimous consent of the soldiers, who knew him to be brave and gentle, of the clergy and people, who believed him to be orthodox, and of the provincials, who yielded a blind and implicit submission to the will of the capital. The elder Justin, as he is distinguished from another emperor of the same family and name, ascended the Byzantine throne at the age of sixty-eight years; and had he been left to his own guidance, every moment of a nine years' reign must have exposed to his subjects the impropriety of their choice [A.D. 518–527]. His ignorance was similar to that of Theodoric; and it is remarkable that in an age not destitute of learning, two contemporary monarchs had never been instructed in the knowledge of the alphabet. But the genius of Justin was far inferior to that of the Gothic king: the experience of a soldier had not qualified him for the government of an empire; and though personally brave, the consciousness of his own weakness was naturally attended with doubt, distrust, and political apprehension. But the official business of the state was diligently and faithfully transacted by the quaestor Proclus; and the aged emperor adopted the talents and ambition of his nephew Justinian, an aspiring youth whom his uncle had drawn from the rustic solitude of Dacia and educated at Constantinople as the heir of his private fortune, and at length of the Eastern empire.

Since the eunuch Amantius had been defrauded of his money, it became necessary to deprive him of his life. The task was easily accomplished by the charge of a real or fictitious conspiracy; and the judges were informed, as an accumulation of guilt, that he was secretly addicted to the Manichaean heresy. Amantius lost his head; three of his companions, the first domestics of the palace, were punished either with death or exile; and their unfortunate candidate for the purple was cast into a deep dungeon, overwhelmed with stones, and ignominiously thrown, without burial, into the sea. The ruin of Vitalian was a work of more difficulty and danger. That Gothic chief had rendered himself popular by the civil war which he boldly waged against Anastasius for the defense of the orthodox faith, and after the conclusion of an advantageous treaty, he still remained in the neighborhood of Constantinople at the head of a formidable and victorious army of Barbarians. By the frail security of oaths, he was tempted to relinquish this advantageous situation and to trust his person within the walls of a city whose inhabitants, particularly the *blue* faction, were artfully incensed against him by the remembrance even of his pious hostilities. The emperor and his nephew embraced him as the faithful and worthy champion of the church and state; and gratefully adorned their favorite with the titles of consul and general; but in the seventh month of his consulship, Vitalian was stabbed with seventeen wounds at the royal banquet; and Justinian, who inherited the spoil, was accused as the assassin of a spiritual brother to whom he had recently pledged his faith in the participation of the Christian mysteries. After the fall of his rival, he was promoted, without any claim of military service, to the office of master-general of the Eastern armies, whom it was his duty to lead into the field against the public enemy. But in the pursuit of fame, Justinian might have lost his present dominion over the age and weakness of his uncle; and instead of acquiring by Scythian or Persian trophies the applause of his countrymen, the prudent warrior solicited their favor in the churches, the circus, and the senate of Constantinople. The Catholics were attached to the nephew of Justin, who, between the Nestorian and Eutychian heresies, trod the narrow path of inflexible and intolerant orthodoxy. In the first days of the new reign, he prompted and gratified the popular enthusiasm against the memory of the deceased emperor. After a schism of thirty-four years, he reconciled the proud and angry spirit of the Roman pontiff, and spread among the Latins a favorable report of his pious respect for the apostolic see. The thrones of the East were filled with Catholic bishops devoted to his interest, the clergy and the monks were gained by his liberality, and the people were taught to pray for their future sovereign, the hope and pillar of the true religion. The magnificence of Justinian was displayed in the superior pomp of his public spectacles, an object not less sacred and important in the eyes of the multitude than the creed of Nice or Chalcedon: the expense of his consulship was esteemed at two hundred and twenty-eight thousand pieces of gold; twenty lions and thirty leopards were produced at the same time in the amphitheater, and a numerous train of horses, with their rich trappings, was bestowed as an extraordinary gift on the victorious charioteers of the circus. While he indulged the people of Constantinople and received the addresses of foreign kings, the nephew of Justin assiduously cultivated the friendship of the senate. . . . The treasures of the state were lavished to procure the voices of the senators, and their unanimous wish that he would be pleased to adopt Justinian for his colleague was communicated to the emperor. But this request, which too clearly admonished him of his approaching end, was unwelcome to the jealous temper of an aged monarch, desirous to retain the power which he was incapable of exercising; and Justin, holding his purple with both his hands, advised them to prefer, since an election was so profitable, some older candidate. Notwithstanding this reproach, the senate proceeded to decorate Justinian with the royal epithet of *nobilissimus;* and their decree was ratified by the affection or the fears of his uncle. After some time the languor of mind and body to which he was reduced by an incurable wound in his thigh indispensably required the aid of a guardian. He summoned the patriarch and senators; and in their presence solemnly placed the diadem on the head of his nephew, who was conducted from the palace to the circus and saluted by the loud and joyful applause of the people. The life of Justin was prolonged about four months; but from the instant of this ceremony, he was considered as dead to the empire, which acknowledged Justinian, in the forty-fifth year of his age, for the lawful sovereign of the East.

From his elevation to his death, Justinian governed the Roman empire thirty-eight years, seven months, and thirteen days [April 1, A.D. 527–November 14, A.D. 565]. The events of his reign, which excite our curious attention by their number, variety, and importance, are diligently related by the secretary of Belisarius, a rhetorician whom eloquence had promoted to the rank of senator and praefect of Constantinople. According to the vicissitudes of courage or servitude, of favor or disgrace, Procopius successively composed the *history,* the *panegyric,* and the *satire* of his own times. The eight books of the Persian, Vandalic, and Gothic wars, which are continued in the five books of Agathias, deserve our esteem as a laborious and successful imitation of the Attic, or at least of the Asiatic, writers of ancient Greece. His facts are collected from the personal experience and free conversation of a soldier, a statesman, and a traveler; his style continually aspires, and often attains, to the merit of strength and elegance; his reflections, more especially in the speeches which he too frequently inserts, contain a rich fund of political knowledge; and the historian, excited by the generous ambition of pleasing and instructing posterity, appears to disdain the prejudices of the people and the flattery of courts. The writings of Procopius were read and applauded by his contemporaries: but although he respectfully laid them at the foot of the throne, the pride of Justinian must have been wounded by the praise of a hero who perpetually eclipses the glory of his inactive sovereign. The conscious dignity of independence was subdued by the hopes and fears of a slave; and the secretary of Belisarius labored for pardon and reward in the six books of the Imperial *edifices*. He had dexterously chosen a subject of apparent splendor, in which he could loudly celebrate the genius, the magnificence, and the piety of a prince, who, both as a conqueror and legislator, had surpassed the puerile virtues of Themistocles and Cyrus. Disappointment might urge the flatterer to secret revenge; and the first glance of favor might again tempt him to suspend and suppress a libel in which the Roman Cyrus is degraded into an odious and contemptible tyrant, in which both the emperor and his consort Theodora are seriously represented as two demons who had assumed a human form for the destruction of mankind. Such base inconsistency must doubtless sully the reputation and detract from the credit of Procopius: yet after the venom of his malignity has been suffered to exhale, the residue of the *anecdotes*, even the most disgraceful facts, some of which had been tenderly hinted in his public history, are established by their internal evidence, or the authentic monuments of the times. From these various materials, I shall now proceed to describe the reign of Justinian, which will deserve and occupy an ample space. The present chapter will explain the elevation and character of Theodora, the factions of the circus, and the peaceful administration of the sovereign of the East. In the three succeeding chapters, I shall relate the wars of Justinian, which achieved the conquest of Africa and Italy; and I shall follow the victories of Belisarius and Narses, without disguising the vanity of their triumphs, or the hostile virtue of the Persian and Gothic heroes. The series of this and the following volume will embrace the jurisprudence and theology of the emperor; the controversies and sects which still divide the Oriental church; the reformation of the Roman law which is obeyed or respected by the nations of modern Europe.

I. In the exercise of supreme power, the first act of Justinian was to divide it with the woman whom he loved, the famous THEODORA, whose strange elevation cannot be applauded as the triumph of female virtue. Under the reign of Anastasius, the care of the wild beasts maintained by the green faction at Constantinople was entrusted to Acacius, a native of the Isle of Cyprus who, from his employment, was surnamed the master of the bears. This honorable office was given after his death to another candidate, notwithstanding the diligence of his widow, who had already provided a husband and a successor. Acacius had left three daughters, Comito, Theodora, and Anastasia, the eldest of whom did not then exceed the age of seven years. On a solemn festival, these helpless orphans were sent by their distressed and indignant mother, in the garb of suppliants, into the midst of the theater: the green faction received them with contempt, the blues with compassion; and this difference, which sunk deep into the mind of Theodora, was felt long afterwards in the administration of the empire. As they improved in age and beauty, the three sisters were successively devoted to the public and private pleasures of the Byzantine people: and Theodora, after following Comito on the stage in the dress of a slave with a stool on her head, was at length permitted to exercise her independent talents. She neither danced, nor sung, nor played on the flute; her skill was confined to the pantomime arts; she excelled in buffoon characters, and as often as the comedian swelled her cheeks and complained with a ridiculous tone and gesture of the blows that were inflicted, the whole theater of Constantinople resounded with laughter and applause. The beauty of Theodora was the subject of more flattering praise, and the source of more exquisite delight. Her features were delicate and regular; her complexion, though somewhat pale, was tinged with a natural color; every sensation was instantly expressed by the vivacity of her eyes; her easy motions displayed the graces of a small but elegant figure; and either love or adulation might proclaim that painting and poetry were incapable of delineating the matchless excellence of her form. But this form was degraded by the facility with which it was exposed to the public eye and prostituted to licentious desire. Her venal charms were abandoned to a promiscuous crowd of citizens and strangers of every rank and of every profession: the fortunate lover who had been promised a night of enjoyment was often driven from her bed by a stronger or more wealthy favorite; and when she passed through the streets, her presence was avoided by all who wished to escape either the scandal or the temptation. The satirical historian has not blushed to describe the naked scenes which Theodora was not ashamed to exhibit in the theater. After exhausting the arts of sensual pleasure, she most ungratefully murmured against the parsimony of nature; but her murmurs, her pleasures, and her arts must be veiled in the obscurity of a learned language. After reigning for some time the delight and contempt of the capital, she condescended to accompany Ecebolus, a native of Tyre who had obtained the government of the African Pentapolis. But this union was frail and transient; Ecebolus soon rejected an expensive or faithless concubine; she was reduced at Alexandria to extreme distress; and in her laborious return to Constantinople, every city of the East admired and enjoyed the fair Cyprian, whose merit appeared to justify her descent from the peculiar island of Venus. The vague commerce of Theodora, and the most detestable precautions, preserved her from the danger which she feared; yet once, and once only, she became a mother. The infant was saved and educated in Arabia by his father, who imparted to him on his deathbed that he was the son of an empress. Filled with ambitious hopes, the unsuspecting youth immediately hastened to the palace of Constantinople and was admitted to the presence of his mother. As he was never more seen, even after the decease of Theodora, she deserves the foul imputation of extinguishing with his life a secret so offensive to her Imperial virtue.

In the most abject state of her fortune and reputation, some vision, either of sleep or of fancy, had whispered to Theodora the pleasing assurance that she was destined to become the spouse of a potent monarch. Conscious of her approaching greatness, she returned from Paphlagonia to Constantinople; assumed, like a skillful actress, a more decent character; relieved her poverty by the laudable industry of spinning wool; and affected a life of chastity and solitude in a small house, which she afterwards changed into a magnificent temple. Her beauty, assisted by art or accident, soon attracted, captivated, and fixed the patrician Justinian, who already reigned with absolute sway under the name of his uncle. Perhaps she contrived to enhance the value of a gift which she had so often lavished on the meanest of mankind; perhaps she inflamed, at first by modest delays and at last by sensual allurements, the desires of a lover who, from nature or devotion, was addicted to long vigils and abstemious diet. When his first transports had subsided, she still maintained the same ascendant over his mind by the more solid merit of temper and understanding. Justinian delighted to ennoble and enrich the object of his affection; the treasures of the East were poured at her feet, and the nephew of Justin was determined, perhaps by religious scruples, to bestow on his concubine the sacred and legal character of a wife. But the laws of Rome expressly prohibited the marriage of a senator with any female who had been dishonored by a servile origin or theatrical profession: the empress Lupicina, or Euphemia, a Barbarian of rustic manners but of irreproachable virtue, refused to accept a prostitute for her niece; and even Vigilantia, the superstitious mother of Justinian, though she acknowledged the wit and beauty of Theodora, was seriously apprehensive lest the levity and arrogance of that artful paramour might corrupt the piety and happiness of her son. These obstacles were removed by the inflexible constancy of Justinian. He patiently expected the death of the empress; he despised the tears of his mother, who soon sunk under the weight of her affliction; and a law was promulgated in the name of the emperor Justin which abolished the rigid jurisprudence of antiquity. A glorious repentance (the words of the edict) was left open for the unhappy females who had prostituted their persons on the theater, and they were permitted to contract a legal union with the most illustrious of the Romans. This indulgence was speedily followed by the solemn nuptials of Justinian and Theodora; her dignity was gradually exalted with that of her lover, and as soon as Justin had invested his nephew with the purple, the patriarch of Constantinople placed the diadem on the heads of the emperor and empress of the East. But the usual honors which the severity of Roman manners had allowed to the wives of princes could not satisfy either the ambition of Theodora or the fondness of Justinian. He seated her on the throne as an equal and independent colleague in the sovereignty of the empire, and an oath of allegiance was imposed on the governors of the provinces in the joint names of Justinian and Theodora. The Eastern world fell prostrate before the genius and fortune of the daughter of Acacius. The prostitute who, in the presence of innumerable spectators, had polluted the theater of Constantinople was adored as a queen in the same city by grave magistrates, orthodox bishops, victorious generals, and captive monarchs.

Those who believe that the female mind is totally depraved by the loss of chastity will eagerly listen to all the invectives of private envy or popular resentment which have dissembled the virtues of Theodora, exaggerated her vices, and condemned with rigor the venal or voluntary sins of the youthful harlot. From a motive of shame or contempt, she often declined the servile homage of the multitude, escaped from the odious light of the capital, and passed the greatest part of the year in the palaces and gardens which were pleasantly seated on the seacoast of the Propontis and the Bosphorus. Her private hours were devoted to the prudent as well as grateful care of her beauty, the luxury of the bath and table, and the long slumber of the evening and the morning. Her secret apartments were occupied by the favorite women and eunuchs whose interests and passions she indulged at the expense of justice; the most illustrious personages of the state were crowded into a dark and sultry antechamber, and when at last, after tedious attendance, they were admitted to kiss the feet of Theodora, they experienced, as her humor might suggest, the silent arrogance of an empress or the capricious levity of a comedian. Her rapacious avarice to accumulate an immense treasure may be excused by the apprehension of her husband's death, which could leave no alternative between ruin and the throne; and fear as well as ambition might exasperate Theodora against two generals who, during the malady of the emperor, had rashly declared that they were not disposed to acquiesce in the choice of the capital. But the reproach of cruelty, so repugnant even to her softer vices, has left an indelible stain on the memory of Theodora. Her numerous spies observed and zealously reported every action or word or look injurious to their royal mistress. Whomsoever they accused were cast into her peculiar prisons, inaccessible to the inquiries of justice; and it was rumored that the torture of the rack, or scourge, had been inflicted in the presence of the female tyrant, insensible to the voice of prayer or of pity. Some of these unhappy victims perished in deep, unwholesome dungeons, while others were permitted, after the loss of their limbs, their reason, or their fortunes, to appear in the world, the living monuments of her vengeance, which was commonly extended to the children of those whom she had suspected or injured. The senator or bishop whose death or exile Theodora had pronounced was delivered to a trusty messenger, and his diligence was quickened by a menace from her own mouth. "If you fail in the execution of my commands, I swear by Him who liveth forever that your skin shall be flayed from your body."

If the creed of Theodora had not been tainted with heresy, her exemplary devotion might have atoned, in the opinion of her contemporaries, for pride, avarice, and cruelty. But if she employed her influence to assuage the intolerant fury of the emperor, the present age will allow some merit to her religion, and much indulgence to her speculative errors. The name of Theodora was introduced with equal honor in all the pious and charitable foundations of Justinian; and the most benevolent institution of his reign may be ascribed to the sympathy of the empress for her less fortunate sisters who had been seduced or compelled to embrace the trade of prostitution. A palace on the Asiatic side of the Bosphorus was converted into a stately and spacious monastery, and a liberal maintenance was assigned to five hundred women who had been collected from the streets and brothels of Constantinople. In this safe and holy retreat, they were devoted to perpetual confinement; and the despair of some who threw themselves headlong into the sea was lost in the gratitude of the penitents who had been delivered from sin and misery by their generous benefactress. The prudence of Theodora is celebrated by Justinian himself; and his laws are attributed to the sage counsels of his most reverend wife, whom he had received as the gift of the Deity. Her courage was displayed amidst the tumult of the people and the terrors of the court. Her chastity, from the moment of her union with Justinian, is founded on the silence of her implacable enemies; and although the daughter of Acacius might be satiated with love, yet some applause is due to the firmness of a mind which could sacrifice pleasure and habit to the stronger sense either of duty or interest. The wishes and prayers of Theodora could never obtain the blessing of a lawful son, and she buried an infant daughter, the sole offspring of her marriage. Notwithstanding this disappointment, her dominion was permanent and absolute; she preserved by art or merit the affections of Justinian; and their seeming dissensions were always fatal to the courtiers who believed them to be sincere. Perhaps her health had been impaired by the licentiousness of her youth; but it was always delicate, and she was directed by her physicians to use the Pythian warm baths. In this journey, the empress was followed by the Praetorian praefect, the great treasurer, several counts and patricians, and a splendid train of four thousand attendants: the highways were repaired at her approach; a palace was erected for her reception; and as she passed through Bithynia, she distributed liberal alms to the churches, the monasteries, and the hospitals that they might implore Heaven for the restoration of her health. At length, in the twenty-fourth year of her marriage, and the twenty-second of her reign, she was consumed by a cancer [June 11, A.D. 548]; and the irreparable loss was deplored by her husband, who, in the room of a theatrical prostitute, might have selected the purest and most noble virgin of the East.

II. A material difference may be observed in the games of antiquity: the most eminent of the Greeks were actors, the Romans were merely spectators. The Olympic stadium was open to wealth, merit, and ambition; and if the candidates could depend on their personal skill and activity, they might pursue the footsteps of Diomede and Menelaus and conduct their own horses in the rapid career. Ten, twenty, forty chariots were allowed to start at the same instant; a crown of leaves was the reward of the victor; and his fame, with that of his family and country, was chanted in lyric strains more durable than monuments of brass and marble. But a senator, or even a citizen conscious of his dignity, would have blushed to expose his person or his horses in the circus of Rome. The games were exhibited at the expense of the republic, the magistrates, or the emperors: but the reins were abandoned to servile hands; and if the profits of a favorite charioteer sometimes exceeded those of an advocate, they must be considered as the effects of popular extravagance, and the high wages of a disgraceful profession. The race, in its first institution, was a simple contest of two chariots whose drivers were distinguished by *white* and *red* liveries: two additional colors, a light *green* and a caerulean *blue*, were afterwards introduced; and as the races were repeated twenty-five times, one hundred chariots contributed in the same day to the pomp of the circus. The four *factions* soon acquired a legal establishment and a mysterious origin, and their fanciful colors were derived from the various appearances of nature in the four seasons of the year; the red dogstar of summer, the snows of winter, the deep shades of autumn, and the cheerful verdure of the spring. Another interpretation preferred the elements to the seasons, and the struggle of the green and blue was supposed to represent the conflict of the earth and sea. Their respective victories announced either a plentiful harvest or a prosperous navigation, and the hostility of the husbandmen and mariners was somewhat less absurd than the blind ardor of the Roman people, who devoted their lives and fortunes to the color which they had espoused. Such folly was disdained and indulged by the wisest princes; but the names of Caligula, Nero, Vitellius, Verus, Commodus, Caracalla, and Elagabalus were enrolled in the blue or green factions of the circus; they frequented their stables, applauded their favorites, chastised their antagonists, and deserved the esteem of the populace by the natural or affected imitation of their manners. The bloody and tumultuous contest continued to disturb the public festivity till the last age of the spectacles of Rome; and Theodoric, from a motive of justice or affection, interposed his authority to protect the greens against the violence of a consul and a patrician who were passionately addicted to the blue faction of the circus.

Constantinople adopted the follies, though not the virtues, of ancient Rome; and the same factions which had agitated the circus raged with redoubled fury in the hippodrome. Under the reign of Anastasius, this popular frenzy was inflamed by religious zeal; and the greens, who had treacherously concealed stones and daggers under baskets of fruit, massacred at a solemn festival three thousand of their blue adversaries. From the capital, the pestilence was diffused into the provinces and cities of the East, and the sportive distinction of two colors produced two strong and irreconcilable factions which shook the foundations of a feeble government. The popular dissensions, founded on the most serious interest or holy pretense, have scarcely equaled the obstinacy of this wanton discord, which invaded the peace of families, divided friends and brothers, and tempted the female sex, though seldom seen in the circus, to espouse the inclinations of their lovers or to contradict the wishes of their husbands. Every law, either human or divine, was trampled under foot, and as long as the party was successful, its deluded followers appeared careless of private distress or public calamity. The license, without the freedom, of democracy was revived at Antioch and Constantinople, and the support of a faction became necessary to every candidate for civil or ecclesiastical honors. A secret attachment to the family or sect of Anastasius was imputed to the greens; the blues were zealously devoted to the cause of orthodoxy and Justinian, and their grateful patron protected, above five years, the disorders of a faction whose seasonable tumults overawed the palace, the senate, and the capitals of the East. Insolent with royal favor, the blues affected to strike terror by a peculiar and Barbaric dress, the long hair of the Huns, their close sleeves and ample garments, a lofty step, and a sonorous voice. In the day they concealed their two-edged poniards, but in the night they boldly assembled in arms and in numerous bands, prepared for every act of violence and rapine. Their adversaries of the green faction, or even inoffensive citizens, were stripped and often murdered by these nocturnal robbers, and it became dangerous to wear any gold buttons or girdles, or to appear at a late hour in the streets of a peaceful capital.†

A sedition which almost laid Constantinople in ashes was excited by the mutual hatred and momentary reconciliation of the two factions.

[*The so-called Nika riot unites blues and greens around the former emperor Anastasius' nephews, Hypatius and Pompey. Justinian considers flight from Constantinople (January* A.D. *532).*]

Justinian was lost if the prostitute whom he raised from the theater had not renounced the timidity, as well as the virtues, of her sex. In the midst of a council where Belisarius was present, Theodora alone displayed the spirit of a hero; and she alone, without apprehending his future hatred, could save the emperor from the imminent danger and his unworthy fears. "If flight," said the consort of Justinian, "were the only means of safety, yet I should disdain to fly. Death is the condition of our birth; but they who have reigned should never survive the loss of dignity and dominion. I implore Heaven that I may never be seen, not a day, without my diadem and purple; that I may no longer behold the light when I cease to be saluted with the name of queen. If you resolve, O Caesar! to fly, you have treasures; behold the sea, you have ships; but tremble lest the desire of life should expose you to wretched exile and ignominious death. For my own part, I adhere to the maxim of antiquity that the throne is a glorious sepulchre." The firmness of a woman restored the courage to deliberate and act, and courage soon discovers the resources of the most desperate situation. It was an easy and a decisive measure to revive the animosity of the factions; the blues were astonished at their own guilt and folly, that a trifling injury should provoke them to conspire with their implacable enemies against a gracious and liberal benefactor; they again proclaimed the majesty of Justinian; and the greens, with their upstart emperor, were left alone in the hippodrome. The fidelity of the guards was doubtful; but the military force of Justinian consisted in three thousand veterans who had been trained to valor and discipline in the Persian and Illyrian wars. Under the command of Belisarius and Mundus, they silently marched in two divisions from the palace, forced their obscure way through narrow passages, expiring flames, and falling edifices, and burst open at the same moment the two opposite gates of the hippodrome. In this narrow space, the disorderly and affrighted crowd was incapable of resisting on either side a firm and regular attack; the blues signalized the fury of their repentance; and it is computed that above thirty thousand persons were slain in the merciless and promiscuous carnage of the day. Hypatius was dragged from his throne and conducted, with his brother Pompey, to the feet of the emperor: they implored his clemency; but their crime was manifest, their innocence uncertain, and Justinian had been too much terrified to forgive. The next morning the two nephews of Anastasius, with eighteen *illustrious* accomplices of patrician or consular rank, were privately executed by the soldiers; their bodies were thrown into the sea, their palaces razed, and their fortunes confiscated. The hippodrome itself was condemned, during several years, to a mournful silence: with the restoration of the games, the same disorders revived; and the blue and green factions continued to afflict the reign of Justinian and to disturb the tranquility of the Eastern empire.

III. That empire, after Rome was barbarous, still embraced the nations whom she had conquered beyond the Adriatic, and as far as the frontiers of Aethiopia and Persia. Justinian reigned over sixty-four provinces and nine hundred and thirty-five cities; his dominions were blessed by nature with the advantages of soil, situation, and climate: and the improvements of human art had been perpetually diffused along the coast of the Mediterranean and the banks of the Nile, from ancient Troy to the Egyptian Thebes.†

I need not explain that *silk* is originally spun from the bowels of a caterpillar, and that it composes the golden tomb from whence a worm emerges in the form of a butterfly. Till the reign of Justinian, the silkworms who feed on the leaves of the white mulberry-tree were confined to China; those of the pine, the oak, and the ash were common in the forests both of Asia and Europe; but as their education is more difficult and their produce more uncertain, they were generally neglected, except in the little island of Ceos, near the coast of Attica. A thin gauze was procured from their webs, and this Cean manufacture, the invention of a woman for female use, was long admired both in the East and at Rome. . . . That rare and elegant luxury was censured in the reign of Tiberius by the gravest of the Romans; and Pliny, in affected though forcible language, has condemned the thirst of gain which explores the last confines of the earth for the pernicious purpose of exposing to the public eye naked draperies and transparent matrons. A dress which showed the turn of the limbs and color of the skin might gratify vanity or provoke desire. . . . Two hundred years after the age of Pliny, the use of pure or even of mixed silks was confined to the female sex, till the opulent citizens of Rome and the provinces were insensibly familiarized with the example of Elagabalus, the first who, by this effeminate habit, had sullied the dignity of an emperor and a man.[†]

As silk became of indispensable use, the emperor Justinian saw with concern that the Persians had occupied by land and sea the monopoly of this important supply, and that the wealth of his subjects was continually drained by a nation of enemies and idolaters. An active government would have restored the trade of Egypt and the navigation of the Red Sea, which had decayed with the prosperity of the empire; and the Roman vessels might have sailed, for the purchase of silk, to the ports of Ceylon, of Malacca, or even of China. Justinian embraced a more humble expedient and solicited the aid of his Christian allies, the Aethiopians of Abyssinia, who had recently acquired the arts of navigation, the spirit of trade, and the seaport of Adulis, still decorated with the trophies of a Grecian conqueror. Along the African coast, they penetrated to the equator in search of gold, emeralds, and aromatics; but they wisely declined an unequal competition in which they must be always prevented by the vicinity of the Persians to the markets of India; and the emperor submitted to the disappointment till his wishes were gratified by an unexpected event. The gospel had been preached to the Indians: a bishop already governed the Christians of St. Thomas on the pepper-coast of Malabar; a church was planted in Ceylon, and the missionaries pursued the footsteps of commerce to the extremities of Asia. Two Persian monks had long resided in China, perhaps in the royal city of Nankin, the seat of a monarch addicted to foreign superstitions, and who actually received an embassy from the

Isle of Ceylon. Amidst their pious occupations, they viewed with a curious eye the common dress of the Chinese, the manufactures of silk, and the myriads of silk-worms, whose education (either on trees or in houses) had once been considered as the labor of queens. They soon discovered that it was impracticable to transport the short-lived insect, but that in the eggs a numerous progeny might be preserved and multiplied in a distant climate. Religion or interest had more power over the Persian monks than the love of their country: after a long journey, they arrived at Constantinople, imparted their project to the emperor, and were liberally encouraged by the gifts and promises of Justinian. To the historians of that prince, a campaign at the foot of Mount Caucasus has seemed more deserving of a minute relation than the labors of these missionaries of commerce, who again entered China, deceived a jealous people by concealing the eggs of the silk-worm in a hollow cane, and returned in triumph with the spoils of the East. Under their direction, the eggs were hatched at the proper season by the artificial heat of dung; the worms were fed with mulberry leaves; they lived and labored in a foreign climate; a sufficient number of butterflies was saved to propagate the race, and trees were planted to supply the nourishment of the rising generations. Experience and reflection corrected the errors of a new attempt, and the Sogdoite ambassadors acknowledged in the succeeding reign that the Romans were not inferior to the natives of China in the education of the insects and the manufactures of silk, in which both China and Constantinople have been surpassed by the industry of modern Europe. I am not insensible of the benefits of elegant luxury; yet I reflect with some pain that if the importers of silk had introduced the art of printing, already practiced by the Chinese, the comedies of Menander and the entire decads of Livy would have been perpetuated in the editions of the sixth century. A larger view of the globe might at least have promoted the improvement of speculative science, but the Christian geography was forcibly extracted from texts of Scripture, and the study of nature was the surest symptom of an unbelieving mind. The orthodox faith confined the habitable world to *one* temperate zone, and represented the earth as an oblong surface, four hundred days' journey in length, two hundred in breadth, encompassed by the ocean, and covered by the solid crystal of the firmament.

IV. The subjects of Justinian were dissatisfied with the times, and with the government. Europe was overrun by the Barbarians, and Asia by the monks: the poverty of the West discouraged the trade and manufactures of the East: the produce of labor was consumed by the unprofitable servants of the church, the state, and the army; and a rapid decrease was felt in the fixed and circulating capitals which constitute the national wealth. The public distress had been alleviated by the economy of Anastasius, and that prudent emperor accumulated an immense treasure, while he delivered his people from the most odious or oppressive taxes. Their gratitude universally applauded the abolition of the *gold of affliction,* a personal tribute on the industry of the poor, but more intolerable, as it should seem, in the form than in the substance, since the flourishing city of Edessa paid only one hundred and forty pounds of gold, which was collected in four years from ten thousand artificers. Yet such was the parsimony which supported this liberal disposition that, in a reign of twenty-seven years, Anastasius saved, from his annual revenue, the enormous sum of . . . three hundred and twenty thousand pounds of gold. His example was neglected, and his treasure was abused, by the nephew of Justin. The riches of Justinian were speedily exhausted by alms and buildings, by ambitious wars and ignominious treaties. His revenues were found inadequate to his expenses. Every art was tried to extort from the people the gold and silver which he scattered with a lavish hand from Persia to France: his reign was marked by the vicissitudes, or rather by the combat, of rapaciousness and avarice, of splendor and poverty; he lived with the reputation of hidden treasures, and bequeathed to his successor the payment of his debts.[†]

V. The *edifices* of Justinian were cemented with the blood and treasure of his people; but those stately structures appeared to announce the prosperity of the empire, and actually displayed the skill of their architects. Both the theory and practice of the arts which depend on mathematical science and mechanical power were cultivated under the patronage of the emperors.[†]

The principal church, which was dedicated by the founder of Constantinople to St. Sophia, or the eternal wisdom, had been twice destroyed by fire; after the exile of John Chrysostom, and during the *Nika* [insurrection] of the blue and green factions. No sooner did the tumult subside than the Christian populace deplored their sacrilegious rashness; but they might have rejoiced in the calamity had they foreseen the glory of the new temple which at the end of forty days was strenuously undertaken by the piety of Justinian. The ruins were cleared away, a more spacious plan was described, and as it required the consent of some proprietors of ground, they obtained the most exorbitant terms from the eager desires and timorous conscience of the monarch. Anthemius formed the design, and his genius directed the hands of ten thousand workmen, whose payment in pieces of fine silver was never delayed beyond the evening. The emperor himself, clad in a linen tunic, surveyed each day their rapid progress, and encouraged their diligence by his familiarity, his zeal, and his rewards. The new Cathedral of St. Sophia was consecrated by the patriarch five years, eleven months, and ten days from the first foundation; and in the midst of the solemn festival Justinian exclaimed with devout vanity, "Glory be to God, who hath thought me worthy to accomplish so great a work; I have vanquished thee, O Solomon!" But the pride of the Roman Solomon, before twenty years had elapsed, was humbled by an earthquake which overthrew the eastern part of the dome. Its splendor was again restored by the perseverance of the same prince; and in the thirty-sixth year of his reign, Justinian celebrated the second dedication of a temple which remains, after twelve centuries, a stately monument of his fame. The architecture of St. Sophia, which is now converted into the principal mosque, has been imitated by the Turkish sultans, and that venerable pile continues to excite the fond admiration of the Greeks and the more rational curiosity of European travelers. The eye of the spectator is disappointed by an irregular prospect of half-domes and shelving roofs: the western front, the principal approach, is destitute of simplicity and magnificence; and the scale of dimensions has been much surpassed by several of the Latin cathedrals. But the architect who first erected an *aerial* cupola is entitled to the praise of bold design and skillful execution. The dome of St. Sophia, illuminated by four-and-twenty windows, is formed with so small a curve that the depth is equal only to one sixth of its diameter; the measure of that diameter is one hundred and fifteen feet, and the lofty center, where a crescent has supplanted the cross, rises to the perpendicular height of one hundred and eighty feet above the pavement.... A variety of ornaments and figures was curiously expressed in mosaic; and the images of Christ, of the Virgin, of saints, and of angels, which have been defaced by Turkish fanaticism, were dangerously exposed to the superstition of the

Greeks. According to the sanctity of each object, the precious metals were distributed in thin leaves or in solid masses. . . . A magnificent temple is a laudable monument of national taste and religion; and the enthusiast who entered the dome of St. Sophia might be tempted to suppose that it was the residence, or even the workmanship, of the Deity. Yet how dull is the artifice, how insignificant is the labor, if it be compared with the formation of the vilest insect that crawls upon the surface of the temple!

[A] description of an edifice which time has respected may attest the truth and excuse the relation of the innumerable works, both in the capital and provinces, which Justinian constructed on a smaller scale and less durable foundations. In Constantinople alone and the adjacent suburbs, he dedicated twenty-five churches to the honor of Christ, the Virgin, and the saints: most of these churches were decorated with marble and gold; and their various situation was skillfully chosen in a populous square or a pleasant grove; on the margin of the sea-shore, or on some lofty eminence which overlooked the continents of Europe and Asia. . . . The pious munificence of the emperor was diffused over the Holy Land; and if reason should condemn the monasteries of both sexes which were built or restored by Justinian, yet charity must applaud the wells which he sunk and the hospitals which he founded for the relief of the weary pilgrims. . . . Almost every saint in the calendar acquired the honors of a temple; almost every city of the empire obtained the solid advantages of bridges, hospitals, and aqueducts; but the severe liberality of the monarch disdained to indulge his subjects in the popular luxury of baths and theaters. While Justinian labored for the public service, he was not unmindful of his own dignity and ease. The Byzantine palace, which had been damaged by the conflagration, was restored with new magnificence.†

VI. The fortifications of Europe and Asia were multiplied by Justinian; but the repetition of those timid and fruitless precautions exposes to a philosophic eye the debility of the empire. From Belgrade to the Euxine, from the conflux of the Save to the mouth of the Danube, a chain of above fourscore fortified places was extended along the banks of the great river. Single watchtowers were changed into spacious citadels; vacant walls, which the engineers contracted or enlarged according to the nature of the ground, were filled with colonies or garrisons; a strong fortress defended the ruins of Trajan's bridge, and several military stations affected to spread beyond the Danube the pride of the Roman name. But that name was divested of its terrors; the Barbarians, in their annual inroads, passed and contemptuously repassed before these useless bulwarks; and the inhabitants of the frontier, instead of reposing under the shadow of the general defense, were compelled to guard, with incessant vigilance, their separate habitations. . . . [T]he unskillful assaults of the Huns and Sclavonians [were] sometimes retarded, and their hopes of rapine were disappointed, by the innumerable castles which, in the provinces of Dacia, Epirus, Thessaly, Macedonia, and Thrace, appeared to cover the whole face of the country. Six hundred of these forts were built or repaired by the emperor; but it seems reasonable to believe that the far greater part consisted only of a stone or brick tower in the midst of a square or circular area, which was surrounded by a wall and ditch, and afforded in a moment of danger some protection to the peasants and cattle of the neighboring villages. Yet these military works, which exhausted the public treasure, could not remove the just apprehensions of Justinian and his European subjects. The warm baths of Anchialus in Thrace were rendered as safe as they were salutary; but the rich pastures of Thessalonica were foraged by the Scythian cavalry; the delicious vale of Tempe, three hundred miles from the Danube, was continually alarmed by the sound of war. . . . The walls of Corinth, overthrown by an earthquake, and the mouldering bulwarks of Athens and Plataea were carefully restored; the Barbarians were discouraged by the prospect of successive and painful sieges: and the naked cities of Peloponnesus were covered by the fortifications of the Isthmus of Corinth. At the extremity of Europe, another peninsula, the Thracian Chersonesus, runs three days' journey into the sea to form, with the adjacent shores of Asia, the Straits of the Hellespont. The intervals between eleven populous towns were filled by lofty woods, fair pastures, and arable lands; and the isthmus, of thirty-seven stadia or furlongs, had been fortified by a Spartan general nine hundred years before the reign of Justinian. In an age of freedom and valor, the slightest rampart may prevent a surprise; and Procopius appears insensible of the superiority of ancient times while he praises the solid construction and double parapet of a wall whose long arms stretched on either side into the sea; but whose strength was deemed insufficient to guard the Chersonesus if each city, and particularly Gallipoli and Sestus, had not been secured by their peculiar fortifications.[†]

VII. Justinian suppressed the schools of Athens and the consulship of Rome, which had given so many sages and heroes to mankind. Both these institutions had long since degenerated from their primitive glory; yet some reproach may be justly inflicted on the avarice and jealousy of a prince by whose hand such venerable ruins were destroyed.

Athens, after her Persian triumphs, adopted the philosophy of Ionia and the rhetoric of Sicily; and these studies became the patrimony of a city whose inhabitants, about thirty thousand males, condensed within the period of a single life the genius of ages and millions. Our sense of the dignity of human nature is exalted by the simple recollection that Isocrates was the companion of Plato and Xenophon; that he assisted, perhaps with the historian Thucydides, at the first representation of the Oedipus of Sophocles and the Iphigenia of Euripides; and that his pupils Aeschines and Demosthenes contended for the crown of patriotism in the presence of Aristotle, the master of Theophrastus, who taught at Athens with the founders of the Stoic and Epicurean sects. The ingenuous youth of Attica enjoyed the benefits of their domestic education, which was communicated without envy to the rival cities. Two thousand disciples heard the lessons of Theophrastus; the schools of rhetoric must have been still more populous than those of philosophy; and a rapid succession of students diffused the fame of their teachers as far as the utmost limits of the Grecian language and name. Those limits were enlarged by the victories of Alexander; the arts of Athens survived her freedom and dominion; and the Greek colonies which the Macedonians planted in Egypt and scattered over Asia undertook long and frequent pilgrimages to worship the Muses in their favorite temple on the banks of the Ilissus. The Latin conquerors respectfully listened to the instructions of their subjects and captives; the names of Cicero and Horace were enrolled in the schools of Athens; and after the perfect settlement of the Roman empire, the natives of Italy, of Africa, and of Britain conversed in the groves of the academy with their fellow-students of the East. The studies of philosophy and eloquence are congenial to a popular state which encourages the freedom of inquiry and submits only to the force of persuasion. In the republics of Greece and Rome, the art of speaking was the powerful engine of patriotism or ambition; and the schools of rhetoric poured forth a colony of statesmen and legislators.

When the liberty of public debate was suppressed, the orator, in the honorable profession of an advocate, might plead the cause of innocence and justice; he might abuse his talents in the more profitable trade of panegyric; and the same precepts continued to dictate the fanciful declamations of the sophist and the chaster beauties of historical composition. The systems which professed to unfold the nature of God, of man, and of the universe entertained the curiosity of the philosophic student; and according to the temper of his mind, he might doubt with the Skeptics or decide with the Stoics, sublimely speculate with Plato or severely argue with Aristotle. The pride of the adverse sects had fixed an unattainable term of moral happiness and perfection; but the race was glorious and salutary; the disciples of Zeno, and even those of Epicurus, were taught both to act and to suffer; and the death of Petronius was not less effectual than that of Seneca to humble a tyrant by the discovery of his impotence. The light of science could not indeed be confined within the walls of Athens. Her incomparable writers address themselves to the human race; the living masters emigrated to Italy and Asia; Beirut, in later times, was devoted to the study of the law; astronomy and physic were cultivated in the museum of Alexandria; but the Attic schools of rhetoric and philosophy maintained their superior reputation from the Peloponnesian war to the reign of Justinian. Athens, though situate in a barren soil, possessed a pure air, a free navigation, and the monuments of ancient art. That sacred retirement was seldom disturbed by the business of trade or government; and the last of the Athenians were distinguished by their lively wit, the purity of their taste and language, their social manners, and some traces, at least in discourse, of the magnanimity of their fathers. In the suburbs of the city, the *academy* of the Platonists, the *lycaeum* of the Peripatetics, the *portico* of the Stoics, and the *garden* of the Epicureans were planted with trees and decorated with statues; and the philosophers, instead of being immured in a cloister, delivered their instructions in spacious and pleasant walks which, at different hours, were consecrated to the exercises of the mind and body. The genius of the founders still lived in those venerable seats; the ambition of succeeding to the masters of human reason excited a generous emulation; and the merit of the candidates was determined, on each vacancy, by the free voices of an enlightened people.[†]

The Gothic arms were less fatal to the schools of Athens than the establishment of a new religion whose ministers superseded the exercise of reason, resolved every question by an article of faith, and condemned the infidel or skeptic to eternal flames. In many a volume of laborious controversy, they exposed the weakness of the understanding and the corruption of the heart, insulted human nature in the sages of antiquity, and proscribed the spirit of philosophical inquiry, so repugnant to the doctrine, or at least to the temper, of an humble believer. The surviving sects of the Platonists, whom Plato would have blushed to acknowledge, extravagantly mingled a sublime theory with the practice of superstition and magic; and as they remained alone in the midst of a Christian world, they indulged a secret rancor against the government of the church and state whose severity was still suspended over their heads. About a century after the reign of Julian, Proclus was permitted to teach in the philosophic chair of the academy; and such was his industry that he frequently in the same day pronounced five lessons and composed seven hundred lines. His sagacious mind explored the deepest questions of morals and metaphysics, and he ventured to urge eighteen arguments against the Christian doctrine of the creation of the world. But in the intervals of study, he *personally* conversed with Pan, Aesculapius, and Minerva, in whose mysteries he was secretly initiated and whose prostrate statues he adored, in the devout persuasion that the philosopher who is a citizen of the universe should be the priest of its various deities. An eclipse of the sun announced his approaching end; and his life, with that of his scholar Isidore, compiled by two of their most learned disciples, exhibits a deplorable picture of the second childhood of human reason. Yet the golden chain, as it was fondly styled, of the Platonic succession continued forty-four years from the death of Proclus to the edict of Justinian [A.D. 485–529], which imposed a perpetual silence on the schools of Athens and excited the grief and indignation of the few remaining votaries of Grecian science and superstition.[†]

About the same time that Pythagoras first invented the appellation of philosopher, liberty and the consulship were founded at Rome by the elder Brutus [509 B.C.]. The revolutions of the consular office, which may be viewed in the successive lights of a substance, a shadow, and a name, have been occasionally mentioned in the present History. The

THE COLUMN OF TRAJAN

A. The Modern Level of Rome; B. S. Maria di Loretto;
C. SS. Nome di Maria

first magistrates of the republic had been chosen by the people to exercise, in the senate and in the camp, the powers of peace and war which were afterwards translated to the emperors. But the tradition of ancient dignity was long revered by the Romans and Barbarians. A Gothic historian applauds the consulship of Theodoric as the height of all temporal glory and greatness; the king of Italy himself congratulated those annual favorites of fortune who, without the cares, enjoyed the splendor of the throne; and at the end of a thousand years, two consuls were created by the sovereigns of Rome and Constantinople for the sole purpose of giving a date to the year and a festival to the people. . . . [The] succession of consuls finally ceased in the thirteenth year of Justinian, whose despotic temper might be gratified by the silent extinction of a title which admonished the Romans of their ancient freedom [A.D. 541]. Yet the annual consulship still lived in the minds of the people; they fondly expected its speedy restoration; they applauded the gracious condescension of successive princes by whom it was assumed in the first year of their reign; and three centuries elapsed after the death of Justinian before that obsolete dignity which had been suppressed by custom could be abolished by law. The imperfect mode of distinguishing each year by the name of a magistrate was usefully supplied by the date of a permanent era: the creation of the world, according to the Septuagint version, was adopted by the Greeks; and the Latins, since the age of Charlemagne, have computed their time from the birth of Christ.

CHAPTER XLI

CONQUESTS OF JUSTINIAN, CHARACTER OF BELISARIUS

Conquests of Justinian in the West. • Character and first campaigns of Belisarius. • He invades and subdues the Vandal kingdom of Africa. • His triumph. • The Gothic war. • He recovers Sicily, Naples, and Rome. • Siege of Rome by the Goths. • Their retreat and losses. • Surrender of Ravenna. • Glory of Belisarius. • His domestic shame and misfortunes.

When Justinian ascended the throne, about fifty years after the fall of the Western empire, the kingdoms of the Goths and Vandals had obtained a solid and, as it might seem, a legal establishment both in Europe and Africa. The titles which Roman victory had inscribed were erased with equal justice by the sword of the Barbarians; and their successful rapine derived a more venerable sanction from time, from treaties, and from the oaths of fidelity, already repeated by a second or third generation of obedient subjects. Experience and Christianity had refuted the superstitious hope that Rome was founded by the gods to reign forever over the nations of the earth. But the proud claim of perpetual and indefeasible dominion, which her soldiers could no longer maintain, was firmly asserted by her statesmen and lawyers, whose opinions have been sometimes revived and propagated in the modern schools of jurisprudence. After Rome herself had been stripped of the Imperial purple, the princes of Constantinople assumed the sole and sacred scepter of the monarchy; demanded as their rightful inheritance the provinces which had been subdued by the consuls or possessed by the Caesars; and feebly aspired to deliver their faithful subjects of the West from the usurpation of heretics and Barbarians. The execution of this splendid design was in some degree reserved for Justinian. During the five first years of his reign, he reluctantly waged a costly and unprofitable war against the Persians; till his pride submitted to his ambition, and he purchased at the price of four hundred and forty thousand pounds sterling the benefit of a precarious truce which, in the language of both nations, was dignified with the appellation of the *endless* peace. The safety of the East enabled the emperor to employ his forces against the Vandals; and the internal state of Africa afforded an honorable motive and promised a powerful support to the Roman arms [A.D. 533].

[*Under the pretext of restoring the Catholic Hilderic to the throne usurped by the Arian Genseric, Justinian dispatches to North Africa a fleet under the command of Belisarius (June A.D. 533).*]

The Africanus of new Rome was born and perhaps educated among the Thracian peasants, without any of those advantages which had formed the virtues of the elder and younger Scipio; a noble origin, liberal studies, and the emulation of a free state. The silence of a loquacious secretary may be admitted to prove that the youth of Belisarius could not afford any subject of praise: he served, most assuredly with valor and reputation, among the private guards of Justinian; and when his patron became emperor, the domestic was promoted to military command. . . . When the African war became the topic of popular discourse and secret deliberation, each of the Roman generals was apprehensive rather than ambitious of the dangerous honor; but as soon as Justinian had declared his preference of superior merit, their envy was rekindled by the unanimous applause which was given to the choice of Belisarius. The temper of the Byzantine court may encourage a suspicion that the hero was darkly assisted by the intrigues of his wife, the fair and subtle Antonina, who alternately enjoyed the confidence and incurred the hatred of the empress Theodora. The birth of Antonina was ignoble; she descended from a family of charioteers; and her chastity has been stained with the foulest reproach. Yet she reigned with long and absolute power over the mind of her illustrious husband; and if Antonina disdained the merit of conjugal fidelity, she expressed a manly friendship to Belisarius, whom she accompanied with undaunted resolution in all the hardships and dangers of a military life.[†]

[Justinian] received the messengers of [Belisarius' African] victory at the time when he was preparing to publish the Pandects of the Roman laws [A.D. 534]; and the devout or jealous emperor celebrated the divine goodness and confessed in silence the merit of his successful general. Impatient to abolish the temporal and spiritual tyranny of the Vandals, he proceeded without delay to the full establishment of the Catholic church. Her jurisdiction, wealth, and immunities, perhaps the most essential part of episcopal religion, were restored and amplified with a liberal hand; the Arian worship was suppressed; the Donatist meetings were proscribed; and the synod of Carthage, by the voice of two hundred and seventeen bishops, applauded the just measure of pious retaliation. On such an occasion, it may not be presumed that many orthodox prelates were absent; but the comparative smallness of their number, which in ancient councils had been twice or even thrice multiplied, most clearly indicates the decay both of the church and state. While Justinian approved himself the defender of the faith, he entertained an ambitious hope that his victorious lieutenant would speedily enlarge the narrow limits of his dominion to the space which they occupied before the invasion of the Moors and Vandals; and Belisarius was instructed to establish five *dukes* or commanders in the convenient stations of Tripoli, Leptis, Cirta, Caesarea, and Sardinia, and to compute the military force of *palatines* or *borderers* that might be sufficient for the defense of Africa. The kingdom of the Vandals was not unworthy of the presence of a Praetorian praefect; and four consulars, three presidents were appointed to administer the seven provinces under his civil jurisdiction. The number of their subordinate officers, clerks, messengers, or assistants was minutely expressed; three hundred and ninety-six for the praefect himself, fifty for each of his vicegerents; and the rigid definition of their fees and salaries was more effectual to confirm the right than to prevent the abuse. These magistrates might be oppressive, but they were not idle; and the subtle questions of justice and revenue were infinitely propagated under the new government, which professed to revive the freedom and equity of the Roman republic. . . . After the departure of Belisarius, . . . the office of Praetorian praefect was entrusted to a soldier; the civil and military powers were united, according to the practice of Justinian, in the chief governor; and the representative of the emperor in Africa, as well as in Italy, was soon distinguished by the appellation of Exarch.[†]

[It is] a vulgar truth that flattery adheres to power, and envy to superior merit. The chiefs of the Roman army presumed to think themselves the rivals of a hero. Their private despatches maliciously affirmed that the conqueror of Africa, strong in his reputation and the public love, conspired to seat himself on the throne of the Vandals.

Justinian listened with too patient an ear; and his silence was the result of jealousy rather than of confidence. An honorable alternative, of remaining in the province or of returning to the capital, was indeed submitted to the discretion of Belisarius; but he wisely concluded, from intercepted letters and the knowledge of his sovereign's temper, that he must either resign his head, erect his standard, or confound his enemies by his presence and submission. Innocence and courage decided his choice; his guards, captives, and treasures were diligently embarked; and so prosperous was the navigation that his arrival at Constantinople preceded any certain account of his departure from the port of Carthage. Such unsuspecting loyalty removed the apprehensions of Justinian; envy was silenced and inflamed by the public gratitude; and the third Africanus obtained the honors of a triumph, a ceremony which the city of Constantine had never seen and which ancient Rome, since the reign of Tiberius, had reserved for the *auspicious* arms of the Caesars. From the palace of Belisarius, the procession was conducted through the principal streets to the hippodrome; and this memorable day seemed to avenge the injuries of Genseric and to expiate the shame of the Romans. The wealth of nations was displayed, the trophies of martial or effeminate luxury; rich armor, golden thrones, and the chariots of state which had been used by the Vandal queen; the massy furniture of the royal banquet, the splendor of precious stones, the elegant forms of statues and vases, the more substantial treasure of gold, and the holy vessels of the Jewish temple, which after their long peregrination were respectfully deposited in the Christian church of Jerusalem. A long train of the noblest Vandals reluctantly exposed their lofty stature and manly countenance. Gelimer slowly advanced: he was clad in a purple robe, and still maintained the majesty of a king. Not a tear escaped from his eyes, not a sigh was heard; but his pride or piety derived some secret consolation from the words of Solomon, which he repeatedly pronounced, VANITY! VANITY! ALL IS VANITY! Instead of ascending a triumphal car drawn by four horses or elephants, the modest conqueror marched on foot at the head of his brave companions; his prudence might decline an honor too conspicuous for a subject; and his magnanimity might justly disdain what had been so often sullied by the vilest of tyrants. The glorious procession entered the gate of the hippodrome; was saluted by the acclamations of the senate and people; and halted before the throne where Justinian and Theodora were seated to receive homage of the captive monarch and the victorious hero. They both performed the customary adoration and, falling prostrate on the ground, respectfully touched the footstool of a prince who had not unsheathed his sword and of a prostitute who had danced on the theater; some gentle violence was used to bend the stubborn spirit of the grandson of Genseric; and however trained to servitude, the genius of Belisarius must have secretly rebelled. He was immediately declared consul for the ensuing year, and the day of his inauguration resembled the pomp of a second triumph [January 1, A.D. 535]: his curule chair was borne aloft on the shoulders of captive Vandals; and the spoils of war, gold cups, and rich girdles were profusely scattered among the populace.†

The experience of past faults, which may sometimes correct the mature age of an individual, is seldom profitable to the successive generations of mankind. The nations of antiquity, careless of each other's safety, were separately vanquished and enslaved by the Romans. This awful lesson might have instructed the Barbarians of the West to oppose, with timely counsels and confederate arms, the unbounded ambition of Justinian. Yet the same error was repeated, the same consequences were felt, and the Goths, both of Italy and Spain, insensible of their approaching danger, beheld with indifference, and even with joy, the rapid downfall of the Vandals.

[Belisarius subdues the Gothic kingdom in Italy (A.D. 535–539).]

After the second victory of Belisarius, envy again whispered, Justinian listened, and the hero was recalled [A.D. 540 ff.]. "The remnant of the Gothic war was no longer worthy of his presence: a gracious sovereign was impatient to reward his services and to consult his wisdom; and he alone was capable of defending the East against the innumerable armies of Persia." Belisarius understood the suspicion, accepted the excuse, embarked at Ravenna his spoils and trophies; and proved by his ready obedience that such an abrupt removal from the government of Italy was not less unjust than it might have been indiscreet. The emperor received with honorable courtesy both Vitiges and his more noble consort; and as the king of the Goths conformed to the Athanasian faith, he obtained, with a rich inheritance of land in Asia, the rank of senator and patrician. Every spectator admired without peril the strength and stature of the young Barbarians: they adored the majesty of the throne and promised to shed their blood in the service of their benefactor. Justinian deposited in the Byzantine palace the treasures of the Gothic monarchy. A flattering senate was sometimes admitted to gaze on the magnificent spectacle; but it was enviously secluded from the public view: and the conqueror of Italy renounced without a murmur, perhaps without a sigh, the well-earned honors of a second triumph. His glory was indeed exalted above all external pomp; and the faint and hollow praises of the court were supplied, even in a servile age, by the respect and admiration of his country.... By the union of liberality and justice, he acquired the love of the soldiers without alienating the affections of the people. The sick and wounded were relieved with medicines and money, and still more efficaciously by the healing visits and smiles of their commander. The loss of a weapon or a horse was instantly repaired, and each deed of valor was rewarded by the rich and honorable gifts of a bracelet or a collar, which were rendered more precious by the judgment of Belisarius. He was endeared to the husbandmen by the peace and plenty which they enjoyed under the shadow of his standard. Instead of being injured, the country was enriched by the march of the Roman armies; and such was the rigid discipline of their camp that not an apple was gathered from the tree, not a path could be traced in the fields of corn. Belisarius was chaste and sober. In the license of a military life, none could boast that they had seen him intoxicated with wine: the most beautiful captives of Gothic or Vandal race were offered to his embraces, but he turned aside from their charms, and the husband of Antonina was never suspected of violating the laws of conjugal fidelity. The spectator and historian of his exploits has observed that amidst the perils of war, he was daring without rashness, prudent without fear, slow or rapid according to the exigencies of the moment; that in the deepest distress he was animated by real or apparent hope, but that he was modest and humble in the most prosperous fortune. By these virtues, he equaled or excelled the ancient masters of the military art. Victory, by sea and land, attended his arms. He subdued Africa, Italy, and the adjacent islands; led away captives the successors of Genseric and Theodoric; filled Constantinople with the spoils of their palaces; and in the space of six years recovered half the provinces of the Western empire. In his fame and merit, in wealth and power, he remained without a rival, the first of the Roman subjects; the voice of envy could only magnify his dangerous importance; and the emperor might applaud his own discerning spirit, which had discovered and raised the genius of Belisarius.[†]

It was the custom of the Roman triumphs that a slave should be placed behind the chariot to remind the conqueror of the instability of fortune and the infirmities of human nature. Procopius, in his Anecdotes, has assumed that servile and ungrateful office. The generous reader may cast away the libel, but the evidence of facts will adhere to his memory; and he will reluctantly confess that the fame and even the virtue of Belisarius were polluted by the lust and cruelty of his wife; and that hero deserved an appellation which may not drop from the pen of the decent historian. The mother of Antonina was a theatrical prostitute, and both her father and grandfather exercised, at Thessalonica and Constantinople, the vile though lucrative profession of charioteers. In the various situations of their fortune she became the companion, the enemy, the servant, and the favorite of the empress Theodora: these loose and ambitious females had been connected by similar pleasures; they were separated by the jealousy of vice, and at length reconciled by the partnership of guilt. Before her marriage with Belisarius, Antonina had one husband and many lovers: Photius, the son of her former nuptials, was of an age to distinguish himself at the siege of Naples; and it was not till the autumn of her age and beauty that she indulged a scandalous attachment to a Thracian youth. Theodosius had been educated in the Eunomian heresy; the African voyage was consecrated by the baptism and auspicious name of the first soldier who embarked; and the proselyte was adopted into the family of his spiritual parents, Belisarius and Antonina. Before they touched the shores of Africa, this holy kindred degenerated into sensual love: and as Antonina soon overleaped the bounds of modesty and caution, the Roman general was alone ignorant of his own dishonor. During their residence at Carthage, he surprised the two lovers in a subterraneous chamber, solitary, warm, and almost naked. Anger flashed from his eyes. "With the help of this young man," said the unblushing Antonina, "I was secreting our most precious effects from the knowledge of Justinian." The youth resumed his garments, and the pious husband consented to disbelieve the evidence of his own senses. From this pleasing and perhaps voluntary delusion, Belisarius was awakened at Syracuse by the officious information of Macedonia; and that female attendant, after requiring an oath for her security, produced two chamberlains who, like herself, had often beheld the adulteries of Antonina. A hasty flight into Asia saved Theodosius from the justice of an injured husband, who had signified to one of his guards the order of his death; but the tears of Antonina, and her artful seductions, assured the credulous hero of her innocence: and he stooped, against his faith and judgment, to abandon those imprudent friends who had presumed to accuse or doubt the chastity of his wife. The revenge of a guilty woman is implacable and bloody: the unfortunate Macedonia, with the two witnesses, were secretly arrested by the minister of her cruelty; their tongues were cut out, their bodies were hacked into small pieces, and their remains were cast into the Sea of Syracuse. A rash though judicious saying of Constantine, "I would sooner have punished the adulteress than the boy," was deeply remembered by Antonina; and two years afterwards, when despair had armed that officer against his general, her sanguinary advice decided and hastened his execution. Even the indignation of Photius was not forgiven by his mother; the exile of her son prepared the recall of her lover; and Theodosius condescended to accept the pressing and humble invitation of the conqueror of Italy. In the absolute direction of his household and in the important commissions of peace and war, the favorite youth most rapidly acquired a fortune of four hundred thousand pounds sterling; and after their return to Constantinople, the passion of Antonina, at least, continued ardent and unabated. But fear, devotion, and lassitude, perhaps, inspired Theodosius with more serious thoughts. He dreaded the busy scandal of the capital and the indiscreet fondness of the wife of Belisarius; escaped from her embraces and, retiring to Ephesus, shaved his head and took refuge in the sanctuary of a monastic life. The despair of the new Ariadne could scarcely have been excused by the death of her husband. She wept, she tore her hair, she filled the palace with her cries; "She had lost the dearest of friends, a tender, a faithful, a laborious friend!" But her warm entreaties, fortified by the prayers of Belisarius, were insufficient to draw the holy monk from the solitude of Ephesus. It was not till the general moved forward for the Persian war that Theodosius could be tempted to return to Constantinople; and the short interval before the departure of Antonina herself was boldly devoted to love and pleasure.

A philosopher may pity and forgive the infirmities of female nature, from which he receives no real injury: but contemptible is the husband who feels, and yet endures, his own infamy in that of his wife. Antonina pursued her son with implacable hatred; and the gallant Photius was exposed to her secret persecutions in the camp beyond the Tigris. Enraged by his own wrongs and by the dishonor of his blood, he cast away in his turn the sentiments of nature and revealed to Belisarius the turpitude of a woman who had violated all the duties of a mother and a wife. From the surprise and indignation of the Roman general, his former credulity appears to have been sincere: he embraced the knees of the son of Antonina, adjured him to remember his obligations rather than his birth, and confirmed at the altar their holy vows of revenge and mutual defense. The dominion of Antonina was impaired by absence; and when she met her husband on his return from the Persian confines, Belisarius, in his first and transient emotions, confined her person and threatened her life. Photius was more resolved to punish and less prompt to pardon: he flew to Ephesus; extorted from a trusty eunuch of his mother the full confession of her guilt; arrested Theodosius and his treasures in the church of St. John the Apostle, and concealed his captives, whose execution was only delayed, in a secure and sequestered fortress of Cilicia. Such a daring outrage against public justice could not pass with impunity; and the cause of Antonina was espoused by the empress, whose favor she had deserved by the recent services of the disgrace of a praefect and the exile and murder of a pope. At the end of the campaign, Belisarius was recalled; he complied as usual with the Imperial mandate. His mind was not prepared for rebellion: his obedience, however adverse to the dictates of honor, was consonant to the wishes of his heart; and when he embraced his wife, at the command and perhaps in the presence of the empress, the tender husband was disposed to forgive or to be forgiven. The bounty of Theodora reserved for her companion a more precious favor. "I have found," she said, "my dearest patrician, a pearl of inestimable value; it has not yet been viewed by any mortal eye; but the sight and the possession of this jewel are destined for my friend." As soon as the curiosity and impatience of Antonina were kindled, the door of a bedchamber was thrown open and she beheld her lover, whom the diligence of the eunuchs had discovered in his secret prison. Her silent wonder burst into passionate exclamations of gratitude and joy, and she named Theodora her queen, her benefactress, and her savior. The monk of Ephesus was nourished in the palace with luxury and ambition; but instead of assuming, as he was promised, the command of the Roman armies, Theodosius expired in the first fatigues of an amorous interview. The grief of Antonina could only be assuaged by the sufferings of her son. A youth of consular rank and a sickly constitution was punished, without a trial, like a malefactor and a slave: yet such was the constancy of his mind that Photius sustained the tortures of the scourge and the rack without violating the faith which he had sworn to Belisarius. After this fruitless cruelty, the son of Antonina, while his mother feasted with the empress, was buried in her subterraneous prisons, which admitted not the distinction of night and day. He twice escaped to the most venerable sanctuaries of Constantinople, the churches of St. Sophia and of the Virgin: but his tyrants were insensible of religion as of pity; and the helpless youth, amidst the clamors of the clergy and people, was twice dragged from the altar to the dungeon. His third attempt was more successful. At the end of three years, the prophet Zachariah, or some mortal friend, indicated the means of an escape: he eluded the spies and guards of the empress, reached the holy sepulchre of Jerusalem, embraced the profession of a monk; and the abbot Photius was employed, after the death of Justinian, to reconcile and regulate the churches of Egypt. The son of Antonina suffered all that an enemy can inflict: her patient husband imposed on himself the more exquisite misery of violating his promise and deserting his friend.

In the succeeding campaign, Belisarius was again sent against the Persians: he saved the East, but he offended Theodora, and perhaps the emperor himself. The malady of Justinian had countenanced the rumor of his death; and the Roman general, on the supposition of that probable event, spoke the free language of a citizen and a soldier. His colleague Buzes, who concurred in the same sentiments, lost his rank, his liberty, and his health by the persecution of the empress: but the disgrace of Belisarius was alleviated by the dignity of his own character and the influence of his wife, who might wish to humble but could not desire to ruin the partner of her fortunes. Even his removal was colored by the assurance that the sinking state of Italy would be retrieved by the single presence of its conqueror. But no sooner had he returned, alone and defenseless, than a hostile commission was sent to the East to seize his treasures and criminate his actions; the guards and veterans who followed his private banner were distributed among the chiefs of the army, and even the eunuchs presumed to cast lots for the partition of his martial domestics. When he passed with a small and sordid retinue through the streets of Constantinople, his forlorn appearance excited the amazement and compassion of the people. Justinian and Theodora received him with cold ingratitude; the servile crowd, with insolence and contempt; and in the evening he retired with trembling steps to his deserted palace. An indisposition, feigned or real, had confined Antonina to her apartment; and she walked disdainfully silent in the adjacent portico while Belisarius threw himself on his bed and expected, in an agony of grief and terror, the death which he had so often braved under the walls of Rome. Long after sunset a messenger was announced from the empress: he opened with anxious curiosity the letter which contained the sentence of his fate. "You cannot be ignorant how much you have deserved my displeasure. I am not insensible of the services of Antonina. To her merits and intercession I have granted your life, and permit you to retain a part of your treasures, which might be justly forfeited to the state. Let your gratitude, where it is due, be displayed not in words but in your future behavior." I know not how to believe or to relate the transports with which the hero is said to have received this ignominious pardon. He fell prostrate before his wife, he kissed the feet of his savior, and he devoutly promised to live the grateful and submissive slave of Antonina. A fine of one hundred and twenty thousand pounds sterling was levied on the fortunes of Belisarius; and with the office of count, or master of the royal stables, he accepted the conduct of the Italian war. At his departure from Constantinople, his friends, and even the public, were persuaded that as soon as he regained his freedom he would renounce his dissimulation, and that his wife, Theodora, and perhaps the emperor himself would be sacrificed to the just revenge of a virtuous rebel. Their hopes were deceived; and the unconquerable patience and loyalty of Belisarius appear either *below* or *above* the character of a MAN.

State of the Barbaric World

Our estimate of personal merit is relative to the common faculties of mankind. The aspiring efforts of genius or virtue, either in active or speculative life, are measured not so much by their real elevation as by the height to which they ascend above the level of their age and country; and the same stature which in a people of giants would pass unnoticed must appear conspicuous in a race of pygmies. Leonidas and his three hundred companions devoted their lives at Thermopylae; but the education of the infant, the boy, and the man had prepared and almost insured this memorable sacrifice; and each Spartan would approve rather than admire an act of duty of which himself and eight thousand of his fellow-citizens were equally capable. The great Pompey might inscribe on his trophies that he had defeated in battle two millions of enemies and reduced fifteen hundred cities from the Lake Maeotis to the Red Sea: but the fortune of Rome flew before his eagles; the nations were oppressed by their own fears, and the invincible legions which he commanded had been formed by the habits of conquest and the discipline of ages. In this view, the character of Belisarius may be deservedly placed above the heroes of the ancient republics. His imperfections flowed from the contagion of the times; his virtues were his own, the free gift of nature or reflection; he raised himself without a master or a rival; and so inadequate were the arms committed to his hand that his sole advantage was derived from the pride and presumption of his adversaries. Under his command, the subjects of Justinian often deserved to be called Romans: but the unwarlike appellation of Greeks was imposed as a term of reproach by the haughty Goths; who affected to blush that they must dispute the kingdom of

Italy with a nation of tragedians, pantomimes, and pirates. The climate of Asia has indeed been found less congenial than that of Europe to military spirit: those populous countries were enervated by luxury, despotism, and superstition; and the monks were more expensive and more numerous than the soldiers of the East. The regular force of the empire had once amounted to six hundred and forty-five thousand men: it was reduced in the time of Justinian to one hundred and fifty thousand; and this number, large as it may seem, was thinly scattered over the sea and land; in Spain and Italy, in Africa and Egypt, on the banks of the Danube, the coast of the Euxine, and the frontiers of Persia. The citizen was exhausted, yet the soldier was unpaid; his poverty was mischievously soothed by the privilege of rapine and indolence; and the tardy payments were detained and intercepted by the fraud of those agents who usurp, without courage or danger, the emoluments of war. Public and private distress recruited the armies of the state; but in the field, and still more in the presence of the enemy, their numbers were always defective. The want of national spirit was supplied by the precarious faith and disorderly service of Barbarian mercenaries. Even military honor, which has often survived the loss of virtue and freedom, was almost totally extinct. The generals, who were multiplied beyond the example of former times, labored only to prevent the success or to sully the reputation of their colleagues; and they had been taught by experience that if merit sometimes provoked the jealousy, error, or even guilt would obtain the indulgence of a gracious emperor. In such an age, the triumphs of Belisarius, and afterwards of Narses, shine with incomparable luster; but they are encompassed with the darkest shades of disgrace and calamity. While the lieutenant of Justinian subdued the kingdoms of the Goths and Vandals, the emperor, timid though ambitious, balanced the forces of the Barbarians, fomented their divisions by flattery and falsehood, and invited by his patience and liberality the repetition of injuries. The keys of Carthage, Rome, and Ravenna were presented to their conqueror, while Antioch was destroyed by the Persians, and Justinian trembled for the safety of Constantinople.

Even the Gothic victories of Belisarius were prejudicial to the state, since they abolished the important barrier of the Upper Danube, which had been so faithfully guarded by Theodoric and his daughter. For the defense of Italy, the Goths evacuated Pannonia and Noricum, which they left in a peaceful and flourishing condition: the sovereignty was claimed by the emperor of the Romans; the actual possession was abandoned to the boldness of the first invader. On the opposite banks of the Danube, the plains of Upper Hungary and the Transylvanian hills were possessed, since the death of Attila, by the tribes of the Gepidae, who respected the Gothic arms and despised not indeed the gold of the Romans but the secret motive of their annual subsidies. The vacant fortifications of the river were instantly occupied by these Barbarians; their standards were planted on the walls of Sirmium and Belgrade; and the ironical tone of their apology aggravated this insult on the majesty of the empire. "So extensive, O Caesar, are your dominions, so numerous are your cities, that you are continually seeking for nations to whom, either in peace or in war, you may relinquish these useless possessions. The Gepidae are your brave and faithful allies; and if they have anticipated your gifts, they have shown a just confidence in your bounty." Their presumption was excused by the mode of revenge which Justinian embraced. Instead of asserting the rights of a sovereign for the protection of his subjects, the emperor invited a strange people to invade and possess the Roman provinces between the Danube and the Alps, and the ambition of the Gepidae was checked by the rising power and fame of the LOMBARDS. This corrupt appellation has been diffused in the thirteenth century by the merchants and bankers, the Italian posterity of these savage warriors: but the original name of *Langobards* is expressive only of the peculiar length and fashion of their beards. I am not disposed either to question or to justify their Scandinavian origin; nor to pursue the migrations of the Lombards through unknown regions and marvelous adventures.... But the arms of the Lombards were more seriously engaged by a contest of thirty years, which was terminated only by the extirpation of the Gepidae.[†]

The wild people who dwelt or wandered in the plains of Russia, Lithuania, and Poland might be reduced, in the age of Justinian, under the two great families of the BULGARIANS and the SCLAVONIANS.... Their numerous tribes, however distant or adverse, used one common language (it was harsh and irregular) and were known by the resemblance of their form, which deviated from the swarthy Tartar and approached without attaining the lofty stature and fair complexion of the German. Four thousand six hundred villages were scattered over the provinces of Russia and Poland, and their huts were hastily built of rough timber, in a country deficient both in stone and iron. Erected, or rather concealed, in the depth of forests, on the banks of rivers, or the edges of morasses, we may, not perhaps without flattery, compare them to the architecture of the beaver; which they resembled in a double issue, to the land and water, for the escape of the savage inhabitant, an animal less clean, less diligent, and less social than that marvelous quadruped. The fertility of the soil, rather than the labor of the natives, supplied the rustic plenty of the Sclavonians. Their sheep and horned cattle were large and numerous, and the fields which they sowed with millet or panic afforded, in place of bread, a coarse and less nutritive food. The incessant rapine of their neighbors compelled them to bury this treasure in the earth; but on the appearance of a stranger, it was freely imparted by a people whose unfavorable character is qualified by the epithets of chaste, patient, and hospitable. As their supreme god, they adored an invisible master of the thunder. The rivers and the nymphs obtained their subordinate honors, and the popular worship was expressed in vows and sacrifice. The Sclavonians disdained to obey a despot, a prince, or even a magistrate; but their experience was too narrow, their passions too headstrong, to compose a system of equal law or general defense. Some voluntary respect was yielded to age and valor; but each tribe or village existed as a separate republic, and all must be persuaded where none could be compelled. They fought on foot, almost naked, and except an unwieldy shield without any defensive armor; their weapons of offense were a bow, a quiver of small poisoned arrows, and a long rope, which they dexterously threw from a distance and entangled their enemy in a running noose. In the field, the Sclavonian infantry was dangerous by their speed, agility, and hardiness: they swam, they dived, they remained under water, drawing their breath through a hollow cane; and a river or lake was often the scene of their unsuspected ambuscade. But these were the achievements of spies or stragglers; the military art was unknown to the Sclavonians; their name was obscure, and their conquests were inglorious.

I have marked the faint and general outline of the Sclavonians and Bulgarians without attempting to define their intermediate boundaries, which were not accurately known or respected by the Barbarians themselves. Their importance was measured by their vicinity to the empire.... The hopes or fears of the Barbarians; their intense union or discord; the accident of a frozen or shallow stream; the prospect of harvest or vintage; the prosperity or distress of the Romans; were the causes which produced the uniform repetition of annual visits, tedious in the narrative and destructive in the event. The same year, and possibly the same month, in which Ravenna surrendered was marked by an invasion of the Huns or Bulgarians so dreadful that it almost effaced the memory of their past inroads. They spread from the suburbs of Constantinople to the Ionian Gulf, destroyed thirty-two cities or castles, erased Potidaea, which Athens had built and Philip had besieged, and repassed the Danube, dragging at their horses' heels one hundred and twenty thousand of the subjects of Justinian. In a subsequent inroad they pierced the wall of the Thracian Chersonesus, extirpated the habitations and the inhabitants, boldly traversed the Hellespont, and returned to their companions laden with the spoils of Asia.... Whatever praise the boldness of the Sclavonians may deserve, it is sullied by the wanton and deliberate cruelty which they are accused of exercising on their prisoners. Without distinction of rank or age or sex, the captives were impaled or flayed alive, or suspended between four posts and beaten with clubs till they expired, or enclosed in some spacious building and left to perish in the flames with the spoil and cattle which might impede the march of these savage victors.[†]

In the midst of these obscure calamities, Europe felt the shock of revolution, which first revealed to the world the name and nation of the TURKS [circa A.D. 545ff.]. Like Romulus, the founder of that martial people was suckled by a she-wolf, who afterwards made him the father of a numerous progeny; and the representation of that animal in the banners of the Turks preserved the memory, or rather suggested the idea, of a fable which was invented, without any mutual intercourse, by the shepherds of Latium and those of Scythia. At the equal distance of two thousand miles from the Caspian, the Icy, the Chinese, and the Bengal Seas, a ridge of mountains is conspicuous, the center and perhaps the summit of Asia; which, in the language of different nations, has been styled Imaus, and Caf, and Altai, and the Golden Mountains, and the Girdle of the Earth. The sides of the hills were productive of minerals; and the iron forges, for the purpose of war, were exercised by the Turks, the most despised portion of the slaves of the great khan of the Geougen. But their servitude could only last till a leader, bold and eloquent, should arise to persuade his countrymen that the same arms which they forged for their masters might become, in their own hands, the instruments of freedom and victory. They sallied from the mountains; a scepter was the reward of his advice; and the annual ceremony in which a piece of iron was heated in the fire and a smith's hammer was successively handled by the prince and his nobles recorded for ages the humble profession and rational pride of the Turkish nation. Bertezena, their first leader, signalized their valor and his own in successful combats against the neighboring tribes. . . . One of the successors of Bertezena was tempted by the luxury and superstition of China; but his design of building cities and temples was defeated by the simple wisdom of a Barbarian counselor. "The Turks," he said, "are not equal in number to one hundredth part of the inhabitants of China. If we balance their power and elude their armies, it is because we wander without any fixed habitations in the exercise of war and hunting. Are we strong? we advance and conquer: are we feeble? we retire and are concealed. Should the Turks confine themselves within the walls of cities, the loss of a battle would be the destruction of their empire. The bonzes preach only patience, humility, and the renunciation of the world. Such, O king! is not the religion of heroes." They entertained with less reluctance the doctrines of Zoroaster; but the greatest part of the nation acquiesced without inquiry in the opinions, or rather in the practice, of their ancestors. The honors of sacrifice were reserved for the Supreme Deity; they acknowledged in rude hymns their obligations to the air, the fire, the water, and the earth; and their priests derived some profit from the art of divination. Their unwritten laws were rigorous and impartial: theft was punished with a tenfold restitution; adultery, treason, and murder with death; and no chastisement could be inflicted too severe for the rare and inexpiable guilt of cowardice. As the subject nations marched under the standard of the Turks, their cavalry, both men and horses, were proudly computed by millions; one of their effective armies consisted of four hundred thousand soldiers, and in less than fifty years they were connected in peace and war with the Romans, the Persians, and the Chinese. . . . This extent of savage empire compelled the Turkish monarch to establish three subordinate princes of his own blood, who soon forgot their gratitude and allegiance. The conquerors were enervated by luxury, which is always fatal except to an industrious people; the policy of China solicited the vanquished nations to resume their independence, and the power of the Turks was limited to a period of two hundred years. The revival of their name and dominion in the southern countries of Asia are the events of a later age; and the dynasties which succeeded to their native realms may sleep in oblivion; since *their* history bears no relation to the decline and fall of the Roman empire.

In the rapid career of conquest, the Turks attacked and subdued the nation of the Ogors or Varchonites on the banks of the River Til, which derived the epithet of Black from its dark water or gloomy forests. The khan of the Ogors was slain with three hundred thousand of his subjects, and their bodies were scattered over the space of four days' journey: their surviving countrymen acknowledged the strength and mercy of the Turks; and a small portion, about twenty thousand warriors, preferred exile to servitude. They followed the well-known road of the Volga, cherished the error of the nations who confounded them with the AVARS, and spread the terror of that false though famous appellation, which had not, however, saved its lawful proprietors from the yoke of the Turks. After a long and victorious march, the new Avars arrived at the foot of Mount Caucasus, in the country of the Alani and Circassians, where they first heard of the splendor and weakness of the Roman empire. They humbly requested their confederate, the prince of the Alani, to lead them to this source of riches; and their ambassador, with the permission of the governor of Lazica, was transported by the Euxine Sea to Constantinople. The whole city was poured forth to behold with curiosity and terror the aspect of a strange people: their long hair, which hung in tresses down their backs, was gracefully bound with ribbons, but the rest of their habit appeared to imitate the fashion of the Huns. When they were admitted to the audience of Justinian, Candish, the first of the ambassadors, addressed the Roman emperor in these terms [A.D. 558]: "You see before you, O mighty prince, the representatives of the strongest and most populous of nations, the invincible, the irresistible Avars. We are willing to devote ourselves to your service: we are able to vanquish and destroy all the enemies who now disturb your repose. But we expect, as the price of our alliance, as the reward of our valor, precious gifts, annual subsidies, and fruitful possessions." At the time of this embassy, Justinian had reigned above thirty, he had lived above seventy-five, years: his mind as well as his body was feeble and languid; and the conqueror of Africa and Italy, careless of the permanent interest of his people, aspired only to end his days in the bosom even of inglorious peace. In a studied oration, he imparted to the senate his resolution to dissemble the insult and to purchase the friendship of the Avars; and the whole senate, like the mandarins of China, applauded the incomparable wisdom and foresight of their sovereign.[†]

[The] justice of kings is understood by themselves, and even by their subjects, with an ample indulgence for the gratification of passion and interest. The virtue of Chosroes [I, the Just, or Nushirvan; king of Persia (A.D. 531–579)] was that of a conqueror, who, in the measures of peace and war, is excited by ambition and restrained by prudence; who confounds the greatness with the happiness of a nation, and calmly devotes the lives of thousands to the fame, or even the amusement, of a single man. In his domestic administration, the just Nushirvan would merit in our feelings the appellation of a tyrant. His two elder brothers had been deprived of their fair expectations of the diadem: their future life, between the supreme rank and the condition of subjects, was anxious to themselves and formidable to their master: fear as well as revenge might tempt them to rebel: the slightest evidence of a conspiracy satisfied the author of their wrongs; and the repose of Chosroes was secured by the death of these unhappy princes, with their families and adherents. . . . But the people, more especially in the East, is disposed to forgive and even to applaud the cruelty which strikes at the loftiest heads; at the slaves of ambition, whose voluntary choice has exposed them to live in the smiles and to perish by the frown of a capricious monarch. In the execution of the laws which he had no temptation to violate; in the punishment of crimes which attacked his own dignity, as well as the happiness of individuals; Nushirvan, or Chosroes, deserved the appellation of *just*. His government was firm, rigorous, and impartial. It was the first labor of his reign to abolish the dangerous theory of common or equal possessions: the lands and women which [rebellious religious sectaries] had usurped were restored to their lawful owners; and the temperate chastisement of the fanatics or impostors confirmed the domestic rights of society. Instead of listening with blind confidence to a favorite minister, he established four viziers over the four great provinces of his empire, Assyria, Media, Persia, and Bactriana. In the choice of judges, praefects, and counselors, he strove to remove the mask which is always worn in the presence of kings: he wished to substitute the natural order of talents for the accidental distinctions of birth and fortune; he professed in specious language his intention to prefer those men who carried the poor in their bosoms, and to banish corruption from the seat of justice, as dogs were excluded from the temples of the Magi. The code of laws of the first Artaxerxes was revived and published as the rule of the magistrates; but the assurance of speedy punishment was the best security of their virtue. Their behavior was inspected by a thousand eyes, their words were overheard by a thousand ears, the secret or public agents of the throne; and the provinces, from the Indian to the Arabian confines, were enlightened by the frequent visits of a sovereign who affected to emulate his celestial brother in his rapid and salutary career. Education and agriculture he viewed as the two objects most deserving of his care. In every city of Persia, orphans and the children of the poor were maintained and instructed at the public expense; the daughters were given in marriage to the richest citizens of their own rank, and the sons, according to their different talents, were employed in mechanic trades or promoted to more honorable service. The deserted villages were relieved by his bounty; to the peasants and farmers who were found incapable of cultivating their lands, he distributed cattle, seed, and the instruments of husbandry; and the rare and inestimable treasure of fresh water was parsimoniously managed and skillfully dispersed over the arid territory of Persia. The prosperity of that kingdom was the effect and evidence of his virtues; his vices are those of Oriental despotism; but in the long competition between Chosroes and Justinian, the advantage both of merit and fortune is almost always on the side of the Barbarian.

To the praise of justice Nushirvan united the reputation of knowledge; and the seven Greek philosophers who visited his court were invited and deceived by the strange assurance that a disciple of Plato was seated on the Persian throne. Did they expect that a prince strenuously exercised in the toils of war and government should agitate, with dexterity like their own, the abstruse and profound questions which amused the leisure of the schools of Athens? Could they hope that the precepts of philosophy should direct the life and control the passions of a despot, whose infancy had been taught to consider *his* absolute and fluctuating will as the only rule of moral obligation? The studies of Chosroes were ostentatious and superficial: but his example awakened the curiosity of an ingenious people, and the light of science was diffused over the dominions of Persia. At Gondi Sapor, in the neighborhood of the royal city of Susa, an academy of physic was founded, which insensibly became a liberal school of poetry, philosophy, and rhetoric. The annals of the monarchy were composed; and while recent and authentic history might afford some useful lessons both to the prince and people, the darkness of the first ages was embellished by the giants, the dragons, and the fabulous heroes of Oriental romance. Every learned or confident stranger was enriched by the bounty and flattered by the conversation of the monarch. . . . Nushirvan believed, or at least respected, the religion of the Magi; and some traces of persecution may be discovered in his reign. Yet he allowed himself freely to compare the tenets of the various sects; and the theological disputes in which he frequently presided diminished the authority of the priest and enlightened the minds of the people. At his command, the most celebrated writers of Greece and India were translated into the Persian language; a smooth and elegant idiom, recommended by Mohammed to the use of paradise; though it is branded with the epithets of savage and unmusical by the ignorance and presumption of [the Greek historian] Agathias.[†]

The son of Kobad found his kingdom involved in a war with the successor of Constantine; and the anxiety of his domestic situation inclined him to grant the suspension of arms, which Justinian was impatient to purchase [A.D. 533–539]. Chosroes saw the Roman ambassadors at his feet. He accepted eleven thousand pounds of gold as the price of an *endless* or indefinite peace: some mutual exchanges were regulated; the Persian assumed the guard of the gates of Caucasus, and the demolition of Dara was suspended, on condition that it should never be made the residence of the general of the East. This interval of repose had been solicited, and was diligently improved, by the ambition of the emperor: his African conquests were the first fruits of the Persian treaty; and the avarice of Chosroes was soothed by a large portion of the spoils of Carthage, which his ambassadors required in a tone of pleasantry and under the color of friendship. But the trophies of Belisarius disturbed the slumbers of the great king; and he heard with astonishment, envy, and fear that Sicily, Italy, and Rome itself had been reduced, in three rapid campaigns, to the obedience of Justinian.[†]

Whatever might be the provocations of Chosroes, he abused the confidence of treaties; and the just reproaches of dissimulation and falsehood could only be concealed by the luster of his victories.

[*Chosroes invades Syria (A.D. 540) and ruins Antioch. Belisarius defends the East (A.D. 541 ff.). Intermittent hostilities and ongoing negotiations remain the general rule.*]

In peace, the king of Persia continually sought the pretenses of a rupture: but no sooner had he taken up arms than he expressed his desire of a safe and honorable treaty. During the fiercest hostilities, the two monarchs entertained a deceitful negotiation; and such was the superiority of Chosroes that whilst he treated the Roman ministers with insolence and contempt, he obtained the most unprecedented honors for his own ambassadors at the Imperial court. The successor of Cyrus assumed the majesty of the Eastern sun, and graciously permitted his younger brother Justinian to reign over the West with the pale and reflected splendor of the moon. . . . Many years of fruitless desolation elapsed before Justinian and Chosroes were compelled, by mutual lassitude, to consult the repose of their declining age. At a conference held on the frontier, each party, without expecting to gain credit, displayed the power, the justice, and the pacific intentions of their respective sovereigns; but necessity and interest dictated the treaty of peace, which was concluded for a term of fifty years, diligently composed in the Greek and Persian languages, and attested by the seals of twelve interpreters [A.D. 562]. The liberty of commerce and religion was fixed and defined; the allies of the emperor and the great king were included in the same benefits and obligations; and the most scrupulous precautions were provided to prevent or determine the accidental disputes that might arise on the confines of two hostile nations. After twenty years of destructive though feeble war, the limits still remained without alteration.†

CHAPTER XLIII

LAST VICTORY AND DEATH OF BELISARIUS, DEATH OF JUSTINIAN

Rebellions of Africa. • Restoration of the Gothic kingdom by Totila. •
Loss and recovery of Rome. • Final conquest of Italy by Narses. •
Extinction of the Ostrogoths. • Defeat of the Franks and Alemanni. •
Last victory, disgrace, and death of Belisarius. • Death and
character of Justinian.[†]

The review of the nations from the Danube to the Nile has exposed, on every side, the weakness of the Romans; and our wonder is reasonably excited that they should presume to enlarge an empire whose ancient limits they were incapable of defending. But the wars, the conquests, and the triumphs of Justinian are the feeble and pernicious efforts of old age, which exhaust the remains of strength and accelerate the decay of the powers of life. He exulted in the glorious act of restoring Africa and Italy to the republic; but the calamities which followed the departure of Belisarius betrayed the impotence of the conqueror, and accomplished the ruin of those unfortunate countries.

From his new acquisitions, Justinian expected that his avarice, as well as pride, should be richly gratified [A.D. 535–545]. A rapacious minister of the finances closely pursued the footsteps of Belisarius; and as the old registers of tribute had been burnt by the Vandals, he indulged his fancy in a liberal calculation and arbitrary assessment of the wealth of Africa. The increase of taxes which were drawn away by a distant sovereign, and a general resumption of the patrimony or crown lands, soon dispelled the intoxication of the public joy: but the emperor was insensible to the modest complaints of the people, till he was awakened and alarmed by the clamors of military discontent.[†]

[Africa] was rapidly sinking into the state of barbarism from whence it had been raised by the Phoenician colonies and Roman laws; and every step of intestine discord was marked by some deplorable victory of savage man over civilized society [A.D. 544–558]. . . . [The] victories and the losses of Justinian were alike pernicious to mankind; and such was the desolation of Africa that in many parts a stranger might wander whole days without meeting the face either of a friend or an enemy. The nation of the Vandals had disappeared: they once amounted to a hundred and sixty thousand warriors, without including the children, the women, or the slaves. Their numbers were infinitely surpassed by the number of the Moorish families extirpated in a relentless war; and the same destruction was retaliated on the Romans and their allies, who perished by the climate, their mutual quarrels, and the rage of the Barbarians. When Procopius first landed, he admired the populousness of the cities and country, strenuously exercised in the labors of commerce and agriculture. In less than twenty years, that busy scene was converted into a silent solitude; the wealthy citizens escaped to Sicily and Constantinople; and the secret historian has confidently affirmed that five millions of Africans were consumed by the wars and government of the emperor Justinian.

The jealousy of the Byzantine court had not permitted Belisarius to achieve the conquest of Italy; and his abrupt departure revived the courage of the Goths [A.D. 540], who respected his genius, his virtue, and even the laudable motive which had urged the servant of Justinian to deceive and reject them. They had lost their king (an inconsiderable loss), their capital, their treasures, the provinces from Sicily to the Alps, and the military force of two hundred thousand Barbarians, magnificently equipped with horses and arms. Yet all was not lost, as long as Pavia was defended by one thousand Goths, inspired by a sense of honor, the love of freedom, and the memory of their past greatness.†

The successors of Belisarius, eleven generals of equal rank, neglected to crush the feeble and disunited Goths till they were roused to action by the progress of Totila and the reproaches of Justinian [A.D. 541–544].... Twenty thousand Romans encountered the forces of Totila near Faenza, and on the hills of Mugello, of the Florentine territory. The ardor of freedmen who fought to regain their country was opposed to the languid temper of mercenary troops, who were even destitute of the merits of strong and well-disciplined servitude. On the first attack, they abandoned their ensigns, threw down their arms, and dispersed on all sides with an active speed which abated the loss, whilst it aggravated the shame, of their defeat. The king of the Goths, who blushed for the baseness of his enemies, pursued with rapid steps the path of honor and victory.... After the reduction of

Naples and Cumae, the provinces of Lucania, Apulia, and Calabria submitted to the king of the Goths. Totila led his army to the gates of Rome, pitched his camp at Tibur, or Tivoli, within twenty miles of the capital, and calmly exhorted the senate and people to compare the tyranny of the Greeks with the blessings of the Gothic reign.

The rapid success of Totila may be partly ascribed to the revolution which three years' experience had produced in the sentiments of the Italians. At the command, or at least in the name, of a Catholic emperor, the pope, their spiritual father, had been torn from the Roman church and either starved or murdered on a desolate island. The virtues of Belisarius were replaced by the various or uniform vices of eleven chiefs, at Rome, Ravenna, Florence, Perugia, Spoleto, etc., who abused their authority for the indulgence of lust or avarice. The improvement of the revenue was committed to Alexander, a subtle scribe long practiced in the fraud and oppression of the Byzantine schools, and whose name of *Psalliction*, the *Scissors*, was drawn from the dexterous artifice with which he reduced the size without defacing the figure of the gold coin. Instead of expecting the restoration of peace and industry, he imposed a heavy assessment on the fortunes of the Italians. Yet his present or future demands were less odious than a prosecution of arbitrary rigor against the persons and property of all those who, under the Gothic kings, had been concerned in the receipt and expenditure of the public money. The subjects of Justinian who escaped these partial vexations were oppressed by the irregular maintenance of the soldiers, whom Alexander defrauded and despised; and their hasty sallies in quest of wealth or subsistence provoked the inhabitants of the country to await or implore their deliverance from the virtues of a Barbarian. Totila was chaste and temperate; and none were deceived, either friends or enemies, who depended on his faith or his clemency. To the husbandmen of Italy the Gothic king issued a welcome proclamation, enjoining them to pursue their important labors and to rest assured that, on the payment of the ordinary taxes, they should be defended by his valor and discipline from the injuries of war. The strong towns he successively attacked; and as soon as they had yielded to his arms, he demolished the fortifications, to save the people from the calamities of a future siege, to deprive the Romans of the arts of defense, and to decide the tedious quarrel of the two nations by an equal and honorable conflict in the field of battle. The Roman captives and deserters were tempted to enlist in the service of a liberal and courteous adversary; the slaves were attracted by the firm and faithful promise that they should never be delivered to their masters; and from the thousand warriors of Pavia, a new people, under the same appellation of Goths, was insensibly formed in the camp of Totila. He sincerely accomplished the articles of capitulation without seeking or accepting any sinister advantage from ambiguous expressions or unforeseen events: the garrison of Naples had stipulated that they should be transported by sea; the obstinacy of the winds prevented their voyage, but they were generously supplied with horses, provisions, and a safe-conduct to the gates of Rome. The wives of the senators, who had been surprised in the villas of Campania, were restored without a ransom to their husbands; the violation of female chastity was inexorably chastised with death; and in the salutary regulation of the edict of the famished Neapolitans, the conqueror assumed the office of a humane and attentive physician. The virtues of Totila are equally laudable, whether they proceeded from true policy, religious principle, or the instinct of humanity: he often harangued his troops; and it was his constant theme that national vice and ruin are inseparably connected; that victory is the fruit of moral as well as military virtue; and that the prince, and even the people, are responsible for the crimes which they neglect to punish.

The return of Belisarius to save the country which he had subdued was pressed with equal vehemence by his friends and enemies; and the Gothic war was imposed as a trust or an exile on the veteran commander [A.D. 544–548]. A hero on the banks of the Euphrates, a slave in the palace of Constantinople, he accepted with reluctance the painful task of supporting his own reputation and retrieving the faults of his successors. The sea was open to the Romans: the ships and soldiers were assembled at Salona, near the palace of Diocletian: he refreshed and reviewed his troops at Pola in Istria, coasted round the head of the Adriatic, entered the port of Ravenna, and despatched orders rather than supplies to the subordinate cities. His first public oration was addressed to the Goths and Romans in the name of the emperor, who had suspended for a while the conquest of Persia and listened to the prayers of his Italian subjects. He gently touched on the causes and the authors of the recent disasters, striving to remove the fear of punishment for the past and the hope of impunity for the future, and laboring, with more zeal than success, to unite all the members of his government in a firm league of affection and obedience. Justinian, his gracious master, was inclined to pardon and reward; and it was their interest as well as duty to reclaim their deluded brethren who had been seduced by the arts of the usurper. Not a man was tempted to desert the standard of the Gothic king. Belisarius soon discovered that he was sent to remain the idle and impotent spectator of the glory of a young Barbarian; and his own epistle exhibits a genuine and lively picture of the distress of a noble mind. "Most excellent prince, we are arrived in Italy, destitute of all the necessary implements of war, men, horses, arms, and money. In our late circuit through the villages of Thrace and Illyricum, we have collected with extreme difficulty about four thousand recruits, naked and unskilled in the use of weapons and the exercises of the camp. The soldiers already stationed in the province are discontented, fearful, and dismayed; at the sound of an enemy, they dismiss their horses and cast their arms on the ground. No taxes can be raised, since Italy is in the hands of the Barbarians; the failure of payment has deprived us of the right of command, or even of admonition. Be assured, dread Sir, that the greater part of your troops have already deserted to the Goths. If the war could be achieved by the presence of Belisarius alone, your wishes are satisfied; Belisarius is in the midst of Italy. But if you desire to conquer, far other preparations are requisite: without a military force, the title of general is an empty name. It would be expedient to restore to my service my own veteran and domestic guards. Before I can take the field, I must receive an adequate supply of light and heavy armed troops; and it is only with ready money that you can procure the indispensable aid of a powerful body of the cavalry of the Huns." An officer in whom Belisarius confided was sent from Ravenna to hasten and conduct the succors; but the message was neglected, and the messenger was detained at Constantinople by an advantageous marriage. After his patience had been exhausted by delay and disappointment, the Roman general repassed the Adriatic and expected at Dyrrachium the arrival of the troops which were slowly assembled among the subjects and allies of the empire. His powers were still inadequate to the deliverance of Rome, which was closely besieged by the Gothic king. The Appian way, a march of forty days, was covered by the Barbarians; and as the prudence of Belisarius declined a battle, he preferred the safe and speedy navigation of five days from the coast of Epirus to the mouth of the Tiber.†

Famine had relaxed the strength and discipline of the garrison of Rome. They could derive no effectual service from a dying people; and the inhuman avarice of the merchant at length absorbed the vigilance of the governor. Four Isaurian sentinels, while their companions slept and their officers were absent, descended by a rope from the wall and secretly proposed to the Gothic king to introduce his troops into the city. The offer was entertained with coldness and suspicion; they returned in safety; they twice repeated their visit; the place was twice examined; the conspiracy was known and disregarded; and no sooner had Totila consented to the attempt than they unbarred the Asinarian gate and gave admittance to the Goths [December 17, A.D. 546]. Till the dawn of day, they halted in order of battle, apprehensive of treachery or ambush; but the [Roman] troops, with their leader [Bessas], had already escaped; and when the king was pressed to disturb their retreat, he prudently replied that no sight could be more grateful than that of a flying enemy. . . . As soon as daylight had displayed the entire victory of the Goths, their monarch devoutly visited the tomb of the prince of the apostles; but while he prayed at the altar, twenty-five soldiers, and sixty citizens, were put to the sword in the vestibule of the temple. The archdeacon Pelagius stood before him, with the gospels in his hand. "O Lord, be merciful to your servant." "Pelagius," said Totila, with an insulting smile, "your pride now condescends to become a suppliant." "I *am* a suppliant," replied the prudent archdeacon; "God has now made us your subjects, and as your subjects, we are entitled to your clemency." At his humble prayer, the lives of the Romans were spared; and the chastity of the maids and matrons was preserved inviolate from the passions of the hungry soldiers. But they were rewarded by the freedom of pillage, after the most precious spoils had been reserved for the royal treasury. The houses of the senators were plentifully stored with gold and silver; and the avarice of Bessas had labored with so much guilt and shame for the benefit of the conqueror. In this revolution, the sons and daughters of Roman consuls tasted the misery which they had spurned or relieved [during the siege], wandered in tattered garments through the streets of the city and begged their bread, perhaps without success, before the gates of their hereditary mansions. . . . The next day [Totila] pronounced two orations, to congratulate and admonish his victorious Goths and to reproach the senate as the vilest of slaves, with their perjury, folly, and ingratitude; sternly declaring that their estates and honors were justly forfeited to the companions of his arms. Yet he consented to forgive their revolt; and the senators repaid his clemency by despatching circular letters to their tenants and vassals in the provinces of Italy, strictly to enjoin them to desert the standard of the Greeks, to cultivate their lands in peace, and to learn from their masters the duty of obedience to a Gothic sovereign. Against the city which had so long delayed the course of his victories, he appeared inexorable: one third of the walls, in different parts, were demolished by his command; fire and engines prepared to consume or subvert the most stately works of antiquity; and the world was astonished by the fatal decree that Rome should be changed into a pasture for cattle. The firm and temperate remonstrance of Belisarius suspended the execution; he warned the Barbarian not to sully his fame by the destruction of those monuments which were the glory of the dead and the delight of the living; and Totila was persuaded by the advice of an enemy to preserve Rome as the ornament of his kingdom, or the fairest pledge of peace and reconciliation. When he had signified to the ambassadors of Belisarius his intention of sparing the city, he stationed an army at the distance of one hundred and twenty furlongs to observe the motions of the Roman general. With the remainder of his forces he marched into Lucania and Apulia, and occupied on the summit of Mount Garganus one of the camps of Hannibal.[†]

The loss of Rome was speedily retrieved by an action to which, according to the event, the public opinion would apply the names of rashness or heroism. After the departure of Totila, the Roman general sallied from the port at the head of a thousand horse, cut in pieces the enemy who opposed his progress, and visited with pity and reverence the vacant space of the *eternal* city. Resolved to maintain a station so conspicuous in the eyes of mankind, he summoned the greatest part of his troops to the standard which he erected on the Capitol: the old inhabitants were recalled by the love of their country and the hopes of food; and the keys of Rome were sent a second time to the emperor Justinian [February A.D. 547]. The walls, as far as they had been demolished by the Goths, were repaired with rude and dissimilar materials; the ditch was restored; iron spikes were profusely scattered in the highways to annoy the feet of the horses; and as new gates could not suddenly be procured, the entrance was guarded by a Spartan rampart of his bravest soldiers. At the expiration of twenty-five days, Totila returned by hasty marches from Apulia to avenge the injury and disgrace. Belisarius expected his approach. The Goths were thrice repulsed in three general assaults; they lost the flower of their troops; the royal standard had almost fallen into the hands of the enemy, and the fame of Totila sunk, as it had risen, with the fortune of his arms. Whatever skill and courage could achieve had been performed by the Roman general: it remained only that Justinian should terminate, by a strong and seasonable effort, the war which he had ambitiously undertaken. The indolence, perhaps the impotence, of a prince who despised his enemies and envied his servants protracted the calamities of Italy.[†]

The five last campaigns of Belisarius might abate the envy of his competitors, whose eyes had been dazzled and wounded by the blaze of his former glory. Instead of delivering Italy from the Goths, he had wandered like a fugitive along the coast, without daring to march into the country or to accept the bold and repeated challenge of Totila. Yet, in the judgment of the few who could discriminate counsels from events and compare the instruments with the execution, he appeared a more consummate master of the art of war than in the season of his prosperity, when he presented two captive kings before the throne of Justinian.

[*Belisarius receives his final recall (September* A.D. *548), and returns to court. Totila again takes Rome (*A.D. *549).*]

Justinian was deaf to the voice of peace: but he neglected the prosecution of war; and the indolence of his temper disappointed in some degree the obstinacy of his passions. From this salutary slumber the emperor was awakened by the pope Vigilius and the patrician Cethegus, who appeared before his throne and adjured him, in the name of God and the people, to resume the conquest and deliverance of Italy. In the choice of the generals, caprice as well as judgment was shown. . . . Belisarius reposed in the shade of his laurels, but the command of the principal army was reserved for Germanus, the emperor's nephew, whose rank and merit had been long depressed by the jealousy of the court.[†]

After the loss of Germanus, the nations were provoked to smile by the strange intelligence that the command of the Roman armies was given to a eunuch [A.D. 552]. But the eunuch Narses is ranked among the few who have rescued that unhappy name from the contempt and hatred of mankind. A feeble, diminutive body concealed the soul of a statesman and a warrior. His youth had been employed in the management of the loom and distaff, in the cares of the household, and the service of female luxury; but while his hands were busy, he secretly exercised the faculties of a vigorous and discerning mind. A stranger to the schools and the camp, he studied in the palace to dissemble, to flatter, and to persuade; and as soon as he approached the person of the emperor, Justinian listened with surprise and pleasure to the manly counsels of his chamberlain and private treasurer. The talents of Narses were tried and improved in frequent embassies: he led an army into Italy, acquired a practical knowledge of the war and the country, and presumed to strive with the genius of Belisarius. Twelve years after his return, the eunuch was chosen to achieve the conquest which had been left imperfect by the first of the Roman generals. Instead of being dazzled by vanity or emulation, he seriously declared that unless he were armed with an adequate force, he would never consent to risk his own glory and that of his sovereign. Justinian granted to the favorite what he might have denied to the hero: the Gothic war was rekindled from its ashes, and the preparations were not unworthy of the ancient majesty of the empire. The key of the public treasure was put into his hand, to collect magazines, to levy soldiers, to purchase arms and horses, to discharge the arrears of pay, and to tempt the fidelity of the fugitives and deserters.

[*Narses defeats Totila (July A.D. 552). Totila is mortally wounded.*]

Neither the fortifications of Hadrian's mole nor of the port could long delay the progress of the conqueror; and Justinian once more received the keys of Rome, which under his reign had been *five* times taken and recovered. But the deliverance of Rome was the last calamity of the Roman people. The Barbarian allies of Narses too frequently confounded the privileges of peace and war. The despair of the flying Goths found some consolation in sanguinary revenge; and three hundred youths of the noblest families, who had been sent as hostages beyond the Po, were inhumanly slain by the successor of Totila. The fate of the senate suggests an awful lesson of the vicissitude of human affairs. Of the senators whom Totila had banished from their country, some were rescued by an officer of Belisarius and transported from Campania to Sicily; while others were too guilty to confide in the clemency of Justinian or too poor to provide horses for their escape to the sea-shore. Their brethren languished five years in a state of indigence and exile: the victory of Narses revived their hopes; but their premature return to the metropolis was prevented by the furious Goths; and all the fortresses of Campania were stained with patrician blood. After a period of thirteen centuries, the institution of Romulus expired; and if the nobles of Rome still assumed the title of senators, few subsequent traces can be discovered of a public council or constitutional order. Ascend six hundred years, and contemplate the kings of the earth soliciting an audience as the slaves or freedmen of the Roman senate!

The Gothic war was yet alive. . . . [But before it could be concluded,] Italy was overwhelmed by a new deluge of Barbarians.

[*Italy is invaded by Franks and Alemanni (A.D. 553), who are also defeated by Narses (A.D. 554), who thereupon returns to court.*]

Narses entered the capital; the arms and treasures of the Goths, the Franks, and the Alemanni were displayed; his soldiers, with garlands in their hands, chanted the praises of the conqueror; and Rome, for the last time, beheld the semblance of a triumph.

After a reign of sixty years, the throne of the Gothic kings was filled by the exarchs of Ravenna, the representatives in peace and war of the emperor of the Romans. Their jurisdiction was soon reduced to the limits of a narrow province: but Narses himself, the first and most powerful of the exarchs, administered above fifteen years the entire kingdom of Italy [A.D. 554–568]. . . . The civil state of Italy, after the agitation of a long tempest, was fixed by a pragmatic sanction which the emperor promulgated at the request of the pope. Justinian introduced his own jurisprudence into the schools and tribunals of the West; he ratified the acts of Theodoric and his immediate successors, but every deed was rescinded and abolished which force had extorted, or fear had subscribed, under the usurpation of Totila. A moderate theory was framed to reconcile the rights of property with the safety of prescription, the claims of the state with the poverty of the people, and the pardon of offenses with the interest of virtue and order of society. Under the exarchs of Ravenna, Rome was degraded to the second rank. Yet the senators were gratified by the permission of visiting their estates in Italy and of approaching without obstacle the throne of Constantinople: the regulation of weights and measures was delegated to the pope and senate; and the salaries of lawyers and physicians, of orators and grammarians, were destined to preserve or rekindle the light of science in the ancient capital. Justinian might dictate benevolent edicts, and Narses might second his wishes by the restoration of cities, and more especially of churches. But the power of kings is most effectual to destroy; and the twenty years of the Gothic war had consummated the distress and depopulation of Italy. As early as the fourth campaign, under the discipline of Belisarius himself, fifty thousand laborers died of hunger in the narrow region of Picenum; and a strict interpretation of the evidence of Procopius would swell the loss of Italy above the total sum of her present inhabitants.

I desire to believe, but I dare not affirm, that Belisarius sincerely rejoiced in the triumph of Narses. Yet the consciousness of his own exploits might teach him to esteem without jealousy the merit of a rival; and the repose of the aged warrior was crowned by a last victory, which saved the emperor and the capital. The Barbarians, who annually visited the provinces of Europe, were less discouraged by some accidental defeats than they were excited by the double hope of spoil and of subsidy. In the thirty-second winter of Justinian's reign, the Danube was deeply frozen: Zabergan led the cavalry of the Bulgarians, and his standard was followed by a promiscuous multitude of Sclavonians [A.D. 558–559]. . . . The report of the fugitives exaggerated the numbers and fierceness of an enemy who had polluted holy virgins and abandoned new-born infants to the dogs and vultures; a crowd of rustics, imploring food and protection, increased the consternation of the city, and the tents of Zabergan were pitched at the distance of twenty miles, on the banks of a small river which encircles Melanthias and afterwards falls into the Propontis. Justinian trembled: and those who had only seen the emperor in his old age were pleased to suppose that he had lost the alacrity and vigor of his youth. By his command the vessels of gold and silver were removed from the churches in the neighborhood, and even the suburbs, of Constantinople; the ramparts were lined with trembling spectators; the golden gate was crowded with useless generals and tribunes, and the senate shared the fatigues and the apprehensions of the populace.

But the eyes of the prince and people were directed to a feeble veteran who was compelled by the public danger to resume the armor in which he had entered Carthage and defended Rome. The horses of the royal stables, of private citizens, and even of the circus were hastily collected; the emulation of the old and young was roused by the name of Belisarius, and his first encampment was in the presence of a victorious enemy. . . . [T]he Bulgarians lost only four hundred horse; but Constantinople was saved; and Zabergan, who felt the hand of a master, withdrew to a respectful distance. But his friends were numerous in the councils of the emperor, and Belisarius obeyed with reluctance the commands of envy and Justinian, which forbade him to achieve the deliverance of his country. On his return to the city, the people, still conscious of their danger, accompanied his triumph with acclamations of joy and gratitude, which were imputed as a crime to the victorious general. But when he entered the palace, the courtiers were silent, and the emperor, after a cold and thankless embrace, dismissed him to mingle with the train of slaves.[†]

About two years after the last victory of Belisarius [A.D. 561], the emperor returned from a Thracian journey of health, or business, or devotion. Justinian was afflicted by a pain in his head; and his private entry countenanced the rumor of his death. Before the third hour of the day, the bakers' shops were plundered of their bread, the houses were shut, and every citizen, with hope or terror, prepared for the impending tumult. The senators themselves, fearful and suspicious, were convened at the ninth hour; and the praefect received their commands to visit every quarter of the city and proclaim a general illumination for the recovery of the emperor's health. The ferment subsided; but every accident betrayed the impotence of the government and the factious temper of the people: the guards were disposed to mutiny as often as their quarters were changed or their pay was withheld: the frequent calamities of fires and earthquakes afforded the opportunities of disorder; the disputes of the blues and greens, of the orthodox and heretics, degenerated into bloody battles; and in the presence of the Persian ambassador, Justinian blushed for himself and for his subjects.

Capricious pardon and arbitrary punishment embittered the irksomeness and discontent of a long reign: a conspiracy was formed in the palace; and unless we are deceived by the names of Marcellus and Sergius, the most virtuous and the most profligate of the courtiers were associated in the same designs. They had fixed the time of the execution; their rank gave them access to the royal banquet; and their black slaves were stationed in the vestibule and porticos to announce the death of the tyrant and to excite a sedition in the capital. But the indiscretion of an accomplice saved the poor remnant of the days of Justinian. The conspirators were detected and seized, with daggers hidden under their garments: Marcellus died by his own hand, and Sergius was dragged from the sanctuary. Pressed by remorse or tempted by the hopes of safety, he accused two officers of the household of Belisarius; and torture forced them to declare that they had acted according to the secret instructions of their patron. Posterity will not hastily believe that a hero who, in the vigor of life, had disdained the fairest offers of ambition and revenge should stoop to the murder of his prince, whom he could not long expect to survive. His followers were impatient to fly; but flight must have been supported by rebellion, and he had lived enough for nature and for glory. Belisarius appeared before the council with less fear than indignation [December 5, A.D. 563]: after forty years' service, the emperor had prejudged his guilt; and injustice was sanctified by the presence and authority of the patriarch. The life of Belisarius was graciously spared; but his fortunes were sequestered, and from December to July, he was guarded as a prisoner in his own palace. At length his innocence was acknowledged; his freedom and honor were restored [July 19, A.D. 564]; and death, which might be hastened by resentment and grief, removed him from the world in about eight months after his deliverance [March 13, A.D. 565]. The name of Belisarius can never die, but instead of the funeral, the monuments, the statues so justly due to his memory, I only read that his treasures, the spoil of the Goths and Vandals, were immediately confiscated by the emperor. Some decent portion was reserved, however, for the use of his widow: and as Antonina had much to repent, she devoted the last remains of her life and fortune to the foundation of a convent. Such is the simple and genuine narrative of the fall of Belisarius and the ingratitude of Justinian. That he was deprived of his eyes and reduced by envy to beg his bread, "Give a penny to Belisarius the general!" is a fiction of later times which has obtained credit, or rather favor, as a strange example of the vicissitudes of fortune.

If the emperor could rejoice in the death of Belisarius, he enjoyed the base satisfaction only eight months, the last period of a reign of thirty-eight years and a life of eighty-three years [d. November 14, A.D. 565]. It would be difficult to trace the character of a prince who is not the most conspicuous object of his own times: but the confessions of an enemy may be received as the safest evidence of his virtues. The resemblance of Justinian to the bust of Domitian is maliciously urged; with the acknowledgment, however, of a well-proportioned figure, a ruddy complexion, and a pleasing countenance. The emperor was easy of access, patient of hearing, courteous and affable in discourse, and a master of the angry passions which rage with such destructive violence in the breast of a despot. Procopius praises his temper to reproach him with calm and deliberate cruelty: but in the conspiracies which attacked his authority and person, a more candid judge will approve the justice or admire the clemency of Justinian. He excelled in the private virtues of chastity and temperance: but the impartial love of beauty would have been less mischievous than his conjugal tenderness for Theodora; and his abstemious diet was regulated not by the prudence of a philosopher but the superstition of a monk. His repasts were short and frugal: on solemn fasts, he contented himself with water and vegetables; and such was his strength, as well as fervor, that he frequently passed two days and as many nights without tasting any food. The measure of his sleep was not less rigorous: after the repose of a single hour, the body was awakened by the soul and, to the astonishment of his chamberlain, Justinian walked or studied till the morning light. Such restless application prolonged his time for the acquisition of knowledge and the despatch of business; and he might seriously deserve the reproach of confounding, by minute and preposterous diligence, the general order of his administration. The emperor professed himself a musician and architect, a poet and philosopher, a lawyer and theologian; and if he failed in the enterprise of reconciling the Christian sects, the review of the Roman jurisprudence is a noble monument of his spirit and industry. In the government of the empire, he was less wise or less successful: the age was unfortunate; the people was oppressed and discontented; Theodora abused her power; a succession of bad ministers disgraced his judgment; and Justinian was neither beloved in his life nor regretted at his death. The love of fame was deeply implanted in his breast, but he condescended to the poor ambition of titles, honors, and contemporary praise; and while he labored to fix the admiration, he forfeited the esteem and affection, of the Romans. The design of the African and Italian wars was boldly conceived and executed; and his penetration discovered the talents of Belisarius in the camp, of Narses in the palace. But the name of the emperor is eclipsed by the names of his victorious generals; and Belisarius still lives, to upbraid the envy and ingratitude of his sovereign. The partial favor of mankind applauds the genius of a conqueror who leads and directs his subjects in the exercise of arms. The characters of Philip the Second and of Justinian are distinguished by the cold ambition which delights in war and declines the dangers of the field. Yet a colossal statue of bronze represented the emperor on horseback, preparing to march against the Persians in the habit and armor of Achilles. In the great square before the church of St. Sophia, this monument was raised on a brass column and a stone pedestal of seven steps; and the pillar of Theodosius, which weighed seven thousand four hundred pounds of silver, was removed from the same place by the avarice and vanity of Justinian. Future princes were more just or indulgent to *his* memory; the elder Andronicus, in the beginning of the fourteenth century, repaired and beautified his equestrian statue: since the fall of the empire it has been melted into cannon by the victorious Turks.†

CHAPTER XLIV

IDEA OF THE ROMAN JURISPRUDENCE

Idea of the Roman jurisprudence. • The laws of the kings. •
The Twelve Tables of the Decemvirs. • The laws of the people. •
The decrees of the senate. • The edicts of the magistrates and
emperors. • Authority of the civilians. • Code, Pandects, Novels, and
Institutes of Justinian: I. Rights of Persons. II. Rights of things.
III. Private injuries and actions. IV. Crimes and punishments.

The vain titles of the victories of Justinian are crumbled into dust; but
the name of the legislator is inscribed on a fair and everlasting monument. Under his reign and by his care, the civil jurisprudence was digested in the immortal works of the CODE, the PANDECTS, and the
INSTITUTES: the public reason of the Romans has been silently or studiously transfused into the domestic institutions of Europe, and the
laws of Justinian still command the respect or obedience of independent nations. Wise or fortunate is the prince who connects his own
reputation with the honor or interest of a perpetual order of men. The
defense of their founder is the first cause which in every age has exercised the zeal and industry of the civilians. They piously commemorate his virtues; dissemble or deny his failings; and fiercely chastise the
guilt or folly of the rebels who presume to sully the majesty of the purple. The idolatry of love has provoked, as it usually happens, the rancor of opposition; the character of Justinian has been exposed to the
blind vehemence of flattery and invective; and the injustice of a sect
(the *Anti-Tribonians*) has refused all praise and merit to the prince, his
ministers, and his laws. Attached to no party, interested only for the
truth and candor of history, and directed by the most temperate and
skillful guides, I enter with just diffidence on the subject of civil law,
which has exhausted so many learned lives and clothed the walls of
such spacious libraries. In a single, if possible in a short, chapter, I shall
trace the Roman jurisprudence from Romulus to Justinian, appreciate
the labors of that emperor, and pause to contemplate the principles of
a science so important to the peace and happiness of society. The laws

of a nation form the most instructive portion of its history; and although I have devoted myself to write the annals of a declining monarchy, I shall embrace the occasion to breathe the pure and invigorating air of the republic.

The primitive government of Rome was composed, with some political skill, of an elective king, a council of nobles, and a general assembly of the people [circa 753 B.C. ff.]. War and religion were administered by the supreme magistrate; and he alone proposed the laws, which were debated in the senate, and finally ratified or rejected by a majority of votes in the thirty *curiae* or parishes of the city. Romulus, Numa, and Servius Tullius are celebrated as the most ancient legislators; and each of them claims his peculiar part in the threefold division of jurisprudence. The laws of marriage, the education of children, and the authority of parents, which may seem to draw their origin from *nature* itself, are ascribed to the untutored wisdom of Romulus. The law of *nations* and of religious worship, which Numa introduced, was derived from his nocturnal converse with the nymph Egeria. The *civil* law is attributed to the experience of Servius: he balanced the rights and fortunes of the seven classes of citizens, and guarded, by fifty new regulations, the observance of contracts and the punishment of crimes. The state, which he had inclined towards a democracy, was changed by the last Tarquin into a lawless despotism; and when the kingly office was abolished, the patricians engrossed the benefits of freedom. The royal laws became odious or obsolete; the mysterious deposit was silently preserved by the priests and nobles; and at the end of sixty years, the citizens of Rome still complained that they were ruled by the arbitrary sentence of the magistrates. Yet the positive institutions of the kings had blended themselves with the public and private manners of the city, some fragments of that venerable jurisprudence were compiled by the diligence of antiquarians, and above twenty texts still speak the rudeness of the Pelasgic idiom of the Latins.

I shall not repeat the well-known story of the Decemvirs, who sullied by their actions the honor of inscribing on brass, or wood, or ivory the TWELVE TABLES of the Roman laws [451–450 B.C.]. They were dictated by the rigid and jealous spirit of an aristocracy, which had yielded with reluctance to the just demands of the people. But the substance of the Twelve Tables was adapted to the state of the city; and the Romans had emerged from barbarism, since they were capable of studying and embracing the institutions of their more enlightened neighbors. A wise Ephesian was driven by envy from his native country: before he could reach the shores of Latium, he had observed the various forms of human nature and civil society: he imparted his knowledge to the legislators of Rome, and a statue was erected in the forum to the perpetual memory of Hermodorus. The names and divisions of the copper money, the sole coin of the infant state, were of Dorian origin: the harvests of Campania and Sicily relieved the wants of a people whose agriculture was often interrupted by war and faction; and since the trade was established, the deputies who sailed from the Tiber might return from the same harbors with a more precious cargo of political wisdom. The colonies of Great Greece had transported and improved the arts of their mother country. Cumae and Rhegium, Crotona and Tarentum, Agrigentum and Syracuse were in the rank of the most flourishing cities.[†]

Whatever might be the origin or the merit of the Twelve Tables, they obtained among the Romans that blind and partial reverence which the lawyers of every country delight to bestow on their municipal institutions. The study is recommended by Cicero as equally pleasant and instructive. "They amuse the mind by the remembrance of old words and the portrait of ancient manners; they inculcate the soundest principles of government and morals; and I am not afraid to affirm that the brief composition of the Decemvirs surpasses in genuine value the libraries of Grecian philosophy. How admirable," says Tully, with honest or affected prejudice, "is the wisdom of our ancestors! We alone are the masters of civil prudence, and our superiority is the more conspicuous if we deign to cast our eyes on the rude and almost ridiculous jurisprudence of Draco, of Solon, and of Lycurgus." The Twelve Tables were committed to the memory of the young and the meditation of the old; they were transcribed and illustrated with learned diligence; they had escaped the flames of the Gauls, they subsisted in the age of Justinian, and their subsequent loss has been imperfectly restored by the labors of modern critics. But although these venerable monuments were considered as the rule of right and the fountain of justice, they were overwhelmed by the weight and variety of new laws, which, at the end of five centuries, became a grievance more intolerable than the vices of the city. Three thousand brass plates, the acts of the senate of the people, were deposited in the Capitol: and some of the acts, as the Julian law against extortion, surpassed the number of a hundred chapters. The Decemvirs had neglected to import the sanction of Zaleucus, which so long maintained the integrity of his republic. A Locrian who proposed any new law stood forth in the assembly of the people with a cord round his neck, and if the law was rejected, the innovator was instantly strangled.

The Decemvirs had been named, and their tables were approved, by an assembly of the *centuries,* in which riches preponderated against numbers. To the first class of Romans, the proprietors of one hundred thousand pounds of copper, ninety-eight votes were assigned, and only ninety-five were left for the six inferior classes, distributed according to their substance by the artful policy of Servius. But the tribunes soon established a more specious and popular maxim, that every citizen has an equal right to enact the laws which he is bound to obey. Instead of the *centuries,* they convened the *tribes;* and the patricians, after an impotent struggle, submitted to the decrees of an assembly in which their votes were confounded with those of the meanest plebeians. Yet as long as the tribes successively passed over narrow *bridges* and gave their voices aloud, the conduct of each citizen was exposed to the eyes and ears of his friends and countrymen. The insolvent debtor consulted the wishes of his creditor; the client would have blushed to oppose the views of his patron; the general was followed by his veterans, and the aspect of a grave magistrate was a living lesson to the multitude. A new method of secret ballot abolished the influence of fear and shame, of honor and interest, and the abuse of freedom accelerated the progress of anarchy and despotism. The Romans had aspired to be equal; they were leveled by the equality of servitude; and the dictates of Augustus were patiently ratified by the formal consent of the tribes or centuries. Once, and once only, he experienced a sincere and strenuous opposition. His subjects had resigned all political liberty; they defended the freedom of domestic life. A law which enforced the obligation and strengthened the bonds of marriage was clamorously rejected; Propertius, in the arms of Delia, applauded the victory of licentious love; and the project of reform was suspended till a new and more tractable generation had arisen in the world. Such an example was not necessary to instruct a prudent usurper of the mischief of popular assemblies; and their abolition, which Augustus had silently prepared, was accomplished without resistance, and almost without notice, on the accession of his successor. Sixty thousand plebeian legislators, whom numbers made formidable and poverty secure, were supplanted by six hundred senators, who held their honors, their fortunes, and their lives by the clemency of the emperor. The loss of executive power was alleviated by the gift of legislative authority; and Ulpian might assert, after the practice of two hundred years, that the decrees of the senate obtained the force and validity of laws. In the times of freedom, the resolves of the people had often been dictated by the passion or error of the moment: the Cornelian, Pompeian, and Julian laws were adapted by a single hand to the prevailing disorders; but the senate, under the reign of the Caesars, was composed of magistrates and lawyers, and in questions of private jurisprudence the integrity of their judgment was seldom perverted by fear or interest.

The silence or ambiguity of the laws was supplied by the occasional EDICTS of those magistrates who were invested with the *honors* of the state. This ancient prerogative of the Roman kings was transferred, in their respective offices, to the consuls and dictators, the censors and praetors; and a similar right was assumed by the tribunes of the people, the aediles, and the proconsuls. At Rome and in the provinces, the duties of the subject and the intentions of the governor were proclaimed; and the civil jurisprudence was reformed by the annual edicts of the supreme judge, the praetor of the city. As soon as he ascended his tribunal, he announced by the voice of the crier, and afterwards inscribed on a white wall, the rules which he proposed to follow in the decision of doubtful cases, and the relief which his equity would afford from the precise rigor of ancient statutes. A principle of discretion more congenial to monarchy was introduced into the republic: the art of respecting the name and eluding the efficacy of the laws was improved by successive praetors; subtleties and fictions were invented to defeat the plainest meaning of the Decemvirs, and where the end was salutary, the means were frequently absurd. The secret or probable wish of the dead was suffered to prevail over the order of succession and the forms of testaments; and the claimant who was excluded from the character of heir accepted with equal pleasure from an indulgent praetor the possession of the goods of his late kinsman or benefactor.

In the redress of private wrongs, compensations and fines were substituted to the obsolete rigor of the Twelve Tables; time and space were annihilated by fanciful suppositions; and the plea of youth or fraud or violence annulled the obligation or excused the performance of an inconvenient contract. A jurisdiction thus vague and arbitrary was exposed to the most dangerous abuse: the substance, as well as the form, of justice were often sacrificed to the prejudices of virtue, the bias of laudable affection, and the grosser seductions of interest or resentment. But the errors or vices of each praetor expired with his annual office; such maxims alone as had been approved by reason and practice were copied by succeeding judges; the rule of proceeding was defined by the solution of new cases; and the temptations of injustice were removed by the Cornelian law which compelled the praetor of the year to adhere to the spirit and letter of his first proclamation. It was reserved for the curiosity and learning of Hadrian to accomplish the design which had been conceived by the genius of Caesar; and the praetorship of Salvius Julian, an eminent lawyer, was immortalized by the composition of the PERPETUAL EDICT. This well-digested code was ratified by the emperor and the senate; the long divorce of law and equity was at length reconciled; and instead of the Twelve Tables, the perpetual edict was fixed as the invariable standard of civil jurisprudence.

From Augustus to Trajan, the modest Caesars were content to promulgate their edicts in the various characters of a Roman magistrate; and in the decrees of the senate, the *epistles* and *orations* of the prince were respectfully inserted. Hadrian appears to have been the first who assumed without disguise the plenitude of legislative power. And this innovation, so agreeable to his active mind, was countenanced by the patience of the times and his long absence from the seat of government. The same policy was embraced by succeeding monarchs and, according to the harsh metaphor of Tertullian, "the gloomy and intricate forest of ancient laws was cleared away by the axe of royal mandates and *constitutions.*" During four centuries, from Hadrian to Justinian, the public and private jurisprudence was molded by the will of the sovereign; and few institutions, either human or divine, were permitted to stand on their former basis. The origin of Imperial legislation was concealed by the darkness of ages and the terrors of armed despotism; and a double fiction was propagated by the servility, or perhaps the ignorance, of the civilians who basked in the sunshine of the Roman and Byzantine courts. 1. To the prayer of the ancient Caesars, the people or the senate had sometimes granted a personal exemption from the obligation and penalty of particular statutes; and each indulgence was an act of jurisdiction exercised by the republic over the first of her citizens. His humble privilege was at length transformed into the prerogative of a tyrant; and the Latin expression of "released from the laws" was supposed to exalt the emperor above *all* human restraints and to leave his conscience and reason as the sacred measure of his conduct. 2. A similar dependence was implied in the decrees of the senate which, in every reign, defined the titles and powers of an elective magistrate. But it was not before the ideas, and even the language, of the Romans had been corrupted that a *royal* law, and an irrevocable gift of the people, were created by the fancy of Ulpian, or more probably of Tribonian himself; and the origin of Imperial power, though false in fact and slavish in its consequence, was supported on a principle of freedom and justice. "The pleasure of the emperor has the vigor and effect of law, since the Roman people, by the royal law, have transferred to their prince the full extent of their own power and sovereignty." The will of a single man, of a child perhaps, was allowed to prevail over the wisdom of ages and the inclinations of millions; and the degenerate Greeks were proud to declare that in his hands alone the arbitrary exercise of legislation could be safely deposited. "What interest or passion," exclaims Theophilus in the court of Justinian, "can reach the calm and sublime elevation of the monarch? He is already master of the lives and fortunes of his subjects; and those who have incurred his displeasure are already numbered with the dead." Disdaining the language of flattery, the historian may confess that in questions of private jurisprudence, the absolute sovereign of a great empire can seldom be influenced by any personal considerations. Virtue, or even reason, will suggest to his impartial mind that he is the guardian of peace and equity, and that the interest of society is inseparably connected with his own. Under the weakest and most vicious reign, the seat of justice was filled by the wisdom and integrity of Papinian and Ulpian; and the purest materials of the Code and Pandects are inscribed with the names of Caracalla and his ministers. The tyrant of Rome was sometimes the benefactor of the provinces. A dagger terminated the crimes of Domitian; but the prudence of Nerva confirmed his acts, which in the joy of their deliverance had been rescinded by an indignant senate. Yet in the *rescripts,* replies to the consultations of the magistrates, the wisest of princes might be deceived by a partial exposition of the case. And this abuse, which placed their hasty decisions on the same level with mature and deliberate acts of legislation, was ineffectually condemned by the sense and example of Trajan. The rescripts of the emperor, his *grants* and *decrees,* his *edicts* and *pragmatic sanctions,* were subscribed in purple ink and transmitted to the provinces as general or special laws which the magistrates were bound to execute and the people to obey. But as their number continually multiplied, the rule of obedience became each day more doubtful and obscure, till the will of the sovereign was fixed and ascertained in the Gregorian, the Hermogenian, and the Theodosian Codes. The two first, of which some fragments have escaped, were framed by two private lawyers to preserve the constitutions of the Pagan emperors from Hadrian to Constantine. The third, which is still extant, was digested in sixteen books by the order of the younger Theodosius to consecrate the laws of the Christian princes from Constantine to his own reign. But the three codes obtained an equal authority in the tribunals; and any act which was not included in the sacred deposit might be disregarded by the judge as spurious or obsolete.

Among savage nations, the want of letters is imperfectly supplied by the use of visible signs, which awaken attention and perpetuate the remembrance of any public or private transaction. The jurisprudence of the first Romans exhibited the scenes of a pantomime; the words were adapted to the gestures, and the slightest error or neglect in the *forms* of proceeding was sufficient to annul the *substance* of the fairest claim. The communion of the marriage-life was denoted by the necessary elements of fire and water; and the divorced wife resigned the bunch of keys, by the delivery of which she had been invested with the government of the family. The manumission of a son or a slave was performed by turning him round with a gentle blow on the cheek; a work was prohibited by the casting of a stone; prescription was interrupted by the breaking of a branch; the clenched fist was the symbol of a pledge or deposit; the right hand was the gift of faith and confidence. The indenture of covenants was a broken straw; weights and scales were introduced into every payment, and the heir who accepted a testament was sometimes obliged to snap his fingers, to cast away his garments, and to leap or dance with real or affected transport. If a citizen pursued any stolen goods into a neighbor's house, he concealed his nakedness with a linen towel and hid his face with a mask or basin, lest he should encounter the eyes of a virgin or a matron. In a civil action the plaintiff touched the ear of his witness, seized his reluctant adversary by the neck, and implored in solemn lamentation the aid of his fellow-citizens. The two competitors grasped each other's hand as if they stood prepared for combat before the tribunal of the praetor; he commanded them to produce the object of the dispute; they went, they returned with measured steps, and a clod of earth was cast at his feet to represent the field for which they contended. This occult science of the words and actions of law was the inheritance of the pontiffs and patricians. Like the Chaldean astrologers, they announced to their clients the days of business and repose; these important trifles were interwoven with the religion of Numa; and after the publication of the Twelve Tables, the Roman people was still enslaved by the ignorance of judicial proceedings. The treachery of some plebeian officers at length revealed the profitable mystery: in a more enlightened age, the legal actions were derided and observed; and the same antiquity which sanctified the practice, obliterated the use and meaning of this primitive language.

A more liberal art was cultivated, however, by the sages of Rome, who in a stricter sense may be considered as the authors of the civil law. The alteration of the idiom and manners of the Romans rendered the style of the Twelve Tables less familiar to each rising generation, and the doubtful passages were imperfectly explained by the study of legal antiquarians. To define the ambiguities, to circumscribe the latitude, to apply the principles, to extend the consequences, to reconcile the real or apparent contradictions was a much nobler and more important task; and the province of legislation was silently invaded by the expounders of ancient statutes. Their subtle interpretations concurred with the equity of the praetor to reform the tyranny of the darker ages: however strange or intricate the means, it was the aim of artificial jurisprudence to restore the simple dictates of nature and reason, and the skill of private citizens was usefully employed to undermine the public institutions of their country.[†]

When Justinian ascended the throne, the reformation of the Roman jurisprudence was an arduous but indispensable task [A.D. 527 ff.]. In the space of ten centuries, the infinite variety of laws and legal opinions had filled many thousand volumes, which no fortune could purchase and no capacity could digest. Books could not easily be found; and the judges, poor in the midst of riches, were reduced to the exercise of their illiterate discretion. The subjects of the Greek provinces were ignorant of the language that disposed of their lives and properties; and the *barbarous* dialect of the Latins was imperfectly studied in the academies of Beirut and Constantinople. As an Illyrian soldier, that idiom was familiar to the infancy of Justinian; his youth had been instructed by the lessons of jurisprudence, and his Imperial choice selected the most learned civilians of the East to labor with their sovereign in the work of reformation. The theory of professors was assisted by the practice of advocates and the experience of magistrates; and the whole undertaking was animated by the spirit of Tribonian [A.D. 527–546]. This extraordinary man, the object of so much praise and censure, was a native of Side in Pamphylia; and his genius, like that of Bacon, embraced as his own all the business and knowledge of the age. Tribonian composed, both in prose and verse, on a strange diversity of curious and abstruse subjects: a double panegyric of Justinian and the life of the philosopher Theodotus; the nature of happiness and the duties of government; Homer's catalogue and the four-and-twenty sorts of meter; the astronomical canon of Ptolemy; the changes of the months; the houses of the planets; and the harmonic system of the world. To the literature of Greece he added the use of the Latin tongue; the Roman civilians were deposited in his library and in his mind; and he most assiduously cultivated those arts which opened the road of wealth and preferment. From the bar of the Praetorian praefects, he raised himself to the honors of quaestor, of consul, and of master of the offices: the council of Justinian listened to his eloquence and wisdom; and envy was mitigated by the gentleness and affability of his manners. The reproaches of impiety and avarice have stained the virtue or the reputation of Tribonian. In a bigoted and persecuting court, the principal minister was accused of a secret aversion to the Christian faith and was supposed to entertain the sentiments of an Atheist and a Pagan, which have been imputed, inconsistently enough, to the last philosophers of Greece. His avarice was more clearly proved and more sensibly felt. If he were swayed by gifts in the administration of justice, the example of

Bacon will again occur; nor can the merit of Tribonian atone for his baseness if he degraded the sanctity of his profession; and if laws were every day enacted, modified, or repealed for the base consideration of his private emolument. In the sedition of Constantinople, his removal was granted to the clamors, perhaps to the just indignation, of the people: but the quaestor was speedily restored, and till the hour of his death he possessed, above twenty years, the favor and confidence of the emperor. His passive and dutiful submission had been honored with the praise of Justinian himself, whose vanity was incapable of discerning how often that submission degenerated into the grossest adulation. Tribonian adored the virtues of his gracious master; the earth was unworthy of such a prince; and he affected a pious fear, that Justinian, like Elijah or Romulus, would be snatched into the air, and translated alive to the mansions of celestial glory.

If Caesar had achieved the reformation of the Roman law, his creative genius, enlightened by reflection and study, would have given to the world a pure and original system of jurisprudence. Whatever flattery might suggest, the emperor of the East was afraid to establish his private judgment as the standard of equity: in the possession of legislative power, he borrowed the aid of time and opinion; and his laborious compilations are guarded by the sages and legislature of past times. Instead of a statue cast in a simple mold by the hand of an artist, the works of Justinian represent a tessellated pavement of antique and costly, but too often of incoherent, fragments. In the first year of his reign, he directed the faithful Tribonian and nine learned associates to revise the ordinances of his predecessors as they were contained, since the time of Hadrian, in the Gregorian, Hermogenian, and Theodosian Codes; to purge the errors and contradictions, to retrench whatever was obsolete or superfluous, and to select the wise and salutary laws best adapted to the practice of the tribunals and the use of his subjects. The work was accomplished in fourteen months [February 13, A.D. 528–April 7, A.D. 529]; and the twelve books, or *tables*, which the new Decemvirs produced might be designed to imitate the labors of their Roman predecessors. The new CODE of Justinian was honored with his name and confirmed by his royal signature: authentic transcripts were multiplied by the pens of notaries and scribes; they were transmitted to the magistrates of the European, the Asiatic, and afterwards the African provinces; and the law of the empire was proclaimed on solemn festivals at the doors of churches. A more arduous operation was still behind—to extract the spirit of jurisprudence from the decisions and conjectures, the questions and disputes, of the Roman civilians. Seventeen lawyers, with Tribonian at their head, were appointed by the emperor to exercise an absolute jurisdiction over the works of their predecessors. If they had obeyed his commands in ten years, Justinian would have been satisfied with their diligence; and the rapid composition of the DIGEST OF PANDECTS in three years [December 15, A.D. 530–December 16, A.D. 533] will deserve praise or censure according to the merit of the execution. From the library of Tribonian they chose forty, the most eminent civilians of former times: two thousand treatises were comprised in an abridgment of fifty books; and it has been carefully recorded that three millions of lines or sentences were reduced in this abstract to the moderate number of one hundred and fifty thousand. The edition of this great work was delayed a month after that of the INSTITUTES; and it seemed reasonable that the elements should precede the digest of the Roman law. As soon as the emperor had approved their labors, he ratified by his legislative power the speculations of these private citizens: their commentaries on the Twelve Tables, the perpetual edict, the laws of the people, and the decrees of the senate succeeded to the authority of the text; and the text was abandoned as a useless though venerable relic of antiquity. The *Code,* the *Pandects,* and the *Institutes* were declared to be the legitimate system of civil jurisprudence; they alone were admitted into the tribunals, and they alone were taught in the academies of Rome, Constantinople, and Beirut. Justinian addressed to the senate and provinces his *eternal oracles;* and his pride, under the mask of piety, ascribed the consummation of this great design to the support and inspiration of the Deity.

Since the emperor declined the fame and envy of original composition, we can only require, at his hands, method, choice, and fidelity, the humble, though indispensable, virtues of a compiler. Among the various combinations of ideas, it is difficult to assign any reasonable preference; but as the order of Justinian is different in his three works, it is possible that all may be wrong; and it is certain that two cannot be right. In the selection of ancient laws, he seems to have viewed his predecessors without jealousy and with equal regard: the series could not ascend above the reign of Hadrian, and the narrow distinction of Paganism and Christianity introduced by the superstition of Theodosius had been abolished by the consent of mankind. But the jurisprudence of the Pandects is circumscribed within a period of a hundred years, from the perpetual edict to the death of Severus Alexander: the civilians who lived under the first Caesars are seldom permitted to speak, and only three names can be attributed to the age of the republic. The favorite of Justinian (it has been fiercely urged) was fearful of encountering the light of freedom and the gravity of Roman sages. Tribonian condemned to oblivion the genuine and native wisdom of Cato, the Scaevolas, and Sulpicius; while he invoked spirits more congenial to his own, the Syrians, Greeks, and Africans, who flocked to the Imperial court to study Latin as a foreign tongue and jurisprudence as a lucrative profession. But the ministers of Justinian were instructed to labor not for the curiosity of antiquarians but for the immediate benefit of his subjects. It was their duty to select the useful and practical parts of the Roman law; and the writings of the old republicans, however curious or excellent, were no longer suited to the new system of manners, religion, and government. Perhaps if the preceptors and friends of Cicero were still alive, our candor would acknowledge that, except in purity of language, their intrinsic merit was excelled by the school of Papinian and Ulpian. The science of the laws is the slow growth of time and experience, and the advantage both of method and materials is naturally assumed by the most recent authors. The civilians of the reign of the Antonines had studied the works of their predecessors: their philosophic spirit had mitigated the rigor of antiquity, simplified the forms of proceeding, and emerged from the jealousy and prejudice of the rival sects. The choice of the authorities that compose the Pandects depended on the judgment of Tribonian: but the power of his sovereign could not absolve him from the sacred obligations of truth and fidelity. As the legislator of the empire, Justinian might repeal the acts of the Antonines, or condemn as seditious the free principles which were maintained by the last of the *Roman* lawyers. But the existence of past facts is placed beyond the reach of despotism; and the emperor was guilty of fraud and forgery when he corrupted the integrity of their text, inscribed with their venerable names the words and ideas of his servile reign, and suppressed by the hand of power the pure and authentic copies of their sentiments. The changes and interpolations of Tribonian and his colleagues are excused by the pretense of uniformity: but their cares have been insufficient, and the *antinomies* or contradictions of the Code and Pandects still exercise the patience and subtlety of modern civilians.

A rumor devoid of evidence has been propagated by the enemies of Justinian; that the jurisprudence of ancient Rome was reduced to ashes by the author of the Pandects, from the vain persuasion that it was now either false or superfluous. Without usurping an office so invidious, the emperor might safely commit to ignorance and time the accomplishments of this destructive wish. Before the invention of printing and paper, the labor and the materials of writing could be purchased only by the rich; and it may reasonably be computed that the price of books was a hundred fold their present value. Copies were slowly multiplied and cautiously renewed: the hopes of profit tempted the sacrilegious scribes to erase the characters of antiquity, and Sophocles or Tacitus were obliged to resign the parchment to missals, homilies, and the golden legend. If such was the fate of the most beautiful compositions of genius, what stability could be expected for the dull and barren works of an obsolete science? The books of jurisprudence were interesting to few and entertaining to none: their value was connected with present use, and they sunk forever as soon as that use was superseded by the innovations of fashion, superior merit, or public authority.†

It is the first care of a reformer to prevent any future reformation. To maintain the text of the Pandects, the Institutes, and the Code, the use of ciphers and abbreviations was rigorously proscribed; and as Justinian recollected that the perpetual edict had been buried under the weight of commentators, he denounced the punishment of forgery against the rash civilians who should presume to interpret or pervert the will of their sovereign. The scholars of Accursius, of Bartolus, of Cujacius should blush for their accumulated guilt, unless they dare to dispute his right of binding the authority of his successors and the native freedom of the mind. But the emperor was unable to fix his own inconstancy.... Six years had not elapsed from the publication of the Code before he condemned the imperfect attempt by a new and more accurate edition of the same work; which he enriched with two hundred of his own laws, and fifty decisions of the darkest and most intricate points of jurisprudence [November 16, A.D. 534]. Every year, or, according to Procopius, each day, of his long reign was marked by some legal innovation. Many of his acts were rescinded by himself; many were rejected by his successors; many have been obliterated by time; but the number of sixteen EDICTS, and one hundred and sixty-eight NOVELS has been admitted into the authentic body of the civil jurisprudence [A.D. 534–565]. In the opinion of a philosopher superior to the prejudices of his profession, these incessant and for the most part trifling alterations can be only explained by the venal spirit of a prince who sold without shame his judgments and his laws. . . . If candor will acquit the emperor himself and transfer the corruption to his wife and favorites, the suspicion of so foul a vice must still degrade the majesty of his laws; and the advocates of Justinian may acknowledge that such levity, whatsoever be the motive, is unworthy of a legislator and a man.

Monarchs seldom condescend to become the preceptors of their subjects; and some praise is due to Justinian, by whose command an ample system was reduced to a short and elementary treatise [November 21, A.D. 533]. Among the various institutes of the Roman law, those of Gaius were the most popular in the East and West; and their use may be considered as an evidence of their merit. They were selected by the Imperial delegates, Tribonian, Theophilus, and Dorotheus; and the freedom and purity of the Antonines was encrusted with the coarser materials of a degenerate age. The same volume which introduced the youth of Rome, Constantinople, and Beirut to the gradual study of the Code and Pandects is still precious to the historian, the philosopher, and the magistrate. The INSTITUTES of Justinian are divided into four books: they proceed, with no contemptible method, from I. *Persons,* to II. *Things,* and from things to III. *Actions;* and the article IV, of *Private Wrongs,* is terminated by the principles of *Criminal Law.*

The distinction of ranks and *persons* is the firmest basis of a mixed and limited government. . . . Two hundred families supply, in lineal descent, the second branch of English legislature, which maintains between the king and commons the balance of the constitution. A gradation of patricians and plebeians, of strangers and subjects, has supported the aristocracy of Genoa, Venice, and ancient Rome. The perfect equality of men is the point in which the extremes of democracy and despotism are confounded; since the majesty of the prince or people would be offended if any heads were exalted above the level of their fellow-slaves or fellow-citizens. In the decline of the Roman empire, the proud distinctions of the republic were gradually abolished, and the reason or instinct of Justinian completed the simple form of an absolute monarchy. The emperor could not eradicate the popular reverence which always waits on the possession of hereditary wealth or the memory of famous ancestors. He delighted to honor, with titles and emoluments, his generals, magistrates, and senators; and his precarious indulgence communicated some rays of their glory to the persons of their wives and children. But in the eye of the law, all Roman citizens were equal, and all subjects of the empire were citizens of Rome. That inestimable character was degraded to an obsolete and empty name. The voice of a Roman could no longer enact his laws or create the annual ministers of his power: his constitutional rights might have checked the arbitrary will of a master: and the bold adventurer from Germany or Arabia was admitted with equal favor to the civil and military command, which the citizen alone had been once entitled to assume over the conquests of his fathers.[†]

The law of nature instructs most animals to cherish and educate their infant progeny. The law of reason inculcates to the human species the returns of filial piety. But the exclusive, absolute, and perpetual dominion of the father over his children is peculiar to the Roman jurisprudence, and seems to be coeval with the foundation of the city. The paternal power was instituted or confirmed by Romulus himself; and after the practice of three centuries, it was inscribed on the fourth table of the Decemvirs. In the forum, the senate, or the camp, the adult son of a Roman citizen enjoyed the public and private rights of a *person:* in his father's house he was a mere *thing,* confounded by the laws with the movables, the cattle, and the slaves, whom the capricious master might alienate or destroy without being responsible to any earthly tribunal. The hand which bestowed the daily sustenance might resume the voluntary gift, and whatever was acquired by the labor or fortune of the son was immediately lost in the property of the father. His stolen goods (his oxen or his children) might be recovered by the same action of theft; and if either had been guilty of a trespass, it was in his own option to compensate the damage or resign to the injured party the obnoxious animal. At the call of indigence or avarice, the master of a family could dispose of his children or his slaves. But the condition of the slave was far more advantageous, since he regained, by the first manumission, his alienated freedom: the son was again restored to his unnatural father; he might be condemned to servitude a second and a third time, and it was not till after the third sale and deliverance that he was enfranchised from the domestic power which had been so repeatedly abused. According to his discretion, a father might chastise the real or imaginary faults of his children by stripes, by imprisonment, by exile, by sending them to the country to work in chains among the meanest of his servants. The majesty of a parent was armed with the power of life and death; and the examples of such bloody executions, which were sometimes praised and never punished, may be traced in the annals of Rome beyond the times of Pompey and Augustus. Neither age, nor rank, nor the consular office, nor the honors of a triumph could exempt the most illustrious citizen from the bonds of filial subjection: his own descendants were included in the family of their common ancestor; and the claims of adoption were not less sacred or less rigorous than those of nature. Without fear, though not without danger of abuse, the Roman legislators had reposed an unbounded confidence in the sentiments of paternal love; and the oppression was tempered by the assurance that each generation must succeed in its turn to the awful dignity of parent and master.[†]

The Roman father, from the license of servile dominion, was reduced [by Augustus] to the gravity and moderation of a judge. The presence and opinion of Augustus confirmed the sentence of exile pronounced against an intentional parricide by the domestic tribunal of Arius. Hadrian transported to an island the jealous parent who, like a robber, had seized the opportunity of hunting to assassinate a youth, the incestuous lover of his step-mother. A private jurisdiction is repugnant to the spirit of monarchy; the parent was again reduced from a judge to an accuser; and the magistrates were enjoined by Severus Alexander to hear his complaints and execute his sentence. He could no longer take the life of a son without incurring the guilt and punishment of murder; and the pains of parricide from which he had been excepted by the Pompeian law were finally inflicted by the justice of Constantine. The same protection was due to every period of existence; and reason must applaud the humanity of Paulus for imputing the crime of murder to the father who strangles, or starves, or abandons his new-born infant, or exposes him in a public place to find the mercy which he himself had denied. But the exposition of children was the prevailing and stubborn vice of antiquity: it was sometimes prescribed, often permitted, almost always practiced with impunity by the nations who never entertained the Roman ideas of paternal power; and the dramatic poets who appeal to the human heart represent with indifference a popular custom which was palliated by the motives of economy and compassion. If the father could subdue his own feelings, he might escape, though not the censure, at least the chastisement, of the laws; and the Roman empire was stained with the blood of infants till such murders were included, by Valentinian and his colleagues, in the letter and spirit of the Cornelian law. The lessons of jurisprudence and Christianity had been insufficient to eradicate this inhuman practice till their gentle influence was fortified by the terrors of capital punishment.

Experience has proved that savages are the tyrants of the female sex, and that the condition of women is usually softened by the refinements of social life. In the hope of a robust progeny, Lycurgus had delayed the season of marriage: it was fixed by Numa at the tender age of twelve years that the Roman husband might educate to his will a pure and obedient virgin. According to the custom of antiquity, he bought his bride of her parents, and she fulfilled the *coemption* by purchasing, with three pieces of copper, a just introduction to his house and household deities. A sacrifice of fruits was offered by the pontiffs in the presence of ten witnesses; the contracting parties were seated on the same sheep-skin; they tasted a salt cake of *far* or rice; and this *confarreation,* which denoted the ancient food of Italy, served as an emblem of their mystic union of mind and body. But this union on the side of the woman was rigorous and unequal; and she renounced the name and worship of her father's house to embrace a new servitude, decorated only by the title of adoption. A fiction of the law, neither rational nor elegant, bestowed on the mother of a family (her proper appellation) the strange characters of sister to her own children and of daughter to her husband or master, who was invested with the plenitude of paternal power. By his judgment or caprice her behavior was approved, or censured, or chastised; he exercised the jurisdiction of life and death; and it was allowed that in the cases of adultery or drunkenness, the sentence might be properly inflicted. She acquired and inherited for the sole profit of her lord; and so clearly was woman defined not as a *person* but as a *thing* that if the original title were deficient, she might be claimed, like other movables, by the use and possession of an entire year. The inclination of the Roman husband discharged or withheld the conjugal debt so scrupulously exacted by the Athenian and Jewish laws: but as polygamy was unknown, he could never admit to his bed a fairer or a more favored partner.

After the Punic triumphs, the matrons of Rome aspired to the common benefits of a free and opulent republic: their wishes were gratified by the indulgence of fathers and lovers, and their ambition was unsuccessfully resisted by the gravity of Cato the Censor. They declined the solemnities of the old nuptials; defeated the annual prescription by an absence of three days; and, without losing their name or independence, subscribed the liberal and definite terms of a marriage contract. Of their private fortunes, they communicated the use and secured the property: the estates of a wife could neither be alienated nor mortgaged by a prodigal husband; their mutual gifts were prohibited by the jealousy of the laws; and the misconduct of either party might afford, under another name, a future subject for an action of theft. To this loose and voluntary compact, religious and civil rights were no longer essential; and between persons of a similar rank, the apparent community of life was allowed as sufficient evidence of their nuptials. The dignity of marriage was restored by the Christians, who derived all spiritual grace from the prayers of the faithful and the benediction of the priest or bishop. The origin, validity, and duties of the holy institution were regulated by the tradition of the synagogue, the precepts of the gospel, and the canons of general or provincial synods; and the conscience of the Christians was awed by the decrees and censures of their ecclesiastical rulers. Yet the magistrates of Justinian were not subject to the authority of the church: the emperor consulted the unbelieving civilians of antiquity, and the choice of matrimonial laws in the Code and Pandects is directed by the earthly motives of justice, policy, and the natural freedom of both sexes.

Besides the agreement of the parties, the essence of every rational contract, the Roman marriage required the previous approbation of the parents. A father might be forced by some recent laws to supply the wants of a mature daughter; but even his insanity was not gradu-

ally allowed to supersede the necessity of his consent. The causes of
the dissolution of matrimony have varied among the Romans; but the
most solemn sacrament, the *confarreation* itself, might always be done
away by rites of a contrary tendency. In the first ages, the father of a
family might sell his children, and his wife was reckoned in the number of his children: the domestic judge might pronounce the death of
the offender, or his mercy might expel her from his bed and house; but
the slavery of the wretched female was hopeless and perpetual, unless
he asserted for his own convenience the manly prerogative of divorce.
The warmest applause has been lavished on the virtue of the Romans,
who abstained from the exercise of this tempting privilege above five
hundred years: but the same fact evinces the unequal terms of a connection in which the slave was unable to renounce her tyrant, and the
tyrant was unwilling to relinquish his slave. When the Roman matrons
became the equal and voluntary companions of their lords, a new jurisprudence was introduced that marriage, like other partnerships,
might be dissolved by the abdication of one of the associates. In three
centuries of prosperity and corruption, this principle was enlarged to
frequent practice and pernicious abuse. Passion, interest, or caprice
suggested daily motives for the dissolution of marriage; a word, a sign,
a message, a letter, the mandate of a freedman declared the separation;
the most tender of human connections was degraded to a transient society of profit or pleasure. According to the various conditions of life,
both sexes alternately felt the disgrace and injury: an inconstant spouse
transferred her wealth to a new family, abandoning a numerous, perhaps a spurious, progeny to the paternal authority and care of her late
husband; a beautiful virgin might be dismissed to the world, old, indigent, and friendless; but the reluctance of the Romans, when they were
pressed to marriage by Augustus, sufficiently marks that the prevailing
institutions were least favorable to the males. A specious theory is confuted by this free and perfect experiment, which demonstrates that the
liberty of divorce does not contribute to happiness and virtue. The facility of separation would destroy all mutual confidence and inflame
every trifling dispute: the minute difference between a husband and a
stranger, which might so easily be removed, might still more easily be
forgotten; and the matron who in five years can submit to the embraces
of eight husbands must cease to reverence the chastity of her own person.[†]

The Christian princes were the first who specified the just causes of a private divorce; their institutions, from Constantine to Justinian, appear to fluctuate between the custom of the empire and the wishes of the church, and the author of the Novels too frequently reforms the jurisprudence of the Code and Pandects. In the most rigorous laws, a wife was condemned to support a gamester, a drunkard, or a libertine unless he were guilty of homicide, poison, or sacrilege, in which cases the marriage, as it should seem, might have been dissolved by the hand of the executioner. But the sacred right of the husband was invariably maintained, to deliver his name and family from the disgrace of adultery: the list of mortal sins, either male or female, was curtailed and enlarged by successive regulations, and the obstacles of incurable impotence, long absence, and monastic profession were allowed to rescind the matrimonial obligation. Whoever transgressed the permission of the law was subject to various and heavy penalties. The woman was stripped of her wealth and ornaments, without excepting the bodkin of her hair: if the man introduced a new bride into his bed, *her* fortune might be lawfully seized by the vengeance of his exiled wife. Forfeiture was sometimes commuted to a fine; the fine was sometimes aggravated by transportation to an island or imprisonment in a monastery; the injured party was released from the bonds of marriage; but the offender, during life or a term of years, was disabled from the repetition of nuptials. The successor of Justinian yielded to the prayers of his unhappy subjects and restored the liberty of divorce by mutual consent: the civilians were unanimous, the theologians were divided, and the ambiguous word which contains the precept of Christ is flexible to any interpretation that the wisdom of a legislator can demand.†

A sin, a vice, a crime are the objects of theology, ethics, and jurisprudence. Whenever their judgments agree, they corroborate each other; but as often as they differ, a prudent legislator appreciates the guilt and punishment according to the measure of social injury. On this principle, the most daring attack on the life and property of a private citizen is judged less atrocious than the crime of treason or rebellion, which invades the *majesty* of the republic: the obsequious civilians unanimously pronounced that the republic is contained in the person of its chief; and the edge of the Julian law was sharpened by the incessant diligence of the emperors. The licentious commerce of the sexes may be tolerated as an impulse of nature or forbidden as a source of disorder and corruption; but the fame, the fortunes, the family of the husband are seriously injured by the adultery of the wife. The wisdom of Augustus, after curbing the freedom of revenge, applied to this domestic offense the animadversion of the laws: and the guilty parties, after the payment of heavy forfeitures and fines, were condemned to long or perpetual exile in two separate islands. Religion pronounces an equal censure against the infidelity of the husband; but as it is not accompanied by the same civil effects, the wife was never permitted to vindicate her wrongs; and the distinction of simple or double adultery, so familiar and so important in the canon law, is unknown to the jurisprudence of the Code and the Pandects. I touch with reluctance and despatch with impatience a more odious vice, of which modesty rejects the name and nature abominates the idea. The primitive Romans were infected by the example of the Etruscans and Greeks: and in the mad abuse of prosperity and power, every pleasure that is innocent was deemed insipid; and the Scatinian law, which had been extorted by an act of violence, was insensibly abolished by the lapse of time and the multitude of criminals. By this law, the rape, perhaps the seduction, of an ingenuous youth was compensated as a personal injury by the poor damages of ten thousand sesterces, or fourscore pounds; the ravisher might be slain by the resistance or revenge of chastity; and I wish to believe that at Rome as in Athens, the voluntary and effeminate deserter of his sex was degraded from the honors and the rights of a citizen. But the practice of vice was not discouraged by the severity of opinion: the indelible stain of manhood was confounded with the more venial transgressions of fornication and adultery, nor was the licentious lover exposed to the same dishonor which he impressed on the male or female partner of his guilt. From Catullus to Juvenal, the poets accuse and celebrate the degeneracy of the times; and the reformation of manners was feebly attempted by the reason and authority of the civilians till the most virtuous of the Caesars proscribed the sin against nature as a crime against society.

A new spirit of legislation, respectable even in its error, arose in the empire with the religion of Constantine. The laws of Moses were received as the divine original of justice, and the Christian princes adapted their penal statutes to the degrees of moral and religious turpitude. Adultery was first declared to be a capital offense: the frailty of the sexes was assimilated to poison or assassination, to sorcery or parricide; the same penalties were inflicted on the passive and active guilt of pederasty; and all criminals of free or servile condition were either drowned or beheaded or cast alive into the avenging flames. The adulterers were spared by the common sympathy of mankind; but the lovers of their own sex were pursued by general and pious indignation: the impure manners of Greece still prevailed in the cities of Asia, and every vice was fomented by the celibacy of the monks and clergy. Justinian relaxed the punishment at least of female infidelity: the guilty spouse was only condemned to solitude and penance, and at the end of two years she might be recalled to the arms of a forgiving husband. But the same emperor declared himself the implacable enemy of unmanly lust, and the cruelty of his persecution can scarcely be excused by the purity of his motives. In defiance of every principle of justice, he stretched to past as well as future offenses the operations of his edicts, with the previous allowance of a short respite for confession and pardon. A painful death was inflicted by the amputation of the sinful instrument, or the insertion of sharp reeds into the pores and tubes of most exquisite sensibility; and Justinian defended the propriety of the execution, since the criminals would have lost their hands had they been convicted of sacrilege. In this state of disgrace and agony, two bishops, Isaiah of Rhodes and Alexander of Diospolis, were dragged through the streets of Constantinople while their brethren were admonished, by the voice of a crier, to observe this awful lesson and not to pollute the sanctity of their character. Perhaps these prelates were innocent. A sentence of death and infamy was often founded on the slight and suspicious evidence of a child or a servant: the guilt of the green faction, of the rich, and of the enemies of Theodora was presumed by the judges, and pederasty became the crime of those to whom no crime could be imputed. A French philosopher [Montesquieu] has dared to remark that whatever is secret must be doubtful, and that our natural horror of vice may be abused as an engine of tyranny. But the favorable persuasion of the same writer that a legislator may confide in the taste and reason of mankind is impeached by the unwelcome discovery of the antiquity and extent of the disease.[†]

[Prior to the extinction of the republic, a] Roman accused of any capital crime might prevent the sentence of the law by voluntary exile or death. Till his guilt had been legally proved, his innocence was presumed, and his person was free: till the votes of the last *century* had been counted and declared, he might peaceably secede to any of the allied cities of Italy, or Greece, or Asia. His fame and fortunes were preserved, at least to his children, by this civil death; and he might still be happy in every rational and sensual enjoyment, if a mind accustomed to the ambitious tumult of Rome could support the uniformity and silence of Rhodes or Athens. A bolder effort was required to escape from the tyranny of the Caesars; but this effort was rendered familiar by the maxims of the Stoics, the example of the bravest Romans, and the legal encouragements of suicide. The bodies of condemned criminals were exposed to public ignominy, and their children, a more serious evil, were reduced to poverty by the confiscation of their fortunes. But if the victims of Tiberius and Nero anticipated the decree of the prince or senate, their courage and despatch were recompensed by the applause of the public, the decent honors of burial, and the validity of their testaments. The exquisite avarice and cruelty of Domitian appear to have deprived the unfortunate of this last consolation, and it was still denied even by the clemency of the Antonines. A voluntary death which, in the case of a capital offense, intervened between the accusation and the sentence was admitted as a confession of guilt, and the spoils of the deceased were seized by the inhuman claims of the treasury. Yet the civilians have always respected the natural right of a citizen to dispose of his life; and the posthumous disgrace invented by Tarquin [of nailing their dead bodies to crosses] to check the despair of his subjects was never revived or imitated by succeeding tyrants. The powers of this world have indeed lost their dominion over him who is resolved on death; and his arm can only be restrained by the religious apprehension of a future state. Suicides are enumerated by Virgil among the unfortunate rather than the guilty; and the poetical fables of the infernal shades could not seriously influence the faith or practice of mankind. But the precepts of the gospel, or the church, have at length imposed a pious servitude on the minds of Christians, and condemn them to expect without a murmur the last stroke of disease or the executioner.

The penal statutes form a very small proportion of the sixty-two books of the Code and Pandects; and in all judicial proceedings, the life or death of a citizen is determined with less caution or delay than the most ordinary question of covenant or inheritance. This singular distinction, though something may be allowed for the urgent necessity of defending the peace of society, is derived from the nature of criminal and civil jurisprudence. Our duties to the state are simple and uniform: the law by which he is condemned is inscribed not only on brass or marble but on the conscience of the offender, and his guilt is commonly proved by the testimony of a single fact. But our relations to each other are various and infinite; our obligations are created, annulled, and modified by injuries, benefits, and promises; and the interpretation of voluntary contracts and testaments, which are often dictated by fraud or ignorance, affords a long and laborious exercise to the sagacity of the judge. The business of life is multiplied by the extent of commerce and dominion, and the residence of the parties in the distant provinces of an empire is productive of doubt, delay, and inevitable appeals from the local to the supreme magistrate. Justinian, the Greek emperor of Constantinople and the East, was the legal successor of the Latin shepherd who had planted a colony on the banks of the Tiber. In a period of thirteen hundred years, the laws had reluctantly followed the changes of government and manners; and the laudable desire of conciliating ancient names with recent institutions destroyed the harmony and swelled the magnitude of the obscure and irregular system. The laws which excuse on any occasions the ignorance of their subjects confess their own imperfections: the civil jurisprudence, as it was abridged by Justinian, still continued a mysterious science and a profitable trade, and the innate perplexity of the study was involved in tenfold darkness by the private industry of the practitioners. The expense of the pursuit sometimes exceeded the value of the prize, and the fairest rights were abandoned by the poverty or prudence of the claimants. Such costly justice might tend to abate the spirit of litigation, but the unequal pressure serves only to increase the influence of the rich and to aggravate the misery of the poor. By these dilatory and expensive proceedings, the wealthy pleader obtains a more certain advantage than he could hope from the accidental corruption of his judge. The experience of an abuse, from which our own age and country are not perfectly exempt, may sometimes provoke a generous indignation and extort the hasty wish of exchanging our elaborate jurisprudence for the simple and summary decrees of a Turkish *cadhi*. Our calmer reflection will suggest that such forms and delays are necessary to guard the person and property of the citizen; that the discretion of the judge is the first engine of tyranny; and that the laws of a free people should foresee and determine every question that may probably arise in the exercise of power and the transactions of industry. But the government of Justinian united the evils of liberty and servitude; and the Romans were oppressed at the same time by the multiplicity of their laws and the arbitrary will of their master.

CHAPTER XLV

STATE OF ITALY
UNDER THE LOMBARDS

Reign of the younger Justin. • Conquest of Italy by the Lombards. •
Adoption and reign of Tiberius. • Of Maurice. • State of Italy
under the Lombards and the Exarchs of Ravenna. • Distress of
Rome. • Character and pontificate of Gregory the First.

During the last years of Justinian, his infirm mind was devoted to
heavenly contemplation, and he neglected the business of the lower
world. His subjects were impatient of the long continuance of his life
and reign: yet all who were capable of reflection apprehended the moment of his death, which might involve the capital in tumult and the
empire in civil war. Seven nephews of the childless monarch, the sons
or grandsons of his brother and sister, had been educated in the splendor of a princely fortune; they had been shown in high commands to
the provinces and armies; their characters were known, their followers
were zealous, and as the jealousy of age postponed the declaration of
a successor, they might expect with equal hopes the inheritance of
their uncle. He expired in his palace after a reign of thirty-eight years
[November 14, A.D. 565]; and the decisive opportunity was embraced
by the friends of Justin, the son of Vigilantia. At the hour of midnight,
his domestics were awakened by an importunate crowd who thundered at his door and obtained admittance by revealing themselves to
be the principal members of the senate. These welcome deputies announced the recent and momentous secret of the emperor's decease;
reported, or perhaps invented, his dying choice of the best beloved and
most deserving of his nephews, and conjured Justin to prevent the disorders of the multitude if they should perceive with the return of light
that they were left without a master. After composing his countenance
to surprise, sorrow, and decent modesty, Justin, by the advice of his
wife Sophia, submitted to the authority of the senate. He was conducted with speed and silence to the palace; the guards saluted their
new sovereign; and the martial and religious rites of his coronation

were diligently accomplished. By the hands of the proper officers he was invested with the Imperial garments, the red buskins, white tunic, and purple robe [November 15, A.D. 565]. A fortunate soldier, whom he instantly promoted to the rank of tribune, encircled his neck with a military collar; four robust youths exalted him on a shield; he stood firm and erect to receive the adoration of his subjects; and their choice was sanctified by the benediction of the patriarch, who imposed the diadem on the head of an orthodox prince. The hippodrome was already filled with innumerable multitudes; and no sooner did the emperor appear on his throne than the voices of the blue and the green factions were confounded in the same loyal acclamations. In the speeches which Justin addressed to the senate and people, he promised to correct the abuses which had disgraced the age of his predecessor, displayed the maxims of a just and beneficent government, and declared that, on the approaching calends of January, he would revive in his own person the name and liberty of a Roman consul.

[*The Lombards conquer much of Italy (A.D. 568–570).*]

When the nephew of Justinian ascended the throne, he proclaimed a new era of happiness and glory. The annals of the second Justin are marked with disgrace abroad and misery at home. In the West, the Roman empire was afflicted by the loss of Italy, the desolation of Africa, and the conquests of the Persians. Injustice prevailed both in the capital and the provinces: the rich trembled for their property, the poor for their safety, the ordinary magistrates were ignorant or venal, the occasional remedies appear to have been arbitrary and violent, and the complaints of the people could no longer be silenced by the splendid names of a legislator and a conqueror. The opinion which imputes to the prince all the calamities of his times may be countenanced by the historian as a serious truth or a salutary prejudice. Yet a candid suspicion will arise that the sentiments of Justin were pure and benevolent, and that he might have filled his station without reproach if the faculties of his mind had not been impaired by disease, which deprived the emperor of the use of his feet and confined him to the palace, a stranger to the complaints of the people and the vices of the government. The tardy knowledge of his own impotence determined him to lay down the weight of the diadem; and in the choice of a worthy substitute, he showed some symptoms of a discerning and even magnanimous spirit. The only son of Justin and Sophia died in his infancy; their daughter Arabia was the wife of Baduarius, superintendent of the palace and afterwards commander of the Italian armies, who vainly aspired to confirm the rights of marriage by those of adoption. While the empire appeared an object of desire, Justin was accustomed to behold with jealousy and hatred his brothers and cousins, the rivals of his hopes; nor could he depend on the gratitude of those who would accept the purple as a restitution rather than a gift. Of these competitors, one had been removed by exile and afterwards by death; and the emperor himself had inflicted such cruel insults on another that he must either dread his resentment or despise his patience. This domestic animosity was refined into a generous resolution of seeking a successor not in his family but in the republic; and the artful Sophia recommended Tiberius, his faithful captain of the guards, whose virtues and fortune the emperor might cherish as the fruit of his judicious choice. The ceremony of his elevation to the rank of Caesar, or Augustus, was performed in the portico of the palace, in the presence of the patriarch and the senate [December A.D. 574]. Justin collected the remaining strength of his mind and body; but the popular belief that his speech was inspired by the Deity betrays a very humble opinion both of the man and of the times. "You behold," said the emperor, "the ensigns of supreme power. You are about to receive them not from my hand, but from the hand of God. Honor them, and from them you will derive honor. Respect the empress your mother: you are now her son; before, you were her servant. Delight not in blood; abstain from revenge; avoid those actions by which I have incurred the public hatred; and consult the experience rather than the example of your predecessor. As a man, I have sinned; as a sinner, even in this life, I have been severely punished: but these servants (and he pointed to his ministers) who have abused my confidence and inflamed my passions will appear with me before the tribunal of Christ. I have been dazzled by the splendor of the diadem: be thou wise and modest; remember what you have been, remember what you are. You see around us your slaves and your children: with the authority assume the tenderness of a parent. Love your people like yourself; cultivate the affections, maintain the discipline of the army; protect the fortunes of the rich, relieve the necessities of the poor." The assembly, in silence and in tears, applauded the counsels and sympathized with the repentance of their prince; the patriarch rehearsed the prayers of the church; Tiberius received the diadem on his knees; and Justin, who in his abdication appeared most worthy to reign, addressed the new monarch in the following words: "If you consent, I live; if you command, I die: may the God of Heaven and earth infuse into your heart whatever I have neglected or forgotten." The four last years of the emperor Justin were passed in tranquil obscurity: his conscience was no longer tormented by the remembrance of those duties which he was incapable of discharging; and his choice was justified by the filial reverence and gratitude of Tiberius.[†]

With the odious name of Tiberius, he assumed the more popular appellation of Constantine, and imitated the purer virtues of the Antonines. After recording the vice or folly of so many Roman princes, it is pleasing to repose for a moment on a character conspicuous by the qualities of humanity, justice, temperance, and fortitude; to contemplate a sovereign [A.D. 578–582] affable in his palace, pious in the church, impartial on the seat of judgment, and victorious, at least by his generals, in the Persian war. The most glorious trophy of his victory consisted in a multitude of captives, whom Tiberius entertained, redeemed, and dismissed to their native homes with the charitable spirit of a Christian hero. The merit or misfortunes of his own subjects had a dearer claim to his beneficence, and he measured his bounty not so much by their expectations as by his own dignity. This maxim, however dangerous in a trustee of the public wealth, was balanced by a principle of humanity and justice which taught him to abhor as of the basest alloy the gold that was extracted from the tears of the people. For their relief, as often as they had suffered by natural or hostile calamities, he was impatient to remit the arrears of the past or the demands of future taxes: he sternly rejected the servile offerings of his ministers, which were compensated by tenfold oppression; and the wise and equitable laws of Tiberius excited the praise and regret of succeeding times. Constantinople believed that the emperor had discovered a treasure: but his genuine treasure consisted in the practice of liberal economy and the contempt of all vain and superfluous expense. The Romans of the East would have been happy if the best gift of Heaven, a patriot king, had been confirmed as a proper and permanent blessing. But in less than four years after the death of Justin, his worthy successor sunk into a mortal disease which left him only sufficient time to restore the diadem, according to the tenure by which he held it, to the most deserving of his fellow-citizens. He selected Maurice from the crowd, a judgment more precious than the purple itself: the patriarch and senate were summoned to the bed of the dying prince: he bestowed his daughter and the empire; and his last advice was solemnly delivered by the voice of the quaestor. Tiberius expressed his hope that the virtues of his son and successor would erect the noblest mausoleum to his memory. His memory was embalmed by the public affliction; but the most sincere grief evaporates in the tumult of a new reign, and the eyes and acclamations of mankind were speedily directed to the rising sun.

The emperor Maurice [who reigned A.D. 582–602] derived his origin from ancient Rome; but his immediate parents were settled at Arabissus in Cappadocia, and their singular felicity preserved them alive to behold and partake the fortune of their *august* son. The youth of Maurice was spent in the profession of arms: Tiberius promoted him to the command of a new and favorite legion of twelve thousand confederates; his valor and conduct were signalized in the Persian war; and he returned to Constantinople to accept as his just reward the inheritance of the empire. Maurice ascended the throne at the mature age of forty-three years; and he reigned above twenty years over the East and over himself; expelling from his mind the wild democracy of passions and establishing (according to the quaint expression of Evagrius) a perfect aristocracy of reason and virtue. Some suspicion will degrade the testimony of a subject, though he protests that his secret praise should never reach the ear of his sovereign, and some failings seem to place the character of Maurice below the purer merit of his predecessor. His cold and reserved demeanor might be imputed to arrogance; his justice was not always exempt from cruelty, nor his clemency from weakness; and his rigid economy too often exposed him to the reproach of avarice. But the rational wishes of an absolute monarch must tend to the happiness of his people. Maurice was endowed with sense and courage to promote that happiness, and his administration was directed by the principles and example of Tiberius. The pusillanimity of the Greeks had introduced so complete a separation between the offices of king and of general that a private soldier who had deserved and obtained the purple seldom or never appeared at the head of his armies. Yet the emperor Maurice enjoyed the glory of restoring the Persian monarch to his throne; his lieutenants waged a doubtful war against the Avars of the Danube; and he cast an eye of pity, of ineffectual pity, on the abject and distressful state of his Italian provinces.

From Italy the emperors were incessantly tormented by tales of misery and demands of succor, which extorted the humiliating confession of their own weakness. The expiring dignity of Rome was only marked by the freedom and energy of her complaints: "If you are incapable," she said, "of delivering us from the sword of the Lombards, save us at least from the calamity of famine." Tiberius forgave the reproach and relieved the distress: a supply of corn was transported from Egypt to the Tiber; and the Roman people, invoking the name not of Camillus but of St. Peter, repulsed the Barbarians from their walls. But the relief was accidental, the danger was perpetual and pressing; and the clergy and senate, collecting the remains of their ancient opulence, a sum of three thousand pounds of gold, despatched the patrician Pamphronius to lay their gifts and their complaints at the foot of the Byzantine throne [A.D. 577]. The attention of the court and the forces of the East were diverted by the Persian war: but the justice of Tiberius applied the subsidy to the defense of the city; and he dismissed the patrician with his best advice, either to bribe the Lombard chiefs or to purchase the aid of the kings of France. Notwithstanding this weak invention, Italy was still afflicted, Rome was again besieged, and the suburb of Classe, only three miles from Ravenna, was pillaged and occupied by the troops of a simple duke of Spoleto [A.D. 579]. Maurice gave audience to a second deputation of priests and senators: the duties and the menaces of religion were forcibly urged in the letters of the Roman pontiff; and his nuncio, the deacon Gregory, was alike qualified to solicit the powers either of Heaven or of the earth. The emperor adopted with stronger effect the measures of his predecessor: some formidable chiefs were persuaded to embrace the friendship of the Romans; and one of them, a mild and faithful Barbarian, lived and died in the service of the exarchs: the passes of the Alps were delivered to the Franks; and the pope encouraged them to violate without scruple their oaths and engagements to the misbelievers.†

During a period of two hundred years, Italy was unequally divided between the kingdom of the Lombards and the exarchate of Ravenna. The offices and professions which the jealousy of Constantine had separated were united by the indulgence of Justinian; and eighteen successive exarchs were invested, in the decline of the empire, with the full remains of civil, of military, and even of ecclesiastical power. Their immediate jurisdiction . . . was afterwards consecrated as the patrimony of St. Peter. . . . On the map of Italy, the measure of the exarchate occupies a very inadequate space, but it included an ample proportion of wealth, industry, and population. The most faithful and valuable subjects escaped from the Barbarian yoke. . . . The remainder of Italy was possessed by the Lombards; and from Pavia, the royal seat, their kingdom was extended to the east, the north, and the west, as far as the confines of the Avars, the Bavarians, and the Franks of Austrasia and Burgundy.†

In comparing the proportion of the victorious and the vanquished people, the change of language will afford the most probable inference. According to this standard, it will appear that the Lombards of Italy and the Visigoths of Spain were less numerous than the Franks or Burgundians; and the conquerors of Gaul must yield in their turn to the multitude of Saxons and Angles who almost eradicated the idioms of Britain. The modern Italian has been insensibly formed by the mixture of nations: the awkwardness of the Barbarians in the nice management of declensions and conjugations reduced them to the use of articles and auxiliary verbs; and many new ideas have been expressed by Teutonic appellations. Yet the principal stock of technical and familiar words is found to be of Latin derivation; and if we were sufficiently conversant with the obsolete, the rustic, and the municipal dialects of ancient Italy, we should trace the origin of many terms which might, perhaps, be rejected by the classic purity of Rome.†

So rapid was the influence of climate and example that the Lombards of the fourth generation surveyed with curiosity and affright the portraits of their savage forefathers. Their heads were shaven behind, but the shaggy locks hung over their eyes and mouth, and a long beard represented the name and character of the nation. Their dress consisted of loose linen garments after the fashion of the Anglo-Saxons which were decorated, in their opinion, with broad stripes or variegated colors. The legs and feet were clothed in long hose and open sandals; and even in the security of peace a trusty sword was constantly girt to their side. Yet this strange apparel and horrid aspect often concealed a gentle and generous disposition; and as soon as the rage of battle had subsided, the captives and subjects were sometimes surprised by the humanity of the victor. The vices of the Lombards were the effect of passion, of ignorance, of intoxication; their virtues are the more laudable as they were not affected by the hypocrisy of social manners nor imposed by the rigid constraint of laws and education.[†]

Amidst the arms of the Lombards and under the despotism of the Greeks, we again inquire into the fate of Rome, which had reached, about the close of the sixth century, the lowest period of her depression. By the removal of the seat of empire and the successive loss of the provinces, the sources of public and private opulence were exhausted: the lofty tree under whose shade the nations of the earth had reposed was deprived of its leaves and branches, and the sapless trunk was left to wither on the ground. The ministers of command and the messengers of victory no longer met on the Appian or Flaminian way; and the hostile approach of the Lombards was often felt and continually feared. The inhabitants of a potent and peaceful capital who visit without an anxious thought the garden of the adjacent country will faintly picture in their fancy the distress of the Romans: they shut or opened their gates with a trembling hand, beheld from the walls the flames of their houses, and heard the lamentations of their brethren, who were coupled together like dogs and dragged away into distant slavery beyond the sea and the mountains. Such incessant alarms must annihilate the pleasures and interrupt the labors of a rural life; and the Campagna of Rome was speedily reduced to the state of a dreary wilderness in which the land is barren, the waters are impure, and the air is infectious. Curiosity and ambition no longer attracted the nations to the capital of the world: but if chance or necessity directed the steps of a wandering stranger, he contemplated with horror the vacancy and solitude of the city, and might be tempted to ask, Where is the senate, and where are the people? In a season of excessive rains, the Tiber swelled above its banks and rushed with irresistible violence into the valleys of the seven hills. A pestilential disease arose from the stagnation of the deluge, and so rapid was the contagion that fourscore persons expired in an hour in the midst of a solemn procession which implored the mercy of Heaven. A society in which marriage is encouraged and industry prevails soon repairs the accidental losses of pestilence and war: but as the far greater part of the Romans was condemned to hopeless indigence and celibacy, the depopulation was constant and visible, and the gloomy enthusiasts might expect the approaching failure of the human race. Yet the number of citizens still exceeded the measure of subsistence: their precarious food was supplied from the harvests of Sicily or Egypt; and the frequent repetition of famine betrays the inattention of the emperor to a distant province. The edifices of Rome were exposed to the same ruin and decay: the moldering fabrics were easily overthrown by inundations, tempests, and earthquakes: and the monks who had occupied the most advantageous stations exulted in their base triumph over the ruins of antiquity. It is commonly believed that Pope Gregory the First attacked the temples and mutilated the statues of the city; that by the command of the Barbarian the Palatine library was reduced to ashes, and that the history of Livy was the peculiar mark of his absurd and mischievous fanaticism. The writings of Gregory himself reveal his implacable aversion to the monuments of classic genius; and he points his severest censure against the profane learning of a bishop who taught the art of grammar, studied the Latin poets, and pronounced with the same voice the praises of Jupiter and those of Christ. But the evidence of his destructive rage is doubtful and recent: the temple of Peace or the theater of Marcellus have been demolished by the slow operation of ages, and a formal proscription would have multiplied the copies of Virgil and Livy in the countries which were not subject to the ecclesiastical dictator.

Like Thebes or Babylon or Carthage, the name of Rome might have been erased from the earth if the city had not been animated by a vital principle which again restored her to honor and dominion. A vague tradition was embraced that two Jewish teachers, a tent-maker and a fisherman, had formerly been executed in the circus of Nero, and at the end of five hundred years their genuine or fictitious relics were adored as the Palladium of Christian Rome. The pilgrims of the East and West resorted to the holy threshold; but the shrines of the apostles were guarded by miracles and invisible terrors; and it was not without fear that the pious Catholic approached the object of his worship. It was fatal to touch, it was dangerous to behold the bodies of the saints; and those who from the purest motives presumed to disturb the repose of the sanctuary were affrighted by visions or punished with sudden death. The unreasonable request of an empress who wished to deprive the Romans of their sacred treasure, the head of St. Paul, was rejected with the deepest abhorrence; and the pope asserted, most probably with truth, that a linen which had been sanctified in the neighborhood of his body, or the filings of his chain, which it was sometimes easy and sometimes impossible to obtain, possessed an equal degree of miraculous virtue. But the power as well as virtue of the apostles resided with living energy in the breast of their successors; and the chair of St. Peter was filled under the reign of Maurice by the first and greatest of the name of Gregory.

The pontificate of Gregory the *Great,* which lasted thirteen years, six months, and ten days, is one of the most edifying periods of the history of the church [February 8, A.D. 590–March 12, A.D. 604]. His virtues and even his faults, a singular mixture of simplicity and cunning, of pride and humility, of sense and superstition, were happily suited to his station and to the temper of the times. In his rival, the patriarch of Constantinople, he condemned the anti-Christian title of universal bishop, which the successor of St. Peter was too haughty to concede and too feeble to assume; and the ecclesiastical jurisdiction of Gregory was confined to the triple character of Bishop of Rome, Primate of Italy, and Apostle of the West. He frequently ascended the pulpit and kindled, by his rude though pathetic eloquence, the congenial passions of his audience: the language of the Jewish prophets was interpreted and applied; and the minds of a people depressed by their present calamities were directed to the hopes and fears of the invisible world. His precepts and example defined the model of the Roman liturgy; the distribution of the parishes, the calendar of the festivals, the order of processions, the service of the priests and deacons, the variety and change of sacerdotal garments. Till the last days of his life, he officiated in the canon of the mass, which continued above three hours: the Gregorian chant has preserved the vocal and instrumental music of the theater, and the rough voices of the Barbarians attempted to imitate the melody of the Roman school. Experience had shown him the efficacy of these solemn and pompous rites to soothe the distress, to confirm the faith, to mitigate the fierceness, and to dispel the dark enthusiasm of the vulgar, and he readily forgave their tendency to promote the reign of priesthood and superstition. The bishops of Italy and the adjacent islands acknowledged the Roman pontiff as their special metropolitan. Even the existence, the union, or the translation of episcopal seats was decided by his absolute discretion: and his successful inroads into the provinces of Greece, of Spain, and of Gaul might countenance the more lofty pretensions of succeeding popes. He interposed to prevent the abuses of popular elections; his jealous care maintained the purity of faith and discipline; and the apostolic shepherd assiduously watched over the faith and discipline of the subordinate pastors. Under his reign, the Arians of Italy and Spain were reconciled to the Catholic church, and the conquest of Britain reflects less glory on the name of Caesar than on that of Gregory the First. Instead of six legions, forty monks were embarked for that distant island, and the pontiff lamented the austere duties which forbade him to partake the perils of their spiritual warfare. In less than two years, he could announce to the archbishop of Alexandria that they had baptized the king of Kent with ten thousand of his Anglo-Saxons, and that the Roman missionaries, like those of the primitive church, were armed only with spiritual and supernatural powers. The credulity or the prudence of Gregory was always disposed to confirm the truths of religion by the evidence of ghosts, miracles, and resurrections; and posterity has paid to *his* memory the same tribute which he freely granted to the virtue of his own or the preceding generation. The celestial honors have been liberally bestowed by the authority of the popes, but Gregory is the last of their own order whom they have presumed to inscribe in the calendar of saints.

Their temporal power insensibly arose from the calamities of the times: and the Roman bishops, who have deluged Europe and Asia with blood, were compelled to reign as the ministers of charity and peace. I. The church of Rome, as it has been formerly observed, was endowed with ample possessions in Italy, Sicily, and the more distant provinces; and her agents, who were commonly sub-deacons, had acquired a civil and even criminal jurisdiction over their tenants and husbandmen. The successor of St. Peter administered his patrimony with the temper of a vigilant and moderate landlord. . . . II. The misfortunes of Rome involved the apostolical pastor in the business of peace and war; and it might be doubtful to himself whether piety or ambition prompted him to supply the place of his absent sovereign. Gregory awakened the emperor from a long slumber; exposed the guilt or incapacity of the exarch and his inferior ministers; complained that the veterans were withdrawn from Rome for the defense of Spoleto; encouraged the Italians to guard their cities and altars; and condescended, in the crisis of danger, to name the tribunes and to direct the operations of the provincial troops.... The merits of Gregory were treated by the Byzantine court with reproach and insult; but in the attachment of a grateful people, he found the purest reward of a citizen, and the best right of a sovereign.

CHAPTER XLVI

TROUBLES IN PERSIA

*Revolutions in Persia after the death of Chosroes or Nushirvan. •
Usurpation of Bahram. • Flight and restoration of Chosroes II. •
His gratitude to the Romans. • The chagan of the Avars. • Revolt of
the army against Maurice. • His death. • Tyranny of Phocas. •
Elevation of Heraclius. • The Persian war. • Chosroes subdues
Syria, Egypt, and Asia Minor. • Persian expeditions. • Victories
and triumph of Heraclius.*[†]

The conflict of Rome and Persia was prolonged from the death of
Crassus to the reign of Heraclius. An experience of seven hundred
years might convince the rival nations of the impossibility of maintaining their conquests beyond the fatal limits of the Tigris and Euphrates. Yet the emulation of Trajan and Julian was awakened by the
trophies of Alexander, and the sovereigns of Persia indulged the ambitious hope of restoring the empire of Cyrus. Such extraordinary efforts
of power and courage will always command the attention of posterity;
but the events by which the fate of nations is not materially changed
leave a faint impression on the page of history, and the patience of the
reader would be exhausted by the repetition of the same hostilities,
undertaken without cause, prosecuted without glory, and terminated
without effect. The arts of negotiation, unknown to the simple greatness of the senate and the Caesars, were assiduously cultivated by the
Byzantine princes; and the memorials of their perpetual embassies repeat, with the same uniform prolixity, the language of falsehood and
declamation, the insolence of the Barbarians, and the servile temper of
the tributary Greeks. Lamenting the barren superfluity of materials, I
have studied to compress the narrative of these uninteresting transactions: but the just Nushirvan is still applauded as the model of Oriental kings, and the ambition of his grandson Chosroes prepared the
revolution of the East which was speedily accomplished by the arms
and the religion of the successors of Mohammed.

[The Persian king Chosroes, or Nushirvan, is succeeded by his son,
Hormouz (A.D. 579). Hormouz is deposed by his most successful general,
Bahram (A.D. 590). Hormouz's son, Chosroes II, rises to take his displaced
father's throne but is driven into exile. He successfully appeals to the
emperor Maurice and, with Roman assistance, is restored to the throne of
Persia (A.D. 591–603).]

While the majesty of the Roman name was revived in the East, the
prospect of Europe is less pleasing and less glorious. By the departure
of the Lombards and the ruin of the Gepidae, the balance of power
was destroyed on the Danube; and the Avars spread their permanent
dominion from the foot of the Alps to the sea-coast of the Euxine. The
reign of Baian is the brightest era of their monarchy [A.D. 570–600 ff.];
their chagan, who occupied the rustic palace of Attila, appears to have
imitated his character and policy; but as the same scenes were repeated in a smaller circle, a minute representation of the copy would
be devoid of the greatness and novelty of the original. The pride of the
second Justin, of Tiberius, and Maurice was humbled by a proud Barbarian more prompt to inflict than exposed to suffer the injuries of
war; and as often as Asia was threatened by the Persian arms, Europe
was oppressed by the dangerous inroads, or costly friendship, of the
Avars. . . . The warfare of Baian was that of a Tartar; yet his mind was
susceptible of a humane and generous sentiment: he spared [the city
of] Anchialus, whose salutary waters had restored the health of the
best beloved of his wives; and the Romans confessed that their starving army was fed and dismissed by the liberality of a foe. His empire
extended over Hungary, Poland, and Prussia, from the mouth of the
Danube to that of the Oder; and his new subjects were divided and
transplanted by the jealous policy of the conqueror. The eastern regions of Germany, which had been left vacant by the emigration of the
Vandals, were replenished with Sclavonian colonists.†

The Persian alliance restored the troops of the East to the defense
of Europe: and Maurice, who had supported ten years the insolence of
the chagan, declared his resolution to march in person against the Barbarians. In the space of two centuries, none of the successors of Theodosius had appeared in the field: their lives were supinely spent in the
palace of Constantinople; and the Greeks could no longer understand
that the name of *emperor* in its primitive sense denoted the chief of the

armies of the republic. The martial ardor of Maurice was opposed by the grave flattery of the senate, the timid superstition of the patriarch, and the tears of the empress Constantina; and they all conjured him to devolve on some meaner general the fatigues and perils of a Scythian campaign. Deaf to their advice and entreaty, the emperor boldly advanced seven miles from the capital [A.D. 591]; the sacred ensign of the cross was displayed in the front; and Maurice reviewed with conscious pride the arms and numbers of the veterans who had fought and conquered beyond the Tigris. Anchialus was the last term of his progress by sea and land; he solicited without success a miraculous answer to his nocturnal prayers; his mind was confounded by the death of a favorite horse, the encounter of a wild boar, a storm of wind and rain, and the birth of a monstrous child; and he forgot that the best of omens is to unsheathe our sword in the defense of our country. Under the pretense of receiving the ambassadors of Persia, the emperor returned to Constantinople, exchanged the thoughts of war for those of devotion, and disappointed the public hope by his absence and the choice of his lieutenants.†

The theory of war was not more familiar to the camps of Caesar and Trajan than to those of Justinian and Maurice. The iron of Tuscany or Pontus still received the keenest temper from the skill of the Byzantine workmen. The magazines were plentifully stored with every species of offensive and defensive arms. In the construction and use of ships, engines, and fortifications, the Barbarians admired the superior ingenuity of a people whom they had so often vanquished in the field. The science of tactics, the order, evolutions, and stratagems of antiquity, was transcribed and studied in the books of the Greeks and Romans. But the solitude or degeneracy of the provinces could no longer supply a race of men to handle those weapons, to guard those walls, to navigate those ships, and to reduce the theory of war into bold and successful practice. The genius of Belisarius and Narses had been formed without a master and expired without a disciple. Neither honor nor patriotism nor generous superstition could animate the lifeless bodies of slaves and strangers who had succeeded to the honors of the legions: it was in the camp alone that the emperor should have exercised a despotic command; it was only in the camps that his authority was disobeyed and insulted: he appeased and inflamed with gold the licentiousness of the troops; but their vices were inherent, their victories were accidental, and their costly maintenance exhausted the substance of a state which they were unable to defend. After a long and pernicious indulgence, the cure of this inveterate evil was undertaken by Maurice; but the rash attempt, which drew destruction on his own head, tended only to aggravate the disease. A reformer should be exempt from the suspicion of interest, and he must possess the confidence and esteem of those whom he proposes to reclaim. The troops of Maurice might listen to the voice of a victorious leader; they disdained the admonitions of statesmen and sophists; and, when they received an edict which deducted from their pay the price of their arms and clothing, they execrated the avarice of a prince insensible of the dangers and fatigues from which he had escaped. The camps both of Asia and Europe were agitated with frequent and furious seditions; the enraged soldiers of Edessa pursued with reproaches, with threats, with wounds their trembling generals; they overturned the statues of the emperor, cast stones against the miraculous image of Christ, and either rejected the yoke of all civil and military laws or instituted a dangerous model of voluntary subordination. The monarch, always distant and often deceived, was incapable of yielding or persisting according to the exigence of the moment. But the fear of a general revolt induced him too readily to accept any act of valor or any expression of loyalty as an atonement for the popular offense; the new reform was abolished as hastily as it had been announced, and the troops, instead of punishment and restraint, were agreeably surprised by a gracious proclamation of immunities and rewards. But the soldiers accepted without gratitude the tardy and reluctant gifts of the emperor: their insolence was elated by the discovery of his weakness and their own strength; and their mutual hatred was inflamed beyond the desire of forgiveness or the hope of reconciliation. The historians of the times adopt the vulgar suspicion that Maurice conspired to destroy the troops whom he had labored to reform; the misconduct and favor of Commentiolus are imputed to this malevolent design; and every age must condemn the inhumanity or avarice of a prince who, by the trifling ransom of six thousand pieces of gold, might have prevented the massacre of twelve thousand prisoners in the hands of the chagan [A.D. 600]. In the just fervor of indignation, an order was signified to the army of the Danube that they should spare the magazines of the province and establish their winter quarters in the hostile country of the Avars [A.D. 601–602]. The measure of their grievances was full: they pronounced Maurice unworthy to reign, expelled or slaughtered his faithful adherents, and under the command of Phocas, a simple centurion, returned by hasty marches to the neighborhood of Constantinople [October A.D. 602]. After a long series of legal succession, the military disorders of the third century were again revived; yet such was the novelty of the enterprise that the insurgents were awed by their own rashness. They hesitated to invest their favorite with the vacant purple; and while they rejected all treaty with Maurice himself, they held a friendly correspondence with his son Theodosius and with Germanus, the father-in-law of the royal youth. So obscure had been the former condition of Phocas that the emperor was ignorant of the name and character of his rival; but as soon as he learned that the centurion, though bold in sedition, was timid in the face of danger, "Alas!" cried the desponding prince, "if he is a coward, he will surely be a murderer."

Yet if Constantinople had been firm and faithful, the murderer might have spent his fury against the walls; and the rebel army would have been gradually consumed or reconciled by the prudence of the emperor. In the games of the circus, which he repeated with unusual pomp, Maurice disguised with smiles of confidence the anxiety of his heart, condescended to solicit the applause of the *factions*, and flattered their pride by accepting from their respective tribunes a list of nine hundred *blues* and fifteen hundred *greens*, whom he affected to esteem as the solid pillars of his throne. Their treacherous or languid support betrayed his weakness and hastened his fall: the green faction were the secret accomplices of the rebels, and the blues recommended lenity and moderation in a contest with their Roman brethren. The rigid and parsimonious virtues of Maurice had long since alienated the hearts of his subjects: as he walked barefoot in a religious procession, he was rudely assaulted with stones, and his guards were compelled to present their iron maces in the defense of his person. A fanatic monk ran through the streets with a drawn sword, denouncing against him the wrath and the sentence of God; and a vile plebeian who represented his countenance and apparel was seated on an ass and pursued by the imprecations of the multitude. The emperor suspected the popularity of Germanus with the soldiers and citizens: he feared, he threatened, but he delayed to strike; the patrician fled to the sanctuary of the church; the people rose in his defense, the walls were deserted by the guards, and the lawless city was abandoned to the flames and rapine of a nocturnal tumult. In a small bark, the unfortunate Maurice, with his wife and nine children, escaped to the Asiatic shore; but the violence of the wind compelled him to land at the church of St. Autonomus, near Chalcedon, from whence he despatched Theodosius, his eldest son, to implore the gratitude and friendship of the Persian monarch. For himself, he refused to fly: his body was tortured with sciatic pains, his mind was enfeebled by superstition; he patiently awaited the event of the revolution, and addressed a fervent and public prayer to the Almighty that the punishment of his sins might be inflicted in this world rather than in a future life. After the abdication of Maurice, the two factions disputed the choice of an emperor; but the favorite of the blues was rejected by the jealousy of their antagonists, and Germanus himself was hurried along by the crowds who rushed to the palace of Hebdomon, seven miles from the city, to adore the majesty of Phocas the centurion. A modest wish of resigning the purple to the rank and merit of Germanus was opposed by *his* resolution, more obstinate and equally sincere; the senate and clergy obeyed his summons; and as soon as the patriarch was assured of his orthodox belief, he consecrated the successful usurper in the church of St. John the Baptist [November 23, A.D. 602]. On the third day, amidst the acclamations of a thoughtless people, Phocas made his public entry in a chariot drawn by four white horses [November 25]: the revolt of the troops was rewarded by a lavish donative; and the new sovereign, after visiting the palace, beheld from his throne the games of the hippodrome. In a dispute of precedency between the two *factions*, his partial judgment inclined in favor of the *greens*. "Remember that Maurice is still alive" resounded from the opposite side; and the indiscreet clamor of the *blues* admonished and stimulated the cruelty of the tyrant. The ministers of death were despatched to Chalcedon: they dragged the emperor from his sanctuary; and the five sons of Maurice were successively murdered before the eyes of their agonizing parent [November 27]. At each stroke, which he felt in his heart, he found strength to rehearse a pious ejaculation: "Thou art just, O Lord! and thy judgments are righteous." And such in the last moments was his rigid attachment to truth and justice that he revealed to the soldiers the pious falsehood of a nurse who presented her own child in the place of a royal infant. The tragic scene was finally closed by the execution of the emperor himself, in the twentieth year of his reign and the sixty-third of his age. The bodies of the father and his five sons were cast into the sea; their heads were exposed at Constantinople to the insults or pity of the multitude; and it was not till some signs of putrefaction had appeared that Phocas connived at the private burial of these venerable remains. In that grave, the faults and errors of Maurice were kindly interred. His fate alone was remembered; and at the end of twenty years, in the recital of the history of Theophylact, the mournful tale was interrupted by the tears of the audience.

Such tears must have flowed in secret, and such compassion would have been criminal, under the reign of Phocas, who was peaceably acknowledged in the provinces of the East and West. The images of the emperor and his wife Leontia were exposed in the Lateran to the veneration of the clergy and senate of Rome, and afterwards deposited in the palace of the Caesars, between those of Constantine and Theodosius. As a subject and a Christian, it was the duty of Gregory to acquiesce in the established government; but the joyful applause with which he salutes the fortune of the assassin has sullied with indelible disgrace the character of the saint. The successor of the apostles might have inculcated with decent firmness the guilt of blood and the necessity of repentance; he is content to celebrate the deliverance of the people and the fall of the oppressor; to rejoice that the piety and benignity of Phocas have been raised by Providence to the Imperial throne; to pray that his hands may be strengthened against all his enemies; and to express a wish, perhaps a prophecy, that after a long and triumphant reign, he may be transferred from a temporal to an everlasting kingdom. I have already traced the steps of a revolution so pleasing, in Gregory's opinion, both to Heaven and earth; and Phocas does not appear less hateful in the exercise than in the acquisition of power. The pencil of an impartial historian has delineated the portrait of a monster: his diminutive and deformed person, the closeness of his shaggy eyebrows, his red hair, his beardless chin, and his cheek disfigured and discolored by a formidable scar. Ignorant of letters, of laws, and even of arms, he indulged in the supreme rank a more ample privilege of lust and drunkenness; and his brutal pleasures were either injurious to his subjects or disgraceful to himself. Without assuming the office of a prince, he renounced the profession of a soldier; and the reign of Phocas afflicted Europe with ignominious peace and Asia with desolating war. His savage temper was inflamed by passion, hardened by fear, and exasperated by resistance of reproach. The flight of Theodosius to the Persian court had been intercepted by a rapid pursuit or a deceitful message: he was beheaded at Nice, and the last hours of the young prince were soothed by the comforts of religion and the consciousness of innocence. Yet his phantom disturbed the repose of the usurper: a whisper was circulated through the East that the son of Maurice was still alive: the people expected their avenger, and the widow and daughters of the late emperor would have adopted as their son and brother the vilest of mankind. In the massacre of the Imperial family, the mercy, or rather the discretion, of Phocas had spared these unhappy females, and they were decently confined to a private house. But the spirit of the empress Constantina, still mindful of her father, her husband, and her sons, aspired to freedom and revenge. At the dead of night, she escaped to the sanctuary of St. Sophia; but her tears, and the gold of her associate Germanus, were insufficient to provoke an insurrection. Her life was forfeited to revenge, and even to justice: but the patriarch obtained and pledged an oath for her safety: a monastery was allotted for her prison, and the widow of Maurice accepted and abused the lenity of his assassin. The discovery or the suspicion of a second conspiracy dissolved the engagements and rekindled the fury of Phocas. A matron who commanded the respect and pity of mankind, the daughter, wife, and mother of emperors, was tortured like the vilest malefactor to force a confession of her designs and associates; and the empress Constantina, with her three innocent daughters, was beheaded at Chalcedon, on the same ground which had been stained with the blood of her husband and five sons [A.D. 605]. After such an example, it would be superfluous to enumerate the names and sufferings of meaner victims. Their condemnation was seldom preceded by the forms of trial, and their punishment was embittered by the refinements of cruelty: their eyes were pierced, their tongues were torn from the root, the hands and feet were amputated; some expired under the lash, others in the flames; others again were transfixed with arrows; and a simple speedy death was mercy which they could rarely obtain. The hippodrome, the sacred asylum of the pleasures and the liberty of the Romans, was polluted with heads and limbs and mangled bodies; and the companions of Phocas were the most sensible that neither his favor nor their services could protect them from a tyrant, the worthy rival of the Caligulas and Domitians of the first age of the empire.

[*Heraclius, exarch of Africa, rebels successfully; Phocas is put to death, and Heraclius reigns (October 5, A.D. 610–February 11, A.D. 642).*]

Even after his death the republic was afflicted by the crimes of Phocas, which armed with a pious cause the most formidable of her enemies.... Chosroes . . . declared himself the avenger of his father and benefactor. The sentiments of grief and resentment, which humanity would feel and honor would dictate, promoted on this occasion the interest of the Persian king; and his interest was powerfully magnified by the national and religious prejudices of the Magi and satraps. In a strain of artful adulation which assumed the language of freedom, they presumed to censure the excess of his gratitude and friendship for the Greeks; a nation with whom it was dangerous to conclude either peace or alliance; whose superstition was devoid of truth and justice, and who must be incapable of any virtue, since they could perpetrate the most atrocious of crimes, the impious murder of their sovereign. For the crime of an ambitious centurion, the nation which he oppressed was chastised with the calamities of war; and the same calamities, at the end of twenty years, were retaliated and redoubled on the heads of the Persians.

[*Chosroes conquers Syria (A.D. 611) and Palestine (A.D. 614).*]

The conquest of Jerusalem, which had been meditated by Nushirvan, was achieved by the zeal and avarice of his grandson; the ruin of the proudest monument of Christianity was vehemently urged by the intolerant spirit of the Magi; and he could enlist for this holy warfare with an army of six-and-twenty thousand Jews, whose furious bigotry might compensate in some degree for the want of valor and discipline. After the reduction of Galilee and the region beyond the Jordan, whose resistance appears to have delayed the fate of the capital, Jerusalem itself was taken by assault. The sepulchre of Christ and the stately churches of Helena and Constantine were consumed, or at least damaged, by the flames; the devout offerings of three hundred years were rifled in one sacrilegious day; the Patriarch Zachariah and the *true cross* were transported into Persia; and the massacre of ninety thousand

Christians is imputed to the Jews and Arabs who swelled the disorder of the Persian march.

[*Chosroes conquers Egypt (A.D. 616–618) and Asia Minor (A.D. 616).*]

From the long-disputed banks of the Tigris and Euphrates, the reign of the grandson of Nushirvan was suddenly extended to the Hellespont and the Nile, the ancient limits of the Persian monarchy. But the provinces which had been fashioned by the habits of six hundred years to the virtues and vices of the Roman government supported with reluctance the yoke of the Barbarians. The idea of a republic was kept alive by the institutions, or at least by the writings, of the Greeks and Romans, and the subjects of Heraclius had been educated to pronounce the words of liberty and law. But it has always been the pride and policy of Oriental princes to display the titles and attributes of their omnipotence; to upbraid a nation of slaves with their true name and abject condition, and to enforce by cruel and insolent threats the rigor of their absolute commands. The Christians of the East were scandalized by the worship of fire and the impious doctrine of the two principles: the Magi were not less intolerant than the bishops; and the martyrdom of some native Persians who had deserted the religion of Zoroaster was conceived to be the prelude of a fierce and general persecution. By the oppressive laws of Justinian, the adversaries of the church were made the enemies of the state; the alliance of the Jews, Nestorians, and Jacobites had contributed to the success of Chosroes, and his partial favor to the sectaries provoked the hatred and fears of the Catholic clergy. Conscious of their fear and hatred, the Persian conqueror governed his new subjects with an iron scepter; and as if he suspected the stability of his dominion, he exhausted their wealth by exorbitant tributes and licentious rapine; despoiled or demolished the temples of the East; and transported to his hereditary realms the gold, the silver, the precious marbles, the arts, and the artists of the Asiatic cities. . . . While the Persian monarch contemplated the wonders of his art and power, he received an epistle from an obscure citizen of Mecca inviting him to acknowledge Mohammed as the apostle of God. He rejected the invitation and tore the epistle. "It is thus," exclaimed the Arabian prophet, "that God will tear the kingdom and reject the supplications of Chosroes." Placed on the verge of the two great empires of the East, Mohammed observed with secret joy the progress of their mutual destruction; and in the midst of the Persian triumphs, he ventured to foretell that before many years should elapse, victory should again return to the banners of the Romans.

At the time when this prediction is said to have been delivered, no prophecy could be more distant from its accomplishment, since the first twelve years of Heraclius announced the approaching dissolution of the empire [A.D. 610−622]. If the motives of Chosroes had been pure and honorable, he must have ended the quarrel with the death of Phocas, and he would have embraced as his best ally the fortunate African who had so generously avenged the injuries of his benefactor Maurice. The prosecution of the war revealed the true character of the Barbarian; and the suppliant embassies of Heraclius to beseech his clemency, that he would spare the innocent, accept a tribute, and give peace to the world, were rejected with contemptuous silence or insolent menace. Syria, Egypt, and the provinces of Asia were subdued by the Persian arms, while Europe, from the confines of Istria to the long wall of Thrace, was oppressed by the Avars, unsatiated with the blood and rapine of the Italian war.†

Of the characters conspicuous in history, that of Heraclius is one of the most extraordinary and inconsistent. In the first and last years of a long reign, the emperor appears to be the slave of sloth, of pleasure, or of superstition, the careless and impotent spectator of the public calamities. But the languid mists of the morning and evening are separated by the brightness of the meridian sun; the Arcadius of the palace arose the Caesar of the camp; and the honor of Rome and Heraclius was gloriously retrieved by the exploits and trophies of six adventurous campaigns. . . . To provide for the expenses of war was the first care of the emperor; and for the purpose of collecting the tribute, he was allowed to solicit the benevolence of the Eastern provinces. But the revenue no longer flowed in the usual channels; the credit of an arbitrary prince is annihilated by his power; and the courage of Heraclius was first displayed in daring to borrow the consecrated wealth of churches under the solemn vow of restoring with usury whatever he had been compelled to employ in the service of religion and the empire. The clergy themselves appear to have sympathized with the public distress; and the discreet patriarch of Alexandria, without admitting the precedent of sacrilege, assisted his sovereign by the miraculous or seasonable revelation of a secret treasure. Of the soldiers who had conspired with Phocas, only two were found to have survived the stroke of time and of the Barbarians; the loss even of these seditious veterans was imperfectly supplied by the new levies of Heraclius, and the gold of the sanctuary united in the same camp the names and arms and languages of the East and West. He would have been content with the neutrality of the Avars; and his friendly entreaty that the chagan would act not as the enemy but as the guardian of the empire was accompanied with a more persuasive donative of two hundred thousand pieces of gold. Two days after the festival of Easter, the emperor, exchanging his purple for the simple garb of a penitent and warrior, gave the signal of his departure. To the faith of the people Heraclius recommended his children; the civil and military powers were vested in the most deserving hands, and the discretion of the patriarch and senate was authorized to save or surrender the city if they should be oppressed in his absence by the superior forces of the enemy.

[*The provinces conquered by Chosroes are recovered by Heraclius* (A.D. 622–627). *His strategy includes an invasion of Persia.*]

Since the days of Scipio and Hannibal, no bolder enterprise has been attempted than that which Heraclius achieved for the deliverance of the empire. He permitted the Persians to oppress for a while the provinces, and to insult with impunity the capital of the East; while the Roman emperor explored his perilous way through the Black Sea and the mountains of Armenia, penetrated into the heart of Persia, and recalled the armies of the great king to the defense of their bleeding country. . . . In the course of this successful inroad, he signalized the zeal and revenge of a Christian emperor: at his command, the soldiers extinguished the fire and destroyed the temples of the Magi; the statues of Chosroes, who aspired to divine honors, were abandoned to the flames; and the ruins of Thebarma or Ormia, which had given birth to Zoroaster himself, made some atonement for the injuries of the holy sepulchre. A purer spirit of religion was shown in the relief and deliverance of fifty thousand captives. Heraclius was rewarded by their tears and grateful acclamations; but this wise measure, which spread the fame of his benevolence, diffused the murmurs of the Persians against the pride and obstinacy of their own sovereign.

[*Chosroes II is deposed (February 25) and murdered by his son Siroes (February 28, A.D. 628).*]

According to the faith and mercy of his Christian enemies, he sunk without hope into a still deeper abyss; and it will not be denied that tyrants of every age and sect are the best entitled to such infernal abodes. The glory of the house of Sassan ended with the life of Chosroes: his unnatural son enjoyed only eight months the fruit of his crimes: and in the space of four years the regal title was assumed by nine candidates, who disputed with the sword or dagger the fragments of an exhausted monarchy. Every province and each city of Persia was the scene of independence, of discord, and of blood; and the state of anarchy prevailed about eight years longer, till the factions were silenced and united under the common yoke of the Arabian caliphs.

As soon as the mountains became passable, the emperor received the welcome news of the success of the conspiracy, the death of Chosroes, and the elevation of his eldest son to the throne of Persia. The authors of the revolution, eager to display their merits in the court or camp of Tauris, preceded the ambassadors of Siroes, who delivered the letters of their master to his *brother* the emperor of the Romans. In the language of the usurpers of every age, he imputes his own crimes to the Deity and, without degrading his equal majesty, he offers to reconcile the long discord of the two nations by a treaty of peace and alliance more durable than brass or iron. The conditions of the treaty were easily defined and faithfully executed. In the recovery of the standards and prisoners which had fallen into the hands of the Persians, the emperor imitated the example of Augustus: their care of the national dignity was celebrated by the poets of the times, but the decay of genius may be measured by the distance between Horace and George of Pisidia: the subjects and brethren of Heraclius were redeemed from persecution, slavery, and exile; but instead of the Roman eagles, the true wood of the holy cross was restored to the importunate demands of the successor of Constantine. The victor was not ambitious of enlarging the weakness of the empire; the son of Chosroes abandoned without regret the conquests of his father; the Persians who evacuated the cities of Syria and Egypt were honorably conducted to the frontier; and a war which had wounded the vitals of the two monarchies produced no change in their external and relative situation. The return of Heraclius from Tauris to Constantinople was a perpetual triumph; and after the exploits of six glorious campaigns, he peaceably enjoyed the Sabbath of his toils. After a long impatience, the senate, the clergy, and the people went forth to meet their hero with tears and acclamations, with olive branches and innumerable lamps; he entered the capital in a chariot drawn by four elephants; and as soon as the emperor could disengage himself from the tumult of public joy, he tasted more genuine satisfaction in the embraces of his mother and his son.

The succeeding year was illustrated by a triumph of a very different kind, the restitution of the true cross to the holy sepulchre. Heraclius performed in person the pilgrimage of Jerusalem, the identity of the relic was verified by the discreet patriarch, and this august ceremony has been commemorated by the annual festival of the exaltation of the cross. Before the emperor presumed to tread the consecrated ground, he was instructed to strip himself of the diadem and purple, the pomp and vanity of the world: but in the judgment of his clergy, the persecution of the Jews was more easily reconciled with the precepts of the gospel. He again ascended his throne to receive the congratulations of the ambassadors of France and India: and the fame of Moses, Alexander, and Hercules was eclipsed in the popular estimation by the superior merit and glory of the great Heraclius. Yet the deliverer of the East was indigent and feeble. Of the Persian spoils, the most valuable portion had been expended in the war, distributed to the soldiers, or buried by an unlucky tempest in the waves of the Euxine. The conscience of the emperor was oppressed by the obligation of restoring the wealth of the clergy, which he had borrowed for their own defense: a perpetual fund was required to satisfy these inexorable creditors; the provinces, already wasted by the arms and avarice of the Persians, were compelled to a second payment of the same taxes; and the arrears of a simple citizen, the treasurer of Damascus, were commuted to a fine of one hundred thousand pieces of gold. The loss of two hundred thousand soldiers who had fallen by the sword was of less fatal importance than the decay of arts, agriculture, and population in this long and destructive war: and although a victorious army had been formed under the standard of Heraclius, the unnatural effort appears to have exhausted rather than exercised their strength. While the emperor triumphed at Constantinople or Jerusalem, an obscure town on the confines of Syria was pillaged by the Saracens, and they cut in pieces some troops who advanced to its relief; an ordinary and trifling occurrence had it not been the prelude of a mighty revolution. These robbers were the apostles of Mohammed; their fanatic valor had emerged from the desert; and in the last eight years of his reign, Heraclius lost to the Arabs the same provinces which he had rescued from the Persians.

CHAPTER XLVII

ECCLESIASTICAL DISCORD

*Theological history of the doctrine of the Incarnation. •
The human and divine nature of Christ. • Enmity of the
patriarchs of Alexandria and Constantinople. • St. Cyril and
Nestorius. • Third general council of Ephesus. • Heresy of
Eutyches. • Fourth general council of Chalcedon. • Civil and
ecclesiastical discord. • Intolerance of Justinian. •
The Three Chapters. • The Monothelite controversy. • State of the
Oriental sects: I. The Nestorians. II. The Jacobites. III. The
Maronites. IV. The Armenians. V. The Copts and Abyssinians.*

After the extinction of Paganism, the Christians in peace and piety
might have enjoyed their solitary triumph. But the principle of discord
was alive in their bosom, and they were more solicitous to explore the
nature than to practice the laws of their founder. I have already observed that the disputes of the TRINITY were succeeded by those of
the INCARNATION; alike scandalous to the church, alike pernicious to
the state, still more minute in their origin, still more durable in their
effects. It is my design to comprise in the present chapter a religious
war of two hundred and fifty years, to represent the ecclesiastical and
political schism of the Oriental sects, and to introduce their clamorous
or sanguinary contests by a modest inquiry into the doctrines of the
primitive church.

I. [A pure man to the Ebionites.] A laudable regard for the honor
of the first proselyte has countenanced the belief, the hope, the wish
that the Ebionites, or at least the Nazarenes, were distinguished only
by their obstinate perseverance in the practice of the Mosaic rites.
Their churches have disappeared, their books are obliterated: their
obscure freedom might allow a latitude of faith, and the softness of
their infant creed would be variously molded by the zeal or prudence
of three hundred years. Yet the most charitable criticism must refuse
these sectaries any knowledge of the pure and proper divinity of Christ.
Educated in the school of Jewish prophecy and prejudice, they had

never been taught to elevate their hopes above a human and temporal Messiah. If they had courage to hail their king when he appeared in a plebeian garb, their grosser apprehensions were incapable of discerning their God who had studiously disguised his celestial character under the name and person of a mortal. The familiar companions of Jesus of Nazareth conversed with their friend and countryman who, in all the actions of rational and animal life, appeared of the same species with themselves. His progress from infancy to youth and manhood was marked by a regular increase in stature and wisdom; and after a painful agony of mind and body, he expired on the cross. He lived and died for the service of mankind: but the life and death of Socrates had likewise been devoted to the cause of religion and justice; and although the stoic or the hero may disdain the humble virtues of Jesus, the tears which he shed over his friend and country may be esteemed the purest evidence of his humanity. The miracles of the gospel could not astonish a people who held with intrepid faith the more splendid prodigies of the Mosaic law. The prophets of ancient days had cured diseases, raised the dead, divided the sea, stopped the sun, and ascended to Heaven in a fiery chariot. And the metaphorical style of the Hebrews might ascribe to a saint and martyr the adoptive title of SON OF GOD.

Yet in the insufficient creed of the Nazarenes and the Ebionites, a distinction is faintly noticed between the heretics, who confounded the generation of Christ in the common order of nature, and the less guilty schismatics, who revered the virginity of his mother and excluded the aid of an earthly father. The incredulity of the former was countenanced by the visible circumstances of his birth, the legal marriage of the reputed parents, Joseph and Mary, and his lineal claim to the kingdom of David and the inheritance of Judah. But the secret and authentic history has been recorded in several copies of the gospel according to St. Matthew, which these sectaries long preserved in the original Hebrew as the sole evidence of their faith. The natural suspicions of the husband, conscious of his own chastity, were dispelled by the assurance (in a dream) that his wife was pregnant of the Holy Ghost: and as this distant and domestic prodigy could not fall under the personal observation of the historian, he must have listened to the same voice which dictated to Isaiah the future conception of a virgin. The son of a virgin, generated by the ineffable operation of the Holy Spirit, was a creature without example or resemblance, superior in every attribute of mind and body to the children of Adam. Since the introduction of the Greek or Chaldean philosophy, the Jews were persuaded of the preexistence, transmigration, and immortality of souls; and providence was justified by a supposition that they were confined in their earthly prisons to expiate the stains which they had contracted in a former state. But the degrees of purity and corruption are almost immeasurable. It might be fairly presumed that the most sublime and virtuous of human spirits was infused into the offspring of Mary and the Holy Ghost; that his abasement was the result of his voluntary choice; and that the object of his mission was to purify not his own but the sins of the world. On his return to his native skies, he received the immense reward of his obedience; the everlasting kingdom of the Messiah, which had been darkly foretold by the prophets, under the carnal images of peace, of conquest, and of dominion. Omnipotence could enlarge the human faculties of Christ to the extent of his celestial office. In the language of antiquity, the title of God has not been severely confined to the first parent, and his incomparable minister, his only-begotten son, might claim without presumption the religious, though secondary, worship of a subject world.

II. [A pure God to the Docetes.] The seeds of the faith, which had slowly arisen in the rocky and ungrateful soil of Judea, were transplanted in full maturity to the happier climes of the Gentiles; and the strangers of Rome or Asia, who never beheld the manhood, were the more readily disposed to embrace the divinity, of Christ. The Polytheist and the philosopher, the Greek and the Barbarian, were alike accustomed to conceive a long succession, an infinite chain of angels or demons, or deities, or aeons, or emanations issuing from the throne of light. Nor could it seem strange or incredible that the first of these aeons, the LOGOS, or Word of God, of the same substance with the Father, should descend upon earth to deliver the human race from vice and error and to conduct them in the paths of life and immortality. But the prevailing doctrine of the eternity and inherent pravity of matter infected the primitive churches of the East. Many among the Gentile proselytes refused to believe that a celestial spirit, an undivided portion of the first essence, had been personally united with a mass of impure and contaminated flesh; and in their zeal for the divinity, they piously abjured the humanity of Christ. While his blood was still recent on Mount Calvary, the *Docetes,* a numerous and learned sect of

Asiatics, invented the *phantastic* system, which was afterwards propagated by the Marcionites, the Manichaeans, and the various names of the Gnostic heresy. They denied the truth and authenticity of the gospels as far as they relate the conception of Mary, the birth of Christ, and the thirty years that preceded the exercise of his ministry. He first appeared on the banks of the Jordan in the form of perfect manhood; but it was a form only, and not a substance; a human figure created by the hand of Omnipotence to imitate the faculties and actions of a man and to impose a perpetual illusion on the senses of his friends and enemies. Articulate sounds vibrated on the ears of the disciples; but the image which was impressed on their optic nerve eluded the more stubborn evidence of the touch; and they enjoyed the spiritual, not the corporeal, presence of the Son of God. The rage of the Jews was idly wasted against an impassive phantom; and the mystic scenes of the passion and death, the resurrection and ascension, of Christ were represented on the theater of Jerusalem for the benefit of mankind. If it were urged that such ideal mimicry, such incessant deception, was unworthy of the God of truth, the Docetes agreed with too many of their orthodox brethren in the justification of pious falsehood. In the system of the Gnostics, the Jehovah of Israel, the Creator of this lower world, was a rebellious, or at least an ignorant, spirit. The Son of God descended upon earth to abolish his temple and his law; and for the accomplishment of this salutary end, he dexterously transferred to his own person the hope and prediction of a temporal Messiah.

One of the most subtle disputants of the Manichaean school has pressed the danger and indecency of supposing that the God of the Christians, in the state of a human fetus, emerged at the end of nine months from a female womb. The pious horror of his antagonists provoked them to disclaim all sensual circumstances of conception and delivery; to maintain that the divinity passed through Mary like a sunbeam through a plate of glass; and to assert that the seal of her virginity remained unbroken even at the moment when she became the mother of Christ. But the rashness of these concessions has encouraged a milder sentiment of those of the Docetes who taught not that Christ was a phantom but that he was clothed with an impassible and incorruptible body. Such indeed, in the more orthodox system, he has acquired since his resurrection, and such he must have always possessed if it were capable of pervading without resistance or injury the density of intermediate matter. Devoid of its most essential properties, it might be exempt from the attributes and infirmities of the flesh. A fetus that could increase from an invisible point to its full maturity, a child that could attain the stature of perfect manhood without deriving any nourishment from the ordinary sources, might continue to exist without repairing a daily waste by a daily supply of external matter. Jesus might share the repasts of his disciples without being subject to the calls of thirst or hunger; and his virgin purity was never sullied by the involuntary stains of sensual concupiscence. Of a body thus singularly constituted, a question would arise, by what means and of what materials it was originally framed; and our sounder theology is startled by an answer which was not peculiar to the Gnostics, that both the form and the substance proceeded from the divine essence. The idea of pure and absolute spirit is a refinement of modern philosophy: the incorporeal essence, ascribed by the ancients to human souls, celestial beings, and even the Deity himself, does not exclude the notion of extended space; and their imagination was satisfied with a subtle nature of air, or fire, or ether, incomparably more perfect than the grossness of the material world. If we define the place, we must describe the figure, of the Deity. Our experience, perhaps our vanity, represents the powers of reason and virtue under a human form. The Anthropomorphites, who swarmed among the monks of Egypt and the Catholics of Africa, could produce the express declaration of Scripture that man was made after the image of his Creator. The venerable Serapion, one of the saints of the Nitrian deserts, relinquished with many a tear his darling prejudice; and bewailed like an infant his unlucky conversion, which had stolen away his God and left his mind without any visible object of faith or devotion.

III. [Double nature according to Cerinthus.] Such were the fleeting shadows of the Docetes. A more substantial though less simple hypothesis was contrived by Cerinthus of Asia, who dared to oppose the last of the apostles. Placed on the confines of the Jewish and Gentile world, he labored to reconcile the Gnostic with the Ebionite by confessing in the same Messiah the supernatural union of a man and a God; and this mystic doctrine was adopted with many fanciful improvements by Carpocrates, Basilides, and Valentine, the heretics of the Egyptian school. In their eyes, Jesus of Nazareth was a mere mortal, the legitimate son of Joseph and Mary: but he was the best and wisest of the human race, selected as the worthy instrument to restore upon earth the worship of the true and supreme Deity. When he was baptized in the Jordan, the CHRIST, the first of the aeons, the Son of God himself, descended on Jesus in the form of a dove to inhabit his mind and direct his actions during the allotted period of his ministry. When the Messiah was delivered into the hands of the Jews, the Christ, an immortal and impassible being, forsook his earthly tabernacle, flew back to the *pleroma* or world of spirits, and left the solitary Jesus to suffer, to complain, and to expire. But the justice and generosity of such a desertion are strongly questionable; and the fate of an innocent martyr, at first impelled and at length abandoned by his divine companion, might provoke the pity and indignation of the profane. Their murmurs were variously silenced by the sectaries who espoused and modified the double system of Cerinthus. It was alleged that when Jesus was nailed to the cross, he was endowed with a miraculous apathy of mind and body which rendered him insensible of his apparent sufferings. It was affirmed that these momentary, though real, pangs would be abundantly repaid by the temporal reign of a thousand years reserved for the Messiah in his kingdom of the new Jerusalem. It was insinuated that if he suffered, he deserved to suffer; that human nature is never absolutely perfect; and that the cross and passion might serve to expiate the venial transgressions of the son of Joseph before his mysterious union with the Son of God.

IV. [Divine incarnation according to Apollinaris.] All those who believe the immateriality of the soul, a specious and noble tenet, must confess from their present experience the incomprehensible union of mind and matter. A similar union is not inconsistent with a much higher, or even with the highest, degree of mental faculties; and the incarnation of an aeon or archangel, the most perfect of created spirits, does not involve any positive contradiction or absurdity. In the age of religious freedom which was determined by the council of Nice, the dignity of Christ was measured by private judgment according to the indefinite rule of Scripture, or reason, or tradition. But when his pure and proper divinity had been established on the ruins of Arianism, the faith of the Catholics trembled on the edge of a precipice where it was impossible to recede, dangerous to stand, dreadful to fall; and the manifold inconveniences of their creed were aggravated by the sublime character of their theology. They hesitated to pronounce *that* God himself, the second person of an equal and consubstantial Trinity, was manifested in the flesh; *that* a being who pervades the universe had been confined in the womb of Mary; *that* his eternal duration had been marked by the days and months and years of human existence; *that* the Almighty had been scourged and crucified; *that* his impassible essence had felt pain and anguish; *that* his omniscience was not exempt from ignorance; and *that* the source of life and immortality expired on Mount Calvary. These alarming consequences were affirmed with unblushing simplicity by Apollinaris, bishop of Laodicea, and one of the luminaries of the church. The son of a learned grammarian, he was skilled in all the sciences of Greece; eloquence, erudition, and philosophy, conspicuous in the volumes of Apollinaris, were humbly devoted to the service of religion. The worthy friend of Athanasius, the worthy antagonist of Julian, he bravely wrestled with the Arians and Polytheists, and though he affected the rigor of geometrical demonstration his commentaries revealed the literal and allegorical sense of the Scriptures. A mystery which had long floated in the looseness of popular belief was defined by his perverse diligence in a technical form; and he first proclaimed the memorable words "One incarnate nature of Christ," which are still reechoed with hostile clamors in the churches of Asia, Egypt, and Aethiopia. He taught that the Godhead was united or mingled with the body of a man; and that the *Logos,* the eternal wisdom, supplied in the flesh the place and office of a human soul. Yet as the profound doctor had been terrified at his own rashness, Apollinaris was heard to mutter some faint accents of excuse and explanation. He acquiesced in the old distinction of the Greek philosophers between the rational and sensitive soul of man, that he might reserve the *Logos* for intellectual functions, and employ the subordinate human principle in the meaner actions of animal life. With the moderate Docetes, he revered Mary as the spiritual rather than as the carnal mother of Christ, whose body either came from Heaven, impassible and incorruptible, or was absorbed, and as it were transformed, into the essence of the Deity. The system of Apollinaris was strenuously encountered by the Asiatic and Syrian divines whose schools are honored by the names of Basil, Gregory, and Chrysostom and tainted by those of Diodorus, Theodore, and Nestorius. But the person of the aged bishop of Laodicea, his character and dignity, remained inviolate; and his rivals, since we may not suspect them of the weakness of toleration, were astonished, perhaps, by the novelty of the argument, and diffident of the final sentence of the Catholic church. Her judgment at length inclined in their favor; the heresy of Apollinaris was condemned, and the separate congregations of his disciples were proscribed by the Imperial laws. But his principles were secretly entertained in the monasteries of Egypt and his enemies felt the hatred of Theophilus and Cyril, the successive patriarchs of Alexandria.

V. [Orthodox consent and verbal disputes.] The groveling Ebionite and the fantastic Docetes were rejected and forgotten: the recent zeal against the errors of Apollinaris reduced the Catholics to a seeming agreement with the double nature of Cerinthus. But instead of a temporary and occasional alliance, *they* established, and *we* still embrace, the substantial, indissoluble, and everlasting union of a perfect God with a perfect man, of the second person of the Trinity with a reasonable soul and human flesh. In the beginning of the fifth century, the *unity* of the *two natures* was the prevailing doctrine of the church. On all sides, it was confessed that the mode of their coexistence could neither be represented by our ideas nor expressed by our language. Yet a secret and incurable discord was cherished between those who were most apprehensive of confounding and those who were most fearful of separating the divinity and the humanity of Christ. Impelled by religious frenzy, they fled with adverse haste from the error which they mutually deemed most destructive of truth and salvation. On either hand they were anxious to guard, they were jealous to defend, the union and the distinction of the two natures, and to invent such forms of speech, such symbols of doctrine, as were least susceptible of doubt or ambiguity. The poverty of ideas and language tempted them to ransack art and nature for every possible comparison, and each comparison misled their fancy in the explanation of an incomparable mystery. In the polemic microscope, an atom is enlarged to a monster, and each party was skillful to exaggerate the absurd or impious conclusions that might be extorted from the principles of their adversaries. To escape from each other, they wandered through many a dark and devious thicket till they were astonished by the horrid phantoms of Cerinthus and Apollinaris, who guarded the opposite issues of the theological labyrinth. As soon as they beheld the twilight of sense and heresy, they started, measured back their steps, and were again involved in the gloom of impenetrable orthodoxy. To purge themselves from the guilt or reproach of damnable error, they disavowed their consequences, explained their principles, excused their indiscretions, and unanimously pronounced the sounds of concord and faith. Yet a latent and almost invisible spark still lurked among the embers of controversy: by the breath of prejudice and passion, it was quickly kindled to a mighty flame, and the verbal disputes of the Oriental sects have shaken the pillars of the church and state.

The name of CYRIL [patriarch] of Alexandria [A.D. 412–444] is famous in controversial story, and the title of *saint* is a mark that his opinions and his party have finally prevailed.[†]

At a distance from the court and at the head of an immense capital, the patriarch ... of Alexandria had gradually usurped the state and authority of a civil magistrate. The public and private charities of the city were blindly obeyed by his numerous and fanatic *parabolani*, familiarized in their daily office with scenes of death; and the praefects of Egypt were awed or provoked by the temporal power of these Christian pontiffs. Ardent in the prosecution of heresy, Cyril auspiciously opened his reign by oppressing the Novatians, the most innocent and harmless of the sectaries. The interdiction of their religious worship appeared in his eyes a just and meritorious act; and he confiscated their holy vessels without apprehending the guilt of sacrilege. The toleration and even the privileges of the Jews, who had multiplied to the number of forty thousand, were secured by the laws of the Caesars and Ptolemies, and a long prescription of seven hundred years since the foundation of Alexandria. Without any legal sentence, without any royal mandate, the patriarch at the dawn of day led a seditious multitude to the attack of the synagogues. Unarmed and unprepared, the Jews were incapable of resistance; their houses of prayer were leveled with the ground, and the episcopal warrior, after rewarding his troops with the plunder of their goods, expelled from the city the remnant of the unbelieving nation. Perhaps he might plead the insolence of their prosperity and their deadly hatred of the Christians, whose blood they had recently shed in a malicious or accidental tumult. Such crimes would have deserved the animadversion of the magistrate; but in this promiscuous outrage, the innocent were confounded with the guilty, and Alexandria was impoverished by the loss of a wealthy and industrious colony. The zeal of Cyril exposed him to the penalties of the Julian law; but in a feeble government and a superstitious age, he was secure of impunity, and even of praise. Orestes complained; but his just complaints were too quickly forgotten by the ministers of Theodosius, and too deeply remembered by a priest who affected to pardon, and continued to hate, the praefect of Egypt. As he passed through the streets, his chariot was assaulted by a band of five hundred of the Nitrian monks; his guards fled from the wild beasts of the desert; his protestations that he was a Christian and a Catholic were answered by a volley of stones, and the face of Orestes was covered with blood. The loyal citizens of Alexandria hastened to his rescue; he instantly satisfied his justice and revenge against the monk by whose hand he had been wounded, and Ammonius expired under the rod of the lictor. At the command of Cyril his body was raised from the ground and transported, in solemn procession, to the cathedral; the name of Ammonius was changed to that of Thaumasius the *wonderful;* his tomb was decorated with the trophies of martyrdom, and the patriarch ascended the pulpit to celebrate the magnanimity of an assassin and a rebel. Such honors might incite the faithful to combat and die under the banners of the saint; and he soon prompted or accepted the sacrifice of a virgin who professed the religion of the Greeks and cultivated the friendship of Orestes. Hypatia, the daughter of Theon the mathematician, was initiated in her father's studies; her learned comments have elucidated the geometry of Apollonius and Diophantus, and she publicly taught, both at Athens and Alexandria, the philosophy of Plato and Aristotle. In the bloom of beauty and in the maturity of wisdom, the modest maid refused her lovers and instructed her disciples; the persons most illustrious for their rank or merit were impatient to visit the female philosopher; and Cyril beheld with a jealous eye the gorgeous train of horses and slaves who crowded the door of her academy. A rumor was spread among the Christians that the daughter of Theon was the only obstacle to the reconciliation of the praefect and the archbishop; and that obstacle was speedily removed. On a fatal day, in the holy season of Lent, Hypatia was torn from her chariot, stripped naked, dragged to the church, and inhumanly butchered by the hands of Peter the reader and a troop of savage and merciless fanatics: her flesh was scraped from her bones with sharp oyster shells, and her quivering limbs were delivered to the flames. The just progress of inquiry and punishment was stopped by seasonable gifts; but the murder of Hypatia has imprinted an indelible stain on the character and religion of Cyril of Alexandria.†

[Cyril's] enmity to the Byzantine pontiffs was a sense of interest, not a sally of passion: he envied their fortunate station in the sunshine of the Imperial court; and he dreaded their upstart ambition which oppressed the metropolitans of Europe and Asia, invaded the provinces of Antioch and Alexandria, and measured their diocese by the limits of the empire. The long moderation of Atticus, the mild usurper of the throne of Chrysostom, suspended the animosities of the Eastern patriarchs; but Cyril was at length awakened by the exaltation of a rival more worthy of his esteem and hatred. After the short and troubled reign of Sisinnius, bishop of Constantinople, the factions of the clergy and people were appeased by the choice of the emperor, who on this occasion consulted the voice of fame and invited the merit of a stranger [April A.D. 428]. Nestorius, native of Germanicia and a monk of Antioch, was recommended by the austerity of his life and the eloquence of his sermons; but the first homily which he preached before the devout Theodosius betrayed the acrimony and impatience of his zeal. "Give me, O Caesar!" he exclaimed, "give me the earth purged of heretics, and I will give you in exchange the kingdom of Heaven. Exterminate with me the heretics; and with you I will exterminate the Persians." On the fifth day as if the treaty had been already signed, the patriarch of Constantinople discovered, surprised, and attacked a secret conventicle of the Arians: they preferred death to submission; the flames that were kindled by their despair soon spread to the neighboring houses, and the triumph of Nestorius was clouded by the name of *incendiary.* On either side of the Hellespont his episcopal vigor imposed a rigid formulary of faith and discipline; a chronological error concerning the festival of Easter was punished as an offense against the church and state. Lydia and Caria, Sardes and Miletus, were purified with the blood of the obstinate Quartodecimans; and the edict of the emperor, or rather of the patriarch, enumerates three-and-twenty degrees and denominations in the guilt and punishment of heresy [A.D. 428]. But the sword of persecution which Nestorius so furiously wielded was soon turned against his own breast. Religion was the pretense; but, in the judgment of a contemporary saint, ambition was the genuine motive of episcopal warfare.

In the Syrian school, Nestorius had been taught to abhor the confusion of the two natures, and nicely to discriminate the humanity of his *master* Christ from the divinity of the *Lord* Jesus. The Blessed Virgin he revered as the mother of Christ, but his ears were offended with the rash and recent title of mother of God, which had been insensibly adopted since the origin of the Arian controversy. From the pulpit of Constantinople, a friend of the patriarch, and afterwards the patriarch himself, repeatedly preached against the use or the abuse of a word unknown to the apostles, unauthorized by the church, and which could only tend to alarm the timorous, to mislead the simple, to amuse the profane, and to justify by a seeming resemblance the old genealogy of Olympus. In his calmer moments Nestorius confessed that it might be tolerated or excused by the union of the two natures and the communication of their *idioms:* but he was exasperated, by contradiction, to disclaim the worship of a new-born, an infant Deity, to draw his inadequate similes from the conjugal or civil partnerships of life, and to describe the manhood of Christ as the robe, the instrument, the tabernacle of his Godhead. At these blasphemous sounds, the pillars of the sanctuary were shaken. The unsuccessful competitors of Nestorius indulged their pious or personal resentment; the Byzantine clergy was secretly displeased with the intrusion of a stranger; whatever is superstitious or absurd might claim the protection of the monks; and the people were interested in the glory of their virgin patroness. The sermons of the archbishop and the service of the altar were disturbed by seditious clamor; his authority and doctrine were renounced by separate congregations; every wind scattered round the empire the leaves of controversy; and the voice of the combatants on a sonorous theater reechoed in the cells of Palestine and Egypt. It was the duty of Cyril to enlighten the zeal and ignorance of his innumerable monks: in the school of Alexandria, he had imbibed and professed the incarnation of one nature; and the successor of Athanasius consulted his pride and ambition when he rose in arms against another Arius, more formidable and more guilty, on the second throne of the hierarchy. After a short correspondence in which the rival prelates disguised their hatred in the hollow language of respect and charity, the patriarch of Alexandria denounced to the prince and people, to the East and to the West, the damnable errors of the Byzantine pontiff. From the East, more especially from Antioch, he obtained the ambiguous counsels of toleration and silence, which were addressed to both parties while they favored the cause of Nestorius. But the Vatican received with open arms the messengers of Egypt. The vanity of Celestine was flattered by the appeal; and the partial version of a monk decided the faith of the pope, who with his Latin clergy was ignorant of the language, the arts, and the theology of the Greeks. At the head of an Italian synod, Celestine weighed the merits of the cause, approved the creed of Cyril, condemned the sentiments and person of Nestorius, degraded the heretic from his episcopal dignity, allowed a respite of ten days for recantation and penance, and delegated to his enemy the execution of this rash and illegal sentence.†

Yet neither the emperor nor the primate of the East were disposed to obey the mandate of an Italian priest; and a synod of the Catholic, or rather of the Greek, church was unanimously demanded as the sole remedy that could appease or decide this ecclesiastical quarrel [the First Council of Ephesus (June–October A.D. 431)]. Ephesus, on all sides accessible by sea and land, was chosen for the place, the festival of Pentecost for the day of the meeting; a writ of summons was despatched to each metropolitan, and a guard was stationed to protect and confine the fathers till they should settle the mysteries of Heaven and the faith of the earth. Nestorius appeared not as a criminal but as a judge; he depended on the weight rather than the number of his prelates, and his sturdy slaves from the baths of Zeuxippus were armed for every service of injury or defense. But his adversary Cyril was more powerful in the weapons both of the flesh and of the spirit. Disobedient to the letter, or at least to the meaning, of the royal summons, he was attended by fifty Egyptian bishops, who expected from their patriarch's nod the inspiration of the Holy Ghost. He had contracted an intimate alliance with Memnon, bishop of Ephesus. The despotic primate of Asia disposed of the ready succors of thirty or forty episcopal votes: a crowd of peasants, the slaves of the church, was poured into the city to support with blows and clamors a metaphysical argument; and the people zealously asserted the honor of the Virgin, whose body reposed within the walls of Ephesus. The fleet which had transported Cyril from Alexandria was laden with the riches of Egypt; and he disembarked a numerous body of mariners, slaves, and fanatics, enlisted with blind obedience under the banner of St. Mark and the mother of God. The fathers and even the guards of the council were awed by this martial array; the adversaries of Cyril and Mary were insulted in the streets or threatened in their houses; his eloquence and liberality made a daily increase in the number of his adherents; and the Egyptian soon computed that he might command the attendance and the voices of two hundred bishops.

[*Cyril procures a condemnation of Nestorius before Nestorius' supporters arrive. Upon the arrival of Nestorius' supporters, Cyril is condemned.*]

Ephesus, the city of the Virgin, was defiled with rage and clamor, with sedition and blood; the rival synods darted anathemas and excommunications from their spiritual engines; and the court of Theodosius was perplexed by the adverse and contradictory narratives of the Syrian and Egyptian factions. During a busy period of three months, the emperor tried every method, except the most effectual means of indifference and contempt, to reconcile this theological quarrel. He attempted to remove or intimidate the leaders by a common sentence of acquittal or condemnation; he invested his representatives at Ephesus with ample power and military force; he summoned from either party eight chosen deputies to a free and candid conference in the neighborhood of the capital, far from the contagion of popular frenzy. But the Orientals refused to yield, and the Catholics, proud of their numbers and of their Latin allies, rejected all terms of union or toleration. The patience of the meek Theodosius was provoked; and he dissolved in anger this episcopal tumult, which at the distance of thirteen centuries assumes the venerable aspect of the third oecumenical council. "God is my witness," said the pious prince, "that I am not the author of this confusion. His Providence will discern and punish the guilty. Return to your provinces, and may your private virtues repair the mischief and scandal of your meeting." They returned to their provinces; but the same passions which had distracted the synod of Ephesus were diffused over the Eastern world.

[*Cyril subsequently labors diligently (A.D. 431–435), and eventually secures the exile of Nestorius.*]

The rash and obstinate Nestorius . . . was oppressed by Cyril, betrayed by the court, and faintly supported by his Eastern friends. A sentiment of fear or indignation prompted him, while it was yet time, to affect the glory of a voluntary abdication: his wish, or at least his request, was readily granted; he was conducted with honor from Ephesus to his old monastery of Antioch; and after a short pause, his successors, Maximian and Proclus, were acknowledged as the lawful bishops of Constantinople [A.D. 435]. But in the silence of his cell, the degraded patriarch could no longer resume the innocence and security of a private monk.... After a residence at Antioch of four years, the hand of Theodosius subscribed an edict which ranked him with Simon the magician, proscribed his opinions and followers, condemned his writings to the flames, and banished his person first to Petra, in Arabia, and at length to Oasis, one of the *islands* of the Libyan desert.... [N]o sooner had Nestorius reached the banks of the Nile than he would gladly have escaped from a Roman and orthodox city to the milder servitude of the savages. His flight was punished as a new crime: the soul of the patriarch inspired the civil and ecclesiastical powers of Egypt; the magistrates, the soldiers, the monks devoutly tortured the enemy of Christ and St. Cyril; and, as far as the confines of Aethiopia, the heretic was alternately dragged and recalled, till his aged body was broken by the hardships and accidents of these reiterated journeys. Yet his mind was still independent and erect; the president of Thebais was awed by his pastoral letters; he survived the Catholic tyrant of Alexandria, and after sixteen years' banishment, the synod of Chalcedon would perhaps have restored him to the honors, or at least to the communion, of the church. The death of Nestorius prevented his obedience to their welcome summons; and his disease might afford some color to the scandalous report that his tongue, the organ of blasphemy, had been eaten by the worms. He was buried in a city of Upper Egypt known by the names of Chemnis, or Panopolis, or Akmim; but the immortal malice of the Jacobites has persevered for ages to cast stones against his sepulchre, and to propagate the foolish tradition that it was never watered by the rain of Heaven, which equally descends on the righteous and the ungodly. Humanity may drop a tear on the fate of Nestorius; yet justice must observe that he suffered the persecution which he had approved and inflicted.

The death of the Alexandrian primate after a reign of thirty-two years abandoned the Catholics to the intemperance of zeal and the abuse of victory. The *monophysite* doctrine (one incarnate nature) was rigorously preached in the churches of Egypt and the monasteries of the East; the primitive creed of Apollinaris was protected by the sanctity of Cyril; and the name of EUTYCHES, his venerable friend, has been applied to the sect most adverse to the Syrian heresy of Nestorius. His rival Eutyches was the abbot, or archimandrite, or superior of three hundred monks, but the opinions of a simple and illiterate recluse might have expired in the cell, where he had slept above seventy years, if the resentment or indiscretion of Flavian, the Byzantine pontiff, had not exposed the scandal to the eyes of the Christian world. His domestic synod was instantly convened, their proceedings were sullied with clamor and artifice, and the aged heretic was surprised into a seeming confession that Christ had not derived his body from the substance of the Virgin Mary. From their partial decree, Eutyches appealed to a general council; and his cause was vigorously asserted by his godson Chrysaphius, the reigning eunuch of the palace, and his accomplice Dioscorus. . . . By the special summons of Theodosius, the second synod of Ephesus was judiciously composed of ten metropolitans and ten bishops from each of the six dioceses of the Eastern empire [the Second Council of Ephesus, August 8–11, A.D. 449]: some exceptions of favor or merit enlarged the number to one hundred and thirty-five; and the Syrian Barsumas, as the chief and representative of the monks, was invited to sit and vote with the successors of the apostles. But the despotism of the Alexandrian patriarch again oppressed the freedom of debate: the same spiritual and carnal weapons were again drawn from the arsenals of Egypt: the Asiatic veterans, a band of archers, served under the orders of Dioscorus; and the more formidable monks, whose minds were inaccessible to reason or mercy, besieged the doors of the cathedral. The general and, as it should seem, the unconstrained voice of the fathers accepted the faith and even the anathemas of Cyril; and the heresy of the two natures was formally condemned in the persons and writings of the most learned Orientals. "May those who divide Christ be divided with the sword, may they be hewn in pieces, may they be burned alive!" were the charitable wishes of a Christian synod. The innocence and sanctity of Eutyches were acknowledged without hesitation; but the prelates, more especially those of Thrace and Asia, were unwilling to depose their patriarch for the use or even the abuse of his lawful jurisdiction. They embraced the knees of Dioscorus as he stood with a threatening aspect on the footstool of his throne, and conjured him to forgive the offenses and to respect the dignity of his brother. "Do you mean to raise a sedition?" exclaimed the relentless tyrant. "Where are the officers?" At these words a furious multitude of monks and soldiers, with staves and swords and chains, burst into the church; the trembling bishops hid themselves behind the altar or under the benches, and as they were not inspired with the zeal of martyrdom, they successively subscribed a blank paper, which was afterwards filled with the condemnation of the Byzantine pontiff. Flavian was instantly delivered to the wild beasts of this spiritual amphitheater: the monks were stimulated by the voice and example of Barsumas to avenge the injuries of Christ: it is said that the patriarch of Alexandria reviled, and buffeted, and kicked, and trampled his brother of Constantinople: it is certain that the victim, before he could reach the place of his exile, expired on the third day of the wounds and bruises which he had received at Ephesus. This second synod has been justly branded as a gang of robbers and assassins; yet the accusers of Dioscorus would magnify his violence, to alleviate the cowardice and inconstancy of their own behavior.

The faith of Egypt had prevailed: but the vanquished party was supported by the same pope who encountered without fear the hostile rage of Attila and Genseric. The theology of Leo, his famous *tome* or epistle on the mystery of the Incarnation, had been disregarded by the synod of Ephesus: his authority and that of the Latin church was insulted in his legates, who escaped from slavery and death to relate the melancholy tale of the tyranny of Dioscorus and the martyrdom of Flavian. His provincial synod annulled the irregular proceedings of Ephesus; but as this step was itself irregular, he solicited the convocation of a general council in the free and orthodox provinces of Italy. From his independent throne, the Roman bishop spoke and acted without danger as the head of the Christians, and his dictates were obsequiously transcribed by Placidia and her son Valentinian; who addressed their Eastern colleague to restore the peace and unity of the church. . . . Perhaps the Greeks would be still involved in the heresy of the Monophysites if the emperor's horse had not fortunately stumbled; Theodosius expired; his orthodox sister Pulcheria, with a nominal husband, succeeded to the throne; Chrysaphius was burnt, Dioscorus was disgraced, the exiles were recalled, and the *tome* of Leo was subscribed by the Oriental bishops. Yet the pope was disappointed in his favorite project of a Latin council: he disdained to preside in the Greek synod which was speedily assembled at Nice in Bithynia; his legates required in a peremptory tone the presence of the emperor; and the weary fathers were transported to Chalcedon [for the Council of Chalcedon, October 8–November 1, A.D. 451]. . . . A tardy repentance was allowed to expiate the guilt or error of the accomplices of Dioscorus: but their sins were accumulated on his head; he neither asked nor hoped for pardon, and the moderation of those who pleaded for a general amnesty was drowned in the prevailing cry of victory and revenge.†

If we fairly peruse the acts of Chalcedon as they are recorded by the orthodox party, we shall find that a great majority of the bishops embraced the simple unity of Christ; and the ambiguous concession that he was formed OF or FROM two natures might imply either their previous existence, or their subsequent confusion, or some dangerous interval between the conception of the man and the assumption of the God. The Roman theology, more positive and precise, adopted the term most offensive to the ears of the Egyptians, that Christ existed IN TWO natures; and this momentous particle (which the memory rather than the understanding must retain) had almost produced a schism among the Catholic bishops. The tome of Leo had been respectfully, perhaps sincerely, subscribed; but they protested in two successive debates that it was neither expedient nor lawful to transgress the sacred landmarks which had been fixed at Nice, Constantinople, and Ephesus according to the rule of Scripture and tradition. At length they yielded to the importunities of their masters; but their infallible decree, after it had been ratified with deliberate votes and vehement acclamations, was overturned in the next session by the opposition of the legates and their Oriental friends. It was in vain that a multitude of episcopal voices repeated in chorus, "The definition of the fathers is orthodox and immutable! The heretics are now discovered! Anathema to the Nestorians! Let them depart from the synod! Let them repair to Rome." The legates threatened, the emperor was absolute, and a committee of eighteen bishops prepared a new decree, which was imposed on the reluctant assembly. In the name of the fourth general council, the Christ in one person but in two natures was announced to the Catholic world: an invisible line was drawn between the heresy of Apollinaris and the faith of St. Cyril; and the road to paradise, a bridge as sharp as a razor, was suspended over the abyss by the master-hand of the theological artist. During ten centuries of blindness and servitude, Europe received her religious opinions from the oracle of the Vatican; and the same doctrine, already varnished with the rust of antiquity, was admitted without dispute into the creed of the reformers who disclaimed the supremacy of the Roman pontiff. The synod of Chalcedon still triumphs in the Protestant churches; but the ferment of controversy has subsided, and the most pious Christians of the present day are ignorant or careless of their own belief concerning the mystery of the Incarnation.

Far different was the temper of the Greeks and Egyptians under the orthodox reigns of Leo and Marcian [A.D. 451–482]. Those pious emperors enforced with arms and edicts the symbol of their faith; and it was declared by the conscience or honor of five hundred bishops that the decrees of the synod of Chalcedon might be lawfully supported, even with blood. The Catholics observed with satisfaction that the same synod was odious both to the Nestorians and the Monophysites; but the Nestorians were less angry or less powerful, and the East was distracted by the obstinate and sanguinary zeal of the Monophysites. Jerusalem was occupied by an army of monks; in the name of the one incarnate nature, they pillaged, they burnt, they murdered; the sepulchre of Christ was defiled with blood; and the gates of the city were guarded in tumultuous rebellion against the troops of the emperor. . . . On the third day before the festival of Easter, the patriarch was besieged in the cathedral and murdered in the baptistery. The remains of his mangled corpse were delivered to the flames, and his ashes to the wind; and the deed was inspired by the vision of a pretended angel: an ambitious monk who, under the name of Timothy the Cat, succeeded to the place and opinions of Dioscorus. This deadly superstition was inflamed on either side by the principle and the practice of retaliation: in the pursuit of a metaphysical quarrel, many thousands were slain, and the Christians of every degree were deprived of the substantial enjoyments of social life and of the invisible gifts of baptism and the holy communion. Perhaps an extravagant fable of the times may conceal an allegorical picture of these fanatics who tortured each other and themselves. "Under the consulship of Venantius and Celer," says a grave bishop, "the people of Alexandria, and all Egypt, were seized with a strange and diabolical frenzy: great and small, slaves and freedmen, monks and clergy, the natives of the land who opposed the synod of Chalcedon lost their speech and reason, barked like dogs, and tore with their own teeth the flesh from their hands and arms."[†]

In the fever of the times, the sense, or rather the sound, of a syllable was sufficient to disturb the peace of an empire [A.D. 508–518]. The TRISAGION (thrice holy), "Holy, holy, holy, Lord God of Hosts!" is supposed by the Greeks to be the identical hymn which the angels and cherubim eternally repeat before the throne of God, and which, about the middle of the fifth century, was miraculously revealed to the church of Constantinople. The devotion of Antioch soon added, "who was crucified for us!" and this grateful address, either to Christ alone or to the whole Trinity, may be justified by the rules of theology, and has been gradually adopted by the Catholics of the East and West. But it had been imagined by a Monophysite bishop; the gift of an enemy was at first rejected as a dire and dangerous blasphemy and the rash innovation had nearly cost the emperor Anastasius his throne and his life. The people of Constantinople was devoid of any rational principles of freedom; but they held, as a lawful cause of rebellion, the color of a livery in the races, or the color of a mystery in the schools. The Trisagion, with and without this obnoxious addition, was chanted in the cathedral by two adverse choirs, and when their lungs were exhausted they had recourse to the more solid arguments of sticks and stones; the aggressors were punished by the emperor and defended by the patriarch; and the crown and mitre were staked on the event of this momentous quarrel.[†]

Justinian has been already seen in the various lights of a prince, a conqueror, and a lawgiver: the theologian still remains, and it affords an unfavorable prejudice that his theology should form a very prominent feature of his portrait [A.D. 519–565]. The sovereign sympathized with his subjects in their superstitious reverence for living and departed saints: his Code, and more especially his Novels, confirm and enlarge the privileges of the clergy; and in every dispute between a monk and a layman, the partial judge was inclined to pronounce that truth and innocence and justice were always on the side of the church. In his public and private devotions, the emperor was assiduous and exemplary. . . . Among the titles of Imperial greatness, the name of *Pious* was most pleasing to his ear; to promote the temporal and spiritual interest of the church was the serious business of his life; and the duty of father of his country was often sacrificed to that of defender of the faith. . . . While the Barbarians invaded the provinces, while the victorious legion marched under the banners of Belisarius and Narses, the successor of Trajan, unknown to the camp, was content to vanquish at the head of a synod. Had he invited to these synods a disinterested and rational spectator, Justinian might have learned "*that* religious controversy is the offspring of arrogance and folly; *that* true piety is most laudably expressed by silence and submission; *that* man, ignorant of his own nature, should not presume to scrutinize the nature of his God; and *that* it is sufficient for us to know that power and benevolence are the perfect attributes of the Deity."

Toleration was not the virtue of the times, and indulgence to rebels has seldom been the virtue of princes. But when the prince descends to the narrow and peevish character of a disputant, he is easily provoked to supply the defect of argument by the plenitude of power, and to chastise without mercy the perverse blindness of those who willfully shut their eyes against the light of demonstration. The reign of Justinian was a uniform yet various scene of persecution; and he appears to have surpassed his indolent predecessors both in the contrivance of his laws and the rigor of their execution. The insufficient term of three months was assigned for the conversion or exile of all heretics; and if he still connived at their precarious stay, they were deprived under his iron yoke not only of the benefits of society but of the common birth-right of men and Christians. At the end of four hundred years, the Montanists of Phrygia still breathed the wild enthusiasm of perfection and prophecy which they had imbibed from their male and female apostles, the special organs of the Paraclete. On the approach of the Catholic priests and soldiers, they grasped with alacrity the crown of martyrdom; the conventicle and the congregation perished in the flames, but these primitive fanatics were not extinguished three hundred years after the death of their tyrant. . . . A secret remnant of Pagans, who still lurked in the most refined and most rustic conditions of mankind, excited the indignation of the Christians, who were perhaps unwilling that any strangers should be the witnesses of their intestine quarrels. A bishop was named as the inquisitor of the faith, and his diligence soon discovered, in the court and city, the magistrates, lawyers, physicians, and sophists who still cherished the superstition of the Greeks. They were sternly informed that they must choose without delay between the displeasure of Jupiter or Justinian, and that their aversion to the gospel could no longer be distinguished under the scandalous mask of indifference or impiety. The patrician Photius, perhaps alone, was resolved to live and to die like his ancestors: he enfranchised himself with the stroke of a dagger, and left his tyrant the poor consolation of exposing with ignominy the lifeless corpse of the fugitive. His weaker brethren submitted to their earthly monarch, underwent the ceremony of baptism, and labored by their extraordinary zeal to erase the suspicion or to expiate the guilt of idolatry. The native country of Homer and the theater of the Trojan war still retained the last sparks of his mythology: by the care of the same bishop, seventy thousand Pagans were detected and converted in Asia, Phrygia, Lydia, and Caria; ninety-six churches were built for the new proselytes; and linen vestments, Bibles, and liturgies, and vases of gold and silver were supplied by the pious munificence of Justinian. The Jews, who had been gradually stripped of their immunities, were oppressed by a vexatious law which compelled them to observe the festival of Easter the same day on which it was celebrated by the Christians. And they might complain with the more reason, since the Catholics themselves did not agree with the astronomical calculations of their sovereign: the people of Constantinople delayed the beginning of their Lent a whole week after it had been ordained by authority; and they had the pleasure of fasting seven days, while meat was exposed for sale by the command of the emperor. The Samaritans of Palestine were a motley race, an ambiguous sect, rejected as Jews by the Pagans, by the Jews as schismatics, and by the Christians as idolaters. The abomination of the cross had already been planted on their holy mount of Garizim, but the persecution of Justinian offered only the alternative of baptism or rebellion. They chose the latter: under the standard of a desperate leader, they rose in arms and retaliated their wrongs on the lives, the property, and the temples of a defenseless people. The Samaritans were finally subdued by the regular forces of the East: twenty thousand were slain, twenty thousand were sold by the Arabs to the infidels of Persia and India, and the remains of that unhappy nation atoned for the crime of treason by the sin of hypocrisy. It has been computed that one hundred thousand Roman subjects were extirpated in the Samaritan war, which converted the once fruitful province into a desolate and smoking wilderness. But in the creed of Justinian, the guilt of murder could not be applied to the slaughter of unbelievers; and he piously labored to establish with fire and sword the unity of the Christian faith.

With these sentiments, it was incumbent on him at least to be always in the right. In the first years of his administration, he signalized his zeal as the disciple and patron of orthodoxy: the reconciliation of the Greeks and Latins established the *tome* of St. Leo as the creed of the emperor and the empire; the Nestorians and Eutychians were exposed, on either side, to the double edge of persecution; and the four synods of Nice, Constantinople, Ephesus, and *Chalcedon* were ratified by the code of a Catholic lawgiver. But while Justinian strove to maintain the uniformity of faith and worship, his wife Theodora, whose vices were not incompatible with devotion, had listened to the Monophysite teachers; and the open or clandestine enemies of the church revived and multiplied at the smile of their gracious patroness. The capital, the palace, the nuptial bed were torn by spiritual discord; yet so doubtful was the sincerity of the royal consorts that their seeming disagreement was imputed by many to a secret and mischievous confederacy against the religion and happiness of their people. The famous dispute of the THREE CHAPTERS [A.D. 532–569], which has filled more volumes than it deserves lines, is deeply marked with this subtle and disingenuous spirit. It was now three hundred years since the body of Origen had been eaten by the worms: his soul, of which he held the preexistence, was in the hands of its Creator; but his writings were eagerly perused by the monks of Palestine. In these writings, the piercing eye of Justinian descried more than ten metaphysical errors; and the primitive doctor, in the company of Pythagoras and Plato, was devoted by the clergy to the *eternity* of hell-fire, which he had presumed to deny. Under the cover of this precedent, a treacherous blow was aimed at the council of Chalcedon. The fathers had listened without impatience to the praise of Theodore of Mopsuestia; and their justice or indulgence had restored both Theodore of Cyrrhus and Ibas of Edessa to the communion of the church. But the characters of these Oriental bishops were tainted with the reproach of heresy; the first had been the master, the two others were the friends, of Nestorius; their most suspicious passages were accused under the title of the *three chapters;* and the condemnation of their memory must involve the honor of a synod whose name was pronounced with sincere or affected reverence by the Catholic world. If these bishops, whether innocent or guilty, were annihilated in the sleep of death, they would not probably be awakened by the clamor which, after a hundred years, was raised over their grave. If they were already in the fangs of the demon, their torments could neither be aggravated nor assuaged by human industry. If in the company of saints and angels they enjoyed the rewards of piety, they must have smiled at the idle fury of the theological insects who still crawled on the surface of the earth. The foremost of these insects, the emperor of the Romans, darted his sting and distilled his venom, perhaps without discerning the true motives of Theodora and her ecclesiastical faction. The victims were no longer subject to his power, and the vehement style of his edicts could only proclaim their damnation and invite the clergy of the East to join in a full chorus of curses and anathemas. The East, with some hesitation, consented to the voice of her sovereign: the fifth general council, of three patriarchs and one hundred and sixty-five bishops, was held at Constantinople [May 4–June 2, A.D. 553]; and the authors as well as the defenders of the three chapters were separated from the communion of the saints and solemnly delivered to the prince of darkness. But the Latin churches were more jealous of the honor of Leo and the synod of Chalcedon: and if they had fought as they usually did under the standard of Rome, they might have prevailed in the cause of reason and humanity. But their chief was a prisoner in the hands of the enemy; the throne of St. Peter, which had been disgraced by the simony, was betrayed by the cowardice, of Vigilius, who yielded after a long and inconsistent struggle to the despotism of Justinian and the sophistry of the Greeks. His apostasy provoked the indignation of the Latins, and no more than two bishops could be found who would impose their hands on his deacon and successor Pelagius. Yet the perseverance of the popes insensibly transferred to their adversaries the appellation of schismatics; the Illyrian, African, and Italian churches were oppressed by the civil and ecclesiastical powers, not without some effort of military force; the distant Barbarians transcribed the creed of the Vatican, and in the period of a century the schism of the three chapters expired in an obscure angle of the Venetian province. But the religious discontent of the Italians had already promoted the conquests of the Lombards, and the Romans themselves were accustomed to suspect the faith and to detest the government of their Byzantine tyrant.

Justinian was neither steady nor consistent in the nice process of fixing his volatile opinions and those of his subjects. In his youth he was offended by the slightest deviation from the orthodox line; in his old age he transgressed the measure of temperate heresy, and the Jacobites not less than the Catholics were scandalized by his declaration that the body of Christ was incorruptible and that his manhood was never subject to any wants and infirmities, the inheritance of our mortal flesh. This fantastic opinion was announced in the last edicts of Justinian; and at the moment of his seasonable departure, the clergy had refused to subscribe, the prince was prepared to persecute, and the people were resolved to suffer or resist. . . . His death restored in some degree the peace of the church, and the reigns of his four successors, Justin, Tiberius, Maurice, and Phocas, are distinguished by a rare though fortunate vacancy in the ecclesiastical history of the East.

The faculties of sense and reason are least capable of acting on themselves; the eye is most inaccessible to the sight, the soul to the thought; yet we think and even feel that *one will*, a sole principle of action, is essential to a rational and conscious being. When Heraclius returned from the Persian war, the orthodox hero consulted his bishops whether the Christ whom he adored, of one person but of two natures, was actuated by a single or a double will [A.D. 629]. They replied in the singular, and the emperor was encouraged to hope that the Jacobites of Egypt and Syria might be reconciled by the profession of a doctrine most certainly harmless and most probably true, since it was taught even by the Nestorians themselves. The experiment was tried without effect, and the timid or vehement Catholics condemned even the semblance of a retreat in the presence of a subtle and audacious enemy. The orthodox (the prevailing) party devised new modes of speech and argument and interpretation: to either nature of Christ they speciously applied a proper and distinct energy; but the difference was no longer visible when they allowed that the human and the divine will were invariably the same. The disease was attended with the customary symptoms: but the Greek clergy, as if satiated with the endless controversy of the incarnation, instilled a healing counsel into the ear of the prince and people. They declared themselves MONOTHELITES (asserters of the unity of will) but they treated the words as new, the questions as superfluous; and recommended a religious silence as the most agreeable to the prudence and charity of the gospel. This law of silence was successively imposed by the *ecthesis* or exposition of Heraclius [A.D. 638], the *type* or model of his grandson Constans [A.D. 648]; and the Imperial edicts were subscribed with alacrity or reluctance by the four patriarchs of Rome, Constantinople, Alexandria, and Antioch. But the bishop and monks of Jerusalem sounded the alarm: in the language, or even in the silence, of the Greeks, the Latin churches detected a latent heresy: and the obedience of Pope Honorius to the commands of his sovereign was retracted and censured by the bolder ignorance of his successors. They condemned the execrable and abominable heresy of the Monothelites, who revived the errors of Manes, Apollinaris, Eutyches, etc.; they signed the sentence of excommunication on the tomb of St. Peter; the ink was mingled with the sacramental wine, the blood of Christ; and no ceremony was omitted that could fill the superstitious mind with horror and affright.... [But in] the next generation ... the fine problems of the Incarnation were forgotten in the more popular and visible quarrel of the worship of images.†

Before the end of the seventh century, the creed of the Incarnation, which had been defined at Rome and Constantinople, was uniformly preached in the remote islands of Britain and Ireland; the same ideas were entertained, or rather the same words were repeated, by all the Christians whose liturgy was performed in the Greek or the Latin tongue. Their numbers and visible splendor bestowed an imperfect claim to the appellation of Catholics: but in the East they were marked with the less honorable name of *Melchites,* or Royalists; of men whose faith, instead of resting on the basis of Scripture, reason, or tradition, had been established and was still maintained by the arbitrary power of a temporal monarch. Their adversaries might allege the words of the fathers of Constantinople, who profess themselves the slaves of the king; and they might relate with malicious joy how the decrees of Chalcedon had been inspired and reformed by the emperor Marcian and his virgin bride. The prevailing faction will naturally inculcate the duty of submission, nor is it less natural that dissenters should feel and assert the principles of freedom. Under the rod of persecution, the Nestorians and Monophysites degenerated into rebels and fugitives; and the most ancient and useful allies of Rome were taught to consider the emperor not as the chief but as the enemy of the Christians. Language, the leading principle which unites or separates the tribes of mankind, soon discriminated the sectaries of the East by a peculiar and perpetual badge which abolished the means of intercourse and the hope of reconciliation. The long dominion of the Greeks, their colonies, and above all their eloquence had propagated a language doubtless the most perfect that has been contrived by the art of man. Yet the body of the people, both in Syria and Egypt, still persevered in the use of their national idioms; with this difference, however, that the Coptic was confined to the rude and illiterate peasants of the Nile, while the Syriac, from the mountains of Assyria to the Red Sea, was adapted to the higher topics of poetry and argument. Armenia and Abyssinia were infected by the speech or learning of the Greeks; and their Barbaric tongues, which have been revived in the studies of modern Europe, were unintelligible to the inhabitants of the Roman empire. The Syriac and the Coptic, the Armenian and the Aethiopic are consecrated in the service of their respective churches: and their theology is enriched by domestic versions both of the Scriptures and of the most popular fathers. After a period of thirteen hundred and sixty years, the spark of controversy, first kindled by a sermon of Nestorius, still burns in the bosom of the East, and the hostile communions still maintain the faith and discipline of their founders. In the most abject state of ignorance, poverty, and servitude, the Nestorians and Monophysites reject the spiritual supremacy of Rome and cherish the toleration of their Turkish masters, which allows them to anathematize on the one hand St. Cyril and the synod of Ephesus: on the other, Pope Leo and the council of Chalcedon. The weight which they cast into the downfall of the Eastern empire demands our notice, and the reader may be amused with the various prospect of, I. The Nestorians; II. The Jacobites; III. The Maronites; IV. The Armenians; V. The Copts; and, VI. The Abyssinians. To the three former, the Syriac is common; but of the latter, each is discriminated by the use of a national idiom. Yet the modern natives of Armenia and Abyssinia would be incapable of conversing with their ancestors; and the Christians of Egypt and Syria, who reject the religion, have adopted the language of the Arabians. The lapse of time has seconded the sacerdotal arts; and in the East as well as in the West, the Deity is addressed in an obsolete tongue, unknown to the majority of the congregation.

I. [The Nestorians.] Both in his native and his episcopal province, the heresy of the unfortunate Nestorius was speedily obliterated . . . ; and as early as the reign of Justinian, it became difficult to find a church of Nestorians within the limits of the Roman empire. Beyond those limits they had discovered a new world in which they might hope for liberty and aspire to conquest. In Persia, notwithstanding the resistance of the Magi, Christianity had struck a deep root, and the nations of the East reposed under its salutary shade.... [The] progress of the schism was grateful to the jealous pride of [the Persian king] Perozes, and he listened to the eloquence of an artful prelate who painted Nestorius as the friend of Persia, and urged him to secure the fidelity of his Christian subjects by granting a just preference to the victims and enemies of the Roman tyrant. The Nestorians composed a large majority of the clergy and people: they were encouraged by the smile and armed with the sword of despotism; yet many of their weaker brethren were startled at the thought of breaking loose from the communion of the Christian world, and the blood of seven thousand seven hundred Monophysites or Catholics confirmed the uniformity of faith and discipline in the churches of Persia. Their ecclesiastical institutions are distinguished by a liberal principle of reason, or at least of policy: the austerity of the cloister was relaxed and gradually forgotten; houses of charity were endowed for the education of orphans and foundlings; the law of celibacy, so forcibly recommended to the Greeks and Latins, was disregarded by the Persian clergy; and the number of the elect was multiplied by the public and reiterated nuptials of the priests, the bishops, and even the patriarch himself. To this standard of natural and religious freedom, myriads of fugitives resorted from all the provinces of the Eastern empire; the narrow bigotry of Justinian was punished by the emigration of his most industrious subjects; they transported into Persia the arts both of peace and war: and those who deserved the favor were promoted in the service of a discerning monarch. The arms of Nushirvan and his fiercer grandson were assisted with advice and money and troops by the desperate sectaries who still lurked in their native cities of the East: their zeal was rewarded with the gift of the Catholic churches; but when those cities and churches were recovered by Heraclius, their open profession of treason and heresy compelled them to seek a refuge in the realm of their foreign ally. But the seeming tranquility of the Nestorians was often endangered and sometimes overthrown. They were involved in the common evils of Oriental despotism: their enmity to Rome could not always atone for their attachment to the gospel: and a colony of three hundred thousand Jacobites, the captives of Apamea and Antioch, was permitted to erect a hostile altar in the face of the Catholic and in the sunshine of the court. In his last treaty, Justinian introduced some conditions which tended to enlarge and fortify the toleration of Christianity in Persia. The emperor, ignorant of the rights of conscience, was incapable of pity or esteem for the heretics who denied the authority of the holy synods: but he flattered himself that they would gradually perceive the temporal benefits of union with the empire and the church of Rome; and if he failed in exciting their gratitude, he might hope to provoke the jealousy of their sovereign. In a later age the Lutherans have been burnt at Paris and protected in Germany by the superstition and policy of the most Christian king.

The desire of gaining souls for God and subjects for the church has excited in every age the diligence of the Christian priests. From the conquest of Persia they carried their spiritual arms to the north, the east, and the south; and the simplicity of the gospel was fashioned and painted with the colors of the Syriac theology. In the sixth century, according to the report of a Nestorian traveler, Christianity was successfully preached to the Bactrians, the Huns, the Persians, the Indians, the Persarmenians, the Medes, and the Elamites: the Barbaric churches, from the Gulf of Persia to the Caspian Sea, were almost infinite; and their recent faith was conspicuous in the number and sanctity of their monks and martyrs. The pepper coast of Malabar and the isles of the ocean, Socotora and Ceylon, were peopled with an increasing multitude of Christians; and the bishops and clergy of those sequestered regions derived their ordination from the Catholic of Babylon.†

According to the legend of antiquity, the gospel was preached in India by St. Thomas [A.D. 883]. At the end of the ninth century his shrine, perhaps in the neighborhood of Madras, was devoutly visited by the ambassadors of Alfred; and their return with a cargo of pearls and spices rewarded the zeal of the English monarch, who entertained the largest projects of trade and discovery. When the Portuguese first opened the navigation of India, the Christians of St. Thomas had been seated for ages on the coast of Malabar, and the difference of their character and color attested the mixture of a foreign race. In arms, in arts, and possibly in virtue, they excelled the natives of Hindostan; the husbandmen cultivated the palm-tree, the merchants were enriched by the pepper trade, the soldiers preceded the *nairs* or nobles of Malabar, and their hereditary privileges were respected by the gratitude or the fear of the king of Cochin and the Zamorin himself. They acknowledged a Gentoo sovereign, but they were governed, even in temporal concerns, by the bishop of Angamala. He still asserted his ancient title of metropolitan of India, but his real jurisdiction was exercised in fourteen hundred churches, and he was entrusted with the care of two hundred thousand souls. Their religion would have rendered them the firmest and most cordial allies of the Portuguese [A.D. 1500 ff.]; but the inquisitors soon discerned in the Christians of St. Thomas the unpardonable guilt of heresy and schism. Instead of owning themselves the subjects of the Roman pontiff, the spiritual and temporal monarch of the globe, they adhered like their ancestors to the communion of the Nestorian patriarch; and the bishops whom he ordained at Mosul traversed the dangers of the sea and land to reach their diocese on the coast of Malabar. In their Syriac liturgy the names of Theodore and Nestorius were piously commemorated: they united their adoration of the two persons of Christ; the title of Mother of God was offensive to their ear, and they measured with scrupulous avarice the honors of the Virgin Mary, whom the superstition of the Latins had *almost* exalted to the rank of a goddess. When her image was first presented to the disciples of St. Thomas, they indignantly exclaimed, "We are Christians, not idolaters!" and their simple devotion was content with the veneration of the cross. Their separation from the Western world had left them in ignorance of the improvements, or corruptions, of a thousand years; and their conformity with the faith and practice of the fifth century would equally disappoint the prejudices of a Papist or a Protestant. It was the first care of the ministers of Rome to intercept all correspondence with the Nestorian patriarch, and several of his bishops expired in the prisons of the holy office. The flock, without a shepherd, was assaulted by the power of the Portuguese, the arts of the Jesuits, and the zeal of Alexis de Menezes, archbishop of Goa, in his personal visitation of the coast of Malabar. The synod of Diamper, at which he presided, consummated the pious work of the reunion; and rigorously imposed the doctrine and discipline of the Roman church without forgetting auricular confession, the strongest engine of ecclesiastical torture. The memory of Theodore and Nestorius was condemned, and Malabar was reduced under the dominion of the pope, of the primate, and of the Jesuits who invaded the see of Angamala or Cranganor. Sixty years of servitude and hypocrisy were patiently endured [A.D. 1599–1663]; but as soon as the Portuguese empire was shaken by the courage and industry of the Dutch, the Nestorians asserted, with vigor and effect, the religion of their fathers. The Jesuits were incapable of defending the power which they had abused; the arms of forty thousand Christians were pointed against their falling tyrants; and the Indian archdeacon assumed the character of bishop till a fresh supply of episcopal gifts and Syriac missionaries could be obtained from the patriarch of Babylon. Since the expulsion of the Portuguese, the Nestorian creed is freely professed on the coast of Malabar.†

II. [The Jacobites.] The history of the Monophysites is less copious and interesting than that of the Nestorians. . . . The rule of the Monophysite faith was defined with exquisite discretion by Severus, patriarch of Antioch: he condemned, in the style of the Henoticon, the adverse heresies of Nestorius; and Eutyches maintained against the latter the reality of the body of Christ, and constrained the Greeks to allow that he was a liar who spoke truth. . . . The successor of Anastasius replanted the orthodox standard in the East [A.D. 518]; Severus fled into Egypt. . . . Fifty-four bishops were swept from their thrones, eight hundred ecclesiastics were cast into prison, and notwithstanding the ambiguous favor of Theodora, the Oriental flocks, deprived of their shepherds, must insensibly have been either famished or poisoned. In this spiritual distress, the expiring faction was revived and united and perpetuated by the labors of a monk; and the name of James Baradaeus has been preserved in the appellation of *Jacobites*, a familiar sound which may startle the ear of an English reader. From the holy confessors in their prison of Constantinople, he received the powers of bishop of Edessa and apostle of the East [A.D. 541], and the ordination of fourscore thousand bishops, priests, and deacons is derived from the same inexhaustible source. The speed of the zealous missionary was promoted by the fleetest dromedaries of a devout chief of the Arabs; the doctrine and discipline of the Jacobites were secretly established in the dominions of Justinian; and each Jacobite was compelled to violate the laws and to hate the Roman legislator. . . . The superstition of the Jacobites is more abject, their fasts more rigid, their intestine divisions are more numerous, and their doctors (as far as I can measure the degrees of nonsense) are more remote from the precincts of reason. Something may possibly be allowed for the rigor of the

Monophysite theology; much more for the superior influence of the monastic order. In Syria, in Egypt, in Aethiopia, the Jacobite monks have ever been distinguished by the austerity of their penance and the absurdity of their legends. Alive or dead, they are worshiped as the favorites of the Deity; the crosier of bishop and patriarch is reserved for their venerable hands; and they assume the government of men while they are yet reeking with the habits and prejudices of the cloister.

III. [The Maronites.] In the style of the Oriental Christians, the Monothelites of every age are described under the appellation of *Maronites,* a name which has been insensibly transferred from a hermit to a monastery, from a monastery to a nation. Maron, a saint or savage of the fifth century, displayed his religious madness in Syria; the rival cities of Apamea and Emesa disputed his relics, a stately church was erected on his tomb, and six hundred of his disciples united their solitary cells on the banks of the Orontes. In the controversies of the Incarnation they nicely threaded the orthodox line between the sects of Nestorians and Eutyches; but the unfortunate question of *one will* or operation in the two natures of Christ was generated by their curious leisure. Their proselyte, the emperor Heraclius, was rejected as a Maronite from the walls of Emesa; he found a refuge in the monastery of his brethren; and their theological lessons were repaid with the gift of a spacious and wealthy domain.... John Maron, one of the most learned and popular of the monks, assumed the character of patriarch of Antioch; his nephew Abraham, at the head of the Maronites, defended their civil and religious freedom against the tyrants of the East. The son of the orthodox Constantine pursued with pious hatred a people of soldiers who might have stood the bulwark of his empire against the common foes of Christ and of Rome. An army of Greeks invaded Syria; the monastery of St. Maron was destroyed with fire; the bravest chieftains were betrayed and murdered, and twelve thousand of their followers were transplanted to the distant frontiers of Armenia and Thrace. Yet the humble nation of the Maronites has survived the empire of Constantinople, and they still enjoy under their Turkish masters a free religion and a mitigated servitude.[†]

IV. [The Armenians.] Since the age of Constantine, the ARMENIANS had signalized their attachment to the religion and empire of the Christians. The disorders of their country and their ignorance of the

Greek tongue prevented their clergy from assisting at the synod of Chalcedon, and they floated eighty-four years in a state of indifference or suspense, till their vacant faith was finally occupied by the missionaries of Julian of Halicarnassus, who in Egypt, their common exile, had been vanquished by the arguments or the influence of his rival Severus, the Monophysite patriarch of Antioch. The Armenians alone are the pure disciples of Eutyches, an unfortunate parent, who has been renounced by the greater part of his spiritual progeny. They alone persevere in the opinion that the manhood of Christ was created, or existed without creation, of a divine and incorruptible substance. Their adversaries reproach them with the adoration of a phantom; and they retort the accusation by deriding or execrating the blasphemy of the Jacobites, who impute to the Godhead the vile infirmities of the flesh, even the natural effects of nutrition and digestion. . . . Under the rod of oppression, the zeal of the Armenians is fervent and intrepid; they have often preferred the crown of martyrdom to the white turban of Mohammed; they devoutly hate the error and idolatry of the Greeks.[†]

V. [The Copts or Egyptians.] In the rest of the Roman empire, the despotism of the prince might eradicate or silence the sectaries of an obnoxious creed. But the stubborn temper of the Egyptians maintained their opposition to the synod of Chalcedon, and the policy of Justinian condescended to expect and to seize the opportunity of discord. . . . A thousand years were now elapsed since Egypt had ceased to be a kingdom, since the conquerors of Asia and Europe had trampled on the ready necks of a people whose ancient wisdom and power ascend beyond the records of history. The conflict of zeal and persecution rekindled some sparks of their national spirit. They abjured with a foreign heresy the manners and language of the Greeks: every Melchite, in their eyes, was a stranger, every Jacobite a citizen; the alliance of marriage, the offices of humanity were condemned as a deadly sin; the natives renounced all allegiance to the emperor; and his orders, at a distance from Alexandria, were obeyed only under the pressure of military force. A generous effort might have redeemed the religion and liberty of Egypt, and her six hundred monasteries might have poured forth their myriads of holy warriors, for whom death should have no terrors, since life had no comfort or delight. But experience has proved the distinction of active and passive courage; the fanatic who endures without a groan the torture of the rack or the stake would tremble and fly before the face of an armed enemy. The pusillanimous temper of the Egyptians could only hope for a change of masters.†

VI. [The Abyssinians and Nubians.] The Coptic patriarch, a rebel to the Caesars or a slave to the khalifs, still gloried in the filial obedience of the kings of Nubia and Aethiopia. He repaid their homage by magnifying their greatness; and it was boldly asserted that they could bring into the field a hundred thousand horse with an equal number of camels; that their hand could pour out or restrain the waters of the Nile; and the peace and plenty of Egypt was obtained, even in this world, by the intercession of the patriarch. In exile at Constantinople, Theodosius recommended to his patroness the conversion of the black nations of Nubia, from the tropic of Cancer to the confines of Abyssinia. Her design was suspected and emulated by the more orthodox emperor. The rival missionaries, a Melchite and a Jacobite, embarked at the same time; but the empress, from a motive of love or fear, was more effectually obeyed; and the Catholic priest was detained by the president of Thebais, while the king of Nubia and his court were hastily baptized in the faith of Dioscorus. The tardy envoy of Justinian was received and dismissed with honor: but when he accused the heresy and treason of the Egyptians, the negro convert was instructed to reply that he would never abandon his brethren, the true believers, to the persecuting ministers of the synod of Chalcedon. During several ages, the bishops of Nubia were named and consecrated by the Jacobite patriarch of Alexandria: as late as the twelfth century, Christianity prevailed; and some rites, some ruins, are still visible in the savage towns of Sennaar and Dongola. But the Nubians at length executed their threats of returning to the worship of idols; the climate required the indulgence of polygamy, and they have finally preferred the triumph of the Koran to the abasement of the Cross. A metaphysical religion may appear too refined for the capacity of the negro race: yet a black or a parrot might be taught to repeat the *words* of the Chalcedonian or Monophysite creed.

Christianity was more deeply rooted in the Abyssinian empire [A.D. 500 ff.]; and although the correspondence has been sometimes interrupted above seventy or a hundred years, the mother-church of Alexandria retains her colony in a state of perpetual pupilage. Seven bishops once composed the Aethiopic synod: had their number amounted to ten, they might have elected an independent primate; and one of their kings was ambitious of promoting his brother to the ecclesiastical throne. But the event was foreseen, the increase was denied: the episcopal office has been gradually confined to the *abuna,* the head and author of the Abyssinian priesthood; the patriarch supplies each vacancy with an Egyptian monk; and the character of a stranger appears more venerable in the eyes of the people, less dangerous in those of the monarch. In the sixth century, when the schism of Egypt was confirmed, the rival chiefs, with their patrons, Justinian and Theodora, strove to outstrip each other in the conquest of a remote and independent province. The industry of the empress was again victorious, and the pious Theodora has established in that sequestered church the faith and discipline of the Jacobites. Encompassed on all sides by the enemies of their religion, the Aethiopians slept near a thousand years, forgetful of the world, by whom they were forgotten. They were awakened by the Portuguese [A.D. 1525–1550 ff.], who, turning the southern promontory of Africa, appeared in India and the Red Sea as if they had descended through the air from a distant planet. In the first moments of their interview, the subjects of Rome and Alexandria observed the resemblance rather than the difference of their faith; and each nation expected the most important benefits from an alliance with their Christian brethren. In their lonely situation, the Aethiopians had almost relapsed into the savage life. Their vessels, which had traded to Ceylon, scarcely presumed to navigate the rivers of Africa; the ruins of Axume were deserted, the nation was scattered in villages, and the emperor, a pompous name, was content both in peace and war with the immovable residence of a camp. Conscious of their own indigence, the Abyssinians had formed the rational project of importing the arts and ingenuity of Europe; and their ambassadors at Rome and Lisbon were instructed to solicit a colony of smiths, carpenters, tilers, masons, printers, surgeons, and physicians for the use of their country. But the public danger soon called for the instant and effectual aid of arms and soldiers to defend an unwarlike people from the Barbarians, who ravaged the inland country, and the Turks and Arabs, who advanced from the sea-coast in more formidable array. Aethiopia was saved by four hundred and fifty Portuguese, who displayed in the field the native valor of Europeans and the artificial power of the musket and cannon. In a moment of terror, the emperor had promised to reconcile himself and his subjects to the Catholic faith; a Latin patriarch represented the supremacy of the pope: the empire, enlarged in a tenfold proportion, was supposed to contain more gold than the mines of America; and the wildest hopes of avarice and zeal were built on the willing submission of the Christians of Africa.

But the vows which pain had extorted were forsworn on the return of health. The Abyssinians still adhered with unshaken constancy to the Monophysite faith; their languid belief was inflamed by the exercise of dispute; they branded the Latins with the names of Arians and Nestorians, and imputed the adoration of *four* gods to those who separated the two natures of Christ. Fremona, a place of worship, or rather of exile, was assigned to the Jesuit missionaries [A.D. 1557]. Their skill in the liberal and mechanic arts, their theological learning, and the decency of their manners inspired a barren esteem; but they were not endowed with the gift of miracles, and they vainly solicited a reinforcement of European troops. The patience and dexterity of forty years at length obtained a more favorable audience, and two emperors of Abyssinia were persuaded that Rome could insure the temporal and everlasting happiness of her votaries. The first of these royal converts lost his crown and his life; and the rebel army was sanctified by the *abuna,* who hurled an anathema at the apostate and absolved his subjects from their oath of fidelity. The fate of Zadenghel was revenged by the courage and fortune of Susneus, who ascended the throne under the name of Segued, and more vigorously prosecuted the pious enterprise of his kinsman. After the amusement of some unequal combats between the Jesuits and his illiterate priests, the emperor declared himself a proselyte to the synod of Chalcedon, presuming that his clergy and people would embrace without delay the religion of their prince. The liberty of choice was succeeded by a law which imposed, under pain of death, the belief of the two natures of Christ: the Abyssinians were enjoined to work and to play on the Sabbath; and Segued, in the face of Europe and Africa, renounced his connection with the Alexandrian church. A Jesuit, Alphonso Mendez, the Catholic patriarch of Aethiopia, accepted, in the name of Urban VIII, the homage and abjuration of the penitent. "I confess," said the emperor on his knees, "I confess that the pope is the vicar of Christ, the successor of St. Peter, and the sovereign of the world. To him I swear true obedience, and at his feet I offer my person and kingdom." A similar oath was repeated by his son, his brother, the clergy, the nobles, and even the ladies of the court: the Latin patriarch was invested with honors and wealth; and his missionaries erected their churches or citadels in the most convenient stations of the empire. The Jesuits themselves deplore the fatal indiscretion of their chief, who forgot the mildness of the gospel and the policy of his order to introduce with hasty violence the liturgy of Rome and the Inquisition of Portugal. He condemned the ancient practice of circumcision, which health rather than superstition had first invented in the climate of Aethiopia. A new baptism, a new ordination, was inflicted on the natives; and they trembled with horror when the most holy of the dead were torn from their graves, when the most illustrious of the living were excommunicated by a foreign priest. In the defense of their religion and liberty, the Abyssinians rose in arms, with desperate but unsuccessful zeal. Five rebellions were extinguished in the blood of the insurgents: two abunas were slain in battle, whole legions were slaughtered in the field or suffocated in their caverns; and neither merit nor rank nor sex could save from an ignominious death the enemies of Rome. But the victorious monarch was finally subdued by the constancy of the nation, of his mother, of his son, and of his most faithful friends. Segued listened to the voice of pity, of reason, perhaps of fear: and his edict of liberty of conscience instantly revealed the tyranny and weakness of the Jesuits. On the death of his father, Basilides expelled the Latin patriarch and restored to the wishes of the nation the faith and the discipline of Egypt [A.D. 1632 ff.]. The Monophysite churches resounded with a song of triumph "that the sheep of Aethiopia were now delivered from the hyaenas of the West"; and the gates of that solitary realm were forever shut against the arts, the science, and the fanaticism of Europe.

END OF THE FOURTH VOLUME [1788].

VOLUME THE FIFTH

[1788]

CHAPTER XLVIII

SUCCESSION AND CHARACTERS OF THE GREEK EMPERORS

Plan of the two last volumes. • Succession and characters of the Greek emperors of Constantinople, from the time of Heraclius to the Latin conquest.

I have now deduced from Trajan to Constantine, from Constantine to Heraclius, the regular series of the Roman emperors; and faithfully exposed the prosperous and adverse fortunes of their reigns. Five centuries of the decline and fall of the empire have already elapsed; but a period of more than eight hundred years still separates me from the term of my labors, the taking of Constantinople by the Turks. Should I persevere in the same course, should I observe the same measure, a prolix and slender thread would be spun through many a volume, nor would the patient reader find an adequate reward of instruction or amusement. At every step, as we sink deeper in the decline and fall of the Eastern empire, the annals of each succeeding reign would impose a more ungrateful and melancholy task. These annals must continue to repeat a tedious and uniform tale of weakness and misery; the natural connection of causes and events would be broken by frequent and hasty transitions, and a minute accumulation of circumstances must destroy the light and effect of those general pictures which compose the use and ornament of a remote history. From the time of Heraclius, the Byzantine theater is contracted and darkened: the line of empire which had been defined by the laws of Justinian and the arms of Belisarius recedes on all sides from our view; the Roman name, the proper subject of our inquiries, is reduced to a narrow corner of Europe, to the lonely suburbs of Constantinople; and the fate of the Greek empire has been compared to that of the Rhine, which loses itself in the sands before its waters can mingle with the ocean. The scale of dominion is diminished to our view by the distance of time and place; nor is the loss of external splendor compensated by the nobler gifts of virtue and genius. In the last moments of her decay, Constantinople was doubtless more opulent and populous than Athens at her most flourishing era, when a scanty sum of six thousand talents, or twelve hundred thousand pounds sterling, was possessed by twenty-one thousand male citizens of an adult age. But each of these citizens was a freeman, who dared to assert the liberty of his thoughts, words, and actions, whose person and property were guarded by equal law; and who exercised his independent vote in the government of the republic. Their numbers seem to be multiplied by the strong and various discriminations of character; under the shield of freedom, on the wings of emulation and vanity, each Athenian aspired to the level of the national dignity; from this commanding eminence, some chosen spirits soared beyond the reach of a vulgar eye; and the chances of superior merit in a great and populous kingdom, as they are proved by experience, would excuse the computation of imaginary millions. The territories of Athens, Sparta, and their allies do not exceed a moderate province of France or England; but after the trophies of Salamis and Platea, they expand in our fancy to the gigantic size of Asia, which had been trampled under the feet of the victorious Greeks. But the subjects of the Byzantine empire, who assume and dishonor the names both of Greeks and Romans, present a dead uniformity of abject vices which are neither softened by the weakness of humanity nor animated by the vigor of memorable crimes. The freemen of antiquity might repeat with generous enthusiasm the sentence of Homer, "that on the first day of his servitude, the captive is deprived of one half of his manly virtue." But the poet had only seen the effects of civil or domestic slavery, nor could he foretell that the second moiety of manhood must be annihilated by the spiritual despotism which shackles not only the actions but even the thoughts of the prostrate votary. By this double yoke, the Greeks were oppressed under the successors of Heraclius; the tyrant, a law of eternal justice, was degraded by the vices of his subjects; and on the throne, in the camp, in the schools we search, perhaps with fruitless diligence, the names and characters that may deserve to be rescued from oblivion. Nor are the defects of the subject compensated by the skill and variety of the painters. Of a space of eight hundred years, the four first centuries are overspread with a cloud interrupted by some faint and broken rays of historic light: in the lives of the emperors from Maurice to Alexius, Basil the Macedonian has alone been the theme of a separate work; and the absence or loss or imperfection of contemporary evidence must be poorly supplied by the doubtful authority of more recent compilers. The four last centuries are exempt from the reproach of penury; and with the Comnenian family, the historic muse of Constantinople again revives, but her apparel is gaudy, her motions are without elegance or grace. A succession of priests or courtiers treads in each other's footsteps in the same path of servitude and superstition: their views are narrow, their judgment is feeble or corrupt; and we close the volume of copious barrenness still ignorant of the causes of events, the characters of the actors, and the manners of the times which they celebrate or deplore. The observation which has been applied to a man may be extended to a whole people, that the energy of the sword is communicated to the pen; and it will be found by experience that the tone of history will rise or fall with the spirit of the age.

From these considerations, I should have abandoned without regret the Greek slaves and their servile historians had I not reflected that the fate of the Byzantine monarchy is *passively* connected with the most splendid and important revolutions which have changed the state of the world. The space of the lost provinces was immediately replenished with new colonies and rising kingdoms: the active virtues of peace and war deserted from the vanquished to the victorious nations; and it is in their origin and conquests, in their religion and government, that we must explore the causes and effects of the decline and fall of the Eastern empire. Nor will this scope of narrative, the riches and variety of these materials, be incompatible with the unity of design and composition. As in his daily prayers the Moslem of Fez or Delhi still turns his face towards the temple of Mecca, the historian's eye shall be always fixed on the city of Constantinople. The excursive line may embrace the wilds of Arabia and Tartary, but the circle will be ultimately reduced to the decreasing limit of the Roman monarchy.

On this principle I shall now establish the plan of the last two volumes of the present work. The first chapter will contain, in a regular series, the emperors who reigned at Constantinople during a period of six hundred years, from the days of Heraclius to the Latin conquest; a rapid abstract which may be supported by a *general* appeal to the order and text of the original historians. In this introduction, I shall confine myself to the revolutions of the throne, the succession of families, the personal characters of the Greek princes, the mode of their life and death, the maxims and influence of their domestic government, and the tendency of their reign to accelerate or suspend the downfall of the Eastern empire. Such a chronological review will serve to illustrate the various arguments of the subsequent chapters; and each circumstance of the eventful story of the Barbarians will adapt itself in a proper place to the Byzantine annals. The internal state of the empire and the dangerous heresy of the Paulicians, which shook the East and enlightened the West, will be the subject of two separate chapters; but these inquiries must be postponed till our further progress shall have opened the view of the world in the ninth and tenth centuries of the Christian aera. After this foundation of Byzantine history, the following nations will pass before our eyes, and each will occupy the space to which it may be entitled by greatness or merit or the degree of connection with the Roman world and the present age. I. The FRANKS, a general appellation which includes all the Barbarians of France, Italy, and Germany who were united by the sword and scepter of Charlemagne. The persecution of images and their votaries separated Rome and Italy from the Byzantine throne, and prepared the restoration of the Roman empire in the West. II. The ARABS or SARACENS. Three ample chapters will be devoted to this curious and interesting object. In the first, after a picture of the country and its inhabitants, I shall investigate the character of Mohammed; the character, religion, and success of the prophet. In the second, I shall lead the Arabs to the conquest of Syria, Egypt, and Africa, the provinces of the Roman empire; nor can I check their victorious career till they have overthrown the monarchies of Persia and Spain. In the third, I shall inquire how Constantinople and Europe were saved by the luxury and arts, the division and decay, of the empire of the caliphs. A single chapter will include III. The BULGARIANS, IV. HUNGARIANS, and V. RUSSIANS, who assaulted by sea or by land the provinces and the capital; but the last of these, so important in their present greatness, will excite some curiosity in their origin and infancy. VI. The NORMANS, or rather the private adventurers of that warlike people, who founded a powerful kingdom in Apulia and Sicily, shook the throne of Constantinople, displayed the trophies of chivalry, and almost realized the wonders of romance. VII. The LATINS, the subjects of the pope, the nations of the West, who enlisted under the banner of the cross for the recovery or relief of the holy sepulchre. The Greek emperors were terrified and preserved by the myriads of pilgrims who marched to Jerusalem with Godfrey of Bouillon and the peers of Christendom. The second and third crusades trod in the footsteps of the first: Asia and Europe were mingled in a sacred war of two hundred years; and the Christian powers were bravely resisted and finally expelled by Saladin and the Mamalukes of Egypt. In these memorable crusades, a fleet and army of French and Venetians were diverted from Syria to the Thracian Bosphorus: they assaulted the capital, they subverted the Greek monarchy: and a dynasty of Latin princes was seated near threescore years on the throne of Constantine. VIII. The GREEKS themselves, during this period of captivity and exile, must be considered as a foreign nation; the enemies and again the sovereigns of Constantinople. Misfortune had rekindled a spark of national virtue; and the Imperial series may be continued with some dignity from their restoration to the Turkish conquest. IX. The MOGULS and TARTARS. By the arms of Zingis and his descendants, the globe was shaken from China to Poland and Greece: the sultans were overthrown: the caliphs fell, and the Caesars trembled on their throne. The victories of Timour suspended above fifty years the final ruin of the Byzantine empire. X. I have already noticed the first appearance of the TURKS; and the names of the fathers, of *Seljuk* and *Othman*, discriminate the two successive dynasties of the nation which emerged in the eleventh century from the Scythian wilderness. The former established a splendid and potent kingdom from the banks of the Oxus to Antioch and Nice; and the first crusade was provoked by the violation of Jerusalem and the danger of Constantinople. From an humble origin, the *Ottomans* arose, the scourge and terror of Christendom. Constantinople was besieged and taken by Mohammed II, and his triumph annihilates the remnant, the image, the title, of the Roman empire in the East. The schism of the Greeks will be connected with their last calamities and the restoration of learning in the Western world. I shall return from the captivity of the new to the ruins of ancient ROME; and the venerable name, the interesting theme, will shed a ray of glory on the conclusion of my labors.

[*We may survey the Byzantine emperors from Heraclius to Theodosius III: 610–641, Heraclius; 641, Constantine III and Heracleonas; 641, Heracleonas; 641–668, Constans II Pogonatus; 668–685, Constantine IV; 685–695, Justinian II Rhinotmetus; 695–698, Leontius; 698–705,*

*Tiberius III; 705–711, Justinian II (again); 711–713, Philippicus
Bardanes; 713–715, Anastasius II; 716–717, Theodosius III.*]

I shall briefly represent the founder of a new dynasty, who is known to
posterity by the invectives of his enemies, and whose public and private life is involved in the ecclesiastical story of the Iconoclasts. Yet in
spite of the clamors of superstition, a favorable prejudice for the character of Leo the Isaurian may be reasonably drawn from the obscurity
of his birth and the duration of his reign.—I. . . . Leo was a native of
Isauria. . . . His first service was in the guards of Justinian, where he
soon attracted the notice, and by degrees the jealousy, of the tyrant.
His valor and dexterity were conspicuous in the Colchian war: from
Anastasius he received the command of the Anatolian legions, and by
the suffrage of the soldiers he was raised to the empire with the general applause of the Roman world.—II. In this dangerous elevation,
Leo the Third supported himself against the envy of his equals, the
discontent of a powerful faction, and the assaults of his foreign and domestic enemies. The Catholics, who accuse his religious innovations,
are obliged to confess that they were undertaken with temper and
conducted with firmness. Their silence respects the wisdom of his administration and the purity of his manners. After a reign of twenty-
four years, he peaceably expired in the palace of Constantinople; and
the purple which he had acquired was transmitted by the right of inheritance to the third generation.

In a long reign of thirty-four years, the son and successor of Leo,
Constantine the Fifth, surnamed Copronymus, attacked with less temperate zeal the images or idols of the church. Their votaries have exhausted the bitterness of religious gall in their portrait of this spotted
panther, this Antichrist, this flying dragon of the serpent's seed, who
surpassed the vices of Elagabalus and Nero. His reign was a long
butchery of whatever was most noble or holy or innocent in his empire. In person, the emperor assisted at the execution of his victims,
surveyed their agonies, listened to their groans, and indulged, without
satiating, his appetite for blood: a plate of noses was accepted as a
grateful offering, and his domestics were often scourged or mutilated
by the royal hand. His surname was derived from his pollution of his
baptismal font. The infant might be excused; but the manly pleasures

of Copronymus degraded him below the level of a brute; his lust confounded the eternal distinctions of sex and species, and he seemed to extract some unnatural delight from the objects most offensive to human sense. In his religion the Iconoclast was a Heretic, a Jew, a Mohammedan, a Pagan, and an Atheist; and his belief of an invisible power could be discovered only in his magic rites, human victims, and nocturnal sacrifices to Venus and the demons of antiquity. His life was stained with the most opposite vices, and the ulcers which covered his body anticipated before his death the sentiment of hell-tortures. Of these accusations, which I have so patiently copied, a part is refuted by its own absurdity; and in the private anecdotes of the life of the princes, the lie is more easy as the detection is more difficult. Without adopting the pernicious maxim that where much is alleged something must be true, I can however discern that Constantine the Fifth was dissolute and cruel. Calumny is more prone to exaggerate than to invent; and her licentious tongue is checked in some measure by the experience of the age and country to which she appeals. Of the bishops and monks, the generals and magistrates, who are said to have suffered under his reign, the numbers are recorded, the names were conspicuous, the execution was public, the mutilation visible and permanent. The Catholics hated the person and government of Copronymus; but even their hatred is a proof of their oppression. They dissembled the provocations which might excuse or justify his rigor, but even these provocations must gradually inflame his resentment and harden his temper in the use or the abuse of despotism. Yet the character of the fifth Constantine was not devoid of merit nor did his government always deserve the curses or the contempt of the Greeks. From the confession of his enemies, I am informed of the restoration of an ancient aqueduct, of the redemption of two thousand five hundred captives, of the uncommon plenty of the times, and of the new colonies with which he repeopled Constantinople and the Thracian cities. They reluctantly praise his activity and courage; he was on horseback in the field at the head of his legions; and although the fortune of his arms was various, he triumphed by sea and land, on the Euphrates and the Danube, in civil and Barbarian war. Heretical praise must be cast into the scale to counterbalance the weight of orthodox invective. The Iconoclasts revered the virtues of the prince: forty years after his death they still prayed before the tomb of the saint. A miraculous vision was propagated by fanaticism or fraud: and the Christian hero appeared on a milk-white steed, brandishing his lance against the Pagans of Bulgaria: "An absurd fable," says the Catholic historian, "since Copronymus is chained with the demons in the abyss of hell."

[*We may continue our survey: 717–740, Leo III the Isaurian;741–775, Constantine V Copronymus; 775–780, Leo IV the Khazar; 780–797, Constantine VI; 797–802, Irene; 802–811, Nicephorus I; 811, Stauracius; 811–813, Michael I Rangabe; 813–820, Leo V the Armenian; 820–829, Michael II the Amorian; 829–842, Theophilus; 842–867, Michael III the Amorian; 867–886, Basil I; 886–912, Leo VI the Wise, or the Philosopher; 912–913, Alexander; 913–959, Constantine VII Porphyrogenitus; 920–944, Romanus I Lecapenus; 959–963, Romanus II; 963–969, Nicephorus II Phocas; 969–976, John I Tzimisces; 976–1025, Basil II Bulgaroctonus; 1025–1028, Constantine VIII; 1028–1034, Romanus III Argyrus; 1034–1041, Michael IV the Paphlagonian; 1041–1042, Michael V Calaphates; 1042, Zoe and Theodora; 1042–1055, Constantine IX Monomachus; 1055–1056, Theodora (again); 1056–1057, Michael VI Stratioticus; 1057–1059, Isaac I Comnenus. The rise of Isaac I Comnenus signals more than the rise of a new dynasty.*]

From this night of slavery, a ray of freedom, or at least of spirit, begins to emerge: the Greeks either preserved or revived the use of surnames, which perpetuate the fame of hereditary virtue: and we now discern the rise, succession, and alliances of the last dynasties of Constantinople and Trebizond. The *Comneni,* who upheld for a while the fate of the sinking empire, assumed the honor of a Roman origin: but the family had been long since transported from Italy to Asia.

[*The writings of Anna Comnena, daughter of Alexius I, serve as a major historical source.*]

The life of the emperor Alexius has been delineated by a favorite daughter, who was inspired by a tender regard for his person and a laudable zeal to perpetuate his virtues. Conscious of the just suspicions of her readers, the princess Anna Comnena repeatedly protests that, besides her personal knowledge, she had searched the discourses and writings of the most respectable veterans: and after an interval of thirty years, forgotten by and forgetful of the world, her mournful solitude was inaccessible to hope and fear; and that truth, the naked perfect truth, was more dear and sacred than the memory of her parent. Yet, instead of the simplicity of style and narrative which wins our belief, an elaborate affectation of rhetoric and science betrays in every page the vanity of a female author. The genuine character of Alexius is lost in a vague constellation of virtues; and the perpetual strain of panegyric and apology awakens our jealousy to question the veracity of the historian and the merit of the hero. We cannot, however, refuse her judicious and important remark that the disorders of the times were the misfortune and the glory of Alexius; and that every calamity which can afflict a declining empire was accumulated on his reign by the justice of Heaven and the vices of his predecessors. In the East, the victorious Turks had spread, from Persia to the Hellespont, the reign of the Koran and the Crescent: the West was invaded by the adventurous valor of the Normans; and in the moments of peace, the Danube poured forth new swarms, who had gained in the science of war what they had lost in the ferociousness of manners. The sea was not less hostile than the land; and while the frontiers were assaulted by an open enemy, the palace was distracted with secret treason and conspiracy. On a sudden, the banner of the cross was displayed by the Latins; Europe was precipitated on Asia; and Constantinople had almost been swept away by this impetuous deluge. In the tempest, Alexius steered the Imperial vessel with dexterity and courage.... Anna is a faithful witness that his happiness was destroyed and his health was broken by the cares of a public life; the patience of Constantinople was fatigued by the length and severity of his reign; and before Alexius expired, he had lost the love and reverence of his subjects. The clergy could not forgive his application of the sacred riches to the defense of the state; but they applauded his theological learning and ardent zeal for the orthodox faith, which he defended with his tongue, his pen, and his sword. His character was degraded by the superstition of the Greeks; and the same inconsistent principle of human nature enjoined the emperor to found a hospital for the poor and infirm, and to direct the execution of a heretic, who was burned alive in the square of

St. Sophia. Even the sincerity of his moral and religious virtues was suspected by the persons who had passed their lives in his familiar confidence. In his last hours, when he was pressed by his wife Irene to alter the succession, he raised his head and breathed a pious ejaculation on the vanity of this world. The indignant reply of the empress may be inscribed as an epitaph on his tomb, "You die as you have lived—A HYPOCRITE!"

[*We may complete our survey: 1057–1059, Isaac I Comnenus; 1059–1067, Constantine X Ducas; 1068–1071, Romanus IV Diogenes; 1071–1078, Michael VII Ducas (Parapinaces); 1078–1081, Nicephorus III Botaniates; 1081–1118, Alexius I Comnenus; 1118–1143, John II Comnenus; 1143–1180, Manuel I Comnenus; 1180–1183, Alexius II Comnenus; 1183–1185, Andronicus I Comnenus; 1185–1195, Isaac II Angelus.*]

If we compute the number and duration of the reigns, it will be found that a period of six hundred years is filled by sixty emperors, including in the Augustan list some female sovereigns; and deducting some usurpers who were never acknowledged in the capital, and some princes who did not live to possess their inheritance. The average proportion will allow ten years for each emperor, far below the chronological rule of Sir Isaac Newton, who, from the experience of more recent and regular monarchies, has defined about eighteen or twenty years as the term of an ordinary reign. The Byzantine empire was most tranquil and prosperous when it could acquiesce in hereditary succession; five dynasties, the Heraclian, Isaurian, Amorian, Basilian, and Comnenian families, enjoyed and transmitted the royal patrimony during their respective series of five, four, three, six, and four generations; several princes number the years of their reign with those of their infancy; and Constantine the Seventh and his two grandsons occupy the space of an entire century. But in the intervals of the Byzantine dynasties, the succession is rapid and broken, and the name of a successful candidate is speedily erased by a more fortunate competitor. Many were the paths that led to the summit of royalty: the fabric of rebellion was overthrown by the stroke of conspiracy or undermined by the silent arts of intrigue: the favorites of the soldiers or people, of the senate or clergy, of the women and eunuchs, were alternately clothed with the purple: the means of their elevation were base, and their end was often contemptible or tragic. A being of the nature of man, endowed with the same faculties but with a longer measure of existence, would cast down a smile of pity and contempt on the crimes and follies of human ambition, so eager in a narrow span to grasp at a precarious and shortlived enjoyment. It is thus that the experience of history exalts and enlarges the horizon of our intellectual view. In a composition of some days, in a perusal of some hours, six hundred years have rolled away, and the duration of a life or reign is contracted to a fleeting moment: the grave is ever beside the throne: the success of a criminal is almost instantly followed by the loss of his prize and our immortal reason survives and disdains the sixty phantoms of kings who have passed before our eyes and faintly dwell on our remembrance. The observation that in every age and climate ambition has prevailed with the same commanding energy may abate the surprise of a philosopher: but while he condemns the vanity, he may search the motive of this universal desire to obtain and hold the scepter of dominion. To the greater part of the Byzantine series, we cannot reasonably ascribe the love of fame and of mankind. The virtue alone of John Comnenus was beneficent and pure: the most illustrious of the princes who precede or follow that respectable name have trod with some dexterity and vigor the crooked and bloody paths of a selfish policy: in scrutinizing the imperfect characters of Leo the Isaurian, Basil the First, and Alexius Comnenus, of Theophilus, the second Basil, and Manuel Comnenus, our esteem and censure are almost equally balanced; and the remainder of the Imperial crowd could only desire and expect to be forgotten by posterity. Was personal happiness the aim and object of their ambition? I shall not descant on the vulgar topics of the misery of kings; but I may surely observe that their condition, of all others, is the most pregnant with fear and the least susceptible of hope. For these opposite passions, a larger scope was allowed in the revolutions of antiquity than in the smooth and solid temper of the modern world, which cannot easily repeat either the triumph of Alexander or the fall of Darius. But the peculiar infelicity of the Byzantine princes exposed them to domestic perils without affording any lively promise of foreign conquest. . . . The army was licentious without spirit, the nation turbulent without freedom: the Barbarians of the East and West pressed on the monarchy, and the loss of the provinces was terminated by the final servitude of the capital.

THE ROMAN EMPIRE
END OF THE SEVENTH CENTURY
A.D. 695

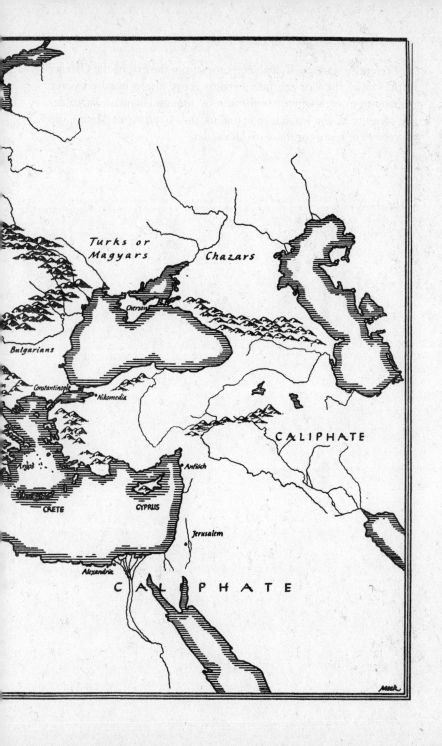

Turks or
Magyars

Chazars

Bulgarians

Cherson

Constantinople

Nikomedia

CALIPHATE

Argos

Antioch

CRETE

CYPRUS

Jerusalem

Alexandria

CALIPHATE

Mock

The entire series of Roman emperors, from the first of the Caesars to the last of the Constantines, extends above fifteen hundred years: and the term of dominion, unbroken by foreign conquest, surpasses the measure of the ancient monarchies, the Assyrians or Medes, the successors of Cyrus or those of Alexander.

CHAPTER XLIX

Conquest of Italy by the Franks

Introduction, worship, and persecution of images. • *Revolt of Italy and Rome.* • *Temporal dominion of the popes.* • *Conquest of Italy by the Franks.* • *Establishment of images.* • *Character and coronation of Charlemagne.* • *Restoration and decay of the Roman empire in the West.* • *Independence of Italy.* • *Constitution of the Germanic body.*

In the connection of the church and state, I have considered the former as subservient only and relative to the latter; a salutary maxim, if in fact as well as in narrative it had ever been held sacred. The Oriental philosophy of the Gnostics, the dark abyss of predestination and grace, and the strange transformation of the Eucharist from the sign to the substance of Christ's body, I have purposely abandoned to the curiosity of speculative divines. But I have reviewed with diligence and pleasure the objects of ecclesiastical history by which the decline and fall of the Roman empire were materially affected, the propagation of Christianity, the constitution of the Catholic church, the ruin of Paganism, and the sects that arose from the mysterious controversies concerning the Trinity and Incarnation. At the head of this class, we may justly rank the worship of images, so fiercely disputed in the eighth and ninth centuries; since a question of popular superstition produced the revolt of Italy, the temporal power of the popes, and the restoration of the Roman empire in the West.

The primitive Christians were possessed with an unconquerable repugnance to the use and abuse of images; and this aversion may be ascribed to their descent from the Jews and their enmity to the Greeks. The Mosaic law had severely proscribed all representations of the Deity; and that precept was firmly established in the principles and practice of the chosen people. The wit of the Christian apologists was pointed against the foolish idolaters who bowed before the workmanship of their own hands; the images of brass and marble which, had *they* been endowed with sense and motion, should have started rather from the pedestal to adore the creative powers of the artist. Perhaps some recent and imperfect converts of the Gnostic tribe might crown the statues of Christ and St. Paul with the profane honors which they paid to those of Aristotle and Pythagoras; but the public religion of the Catholics was uniformly simple and spiritual; and the first notice of the use of pictures is in the censure of the council of Illiberis, three hundred years after the Christian era. Under the successors of Constantine, in the peace and luxury of the triumphant church, the more prudent bishops condescended to indulge a visible superstition for the benefit of the multitude; and after the ruin of Paganism, they were no longer restrained by the apprehension of an odious parallel. The first introduction of a symbolic worship was in the veneration of the cross and of relics. The saints and martyrs whose intercession was implored were seated on the right hand of God; but the gracious and often supernatural favors which, in the popular belief, were showered round their tomb conveyed an unquestionable sanction of the devout pilgrims who visited and touched and kissed these lifeless remains, the memorials of their merits and sufferings. But a memorial more interesting than the skull or the sandals of a departed worthy is the faithful copy of his person and features, delineated by the arts of painting or sculpture. In every age, such copies, so congenial to human feelings, have been cherished by the zeal of private friendship or public esteem: the images of the Roman emperors were adored with civil and almost religious honors; a reverence less ostentatious but more sincere was applied to the statues of sages and patriots; and these profane virtues, these splendid sins, disappeared in the presence of the holy men who had died for their celestial and everlasting country. At first, the experiment was made with caution and scruple; and the venerable pictures were discreetly allowed to instruct the ignorant, to awaken the cold, and to gratify the prejudices of the heathen proselytes. By a slow though inevitable progression, the honors of the original were transferred to the copy: the devout Christian prayed before the image of a saint; and the Pagan rites of genuflection, luminaries, and incense again stole into the Catholic church. The scruples of reason or piety were silenced by the strong evidence of visions and miracles; and the pictures which speak and move and bleed must be endowed with a divine energy, and may be considered as the proper objects of religious adoration. The most audacious pencil might tremble in the rash attempt of defining, by forms and colors, the infinite Spirit, the eternal Father, who pervades and sustains the universe. But the superstitious mind was more easily reconciled to paint and to worship the angels and, above all, the Son of God under the human shape which on earth they have condescended to assume. The second person of the Trinity had been clothed with a real and mortal body; but that body had ascended into Heaven: and, had not some similitude been presented to the eyes of his disciples, the spiritual worship of Christ might have been obliterated by the visible relics and representations of the saints. A similar indulgence was requisite and propitious for the Virgin Mary: the place of her burial was unknown; and the assumption of her soul and body into Heaven was adopted by the credulity of the Greeks and Latins. The use and even the worship of images was firmly established before the end of the sixth century: they were fondly cherished by the warm imagination of the Greeks and Asiatics: the Pantheon and Vatican were adorned with the emblems of a new superstition; but this semblance of idolatry was more coldly entertained by the rude Barbarians and the Arian clergy of the West. The bolder forms of sculpture, in brass or marble, which peopled the temples of antiquity were offensive to the fancy or conscience of the Christian Greeks: and a smooth surface of colors has ever been esteemed a more decent and harmless mode of imitation.[†]

The worship of images had stolen into the church by insensible degrees, and each petty step was pleasing to the superstitious mind as productive of comfort and innocent of sin. But in the beginning of the eighth century, in the full magnitude of the abuse, the more timorous Greeks were awakened by an apprehension that under the mask of Christianity, they had restored the religion of their fathers: they heard with grief and impatience the name of idolaters, the incessant charge of the Jews and Mohammedans, who derived from the law and the Koran an immortal hatred to graven images and all relative worship. The servitude of the Jews might curb their zeal and depreciate their authority; but the triumphant Moslems, who reigned at Damascus and threatened Constantinople, cast into the scale of reproach the accumulated weight of truth and victory. The cities of Syria, Palestine, and Egypt had been fortified with the images of Christ, his mother, and his saints; and each city presumed on the hope or promise of miraculous defense. In a rapid conquest of ten years, the Arabs subdued those cities and these images; and in their opinion, the Lord of Hosts pronounced a decisive judgment between the adoration and contempt of these mute and inanimate idols. . . . In this season of distress and dismay, the eloquence of the monks was exercised in the defense of images; and they attempted to prove that the sin and schism of the greatest part of the Orientals had forfeited the favor and annihilated the virtue of these precious symbols. But they were now opposed by the murmurs of many simple or rational Christians, who appealed to the evidence of texts, of facts, and of the primitive times, and secretly desired the reformation of the church. As the worship of images had never been established by any general or positive law, its progress in the Eastern empire had been retarded or accelerated by the differences of men and manners, the local degrees of refinement, and the personal characters of the bishops. The splendid devotion was fondly cherished by the levity of the capital and the inventive genius of the Byzantine clergy; while the rude and remote districts of Asia were strangers to this innovation of sacred luxury. Many large congregations of Gnostics and Arians maintained after their conversion the simple worship which had preceded their separation; and the Armenians, the most warlike subjects of Rome, were not reconciled in the twelfth century to the sight of images. These various denominations of men afforded a fund of prejudice and aversion, of small account in the villages of Anatolia or Thrace but which, in the fortune of a soldier, a prelate, or a eunuch, might be often connected with the powers of the church and state.

Of such adventurers, the most fortunate was the emperor Leo the Third, who from the mountains of Isauria ascended the throne of the East. He was ignorant of sacred and profane letters; but his education, his reason, perhaps his intercourse with the Jews and Arabs had inspired the martial peasant with a hatred of images; and it was held to be the duty of a prince to impose on his subjects the dictates of his own conscience. . . . [H]e proscribed the existence as well as the use of religious pictures; the churches of Constantinople and the provinces were cleansed from idolatry; the images of Christ, the Virgin, and the saints were demolished, or a smooth surface of plaster was spread over the walls of the edifice [A.D. 729]. The sect of the Iconoclasts was supported by the zeal and despotism of six emperors, and the East and West were involved in a noisy conflict of one hundred and twenty

years [A.D. 726–840]. It was the design of Leo the Isaurian to pronounce the condemnation of images as an article of faith, and by the
authority of a general council: but the convocation of such an assembly was reserved for his son Constantine; and though it is stigmatized
by triumphant bigotry as a meeting of fools and atheists, their own
partial and mutilated acts betray many symptoms of reason and piety
[A.D. 754]. The debates and decrees of many provincial synods introduced the summons of the general council, which met in the suburbs
of Constantinople, and was composed of the respectable number of
three hundred and thirty-eight bishops of Europe and Anatolia; for
the patriarchs of Antioch and Alexandria were the slaves of the caliph,
and the Roman pontiff had withdrawn the churches of Italy and the
West from the communion of the Greeks. This Byzantine synod assumed the rank and powers of the seventh general council; yet even
this title was a recognition of the six preceding assemblies, which had
laboriously built the structure of the Catholic faith. After a serious deliberation of six months, the three hundred and thirty-eight bishops
pronounced and subscribed a unanimous decree that all visible symbols of Christ, except in the Eucharist, were either blasphemous or
heretical; that image-worship was a corruption of Christianity and a
renewal of Paganism; that all such monuments of idolatry should be
broken or erased; and that those who should refuse to deliver the objects of their private superstition were guilty of disobedience to the
authority of the church and of the emperor. In their loud and loyal acclamations, they celebrated the merits of their temporal redeemer;
and to his zeal and justice they entrusted the execution of their spiritual censures. At Constantinople, as in the former councils, the will of
the prince was the rule of episcopal faith; but on this occasion, I am inclined to suspect that a large majority of the prelates sacrificed their
secret conscience to the temptations of hope and fear. In the long night
of superstition, the Christians had wandered far away from the simplicity of the gospel: nor was it easy for them to discern the clue and
tread back the mazes of the labyrinth. The worship of images was inseparably blended, at least to a pious fancy, with the cross, the Virgin,
the saints and their relics; the holy ground was involved in a cloud of
miracles and visions; and the nerves of the mind, curiosity and skepticism, were benumbed by the habits of obedience and belief.[†]

The scandal of an abstract heresy can be only proclaimed to the people by the blast of the ecclesiastical trumpet; but the most ignorant can perceive, the most torpid must feel, the profanation and downfall of their visible deities [A.D. 726–775]. The first hostilities of Leo were directed against a lofty Christ on the vestibule and above the gate of the palace. A ladder had been planted for the assault, but it was furiously shaken by a crowd of zealots and women: they beheld with pious transport the ministers of sacrilege tumbling from on high and dashed against the pavement: and the honors of the ancient martyrs were prostituted to these criminals, who justly suffered for murder and rebellion. The execution of the Imperial edicts was resisted by frequent tumults in Constantinople and the provinces: the person of Leo was endangered, his officers were massacred, and the popular enthusiasm was quelled by the strongest efforts of the civil and military power.... I am not at leisure to examine how far the monks provoked nor how much they have exaggerated their real and pretended sufferings, nor how many lost their lives or limbs, their eyes or their beards, by the cruelty of the emperor. From the chastisement of individuals, he proceeded to the abolition of the order; and as it was wealthy and useless, his resentment might be stimulated by avarice and justified by patriotism. The formidable name and mission of the *Dragon,* his visitor-general, excited the terror and abhorrence of the *black* nation: the religious communities were dissolved, the buildings were converted into magazines or barracks; the lands, movables, and cattle were confiscated; and our modern precedents will support the charge that much wanton or malicious havoc was exercised against the relics and even the books of the monasteries. With the habit and profession of monks, the public and private worship of images was rigorously proscribed; and it should seem that a solemn abjuration of idolatry was exacted from the subjects, or at least from the clergy, of the Eastern empire.

The patient East abjured with reluctance her sacred images; they were fondly cherished and vigorously defended by the independent zeal of the Italians. In ecclesiastical rank and jurisdiction, the patriarch of Constantinople and the pope of Rome were nearly equal. But the Greek prelate was a domestic slave under the eye of his master, at whose nod he alternately passed from the convent to the throne, and from the throne to the convent. A distant and dangerous station amidst the Barbarians of the West excited the spirit and freedom of the Latin bishops. Their popular election endeared them to the Romans: the public and private indigence was relieved by their ample revenue; and the weakness or neglect of the emperors compelled them to consult, both in peace and war, the temporal safety of the city. In the school of adversity the priest insensibly imbibed the virtues and the ambition of a prince; the same character was assumed, the same policy was adopted, by the Italian, the Greek, or the Syrian who ascended the chair of St. Peter; and, after the loss of her legions and provinces, the genius and fortune of the popes again restored the supremacy of Rome. It is agreed that in the eighth century their dominion was founded on rebellion, and that the rebellion was produced, and justified by the heresy of the Iconoclasts.[†]

The first assault of Leo against the images of Constantinople had been witnessed by a crowd of strangers from Italy and the West, who related with grief and indignation the sacrilege of the emperor [A.D. 728 ff.]. But on the reception of his proscriptive edict, they trembled for their domestic deities: the images of Christ and the Virgin, of the angels, martyrs, and saints, were abolished in all the churches of Italy; and a strong alternative was proposed to the Roman pontiff, the royal favor as the price of his compliance, degradation and exile as the penalty of his disobedience. Neither zeal nor policy allowed him to hesitate; and the haughty strain in which Gregory addressed the emperor displays his confidence in the truth of his doctrine or the powers of resistance. Without depending on prayers or miracles, he boldly armed against the public enemy, and his pastoral letters admonished the Italians of their danger and their duty. At this signal, Ravenna, Venice, and the cities of the Exarchate and Pentapolis adhered to the cause of religion; their military force by sea and land consisted for the most part of the natives; and the spirit of patriotism and zeal was transfused into the mercenary strangers. The Italians swore to live and die in the defense of the pope and the holy images; the Roman people was devoted to their father, and even the Lombards were ambitious to share the merit and advantage of this holy war. The most treasonable act, but the most obvious revenge, was the destruction of the statues of Leo himself: the most effectual and pleasing measure of rebellion was the withholding of the tribute of Italy, and depriving him of a power which he had recently abused by the imposition of a new capitation. A form of administration was preserved by the election of magistrates and governors; and so high was the public indignation that the Italians were prepared to create an orthodox emperor and to conduct him with a fleet and army to the palace of Constantinople. In that palace the Roman bishops, the second and third Gregory, were condemned as the authors of the revolt, and every attempt was made, either by fraud or force, to seize their persons and to strike at their lives. The city was repeatedly visited or assaulted by captains of the guards and dukes and exarchs of high dignity or secret trust; they landed with foreign troops, they obtained some domestic aid, and the superstition of Naples may blush that her fathers were attached to the cause of heresy. But these clandestine or open attacks were repelled by the courage and vigilance of the Romans; the Greeks were overthrown and massacred, their leaders suffered an ignominious death, and the popes, however inclined to mercy, refused to intercede for these guilty victims. . . . Amidst the triumph of the Catholic arms, the Roman pontiff convened a synod of ninety-three bishops against the heresy of the Iconoclasts. With their consent, he pronounced a general excommunication against all who by word or deed should attack the tradition of the fathers and the images of the saints: in this sentence the emperor was tacitly involved, but the vote of a last and hopeless remonstrance may seem to imply that the anathema was yet suspended over his guilty head. No sooner had they confirmed their own safety, the worship of images, and the freedom of Rome and Italy than the popes appear to have relaxed their severity and to have spared the relics of the Byzantine dominion. Their moderate councils delayed and prevented the election of a new emperor, and they exhorted the Italians not to separate from the body of the Roman monarchy. The exarch was permitted to reside within the walls of Ravenna, a captive rather than a master; and till the Imperial coronation of Charlemagne, the government of Rome and Italy was exercised in the name of the successors of Constantine.

The liberty of Rome, which had been oppressed by the arms and arts of Augustus, was rescued after seven hundred and fifty years of servitude from the persecution of Leo the Isaurian. By the Caesars, the triumphs of the consuls had been annihilated: in the decline and fall of the empire, the god Terminus, the sacred boundary, had insensibly receded from the Ocean, the Rhine, the Danube, and the Euphrates; and Rome was reduced to her ancient territory from Viterbo to Terracina, and from Narni to the mouth of the Tiber. When the kings were banished, the republic reposed on the firm basis which had been founded by their wisdom and virtue. Their perpetual jurisdiction was divided between two annual magistrates: the senate continued to exercise the powers of administration and counsel; and the legislative authority was distributed in the assemblies of the people by a well-proportioned scale of property and service. Ignorant of the arts of luxury, the primitive Romans had improved the science of government and war: the will of the community was absolute: the rights of individuals were sacred: one hundred and thirty thousand citizens were armed for defense or conquest; and a band of robbers and outlaws was molded into a nation deserving of freedom and ambitious of glory. When the sovereignty of the Greek emperors was extinguished, the ruins of Rome presented the sad image of depopulation and decay: her slavery was a habit, her liberty an accident, the effect of superstition and the object of her own amazement and terror. The last vestige of the substance, or even the forms, of the constitution was obliterated from the practice and memory of the Romans; and they were devoid of knowledge or virtue again to build the fabric of a commonwealth. Their scanty remnant, the offspring of slaves and strangers, was despicable in the eyes of the victorious Barbarians. As often as the Franks or Lombards expressed their most bitter contempt of a foe, they called him a Roman; "and in this name," says the bishop Liutprand, "we include whatever is base, whatever is cowardly, whatever is perfidious, the extremes of avarice and luxury, and every vice that can prostitute the dignity of human nature." By the necessity of their situation, the inhabitants of Rome were cast into the rough model of a republican government: they were compelled to elect some judges in peace and some leaders in war: the nobles assembled to deliberate, and their resolves could not be executed without the union and consent of the multitude. The style of the Roman senate and people was revived, but the spirit was fled; and their new independence was disgraced by the tumultuous conflict of licentiousness and oppression. The want of laws could only be supplied by the influence of religion, and their foreign and domestic counsels were moderated by the authority of the bishop. His alms, his sermons, his correspondence with the kings and prelates of the West, his recent services, their gratitude and oath accustomed the Romans to consider him as the first magistrate or prince of the city. The Christian humility of the popes was not offended by the name of *Dominus,* or Lord; and their face and inscription are still apparent on the most ancient coins. Their temporal dominion is now confirmed by the reverence of a thousand years; and their noblest title is the free choice of a people whom they had redeemed from slavery.

In the quarrels of ancient Greece, the holy people of Elis enjoyed a perpetual peace under the protection of Jupiter and in the exercise of the Olympic games. Happy would it have been for the Romans if a similar privilege had guarded the patrimony of St. Peter from the calamities of war; if the Christians who visited the holy threshold would have sheathed their swords in the presence of the apostle and his successor. But this mystic circle could have been traced only by the wand of a legislator and a sage: this pacific system was incompatible with the zeal and ambition of the popes; the Romans were not addicted, like the inhabitants of Elis, to the innocent and placid labors of agriculture; and the Barbarians of Italy, though softened by the climate, were far below the Grecian states in the institutions of public and private life.

[*The Lombards attack Rome (A.D. 730–752). In defense of their temporal possessions, the popes of Rome appeal to the Franks for aid against the Lombards. Rome is delivered by Pepin (A.D. 754), and Charlemagne conquers Lombardy (A.D. 774).*]

The mutual obligations of the popes and the Carlovingian family form the important link of ancient and modern, of civil and ecclesiastical, history. In the conquest of Italy, the champions of the Roman church obtained a favorable occasion, a specious title, the wishes of the people, the prayers and intrigues of the clergy. But the most essential gifts of the popes to the Carlovingian race were the dignities of king of France, and of patrician of Rome. Under the sacerdotal monarchy of St. Peter, the nations began to resume the practice of seeking on the banks of the Tiber their kings, their laws, and the oracles of their fate. The Franks were perplexed between the name and substance of their government. All the powers of royalty were exercised by Pepin, mayor of the palace; and nothing except the regal title was wanting to his ambition. His enemies were crushed by his valor; his friends were multiplied by his liberality; his father had been the savior of Christendom; and the claims of personal merit were repeated and ennobled in a descent of four generations. The name and image of royalty was still preserved in the last descendant of Clovis, the feeble Childeric; but his obsolete right could only be used as an instrument of sedition: the nation was desirous of restoring the simplicity of the constitution; and Pepin, a subject and a prince, was ambitious to ascertain his own rank and the fortune of his family. The mayor and the nobles were bound by an oath of fidelity to the royal phantom: the blood of Clovis was pure and sacred in their eyes; and their common ambassadors addressed the Roman pontiff, to dispel their scruples or to absolve their promise. The interest of Pope Zachary, the successor of the two Gregories, prompted him to decide, and to decide in their favor: he pronounced that the nation might lawfully unite in the same person the title and authority of king; and that the unfortunate Childeric, a victim of the public safety, should be degraded, shaved, and confined in a monastery for the remainder of his days. An answer so agreeable to their wishes was accepted by the Franks as the opinion of a casuist, the sentence of a judge, or the oracle of a prophet: the Merovingian race disappeared from the earth; and Pepin was exalted on a buckler by the suffrage of a free people, accustomed to obey his laws and to march under his standard. His coronation was twice performed, with the sanction of the popes, by their most faithful servant St. Boniface, the apostle of Germany, and by the grateful hands of Stephen the Third, who in the monastery of St. Denys placed the diadem on the head of his benefactor. The royal unction of the kings of Israel was dexterously applied: the successor of St. Peter assumed the character of a divine ambassador: a German chieftain was transformed into the Lord's anointed; and this Jewish rite has been diffused and maintained by the superstition and vanity of modern Europe. The Franks were absolved from their ancient oath; but a dire anathema was thundered against them and their posterity if they should dare to renew the same freedom of choice, or to elect a king, except in the holy and meritorious race of the Carlovingian princes. Without apprehending the future danger, these princes gloried in their present security: the secretary of Charlemagne affirms that the French scepter was transferred by the authority of the popes; and in their boldest enterprises, they insist with confidence on this signal and successful act of temporal jurisdiction.†

The gratitude of the Carlovingians was adequate to these obligations, and their names are consecrated as the saviors and benefactors of the Roman church. Her ancient patrimony of farms and houses was transformed by their bounty into the temporal dominion of cities and provinces; and the donation of the Exarchate was the first-fruits of the conquests of Pepin. . . . In this transaction, the ambition and avarice of the popes have been severely condemned. Perhaps the humility of a Christian priest should have rejected an earthly kingdom, which it was not easy for him to govern without renouncing the virtues of his profession. . . . But in the rigid interpretation of the laws, everyone may accept without injury whatever his benefactor can bestow without injustice. The Greek emperor had abdicated or forfeited his right to the Exarchate; and [his] sword . . . was broken by the stronger sword of the Carlovingian. It was not in the cause of the Iconoclast that Pepin had exposed his person and army in a double expedition beyond the Alps: he possessed and might lawfully alienate his conquests: and to the importunities of the Greeks he piously replied that no human consideration should tempt him to resume the gift which he had conferred on the Roman pontiff for the remission of his sins and the salvation of his soul. The splendid donation was granted in supreme and absolute dominion, and the world beheld for the first time a Christian bishop invested with the prerogatives of a temporal prince: the choice of magistrates, the exercise of justice, the imposition of taxes, and the wealth of the palace of Ravenna.[†]

Fraud is the resource of weakness and cunning; and the strong though ignorant Barbarian was often entangled in the net of sacerdotal policy. The Vatican and Lateran were an arsenal and manufacture which, according to the occasion, have produced or concealed a various collection of false or genuine, of corrupt or suspicious, acts as they tended to promote the interest of the Roman church. Before the end of the eighth century, some apostolic scribe, perhaps the notorious Isidore, composed the decretals, and the DONATION OF CONSTANTINE, the two magic pillars of the spiritual and temporal monarchy of the popes. This memorable donation was introduced to the world by an epistle of Hadrian the First, who exhorts Charlemagne to imitate the liberality and revive the name of the great Constantine. According to the legend, the first of the Christian emperors was healed of the leprosy and purified in the waters of baptism by St. Silvester, the Roman bishop; and never was physician more gloriously recompensed. His royal proselyte withdrew from the seat and patrimony of St. Peter; declared his resolution of founding a new capital in the East; and resigned to the popes the free and perpetual sovereignty of Rome, Italy, and the provinces of the West. This fiction was productive of the most beneficial effects. The Greek princes were convicted of the guilt of usurpation; and the revolt of Gregory was the claim of his lawful in- heritance. The popes were delivered from their debt of gratitude; and the nominal gifts of the Carlovingians were no more than the just and irrevocable restitution of a scanty portion of the ecclesiastical state. The sovereignty of Rome no longer depended on the choice of a fickle people; and the successors of St. Peter and Constantine were invested with the purple and prerogatives of the Caesars. So deep was the ig- norance and credulity of the times that the most absurd of fables was received with equal reverence in Greece and in France, and is still en- rolled among the decrees of the canon law.†

While the popes established in Italy their freedom and dominion, the images, the first cause of their revolt, were restored in the Eastern empire [A.D. 780 ff.]. Under the reign of Constantine the Fifth, the union of civil and ecclesiastical power had overthrown the tree with- out extirpating the root of superstition. The idols (for such they were now held) were secretly cherished by the order and the sex most prone to devotion; and the fond alliance of the monks and females obtained a final victory over the reason and authority of man. Leo the Fourth maintained with less rigor the religion of his father and grandfather; but his wife, the fair and ambitious Irene, had imbibed the zeal of the Athenians, the heirs of the idolatry, rather than the philosophy of their ancestors. During the life of her husband, these sentiments were in- flamed by danger and dissimulation, and she could only labor to pro- tect and promote some favorite monks whom she drew from their caverns and seated on the metropolitan thrones of the East. But as soon as she reigned in her own name and that of her son, Irene more seriously undertook the ruin of the Iconoclasts; and the first step of her future persecution was a general edict for liberty of conscience. In the restoration of the monks, a thousand images were exposed to the public veneration; a thousand legends were invented of their sufferings and miracles. By the opportunities of death or removal, the episcopal seats were judiciously filled; the most eager competitors for earthly or celestial favor anticipated and flattered the judgment of their sover- eign; and the promotion of her secretary Tarasius gave Irene the pa- triarch of Constantinople and the command of the Oriental church.

But the decrees of a general council could only be repealed by a similar assembly: the Iconoclasts whom she convened were bold in possession and averse to debate; and the feeble voice of the bishops was reechoed by the more formidable clamor of the soldiers and people of Constantinople. The delay and intrigues of a year, the separation of the disaffected troops, and the choice of Nice for a second orthodox synod removed these obstacles [September 24–October 23, A.D. 787]; and the episcopal conscience was again, after the Greek fashion, in the hands of the prince. No more than eighteen days were allowed for the consummation of this important work: the Iconoclasts appeared not as judges but as criminals or penitents: the scene was decorated by the legates of Pope Hadrian and the Eastern patriarchs, the decrees were framed by the president Taracius and ratified by the acclamations and subscriptions of three hundred and fifty bishops. They unanimously pronounced that the worship of images is agreeable to Scripture and reason, to the fathers and councils of the church: but they hesitate whether that worship be relative or direct; whether the Godhead and the figure of Christ be entitled to the same mode of adoration. Of this second Nicene council the acts are still extant; a curious monument of superstition and ignorance, of falsehood and folly. I shall only notice the judgment of the bishops on the comparative merit of image-worship and morality. A monk had concluded a truce with the demon of fornication, on condition of interrupting his daily prayers to a picture that hung in his cell. His scruples prompted him to consult the abbot. "Rather than abstain from adoring Christ and his Mother in their holy images, it would be better for you," replied the casuist, "to enter every brothel and visit every prostitute in the city."

For the honor of orthodoxy, at least the orthodoxy of the Roman church, it is somewhat unfortunate that the two princes who convened the two councils of Nice are both stained with the blood of their sons. The second of these assemblies was approved and rigorously executed by the despotism of Irene, and she refused her adversaries the toleration which at first she had granted to her friends. During the five succeeding reigns, a period of thirty-eight years, the contest was maintained, with unabated rage and various success, between the worshipers and the breakers of the images; but I am not inclined to pursue with minute diligence the repetition of the same events.... After the death of Theophilus, the final victory of the images was achieved by a second female, his widow Theodora, whom he left the guardian of the empire. Her measures were bold and decisive. The fiction of a tardy repentance absolved the fame and the soul of her deceased husband; the sentence of the Iconoclast patriarch was commuted from the loss of his eyes to a whipping of two hundred lashes: the bishops trembled, the monks shouted, and the festival of orthodoxy preserves the annual memory of the triumph of the images [March 11, A.D. 843]. A single question yet remained, whether they are endowed with any proper and inherent sanctity; it was agitated by the Greeks of the eleventh century; and as this opinion has the strongest recommendation of absurdity, I am surprised that it was not more explicitly decided in the affirmative. In the West, Pope Hadrian the First accepted and announced the decrees of the Nicene assembly, which is now revered by the Catholics as the seventh in rank of the general councils. Rome and Italy were docile to the voice of their father; but the greatest part of the Latin Christians were far behind in the race of superstition. The churches of France, Germany, England, and Spain steered a middle course between the adoration and the destruction of images, which they admitted into their temples not as objects of worship but as lively and useful memorials of faith and history.†

It was after the Nycene synod, and under the reign of the pious Irene, that the popes consummated the separation of Rome and Italy by the translation of the empire to the less orthodox Charlemagne [A.D. 774–800]. They were compelled to choose between the rival nations: religion was not the sole motive of their choice; and while they dissembled the failings of their friends, they beheld with reluctance and suspicion the Catholic virtues of their foes. The difference of language and manners had perpetuated the enmity of the two capitals; and they were alienated from each other by the hostile opposition of seventy years. In that schism the Romans had tasted of freedom, and the popes of sovereignty: their submission would have exposed them to the revenge of a jealous tyrant; and the revolution of Italy had betrayed the impotence as well as the tyranny of the Byzantine court. . . . The Greeks were now orthodox; but their religion might be tainted by the breath of the reigning monarch: the Franks were now contumacious; but a discerning eye might discern their approaching conversion from the use to the adoration of images. The name of Charlemagne was stained by the polemic acrimony of his scribes; but the conqueror himself conformed, with the temper of a statesman, to the various practices of France and Italy. In his four pilgrimages or visits to the Vatican, he embraced the popes in the communion of friendship and piety; knelt before the tomb, and consequently before the image, of the apostle; and joined without scruple in all the prayers and processions of the Roman liturgy. Would prudence or gratitude allow the pontiffs to renounce their benefactor? Had they a right to alienate his gift of the Exarchate? Had they power to abolish his government of Rome? . . . [I]t was only by reviving the Western empire that they could pay their obligations or secure their establishment. By this decisive measure they would finally eradicate the claims of the Greeks; from the debasement of a provincial town, the majesty of Rome would be restored: the Latin Christians would be united, under a supreme head, in their ancient metropolis; and the conquerors of the West would receive their crown from the successors of St. Peter. The Roman church would acquire a zealous and respectable advocate; and under the shadow of the Carlovingian power, the bishop might exercise with honor and safety the government of the city.†

On the festival of Christmas, the last year of the eighth century [A.D. 800], Charlemagne appeared in the church of St. Peter; and to gratify the vanity of Rome, he had exchanged the simple dress of his country for the habit of a patrician. After the celebration of the holy mysteries, Leo suddenly placed a precious crown on his head, and the dome resounded with the acclamations of the people, "Long life and victory to Charles, the most pious Augustus, crowned by God the great and pacific emperor of the Romans!" The head and body of Charlemagne were consecrated by the royal unction: after the example of the Caesars, he was saluted or adored by the pontiff: his coronation oath represents a promise to maintain the faith and privileges of the church; and the first-fruits were paid in his rich offerings to the shrine of his apostle.†

The appellation of *great* has been often bestowed, and sometimes deserved; but CHARLEMAGNE [who reigned A.D. 768–814] is the only prince in whose favor the title has been indissolubly blended with the name. That name, with the addition of *saint,* is inserted in the Roman calendar; and the *saint,* by a rare felicity, is crowned with the praises of the historians and philosophers of an enlightened age. His *real* merit is doubtless enhanced by the barbarism of the nation and the times from which he emerged: but the *apparent* magnitude of an object is likewise enlarged by an unequal comparison; and the ruins of Palmyra derive a casual splendor from the nakedness of the surrounding desert. Without injustice to his fame, I may discern some blemishes in the sanctity and greatness of the restorer of the Western empire. Of his moral virtues, chastity is not the most conspicuous: but the public happiness could not be materially injured by his nine wives or concubines, the various indulgence of meaner or more transient amours, the multitude of his bastards, whom he bestowed on the church, and the long celibacy and licentious manners of his daughters, whom the father was suspected of loving with too fond a passion. I shall be scarcely permitted to accuse the ambition of a conqueror; but in a day of equal retribution, the sons of his brother Carloman, the Merovingian princes of Aquitain, and the four thousand five hundred Saxons who were beheaded on the same spot would have something to allege against the justice and humanity of Charlemagne. His treatment of the vanquished Saxons was an abuse of the right of conquest; his laws were not less sanguinary than his arms, and in the discussion of his motives, whatever is subtracted from bigotry must be imputed to temper.... His military renown must be tried by the scrutiny of his troops, his enemies, and his actions. . . . At the head of his veteran and superior armies, he oppressed the savage or degenerate nations who were incapable of confederating for their common safety: nor did he ever encounter an equal antagonist in numbers, in discipline, or in arms. The science of war has been lost and revived with the arts of peace; but his campaigns are not illustrated by any siege or battle of singular difficulty and success.... I touch with reverence the laws of Charlemagne, so highly applauded by a respectable judge. They compose not a system but a series of occasional and minute edicts for the correction of abuses, the reformation of manners, the economy of his farms, the care of his poultry, and even the sale of his eggs. He wished to improve the laws and the character of the Franks; and his attempts, however feeble and imperfect, are deserving of praise: the inveterate evils of the times were suspended or mollified by his government; but in his institutions I can seldom discover the general views and the immortal spirit of a legislator who survives himself for the benefit of posterity. The union and stability of his empire depended on the life of a single man: he imitated the dangerous practice of dividing his kingdoms among his sons;

and after his numerous diets, the whole constitution was left to fluctuate between the disorders of anarchy and despotism. His esteem for the piety and knowledge of the clergy tempted him to entrust that aspiring order with temporal dominion and civil jurisdiction; and his son Lewis, when he was stripped and degraded by the bishops, might accuse in some measure the imprudence of his father. His laws enforced the imposition of tithes, because the demons had proclaimed in the air that the default of payment had been the cause of the last scarcity. The literary merits of Charlemagne are attested by the foundation of schools, the introduction of arts, the works which were published in his name, and his familiar connection with the subjects and strangers whom he invited to his court to educate both the prince and people. His own studies were tardy, laborious, and imperfect; if he spoke Latin and understood Greek, he derived the rudiments of knowledge from conversation rather than from books; and in his mature age, the emperor strove to acquire the practice of writing, which every peasant now learns in his infancy. The grammar and logic, the music and astronomy of the times, were only cultivated as the handmaids of superstition; but the curiosity of the human mind must ultimately tend to its improvement, and the encouragement of learning reflects the purest and most pleasing luster on the character of Charlemagne. The dignity of his person, the length of his reign, the prosperity of his arms, the vigor of his government, and the reverence of distant nations distinguish him from the royal crowd; and Europe dates a new era from his restoration of the Western empire.

That empire was not unworthy of its title; and some of the fairest kingdoms of Europe were the patrimony or conquest of a prince who reigned at the same time in France, Spain, Italy, Germany, and Hungary.[†]

If we retrace the outlines of this geographical picture, it will be seen that the empire of the Franks extended, between east and west, from the Ebro to the Elbe or Vistula; between the north and south, from the duchy of Beneventum to the River Eyder, the perpetual boundary of Germany and Denmark. . . . Two thirds of the Western empire of Rome were subject to Charlemagne, and the deficiency was amply supplied by his command of the inaccessible or invincible nations of Germany. But in the choice of his enemies, we may be reasonably surprised that he so often preferred the poverty of the north to the riches of the south. The three-and-thirty campaigns laboriously consumed in the woods and morasses of Germany would have sufficed to assert the amplitude of his title by the expulsion of the Greeks from Italy and the Saracens from Spain. The weakness of the Greeks would have insured an easy victory; and the holy crusade against the Saracens would have been prompted by glory and revenge, and loudly justified by religion and policy. Perhaps, in his expeditions beyond the Rhine and the Elbe, he aspired to save his monarchy from the fate of the Roman empire, to disarm the enemies of civilized society, and to eradicate the seed of future emigrations. But it has been wisely observed that in a light of precaution, all conquest must be ineffectual unless it could be universal, since the increasing circle must be involved in a larger sphere of hostility. The subjugation of Germany withdrew the veil which had so long concealed the continent or islands of Scandinavia from the knowledge of Europe, and awakened the torpid courage of their barbarous natives. The fiercest of the Saxon idolaters escaped from the Christian tyrant to their brethren of the North; the Ocean and Mediterranean were covered with their piratical fleets; and Charlemagne beheld with a sigh the destructive progress of the Normans, who in less than seventy years precipitated the fall of his race and monarchy.

Had the pope and the Romans revived the primitive constitution, the titles of emperor and Augustus were conferred on Charlemagne for the term of his life; and his successors, on each vacancy, must have ascended the throne by a formal or tacit election. But the association of his son Lewis the Pious asserts the independent right of monarchy and conquest, and the emperor seems on this occasion to have foreseen and prevented the latent claims of the clergy. The royal youth was commanded to take the crown from the altar and with his own hands to place it on his head, as a gift which he held from God, his father, and the nation. The same ceremony was repeated, though with less energy, in the subsequent associations of Lothaire and Lewis the Second: the Carlovingian scepter was transmitted from father to son in a lineal descent of four generations; and the ambition of the popes was reduced to the empty honor of crowning and anointing these hereditary princes who were already invested with their power and dominions. The pious Lewis survived his brothers and embraced the whole empire of Charlemagne [A.D. 814–840]; but the nations and the nobles, his bishops and his children, quickly discerned that this mighty mass was no longer inspired by the same soul; and the foundations were undermined to the center while the external surface was yet fair and entire. After a war or battle which consumed one hundred thousand Franks, the empire was divided by treaty between his three sons, who had violated every filial and fraternal duty. The kingdoms of Germany and France were forever separated; the provinces of Gaul, between the Rhone and the Alps, the Meuse and the Rhine, were assigned with Italy to the Imperial dignity of Lothaire [A.D. 840–855]. In the partition of his share, Lorraine and Arles, two recent and transitory kingdoms, were bestowed on the younger children; and Lewis the Second, his eldest son, was content with the realm of Italy, the proper and sufficient patrimony of a Roman emperor [A.D. 856–875]. On his death without any male issue, the vacant throne was disputed by his uncles and cousins, and the popes most dexterously seized the occasion of judging the claims and merits of the candidates and of bestowing on the most obsequious, or most liberal, the Imperial office of advocate of the Roman church. The dregs of the Carlovingian race no longer exhibited any symptoms of virtue or power, and the ridiculous epithets of the *bald,* the *stammerer,* the *fat,* and the *simple* distinguished the tame and uniform features of a crowd of kings alike deserving of oblivion. By the failure of the collateral branches, the whole inheritance devolved to Charles the Fat, the last emperor of his family [A.D. 884]: his insanity authorized the desertion of Germany, Italy, and France: he was deposed in a diet and solicited his daily bread from the rebels by whose contempt his life and liberty had been spared [A.D. 888]. According to the measure of their force, the governors, the bishops, and the lords usurped the fragments of the falling empire; and some preference was shown to the female or illegitimate blood of Charlemagne. Of the greater part, the title and possession were alike doubtful, and the merit was adequate to the contracted scale of their dominions. Those who could appear with an army at the gates of Rome were crowned emperors in the Vatican; but their modesty was more frequently satisfied with the appellation of kings of Italy: and the whole term of seventy-four years may be deemed a vacancy, from the abdication of Charles the Fat to the establishment of Otho the First.

Otho was of the noble race of the dukes of Saxony; and if he truly descended from Witikind, the adversary and proselyte of Charlemagne, the posterity of a vanquished people was exalted to reign over their conquerors [A.D. 962]. . . . At the head of a victorious army, he passed the Alps, subdued the kingdom of Italy, delivered the pope, and forever fixed the Imperial crown in the name and nation of Germany. From that memorable era, two maxims of public jurisprudence were introduced by force and ratified by time. I. *That* the prince who was elected in the German diet acquired from that instant the subject kingdoms of Italy and Rome. II. But that he might not legally assume the titles of emperor and Augustus till he had received the crown from the hands of the Roman pontiff.[†]

The Greeks affected to despise the poverty and ignorance of the Franks and Saxons; and in their last decline refused to prostitute to the kings of Germany the title of Roman emperors. [But] these emperors, in the election of the popes, continued to exercise the powers which had been assumed by the Gothic and Grecian princes [A.D. 800–1060]; and the importance of this prerogative increased with the temporal estate and spiritual jurisdiction of the Roman church. In the Christian aristocracy, the principal members of the clergy still formed a senate to assist the administration and to supply the vacancy of the bishop. . . . [And] their choice was ratified or rejected by the applause or clamor of the Roman people. But the election was imperfect; nor could the pontiff be legally consecrated till the emperor, the advocate of the church, had graciously signified his approbation and consent. The royal commissioner examined on the spot the form and freedom of the proceedings; nor was it till after a previous scrutiny into the qualifications of the candidates that he accepted an oath of fidelity and confirmed the donations which had successively enriched the patrimony of St. Peter. In the frequent schisms, the rival claims were submitted to the sentence of the emperor; and in a synod of bishops he presumed to judge, to condemn, and to punish the crimes of a guilty pontiff. Otho the First imposed a treaty on the senate and people, who engaged to prefer the candidate most acceptable to his majesty: his successors anticipated or prevented their choice: they bestowed the Roman benefice, like the bishoprics of Cologne or Bamberg, on their chancellors or preceptors; and whatever might be the merit of a Frank or Saxon, his name sufficiently attests the interposition of foreign power. These acts of prerogative were most speciously excused by the vices of a popular election. The competitor who had been excluded by the cardinals appealed to the passions or avarice of the multitude; the Vatican and the Lateran were stained with blood; and the most powerful senators, the marquises of Tuscany and the counts of Tusculum, held the apostolic see in a long and disgraceful servitude. The Roman pontiffs of the ninth and tenth centuries were insulted, imprisoned, and murdered by their tyrants; and such was their indigence, after the loss and usurpation of the ecclesiastical patrimonies, that they could neither support the state of a prince nor exercise the charity of a priest. The influence of two sister prostitutes, Marozia and Theodora, was founded on their wealth and beauty, their political and amorous intrigues: the most strenuous of their lovers were rewarded with the Roman mitre, and their reign may have suggested to the darker ages the fable of a female pope. The bastard son, the grandson, and the great-grandson of Marozia, a rare genealogy, were seated in the chair of St. Peter, and it was at the age of nineteen years that the second of these became the head of the Latin church. His youth and manhood were of a suitable complexion; and the nations of pilgrims could bear testimony to the charges that were urged against him in a Roman synod, and in the presence of Otho the Great. As John XII had renounced the dress and decencies of his profession, the *soldier* may not perhaps be dishonored by the wine which he drank, the blood that he spilt, the flames that he kindled, or the licentious pursuits of gaming and hunting. His open simony might be the consequence of distress; and his blasphemous invocation of Jupiter and Venus, if it be true, could not possibly be serious. But we read with some surprise that the worthy grandson of Marozia lived in public adultery with the matrons of Rome; that the Lateran palace was turned into a school for prostitution, and that his rapes of virgins and widows had deterred the female pilgrims from visiting the tomb of St. Peter lest in the devout act they should be violated by his successor. The Protestants have dwelt with malicious pleasure on these characters of Antichrist; but to a philosophic eye, the vices of the clergy are far less dangerous than their virtues. After a long series of scandal, the apostolic see was reformed and exalted by the austerity and zeal of Gregory VII [A.D. 1073 ff.]. That ambitious monk devoted his life to the execution of two projects. I. To fix in the college of cardinals the freedom and independence of election, and forever to abolish the right or usurpation of the emperors and the Roman people. II. To bestow and resume the Western empire as a fief or benefice of the church, and to extend his temporal dominion over the kings and kingdoms of the earth. After a contest of fifty years, the first of these designs was accomplished by the firm support of the ecclesiastical order, whose liberty was connected with that of their chief. But the second attempt, though it was crowned with some partial and apparent success, has been vigorously resisted by the secular power, and finally extinguished by the improvement of human reason.

[*Frederic the Second* (A.D. *1198–1252*) *fails in his attempt to assert an absolute temporal sovereignty. Western Europe yields to the anarchy of feudalism under the titular reign of the German "Emperor of Rome."*]

After the death of Frederic the Second, Germany was left a monster with a hundred heads. A crowd of princes and prelates disputed the ruins of the empire: the lords of innumerable castles were less prone to obey than to imitate their superiors; and according to the measure of their strength, their incessant hostilities received the names of conquest or robbery. Such anarchy was the inevitable consequence of the laws and manners of Europe; and the kingdoms of France and Italy were shivered into fragments by the violence of the same tempest.†

It is in the fourteenth century that we may view in the strongest light the state and contrast of the Roman empire of Germany, which no longer held, except on the borders of the Rhine and Danube, a single province of Trajan or Constantine. Their unworthy successors were the counts of Hapsburgh, of Nassau, of Luxemburgh, and Schwartzenburgh. . . . From this humiliating scene, let us turn to the apparent majesty of . . . Charles the Fourth [A.D. 1347–1378]. . . . His school resounded with the doctrine that the Roman emperor was the rightful sovereign of the earth, from the rising to the setting sun. The contrary opinion was condemned not as an error but as a heresy, since even the gospel had pronounced, "And there went forth a decree from Caesar Augustus that *all the world* should be taxed."

If we annihilate the interval of time and space between Augustus and Charles, strong and striking will be the contrast between the two Caesars; the Bohemian who concealed his weakness under the mask of ostentation, and the Roman who disguised his strength under the semblance of modesty. At the head of his victorious legions, in his reign over the sea and land from the Nile and Euphrates to the Atlantic

Ocean, Augustus professed himself the servant of the state and the equal of his fellow-citizens. The conqueror of Rome and her provinces assumed a popular and legal form of a censor, a consul, and a tribune. His will was the law of mankind, but in the declaration of his laws he borrowed the voice of the senate and people; and from their decrees their master accepted and renewed his temporary commission to administer the republic. In his dress, his domestics, his titles, in all the offices of social life, Augustus maintained the character of a private Roman; and his most artful flatterers respected the secret of his absolute and perpetual monarchy.

CHAPTER L

DESCRIPTION OF ARABIA AND ITS INHABITANTS

Description of Arabia and its inhabitants. • Birth, character, and doctrine of Mohammed. • He preaches at Mecca. • Flies to Medina. • Propagates his religion by the sword. • Voluntary or reluctant submission of the Arabs. • His death and successors. • The claims and fortunes of Ali and his descendants.

After pursuing above six hundred years the fleeting Caesars of Constantinople and Germany, I now descend, in the reign of Heraclius, on the eastern borders of the Greek monarchy. While the state was exhausted by the Persian war and the church was distracted by the Nestorian and Monophysite sects, Mohammed, with the sword in one hand and the Koran in the other, erected his throne on the ruins of Christianity and of Rome. The genius of the Arabian prophet, the manners of his nation, and the spirit of his religion involve the causes of the decline and fall of the Eastern empire; and our eyes are curiously intent on one of the most memorable revolutions which have impressed a new and lasting character on the nations of the globe.[†]

The perpetual independence of the Arabs has been the theme of praise among strangers and natives; and the arts of controversy transform this singular event into a prophecy and a miracle in favor of the posterity of Ismael. Some exceptions that can neither be dismissed nor eluded render this mode of reasoning as indiscreet as it is superfluous; the kingdom of Yemen has been successively subdued by the Abyssinians, the Persians, the sultans of Egypt, and the Turks; the holy cities of Mecca and Medina have repeatedly bowed under a Scythian tyrant; and the Roman province of Arabia embraced the peculiar wilderness in which Ismael and his sons must have pitched their tents in the face of their brethren. Yet these exceptions are temporary or local; the body of the nation has escaped the yoke of the most powerful monarchies: the arms of Sesostris and Cyrus, of Pompey and Trajan, could never achieve the conquest of Arabia; the present sovereign of the

Turks may exercise a shadow of jurisdiction, but his pride is reduced to solicit the friendship of a people whom it is dangerous to provoke and fruitless to attack. The obvious causes of their freedom are inscribed on the character and country of the Arabs. Many ages before Mohammed, their intrepid valor had been severely felt by their neighbors in offensive and defensive war. The patient and active virtues of a soldier are insensibly nursed in the habits and discipline of a pastoral life. The care of the sheep and camels is abandoned to the women of the tribe; but the martial youth, under the banner of the emir, is ever on horseback and in the field, to practice the exercise of the bow, the javelin, and the cimeter. The long memory of their independence is the firmest pledge of its perpetuity, and succeeding generations are animated to prove their descent and to maintain their inheritance. . . . Their service in the field was speedy and vigorous; but their friendship was venal, their faith inconstant, their enmity capricious: it was an easier task to excite than to disarm these roving Barbarians; and in the familiar intercourse of war, they learned to see and to despise the splendid weakness both of Rome and of Persia. From Mecca to the Euphrates, the Arabian tribes were confounded by the Greeks and Latins under the general appellation of SARACENS, a name which every Christian mouth has been taught to pronounce with terror and abhorrence.

The slaves of domestic tyranny may vainly exult in their national independence: but the Arab is personally free. . . . In private life every man, at least every family, was the judge and avenger of his own cause. The nice sensibility of honor which weighs the insult rather than the injury sheds its deadly venom on the quarrels of the Arabs: the honor of their women, and of their *beards*, is most easily wounded; an indecent action, a contemptuous word, can be expiated only by the blood of the offender; and such is their patient inveteracy that they expect whole months and years the opportunity of revenge. A fine or compensation for murder is familiar to the Barbarians of every age: but in Arabia the kinsmen of the dead are at liberty to accept the atonement or to exercise with their own hands the law of retaliation. The refined malice of the Arabs refuses even the head of the murderer, substitutes an innocent for the guilty person, and transfers the penalty to the best and most considerable of the race by whom they have been injured. If he falls by their hands, they are exposed in their turn to the danger of reprisals; the interest and principal of the bloody debt are accumulated; the individuals of either family lead a life of malice and suspicion, and fifty years may sometimes elapse before the account of vengeance be finally settled. This sanguinary spirit, ignorant of pity or forgiveness, has been moderated, however, by the maxims of honor, which require in every private encounter some decent equality of age and strength, of numbers and weapons. An annual festival of two, perhaps of four, months was observed by the Arabs before the time of Mohammed, during which their swords were religiously sheathed both in foreign and domestic hostility; and this partial truce is more strongly expressive of the habits of anarchy and warfare.

But the spirit of rapine and revenge was attempered by the milder influence of trade and literature. The solitary peninsula is encompassed by the most civilized nations of the ancient world; the merchant is the friend of mankind; and the annual caravans imported the first seeds of knowledge and politeness into the cities, and even the camps of the desert. Whatever may be the pedigree of the Arabs, their language is derived from the same original stock with the Hebrew, the Syriac, and the Chaldean tongues; the independence of the tribes was marked by their peculiar dialects; but each, after their own, allowed a just preference to the pure and perspicuous idiom of Mecca. In Arabia as well as in Greece, the perfection of language outstripped the refinement of manners; and her speech could diversify the fourscore names of honey, the two hundred of a serpent, the five hundred of a lion, the thousand of a sword, at a time when this copious dictionary was entrusted to the memory of an illiterate people. The monuments of the Homerites were inscribed with an obsolete and mysterious character; but the Cufic letters, the groundwork of the present alphabet, were invented on the banks of the Euphrates; and the recent invention was taught at Mecca by a stranger who settled in that city after the birth of Mohammed. The arts of grammar, of meter, and of rhetoric were unknown to the freeborn eloquence of the Arabians; but their penetration was sharp, their fancy luxuriant, their wit strong and sententious, and their more elaborate compositions were addressed with energy and effect to the minds of their hearers. The genius and merit of a rising poet was celebrated by the applause of his own and the kindred tribes. A solemn banquet was prepared, and a chorus of women, striking their tymbals and displaying the pomp of their nuptials, sung in the presence of their sons and husbands the felicity of their native tribe; that a champion had now appeared to vindicate their rights; that a herald had raised his voice to immortalize their renown. The distant or hostile tribes resorted to an annual fair, which was abolished by the fanaticism of the first Moslems; a national assembly that must have contributed to refine and harmonize the Barbarians. Thirty days were employed in the exchange not only of corn and wine, but of eloquence and poetry. The prize was disputed by the generous emulation of the bards; the victorious performance was deposited in the archives of princes and emirs; and we may read in our own language the seven original poems which were inscribed in letters of gold and suspended in the temple of Mecca. The Arabian poets were the historians and moralists of the age; and if they sympathized with the prejudices, they inspired and crowned the virtues, of their countrymen. The indissoluble union of generosity and valor was the darling theme of their song; and when they pointed their keenest satire against a despicable race, they affirmed in the bitterness of reproach that the men knew not how to give, nor the women to deny. The same hospitality which was practiced by Abraham and celebrated by Homer is still renewed in the camps of the Arabs. The ferocious Bedoweens, the terror of the desert, embrace without inquiry or hesitation the stranger who dares to confide in their honor and to enter their tent. His treatment is kind and respectful: he shares the wealth or the poverty of his host; and after a needful repose, he is dismissed on his way, with thanks, with blessings, and perhaps with gifts.†

The religion of the Arabs, as well as of the Indians, consisted in the worship of the sun, the moon, and the fixed stars; a primitive and specious mode of superstition. The bright luminaries of the sky display the visible image of a Deity: their number and distance convey to a philosophic or even a vulgar eye the idea of boundless space: the character of eternity is marked on these solid globes that seem incapable of corruption or decay: the regularity of their motions may be ascribed to a principle of reason or instinct; and their real or imaginary influence encourages the vain belief that the earth and its inhabitants are the object of their peculiar care. The science of astronomy was cultivated at Babylon; but the school of the Arabs was a clear firmament and a naked plain. In their nocturnal marches, they steered by the guidance of the stars: their names and order and daily station were familiar to the curiosity and devotion of the Bedoween; and he was taught by experience to divide in twenty-eight parts the zodiac of the moon, and to bless the constellations who refreshed with salutary rains the thirst of the desert. The reign of the heavenly orbs could not be extended beyond the visible sphere; and some metaphysical powers were necessary to sustain the transmigration of souls and the resurrection of bodies: a camel was left to perish on the grave that he might serve his master in another life; and the invocation of departed spirits implies that they were still endowed with consciousness and power. I am ignorant, and I am careless, of the blind mythology of the Barbarians; of the local deities of the stars, the air, and the earth, of their sex or titles, their attributes or subordination. Each tribe, each family, each independent warrior created and changed the rites and the object of his *phantastic* worship; but the nation, in every age, has bowed to the religion as well as to the language of Mecca. The genuine antiquity of the CAABA ascends beyond the Christian era. . . . The precincts of Mecca enjoyed the rights of sanctuary; and in the last month of each year, the city and the temple were crowded with a long train of pilgrims who presented their vows and offerings in the house of God. The same rites which are now accomplished by the faithful Moslem were invented and practiced by the superstition of the idolaters. At an awful distance they cast away their garments: seven times, with hasty steps, they encircled the Caaba and kissed the black stone: seven times they visited and adored the adjacent mountains; seven times they threw stones into the valley of Mina; and the pilgrimage was achieved, as at the present hour, by a sacrifice of sheep and camels, and the burial of their hair and nails in the consecrated ground. Each tribe either found or introduced in the Caaba their domestic worship: the temple was adorned or defiled with three hundred and sixty idols of men, eagles, lions, and antelopes; and most conspicuous was the statue of Hebal, of red agate, holding in his hand seven arrows without heads or feathers, the instruments and symbols of profane divination. But this statue was a monument of Syrian arts: the devotion of the ruder ages was content with a pillar or a tablet; and the rocks of the desert were hewn into gods or altars in imitation of the black stone of Mecca, which is deeply tainted with the reproach of an idolatrous origin. From Japan to Peru, the use of sacrifice has universally prevailed; and the votary has expressed his gratitude or fear by destroying or consuming, in honor of the gods, the dearest and most precious of their gifts. The life of a man is the most precious oblation to deprecate a public calamity: the altars of Phoenicia and Egypt, of Rome and Carthage, have been polluted with human gore: the cruel practice was long preserved among the Arabs; in the third century, a boy was annually sacrificed by the tribe of the Dumatians; and a royal captive was piously slaughtered by the prince of the Saracens, the ally and soldier of the emperor Justinian. A parent who drags his son to the altar exhibits the most painful and sublime effort of fanaticism: the deed, or the intention, was sanctified by the example of saints and heroes; and the father of Mohammed himself was devoted by a rash vow, and hardly ransomed for the equivalent of a hundred camels. In the time of ignorance, the Arabs, like the Jews and Egyptians, abstained from the taste of swine's flesh; they circumcised their children at the age of puberty: the same customs, without the censure or the precept of the Koran, have been silently transmitted to their posterity and proselytes. It has been sagaciously conjectured that the artful legislator indulged the stubborn prejudices of his countrymen. It is more simple to believe that he adhered to the habits and opinions of his youth without foreseeing that a practice congenial to the climate of Mecca might become useless or inconvenient on the banks of the Danube or the Volga.

Arabia was free: the adjacent kingdoms were shaken by the storms of conquest and tyranny, and the persecuted sects fled to the happy land where they might profess what they thought and practice what they professed. The religions of the Sabians and Magians, of the Jews and Christians, were disseminated from the Persian Gulf to the Red Sea. In a remote period of antiquity, Sabianism was diffused over Asia by the science of the Chaldeans and the arms of the Assyrians. From the observations of two thousand years, the priests and astronomers of Babylon deduced the eternal laws of nature and providence. They adored the seven gods or angels who directed the course of the seven planets and shed their irresistible influence on the earth. The attributes of the seven planets, with the twelve signs of the zodiac and the twenty-four constellations of the northern and southern hemisphere, were represented by images and talismans; the seven days of the week were dedicated to their respective deities; the Sabians prayed thrice each day; and the temple of the moon at Haran was the term of their pilgrimage. But the flexible genius of their faith was always ready either to teach or to learn: in the tradition of the creation, the deluge, and the patriarchs, they held a singular agreement with their Jewish captives; they appealed to the secret books of Adam, Seth, and Enoch; and a slight infusion of the gospel has transformed the last remnant of the Polytheists into the Christians of St. John, in the territory of Bassora. The altars of Babylon were overturned by the Magians; but the injuries of the Sabians were revenged by the sword of Alexander; Persia groaned above five hundred years under a foreign yoke; and the purest disciples of Zoroaster escaped from the contagion of idolatry and breathed with their adversaries the freedom of the desert. Seven hundred years before the death of Mohammed, the Jews were settled in Arabia; and a far greater multitude was expelled from the Holy Land in the wars of Titus and Hadrian. The industrious exiles aspired to liberty and power: they erected synagogues in the cities and castles in the wilderness, and their Gentile converts were confounded with the children of Israel, whom they resembled in the outward mark of circumcision. The Christian missionaries were still more active and successful: the Catholics asserted their universal reign; the sects whom they oppressed successively retired beyond the limits of the Roman empire; the Marcionites and Manichaeans dispersed their *phantastic* opinions and apocryphal gospels; the churches of Yemen and the princes of Hira and Gassan were instructed in a purer creed by the Jacobite and Nestorian bishops. The liberty of choice was presented to the tribes: each Arab was free to elect or to compose his private religion: and the rude superstition of his house was mingled with the sublime theology of saints and philosophers. A fundamental article of faith was inculcated by the consent of the learned strangers; the existence of one supreme God who is exalted above the powers of Heaven and earth, but who has often revealed himself to mankind by the ministry of his angels and prophets, and whose grace or justice has interrupted, by seasonable miracles, the order of nature. The most rational of the Arabs acknowledged his power, though they neglected his worship; and it was habit rather than conviction that still attached them to the relics of idolatry. The Jews and Christians were the people of the *Book;* the Bible was already translated into the Arabic language, and the volume of the Old Testament was accepted by the concord of these implacable enemies. In the story of the Hebrew patriarchs, the Arabs were pleased to discover the fathers of their nation. They applauded the birth and promises of Ismael; revered the faith and virtue of Abraham;

traced his pedigree and their own to the creation of the first man, and imbibed, with equal credulity, the prodigies of the holy text and the dreams and traditions of the Jewish rabbis.

The base and plebeian origin of Mohammed is an unskillful calumny of the Christians, who exalt instead of degrading the merit of their adversary. His descent from Ismael was a national privilege or fable; but if the first steps of the pedigree are dark and doubtful, he could produce many generations of pure and genuine nobility: he sprung from the tribe of Koreish and the family of Hashem, the most illustrious of the Arabs, the princes of Mecca and the hereditary guardians of the Caaba. The grandfather of Mohammed was Abdol Motalleb, the son of Hashem, a wealthy and generous citizen who relieved the distress of famine with the supplies of commerce. Mecca, which had been fed by the liberality of the father, was saved by the courage of the son. The kingdom of Yemen was subject to the Christian princes of Abyssinia; their vassal Abrahah was provoked by an insult to avenge the honor of the cross; and the holy city was invested by a train of elephants and an army of Africans. A treaty was proposed; and in the first audience, the grandfather of Mohammed demanded the restitution of his cattle. "And why," said Abrahah, "do you not rather implore my clemency in favor of your temple, which I have threatened to destroy?" "Because," replied the intrepid chief, "the cattle is my own; the Caaba belongs to the gods, and *they* will defend their house from injury and sacrilege." The want of provisions, or the valor of the Koreish, compelled the Abyssinians to a disgraceful retreat: their discomfiture has been adorned with a miraculous flight of birds who showered down stones on the heads of the infidels; and the deliverance was long commemorated by the era of the elephant. The glory of Abdol Motalleb was crowned with domestic happiness; his life was prolonged to the age of one hundred and ten years; and he became the father of six daughters and thirteen sons. His best beloved Abdallah was the most beautiful and modest of the Arabian youth; and in the first night when he consummated his marriage with Amina, of the noble race of the Zahrites, two hundred virgins are said to have expired of jealousy and despair. . . . Mohammed, the only son of Abdallah and Amina, was born at Mecca four years after the death of Justinian and two months after the defeat of the Abyssinians, whose victory would have introduced into the Caaba the religion of the Christians. In his early infancy he was deprived of his father, his mother, and his grandfather; his uncles were strong and numerous; and in the division of the inheritance, the orphan's share was reduced to five camels and an Aethiopian maidservant. At home and abroad, in peace and war, Abu Taleb, the most respectable of his uncles, was the guide and guardian of his youth; in his twenty-fifth year, he entered into the service of Cadijah, a rich and noble widow of Mecca, who soon rewarded his fidelity with the gift of her hand and fortune. The marriage contract, in the simple style of antiquity, recites the mutual love of Mohammed and Cadijah; describes him as the most accomplished of the tribe of Koreish; and stipulates a dowry of twelve ounces of gold and twenty camels, which was supplied by the liberality of his uncle. By this alliance, the son of Abdallah was restored to the station of his ancestors; and the judicious matron was content with his domestic virtues, till, in the fortieth year of his age, he assumed the title of a prophet and proclaimed the religion of the Koran.

According to the tradition of his companions, Mohammed was distinguished by the beauty of his person, an outward gift which is seldom despised, except by those to whom it has been refused. Before he spoke, the orator engaged on his side the affections of a public or private audience. They applauded his commanding presence, his majestic aspect, his piercing eye, his gracious smile, his flowing beard, his countenance that painted every sensation of the soul, and his gestures that enforced each expression of the tongue. In the familiar offices of life he scrupulously adhered to the grave and ceremonious politeness of his country: his respectful attention to the rich and powerful was dignified by his condescension and affability to the poorest citizens of Mecca: the frankness of his manner concealed the artifice of his views; and the habits of courtesy were imputed to personal friendship or universal benevolence. His memory was capacious and retentive; his wit easy and social; his imagination sublime; his judgment clear, rapid, and decisive. He possessed the courage both of thought and action; and although his designs might gradually expand with his success, the first idea which he entertained of his divine mission bears the stamp of an original and superior genius. The son of Abdallah was educated in the bosom of the noblest race, in the use of the purest dialect of Arabia; and the fluency of his speech was corrected and enhanced by the practice of discreet and seasonable silence. With these powers of eloquence, Mohammed was an illiterate Barbarian: his youth had never been instructed in the arts of reading and writing; the common ignorance exempted him from shame or reproach, but he was reduced to a narrow circle of existence and deprived of those faithful mirrors which reflect to our mind the minds of sages and heroes. Yet the book of nature and of man was open to his view; and some fancy has been indulged in the political and philosophical observations which are ascribed to the Arabian *traveler*. He compares the nations and the regions of the earth; discovers the weakness of the Persian and Roman monarchies; beholds, with pity and indignation, the degeneracy of the times; and resolves to unite under one God and one king the invincible spirit and primitive virtues of the Arabs. Our more accurate inquiry will suggest that, instead of visiting the courts, the camps, the temples of the East, the two journeys of Mohammed into Syria were confined to the fairs of Bostra and Damascus; that he was only thirteen years of age when he accompanied the caravan of his uncle; and that his duty compelled him to return as soon as he had disposed of the merchandise of Cadijah. In these hasty and superficial excursions, the eye of genius might discern some objects invisible to his grosser companions; some seeds of knowledge might be cast upon a fruitful soil; but his ignorance of the Syriac language must have checked his curiosity; and I cannot perceive, in the life or writings of Mohammed, that his prospect was far extended beyond the limits of the Arabian world. From every region of that solitary world, the pilgrims of Mecca were annually assembled by the calls of devotion and commerce: in the free concourse of multitudes, a simple citizen, in his native tongue, might study the political state and character of the tribes, the theory and practice of the Jews and Christians. Some useful strangers might be tempted, or forced, to implore the rights of hospitality; and the enemies of Mohammed have named the Jew, the Persian, and the Syrian monk whom they accuse of lending their secret aid to the composition of the Koran. Conversation enriches the understanding, but solitude is the school of genius; and the uniformity of a work denotes the hand of a single artist. From his earliest youth Mohammed was addicted to religious contemplation; each year, during the month of Ramadan, he withdrew from the world and from the arms of Cadijah: in the cave of Hera, three miles from Mecca, he consulted the spirit of fraud or enthusiasm, whose abode is not in the heavens but in the mind of the prophet. The faith which, under the name of *Islam,* he preached to his family and nation is compounded of an eternal truth and a necessary fiction, THAT THERE IS ONLY ONE GOD, AND THAT MOHAMMED IS THE APOSTLE OF GOD.

It is the boast of the Jewish apologists that while the learned nations of antiquity were deluded by the fables of Polytheism, their simple ancestors of Palestine preserved the knowledge and worship of the true God. The moral attributes of Jehovah may not easily be reconciled with the standard of *human* virtue: his metaphysical qualities are darkly expressed; but each page of the Pentateuch and the Prophets is an evidence of his power: the unity of his name is inscribed on the first table of the law; and his sanctuary was never defiled by any visible image of the invisible essence. After the ruin of the temple, the faith of the Hebrew exiles was purified, fixed, and enlightened by the spiritual devotion of the synagogue; and the authority of Mohammed will not justify his perpetual reproach that the Jews of Mecca or Medina adored Ezra as the son of God. But the children of Israel had ceased to be a people; and the religions of the world were guilty, at least in the eyes of the prophet, of giving sons or daughters or companions to the supreme God. In the rude idolatry of the Arabs, the crime is manifest and audacious: the Sabians are poorly excused by the preeminence of the first planet, or intelligence, in their celestial hierarchy; and in the Magian system the conflict of the two principles betrays the imperfection of the conqueror. The Christians of the seventh century had insensibly relapsed into a semblance of Paganism: their public and private vows were addressed to the relics and images that disgraced the temples of the East: the throne of the Almighty was darkened by a cloud of martyrs and saints and angels, the objects of popular veneration; and the Collyridian heretics, who flourished in the fruitful soil of Arabia, invested the Virgin Mary with the name and honors of a goddess. The mysteries of the Trinity and Incarnation *appear* to contradict the principle of the divine unity. In their obvious sense, they introduce three equal deities and transform the man Jesus into the substance of the Son of God: an orthodox commentary will satisfy only a believing mind: intemperate curiosity and zeal had torn the veil of the sanctuary; and each of the Oriental sects was eager to confess that all except themselves deserved the reproach of idolatry and Polytheism. The creed of Mohammed is free from suspicion or ambiguity; and the Koran is a glorious testimony to the unity of God. The prophet of Mecca rejected the worship of idols and men, of stars and planets, on the rational principle that whatever rises must set, that whatever is born must die, that whatever is corruptible must decay and perish. In the Author of the universe, his rational enthusiasm confessed and adored an infinite and eternal being without form or place, without issue or similitude, present to our most secret thoughts, existing by the necessity of his own nature, and deriving from himself all moral and intellectual perfection. These sublime truths, thus announced in the language of the prophet, are firmly held by his disciples, and defined with metaphysical precision by the interpreters of the Koran. A philosophic theist might subscribe the popular creed of the Mohammedans; a creed too sublime, perhaps, for our present faculties. What object remains for the fancy, or even the understanding, when we have abstracted from the unknown substance all ideas of time and space, of motion and matter, of sensation and reflection? The first principle of reason and revolution was confirmed by the voice of Mohammed: his proselytes, from India to Morocco, are distinguished by the name of *Unitarians;* and the danger of idolatry has been prevented by the interdiction of images. The doctrine of eternal decrees and absolute predestination is strictly embraced by the Mohammedans; and they struggle, with the common difficulties, *how* to reconcile the prescience of God with the freedom and responsibility of man; *how* to explain the permission of evil under the reign of infinite power and infinite goodness.

The God of nature has written his existence on all his works, and his law in the heart of man. To restore the knowledge of the one and the practice of the other has been the real or pretended aim of the prophets of every age: the liberality of Mohammed allowed to his predecessors the same credit which he claimed for himself; and the chain of inspiration was prolonged from the fall of Adam to the promulgation of the Koran. During that period, some rays of prophetic light had been imparted to one hundred and twenty-four thousand of the elect, discriminated by their respective measure of virtue and grace; three hundred and thirteen apostles were sent with a special commission to recall their country from idolatry and vice; one hundred and four volumes have been dictated by the Holy Spirit; and six legislators of transcendent brightness have announced to mankind the six successive revelations of various rites but of one immutable religion. The authority and station of Adam, Noah, Abraham, Moses, Christ, and Mohammed rise in just gradation above each other; but whosoever hates or rejects any one of the prophets is numbered with the infidels. . . . [T]he remnant of the inspired writings was comprised in the books of the Old and the New Testament. The miraculous story of Moses is consecrated and embellished in the Koran; and the captive Jews enjoy the secret revenge of imposing their own belief on the nations whose recent creeds they deride. For the author of Christianity, the Mohammedans are taught by the prophet to entertain a high and mysterious reverence. "Verily, Christ Jesus, the son of Mary, is the apostle of God, and his word, which he conveyed unto Mary, and a Spirit proceeding from him; honorable in this world, and in the world to come, and one of those who approach near to the presence of God." The wonders of the genuine and apocryphal gospels are profusely heaped on his head; and the Latin church has not disdained to borrow from the Koran the immaculate conception of his virgin mother. Yet Jesus was a mere mortal; and at the day of judgment, his testimony will serve to condemn both the Jews, who reject him as a prophet, and the Christians, who adore him as the Son of God. The malice of his enemies aspersed his reputation and conspired against his life; but their intention only was guilty; a phantom or a criminal was substituted on the cross; and the innocent saint was translated to the seventh heaven. During six hundred years the gospel was the way of truth and salvation; but the Christians insensibly forgot both the laws and example of their founder; and Mohammed was instructed by the Gnostics to accuse the church as well as the synagogue of corrupting the integrity of the sacred text. The piety of Moses and of Christ rejoiced in the assurance of a future prophet more illustrious than themselves: the evangelical promise of the *Paraclete,* or Holy Ghost, was prefigured in the name and accomplished in the person of Mohammed, the greatest and the last of the apostles of God.[†]

[T]he substance of the Koran, according to [Mohammed] himself or his disciples, is uncreated and eternal; subsisting in the essence of the Deity, and inscribed with a pen of light on the table of his everlasting decrees. A paper copy, in a volume of silk and gems, was brought down to the lowest heaven by the angel Gabriel, who, under the Jewish economy, had indeed been despatched on the most important errands; and this trusty messenger successively revealed the chapters and verses to the Arabian prophet. Instead of a perpetual and perfect measure of the divine will, the fragments of the Koran were produced at the discretion of Mohammed; each revelation is suited to the emergencies of his policy or passion; and all contradiction is removed by the saving maxim that any text of Scripture is abrogated or modified by any subsequent passage. The word of God, and of the apostle, was diligently recorded by his disciples on palm-leaves and the shoulder-bones of mutton; and the pages, without order or connection, were cast into a domestic chest in the custody of one of his wives. Two years after the death of Mohammed, the sacred volume was collected and published by his friend and successor Abubeker: the work was revised by the caliph Othman in the thirtieth year of the Hegira; and the various editions of the Koran assert the same miraculous privilege of a uniform and incorruptible text. In the spirit of enthusiasm or vanity, the prophet rests the truth of his mission on the merit of his book; audaciously challenges both men and angels to imitate the beauties of a single page; and presumes to assert that God alone could dictate this incomparable performance. This argument is most powerfully addressed to a devout Arabian whose mind is attuned to faith and rapture; whose ear is delighted by the music of sounds; and whose ignorance is incapable of comparing the productions of human genius. The harmony and copiousness of style will not reach, in a [translated] version, the European infidel: he will peruse with impatience the endless incoherent rhapsody of fable and precept and declamation which seldom excites a sentiment or an idea, which sometimes crawls in the dust and is sometimes lost in the clouds. The divine attributes exalt the fancy of the Arabian missionary; but his loftiest strains must yield to the sublime simplicity of the book of Job, composed in a remote age in the same country and in the same language. If the composition of the Koran exceed the faculties of a man, to what superior intelligence should we ascribe the Iliad of Homer, or the Philippics of Demosthenes? In all religions, the life of the founder supplies the silence of his written revelation: the sayings of Mohammed were so many lessons of truth; his actions so many examples of virtue; and the public and private memorials were preserved by his wives and companions. At the end of two hundred years, the *Sonna,* or oral law, was fixed and consecrated by the labors of Al Bochari, who discriminated seven thousand two hundred and seventy-five genuine traditions from a mass of three hundred thousand reports of a more doubtful or spurious character. Each day the pious author prayed in the temple of Mecca, and performed his ablutions with the water of Zemzem: the pages were successively deposited on the pulpit and the sepulchre of the apostle; and the work has been approved by the four orthodox sects of the Sonnites.

The mission of the ancient prophets, of Moses and of Jesus, had been confirmed by many splendid prodigies; and Mohammed was repeatedly urged, by the inhabitants of Mecca and Medina, to produce a similar evidence of his divine legation; to call down from Heaven the angel or the volume of his revelation, to create a garden in the desert, or to kindle a conflagration in the unbelieving city. As often as he is pressed by the demands of the Koreish, he involves himself in the obscure boast of vision and prophecy, appeals to the internal proofs of his doctrine, and shields himself behind the providence of God, who refuses those signs and wonders that would depreciate the merit of faith and aggravate the guilt of infidelity. But the modest or angry tone of his apologies betrays his weakness and vexation; and these passages of scandal established beyond suspicion the integrity of the Koran. The votaries of Mohammed are more assured than himself of his miraculous gifts; and their confidence and credulity increase as they are farther removed from the time and place of his spiritual exploits. They believe or affirm that trees went forth to meet him; that he was saluted by stones; that water gushed from his fingers; that he fed the hungry, cured the sick, and raised the dead; that a beam groaned to him; that a camel complained to him; that a shoulder of mutton informed him of its being poisoned; and that both animate and inanimate nature were equally subject to the apostle of God. His dream of a nocturnal journey is seriously described as a real and corporeal transaction. A mysterious animal, the Borak, conveyed him from the temple of Mecca to that of Jerusalem: with his companion Gabriel he successively ascended the seven heavens, and received and repaid the salutations of the patriarchs, the prophets, and the angels in their respective mansions. Beyond the seventh heaven, Mohammed alone was permitted to proceed; he passed the veil of unity, approached within two bow-shots of the throne, and felt a cold that pierced him to the heart when his shoulder was touched by the hand of God. After this familiar though important conversation, he again descended to Jerusalem, remounted the Borak, returned to Mecca, and performed in the tenth part of a night the journey of many thousand years. According to another legend, the apostle confounded in a national assembly the malicious challenge of the Koreish. His resistless word split asunder the orb of the moon: the obedient planet stooped from her station in the sky, accomplished the seven revolutions round the Caaba, saluted Mohammed in the Arabian tongue, and, suddenly contracting her dimensions, entered at the collar and issued forth through the sleeve of his shirt. The vulgar are amused with these marvelous tales; but the gravest of the Moslem doctors imitate the modesty of their master and indulge a latitude of faith or interpretation. They might speciously allege that in preaching the religion it was needless to violate the harmony of nature; that a creed unclouded with mystery may be excused from miracles; and that the sword of Mohammed was not less potent than the rod of Moses.

The Polytheist is oppressed and distracted by the variety of superstition: a thousand rites of Egyptian origin were interwoven with the essence of the Mosaic law; and the spirit of the gospel had evaporated in the pageantry of the church. The prophet of Mecca was tempted by prejudice or policy or patriotism to sanctify the rites of the Arabians and the custom of visiting the holy stone of the Caaba. But the precepts of Mohammed himself inculcate a more simple and rational piety: prayer, fasting, and alms are the religious duties of a Moslem; and he is encouraged to hope that prayer will carry him half way to God, fasting will bring him to the door of his palace, and alms will gain him admittance. I. According to the tradition of the nocturnal journey, the apostle, in his personal conference with the Deity, was commanded to impose on his disciples the daily obligation of fifty prayers. By the advice of Moses, he applied for an alleviation of this intolerable burden; the number was gradually reduced to five, without any dispensation of business or pleasure, or time or place: the devotion of the faithful is repeated at daybreak, at noon, in the afternoon, in the evening, and at the first watch of the night. . . . Cleanliness is the key of prayer: the frequent lustration of the hands, the face, and the body, which was practiced of old by the Arabs, is solemnly enjoined by the Koran; and a permission is formally granted to supply with sand the scarcity of water. The words and attitudes of supplication, as it is performed either sitting or standing or prostrate on the ground, are prescribed by custom or authority; but the prayer is poured forth in short and fervent ejaculations; the measure of zeal is not exhausted by a tedious liturgy; and each Moslem for his own person is invested with the character of a priest. Among the theists, who reject the use of images, it has been found necessary to restrain the wanderings of the fancy by directing the eye and the thought towards a *kebla,* or visible point of the horizon. The prophet was at first inclined to gratify the Jews by the choice of Jerusalem; but he soon returned to a more natural partiality; and five times every day the eyes of the nations at Astracan, at Fez, at Delhi are devoutly turned to the holy temple of Mecca. Yet every spot for the service of God is equally pure: the Mohammedans indifferently pray in their chamber or in the street. As a distinction from the Jews and Christians, the Friday in each week is set apart for the useful institution of public worship: the people is assembled in the mosque; and the imam, some respectable elder, ascends the pulpit to begin the prayer and pronounce the sermon. But the Mohammedan religion is destitute of priesthood or sacrifice; and the independent spirit of fanaticism looks down with contempt on the ministers and the slaves of superstition. II. The voluntary penance of the ascetics, the torment and glory of their lives, was odious to a prophet who censured in his companions a rash vow of abstaining from flesh and women and sleep; and firmly declared that he would suffer no monks in his religion. Yet he instituted, in each year, a fast of thirty days; and strenuously recommended the observance as a discipline which purifies the soul and subdues the body, as a salutary exercise of obedience to the will of God and his apostle. During the month of Ramadan, from the rising to the setting of the sun, the Moslem abstains from eating, and drinking, and women, and baths, and perfumes; from all nourishment that can restore his strength, from all pleasure that can gratify his senses. In the revolution of the lunar year, the Ramadan coincides, by turns, with the winter cold and the summer heat; and the patient martyr, without assuaging his thirst with a drop of water, must expect the close of a tedious and sultry day. The interdiction of wine, peculiar to some orders of priests or hermits, is converted by Mohammed alone into a positive and general law; and a considerable portion of the globe has abjured at his command the use of that salutary though dangerous liquor. These painful restraints are doubtless infringed by the libertine, and eluded by the hypocrite; but the legislator by whom they are enacted cannot surely be accused of alluring his proselytes by the indulgence of their sensual appetites. III. The charity of the Mohammedans descends to the animal creation; and the Koran repeatedly inculcates, not as a merit but as a strict and indispensable duty, the relief of the indigent and unfortunate. Mohammed, perhaps, is the only lawgiver who has defined the precise measure of charity: the standard may vary with the degree and nature of property, as it consists either in money, in corn or cattle, in fruits or merchandise; but the Moslem does not accomplish the law unless he bestows a *tenth* of his revenue; and if his conscience accuses him of fraud or extortion, the tenth, under the idea of restitution, is enlarged to a *fifth*. Benevolence is the foundation of justice, since we are forbid to injure those whom we are bound to assist. A prophet may reveal the secrets of Heaven and of futurity; but in his moral precepts he can only repeat the lessons of our own hearts.

The two articles of belief and the four practical duties of Islam are guarded by rewards and punishments; and the faith of the Moslem is devoutly fixed on the event of the judgment and the last day. The prophet has not presumed to determine the moment of that awful catastrophe, though he darkly announces the signs, both in Heaven and earth, which will precede the universal dissolution, when life shall be destroyed and the order of creation shall be confounded in the primitive chaos. At the blast of the trumpet, new worlds will start into being: angels, genii, and men will arise from the dead, and the human soul will again be united to the body. The doctrine of the resurrection was first entertained by the Egyptians; and their mummies were embalmed, their pyramids were constructed, to preserve the ancient mansion of the soul during a period of three thousand years. But the attempt is partial and unavailing; and it is with a more philosophic spirit that Mohammed relies on the omnipotence of the Creator, whose word can reanimate the breathless clay and collect the innumerable atoms that no longer retain their form or substance. The intermediate state of the soul it is hard to decide; and those who most firmly believe her immaterial nature are at a loss to understand how she can think or act without the agency of the organs of sense.

The reunion of the soul and body will be followed by the final judgment of mankind; and in his copy of the Magian picture, the prophet has too faithfully represented the forms of proceeding, and even the slow and successive operations, of an earthly tribunal. By his intolerant adversaries he is upbraided for extending, even to themselves, the hope of salvation, for asserting the blackest heresy, that every man who believes in God and accomplishes good works may expect in the last day a favorable sentence. Such rational indifference is ill adapted to the character of a fanatic; nor is it probable that a messenger from Heaven should depreciate the value and necessity of his own revelation. In the idiom of the Koran, the belief of God is inseparable from that of Mohammed: the good works are those which he has enjoined, and the two qualifications imply the profession of Islam, to which all nations and all sects are equally invited. Their spiritual blindness, though excused by ignorance and crowned with virtue, will be scourged with everlasting torments; and the tears which Mohammed shed over the tomb of his mother, for whom he was forbidden to pray, display a striking contrast of humanity and enthusiasm. The doom of the infidels is common: the measure of their guilt and punishment is determined by the degree of evidence which they have rejected, by the magnitude of the errors which they have entertained: the eternal mansions of the Christians, the Jews, the Sabians, the Magians, and idolaters are sunk below each other in the abyss; and the lowest hell is reserved for the faithless hypocrites who have assumed the mask of religion. After the greater part of mankind has been condemned for their opinions, the true believers only will be judged by their actions. The good and evil of each Moslem will be accurately weighed in a real or allegorical balance; and a singular mode of compensation will be allowed for the payment of injuries: the aggressor will refund an equivalent of his own good actions for the benefit of the person whom he has wronged; and if he should be destitute of any moral property, the weight of his sins will be loaded with an adequate share of the demerits of the sufferer. According as the shares of guilt or virtue shall preponderate, the sentence will be pronounced, and all, without distinction, will pass over the sharp and perilous bridge of the abyss; but the innocent, treading in the footsteps of Mohammed, will gloriously enter the gates of paradise, while the guilty will fall into the first and mildest of the seven hells. The term of expiation will vary from nine hundred to seven thousand years; but the prophet has judiciously promised that *all* his disciples, whatever may be their sins, shall be saved by their own faith and his intercession from eternal damnation. It is not surprising that superstition should act most powerfully on the fears of her votaries, since the human fancy can paint with more energy the misery than the bliss of a future life. With the two simple elements of darkness and fire, we create a sensation of pain, which may be aggravated to an infinite degree by the idea of endless duration. But the same idea operates with an opposite effect on the continuity of pleasure; and too much of our present enjoyments is obtained from the relief or the comparison of evil. It is natural enough that an Arabian prophet should dwell with rapture on the groves, the fountains, and the rivers of paradise; but instead of inspiring the blessed inhabitants with a liberal taste for harmony and science, conversation and friendship, he idly celebrates the pearls and diamonds, the robes of silk, palaces of marble, dishes of gold, rich wines, artificial dainties, numerous attendants, and the whole train of sensual and costly luxury which becomes insipid to the owner, even in the short period of this mortal life. Seventy-two *Houris,* or black-eyed girls, of resplendent beauty, blooming youth, virgin purity, and exquisite sensibility will be created for the use of the meanest believer; a moment of pleasure will be prolonged to a thousand years; and his faculties will be increased a hundredfold to render him worthy of his felicity. Notwithstanding a vulgar prejudice, the gates of Heaven will be open to both sexes; but Mohammed has not specified the male companions of the female elect, lest he should either alarm the jealousy of their former husbands or disturb their felicity by the suspicion of an everlasting marriage. This image of a carnal paradise has provoked the indignation, perhaps the envy, of the monks: they declaim against the impure religion of Mohammed; and his modest apologists are driven to the poor excuse of figures and allegories. But the sounder and more consistent party adhere without shame to the literal interpretation of the Koran: useless would be the resurrection of the body unless it were restored to the possession and exercise of its worthiest faculties; and the union of sensual and intellectual enjoyment is requisite to complete the happiness of the double animal, the perfect man. Yet the joys of the Mohammedan paradise will not be confined to the indulgence of luxury and appetite; and the prophet has expressly declared that all meaner happiness will be forgotten and despised by the saints and martyrs, who shall be admitted to the beatitude of the divine vision.

The first and most arduous conquests of Mohammed were those of his wife, his servant, his pupil, and his friend; since he presented himself as a prophet to those who were most conversant with his infirmities as a man [A.D. 609]. Yet Cadijah believed the words and cherished the glory of her husband; the obsequious and affectionate Zeid was tempted by the prospect of freedom; the illustrious Ali, the son of Abu Taleb, embraced the sentiments of his cousin with the spirit of a youthful hero; and the wealth, the moderation, the veracity of Abubeker confirmed the religion of the prophet whom he was destined to succeed. By his persuasion, ten of the most respectable citizens of Mecca were introduced to the private lessons of Islam; they yielded to the voice of reason and enthusiasm; they repeated the fundamental creed, "There is but one God, and Mohammed is the apostle of God"; and their faith, even in this life, was rewarded with riches and honors, with the command of armies and the government of kingdoms. Three years were silently employed in the conversion of fourteen proselytes, the first-fruits of his mission; but in the fourth year he assumed the prophetic office, and resolving to impart to his family the light of divine truth, he prepared a banquet, a lamb, as it is said, and a bowl of milk, for the entertainment of forty guests of the race of Hashem. "Friends and kinsmen," said Mohammed to the assembly, "I offer you, and I alone can offer, the most precious of gifts, the treasures of this world and of the world to come. God has commanded me to call you to his service. Who among you will support my burden? Who among you will be my companion and my vizier?" No answer was returned, till the silence of astonishment and doubt and contempt was at length broken by the impatient courage of Ali, a youth in the fourteenth year of his age. "O prophet, I am the man: whosoever rises against thee, I will dash out his teeth, tear out his eyes, break his legs, rip up his belly. O prophet, I will be thy vizier over them." Mohammed accepted his offer with transport, and Abu Taled was ironically exhorted to respect the superior dignity of his son. In a more serious tone, the father of Ali advised his nephew to relinquish his impracticable design. "Spare your remonstrances," replied the intrepid fanatic to his uncle and benefactor; "if they should place the sun on my right hand, and the moon on my left, they should not divert me from my course." He persevered ten years in the exercise of his mission; and the religion which has overspread the East and the West advanced with a slow and painful progress within the walls of Mecca. Yet Mohammed enjoyed the satisfaction of beholding the increase of his infant congregation of Unitarians, who revered him as a prophet and to whom he seasonably dispensed the spiritual nourishment of the Koran. The number of proselytes may be esteemed by the absence of eighty-three men and eighteen women who retired to Aethiopia in the seventh year of his mission; and his party was fortified by the timely conversion of his uncle Hamza and of the fierce and inflexible Omar, who signalized in the cause of Islam the same zeal which he had exerted for its destruction. Nor was the charity of Mohammed confined to the tribe of Koreish or the precincts of Mecca: on solemn festivals, in the days of pilgrimage, he frequented the Caaba, accosted the strangers of every tribe, and urged, both in private converse and public discourse, the belief and worship of a sole Deity. Conscious of his reason and of his weakness, he asserted the liberty of conscience and disclaimed the use of religious violence: but he called the Arabs to repentance, and conjured them to remember the ancient idolaters of Ad and Thamud, whom the divine justice had swept away from the face of the earth.

The people of Mecca were hardened in their unbelief by superstition and envy [A.D. 613–622]. The elders of the city, the uncles of the prophet, affected to despise the presumption of an orphan, the reformer of his country: the pious orations of Mohammed in the Caaba were answered by the clamors of Abu Taleb. "Citizens and pilgrims, listen not to the tempter, hearken not to his impious novelties. Stand fast in the worship of Al Lata and Al Uzzah." Yet the son of Abdallah was ever dear to the aged chief: and he protected the fame and person of his nephew against the assaults of the Koreishites, who had long been jealous of the preeminence of the family of Hashem. Their malice was colored with the pretense of religion: in the age of Job, the crime of impiety was punished by the Arabian magistrate; and Mohammed was guilty of deserting and denying the national deities. But so loose was the policy of Mecca that the leaders of the Koreish, instead of accusing a criminal, were compelled to employ the measures of persuasion or violence. They repeatedly addressed Abu Taleb in the style of reproach and menace. "Thy nephew reviles our religion; he accuses our wise forefathers of ignorance and folly; silence him quickly, lest he kindle tumult and discord in the city. If he perseveres, we shall draw our swords against him and his adherents, and thou wilt be responsible for the blood of thy fellow-citizens." The weight and moderation of Abu Taleb eluded the violence of religious faction; the most helpless or timid of the disciples retired to Aethiopia, and the prophet withdrew himself to various places of strength in the town and country. As he was still supported by his family, the rest of the tribe of Koreish engaged themselves to renounce all intercourse with the children of Hashem, neither to buy nor sell, neither to marry nor to give in marriage, but to pursue them with implacable enmity till they should deliver the person of Mohammed to the justice of the gods. The decree was suspended in the Caaba before the eyes of the nation; the messengers of the Koreish pursued the Moslem exiles in the heart of Africa: they besieged the prophet and his most faithful followers, intercepted their water, and inflamed their mutual animosity by the retaliation of injuries and insults [A.D. 619–620]. A doubtful truce restored the appearances of concord till the death of Abu Taleb abandoned Mohammed to the power of his enemies, at the moment when he was deprived of his domestic comforts by the loss of his faithful and generous Cadijah. Abu Sophian, the chief of the branch of Ommiyah, succeeded to the principality of the republic of Mecca. A zealous votary of the idols, a mortal foe of the line of Hashem, he convened an assembly of the Koreishites and their allies to decide the fate of the apostle. His imprisonment might provoke the despair of his enthusiasm; and the exile of an eloquent and popular fanatic would diffuse the mischief through the provinces of Arabia. His death was resolved; and they agreed that a sword from each tribe should be buried in his heart, to divide the guilt of his blood and baffle the vengeance of the Hashemites. An angel or a spy revealed their conspiracy; and flight was the only resource of Mohammed [A.D. 622]. At the dead of night, accompanied by his friend Abubeker, he silently escaped from his house: the assassins watched at the door; but they were deceived by the figure of Ali, who reposed on the bed and was covered with the green vestment of the apostle. The Koreish respected the piety of the heroic youth; but some verses of Ali, which are still extant, exhibit an interesting picture of his anxiety, his tenderness, and his religious confidence. Three days Mohammed and his companion were concealed in the cave of Thor, at the distance of a league from Mecca; and in the close of each evening, they received from the son and daughter of Abubeker a secret supply of intelligence and food. The diligence of the Koreish explored every haunt in the neighborhood of the city: they arrived at the entrance of the cavern; but the providential deceit of a spider's web and a pigeon's nest is supposed to convince them that the place was solitary and inviolate. "We are only two," said the trembling Abubeker. "There is a third," replied the prophet; "it is God himself." No sooner was the pursuit abated than the two fugitives issued from the rock and mounted their camels: on the road to Medina, they were overtaken by the emissaries of the Koreish; they redeemed themselves with prayers and promises from their hands. In this eventful moment, the lance of an Arab might have changed the history of the world. The flight of the prophet from Mecca to Medina has fixed the memorable era of the *Hegira*, which, at the end of twelve centuries, still discriminates the lunar years of the Mohammedan nations.

The religion of the Koran might have perished in its cradle had not Medina embraced with faith and reverence the holy outcasts of Mecca. Medina, or the *city*, known under the name of Yathreb before it was sanctified by the throne of the prophet, was divided between the tribes of the Charegites and the Awsites, whose hereditary feud was rekindled by the slightest provocations: two colonies of Jews, who boasted a sacerdotal race, were their humble allies, and without converting the Arabs they introduced the taste of science and religion, which distinguished Medina as the city of the Book. Some of her noblest citizens, in a pilgrimage to the Caaba, were converted by the preaching of Mohammed; on their return, they diffused the belief of God and his prophet, and the new alliance was ratified by their deputies in two secret and nocturnal interviews on a hill in the suburbs of Mecca [A.D. 620–621]. In the first, ten Charegites and two Awsites, united in faith and love, protested in the name of their wives, their children, and their absent brethren that they would forever profess the creed and observe the precepts of the Koran. The second was a political association, the first vital spark of the empire of the Saracens [A.D. 622]. Seventy-three men and two women of Medina held a solemn conference with Mohammed, his kinsman, and his disciples; and pledged themselves to each other by a mutual oath of fidelity. They promised in the name of the city that if he should be banished, they would receive him as a confederate, obey him as a leader, and defend him to the last extremity, like their wives and children. "But if you are recalled by your country," they asked with a flattering anxiety, "will you not abandon your new allies?" "All things," replied Mohammed with a smile, "are now common between us; your blood is as my blood, your ruin as my ruin. We are bound to each other by the ties of honor and interest. I am your friend, and the enemy of your foes." "But if we are killed in your service, what," exclaimed the deputies of Medina, "will be our reward?" "PARADISE," replied the prophet. "Stretch forth thy hand." He stretched it forth, and they reiterated the oath of allegiance and fidelity. Their treaty was ratified by the people, who unanimously embraced the profession of Islam; they rejoiced in the exile of the apostle, but they trembled for his safety and impatiently expected his arrival. After a perilous and rapid journey along the sea-coast, he halted at Koba, two miles from the city, and made his public entry into Medina, sixteen days after his flight from Mecca [September 24]. Five hundred of the citizens advanced to meet him; he was hailed with acclamations of loyalty and devotion; Mohammed was mounted on a she-camel, an umbrella shaded his head, and a turban was unfurled before him to supply the deficiency of a standard. His bravest disciples, who had been scattered by the storm, assembled round his person; and the equal though various merit of the Moslems was distinguished by the names of *Mohagerians* and *Ansars,* the fugitives of Mecca and the auxiliaries of Medina. To eradicate the seeds of jealousy, Mohammed judiciously coupled his principal followers with the rights and obligations of brethren; and when Ali found himself without a peer, the prophet tenderly declared that *he* would be the companion and brother of the noble youth. The expedient was crowned with success; the holy fraternity was respected in peace and war, and the two parties vied with each other in a generous emulation of courage and fidelity. Once only the concord was slightly ruffled by an accidental quarrel: a patriot of Medina arraigned the insolence of the strangers, but the hint of their expulsion was heard with abhorrence; and his own son most eagerly offered to lay at the apostle's feet the head of his father.

From his establishment at Medina, Mohammed assumed the exercise of the regal and sacerdotal office [A.D. 622–632]; and it was impious to appeal from a judge whose decrees were inspired by the divine wisdom. A small portion of ground, the patrimony of two orphans, was acquired by gift or purchase; on that chosen spot he built a house and a mosque, more venerable in their rude simplicity than the palaces and temples of the Assyrian caliphs. His seal of gold or silver was inscribed with the apostolic title; when he prayed and preached in the weekly assembly, he leaned against the trunk of a palm-tree; and it was long before he indulged himself in the use of a chair or pulpit of rough timber. After a reign of six years, fifteen hundred Moslems, in arms and in the field, renewed their oath of allegiance; and their chief repeated the assurance of protection till the death of the last member or the final dissolution of the party. It was in the same camp that the deputy of Mecca was astonished by the attention of the faithful to the words and looks of the prophet, by the eagerness with which they collected his spittle, a hair that dropped on the ground, the refuse water of his lustrations, as if they participated in some degree of the prophetic virtue. "I have seen," said he, "the Chosroes of Persia and the Caesar of Rome, but never did I behold a king among his subjects like Mohammed among his companions." The devout fervor of enthusiasm acts with more energy and truth than the cold and formal servility of courts.

In the state of nature, every man has a right to defend by force of arms his person and his possessions; to repel, or even to prevent, the violence of his enemies; and to extend his hostilities to a reasonable measure of satisfaction and retaliation. In the free society of the Arabs, the duties of subject and citizen imposed a feeble restraint; and Mohammed, in the exercise of a peaceful and benevolent mission, had been despoiled and banished by the injustice of his countrymen. The choice of an independent people had exalted the fugitive of Mecca to the rank of a sovereign; and he was invested with the just prerogative of forming alliances and of waging offensive or defensive war. The imperfection of human rights was supplied and armed by the plenitude of divine power: the prophet of Medina assumed in his new revelations a fiercer and more sanguinary tone, which proves that his former moderation was the effect of weakness: the means of persuasion had been tried, the season of forbearance was elapsed, and he was now commanded to propagate his religion by the sword, to destroy the monuments of idolatry, and, without regarding the sanctity of days or months, to pursue the unbelieving nations of the earth. The same bloody precepts, so repeatedly inculcated in the Koran, are ascribed by the author to the Pentateuch and the gospel. But the mild tenor of the evangelic style may explain an ambiguous text that Jesus did not bring peace on the earth but a sword: his patient and humble virtues should not be confounded with the intolerant zeal of princes and bishops who have disgraced the name of his disciples. In the prosecution of religious war, Mohammed might appeal with more propriety to the example of Moses, of the Judges, and the kings of Israel. The military laws of the Hebrews are still more rigid than those of the Arabian legislator. The Lord of Hosts marched in person before the Jews: if a city resisted their summons, the males, without distinction, were put to the sword: the seven nations of Canaan were devoted to destruction; and neither repentance nor conversion could shield them from the inevitable doom that no creature within their precincts should be left alive. The fair option of friendship or submission or battle was proposed to the enemies of Mohammed. If they professed the creed of Islam, they were admitted to all the temporal and spiritual benefits of his primitive disciples, and marched under the same banner to extend the religion which they had embraced. The clemency of the prophet was decided by his interest: yet he seldom trampled on a prostrate enemy; and he seems to promise that on the payment of a tribute, the least guilty of his unbelieving subjects might be indulged in their worship, or at least in their imperfect faith. In the first months of his reign he practiced the lessons of holy warfare and displayed his white banner before the gates of Medina: the martial apostle fought in person at nine battles or sieges; and fifty enterprises of war were achieved in ten years by himself or his lieutenants. The Arab continued to unite the professions of a merchant and a robber; and his petty excursions for the defense or the attack of a caravan insensibly prepared his troops for the conquest of Arabia. The distribution of the spoil was regulated by a divine law: the whole was faithfully collected in one common mass: a fifth of the gold and silver, the prisoners and cattle, the movables and immovables was reserved by the prophet for pious and charitable uses; the remainder was shared in adequate portions by the soldiers who had obtained the victory or guarded the camp: the rewards of the slain devolved to their widows and orphans; and the increase of cavalry was encouraged by the allotment of a double share to the horse and to the man. From all sides the roving Arabs were allured to the standard of religion and plunder: the apostle sanctified the license of embracing the female captives as their wives or concubines, and the enjoyment of wealth and beauty was a feeble type of the joys of paradise prepared for the valiant martyrs of the faith. "The sword," says Mohammed, "is the key of heaven and of hell; a drop of blood shed in the cause of God, a night spent in arms, is of more avail than two months of fasting or prayer: whosoever falls in battle, his sins are forgiven: at the day of judgment his wounds shall be resplendent as vermilion and odoriferous as musk; and the loss of his limbs shall be supplied by the wings of angels and cherubim." The intrepid souls of the Arabs were fired with enthusiasm: the picture of the invisible world was strongly painted on their imagination; and the death which they had always despised became an object of hope and desire. The Koran inculcates in the most absolute sense the tenets of fate and predestination, which would extinguish both industry and virtue if the actions of man were governed by his speculative belief. Yet their influence in every age has exalted the courage of the Saracens and Turks. The first companions of Mohammed advanced to battle with a fearless confidence: there is no danger where there is no chance: they were ordained to perish in their beds, or they were safe and invulnerable amidst the darts of the enemy.

Perhaps the Koreish would have been content with the flight of Mohammed, had they not been provoked and alarmed by the vengeance of an enemy who could intercept their Syrian trade as it passed and repassed through the territory of Medina. Abu Sophian himself, with only thirty or forty followers, conducted a wealthy caravan of a thousand camels; the fortune or dexterity of his march escaped the vigilance of Mohammed; but the chief of the Koreish was informed that the holy robbers were placed in ambush to await his return. He despatched a messenger to his brethren of Mecca, and they were roused by the fear of losing their merchandise and their provisions unless they hastened to his relief with the military force of the city. The sacred band of Mohammed was formed of three hundred and thirteen Moslems, of whom seventy-seven were fugitives and the rest auxiliaries; they mounted by turns a train of seventy camels (the camels of Yathreb were formidable in war); but such was the poverty of his first disciples that only two could appear on horseback in the field. In the fertile and famous vale of Beder, three stations from Medina, he was informed by his scouts of the caravan that approached on one side; of the Koreish, one hundred horse, eight hundred and fifty foot, who advanced on the other. After a short debate, he sacrificed the prospect of wealth to the pursuit of glory and revenge, and a slight entrenchment was formed to cover his troops and a stream of fresh water that glided through the valley [A.D. 624]. "O God," he exclaimed, as the numbers of the Koreish descended from the hills, "O God, if these are destroyed, by whom wilt thou be worshiped on the earth? Courage, my children; close your ranks; discharge your arrows and the day is your own." At these words he placed himself, with Abubeker, on a throne or pulpit, and instantly demanded the succor of Gabriel and three thousand angels. His eye was fixed on the field of battle: the Moslems fainted and were pressed: in that decisive moment the prophet started from his throne, mounted his horse, and cast a handful of sand into the air: "Let their faces be covered with confusion." Both armies heard the thunder of his voice: their fancy beheld the angelic warriors: the Koreish trembled and fled: seventy of the bravest were slain; and seventy captives adorned the first victory of the faithful. The dead bodies of the Koreish were despoiled and insulted: two of the most obnoxious prisoners were punished with death; and the ransom of the others, four thousand drams of silver, compensated in some degree the escape of the caravan. But it was in vain that the camels of Abu Sophian explored a new road through the desert and along the Euphrates: they were overtaken by the diligence of the Moslems; and wealthy must have been the prize, if twenty thousand drams could be set apart for the fifth of the apostle. The resentment of the public and private loss stimulated Abu Sophian to collect a body of three thousand men, seven hundred of whom were armed with cuirasses and two hundred were mounted on horseback; three thousand camels attended his march; and his wife Henda, with fifteen matrons of Mecca, incessantly sounded their timbrels to animate the troops and to magnify the greatness of Hobal, the most popular deity of the Caaba. The standard of God and Mohammed was upheld by nine hundred and fifty believers [A.D. 625]: the disproportion of numbers was not more alarming than in the field of Beder; and their presumption of victory prevailed against the divine and human sense of the apostle. The second battle was fought on Mount Ohud, six miles to the north of Medina; the Koreish advanced in the form of a crescent; and the right wing of cavalry was led by Caled, the fiercest and most successful of the Arabian warriors. The troops of Mohammed were skillfully posted on the declivity of the hill; and their rear was guarded by a detachment of fifty archers. The weight of their charge impelled and broke the center of the idolaters: but in the pursuit they lost the advantage of their ground: the archers deserted their station: the Moslems were tempted by the spoil, disobeyed their general, and disordered their ranks. The intrepid Caled, wheeling his cavalry on their flank and rear, exclaimed with a loud voice that Mohammed was slain. He was indeed wounded in the face with a javelin: two of his teeth were shattered with a stone; yet in the midst of tumult and dismay, he reproached the infidels with the murder of a prophet; and blessed the friendly hand that stanched his blood and conveyed him to a place of safety. Seventy martyrs died for the sins of the people; they fell, said the apostle, in pairs, each brother embracing his lifeless companion; their bodies were mangled by the inhuman females of Mecca; and the wife of Abu Sophian tasted the entrails of Hamza, the uncle of Mohammed. They might applaud their superstition and satiate their fury; but the Moslems soon rallied in the field, and the Koreish wanted strength or courage to undertake the siege of Medina. It was attacked the ensuing year by an army of ten thousand enemies; and this third expedition is variously named from the *nations* which marched under the banner of Abu Sophian, from the *ditch* which was drawn before the city, and a camp of three thousand Moslems [A.D. 627]. The prudence of Mohammed declined a general engagement: the valor of Ali was signalized in single combat; and the war was protracted twenty days, till the final separation of the confederates. A tempest of wind, rain, and hail overturned their tents: their private quarrels were fomented by an insidious adversary; and the Koreish, deserted by their allies, no longer hoped to subvert the throne or to check the conquests of their invincible exile.

The choice of Jerusalem for the first kebla of prayer discovers the early propensity of Mohammed in favor of the Jews; and happy would it have been for their temporal interest had they recognized in the Arabian prophet the hope of Israel and the promised Messiah. Their obstinacy converted his friendship into implacable hatred, with which he pursued that unfortunate people to the last moment of his life; and in the double character of an apostle and a conqueror, his persecution was extended to both worlds. The Kainoka dwelt at Medina under the protection of the city; he seized the occasion of an accidental tumult and summoned them to embrace his religion or contend with him in battle. "Alas!" replied the trembling Jews, "we are ignorant of the use of arms, but we persevere in the faith and worship of our fathers; why wilt thou reduce us to the necessity of a just defense?" The unequal conflict was terminated in fifteen days; and it was with extreme reluctance that Mohammed yielded to the importunity of his allies and consented to spare the lives of the captives. But their riches were confiscated, their arms became more effectual in the hands of the Moslems; and a wretched colony of seven hundred exiles was driven, with their wives and children, to implore a refuge on the confines of Syria. The Nadhirites were more guilty, since they conspired in a friendly interview to assassinate the prophet. He besieged their castle, three miles from Medina; but their resolute defense obtained an honorable capitulation [A.D. 625]; and the garrison, sounding their trumpets and beating their drums, was permitted to depart with the honors of war. The Jews had excited and joined the war of the Koreish: no sooner had the *nations* retired from the *ditch* than Mohammed, without laying aside his armor, marched on the same day to extirpate the hostile race of the children of Koraidha [A.D. 627]. After a resistance of twenty-five days, they surrendered at discretion. They trusted to the intercession of their old allies of Medina; they could not be ignorant that fanaticism obliterates the feelings of humanity. A venerable elder to whose judgment they appealed pronounced the sentence of their death; seven hundred Jews were dragged in chains to the market-place of the city; they descended alive into the grave prepared for their execution and burial; and the apostle beheld with an inflexible eye the slaughter of his helpless enemies. Their sheep and camels were inherited by the Moslems: three hundred cuirasses, five hundred piles, a thousand lances composed the most useful portion of the spoil. Six days' journey to the north-east of Medina, the ancient and wealthy town of Chaibar was the seat of the Jewish power in Arabia: the territory, a fertile spot in the desert, was covered with plantations and cattle and protected by eight castles, some of which were esteemed of impregnable strength. The forces of Mohammed consisted of two hundred horse and fourteen hundred foot [A.D. 628]: in the succession of eight regular and painful sieges they were exposed to danger and fatigue and hunger; and the most undaunted chiefs despaired of the event. The apostle revived their faith and courage by the example of Ali, on whom he bestowed the surname of the Lion of God: perhaps we may believe that a Hebrew champion of gigantic stature was cloven to the chest by his irresistible cimeter; but we cannot praise the modesty of romance, which represents him as tearing from its hinges the gate of a fortress and wielding the ponderous buckler in his left hand. After the reduction of the castles, the town of Chaibar submitted to the yoke. The chief of the tribe was tortured, in the presence of Mohammed, to force a confession of his hidden treasure: the industry of the shepherds and husbandmen was rewarded with a precarious toleration: they were permitted, so long as it should please the conqueror, to improve their patrimony, in equal shares, for *his* emolument and their own. Under the reign of Omar, the Jews of Chaibar were transported to Syria; and the caliph alleged the injunction of his dying master that one and the true religion should be professed in his native land of Arabia.

Five times each day the eyes of Mohammed were turned towards Mecca, and he was urged by the most sacred and powerful motives to revisit as a conqueror the city and the temple from whence he had been driven as an exile. The Caaba was present to his waking and sleeping fancy: an idle dream was translated into vision and prophecy; he unfurled the holy banner; and a rash promise of success too hastily dropped from the lips of the apostle. His march from Medina to Mecca displayed the peaceful and solemn pomp of a pilgrimage: seventy camels, chosen and bedecked for sacrifice, preceded the van; the sacred territory was respected; and the captives were dismissed without ransom to proclaim his clemency and devotion. But no sooner did Mohammed descend into the plain within a day's journey of the city than he exclaimed, "They have clothed themselves with the skins of tigers": the numbers and resolution of the Koreish opposed his progress; and the roving Arabs of the desert might desert or betray a leader whom they had followed for the hopes of spoil. The intrepid fanatic sunk into a cool and cautious politician: he waived in the treaty his title of apostle of God; concluded with the Koreish and their allies a truce of ten years; engaged to restore the fugitives of Mecca who should embrace his religion; and stipulated only for the ensuing year the humble privilege of entering the city as a friend, and of remaining three days to accomplish the rites of the pilgrimage [A.D. 628]. A cloud of shame and sorrow hung on the retreat of the Moslems, and their disappointment might justly accuse the failure of a prophet who had so often appealed to the evidence of success. The faith and hope of the pilgrims were rekindled by the prospect of Mecca: their swords were sheathed; seven times in the footsteps of the apostle they encompassed the Caaba: the Koreish had retired to the hills, and Mohammed, after the customary sacrifice, evacuated the city on the fourth day [A.D. 629]. The people was edified by his devotion; the hostile chiefs were awed, or divided, or seduced; and both Kaled and Amrou, the future conquerors of Syria and Egypt, most seasonably deserted the sinking cause of idolatry. The power of Mohammed was increased by the submission of the Arabian tribes; ten thousand soldiers were assembled for the conquest of Mecca; and the idolaters, the weaker party, were easily convicted of violating the truce [A.D. 630]. Enthusiasm and discipline impelled the march, and preserved the secret till the blaze of ten thousand fires proclaimed to the astonished Koreish the design, the approach, and the irresistible force of the enemy. The haughty Abu Sophian presented the keys of the city, admired the variety of arms and ensigns that passed before him in review, observed that the son of Abdallah had acquired a mighty kingdom, and confessed, under the cimeter of Omar, that he was the apostle of the true God. The return of Marius and Sulla was stained with the blood of the Romans: the revenge of Mohammed was stimulated by religious zeal, and his injured followers were eager to execute or to prevent the order of a massacre. Instead of indulging their passions and his own, the victorious exile forgave the guilt and united the factions of Mecca. His troops, in three divisions, marched into the city: eight-and-twenty of the inhabitants were slain by the sword of Caled; eleven men and six women were proscribed by the sentence of Mohammed; but he blamed the cruelty of his lieutenant; and several of the most obnoxious victims were indebted for their lives to his clemency or contempt. The chiefs of the Koreish were prostrate at his feet. "What mercy can you expect from the man whom you have wronged?" "We confide in the generosity of our kinsman." "And you shall not confide in vain: begone! you are safe, you are free." The people of Mecca deserved their pardon by the profession of Islam; and after an exile of seven years, the fugitive missionary was enthroned as the prince and prophet of his native country. But the three hundred and sixty idols of the Caaba were ignominiously broken: the house of God was purified and adorned: as an example to future times, the apostle again fulfilled the duties of a pilgrim; and a perpetual law was enacted that no unbeliever should dare to set his foot on the territory of the holy city.

The conquest of Mecca determined the faith and obedience of the Arabian tribes who, according to the vicissitudes of fortune, had obeyed or disregarded the eloquence or the arms of the prophet.

[*The conquest of Arabia proceeds rapidly (A.D. 629–632).*]

When Heraclius returned in triumph from the Persian war, he entertained at Emesa one of the ambassadors of Mohammed, who invited the princes and nations of the earth to the profession of Islam. On this foundation the zeal of the Arabians has supposed the secret conversion of the Christian emperor: the vanity of the Greeks has feigned a personal visit of the prince of Medina, who accepted from the royal bounty a rich domain and a secure retreat in the province of Syria. But the friendship of Heraclius and Mohammed was of short continuance: the new religion had inflamed rather than assuaged the rapacious spirit of the Saracens, and the murder of an envoy afforded a decent pretense for invading, with three thousand soldiers, the territory of Palestine that extends to the eastward of the Jordan [A.D. 629]. The holy banner was entrusted to Zeid; and such was the discipline or enthusiasm of the rising sect that the noblest chiefs served without reluctance under the slave of the prophet. On the event of his decease, Jaafar and Abdallah were successively substituted to the command; and if the three should perish in the war, the troops were authorized to elect their general. The three leaders were slain in the battle of Muta, the first military action which tried the valor of the Moslems against a foreign enemy. Zeid fell, like a soldier, in the foremost ranks: the death of Jaafar was heroic and memorable: he lost his right hand: he shifted the standard to his left: the left was severed from his body: he embraced the standard with his bleeding stumps, till he was transfixed to the ground with fifty honorable wounds. "Advance," cried Abdallah, who stepped into the vacant place, "advance with confidence: either victory or paradise is our own." The lance of a Roman decided the alternative; but the falling standard was rescued by Caled, the proselyte of Mecca: nine swords were broken in his hand; and his valor withstood and repulsed the superior numbers of the Christians. In the nocturnal council of the camp he was chosen to command: his skillful evolutions of the ensuing day secured either the victory or the retreat of the Saracens; and Caled is renowned among his brethren and his enemies by the glorious appellation of the *Sword of God.* In the pulpit, Mohammed described with prophetic rapture the crowns of the blessed martyrs; but in private he betrayed the feelings of human nature: he was surprised as he wept over the daughter of Zeid: "What do I see?" said the astonished votary. "You see," replied the apostle, "a friend who is deploring the loss of his most faithful friend." After the conquest of Mecca, the sovereign of Arabia affected to prevent the hostile preparations of Heraclius; and solemnly proclaimed war against the Romans, without attempting to disguise the hardships and dangers of the enterprise. The Moslems were discouraged: they alleged the want of money, or horses, or provisions; the season of harvest, and the intolerable heat of the summer: "Hell is much hotter," said the indignant prophet. He disdained to compel their service: but on his return he admonished the most guilty by an excommunication of fifty days. Their desertion enhanced the merit of Abubeker, Othman, and the faithful companions who devoted their lives and fortunes; and Mohammed displayed his banner at the head of ten thousand horse and twenty thousand foot [A.D. 630]. Painful indeed was the distress of the march: lassitude and thirst were aggravated by the scorching and pestilential winds of the desert: ten men rode by turns on one camel; and they were reduced to the shameful necessity of drinking the water from the belly of that useful animal. In the mid-way, ten days' journey from Medina and Damascus, they reposed near the grove and fountain of Tabuc. Beyond that place Mohammed declined the prosecution of the war: he declared himself satisfied with the peaceful intentions, he was more probably daunted by the martial array, of the emperor of the East. But the active and intrepid Caled spread around the terror of his name; and the prophet received the submission of the tribes and cities from the Euphrates to Ailah, at the head of the Red Sea. To his Christian subjects, Mohammed readily granted the security of their persons, the freedom of their trade, the property of their goods, and the toleration of their worship. The weakness of their Arabian brethren had restrained them from opposing his ambition; the disciples of Jesus were endeared to the enemy of the Jews; and it was the interest of a conqueror to propose a fair capitulation to the most powerful religion of the earth.

Till the age of sixty-three years, the strength of Mohammed was equal to the temporal and spiritual fatigues of his mission. His epileptic fits, an absurd calumny of the Greeks, would be an object of pity rather than abhorrence; but he seriously believed that he was poisoned at Chaibar by the revenge of a Jewish female. During four years, the health of the prophet declined; his infirmities increased; but his mortal disease was a fever of fourteen days, which deprived him by intervals of the use of reason. As soon as he was conscious of his danger, he edified his brethren by the humility of his virtue or penitence. "If there be any man," said the apostle from the pulpit, "whom I have unjustly scourged, I submit my own back to the lash of retaliation. Have I aspersed the reputation of a Moslem? let him proclaim *my faults* in the face of the congregation. Has any one been despoiled of his goods? the little that I possess shall compensate the principal and the interest of the debt." "Yes," replied a voice from the crowd, "I am entitled to three drams of silver." Mohammed heard the complaint, satisfied the demand, and thanked his creditor for accusing him in this world rather than at the day of judgment. He beheld with temperate firmness the approach of death; enfranchised his slaves (seventeen men, as they are named, and eleven women); minutely directed the order of his funeral; and moderated the lamentations of his weeping friends, on whom he bestowed the benediction of peace. Till the third day before his death, he regularly performed the function of public prayer: the choice of Abubeker to supply his place appeared to mark that ancient and faithful friend as his successor in the sacerdotal and regal office; but he prudently declined the risk and envy of a more explicit nomination. At a moment when his faculties were visibly impaired, he called for pen and ink to write, or more properly to dictate, a divine book, the sum and accomplishment of all his revelations: a dispute arose in the chamber whether he should be allowed to supersede the authority of the Koran; and the prophet was forced to reprove the indecent vehemence of his disciples. If the slightest credit may be afforded to the traditions of his wives and companions, he maintained, in the bosom of his family and to the last moments of his life, the dignity of an apostle and the faith of an enthusiast; described the visits of Gabriel, who bade an everlasting farewell to the earth; and expressed his lively confidence not only of the mercy but of the favor of the Supreme Being. In a familiar discourse he had mentioned his special prerogative that the angel of death was not allowed to take his soul till he had respectfully asked the permission of the prophet. The request was granted; and Mohammed immediately fell into the agony of his dissolution [June 8, A.D. 632]: his head was reclined on the lap of Ayesha, the best beloved of all his wives; he fainted with the violence of pain; recovering his spirits, he raised his eyes towards the roof of the house, and with a steady look, though a faltering voice, uttered the last broken though articulate words: "O God! . . . pardon my sins. . . . Yes, . . . I come, . . . among my fellow-citizens on high"; and thus peaceably expired on a carpet spread upon the floor. An expedition for the conquest of Syria was stopped by this mournful event; the army halted at the gates of Medina; the chiefs were assembled round their dying master. The city, more especially the house, of the prophet was a scene of clamorous sorrow, of silent despair: fanaticism alone could suggest a ray of hope and consolation. "How can he be dead, our witness, our intercessor, our mediator with God? By God he is not dead: like Moses and Jesus, he is wrapped in a holy trance, and speedily will he return to his faithful people." The evidence of sense was disregarded; and Omar, unsheathing his cimeter, threatened to strike off the heads of the infidels who should dare to affirm that the prophet was no more. The tumult was appeased by the weight and moderation of Abubeker. "Is it Mohammed," said he to Omar and the multitude, "or the God of Mohammed whom you worship? The God of Mohammed liveth forever; but the apostle was a mortal like ourselves, and according to his own prediction he has experienced the common fate of mortality." He was piously interred by the hands of his nearest kinsman on the same spot on which he expired: Medina has been sanctified by the death and burial of Mohammed; and the innumerable pilgrims of Mecca often turn aside from the way to bow in voluntary devotion before the simple tomb of the prophet.

At the conclusion of the life of Mohammed, it may perhaps be expected that I should balance his faults and virtues, that I should decide whether the title of enthusiast or impostor more properly belongs to that extraordinary man. Had I been intimately conversant with the son of Abdallah, the task would still be difficult and the success uncertain: at the distance of twelve centuries, I darkly contemplate his shade through a cloud of religious incense; and could I truly delineate the portrait of an hour, the fleeting resemblance would not equally apply to the solitary of Mount Hera, to the preacher of Mecca, and to the conqueror of Arabia. The author of a mighty revolution appears to have been endowed with a pious and contemplative disposition: so soon as marriage had raised him above the pressure of want, he avoided the paths of ambition and avarice; and till the age of forty he lived with innocence and would have died without a name. The unity of God is an idea most congenial to nature and reason; and a slight conversation with the Jews and Christians would teach him to despise and detest the idolatry of Mecca. It was the duty of a man and a citizen to impart the doctrine of salvation, to rescue his country from the dominion of sin and error. The energy of a mind incessantly bent on the same object would convert a general obligation into a particular call; the warm suggestions of the understanding or the fancy would be felt as the inspirations of Heaven; the labor of thought would expire in rapture and vision; and the inward sensation, the invisible monitor, would be described with the form and attributes of an angel of God. From enthusiasm to imposture, the step is perilous and slippery: the demon of Socrates affords a memorable instance how a wise man may deceive himself, how a good man may deceive others, how the conscience may slumber in a mixed and middle state between self-illusion and voluntary fraud. Charity may believe that the original motives of Mohammed were those of pure and genuine benevolence; but a human missionary is incapable of cherishing the obstinate unbelievers who reject his claims, despise his arguments, and persecute his life; he might forgive his personal adversaries, he may lawfully hate the enemies of God; the stern passions of pride and revenge were kindled in the bosom of Mohammed, and he sighed, like the prophet of Nineveh, for the destruction of the rebels whom he had condemned. The injustice of Mecca and the choice of Medina transformed the citizen into a prince, the humble preacher into the leader of armies; but his sword was consecrated by the example of the saints; and the same God who afflicts a sinful world with pestilence and earthquakes might inspire for their conversion or chastisement the valor of his servants. In the exercise of political government, he was compelled to abate of the stern rigor of fanaticism, to comply in some measure with the prejudices and passions of his followers, and to employ even the vices of mankind as the instruments of their salvation. The use of fraud and perfidy, of cruelty and injustice, were often subservient to the propagation of the faith; and Mohammed commanded or approved the assassination of the Jews and idolaters who had escaped from the field of battle. By the repetition of such acts, the character of Mohammed must have been gradually stained; and the influence of such pernicious habits would be poorly compensated by the practice of the personal and social virtues which are necessary to maintain the reputation of a prophet among his sectaries and friends. Of his last years, ambition was the ruling passion; and a politician will suspect that he secretly smiled (the victorious impostor!) at the enthusiasm of his youth and the credulity of his proselytes. A philosopher will observe that *their* credulity and *his* success would tend more strongly to fortify the assurance of his divine mission, that his interest and religion were inseparably connected, and that his conscience would be soothed by the persuasion that he alone was absolved by the Deity from the obligation of positive and moral laws. If he retained any vestige of his native innocence, the sins of Mohammed may be allowed as an evidence of his sincerity. In the support of truth, the arts of fraud and fiction may be deemed less criminal; and he would have started at the foulness of the means, had he not been satisfied of the importance and justice of the end. Even in a conqueror or a priest, I can surprise a word or action of unaffected humanity; and the decree of Mohammed that, in the sale of captives, the mothers should never be separated from their children may suspend or moderate the censure of the historian.

The good sense of Mohammed despised the pomp of royalty: the apostle of God submitted to the menial offices of the family: he kindled the fire, swept the floor, milked the ewes, and mended with his own hands his shoes and his woolen garment. Disdaining the penance and merit of a hermit, he observed, without effort or vanity, the abstemious diet of an Arab and a soldier. On solemn occasions he feasted his companions with rustic and hospitable plenty; but in his domestic life, many weeks would elapse without a fire being kindled on the hearth of the prophet. The interdiction of wine was confirmed by his example; his hunger was appeased with a sparing allowance of barley-bread: he delighted in the taste of milk and honey; but his ordinary food consisted of dates and water. Perfumes and women were the two sensual enjoyments which his nature required and his religion did not forbid; and Mohammed affirmed that the fervor of his devotion was increased by these innocent pleasures. The heat of the climate inflames the blood of the Arabs; and their libidinous complexion has been noticed by the writers of antiquity. Their incontinence was regulated by the civil and religious laws of the Koran: their incestuous alliances were blamed; the boundless license of polygamy was reduced to four legitimate wives or concubines; their rights both of bed and of dowry were equitably determined; the freedom of divorce was discouraged, adultery was condemned as a capital offense; and fornication, in either sex, was punished with a hundred stripes. Such were the calm and rational precepts of the legislator: but in his private conduct, Mohammed indulged the appetites of a man, and abused the claims of a prophet. A special revelation dispensed him from the laws which he had imposed on his nation: the female sex, without reserve, was abandoned to his desires; and this singular prerogative excited the envy rather than the scandal, the veneration rather than the envy, of the devout Moslems. If we remember the seven hundred wives and three hundred concubines of the wise Solomon, we shall applaud the modesty of the Arabian, who espoused no more than seventeen or fifteen wives; eleven are enumerated who occupied at Medina their separate apartments round the house of the apostle and enjoyed in their turns the favor of his conjugal society. What is singular enough, they were all widows, excepting only Ayesha, the daughter of Abubeker. *She* was doubtless a virgin, since Mohammed consummated his nuptials (such is the premature ripeness of the climate) when she was only nine years of age. The youth, the beauty, the spirit of Ayesha gave her a superior ascendant: she was beloved and trusted by the prophet; and after his death, the daughter of Abubeker was long revered as the mother of the faithful. Her behavior had been ambiguous and indiscreet: in a nocturnal march she was accidentally left behind; and in the morning Ayesha returned to the camp with a man. The temper of Mohammed was inclined to jealousy; but a divine revelation assured him of her innocence: he chastised her accusers and published a law of domestic peace, that no woman should be condemned unless four male witnesses had seen her in the act of adultery. In his adventures with Zeineb, the wife of Zeid, and with Mary, an Egyptian captive, the amorous prophet forgot the interest of his reputation. At the house of Zeid, his freedman and adopted son, he beheld in a loose undress the beauty of Zeineb and burst forth into an ejaculation of devotion and desire. The servile, or grateful, freedman understood the hint, and yielded without hesitation to the love of his benefactor. But as the filial relation had excited some doubt and scandal, the angel Gabriel descended from Heaven to ratify the deed, to annul the adoption, and gently to reprove the apostle for distrusting the indulgence of his God. One of his wives, Hafna, the daughter of Omar, surprised him on her own bed in the embraces of his Egyptian captive: she promised secrecy and forgiveness, he swore that he would renounce the possession of Mary. Both parties forgot their engagements; and Gabriel again descended with a chapter of the Koran, to absolve him from his oath and to exhort him freely to enjoy his captives and concubines without listening to the clamors of his wives. In a solitary retreat of thirty days he labored, alone with Mary, to fulfill the commands of the angel. When his love and revenge were satiated, he summoned to his presence his eleven wives, reproached their disobedience and indiscretion, and threatened them with a sentence of divorce, both in this world and in the next; a dreadful sentence, since those who had ascended the bed of the prophet were forever excluded from the hope of a second marriage. Perhaps the incontinence of Mohammed may be palliated by the tradition of his natural or preternatural gifts; he united the manly virtue of thirty of the children of Adam: and the apostle might rival the thirteenth labor of the Grecian Hercules. A more serious and decent excuse may be drawn from his fidelity to Cadijah. During the twenty-four years of their marriage, her youthful husband abstained from the right of polygamy, and the pride or tenderness of the venerable matron was never insulted by the society of a rival. After her death, he placed her in the rank of the four perfect women, with the sister of Moses, the mother of Jesus, and Fatima, the best beloved of his daughters. "Was she not old?" said Ayesha, with the insolence of a blooming beauty; "has not God given you a better in her place?" "No, by God," said Mohammed, with an effusion of honest gratitude, "there never can be a better! She believed in me when men despised me; she relieved my wants when I was poor and persecuted by the world."

In the largest indulgence of polygamy, the founder of a religion and empire might aspire to multiply the chances of a numerous posterity and a lineal succession. The hopes of Mohammed were fatally disappointed. The virgin Ayesha, and his ten widows of mature age and approved fertility, were barren in his potent embraces. The four sons of Cadijah died in their infancy. Mary, his Egyptian concubine, was endeared to him by the birth of Ibrahim. At the end of fifteen months the prophet wept over his grave; but he sustained with firmness the raillery of his enemies, and checked the adulation or credulity of the Moslems, by the assurance that an eclipse of the sun was not occasioned by the death of the infant. Cadijah had likewise given him four daughters, who were married to the most faithful of his disciples: the three eldest died before their father; but Fatima, who possessed his confidence and love, became the wife of her cousin Ali and the mother of an illustrious progeny. The merit and misfortunes of Ali and his descendants will lead me to anticipate, in this place, the series of the Saracen caliphs, a title which describes the commanders of the faithful as the vicars and successors of the apostle of God.

The birth, the alliance, the character of Ali, which exalted him above the rest of his countrymen, might justify his claim to the vacant throne of Arabia. The son of Abu Taleb was in his own right the chief of the family of Hashem, and the hereditary prince or guardian of the city and temple of Mecca. The light of prophecy was extinct; but the husband of Fatima might expect the inheritance and blessing of her father: the Arabs had sometimes been patient of a female reign; and the two grandsons of the prophet had often been fondled in his lap, and shown in his pulpit as the hope of his age, and the chief of the youth of paradise. The first of the true believers might aspire to march before them in this world and in the next; and if some were of a graver and more rigid cast, the zeal and virtue of Ali were never outstripped by any recent proselyte. He united the qualifications of a poet, a soldier, and a saint: his wisdom still breathes in a collection of moral and religious sayings; and every antagonist, in the combats of the tongue or of the sword, was subdued by his eloquence and valor. From the first hour of his mission to the last rites of his funeral, the apostle was never forsaken by a generous friend whom he delighted to name his brother, his vicegerent, and the faithful Aaron of a second Moses. The son of Abu Taleb was afterwards reproached for neglecting to secure his interest by a solemn declaration of his right, which would have silenced all competition and sealed his succession by the decrees of Heaven. But the unsuspecting hero confided in himself: the jealousy of empire, and perhaps the fear of opposition, might suspend the resolutions of Mohammed; and the bed of sickness was besieged by the artful Ayesha, the daughter of Abubeker and the enemy of Ali.

The silence and death of the prophet restored the liberty of the people; and his companions convened an assembly to deliberate on the choice of his successor. The hereditary claim and lofty spirit of Ali were offensive to an aristocracy of elders desirous of bestowing and resuming the scepter by a free and frequent election: the Koreish could never be reconciled to the proud preeminence of the line of Hashem; the ancient discord of the tribes was rekindled, the *fugitives* of Mecca and the *auxiliaries* of Medina asserted their respective merits; and the rash proposal of choosing two independent caliphs would have crushed in their infancy the religion and empire of the Saracens. The tumult was appeased by the disinterested resolution of Omar, who, suddenly renouncing his own pretensions, stretched forth his hand and declared himself the first subject of the mild and venerable Abubeker [June 8, A.D. 632]. The urgency of the moment and the acquiescence of the people might excuse this illegal and precipitate measure; but Omar himself confessed from the pulpit that if any Moslem should hereafter presume to anticipate the suffrage of his brethren, both the elector and the elected would be worthy of death. After the simple inauguration of Abubeker, he was obeyed in Medina, Mecca, and the provinces of Arabia: the Hashemites alone declined the oath of fidelity; and their chief, in his own house, maintained above six months a sullen and independent reserve, without listening to the threats of Omar, who attempted to consume with fire the habitation of the daughter of the apostle. The death of Fatima and the decline of his party subdued the indignant spirit of Ali: he condescended to salute the commander of the faithful, accepted his excuse of the necessity of preventing their common enemies, and wisely rejected his courteous offer of abdicating the government of the Arabians. After a reign of two years, the aged caliph was summoned by the angel of death [August 22, A.D. 634]. In his testament, with the tacit approbation of his companions, he bequeathed the scepter to the firm and intrepid virtue of Omar [August 23, A.D. 634]. "I have no occasion," said the modest candidate, "for the place." "But the place has occasion for you," replied Abubeker; who expired with a fervent prayer that the God of Mohammed would ratify his choice and direct the Moslems in the way of concord and obedience. The prayer was not ineffectual, since Ali himself, in a life of privacy and prayer, professed to revere the superior worth and dignity of his rival; who comforted him for the loss of empire by the most flattering marks of confidence and esteem. In the twelfth year of his reign, Omar received a mortal wound from the hand of an assassin: he rejected with equal impartiality the names of his son and of Ali, refused to load his conscience with the sins of his successor, and devolved on six of the most respectable companions the arduous task of electing a commander of the faithful. On this occasion, Ali was again blamed by his friends for submitting his right to the judgment of men, for recognizing their jurisdiction by accepting a place among the six electors. He might have obtained their suffrage had he deigned to promise a strict and servile conformity, not only to the Koran and tradition, but likewise to the determinations of two seniors. With these limitations, Othman, the secretary of Mohammed, accepted the government [November 7, A.D. 644]; nor was it till after the third caliph, twenty-four years after the death of the prophet, that Ali was invested, by the popular choice, with the regal and sacerdotal office. The manners of the Arabians retained their primitive simplicity, and the son of Abu Taleb despised the pomp and vanity of this world. At the hour of prayer, he repaired to the mosque of Medina, clothed in a thin cotton gown, a coarse turban on his head, his slippers in one hand, and his bow in the other, instead of a walking-staff. The companions of the prophet and the chiefs of the tribes saluted their new sovereign and gave him their right hands as a sign of fealty and allegiance.

The mischiefs that flow from the contests of ambition are usually confined to the times and countries in which they have been agitated. But the religious discord of the friends and enemies of Ali has been renewed in every age of the Hegira, and is still maintained in the immortal hatred of the Persians and Turks. The former, who are branded with the appellation of *Shiites* or sectaries, have enriched the Mohammedan creed with a new article of faith; and if Mohammed be the apostle, his companion Ali is the vicar, of God. In their private converse, in their public worship, they bitterly execrate the three usurpers who intercepted his indefeasible right to the dignity of Imam and Caliph; and the name of Omar expresses in their tongue the perfect accomplishment of wickedness and impiety. The *Sonnites*, who are supported by the general consent and orthodox tradition of the Moslems, entertain a more impartial, or at least a more decent, opinion. They respect the memory of Abubeker, Omar, Othman, and Ali, the holy and legitimate successors of the prophet. But they assign the last and most humble place to the husband of Fatima, in the persuasion that the order of succession was determined by the degrees of sanctity. An historian who balances the four caliphs with a hand unshaken by superstition will calmly pronounce that their manners were alike pure and exemplary; that their zeal was fervent, and probably sincere; and that, in the midst of riches and power, their lives were devoted to the practice of moral and religious duties. But the public virtues of Abubeker and Omar, the prudence of the first, the severity of the second, maintained the peace and prosperity of their reigns. The feeble temper and declining age of Othman were incapable of sustaining the weight of conquest and empire. He chose, and he was deceived; he trusted, and he was betrayed: the most deserving of the faithful became useless or hostile to his government, and his lavish bounty was productive only of ingratitude and discontent. The spirit of discord went forth in the provinces: their deputies assembled at Medina; and the Charegites, the desperate fanatics who disclaimed the yoke of subordination and reason, were confounded among the free-born Arabs, who demanded the redress of their wrongs and the punishment of their oppressors. From Cufa, from Bassora, from Egypt, from the tribes of the desert, they rose in arms, encamped about a league from Medina, and despatched a haughty mandate to their sovereign, requiring him to execute justice or to descend from the throne. His repentance began to disarm and disperse the insurgents; but their fury was rekindled by the arts of his enemies; and the forgery of a perfidious secretary was contrived to blast his reputation and precipitate his fall. The caliph had lost the only guard of his predecessors, the esteem and confidence of the Moslems: during a siege of six weeks his water and provisions were intercepted, and the feeble gates of the palace were protected only by the scruples of the more timorous rebels. Forsaken by those who had abused his simplicity, the hopeless and venerable caliph expected the approach of death: the brother of Ayesha marched at the head of the assassins; and Othman, with the Koran in his lap, was pierced with a multitude of wounds [June 17, A.D. 656]. A tumultuous anarchy of five days was appeased by the inauguration of Ali: his refusal would have provoked a general massacre. In this painful situation he supported the becoming pride of the chief of the Hashemites; declared that he would rather serve than reign; rebuked the presumption of the strangers; and required the formal, if not the voluntary, assent of the chiefs of the nation. He has never been accused of prompting the assassin of Omar;

though Persia indiscreetly celebrates the festival of that holy martyr. The quarrel between Othman and his subjects was assuaged by the early mediation of Ali; and Hassan, the eldest of his sons, was insulted and wounded in the defense of the caliph. Yet it is doubtful whether the father of Hassan was strenuous and sincere in his opposition to the rebels; and it is certain that he enjoyed the benefit of their crime. The temptation was indeed of such magnitude as might stagger and corrupt the most obdurate virtue. The ambitious candidate no longer aspired to the barren scepter of Arabia; the Saracens had been victorious in the East and West; and the wealthy kingdoms of Persia, Syria, and Egypt were the patrimony of the commander of the faithful.

A life of prayer and contemplation had not chilled the martial activity of Ali; but in a mature age, after a long experience of mankind, he still betrayed in his conduct the rashness and indiscretion of youth. In the first days of his reign [A.D. 656–661], he neglected to secure, either by gifts or fetters, the doubtful allegiance of Telha and Zobeir, two of the most powerful of the Arabian chiefs. They escaped from Medina to Mecca, and from thence to Bassora; erected the standard of revolt; and usurped the government of Irak, or Assyria, which they had vainly solicited as the reward of their services. The mask of patriotism is allowed to cover the most glaring inconsistencies; and the enemies, perhaps the assassins, of Othman now demanded vengeance for his blood. They were accompanied in their flight by Ayesha, the widow of the prophet, who cherished to the last hour of her life an implacable hatred against the husband and the posterity of Fatima. The most reasonable Moslems were scandalized that the mother of the faithful should expose in a camp her person and character; but the superstitious crowd was confident that her presence would sanctify the justice and assure the success of their cause. At the head of twenty thousand of his loyal Arabs and nine thousand valiant auxiliaries of Cufa, the caliph encountered and defeated the superior numbers of the rebels under the walls of Bassora. Their leaders, Telha and Zobeir, were slain in the first battle that stained with civil blood the arms of the Moslems. After passing through the ranks to animate the troops, Ayesha had chosen her post amidst the dangers of the field. In the heat of the action, seventy men who held the bridle of her camel were successively killed or wounded; and the cage or litter in which she sat was stuck with javelins and darts like the quills of a porcupine. The venerable captive sustained with firmness the reproaches of the conqueror and was speedily dismissed to her proper station at the tomb of Mohammed, with the respect and tenderness that was still due to the widow of the apostle. After this victory, which was styled the Day of the Camel, Ali marched against a more formidable adversary; against Moawiyah, the son of Abu Sophian, who had assumed the title of caliph, and whose claim was supported by the forces of Syria and the interest of the house of Ommiyah. From the passage of Thapsacus, the plain of Siffin extends along the western bank of the Euphrates. On this spacious and level theater, the two competitors waged a desultory war of one hundred and ten days. In the course of ninety actions or skirmishes, the loss of Ali was estimated at twenty-five, that of Moawiyah at forty-five, thousand soldiers; and the list of the slain was dignified with the names of five-and-twenty veterans who had fought at Beder under the standard of Mohammed. In this sanguinary contest the lawful caliph displayed a superior character of valor and humanity. His troops were strictly enjoined to await the first onset of the enemy, to spare their flying brethren, and to respect the bodies of the dead and the chastity of the female captives. He generously proposed to save the blood of the Moslems by a single combat; but his trembling rival declined the challenge as a sentence of inevitable death. The ranks of the Syrians were broken by the charge of a hero who was mounted on a piebald horse and wielded with irresistible force his ponderous and two-edged sword. As often as he smote a rebel, he shouted the *Allah Acbar,* "God is victorious!," and in the tumult of a nocturnal battle he was heard to repeat four hundred times that tremendous exclamation. The prince of Damascus already meditated his flight; but the certain victory was snatched from the grasp of Ali by the disobedience and enthusiasm of his troops. Their conscience was awed by the solemn appeal to the books of the Koran which Moawiyah exposed on the foremost lances; and Ali was compelled to yield to a disgraceful truce and an insidious compromise. He retreated with sorrow and indignation to Cufa; his party was discouraged; the distant provinces of Persia, of Yemen, and of Egypt were subdued or seduced by his crafty rival; and the stroke of fanaticism, which was aimed against the three chiefs of the nation, was fatal only to the cousin of Mohammed. In the temple of Mecca, three Charegites or enthusiasts discoursed of the disorders of the church and state: they soon agreed that the deaths of Ali, of Moawiyah, and of his friend Amrou, the viceroy of Egypt, would restore the peace and unity of religion. Each of the assassins chose his victim, poisoned his dagger, devoted his life, and secretly repaired to the scene of action. Their resolution was equally desperate: but the first mistook the person of Amrou, and stabbed the deputy who occupied his seat; the prince of Damascus was dangerously hurt by the second; the lawful caliph, in the mosque of Cufa, received a mortal wound from the hand of the third. He expired in the sixty-third year of his age [January 21, A.D. 661] and mercifully recommended to his children that they would despatch the murderer by a single stroke. The sepulchre of Ali was concealed from the tyrants of the house of Ommiyah; but in the fourth age of the Hegira, a tomb, a temple, a city, arose near the ruins of Cufa. Many thousands of the Shiites repose in holy ground at the feet of the vicar of God; and the desert is vivified by the numerous and annual visits of the Persians, who esteem their devotion not less meritorious than the pilgrimage of Mecca.

The persecutors of Mohammed usurped the inheritance of his children; and the champions of idolatry became the supreme heads of his religion and empire. The opposition of Abu Sophian had been fierce and obstinate; his conversion was tardy and reluctant; his new faith was fortified by necessity and interest; he served, he fought, perhaps he believed; and the sins of the time of ignorance were expiated by the recent merits of the family of Ommiyah.

[*Moawiyah reigns (A.D. 665 or 661–680). The caliphate becomes hereditary rather than elective. The family of Ali experiences martyrdom. His descendants, however, represent "the twelve IMAMS or pontiffs of the Persian creed." Their followers are distinguished by a green turban.*]

The talents of Mohammed are entitled to our applause; but his success has perhaps too strongly attracted our admiration. Are we surprised that a multitude of proselytes should embrace the doctrine and the passions of an eloquent fanatic? In the heresies of the church, the same seduction has been tried and repeated from the time of the apostles to that of the reformers. Does it seem incredible that a private citizen should grasp the sword and the scepter, subdue his native country, and erect a monarchy by his victorious arms? In the moving picture of the dynasties of the East, a hundred fortunate usurpers have arisen from a baser origin, surmounted more formidable obstacles, and filled a larger scope of empire and conquest. Mohammed was alike instructed to preach and to fight; and the union of these opposite qualities, while it enhanced his merit, contributed to his success: the operation of force and persuasion, of enthusiasm and fear, continually acted on each other, till every barrier yielded to their irresistible power. His voice invited the Arabs to freedom and victory, to arms and rapine, to the indulgence of their darling passions in this world and the other: the restraints which he imposed were requisite to establish the credit of the prophet and to exercise the obedience of the people; and the only objection to his success was his rational creed of the unity and perfections of God. It is not the propagation but the permanency of his religion that deserves our wonder: the same pure and perfect impression which he engraved at Mecca and Medina is preserved, after the revolutions of twelve centuries, by the Indian, the African, and the Turkish proselytes of the Koran. If the Christian apostles, St. Peter or St. Paul, could return to the Vatican, they might possibly inquire the name of the Deity who is worshiped with such mysterious rites in that magnificent temple: at Oxford or Geneva, they would experience less surprise; but it might still be incumbent on them to peruse the catechism of the church and to study the orthodox commentators on their own writings and the words of their Master. But the Turkish dome of St. Sophia, with an increase of splendor and size, represents the humble tabernacle erected at Medina by the hands of Mohammed. The Mohammedans have uniformly withstood the temptation of reducing the object of their faith and devotion to a level with the senses and imagination of man. "I believe in one God, and Mohammed the apostle of God," is the simple and invariable profession of Islam. The intellectual image of the Deity has never been degraded by any visible idol; the honors of the prophet have never transgressed the measure of human virtue; and his living precepts have restrained the gratitude of his disciples within the bounds of reason and religion. The votaries of Ali have indeed consecrated the memory of their hero, his wife, and his children; and some of the Persian doctors pretend that the divine essence was incarnate in the person of the Imams; but their superstition is universally condemned by the Sonnites; and their impiety has afforded a seasonable warning against the worship of saints and martyrs. The metaphysical questions on the attributes of God and the liberty of man have been agitated in the schools of the Mohammedans as well as in those of the Christians; but among the former they have never engaged the passions of the people or disturbed the tranquility of the state. The cause of this important difference may be found in the separation or union of the regal and sacerdotal characters. It was the interest of the caliphs, the successors of the prophet and commanders of the faithful, to repress and discourage all religious innovations: the order, the discipline, the temporal and spiritual ambition of the clergy are unknown to the Moslems; and the sages of the law are the guides of their conscience and the oracles of their faith. From the Atlantic to the Ganges, the Koran is acknowledged as the fundamental code not only of theology but of civil and criminal jurisprudence; and the laws which regulate the actions and the property of mankind are guarded by the infallible and immutable sanction of the will of God. This religious servitude is attended with some practical disadvantage; the illiterate legislator had been often misled by his own prejudices and those of his country; and the institutions of the Arabian desert may be ill adapted to the wealth and numbers of Ispahan and Constantinople. On these occasions, the Cadhi respectfully places on his head the holy volume, and substitutes a dexterous interpretation more apposite to the principles of equity and the manners and policy of the times.

His beneficial or pernicious influence on the public happiness is the last consideration in the character of Mohammed. The most bitter or most bigoted of his Christian or Jewish foes will surely allow that he assumed a false commission to inculcate a salutary doctrine, less perfect only than their own. He piously supposed, as the basis of his religion, the truth and sanctity of *their* prior revolutions, the virtues and miracles of their founders. The idols of Arabia were broken before the throne of God; the blood of human victims was expiated by prayer and fasting and alms, the laudable or innocent arts of devotion; and his rewards and punishments of a future life were painted by the images most congenial to an ignorant and carnal generation. Mohammed was perhaps incapable of dictating a moral and political system for the use of his countrymen: but he breathed among the faithful a spirit of charity and friendship; recommended the practice of the social virtues; and checked, by his laws and precepts, the thirst of revenge and the oppression of widows and orphans. The hostile tribes were united in faith and obedience, and the valor which had been idly spent in domestic quarrels was vigorously directed against a foreign enemy. Had the impulse been less powerful, Arabia, free at home and formidable abroad, might have flourished under a succession of her native monarchs. Her sovereignty was lost by the extent and rapidity of conquest. The colonies of the nation were scattered over the East and West, and their blood was mingled with the blood of their converts and captives. After the reign of three caliphs, the throne was transported from Medina to the valley of Damascus and the banks of the Tigris; the holy cities were violated by impious war; Arabia was ruled by the rod of a subject, perhaps of a stranger; and the Bedoweens of the desert, awakening from their dream of dominion, resumed their old and solitary independence.

CHAPTER LI

CONQUESTS BY THE ARABS

*The conquest of Persia, Syria, Egypt, Africa, and Spain by the
Arabs or Saracens. • Empire of the caliphs, or successors of
Mohammed. • State of the Christians, etc., under their government.*

The revolution of Arabia had not changed the character of the Arabs:
the death of Mohammed was the signal of independence; and the
hasty structure of his power and religion tottered to its foundations
[A.D. 632]. A small and faithful band of his primitive disciples had listened to his eloquence and shared his distress; had fled with the apostle from the persecution of Mecca, or had received the fugitive in the
walls of Medina. The increasing myriads who acknowledged Mohammed as their king and prophet had been compelled by his arms or
allured by his prosperity. The Polytheists were confounded by the
simple idea of a solitary and invisible God; the pride of the Christians
and Jews disdained the yoke of a mortal and contemporary legislator.
The habits of faith and obedience were not sufficiently confirmed; and
many of the new converts regretted the venerable antiquity of the law
of Moses, or the rites and mysteries of the Catholic church; or the
idols, the sacrifices, the joyous festivals of their Pagan ancestors. The
jarring interests and hereditary feuds of the Arabian tribes had not yet
coalesced in a system of union and subordination; and the Barbarians
were impatient of the mildest and most salutary laws that curbed their
passions or violated their customs. They submitted with reluctance to
the religious precepts of the Koran, the abstinence from wine, the fast
of the Ramadan, and the daily repetition of five prayers; and the alms
and tithes which were collected for the treasury of Medina could be
distinguished only by a name from the payment of a perpetual and ignominious tribute. The example of Mohammed had excited a spirit of
fanaticism or imposture, and several of his rivals presumed to imitate
the conduct and defy the authority of the living prophet. At the head
of the *fugitives* and *auxiliaries,* the first caliph was reduced to the cities
of Mecca, Medina, and Tayef; and perhaps the Koreish would have restored the idols of the Caaba if their levity had not been checked by a

seasonable reproof. "Ye men of Mecca, will ye be the last to embrace and the first to abandon the religion of Islam?" After exhorting the Moslems to confide in the aid of God and his apostle, Abubeker resolved by a vigorous attack to prevent the junction of the rebels. The women and children were safely lodged in the cavities of the mountains: the warriors, marching under eleven banners, diffused the terror of their arms; and the appearance of a military force revived and confirmed the loyalty of the faithful. The inconstant tribes accepted with humble repentance the duties of prayer and fasting and alms; and after some examples of success and severity, the most daring apostates fell prostrate before the sword. . . . Yet the spoils of unknown nations were continually laid at the foot of their throne, and the uniform ascent of the Arabian greatness must be ascribed to the spirit of the nation rather than the abilities of their chiefs. A large deduction must be allowed for the weakness of their enemies. The birth of Mohammed was fortunately placed in the most degenerate and disorderly period of the Persians, the Romans, and the Barbarians of Europe: the empires of Trajan, or even of Constantine or Charlemagne, would have repelled the assault of the naked Saracens, and the torrent of fanaticism might have been obscurely lost in the sands of Arabia.

In the victorious days of the Roman republic, it had been the aim of the senate to confine their councils and legions to a single war, and completely to suppress a first enemy before they provoked the hostilities of a second. These timid maxims of policy were disdained by the magnanimity or enthusiasm of the Arabian caliphs. With the same vigor and success they invaded the successors of Augustus and those of Artaxerxes; and the rival monarchies at the same instant became the prey of an enemy whom they had been so long accustomed to despise. In the ten years of the administration of Omar, the Saracens reduced to his obedience thirty-six thousand cities or castles, destroyed four thousand churches or temples of the unbelievers, and edified fourteen hundred mosques for the exercise of the religion of Mohammed. One hundred years after his flight from Mecca, the arms and the reign of his successors extended from India to the Atlantic Ocean, over the various and distant provinces which may be comprised under the names of I. Persia; II. Syria; III. Egypt; IV. Africa; and V. Spain. Under this general division, I shall proceed to unfold these memorable transactions; despatching with brevity the remote and less interesting conquests of the East, and reserving a fuller narrative for those domestic countries which had been included within the pale of the Roman empire. Yet I must excuse my own defects by a just complaint of the blindness and insufficiency of my guides. The Greeks, so loquacious in controversy, have not been anxious to celebrate the triumphs of their enemies. After a century of ignorance, the first annals of the Moslems were collected in a great measure from the voice of tradition. Among the numerous productions of Arabic and Persian literature, our interpreters have selected the imperfect sketches of a more recent age. The art and genius of history have ever been unknown to the Asiatics; they are ignorant of the laws of criticism; and our monkish chronicle of the same period may be compared to their most popular works, which are never vivified by the spirit of philosophy and freedom. The *Oriental library* of a Frenchman would instruct the most learned mufti of the East; and perhaps the Arabs might not find in a single historian so clear and comprehensive a narrative of their own exploits as that which will be deduced in the ensuing sheets.

I. [Invasion and conquest of Persia, A.D. 633–651.] In the first year of the first caliph, his lieutenant Caled, the Sword of God and the scourge of the infidels, advanced to the banks of the Euphrates.[†]

[A] country intersected by rivers and canals might have opposed an insuperable barrier to the victorious cavalry; and the walls of Ctesiphon or Madayn, which had resisted the battering-rams of the Romans, would not have yielded to the darts of the Saracens. But the flying Persians were overcome by the belief that the last day of their religion and empire was at hand; the strongest posts were abandoned by treachery or cowardice. . . . In the public anarchy, the independent governors of the cities and castles obtained their separate capitulations: the terms were granted or imposed by the esteem, the prudence, or the compassion of the victors; and a simple profession of faith established the distinction between a brother and a slave.[†]

After the fall of the Persian kingdom, the River Oxus divided the territories of the Saracens and of the Turks. This narrow boundary was soon overleaped by the spirit of the Arabs; the governors of Chorasan extended their successive inroads; and one of their triumphs was adorned with the buskin of a Turkish queen, which she dropped in her precipitate flight beyond the hills of Bochara. But the final conquest of Transoxiana, as well as of Spain, was reserved for the glorious reign of the inactive Walid; and the name of Catibah, the camel driver, declares the origin and merit of his successful lieutenant. While one of his colleagues displayed the first Mohammedan banner on the banks of the Indus, the spacious regions between the Oxus, the Jaxartes, and the Caspian Sea were reduced by the arms of Catibah to the obedience of the prophet and of the caliph. A tribute of two millions of pieces of gold was imposed on the infidels; their idols were burnt or broken; the Moslem chief pronounced a sermon in the new mosque of Carizme; after several battles, the Turkish hordes were driven back to the desert; and the emperors of China solicited the friendship of the victorious Arabs [A.D. 710].[†]

II. [Invasion and conquest of Syria, A.D. 633–639.] No sooner had Abubeker restored the unity of faith and government than he despatched a circular letter to the Arabian tribes. "In the name of the most merciful God, to the rest of the true believers. Health and happiness and the mercy and blessing of God be upon you. I praise the most high God, and I pray for his prophet Mohammed. This is to acquaint you that I intend to send the true believers into Syria to take it out of the hands of the infidels. And I would have you know that the fighting for religion is an act of obedience to God."[†]

About four years after the triumphs of the Persian war, the repose of Heraclius and the empire was again disturbed by a new enemy, the power of whose religion was more strongly felt than it was clearly understood by the Christians of the East. In his palace of Constantinople or Antioch, he was awakened by the invasion of Syria, the loss of Bosra, and the danger of Damascus. An army of seventy thousand veterans or new levies was assembled at Hems or Emesa, under the command of his general Werdan: and these troops, consisting chiefly of cavalry, might be indifferently styled either Syrians, or Greeks, or Romans: *Syrians,* from the place of their birth or warfare; *Greeks,* from the religion and language of their sovereign; and *Romans,* from the proud appellation which was still profaned by the successors of Constantine. On the plain of Aiznadin, as Werdan rode on a white mule decorated with gold chains, and surrounded with ensigns and standards, he was surprised by the near approach of a fierce and naked warrior, who had undertaken to view the state of the enemy. The adventurous valor of Derar was inspired, and has perhaps been adorned, by the enthusiasm of his age and country. The hatred of the Christians, the love of spoil, and the contempt of danger were the ruling passions of the audacious Saracen; and the prospect of instant death could never shake his religious confidence, or ruffle the calmness of his resolution, or even suspend the frank and partial pleasantry of his humor. In the most hopeless enterprises he was bold and prudent and fortunate: after innumerable hazards, after being thrice a prisoner in the hands of the infidels, he still survived to relate the achievements and to enjoy the rewards of the Syrian conquest. On this occasion his single lance maintained a flying fight against thirty Romans who were detached by Werdan; and after killing or unhorsing seventeen of their number, Derar returned in safety to his applauding brethren. When his rashness was mildly censured by the general, he excused himself with the simplicity of a soldier. "Nay," said Derar, "I did not begin first: but they came out to take me, and I was afraid that God should see me turn my back: and indeed I fought in good earnest, and without doubt God assisted me against them; and had I not been apprehensive of disobeying your orders, I should not have come away as I did; and I perceive already that they will fall into our hands." In the presence of both armies, a venerable Greek advanced from the ranks with a liberal offer of peace; and the departure of the Saracens would have been purchased by a gift to each soldier of one turban, a robe, and a piece of gold; ten robes and a hundred pieces to their leader; one hundred robes and a thousand pieces to the caliph. A smile of indignation expressed the refusal of Chaled. "Ye Christian dogs, you know your option; the Koran, the tribute, or the sword. . . ."[†]

In the life of Heraclius, the glories of the Persian war are clouded on either hand by the disgrace and weakness of his more early and his later days. When the successors of Mohammed unsheathed the sword of war and religion, he was astonished at the boundless prospect of toil and danger; his nature was indolent, nor could the infirm and frigid age of the emperor be kindled to a second effort. The sense of shame and the importunities of the Syrians prevented the hasty departure from the scene of action; but the hero was no more; and the loss of Damascus and Jerusalem, the bloody fields of Aiznadin and Yermuk, may be imputed in some degree to the absence or misconduct of the sovereign. Instead of defending the sepulchre of Christ, he involved the church and state in a metaphysical controversy for the unity of his will; and while Heraclius crowned the offspring of his second nuptials, he was tamely stripped of the most valuable part of their inheritance. In the cathedral of Antioch, in the presence of the bishops, at the foot of the crucifix, he bewailed the sins of the prince and people; but his confession instructed the world that it was vain and perhaps impious to resist the judgment of God. The Saracens were invincible in fact, since they were invincible in opinion; and the desertion of Youkinna [at Aleppo], his false repentance and repeated perfidy, might justify the suspicion of the emperor that he was encompassed by traitors and apostates who conspired to betray his person and their country to the enemies of Christ.[†]

The sieges and battles of six campaigns had consumed many thousands of the Moslems. They died with the reputation and the cheerfulness of martyrs; and the simplicity of their faith may be expressed in the words of an Arabian youth when he embraced for the last time his sister and mother: "It is not," said he, "the delicacies of Syria or the fading delights of this world that have prompted me to devote my life in the cause of religion. But I seek the favor of God and his apostle; and I have heard from one of the companions of the prophet that the spirits of the martyrs will be lodged in the crops of green birds, who shall taste the fruits and drink of the rivers of paradise. Farewell, we shall meet again among the groves and fountains which God has provided for his elect."[†]

III. [Invasion and conquest of Egypt, A.D. 639–641.] Yet the Arabs . . . must have retreated to the desert had they not found a powerful alliance in the heart of [Egypt]. The rapid conquest of Alexander was assisted by the superstition and revolt of the natives: they abhorred their Persian oppressors, the disciples of the Magi who had burnt the temples of Egypt and feasted with sacrilegious appetite on the flesh of the god Apis. After a period of ten centuries, the same revolution was renewed by a similar cause; and in the support of an incomprehensible creed, the zeal of the Coptic Christians was equally ardent. I have already explained the origin and progress of the Monophysite controversy and the persecution of the emperors, which converted a sect into a nation and alienated Egypt from their religion and government. The Saracens were received as the deliverers of the Jacobite church; and a secret and effectual treaty was opened during the siege of Memphis between a victorious army and a people of slaves. A rich and noble Egyptian of the name of Mokawkas had dissembled his faith to obtain the administration of his province: in the disorders of the Persian war he aspired to independence: the embassy of Mohammed ranked him among princes; but he declined, with rich gifts and ambiguous compliments, the proposal of a new religion. The abuse of his trust exposed him to the resentment of Heraclius: his submission was delayed by arrogance and fear; and his conscience was prompted by interest to throw himself on the favor of the nation and the support of the Saracens. In his first conference with Amrou, he heard without indignation the usual option of the Koran, the tribute, or the sword. "The Greeks," replied Mokawkas, "are determined to abide the determination of the sword; but with the Greeks I desire no communion, either in this world or in the next, and I abjure forever the Byzantine tyrant, his synod of Chalcedon, and his Melchite slaves. For myself and my brethren, we are resolved to live and die in the profession of the gospel and unity of Christ. It is impossible for us to embrace the revelations of your prophet; but we are desirous of peace, and cheerfully submit to pay tribute and obedience to his temporal successors." The tribute was ascertained at two pieces of gold for the head of every Christian; but old men, monks, women, and children of both sexes under sixteen years of age were exempted from this personal assessment: the Copts above and below Memphis swore allegiance to the caliph, and promised a hospitable entertainment of three days to every Moslem who should travel through their country. By this charter of security, the ecclesiastical and civil tyranny of the Melchites was destroyed: the anathemas of St. Cyril were thundered from every pulpit; and the sacred edifices, with the patrimony of the church, were restored to the national communion of the Jacobites, who enjoyed without moderation the moment of triumph and revenge. At the pressing summons of Amrou, their patriarch Benjamin emerged from his desert; and after the first interview, the courteous Arab affected to declare that he had never conversed with a Christian priest of more innocent manners and a more venerable aspect. In the march from Memphis to Alexandria, the lieutenant of Omar entrusted his safety to the zeal and gratitude of the Egyptians: the roads and bridges were diligently repaired; and in every step of his progress, he could depend on a constant supply of provisions and intelligence. The Greeks of Egypt, whose numbers could scarcely equal a tenth of the natives, were overwhelmed by the universal defection: they had ever been hated, they were no longer feared: the magistrate fled from his tribunal, the bishop from his altar; and the distant garrisons were surprised or starved by the surrounding multitudes. Had not the Nile afforded a safe and ready conveyance to the sea, not an individual could have escaped who by birth or language or office or religion was connected with their odious name.†

I should deceive the expectation of the reader if I passed in silence the fate of the Alexandrian library, as it is described by the learned Abulpharagius. The spirit of Amrou was more curious and liberal than that of his brethren, and in his leisure hours the Arabian chief was pleased with the conversation of John, the last disciple of Ammonius, and who derived the surname of *Philoponus* from his laborious studies of grammar and philosophy. Emboldened by this familiar intercourse, Philoponus presumed to solicit a gift, inestimable in his opinion, contemptible in that of the Barbarians—the royal library, which alone among the spoils of Alexandria had not been appropriated by the visit and the seal of the conqueror. Amrou was inclined to gratify the wish of the grammarian, but his rigid integrity refused to alienate the minutest object without the consent of the caliph; and the well-known answer of Omar was inspired by the ignorance of a fanatic. "If these writings of the Greeks agree with the book of God, they are useless, and need not be preserved: if they disagree, they are pernicious, and ought to be destroyed." The sentence was executed with blind obedience: the volumes of paper or parchment were distributed to the four thousand baths of the city; and such was their incredible multitude that six months were barely sufficient for the consumption of this precious fuel. Since the Dynasties of Abulpharagius have been given to the world in a Latin version, the tale has been repeatedly transcribed; and every scholar, with pious indignation, has deplored the irreparable shipwreck of the learning, the arts, and the genius of antiquity. For my own part, I am strongly tempted to deny both the fact and the consequences. The fact is indeed marvelous. "Read and wonder!" says the historian himself: and the solitary report of a stranger who wrote at the end of six hundred years on the confines of Media is overbalanced by the silence of two annalists of a more early date, both Christians, both natives of Egypt, and the most ancient of whom, the patriarch Eutychius, has amply described the conquest of Alexandria. The rigid sentence of Omar is repugnant to the sound and orthodox precept of the Mohammedan casuists; they expressly declare that the religious books of the Jews and Christians which are acquired by the right of war should never be committed to the flames; and that the works of profane science, historians or poets, physicians or philosophers, may be lawfully applied to the use of the faithful. A more destructive zeal may perhaps be attributed to the first successors of Mohammed; yet in this instance, the conflagration would have speedily expired in the deficiency of materials. I should not recapitulate the disasters of the Alexandrian library, the involuntary flame that was kindled by Caesar in his own defense, or the mischievous bigotry of the Christians who studied to destroy the monuments of idolatry. But if we gradually descend from the age of the Antonines to that of Theodosius, we shall learn from a chain of contemporary witnesses that the royal palace and the temple of Serapis no longer contained the four, or the seven, hundred thousand volumes which had been assembled by the curiosity and magnificence of the Ptolemies. Perhaps the church and seat of the patriarchs might be enriched with a repository of books; but if the ponderous mass of Arian and Monophysite controversy were indeed consumed in the public baths, a philosopher may allow, with a smile, that it was ultimately devoted to the benefit of mankind. I sincerely regret the more valuable libraries which have been involved in the ruin of the Roman empire; but when I seriously compute the lapse of ages, the waste of ignorance, and the calamities of war, our treasures rather than our losses are the objects of my surprise. Many curious and interesting facts are buried in oblivion: the three great historians of Rome have been transmitted to our hands in a mutilated state, and we are deprived of many pleasing compositions of the lyric, iambic, and dramatic poetry of the Greeks. Yet we should gratefully remember that the mischances of time and accident have spared the classic works to which the suffrage of antiquity had adjudged the first place of genius and glory: the teachers of ancient knowledge who are still extant had perused and compared the writings of their predecessors; nor can it fairly be presumed that any important truth, any useful discovery in art or nature, has been snatched away from the curiosity of modern ages.[†]

IV. [Invasion and final conquest of North Africa, A.D. 647–709.] The western conquests of the Saracens were suspended near twenty years, till their dissensions were composed by the establishment of the house of Ommiyah; and the caliph Moawiyah was invited by the cries of the

Africans themselves. The successors of Heraclius had been informed of the tribute which they had been compelled to stipulate with the Arabs, but instead of being moved to pity and relieve their distress, they imposed, as an equivalent or a fine, a second tribute of a similar amount. The ears of the Byzantine ministers were shut against the complaints of their poverty and ruin; their despair was reduced to prefer the dominion of a single master; and the extortions of the patriarch of Carthage, who was invested with civil and military power, provoked the sectaries and even the Catholics of the Roman province to abjure the religion as well as the authority of their tyrants. . . . The career, though not the zeal, of [the Moslem commander] Akbah was checked by the prospect of a boundless ocean. He spurred his horse into the waves and, raising his eyes to Heaven, exclaimed with the tone of a fanatic, "Great God! if my course were not stopped by this sea, I would still go on, to the unknown kingdoms of the West, preaching the unity of thy holy name, and putting to the sword the rebellious nations who worship any other gods than thee."[†]

V. [Invasion and conquest of Spain, A.D. 709–713.] The most zealous of the Catholics had escaped [from Toledo] with the relics of their saints; and if the gates were shut, it was only till the victor had subscribed a fair and reasonable capitulation. The voluntary exiles were allowed to depart with their effects; seven churches were appropriated to the Christian worship; the archbishop and his clergy were at liberty to exercise their functions, the monks to practice or neglect their penance—and the Goths and Romans were left in all civil and criminal cases to the subordinate jurisdiction of their own laws and magistrates. But if the justice of [the Moslem commander] Tarik protected the Christians, his gratitude and policy rewarded the Jews, to whose secret or open aid he was indebted for his most important acquisitions. Persecuted by the kings and synods of Spain, who had often pressed the alternative of banishment or baptism, that outcast nation embraced the moment of revenge: the comparison of their past and present state was the pledge of their fidelity; and the alliance between the disciples of Moses and of Mohammed was maintained till the final era of their common expulsion.[†]

In this revolution, many partial calamities were inflicted by the carnal or religious passions of the enthusiasts: some churches were profaned by the new worship: some relics or images were confounded with idols: the rebels were put to the sword; and one town (an obscure place between Cordova and Seville) was razed to its foundations. Yet if we compare the invasion of Spain by the Goths, or its recovery by the kings of Castile and Arragon, we must applaud the moderation and discipline of the Arabian conquerors.

The exploits of [the Moslem commander] Musa were performed in the evening of life, though he affected to disguise his age by coloring with a red powder the whiteness of his beard. But in the love of action and glory, his breast was still fired with the ardor of youth; and the possession of Spain was considered only as the first step to the monarchy of Europe. With a powerful armament by sea and land, he was preparing to repass the Pyrenees, to extinguish in Gaul and Italy the declining kingdoms of the Franks and Lombards, and to preach the unity of God on the altar of the Vatican. From thence, subduing the Barbarians of Germany, he proposed to follow the course of the Danube from its source to the Euxine Sea, to overthrow the Greek or Roman empire of Constantinople, and, returning from Europe to Asia, to unite his new acquisitions with Antioch and the provinces of Syria. But his vast enterprise, perhaps of easy execution, must have seemed extravagant to vulgar minds; and the visionary conqueror was soon reminded of his dependence and servitude.

[*Musa is recalled by the caliph Walid; Musa is disgraced.*]

A province is assimilated to the victorious state by the introduction of strangers and the imitative spirit of the natives; and Spain, which had been successively tinctured with Punic, and Roman, and Gothic blood, imbibed in a few generations the name and manners of the Arabs. . . . Ten years after the conquest, a map of the province was presented to the caliph: the seas, the rivers, and the harbors, the inhabitants and cities, the climate, the soil, and the mineral productions of the earth. In the space of two centuries, the gifts of nature were improved by the agriculture, the manufactures, and the commerce of an industrious people; and the effects of their diligence have been magnified by the idleness of their fancy. The first of the Ommiades who reigned in Spain solicited the support of the Christians; and in his edict of peace and protection, he contents himself with a modest imposition of ten thousand ounces of gold, ten thousand pounds of silver, ten thousand horses, as many mules, one thousand cuirasses, with an equal number of helmets and lances. The most powerful of his successors derived from the same kingdom the annual tribute of twelve millions and forty-five thousand dinars or pieces of gold, about six millions of sterling money; a sum which, in the tenth century, most probably surpassed the united revenues of the Christian monarchs. His royal seat of Cordova contained six hundred mosques, nine hundred baths, and two hundred thousand houses; he gave laws to eighty cities of the first, to three hundred of the second and third order; and the fertile banks of the Guadalquivir were adorned with twelve thousand villages and hamlets. The Arabs might exaggerate the truth, but they created and they describe the most prosperous era of the riches, the cultivation, and the populousness of Spain.

The wars of the Moslems were sanctified by the prophet; but among the various precepts and examples of his life, the caliphs selected the lessons of toleration that might tend to disarm the resistance of the unbelievers. Arabia was the temple and patrimony of the God of Mohammed; but he beheld with less jealousy and affection the nations of the earth. The Polytheists and idolaters who were ignorant of his name might be lawfully extirpated by his votaries; but a wise policy supplied the obligation of justice; and after some acts of intolerant zeal, the Mohammedan conquerors of Hindostan have spared the pagodas of that devout and populous country. The disciples of Abraham, of Moses, and of Jesus were solemnly invited to accept the more *perfect* revelation of Mohammed; but if they preferred the payment of a moderate tribute, they were entitled to the freedom of conscience and religious worship. In a field of battle the forfeit lives of the prisoners were redeemed by the profession of *Islam;* the females were bound to embrace the religion of their masters, and a race of sincere proselytes was gradually multiplied by the education of the infant captives. But the millions of African and Asiatic converts who swelled the native band of the faithful Arabs must have been allured, rather than constrained, to declare their belief in one God and the apostle of God. By the repetition of a sentence and the loss of a foreskin, the subject or the slave, the captive or the criminal arose in a moment the free and equal companion of the victorious Moslems. Every sin was expiated, every engagement was dissolved: the vow of celibacy was superseded by the indulgence of nature; the active spirits who slept in the cloister were awakened by the trumpet of the Saracens; and in the convulsion of the world, every member of a new society ascended to the natural level of his capacity and courage. The minds of the multitude were tempted by the invisible as well as temporal blessings of the Arabian prophet; and charity will hope that many of his proselytes entertained a serious conviction of the truth and sanctity of his revelation. In the eyes of an inquisitive Polytheist, it must appear worthy of the human and the divine nature. More pure than the system of Zoroaster, more liberal than the law of Moses, the religion of Mohammed might seem less inconsistent with reason than the creed of mystery and superstition which in the seventh century disgraced the simplicity of the gospel.

In the extensive provinces of Persia and Africa, the national religion has been eradicated by the Mohammedan faith. The ambiguous theology of the Magi stood alone among the sects of the East; but the profane writings of Zoroaster might, under the reverend name of Abraham, be dexterously connected with the chain of divine revelation. Their evil principle, the demon Ahriman, might be represented as the rival or as the creature of the God of light. The temples of Persia were devoid of images; but the worship of the sun and of fire might be stigmatized as a gross and criminal idolatry. The milder sentiment was consecrated by the practice of Mohammed and the prudence of the caliphs; the Magians or Ghebers were ranked with the Jews and Christians among the people of the written law; and as late as the third century of the Hegira, the city of Herat will afford a lively contrast of private zeal and public toleration. Under the payment of an annual tribute, the Mohammedan law secured to the Ghebers of Herat their civil and religious liberties: but the recent and humble mosque was overshadowed by the antique splendor of the adjoining temple of fire. A fanatic Imam deplored in his sermons the scandalous neighborhood, and accused the weakness or indifference of the faithful. Excited by his voice, the people assembled in tumult; the two houses of prayer were consumed by the flames, but the vacant ground was immediately occupied by the foundations of a new mosque. The injured Magi appealed to the sovereign of Chorasan; he promised justice and relief; when, behold! four thousand citizens of Herat, of a grave character and mature age, unanimously swore that the idolatrous fane had *never* existed; the inquisition was silenced and their conscience was satisfied (says the historian Mirchond) with this holy and meritorious perjury. But the greatest part of the temples of Persia were ruined by the insensible and general desertion of their votaries. It was *insensible*, since it is not accompanied with any memorial of time or place, of persecution or resistance. It was *general*, since the whole realm, from Shiraz to Samarcand, imbibed the faith of the Koran; and the preservation of the native tongue reveals the descent of the Mohammedans of Persia. In the mountains and deserts, an obstinate race of unbelievers adhered to the superstition of their fathers; and a faint tradition of the Magian theology is kept alive in the province of Kirman, along the banks of the Indus, among the exiles of Surat, and in the colony which, in the last century, was planted by Shaw Abbas at the gates of Ispahan. The chief pontiff has retired to Mount Elbourz, eighteen leagues from the city of Yezd: the perpetual fire (if it continues to burn) is inaccessible to the profane; but his residence is the school, the oracle, and the pilgrimage of the Ghebers, whose hard and uniform features attest the unmingled purity of their blood. Under the jurisdiction of their elders, eighty thousand families maintain an innocent and industrious life: their subsistence is derived from some curious manufactures and mechanic trades; and they cultivate the earth with the fervor of a religious duty. Their ignorance withstood the despotism of Shaw Abbas, who demanded with threats and tortures the prophetic books of Zoroaster; and this obscure remnant of the Magians is spared by the moderation or contempt of their present sovereigns.

The northern coast of Africa is the only land in which the light of the gospel, after a long and perfect establishment, has been totally extinguished. The arts, which had been taught by Carthage and Rome, were involved in a cloud of ignorance; the doctrine of Cyprian and Augustine was no longer studied. Five hundred episcopal churches were overturned by the hostile fury of the Donatists, the Vandals, and the Moors. The zeal and numbers of the clergy declined; and the people, without discipline or knowledge or hope, submissively sunk under the yoke of the Arabian prophet. Within fifty years after the expulsion of the Greeks [A.D. 749], a lieutenant of Africa informed the caliph that the tribute of the infidels was abolished by their conversion; and though he sought to disguise his fraud and rebellion, his specious pretense was drawn from the rapid and extensive progress of the Mohammedan faith. In the next age, an extraordinary mission of five bishops was detached from Alexandria to Cairo [A.D. 837]. They were ordained by the Jacobite patriarch to cherish and revive the dying embers of Christianity: but the interposition of a foreign prelate, a stranger to the Latins, an enemy to the Catholics, supposes the decay and dissolution of the African hierarchy. It was no longer the time when the successor of St. Cyprian, at the head of a numerous synod, could maintain an equal contest with the ambition of the Roman pontiff. In the eleventh century, the unfortunate priest who was seated on the ruins of Carthage implored the arms and the protection of the Vatican; and he bitterly complains that his naked body had been scourged by the Saracens and that his authority was disputed by the four suffragans, the tottering pillars of his throne [A.D. 1053–1076]. Two epistles of Gregory the Seventh are destined to soothe the distress of the Catholics and the pride of a Moorish prince. The pope assures the sultan that they both worship the same God and may hope to meet in the bosom of Abraham; but the complaint that three bishops could no longer be found to consecrate a brother announces the speedy and inevitable ruin of the episcopal order. The Christians of Africa and Spain had long since submitted to the practice of circumcision and the legal abstinence from wine and pork; and the name of *Mozarabes* (adoptive Arabs) was applied to their civil or religious conformity [A.D. 1149 ff.]. About the middle of the twelfth century, the worship of Christ and the succession of pastors were abolished along the coast of Barbary and in the kingdoms of Cordova and Seville, of Valencia and Grenada. The throne of the Almohades, or Unitarians, was founded on the blindest fanaticism, and their extraordinary rigor might be provoked or justified by the recent victories and intolerant zeal of the princes of Sicily and Castille, of Arragon and Portugal. The faith of the Mozarabes was occasionally revived by the papal missionaries; and on the landing of Charles the Fifth, some families of Latin Christians were encouraged to rear their heads at Tunis and Algiers [A.D. 1535]. But the seed of the gospel was quickly eradicated, and the long province from Tripoli to the Atlantic has lost all memory of the language and religion of Rome.

After the revolution of eleven centuries, the Jews and Christians of the Turkish empire enjoy the liberty of conscience which was granted by the Arabian caliphs. During the first age of the conquest, they suspected the loyalty of the Catholics, whose name of Melchites betrayed their secret attachment to the Greek emperor, while the Nestorians and Jacobites, his inveterate enemies, approved themselves the sincere and voluntary friends of the Mohammedan government. Yet this partial jealousy was healed by time and submission; the churches of Egypt were shared with the Catholics; and all the Oriental sects were included in the common benefits of toleration. The rank, the immunities, the domestic jurisdiction of the patriarchs, the bishops, and the clergy were protected by the civil magistrate: the learning of individuals recommended them to the employments of secretaries and physicians: they were enriched by the lucrative collection of the revenue; and their merit was sometimes raised to the command of cities and provinces. A caliph of the house of Abbas was heard to declare that the Christians were most worthy of trust in the administration of Persia. "The Moslems," said he, "will abuse their present fortune; the Magians regret their fallen greatness; and the Jews are impatient for their approaching deliverance." But the slaves of despotism are exposed to the alternatives of favor and disgrace. The captive churches of the East have been afflicted in every age by the avarice or bigotry of their rulers; and the ordinary and legal restraints must be offensive to the pride or the zeal of the Christians. About two hundred years after Mohammed, they were separated from their fellow-subjects by a turban or girdle of a less honorable color; instead of horses or mules, they were condemned to ride on asses, in the attitude of women. Their public and private building were measured by a diminutive standard; in the streets or the baths it is their duty to give way or bow down before the meanest of the people; and their testimony is rejected if it may tend to the prejudice of a true believer. The pomp of processions, the sound of bells or of psalmody, is interdicted in their worship; a decent reverence for the national faith is imposed on their sermons and conversations; and the sacrilegious attempt to enter a mosque or to seduce a Moslem will not be suffered to escape with impunity. In a time, however, of tranquility and justice, the Christians have never been compelled to renounce the gospel or to embrace the Koran; but the punishment of death is inflicted upon the apostates who have professed and deserted the law of Mohammed. The martyrs of Cordova provoked the sentence of the cadhi by the public confession of their inconstancy, or their passionate invectives against the person and religion of the prophet.

At the end of the first century of the Hegira, the caliphs were the most potent and absolute monarchs of the globe [A.D. 718]. Their prerogative was not circumscribed, either in right or in fact, by the power of the nobles, the freedom of the commons, the privileges of the church, the votes of a senate, or the memory of a free constitution. The authority of the companions of Mohammed expired with their lives; and the chiefs or emirs of the Arabian tribes left behind in the desert the spirit of equality and independence. The regal and sacerdotal characters were united in the successors of Mohammed; and if the Koran was the rule of their actions, they were the supreme judges and interpreters of that divine book. They reigned by the right of conquest over the nations of the East, to whom the name of liberty was unknown, and who were accustomed to applaud in their tyrants the acts of violence and severity that were exercised at their own expense. Under the last of the Ommiades, the Arabian empire extended two hundred days' journey from east to west, from the confines of Tartary and India to the shores of the Atlantic Ocean. And if we retrench the sleeve of the robe, as it is styled by their writers, the long and narrow province of Africa, the solid and compact dominion from Fargana to Aden, from Tarsus to Surat, will spread on every side to the measure of four or five months of the march of a caravan. We should vainly seek the indissoluble union and easy obedience that pervaded the government of Augustus and the Antonines; but the progress of the Mohammedan religion diffused over this ample space a general resemblance of manners and opinions. The language and laws of the Koran were studied with equal devotion at Samarcand and Seville: the Moor and the Indian embraced as countrymen and brothers in the pilgrimage of Mecca; and the Arabian language was adopted as the popular idiom in all the provinces to the westward of the Tigris.

CHAPTER LII

More Conquests by the Arabs

The two sieges of Constantinople by the Arabs. • Their invasion of France and defeat by Charles Martel. • Civil war of the Ommiades and Abbassides. • Learning of the Arabs. • Luxury of the caliphs. • Naval enterprises on Crete, Sicily, and Rome. • Decay and division of the empire of the caliphs. • Defeats and victories of the Greek emperors.

When the Arabs first issued from the desert, they must have been surprised at the ease and rapidity of their own success. But when they advanced in the career of victory to the banks of the Indus and the summit of the Pyrenees, when they had repeatedly tried the edge of their cimeters and the energy of their faith, they might be equally astonished that any nation could resist their invincible arms; that any boundary should confine the dominion of the successor of the prophet. The confidence of soldiers and fanatics may indeed be excused, since the calm historian of the present hour who strives to follow the rapid course of the Saracens must study to explain by what means the church and state were saved from this impending and, as it should seem, from this inevitable danger. The deserts of Scythia and Sarmatia might be guarded by their extent, their climate, their poverty, and the courage of the Northern shepherds; China was remote and inaccessible; but the greatest part of the temperate zone was subject to the Mohammedan conquerors, the Greeks were exhausted by the calamities of war and the loss of their fairest provinces, and the Barbarians of Europe might justly tremble at the precipitate fall of the Gothic monarchy. In this inquiry I shall unfold the events that rescued our ancestors of Britain and our neighbors of Gaul from the civil and religious yoke of the Koran; that protected the majesty of Rome and delayed the servitude of Constantinople; that invigorated the defense of the Christians, and scattered among their enemies the seeds of division and decay.

Forty-six years after the flight of Mohammed from Mecca, his disciples appeared in arms under the walls of Constantinople [A.D. 668–675].

They were animated by a genuine or fictitious saying of the prophet that to the first army which besieged the city of the Caesars, their sins were forgiven: the long series of Roman triumphs would be meritoriously transferred to the conquerors of New Rome; and the wealth of nations was deposited in this well-chosen seat of royalty and commerce. No sooner had the caliph Moawiyah suppressed his rivals and established his throne than he aspired to expiate the guilt of civil blood by the success and glory of this holy expedition; his preparations by sea and land were adequate to the importance of the object; his standard was entrusted to Sophian, a veteran warrior, but the troops were encouraged by the example and presence of Yezid, the son and presumptive heir of the commander of the faithful. The Greeks had little to hope, nor had their enemies any reason of fear, from the courage and vigilance of the reigning emperor, who disgraced the name of Constantine [IV] and imitated only the inglorious years of his grandfather Heraclius. Without delay or opposition, the naval forces of the Saracens passed through the unguarded channel of the Hellespont, which even now, under the feeble and disorderly government of the Turks, is maintained as the natural bulwark of the capital. The Arabian fleet cast anchor, and the troops were disembarked near the palace of Hebdomon, seven miles from the city. During many days, from the dawn of light to the evening, the line of assault was extended from the golden gate to the eastern promontory, and the foremost warriors were impelled by the weight and effort of the succeeding columns. But the besiegers had formed an insufficient estimate of the strength and resources of Constantinople. The solid and lofty walls were guarded by numbers and discipline: the spirit of the Romans was rekindled by the last danger of their religion and empire: the fugitives from the conquered provinces more successfully renewed the defense of Damascus and Alexandria; and the Saracens were dismayed by the strange and prodigious effects of artificial fire. This firm and effectual resistance diverted their arms to the more easy attempt of plundering the European and Asiatic coasts of the Propontis; and after keeping the sea from the month of April to that of September, on the approach of winter they retreated fourscore miles from the capital to the Isle of Cyzicus, in which they had established their magazine of spoil and provisions. So patient was their perseverance, or so languid were their operations, that they repeated in the six following summers the same attack and retreat, with a gradual abatement of hope and vigor, till the mischances of shipwreck and disease, of the sword and of fire, compelled them to relinquish the fruitless enterprise. They might bewail the loss or commemorate the martyrdom of thirty thousand Moslems who fell in the siege of Constantinople; and the solemn funeral of Abu Ayub, or Job, excited the curiosity of the Christians themselves. That venerable Arab, one of the last of the companions of Mohammed, was numbered among the *ansars,* or auxiliaries, of Medina, who sheltered the head of the flying prophet. In his youth he fought, at Beder and Ohud, under the holy standard: in his mature age he was the friend and follower of Ali; and the last remnant of his strength and life was consumed in a distant and dangerous war against the enemies of the Koran. His memory was revered; but the place of his burial was neglected and unknown during a period of seven hundred and eighty years, till the conquest of Constantinople by Mohammed the Second. A seasonable vision (for such are the manufacture of every religion) revealed the holy spot at the foot of the walls and the bottom of the harbor; and the mosque of Ayub has been deservedly chosen for the simple and martial inauguration of the Turkish sultans.

The event of the siege revived, both in the East and West, the reputation of the Roman arms, and cast a momentary shade over the glories of the Saracens. The Greek ambassador was favorably received at Damascus, a general council of the emirs or Koreish: a peace or truce of thirty years was ratified between the two empires; and the stipulation of an annual tribute, fifty horses of a noble breed, fifty slaves, and three thousand pieces of gold, degraded the majesty of the commander of the faithful [A.D. 677]. The aged caliph was desirous of possessing his dominions and ending his days in tranquility and repose: while the Moors and Indians trembled at his name, his palace and city of Damascus was insulted by the Mardaites, or Maronites, of Mount Libanus, the firmest barrier of the empire, till they were disarmed and transplanted by the suspicious policy of the Greeks.[†]

Whilst the caliph Walid sat idle on the throne of Damascus, whilst his lieutenants achieved the conquest of Transoxiana and Spain, a third army of Saracens overspread the provinces of Asia Minor and approached the borders of the Byzantine capital. But the attempt and disgrace of the second siege was reserved for his brother Soliman [A.D. 716–718].[†]

Constantinople . . . might exclude the Arabs from the eastern entrance of Europe; but in the west, on the side of the Pyrenees, the
provinces of Gaul were threatened and invaded by the conquerors of
Spain [A.D. 721 ff.]. The decline of the French monarchy invited the
attack of these insatiate fanatics. The descendants of Clovis had lost
the inheritance of his martial and ferocious spirit; and their misfortune
or demerit has affixed the epithet of lazy to the last kings of the
Merovingian race. They ascended the throne without power and sunk
into the grave without a name . . . ; and the south of France, from the
mouth of the Garonne to that of the Rhone, assumed the manners and
religion of Arabia.

But these narrow limits were scorned by the spirit of Abdalraman,
or Abderame, who had been restored by the caliph Hashem to the
wishes of the soldiers and people of Spain. That veteran and daring
commander adjudged to the obedience of the prophet whatever yet
remained of France or of Europe; and prepared to execute the sentence at the head of a formidable host, in the full confidence of sur-
mounting all opposition either of nature or of man [A.D. 731]. . . . In the
decline of society and art, the deserted cities could supply a slender
booty to the Saracens; their richest spoil was found in the churches and
monasteries, which they stripped of their ornaments and delivered to
the flames: and the tutelar saints, both Hilary of Poitiers and Martin of
Tours, forgot their miraculous powers in the defense of their own
sepulchres. A victorious line of march had been prolonged above a
thousand miles from the rock of Gibraltar to the banks of the Loire;
the repetition of an equal space would have carried the Saracens to the
confines of Poland and the highlands of Scotland; the Rhine is not
more impassable than the Nile or Euphrates, and the Arabian fleet
might have sailed without a naval combat into the mouth of the Thames.
Perhaps the interpretation of the Koran would now be taught in the
schools of Oxford, and her pulpits might demonstrate to a circumcised
people the sanctity and truth of the revelation of Mohammed.

From such calamities was Christendom delivered by the genius and
fortune of one man [A.D. 732]. Charles, the illegitimate son of the elder
Pepin, was content with the titles of mayor or duke of the Franks; but
he deserved to become the father of a line of kings. In a laborious administration of twenty-four years, he restored and supported the dignity
of the throne, and the rebels of Germany and Gaul were successively

crushed by the activity of a warrior who, in the same campaign, could display his banner on the Elbe, the Rhone, and the shores of the Ocean. In the public danger he was summoned by the voice of his country; and his rival, the duke of Aquitain, was reduced to appear among the fugitives and suppliants. "Alas!" exclaimed the Franks, "what a misfortune! what an indignity! We have long heard of the name and conquests of the Arabs: we were apprehensive of their attack from the east; they have now conquered Spain, and invade our country on the side of the west. Yet their numbers, and (since they have no buckler) their arms, are inferior to our own." "If you follow my advice," replied the prudent mayor of the palace, "you will not interrupt their march nor precipitate your attack. They are like a torrent which it is dangerous to stem in its career. The thirst of riches and the consciousness of success redouble their valor, and valor is of more avail than arms or numbers. Be patient till they have loaded themselves with the encumbrance of wealth. The possession of wealth will divide their councils and assure your victory." This subtle policy is perhaps a refinement of the Arabian writers; and the situation of Charles will suggest a more narrow and selfish motive of procrastination—the secret desire of humbling the pride and wasting the provinces of the rebel duke of Aquitain. It is yet more probable that the delays of Charles were inevitable and reluctant. A standing army was unknown under the first and second race; more than half the kingdom was now in the hands of the Saracens: according to their respective situation, the Franks of Neustria and Austrasia were too conscious or too careless of the impending danger; and the voluntary aids of the Gepidae and Germans were separated by a long interval from the standard of the Christian general. No sooner had he collected his forces than he sought and found the enemy in the center of France, between Tours and Poitiers. His well-conducted march was covered with a range of hills, and Abderame appears to have been surprised by his unexpected presence. The nations of Asia, Africa, and Europe advanced with equal ardor to an encounter which would change the history of the world [October, A.D. 732]. In the six first days of desultory combat, the horsemen and archers of the East maintained their advantage: but in the closer onset of the seventh day, the Orientals were oppressed by the strength and stature of the Germans, who, with stout hearts and *iron* hands, asserted the civil and religious freedom of their posterity. The epithet of *Mar-*

tel, the *Hammer,* which has been added to the name of Charles, is expressive of his weighty and irresistible strokes: the valor of Eudes was excited by resentment and emulation; and their companions in the eye of history are the true Peers and Paladins of French chivalry. After a bloody field in which Abderame was slain, the Saracens, in the close of the evening, retired to their camp. In the disorder and despair of the night, the various tribes of Yemen and Damascus, of Africa and Spain, were provoked to turn their arms against each other: the remains of their host were suddenly dissolved, and each *emir* consulted his safety by a hasty and separate retreat. At the dawn of the day, the stillness of a hostile camp was suspected by the victorious Christians: on the report of their spies, they ventured to explore the riches of the vacant tents; but if we except some celebrated relics, a small portion of the spoil was restored to the innocent and lawful owners. The joyful tidings were soon diffused over the Catholic world, and the monks of Italy could affirm and believe that three hundred and fifty, or three hundred and seventy-five, thousand of the Mohammedans had been crushed by the hammer of Charles, while no more than fifteen hundred Christians were slain in the field of Tours. But this incredible tale is sufficiently disproved by the caution of the French general, who apprehended the snares and accidents of a pursuit, and dismissed his German allies to their native forests. The inactivity of a conqueror betrays the loss of strength and blood, and the most cruel execution is inflicted not in the ranks of battle, but on the backs of a flying enemy. Yet the victory of the Franks was complete and final; Aquitain was recovered by the arms of Eudes; the Arabs never resumed the conquest of Gaul, and they were soon driven beyond the Pyrenees by Charles Martel and his valiant race. It might have been expected that the savior of Christendom would have been canonized, or at least applauded, by the gratitude of the clergy, who are indebted to his sword for their present existence. But in the public distress, the mayor of the palace had been compelled to apply the riches, or at least the revenues, of the bishops and abbots to the relief of the state and the reward of the soldiers. His merits were forgotten, his sacrilege alone was remembered, and in an epistle to a Carlovingian prince, a Gallic synod presumes to declare that his ancestor was damned; that on the opening of his tomb, the spectators were affrighted by a smell of fire and the aspect of a horrid dragon; and that a saint of the times was indulged with a pleasant vision of the soul and body of Charles Martel, burning to all eternity in the abyss of hell.

The loss of an army, or a province, in the Western world was less painful to the court of Damascus than the rise and progress of a domestic competitor [A.D. 746–750]. Except among the Syrians, the caliphs of the house of Ommiyah had never been the objects of the public favor. The life of Mohammed recorded their perseverance in idolatry and rebellion: their conversion had been reluctant, their elevation irregular and factious, and their throne was cemented with the most holy and noble blood of Arabia. The best of their race, the pious Omar, was dissatisfied with his own title: their personal virtues were insufficient to justify a departure from the order of succession; and the eyes and wishes of the faithful were turned towards the line of Hashem and the kindred of the apostle of God. Of these the Fatimites were either rash or pusillanimous; but the descendants of Abbas cherished, with courage and discretion, the hopes of their rising fortunes. From an obscure residence in Syria, they secretly despatched their agents and missionaries, who preached in the Eastern provinces their hereditary indefeasible right; and Mohammed, the son of Ali, the son of Abdallah, the son of Abbas, the uncle of the prophet, gave audience to the deputies of Chorasan, and accepted their free gift of four hundred thousand pieces of gold. After the death of Mohammed, the oath of allegiance was administered in the name of his son Ibrahim to a numerous band of votaries, who expected only a signal and a leader; and the governor of Chorasan continued to deplore his fruitless admonitions and the deadly slumber of the caliphs of Damascus, till he himself, with all his adherents, was driven from the city and palace of Meru by the rebellious arms of Abu Moslem. That maker of kings, the author, as he is named, of the *call* of the Abbassides, was at length rewarded for his presumption of merit with the usual gratitude of courts. A mean, perhaps a foreign, extraction could not repress the aspiring energy of Abu Moslem. Jealous of his wives, liberal of his wealth, prodigal of his own blood and of that of others, he could boast with pleasure, and possibly with truth, that he had destroyed six hundred thousand of his enemies; and such was the intrepid gravity of his mind and countenance that he was never seen to smile except on a day of battle. In the visible separation of parties, the *green* was consecrated to the Fatimites; the Ommiades were distinguished by the *white;* and the *black,* as the most adverse, was naturally adopted by the Abbassides. Their turbans and garments were stained with that gloomy color: two black standards, on pike staves nine cubits long, were borne aloft in the van of Abu Moslem; and their allegorical names of the *night* and the *shadow* obscurely represented the indissoluble union and perpetual succession of the line of Hashem. From the Indus to the Euphrates, the East was convulsed by the quarrel of the white and the black factions: the Abbassides were most frequently victorious. . . . By the event of the civil war, the dynasty of the Abbassides was firmly established [A.D. 750]; but the Christians only could triumph in the mutual hatred and common loss of the disciples of Mohammed.

Yet the thousands who were swept away by the sword of war might have been speedily retrieved in the succeeding generation if the consequences of the revolution had not tended to dissolve the power and unity of the empire of the Saracens.

[*Spain revolts (A.D. 755). The caliphate is eventually divided between the three contending confessions of Fatimites, Ommiades, and Abbassides.*]

In the tenth century, the chair of Mohammed was disputed by three caliphs or commanders of the faithful, who reigned at Baghdad, Cairo, and Cordova, excommunicating each other and agreed only in a principle of discord, that a sectary is more odious and criminal than an unbeliever.

Mecca was the patrimony of the line of Hashem, yet the Abbassides were never tempted to reside either in the birthplace or the city of the prophet. Damascus was disgraced by the choice, and polluted with the blood, of the Ommiades; and after some hesitation, Almansor, the brother and successor of Saffah, laid the foundations of Baghdad, the Imperial seat of his posterity during a reign of five hundred years. . . . In this *city of peace*, amidst the riches of the East, the Abbassides soon disdained the abstinence and frugality of the first caliphs and aspired to emulate the magnificence of the Persian kings [A.D. 750–960]. . . . In the West, the Ommiades of Spain supported with equal pomp the title of commander of the faithful. Three miles from Cordova, in honor of his favorite sultana, the third and greatest of the Abdalrahmans constructed the city, palace, and gardens of Zehra. Twenty-five years, and above three millions sterling, were employed by the founder: his liberal taste invited the artists of Constantinople, the most skillful sculptors and architects of the age; and the buildings were sustained or adorned by twelve hundred columns of Spanish and African, of Greek and Italian marble. The hall of audience was incrusted with gold and pearls, and a great basin in the center was surrounded with the curious and costly figures of birds and quadrupeds. In a lofty pavilion of the gardens, one of these basins and fountains, so delightful in a sultry climate, was replenished not with water but with the purest quicksilver. The seraglio of Abdalrahman, his wives, concubines, and black eunuchs, amounted to six thousand three hundred persons: and he was attended to the field by a guard of twelve thousand horse, whose belts and cimeters were studded with gold.

In a private condition, our desires are perpetually repressed by poverty and subordination; but the lives and labors of millions are devoted to the service of a despotic prince, whose laws are blindly obeyed and whose wishes are instantly gratified. Our imagination is dazzled by the splendid picture; and whatever may be the cool dictates of reason, there are few among us who would obstinately refuse a trial of the comforts and the cares of royalty. It may therefore be of some use to borrow the experience of the same Abdalrahman, whose magnificence has perhaps excited our admiration and envy, and to transcribe an authentic memorial which was found in the closet of the deceased caliph. "I have now reigned above fifty years in victory or peace; beloved by my subjects, dreaded by my enemies, and respected by my allies. Riches and honors, power and pleasure, have waited on my call, nor does any earthly blessing appear to have been wanting to my felicity. In this situation, I have diligently numbered the days of pure and genuine happiness which have fallen to my lot: they amount to FOURTEEN:—O man! place not thy confidence in this present world!" The luxury of the caliphs, so useless to their private happiness, relaxed the nerves and terminated the progress of the Arabian empire. Temporal and spiritual conquest had been the sole occupation of the first successors of Mohammed; and after supplying themselves with the necessaries of life, the whole revenue was scrupulously devoted to that salutary work. The Abbassides were impoverished by the multitude of their wants and their contempt of economy. Instead of pursuing the great object of ambition, their leisure, their affections, the powers of their mind were diverted by pomp and pleasure: the rewards of valor were embezzled by women and eunuchs, and the royal camp was encumbered by the luxury of the palace. A similar temper was diffused among the subjects of the caliph. Their stern enthusiasm was softened by time and prosperity; they sought riches in the occupations of industry, fame in the pursuits of literature, and happiness in the tranquility of domestic life. War was no longer the passion of the Saracens; and the increase of pay, the repetition of donatives, were insufficient to allure the posterity of those voluntary champions who had crowded to the standard of Abubeker and Omar for the hopes of spoil and of paradise.

Under the reign of the Ommiades, the studies of the Moslems were confined to the interpretation of the Koran and the eloquence and poetry of their native tongue. A people continually exposed to the dangers of the field must esteem the healing powers of medicine, or rather of surgery; but the starving physicians of Arabia murmured a complaint that exercise and temperance deprived them of the greatest part of their practice. After their civil and domestic wars, the subjects of the Abbassides, awakening from this mental lethargy, found leisure and felt curiosity for the acquisition of profane science. This spirit was first encouraged by the caliph Almansor, who, besides his knowledge of the Mohammedan law, had applied himself with success to the study of astronomy. But when the scepter devolved to Almamon, the seventh of the Abbassides, he completed the designs of his grandfather and invited the muses from their ancient seats. His ambassadors at Constantinople, his agents in Armenia, Syria, and Egypt, collected the volumes of Grecian science; at his command they were translated by the most skillful interpreters into the Arabic language: his subjects were exhorted assiduously to peruse these instructive writings; and the successor of Mohammed assisted with pleasure and modesty at the assemblies and disputations of the learned. "He was not ignorant," says Abulpharagius, "that they are the elect of God, his best and most useful servants, whose lives are devoted to the improvement of their rational faculties. The mean ambition of the Chinese or the Turks may glory in the industry of their hands or the indulgence of their brutal appetites. Yet these dexterous artists must view with hopeless emulation the hexagons and pyramids of the cells of a beehive: these fortitudinous heroes are awed by the superior fierceness of the lions and tigers; and in their amorous enjoyments they are much inferior to the vigor of the grossest and most sordid quadrupeds. The teachers of wisdom are the true luminaries and legislators of a world which, without their aid, would again sink in ignorance and barbarism." The zeal and curiosity of Al- mamon were imitated by succeeding princes of the line of Abbas: their rivals, the Fatimites of Africa and the Ommiades of Spain, were the patrons of the learned as well as the commanders of the faithful; the same royal prerogative was claimed by their independent emirs of the provinces; and their emulation diffused the taste and the rewards of science from Samarcand and Bochara to Fez and Cordova. The vizier of a sultan consecrated a sum of two hundred thousand pieces of gold to the foundation of a college at Baghdad, which he endowed with an annual revenue of fifteen thousand dinars. The fruits of instruction were communicated, perhaps at different times, to six thousand disci- ples of every degree, from the son of the noble to that of the mechanic: a sufficient allowance was provided for the indigent scholars; and the merit or industry of the professors was repaid with adequate stipends. In every city the productions of Arabic literature were copied and col- lected by the curiosity of the studious and the vanity of the rich. A pri- vate doctor refused the invitation of the sultan of Bochara because the carriage of his books would have required four hundred camels. The royal library of the Fatimites consisted of one hundred thousand man- uscripts, elegantly transcribed and splendidly bound, which were lent without jealousy or avarice to the students of Cairo. Yet this collection must appear moderate if we can believe that the Ommiades of Spain had formed a library of six hundred thousand volumes, forty-four of which were employed in the mere catalogue. Their capital, Cordova, with the adjacent towns of Malaga, Almeria, and Murcia, had given birth to more than three hundred writers, and above seventy public li- braries were opened in the cities of the Andalusian kingdom. The age of Arabian learning continued about five hundred years, till the great eruption of the Moguls, and was coeval with the darkest and most slothful period of European annals; but since the sun of science has arisen in the West, it should seem that the Oriental studies have lan- guished and declined.[†]

But the Moslems deprived themselves of the principal benefits of a familiar intercourse with Greece and Rome, the knowledge of antiq- uity, the purity of taste, and the freedom of thought. Confident in the riches of their native tongue, the Arabians disdained the study of any foreign idiom. The Greek interpreters were chosen among their Christian subjects; they formed their translations sometimes on the original text, more frequently perhaps on a Syriac version; and in the crowd of astronomers and physicians, there is no example of a poet, an orator, or even an historian being taught to speak the language of the Saracens. The mythology of Homer would have provoked the abhorrence of those stern fanatics: they possessed in lazy ignorance the colonies of the Macedonians and the provinces of Carthage and Rome: the heroes of Plutarch and Livy were buried in oblivion; and the history of the world before Mohammed was reduced to a short legend of the patriarchs, the prophets, and the Persian kings. Our education in the Greek and Latin schools may have fixed in our minds a standard of exclusive taste; and I am not forward to condemn the literature and judgment of nations of whose language I am ignorant. Yet I *know* that the classics have much to teach, and I *believe* that the Orientals have much to learn; the temperate dignity of style, the graceful proportions of art, the forms of visible and intellectual beauty, the just delineation of character and passion, the rhetoric of narrative and argument, the regular fabric of epic and dramatic poetry. The influence of truth and reason is of a less ambiguous complexion. The philosophers of Athens and Rome enjoyed the blessings and asserted the rights of civil and religious freedom. Their moral and political writings might have gradually unlocked the fetters of Eastern despotism, diffused a liberal spirit of inquiry and toleration, and encouraged the Arabian sages to suspect that their caliph was a tyrant and their prophet an impostor. The instinct of superstition was alarmed by the introduction even of the abstract sciences; and the more rigid doctors of the law condemned the rash and pernicious curiosity of Almamon. To the thirst of martyrdom, the vision of paradise, and the belief of predestination, we must ascribe the invincible enthusiasm of the prince and people. And the sword of the Saracens became less formidable when their youth was drawn away from the camp to the college, when the armies of the faithful presumed to read and to reflect. Yet the foolish vanity of the Greeks was jealous of their studies, and reluctantly imparted the sacred fire to the Barbarians of the East.[†]

Under the reign of Almamon at Baghdad, of Michael the Stammerer at Constantinople, the islands of Crete [A.D. 823] and Sicily [A.D. 827–878] were subdued by the Arabs. . . . The hundred cities of the age of Minos were diminished to thirty; and of these only one, most probably Cydonia, had courage to retain the substance of freedom and the profession of Christianity.... During a hostile period of one hundred and thirty-eight years, the princes of Constantinople attacked these licentious corsairs with fruitless curses and ineffectual arms.†

In Sicily, the religion and language of the Greeks were eradicated; and such was the docility of the rising generation that fifteen thousand boys were circumcised and clothed on the same day with the son of the Fatimite caliph. The Arabian squadrons issued from the harbors of Palermo, Biserta, and Tunis; a hundred and fifty towns of Calabria and Campania were attacked and pillaged; nor could the suburbs of Rome be defended by the name of the Caesars and apostles. Had the Mohammedans been united, Italy must have fallen an easy and glorious accession to the empire of the prophet. But the caliphs of Baghdad had lost their authority in the West; the Aglabites and Fatimites usurped the provinces of Africa, their emirs of Sicily aspired to independence; and the design of conquest and dominion was degraded to a repetition of predatory inroads.

In the sufferings of prostrate Italy, the name of Rome awakens a solemn and mournful recollection. A fleet of Saracens from the African coast presumed to enter the mouth of the Tiber and to approach a city which even yet, in her fallen state, was revered as the metropolis of the Christian world [A.D. 846]. The gates and ramparts were guarded by a trembling people; but the tombs and temples of St. Peter and St. Paul were left exposed in the suburbs of the Vatican and of the Ostian way. Their invisible sanctity had protected them against the Goths, the Vandals, and the Lombards; but the Arabs disdained both the gospel and the legend; and their rapacious spirit was approved and animated by the precepts of the Koran. The Christian *idols* were stripped of their costly offerings; a silver altar was torn away from the shrine of St. Peter; and if the bodies or the buildings were left entire, their deliverance must be imputed to the haste rather than the scruples of the Saracens. In their course along the Appian way, they pillaged Fundi and besieged Gayeta; but they had turned aside from the walls of Rome, and by their divisions the Capitol was saved from the yoke of the prophet of Mecca. The same danger still impended on the heads of the Roman people; and their domestic force was unequal to the assault of an African emir. They claimed the protection of their Latin sovereign; but the Carlovingian standard was overthrown by a detachment of the Barbarians: they meditated the restoration of the Greek emperors; but the attempt was treasonable, and the succor remote and precarious. Their distress appeared to receive some aggravation from the death of their spiritual and temporal chief; but the pressing emergency superseded the forms and intrigues of an election; and the unanimous choice of Pope Leo the Fourth was the safety of the church and city [A.D. 847]. This pontiff was born a Roman; the courage of the first ages of the republic glowed in his breast; and amidst the ruins of his country he stood erect, like one of the firm and lofty columns that rear their heads above the fragments of the Roman forum. The first days of his reign were consecrated to the purification and removal of relics, to prayers and processions, and to all the solemn offices of religion, which served at least to heal the imagination and restore the hopes of the multitude. The public defense had been long neglected, not from the presumption of peace but from the distress and poverty of the times. As far as the scantiness of his means and the shortness of his leisure would allow, the ancient walls were repaired by the command of Leo; fifteen towers, in the most accessible stations, were built or renewed; two of these commanded on either side of the Tiber; and an iron chain was drawn across the stream to impede the ascent of a hostile navy.[†]

The city bands, in arms, attended their father to Ostia, where he reviewed and blessed his generous deliverers. They kissed his feet, received the communion with martial devotion, and listened to the prayer of Leo that the same God who had supported St. Peter and St. Paul on the waves of the sea would strengthen the hands of his champions against the adversaries of his holy name. After a similar prayer, and with equal resolution, the Moslems advanced to the attack of the Christian galleys, which preserved their advantageous station along the coast. The victory inclined to the side of the allies when it was less gloriously decided in their favor by a sudden tempest, which confounded the skill and courage of the stoutest mariners. The Christians were sheltered in a friendly harbor, while the Africans were scattered and dashed in pieces among the rocks and islands of a hostile shore. Those who escaped from shipwreck and hunger neither found nor deserved mercy at the hands of their implacable pursuers. The sword and the gibbet reduced the dangerous multitude of captives; and the remainder was more usefully employed to restore the sacred edifices which they had attempted to subvert. The pontiff, at the head of the citizens and allies, paid his grateful devotion at the shrines of the apostles; and among the spoils of this naval victory, thirteen Arabian bows of pure and massy silver were suspended round the altar of the fishermen of Galilee. The reign of Leo the Fourth was employed in the defense and ornament of the Roman state.

[*War between the Christian Theophilus and Moslem Motassem also afflicts the East (A.D. 838).*]

Mutual necessity could sometimes extort the exchange or ransom of prisoners: but in the national and religious conflict of the two empires, peace was without confidence and war without mercy. Quarter was seldom given in the field; those who escaped the edge of the sword were condemned to hopeless servitude or exquisite torture; and a Catholic emperor relates, with visible satisfaction, the execution of the Saracens of Crete, who were flayed alive or plunged into caldrons of boiling oil.[†]

When the Arabian conquerors had spread themselves over the East and were mingled with the servile crowds of Persia, Syria, and Egypt, they insensibly lost the freeborn and martial virtues of the desert. The courage of the South is the artificial fruit of discipline and prejudice; the active power of enthusiasm had decayed, and the mercenary forces of the caliphs were recruited in those climates of the North, of which valor is the hardy and spontaneous production. Of the Turks who dwelt beyond the Oxus and Jaxartes, the robust youths either taken in war or purchased in trade were educated in the exercises of the field and the profession of the Mohammedan faith. The Turkish guards stood in arms round the throne of their benefactor, and their chiefs usurped the dominion of the palace and the provinces [A.D. 841–870 ff.]. Motassem, the first author of this dangerous example, introduced into the capital above fifty thousand Turks: their licentious conduct provoked the public indignation, and the quarrels of the soldiers and people induced the caliph to retire from Baghdad and establish his own residence and the camp of his Barbarian favorites at Samara on the Tigris, about twelve leagues above the city of Peace. His son Motawakkel was a jealous and cruel tyrant [A.D. 847–861]: odious to his subjects, he cast himself on the fidelity of the strangers, and these strangers, ambitious and apprehensive, were tempted by the rich promise of a revolution. At the instigation or at least in the cause of his son, they burst into his apartment at the hour of supper, and the caliph was cut into seven pieces by the same swords which he had recently distributed among the guards of his life and throne. To this throne, yet streaming with a father's blood, Montasser was triumphantly led; but in a reign of six months [A.D. 861–862], he found only the pangs of a guilty conscience. If he wept at the sight of an old tapestry which represented the crime and punishment of the son of Chosroes, if his days were abridged by grief and remorse, we may allow some pity to a parricide who exclaimed in the bitterness of death that he had lost both this world and the world to come. After this act of treason, the ensigns of royalty, the garment and walking-staff of Mohammed, were given and torn away by the foreign mercenaries, who in four years created, deposed, and murdered three commanders of the faithful. As often as the Turks were inflamed by fear or rage or avarice, these caliphs were dragged by the feet, exposed naked to the scorching sun, beaten with iron clubs, and compelled to purchase, by the abdication of their dignity, a short reprieve of inevitable fate. At length, however, the fury of the tempest was spent or diverted: the Abbassides returned to the less turbulent residence of Baghdad; the insolence of the Turks was curbed with a firmer and more skillful hand, and their numbers were divided and destroyed in foreign warfare. But the nations of the East had been taught to trample on the successors of the prophet; and the blessings of domestic peace were obtained by the relaxation of strength and discipline. So uniform are the mischiefs of military despotism that I seem to repeat the story of the Praetorians of Rome.

While the flame of enthusiasm was damped by the business, the pleasure, and the knowledge of the age, it burnt with concentrated heat in the breasts of the chosen few, the congenial spirits who were ambitious of reigning either in this world or in the next [A.D. 890–951]. How carefully soever the book of prophecy had been sealed by the apostle of Mecca, the wishes and (if we may profane the word) even the reason of fanaticism might believe that, after the successive missions of Adam, Noah, Abraham, Moses, Jesus, and Mohammed, the same God, in the fullness of time, would reveal a still more perfect and permanent law. In the two hundred and seventy-seventh year of the Hegira, and in the neighborhood of Cufa, an Arabian preacher of the name of Carmath assumed the lofty and incomprehensible style of the Guide, the Director, the Demonstration, the Word, the Holy Ghost, the Camel, the Herald of the Messiah, who had conversed with him in a human shape, and the representative of Mohammed the son of Ali, of St. John the Baptist, and of the angel Gabriel. In his mystic volume, the precepts of the Koran were refined to a more spiritual sense: he relaxed the duties of ablution, fasting, and pilgrimage; allowed the indiscriminate use of wine and forbidden food; and nourished the fervor of his disciples by the daily repetition of fifty prayers. The idleness and ferment of the rustic crowd awakened the attention of the magistrates of Cufa; a timid persecution assisted the progress of the new sect; and the name of the prophet became more revered after his person had been withdrawn from the world. His twelve apostles dispersed themselves among the Bedoweens, "a race of men," says Abulfeda, "equally devoid of reason and of religion"; and the success of their preaching seemed to threaten Arabia with a new revolution. The Carmathians were ripe for rebellion, since they disclaimed the title of the house of Abbas and abhorred the worldly pomp of the caliphs of Baghdad. They were susceptible of discipline, since they vowed a blind and absolute submission to their imam, who was called to the prophetic office by the voice of God and the people. Instead of the legal tithes, he claimed the fifth of their substance and spoil; the most flagitious sins were no more than the type of disobedience; and the brethren were united and concealed by an oath of secrecy. After a bloody conflict, they prevailed in the province of Bahrein, along the Persian Gulf [A.D. 900 ff.]: far and wide, the tribes of the desert were subject to the scepter, or rather to the sword, of Abu Said and his son Abu Taher; and these rebellious imams could muster in the field a hundred and seven thousand fanatics. The mercenaries of the caliph were dismayed at the approach of an enemy who neither asked nor accepted quarter; and the difference between them, in fortitude and patience, is expressive of the change which three centuries of prosperity had effected in the character of the Arabians. Such troops were discomfited in every action; the cities of Racca and Baalbec, of Cufa and Bassora, were taken and pillaged; Baghdad was filled with consternation; and the caliph trembled behind the veils of his palace. In a daring inroad beyond the Tigris, Abu Taher advanced to the gates of the capital with no more than five hundred horse.

By the special order of Moctader, the bridges had been broken down, and the person or head of the rebel was expected every hour by the commander of the faithful. His lieutenant, from a motive of fear or pity, apprised Abu Taher of his danger and recommended a speedy escape. "Your master," said the intrepid Carmathian to the messenger, "is at the head of thirty thousand soldiers: three such men as these are wanting in his host": at the same instant, turning to three of his companions, he commanded the first to plunge a dagger into his breast, the second to leap into the Tigris, and the third to cast himself headlong down a precipice. They obeyed without a murmur. "Relate," continued the imam, "what you have seen: before the evening your general shall be chained among my dogs." Before the evening, the camp was surprised and the menace was executed. The rapine of the Carmathians was sanctified by their aversion to the worship of Mecca: they robbed a caravan of pilgrims, and twenty thousand devout Moslems were abandoned on the burning sands to a death of hunger and thirst. Another year they suffered the pilgrims to proceed without interruption; but in the festival of devotion, Abu Taher stormed the holy city and trampled on the most venerable relics of the Mohammedan faith [A.D. 929]. Thirty thousand citizens and strangers were put to the sword; the sacred precincts were polluted by the burial of three thousand dead bodies; the well of Zemzem overflowed with blood; the golden spout was forced from its place; the veil of the Caaba was divided among these impious sectaries; and the black stone, the first monument of the nation, was borne away in triumph to their capital. After this deed of sacrilege and cruelty, they continued to infest the confines of Irak, Syria, and Egypt: but the vital principle of enthusiasm had withered at the root. Their scruples, or their avarice, again opened the pilgrimage of Mecca and restored the black stone of the Caaba; and it is needless to inquire into what factions they were broken or by whose swords they were finally extirpated. The sect of the Carmathians may be considered as the second visible cause of the decline and fall of the empire of the caliphs.

The third and most obvious cause was the weight and magnitude of the empire itself [A.D. 800–936]. The caliph Almamon might proudly assert that it was easier for him to rule the East and the West than to manage a chess-board of two feet square: yet I suspect that in both those games he was guilty of many fatal mistakes; and I perceive that in the distant provinces the authority of the first and most powerful of the Abbassides was already impaired. The analogy of despotism invests the representative with the full majesty of the prince; the division and balance of powers might relax the habits of obedience, might encourage the passive subject to inquire into the origin and administration of civil government. He who is born in the purple is seldom worthy to reign; but the elevation of a private man, of a peasant, perhaps, or a slave, affords a strong presumption of his courage and capacity. The viceroy of a remote kingdom aspires to secure the property and inheritance of his precarious trust; the nations must rejoice in the presence of their sovereign; and the command of armies and treasures are at once the object and the instrument of his ambition. A change was scarcely visible as long as the lieutenants of the caliph were content with their vicarious title; while they solicited for themselves or their sons a renewal of the Imperial grant, and still maintained on the coin and in the public prayers the name and prerogative of the commander of the faithful. But in the long and hereditary exercise of power, they assumed the pride and attributes of royalty; the alternative of peace or war, of reward or punishment, depended solely on their will; and the revenues of their government were reserved for local services or private magnificence.[†]

In the declining age of the caliphs, in the century which elapsed after the war of Theophilus and Motassem, the hostile transactions of the two nations were confined to some inroads by sea and land, the fruits of their close vicinity and indelible hatred. But when the Eastern world was convulsed and broken, the Greeks were roused from their lethargy by the hopes of conquest and revenge. The Byzantine empire, since the accession of the Basilian race, had reposed in peace and dignity; and they might encounter with their entire strength the front of some petty emir whose rear was assaulted and threatened by his national foes of the Mohammedan faith. The lofty titles of the morning star and the death of the Saracens were applied in the public acclamations to Nicephorus Phocas, a prince as renowned in the camp as he was unpopular in the city. In the subordinate station of great domestic, or general of the East, he reduced the Island of Crete and extirpated the nest of pirates who had so long defied with impunity the majesty of the empire [A.D. 960]. His military genius was displayed in the conduct and success of the enterprise, which had so often failed with loss and dishonor. The Saracens were confounded by the landing of his troops on safe and level bridges, which he cast from the vessels to the shore. Seven months were consumed in the siege of Candia; the despair of the native Cretans was stimulated by the frequent aid of their brethren of Africa and Spain; and after the massy wall and double ditch had been stormed by the Greeks, a hopeless conflict was still maintained in the streets and houses of the city. The whole island was subdued in the capital, and a submissive people accepted without resistance the baptism of the conqueror. Constantinople applauded the long-forgotten pomp of a triumph; but the Imperial diadem was the sole reward that could repay the services or satisfy the ambition of Nicephorus.

After the death of the younger Romanus, the fourth in lineal descent of the Basilian race, his widow Theophania successively married Nicephorus Phocas and his assassin John Zimisces, the two heroes of the age. They reigned as the guardians and colleagues of her infant sons; and the twelve years of their military command form the most splendid period of the Byzantine annals. [A.D. 963–975]. . . . After they had forced and secured the narrow passes of Mount Amanus, the two Roman princes repeatedly carried their arms into the heart of Syria. Yet instead of assaulting the walls of Antioch, the humanity or superstition of Nicephorus appeared to respect the ancient metropolis of the East: he contented himself with drawing round the city a line of circumvallation; left a stationary army; and instructed his lieutenant to expect without impatience the return of spring. But in the depth of winter, in a dark and rainy night, an adventurous subaltern with three hundred soldiers approached the rampart, applied his scaling-ladders, occupied two adjacent towers, stood firm against the pressure of multitudes, and bravely maintained his post till he was relieved by the tardy though effectual support of his reluctant chief. The first tumult of slaughter and rapine subsided; the reign of Caesar and of Christ was restored; and the efforts of a hundred thousand Saracens, of the armies of Syria and the fleets of Africa, were consumed without effect before the walls of Antioch. The royal city of Aleppo was subject to Seifeddowlat of the dynasty of Hamadan, who clouded his past glory by the precipitate retreat which abandoned his kingdom and capital to the Roman invaders. In his stately palace that stood without the walls of Aleppo, they joyfully seized a well-furnished magazine of arms, a stable of fourteen hundred mules, and three hundred bags of silver and gold. But the walls of the city withstood the strokes of their battering-rams: and the besiegers pitched their tents on the neighboring mountain of Jaushan. . . . In their Syrian inroads [the Romans] commanded the husbandmen to cultivate their lands, that they themselves, in the ensuing season, might reap the benefit; more than a hundred cities were reduced to obedience; and eighteen pulpits of the principal mosques were committed to the flames to expiate the sacrilege of the disciples of Mohammed. . . . [T]he torrent was only stopped by the impregnable fortress of Tripoli, on the sea-coast of Phoenicia. Since the days of Heraclius, the Euphrates, below the passage of Mount Taurus, had been impervious and almost invisible to the Greeks. The river yielded a free passage to the victorious Zimisces. . . . But the apprehensions of Baghdad were relieved by the retreat of the Greeks: thirst and hunger guarded the desert of Mesopotamia; and the emperor, satiated with glory and laden with Oriental spoils, returned to Constantinople and displayed in his triumph the silk, the aromatics, and three hundred myriads of gold and silver. Yet the powers of the East had been bent, not broken, by this transient hurricane. After the departure of the Greeks, the fugitive princes returned to their capitals; the subjects disclaimed their involuntary oaths of allegiance; the Moslems again purified their temples and overturned the idols of the saints and martyrs; the Nestorians and Jacobites preferred a Saracen to an orthodox master; and the numbers and spirit of the Melchites were inadequate to the support of the church and state. Of these extensive conquests, Antioch, with the cities of Cilicia and the Isle of Cyprus, was alone restored, a permanent and useful accession to the Roman empire.

CHAPTER LIII

Fate of the Eastern Empire

Fate of the Eastern empire in the tenth century. • Extent and division. • Wealth and revenue. • Palace of Constantinople. • Titles and offices. • Pride and power of the emperors. • Tactics of the Greeks, Arabs, and Franks. • Loss of the Latin tongue. • Studies and solitude of the Greeks.

A ray of historic light seems to beam from the darkness of the tenth century. We open with curiosity and respect the royal volumes of Constantine Porphyrogenitus which he composed at a mature age for the instruction of his son and which promise to unfold the state of the Eastern empire, both in peace and war, both at home and abroad. In the first of these works he minutely describes the pompous ceremonies of the church and palace of Constantinople, according to his own practice and that of his predecessors. In the second, he attempts an accurate survey of the provinces, the *themes,* as they were then denominated, both of Europe and Asia. The system of Roman tactics, the discipline and order of the troops, and the military operations by land and sea are explained in the third of these didactic collections, which may be ascribed to Constantine or his father Leo. In the fourth, of the administration of the empire, he reveals the secrets of the Byzantine policy, in friendly or hostile intercourse with the nations of the earth. The literary labors of the age, the practical systems of law, agriculture, and history, might redound to the benefit of the subject and the honor of the Macedonian princes. The sixty books of the *Basilics,* the code and pandects of civil jurisprudence, were gradually framed in the three first reigns of that prosperous dynasty. The art of agriculture had amused the leisure and exercised the pens of the best and wisest of the ancients; and their chosen precepts are comprised in the twenty books of the *Geoponics* of Constantine. At his command, the historical examples of vice and virtue were methodized in fifty-three books, and every citizen might apply to his contemporaries or himself the lesson or the warning of past times. From the august character of a legislator, the sovereign of the East descends to the more humble office of a teacher and a scribe; and if his successors and subjects were regardless of his paternal cares, *we* may inherit and enjoy the everlasting legacy.

A closer survey will indeed reduce the value of the gift and the gratitude of posterity: in the possession of these Imperial treasures we may still deplore our poverty and ignorance; and the fading glories of their authors will be obliterated by indifference or contempt. The Basilics will sink to a broken copy, a partial and mutilated version in the Greek language, of the laws of Justinian; but the sense of the old civilians is often superseded by the influence of bigotry: and the absolute prohibition of divorce, concubinage, and interest for money enslaves the freedom of trade and the happiness of private life. In the historical book, a subject of Constantine might admire the inimitable virtues of Greece and Rome: he might learn to what a pitch of energy and elevation the human character had formerly aspired. But a contrary effect must have been produced by a new edition of the lives of the saints which the great *logothete*, or chancellor of the empire, was directed to prepare; and the dark fund of superstition was enriched by the fabulous and florid legends of Simon the *Metaphrast*. The merits and miracles of the whole calendar are of less account in the eyes of a sage than the toil of a single husbandman, who multiplies the gifts of the Creator and supplies the food of his brethren. Yet the royal authors of the *Geoponics* were more seriously employed in expounding the precepts of the destroying art, which had been taught since the days of Xenophon as the art of heroes and kings. But the *Tactics* of Leo and Constantine are mingled with the baser alloy of the age in which they lived. It was destitute of original genius; they implicitly transcribe the rules and maxims which had been confirmed by victories. It was unskilled in the propriety of style and method; they blindly confound the most distant and discordant institutions, the phalanx of Sparta and that of Macedon, the legions of Cato and Trajan, of Augustus and Theodosius. Even the use, or at least the importance, of these military rudiments may be fairly questioned: their general theory is dictated by reason; but the merit as well as difficulty consists in the application. The discipline of a soldier is formed by exercise rather than by study: the talents of a commander are appropriated to those calm though rapid minds which nature produces to decide the fate of armies and nations: the former is the habit of a life, the latter the glance of a moment; and the battles won by lessons of tactics may be numbered with

the epic poems created from the rules of criticism. The book of ceremonies is a recital, tedious yet imperfect, of the despicable pageantry
which had infected the church and state since the gradual decay of the
purity of the one and the power of the other. A review of the themes
or provinces might promise such authentic and useful information as
the curiosity of government only can obtain, instead of traditionary
fables on the origin of the cities and malicious epigrams on the vices
of their inhabitants. Such information the historian would have been
pleased to record; nor should his silence be condemned if the most interesting objects, the population of the capital and provinces, the
amount of the taxes and revenues, the numbers of subjects and strangers
who served under the Imperial standard, have been unnoticed by Leo
the philosopher and his son Constantine. His treatise of the public administration is stained with the same blemishes; yet it is discriminated
by peculiar merit; the antiquities of the nations may be doubtful or
fabulous; but the geography and manners of the Barbaric world are
delineated with curious accuracy. Of these nations, the Franks alone
were qualified to observe in their turn, and to describe, the metropolis
of the East. The ambassador of the great Otho, a bishop of Cremona,
has painted the state of Constantinople about the middle of the tenth
century: his style is glowing, his narrative lively, his observation keen;
and even the prejudices and passions of Liutprand are stamped with
an original character of freedom and genius. From this scanty fund of
foreign and domestic materials, I shall investigate the form and substance of the Byzantine empire; the provinces and wealth, the civil
government and military force, the character and literature, of the
Greeks in a period of six hundred years, from the reign of Heraclius
to his successful invasion of the Franks or Latins.

After the final division between the sons of Theodosius, the swarms
of Barbarians from Scythia and Germany overspread the provinces
and extinguished the empire of ancient Rome. The weakness of Constantinople was concealed by the extent of dominion: her limits were
inviolate, or at least entire; and the kingdom of Justinian was enlarged
by the splendid acquisition of Africa and Italy. But the possession of
these new conquests was transient and precarious; and almost a moiety
of the Eastern empire was torn away by the arms of the Saracens. Syria
and Egypt were oppressed by the Arabian caliphs; and after the reduction of Africa, their lieutenants invaded and subdued the Roman prov-

ince which had been changed into the Gothic monarchy of Spain. The islands of the Mediterranean were not inaccessible to their naval powers; and it was from their extreme stations, the harbors of Crete and the fortresses of Cilicia, that the faithful or rebel emirs insulted the majesty of the throne and capital. The remaining provinces, under the obedience of the emperors, were cast into a new mold; and the jurisdiction of the presidents, the consulars, and the counts was superseded by the institution of the *themes,* or military governments, which prevailed under the successors of Heraclius and are described by the pen of the royal author. Of the twenty-nine themes, twelve in Europe and seventeen in Asia, the origin is obscure, the etymology doubtful or capricious: the limits were arbitrary and fluctuating; but some particular names that sound the most strangely to our ear were derived from the character and attributes of the troops that were maintained at the expense and for the guard of the respective divisions. The vanity of the Greek princes most eagerly grasped the shadow of conquest and the memory of lost dominion. A new Mesopotamia was created on the western side of the Euphrates: the appellation and praetor of Sicily were transferred to a narrow slip of Calabria; and a fragment of the duchy of Beneventum was promoted to the style and title of the theme of Lombardy. In the decline of the Arabian empire, the successors of Constantine might indulge their pride in more solid advantages. The victories of Nicephorus, John Zimisces, and Basil the Second revived the fame and enlarged the boundaries of the Roman name: the province of Cilicia, the metropolis of Antioch, the islands of Crete and Cyprus were restored to the allegiance of Christ and Caesar: one third of Italy was annexed to the throne of Constantinople: the kingdom of Bulgaria was destroyed; and the last sovereigns of the Macedonian dynasty extended their sway from the sources of the Tigris to the neighborhood of Rome. In the eleventh century, the prospect was again clouded by new enemies and new misfortunes: the relics of Italy were swept away by the Norman adventurers; and almost all the Asiatic branches were dissevered from the Roman trunk by the Turkish conquerors. After these losses, the emperors of the Comnenian family continued to reign from the Danube to Peloponnesus, and from Belgrade to Nice, Trebizond, and the winding stream of the Meander. The spacious provinces of Thrace, Macedonia, and Greece were obedient to their scepter; the possession of Cyprus, Rhodes, and Crete was accompanied by the fifty islands of the Aegean or Holy Sea; and the remnant of their empire transcends the measure of the largest of the European kingdoms.

The same princes might assert, with dignity and truth, that of all the monarchs of Christendom they possessed the greatest city, the most ample revenue, the most flourishing and populous state. With the decline and fall of the empire, the cities of the West had decayed and fallen; nor could the ruins of Rome, or the mud walls, wooden hovels, and narrow precincts of Paris and London, prepare the Latin stranger to contemplate the situation and extent of Constantinople, her stately palaces and churches, and the arts and luxury of an innumerable people. Her treasures might attract, but her virgin strength had repelled and still promised to repel, the audacious invasion of the Persian and Bulgarian, the Arab and the Russian. The provinces were less fortunate and impregnable; and few districts, few cities, could be discovered which had not been violated by some fierce Barbarian, impatient to despoil because he was hopeless to possess. From the age of Justinian the Eastern empire was sinking below its former level; the powers of destruction were more active than those of improvement; and the calamities of war were embittered by the more permanent evils of civil and ecclesiastical tyranny. The captive who had escaped from the Barbarians was often stripped and imprisoned by the ministers of his sovereign: the Greek superstition relaxed the mind by prayer and emaciated the body by fasting; and the multitude of convents and festivals diverted many hands and many days from the temporal service of mankind. Yet the subjects of the Byzantine empire were still the most dexterous and diligent of nations; their country was blessed by nature with every advantage of soil, climate, and situation; and in the support and restoration of the arts, their patient and peaceful temper was more useful than the warlike spirit and feudal anarchy of Europe. The provinces that still adhered to the empire were repeopled and enriched by the misfortunes of those which were irrecoverably lost. From the yoke of the caliphs, the Catholics of Syria, Egypt, and Africa retired to the allegiance of their prince, to the society of their brethren: the movable wealth which eludes the search of oppression accompanied and alleviated their exile, and Constantinople received into her bosom the fugitive trade of Alexandria and Tyre. The chiefs of Armenia and Scythia, who fled from hostile or religious persecution, were hospitably entertained: their followers were encouraged to build new cities and to cultivate waste lands; and many spots, both in Europe and Asia, preserved the name, the manners, or at least the memory of these national colonies. Even the tribes of Barbarians who had seated themselves in arms on the territory of the empire were gradually reclaimed to the laws of the church and state; and as long as they were separated from the Greeks, their posterity supplied a race of faithful and obedient soldiers.†

In an absolute government, which levels the distinctions of noble and plebeian birth, the sovereign is the sole fountain of honor; and the rank, both in the palace and the empire, depends on the titles and offices which are bestowed and resumed by his arbitrary will. Above a thousand years, from Vespasian to Alexius Comnenus, the *Caesar* was the second person, or at least the second degree, after the supreme title of *Augustus* was more freely communicated to the sons and brothers of the reigning monarch. To elude without violating his promise to a powerful associate, the husband of his sister, and, without giving himself an equal, to reward the piety of his brother Isaac, the crafty Alexius interposed a new and supereminent dignity. The happy flexibility of the Greek tongue allowed him to compound the names of Augustus and Emperor (Sebastos and Autocrator), and the union produces the sonorous title of *Sebastocrator*. He was exalted above the Caesar on the first step of the throne: the public acclamations repeated his name; and he was only distinguished from the sovereign by some peculiar ornaments of the head and feet. The emperor alone could assume the purple or red buskins and the close diadem or tiara which imitated the fashion of the Persian kings. It was a high pyramidal cap of cloth or silk, almost concealed by a profusion of pearls and jewels: the crown was formed by a horizontal circle and two arches of gold: at the summit, the point of their intersection, was placed a globe or cross, and two strings or lappets of pearl depended on either cheek. Instead of red, the buskins of the Sebastocrator and Caesar were green; and on their *open* coronets or crowns, the precious gems were more sparingly distributed. Beside and below the Caesar the fancy of Alexius created the *Panhypersebastos* and the *Protosebastos,* whose sound and signification will satisfy a Grecian ear. They imply a superiority and a priority above the simple name of Augustus; and this sacred and primitive title of the Roman prince was degraded to the kinsmen and servants of the

Byzantine court. The daughter of Alexius applauds with fond complacency this artful gradation of hopes and honors; but the science of words is accessible to the meanest capacity; and this vain dictionary was easily enriched by the pride of his successors. To their favorite sons or brothers, they imparted the more lofty appellation of Lord or *Despot*, which was illustrated with new ornaments and prerogatives and placed immediately after the person of the emperor himself. The five titles of 1. *Despot*; 2. *Sebastocrator*; 3. *Caesar*; 4. *Panhypersebastos*; and 5. *Protosebastos* were usually confined to the princes of his blood: they were the emanations of his majesty; but as they exercised no regular functions, their existence was useless and their authority precarious.

But in every monarchy the substantial powers of government must be divided and exercised by the ministers of the palace and treasury, the fleet and army. The titles alone can differ; and in the revolution of ages, the counts and praefects, the praetor and quaestor, insensibly descended, while their servants rose above their heads to the first honors of the state. . . . Their honors and emoluments, their dress and titles, their mutual salutations and respective preeminence, were balanced with more exquisite labor than would have fixed the constitution of a free people; and the code was almost perfect when this baseless fabric, the monument of pride and servitude, was forever buried in the ruins of the empire.

The most lofty titles and the most humble postures which devotion has applied to the Supreme Being have been prostituted by flattery and fear to creatures of the same nature with ourselves. The mode of *adoration*, of falling prostrate on the ground and kissing the feet of the emperor, was borrowed by Diocletian from Persian servitude; but it was continued and aggravated till the last age of the Greek monarchy. Excepting only on Sundays, when it was waived from a motive of religious pride, this humiliating reverence was exacted from all who entered the royal presence, from the princes invested with the diadem and purple and from the ambassadors who represented their independent sovereigns, the caliphs of Asia, Egypt, or Spain, the kings of France and Italy, and the Latin emperors of ancient Rome. In his transactions of business, Liutprand, bishop of Cremona, asserted the free spirit of a Frank and the dignity of his master Otho. Yet his sincerity cannot disguise the abasement of his first audience. When he approached the throne, the birds of the golden tree began to warble their notes, which were accompanied by the roarings of the two lions of gold. With his two companions, Liutprand was compelled to bow and to fall prostrate, and thrice to touch the ground with his forehead. He arose, but in the short interval the throne had been hoisted from the floor to the ceiling, the Imperial figure appeared in new and more gorgeous apparel, and the interview was concluded in haughty and majestic silence. In this honest and curious narrative, the bishop of Cremona represents the ceremonies of the Byzantine court, which . . . were preserved in the last age by the dukes of Muscovy or Russia. After a long journey by sea and land, from Venice to Constantinople, the ambassador halted at the golden gate till he was conducted by the formal officers to the hospitable palace prepared for his reception; but this palace was a prison, and his jealous keepers prohibited all social intercourse either with strangers or natives. At his first audience, he offered the gifts of his master, slaves and golden vases and costly armor. The ostentatious payment of the officers and troops displayed before his eyes the riches of the empire: he was entertained at a royal banquet in which the ambassadors of the nations were marshaled by the esteem or contempt of the Greeks: from his own table the emperor, as the most signal favor, sent the plates which he had tasted; and his favorites were dismissed with a robe of honor. In the morning and evening of each day, his civil and military servants attended their duty in the palace; their labors were repaid by the sight, perhaps by the smile, of their lord; his commands were signified by a nod or a sign: but all earthly greatness *stood* silent and submissive in his presence. In his regular or extraordinary processions through the capital, he unveiled his person to the public view: the rites of policy were connected with those of religion, and his visits to the principal churches were regulated by the festivals of the Greek calendar. On the eve of these processions, the gracious or devout intention of the monarch was proclaimed by the heralds. The streets were cleared and purified; the pavement was strewed with flowers; the most precious furniture, the gold and silver plate, and silken hangings were displayed from the windows and balconies, and a severe discipline restrained and silenced the tumult of the populace. The march was opened by the military officers at the head of their troops: they were followed in long order by the magistrates and ministers of the civil government: the person of the emperor was guarded by his eunuchs and domestics, and at the church door he was solemnly received by the patriarch and his clergy. The task of applause was not abandoned to the rude and spontaneous voices of the crowd. The most convenient stations were occupied by the bands of the blue and green factions of the circus; and their furious conflicts, which had shaken the capital, were insensibly sunk to an emulation of servitude. From either side they echoed in responsive melody the praises of the emperor; their poets and musicians directed the choir, and *long life* and victory were the burden of every song. The same acclamations were performed at the audience, the banquet, and the church; and as an evidence of boundless sway, they were repeated in the Latin, Gothic, Persian, French, and even English language by the mercenaries who sustained the real or fictitious character of those nations. By the pen of Constantine Porphyrogenitus, this science of form and flattery has been reduced into a pompous and trifling volume, which the vanity of succeeding times might enrich with an ample supplement. Yet the calmer reflection of a prince would surely suggest that the same acclamations were applied to every character and every reign: and if he had risen from a private rank, he might remember that his own voice had been the loudest and most eager in applause at the very moment when he envied the fortune, or conspired against the life, of his predecessor.

The princes of the North, of the nations, says Constantine, without faith or fame, were ambitious of mingling their blood with the blood of the Caesars by their marriage with a royal virgin, or by the nuptials of their daughters with a Roman prince. The aged monarch, in his instructions to his son, reveals the secret maxims of policy and pride; and suggests the most decent reasons for refusing these insolent and unreasonable demands. Every animal, says the discreet emperor, is prompted by the distinction of language, religion, and manners. A just regard to the purity of descent preserves the harmony of public and private life; but the mixture of foreign blood is the fruitful source of disorder and discord. Such had ever been the opinion and practice of the sage Romans: their jurisprudence proscribed the marriage of a citizen and a stranger: in the days of freedom and virtue, a senator would have scorned to match his daughter with a king: the glory of Mark Antony was sullied by an Egyptian wife: and the emperor Titus was compelled, by popular censure, to dismiss with reluctance the reluctant Berenice. This perpetual interdict was ratified by the fabulous sanction of the great Constantine. The ambassadors of the nations, more especially of the unbelieving nations, were solemnly admonished that such strange alliances had been condemned by the founder of the church and city. The irrevocable law was inscribed on the altar of St. Sophia; and the impious prince who should stain the majesty of the purple was excluded from the civil and ecclesiastical communion of the Romans.

[*Various exceptions were of course sometimes made to the rigors of this law.*]

In the Byzantine palace, the emperor was the first slave of the ceremonies which he imposed, of the rigid forms which regulated each word and gesture, besieged him in the palace, and violated the leisure of his rural solitude. But the lives and fortunes of millions hung on his arbitrary will; and the firmest minds, superior to the allurements of pomp and luxury, may be seduced by the more active pleasure of commanding their equals. The legislative and executive powers were centered in the person of the monarch, and the last remains of the authority of the senate were finally eradicated by Leo the philosopher. A lethargy of servitude had benumbed the minds of the Greeks: in the wildest tumults of rebellion they never aspired to the idea of a free constitution; and the private character of the prince was the only source and measure of their public happiness. Superstition riveted their chains; in the church of St. Sophia he was solemnly crowned by the patriarch; at the foot of the altar, they pledged their passive and unconditional obedience to his government and family. On his side he engaged to abstain as much as possible from the capital punishments of death and mutilation; his orthodox creed was subscribed with his own hand, and he promised to obey the decrees of the seven synods and the canons of the holy church. But the assurance of mercy was loose and indefinite: he swore not to his people but to an invisible judge; and except in the inexpiable guilt of heresy, the ministers of Heaven were always prepared to preach the indefeasible right, and to absolve the venial transgressions, of their sovereign. The Greek ecclesiastics were themselves the subjects of the civil magistrate: at the nod of a tyrant, the bishops were created, or transferred, or deposed, or punished with an ignominious death: whatever might be their wealth or influence, they could never succeed like the Latin clergy in the establishment of an independent republic; and the patriarch of Constantinople condemned what he secretly envied, the temporal greatness of his Roman brother. Yet the exercise of boundless despotism is happily checked by the laws of nature and necessity. In proportion to his wisdom and virtue, the master of an empire is confined to the path of his sacred and laborious duty. In proportion to his vice and folly, he drops the scepter too weighty for his hands; and the motions of the royal image are ruled by the imperceptible thread of some minister or favorite who undertakes for his private interest to exercise the task of the public oppression. In some fatal moment, the most absolute monarch may dread the reason or the caprice of a nation of slaves; and experience has proved that whatever is gained in the extent, is lost in the safety and solidity, of regal power.

Whatever titles a despot may assume, whatever claims he may assert, it is on the sword that he must ultimately depend to guard him against his foreign and domestic enemies. From the age of Charlemagne to that of the Crusades, the world (for I overlook the remote monarchy of China) was occupied and disputed by the three great empires or nations of the Greeks, the Saracens, and the Franks. Their military strength may be ascertained by a comparison of their courage, their arts and riches, and their obedience to a supreme head who might call into action all the energies of the state. The Greeks, far inferior to their rivals in the first, were superior to the Franks, and at least equal to the Saracens, in the second and third of these warlike qualifications.

The wealth of the Greeks enabled them to purchase the service of the poorer nations and to maintain a naval power for the protection of their coasts and the annoyance of their enemies. A commerce of mutual benefit exchanged the gold of Constantinople for the blood of Sclavonians and Turks, the Bulgarians and Russians: their valor contributed to the victories of Nicephorus and Zimisces; and if a hostile people pressed too closely on the frontier, they were recalled to the defense of their country and the desire of peace by the well-managed attack of a more distant tribe. The command of the Mediterranean, from the mouth of the Tanais to the columns of Hercules, was always claimed and often possessed by the successors of Constantine. Their capital was filled with naval stores and dexterous artificers: the situation of Greece and Asia, the long coasts, deep gulfs, and numerous islands, accustomed their subjects to the exercise of navigation; and the trade of Venice and Amalfi supplied a nursery of seamen to the Imperial fleet.[†]

The invention of the Greek fire did not, like that of gunpowder, produce a total revolution in the art of war. To these liquid combustibles the city and empire of Constantine owed their deliverance; and they were employed in sieges and sea-fights with terrible effect. But they were either less improved or less susceptible of improvement: the engines of antiquity, the catapultae, balistae, and battering-rams, were still of most frequent and powerful use in the attack and defense of fortifications; nor was the decision of battles reduced to the quick and heavy *fire* of a line of infantry, whom it were fruitless to protect with armor against a similar fire of their enemies. Steel and iron were still the common instruments of destruction and safety; and the helmets, cuirasses, and shields of the tenth century did not, either in form or substance, essentially differ from those which had covered the companions of Alexander or Achilles. . . . Whatever authority could enact was accomplished, at least in theory, by the camps and marches, the exercises and evolutions, the edicts and books of the Byzantine monarch. Whatever art could produce from the forge, the loom, or the laboratory was abundantly supplied by the riches of the prince and the industry of his numerous workmen. But neither authority nor art could frame the most important machine, the soldier himself; and if the *ceremonies* of Constantine always suppose the safe and triumphal return of the emperor, his *tactics* seldom soar above the means of escaping a defeat and procrastinating the war. Notwithstanding some transient success, the Greeks were sunk in their own esteem and that of their neighbors. A cold hand and a loquacious tongue was the vulgar description of the nation: the author of the tactics was besieged in his capital; and the last of the Barbarians, who trembled at the name of the Saracens or Franks, could proudly exhibit the medals of gold and silver which they had extorted from the feeble sovereign of Constantinople. What spirit their government and character denied might have been inspired in some degree by the influence of religion; but the religion of the Greeks could only teach them to suffer and to yield. The emperor Nicephorus, who restored for a moment the discipline and glory of the Roman name, was desirous of bestowing the honors of martyrdom on the Christians who lost their lives in a holy war against the infidels. But this political law was defeated by the opposition of the patriarch, the bishops, and the principal senators; and they strenuously urged the canons of St. Basil, that all who were polluted by the bloody trade of a soldier should be separated during three years from the communion of the faithful.

These scruples of the Greeks have been compared with the tears of the primitive Moslems when they were held back from battle; and this contrast of base superstition and high-spirited enthusiasm unfolds to a philosophic eye the history of the rival nations. The subjects of the last caliphs had undoubtedly degenerated from the zeal and faith of the companions of the prophet. Yet their martial creed still represented the Deity as the author of war: the vital though latent spark of fanaticism still glowed in the heart of their religion, and among the Saracens, who dwelt on the Christian borders, it was frequently rekindled to a lively and active flame. Their regular force was formed of the valiant slaves who had been educated to guard the person and accompany the standard of their lord: but the Moslem people of Syria and Cilicia, of Africa and Spain, was awakened by the trumpet which proclaimed a holy war against the infidels. The rich were ambitious of death or victory in the cause of God; the poor were allured by the hopes of plunder; and the old, the infirm, and the women assumed their share of meritorious service by sending their substitutes, with arms and horses, into the field. These offensive and defensive arms were similar in strength and temper to those of the Romans, whom they far excelled in the management of the horse and the bow: the massy silver of their belts, their bridles, and their swords displayed the magnificence of a prosperous nation; and except some black archers of the South, the Arabs disdained the naked bravery of their ancestors. Instead of wagons, they were attended by a long train of camels, mules, and asses: the multitude of these animals, whom they bedecked with flags and streamers, appeared to swell the pomp and magnitude of their host; and the horses of the enemy were often disordered by the uncouth figure and odious smell of the camels of the East. Invincible by their patience of thirst and heat, their spirits were frozen by a winter's cold, and the consciousness of their propensity to sleep exacted the most rigorous precautions against the surprises of the night. Their order of battle was a long square of two deep and solid lines; the first of archers, the second of cavalry. In their engagements by sea and land, they sustained with patient firmness the fury of the attack, and seldom advanced to the charge till they could discern and oppress the lassitude of their foes. But if they were repulsed and broken, they knew not how to rally or renew the combat; and their dismay was heightened by the superstitious prejudice that God had declared himself on the side of their enemies. The decline and fall of the caliphs countenanced this fearful opinion; nor were there wanting, among the Mohammedans and Christians, some obscure prophecies which prognosticated their alternate defeats. The unity of the Arabian empire was dissolved, but the independent fragments were equal to populous and powerful kingdoms; and in their naval and military armaments, an emir of Aleppo or Tunis might command no despicable fund of skill and industry and treasure. In their transactions of peace and war with the Saracens, the princes of Constantinople too often felt that these Barbarians had nothing barbarous in their discipline; and that if they were destitute of original genius, they had been endowed with a quick spirit of curiosity and imitation. The model was indeed more perfect than the copy; their ships and engines and fortifications were of a less skillful construction; and they confess without shame that the same God who has given a tongue to the Arabians had more nicely fashioned the hands of the Chinese and the heads of the Greeks.

A name of some German tribes between the Rhine and the Weser had spread its victorious influence over the greatest part of Gaul, Germany, and Italy; and the common appellation of FRANKS was applied by the Greeks and Arabians to the Christians of the Latin church, the nations of the West, who stretched beyond *their* knowledge to the shores of the Atlantic Ocean. The vast body had been inspired and united by the soul of Charlemagne; but the division and degeneracy of his race soon annihilated the Imperial power which would have rivaled the Caesars of Byzantium and revenged the indignities of the Christian name. The enemies no longer feared, nor could the subjects any longer trust, the application of a public revenue, the labors of trade and manufactures in the military service, the mutual aid of provinces and armies, and the naval squadrons which were regularly stationed from the mouth of the Elbe to that of the Tiber. In the beginning of the tenth century, the family of Charlemagne had almost disappeared; his monarchy was broken into many hostile and independent states; the regal title was assumed by the most ambitious chiefs;

their revolt was imitated in a long subordination of anarchy and discord, and the nobles of every province disobeyed their sovereign, oppressed their vassals, and exercised perpetual hostilities against their equals and neighbors. Their private wars, which overturned the fabric of government, fomented the martial spirit of the nation.... In the disorders of the tenth and eleventh centuries, every peasant was a soldier and every village a fortification; each wood or valley was a scene of murder and rapine; and the lords of each castle were compelled to assume the character of princes and warriors. To their own courage and policy they boldly trusted for the safety of their family, the protection of their lands, and the revenge of their injuries; and like the conquerors of a larger size, they were too apt to transgress the privilege of defensive war. The powers of the mind and body were hardened by the presence of danger and necessity of resolution: the same spirit refused to desert a friend and to forgive an enemy; and instead of sleeping under the guardian care of a magistrate, they proudly disdained the authority of the laws. In the days of feudal anarchy, the instruments of agriculture and art were converted into the weapons of bloodshed: the peaceful occupations of civil and ecclesiastical society were abolished or corrupted; and the bishop who exchanged his mitre for a helmet was more forcibly urged by the manners of the times than by the obligation of his tenure.

The love of freedom and of arms was felt with conscious pride by the Franks themselves, and is observed by the Greeks with some degree of amazement and terror. "The Franks," says the emperor Constantine, "are bold and valiant to the verge of temerity; and their dauntless spirit is supported by the contempt of danger and death. In the field and in close onset, they press to the front and rush headlong against the enemy, without deigning to compute either his numbers or their own. Their ranks are formed by the firm connections of consanguinity and friendship; and their martial deeds are prompted by the desire of saving or revenging their dearest companions. In their eyes, a retreat is a shameful flight; and flight is indelible infamy." A nation endowed with such high and intrepid spirit must have been secure of victory if these advantages had not been counterbalanced by many weighty defects. The decay of their naval power left the Greeks and Saracens in possession of the sea, for every purpose of annoyance and supply. In the age which preceded the institution of knighthood, the

Franks were rude and unskillful in the service of cavalry; and in all perilous emergencies, their warriors were so conscious of their ignorance that they chose to dismount from their horses and fight on foot. Unpracticed in the use of pikes or of missile weapons, they were encumbered by the length of their swords, the weight of their armor, the magnitude of their shields, and, if I may repeat the satire of the meager Greeks, by their unwieldy intemperance. Their independent spirit disdained the yoke of subordination, and abandoned the standard of their chief if he attempted to keep the field beyond the term of their stipulation or service. On all sides they were open to the snares of an enemy less brave but more artful than themselves. They might be bribed, for the Barbarians were venal; or surprised in the night, for they neglected the precautions of a close encampment or vigilant sentinels. The fatigues of a summer's campaign exhausted their strength and patience, and they sunk in despair if their voracious appetite was disappointed of a plentiful supply of wine and of food.†

By the well-known edict of Caracalla, his subjects, from Britain to Egypt, were entitled to the name and privileges of Romans, and their national sovereign might fix his occasional or permanent residence in any province of their common country. In the division of the East and West, an ideal unity was scrupulously observed, and in their titles, laws, and statutes, the successors of Arcadius and Honorius announced themselves as the inseparable colleagues of the same office, as the joint sovereigns of the Roman world and city, which were bounded by the same limits. After the fall of the Western monarchy, the majesty of the purple resided solely in the princes of Constantinople; and of these, Justinian was the first who, after a divorce of sixty years, regained the dominion of ancient Rome and asserted, by the right of conquest, the august title of Emperor of the Romans. . . . The final revolt and separation of Italy was accomplished about two centuries after the conquests of Justinian, and from his reign we may date the gradual oblivion of the Latin tongue. That legislator had composed his Institutes, his Code, and his Pandects in a language which he celebrates as the proper and public style of the Roman government, the consecrated idiom of the palace and senate of Constantinople, of the campus and tribunals of the East. But this foreign dialect was unknown to the people and soldiers of the Asiatic provinces, it was imperfectly understood by the greater part of the interpreters of the laws and the ministers of the state. After a short conflict, nature and habit prevailed over the obsolete institutions of human power: for the general benefit of his subjects, Justinian promulgated his Novels in the two languages: the several parts of his voluminous jurisprudence were successively translated; the original was forgotten, the version was studied; and the Greek, whose intrinsic merit deserved indeed the preference, obtained a legal as well as popular establishment in the Byzantine monarchy. The birth and residence of succeeding princes estranged them from the Roman idiom . . . ; and the ruins of the Latin speech were darkly preserved in the terms of jurisprudence and the acclamations of the palace. After the restoration of the Western empire by Charlemagne and the Othos, the names of Franks and Latins acquired an equal signification and extent; and these haughty Barbarians asserted, with some justice, their superior claim to the language and dominion of Rome. They insulted the alien of the East who had renounced the dress and idiom of Romans; and their reasonable practice will justify the frequent appellation of Greeks. But this contemptuous appellation was indignantly rejected by the prince and people to whom it was applied. Whatsoever changes had been introduced by the lapse of ages, they alleged a lineal and unbroken succession from Augustus and Constantine; and, in the lowest period of degeneracy and decay, the name of ROMANS adhered to the last fragments of the empire of Constantinople.

While the government of the East was transacted in Latin, the Greek was the language of literature and philosophy; nor could the masters of this rich and perfect idiom be tempted to envy the borrowed learning and imitative taste of their Roman disciples. After the fall of Paganism, the loss of Syria and Egypt, and the extinction of the schools of Alexandria and Athens, the studies of the Greeks insensibly retired to some regular monasteries, and above all to the royal college of Constantinople, which was burnt in the reign of Leo the Isaurian. In the pompous style of the age, the president of that foundation was named the Sun of Science: his twelve associates, the professors in the different arts and faculties, were the twelve signs of the zodiac; a library of thirty-six thousand five hundred volumes was open to their inquiries; and they could show an ancient manuscript of Homer on a roll of parchment one hundred and twenty feet in length, the intestines, as it was fabled, of a prodigious serpent. But the seventh and eighth centuries were a period of discord and darkness: the library was burnt, the college was abolished, the Iconoclasts are represented as the foes of antiquity; and a savage ignorance and contempt of letters has disgraced the princes of the Heraclean and Isaurian dynasties.

In the ninth century we trace the first dawnings of the restoration of science. After the fanaticism of the Arabs had subsided, the caliphs aspired to conquer the arts rather than the provinces of the empire: their liberal curiosity rekindled the emulation of the Greeks, brushed away the dust from their ancient libraries, and taught them to know and reward the philosophers, whose labors had been hitherto repaid by the pleasure of study and the pursuit of truth. The Caesar Bardas, the uncle of Michael the Third, was the generous protector of letters, a title which alone has preserved his memory and excused his ambition. . . . At the pressing entreaty of the Caesar, his friend, the celebrated Photius, renounced the freedom of a secular and studious life, ascended the patriarchal throne, and was alternately excommunicated and absolved by the synods of the East and West. By the confession even of priestly hatred, no art or science, except poetry, was foreign to this universal scholar, who was deep in thought, indefatigable in reading, and eloquent in diction. Whilst he exercised the office of *protospathaire,* or captain of the guards, Photius was sent as an ambassador to the caliph of Baghdad. The tedious hours of exile, perhaps of confinement, were beguiled by the hasty composition of his *Library,* a living monument of erudition and criticism. Two hundred and fourscore writers, historians, orators, philosophers, theologians are reviewed without any regular method: he abridges their narrative or doctrine, appreciates their style and character, and judges even the fathers of the church with a discreet freedom which often breaks through the superstition of the times. The emperor Basil, who lamented the defects of his own education, entrusted to the care of Photius his son and successor, Leo the philosopher; and the reign of that prince and of his son Constantine Porphyrogenitus forms one of the most prosperous eras of the Byzantine literature. By their munificence the treasures of antiquity were deposited in the Imperial library; by their pens or those of their associates, they were imparted in such extracts and abridgments as might amuse the curiosity without oppressing the indolence of the public. Besides the *Basilics,* or code of laws, the arts of husbandry and war, of feeding or destroying the human species, were propagated with equal diligence; and the history of Greece and Rome was digested into fifty-three heads or titles, of which two only (of embassies and of virtues and vices) have escaped the injuries of time. In every station, the reader might contemplate the image of the past world, apply the lesson or warning of each page, and learn to admire, perhaps to imitate, the examples of a brighter period. I shall not expatiate on the works of the Byzantine Greeks who, by the assiduous study of the ancients, have deserved in some measure the remembrance and gratitude of the moderns. The scholars of the present age may still enjoy the benefit of the philosophical commonplace book of Stobaeus, the grammatical and historical lexicon of Suidas, the Chiliads of Tzetzes, which comprise six hundred narratives in twelve thousand verses, and the commentaries on Homer of Eustathius, archbishop of Thessalonica, who from his horn of plenty has poured the names and authorities of four hundred writers. From these originals, and from the numerous tribe of scholiasts and critics, some estimate may be formed of the literary wealth of the twelfth century: Constantinople was enlightened by the genius of Homer and Demosthenes, of Aristotle and Plato: and in the enjoyment or neglect of our present riches, we must envy the generation that could still peruse the history of Theopompus, the orations of Hyperides, the comedies of Menander, and the odes of Alcaeus and Sappho. The frequent labor of illustration attests not only the existence but the popularity of the Grecian classics: the general knowledge of the age may be deduced from the example of two learned females, the empress Eudocia and the princess Anna Comnena, who cultivated in the purple the arts of rhetoric and philosophy. The vulgar dialect of the city was gross and barbarous: a more correct and elaborate style distinguished the discourse, or at least the compositions, of the church and palace, which sometimes affected to copy the purity of the Attic models.

In our modern education, the painful though necessary attainment of two languages which are no longer living may consume the time and damp the ardor of the youthful student. The poets and orators were long imprisoned in the barbarous dialects of our Western ancestors, devoid of harmony or grace; and their genius, without precept or example, was abandoned to the rude and native powers of their judgment and fancy. But the Greeks of Constantinople, after purging away the impurities of their vulgar speech, acquired the free use of their ancient language, the most happy composition of human art, and a familiar knowledge of the sublime masters who had pleased or instructed the first of nations. But these advantages only tend to aggravate the reproach and shame of a degenerate people. They held in their lifeless hands the riches of their fathers without inheriting the spirit which had created and improved that sacred patrimony: they read, they praised, they compiled, but their languid souls seemed alike incapable of thought and action. In the revolution of ten centuries, not a single discovery was made to exalt the dignity or promote the happiness of mankind. Not a single idea has been added to the speculative systems of antiquity, and a succession of patient disciples became in their turn the dogmatic teachers of the next servile generation. Not a single composition of history, philosophy, or literature has been saved from oblivion by the intrinsic beauties of style or sentiment, of original fancy, or even of successful imitation. In prose, the least offensive of the Byzantine writers are absolved from censure by their naked and unpresuming simplicity: but the orators most eloquent in their own conceit are the farthest removed from the models whom they affect to emulate. In every page our taste and reason are wounded by the choice of gigantic and obsolete words, a stiff and intricate phraseology, the discord of images, the childish play of false or unseasonable ornament, and the painful attempt to elevate themselves, to astonish the reader, and to involve a trivial meaning in the smoke of obscurity and exaggeration. Their prose is soaring to the vicious affectation of poetry: their poetry is sinking below the flatness and insipidity of prose. The tragic, epic, and lyric muses were silent and inglorious: the bards of Constantinople seldom rose above a riddle or epigram, a panegyric or tale; they forgot even the rules of prosody; and with the melody of Homer yet sounding in their ears, they confound all measure of feet and syllables in the impotent strains which have received the name of *political* or city verses. The minds of the Greek were bound in the fetters of a base and imperious superstition which extends her dominion round the circle of profane science. Their understandings were bewildered in metaphysical controversy: in the belief of visions and miracles, they had lost all principles of moral evidence, and their taste was vitiated by the homilies of the monks, an absurd medley of declamation and Scripture. Even these contemptible studies were no longer dignified by the abuse of superior talents: the leaders of the Greek church were humbly content to admire and copy the oracles of antiquity, nor did the schools of pulpit produce any rivals of the fame of Athanasius and Chrysostom.

In all the pursuits of active and speculative life, the emulation of states and individuals is the most powerful spring of the efforts and improvements of mankind. The cities of ancient Greece were cast in the happy mixture of union and independence, which is repeated on a larger scale but in a looser form by the nations of modern Europe: the union of language, religion, and manners, which renders them the spectators and judges of each other's merit; the independence of government and interest, which asserts their separate freedom and excites them to strive for preeminence in the career of glory. The situation of the Romans was less favorable; yet in the early ages of the republic, which fixed the national character, a similar emulation was kindled among the states of Latium and Italy; and in the arts and sciences, they aspired to equal or surpass their Grecian masters. The empire of the Caesars undoubtedly checked the activity and progress of the human mind; its magnitude might indeed allow some scope for domestic competition; but when it was gradually reduced, at first to the East and at last to Greece and Constantinople, the Byzantine subjects were degraded to an abject and languid temper, the natural effect of their solitary and insulated state. From the North they were oppressed by nameless tribes of Barbarians, to whom they scarcely imparted the appellation of men. The language and religion of the more polished Arabs were an insurmountable bar to all social intercourse. The conquerors of Europe were their brethren in the Christian faith; but the speech of the Franks or Latins was unknown, their manners were rude, and they were rarely connected in peace or war with the successors of Heraclius. Alone in the universe, the self-satisfied pride of the Greeks was not disturbed by the comparison of foreign merit; and it is no wonder if they fainted in the race, since they had neither competitors to urge their speed nor judges to crown their victory. The nations of Europe and Asia were mingled by the expeditions to the Holy Land; and it is under the Comnenian dynasty that a faint emulation of knowledge and military virtue was rekindled in the Byzantine empire.

CHAPTER LIV

Origin and Doctrine of the Paulicians

Origin and doctrine of the Paulicians. • *Their persecution by the Greek emperors.* • *Revolt in Armenia, etc.* • *Propagation in the West.* • *The seeds, character, and consequences of the Reformation.*[†]

In the profession of Christianity, the variety of national characters may be clearly distinguished. The natives of Syria and Egypt abandoned their lives to lazy and contemplative devotion: Rome again aspired to the dominion of the world; and the wit of the lively and loquacious Greeks was consumed in the disputes of metaphysical theology. The incomprehensible mysteries of the Trinity and Incarnation, instead of commanding their silent submission, were agitated in vehement and subtle controversies which enlarged their faith at the expense, perhaps, of their charity and reason. From the council of Nice to the end of the seventh century, the peace and unity of the church was invaded by these spiritual wars; and so deeply did they affect the decline and fall of the empire that the historian has too often been compelled to attend the synods, to explore the creeds, and to enumerate the sects of this busy period of ecclesiastical annals. From the beginning of the eighth century to the last ages of the Byzantine empire, the sound of controversy was seldom heard: curiosity was exhausted, zeal was fatigued, and in the decrees of six councils, the articles of the Catholic faith had been irrevocably defined. The spirit of dispute, however vain and pernicious, requires some energy and exercise of the mental faculties; and the prostrate Greeks were content to fast, to pray, and to believe in blind obedience to the patriarch and his clergy. During a long dream of superstition, the Virgin and the saints, their visions and miracles, their relics and images, were preached by the monks and worshiped by the people; and the appellation of people might be extended without injustice to the first ranks of civil society. At an unseasonable moment, the Isaurian emperors attempted somewhat rudely to awaken their subjects: under their influence reason might obtain some proselytes; a far greater number was swayed by interest or fear; but the Eastern world embraced or deplored their visible deities, and the restoration of images was celebrated as the feast of orthodoxy [A.D. 843]. In this passive and unanimous state the ecclesiastical rulers were relieved from the toil, or deprived of the pleasure, of persecution. The Pagans had disappeared; the Jews were silent and obscure; the disputes with the Latins were rare and remote hostilities against a national enemy; and the sects of Egypt and Syria enjoyed a free toleration under the shadow of the Arabian caliphs. About the middle of the seventh century, a branch of Manichaeans was selected as the victims of spiritual tyranny; their patience was at length exasperated to despair and rebellion; and their exile has scattered over the West the seeds of reformation. These important events will justify some inquiry into the doctrine and story of the PAULICIANS; and as they cannot plead for themselves, our candid criticism will magnify the *good* and abate or suspect the *evil* that is reported by their adversaries.

The Gnostics, who had distracted the infancy, were oppressed by the greatness and authority, of the church. Instead of emulating or surpassing the wealth, learning, and numbers of the Catholics, their obscure remnant was driven from the capitals of the East and West and confined to the villages and mountains along the borders of the Euphrates. Some vestige of the Marcionites may be detected in the fifth century; but the numerous sects were finally lost in the odious name of the Manichaeans; and these heretics, who presumed to reconcile the doctrines of Zoroaster and Christ, were pursued by the two religions with equal and unrelenting hatred. Under the grandson of Heraclius, in the neighborhood of Samosata, more famous for the birth of Lucian than for the title of a Syrian kingdom, a reformer arose, esteemed by the *Paulicians* as the chosen messenger of truth [A.D. 660 ff.]. In his humble dwelling of Mananalis, Constantine entertained a deacon who returned from Syrian captivity and received the inestimable gift of the New Testament, which was already concealed from the vulgar by the prudence of the Greek, and perhaps of the Gnostic, clergy. These books became the measure of his studies and the rule of his faith; and the Catholics, who dispute his interpretation, acknowledge that his text was genuine and sincere. But he attached himself with peculiar devotion to the writings and character of St. Paul: the name of the Paulicians is derived by their enemies from some unknown and domestic teacher; but I am confident that they gloried in their affinity to the apostle of the Gentiles. His disciples, Titus, Timothy, Sylvanus, Tychicus, were represented by Constantine and his fellow-laborers: the names of the apostolic churches were applied to the congregations which they assembled in Armenia and Cappadocia; and this innocent allegory revived the example and memory of the first ages. In the Gospel and the Epistles of St. Paul, his faithful follower investigated the creed of primitive Christianity; and, whatever might be the success, a Protestant reader will applaud the spirit of the inquiry. But if the Scriptures of the Paulicians were pure, they were not perfect. Their founders rejected the two Epistles of St. Peter, the apostle of the circumcision, whose dispute with their favorite for the observance of the law could not easily be forgiven. They agreed with their Gnostic brethren in the universal contempt for the Old Testament, the books of Moses and the prophets, which have been consecrated by the decrees of the Catholic church.[†]

Of the ecclesiastical chain, many links had been broken by the Paulician reformers; and their liberty was enlarged as they reduced the number of masters at whose voice profane reason must bow to mystery and miracle. The early separation of the Gnostics had preceded the establishment of the Catholic worship; and against the gradual innovations of discipline and doctrine they were as strongly guarded by habit and aversion as by the silence of St. Paul and the evangelists. The objects which had been transformed by the magic of superstition appeared to the eyes of the Paulicians in their genuine and naked colors. An image made without hands was the common workmanship of a mortal artist, to whose skill alone the wood and canvas must be indebted for their merit or value. The miraculous relics were a heap of bones and ashes, destitute of life or virtue, or of any relation, perhaps, with the person to whom they were ascribed. The true and vivifying cross was a piece of sound or rotten timber, the body and blood of Christ a loaf of bread and a cup of wine, the gifts of nature and the symbols of grace. The mother of God was degraded from her celestial honors and immaculate virginity; and the saints and angels were no longer solicited to exercise the laborious office of meditation in Heaven and ministry upon earth. In the practice, or at least in the theory, of the sacraments, the Paulicians were inclined to abolish all visible objects of worship, and the words of the gospel were in their judgment the baptism and communion of the faithful. They indulged a convenient latitude for the interpretation of Scripture: and as often as they were pressed by the literal sense, they could escape to the intricate mazes of figure and allegory. Their utmost diligence must have been employed to dissolve the connection between the Old and the New Testament; since they adored the latter as the oracles of God, and abhorred the former as the fabulous and absurd invention of men or demons. We cannot be surprised that they should have found in the gospel the orthodox mystery of the Trinity: but instead of confessing the human nature and substantial sufferings of Christ, they amused their fancy with a celestial body that passed through the virgin like water through a pipe; with a fantastic crucifixion that eluded the vain and impotent malice of the Jews. A creed thus simple and spiritual was not adapted to the genius of the times; and the rational Christian who might have been contented with the light yoke and easy burden of Jesus and his apostles was justly offended that the Paulicians should dare to violate the unity of God, the first article of natural and revealed religion. Their belief and their trust was in the Father of Christ, of the human soul, and of the invisible world. But they likewise held the eternity of matter, a stubborn and rebellious substance, the origin of a second principle of an active being who has created this visible world and exercises his temporal reign till the final consummation of death and sin. The appearances of moral and physical evil had established the two principles in the ancient philosophy and religion of the East; from whence this doctrine was transfused to the various swarms of the Gnostics. A thousand shades may be devised in the nature and character of *Ahriman,* from a rival god to a subordinate demon, from passion and frailty to pure and perfect malevolence: but in spite of our efforts, the goodness and the power of Ormusd are placed at the opposite extremities of the line; and every step that approaches the one must recede in equal proportion from the other.[†]

The most furious and desperate of rebels are the sectaries of a religion long persecuted and at length provoked. In a holy cause they are no longer susceptible of fear or remorse: the justice of their arms hardens them against the feelings of humanity; and they revenge their fathers' wrongs on the children of their tyrants. Such have been the

Hussites of Bohemia and the Calvinists of France, and such in the ninth century were the Paulicians of Armenia and the adjacent provinces [A.D. 845–880]. . . . During more than thirty years, Asia was afflicted by the calamities of foreign and domestic war; in their hostile inroads, the disciples of St. Paul were joined with those of Mohammed; and the peaceful Christians, the aged parent and tender virgin, who were delivered into barbarous servitude, might justly accuse the intolerant spirit of their sovereign [whose conduct had provoked the rebellion]. . . . In alliance with [the] faithful Moslems, [the Paulicians] boldly penetrated into the heart of Asia; the troops of the frontier and the palace were repeatedly overthrown; the edicts of persecution were answered by the pillage of Nice and Nicomedia, of Ancyra and Ephesus; nor could the apostle St. John protect from violation his city and sepulchre. The cathedral of Ephesus was turned into a stable for mules and horses; and the Paulicians vied with the Saracens in their contempt and abhorrence of images and relics. It is not unpleasing to observe the triumph of rebellion over the same despotism which had disdained the prayers of an injured people. The emperor Basil, the Macedonian, was reduced to sue for peace, to offer a ransom for the captives, and to request, in the language of moderation and charity, that Chrysocheir would spare his fellow-Christians and content himself with a royal donative of gold and silver and silk garments. "If the emperor," replied the insolent fanatic, "be desirous of peace, let him abdicate the East and reign without molestation in the West. If he refuse, the servants of the Lord will precipitate him from the throne." The reluctant Basil suspended the treaty, accepted the defiance, and led his army into the land of heresy, which he wasted with fire and sword. The open country of the Paulicians was exposed to the same calamities which they had inflicted [circa A.D. 871–872]; . . . [but they] defended, above a century, their religion and liberty, infested the Roman limits, and maintained their perpetual alliance with the enemies of the empire and the gospel.[†]

In the West . . . [three] different roads might introduce the Paulicians into the heart of Europe. After the conversion of Hungary, the pilgrims who visited Jerusalem might safely follow the course of the Danube: in their journey and return they passed through Philippopolis; and the sectaries, disguising their name and heresy, might accompany the French or German caravans to their respective countries.

The trade and dominion of *Venice* pervaded the coast of the Adriatic, and the hospitable republic opened her bosom to foreigners of every climate and religion. Under the Byzantine standard, the Paulicians were often transported to the Greek provinces of Italy and Sicily: in peace and war, they freely conversed with strangers and natives, and their opinions were silently propagated in Rome, Milan, and the kingdoms beyond the Alps. It was soon discovered that many thousand Catholics of every rank and of either sex had embraced the Manichaean heresy; and the flames which consumed the twelve canons of Orleans was the first act and signal of persecution.... United in common hatred of idolatry and Rome, they were connected by a form of episcopal and presbyterian government; their various sects were discriminated by some fainter or darker shades of theology; but they generally agreed in the two principles, the contempt of the Old Testament and the denial of the body of Christ, either on the cross or in the Eucharist. A confession of simple worship and blameless manners is extorted from their enemies; and so high was their standard of perfection that the increasing congregations were divided into two classes of disciples, of those who practiced and of those who aspired. It was in the country of the Albigeois, in the southern provinces of France, that the Paulicians were most deeply implanted [A.D. 1200 ff.]; and the same vicissitudes of martyrdom and revenge which had been displayed in the neighborhood of the Euphrates were repeated in the thirteenth century on the banks of the Rhone.... Pope Innocent III surpassed the sanguinary fame of Theodora. It was in cruelty alone that her soldiers could equal the heroes of the Crusades, and the cruelty of her priests was far excelled by the founders of the Inquisition, an office more adapted to confirm than to refute the belief of an evil principle. The visible assemblies of the Paulicians, or Albigeois, were extirpated by fire and sword; and the bleeding remnant escaped by flight, concealment, or Catholic conformity. But the invincible spirit which they had kindled still lived and breathed in the Western world. In the state, in the church, and even in the cloister, a latent succession was preserved of the disciples of St. Paul, who protested against the tyranny of Rome, embraced the Bible as the rule of faith, and purified their creed from all the visions of the Gnostic theology. The struggles of Wickliff in England, of Huss in Bohemia, were premature and ineffectual; but the names of Zuinglius, Luther, and Calvin are pronounced with gratitude as the deliverers of nations.

A philosopher who calculates the degree of their merit and the value of their reformation will prudently ask from what articles of faith, *above* or *against* our reason, they have enfranchised the Christians; for such enfranchisement is doubtless a benefit so far as it may be compatible with truth and piety. After a fair discussion, we shall rather be surprised by the timidity than scandalized by the freedom of our first reformers. With the Jews, they adopted the belief and defense of all the Hebrew Scriptures, with all their prodigies, from the garden of Eden to the visions of the prophet Daniel; and they were bound, like the Catholics, to justify against the Jews the abolition of a divine law. In the great mysteries of the Trinity and Incarnation the reformers were severely orthodox: they freely adopted the theology of the four, or the six, first councils; and with the Athanasian creed, they pronounced the eternal damnation of all who did not believe the Catholic faith. Transubstantiation, the invisible change of the bread and wine into the body and blood of Christ, is a tenet that may defy the power of argument and pleasantry; but instead of consulting the evidence of their senses, of their sight, their feeling, and their taste, the first Protestants were entangled in their own scruples, and awed by the words of Jesus in the institution of the sacrament. Luther maintained a *corporeal* and Calvin a *real* presence of Christ in the eucharist; and the opinion of Zuinglius that it is no more than a spiritual communion, a simple memorial, has slowly prevailed in the reformed churches. But the loss of one mystery was amply compensated by the stupendous doctrines of original sin, redemption, faith, grace, and predestination, which have been strained from the epistles of St. Paul. These subtle questions had most assuredly been prepared by the fathers and schoolmen; but the final improvement and popular use may be attributed to the first reformers, who enforced them as the absolute and essential terms of salvation. Hitherto the weight of supernatural belief inclines against the Protestants; and many a sober Christian would rather admit that a wafer is God than that God is a cruel and capricious tyrant.

Yet the services of Luther and his rivals are solid and important; and the philosopher must own his obligations to these fearless enthusiasts. I. By their hands the lofty fabric of superstition, from the abuse of indulgences to the intercession of the Virgin, has been leveled with the ground. Myriads of both sexes of the monastic profession were restored to the liberty and labors of social life. A hierarchy of saints and angels, of imperfect and subordinate deities, were stripped of their temporal power and reduced to the enjoyment of celestial happiness; their images and relics were banished from the church; and the credulity of the people was no longer nourished with the daily repetition of miracles and visions. The imitation of Paganism was supplied by a pure and spiritual worship of prayer and thanksgiving, the most worthy of man, the least unworthy of the Deity. It only remains to observe whether such sublime simplicity be consistent with popular devotion; whether the vulgar, in the absence of all visible objects, will not be inflamed by enthusiasm, or insensibly subside in languor and indifference. II. The chain of authority was broken which restrains the bigot from thinking as he pleases and the slave from speaking as he thinks: the popes, fathers, and councils were no longer the supreme and infallible judges of the world; and each Christian was taught to acknowledge no law but the Scriptures, no interpreter but his own conscience. This freedom, however, was the consequence rather than the design of the Reformation. The patriot reformers were ambitious of succeeding the tyrants whom they had dethroned. They imposed with equal rigor their creeds and confessions; they asserted the right of the magistrate to punish heretics with death. The pious or personal animosity of Calvin proscribed in Servetus the guilt of his own rebellion; and the flames of Smithfield, in which he was afterwards consumed, had been kindled for the Anabaptists by the zeal of Cranmer. The nature of the tiger was the same, but he was gradually deprived of his teeth and fangs. A spiritual and temporal kingdom was possessed by the Roman pontiff; the Protestant doctors were subjects of an humble rank, without revenue or jurisdiction. *His* decrees were consecrated by the antiquity of the Catholic church: *their* arguments and disputes were submitted to the people; and their appeal to private judgment was accepted beyond their wishes, by curiosity and enthusiasm. Since the days of Luther and Calvin, a secret reformation has been silently working in the bosom of the reformed churches; many weeds of prejudice were eradicated; and the disciples of Erasmus diffused a spirit of freedom and moderation. The liberty of conscience has been claimed as a common benefit, an inalienable right: the free governments of

Holland and England introduced the practice of toleration; and the narrow allowance of the laws has been enlarged by the prudence and humanity of the times. In the exercise, the mind has understood the limits of its powers, and the words and shadows that might amuse the child can no longer satisfy his manly reason. The volumes of controversy are overspread with cobwebs: the doctrine of a Protestant church is far removed from the knowledge or belief of its private members; and the forms of orthodoxy, the articles of faith, are subscribed with a sigh or a smile by the modern clergy. Yet the friends of Christianity are alarmed at the boundless impulse of inquiry and skepticism. The predictions of the Catholics are accomplished: the web of mystery is unraveled by the Armenians, Arians, and Socinians, whose number must not be computed from their separate congregations; and the pillars of Revelation are shaken by those men who preserve the name without the substance of religion, who indulge the license without the temper of philosophy.

CHAPTER LV

The Bulgarians, the Hungarians, and the Russians

The Bulgarians. • Origin, migrations, and settlement of the Hungarians. • The monarchy of Russia. • Wars of the Russians against the Greek empire. • Conversion of the Barbarians.[†]

Under the reign of Constantine, the grandson of Heraclius, the ancient barrier of the Danube, so often violated and so often restored, was irretrievably swept away by a new deluge of Barbarians. Their progress was favored by the caliphs, their unknown and accidental auxiliaries: the Roman legions were occupied in Asia; and after the loss of Syria, Egypt, and Africa, the Caesars were twice reduced to the danger and disgrace of defending their capital against the Saracens. If in the account of this interesting people I have deviated from the strict and original line of my undertaking, the merit of the subject will hide my transgression, or solicit my excuse. In the East, in the West, in war, in religion, in science, in their prosperity, and in their decay, the Arabians press themselves on our curiosity: the first overthrow of the church and empire of the Greeks may be imputed to their arms; and the disciples of Mohammed still hold the civil and religious scepter of the Oriental world. But the same labor would be unworthily bestowed on the swarms of savages who, between the seventh and the twelfth century, descended from the plains of Scythia, in transient inroad or perpetual emigration. Their names are uncouth, their origins doubtful, their actions obscure; their superstition was blind, their valor brutal, and the uniformity of their public and private lives was neither softened by innocence nor refined by policy. The majesty of the Byzantine throne repelled and survived their disorderly attacks; the greater part of these Barbarians has disappeared without leaving any memorial of their existence, and the despicable remnant continues, and may long continue, to groan under the dominion of a foreign tyrant. From the antiquities of I. *Bulgarians,* II. *Hungarians,* and III. *Russians,* I shall content myself with selecting such facts as yet deserve to be remembered. The conquests of the IV. *Normans,* and the monarchy of the V. *Turks,* will naturally terminate in the memorable Crusades to the Holy Land, and the double fall of the city and empire of Constantine.[†]

I. The glory of the Bulgarians was confined to a narrow scope both of time and place. In the ninth and tenth centuries, they reigned to the south of the Danube; but the more powerful nations that had followed their emigration repelled all return to the north and all progress to the west. . . . [I]n the beginning of the eleventh century, the second Basil, who was born in the purple, deserved the appellation of conqueror of the Bulgarians [A.D. 1014]. . . . His cruelty inflicted a cool and exquisite vengeance on fifteen thousand captives who had been guilty of the defense of their country. They were deprived of sight; but to one of each hundred a single eye was left, that he might conduct his blind century to the presence of their king. Their king is said to have expired of grief and horror; the nation was awed by this terrible example; the Bulgarians were swept away from their settlements and circumscribed within a narrow province; the surviving chiefs bequeathed to their children the advice of patience and the duty of revenge.

II. When the black swarm of Hungarians first hung over Europe, above nine hundred years after the Christian era, they were mistaken by fear and superstition for the Gog and Magog of the Scriptures, the signs and forerunners of the end of the world. Since the introduction of letters, they have explored their own antiquities with a strong and laudable impulse of patriotic curiosity. Their rational criticism can no longer be amused with a vain pedigree of Attila and the Huns; but they complain that their primitive records have perished in the Tartar war; that the truth or fiction of their rustic songs is long since forgotten; and that the fragments of a rude chronicle must be painfully reconciled with the contemporary though foreign intelligence of the Imperial geographer. *Magiar* is the national and Oriental denomination of the Hungarians; but among the tribes of Scythia, they are distinguished by the Greeks under the proper and peculiar name of *Turks,* as the descendants of that mighty people who had conquered and reigned from China to the Volga.[†]

III. The name of RUSSIANS was first divulged in the ninth century by an embassy of Theophilus, emperor of the East, to the emperor of the West, Lewis, the son of Charlemagne. The Greeks were accompanied by the envoys of the great duke, or chagan, or *czar* of the Russians. In their journey to Constantinople, they had traversed many hostile nations [A.D. 839]; and they hoped to escape the dangers of their return by requesting the French monarch to transport them by sea to their native country. A closer examination detected their origin: they were the brethren of the Swedes and Normans, whose name was already odious and formidable in France; and it might justly be apprehended that these Russian strangers were not the messengers of peace but the emissaries of war. They were detained, while the Greeks were dismissed; and Lewis expected a more satisfactory account, that he might obey the laws of hospitality or prudence, according to the interest of both empires. This Scandinavian origin of the people, or at least the princes, of Russia may be confirmed and illustrated by the national annals and the general history of the North. The Normans, who had so long been concealed by a veil of impenetrable darkness, suddenly burst forth in the spirit of naval and military enterprise. The vast and, as it is said, the populous regions of Denmark, Sweden, and Norway were crowded with independent chieftains and desperate adventurers who sighed in the laziness of peace and smiled in the agonies of death. Piracy was the exercise, the trade, the glory, and the virtue of the Scandinavian youth. Impatient of a bleak climate and narrow limits, they started from the banquet, grasped their arms, sounded their horn, ascended their vessels, and explored every coast that promised either spoil or settlement. The Baltic was the first scene of their naval achievements; they visited the eastern shores, the silent residence of Fennic and Sclavonic tribes, and the primitive Russians of the Lake Ladoga paid a tribute, the skins of white squirrels, to these strangers, whom they saluted with the title of *Varangians* or Corsairs. Their superiority in arms, discipline, and renown commanded the fear and reverence of the natives. In their wars against the more inland savages, the Varangians condescended to serve as friends and auxiliaries, and gradually, by choice or conquest, obtained the dominion of a people whom they were qualified to protect. Their tyranny was expelled, their valor was again recalled, till at length Ruric, a Scandinavian chief, became the father of a dynasty which reigned above seven hundred years [A.D. 862]. His brothers extended his influence: the example of service and usurpation was imitated by his companions in the southern provinces of Russia; and their establishments, by the usual methods of war and assassination, were cemented into the fabric of a powerful monarchy.

As long as the descendants of Ruric were considered as aliens and conquerors, they ruled by the sword of the Varangians, distributed estates and subjects to their faithful captains, and supplied their numbers with fresh streams of adventurers from the Baltic coast. But when the Scandinavian chiefs had struck a deep and permanent root into the soil, they mingled with the Russians in blood, religion, and language.†

In a period of one hundred and ninety years, the Russians made four attempts to plunder the treasures of Constantinople: the event was various, but the motive, the means, and the object were the same in these naval expeditions. The Russian traders had seen the magnificence and tasted the luxury of the city of the Caesars. A marvelous tale and a scanty supply excited the desires of their savage countrymen: they envied the gifts of nature which their climate denied; they coveted the works of art which they were too lazy to imitate and too indigent to purchase; the Varangian princes unfurled the banners of piratical adventure, and their bravest soldiers were drawn from the nations that dwelt in the northern isles of the ocean. . . . Had the Greek emperors been endowed with foresight to discern and vigor to prevent, perhaps they might have sealed with a maritime force the mouth of the Borysthenes. Their indolence abandoned the coast of Anatolia to the calamities of a piratical war which, after an interval of six hundred years, again infested the Euxine; but as long as the capital was respected, the sufferings of a distant province escaped the notice both of the prince and the historian.†

Photius of Constantinople, a patriarch whose ambition was equal to his curiosity, congratulates himself and the Greek church on the conversion of the Russians [A.D. 864]. Those fierce and bloody Barbarians had been persuaded, by the voice of reason and religion, to acknowledge Jesus for their God, the Christian missionaries for their teachers, and the Romans for their friends and brethren. His triumph was transient and premature. In the various fortune of their piratical adventures, some Russian chiefs might allow themselves to be sprinkled with the waters of baptism; and a Greek bishop with the name of metropolitan might administer the sacraments in the church of Kiow to a congregation of slaves and natives. But the seed of the gospel was sown on a barren soil: many were the apostates, the converts were few; and the baptism of Olga may be fixed as the era of Russian Christianity [A.D. 957]. A female, perhaps of the basest origin, who could revenge the death and assume the scepter of her husband Igor must have been endowed with those active virtues which command the fear and obedience of Barbarians. In a moment of foreign and domestic peace, she sailed from Kiow to Constantinople; and the emperor Constantine Porphyrogenitus has described with minute diligence the ceremonial of her reception in his capital and palace. The steps, the titles, the salutations, the banquet, the presents were exquisitely adjusted to gratify the vanity of the stranger, with due reverence to the superior majesty of the purple. In the sacrament of baptism, she received the venerable name of the empress Helena; and her conversion might be preceded or followed by her uncle, two interpreters, sixteen damsels of a higher, and eighteen of a lower, rank, twenty-two domestics or ministers, and forty-four Russian merchants, who composed the retinue of the great princess Olga. After her return to Kiow and Novogorod, she firmly persisted in her new religion; but her labors in the propagation of the gospel were not crowned with success; and both her family and nation adhered with obstinacy or indifference to the gods of their fathers. Her son Swatoslaus was apprehensive of the scorn and ridicule of his companions; and her grandson Wolodomir devoted his youthful zeal to multiply and decorate the monuments of ancient worship. The savage deities of the North were still propitiated with human sacrifices: in the choice of the victim, a citizen was preferred to a stranger, a Christian to an idolater; and the father who defended his son from the sacerdotal knife was involved in the same doom by the rage of a fanatic tumult. Yet the lessons and example of the pious Olga had made a deep, though secret, impression in the minds of the prince and people: the Greek missionaries continued to preach, to dispute, and to baptize: and the ambassadors or merchants of Russia compared the idolatry of the woods with the elegant superstition of Constantinople. They had gazed with admiration on the dome of St. Sophia: the lively pictures of saints and martyrs, the riches of the altar, the number and vestments of the priests, the pomp and order of the ceremonies; they were edified by the alternate succession of devout silence and harmonious song; nor was it difficult to persuade them that a choir of angels descended each day from Heaven to join in the devotion of the Christians. But the conversion of Wolodomir was determined, or hastened, by his desire of a Roman bride [A.D. 989]. At the same time, and in the city of Cherson, the rites of baptism and marriage were celebrated by the Christian pontiff: the city he restored to the emperor Basil, the brother of his spouse; but the brazen gates were transported, as it is said, to Novogorod, and erected before the first church as a trophy of his victory and faith. At his despotic command, Peround, the god of thunder whom he had so long adored, was dragged through the streets of Kiow; and twelve sturdy Barbarians battered with clubs the misshapen image, which was indignantly cast into the waters of the Borysthenes. The edict of Wolodomir had proclaimed that all who should refuse the rites of baptism would be treated as the enemies of God and their prince; and the rivers were instantly filled with many thousands of obedient Russians who acquiesced in the truth and excellence of a doctrine which had been embraced by the great duke and his boyars. In the next generation, the relics of Paganism were finally extirpated; but as the two brothers of Wolodomir had died without baptism, their bones were taken from the grave and sanctified by an irregular and posthumous sacrament.

In the ninth, tenth, and eleventh centuries of the Christian era, the reign of the gospel and of the church was extended over Bulgaria, Hungary, Bohemia, Saxony, Denmark, Norway, Sweden, Poland, and Russia. The triumphs of apostolic zeal were repeated in the iron age of Christianity; and the northern and eastern regions of Europe submitted to a religion more different in theory than in practice from the worship of their native idols. A laudable ambition excited the monks both of Germany and Greece to visit the tents and huts of the Barbarians: poverty, hardships, and dangers were the lot of the first missionaries; their courage was active and patient; their motive pure and meritorious; their present reward consisted in the testimony of their conscience and the respect of a grateful people; but the fruitful harvest of their toils was inherited and enjoyed by the proud and wealthy prelates of succeeding times. The first conversions were free and spontaneous: a holy life and an eloquent tongue were the only arms of the missionaries; but the domestic fables of the Pagans were silenced by the miracles and visions of the strangers; and the favorable temper of the chiefs was accelerated by the dictates of vanity and interest. The leaders of nations, who were saluted with the titles of kings and saints, held it lawful and pious to impose the Catholic faith on their subjects and neighbors; the coast of the Baltic, from Holstein to the Gulf of Finland, was invaded under the standard of the cross; and the reign of idolatry was closed by the conversion of Lithuania in the fourteenth century. Yet truth and candor must acknowledge that the conversion of the North imparted many temporal benefits both to the old and the new Christians. The rage of war, inherent to the human species, could not be healed by the evangelic precepts of charity and peace; and the ambition of Catholic princes has renewed in every age the calamities of hostile contention. But the admission of the Barbarians into the pale of civil and ecclesiastical society delivered Europe from the depredations, by sea and land, of the Normans, the Hungarians, and the Russians, who learned to spare their brethren and cultivate their possessions. The establishment of law and order was promoted by the influence of the clergy; and the rudiments of art and science were introduced into the savage countries of the globe. The liberal piety of the Russian princes engaged in their service the most skillful of the Greeks to decorate the cities and instruct the inhabitants: the dome and the paintings of St. Sophia were rudely copied in the churches of Kiow and Novogorod: the writings of the fathers were translated into the Sclavonic idiom; and three hundred noble youths were invited or compelled to attend the lessons of the college of Jaroslaus. It should appear that Russia might have derived an early and rapid improvement from her peculiar connection with the church and state of Constantinople, which at that age so justly despised the ignorance of the Latins. But the Byzantine nation was servile, solitary, and verging to a hasty decline: after the fall of Kiow, the navigation of the Borysthenes was forgotten; the great princes of Wolodomir and Moscow were separated from the sea and Christendom; and the divided monarchy was oppressed by the ignominy and blindness of Tartar servitude. The Sclavonic and Scandinavian kingdoms, which had been converted by the Latin missionaries, were exposed, it is true, to the spiritual jurisdiction and temporal claims of the popes; but they were united in language and religious worship with each other and with Rome; they imbibed the free and generous spirit of the European republic, and gradually shared the light of knowledge which arose on the Western world.

CHAPTER LVI

The Saracens, the Franks, and the Normans

The Saracens, Franks, and Greeks in Italy. • First adventures and settlement of the Normans. • Character and conquest of Robert Guiscard, duke of Apulia. • Deliverance of Sicily by his brother Roger. • Victories of Robert over the emperors of the East and West. • Roger, king of Sicily, invades Africa and Greece. • Wars of the Greeks and Normans. • Extinction of the Normans.[†]

The three great nations of the world, the Greeks, the Saracens, and the Franks, encountered each other on the theater of Italy [A.D. 840–1017]. The southern provinces, which now compose the kingdom of Naples, were subject for the most part to the Lombard dukes and princes of Beneventum; so powerful in war that they checked for a moment the genius of Charlemagne; so liberal in peace that they maintained in their capital an academy of thirty-two philosophers and grammarians. The division of this flourishing state produced the rival principalities of Benevento, Salerno, and Capua; and the thoughtless ambition or revenge of the competitors invited the Saracens to the ruin of their common inheritance. During a calamitous period of two hundred years, Italy was exposed to a repetition of wounds which the invaders were not capable of healing by the union and tranquility of a perfect conquest. Their frequent and almost annual squadrons issued from the port of Palermo and were entertained with too much indulgence by the Christians of Naples: the more formidable fleets were prepared on the African coast; and even the Arabs of Andalusia were sometimes tempted to assist or oppose the Moslems of an adverse sect. In the revolution of human events, a new ambuscade was concealed in the Caudine Forks, the fields of Cannae were bedewed a second time with the blood of the Africans, and the sovereign of Rome again attacked or defended the walls of Capua and Tarentum.[†]

The revolution of human affairs had produced in Apulia and Calabria a melancholy contrast between the age of Pythagoras and the

tenth century of the Christian era. At the former period, the coast of
Great Greece (as it was then styled) was planted with free and opulent
cities: these cities were peopled with soldiers, artists, and philosophers; and the military strength of Tarentum, Sybaris, or Crotona was
not inferior to that of a powerful kingdom. At the second era, these
once flourishing provinces were clouded with ignorance, impoverished by tyranny, and depopulated by Barbarian war; nor can we
severely accuse the exaggeration of a contemporary that a fair and
ample district was reduced to the same desolation which had covered
the earth after the general deluge. Among the hostilities of the Arabs,
the Franks, and the Greeks in the southern Italy, I shall select two
or three anecdotes expressive of their national manners. 1. It was the
amusement of the Saracens to profane as well as to pillage the monasteries and churches. At the siege of Salerno [A.D. 872], a Moslem chief
spread his couch on the communion-table, and on that altar sacrificed
each night the virginity of a Christian nun. As he wrestled with a
reluctant maid, a beam in the roof was accidentally or dexterously
thrown down on his head; and the death of the lustful emir was imputed to the wrath of Christ, which was at length awakened to the
defense of his faithful spouse. 2. The Saracens besieged the cities of
Beneventum and Capua [A.D. 874]: after a vain appeal to the successors
of Charlemagne, the Lombards implored the clemency and aid of the
Greek emperor. A fearless citizen dropped from the walls, passed the
entrenchments, accomplished his commission, and fell into the hands
of the Barbarians as he was returning with the welcome news. They
commanded him to assist their enterprise and deceive his countrymen,
with the assurance that wealth and honors should be the reward of his
falsehood, and that his sincerity would be punished with immediate
death. He affected to yield, but as soon as he was conducted within
hearing of the Christians on the rampart, "Friends and brethren," he
cried with a loud voice, "be bold and patient, maintain the city; your
sovereign is informed of your distress, and your deliverers are at hand.
I know my doom, and commit my wife and children to your gratitude."
The rage of the Arabs confirmed his evidence; and the self-devoted
patriot was transpierced with a hundred spears. He deserves to live in
the memory of the virtuous, but the repetition of the same story in ancient and modern times may sprinkle some doubts on the reality of
this generous deed. 3. The recital of a third incident may provoke a

smile amidst the horrors of war. Theobald, marquis of Camerino and Spoleto, supported the rebels of Beneventum [A.D. 930]; and his wanton cruelty was not incompatible in that age with the character of a hero. His captives of the Greek nation or party were castrated without mercy, and the outrage was aggravated by a cruel jest that he wished to present the emperor with a supply of eunuchs, the most precious ornaments of the Byzantine court. The garrison of a castle had been defeated in a sally, and the prisoners were sentenced to the customary operation. But the sacrifice was disturbed by the intrusion of a frantic female who, with bleeding cheeks, disheveled hair, and importunate clamors, compelled the marquis to listen to her complaint. "Is it thus," she cried, "ye magnanimous heroes, that ye wage war against women, against women who have never injured ye, and whose only arms are the distaff and the loom?" Theobald denied the charge and protested that, since the Amazons, he had never heard of a female war. "And how," she furiously exclaimed, "can you attack us more directly, how can you wound us in a more vital part, than by robbing our husbands of what we most dearly cherish, the source of our joys and the hope of our posterity? The plunder of our flocks and herds I have endured without a murmur, but this fatal injury, this irreparable loss, subdues my patience and calls aloud on the justice of Heaven and earth." A general laugh applauded her eloquence; the savage Franks, inaccessible to pity, were moved by her ridiculous yet rational despair; and with the deliverance of the captives, she obtained the restitution of her effects. As she returned in triumph to the castle, she was overtaken by a messenger, to inquire in the name of Theobald what punishment should be inflicted on her husband were he again taken in arms. "Should such," she answered without hesitation, "be his guilt and misfortune, he has eyes, and a nose, and hands, and feet. These are his own, and these he may deserve to forfeit by his personal offenses. But let my lord be pleased to spare what his little handmaid presumes to claim as her peculiar and lawful property."

The establishment of the Normans in the kingdoms of Naples and Sicily is an event most romantic in its origin, and in its consequences most important both to Italy and the Eastern empire [A.D. 1016]. The broken provinces of the Greeks, Lombards, and Saracens were exposed to every invader and every sea and land were invaded by the adventurous spirit of the Scandinavian pirates. After a long indulgence of rapine and slaughter a fair and ample territory was accepted, occupied, and named by the Normans of France: they renounced their gods for the God of the Christians; and the dukes of Normandy acknowledged themselves the vassals of the successors of Charlemagne and Capet. The savage fierceness which they had brought from the snowy mountains of Norway was refined, without being corrupted, in a warmer climate; the companions of Rollo insensibly mingled with the natives; they imbibed the manners, language, and gallantry of the French nation; and in a martial age, the Normans might claim the palm of valor and glorious achievements. Of the fashionable superstitions, they embraced with ardor the pilgrimages of Rome, Italy, and the Holy Land. In this active devotion, the minds and bodies were invigorated by exercise: danger was the incentive, novelty the recompense; and the prospect of the world was decorated by wonder, credulity, and ambitious hope. They confederated for their mutual defense; and the robbers of the Alps who had been allured by the garb of a pilgrim were often chastised by the arm of a warrior.

[*The Normans establish themselves in Apulia (*A.D. *1040 ff.). Pope Leo IX leads an army against these Normans (*A.D. *1053) and acquires temporal jurisdictions while conferring papal investitures.*]

In his long progress from Mantua to Beneventum, a vile and promiscuous multitude of Italians was enlisted under the holy standard [of Pope Leo IX]: the priest and the robber slept in the same tent; the pikes and crosses were intermingled in the front; and the martial saint repeated the lessons of his youth in the order of march, of encampment, and of combat. The Normans of Apulia could muster in the field no more than three thousand horse, with a handful of infantry: the defection of the natives intercepted their provisions and retreat; and their spirit, incapable of fear, was chilled for a moment by superstitious awe. On the hostile approach of Leo, they knelt without disgrace or reluctance before their spiritual father. But the pope was inexorable; his lofty Germans affected to deride the diminutive stature of their adversaries; and the Normans were informed that death or exile was their only alternative. Flight they disdained, and as many of them had been three days without tasting food, they embraced the assurance of a more easy and honorable death. They climbed the hill of

Civitella, descended into the plain, and charged in three divisions the army of the pope. On the left and in the center, Richard, count of Aversa, and Robert, the famous Guiscard, attacked, broke, routed, and pursued the Italian multitudes, who fought without discipline and fled without shame. A harder trial was reserved for the valor of Count Humphrey, who led the cavalry of the right wing. The Germans have been described as unskillful in the management of the horse and the lance, but on foot they formed a strong and impenetrable phalanx; and neither man nor steed nor armor could resist the weight of their long and two-handed swords. After a severe conflict, they were encompassed by the squadrons returning from the pursuit; and died in the ranks with the esteem of their foes and the satisfaction of revenge. The gates of Civitella were shut against the flying pope, and he was overtaken by the pious conquerors, who kissed his feet to implore his blessing and the absolution of their sinful victory. The soldiers beheld in their enemy and captive the vicar of Christ; and though we may suppose the policy of the chiefs, it is probable that they were infected by the popular superstition. In the calm of retirement, the well-meaning pope deplored the effusion of Christian blood, which must be imputed to his account: he felt that he had been the author of sin and scandal; and as his undertaking had failed, the indecency of his military character was universally condemned. With these dispositions, he listened to the offers of a beneficial treaty; deserted an alliance which he had preached as the cause of God; and ratified the past and future conquests of the Normans. By whatever hands they had been usurped, the provinces of Apulia and Calabria were a part of the donation of Constantine and the patrimony of St. Peter: the grant and the acceptance confirmed the mutual claims of the pontiff and the adventurers. They promised to support each other with spiritual and temporal arms; a tribute or quitrent of twelve pence was afterwards stipulated for every ploughland; and since this memorable transaction, the kingdom of Naples has remained above seven hundred years a fief of the holy see.

[*Under Robert Guiscard, the Normans establish the kingdom of Naples (A.D. 1054–1080). Under Count Roger (the twelfth), the Normans conquer Sicily (A.D. 1060–1090).*]

After a war of thirty years, Roger, with the title of great count, obtained the sovereignty of the largest and most fruitful island of the Mediterranean; and his administration displays a liberal and enlightened mind, above the limits of his age and education. The Moslems were maintained in the free enjoyment of their religion and property: a philosopher and physician of Mazara, of the race of Mohammed, harangued the conqueror and was invited to court; his geography of the seven climates was translated into Latin; and Roger, after a diligent perusal, preferred the work of the Arabian to the writings of the Grecian Ptolemy. A remnant of Christian natives had promoted the success of the Normans: they were rewarded by the triumph of the cross. The island was restored to the jurisdiction of the Roman pontiff; new bishops were planted in the principal cities; and the clergy was satisfied by a liberal endowment of churches and monasteries. Yet the Catholic hero asserted the rights of the civil magistrate. Instead of resigning the investiture of benefices, he dexterously applied to his own profit the papal claims: the supremacy of the crown was secured and enlarged by the singular bull which declares the princes of Sicily hereditary and perpetual legates of the holy see.

[*Robert Guiscard invades the Eastern empire with mixed results*
(A.D. 1081). Robert besieges Rome (A.D. 1084) in order to restore Pope
Gregory, who had been deposed by the German king, Henry IV.]

[T]he anti-pope, Clement the Third, was consecrated in the Lateran: the grateful pontiff crowned his protector in the Vatican; and the emperor Henry fixed his residence in the Capitol, as the lawful successor of Augustus and Charlemagne. The ruins of the Septizonium were still defended by the nephew of Gregory: the pope himself was invested in the castle of St. Angelo; and his last hope was in the courage and fidelity of his Norman vassal. Their friendship had been interrupted by some reciprocal injuries and complaints; but on this pressing occasion, Guiscard was urged by the obligation of his oath, by his interest, more potent than oaths, by the love of fame, and his enmity to the two emperors. Unfurling the holy banner, he resolved to fly to the relief of the prince of the apostles: the most numerous of his armies, six thousand horse and thirty thousand foot, was instantly assembled;

and his march from Salerno to Rome was animated by the public applause and the promise of the divine favor. Henry, invincible in sixty-six battles, trembled at his approach; recollected some indispensable affairs that required his presence in Lombardy; exhorted the Romans to persevere in their allegiance; and hastily retreated three days before the entrance of the Normans. In less than three years, the son of Tancred of Hauteville enjoyed the glory of delivering the pope and of compelling the two emperors, of the East and West, to fly before his victorious arms. But the triumph of Robert was clouded by the calamities of Rome. By the aid of the friends of Gregory, the walls had been perforated or scaled; but the Imperial faction was still powerful and active; on the third day, the people rose in a furious tumult; and a hasty word of the conqueror, in his defense or revenge, was the signal of fire and pillage. The Saracens of Sicily, the subjects of Roger and auxiliaries of his brother, embraced this fair occasion of rifling and profaning the holy city of the Christians: many thousands of the citizens, in the sight and by the allies of their spiritual father, were exposed to violation, captivity, or death; and a spacious quarter of the city, from the Lateran to the Colosseum, was consumed by the flames and devoted to perpetual solitude. From a city where he was now hated, and might be no longer feared, Gregory retired to end his days in the palace of Salerno. The artful pontiff might flatter the vanity of Guiscard with the hope of a Roman or Imperial crown; but this dangerous measure, which would have inflamed the ambition of the Norman, must forever have alienated the most faithful princes of Germany.

The deliverer and scourge of Rome might have indulged himself in a season of repose; but in the same year of the flight of the German emperor, the indefatigable Robert resumed the design of his Eastern conquests. . . . But in the Isle of Cephalonia, his projects were fatally blasted by an epidemical disease: Robert himself, in the seventieth year of his age, expired in his tent [July 17, A.D. 1085]; and a suspicion of poison was imputed by public rumor to his wife, or to the Greek emperor. This premature death might allow a boundless scope for the imagination of his future exploits; and the event sufficiently declares that the Norman greatness was founded on his life. Without the appearance of an enemy, a victorious army dispersed or retreated in disorder and consternation; and Alexius, who had trembled for his empire, rejoiced in his deliverance. The galley which transported the remains of Guiscard was shipwrecked on the Italian shore; but the duke's body was recovered from the sea and deposited in the sepulchre of Venusia, a place more illustrious for the birth of Horace than for the burial of the Norman heroes. Roger, his second son and successor, immediately sunk to the humble station of a duke of Apulia: the esteem or partiality of his father left the valiant Bohemond to the inheritance of his sword. The national tranquility was disturbed by his claims, till the first crusade against the infidels of the East opened a more splendid field of glory and conquest.

Of human life, the most glorious or humble prospects are alike and soon bounded by the sepulchre. The male line of Robert Guiscard was extinguished, both in Apulia and at Antioch, in the second generation; but his younger brother became the father of a line of kings; and the son of the great count was endowed with the name, the conquests, and the spirit of the first Roger. The heir of that Norman adventurer was born in Sicily; and at the age of only four years he succeeded to the sovereignty of the island, a lot which reason might envy, could she indulge for a moment the visionary though virtuous wish of dominion. Had Roger been content with his fruitful patrimony, a happy and grateful people might have blessed their benefactor; and if a wise administration could have restored the prosperous times of the Greek colonies, the opulence and power of Sicily alone might have equaled the widest scope that could be acquired and desolated by the sword of war. But the ambition of the great count was ignorant of these noble pursuits; it was gratified by the vulgar means of violence and artifice.

[*Roger reigns in Sicily,* A.D. *1101–1154. His successors continue to wage war. The German king, Henry VI, conquers Sicily and extinguishes the Norman kingdom* (A.D. *1194).*]

Henry pursued his victorious march from Capua to Palermo. The political balance of Italy was destroyed by his success; and if the pope and the free cities had consulted their obvious and real interest, they would have combined the powers of earth and Heaven to prevent the dangerous union of the German empire with the kingdom of Sicily. But the subtle policy for which the Vatican has so often been praised or arraigned was on this occasion blind and inactive; and if it were true that Celestine the Third had kicked away the Imperial crown from the head of the prostrate Henry, such an act of impotent pride could serve only to cancel an obligation and provoke an enemy. The Genoese, who enjoyed a beneficial trade and establishment in Sicily, listened to the promise of his boundless gratitude and speedy departure: their fleet commanded the straits of Messina and opened the harbor of Palermo; and the first act of his government was to abolish the privileges and to seize the property of these imprudent allies. The last hope of [the Norman historian] Falcandus was defeated by the discord of the Christians and Mohammedans: they fought in the capital; several thousands of the latter were slain; but their surviving brethren fortified the mountains and disturbed above thirty years the peace of the island. By the policy of Frederic the Second, sixty thousand Saracens were transplanted to Nocera in Apulia. In their wars against the Roman church, the emperor and his son Mainfroy were strengthened and disgraced by the service of the enemies of Christ; and this national colony maintained their religion and manners in the heart of Italy till they were extirpated, at the end of the thirteenth century, by the zeal and revenge of the house of Anjou. All the calamities which the prophetic orator had deplored were surpassed by the cruelty and avarice of the German conqueror. He violated the royal sepulchres and explored the secret treasures of the palace, Palermo, and the whole kingdom: the pearls and jewels, however precious, might be easily removed; but one hundred and sixty horses were laden with the gold and silver of Sicily. The young king, his mother and sisters, and the nobles of both sexes were separately confined in the fortresses of the Alps; and on the slightest rumor of rebellion, the captives were deprived of life, of their eyes, or of the hope of posterity. Constantia herself was touched with sympathy for the miseries of her country; and the heiress of the Norman line might struggle to check her despotic husband and to save the patrimony of her new-born son, of an emperor so famous in the next age under the name of Frederic the Second. Ten years after this revolution, the French monarchs annexed to their crown the duchy of Normandy: the scepter of her ancient dukes had been transmitted by a granddaughter of William the Conqueror to the house of Plantagenet; and the adventurous Normans, who had raised so many trophies in France, England, and Ireland, in Apulia, Sicily, and the East, were lost, either in victory or servitude, among the vanquished nations [A.D. 1204].

CHAPTER LVII

THE TURKS

*The Turks of the house of Seljuk. • Their revolt against Mahmud,
conqueror of Hindostan. • Togrul subdues Persia and protects the
caliphs. • Defeat and captivity of the emperor Romanus Diogenes
by Alp Arslan. • Power and magnificence of Malek Shah. •
Conquest of Asia Minor and Syria. • State and oppression of
Jerusalem. • Pilgrimages to the holy sepulchre.*

From the Isle of Sicily, the reader must transport himself beyond the
Caspian Sea to the original seat of the Turks or Turkmans, against
whom the first crusade was principally directed. Their Scythian empire of the sixth century was long since dissolved; but the name was
still famous among the Greeks and Orientals; and the fragments of the
nation, each a powerful and independent people, were scattered over
the desert from China to the Oxus and the Danube: the colony of
Hungarians was admitted into the republic of Europe, and the thrones
of Asia were occupied by slaves and soldiers of Turkish extraction.
While Apulia and Sicily were subdued by the Norman lance, a swarm
of these Northern shepherds overspread the kingdoms of Persia; their
princes of the race of Seljuk erected a splendid and solid empire from
Samarcand to the confines of Greece and Egypt; and the Turks have
maintained their dominion in Asia Minor, till the victorious crescent
has been planted on the dome of St. Sophia.

One of the greatest of the Turkish princes was Mahmood, or Mahmud, the Gaznevide, who reigned in the eastern provinces of Persia
one thousand years after the birth of Christ [A.D. 997–1028]. His father
Sebectagi was the slave of the slave of the slave of the commander of
the faithful. . . . The falling dynasty of the Samanides was at first protected and at last overthrown by their servants; and in the public disorders, the fortune of Mahmud continually increased. From him the
title of *Sultan* was first invented; and his kingdom was enlarged from
Transoxiana to the neighborhood of Ispahan, from the shores of the
Caspian to the mouth of the Indus. But the principal source of his

fame and riches was the holy war which he waged against the Gentoos of Hindostan. In this foreign narrative I may not consume a page; and a volume would scarcely suffice to recapitulate the battles and sieges of his twelve expeditions. Never was the Moslem hero dismayed by the inclemency of the seasons, the height of the mountains, the breadth of the rivers, the barrenness of the desert, the multitudes of the enemy, or the formidable array of their elephants of war. The sultan of Gazna surpassed the limits of the conquests of Alexander: after a march of three months over the hills of Cashmir and Thibet, he reached the famous city of Kinnoge, on the Upper Ganges; and in a naval combat on one of the branches of the Indus, he fought and vanquished four thousand boats of the natives. Delhi, Lahor, and Multan were compelled to open their gates: the fertile kingdom of Guzarat attracted his ambition and tempted his stay; and his avarice indulged the fruitless project of discovering the golden and aromatic isles of the Southern Ocean. On the payment of a tribute, the *rajahs* preserved their dominions; the people, their lives and fortunes; but to the religion of Hindostan the zealous Moslem was cruel and inexorable: many hundred temples, or pagodas, were leveled with the ground; many thousand idols were demolished; and the servants of the prophet were stimulated and rewarded by the precious materials of which they were composed. The pagoda of Sumnat was situate on the promontory of Guzarat, in the neighborhood of Diu [A.D. 1024]. . . . It was endowed with the revenue of two thousand villages; two thousand Brahmins were consecrated to the service of the Deity, whom they washed each morning and evening in water from the distant Ganges: the subordinate ministers consisted of three hundred musicians, three hundred barbers, and five hundred dancing girls conspicuous for their birth or beauty. Three sides of the temple were protected by the ocean; the narrow isthmus was fortified by a natural or artificial precipice; and the city and adjacent country were peopled by a nation of fanatics. They confessed the sins and the punishment of Kinnoge and Delhi; but if the impious stranger should presume to approach *their* holy precincts, he would surely be overwhelmed by a blast of the divine vengeance. By this challenge, the faith of Mahmud was animated to a personal trial of the strength of this Indian deity. Fifty thousand of his worshipers were pierced by the spear of the Moslems; the walls were scaled; the sanctuary was profaned; and the conqueror aimed a blow of his iron mace at the head of the idol. The trembling Brahmins are said to have offered ten millions sterling for his ransom; and it was urged by the wisest counselors that the destruction of a stone image would not change the hearts of the Gentoos; and that such a sum might be dedicated to the relief of the true believers. "Your reasons," replied the sultan, "are specious and strong; but never in the eyes of posterity shall Mahmud appear as a merchant of idols." He repeated his blows, and a treasure of pearls and rubies, concealed in the belly of the statue, explained in some degree the devout prodigality of the Brahmins. The fragments of the idol were distributed to Gazna, Mecca, and Medina. Baghdad listened to the edifying tale; and Mahmud was saluted by the caliph with the title of guardian of the fortune and faith of Mohammed.

From the paths of blood (and such is the history of nations) I cannot refuse to turn aside to gather some flowers of science or virtue. The name of Mahmud the Gaznevide is still venerable in the East: his subjects enjoyed the blessings of prosperity and peace; his vices were concealed by the veil of religion; and two familiar examples will testify his justice and magnanimity. I. As he sat in the Divan, an unhappy subject bowed before the throne to accuse the insolence of a Turkish soldier who had driven him from his house and bed. "Suspend your clamors," said Mahmud; "inform me of his next visit, and ourself in person will judge and punish the offender." The sultan followed his guide, invested the house with his guards, and, extinguishing the torches, pronounced the death of the criminal, who had been seized in the act of rapine and adultery. After the execution of his sentence, the lights were rekindled, Mahmud fell prostrate in prayer, and, rising from the ground, demanded some homely fare, which he devoured with the voraciousness of hunger. The poor man whose injury he had avenged was unable to suppress his astonishment and curiosity; and the courteous monarch condescended to explain the motives of this singular behavior. "I had reason to suspect that none except one of my sons could dare to perpetrate such an outrage; and I extinguished the lights that my justice might be blind and inexorable. My prayer was a thanksgiving on the discovery of the offender; and so painful was my anxiety that I had passed three days without food since the first moment of your complaint." II. The sultan of Gazna had declared war against the dynasty of the Bowides, the sovereigns of western Persia: he was disarmed by an epistle of the sultana mother and delayed his invasion till the manhood of her son. "During the life of my husband," said the artful regent, "I was ever apprehensive of your ambition: he was a prince and a soldier worthy of your arms. He is now no more; his scepter has passed to a woman and a child, and you *dare not* attack their infancy and weakness. How inglorious would be your conquest, how shameful your defeat! and yet the event of war is in the hand of the Almighty." Avarice was the only defect that tarnished the illustrious character of Mahmud; and never has that passion been more richly satiated. The Orientals exceed the measure of credibility in the account of millions of gold and silver such as the avidity of man has never accumulated; in the magnitude of pearls, diamonds, and rubies, such as have never been produced by the workmanship of nature. Yet the soil of Hindostan is impregnated with precious minerals: her trade in every age has attracted the gold and silver of the world; and her virgin spoils were rifled by the first of the Mohammedan conquerors. His behavior in the last days of his life evinces the vanity of these possessions, so laboriously won, so dangerously held, and so inevitably lost. He surveyed the vast and various chambers of the treasury of Gazna, burst into tears, and again closed the doors without bestowing any portion of the wealth which he could no longer hope to preserve. The following day he reviewed the state of his military force; one hundred thousand foot, fifty-five thousand horse, and thirteen hundred elephants of battle. He again wept the instability of human greatness; and his grief was embittered by the hostile progress of the Turkmans, whom he had introduced into the heart of his Persian kingdom.

In the modern depopulation of Asia, the regular operation of government and agriculture is confined to the neighborhood of cities; and the distant country is abandoned to the pastoral tribes of Arabs, Curds, and *Turkmans.* Of the last-mentioned people, two considerable branches extend on either side of the Caspian Sea: the western colony can muster forty thousand soldiers; the eastern, less obvious to the traveler but more strong and populous, has increased to the number of one hundred thousand families. In the midst of civilized nations, they preserve the manners of the Scythian desert, remove their encampments with a change of seasons, and feed their cattle among the ruins of palaces and temples. Their flocks and herds are their only riches; their tents, either black or white according to the color of the banner, are covered with felt and of a circular form; their winter apparel is a sheep-skin; a robe of cloth or cotton their summer garment: the features of the men are harsh and ferocious; the countenance of their women is soft and pleasing. Their wandering life maintains the spirit and exercise of arms; they fight on horseback; and their courage is displayed in frequent contests with each other and with their neighbors. For the license of pasture they pay a slight tribute to the sovereign of the land; but the domestic jurisdiction is in the hands of the chiefs and elders. The first emigration of the eastern Turkmans, the most ancient of the race, may be ascribed to the tenth century of the Christian era. In the decline of the caliphs and the weakness of their lieutenants, the barrier of the Jaxartes was often violated; in each invasion, after the victory or retreat of their countrymen, some wandering tribe, embracing the Mohammedan faith, obtained a free encampment in the spacious plains and pleasant climate of Transoxiana and Carizme. The Turkish slaves who aspired to the throne encouraged these emigrations which recruited their armies, awed their subjects and rivals, and protected the frontier against the wilder natives of Turkestan; and this policy was abused by Mahmud the Gaznevide beyond the example of former times. He was admonished of his error by the chief of the race of Seljuk, who dwelt in the territory of Bochara. The sultan had inquired what supply of men he could furnish for military service. "If you send," replied Ismael, "one of these arrows into our camp, fifty thousand of your servants will mount on horseback."—"And if that number," continued Mahmud, "should not be sufficient?"—"Send this second arrow to the horde of Balik, and you will find fifty thousand more."—"But," said the Gaznevide, dissembling his anxiety, "if I should stand in need of the whole force of your kindred tribes?"— "Despatch my bow," was the last reply of Ismael, "and as it is circulated around, the summons will be obeyed by two hundred thousand horse." The apprehension of such formidable friendship induced Mahmud to transport the most obnoxious tribes into the heart of Chorasan, where they would be separated from their brethren of the River Oxus and enclosed on all sides by the walls of obedient cities. But the face of the country was an object of temptation rather than terror; and the vigor of government was relaxed by the absence and death of the sultan of Gazna. The shepherds were converted into robbers; the bands of robbers were collected into an army of conquerors: as far as Ispahan and the Tigris, Persia was afflicted by their predatory inroads; and the Turkmans were not ashamed or afraid to measure their courage and numbers with the proudest sovereigns of Asia. Massoud, the son and successor of Mahmud, had too long neglected the advice of his wisest Omrahs. "Your enemies," they repeatedly urged, "were in their origin a swarm of ants; they are now little snakes; and unless they be instantly crushed, they will acquire the venom and magnitude of serpents." After some alternatives of truce and hostility, after the repulse or partial success of his lieutenants, the sultan marched in person against the Turkmans, who attacked him on all sides with barbarous shouts and irregular onset. "Massoud," says the Persian historian, "plunged singly to oppose the torrent of gleaming arms, exhibiting such acts of gigantic force and valor as never a king had before displayed. A few of his friends, roused by his words and actions and that innate honor which inspires the brave, seconded their lord so well that wheresoever he turned his fatal sword the enemies were mowed down, or retreated before him. But now, when victory seemed to blow on his standard, misfortune was active behind it; for when he looked round, he beheld almost his whole army, excepting that body he commanded in person, devouring the paths of flight." The Gaznevide was abandoned by the cowardice or treachery of some generals of Turkish race; and this memorable day of Zendecan founded in Persia the dynasty of the shepherd kings [A.D. 1038].

The victorious Turkmans immediately proceeded to the election of a king; and if the probable tale of a Latin historian deserves any credit, they determined by lot the choice of their new master. A number of arrows were successively inscribed with the name of a tribe, a family, and a candidate; they were drawn from the bundle by the hand of a child; and the important prize was obtained by Togrul Beg, the son of Michael the son of Seljuk, whose surname was immortalized in the greatness of his posterity [the dynasty of the Seljukians, A.D. 1038–1152]. . . . The blind determination of chance was justified by the virtues of the successful candidate. It would be superfluous to praise the valor of a Turk; and the ambition of Togrul was equal to his valor. By his arms, the Gaznevides were expelled from the eastern kingdoms of Persia and gradually driven to the banks of the Indus in search of a softer and more wealthy conquest. In the west he annihilated the dynasty of the Bowides; and the scepter of Irak passed from the Persian to the Turk-

ish nation. The princes who had felt, or who feared, the Seljukian arrows bowed their heads in the dust; by the conquest of Aderbijan, or
Media, he approached the Roman confines; and the shepherd presumed to despatch an ambassador or herald to demand the tribute and
obedience of the emperor of Constantinople. In his own dominions,
Togrul was the father of his soldiers and people; by a firm and equal
administration, Persia was relieved from the evils of anarchy; and the
same hands which had been imbrued in blood became the guardians of
justice and the public peace. The more rustic, perhaps the wisest, portion of the Turkmans continued to dwell in the tents of their ancestors; and from the Oxus to the Euphrates, these military colonies were
protected and propagated by their native princes. But the Turks of the
court and city were refined by business and softened by pleasure: they
imitated the dress, language, and manners of Persia; and the royal
palaces of Nishabur and Rei displayed the order and magnificence of
a great monarchy. The most deserving of the Arabians and Persians
were promoted to the honors of the state; and the whole body of the
Turkish nation embraced, with fervor and sincerity, the religion of Mohammed. The Northern swarms of Barbarians who overspread both
Europe and Asia have been irreconcilably separated by the consequences of a similar conduct. Among the Moslems, as among the Christians, their vague and local traditions have yielded to the reason and
authority of the prevailing system, to the fame of antiquity, and the
consent of nations. But the triumph of the Koran is more pure and
meritorious, as it was not assisted by any visible splendor of worship
which might allure the Pagans by some resemblance of idolatry. The
first of the Seljukian sultans was conspicuous by his zeal and faith: each
day he repeated the five prayers which are enjoined to the true believers; of each week, the two first days were consecrated by an extraordinary fast; and in every city a mosque was completed before Togrul
presumed to lay the foundations of a palace.

[*Togrul relieves the caliph of Baghdad, who invests Togrul as "temporal
lieutenant of the vicar of the prophet"* (A.D. 1053).]

Since the fall of the caliphs, the discord and degeneracy of the Saracens respected the Asiatic provinces of Rome; which, by the victories
of Nicephorus, Zimisces, and Basil, had been extended as far as Anti-

och and the eastern boundaries of Armenia. Twenty-five years after the death of Basil, his successors were suddenly assaulted by an unknown race of Barbarians who united the Scythian valor with the fanaticism of new proselytes and the art and riches of a powerful monarchy. The myriads of Turkish horse overspread a frontier of six hundred miles from Tauris to Arzeroum, and the blood of one hundred and thirty thousand Christians was a grateful sacrifice to the Arabian prophet. Yet the arms of Togrul did not make any deep or lasting impression on the Greek empire. The torrent rolled away from the open country; the sultan retired without glory or success from the siege of an Armenian city; the obscure hostilities were continued or suspended with a vicissitude of events; and the bravery of the Macedonian legions renewed the fame of the conqueror of Asia.

[*Alp Arslan succeeds Togrul Beg; he conquers Armenia and Georgia (A.D. 1065–1068).*]

The false or genuine magnanimity of Mahmud the Gaznevide was not imitated by Alp Arslan; and he attacked without scruple the Greek empress Eudocia and her children. His alarming progress compelled her to give herself and her scepter to the hand of a soldier; and Romanus Diogenes was invested with the Imperial purple. His patriotism, and perhaps his pride, urged him from Constantinople within two months after his accession; and the next campaign he most scandalously took the field during the holy festival of Easter. In the palace, Diogenes was no more than the husband of Eudocia: in the camp, he was the emperor of the Romans, and he sustained that character with feeble resources and invincible courage. By his spirit and success the soldiers were taught to act, the subjects to hope, and the enemies to fear. The Turks had penetrated into the heart of Phrygia; but the sultan himself had resigned to his emirs the prosecution of the war; and their numerous detachments were scattered over Asia in the security of conquest. Laden with spoil and careless of discipline, they were separately surprised and defeated by the Greeks: the activity of the emperor seemed to multiply his presence: and while they heard of his expedition to Antioch, the enemy felt his sword on the hills of Trebizond. In three laborious campaigns, the Turks were driven beyond the

Euphrates; in the fourth and last, Romanus undertook the deliverance of Armenia.

[The Roman emperor Romanus is not only defeated in Armenia, he is captured (August A.D. 1071).]

The Byzantine writers deplore the loss of an inestimable pearl: they forgot to mention that in this fatal day the Asiatic provinces of Rome were irretrievably sacrificed.

As long as a hope survived, Romanus attempted to rally and save the relics of his army. When the center, the Imperial station, was left naked on all sides and encompassed by the victorious Turks, he still, with desperate courage, maintained the fight till the close of day, at the head of the brave and faithful subjects who adhered to his standard. They fell around him; his horse was slain; the emperor was wounded; yet he stood alone and intrepid, till he was oppressed and bound by the strength of multitudes. The glory of this illustrious prize was disputed by a slave and a soldier; a slave who had seen him on the throne of Constantinople, and a soldier whose extreme deformity had been excused on the promise of some signal service. Despoiled of his arms, his jewels, and his purple, Romanus spent a dreary and perilous night on the field of battle, amidst a disorderly crowd of the meaner Barbarians. In the morning the royal captive was presented to Alp Arslan, who doubted of his fortune, till the identity of the person was ascertained by the report of his ambassadors and by the more pathetic evidence of Basilacius, who embraced with tears the feet of his unhappy sovereign. The successor of Constantine, in a plebeian habit, was led into the Turkish divan and commanded to kiss the ground before the lord of Asia. He reluctantly obeyed; and Alp Arslan, starting from his throne, is said to have planted his foot on the neck of the Roman emperor. But the fact is doubtful; and if in this moment of insolence the sultan complied with the national custom, the rest of his conduct has extorted the praise of his bigoted foes, and may afford a lesson to the most civilized ages. He instantly raised the royal captive from the ground; and thrice clasping his hand with tender sympathy, assured him that his life and dignity should be inviolate in the hands of a prince who had learned to respect the majesty of his equals and the vicissitudes of fortune. From the divan, Romanus was conducted to an adjacent tent, where he was served with pomp and reverence by the officers of the sultan, who twice each day seated him in the place of honor at his own table. In a free and familiar conversation of eight days, not a word, not a look of insult escaped from the conqueror; but he severely censured the unworthy subjects who had deserted their valiant prince in the hour of danger, and gently admonished his antagonist of some errors which he had committed in the management of the war. In the preliminaries of negotiation, Alp Arslan asked him what treatment he expected to receive, and the calm indifference of the emperor displays the freedom of his mind. "If you are cruel," said he, "you will take my life; if you listen to pride, you will drag me at your chariot-wheels; if you consult your interest, you will accept a ransom and restore me to my country." "And what," continued the sultan, "would have been your own behavior, had fortune smiled on your arms?" The reply of the Greek betrays a sentiment which prudence, and even gratitude, should have taught him to suppress. "Had I vanquished," he fiercely said, "I would have inflicted on thy body many a stripe." The Turkish conqueror smiled at the insolence of his captive; observed that the Christian law inculcated the love of enemies and forgiveness of injuries; and nobly declared that he would not imitate an example which he condemned. After mature deliberation, Alp Arslan dictated the terms of liberty and peace, a ransom of a million, an annual tribute of three hundred and sixty thousand pieces of gold, the marriage of the royal children, and the deliverance of all the Moslems who were in the power of the Greeks. Romanus, with a sigh, subscribed this treaty, so disgraceful to the majesty of the empire; he was immediately invested with a Turkish robe of honor; his nobles and patricians were restored to their sovereign; and the sultan, after a courteous embrace, dismissed him with rich presents and a military guard. No sooner did he reach the confines of the empire than he was informed that the palace and provinces had disclaimed their allegiance to a captive: a sum of two hundred thousand pieces was painfully collected; and the fallen monarch transmitted this part of his ransom, with a sad confession of his impotence and disgrace. The generosity, or perhaps the ambition, of the sultan prepared to espouse the cause of his ally; but his designs were prevented by the defeat, imprisonment, and death of Romanus Diogenes.

[*Alp Arslan is succeeded by Malek Shah, who reigns* A.D. *1072–1092.*]

The greatness and unity of the Turkish empire expired in the person of Malek Shah. His vacant throne was disputed by his brother and his four sons; and after a series of civil wars, the treaty which reconciled the surviving candidates confirmed a lasting separation in the *Persian* dynasty, the eldest and principal branch of the house of Seljuk. The three younger dynasties were those of *Kerman,* of *Syria,* and of *Roum:* the first of these commanded an extensive though obscure dominion on the shores of the Indian Ocean: the second expelled the Arabian princes of Aleppo and Damascus; and the third, our peculiar care, invaded the Roman provinces of Asia Minor. The generous policy of Malek contributed to their elevation: he allowed the princes of his blood, even those whom he had vanquished in the field, to seek new kingdoms worthy of their ambition; nor was he displeased that they should draw away the more ardent spirits, who might have disturbed the tranquility of his reign. As the supreme head of his family and nation, the great sultan of Persia commanded the obedience and tribute of his royal brethren: the thrones of Kerman and Nice, of Aleppo and Damascus; the Atabeks, and emirs of Syria and Mesopotamia, erected their standards under the shadow of his scepter: and the hordes of Turkmans overspread the plains of western Asia. After the death of Malek, the bands of union and subordination were relaxed and finally dissolved: the indulgence of the house of Seljuk invested their slaves with the inheritance of kingdoms; and in the Oriental style, a crowd of princes arose from the dust of their feet.

A prince of the royal line, Cutulmish, the son of Izrail the son of Seljuk, had fallen in a battle against Alp Arslan, and the humane victor had dropped a tear over his grave. His five sons, strong in arms, ambitious of power, and eager for revenge, unsheathed their cimeters against the son of Alp Arslan. The two armies expected the signal when the caliph, forgetful of the majesty which secluded him from vulgar eyes, interposed his venerable mediation. "Instead of shedding the blood of your brethren, your brethren both in descent and faith, unite your forces in a holy war against the Greeks, the enemies of God and his apostle." They listened to his voice; the sultan embraced his rebellious kinsmen; and the eldest, the valiant Soliman, accepted the royal standard, which gave him the free conquest and hereditary command of the provinces of the Roman empire, from Arzeroum to Constantinople, and the unknown regions of the West.

[*The Turks conquer Asia Minor (A.D. 1074–1084).*]

Since the first conquests of the caliphs, the establishment of the Turks in Anatolia or Asia Minor was the most deplorable loss which the church and empire had sustained. By the propagation of the Moslem faith, Soliman deserved the name of *Gazi*, a holy champion; and his new kingdom of the Romans, or of *Roum*, was added to the tables of Oriental geography. It is described as extending from the Euphrates to Constantinople, from the Black Sea to the confines of Syria; pregnant with mines of silver and iron, of alum and copper, fruitful in corn and wine, and productive of cattle and excellent horses. The wealth of Lydia, the arts of the Greeks, the splendor of the Augustan age existed only in books and ruins, which were equally obscure in the eyes of the Scythian conquerors. Yet in the present decay, Anatolia still contains *some* wealthy and populous cities; and under the Byzantine empire, they were far more flourishing in numbers, size, and opulence. By the choice of the sultan, Nice, the metropolis of Bithynia, was preferred for his palace and fortress: the seat of the Seljukian dynasty of Roum was planted one hundred miles from Constantinople; and the divinity of Christ was denied and derided in the same temple in which it had been pronounced by the first general synod of the Catholics. The unity of God and the mission of Mohammed were preached in the mosques; the Arabian learning was taught in the schools; the Cadhis judged according to the law of the Koran; the Turkish manners and language prevailed in the cities; and Turkman camps were scattered over the plains and mountains of Anatolia. On the hard conditions of tribute and servitude, the Greek Christians might enjoy the exercise of their religion; but their most holy churches were profaned; their priests and bishops were insulted; they were compelled to suffer the triumph of the *Pagans* and the apostasy of their brethren; many thousand children were marked by the knife of circumcision; and many thousand captives were devoted to the service or the pleasures of their masters. After the loss of Asia, Antioch still maintained her primitive allegiance to Christ and Caesar; but the solitary province was separated from all Roman aid and surrounded on all sides by the Mohammedan powers. The despair of Philaretus the governor prepared the sacrifice of his religion and loyalty, had not his guilt been prevented by his son, who hastened to the Nicene palace and offered to deliver this valuable prize into the hands of Soliman. The ambitious sultan mounted on horseback, and in twelve nights (for he reposed in the day) performed a march of six hundred miles. Antioch was oppressed by the speed and secrecy of his enterprise; and the dependent cities, as far as Laodicea and the confines of Aleppo, obeyed the example of the metropolis. From Laodicea to the Thracian Bosphorus, or arm of St. George, the conquests and reign of Soliman extended thirty days' journey in length, and in breadth about ten or fifteen, between the rocks of Lycia and the Black Sea. The Turkish ignorance of navigation protected for a while the inglorious safety of the emperor; but no sooner had a fleet of two hundred ships been constructed by the hands of the captive Greeks than Alexius trembled behind the walls of his capital. His plaintive epistles were dispersed over Europe to excite the compassion of the Latins and to paint the danger, the weakness, and the riches of the city of Constantine.

But the most interesting conquest of the Seljukian Turks was that of Jerusalem, which soon became the theater of nations. In their capitulation with Omar, the inhabitants had stipulated the assurance of their religion and property; but the articles were interpreted by a master against whom it was dangerous to dispute; and in the four hundred years of the reign of the caliphs, the political climate of Jerusalem was exposed to the vicissitudes of storm and sunshine. By the increase of proselytes and population, the Mohammedans might excuse the usurpation of three fourths of the city: but a peculiar quarter was resolved for the patriarch with his clergy and people; a tribute of two pieces of gold was the price of protection; and the sepulchre of Christ, with the church of the Resurrection, was still left in the hands of his votaries. Of these votaries, the most numerous and respectable portion were strangers to Jerusalem: the pilgrimages to the Holy Land had been stimulated rather than suppressed by the conquest of the Arabs; and the enthusiasm which had always prompted these perilous journeys was nourished by the congenial passions of grief and indignation. A crowd of pilgrims from the East and West continued to visit the holy sepulchre and the adjacent sanctuaries, more especially at the festival of Easter; and the

Greeks and Latins, the Nestorians and Jacobites, the Copts and Abyssinians, the Armenians and Georgians, maintained the chapels, the clergy, and the poor of their respective communions. The harmony of prayer in so many various tongues, the worship of so many nations in the common temple of their religion, might have afforded a spectacle of edification and peace; but the zeal of the Christian sects was embittered by hatred and revenge; and in the kingdom of a suffering Messiah who had pardoned his enemies, they aspired to command and persecute their spiritual brethren.... [And had] the Christian pilgrims been content to revere the tomb of a prophet, the disciples of Mohammed, instead of blaming, would have imitated, their piety: but these rigid *Unitarians* were scandalized by a worship which represents the birth, death, and resurrection of a God; the Catholic images were branded with the name of idols; and the Moslems smiled with indignation at the miraculous flame which was kindled on the eve of Easter in the holy sepulchre. This pious fraud, first devised in the ninth century, was devoutly cherished by the Latin crusaders and is annually repeated by the clergy of the Greek, Armenian, and Coptic sects, who impose on the credulous spectators for their own benefit and that of their tyrants. In every age, a principle of toleration has been fortified by a sense of interest: and the revenue of the prince and his emir was increased each year by the expense and tribute of so many thousand strangers.†

The house of Seljuk reigned about twenty years in Jerusalem [A.D. 1076–1096]; but the hereditary command of the holy city and territory was entrusted or abandoned to the emir Ortok, the chief of a tribe of Turkmans, whose children, after their expulsion from Palestine, formed two dynasties on the borders of Armenia and Assyria. The Oriental Christians and the Latin pilgrims deplored a revolution which, instead of the regular government and old alliance of the caliphs, imposed on their necks the iron yoke of the strangers of the North. In his court and camp the great sultan had adopted in some degree the arts and manners of Persia; but the body of the Turkish nation, and more especially the pastoral tribes, still breathed the fierceness of the desert. From Nice to Jerusalem, the western countries of Asia were a scene of foreign and domestic hostility; and the shepherds of Palestine, who held a precarious sway on a doubtful frontier, had neither leisure nor capacity to await the slow profits of commercial and religious freedom. The pilgrims who, through innumerable perils, had reached the gates of Jerusalem were the victims of private rapine or public oppression, and often sunk under the pressure of famine and disease before they were permitted to salute the holy sepulchre. A spirit of native barbarism or recent zeal prompted the Turkmans to insult the clergy of every sect: the patriarch was dragged by the hair along the pavement and cast into a dungeon to extort a ransom from the sympathy of his flock; and the divine worship in the Church of the Resurrection was often disturbed by the savage rudeness of its masters. The pathetic tale excited the millions of the West to march under the standard of the cross to the relief of the Holy Land; and yet how trifling is the sum of these accumulated evils if compared with the single act of the sacrilege of Hakem [who in A.D. 1009 had destroyed the Church of the Resurrection and attempted to destroy the cave in the rock, the holy sepulchre proper], which had been so patiently endured by the Latin Christians! A slighter provocation inflamed the more irascible temper of their descendants: a new spirit had arisen of religious chivalry and papal dominion; a nerve was touched of exquisite feeling; and the sensation vibrated to the heart of Europe.

END OF THE FIFTH VOLUME [1788].

VOLUME THE SIXTH

[1788]

CHAPTER LVIII

THE FIRST CRUSADE

*Origin and numbers of the first crusade. • Characters of the Latin
princes. • Their march to Constantinople. • Policy of the Greek
emperor Alexius. • Conquest of Nice, Antioch, and Jerusalem by the
Franks. • Deliverance of the holy sepulchre. • Godfrey of
Bouillon, first king of Jerusalem. • Institutions of the
French or Latin kingdom.*

About twenty years after the conquest of Jerusalem by the Turks, the
holy sepulchre was visited by a hermit of the name of Peter, a native of
Amiens in the province of Picardy in France [A.D. 1095–1096]. His resentment and sympathy were excited by his own injuries and the oppression of the Christian name; he mingled his tears with those of the
patriarch, and earnestly inquired if no hopes of relief could be entertained from the Greek emperors of the East. The patriarch exposed
the vices and weakness of the successors of Constantine. "I will rouse,"
exclaimed the hermit, "the martial nations of Europe in your cause";
and Europe was obedient to the call of the hermit. The astonished patriarch dismissed him with epistles of credit and complaint; and no
sooner did he land at Bari than Peter hastened to kiss the feet of the
Roman pontiff. His stature was small, his appearance contemptible,
but his eye was keen and lively; and he possessed that vehemence of
speech which seldom fails to impart the persuasion of the soul. He was
born of a gentleman's family (for we must now adopt a modern idiom)
and his military service was under the neighboring counts of Boulogne,
the heroes of the first crusade. But he soon relinquished the sword and
the world; and if it be true that his wife, however noble, was aged and
ugly, he might withdraw with the less reluctance from her bed to a
convent and at length to a hermitage. In this austere solitude, his body
was emaciated, his fancy was inflamed; whatever he wished, he believed; whatever he believed, he *saw* in dreams and revelations. From
Jerusalem the pilgrim returned an accomplished fanatic; but as he excelled in the popular madness of the times, Pope Urban the Second re-

ceived him as a prophet, applauded his glorious design, promised to support it in a general council, and encouraged him to proclaim the deliverance of the Holy Land. Invigorated by the approbation of the pontiff, his zealous missionary traversed, with speed and success, the provinces of Italy and France. His diet was abstemious, his prayers long and fervent, and the alms which he received with one hand he distributed with the other: his head was bare, his feet naked, his meager body was wrapped in a coarse garment; he bore and displayed a weighty crucifix; and the ass on which he rode was sanctified in the public eye by the service of the man of God. He preached to innumerable crowds in the churches, the streets, and the highways: the hermit entered with equal confidence the palace and the cottage; and the people (for all was people) was impetuously moved by his call to repentance and arms. When he painted the sufferings of the natives and pilgrims of Palestine, every heart was melted to compassion; every breast glowed with indignation when he challenged the warriors of the age to defend their brethren and rescue their Savior: his ignorance of art and language was compensated by sighs and tears and ejaculations; and Peter supplied the deficiency of reason by loud and frequent appeals to Christ and his mother, to the saints and angels of Paradise, with whom he had personally conversed. The most perfect orator of Athens might have envied the success of his eloquence; the rustic enthusiast inspired the passions which he felt, and Christendom expected with impatience the counsels and decrees of the supreme pontiff.

The magnanimous spirit of Gregory the Seventh had already embraced the design of arming Europe against Asia; the ardor of his zeal and ambition still breathes in his epistles: from either side of the Alps, fifty thousand Catholics had enlisted under the banner of St. Peter; and his successor reveals *his* intention of marching at their head against the impious sectaries of Mohammed. But the glory or reproach of executing, though not in person, this holy enterprise was reserved for Urban the Second, the most faithful of his disciples.... So popular was the cause of Urban, so weighty was his influence, that the council which he summoned at Placentia was composed of two hundred bishops of Italy, France, Burgundy, Swabia, and Bavaria [March A.D. 1095]. Four thousand of the clergy and thirty thousand of the laity attended this important meeting; and as the most spacious cathedral would have been inadequate to the multitude, the session of seven days was held in a plain adjacent to the city. The ambassadors of the Greek emperor, Alexius Comnenus, were introduced to plead the distress of their sovereign and the danger of Constantinople, which was divided only by a narrow sea from the victorious Turks, the common enemies of the Christian name. In their suppliant address they flattered the pride of the Latin princes and, appealing at once to their policy and religion, exhorted them to repel the Barbarians on the confines of Asia rather than to expect them in the heart of Europe. At the sad tale of the misery and perils of their Eastern brethren, the assembly burst into tears; the most eager champions declared their readiness to march; and the Greek ambassadors were dismissed with the assurance of a speedy and powerful succor. The relief of Constantinople was included in the larger and most distant project of the deliverance of Jerusalem; but the prudent Urban adjourned the final decision to a second synod, which he proposed to celebrate in some city of France in the autumn of the same year. The short delay would propagate the flame of enthusiasm; and his firmest hope was in a nation of soldiers still proud of the preeminence of their name and ambitious to emulate their hero Charlemagne, who in the popular romance of Turpin had achieved the conquest of the Holy Land. A latent motive of affection or vanity might influence the choice of Urban: he was himself a native of France, a monk of Clugny, and the first of his countrymen who ascended the throne of St. Peter. The pope had illustrated his family and province; nor is there perhaps a more exquisite gratification than to revisit, in a conspicuous dignity, the humble and laborious scenes of our youth.[†]

[T]he council which he convened [at Clermont] was not less numerous or respectable than the synod of Placentia [November A.D. 1095]. Besides his court and council of Roman cardinals, he was supported by thirteen archbishops and two hundred and twenty-five bishops: the number of mitred prelates was computed at four hundred; and the fathers of the church were blessed by the saints and enlightened by the doctors of the age. From the adjacent kingdoms, a martial train of lords and knights of power and renown attended the council, in high expectation of its resolves; and such was the ardor of zeal and curiosity that the city was filled, and many thousands, in the month of November, erected their tents or huts in the open field. A session of eight days produced some useful or edifying canons for the reformation of manners; a severe censure was pronounced against the license of private war; the Truce of God was confirmed, a suspension of hostilities during four days of the week; women and priests were placed under the safeguard of the church; and a protection of three years was extended to husbandmen and merchants, the defenseless victims of military rapine. But a law, however venerable be the sanction, cannot suddenly transform the temper of the times; and the benevolent efforts of Urban deserve the less praise, since he labored to appease some domestic quarrels that he might spread the flames of war from the Atlantic to the Euphrates. From the synod of Placentia, the rumor of his great design had gone forth among the nations: the clergy on their return had preached in every diocese the merit and glory of the deliverance of the Holy Land; and when the pope ascended a lofty scaffold in the market-place of Clermont, his eloquence was addressed to a well-prepared and impatient audience. His topics were obvious, his exhortation was vehement, his success inevitable. The orator was interrupted by the shout of thousands, who with one voice and in their rustic idiom exclaimed aloud, "God wills it, God wills it." "It is indeed the will of God," replied the pope; "and let this memorable word, the inspiration surely of the Holy Spirit, be forever adopted as your cry of battle, to animate the devotion and courage of the champions of Christ. His cross is the symbol of your salvation; wear it, a red, a bloody cross, as an external mark on your breasts or shoulders, as a pledge of your sacred and irrevocable engagement." The proposal was joyfully accepted; great numbers, both of the clergy and laity, impressed on their garments the sign of the cross and solicited the pope to march at their head. This dangerous honor was declined by the more prudent successor of Gregory, who alleged the schism of the church and the duties of his pastoral office, recommending to the faithful who were disqualified by sex or profession, by age or infirmity, to aid with their prayers and alms the personal service of their robust brethren. The name and powers of his legate he devolved on Adhemar, bishop of Puy, the first who had received the cross at his hands. The foremost of the temporal chiefs was Raymond, count of Toulouse, whose ambassadors in the council excused the absence and pledged the honor of their master. After the confession and absolution of their sins, the champions of the cross were dismissed with a superfluous admonition to invite their countrymen and friends; and their departure for the Holy

Land was fixed to the festival of the Assumption, the fifteenth of August, of the ensuing year.

So familiar and, as it were, so natural to man is the practice of violence that our indulgence allows the slightest provocation, the most disputable right, as a sufficient ground of national hostility. But the name and nature of a *holy war* demands a more rigorous scrutiny; nor can we hastily believe that the servants of the Prince of Peace would unsheathe the sword of destruction unless the motive were pure, the quarrel legitimate, and the necessity inevitable. The policy of an action may be determined from the tardy lessons of experience; but before we act, our conscience should be satisfied of the justice and propriety of our enterprise. In the age of the crusades, the Christians, both of the East and West, were persuaded of their lawfulness and merit; their arguments are clouded by the perpetual abuse of Scripture and rhetoric; but they seem to insist on the right of natural and religious defense, their peculiar title to the Holy Land, and the impiety of their Pagan and Mohammedan foes.

I. The right of a just defense may fairly include our civil and spiritual allies: it depends on the existence of danger; and that danger must be estimated by the twofold consideration of the malice and the power of our enemies. A pernicious tenet has been imputed to the Mohammedans, the duty of *extirpating* all other religions by the sword. This charge of ignorance and bigotry is refuted by the Koran, by the history of the Moslem conquerors, and by their public and legal toleration of the Christian worship. But it cannot be denied that the Oriental churches are depressed under their iron yoke; that in peace and war they assert a divine and indefeasible claim of universal empire; and that in their orthodox creed the unbelieving nations are continually threatened with the loss of religion or liberty. In the eleventh century, the victorious arms of the Turks presented a real and urgent apprehension of these losses. They had subdued in less than thirty years the kingdoms of Asia as far as Jerusalem and the Hellespont; and the Greek empire tottered on the verge of destruction. Besides an honest sympathy for their brethren, the Latins had a right and interest in the support of Constantinople, the most important barrier of the West; and the privilege of defense must reach to prevent as well as to repel an impending assault. But this salutary purpose might have been accomplished by a moderate succor; and our calmer reason must disclaim the innumerable hosts and remote operations which overwhelmed Asia and depopulated Europe.

II. Palestine could add nothing to the strength or safety of the Latins; and fanaticism alone could pretend to justify the conquest of that distant and narrow province. The Christians affirmed that their inalienable title to the promised land had been sealed by the blood of their divine Savior; it was their right and duty to rescue their inheritance from the unjust possessors who profaned his sepulchre and oppressed the pilgrimage of his disciples. Vainly would it be alleged that the preeminence of Jerusalem and the sanctity of Palestine have been abolished with the Mosaic law; that the God of the Christians is not a local deity, and that the recovery of Bethlehem or Calvary, his cradle or his tomb, will not atone for the violation of the moral precepts of the gospel. Such arguments glance aside from the leaden shield of superstition; and the religious mind will not easily relinquish its hold on the sacred ground of mystery and miracle.

III. But the holy wars which have been waged in every climate of the globe, from Egypt to Livonia and from Peru to Hindostan, require the support of some more general and flexible tenet. It has been often supposed, and sometimes affirmed, that a difference of religion is a worthy cause of hostility; that obstinate unbelievers may be slain or subdued by the champions of the cross; and that grace is the sole fountain of dominion as well as of mercy. Above four hundred years before the first crusade, the Eastern and Western provinces of the Roman empire had been acquired about the same time, and in the same manner, by the Barbarians of Germany and Arabia. Time and treaties had legitimated the conquest of the *Christian* Franks; but in the eyes of their subjects and neighbors, the Mohammedan princes were still tyrants and usurpers who, by the arms of war or rebellion, might be lawfully driven from their unlawful possession.

As the manners of the Christians were relaxed, their discipline of penance was enforced; and with the multiplication of sins, the remedies were multiplied. In the primitive church, a voluntary and open confession prepared the work of atonement. In the middle ages, the bishops and priests interrogated the criminal; compelled him to account for his thoughts, words, and actions; and prescribed the terms of his reconciliation with God. But as this discretionary power might alternately be abused by indulgence and tyranny, a rule of discipline was framed to inform and regulate the spiritual judges. This mode of legislation was invented by the Greeks; their *penitentials* were translated, or imitated, in the Latin church; and in the time of Charlemagne, the clergy of every diocese were provided with a code, which they prudently concealed from the knowledge of the vulgar. In this dangerous estimate of crimes and punishments, each case was supposed, each difference was remarked, by the experience or penetration of the monks; some sins are enumerated which innocence could not have suspected, and others which reason cannot believe; and the more ordinary offenses of fornication and adultery, of perjury and sacrilege, of rapine and murder, were expiated by a penance which, according to the various circumstances, was prolonged from forty days to seven years. During this term of mortification, the patient was healed, the criminal was absolved, by a salutary regimen of fasts and prayers: the disorder of his dress was expressive of grief and remorse; and he humbly abstained from all the business and pleasure of social life. But the rigid execution of these laws would have depopulated the palace, the camp, and the city; the Barbarians of the West believed and trembled; but nature often rebelled against principle; and the magistrate labored without effect to enforce the jurisdiction of the priest. A literal accomplishment of penance was indeed impracticable: the guilt of adultery was multiplied by daily repetition; that of homicide might involve the massacre of a whole people; each act was separately numbered; and in those times of anarchy and vice, a modest sinner might easily incur a debt of three hundred years. His insolvency was relieved by a commutation, or *indulgence:* a year of penance was appreciated at twenty-six *solidi* of silver, about four pounds sterling, for the rich; at three solidi, or nine shillings, for the indigent: and these alms were soon appropriated to the use of the church, which derived from the redemption of sins an inexhaustible source of opulence and dominion. A debt of three hundred years, or twelve hundred pounds, was enough to impoverish a plentiful fortune; the scarcity of gold and silver was supplied by the alienation of land; and the princely donations of Pepin and Charlemagne are expressly given for the *remedy* of their soul. It is a maxim of the civil law that whosoever cannot pay with his purse must pay with his body; and the practice of flagellation was adopted by the monks, a cheap though painful equivalent. By a fantastic arithmetic, a year of penance was taxed at three thousand lashes; and such was the skill and patience of a famous hermit, St. Dominic of the Iron Cuirass, that in six days he could discharge an entire century by a whipping of three hundred thousand stripes. His example was followed by many penitents of both sexes; and as a vicarious sacrifice was accepted, a sturdy disciplinarian might expiate on his own back the sins of his benefactors. These compensations of the purse and the person introduced in the eleventh century a more honorable mode of satisfaction. The merit of military service against the Saracens of Africa and Spain had been allowed by the predecessors of Urban the Second. In the council of Clermont, that pope proclaimed a *plenary indulgence* to those who should enlist under the banner of the cross; the absolution of *all* their sins, and a full receipt for *all* that might be due of canonical penance. The cold philosophy of modern times is incapable of feeling the impression that was made on a sinful and fanatic world. At the voice of their pastor, the robber, the incendiary, the homicide arose by thousands to redeem their souls by repeating on the infidels the same deeds which they had exercised against their Christian brethren; and the terms of atonement were eagerly embraced by offenders of every rank and denomination. None were pure; none were exempt from the guilt and penalty of sin; and those who were the least amenable to the justice of God and the church were the best entitled to the temporal and eternal recompense of their pious courage. If they fell, the spirit of the Latin clergy did not hesitate to adorn their tomb with the crown of martyrdom; and should they survive, they could expect without impatience the delay and increase of their heavenly reward. They offered their blood to the Son of God, who had laid down his life for their salvation: they took up the cross, and entered with confidence into the way of the Lord. His providence would watch over their safety; perhaps his visible and miraculous power would smooth the difficulties of their holy enterprise. The cloud and pillar of Jehovah had marched before the Israelites into the promised land. Might not the Christians more reasonably hope that the rivers would open for their passage; that the walls of their strongest cities would fall at the sound of their trumpets; and that the sun would be arrested in his mid-career, to allow them time for the destruction of the infidels?

Of the chiefs and soldiers who marched to the holy sepulchre, I will dare to affirm that *all* were prompted by the spirit of enthusiasm; the belief of merit, the hope of reward, and the assurance of divine aid. But I am equally persuaded that in *many* it was not the sole, that in *some* it was not the leading, principle of action. The use and abuse of religion are feeble to stem, they are strong and irresistible to impel, the stream of national manners. Against the private wars of the Barbarians, their bloody tournaments, licentious love, and judicial duels, the popes and synods might ineffectually thunder. It is a more easy task to provoke the metaphysical disputes of the Greeks, to drive into the cloister the victims of anarchy or despotism, to sanctify the patience of slaves and cowards, or to assume the merit of the humanity and benevolence of modern Christians. War and exercise were the reigning passions of the Franks or Latins; they were enjoined as a penance to gratify those passions, to visit distant lands, and to draw their swords against the nations of the East. Their victory, or even their attempt, would immortalize the names of the intrepid heroes of the cross; and the purest piety could not be insensible to the most splendid prospect of military glory. In the petty quarrels of Europe, they shed the blood of their friends and countrymen for the acquisition perhaps of a castle or a village. They could march with alacrity against the distant and hostile nations who were devoted to their arms; their fancy already grasped the golden scepters of Asia; and the conquest of Apulia and Sicily by the Normans might exalt to royalty the hopes of the most private adventurer. Christendom in her rudest state must have yielded to the climate and cultivation of the Mohammedan countries; and their natural and artificial wealth had been magnified by the tales of pilgrims and the gifts of an imperfect commerce. The vulgar, both the great and small, were taught to believe every wonder, of lands flowing with milk and honey, of mines and treasures, of gold and diamonds, of palaces of marble and jasper, and of odoriferous groves of cinnamon and frankincense. In this earthly paradise, each warrior depended on his sword to carve a plenteous and honorable establishment, which he measured only by the extent of his wishes. Their vassals and soldiers trusted their fortunes to God and their master: the spoils of a Turkish emir might enrich the meanest follower of the camp; and the flavor of the wines, the beauty of the Grecian women, were temptations more adapted to the nature than to the profession of the champions of the cross. The love of freedom was a powerful incitement to the multitudes who were oppressed by feudal or ecclesiastical tyranny. Under this holy sign, the peasants and burghers who were attached to the servitude of the glebe might escape from a haughty lord and transplant themselves and their families to a land of liberty. The monk might release himself from the discipline of his convent: the debtor might suspend the accumulation of usury and the pursuit of his creditors; and outlaws and malefactors of every cast might continue to brave the laws and elude the punishment of their crimes.

These motives were potent and numerous: when we have singly computed their weight on the mind of each individual, we must add the infinite series, the multiplying powers, of example and fashion. The first proselytes became the warmest and most effectual missionaries of the cross: among their friends and countrymen they preached the duty, the merit, and the recompense of their holy vow; and the most reluctant hearers were insensibly drawn within the whirlpool of persuasion and authority. The martial youths were fired by the reproach or suspicion of cowardice; the opportunity of visiting with an army the sepulchre of Christ was embraced by the old and infirm, by women and children, who consulted rather their zeal than their strength; and those who in the evening had derided the folly of their companions were the most eager the ensuing day to tread in their footsteps. The ignorance which magnified the hopes diminished the perils of the enterprise. Since the Turkish conquest, the paths of pilgrimage were obliterated; the chiefs themselves had an imperfect notion of the length of the way and the state of their enemies; and such was the stupidity of the people that, at the sight of the first city or castle beyond the limits of their knowledge, they were ready to ask whether that was not the Jerusalem, the term and object of their labors. Yet the more prudent of the crusaders, who were not sure that they should be fed from Heaven with a shower of quails or manna, provided themselves with those precious metals which in every country are the representatives of every commodity. To defray according to their rank the expenses of the road, princes alienated their provinces, nobles their lands and castles, peasants their cattle and the instruments of husbandry. The value of property was depreciated by the eager competition of multitudes; while the price of arms and horses was raised to an exorbitant height by the wants and impatience of the buyers. Those who remained at home, with sense and money, were enriched by the epidemical disease: the sovereigns acquired at a cheap rate the domains of their vassals; and the ecclesiastical purchasers completed the payment by the assurance of their prayers. The cross, which was commonly sewed on the garment in cloth or silk, was inscribed by some zealots on their skin: a hot iron or indelible liquor was applied to perpetuate the mark; and a crafty monk who showed the miraculous impression on his breast was repaid with the popular veneration and the richest benefices of Palestine.

The fifteenth of August had been fixed in the council of Clermont for the departure of the pilgrims [A.D. 1096]; but the day was anticipated by the thoughtless and needy crowd of plebeians, and I shall briefly despatch the calamities which they inflicted and suffered before I enter on the more serious and successful enterprise of the chiefs. Early in the spring, from the confines of France and Lorraine, above sixty thousand of the populace of both sexes flocked round the first missionary of the crusade and pressed him with clamorous importunity to lead them to the holy sepulchre. The hermit, assuming the character, without the talents or authority, of a general, impelled or obeyed the forward impulse of his votaries along the banks of the Rhine and Danube. Their wants and numbers soon compelled them to separate, and his lieutenant, Walter the Penniless, a valiant though needy soldier, conducted a vanguard of pilgrims whose condition may be determined from the proportion of eight horsemen to fifteen thousand foot. The example and footsteps of Peter were closely pursued by another fanatic, the monk Godescal, whose sermons had swept away fifteen or twenty thousand peasants from the villages of Germany. Their rear was again pressed by a herd of two hundred thousand, the most stupid and savage refuse of the people, who mingled with their devotion a brutal license of rapine, prostitution, and drunkenness. Some counts and gentlemen, at the head of three thousand horse, attended the motions of the multitude to partake in the spoil; but their genuine leaders (may we credit such folly?) were a goose and a goat, who were carried in the front, and to whom these worthy Christians ascribed an infusion of the divine spirit. Of these and of other bands of enthusiasts, the first and most easy warfare was against the Jews, the murderers of the Son of God. In the trading cities of the Moselle and the Rhine, their colonies were numerous and rich; and they enjoyed, under the protection of the emperor and the bishops, the free exercise of their religion. At Verdun, Treves, Mentz, Spires, Worms, many thousands of that unhappy people were pillaged and massacred: nor had they felt a more bloody stroke since the persecution of Hadrian. A remnant was saved by the firmness of their bishops, who accepted a feigned and transient conversion; but the more obstinate Jews opposed their fanaticism to the fanaticism of the Christians, barricaded their houses, and, precipitating themselves, their families, and their wealth into the rivers or the flames, disappointed the malice, or at least the avarice, of their implacable foes.

Between the frontiers of Austria and the seat of the Byzantine monarchy, the crusaders were compelled to traverse an interval of six hundred miles; the wild and desolate countries of Hungary and Bulgaria [A.D. 1096]. The soil is fruitful and intersected with rivers; but it was then covered with morasses and forests, which spread to a boundless extent whenever man has ceased to exercise his dominion over the earth. Both nations had imbibed the rudiments of Christianity; the Hungarians were ruled by their native princes, the Bulgarians by a lieutenant of the Greek emperor; but on the slightest provocation their ferocious nature was rekindled, and ample provocation was afforded by the disorders of the first pilgrims. Agriculture must have been unskillful and languid among a people whose cities were built of reeds and timber, which were deserted in the summer season for the tents of hunters and shepherds. A scanty supply of provisions was rudely demanded, forcibly seized, and greedily consumed; and on the first quarrel, the crusaders gave a loose to indignation and revenge. But their ignorance of the country, of war, and of discipline exposed them to every snare. The Greek praefect of Bulgaria commanded a regular force; at the trumpet of the Hungarian king, the eighth or the tenth of his martial subjects bent their bows and mounted on horseback; their policy was insidious, and their retaliation on these pious robbers was unrelenting and bloody. About a third of the naked fugitives (and the hermit Peter was of the number) escaped to the Thracian mountains; and the emperor, who respected the pilgrimage and succor of the Latins, conducted them by secure and easy journeys to Constantinople and advised them to await the arrival of their brethren. For a while they remembered their faults and losses; but no sooner were they revived by the hospitable entertainment than their venom was again inflamed; they stung their benefactor, and neither gardens nor palaces nor churches were safe from their depredations. For his own safety,

Alexius allured them to pass over to the Asiatic side of the Bosphorus; but their blind impetuosity soon urged them to desert the station which he had assigned and to rush headlong against the Turks who occupied the road to Jerusalem. The hermit, conscious of his shame, had withdrawn from the camp to Constantinople; and his lieutenant, Walter the Penniless, who was worthy of a better command, attempted without success to introduce some order and prudence among the herd of savages. They separated in quest of prey, and themselves fell an easy prey to the arts of the sultan. By a rumor that their foremost companions were rioting in the spoils of his capital, Soliman tempted the main body to descend into the plain of Nice: they were overwhelmed by the Turkish arrows; and a pyramid of bones informed their companions of the place of their defeat. Of the first crusaders, three hundred thousand had already perished before a single city was rescued from the infidels, before their graver and more noble brethren had completed the preparations of their enterprise.

None of the great sovereigns of Europe embarked their persons in the first crusade. . . . The religious ardor was more strongly felt by the princes of the second order, who held an important place in the feudal system. Their situation will naturally cast under four distinct heads the review of their names and characters; but I may escape some needless repetition by observing at once that courage and the exercise of arms are the common attribute of these Christian adventurers. I. The first rank both in war and council is justly due to Godfrey of Bouillon; and happy would it have been for the crusaders if they had trusted themselves to the sole conduct of that accomplished hero, a worthy representative of Charlemagne, from whom he was descended in the female line. . . . His valor was matured by prudence and moderation; his piety, though blind, was sincere; and in the tumult of a camp, he practiced the real and fictitious virtues of a convent. Superior to the private factions of the chiefs, he reserved his enmity for the enemies of Christ; and though he gained a kingdom by the attempt, his pure and disinterested zeal was acknowledged by his rivals. . . . II. In the parliament that was held at Paris, in the king's presence, about two months after the council of Clermont, Hugh, count of Vermandois, was the most conspicuous of the princes who assumed the cross. But the appellation of the Great was applied not so much to his merit or possessions (though neither were contemptible) as to the royal birth of the brother of the king of France. Robert, duke of Normandy, was the eldest son of William the Conqueror; but on his father's death he was deprived of the kingdom of England by his own indolence and the activity of his brother Rufus. . . . Another Robert was count of Flanders, a royal province which in this century gave three queens to the thrones of France, England, and Denmark: he was surnamed the Sword and Lance of the Christians; but in the exploits of a soldier he sometimes forgot the duties of a general. Stephen, count of Chartres, of Blois, and of Troyes, was one of the richest princes of the age. . . . His mind was improved by literature; and in the council of the chiefs, the eloquent Stephen was chosen to discharge the office of their president. These four were the principal leaders of the French, the Normans, and the pilgrims of the British isles: but the list of the barons who were possessed of three or four towns would exceed, says a contemporary, the catalogue of the Trojan war. III. In the south of France, the command was assumed by Adhemar, bishop of Puy, the pope's legate, and by Raymond, count of St. Giles and Toulouse, who added the prouder titles of duke of Narbonne and marquis of Provence. . . . IV. The name of Bohemond, the son of Robert Guiscard, was already famous by his double victory over the Greek emperor; but his father's will had reduced him to the principality of Tarentum and the remembrance of his Eastern trophies, till he was awakened by the rumor and passage of the French pilgrims. It is in the person of this Norman chief that we may seek for the coolest policy and ambition, with a small alloy of religious fanaticism. . . . Several princes of the Norman race accompanied this veteran general; and his cousin Tancred was the partner rather than the servant of the war. In the accomplished character of Tancred we discover all the virtues of a perfect knight, the true spirit of chivalry, which inspired the generous sentiments and social offices of man far better than the base philosophy or the baser religion of the times.

Between the age of Charlemagne and that of the crusades, a revolution had taken place among the Spaniards, the Normans, and the French, which was gradually extended to the rest of Europe. The service of the infantry was degraded to the plebeians; the cavalry formed the strength of the armies, and the honorable name of *miles,* or soldier, was confined to the gentlemen who served on horseback and were invested with the character of knighthood. The dukes and counts who had usurped the rights of sovereignty divided the provinces among their faithful barons: the barons distributed among their vassals the fiefs or benefices of their jurisdiction; and these military tenants, the peers of each other and of their lord, composed the noble or equestrian order, which disdained to conceive the peasant or burgher as of the same species with themselves. The dignity of their birth was preserved by pure and equal alliances; their sons alone who could produce four quarters or lines of ancestry without spot or reproach might legally pretend to the honor of knighthood; but a valiant plebeian was sometimes enriched and ennobled by the sword and became the father of a new race. A single knight could impart according to his judgment the character which he received; and the warlike sovereigns of Europe derived more glory from this personal distinction than from the luster of their diadem. This ceremony, of which some traces may be found in Tacitus and the woods of Germany, was in its origin simple and profane; the candidate, after some previous trial, was invested with the sword and spurs; and his cheek or shoulder was touched with a slight blow, as an emblem of the last affront which it was lawful for him to endure. But superstition mingled in every public and private action of life: in the holy wars, it sanctified the profession of arms; and the order of chivalry was assimilated in its rights and privileges to the sacred orders of priesthood. The bath and white garment of the novice were an indecent copy of the regeneration of baptism: his sword, which he offered on the altar, was blessed by the ministers of religion: his solemn reception was preceded by fasts and vigils; and he was created a knight in the name of God, of St. George, and of St. Michael the archangel. He swore to accomplish the duties of his profession; and education, example, and the public opinion were the inviolable guardians of his oath. As the champion of God and the ladies (I blush to unite such discordant names) he devoted himself to speak the truth; to maintain the right; to protect the distressed; to practice *courtesy*, a virtue less familiar to the ancients; to pursue the infidels; to despise the allurements of ease and safety; and to vindicate in every perilous adventure the honor of his character. The abuse of the same spirit provoked the illiterate knight to disdain the arts of industry and peace; to esteem himself the sole judge and avenger of his own injuries; and proudly to neglect the laws of civil society and military discipline. Yet the benefits of this institution, to refine the temper of Barbarians and to infuse some principles of faith, justice, and humanity, were strongly felt, and have been often observed. The asperity of national prejudice was softened; and the community of religion and arms spread a similar color and generous emulation over the face of Christendom. Abroad in enterprise and pilgrimage, at home in martial exercise, the warriors of every country were perpetually associated; and impartial taste must prefer a Gothic tournament to the Olympic games of classic antiquity. Instead of the naked spectacles which corrupted the manners of the Greeks and banished from the stadium the virgins and matrons, the pompous decoration of the lists was crowned with the presence of chaste and high-born beauty, from whose hands the conqueror received the prize of his dexterity and courage. The skill and strength that were exerted in wrestling and boxing bear a distant and doubtful relation to the merit of a soldier; but the tournaments, as they were invented in France and eagerly adopted both in the East and West, presented a lively image of the business of the field. The single combats, the general skirmish, the defense of a pass or castle, were rehearsed as in actual service; and the contest, both in real and mimic war, was decided by the superior management of the horse and lance. The lance was the proper and peculiar weapon of the knight: his horse was of a large and heavy breed; but this charger, till he was roused by the approaching danger, was usually led by an attendant, and he quietly rode a pad or palfrey of a more easy pace. His helmet and sword, his greaves and buckler, it would be superfluous to describe; but I may remark that at the period of the crusades, the armor was less ponderous than in later times; and that instead of a massy cuirass, his breast was defended by a hauberk or coat of mail. When their long lances were fixed in the rest, the warriors furiously spurred their horses against the foe; and the light cavalry of the Turks and Arabs could seldom stand against the direct and impetuous weight of their charge. Each knight was attended to the field by his faithful squire, a youth of equal birth and similar hopes; he was followed by his archers and men at arms, and four or five or six soldiers were computed as the furniture of a complete *lance.* In the expeditions to the neighboring kingdoms or the Holy Land, the duties of the feudal tenure no longer subsisted; the voluntary service of the knights and their followers were either prompted by zeal or attachment, or purchased with rewards and promises; and the numbers of each squadron were measured by the power, the wealth, and the fame of each independent chieftain. They were distinguished by his banner, his armorial coat, and his cry of war; and the most ancient families of Europe must seek in these achievements the origin and proof of their nobility. In this rapid portrait of chivalry I have been urged to anticipate on the story of the crusades, at once an effect and a cause of this memorable institution.

Such were the troops and such the leaders who assumed the cross for the deliverance of the holy sepulchre. As soon as they were relieved by the absence of the plebeian multitude, they encouraged each other, by interviews and messages, to accomplish their vow and hasten their departure. Their wives and sisters were desirous of partaking the danger and merit of the pilgrimage: their portable treasures were conveyed in bars of silver and gold; and the princes and barons were attended by their equipage of hounds and hawks to amuse their leisure and to supply their table. The difficulty of procuring subsistence for so many myriads of men and horses engaged them to separate their forces: their choice or situation determined the road; and it was agreed to meet in the neighborhood of Constantinople, and from thence to begin their operations against the Turks. . . . They separately accomplished their passage, regardless of safety or dignity; and within nine months from the feast of the Assumption, the day appointed by Urban, all the Latin princes had reached Constantinople [August 15, A.D. 1096–May A.D. 1097].†

In some Oriental tale I have read the fable of a shepherd who was ruined by the accomplishment of his own wishes: he had prayed for water; the Ganges was turned into his grounds, and his flock and cottage were swept away by the inundation. Such was the fortune, or at least the apprehension, of the Greek emperor Alexius Comnenus, whose name has already appeared in this history, and whose conduct is so differently represented by his daughter Anne and by the Latin writers. In the council of Placentia, his ambassadors had solicited a moderate succor, perhaps of ten thousand soldiers, but he was astonished by the approach of so many potent chiefs and fanatic nations. The emperor fluctuated between hope and fear, between timidity and courage; but in the crooked policy which he mistook for wisdom, I cannot believe, I cannot discern, that he maliciously conspired against the life or honor of the French heroes. The promiscuous multitudes of Peter the Hermit were savage beasts, alike destitute of humanity and reason: nor was it possible for Alexius to prevent or deplore their destruction. The troops of Godfrey and his peers were less contemptible but not less suspicious to the Greek emperor. Their motives *might* be pure and pious: but he was equally alarmed by his knowledge of the ambitious Bohemond and his ignorance of the Transalpine chiefs: the courage of the French was blind and headstrong; they might be tempted by the luxury and wealth of Greece and elated by the view and opinion of their invincible strength: and Jerusalem might be forgotten in the prospect of Constantinople.†

Alexius indulged or affected the ambitious hope of leading his new allies to subvert the thrones of the East; but the calmer dictates of reason and temper dissuaded him from exposing his royal person to the faith of unknown and lawless Barbarians. His prudence or his pride was content with extorting from the French princes an oath of homage and fidelity, and a solemn promise that they would either restore or hold their Asiatic conquests as the humble and loyal vassals of the Roman empire. Their independent spirit was fired at the mention of this foreign and voluntary servitude: they successively yielded to the dexterous application of gifts and flattery; and the first proselytes became the most eloquent and effectual missionaries to multiply the companions of their shame. . . . The spirit of chivalry was . . . subdued. . . . The best and most ostensible reason was the impossibility of passing the sea and accomplishing their vow without the license and the vessels of Alexius; but they cherished a secret hope that as soon as they trod the continent of Asia, their swords would obliterate their shame and dissolve the engagement, which on his side might not be very faithfully performed. The ceremony of their homage was grateful to a people who had long since considered pride as the substitute of power. High on his throne, the emperor sat mute and immovable: his majesty was adored by the Latin princes; and they submitted to kiss either his feet or his knees, an indignity which their own writers are ashamed to confess and unable to deny.†

The conquest of Asia was undertaken and achieved by Alexander with thirty-five thousand Macedonians and Greeks; and his best hope was in the strength and discipline of his phalanx of infantry. The principal force of the crusaders consisted in their cavalry; and when that force was mustered in the plains of Bithynia, the knights and their martial attendants on horseback amounted to one hundred thousand fighting men, completely armed with the helmet and coat of mail

[May A.D. 1097]. The value of these soldiers deserved a strict and authentic account; and the flower of European chivalry might furnish, in a first effort, this formidable body of heavy horse. A part of the infantry might be enrolled for the service of scouts, pioneers, and archers; but the promiscuous crowd were lost in their own disorder; and we depend not on the eyes and knowledge but on the belief and fancy of a chaplain of Count Baldwin in the estimate of six hundred thousand pilgrims able to bear arms, besides the priests and monks, the women and children of the Latin camp. The reader starts; and before he is recovered from his surprise, I shall add, on the same testimony, that if all who took the cross had accomplished their vow, above SIX MILLIONS would have migrated from Europe to Asia. Under this oppression of faith, I derive some relief from a more sagacious and thinking writer, who, after the same review of the cavalry, accuses the credulity of the priest of Chartres, and even doubts whether the *Cisalpine* regions (in the geography of a Frenchman) were sufficient to produce and pour forth such incredible multitudes. The coolest skepticism will remember that of these religious volunteers, great numbers never beheld Constantinople and Nice. Of enthusiasm the influence is irregular and transient: many were detained at home by reason or cowardice, by poverty or weakness; and many were repulsed by the obstacles of the way, the more insuperable as they were unforeseen to these ignorant fanatics. The savage countries of Hungary and Bulgaria were whitened with their bones: their vanguard was cut in pieces by the Turkish sultan; and the loss of the first adventure, by the sword or climate or fatigue, has already been stated at three hundred thousand men. Yet the myriads that survived, that marched, that pressed forwards on the holy pilgrimage, were a subject of astonishment to themselves and to the Greeks. The copious energy of her language sinks under the efforts of the princess Anne: the images of locusts, of leaves and flowers, of the sands of the sea or the stars of Heaven, imperfectly represent what she had seen and heard; and the daughter of Alexius exclaims that Europe was loosened from its foundations and hurled against Asia. The ancient hosts of Darius and Xerxes labor under the same doubt of a vague and indefinite magnitude; but I am inclined to believe that a larger number has never been contained within the lines of a single camp than at the siege of Nice, the first operation of the Latin princes. Their motives, their characters, and their arms have been already displayed.

Of their troops the most numerous portion were natives of France: the Low Countries, the banks of the Rhine, and Apulia sent a powerful reinforcement: some bands of adventurers were drawn from Spain, Lombardy, and England; and from the distant bogs and mountains of Ireland or Scotland issued some naked and savage fanatics, ferocious at home but unwarlike abroad. Had not superstition condemned the sacrilegious prudence of depriving the poorest or weakest Christian of the merit of the pilgrimage, the useless crowd, with mouths but without hands, might have been stationed in the Greek empire till their companions had opened and secured the way of the Lord. A small remnant of the pilgrims who passed the Bosphorus was permitted to visit the holy sepulchre. Their Northern constitution was scorched by the rays and infected by the vapors of a Syrian sun. They consumed with heedless prodigality their stores of water and provision: their numbers exhausted the inland country: the sea was remote, the Greeks were unfriendly, and the Christians of every sect fled before the voracious and cruel rapine of their brethren. In the dire necessity of famine, they sometimes roasted and devoured the flesh of their infant or adult captives. Among the Turks and Saracens, the idolaters of Europe were rendered more odious by the name and reputation of Cannibals; the spies who introduced themselves into the kitchen of Bohemond were shown several human bodies turning on the spit: and the artful Norman encouraged a report which increased at the same time the abhorrence and the terror of the infidels.

I have expatiated with pleasure on the first steps of the crusaders as they paint the manners and character of Europe: but I shall abridge the tedious and uniform narrative of their blind achievements, which were performed by strength and are described by ignorance.

[*The crusaders successfully besiege Nice (May 14–June 20, A.D. 1097) and then Antioch (October 21, A.D. 1097–June 3, A.D. 1098).*]

In the eventful period of the siege and defense of Antioch, the crusaders were alternately exalted by victory or sunk in despair; either swelled with plenty or emaciated with hunger. A speculative reasoner might suppose that their faith had a strong and serious influence on their practice; and that the soldiers of the cross, the deliverers of the holy sepulchre, prepared themselves by a sober and virtuous life for the daily contemplation of martyrdom. Experience blows away this charitable illusion; and seldom does the history of profane war display such scenes of intemperance and prostitution as were exhibited under the walls of Antioch. The grove of Daphne no longer flourished; but the Syrian air was still impregnated with the same vices; the Christians were seduced by every temptation that nature either prompts or reprobates; the authority of the chiefs was despised; and sermons and edicts were alike fruitless against those scandalous disorders not less pernicious to military discipline than repugnant to evangelic purity. In the first days of the siege and the possession of Antioch, the Franks consumed with wanton and thoughtless prodigality the frugal subsistence of weeks and months: the desolate country no longer yielded a supply; and from that country they were at length excluded by the arms of the besieging Turks. Disease, the faithful companion of want, was envenomed by the rains of the winter, the summer heats, unwholesome food, and the close imprisonment of multitudes. The pictures of famine and pestilence are always the same, and always disgustful; and our imagination may suggest the nature of their sufferings and their resources. The remains of treasure or spoil were eagerly lavished in the purchase of the vilest nourishment; and dreadful must have been the calamities of the poor, since, after paying three marks of silver for a goat and fifteen for a lean camel, the count of Flanders was reduced to beg a dinner, and Duke Godfrey to borrow a horse. Sixty thousand horse had been reviewed in the camp: before the end of the siege they were diminished to two thousand, and scarcely two hundred fit for service could be mustered on the day of battle. Weakness of body and terror of mind extinguished the ardent enthusiasm of the pilgrims; and every motive of honor and religion was subdued by the desire of life. Among the chiefs, three heroes may be found without fear or reproach: Godfrey of Bouillon was supported by his magnanimous piety; Bohemond by ambition and interest; and Tancred declared, in the true spirit of chivalry, that as long as he was at the head of forty knights, he would never relinquish the enterprise of Palestine. But the count of Toulouse and Provence was suspected of a voluntary indisposition; the duke of Normandy was recalled from the sea-shore by the censures of the church; Hugh the Great, though he led the vanguard of the battle, embraced an ambiguous opportunity of returning to France; and Stephen, count of Chartres, basely deserted the standard which he bore and the council in which he presided. The soldiers were discouraged by the flight of William, viscount of Melun, surnamed the *Carpenter* from the weighty strokes of his axe; and the saints were scandalized by the fall of Peter the Hermit, who, after arming Europe against Asia, attempted to escape from the penance of a necessary fast. Of the multitude of recreant warriors, the names (says an historian) are blotted from the book of life; and the opprobrious epithet of the rope-dancers was applied to the deserters who dropped in the night from the walls of Antioch. The emperor Alexius, who seemed to advance to the succor of the Latins, was dismayed by the assurance of their hopeless condition. They expected their fate in silent despair; oaths and punishments were tried without effect; and to rouse the soldiers to the defense of the walls, it was found necessary to set fire to their quarters.

For their salvation and victory, they were indebted to the same fanaticism which had led them to the brink of ruin. In such a cause and in such an army, visions, prophecies, and miracles were frequent and familiar. In the distress of Antioch, they were repeated with unusual energy and success: St. Ambrose had assured a pious ecclesiastic that two years of trial must precede the season of deliverance and grace; the deserters were stopped by the presence and reproaches of Christ himself; the dead had promised to arise and combat with their brethren; the Virgin had obtained the pardon of their sins; and their confidence was revived by a visible sign, the seasonable and splendid discovery of the HOLY LANCE. The policy of their chiefs has on this occasion been admired, and might surely be excused; but a pious fraud is seldom produced by the cool conspiracy of many persons; and a voluntary impostor might depend on the support of the wise and the credulity of the people. Of the diocese of Marseilles, there was a priest of low cunning and loose manners, and his name was Peter Bartholemy. He presented himself at the door of the council-chamber to disclose an apparition of St. Andrew, which had been thrice reiterated in his sleep with a dreadful menace if he presumed to suppress the commands of Heaven. "At Antioch," said the apostle, "in the church of my brother St. Peter, near the high altar, is concealed the steel head of the lance that pierced the side of our Redeemer. In three days that instrument of eternal and now of temporal salvation will be manifested to his disciples. Search and ye shall find: bear it aloft in battle; and that mystic weapon shall penetrate the souls of the miscreants." The pope's legate, the bishop of Puy, affected to listen with coldness and distrust; but the revelation was eagerly accepted by Count Raymond, whom his faithful subject, in the name of the apostle, had chosen for the guardian of the holy lance. The experiment was resolved; and on the third day, after a due preparation of prayer and fasting, the priest of Marseilles introduced twelve trusty spectators, among whom were the count and his chaplain; and the church doors were barred against the impetuous multitude. The ground was opened in the appointed place; but the workmen, who relieved each other, dug to the depth of twelve feet without discovering the object of their search. In the evening, when Count Raymond had withdrawn to his post and the weary assistants began to murmur, Bartholemy, in his shirt and without his shoes, boldly descended into the pit; the darkness of the hour and of the place enabled him to secrete and deposit the head of a Saracen lance; and the first sound, the first gleam, of the steel was saluted with a devout rapture. The holy lance was drawn from its recess, wrapped in a veil of silk and gold and exposed to the veneration of the crusaders; their anxious suspense burst forth in a general shout of joy and hope, and the desponding troops were again inflamed with the enthusiasm of valor. Whatever had been the arts and whatever might be the sentiments of the chiefs, they skillfully improved this fortunate revolution by every aid that discipline and devotion could afford. The soldiers were dismissed to their quarters with an injunction to fortify their minds and bodies for the approaching conflict, freely to bestow their last pittance on themselves and their horses, and to expect with the dawn of day the signal of victory. On the festival of St. Peter and St. Paul, the gates of Antioch were thrown open: a martial psalm, "Let the Lord arise and let his enemies be scattered!," was chanted by a procession of priests and monks; the battle array was marshaled in twelve divisions, in honor of the twelve apostles; and the holy lance, in the absence of Raymond, was entrusted to the hands of his chaplain. The influence of this relic or trophy was felt by the servants, and perhaps by the enemies, of Christ; and its potent energy was heightened by an accident, a stratagem, or a rumor of a miraculous complexion. Three knights, in white garments and resplendent arms, either issued or seemed to issue from the hills: the voice of Adhemar, the pope's legate, proclaimed them as the martyrs St. George, St. Theodore, and St. Maurice: the tumult of battle allowed no time for doubt or scrutiny; and the welcome apparition dazzled the eyes or the imagination of a fanatic army. In the season of danger and triumph, the revelation of Bartholemy of Marseilles was unanimously asserted; but as soon as the temporary service was accomplished, the personal dignity and liberal arms which the count of Toulouse derived from the custody of the holy lance, provoked the envy and awakened the reason of his rivals. A Norman clerk presumed to sift, with a philosophic spirit, the truth of the legend, the circumstances of the discovery, and the character of the prophet; and the pious Bohemond ascribed their deliverance to the merits and intercession of Christ alone. For a while, the Provincials defended their national palladium with clamors and arms, and new visions condemned to death and Hell the profane skeptics who presumed to scrutinize the truth and merit of the discovery. The prevalence of incredulity compelled the author to submit his life and veracity to the judgment of God. A pile of dry faggots, four feet high and fourteen long, was erected in the midst of the camp; the flames burnt fiercely to the elevation of thirty cubits; and a narrow path of twelve inches was left for the perilous trial. The unfortunate priest of Marseilles traversed the fire with dexterity and speed; but the thighs and belly were scorched by the intense heat; he expired the next day; and the logic of believing minds will pay some regard to his dying protestations of innocence and truth. Some efforts were made by the Provincials to substitute a cross, a ring, or a tabernacle in the place of the holy lance, which soon vanished in contempt and oblivion. Yet the revelation of Antioch is gravely asserted by succeeding historians: and such is the progress of credulity that miracles most doubtful on the spot and at the moment will be received with implicit faith at a convenient distance of time and space.

[*The crusaders besiege and conquer Jerusalem
(June 7–July 15, A.D. 1099).*]

[A]bout four hundred and sixty years after the conquest of Omar, the holy city was rescued from the Mohammedan yoke. In the pillage of public and private wealth, the adventurers had agreed to respect the exclusive property of the first occupant; and the spoils of the great mosque, seventy lamps and massy vases of gold and silver, rewarded

the diligence and displayed the generosity of Tancred. A bloody sacrifice was offered by his mistaken votaries to the God of the Christians:
resistance might provoke but neither age nor sex could mollify their
implacable rage: they indulged themselves three days in a promiscuous massacre; and the infection of the dead bodies produced an epidemical disease. After seventy thousand Moslems had been put to the
sword and the harmless Jews had been burnt in their synagogue, they
could still reserve a multitude of captives whom interest or lassitude
persuaded them to spare. Of these savage heroes of the cross, Tancred
alone betrayed some sentiments of compassion; yet we may praise the
more selfish lenity of Raymond, who granted a capitulation and safe-
conduct to the garrison of the citadel. The holy sepulchre was now
free; and the bloody victors prepared to accomplish their vow. Bare-
headed and barefoot, with contrite hearts and in an humble posture,
they ascended the hill of Calvary amidst the loud anthems of the
clergy; kissed the stone which had covered the Savior of the world;
and bedewed with tears of joy and penitence the monument of their
redemption. This union of the fiercest and most tender passions has
been variously considered by two philosophers; by the one, as easy and
natural; by the other, as absurd and incredible. Perhaps it is too rigorously applied to the same persons and the same hour; the example of
the virtuous Godfrey awakened the piety of his companions; while
they cleansed their bodies, they purified their minds; nor shall I believe that the most ardent in slaughter and rapine were the foremost in
the procession to the holy sepulchre.†

The revenue and jurisdiction of the lawful patriarch were usurped
by the Latin clergy: the exclusion of the Greeks and Syrians was justified by the reproach of heresy or schism; and under the iron yoke of
their deliverers, the Oriental Christians regretted the tolerating government of the Arabian caliphs. Daimbert, archbishop of Pisa, had
long been trained in the secret policy of Rome: he brought a fleet of
his countrymen to the succor of the Holy Land and was installed,
without a competitor, the spiritual and temporal head of the church.
The new patriarch immediately grasped the scepter which had been
acquired by the toil and blood of the victorious pilgrims; and both
Godfrey and Bohemond submitted to receive at his hands the investiture of their feudal possessions. Nor was this sufficient; Daimbert
claimed the immediate property of Jerusalem and Jaffa; instead of a

firm and generous refusal, the hero negotiated with the priest; a quarter of either city was ceded to the church; and the modest bishop was satisfied with an eventual reversion of the rest on the death of Godfrey without children, or on the future acquisition of a new seat at Cairo or Damascus.

Without this indulgence, the conqueror would have almost been stripped of his infant kingdom, which consisted only of Jerusalem and Jaffa, with about twenty villages and towns of the adjacent country. Within this narrow verge, the Mohammedans were still lodged in some impregnable castles: and the husbandman, the trader, and the pilgrim were exposed to daily and domestic hostility. By the arms of Godfrey himself and of the two Baldwins, his brother and cousin, who succeeded to the throne, the Latins breathed with more ease and safety; and at length they equaled in the extent of their dominions, though not in the millions of their subjects, the ancient princes of Judah and Israel [A.D. 1099–1187]. . . . The laws and language, the manners and titles, of the French nation and Latin church were introduced into these transmarine colonies. According to the feudal jurisprudence, the principal states and subordinate baronies descended in the line of male and female succession: but the children of the first conquerors, a motley and degenerate race, were dissolved by the luxury of the climate; the arrival of new crusaders from Europe was a doubtful hope and a casual event. . . . [T]he firmest bulwark of Jerusalem was founded on the knights of the Hospital of St. John, and of the temple of Solomon; on the strange association of a monastic and military life, which fanaticism might suggest but which policy must approve. The flower of the nobility of Europe aspired to wear the cross and to profess the vows of these respectable orders; their spirit and discipline were immortal; and the speedy donation of twenty-eight thousand farms or manors enabled them to support a regular force of cavalry and infantry for the defense of Palestine. The austerity of the convent soon evaporated in the exercise of arms; the world was scandalized by the pride, avarice, and corruption of these Christian soldiers; their claims of immunity and jurisdiction disturbed the harmony of the church and state; and the public peace was endangered by their jealous emulation. But in their most dissolute period, the knights of their hospital and temple maintained their fearless and fanatic character: they neglected to live, but they were prepared to die, in the service of Christ.[†]

The spirit of freedom which pervades the feudal institutions was felt in its strongest energy by the volunteers of the cross, who elected for their chief the most deserving of his peers. Amidst the slaves of Asia, unconscious of the lesson or example, a model of political liberty was introduced; and the laws of the French kingdom are derived from the purest source of equality and justice. Of such laws, the first and indispensable condition is the assent of those whose obedience they require and for whose benefit they are designed. No sooner had Godfrey of Bouillon accepted the office of supreme magistrate than he solicited the public and private advice of the Latin pilgrims who were the best skilled in the statutes and customs of Europe. From these materials, with the counsel and approbation of the patriarch and barons, of the clergy and laity, Godfrey composed the ASSISE OF JERUSALEM, a precious monument of feudal jurisprudence. The new code, attested by the seals of the king, the patriarch, and the viscount of Jerusalem, was deposited in the holy sepulchre, enriched with the improvements of succeeding times, and respectfully consulted as often as any doubtful question arose in the tribunals of Palestine [A.D. 1099–1369].[†]

Among the causes which enfranchised the plebeians from the yoke of feudal tyranny, the institution of cities and corporations is one of the most powerful; and if those of Palestine are coeval with the first crusade, they may be ranked with the most ancient of the Latin world. Many of the pilgrims had escaped from their lords under the banner of the cross; and it was the policy of the French princes to tempt their stay by the assurance of the rights and privileges of freemen. It is expressly declared in the Assise of Jerusalem that after instituting for his knights and barons the court of peers, in which he presided himself, Godfrey of Bouillon established a second tribunal in which his person was represented by his viscount. The jurisdiction of this inferior court extended over the burgesses of the kingdom; and it was composed of a select number of the most discreet and worthy citizens, who were sworn to judge according to the laws of the actions and fortunes of their equals. In the conquest and settlement of new cities, the example of Jerusalem was imitated by the kings and their great vassals; and above thirty similar corporations were founded before the loss of the

Holy Land. Another class of subjects, the Syrians or Oriental Christians, were oppressed by the zeal of the clergy and protected by the toleration of the state. Godfrey listened to their reasonable prayer that they might be judged by their own national laws. A third court was instituted for their use, of limited and domestic jurisdiction: the sworn members were Syrians, in blood, language, and religion; but the office of the president (in Arabic, of the *rais*) was sometimes exercised by the viscount of the city. At an immeasurable distance below the *nobles,* the *burgesses,* and the *strangers,* the Assise of Jerusalem condescends to mention the *villains* and *slaves,* the peasants of the land and the captives of war, who were almost equally considered as the objects of property. The relief or protection of these unhappy men was not esteemed worthy of the care of the legislator; but he diligently provides for the recovery, though not indeed for the punishment, of the fugitives. Like hounds or hawks who had strayed from the lawful owner, they might be lost and claimed: the slave and falcon were of the same value; but three slaves or twelve oxen were accumulated to equal the price of the war-horse; and a sum of three hundred pieces of gold was fixed in the age of chivalry as the equivalent of the more noble animal.

CHAPTER LIX

The Crusades

*Preservation of the Greek empire. • Numbers, passage, and event of
the second and third crusades. • St. Bernard. • Reign of
Saladin in Egypt and Syria. • His conquest of Jerusalem. •
Naval crusades. • Richard the First of England. • Pope Innocent
the Third; and the fourth and fifth crusades. • The emperor
Frederic the Second. • Louis the Ninth of France; and the two last
crusades. • Expulsion of the Latins or Franks by the Mamalukes.*

In a style less grave than that of history, I should perhaps compare the
emperor Alexius [who reigned A.D. 1097–1118] to the jackal who is
said to follow the steps and to devour the leavings of the lion. Whatever had been his fears and toils in the passage of the first crusade, they
were amply recompensed by the subsequent benefits which he derived
from the exploits of the Franks. His dexterity and vigilance secured
their first conquest of Nice; and from this threatening station the
Turks were compelled to evacuate the neighborhood of Constantinople. While the crusaders, with blind valor, advanced into the midland
countries of Asia, the crafty Greek improved the favorable occasion
when the emirs of the sea-coast were recalled to the standard of the
sultan. The Turks were driven from the isles of Rhodes and Chios: the
cities of Ephesus and Smyrna, of Sardes, Philadelphia, and Laodicea
were restored to the empire, which Alexius enlarged from the Hellespont to the banks of the Maeander and the rocky shores of Pamphylia.
The churches resumed their splendor: the towns were rebuilt and fortified; and the desert country was peopled with colonies of Christians,
who were gently removed from the more distant and dangerous frontier. In these paternal cares, we may forgive Alexius if he forgot the deliverance of the holy sepulchre; but by the Latins, he was stigmatized
with the foul reproach of treason and desertion. They had sworn fidelity and obedience to his throne; but he had promised to assist their
enterprise in person, or at least with his troops and treasures: his base
retreat dissolved their obligations; and the sword, which had been the

instrument of their victory, was the pledge and title of their just independence. It does not appear that the emperor attempted to revive his obsolete claims over the kingdom of Jerusalem; but the borders of Cilicia and Syria were more recent in his possession and more accessible to his arms.... The Seljukian dynasty of Roum was separated on all sides from the sea and their Moslem brethren; the power of the sultan was shaken by the victories and even the defeats of the Franks; and after the loss of Nice, they removed their throne to Cogni or Iconium, an obscure and inland town above three hundred miles from Constantinople. Instead of trembling for their capital, the Comnenian princes waged an offensive war against the Turks, and the first crusade prevented the fall of the declining empire.

In the twelfth century, three great emigrations marched by land from the West for the relief of Palestine. The soldiers and pilgrims of Lombardy, France, and Germany were excited by the example and success of the first crusade [A.D. 1101]. Forty-eight years after the deliverance of the holy sepulchre, the emperor and the French king, Conrad the Third and Louis the Seventh, undertook the second crusade to support the falling fortunes of the Latins [A.D. 1147]. A grand division of the third crusade was led by the emperor Frederic Barbarossa, who sympathized with his brothers of France and England in the common loss of Jerusalem [A.D. 1189]. These three expeditions may be compared in their resemblance of the greatness of numbers, their passage through the Greek empire, and the nature and event of their Turkish warfare, and a brief parallel may save the repetition of a tedious narrative. However splendid it may seem, a regular story of the crusades would exhibit the perpetual return of the same causes and effects; and the frequent attempts for the defense or recovery of the Holy Land would appear so many faint and unsuccessful copies of the original.

I. Of the swarms that so closely trod in the footsteps of the first pilgrims, the chiefs were equal in rank, though unequal in fame and merit, to Godfrey of Bouillon and his fellow-adventurers.... The armies of the second crusade might have claimed the conquest of Asia; the nobles of France and Germany were animated by the presence of their sovereigns; and both the rank and personal character of Conrad and Louis gave a dignity to their cause and a discipline to their force which might be vainly expected from the feudatory chiefs.... In the third crusade, as the French and English preferred the navigation of the Mediterranean, the host of Frederic Barbarossa was less numerous. . . . [E]xtravagant reckonings prove only the astonishment of contemporaries; but their astonishment most strongly bears testimony to the existence of an enormous, though indefinite, multitude. The Greeks might applaud their superior knowledge of the arts and stratagems of war, but they confessed the strength and courage of the French cavalry and the infantry of the Germans; and the strangers are described as an iron race, of gigantic stature, who darted fire from their eyes and spilt blood like water on the ground. Under the banners of Conrad, a troop of females rode in the attitude and armor of men; and the chief of these Amazons, from her gilt spurs and buskins, obtained the epithet of the Goldenfooted Dame.

II. The number and character of the strangers was an object of terror to the effeminate Greeks, and the sentiment of fear is nearly allied to that of hatred. This aversion was suspended or softened by the apprehension of the Turkish power; and the invectives of the Latins will not bias our more candid belief that the emperor Alexius dissembled their insolence, eluded their hostilities, counseled their rashness, and opened to their ardor the road of pilgrimage and conquest. But when the Turks had been driven from Nice and the sea-coast, when the Byzantine princes no longer dreaded the distant sultans of Cogni, they felt with purer indignation the free and frequent passage of the Western Barbarians, who violated the majesty and endangered the safety of the empire. The second and third crusades were undertaken under the reign of Manuel Comnenus and Isaac Angelus. Of the former, the passions were always impetuous and often malevolent; and the natural union of a cowardly and a mischievous temper was exemplified in the latter, who, without merit or mercy, could punish a tyrant and occupy his throne. It was secretly and perhaps tacitly resolved by the prince and people to destroy, or at least to discourage, the pilgrims by every species of injury and oppression; and their want of prudence and discipline continually afforded the pretense or the opportunity. The Western monarchs had stipulated a safe passage and fair market in the country of their Christian brethren; the treaty had been ratified by oaths and hostages; and the poorest soldier of Frederic's army was furnished with three marks of silver to defray his expenses on the road. But every engagement was violated by treachery and injustice; and the complaints of the Latins are attested by the honest confession of a Greek historian, who has dared to prefer truth to his country. Instead of a hospitable reception, the gates of the cities, both in Europe and Asia, were closely barred against the crusaders; and the scanty pittance of food was let down in baskets from the walls. Experience or foresight might excuse this timid jealousy; but the common duties of humanity prohibited the mixture of chalk or other poisonous ingredients in the bread; and should Manuel be acquitted of any foul connivance, he is guilty of coining base money for the purpose of trading with the pilgrims. In every step of their march they were stopped or misled: the governors had private orders to fortify the passes and break down the bridges against them: the stragglers were pillaged and murdered: the soldiers and horses were pierced in the woods by arrows from an invisible hand; the sick were burnt in their beds; and the dead bodies were hung on gibbets along the highways. These injuries exasperated the champions of the cross, who were not endowed with evangelical patience; and the Byzantine princes who had provoked the unequal conflict promoted the embarkation and march of these formidable guests. On the verge of the Turkish frontier Barbarossa spared the guilty Philadelphia, rewarded the hospitable Laodicea, and deplored the hard necessity that had stained his sword with any drops of Christian blood. . . . While they viewed with hatred and suspicion the Latin pilgrims, the Greek emperors maintained a strict, though secret, alliance with the Turks and Saracens. Isaac Angelus complained that by his friendship for the great Saladin he had incurred the enmity of the Franks; and a mosque was founded at Constantinople for the public exercise of the religion of Mohammed.

III. The swarms that followed the first crusade were destroyed in Anatolia by famine, pestilence, and the Turkish arrows; and the princes only escaped with some squadrons of horse to accomplish their lamentable pilgrimage. A just opinion may be formed of their knowledge and humanity; of their knowledge, from the design of subduing Persia and Chorasan in their way to Jerusalem; of their humanity, from the massacre of the Christian people, a friendly city, who came out to meet them with palms and crosses in their hands. The arms of Conrad and Louis were less cruel and imprudent; but the event of the second crusade was still more ruinous to Christendom; and the Greek Manuel is accused by his own subjects of giving seasonable intelligence to the sultan and treacherous guides to the Latin princes.

[*Conrad and Louis arrive at Jerusalem with only the sad remnants of their forces. Frederic Barbarossa drowns while crossing a river in Asia Minor. His forces are overwhelmed.*]

The enthusiasm of the first crusade is a natural and simple event, while hope was fresh, danger untried, and enterprise congenial to the spirit of the times. But the obstinate perseverance of Europe may indeed excite our pity and admiration; that no instruction should have been drawn from constant and adverse experience; that the same confidence should have repeatedly grown from the same failures; that six succeeding generations should have rushed headlong down the precipice that was open before them; and that men of every condition should have staked their public and private fortunes on the desperate adventure of possessing or recovering a tombstone two thousand miles from their country. In a period of two centuries after the council of Clermont, each spring and summer produced a new emigration of pilgrim warriors for the defense of the Holy Land; but the seven great armaments or crusades were excited by some impending or recent calamity: the nations were moved by the authority of their pontiffs, and the example of their kings: their zeal was kindled and their reason was silenced by the voice of their holy orators; and among these Bernard, the monk or the saint, may claim the most honorable place [A.D. 1091–1153]. About eight years before the first conquest of Jerusalem, he was born of a noble family in Burgundy; at the age of three-and-twenty he buried himself in the monastery of Citeaux, then in the primitive fervor of the institution; at the end of two years he led forth her third colony, or daughter, to the valley of Clairvaux in Champagne; and was content till the hour of his death with the humble station of abbot of his own community. A philosophic age has abolished, with too liberal and indiscriminate disdain, the honors of these spiritual heroes. The meanest among them are distinguished by some energies of the mind; they were at least superior to their votaries and disciples; and in the race of superstition, they attained the prize for which such numbers contended. In speech, in writing, in action, Bernard stood high above his rivals and contemporaries; his compositions are not devoid of wit and eloquence; and he seems to have preserved as much reason and humanity as may be reconciled with the character of a saint. In a secular life, he would have shared the seventh part of a private inheritance; by a vow of poverty and penance, by closing his eyes against the visible world, by the refusal of all ecclesiastical dignities, the abbot of Clairvaux became the oracle of Europe, and the founder of one hundred and sixty convents. Princes and pontiffs trembled at the freedom of his apostolical censures: France, England, and Milan consulted and obeyed his judgment in a schism of the church: the debt was repaid by the gratitude of Innocent the Second; and his successor, Eugenius the Third, was the friend and disciple of the holy Bernard. It was in the proclamation of the second crusade that he shone as the missionary and prophet of God, who called the nations to the defense of his holy sepulchre. At the parliament of Vezelay he spoke before the king; and Louis the Seventh, with his nobles, received their crosses from his hand. The abbot of Clairvaux then marched to the less easy conquest of the emperor Conrad: a phlegmatic people, ignorant of his language, was transported by the pathetic vehemence of his tone and gestures; and his progress from Constance to Cologne was the triumph of eloquence and zeal. Bernard applauds his own success in the depopulation of Europe; affirms that cities and castles were emptied of their inhabitants; and computes that only one man was left behind for the consolation of seven widows. The blind fanatics were desirous of electing him for their general; but the example of the hermit Peter was before his eyes; and while he assured the crusaders of the divine favor, he prudently declined a military command, in which failure and victory would have been almost equally disgraceful to his character. Yet, after the calamitous event, the abbot of Clairvaux was loudly accused as a false prophet, the author of the public and private mourning; his enemies exulted, his friends blushed, and his apology was slow and unsatisfactory. He justifies his obedience to the commands of the pope; expatiates on the mysterious ways of Providence; imputes the misfortunes of the pilgrims to their own sins; and modestly insinuates that his mission had been approved by signs and wonders. Had the fact been certain, the argument would be decisive; and his faithful disciples, who enumerate twenty or thirty miracles in a day, appeal to the public assemblies of France and Germany, in which they were performed. At the present hour, such prodigies will not obtain credit beyond the precincts of Clairvaux; but in the preternatural cures of the blind, the lame, and the sick who were presented to the man of God, it is impossible for us to ascertain the separate shares of accident, of fancy, of imposture, and of fiction.

Omnipotence itself cannot escape the murmurs of its discordant votaries; since the same dispensation which was applauded as a deliverance in Europe was deplored, and perhaps arraigned, as a calamity in Asia. After the loss of Jerusalem, the Syrian fugitives diffused their consternation and sorrow; Baghdad mourned in the dust; the cadhi Zeineddin of Damascus tore his beard in the caliph's presence; and the whole divan shed tears at his melancholy tale. But the commanders of the faithful could only weep; they were themselves captives in the hands of the Turks: some temporal power was restored to the last age of the Abbassides; but their humble ambition was confined to Baghdad and the adjacent province. Their tyrants, the Seljukian sultans, had followed the common law of the Asiatic dynasties, the unceasing round of valor, greatness, discord, degeneracy, and decay; their spirit and power were unequal to the defense of religion. . . . While the sultans were involved in the silken web of the harem, . . . Noureddin gradually united the Mohammedan powers [A.D. 1145–1174]; added the kingdom of Damascus to that of Aleppo, and waged a long and successful war against the Christians of Syria; he spread his ample reign from the Tigris to the Nile, and the Abbassides rewarded their faithful servant with all the titles and prerogatives of royalty. The Latins themselves were compelled to own the wisdom and courage, and even the justice and piety, of this implacable adversary. In his life and government the holy warrior revived the zeal and simplicity of the first caliphs. Gold and silk were banished from his palace, the use of wine from his dominions; the public revenue was scrupulously applied to the public service; and the frugal household of Noureddin was maintained from his legitimate share of the spoil which he vested in the purchase of a private estate.

[*Noureddin conquers Egypt (A.D. 1163–1169) and deposes the Fatimite caliphs of Cairo (A.D. 1171).*]

By the command of Noureddin and the sentence of the doctors, the holy names of Abubeker, Omar, and Othman were solemnly restored:

the caliph Mosthadi, of Baghdad, was acknowledged in the public prayers as the true commander of the faithful; and the green livery of the sons of Ali was exchanged for the black color of the Abbassides . . . ; and in all subsequent revolutions, Egypt has never departed from the orthodox tradition of the Moslems.

[*Saladin, son of Ayub, rises to power and rule* (A.D. *1171–1193*).]

The hilly country beyond the Tigris is occupied by the pastoral tribes of the Curds; a people hardy, strong, savage, impatient of the yoke, addicted to rapine, and tenacious of the government of their national chiefs. The resemblance of name, situation, and manners seems to identify them with the Carduchians of the Greeks; and they still defend against the Ottoman *Porte* the antique freedom which they asserted against the successors of Cyrus. Poverty and ambition prompted them to embrace the profession of mercenary soldiers: the service of his father and uncle prepared the reign of the great Saladin; and the son of Job or Ayub, a simple Curd, magnanimously smiled at his pedigree, which flattery deduced from the Arabian caliphs. . . . While Noureddin lived, these ambitious Curds were the most humble of his slaves; and the indiscreet murmurs of the divan were silenced by the prudent Ayub, who loudly protested that at the command of the sultan he himself would lead his sons in chains to the foot of the throne. "Such language," he added in private, "was prudent and proper in an assembly of your rivals; but we are now above fear and obedience; and the threats of Noureddin shall not extort the tribute of a sugar-cane." His seasonable death relieved them from the odious and doubtful conflict: his son, a minor of eleven years of age, was left for a while to the emirs of Damascus; and the new lord of Egypt was decorated by the caliph with every title that could sanctify his usurpation in the eyes of the people. Nor was Saladin long content with the possession of Egypt; he despoiled the Christians of Jerusalem and the Atabeks of Damascus, Aleppo, and Diarbekir: Mecca and Medina acknowledged him for their temporal protector: his brother subdued the distant regions of Yemen or the happy Arabia; and at the hour of his death, his empire was spread from the African Tripoli to the Tigris, and from the Indian Ocean to the mountains of Armenia. In the judgment of his character, the reproaches of treason and ingratitude strike forcibly on *our* minds, impressed as they are with the principle and experience of law and loyalty. But his ambition may in some measure be excused by the revolutions of Asia, which had erased every notion of legitimate succession ... ; by the approbation of the caliph, the sole source of all legitimate power; and above all by the wishes and interest of the people, whose happiness is the first object of government. In *his* virtues and in those of his patron, they admired the singular union of the hero and the saint; for both Noureddin and Saladin are ranked among the Mohammedan saints; and the constant meditation of the holy war appears to have shed a serious and sober color over their lives and actions. The youth of the latter was addicted to wine and women: but his aspiring spirit soon renounced the temptations of pleasure for the graver follies of fame and dominion: the garment of Saladin was of coarse woollen; water was his only drink; and while he emulated the temperance he surpassed the chastity of his Arabian prophet. Both in faith and practice he was a rigid Moslem: he ever deplored that the defense of religion had not allowed him to accomplish the pilgrimage of Mecca; but at the stated hours, five times each day, the sultan devoutly prayed with his brethren: the involuntary omission of fasting was scrupulously repaid; and his perusal of the Koran, on horseback between the approaching armies, may be quoted as a proof, however ostentatious, of piety and courage. The superstitious doctrine of the sect of Shafei was the only study that he deigned to encourage: the poets were safe in his contempt; but all profane science was the object of his aversion; and a philosopher who had invented some speculative novelties was seized and strangled by the command of the royal saint. The justice of his divan was accessible to the meanest suppliant against himself and his ministers; and it was only for a kingdom that Saladin would deviate from the rule of equity. While the descendants of Seljuk ... held his stirrup and smoothed his garments, he was affable and patient with the meanest of his servants. So boundless was his liberality that he distributed twelve thousand horses at the siege of Acre; and at the time of his death, no more than forty-seven drams of silver and one piece of gold coin were found in the treasury; yet in a martial reign the tributes were diminished, and the wealthy citizens enjoyed without fear or danger the fruits of their industry. Egypt, Syria, and Arabia were adorned by the royal foundations of hospitals, colleges, and mosques; and Cairo was fortified with a wall and citadel; but his works were consecrated to public use: nor did the sultan indulge himself in a garden or palace of private luxury. In a fanatic age, himself a fanatic, the genuine virtues of Saladin commanded the esteem of the Christians; the emperor of Germany gloried in his friendship; the Greek emperor solicited his alliance; and the conquest of Jerusalem diffused and perhaps magnified his fame both in the East and West.[†]

[Saladin] might expect that the siege of [Jerusalem (A.D. 1187),] a city so venerable on earth and in Heaven, so interesting to Europe and Asia, would rekindle the last sparks of enthusiasm; and that, of sixty thousand Christians, every man would be a soldier, and every soldier a candidate for martyrdom. . . . [But the] most numerous portion of the inhabitants was composed of the Greek and Oriental Christians, whom experience had taught to prefer the Mohammedan before the Latin yoke; and the holy sepulchre attracted a base and needy crowd, without arms or courage, who subsisted only on the charity of the pilgrims. Some feeble and hasty efforts were made for the defense of Jerusalem: but in the space of fourteen days, a victorious army drove back the sallies of the besieged, planted their engines, opened the wall to the breadth of fifteen cubits, applied their scaling-ladders, and erected on the breach twelve banners of the prophet and the sultan. It was in vain that a barefoot procession of the queen, the women, and the monks implored the Son of God to save his tomb and his inheritance from impious violation. Their sole hope was in the mercy of the conqueror, and to their first suppliant deputation that mercy was sternly denied. "He had sworn to avenge the patience and long suffering of the Moslems; the hour of forgiveness was elapsed, and the moment was now arrived to expiate in blood the innocent blood which had been spilt by Godfrey and the first crusaders." But a desperate and successful struggle of the Franks admonished the sultan that his triumph was not yet secure; he listened with reverence to a solemn adjuration in the name of the common Father of mankind; and a sentiment of human sympathy mollified the rigor of fanaticism and conquest. He consented to accept the city and to spare the inhabitants. The Greek and Oriental Christians were permitted to live under his dominion, but it was stipulated that in forty days all the Franks and Latins should evacuate Jerusalem and be safely conducted to the seaports of Syria and Egypt; that ten pieces of gold should be paid for each man, five for each woman, and one for every child; and that those who were unable to purchase their freedom should be detained in perpetual slavery. Of some writers it is a favorite and invidious theme to compare the humanity of Saladin with the massacre of the first crusade. The difference would be merely personal; but we should not forget that the Christians had offered to capitulate, and that the Mohammedans of Jerusalem sustained the last extremities of an assault and storm. Justice is indeed due to the fidelity with which the Turkish conqueror fulfilled the conditions of the treaty; and he may be deservedly praised for the glance of pity which he cast on the misery of the vanquished. Instead of a rigorous exaction of his debt, he accepted a sum of thirty thousand byzants for the ransom of seven thousand poor; two or three thousand more were dismissed by his gratuitous clemency; and the number of slaves was reduced to eleven or fourteen thousand persons. In his interview with the queen, his words and even his tears suggested the kindest consolations; his liberal alms were distributed among those who had been made orphans or widows by the fortune of war; and while the knights of the hospital were in arms against him, he allowed their more pious brethren to continue, during the term of a year, the care and service of the sick. In these acts of mercy the virtue of Saladin deserves our admiration and love: he was above the necessity of dissimulation, and his stern fanaticism would have prompted him to dissemble rather than to affect this profane compassion for the enemies of the Koran. After Jerusalem had been delivered from the presence of the strangers, the sultan made his triumphal entry, his banners waving in the wind, and to the harmony of martial music. The great mosque of Omar, which had been converted into a church, was again consecrated to one God and his prophet Mohammed: the walls and pavement were purified with rose-water; and a pulpit, the labor of Noureddin, was erected in the sanctuary. But when the golden cross that glittered on the dome was cast down and dragged through the streets, the Christians of every sect uttered a lamentable groan, which was answered by the joyful shouts of the Moslems. In four ivory chests the patriarch had collected the crosses, the images, the vases, and the relics of the holy place; they were seized by the conqueror, who was desirous of presenting the caliph with the trophies of Christian idolatry. He was persuaded, however, to entrust them to the patriarch and prince of Antioch; and the pious pledge was redeemed by Richard of England at the expense of fifty-two thousand byzants of gold.

[*Richard Plantagenet, the lion-hearted (Coeur de Lion), fails to take Jerusalem, and so comes to terms with Saladin (A.D. 1192).*]

During these hostilities, a languid and tedious negotiation between the Franks and Moslems was started, and continued, and broken, and again resumed, and again broken. Some acts of royal courtesy, the gift of snow and fruit, the exchange of Norway hawks and Arabian horses, softened the asperity of religious war: from the vicissitude of success, the monarchs might learn to suspect that Heaven was neutral in the quarrel; nor, after the trial of each other, could either hope for a decisive victory. The health both of Richard and Saladin appeared to be in a declining state; and they respectively suffered the evils of distant and domestic warfare: Plantagenet was impatient to punish a perfidious rival who had invaded Normandy in his absence; and the indefatigable sultan was subdued by the cries of the people who was the victim, and of the soldiers who were the instruments, of his martial zeal. The first demands of the king of England were the restitution of Jerusalem, Palestine, and the true cross; and he firmly declared that himself and his brother pilgrims would end their lives in the pious labor, rather than return to Europe with ignominy and remorse. But the conscience of Saladin refused, without some weighty compensation, to restore the idols or promote the idolatry of the Christians; he asserted with equal firmness his religious and civil claim to the sovereignty of Palestine; descanted on the importance and sanctity of Jerusalem; and rejected all terms of the establishment or partition of the Latins. The marriage which Richard proposed, of his sister with the sultan's brother, was defeated by the difference of faith; the princess abhorred the embraces of a Turk; and Adel, or Saphadin, would not easily renounce a plurality of wives. A personal interview was declined by Saladin, who alleged their mutual ignorance of each other's language; and the negotiation was managed with much art and delay by their interpreters and envoys. The final agreement was equally disapproved by the zealots of both parties, by the Roman pontiff and the caliph of Baghdad. It was stipulated that Jerusalem and the holy sepulchre should be open, without tribute or vexation, to the pilgrimage of the Latin Christians; that after the demolition of Ascalon, they should inclusively possess the sea-coast from Jaffa to Tyre; that the count of Tripoli and the prince of Antioch should be comprised in the truce; and that, during three years and three months, all hostilities should cease. The principal chiefs of the two armies swore to the observance of the treaty; but the monarchs were satisfied with giving their word and their right hand; and the royal majesty was excused from an oath, which always implies some suspicion of falsehood and dishonor. Richard embarked for Europe to seek a long captivity and a premature grave; and the space of a few months concluded the life and glories of Saladin [March 4, A.D. 1193].[†]

The noblest monument of a conqueror's fame, and of the terror which he inspired, is the Saladine tenth, a general tax which was imposed on the laity and even the clergy of the Latin church for the service of the holy war. The practice was too lucrative to expire with the occasion: and this tribute became the foundation of all the tithes and tenths on ecclesiastical benefices which have been granted by the Roman pontiffs to Catholic sovereigns, or reserved for the immediate use of the apostolic see. This pecuniary emolument must have tended to increase the interest of the popes in the recovery of Palestine: after the death of Saladin, they preached the crusade, by their epistles, their legates, and their missionaries; and the accomplishment of the pious work might have been expected from the zeal and talents of Innocent the Third. Under that young and ambitious priest, the successors of St. Peter attained the full meridian of their greatness: and in a reign of eighteen years [A.D. 1198–1216], he exercised a despotic command over the emperors and kings, whom he raised and deposed; over the nations, whom an interdict of months or years deprived, for the offense of their rulers, of the exercise of Christian worship. In the council of the Lateran he acted as the ecclesiastical, almost as the temporal, sovereign of the East and West. It was at the feet of his legate that John of England surrendered his crown; and Innocent may boast of the two most signal triumphs over sense and humanity, the establishment of transubstantiation and the origin of the Inquisition. At his voice, two crusades, the fourth and the fifth, were undertaken; but, except a king of Hungary, the princes of the second order were at the head of the pilgrims: the forces were inadequate to the design; nor did the effects correspond with the hopes and wishes of the pope and the people. The fourth crusade was diverted from Syria to Constantinople [A.D. 1203]; and the conquest of the Greek or Roman empire by the Latins will form the proper and important subject of the next chapter. In the fifth

[A.D. 1218], two hundred thousand Franks were landed at the eastern mouth of the Nile. They reasonably hoped that Palestine must be subdued in Egypt, the seat and storehouse of the sultan; and after a siege of sixteen months, the Moslems deplored the loss of Damietta. But the Christian army was ruined by the pride and insolence of the legate Pelagius, who, in the pope's name, assumed the character of general: the sickly Franks were encompassed by the waters of the Nile and the Oriental forces; and it was by the evacuation of Damietta that they obtained a safe retreat, some concessions for the pilgrims, and the tardy restitution of the doubtful relic of the true cross. The failure may in some measure be ascribed to the abuse and multiplication of the crusades, which were preached at the same time against the Pagans of Livonia, the Moors of Spain, the Albigeois of France, and the kings of Sicily of the Imperial family. In these meritorious services, the volunteers might acquire at home the same spiritual indulgence, and a larger measure of temporal rewards; and even the popes, in their zeal against a domestic enemy, were sometimes tempted to forget the distress of their Syrian brethren. From the last age of the crusades they derived the occasional command of an army and revenue; and some deep reasoners have suspected that the whole enterprise, from the first synod of Placentia, was contrived and executed by the policy of Rome. The suspicion is not founded either in nature or in fact. The successors of St. Peter appear to have followed rather than guided the impulse of manners and prejudice; without much foresight of the seasons or cultivation of the soil, they gathered the ripe and spontaneous fruits of the superstition of the times. They gathered these fruits without toil or personal danger: in the council of the Lateran, Innocent the Third declared an ambiguous resolution of animating the crusaders by his example; but the pilot of the sacred vessel could not abandon the helm; nor was Palestine ever blessed with the presence of a Roman pontiff.

The persons, the families, and estates of the pilgrims were under the immediate protection of the popes; and these spiritual patrons soon claimed the prerogative of directing their operations and enforcing, by commands and censures, the accomplishment of their vow. Frederic the Second, the grandson of Barbarossa, was successively the pupil, the enemy, and the victim of the church. At the age of twenty-one years, and in obedience to his guardian Innocent the Third, he assumed the cross; the same promise was repeated at his royal and imperial coronations; and his marriage with the heiress of Jerusalem [A.D. 1225] forever bound him to defend the kingdom of his son Conrad. But as Frederic advanced in age and authority, he repented of the rash engagements of his youth: his liberal sense and knowledge taught him to despise the phantoms of superstition and the crowns of Asia: he no longer entertained the same reverence for the successors of Innocent: and his ambition was occupied by the restoration of the Italian monarchy from Sicily to the Alps. But the success of this project would have reduced the popes to their primitive simplicity; and after the delays and excuses of twelve years, they urged the emperor, with entreaties and threats, to fix the time and place of his departure for Palestine. In the harbors of Sicily and Apulia, he prepared a fleet of one hundred galleys and of one hundred vessels that were framed to transport and land two thousand five hundred knights, with their horses and attendants; his vassals of Naples and Germany formed a powerful army; and the number of English crusaders was magnified to sixty thousand by the report of fame. But the inevitable or affected slowness of these mighty preparations consumed the strength and provisions of the more indigent pilgrims: the multitude was thinned by sickness and desertion; and the sultry summer of Calabria anticipated the mischiefs of a Syrian campaign. At length the emperor hoisted sail at Brundisium [A.D. 1227], with a fleet and army of forty thousand men: but he kept the sea no more than three days; and his hasty retreat, which was ascribed by his friends to a grievous indisposition, was accused by his enemies as a voluntary and obstinate disobedience. For suspending his vow was Frederic excommunicated by Gregory the Ninth; for presuming the next year to accomplish his vow, he was again excommunicated by the same pope. While he served under the banner of the cross, a crusade was preached against him in Italy; and after his return he was compelled to ask pardon for the injuries which he had suffered. The clergy and military orders of Palestine were previously instructed to renounce his communion and dispute his commands; and in his own kingdom, the emperor was forced to consent that the orders of the camp should be issued in the name of God and of the Christian republic. Frederic entered Jerusalem in triumph [March 18, A.D. 1229];

and with his own hands (for no priest would perform the office) he took the crown from the altar of the holy sepulchre. But the patriarch cast an interdict on the church which his presence had profaned; and the knights of the hospital and temple informed the sultan how easily he might be surprised and slain in his unguarded visit to the River Jordan. In such a state of fanaticism and faction, victory was hopeless and defense was difficult; but the conclusion of an advantageous peace may be imputed to the discord of the Mohammedans and their personal esteem for the character of Frederic. The enemy of the church is accused of maintaining with the miscreants an intercourse of hospitality and friendship unworthy of a Christian; of despising the barrenness of the land; and of indulging a profane thought, that if Jehovah had seen the kingdom of Naples he never would have selected Palestine for the inheritance of his chosen people. Yet Frederic obtained from the sultan the restitution of Jerusalem, of Bethlehem and Nazareth, of Tyre and Sidon; the Latins were allowed to inhabit and fortify the city; an equal code of civil and religious freedom was ratified for the sectaries of Jesus and those of Mohammed; and while the former worshiped at the holy sepulchre, the latter might pray and preach in the mosque of the temple from whence the prophet undertook his nocturnal journey to Heaven. The clergy deplored this scandalous toleration; and the weaker Moslems were gradually expelled; but every rational object of the crusades was accomplished without bloodshed; the churches were restored, the monasteries were replenished; and in the space of fifteen years, the Latins of Jerusalem exceeded the number of six thousand. This peace and prosperity, for which they were ungrateful to their benefactor, was terminated by the irruption of the strange and savage hordes of Carizmians [A.D. 1243]. Flying from the arms of the Moguls, those shepherds of the Caspian rolled headlong on Syria; and the union of the Franks with the sultans of Aleppo, Hems, and Damascus was insufficient to stem the violence of the torrent. Whatever stood against them was cut off by the sword or dragged into captivity: the military orders were almost exterminated in a single battle; and in the pillage of the city, in the profanation of the holy sepulchre, the Latins confess and regret the modesty and discipline of the Turks and Saracens.

Of the seven crusades, the two last were undertaken by Louis the Ninth, king of France.

[The sixth crusade fails (A.D. 1248–1254), and Louis eventually returns to France.]

The memory of his defeat excited Louis, after sixteen years of wisdom and repose, to undertake the seventh and last of the crusades. His finances were restored, his kingdom was enlarged; a new generation of warriors had arisen, and he advanced with fresh confidence at the head of six thousand horse and thirty thousand foot. The loss of Antioch had provoked the enterprise; a wild hope of baptizing the king of Tunis tempted him to steer for the African coast; and the report of an immense treasure reconciled his troops to the delay of their voyage to the Holy Land. Instead of a proselyte, he found a siege: the French panted and died on the burning sands: St. Louis expired in his tent; and no sooner had he closed his eyes than his son and successor gave the signal of the retreat [August 25, A.D. 1270]. "It is thus," says a lively writer, "that a Christian king died near the ruins of Carthage, waging war against the sectaries of Mohammed, in a land to which Dido had introduced the deities of Syria."

[The Moslems gradually reconquer the Holy Land and extirpate all remnants of the Latin kingdoms.]

Antioch, whose situation had been less exposed to the calamities of the holy war, was finally occupied and ruined by Bondocdar, or Bibars, sultan of Egypt and Syria [June 12, A.D. 1268]; the Latin principality was extinguished; and the first seat of the Christian name was dispeopled by the slaughter of seventeen, and the captivity of one hundred, thousand of her inhabitants. The maritime towns of Laodicea, Gabala, Tripoli, Beirut, Sidon, Tyre, and Jaffa, and the stronger castles of the Hospitallers and Templars, successively fell; and the whole existence of the Franks was confined to the city and colony of St. John of Acre, which is sometimes described by the more classic title of Ptolemais.

After the loss of Jerusalem, Acre, which is distant about seventy miles, became the metropolis of the Latin Christians, and was adorned with strong and stately buildings, with aqueducts, an artificial port, and a double wall. The population was increased by the incessant streams of pilgrims and fugitives: in the pauses of hostility the trade of the East and West was attracted to this convenient station; and the market could offer the produce of every clime and the interpreters of every tongue. But in this conflux of nations, every vice was propagated and practiced: of all the disciples of Jesus and Mohammed, the male and female inhabitants of Acre were esteemed the most corrupt; nor could the abuse of religion be corrected by the discipline of law. The city had many sovereigns and no government. The kings of Jerusalem and Cyprus, of the house of Lusignan, the princes of Antioch, the counts of Tripoli and Sidon, the great masters of the hospital, the temple, and the Teutonic order, the republics of Venice, Genoa, and Pisa, the pope's legate, the kings of France and England, assumed an independent command: seventeen tribunals exercised the power of life and death; every criminal was protected in the adjacent quarter; and the perpetual jealousy of the nations often burst forth in acts of violence and blood. Some adventurers who disgraced the ensign of the cross compensated their want of pay by the plunder of the Mohammedan villages: nineteen Syrian merchants, who traded under the public faith, were despoiled and hanged by the Christians; and the denial of satisfaction justified the arms of the sultan Khalil. He marched against Acre at the head of sixty thousand horse and one hundred and forty thousand foot: his train of artillery (if I may use the word) was numerous and weighty: the separate timbers of a single engine were transported in one hundred wagons; and the royal historian Abulfeda, who served with the troops of Hamah, was himself a spectator of the holy war. Whatever might be the vices of the Franks, their courage was rekindled by enthusiasm and despair; but they were torn by the discord of seventeen chiefs, and overwhelmed on all sides by the powers of the sultan. After a siege of thirty-three days, the double wall was forced by the Moslems; the principal tower yielded to their engines; the Mamalukes made a general assault; the city was stormed; and death or slavery was the lot of sixty thousand Christians [May 18, A.D. 1291]. The convent, or rather fortress, of the Templars resisted three days longer; but the great master was pierced with an arrow; and of five hundred knights, only ten were left alive, less happy than the victims of the sword if they lived to suffer on a scaffold in the unjust and cruel proscription of the whole order. The king of Jerusalem, the patriarch and the great master of the hospital, effected their retreat to the shore; but the sea was rough, the vessels were insufficient; and great numbers of the fugitives were drowned before they could reach the Isle of Cyprus, which might comfort Lusignan for the loss of Palestine. By the command of the sultan, the churches and fortifications of the Latin cities were demolished: a motive of avarice or fear still opened the holy sepulchre to some devout and defenseless pilgrims; and a mournful and solitary silence prevailed along the coast which had so long resounded with the WORLD'S DEBATE.

CHAPTER LX

THE FOURTH CRUSADE

Schism of the Greeks and Latins. • State of Constantinople. •
Isaac Angelus dethroned by his brother Alexius. • Origin of the
fourth crusade. • Alliance of the French and Venetians with the
son of Isaac. • Their naval expedition to Constantinople. •
The two sieges and final conquest of the city by the Latins.

The restoration of the Western empire by Charlemagne was speedily
followed by the separation of the Greek and Latin churches. A religious and national animosity still divides the two largest communions
of the Christian world; and the schism of Constantinople, by alienating her most useful allies and provoking her most dangerous enemies,
has precipitated the decline and fall of the Roman empire in the East.

In the course of the present History, the aversion of the Greeks for
the Latins has been often visible and conspicuous. It was originally derived from the disdain of servitude; inflamed, after the time of Constantine, by the pride of equality or dominion; and finally exasperated
by the preference which their rebellious subjects had given to the alliance of the Franks. In every age the Greeks were proud of their superiority in profane and religious knowledge: they had first received
the light of Christianity; they had pronounced the decrees of the
seven general councils; they alone possessed the language of Scripture
and philosophy; nor should the Barbarians, immersed in the darkness
of the West, presume to argue on the high and mysterious questions of
theological science. These Barbarians despised, in their turn, the restless and subtle levity of the Orientals, the authors of every heresy; and
blessed their own simplicity, which was content to hold the tradition of
the apostolic church. Yet in the seventh century, the synods of Spain,
and afterwards of France, improved or corrupted the Nicene creed on
the mysterious subject of the third person of the Trinity. In the long
controversies of the East, the nature and generation of the Christ had
been scrupulously defined; and the well-known relation of father and
son seemed to convey a faint image to the human mind. The idea of
birth was less analogous to the Holy Spirit, who, instead of a divine gift

or attribute, was considered by the Catholics as a substance, a person, a god; he was not begotten, but in the orthodox style he *proceeded*. Did he proceed from the Father alone, perhaps *by* the Son? or from the Father *and* the Son? The first of these opinions was asserted by the Greeks, the second by the Latins; and the addition to the Nicene creed of the word *filioque* ["and the Son"] kindled the flame of discord between the Oriental and the Gallic churches. In the origin of the disputes the Roman pontiffs affected a character of neutrality and moderation: they condemned the innovation but they acquiesced in the sentiment of their Transalpine brethren: they seemed desirous of casting a veil of silence and charity over the superfluous research; and in the correspondence of Charlemagne and Leo the Third, the pope assumes the liberality of a statesman and the prince descends to the passions and prejudices of a priest. But the orthodoxy of Rome spontaneously obeyed the impulse of the temporal policy; and the *filioque,* which Leo wished to erase, was transcribed in the symbol and chanted in the liturgy of the Vatican. The Nicene and Athanasian creeds are held as the Catholic faith, without which none can be saved; and both Papists and Protestants must now sustain and return the anathemas of the Greeks, who deny the procession of the Holy Ghost from the Son, as well as from the Father. Such articles of faith are not susceptible of treaty; but the rules of discipline will vary in remote and independent churches; and the reason, even of divines, might allow that the difference is inevitable and harmless. The craft or superstition of Rome has imposed on her priests and deacons the rigid obligation of celibacy; among the Greeks it is confined to the bishops; the loss is compensated by dignity or annihilated by age; and the parochial clergy, the *papas,* enjoy the conjugal society of the wives whom they have married before their entrance into holy orders. A question concerning the *Azyms* [the "elements" of the sacrament of communion] was fiercely debated in the eleventh century, and the essence of the Eucharist was supposed in the East and West to depend on the use of leavened or unleavened bread. Shall I mention in a serious history the furious reproaches that were urged against the Latins, who for a long while remained on the defensive? They neglected to abstain, according to the apostolical decree, from things strangled and from blood; they fasted (a Jewish observance!) on the Saturday of each week; during the first week of Lent they permitted the use of milk and cheese; their infirm monks were indulged in the taste of flesh, and animal grease was substituted for the want of vegetable oil; the holy chrism or unction in baptism was reserved to the episcopal order; the bishops, as the bridegrooms of their churches, were decorated with rings; their priests shaved their faces and baptized by a single immersion. Such were the crimes which provoked the zeal of the patriarchs of Constantinople; and which were justified with equal zeal by the doctors of the Latin church.

Bigotry and national aversion are powerful magnifiers of every object of dispute; but the immediate cause of the schism of the Greeks may be traced in the emulation of the leading prelates, who maintained the supremacy of the old metropolis superior to all, and of the reigning capital inferior to none, in the Christian world. About the middle of the ninth century, Photius, an ambitious layman, the captain of the guards and principal secretary, was promoted by merit and favor to the more desirable office of patriarch of Constantinople [December 25, A.D. 858]. In science, even ecclesiastical science, he surpassed the clergy of the age; and the purity of his morals has never been impeached: but his ordination was hasty, his rise was irregular; and Ignatius, his abdicated predecessor, was yet supported by the public compassion and the obstinacy of his adherents. They appealed to the tribunal of Nicholas the First, one of the proudest and most aspiring of the Roman pontiffs, who embraced the welcome opportunity of judging and condemning his rival of the East. Their quarrel was embittered by a conflict of jurisdiction over the king and nation of the Bulgarians; nor was their recent conversion to Christianity of much avail to either prelate, unless he could number the proselytes among the subjects of his power. With the aid of his court the Greek patriarch was victorious; but in the furious contest he deposed in his turn the successor of St. Peter and involved the Latin church in the reproach of heresy and schism. Photius sacrificed the peace of the world to a short and precarious reign: he fell with his patron, the Caesar Bardas [A.D. 867]; and Basil the Macedonian performed an act of justice in the restoration of Ignatius, whose age and dignity had not been sufficiently respected. From his monastery or prison, Photius solicited the favor of the emperor by pathetic complaints and artful flattery; and the eyes of his rival were scarcely closed when he was again restored to the throne of Constantinople [A.D. 877]. After the death of Basil he experienced the vicissitudes of courts and the ingratitude of a royal pupil: the patriarch was again deposed [A.D. 886], and in his last solitary hours he might regret the freedom of a secular and studious life [d. circa A.D. 891]. In each revolution, the breath, the nod, of the sovereign had been accepted by a submissive clergy; and a synod of three hundred bishops was always prepared to hail the triumph or to stigmatize the fall of the holy, or the execrable, Photius. By a delusive promise of succor or reward, the popes were tempted to countenance these various proceedings; and the synods of Constantinople were ratified by their epistles or legates. But the court and the people, Ignatius and Photius, were equally adverse to their claims; their ministers were insulted or imprisoned; the procession of the Holy Ghost was forgotten; Bulgaria was forever annexed to the Byzantine throne; and the schism was prolonged by their rigid censure of all the multiplied ordinations of an irregular patriarch. The darkness and corruption of the tenth century suspended the intercourse, without reconciling the minds, of the two nations. But when the Norman sword restored the churches of Apulia to the jurisdiction of Rome, the departing flock was warned, by a petulant epistle of the Greek patriarch, to avoid and abhor the errors of the Latins. The rising majesty of Rome could no longer brook the insolence of a rebel; and Michael Cerularius was excommunicated in the heart of Constantinople by the pope's legates [July 16, A.D. 1054]. Shaking the dust from their feet, they deposited on the altar of St. Sophia a direful anathema which enumerates the seven mortal heresies of the Greeks and devotes the guilty teachers and their unhappy sectaries to the eternal society of the devil and his angels. According to the emergencies of the church and state, a friendly correspondence was sometimes resumed; the language of charity and concord was sometimes affected; but the Greeks have never recanted their errors; the popes have never repealed their sentence; and from this thunderbolt we may date the consummation of the schism. It was enlarged by each ambitious step of the Roman pontiffs: the emperors blushed and trembled at the ignominious fate of their royal brethren of Germany; and the people were scandalized by the temporal power and military life of the Latin clergy.

The aversion of the Greeks and Latins was nourished and manifested in the three first expeditions to the Holy Land [A.D. 1100–1200].

Alexius Comnenus contrived the absence at least of the formidable pilgrims: his successors, Manuel and Isaac Angelus, conspired with the Moslems for the ruin of the greatest princes of the Franks; and their crooked and malignant policy was seconded by the active and voluntary obedience of every order of their subjects. Of this hostile temper, a large portion may doubtless be ascribed to the difference of language, dress, and manners which severs and alienates the nations of the globe. The pride as well as the prudence of the sovereign was deeply wounded by the intrusion of foreign armies that claimed a right of traversing his dominions and passing under the walls of his capital: his subjects were insulted and plundered by the rude strangers of the West: and the hatred of the pusillanimous Greeks was sharpened by secret envy of the bold and pious enterprises of the Franks. But these profane causes of national enmity were fortified and inflamed by the venom of religious zeal. Instead of a kind embrace, a hospitable reception from their Christian brethren of the East, every tongue was taught to repeat the names of schismatic and heretic, more odious to an orthodox ear than those of pagan and infidel: instead of being loved for the general conformity of faith and worship, they were abhorred for some rules of discipline, some questions of theology, in which themselves or their teachers might differ from the Oriental church. In the crusade of Louis the Seventh, the Greek clergy washed and purified the altars which had been defiled by the sacrifice of a French priest. The companions of Frederic Barbarossa deplored the injuries which they endured, both in word and deed, from the peculiar rancor of the bishops and monks. Their prayers and sermons excited the people against the impious Barbarians; and the patriarch is accused of declaring that the faithful might obtain the redemption of all their sins by the extirpation of the schismatics. An enthusiast named Dorotheus alarmed the fears and restored the confidence of the emperor by a prophetic assurance that the German heretic, after assaulting the gate of Blachernes, would be made a signal example of the divine vengeance. The passage of these mighty armies were rare and perilous events; but the crusades introduced a frequent and familiar intercourse between the two nations, which enlarged their knowledge without abating their prejudices. The wealth and luxury of Constantinople demanded the productions of every climate; these imports were balanced by the art and labor of her numerous inhabitants; her situation invites the commerce of the world; and in every period of her existence, that commerce has been in the hands of foreigners. After the decline of Amalphi, the Venetians, Pisans, and Genoese introduced their factories and settlements into the capital of the empire: their services were rewarded with honors and immunities; they acquired the possession of lands and houses; their families were multiplied by marriages with the natives; and after the toleration of a Mohammedan mosque, it was impossible to interdict the churches of the Roman rite. The two wives of Manuel Comnenus were of the race of the Franks. . . . [He] esteemed the valor and trusted the fidelity of the Franks; their military talents were unfitly recompensed by the lucrative offices of judges and treasurers; the policy of Manuel had solicited the alliance of the pope; and the popular voice accused him of a partial bias to the nation and religion of the Latins. During his reign and that of his successor Alexius, they were exposed at Constantinople to the reproach of foreigners, heretics, and favorites; and this triple guilt was severely expiated in the tumult which announced the return and elevation of Andronicus. The people rose in arms [A.D. 1183]: from the Asiatic shore the tyrant despatched his troops and galleys to assist the national revenge; and the hopeless resistance of the strangers served only to justify the rage and sharpen the daggers of the assassins. Neither age nor sex nor the ties of friendship or kindred could save the victims of national hatred and avarice and religious zeal; the Latins were slaughtered in their houses and in the streets; their quarter was reduced to ashes; the clergy were burnt in their churches and the sick in their hospitals; and some estimate may be formed of the slain from the clemency which sold above four thousand Christians in perpetual slavery to the Turks. The priests and monks were the loudest and most active in the destruction of the schismatics; and they chanted a thanksgiving to the Lord when the head of a Roman cardinal, the pope's legate, was severed from his body, fastened to the tail of a dog, and dragged with savage mockery through the city. The more diligent of the strangers had retreated on the first alarm to their vessels and escaped through the Hellespont from the scene of blood. In their flight, they burnt and ravaged two hundred miles of the sea-coast; inflicted a severe revenge on the guiltless subjects of the empire; marked the priests and monks as their peculiar enemies; and compensated, by the accumulation of plunder, the loss of their property and friends. On their return, they exposed to Italy and Europe the wealth and weakness, the perfidy and malice, of the Greeks, whose vices were painted as the genuine characters of heresy and schism. The scruples of the first crusaders had neglected the fairest opportunities of securing, by the possession of Constantinople, the way to the Holy Land: domestic revolution invited and almost compelled the French and Venetians to achieve the conquest of the Roman empire of the East.

[*An illiterate French priest of Paris raises the call for a fourth crusade (A.D. 1198). Under the direction of the doge of Venice, French and Venetian forces are diverted from Jerusalem to Constantinople (A.D. 1202), which they besiege. Dynastic politics provide a pretext for intervention. The Latins restore Isaac Angelus to the throne usurped by Alexius Angelus. Isaac, however, is killed, and replaced by Mourzoufle (A.D. 1204). The Latins besiege Constantinople a second time, and take it (A.D. 1204).*]

[T]he empire, which still bore the name of Constantine and the title of Roman, was subverted by the arms of the Latin pilgrims. Constantinople had been taken by storm; and no restraints, except those of religion and humanity, were imposed on the conquerors by the laws of war.[†]

In this great revolution we enjoy the singular felicity of comparing the narratives of Villehardouin and Nicetas, the opposite feelings of the marshal of Champagne and the Byzantine senator. At the first view it should seem that the wealth of Constantinople was only transferred from one nation to another; and that the loss and sorrow of the Greeks is exactly balanced by the joy and advantage of the Latins. But in the miserable account of war, the gain is never equivalent to the loss, the pleasure to the pain; the smiles of the Latins were transient and fallacious; the Greeks forever wept over the ruins of their country; and their real calamities were aggravated by sacrilege and mockery. What benefits accrued to the conquerors from the three fires which annihilated so vast a portion of the buildings and riches of the city? What a stock of such things as could neither be used nor transported was maliciously or wantonly destroyed! How much treasure was idly wasted in gaming, debauchery, and riot! And what precious objects were bar-tered for a vile price by the impatience or ignorance of the soldiers whose reward was stolen by the base industry of the last of the Greeks! These alone, who had nothing to lose, might derive some profit from the revolution; but the misery of the upper ranks of society is strongly painted in the personal adventures of Nicetas himself. His stately palace had been reduced to ashes in the second conflagration; and the senator, with his family and friends, found an obscure shelter in another house which he possessed near the church of St. Sophia. It was the door of this mean habitation that his friend, the Venetian merchant, guarded in the disguise of a soldier till Nicetas could save, by a precipitate flight, the relics of his fortune and the chastity of his daughter. In a cold, wintry season, these fugitives, nursed in the lap of prosperity, departed on foot; his wife was with child; the desertion of their slaves compelled them to carry their baggage on their own shoulders; and their women, whom they placed in the center, were exhorted to conceal their beauty with dirt instead of adorning it with paint and jewels. Every step was exposed to insult and danger: the threats of the strangers were less painful than the taunts of the plebeians, with whom they were now leveled; nor did the exiles breathe in safety till their mournful pilgrimage was concluded at Selymbria, above forty miles from the capital. On the way they overtook the patriarch, without attendance and almost without apparel, riding on an ass and reduced to a state of apostolical poverty which, had it been voluntary, might perhaps have been meritorious. In the meanwhile, his desolate churches were profaned by the licentiousness and party zeal of the Latins. After stripping the gems and pearls, they converted the chalices into drinking-cups; their tables, on which they gamed and feasted, were covered with the pictures of Christ and the saints; and they trampled under foot the most venerable objects of the Christian worship. In the cathedral of St. Sophia, the ample veil of the sanctuary was rent asunder for the sake of the golden fringe; and the altar, a monument of art and riches, was broken in pieces and shared among the captors. Their mules and horses were laden with the wrought silver and gilt carvings, which they tore down from the doors and pulpit; and if the beasts stumbled under the burden, they were stabbed by their impatient drivers, and the holy pavement streamed with their impure blood. A prostitute was seated on the throne of the patriarch; and that daughter of Belial, as she is styled, sung and danced in the church to ridicule the hymns and processions of the Orientals. Nor were the repositories of the royal dead secure from violation: in the church of the Apostles, the tombs of the emperors were rifled; and it is said that after six centuries the corpse of Justinian was found without any signs of decay or putrefaction. In the streets, the French and Flemings clothed themselves and their horses in painted robes and flowing head-dresses of linen; and the coarse intemperance of their feasts insulted the splendid sobriety of the East. To expose the arms of a people of scribes and scholars, they affected to display a pen, an inkhorn, and a sheet of paper, without discerning that the instruments of science and valor were alike feeble and useless in the hands of the modern Greeks.

Their reputation and their language encouraged them, however, to despise the ignorance and to overlook the progress of the Latins. In the love of the arts, the national difference was still more obvious and real; the Greeks preserved with reverence the works of their ancestors, which they could not imitate; and in the destruction of the statues of Constantinople, we are provoked to join in the complaints and invectives of the Byzantine historian. We have seen how the rising city was adorned by the vanity and despotism of the Imperial founder: in the ruins of Paganism, some gods and heroes were saved from the axe of superstition; and the forum and hippodrome were dignified with the relics of a better age. . . . The [Classical] statues of brass . . . were broken and melted by the unfeeling avarice of the crusaders: the cost and labor were consumed in a moment; the soul of genius evaporated in smoke; and the remnant of base metal was coined into money for the payment of the troops. Bronze is not the most durable of monuments: from the marble forms of Phidias and Praxiteles, the Latins might turn aside with stupid contempt; but unless they were crushed by some accidental injury, those useless stones stood secure on their pedestals. The most enlightened of the strangers, above the gross and sensual pursuits of their countrymen, more piously exercised the right of conquest in the search and seizure of the relics of the saints. Immense was the supply of heads and bones, crosses and images, that were scattered by this revolution over the churches of Europe; and such was the increase of pilgrimage and oblation that no branch, perhaps, of more lucrative plunder was imported from the East. Of the writings of antiquity, many that still existed in the twelfth century are now lost. But the pilgrims were not solicitous to save or transport the volumes of an unknown tongue: the perishable substance of paper or parchment can only be preserved by the multiplicity of copies; the literature of the Greeks had almost centered in the metropolis; and without computing the extent of our loss, we may drop a tear over the libraries that have perished in the triple fire of Constantinople.

CHAPTER LXI

PARTITION OF THE EMPIRE BY THE FRENCH AND VENETIANS

Weakness and poverty of the Latin empire. • Recovery of Constantinople by the Greeks. • General consequences of the crusades.[†]

[*The French and Venetians divide the Eastern empire.*]

The Greeks were oppressed by the double weight of the priest, who was invested with temporal power, and of the soldier, who was inflamed by fanatic hatred; and the insuperable bar of religion and language forever separated the stranger and the native. As long as the crusaders were united at Constantinople, the memory of their conquest and the terror of their arms imposed silence on the captive land: their dispersion betrayed the smallness of their numbers and the defects of their discipline; and some failures and mischances revealed the secret that they were not invincible. As the fears of the Greeks abated, their hatred increased. They murdered; they conspired; and before a year of slavery had elapsed, they implored or accepted the succor of a Barbarian, whose power they had felt and whose gratitude they trusted.[†]

[*After over fifty years of struggle, the Greeks recover Constantinople on July 25, A.D. 1261.*]

After this narrative of the expeditions of the Latins to Palestine and Constantinople, I cannot dismiss the subject without resolving the general consequences on the countries that were the scene, and on the nations that were the actors, of these memorable crusades. As soon as the arms of the Franks were withdrawn, the impression, though not the memory, was erased in the Mohammedan realms of Egypt and Syria. The faithful disciples of the prophet were never tempted by a profane desire to study the laws or language of the idolaters; nor did the simplicity of their primitive manners receive the slightest alteration from their intercourse in peace and war with the unknown strangers of the West. The Greeks, who thought themselves proud but who were only vain, showed a disposition somewhat less inflexible. In the efforts for the recovery of their empire, they emulated the valor, discipline, and tactics of their antagonists. The modern literature of the West they might justly despise; but its free spirit would instruct them in the rights of man; and some institutions of public and private life were adopted from the French. The correspondence of Constantinople and Italy diffused the knowledge of the Latin tongue; and several of the fathers and classics were at length honored with a Greek version. But the national and religious prejudices of the Orientals were inflamed by persecution, and the reign of the Latins confirmed the separation of the two churches.

If we compare the era of the crusades, the Latins of Europe with the Greeks and Arabians, their respective degrees of knowledge, industry, and art, our rude ancestors must be content with the third rank in the scale of nations. Their successive improvement and present superiority may be ascribed to a peculiar energy of character, to an active and imitative spirit, unknown to their more polished rivals, who at that time were in a stationary or retrograde state. With such a disposition, the Latins should have derived the most early and essential benefits from a series of events which opened to their eyes the prospect of the world and introduced them to a long and frequent intercourse with the more cultivated regions of the East. The first and most obvious progress was in trade and manufactures, in the arts which are strongly prompted by the thirst of wealth, the calls of necessity, and the gratification of the sense or vanity. Among the crowd of unthinking fanatics, a captive or a pilgrim might sometimes observe the superior refinements of Cairo and Constantinople: the first importer of windmills was the benefactor of nations; and if such blessings are enjoyed without any grateful remembrance, history has condescended to notice the more apparent luxuries of silk and sugar, which were transported into Italy from Greece and Egypt. But the intellectual wants of the Latins were more slowly felt and supplied; the ardor of studious curiosity was awakened in Europe by different causes and more recent events; and in the age of the crusades, they viewed with careless indifference the literature of the Greeks and Arabians. Some rudiments of mathematical and medicinal knowledge might be imparted in practice and in figures; necessity might produce some interpreters for the grosser business of merchants and soldiers; but the commerce of the Orientals had not diffused the study and knowledge of their languages in the schools of Europe. If a similar principle of religion repulsed the idiom of the Koran, it should have excited their patience and curiosity to understand the original text of the gospel; and the same grammar would have unfolded the sense of Plato and the beauties of Homer. Yet in a reign of sixty years, the Latins of Constantinople disdained the speech and learning of their subjects; and the manuscripts were the only treasures which the natives might enjoy without rapine or envy. Aristotle was indeed the oracle of the Western universities, but it was a barbarous Aristotle; and instead of ascending to the fountainhead, his Latin votaries humbly accepted a corrupt and remote version from the Jews and Moors of Andalusia. The principle of the crusades was a savage fanaticism; and the most important effects were analogous to the cause. Each pilgrim was ambitious to return with his sacred spoils, the relics of Greece and Palestine; and each relic was preceded and followed by a train of miracles and visions. The belief of the Catholics was corrupted by new legends, their practice by new superstitions; and the establishment of the Inquisition, the mendicant orders of monks and friars, the last abuse of indulgences, and the final progress of idolatry flowed from the baleful fountain of the holy war. The active spirit of the Latins preyed on the vitals of their reason and religion; and if the ninth and tenth centuries were the times of darkness, the thirteenth and fourteenth were the age of absurdity and fable.

In the profession of Christianity, in the cultivation of a fertile land, the Northern conquerors of the Roman empire insensibly mingled with the provincials and rekindled the embers of the arts of antiquity. Their settlements about the age of Charlemagne had acquired some degree of order and stability when they were overwhelmed by new swarms of invaders, the Normans, Saracens, and Hungarians, who re-plunged the western countries of Europe into their former state of anarchy and barbarism. About the eleventh century, the second tempest had subsided by the expulsion or conversion of the enemies of Christendom: the tide of civilization, which had so long ebbed, began to flow with a steady and accelerated course; and a fairer prospect was opened to the hopes and efforts of the rising generations. Great was the increase and rapid the progress during the two hundred years of the crusades; and some philosophers have applauded the propitious influence of these holy wars, which appear to me to have checked rather than forwarded the maturity of Europe. The lives and labors of millions which were buried in the East would have been more profitably employed in the improvement of their native country: the accumulated stock of industry and wealth would have overflowed in navigation and trade; and the Latins would have been enriched and enlightened by a pure and friendly correspondence with the climates of the East. In one respect I can indeed perceive the accidental operation of the crusades, not so much in producing a benefit as in removing an evil. The larger portion of the inhabitants of Europe was chained to the soil, without freedom or property or knowledge; and the two orders of ecclesiastics and nobles, whose numbers were comparatively small, alone deserved the name of citizens and men. This oppressive system was supported by the arts of the clergy and the swords of the barons. The authority of the priests operated in the darker ages as a salutary antidote: they prevented the total extinction of letters, mitigated the fierceness of the times, sheltered the poor and defenseless, and preserved or revived the peace and order of civil society. But the independence, rapine, and discord of the feudal lords were unmixed with any semblance of good; and every hope of industry and improvement was crushed by the iron weight of the martial aristocracy. Among the causes that undermined that Gothic edifice, a conspicuous place must be allowed to the crusades. The estates of the barons were dissipated, and their race was often extinguished, in these costly and perilous expeditions. Their poverty extorted from their pride those charters of freedom which unlocked the fetters of the slave, secured the farm of the peasant and the shop of the artificer, and gradually restored a substance and a soul to the most numerous and useful part of the community. The conflagration which destroyed the tall and barren trees of the forest gave air and scope to the vegetation of the smaller and nutritive plants of the soil.[†]

CHAPTER LXII

GREEK EMPERORS OF NICE AND CONSTANTINOPLE

The Greek emperors of Nice and Constantinople. • Elevation and reign of Michael Palaeologus. • His false union with the pope and the Latin church.[†]

The loss of Constantinople restored a momentary vigor to the Greeks. From their palaces, the princes and nobles were driven into the field; and the fragments of the falling monarchy were grasped by the hands of the most vigorous or the most skillful candidates. In the long and barren pages of the Byzantine annals, it would not be an easy task to equal the two characters of Theodore Lascaris and John Ducas Vataces, who replanted and upheld the Roman standard at Nice in Bithynia. The difference of their virtues was happily suited to the diversity of their situation. In his first efforts, the fugitive Lascaris commanded only three cities and two thousand soldiers: his reign was the season of generous and active despair [A.D. 1204–1222]: in every military operation he staked his life and crown; and his enemies of the Hellespont and the Maeander were surprised by his celerity and subdued by his boldness. A victorious reign of eighteen years expanded the principality of Nice to the magnitude of an empire. The throne of his successor and son-in-law Vataces was founded on a more solid basis, a larger scope, and more plentiful resources; and it was the temper as well as the interest of Vataces to calculate the risk, to expect the moment, and to insure the success of his ambitious designs [A.D. 1222–1255]. In the decline of the Latins, I have briefly exposed the progress of the Greeks; the prudent and gradual advances of a conqueror who, in a reign of thirty-three years, rescued the provinces from national and foreign usurpers, till he pressed on all sides the Imperial city, a leafless and sapless trunk, which must fall at the first stroke of the axe. But his interior and peaceful administration is still more deserving of notice and praise. The calamities of the times had wasted the numbers and the substance of the Greeks; the motives and the means of agriculture were extirpated; and the most fertile lands were left without cultivation or inhabitants. A portion of this vacant property was occupied and improved by the command and for the benefit of the emperor: a powerful hand and a vigilant eye supplied and surpassed, by a skillful management, the minute diligence of a private farmer: the royal domain became the garden and granary of Asia; and without impoverishing the people, the sovereign acquired a fund of innocent and productive wealth. According to the nature of the soil, his lands were sown with corn or planted with vines; the pastures were filled with horses and oxen, with sheep and hogs; and when Vataces presented to the empress a crown of diamonds and pearls, he informed her with a smile that this precious ornament arose from the sale of the eggs of his innumerable poultry. The produce of his domain was applied to the maintenance of his palace and hospitals, the calls of dignity and benevolence: the lesson was still more useful than the revenue: the plough was restored to its ancient security and honor; and the nobles were taught to seek a sure and independent revenue from their estates instead of adorning their splendid beggary by the oppression of the people or (what is almost the same) by the favors of the court. The superfluous stock of corn and cattle was eagerly purchased by the Turks, with whom Vataces preserved a strict and sincere alliance; but he discouraged the importation of foreign manufactures, the costly silks of the East, and the curious labors of the Italian looms. "The demands of nature and necessity," was he accustomed to say, "are indispensable; but the influence of fashion may rise and sink at the breath of a monarch"; and both his precept and example recommended simplicity of manners and the use of domestic industry. The education of youth and the revival of learning were the most serious objects of his care; and without deciding the precedency, he pronounced with truth that a prince and a philosopher are the two most eminent characters of human society. His first wife was Irene, the daughter of Theodore Lascaris, a woman more illustrious by her personal merit, the milder virtues of her sex, than by the blood of the Angeli and Comneni that flowed in her veins and transmitted the inheritance of the empire. After her death he was contracted to Anne, or Constance, a natural daughter of the emperor Frederic the Second; but as the bride had not attained the years of puberty, Vataces placed in his solitary bed an Italian damsel of her train; and his amorous weakness bestowed on the concubine the honors, though not the title, of a lawful empress. His frailty was censured as a flagitious and damnable sin by the monks; and their rude invectives exercised and displayed the patience of the royal lover. A philosophic age may excuse a single vice which was redeemed by a crowd of virtues; and in the review of his faults and the more intemperate passions of Lascaris, the judgment of their contemporaries was softened by gratitude to the second founders of the empire. The slaves of the Latins, without law or peace, applauded the happiness of their brethren who had resumed their national freedom; and Vataces employed the laudable policy of convincing the Greeks of every dominion that it was their interest to be enrolled in the number of his subjects.

A strong shade of degeneracy is visible between John Vataces and his son Theodore; between the founder who sustained the weight and the heir who enjoyed the splendor of the Imperial crown [A.D. 1255–1259]. Yet the character of Theodore was not devoid of energy; he had been educated in the school of his father in the exercise of war and hunting; Constantinople was yet spared; but in the three years of a short reign, he thrice led his armies into the heart of Bulgaria. His virtues were sullied by a choleric and suspicious temper: the first of these may be ascribed to the ignorance of control; and the second might naturally arise from a dark and imperfect view of the corruption of mankind. On a march in Bulgaria, he consulted on a question of policy his principal ministers; and the Greek logothete, George Acropolita, presumed to offend him by the declaration of a free and honest opinion. The emperor half unsheathed his cimeter; but his more deliberate rage reserved Acropolita for a baser punishment. One of the first officers of the empire was ordered to dismount, stripped of his robes, and extended on the ground in the presence of the prince and army. In this posture he was chastised with so many and such heavy blows from the clubs of two guards or executioners that when Theodore commanded them to cease, the great logothete was scarcely able to rise and crawl away to his tent. After a seclusion of some days, he was recalled by a peremptory mandate to his seat in council; and so dead were the Greeks to the sense of honor and shame that it is from the narrative of the sufferer himself that we acquire the knowledge of his disgrace. The cruelty of the emperor was exasperated by the pangs of sickness, the approach of a premature end, and the suspicion of poison and magic. The lives and fortunes, the eyes and limbs, of his kinsmen and nobles were sacrificed to each sally of passion; and before he died, the son of Vataces might deserve from the people, or at least from the court, the appellation of tyrant. A matron of the family of the Palaeologi had provoked his anger by refusing to bestow her beauteous daughter on the vile plebeian who was recommended by his caprice. Without regard to her birth or age, her body, as high as the neck, was enclosed in a sack with several cats, who were pricked with pins to irritate their fury against their unfortunate fellow-captive. In his last hours the emperor testified a wish to forgive and be forgiven, a just anxiety for the fate of John, his son and successor, who at the age of eight years was condemned to the dangers of a long minority. His last choice entrusted the office of guardian to the sanctity of the patriarch Arsenius and to the courage of George Muzalon, the great domestic, who was equally distinguished by the royal favor and the public hatred. Since their connection with the Latins, the names and privileges of hereditary rank had insinuated themselves into the Greek monarchy; and the noble families were provoked by the elevation of a worthless favorite, to whose influence they imputed the errors and calamities of the late reign. In the first council after the emperor's death, Muzalon, from a lofty throne, pronounced a labored apology of his conduct and intentions: his modesty was subdued by a unanimous assurance of esteem and fidelity; and his most inveterate enemies were the loudest to salute him as the guardian and savior of the Romans. Eight days were sufficient to prepare the execution of the conspiracy. On the ninth, the obsequies of the deceased monarch were solemnized in the cathedral of Magnesia, an Asiatic city, where he expired on the banks of the Hermus and at the foot of Mount Sipylus. The holy rites were interrupted by a sedition of the guards; Muzalon, his brothers, and his adherents were massacred at the foot of the altar; and the absent patriarch was associated with a new colleague, with Michael Palaeologus, the most illustrious, in birth and merit, of the Greek nobles.

Of those who are proud of their ancestors, the far greater part must be content with local or domestic renown; and few there are who dare trust the memorials of their family to the public annals of their country. As early as the middle of the eleventh century, the noble race of the Palaeologi stands high and conspicuous in the Byzantine history: it was the valiant George Palaeologus who placed the father of the Comneni on the throne; and his kinsmen or descendants continue, in each generation, to lead the armies and councils of the state.... In his person, the splendor of birth was dignified by the merit of the soldier and statesman: in his early youth he was promoted to the office of *constable* or commander of the French mercenaries; the private expense of a day never exceeded three pieces of gold; but his ambition was rapacious and profuse; and his gifts were doubled by the graces of his conversation and manners. The love of the soldiers and people excited the jealousy of the court, [but] Michael ... escaped from the dangers in which he was involved by his own imprudence.... Under the reign of Justice and Vataces, a dispute arose between two officers, one of whom accused the other of maintaining the hereditary right of the Palaeologi. The cause was decided, according to the new jurisprudence of the Latins, by single combat; the defendant was overthrown; but he persisted in declaring that himself alone was guilty; and that he had uttered these rash or treasonable speeches without the approbation or knowledge of his patron. Yet a cloud of suspicion hung over the innocence of the constable; he was still pursued by the whispers of malevolence; and a subtle courtier, the archbishop of Philadelphia, urged him to accept the judgment of God in the fiery proof of the ordeal. Three days before the trial, the patient's arm was enclosed in a bag and secured by the royal signet; and it was incumbent on him to bear a redhot ball of iron three times from the altar to the rails of the sanctuary, without artifice and without injury. Palaeologus eluded the dangerous experiment with sense and pleasantry. "I am a soldier," said he, "and will boldly enter the lists with my accusers; but a layman, a sinner like myself, is not endowed with the gift of miracles. *Your* piety, most holy prelate, may deserve the interposition of Heaven, and from your hands I will receive the fiery globe, the pledge of my innocence." The archbishop started; the emperor smiled; and the absolution or pardon of Michael was approved by new rewards and new services.[†]

In the council, after the death of Theodore, he was the first to pronounce and the first to violate the oath of allegiance to Muzalon; and so dexterous was his conduct that he reaped the benefit without incurring the guilt, or at least the reproach, of the subsequent massacre. In the choice of a regent, he balanced the interests and passions of the candidates; turned their envy and hatred from himself against each other, and forced every competitor to own that after his own claims, those of Palaeologus were best entitled to the preference. Under the title of great duke, he accepted or assumed, during a long minority, the active powers of government; the patriarch was a venerable name; and the factious nobles were seduced or oppressed by the ascendant of his genius. The fruits of the economy of Vataces were deposited in a strong castle on the banks of the Hermus, in the custody of the faithful Varangians: the *constable* retained his command or influence over the foreign troops; he employed the guards to possess the treasure, and the treasure to corrupt the guards; and whatsoever might be the abuse of the public money, his character was above the suspicion of private avarice. By himself or by his emissaries, he strove to persuade every rank of subjects that their own prosperity would rise in just proportion to the establishment of his authority. The weight of taxes was suspended, the perpetual theme of popular complaint; and he prohibited the trials by the ordeal and judicial combat. These Barbaric institutions were already abolished or undermined in France and England; and the appeal to the sword offended the sense of a civilized, and the temper of an unwarlike, people. For the future maintenance of their wives and children, the veterans were grateful: the priests and the philosophers applauded his ardent zeal for the advancement of religion and learning; and his vague promise of rewarding merit was applied by every candidate to his own hopes. Conscious of the influence of the clergy, Michael successfully labored to secure the suffrage of that powerful order. Their expensive journey from Nice to Magnesia afforded a decent and ample pretense: the leading prelates were tempted by the liberality of his nocturnal visits; and the incorruptible patriarch was flattered by the homage of his new colleague, who led his mule by the bridle into the town, and removed to a respectful distance the importunity of the crowd. Without renouncing his title by royal descent, Palaeologus encouraged a free discussion into the advantages of elective monarchy; and his adherents asked, with the insolence of triumph, what patient would trust his health, or what merchant would abandon his vessel, to the *hereditary* skill of a physician or a pilot? The youth of the emperor, and the impending dangers of a minority, required the support of a mature and experienced guardian; of an associate raised above the envy of his equals and invested with the name and prerogatives of royalty. For the interest of the prince and people, without any selfish views for himself or his family, the great duke consented to guard and instruct the son of Theodore; but he sighed for the happy moment when he might restore to his firmer hands the administration of his patrimony and enjoy the blessings of a private station. He was first invested with the title and prerogatives of *despot*, which bestowed the purple ornaments and the second place in the Roman monarchy. It was afterwards agreed that John and Michael should be proclaimed as joint emperors and raised on the buckler, but that the preeminence should be reserved for the birthright of the former. A mutual league of amity was pledged between the royal partners; and in case of a rupture, the subjects were bound, by their oath of allegiance, to declare themselves against the aggressor; an ambiguous name, the seed of discord and civil war. Palaeologus was content; but on the day of the coronation and in the cathedral of Nice, his zealous adherents most vehemently urged the just priority of his age and merit. The unseasonable dispute was eluded by postponing to a more convenient opportunity the coronation of John Lascaris; and he walked with a slight diadem in the train of his guardian, who alone received the Imperial crown from the hands of the patriarch [January 1, 1260]. It was not without extreme reluctance that Arsenius abandoned the cause of his pupil; but the Varangians brandished their battle-axes; a sign of assent was extorted from the trembling youth; and some voices were heard that the life of a child should no longer impede the settlement of the nation. A full harvest of honors and employments was distributed among his friends by the grateful Palaeologus. In his own family he created a despot and two sebastocrators; Alexius Strategopulus was decorated with the title of Caesar; and that veteran commander soon repaid the obligation by restoring Constantinople to the Greek emperor.

It was in the second year of his reign, while he resided in the palace and gardens of Nymphaeum, near Smyrna, that the first messenger arrived at the dead of night; and the stupendous intelligence was imparted to Michael after he had been gently waked by the tender precaution of his sister Eulogia. The man was unknown or obscure; he produced no letters from the victorious Caesar; nor could it easily be credited, after the defeat of Vataces and the recent failure of Palaeologus himself, that the capital had been surprised by a detachment of eight hundred soldiers [July 25, 1261]. As a hostage, the doubtful author was confined, with the assurance of death or an ample recompense; and the court was left some hours in the anxiety of hope and fear, till the messengers of Alexius arrived with the authentic intelligence and displayed the trophies of the conquest, the sword and scepter, the buskins and bonnet, of the usurper Baldwin, which he had dropped in his precipitate flight. A general assembly of the bishops, senators, and nobles was immediately convened, and never perhaps was an event received with more heartfelt and universal joy. In a studied oration, the new sovereign of Constantinople congratulated his own and the public fortune. "There was a time," said he, "a far distant time, when the Roman empire extended to the Adriatic, the Tigris, and the confines of Aethiopia. After the loss of the provinces, our capital itself, in these last and calamitous days, has been wrested from our hands by the Barbarians of the West. From the lowest ebb, the tide of prosperity has again returned in our favor; but our prosperity was that of fugitives and exiles: and when we were asked which was the country of the Romans, we indicated with a blush the climate of the globe, and the quarter of the heavens. The divine Providence has now restored to our arms the city of Constantine, the sacred seat of religion and empire; and it will depend on our valor and conduct to render this important acquisition the pledge and omen of future victories." So eager was the impatience of the prince and people that Michael made his triumphal entry into Constantinople only twenty days after the expulsion of the Latins [August 14, 1261]. The golden gate was thrown open at his approach; the devout conqueror dismounted from his horse; and a miraculous image of Mary the Conductress was borne before him, that the divine Virgin in person might appear to conduct him to the temple of her Son, the cathedral of St. Sophia. But after the first transport of devotion and pride, he sighed at the dreary prospect of solitude and ruin. The palace was defiled with smoke and dirt and the gross intemperance of the Franks; whole streets had been consumed by fire or were decayed by the injuries of time; the sacred and profane edifices were stripped of their ornaments: and as if they were conscious of their approaching exile, the industry of the Latins had been confined to the work of pillage and destruction. Trade had expired under the pressure of anarchy and distress, and the numbers of inhabitants had decreased with the opulence of the city. It was the first care of the Greek monarch to reinstate the nobles in the palaces of their fathers; and the houses or the ground which they occupied were restored to the families that could exhibit a legal right of inheritance.

But the far greater part was extinct or lost; the vacant property had devolved to the lord; he repeopled Constantinople by a liberal invitation to the provinces; and the brave volunteers were seated in the capital which had been recovered by their arms. The French barons and the principal families had retired with their emperor; but the patient and humble crowd of Latins was attached to the country and indifferent to the change of masters. Instead of banishing the factories of the Pisans, Venetians, and Genoese, the prudent conqueror accepted their oaths of allegiance, encouraged their industry, confirmed their privileges, and allowed them to live under the jurisdiction of their proper magistrates. Of these nations, the Pisans and Venetians preserved their respective quarters in the city; but the services and power of the Genoese deserved at the same time the gratitude and the jealousy of the Greeks. Their independent colony was first planted at the seaport town of Heraclea in Thrace. They were speedily recalled and settled in the exclusive possession of the suburb of Galata, an advantageous post, in which they revived the commerce and insulted the majesty of the Byzantine empire.

The recovery of Constantinople was celebrated as the era of a new empire: the conqueror, alone and by the right of the sword, renewed his coronation in the church of St. Sophia; and the name and honors of John Lascaris, his pupil and lawful sovereign, were insensibly abolished. But his claims still lived in the minds of the people; and the royal youth must speedily attain the years of manhood and ambition. By fear or conscience, Palaeologus was restrained from dipping his hands in innocent and royal blood; but the anxiety of a usurper and a parent urged him to secure his throne by one of those imperfect crimes so familiar to the modern Greeks. The loss of sight incapacitated the young prince for the active business of the world; instead of the brutal violence of tearing out his eyes, the visual nerve was destroyed by the intense glare of a red-hot basin [December 25, A.D. 1261]; and John Lascaris was removed to a distant castle, where he spent many years in privacy and oblivion. Such cool and deliberate guilt may seem incompatible with remorse; but if Michael could trust the mercy of Heaven, he was not inaccessible to the reproaches and vengeance of mankind, which he had provoked by cruelty and treason. His cruelty imposed on a servile court the duties of applause or silence; but the clergy had a right to speak in the name of their invisible

Master; and their holy legions were led by a prelate whose character was above the temptations of hope or fear. After a short abdication of his dignity, Arsenius had consented to ascend the ecclesiastical throne of Constantinople and to preside in the restoration of the church. His pious simplicity was long deceived by the arts of Palaeologus; and his patience and submission might soothe the usurper and protect the safety of the young prince. On the news of his inhuman treatment, the patriarch unsheathed the spiritual sword; and superstition, on this occasion, was enlisted in the cause of humanity and justice. In a synod of bishops, who were stimulated by the example of his zeal, the patriarch pronounced a sentence of excommunication; though his prudence still repeated the name of Michael in the public prayers [A.D. 1262–1268]. The Eastern prelates had not adopted the dangerous maxims of ancient Rome; nor did they presume to enforce their censures by deposing princes or absolving nations from their oaths of allegiance. But the Christian who had been separated from God and the church became an object of horror; and in a turbulent and fanatic capital, that horror might arm the hand of an assassin or inflame a sedition of the people. Palaeologus felt his danger, confessed his guilt, and deprecated his judge: the act was irretrievable; the prize was obtained; and the most rigorous penance, which he solicited, would have raised the sinner to the reputation of a saint. The unrelenting patriarch refused to announce any means of atonement or any hopes of mercy; and condescended only to pronounce that for so great a crime, great indeed must be the satisfaction. "Do you require," said Michael, "that I should abdicate the empire?" and at these words he offered, or seemed to offer, the sword of state. Arsenius eagerly grasped this pledge of sovereignty; but when he perceived that the emperor was unwilling to purchase absolution at so dear a rate, he indignantly escaped to his cell, and left the royal sinner kneeling and weeping before the door.

The danger and scandal of this excommunication subsisted above three years, till the popular clamor was assuaged by time and repentance; till the brethren of Arsenius condemned his inflexible spirit, so repugnant to the unbounded forgiveness of the gospel. The emperor had artfully insinuated that if he were still rejected at home, he might seek in the Roman pontiff a more indulgent judge; but it was far more easy and effectual to find or to place that judge at the head of the Byzantine church. Arsenius was involved in a vague rumor of conspiracy and disaffection; some irregular steps in his ordination and government were liable to censure; a synod deposed him from the episcopal office; and he was transported under a guard of soldiers to a small island of the Propontis. Before his exile, he sullenly requested that a strict account might be taken of the treasures of the church; boasted that his sole riches, three pieces of gold, had been earned by transcribing the psalms; continued to assert the freedom of his mind; and denied with his last breath the pardon which was implored by the royal sinner. After some delay, Gregory, bishop of Hadrianople, was translated to the Byzantine throne; but his authority was found insufficient to support the absolution of the emperor; and Joseph, a reverend monk, was substituted to that important function. This edifying scene was represented in the presence of the senate and the people; at the end of six years the humble penitent was restored to the communion of the faithful; and humanity will rejoice that a milder treatment of the captive Lascaris was stipulated as a proof of his remorse. But the spirit of Arsenius still survived in a powerful faction of the monks and clergy, who persevered about forty-eight years in an obstinate schism [A.D. 1266–1312]. Their scruples were treated with tenderness and respect by Michael and his son; and the reconciliation of the Arsenites was the serious labor of the church and state. In the confidence of fanaticism, they had proposed to try their cause by a miracle; and when the two papers that contained their own and the adverse cause were cast into a fiery brazier, they expected that the Catholic verity would be respected by the flames. Alas! the two papers were indiscriminately consumed, and this unforeseen accident produced the union of a day, and renewed the quarrel of an age. The final treaty displayed the victory of the Arsenites: the clergy abstained during forty days from all ecclesiastical functions; a slight penance was imposed on the laity; the body of Arsenius was deposited in the sanctuary; and in the name of the departed saint, the prince and people were released from the sins of their fathers.

The establishment of his family was the motive, or at least the pretense, of the crime of Palaeologus; and he was impatient to confirm the succession by sharing with his eldest son the honors of the purple. Andronicus, afterwards surnamed the Elder, was proclaimed and crowned emperor of the Romans in the fifteenth year of his age; and from the first era of a prolix and inglorious reign, he held that august title nine years as the colleague, and fifty as the successor, of his father [Michael Palaeologus reigned A.D. 1259–1282; Andronicus A.D. 1273–1332]. Michael himself, had he died in a private station, would have been thought more worthy of the empire; and the assaults of his temporal and spiritual enemies left him few moments to labor for his own fame or the happiness of his subjects. He wrested from the Franks several of the noblest islands of the archipelago, Lesbos, Chios, and Rhodes: his brother Constantine was sent to command in Malvasia and Sparta; and the eastern side of the Morea, from Argos and Napoli to Cape Taenarus, was repossessed by the Greeks. This effusion of Christian blood was loudly condemned by the patriarch; and the insolent priest presumed to interpose his fears and scruples between the arms of princes. But in the prosecution of these Western conquests, the countries beyond the Hellespont were left naked to the Turks; and their depredations verified the prophecy of a dying senator that the recovery of Constantinople would be the ruin of Asia. The victories of Michael were achieved by his lieutenants; his sword rusted in the palace; and in the transactions of the emperor with the popes and the king of Naples, his political acts were stained with cruelty and fraud.

I. The Vatican was the most natural refuge of a Latin emperor who had been driven from his throne; and Pope Urban the Fourth appeared to pity the misfortunes and vindicate the cause of the fugitive Baldwin. A crusade, with plenary indulgence, was preached by his command against the schismatic Greeks: he excommunicated their allies and adherents; solicited Louis the Ninth in favor of his kinsman; and demanded a tenth of the ecclesiastical revenues of France and England for the service of the holy war. The subtle Greek, who watched the rising tempest of the West, attempted to suspend or soothe the hostility of the pope by suppliant embassies and respectful letters; but he insinuated that the establishment of peace must prepare the reconciliation and obedience of the Eastern church. The Roman court could not be deceived by so gross an artifice; and Michael was admonished that the repentance of the son should precede the forgiveness of the father; and that *faith* (an ambiguous word) was the only basis of friendship and alliance. After a long and affected delay, the approach of danger, and the importunity of Gregory the Tenth, compelled him to enter on a more serious negotiation: he alleged the example of the great Vataces;

and the Greek clergy, who understood the intentions of their prince, were not alarmed by the first steps of reconciliation and respect. But when he pressed the conclusion of the treaty, they strenuously declared that the Latins, though not in name, were heretics in fact, and that they despised those strangers as the vilest and most despicable portion of the human race. It was the task of the emperor to persuade, to corrupt, to intimidate the most popular ecclesiastics, to gain the vote of each individual, and alternately to urge the arguments of Christian charity and the public welfare. The texts of the fathers and the arms of the Franks were balanced in the theological and political scale; and without approving the addition to the Nicene creed, the most moderate were taught to confess that the two hostile propositions of proceeding from the Father BY the Son and of proceeding from the Father AND the Son might be reduced to a safe and Catholic sense. The supremacy of the pope was a doctrine more easy to conceive but more painful to acknowledge: yet Michael represented to his monks and prelates that they might submit to name the Roman bishop as the first of the patriarchs; and that their distance and discretion would guard the liberties of the Eastern church from the mischievous consequences of the right of appeal. He protested that he would sacrifice his life and empire rather than yield the smallest point of orthodox faith or national independence; and this declaration was sealed and ratified by a golden bull. The patriarch Joseph withdrew to a monastery to resign or resume his throne, according to the event of the treaty: the letters of union and obedience were subscribed by the emperor, his son Andronicus, and thirty-five archbishops and metropolitans, with their respective synods; and the episcopal list was multiplied by many dioceses which were annihilated under the yoke of the infidels. An embassy was composed of some trusty ministers and prelates: they embarked for Italy with rich ornaments and rare perfumes for the altar of St. Peter; and their secret orders authorized and recommended a boundless compliance. They were received in the general council of Lyons by Pope Gregory the Tenth, at the head of five hundred bishops. He embraced with tears his long-lost and repentant children; accepted the oath of the ambassadors, who abjured the schism in the name of the two emperors; adorned the prelates with the ring and mitre; chanted in Greek and Latin the Nicene creed with the addition of *filioque* ["and the Son"]; and rejoiced in the union of the East and West, which had been reserved for his reign [A.D. 1274 ff.]. To consummate this pious work, the Byzantine deputies were speedily followed by the pope's nuncios; and their instruction discloses the policy of the Vatican, which could not be satisfied with the vain title of supremacy. After viewing the temper of the prince and people, they were enjoined to absolve the schismatic clergy, who should subscribe and swear their abjuration and obedience; to establish in all the churches the use of the perfect creed; to prepare the entrance of a cardinal legate, with the full powers and dignity of his office; and to instruct the emperor in the advantages which he might derive from the temporal protection of the Roman pontiff.

But they found a country without a friend, a nation in which the names of Rome and Union were pronounced with abhorrence. The patriarch Joseph was indeed removed: his place was filled by Veccus, an ecclesiastic of learning and moderation; and the emperor was still urged by the same motives to persevere in the same professions. But in his private language Palaeologus affected to deplore the pride and to blame the innovations of the Latins; and while he debased his character by this double hypocrisy, he justified and punished the opposition of his subjects [A.D. 1277–1282]. By the joint suffrage of the new and the ancient Rome, a sentence of excommunication was pronounced against the obstinate schismatics; the censures of the church were executed by the sword of Michael; on the failure of persuasion, he tried the arguments of prison and exile, of whipping and mutilation; those touchstones, says an historian, of cowards and the brave. Two Greeks still reigned in Aetolia, Epirus, and Thessaly with the appellation of despots: they had yielded to the sovereign of Constantinople, but they rejected the chains of the Roman pontiff, and supported their refusal by successful arms. Under their protection, the fugitive monks and bishops assembled in hostile synods; and retorted the name of heretic with the galling addition of apostate: the prince of Trebizond was tempted to assume the forfeit title of emperor; and even the Latins of Negropont, Thebes, Athens, and the Morea forgot the merits of the convert to join, with open or clandestine aid, the enemies of Palaeologus. His favorite generals, of his own blood and family, successively deserted or betrayed the sacrilegious trust. His sister Eulogia, a niece, and two female cousins conspired against him; another niece, Mary, queen of Bulgaria, negotiated his ruin with the sultan of Egypt; and in the public eye, their treason was consecrated as the most sublime virtue. To the pope's nuncios, who urged the consummation of the work, Palaeologus exposed a naked recital of all that he had done and suffered for their sake. They were assured that the guilty sectaries, of both sexes and every rank, had been deprived of their honors, their fortunes, and their liberty; a spreading list of confiscation and punishment which involved many persons, the dearest to the emperor or the best deserving of his favor. They were conducted to the prison to behold four princes of the royal blood chained in the four corners, and shaking their fetters in an agony of grief and rage. Two of these captives were afterwards released; the one by submission, the other by death: but the obstinacy of their two companions was chastised by the loss of their eyes; and the Greeks, the least adverse to the union, deplored that cruel and inauspicious tragedy. Persecutors must expect the hatred of those whom they oppress; but they commonly find some consolation in the testimony of their conscience, the applause of their party, and, perhaps, the success of their undertaking. But the hypocrisy of Michael, which was prompted only by political motives, must have forced him to hate himself, to despise his followers, and to esteem and envy the rebel champions by whom he was detested and despised. While his violence was abhorred at Constantinople, at Rome his slowness was arraigned and his sincerity suspected; till at length Pope Martin the Fourth excluded the Greek emperor from the pale of a church into which he was striving to reduce a schismatic people [A.D. 1280]. No sooner had the tyrant expired than the union was dissolved, and abjured by unanimous consent; the churches were purified; the penitents were reconciled; and his son Andronicus, after weeping the sins and errors of his youth, most piously denied his father the burial of a prince and a Christian [A.D. 1283].

CHAPTER LXIII

CIVIL WARS AND THE RUIN OF THE GREEK EMPIRE

Civil wars and ruin of the Greek empire. • Reigns of Andronicus, the elder and younger, and John Palaeologus. • Regency, revolt, reign, and abdication of John Cantacuzene.[†]

The long reign of Andronicus the elder is chiefly memorable by the disputes of the Greek church, the invasion of the Catalans, and the rise of the Ottoman power [A.D. 1282–1320]. He is celebrated as the most learned and virtuous prince of the age; but such virtue, and such learning, contributed neither to the perfection of the individual nor to the happiness of society. A slave of the most abject superstition, he was surrounded on all sides by visible and invisible enemies; nor were the flames of hell less dreadful to his fancy than those of a Catalan or Turkish war. Under the reign of the Palaeologi, the choice of the patriarch was the most important business of the state; the heads of the Greek church were ambitious and fanatic monks; and their vices or virtues, their learning or ignorance, were equally mischievous or contemptible. By his intemperate discipline, the patriarch Athanasius excited the hatred of the clergy and people: he was heard to declare that the sinner should swallow the last dregs of the cup of penance; and the foolish tale was propagated of his punishing a sacrilegious ass that had tasted the lettuce of a convent garden. Driven from the throne by the universal clamor [A.D. 1294], Athanasius composed before his retreat two papers of a very opposite cast. His public testament was in the tone of charity and resignation; the private codicil breathed the direst anathemas against the authors of his disgrace, whom he excluded forever from the communion of the Holy Trinity, the angels, and the saints. This last paper he enclosed in an earthen pot, which was placed by his order on the top of one of the pillars in the dome of St. Sophia, in the distant hope of discovery and revenge. At the end of four years, some youths, climbing by a ladder in search of pigeons' nests, detected the fatal secret; and as Andronicus felt himself touched and bound by the excommunication, he trembled on the brink of the abyss which had been so treacherously dug under his feet. A synod of bishops was instantly convened to debate this important question: the rashness of these clandestine anathemas was generally condemned; but as the knot could be untied only by the same hand, as that hand was now deprived of the crosier, it appeared that this posthumous decree was irrevocable by any earthly power. Some faint testimonies of repentance and pardon were extorted from the author of the mischief; but the conscience of the emperor was still wounded, and he desired, with no less ardor than Athanasius himself, the restoration of a patriarch by whom alone he could be healed. At the dead of night, a monk rudely knocked at the door of the royal bed-chamber, announcing a revelation of plague and famine, of inundations and earthquakes. Andronicus started from his bed and spent the night in prayer, till he felt, or thought that he felt, a slight motion of the earth. The emperor on foot led the bishops and monks to the cell of Athanasius; and after a proper resistance, the saint from whom this message had been sent consented to absolve the prince and govern the church of Constantinople [A.D. 1303]. Untamed by disgrace and hardened by solitude, the shepherd was again odious to the flock, and his enemies contrived a singular, and as it proved a successful, mode of revenge. In the night, they stole away the footstool or foot-cloth of his throne, which they secretly replaced with the decoration of a satirical picture. The emperor was painted with a bridle in his mouth, and Athanasius leading the tractable beast to the feet of Christ. The authors of the libel were detected and punished [A.D. 1311]; but as their lives had been spared, the Christian priest in sullen indignation retired to his cell; and the eyes of Andronicus, which had been opened for a moment, were again closed by his successor.

If this transaction be one of the most curious and important of a reign of fifty years, I cannot at least accuse the brevity of my materials, since I reduce into some few pages the enormous folios of Pachymer, Cantacuzene, and Nicephorus Gregoras, who have composed the prolix and languid story of the times. The name and situation of the emperor John Cantacuzene might inspire the most lively curiosity. His memorials of forty years extend from the revolt of the younger Andronicus to his own abdication of the empire; and it is observed that, like Moses and Caesar, he was the principal actor in the scenes which he describes. But in this eloquent work we should vainly seek the sincerity of a hero or a penitent. Retired in a cloister from the vices and passions of the world, he presents not a confession but an apology of the life of an ambitious statesman. Instead of unfolding the true counsels and characters of men, he displays the smooth and specious surface of events, highly varnished with his own praises and those of his friends. Their motives are always pure; their ends always legitimate: they conspire and rebel without any views of interest; and the violence which they inflict or suffer is celebrated as the spontaneous effect of reason and virtue.

After the example of the first of the Palaeologi, the elder Andronicus associated his son Michael to the honors of the purple; and from the age of eighteen to his premature death, that prince was acknowledged, above twenty-five years, as the second emperor of the Greeks. At the head of an army, he excited neither the fears of the enemy nor the jealousy of the court; his modesty and patience were never tempted to compute the years of his father; nor was that father compelled to repent of his liberality either by the virtues or vices of his son. The son of Michael was named Andronicus from his grandfather, to whose early favor he was introduced by that nominal resemblance. The blossoms of wit and beauty increased the fondness of the elder Andronicus; and with the common vanity of age, he expected to realize in the second the hope which had been disappointed in the first generation. The boy was educated in the palace as an heir and a favorite; and in the oaths and acclamations of the people, the *august triad* was formed by the names of the father, the son, and the grandson. But the younger Andronicus was speedily corrupted by his infant greatness, while he beheld with puerile impatience the double obstacle that hung, and might long hang, over his rising ambition. It was not to acquire fame or to diffuse happiness that he so eagerly aspired: wealth and impunity were in his eyes the most precious attributes of a monarch; and his first indiscreet demand was the sovereignty of some rich and fertile island where he might lead a life of independence and pleasure. The emperor was offended by the loud and frequent intemperance which disturbed his capital; the sums which his parsimony denied were supplied by the Genoese usurers of Pera; and the oppressive debt, which consolidated the interest of a faction, could be discharged only by a revolution. A beautiful female, a matron in rank, a prostitute in manners, had instructed the younger Andronicus in the rudiments of love; but he had reason to suspect the nocturnal visits of a rival; and a stranger passing through the street was pierced by the arrows of his guards, who were placed in ambush at her door. That stranger was his brother, Prince Manuel, who languished and died of his wound; and the emperor Michael, their common father, whose health was in a declining state, expired on the eighth day, lamenting the loss of both his children [A.D. 1320]. However guiltless in his intention, the younger Andronicus might impute a brother's and a father's death to the consequence of his own vices; and deep was the sigh of thinking and feeling men when they perceived, instead of sorrow and repentance, his ill-dissembled joy on the removal of two odious competitors. By these melancholy events and the increase of his disorders, the mind of the elder emperor was gradually alienated; and after many fruitless reproofs, he transferred on another grandson his hopes and affection. The change was announced by the new oath of allegiance to the reigning sovereign, and the *person* whom he should appoint for his successor; and the acknowledged heir, after a repetition of insults and complaints, was exposed to the indignity of a public trial. Before the sentence, which would probably have condemned him to a dungeon or a cell, the emperor was informed that the palace courts were filled with the armed followers of his grandson; the judgment was softened to a treaty of reconciliation; and the triumphant escape of the prince encouraged the ardor of the younger faction.

Yet the capital, the clergy, and the senate adhered to the person, or at least to the government, of the old emperor; and it was only in the provinces, by flight and revolt and foreign succor, that the malcontents could hope to vindicate their cause and subvert his throne. The soul of the enterprise was the great domestic John Cantacuzene; the sally from Constantinople is the first date of his actions and memorials; and if his own pen be most descriptive of his patriotism, an unfriendly historian has not refused to celebrate the zeal and ability which he displayed in the service of the young emperor. That prince escaped from the capital under the pretense of hunting; erected his standard at Hadrianople; and in a few days assembled fifty thousand horse and foot, whom neither honor nor duty could have armed against the Barbarians. Such a force might have saved or commanded the empire; but their counsels were discordant, their motions were slow and doubtful, and their progress was checked by intrigue and negotiation. The quarrel of the two Andronici was protracted, and suspended, and renewed, during a ruinous period of seven years [A.D. 1321–1328]. In the first treaty, the relics of the Greek empire were divided: Constantinople, Thessalonica, and the islands were left to the elder, while the younger acquired the sovereignty of the greatest part of Thrace, from Philippi to the Byzantine limit. By the second treaty, he stipulated the payment of his troops, his immediate coronation, and an adequate share of the power and revenue of the state [A.D. 1325]. The third civil war was terminated by the surprise of Constantinople, the final retreat of the old emperor, and the sole reign of his victorious grandson. The reasons of this delay may be found in the characters of the men and of the times. When the heir of the monarchy first pleaded his wrongs and his apprehensions, he was heard with pity and applause: and his adherents repeated on all sides the inconsistent promise that he would increase the pay of the soldiers and alleviate the burdens of the people. The grievances of forty years were mingled in his revolt; and the rising generation was fatigued by the endless prospect of a reign whose favorites and maxims were of other times. The youth of Andronicus had been without spirit, his age was without reverence: his taxes produced an unusual revenue of five hundred thousand pounds; yet the richest of the sovereigns of Christendom was incapable of maintaining three thousand horse and twenty galleys to resist the destructive progress of the Turks. "How different," said the younger Andronicus, "is my situation from that of the son of Philip! Alexander might complain that his father would leave him nothing to conquer: alas! my grandsire will leave me nothing to lose." But the Greeks were soon admonished that the public disorders could not be healed by a civil war, and that their young favorite was not destined to be the savior of a falling empire. On the first repulse, his party was broken by his own levity, their intestine discord, and the intrigues of the ancient court, which tempted each malcontent to desert or betray the cause of the rebellion. Andronicus the younger was touched with remorse, or fatigued with business, or deceived by negotiation: pleasure rather than power was his aim; and the license of maintaining a thousand hounds, a thousand hawks, and a thousand huntsmen was sufficient to sully his fame and disarm his ambition.

Let us now survey the catastrophe of this busy plot, and the final situation of the principal actors. The age of Andronicus was consumed in civil discord; and amidst the events of war and treaty, his power and reputation continually decayed, till the fatal night in which the gates of the city and palace were opened without resistance to his grandson. His principal commander scorned the repeated warnings of danger and, retiring to rest in the vain security of ignorance, abandoned the feeble monarch, with some priests and pages, to the terrors of a sleepless night. These terrors were quickly realized by the hostile shouts which proclaimed the titles and victory of Andronicus the younger; and the aged emperor, falling prostrate before an image of the Virgin, despatched a suppliant message to resign the scepter and to obtain his life at the hands of the conqueror [May 24, A.D. 1328]. The answer of his grandson was decent and pious; at the prayer of his friends, the younger Andronicus assumed the sole administration; but the elder still enjoyed the name and preeminence of the first emperor, the use of the great palace, and a pension of twenty-four thousand pieces of gold, one half of which was assigned on the royal treasury and the other on the fishery of Constantinople. But his impotence was soon exposed to contempt and oblivion; the vast silence of the palace was disturbed only by the cattle and poultry of the neighborhood, which roved with impunity through the solitary courts; and a reduced allowance of ten thousand pieces of gold was all that he could ask, and more than he could hope. His calamities were embittered by the gradual extinction of sight; his confinement was rendered each day more rigorous; and during the absence and sickness of his grandson, his inhuman keepers, by the threats of instant death, compelled him to exchange the purple for the monastic habit and profession [A.D. 1330]. The monk *Antony* had renounced the pomp of the world; yet he had occasion for a coarse fur in the winter season, and as wine was forbidden by his confessor and water by his physician, the sherbet of Egypt was his common drink. It was not without difficulty that the late emperor could procure three or four pieces to satisfy these simple wants; and if he bestowed the gold to relieve the more painful distress of a friend, the sacrifice is of some weight in the scale of humanity and religion. Four years after his abdication, Andronicus or Antony expired in a cell in the seventy-fourth year of his age [February 13, 1332]: and the last strain of adulation could only promise a more splendid crown of glory in Heaven than he had enjoyed upon earth.

Nor was the reign of the younger [A.D. 1328–1341] more glorious or fortunate than that of the elder Andronicus. He gathered the fruits of ambition; but the taste was transient and bitter: in the supreme station he lost the remains of his early popularity; and the defects of his character became still more conspicuous to the world. The public reproach urged him to march in person against the Turks; nor did his courage fail in the hour of trial; but a defeat and a wound were the only trophies of his expedition in Asia, which confirmed the establishment of the Ottoman monarchy. The abuses of the civil government attained their full maturity and perfection: his neglect of forms, and the confusion of national dresses, are deplored by the Greeks as the fatal symptoms of the decay of the empire. Andronicus was old before his time; the intemperance of youth had accelerated the infirmities of age; and after being rescued from a dangerous malady by nature, or physic, or the Virgin, he was snatched away before he had accomplished his forty-fifth year. He was twice married; and, as the progress of the Latins in arms and arts had softened the prejudices of the Byzantine court, his two wives were chosen in the princely houses of Germany and Italy. The first, Agnes at home, Irene in Greece, was daughter of the duke of Brunswick. Her father was a petty lord in the poor and savage regions of the north of Germany: yet he derived some revenue from his silver mines; and his family is celebrated by the Greeks as the most ancient and noble of the Teutonic name. After the death of this childish princess, Andronicus sought in marriage Jane, the sister of the count of Savoy; and his suit was preferred to that of the French king. The count respected in his sister the superior majesty of a Roman empress: her retinue was composed of knights and ladies; she was regenerated and crowned in St. Sophia under the more orthodox appellation of Anne; and at the nuptial feast, the Greeks and Italians vied with each other in the martial exercises of tilts and tournaments.

The empress Anne of Savoy survived her husband: their son, John Palaeologus, was left an orphan and an emperor in the ninth year of his age [he reigned A.D. 1341–1391]; and his weakness was protected by the first and most deserving of the Greeks. The long and cordial friendship of his father for John Cantacuzene is alike honorable to the prince and the subject. It had been formed amidst the pleasures of their youth: their families were almost equally noble; and the recent luster of the purple was amply compensated by the energy of a private education. We have seen that the young emperor was saved by Cantacuzene from the power of his grandfather; and after six years of civil war, the same favorite brought him back in triumph to the palace of Constantinople. Under the reign of Andronicus the younger, the great domestic ruled the emperor and the empire; and it was by his valor and conduct that the Isle of Lesbos and the principality of Aetolia were restored to their ancient allegiance. His enemies confess that, among the public robbers, Cantacuzene alone was moderate and abstemious; and the free and voluntary account which he produces of his own wealth may sustain the presumption that it was devolved by inheritance and not accumulated by rapine.... The favor of Cantacuzene was above his fortune. In the moments of familiarity, in the hour of sickness, the emperor was desirous to level the distance between them and pressed his friend to accept the diadem and purple. The virtue of the great domestic, which is attested by his own pen, resisted the dangerous proposal; but the last testament of Andronicus the younger named him the guardian of his son and the regent of the empire.

Had the regent found a suitable return of obedience and gratitude, perhaps he would have acted with pure and zealous fidelity in the service of his pupil. A guard of five hundred soldiers watched over his person and the palace; the funeral of the late emperor was decently performed; the capital was silent and submissive; and five hundred letters which Cantacuzene despatched in the first month informed the provinces of their loss and their duty. The prospect of a tranquil minority was blasted by the great duke or admiral Apocaucus, and to exaggerate *his* perfidy, the Imperial historian is pleased to magnify his own imprudence in raising him to that office against the advice of his more sagacious sovereign. Bold and subtle, rapacious and profuse, the avarice and ambition of Apocaucus were by turns subservient to each other; and his talents were applied to the ruin of his country. His arrogance was heightened by the command of a naval force and an impregnable castle, and under the mask of oaths and flattery he secretly conspired against his benefactor. The female court of the empress was bribed and directed; he encouraged Anne of Savoy to assert, by the law of nature, the tutelage of her son; the love of power was disguised by the anxiety of maternal tenderness: and the founder of the Palaeologi had instructed his posterity to dread the example of a perfidious guardian. The patriarch John of Apri was a proud and feeble old man encompassed by a numerous and hungry kindred. He produced an obsolete epistle of Andronicus which bequeathed the prince and people to his pious care: the fate of his predecessor Arsenius prompted him to prevent rather than punish the crimes of a usurper; and Apocaucus smiled at the success of his own flattery when he beheld the Byzantine priest assuming the state and temporal claims of the Roman pontiff. Between three persons so different in their situation and character, a private league was concluded: a shadow of authority was restored to the senate; and the people was tempted by the name of freedom. By this powerful confederacy, the great domestic was assaulted at first with clandestine, at length with open, arms. His prerogatives were disputed; his opinions slighted; his friends persecuted; and his safety was threatened both in the camp and city. In his absence on the public service, he was accused of treason; proscribed as an enemy of the church and state; and delivered with all his adherents to the sword of justice, the vengeance of the people, and the power of the devil; his fortunes were confiscated; his aged mother was cast into prison; all his past services were buried in oblivion; and he was driven by injustice to perpetrate the crime of which he was accused. From the review of his preceding conduct, Cantacuzene appears to have been guiltless of any treasonable designs; and the only suspicion of his innocence must arise from the vehemence of his protestations and the sublime purity which he ascribes to his own virtue. While the empress and the patriarch still affected the appearances of harmony, he repeatedly solicited the permission of retiring to a private, and even a monastic, life. After he had been declared a public enemy, it was his fervent wish to throw himself at the feet of the young emperor and to receive without a murmur the stroke of the executioner: it was not without reluctance that he listened to the voice of reason, which inculcated the sacred duty of saving his family and friends, and proved that he could only save them by drawing the sword and assuming the Imperial title.

In the strong city of Demotica, his peculiar domain, the emperor John Cantacuzene was invested with the purple buskins: his right leg was clothed by his noble kinsmen, the left by the Latin chiefs, on whom he conferred the order of knighthood [October 26, A.D. 1341]. But even in this act of revolt, he was still studious of loyalty; and the titles of John Palaeologus and Anne of Savoy were proclaimed before his own name and that of his wife Irene. Such vain ceremony is a thin disguise of rebellion, nor are there perhaps any personal wrongs that can authorize a subject to take arms against his sovereign: but the want of preparation and success may confirm the assurance of the usurper that this decisive step was the effect of necessity rather than of choice.... Near six years the flame of discord burnt with various success and unabated rage [A.D. 1341–1347]: the cities were distracted by the faction of the nobles and the plebeians; the Cantacuzeni and Palaeologi: and the Bulgarians, the Servians, and the Turks were invoked on both sides as the instruments of private ambition and the common ruin. The regent deplored the calamities of which he was the author and victim: and his own experience might dictate a just and lively remark on the different nature of foreign and civil war. "The former," said he, "is the external warmth of summer, always tolerable and often beneficial; the latter is the deadly heat of a fever, which consumes without a remedy the vitals of the constitution."

The introduction of Barbarians and savages into the contests of civilized nations is a measure pregnant with shame and mischief; which the interest of the moment may compel, but which is reprobated by the best principles of humanity and reason. It is the practice of both sides to accuse their enemies of the guilt of the first alliances; and those who fail in their negotiations are loudest in their censure of the example which they envy and would gladly imitate. The Turks of Asia were less barbarous perhaps than the shepherds of Bulgaria and Servia; but their religion rendered them implacable foes of Rome and Christianity. To acquire the friendship of their emirs, the two factions vied with each other in baseness and profusion: the dexterity of Cantacuzene obtained the preference: but the succor and victory were dearly purchased by the marriage of his daughter with an infidel, the captivity of many thousand Christians, and the passage of the Ottomans into Europe, the last and fatal stroke in the fall of the Roman empire.... [The] civil war was protracted by the weakness of both parties; and the moderation of Cantacuzene has not escaped the reproach of timidity and indolence. He successively recovered the provinces and cities; and the realm of his pupil was measured by the walls of Constantinople; but the metropolis alone counterbalanced the rest of the empire; nor could he attempt that important conquest till he had secured in his favor the public voice and a private correspondence. An Italian of the name of Facciolati had succeeded to the office of great duke: the ships, the guards, and the golden gate were subject to his command; but his humble ambition was bribed to become the instrument of treachery; and the revolution was accomplished without danger or bloodshed. Destitute of the powers of resistance or the hope of relief, the inflexible Anne would have still defended the palace, and have smiled to behold the capital in flames rather than in the possession of a rival. She yielded to the prayers of her friends and enemies; and the treaty was dictated by the conqueror, who professed a loyal and zealous attachment to the son of his benefactor. The marriage of his daughter with John Palaeologus was at length consummated: the hereditary right of the pupil was acknowledged; but the sole administration during ten years was vested in the guardian. Two emperors and three empresses were seated on the Byzantine throne; and a general amnesty quieted the apprehensions and confirmed the property of the most guilty subjects. The festival of the coronation and nuptials was celebrated with the appearances of concord and magnificence, and both were equally fallacious. During the late troubles, the treasures of the state, and even the furniture of the palace, had been alienated or embezzled; the royal banquet was served in pewter or earthenware; and such was the proud poverty of the times that the absence of gold and jewels was supplied by the paltry artifices of glass and gilt-leather.

I hasten to conclude the personal history of John Cantacuzene. He triumphed and reigned [A.D. 1347–1355]; but his reign and triumph were clouded by the discontent of his own and the adverse faction. His followers might style the general amnesty an act of pardon for his enemies, and of oblivion for his friends: in his cause their estates had been forfeited or plundered; and as they wandered naked and hungry through the streets, they cursed the selfish generosity of a leader, who, on the throne of the empire, might relinquish without merit his private inheritance. The adherents of the empress blushed to hold their lives and fortunes by the precarious favor of a usurper; and the thirst of revenge was concealed by a tender concern for the succession, and even the safety, of her son. They were justly alarmed by a petition of the friends of Cantacuzene that they might be released from their oath of allegiance to the Palaeologi and entrusted with the defense of some cautionary towns; a measure supported with argument and eloquence; and which was rejected (says the Imperial historian) "by *my* sublime and almost incredible virtue." His repose was disturbed by the sound of plots and seditions; and he trembled lest the lawful prince should be stolen away by some foreign or domestic enemy, who would inscribe his name and his wrongs in the banners of rebellion. As the son of Andronicus advanced in the years of manhood, he began to feel and to act for himself; and his rising ambition was rather stimulated than checked by the imitation of his father's vices. If we may trust his own professions, Cantacuzene labored with honest industry to correct these sordid and sensual appetites, and to raise the mind of the young prince to a level with his fortune. In the Servian expedition, the two emperors showed themselves in cordial harmony to the troops and provinces; and the younger colleague was initiated by the elder in the mysteries of war and government. After the conclusion of the peace, Palaeologus was left at Thessalonica, a royal residence and a frontier station, to secure by his absence the peace of Constantinople, and to withdraw his youth from the temptations of a luxurious capital. But the distance weakened the powers of control, and the son of Andronicus was surrounded with artful or unthinking companions who taught him to hate his guardian, to deplore his exile, and to vindicate his rights. A private treaty with the *cral* or despot of Servia was soon followed by an open revolt; and Cantacuzene, on the throne of the elder Andronicus, defended the cause of age and prerogative, which in his youth he had so vigorously attacked. At his request the empress-mother undertook the voyage to Thessalonica and the office of mediation: she returned without success; and unless Anne of Savoy was instructed by adversity, we may doubt the sincerity, or at least the fervor, of her zeal. While the regent grasped the scepter with a firm and vigorous hand, she had been instructed to declare that the ten years of his legal administration would soon elapse; and that, after a full trial of the vanity of the world, the emperor Cantacuzene sighed for the repose of a cloister and was ambitious only of a heavenly crown. Had these sentiments been genuine, his voluntary abdication would have restored the peace of the empire, and his conscience would have been relieved by an act of justice. Palaeologus alone was responsible for his future government; and whatever might be his vices, they were surely less formidable than the calamities of a civil war in which the Barbarians and infidels were again invited to assist the Greeks in their mutual destruction [A.D. 1353]. By the arms of the Turks, who now struck a deep and everlasting root in Europe, Cantacuzene prevailed in the third contest in which he had been involved; and the young emperor, driven from the sea and land, was compelled to take shelter among the Latins of the Isle of Tenedos. His insolence and obstinacy provoked the victor to a step which must render the quarrel irreconcilable; and the association of his son Matthew, whom he invested with the purple, established the succession in the family of the Cantacuzeni. But Constantinople was still attached to the blood of her ancient princes; and this last injury accelerated the restoration of the rightful heir. A noble Genoese espoused the cause of Palaeologus, obtained a promise of his sister, and achieved the revolution with two galleys and two thousand five hundred auxiliaries. Under the pretense of distress, they were admitted into the lesser port; a gate was opened, and the Latin shout of "Long life and victory to the emperor, John Palaeologus!" was answered by a general rising in his favor. A numerous and loyal party yet adhered to the standard of Cantacuzene: but he asserts in his history (does he hope for belief?) that his tender conscience rejected the assurance of conquest; that in free obedience to the voice of religion and philosophy, he descended from the throne and embraced with pleasure the monastic habit and profession [January A.D. 1355]. So soon as he ceased to be a prince, his successor was not unwilling that he should be a saint: the remainder of his life was devoted to piety and learning; in the cells of Constantinople and Mount Athos, the monk Joasaph was respected as the temporal and spiritual father of the emperor; and if he issued from his retreat, it was as the minister of peace, to subdue the obstinacy and solicit the pardon of his rebellious son.[†]

CHAPTER LXIV

Moguls, Ottoman Turks

*Conquests of Zingis Khan and the Moguls from China to Poland. •
Escape of Constantinople and the Greeks. • Origin of the Ottoman
Turks in Bithynia. • Reigns and victories of Othman, Orchan,
Amurath the First, and Bajazet the First. • Foundation and
progress of the Turkish monarchy in Asia and Europe. • Danger of
Constantinople and the Greek empire.*

From the petty quarrels of a city and her suburbs, from the cowardice
and discord of the falling Greeks, I shall now ascend to the victorious
Turks; whose domestic slavery was ennobled by martial discipline, religious enthusiasm, and the energy of the national character. The rise
and progress of the Ottomans, the present sovereigns of Constantinople, are connected with the most important scenes of modern history;
but they are founded on a previous knowledge of the great eruption of
the Moguls [or Mongols] and Tartars; whose rapid conquests may be
compared with the primitive convulsions of nature which have agitated and altered the surface of the globe. I have long since asserted
my claim to introduce the nations, the immediate or remote authors of
the fall of the Roman empire; nor can I refuse myself to those events
which, from their uncommon magnitude, will interest a philosophic
mind in the history of blood.

From the spacious highlands between China, Siberia, and the Caspian Sea, the tide of emigration and war has repeatedly been poured.
These ancient seats of the Huns and Turks were occupied in the
twelfth century by many pastoral tribes, of the same descent and similar manners, which were united and led to conquest by the formidable
Zingis [or Genghis Khan, first emperor of the Moguls and Tartars,
A.D. 1206–1227]. In his ascent to greatness, that Barbarian (whose private appellation was Temugin) had trampled on the necks of his
equals. His birth was noble; but it was in the pride of victory that the
prince or people deduced his seventh ancestor from the immaculate
conception of a virgin. . . . The ambition of Temugin condescended to

employ the arts of superstition; and it was from a naked prophet, who could ascend to Heaven on a white horse, that he accepted the title of Zingis, the *Most Great;* and a divine right to the conquest and dominion of the earth. In a general *couroultai,* or diet, he was seated on a felt, which was long afterwards revered as a relic, and solemnly proclaimed great *khan,* or emperor of the Moguls and Tartars. Of these kindred though rival names, the former had given birth to the imperial race; and the latter has been extended by accident or error over the spacious wilderness of the North.

The code of laws which Zingis dictated to his subjects was adapted to the preservation of a domestic peace and the exercise of foreign hostility. The punishment of death was inflicted on the crimes of adultery, murder, perjury, and the capital thefts of a horse or ox; and the fiercest of men were mild and just in their intercourse with each other. The future election of the great khan was vested in the princes of his family and the heads of the tribes; and the regulations of the chase were essential to the pleasures and plenty of a Tartar camp. The victorious nation was held sacred from all servile labors, which were abandoned to slaves and strangers; and every labor was servile except the profession of arms. The service and discipline of the troops, who were armed with bows, cimeters, and iron maces and divided by hundreds, thousands, and ten thousands, were the institutions of a veteran commander. Each officer and soldier was made responsible, under pain of death, for the safety and honor of his companions; and the spirit of conquest breathed in the law that peace should never be granted unless to a vanquished and suppliant enemy. But it is the religion of Zingis that best deserves our wonder and applause. The Catholic inquisitors of Europe, who defended nonsense by cruelty, might have been confounded by the example of a Barbarian who anticipated the lessons of philosophy and established by his laws a system of pure theism and perfect toleration. His first and only article of faith was the existence of one God, the Author of all good; who fills by his presence the heavens and earth, which he has created by his power. The Tartars and Moguls were addicted to the idols of their peculiar tribes; and many of them had been converted by the foreign missionaries to the religions of Moses, of Mohammed, and of Christ. These various systems in freedom and concord were taught and practiced within the precincts of the same camp; and the bonze, the imam, the rabbi, the

Nestorian, and the Latin priest enjoyed the same honorable exemption from service and tribute: in the mosque of Bochara, the insolent victor might trample the Koran under his horse's feet, but the calm legislator respected the prophets and pontiffs of the most hostile sects. The reason of Zingis was not informed by books: the khan could neither read nor write; and except the tribe of the Igours, the greatest part of the Moguls and Tartars were as illiterate as their sovereign. The memory of their exploits was preserved by tradition: sixty-eight years after the death of Zingis, these traditions were collected and transcribed; the brevity of their domestic annals may be supplied by the Chinese, Persians, Armenians, Syrians, Arabians, Greeks, Russians, Poles, Hungarians, and Latins; and each nation will deserve credit in the relation of their own disasters and defeats.

The arms of Zingis and his lieutenants successively reduced the hordes of the desert who pitched their tents between the wall of China and the Volga; and the Mogul emperor became the monarch of the pastoral world, the lord of many millions of shepherds and soldiers, who felt their united strength and were impatient to rush on the mild and wealthy climates of the South. His ancestors had been the tributaries of the Chinese emperors; and Temugin himself had been disgraced by a title of honor and servitude. The court of Peking was astonished by an embassy from its former vassal, who, in the tone of the king of nations, exacted the tribute and obedience which he had paid, and who affected to treat the *Son of Heaven* as the most contemptible of mankind. A haughty answer disguised their secret apprehensions; and their fears were soon justified by the march of innumerable squadrons, who pierced on all sides the feeble rampart of the great wall. Ninety cities were stormed or starved by the Moguls; ten only escaped; and Zingis, from a knowledge of the filial piety of the Chinese, covered his vanguard with their captive parents; an unworthy, and by degrees a fruitless, abuse of the virtue of his enemies. His invasion [A.D. 1210–1214] was supported by the revolt of a hundred thousand Khitans, who guarded the frontier: yet he listened to a treaty [A.D. 1215]; and a princess of China, three thousand horses, five hundred youths and as many virgins, and a tribute of gold and silk were the price of his retreat. In his second expedition, he compelled the Chinese emperor to retire beyond the yellow river to a more southern residence. The siege of Peking was long and laborious: the inhabitants were reduced by famine to decimate and devour their fellow-citizens; when their ammunition was spent, they discharged ingots of gold and silver from their engines; but the Moguls introduced a mine to the center of the capital; and the conflagration of the palace burnt above thirty days [A.D. 1216]. China was desolated by Tartar war and domestic faction; and the five northern provinces were added to the empire of Zingis.

In the West [A.D. 1218–1224], he touched the dominions of Mohammed, sultan of Carizime, who reigned from the Persian Gulf to the borders of India and Turkestan; and who, in the proud imitation of Alexander the Great, forgot the servitude and ingratitude of his fathers to the house of Seljuk. It was the wish of Zingis to establish a friendly and commercial intercourse with the most powerful of the Moslem princes: nor could he be tempted by the secret solicitations of the caliph of Baghdad, who sacrificed to his personal wrongs the safety of the church and state. A rash and inhuman deed provoked and justified the Tartar arms in the invasion of southern Asia. A caravan of three ambassadors and one hundred and fifty merchants were arrested and murdered at Otrar, by the command of Mohammed; nor was it till after a demand and denial of justice, till he had prayed and fasted three nights on a mountain, that the Mogul emperor appealed to the judgment of God and his sword. Our European battles, says a philosophic writer, are petty skirmishes if compared to the numbers that have fought and fallen in the fields of Asia. Seven hundred thousand Moguls and Tartars are said to have marched under the standard of Zingis and his four sons. In the vast plains that extend to the north of the Sihon or Jaxartes, they were encountered by four hundred thousand soldiers of the sultan; and in the first battle, which was suspended by the night, one hundred and sixty thousand Carizmians were slain. Mohammed was astonished by the multitude and valor of his enemies: he withdrew from the scene of danger and distributed his troops in the frontier towns; trusting that the Barbarians, invincible in the field, would be repulsed by the length and difficulty of so many regular sieges. But the prudence of Zingis had formed a body of Chinese engineers, skilled in the mechanic arts, informed perhaps of the secret of gunpowder, and capable, under his discipline, of attacking a foreign country with more vigor and success than they had defended their own. The Persian historians will relate the sieges and reduction of Otrar, Cogende, Bochara, Samarcand, Carizme, Herat, Merou, Nisabour, Balch, and Candahar, and the conquest of the rich and populous countries of Transoxiana, Carizme, and Chorasan. The destructive hostilities of Attila and the Huns have long since been elucidated by the example of Zingis and the Moguls; and in this more proper place I shall be content to observe that, from the Caspian to the Indus, they ruined a tract of many hundred miles which was adorned with the habitations and labors of mankind, and that five centuries have not been sufficient to repair the ravages of four years. The Mogul emperor encouraged or indulged the fury of his troops: the hope of future possession was lost in the ardor of rapine and slaughter; and the cause of the war exasperated their native fierceness by the pretense of justice and revenge. The downfall and death of the sultan Mohammed, who expired, unpitied and alone, in a desert island of the Caspian Sea, is a poor atonement for the calamities of which he was the author.... The return of Zingis was signalized by the overthrow of the rebellious or independent kingdoms of Tartary; and he died in the fullness of years and glory, with his last breath exhorting and instructing his sons to achieve the conquest of the Chinese empire [A.D. 1227].

The harem of Zingis was composed of five hundred wives and concubines; and of his numerous progeny, four sons, illustrious by their birth and merit, exercised under their father the principal offices of peace and war. Toushi was his great huntsman, Zagatai his judge, Octai his minister, and Tuli his general; and their names and actions are often conspicuous in the history of his conquests. Firmly united for their own and the public interest, the three brothers and their families were content with dependent scepters; and Octai, by general consent, was proclaimed great khan, or emperor of the Moguls and Tartars. He was succeeded by his son Gayuk, after whose death the empire devolved to his cousins Mangou and Cublai, the sons of Tuli and the grandsons of Zingis. In the sixty-eight years of his four first successors [A.D. 1227–1295], the Moguls subdued almost all of Asia and a large portion of Europe.†

No sooner had Octai subverted the northern empire of China than he resolved to visit with his arms the most remote countries of the West [A.D. 1235–1245].... In his rapid progress, he overran the kingdoms, as they are now styled, of Astracan and Cazan; and the troops which he detached towards Mount Caucasus explored the most secret recesses of Georgia and Circassia. The civil discord of the great dukes or princes of Russia betrayed their country to the Tartars. They spread from Livonia to the Black Sea, and both Moscow and Kiow, the modern and the ancient capitals, were reduced to ashes; a temporary ruin, less fatal than the deep and perhaps indelible mark which a servitude of two hundred years has imprinted on the character of the Russians. The Tartars ravaged with equal fury the countries which they hoped to possess and those which they were hastening to leave. From the permanent conquest of Russia they made a deadly, though transient, inroad into the heart of Poland, and as far as the borders of Germany. The cities of Lublin and Cracow were obliterated: they approached the shores of the Baltic; and in the battle of Lignitz [April 9, 1241] they defeated the dukes of Silesia, the Polish palatines, and the great master of the Teutonic order, and filled nine sacks with the right ears of the slain. From Lignitz, the extreme point of their western march, they turned aside to the invasion of Hungary; and the presence or spirit of Batou inspired the host of five hundred thousand men: the Carpathian hills could not be long impervious to their divided columns; and their approach had been fondly disbelieved till it was irresistibly felt. The king, Bela the Fourth, assembled the military force of his counts and bishops; but he had alienated the nation by adopting a vagrant horde of forty thousand families of Comans, and these savage guests were provoked to revolt by the suspicion of treachery and the murder of their prince. The whole country north of the Danube was lost in a day and depopulated in a summer; and the ruins of cities and churches were overspread with the bones of the natives, who expiated the sins of their Turkish ancestors. An ecclesiastic who fled from the sack of Waradin describes the calamities which he had seen or suffered; and the sanguinary rage of sieges and battles is far less atrocious than the treatment of the fugitives, who had been allured from the woods under a promise of peace and pardon and who were coolly slaughtered as soon as they had performed the labors of the harvest and vintage. In the winter the Tartars passed the Danube on the ice and advanced to Gran or Strigonium, a German colony and the metropolis of the kingdom. Thirty engines were planted against the walls; the ditches were filled with sacks of earth and dead bodies; and after a promiscuous massacre, three hundred noble matrons were slain in the presence of the khan.

Of all the cities and fortresses of Hungary, three alone survived the Tartar invasion, and the unfortunate Bela hid his head among the islands of the Adriatic.

The Latin world was darkened by this cloud of savage hostility: a Russian fugitive carried the alarm to Sweden; and the remote nations of the Baltic and the Ocean trembled at the approach of the Tartars, whom their fear and ignorance were inclined to separate from the human species. Since the invasion of the Arabs in the eighth century, Europe had never been exposed to a similar calamity: and if the disciples of Mohammed would have oppressed her religion and liberty, it might be apprehended that the shepherds of Scythia would extinguish her cities, her arts, and all the institutions of civil society. The Roman pontiff attempted to appease and convert these invincible Pagans by a mission of Franciscan and Dominican friars; but he was astonished by the reply of the khan that the sons of God and of Zingis were invested with a divine power to subdue or extirpate the nations; and that the pope would be involved in the universal destruction unless he visited in person, and as a suppliant, the royal horde. The emperor Frederic the Second embraced a more generous mode of defense; and his letters to the kings of France and England and the princes of Germany represented the common danger, and urged them to arm their vassals in this just and rational crusade. The Tartars themselves were awed by the fame and valor of the Franks; the town of Newstadt in Austria was bravely defended against them by fifty knights and twenty crossbows; and they raised the siege on the appearance of a German army. After wasting the adjacent kingdoms of Servia, Bosnia, and Bulgaria, Batou slowly retreated from the Danube to the Volga to enjoy the rewards of victory in the city and palace of Serai, which started at his command from the midst of the desert.

Even the poor and frozen regions of the north attracted the arms of the Moguls: Sheibani Khan, the brother of the great Batou, led a horde of fifteen thousand families into the wilds of Siberia; and his descendants reigned at Tobolskoi above three centuries, till the Russian conquest.... The conquests of Russia and Syria might amuse the vanity of the great khans; but they were seated on the borders of China; the acquisition of that empire was the nearest and most interesting object; and they might learn from their pastoral economy that it is for the advantage of the shepherd to protect and propagate his flock.... The northern, and by degrees the southern, empire acquiesced in the government of Cublai, the lieutenant and afterwards the successor of Mangou; and the nation was loyal to a prince who had been educated in the manners of China. He restored the forms of her venerable constitution; and the victors submitted to the laws, the fashions, and even the prejudices of the vanquished people. This peaceful triumph, which has been more than once repeated, may be ascribed in a great measure to the numbers and servitude of the Chinese. The Mogul army was dissolved in a vast and populous country; and their emperors adopted with pleasure a political system which gives to the prince the solid substance of despotism, and leaves to the subject the empty names of philosophy, freedom, and filial obedience. Under the reign of Cublai, letters and commerce, peace and justice, were restored; the great canal of five hundred miles was opened from Nankin to the capital: he fixed his residence at Peking; and displayed in his court the magnificence of the greatest monarch of Asia. Yet this learned prince declined from the pure and simple religion of his great ancestor: he sacrificed to the idol Fo; and his blind attachment to the lamas of Thibet and the bonzes of China provoked the censure of the disciples of Confucius. His successors polluted the palace with a crowd of eunuchs, physicians, and astrologers, while thirteen millions of their subjects were consumed in the provinces by famine. One hundred and forty years after the death of Zingis, his degenerate race, the dynasty of the Yuen, was expelled by a revolt of the native Chinese [A.D. 1368]; and the Mogul emperors were lost in the oblivion of the desert. Before this revolution, they had forfeited their supremacy over the dependent branches of their house, the khans of Kipzak and Russia, the khans of Zagatai or Transoxiana, and the khans of Iran or Persia [A.D. 1259–1300]. By their distance and power, these royal lieutenants had soon been released from the duties of obedience; and after the death of Cublai, they scorned to accept a scepter or a title from his unworthy successors. According to their respective situations, they maintained the simplicity of the pastoral life or assumed the luxury of the cities of Asia; but the princes and their hordes were alike disposed for the reception of a foreign worship. After some hesitation between the gospel and the Koran, they conformed to the religion of Mohammed; and while they adopted for their brethren the Arabs and Persians, they renounced all intercourse with the ancient Moguls, the idolaters of China.

In this shipwreck of nations, some surprise may be excited by the escape of the Roman empire, whose relics, at the time of the Mogul invasion, were dismembered by the Greeks and Latins [A.D. 1240–1304]. Less potent than Alexander, they were pressed like the Macedonian, both in Europe and Asia, by the shepherds of Scythia; and had the Tartars undertaken the siege, Constantinople must have yielded to the fate of Peking, Samarcand, and Baghdad.... The first terror of [Mogul] arms secured rather than disturbed the peace of the Roman Asia. The sultan of Iconium solicited a personal interview with John Vataces; and his artful policy encouraged the Turks to defend their barrier against the common enemy. That barrier indeed was soon overthrown; and the servitude and ruin of the Seljukians exposed the nakedness of the Greeks. The formidable Holagou threatened to march to Constantinople at the head of four hundred thousand men.... But the ambition of Holagou and his successors was fortunately diverted by the conquest of Baghdad and a long vicissitude of Syrian wars; their hostility to the Moslems inclined them to unite with the Greeks and Franks; and their generosity or contempt had offered the kingdom of Anatolia as the reward of an Armenian vassal. The fragments of the Seljukian monarchy were disputed by the emirs who had occupied the cities or the mountains; but they all confessed the supremacy of the khans of Persia; and he often interposed his authority, and sometimes his arms, to check their depredations and to preserve the peace and balance of his Turkish frontier. The death of Cazan, one of the greatest and most accomplished princes of the house of Zingis, removed this salutary control [May 31, A.D. 1304]; and the decline of the Moguls gave a free scope to the rise and progress of the OTTOMAN EMPIRE.†

The Seljukian dynasty was no more; and the distance and decline of the Mogul khans soon enfranchised [Othman, also Thaman or Athman, son of Orthogul, who ruled Surgut on the banks of the Sangar] from the control of a superior. He was situate on the verge of the Greek empire: the Koran sanctified his *gazi,* or holy war, against the infidels; and their political errors unlocked the passes of Mount Olympus and invited him to descend into the plains of Bithynia. Till the reign of Palaeologus, these passes had been vigilantly guarded by the militia of the country, who were repaid by their own safety and an exemption from taxes. The emperor abolished their privilege and assumed their office; but the tribute was rigorously collected, the custody of the passes was neglected, and the hardy mountaineers degenerated into a trembling crowd of peasants without spirit or discipline. It was on the twenty-seventh of July, in the year twelve hundred and ninety-nine of the Christian era, that Othman first invaded the territory of Nicomedia; and the singular accuracy of the date seems to disclose some foresight of the rapid and destructive growth of the monster. The annals of the twenty-seven years of his reign [A.D. 1299–1326] would exhibit a repetition of the same inroads; and his hereditary troops were multiplied in each campaign by the accession of captives and volunteers. Instead of retreating to the hills, he maintained the most useful and defensive posts; fortified the towns and castles which he had first pillaged; and renounced the pastoral life for the baths and palaces of his infant capitals. But it was not till Othman was oppressed by age and infirmities that he received the welcome news of the conquest of Prusa, which had been surrendered by famine or treachery to the arms of his son Orchan [A.D. 1326]. The glory of Othman is chiefly founded on that of his descendants; but the Turks have transcribed or composed a royal testament of his last counsels of justice and moderation.

From the conquest of Prusa, we may date the true era of the Ottoman empire. The lives and possessions of the Christian subjects were redeemed by a tribute or ransom of thirty thousand crowns of gold; and the city, by the labors of Orchan, assumed the aspect of a Mohammedan capital [A.D. 1326–1360]; Prusa was decorated with a mosque, a college, and a hospital of royal foundation; the Seljukian coin was changed for the name and impression of the new dynasty: and the most skillful professors, of human and divine knowledge, attracted the Persian and Arabian students from the ancient schools of Oriental learning. The office of vizier was instituted for Aladin, the brother of Orchan; and a different habit distinguished the citizens from the peasants, the Moslems from the infidels. All the troops of Othman had consisted of loose squadrons of Turkman cavalry, who served without pay and fought without discipline: but a regular body of infantry was first established and trained by the prudence of his son. A great number of volunteers was enrolled with a small stipend, but with the permission of living at home unless they were summoned to the field: their rude manners and seditious temper disposed Orchan to educate his young captives as his soldiers and those of the prophet; but the Turkish peasants were still allowed to mount on horseback and follow his standard, with the appellation and the hopes of *freebooters*. By these arts he formed an army of twenty-five thousand Moslems: a train of battering engines was framed for the use of sieges; and the first successful experiment was made on the cities of Nice and Nicomedia. Orchan granted a safe-conduct to all who were desirous of departing with their families and effects; but the widows of the slain were given in marriage to the conquerors; and the sacrilegious plunder, the books, the vases, and the images, were sold or ransomed at Constantinople. The emperor Andronicus the Younger was vanquished and wounded by the son of Othman: he subdued the whole province or kingdom of Bithynia, as far as the shores of the Bosphorus and Hellespont [A.D. 1326–1339]; and the Christians confessed the justice and clemency of a reign which claimed the voluntary attachment of the Turks of Asia. Yet Orchan was content with the modest title of emir; and in the list of his compeers, the princes of Roum or Anatolia, his military forces were surpassed by the emirs of Ghermian and Caramania, each of whom could bring into the field an army of forty thousand men. Their domains were situate in the heart of the Seljukian kingdom; but the holy warriors, though of inferior note, who formed new principalities on the Greek empire are more conspicuous in the light of history. The maritime country from the Propontis to the Maeander and the Isle of Rhodes, so long threatened and so often pillaged, was finally lost about the thirteenth year of Andronicus the Elder. Two Turkish chieftains, Sarukhan and Aidin, left their names to their conquests, and their conquests to their posterity. The captivity or ruin of the *seven* churches of Asia was consummated; and the barbarous lords of Ionia and Lydia still trample on the monuments of classic and Christian antiquity. In the loss of Ephesus, the Christians deplored the fall of the first angel, the extinction of the first candlestick, of the Revelations; the desolation is complete; and the temple of Diana or the church of Mary will equally elude the search of the curious traveler. The circus and three stately theaters of Laodicea are now peopled with wolves and foxes; Sardes is reduced to a miserable village; the God of Mohammed, without a rival or a son, is invoked in the mosques of Thyatira and Pergamus.[†]

The Greeks, by their intestine divisions, were the authors of their final ruin. During the civil wars of the elder and younger Andronicus, the son of Othman achieved, almost without resistance, the conquest of Bithynia; and the same disorders encouraged the Turkish emirs of Lydia and Ionia to build a fleet and to pillage the adjacent islands and the sea-coast of Europe [A.D. 1341–1347]. In the defense of his life and honor, Cantacuzene was tempted to prevent, or imitate, his adversaries by calling to his aid the public enemies of his religion and country. . . . [T]he Turkish prince of Bithynia was detached from his engagements with Anne of Savoy; and the pride of Orchan dictated the most solemn protestations that if he could obtain the daughter of Cantacuzene, he would invariably fulfill the duties of a subject and a son. Parental tenderness was silenced by the voice of ambition: the Greek clergy connived at the marriage of a Christian princess with a sectary of Mohammed [A.D. 1346]; and the father of Theodora describes, with shameful satisfaction, the dishonor of the purple. A body of Turkish cavalry attended the ambassadors who disembarked from thirty vessels before his camp of Selybria. A stately pavilion was erected, in which the empress Irene passed the night with her daughters. In the morning, Theodora ascended a throne, which was surrounded with curtains of silk and gold: the troops were under arms; but the emperor alone was on horseback. At a signal the curtains were suddenly withdrawn to disclose the bride, or the victim, encircled by kneeling eunuchs and hymeneal torches: the sound of flutes and trumpets proclaimed the joyful event; and her pretended happiness was the theme of the nuptial song, which was chanted by such poets as the age could produce. Without the rites of the church, Theodora was delivered to her barbarous lord: but it had been stipulated that she should preserve her religion in the harem of Bursa; and her father celebrates her charity and devotion in this ambiguous situation. After his peaceful establishment on the throne of Constantinople, the Greek emperor visited his Turkish ally, who with four sons, by various wives, expected him at Scutari, on the Asiatic shore. The two princes partook with seeming cordiality of the pleasures of the banquet and the chase; and Theodora was permitted to repass the Bosphorus and to enjoy some days in the society of her mother. But the friendship of Orchan was subservient to his religion and interest; and in the Genoese war he joined without a blush the enemies of Cantacuzene.[†]

It was in his last quarrel with his pupil that Cantacuzene inflicted the deep and deadly wound which could never be healed by his successors, and which is poorly expiated by his theological dialogues against the prophet Mohammed. . . . Soliman [the son of Orchan], at the head of ten thousand horse, was transported in the vessels, and entertained as the friend, of the Greek emperor. In the civil wars of Romania, he performed some service and perpetrated more mischief; but the Chersonesus was insensibly filled with a Turkish colony; and the Byzantine court solicited in vain the restitution of the fortresses of Thrace. After some artful delays between the Ottoman prince and his son, their ransom was valued at sixty thousand crowns, and the first payment had been made when an earthquake shook the walls and cities of the provinces; the dismantled places were occupied by the Turks; and Gallipoli, the key of the Hellespont, was rebuilt and repeopled by the policy of Soliman. The abdication of Cantacuzene dissolved the feeble bands of domestic alliance; and his last advice admonished his countrymen to decline a rash contest and to compare their own weakness with the numbers and valor, the discipline and enthusiasm, of the Moslems. His prudent counsels were despised by the headstrong vanity of youth, and soon justified by the victories of the Ottomans. But as he practiced in the field the exercise of the *jerid,* Soliman was killed by a fall from his horse; and the aged Orchan wept and expired on the tomb of his valiant son [A.D. 1360].

But the Greeks had not time to rejoice in the death of their enemies; and the Turkish cimeter was wielded with the same spirit by Amurath the First, the son of Orchan and the brother of Soliman. By the pale and fainting light of the Byzantine annals, we can discern that he subdued without resistance the whole province of Romania or Thrace, from the Hellespont to Mount Haemus, and the verge of the capital; and that Hadrianople was chosen for the royal seat of his government and religion in Europe [A.D. 1360–1389]. Constantinople, whose decline is almost coeval with her foundation, had often, in the lapse of a thousand years, been assaulted by the Barbarians of the East and West; but never till this fatal hour had the Greeks been surrounded, both in Asia and Europe, by the arms of the same hostile monarchy. Yet the prudence or generosity of Amurath postponed for a while this easy conquest; and his pride was satisfied with the frequent and humble attendance of the emperor John Palaeologus and his four sons, who followed at his summons the court and camp of the Ottoman prince. He marched against the Sclavonian nations between the

Danube and the Adriatic, the Bulgarians, Servians, Bosnians, and Albanians; and these warlike tribes, who had so often insulted the majesty of the empire, were repeatedly broken by his destructive inroads. Their countries did not abound either in gold or silver; nor were their rustic hamlets and townships enriched by commerce or decorated by the arts of luxury. But the natives of the soil have been distinguished in every age by their hardiness of mind and body; and they were converted by a prudent institution into the firmest and most faithful supporters of the Ottoman greatness. The vizier of Amurath reminded his sovereign that, according to the Mohammedan law, he was entitled to a fifth part of the spoil and captives; and that the duty might easily be levied if vigilant officers were stationed in Gallipoli to watch the passage, and to select for his use the stoutest and most beautiful of the Christian youth. The advice was followed: the edict was proclaimed; many thousands of the European captives were educated in religion and arms; and the new militia was consecrated and named by a celebrated *dervish*. Standing in the front of their ranks, he stretched the sleeve of his gown over the head of the foremost soldier, and his blessing was delivered in these words: "Let them be called Janizaries (*Yengi cheri*, or new soldiers); may their countenance be ever bright! their hand victorious! their sword keen! may their spear always hang over the heads of their enemies! and wheresoever they go, may they return with a *white face*!" [*White* and *black* face are common and proverbial expressions of praise and blame in the Turkish language.] Such was the origin of these haughty troops, the terror of the nations, and sometimes of the sultans themselves. . . . The Janizaries fought with the zeal of proselytes against their *idolatrous* countryman.[†]

The character of Bajazet, the son and successor of Amurath, is strongly expressed in his surname of *Ilderim*, or the lightning; and he might glory in an epithet which was drawn from the fiery energy of his soul and the rapidity of his destructive march. In the fourteen years of his reign [A.D. 1389–1403], he incessantly moved at the head of his armies, from Boursa to Hadrianople, from the Danube to the Euphrates; and though he strenuously labored for the propagation of the law, he invaded with impartial ambition the Christian and Mohammedan princes of Europe and Asia. . . . In the pride of victory, Bajazet threatened that he would besiege Buda; that he would subdue the adjacent countries of Germany and Italy, and that he would feed his horse with a bushel of oats on the altar of St. Peter at Rome. His progress was checked not by the miraculous interposition of the apostle, not by a crusade of the Christian powers, but by a long and painful fit of the gout. The disorders of the moral, are sometimes corrected by those of the physical, world; and an acrimonious humor falling on a single fiber of one man may prevent or suspend the misery of nations.[†]

After his enfranchisement from an oppressive guardian, John Palaeologus remained thirty-six years the helpless and, as it should seem, the careless spectator of the public ruin [A.D. 1355–1391]. Love, or rather lust, was his only vigorous passion; and in the embraces of the wives and virgins of the city, the Turkish slave forgot the dishonor of the emperor of the *Romans*. Andronicus, his eldest son, had formed at Hadrianople an intimate and guilty friendship with Sauzes, the son of Amurath; and the two youths conspired against the authority and lives of their parents. The presence of Amurath in Europe soon discovered and dissipated their rash counsels; and after depriving Sauzes of his sight, the Ottoman threatened his vassal with the treatment of an accomplice and an enemy unless he inflicted a similar punishment on his own son. Palaeologus trembled and obeyed; and a cruel precaution involved in the same sentence the childhood and innocence of John, the son of the criminal. But the operation was so mildly, or so unskillfully, performed that the one retained the sight of an eye, and the other was afflicted only with the infirmity of squinting. Thus excluded from the succession, the two princes were confined in the tower of Anema; and the piety of Manuel, the second son of the reigning monarch, was rewarded with the gift of the Imperial crown. But at the end of two years, the turbulence of the Latins and the levity of the Greeks produced a revolution; and the two emperors were buried in the tower from whence the two prisoners were exalted to the throne. Another period of two years afforded Palaeologus and Manuel the means of escape: it was contrived by the magic or subtlety of a monk, who was alternately named the angel or the devil: they fled to Scutari; their adherents armed in their cause; and the two Byzantine factions displayed the ambition and animosity with which Caesar and Pompey had disputed the empire of the world. The Roman world was now contracted to a corner of Thrace, between the Propontis and the Black Sea, about fifty miles in length and thirty in breadth; a space of ground not more extensive than the lesser principalities of Germany or Italy, if the re-

mains of Constantinople had not still represented the wealth and populousness of a kingdom. To restore the public peace, it was found necessary to divide this fragment of the empire; and while Palaeologus
and Manuel were left in possession of the capital, almost all that lay
without the walls was ceded to the blind princes, who fixed their residence at Rhodosto and Selybria. In the tranquil slumber of royalty, the
passions of John Palaeologus survived his reason and his strength: he
deprived his favorite and heir of a blooming princess of Trebizond;
and while the feeble emperor labored to consummate his nuptials,
Manuel, with a hundred of the noblest Greeks, was sent on a peremptory summons to the Ottoman *porte.* They served with honor in the
wars of Bajazet; but a plan of fortifying Constantinople excited his
jealousy: he threatened their lives; the new works were instantly demolished; and we shall bestow a praise perhaps above the merit of
Palaeologus if we impute this last humiliation as the cause of his
death.

The earliest intelligence of that event was communicated to
Manuel, who escaped with speed and secrecy from the palace of
Boursa to the Byzantine throne [and reigned A.D. 1391–1425]. Bajazet
affected a proud indifference at the loss of this valuable pledge; and
while he pursued his conquests in Europe and Asia, he left the emperor to struggle with his blind cousin John of Selybria, who in eight
years of civil war asserted his right of primogeniture. At length, the
ambition of the victorious sultan pointed to the conquest of Constantinople; but he listened to the advice of his vizier, who represented
that such an enterprise might unite the powers of Christendom in a
second and more formidable crusade. His epistle to the emperor was
conceived in these words: "By the divine clemency, our invincible
cimeter has reduced to our obedience almost all Asia, with many and
large countries in Europe, excepting only the city of Constantinople;
for beyond the walls thou hast nothing left. Resign that city; stipulate
thy reward; or tremble, for thyself and thy unhappy people, at the consequences of a rash refusal." But his ambassadors were instructed to
soften their tone and to propose a treaty, which was subscribed with
submission and gratitude. A truce of ten years was purchased by an annual tribute of thirty thousand crowns of gold; the Greeks deplored
the public toleration of the law of Mohammed, and Bajazet enjoyed
the glory of establishing a Turkish cadhi and founding a royal mosque

in the metropolis of the Eastern church. Yet this truce was soon violated by the restless sultan: in the cause of the prince of Selybria, the lawful emperor, an army of Ottomans again threatened Constantinople; and the distress of Manuel implored the protection of the king of France. His plaintive embassy obtained much pity and some relief; and the conduct of the succor was entrusted to the marshal Boucicault, whose religious chivalry was inflamed by the desire of revenging his captivity on the infidels. He sailed with four ships of war [A.D. 1399] from Aiguesmortes to the Hellespont; forced the passage, which was guarded by seventeen Turkish galleys; landed at Constantinople a supply of six hundred men-at-arms and sixteen hundred archers; and reviewed them in the adjacent plain, without condescending to number or array the multitude of Greeks. By his presence, the blockade was raised both by sea and land; the flying squadrons of Bajazet were driven to a more respectful distance; and several castles in Europe and Asia were stormed by the emperor and the marshal, who fought with equal valor by each other's side. But the Ottomans soon returned with an increase of numbers; and the intrepid Boucicault, after a year's struggle, resolved to evacuate a country which could no longer afford either pay or provisions for his soldiers. The marshal offered to conduct Manuel to the French court, where he might solicit in person a supply of men and money; and advised in the meanwhile that, to extinguish all domestic discord, he should leave his blind competitor on the throne. The proposal was embraced: the prince of Selybria was introduced to the capital; and such was the public misery that the lot of the exile seemed more fortunate than that of the sovereign. Instead of applauding the success of his vassal, the Turkish sultan claimed the city as his own; and on the refusal of the emperor John, Constantinople was more closely pressed by the calamities of war and famine. Against such an enemy prayers and resistance were alike unavailing; and the savage would have devoured his prey if, in the fatal moment, he had not been overthrown by another savage stronger than himself. By the victory of Timour or Tamerlane, the fall of Constantinople was delayed about fifty years; and this important though accidental service may justly introduce the life and character of the Mogul conqueror.

CHAPTER LXV

TIMOUR OR TAMERLANE

*Elevation of Timour or Tamerlane to the throne of Samarcand. •
His conquests in Persia, Georgia, Tartary, Russia, India, Syria,
and Anatolia. • His Turkish war. • Defeat and captivity of
Bajazet. • Death of Timour. • Civil war of the sons of Bajazet. •
Restoration of the Turkish monarchy by Mohammed the First. •
Siege of Constantinople by Amurath the Second.*

The conquest and monarchy of the world was the first object of the
ambition of TIMOUR. To live in the memory and esteem of future ages
was the second wish of his magnanimous spirit. All the civil and military transactions of his reign were diligently recorded in the journals
of his secretaries: the authentic narrative was revised by the persons
best informed of each particular transaction; and it is believed in the
empire and family of Timour that the monarch himself composed the
Commentaries of his life and the *Institutions* of his government. But these
cares were ineffectual for the preservation of his fame, and these precious memorials in the Mogul or Persian language were concealed
from the world, or at least from the knowledge of Europe. The nations
which he vanquished exercised a base and impotent revenge; and ignorance has long repeated the tale of calumny which had disfigured
the birth and character, the person, and even the name of *Tamerlane*.
Yet his real merit would be enhanced rather than debased by the elevation of a peasant to the throne of Asia; nor can his lameness be a
theme of reproach, unless he had the weakness to blush at a natural, or
perhaps an honorable, infirmity.

In the eyes of the Moguls, who held the indefeasible succession of
the house of Zingis, he was doubtless a rebel subject; yet he sprang
from the noble tribe of Berlass . . . ; and in the ascent of some generations, the branch of Timour is confounded, at least by the females,
with the Imperial stem. He was born forty miles to the south of Samarcand in the village of Sebzar, in the fruitful territory of Cash, of which
his fathers were the hereditary chiefs, as well as of a *toman* of ten

thousand horse. His birth [A.D. 1335] was cast on one of those periods of anarchy which announce the fall of the Asiatic dynasties and open a new field to adventurous ambition. The khans of Zagatai were extinct; the emirs aspired to independence; and their domestic feuds could only be suspended by the conquest and tyranny of the khans of Kashgar, who, with an army of Getes or Calmucks, invaded the Transoxian kingdom. From the twelfth year of his age, Timour had entered the field of action; in the twenty-fifth he stood forth as the deliverer of his country; and the eyes and wishes of the people were turned towards a hero who suffered in their cause. The chiefs of the law and of the army had pledged their salvation to support him with their lives and fortunes; but in the hour of danger they were silent and afraid; and after waiting seven days on the hills of Samarcand, he retreated to the desert with only sixty horsemen. The fugitives were overtaken by a thousand Getes, whom he repulsed with incredible slaughter, and his enemies were forced to exclaim, "Timour is a wonderful man: fortune and the divine favor are with him." But in this bloody action his own followers were reduced to ten, a number which was soon diminished by the desertion of three Carizmians. He wandered in the desert with his wife, seven companions, and four horses; and sixty-two days was he plunged in a loathsome dungeon, from whence he escaped by his own courage and the remorse of the oppressor. After swimming the broad and rapid steam of the Jihoon, or Oxus, he led, during some months, the life of a vagrant and outlaw, on the borders of the adjacent states. But his fame shone brighter in adversity; he learned to distinguish the friends of his person, the associates of his fortune, and to apply the various characters of men for their advantage, and above all for his own. On his return to his native country, Timour was successively joined by the parties of his confederates, who anxiously sought him in the desert; nor can I refuse to describe, in his pathetic simplicity, one of their fortunate encounters. He presented himself as a guide to three chiefs, who were at the head of seventy horse. "When their eyes fell upon me," says Timour, "they were overwhelmed with joy; and they alighted from their horses; and they came and kneeled; and they kissed my stirrup. I also came down from my horse and took each of them in my arms. And I put my turban on the head of the first chief; and my girdle, rich in jewels and wrought with gold, I bound on the loins of the second; and the third I clothed in my own coat. And they wept, and

I wept also; and the hour of prayer was arrived, and we prayed. And we mounted our horses, and came to my dwelling; and I collected my people and made a feast." His trusty bands were soon increased by the bravest of the tribes; he led them against a superior foe; and after some vicissitudes of war the Getes were finally driven from the kingdom of Transoxiana. He had done much for his own glory; but much remained to be done, much art to be exerted and some blood to be spilt, before he could teach his equals to obey him as their master. The birth and power of emir Houssein compelled him to accept a vicious and unworthy colleague, whose sister was the best beloved of his wives. Their union was short and jealous; but the policy of Timour, in their frequent quarrels, exposed his rival to the reproach of injustice and perfidy; and after a final defeat, Houssein was slain by some sagacious friends who presumed, for the last time, to disobey the commands of their lord. At the age of thirty-four and in a general diet or *couroultai,* he was invested with *Imperial* command [A.D. 1370], but he affected to revere the house of Zingis; and while the emir Timour reigned over Zagatai and the East, a nominal khan served as a private officer in the armies of his servant. A fertile kingdom, five hundred miles in length and in breadth, might have satisfied the ambition of a subject; but Timour aspired to the dominion of the world; and before his death, the crown of Zagatai was one of the twenty-seven crowns which he had placed on his head. [The] victories of thirty-five campaigns, . . . which he repeatedly traced over the continent of Asia [brought him] conquests in I. Persia, II. Tartary, and III. India.†

It was on the banks of the Ganges that Timour was informed by his speedy messengers of the disturbances which had arisen on the confines of Georgia and Anatolia, of the revolt of the Christians, and the ambitious designs of the [Ottoman] sultan Bajazet [September 1, A.D. 1400]. His vigor of mind and body was not impaired by sixty-three years and innumerable fatigues; and after enjoying some tranquil months in the palace of Samarcand, he proclaimed a new expedition of seven years into the western countries of Asia. To the soldiers who had served in the Indian war he granted the choice of remaining at home or following their prince; but the troops of all the provinces and kingdoms of Persia were commanded to assemble at Ispahan and wait the arrival of the Imperial standard. It was first directed against the Christians of Georgia, who were strong only in their rocks, their castles, and the winter season; but these obstacles were overcome by the zeal and perseverance of Timour: the rebels submitted to the tribute or the Koran; and if both religions boasted of their martyrs, that name is more justly due to the Christian prisoners, who were offered the choice of abjuration or death. On his descent from the hills, the emperor gave audience to the first ambassadors of Bajazet and opened the hostile correspondence of complaints and menaces, which fermented two years before the final explosion. Between two jealous and haughty neighbors, the motives of quarrel will seldom be wanting. The Mogul and Ottoman conquests now touched each other in the neighborhood of Erzerum and the Euphrates; nor had the doubtful limit been ascertained by time and treaty. Each of these ambitious monarchs might accuse his rival of violating his territory, of threatening his vassals and protecting his rebels; and by the name of rebels, each understood the fugitive princes whose kingdoms he had usurped and whose life or liberty he implacably pursued. The resemblance of character was still more dangerous than the opposition of interest; and in their victorious career, Timour was impatient of an equal, and Bajazet was ignorant of a superior. The first epistle of the Mogul emperor must have provoked instead of reconciling the Turkish sultan, whose family and nation he affected to despise. "Dost thou not know that the greatest part of Asia is subject to our arms and our laws? that our invincible forces extend from one sea to the other? that the potentates of the earth form a line before our gate? and that we have compelled Fortune herself to watch over the prosperity of our empire? What is the foundation of thy insolence and folly? Thou hast fought some battles in the woods of Anatolia; contemptible trophies! Thou hast obtained some victories over the Christians of Europe; thy sword was blessed by the apostle of God; and thy obedience to the precept of the Koran in waging war against the infidels is the sole consideration that prevents us from destroying thy country, the frontier and bulwark of the Moslem world. Be wise in time; reflect; repent; and avert the thunder of our vengeance, which is yet suspended over thy head. Thou art no more than a pismire; why wilt thou seek to provoke the elephants? Alas! they will trample thee under their feet." In his replies, Bajazet poured forth the indignation of a soul which was deeply stung by such unusual contempt. After retorting the basest reproaches on the thief and rebel of the desert, the Ottoman recapitulates his boasted victories in Iran, Touran, and the

Indies; and labors to prove that Timour had never triumphed unless by his own perfidy and the vices of his foes. "Thy armies are innumerable: be they so; but what are the arrows of the flying Tartar against the cimeters and battle-axes of my firm and invincible Janizaries? I will guard the princes who have implored my protection: seek them in my tents. The cities of Arzingan and Erzeroum are mine; and unless the tribute be duly paid, I will demand the arrears under the walls of Tauris and Sultania." The ungovernable rage of the sultan at length betrayed him to an insult of a more domestic kind. "If I fly from thy arms," said he, "may *my* wives be thrice divorced from my bed: but if thou hast not courage to meet me in the field, mayest thou again receive *thy* wives after they have thrice endured the embraces of a stranger." Any violation by word or deed of the secrecy of the harem is an unpardonable offense among the Turkish nations; and the political quarrel of the two monarchs was embittered by private and personal resentment. Yet in his first expedition, Timour was satisfied with the siege and destruction of Siwas or Sebaste, a strong city on the borders of Anatolia; and he revenged the indiscretion of the Ottoman on a garrison of four thousand Armenians, who were buried alive for the brave and faithful discharge of their duty. As a Moslem, he seemed to respect the pious occupation of Bajazet, who was still engaged in the blockade of Constantinople; and after this salutary lesson, the Mogul conqueror checked his pursuit and turned aside to the invasion of Syria and Egypt. In these transactions, the Ottoman prince, by the Orientals and even by Timour, is styled the *Kaissar of Roum,* the Caesar of the Romans; a title which, by a small anticipation, might be given to a monarch who possessed the provinces and threatened the city of the successors of Constantine.

[*Timour invades Syria and on November 11, A.D. 1400, sacks Aleppo.*]

Among the suppliants and captives, Timour distinguished the doctors of the law, whom he invited to the dangerous honor of a personal conference. The Mogul prince was a zealous Moslem; but his Persian schools had taught him to revere the memory of Ali and Hosein; and he had imbibed a deep prejudice against the Syrians as the enemies of the son of the daughter of the apostle of God. To these doctors he proposed a captious question, which the casuists of Bochara, Samarcand, and Herat were incapable of resolving. "Who are the true martyrs, of those who are slain on my side, or on that of my enemies?" But he was silenced or satisfied by the dexterity of one of the cadhis of Aleppo, who replied, in the words of Mohammed himself, that the motive, not the ensign, constitutes the martyr; and that the Moslems of either party who fight only for the glory of God may deserve that sacred appellation. The true succession of the caliphs was a controversy of a still more delicate nature; and the frankness of a doctor, too honest for his situation, provoked the emperor to exclaim, "Ye are as false as those of Damascus: Moawiyah was a usurper, Yezid a tyrant, and Ali alone is the lawful successor of the prophet." A prudent explanation restored his tranquility; and he passed to a more familiar topic of conversation. "What is your age?" said he to the cadhi. "Fifty years."—"It would be the age of my eldest son: you see me here (continued Timour) a poor lame, decrepit mortal. Yet by my arm has the Almighty been pleased to subdue the kingdoms of Iran, Touran, and the Indies. I am not a man of blood; and God is my witness that in all my wars I have never been the aggressor, and that my enemies have always been the authors of their own calamity." During this peaceful conversation the streets of Aleppo streamed with blood and reechoed with the cries of mothers and children, with the shrieks of violated virgins. The rich plunder that was abandoned to his soldiers might stimulate their avarice; but their cruelty was enforced by the peremptory command of producing an adequate number of heads, which, according to his custom, were curiously piled in columns and pyramids: the Moguls celebrated the feast of victory, while the surviving Moslems passed the night in tears and in chains. I shall not dwell on the march of the destroyer from Aleppo to Damascus, where he was rudely encountered and almost overthrown by the armies of Egypt [January 23, A.D. 1401]. A retrograde motion was imputed to his distress and despair: one of his nephews deserted to the enemy; and Syria rejoiced in the tale of his defeat, when the sultan was driven by the revolt of the Mamalukes to escape with precipitation and shame to his palace of Cairo. Abandoned by their prince, the inhabitants of Damascus still defended their walls; and Timour consented to raise the siege if they would adorn his retreat with a gift or ransom; each article of nine pieces. But no sooner had he introduced himself into the city, under color of a truce, than he perfidiously violated the treaty [January 23, A.D. 1401]; imposed a contribution of ten millions of gold; and animated his troops to chastise the posterity of those Syrians who had executed or approved the murder of the grandson of Mohammed. A family which had given honorable burial to the head of Hosein, and a colony of artificers whom he sent to labor at Samarcand, were alone reserved in the general massacre, and after a period of seven centuries, Damascus was reduced to ashes because a Tartar was moved by religious zeal to avenge the blood of an Arab. The losses and fatigues of the campaign obliged Timour to renounce the conquest of Palestine and Egypt; but in his return to the Euphrates he delivered Aleppo to the flames; and justified his pious motive by the pardon and reward of two thousand sectaries of Ali, who were desirous to visit the tomb of his son. I have expatiated on the personal anecdotes which mark the character of the Mogul hero; but I shall briefly mention that he erected on the ruins of Baghdad a pyramid of ninety thousand heads [July 23, A.D. 1401]; again visited Georgia; encamped on the banks of Araxes; and proclaimed his resolution of marching against the Ottoman emperor.

[*Timour invades Anatolia (A.D. 1402). Soliman, the son of Bajazet, escapes to Bajazet's European possessions with the royal treasure. Bajazet is captured and dies in captivity. Timour establishes Bajazet's son Mousa on the vacant throne of Boursa in Anatolia.*]

From the Irtish and Volga to the Persian Gulf, and from the Ganges to Damascus and the Archipelago, Asia was in the hand of Timour [A.D. 1403]: his armies were invincible, his ambition was boundless, and his zeal might aspire to conquer and convert the Christian kingdoms of the West, which already trembled at his name. He touched the utmost verge of the land; but an insuperable, though narrow, sea rolled between the two continents of Europe and Asia; and the lord of so many *tomans,* or myriads, of horse was not master of a single galley. The two passages of the Bosphorus and Hellespont, of Constantinople and Gallipoli, were possessed, the one by the Christians, the other by the Turks. On this great occasion, they forgot the difference of religion to act with union and firmness in the common cause: the double straits were guarded with ships and fortifications; and they separately withheld the transports which Timour demanded of either nation, under the pretense of attacking their enemy. At the same time, they soothed his pride with tributary gifts and suppliant embassies, and prudently tempted him to retreat with the honors of victory. Soliman, the son of Bajazet, implored his clemency for his father and himself; accepted, by a red patent, the investiture of the kingdom of Romania, which he already held by the sword; and reiterated his ardent wish of casting himself in person at the feet of the king of the world. The Greek emperor (either John or Manuel) submitted to pay the same tribute which he had stipulated with the Turkish sultan, and ratified the treaty by an oath of allegiance, from which he could absolve his conscience so soon as the Mogul arms had retired from Anatolia.†

On the throne of Samarcand, [Timour] displayed, in a short repose [July A.D. 1404–January 1405], his magnificence and power; listened to the complaints of the people; distributed a just measure of rewards and punishments; employed his riches in the architecture of palaces and temples; and gave audience to the ambassadors of Egypt, Arabia, India, Tartary, Russia, and Spain, the last of whom presented a suit of tapestry which eclipsed the pencil of the Oriental artists. The marriage of six of the emperor's grandsons was esteemed an act of religion as well as of paternal tenderness; and the pomp of the ancient caliphs was revived in their nuptials. They were celebrated in the gardens of Canighul, decorated with innumerable tents and pavilions, which displayed the luxury of a great city and the spoils of a victorious camp. Whole forests were cut down to supply fuel for the kitchens; the plain was spread with pyramids of meat and vases of every liquor, to which thousands of guests were courteously invited: the orders of the state and the nations of the earth were marshaled at the royal banquet; nor were the ambassadors of Europe (says the haughty Persian) excluded from the feast; since even the *casses,* the smallest of fish, find their place in the ocean. The public joy was testified by illuminations and masquerades; the trades of Samarcand passed in review; and every trade was emulous to execute some quaint device, some marvelous pageant, with the materials of their peculiar art. After the marriage contracts had been ratified by the cadhis, the bridegrooms and their brides retired to the nuptial chambers: nine times, according to the Asiatic fashion, they were dressed and undressed; and at each change of apparel, pearls and rubies were showered on their heads, and contemptuously abandoned to their attendants. A general indulgence was proclaimed: every law was relaxed, every pleasure was allowed; the people was free, the sovereign was idle; and the historian of Timour may remark that, after devoting fifty years to the attainment of empire, the only happy period of his life were the two months in which he ceased to exercise his power. But he was soon awakened to the cares of government and war. The standard was unfurled for the invasion of China: the emirs made their report of two hundred thousand, the select and veteran soldiers of Iran and Touran: their baggage and provisions were transported by five hundred great wagons and an immense train of horses and camels; and the troops might prepare for a long absence, since more than six months were employed in the tranquil journey of a caravan from Samarcand to Peking. Neither age nor the severity of the winter could retard the impatience of Timour; he mounted on horseback, passed the Sihoon on the ice, marched . . . three hundred miles from his capital, and pitched his last camp in the neighborhood of Otrar, where he was expected by the angel of death [April 1, A.D. 1405]. Fatigue and the indiscreet use of iced water accelerated the progress of his fever; and the conqueror of Asia expired in the seventieth year of his age, thirty-five years after he had ascended the throne of Zagatai. His designs were lost; his armies were disbanded; China was saved; and fourteen years after his decease, the most powerful of his children sent an embassy of friendship and commerce to the court of Peking.

The fame of Timour has pervaded the East and West: his posterity is still invested with the Imperial *title*; and the admiration of his subjects, who revered him almost as a deity, may be justified in some degree by the praise or confession of his bitterest enemies. Although he was lame of a hand and foot, his form and stature were not unworthy of his rank; and his vigorous health, so essential to himself and to the world, was corroborated by temperance and exercise. In his familiar discourse he was grave and modest, and if he was ignorant of the Arabic language, he spoke with fluency and elegance the Persian and Turkish idioms. It was his delight to converse with the learned on topics of history and science; and the amusement of his leisure hours was the game of chess, which he improved or corrupted with new refinements. In his religion he was a zealous, though not perhaps an orthodox, Moslem; but his sound understanding may tempt us to believe that a superstitious reverence for omens and prophecies, for saints and astrologers, was only affected as an instrument of policy. In the government of a vast empire, he stood alone and absolute, without a rebel to oppose his power, a favorite to seduce his affections, or a minister to mislead his judgment. It was his firmest maxim that whatever might be the consequence, the word of the prince should never be disputed or recalled; but his foes have maliciously observed that the commands of anger and destruction were more strictly executed than those of beneficence and favor. His sons and grandsons, of whom Timour left six-and-thirty at his decease, were his first and most submissive subjects; and whenever they deviated from their duty, they were corrected, according to the laws of Zingis, with the bastinade, and afterwards restored to honor and command. Perhaps his heart was not devoid of the social virtues; perhaps he was not incapable of loving his friends and pardoning his enemies; but the rules of morality are founded on the public interest; and it may be sufficient to applaud the *wisdom* of a monarch for the liberality by which he is not impoverished, and for the justice by which he is strengthened and enriched. To maintain the harmony of authority and obedience, to chastise the proud, to protect the weak, to reward the deserving, to banish vice and idleness from his dominions, to secure the traveler and merchant, to restrain the depredations of the soldier, to cherish the labors of the husbandman, to encourage industry and learning, and, by an equal and moderate assessment, to increase the revenue without increasing the taxes, are indeed the duties of a prince; but in the discharge of these duties, he finds an ample and immediate recompense. Timour might boast that at his accession to the throne Asia was the prey of anarchy and rapine, whilst under his prosperous monarchy a child, fearless and unhurt, might carry a purse of gold from the East to the West. Such was his confidence of merit that from this reformation he derived an excuse for his victories and a title to universal dominion. The four following observations will serve to appreciate his claim to the public gratitude; and perhaps we shall conclude that the Mogul emperor was rather the scourge than the benefactor of mankind. 1. If some partial disorders, some local oppressions, were healed by the sword of Timour, the remedy was far more pernicious than the disease. By their rapine, cruelty, and discord, the petty tyrants of Persia might afflict their subjects; but whole nations were crushed under the footsteps of the reformer. The ground which had been occupied by flourishing cities was often marked by his abominable trophies, by columns or pyramids of human heads. Astracan, Carizme, Delhi, Ispahan, Baghdad, Aleppo, Damascus, Boursa, Smyrna, and a thousand others were sacked or burnt or utterly destroyed in his presence, and by his troops: and perhaps his conscience would have been startled if a priest or philosopher had dared to number the millions of victims whom he had sacrificed to the establishment of peace and order. 2. His most destructive wars were rather inroads than conquests. He invaded Turkestan, Kipzak, Russia, Hindostan, Syria, Anatolia, Armenia, and Georgia without a hope or a desire of preserving those distant provinces. From thence he departed laden with spoil; but he left behind him neither troops to awe the contumacious, nor magistrates to protect the obedient, natives. When he had broken the fabric of their ancient government, he abandoned them to the evils which his invasion had aggravated or caused; nor were these evils compensated by any present or possible benefits. 3. The kingdoms of Transoxiana and Persia were the proper field which he labored to cultivate and adorn, as the perpetual inheritance of his family. But his peaceful labors were often interrupted, and sometimes blasted, by the absence of the conqueror. While he triumphed on the Volga or the Ganges, his servants and even his sons forgot their master and their duty. The public and private injuries were poorly redressed by the tardy rigor of inquiry and punishment; and we must be content to praise the *Institutions* of Timour as the specious idea of a perfect monarchy. 4. Whatsoever might be the blessings of his administration, they evaporated with his life. To reign, rather than to govern, was the ambition of his children and grandchildren; the enemies of each other and of the people. A fragment of the empire was upheld with some glory by Sharokh, his youngest son; but after *his* decease, the scene was again involved in darkness and blood.[†]

If Timour had generously marched at the request and to the relief of the Greek emperor, he might be entitled to the praise and gratitude of the Christians. But a Moslem who carried into Georgia the sword of persecution and respected the holy warfare of Bajazet was not disposed to pity or succor the *idolaters* of Europe. The Tartar followed the impulse of ambition; and the deliverance of Constantinople was the accidental [and temporary] consequence.

[*The Ottoman empire is reunited under Amurath II (A.D. 1421). He besieges Constantinople (June 10–August 24, A.D. 1422).*]

The religious merit of subduing the city of the Caesars attracted from Asia a crowd of volunteers who aspired to the crown of martyrdom: their military ardor was inflamed by the promise of rich spoils and beautiful females; and the sultan's ambition was consecrated by the presence and prediction of Seid Bechar, a descendant of the prophet, who arrived in the camp on a mule with a venerable train of five hundred disciples. But he might blush, if a fanatic could blush, at the failure of his assurances. The strength of the walls resisted an army of two hundred thousand Turks; their assaults were repelled by the sallies of the Greeks and their foreign mercenaries; the old resources of defense were opposed to the new engines of attack; and the enthusiasm of the dervish, who was snatched to Heaven in visionary converse with Mohammed, was answered by the credulity of the Christians, who *beheld* the Virgin Mary, in a violet garment, walking on the rampart and animating their courage. After a siege of two months, Amurath was recalled to Boursa by a domestic revolt, which had been kindled by Greek treachery and was soon extinguished by the death of a guiltless brother. While he led his Janizaries to new conquests in Europe and Asia, the Byzantine empire was indulged in a servile and precarious respite of thirty years. Manuel sank into the grave; and John Palaeologus was permitted to reign [A.D. 1425–1448] for an annual tribute of three hundred thousand aspers, and the dereliction of almost all that he held beyond the suburbs of Constantinople.

In the establishment and restoration of the Turkish empire, the first merit must doubtless be assigned to the personal qualities of the sultans; since in human life the most important scenes will depend on the character of a single actor. By some shades of wisdom and virtue, they may be discriminated from each other; but except in a single instance, a period of nine reigns and two hundred and sixty-five years is occupied, from the elevation of Othman to the death of Soliman [A.D. 1299–1566], by a rare series of warlike and active princes, who impressed their subjects with obedience and their enemies with terror. Instead of the slothful luxury of the seraglio, the heirs of royalty were educated in the council and the field: from early youth they were entrusted by their fathers with the command of provinces and armies; and this manly institution, which was often productive of civil war, must have essentially contributed to the discipline and vigor of the monarchy. The Ottomans cannot style themselves, like the Arabian caliphs, the descendants or successors of the apostle of God; and the kindred which they claim with the Tartar khans of the house of Zingis appears to be founded in flattery rather than in truth. Their origin is obscure; but their sacred and indefeasible right, which no time can erase and no violence can infringe, was soon and unalterably implanted in the minds of their subjects. A weak or vicious sultan may be deposed and strangled; but his inheritance devolves to an infant or an idiot: nor has the most daring rebel presumed to ascend the throne of his lawful sovereign. While the transient dynasties of Asia have been continually subverted by a crafty vizier in the palace, or a victorious general in the camp, the Ottoman succession has been confirmed by the practice of five centuries, and is now incorporated with the vital principle of the Turkish nation.

To the spirit and constitution of that nation, a strong and singular influence may, however, be ascribed. The primitive subjects of Othman were the four hundred families of wandering Turkmans, who had followed his ancestors from the Oxus to the Sangar; and the plains of Anatolia are still covered with the white and black tents of their rustic brethren. But this original drop was dissolved in the mass of voluntary and vanquished subjects who, under the name of Turks, are united by the common ties of religion, language, and manners. In the cities from Erzeroum to Belgrade, that national appellation is common to all the Moslems, the first and most honorable inhabitants; but they have abandoned, at least in Romania, the villages and the cultivation of the land to the Christian peasants. In the vigorous age of the Ottoman government, the Turks were themselves excluded from all civil and military honors; and a servile class, an artificial people, was raised by the discipline of education to obey, to conquer, and to command. From the time of Orchan and the first Amurath, the sultans were persuaded that a government of the sword must be renewed in each generation with new soldiers; and that such soldiers must be sought not in effeminate Asia but among the hardy and warlike natives of Europe. The provinces of Thrace, Macedonia, Albania, Bulgaria, and Servia became the perpetual seminary of the Turkish army; and when the royal fifth of the captives was diminished by conquest, an inhuman tax of the fifth child, or of every fifth year, was rigorously levied on the Christian families. At the age of twelve or fourteen years, the most robust youths were torn from their parents; their names were enrolled in a book; and from that moment they were clothed, taught, and maintained for the public service. According to the promise of their appearance, they were selected for the royal schools of Boursa, Pera, and Hadrianople, entrusted to the care of the *bashaws,* or dispersed in the houses of the Anatolian peasantry. It was the first care of their masters to instruct them in the Turkish language: their bodies were exercised by every labor that could fortify their strength; they learned to wrestle, to leap, to run, to shoot with the bow and afterwards with the musket; till they were drafted into the chambers and companies of the Janizaries, and severely trained in the military or monastic discipline of the order. The youths most conspicuous for birth, talents, and beauty were admitted into the inferior class of *Agiamoglans,* or the more liberal rank of *Ichoglans,* of whom the former were attached to the palace, and the latter to the person, of the prince. In four successive schools, under the rod of the white eunuchs, the arts of horsemanship and of darting the javelin were their daily exercise, while those of a more studious cast applied themselves to the study of the Koran and the knowledge of the Arabic and Persian tongues. As they advanced in seniority and merit, they were gradually dismissed to military, civil, and even ecclesiastical employments: the longer their stay, the higher was their expectation; till, at a mature period, they were admitted into the number of the forty *agas,* who stood before the sultan and were promoted by his choice to the government of provinces and the first honors of the empire. Such a mode of institution was admirably adapted to the form and spirit of a despotic monarchy. The ministers and generals were, in the strictest sense, the slaves of the emperor, to whose bounty they were indebted for their instruction and support. When they left the seraglio and suffered their beards to grow as the symbol of enfranchisement, they found themselves in an important office, without faction or friendship, without parents and without heirs, dependent on the hand which had raised them from the dust and which, on the slightest displeasure, could break in pieces these statues of glass, as they were aptly termed by the Turkish proverb. In the slow and painful steps of education, their characters and talents were unfolded to a discerning eye: the *man,* naked and alone, was reduced to the standard of his personal merit; and if the sovereign had wisdom to choose, he possessed a pure and boundless liberty of choice. The Ottoman candidates were trained by the virtues of abstinence to those of action; by the habits of submission to those of command. A similar spirit was diffused among the troops; and their silence and sobriety, their patience and modesty, have extorted the reluctant praise of their Christian enemies. Nor can the victory appear doubtful if we compare the discipline and exercise of the Janizaries with the pride of birth, the independence of chivalry, the ignorance of the new levies, the mutinous temper of the veterans, and the vices of intemperance and disorder which so long contaminated the armies of Europe.

The only hope of salvation for the Greek empire and the adjacent kingdoms would have been some more powerful weapon, some discovery in the art of war, that would give them a decisive superiority over their Turkish foes. Such a weapon was in their hands; such a discovery had been made in the critical moment of their fate. The chemists of China or Europe had found, by casual or elaborate experiments, that a mixture of saltpeter, sulphur, and charcoal produces, with a spark of fire, a tremendous explosion. It was soon observed that if the expansive force were compressed in a strong tube, a ball of stone or iron might be expelled with irresistible and destructive velocity. The precise era of the invention and application of gunpowder is involved in doubtful traditions and equivocal language; yet we may clearly discern that it was known before the middle of the fourteenth century; and that before the end of the same, the use of artillery in battles and sieges, by sea and land, was familiar to the states of Germany, Italy, Spain, France, and England. The priority of nations is of small account; none could derive any exclusive benefit from their previous or superior knowledge; and in the common improvement, they stood on the same level of relative power and military science. Nor was it possible to circumscribe the secret within the pale of the church; it was disclosed to the Turks by the treachery of apostates and the selfish policy of rivals; and the sultans had sense to adopt, and wealth to reward, the talents of a Christian engineer. The Genoese, who transported Amurath into Europe, must be accused as his preceptors; and it was probably by their hands that his cannon was cast and directed at the siege of Constantinople. The first attempt was indeed unsuccessful; but in the general warfare of the age, the advantage was on *their* side, who were most commonly the assailants: for a while the proportion of the attack and defense was suspended; and this thundering artillery was pointed against the walls and towers which had been erected only to resist the less potent engines of antiquity. By the Venetians, the use of gunpowder was communicated without reproach to the sultans of Egypt and Persia, their allies against the Ottoman power; the secret was soon propagated to the extremities of Asia; and the advantage of the European was confined to his easy victories over the savages of the new world. If we contrast the rapid progress of this mischievous discovery with the slow and laborious advances of reason, science, and the arts of peace, a philosopher, according to his temper, will laugh or weep at the folly of mankind.

CHAPTER LXVI

UNION OF THE GREEK AND LATIN CHURCHES

Applications of the Eastern emperors to the popes. • Visits to the West of John the First, Manuel, and John the Second, Palaeologus. • Union of the Greek and Latin churches, promoted by the council of Basel and concluded at Ferrara and Florence. • State of literature at Constantinople. • Its revival in Italy by the Greek fugitives. • Curiosity and emulation of the Latins.

In the four last centuries of the Greek emperors, their friendly or hostile aspect towards the pope and the Latins may be observed as the thermometer of their prosperity or distress; as the scale of the rise and fall of the Barbarian dynasties. When the Turks of the house of Seljuk pervaded Asia and threatened Constantinople, we have seen, at the council of Placentia, the suppliant ambassadors of Alexius imploring the protection of the common father of the Christians. No sooner had the arms of the French pilgrims removed the sultan from Nice to Iconium than the Greek princes resumed, or avowed, their genuine hatred and contempt for the schismatics of the West, which precipitated the first downfall of their empire. The date of the Mogul invasion is marked in the soft and charitable language of John Vataces. After the recovery of Constantinople, the throne of the first Palaeologus was encompassed by foreign and domestic enemies; as long as the sword of Charles was suspended over his head, he basely courted the favor of the Roman pontiff, and sacrificed to the present danger his faith, his virtue, and the affection of his subjects. On the decease of Michael, the prince and people asserted the independence of their church and the purity of their creed: the elder Andronicus neither feared nor loved the Latins; in his last distress, pride was the safeguard of superstition; nor could he decently retract in his age the firm and orthodox declarations of his youth. His grandson, the younger Andronicus, was less a slave in his temper and situation; and the conquest of Bithynia by the Turks admonished him to seek a temporal and spiritual alliance with the Western princes. After a separation and silence of fifty years, a secret agent, the monk Barlaam, was despatched to Pope Benedict the Twelfth; and his artful instructions appear to have been drawn by the master-hand of the great domestic [A.D. 1339]. "Most holy father," was he commissioned to say, "the emperor is not less desirous than yourself of a union between the two churches: but in this delicate transaction, he is obliged to respect his own dignity and the prejudices of his subjects. The ways of union are twofold: force and persuasion. Of force, the inefficacy has been already tried; since the Latins have subdued the empire without subduing the minds of the Greeks. The method of persuasion, though slow, is sure and permanent. A deputation of thirty or forty of our doctors would probably agree with those of the Vatican, in the love of truth and the unity of belief; but on their return, what would be the use, the recompense, of such an agreement? the scorn of their brethren and the reproaches of a blind and obstinate nation. Yet that nation is accustomed to reverence the general councils which have fixed the articles of our faith; and if they reprobate the decrees of Lyons, it is because the Eastern churches were neither heard nor represented in that arbitrary meeting. For this salutary end, it will be expedient, and even necessary, that a well-chosen legate should be sent into Greece to convene the patriarchs of Constantinople, Alexandria, Antioch, and Jerusalem; and with their aid, to prepare a free and universal synod. But at this moment," continued the subtle agent, "the empire is assaulted and endangered by the Turks, who have occupied four of the greatest cities of Anatolia. The Christian inhabitants have expressed a wish of returning to their allegiance and religion; but the forces and revenues of the emperor are insufficient for their deliverance: and the Roman legate must be accompanied or preceded by an army of Franks, to expel the infidels and open a way to the holy sepulchre." If the suspicious Latins should require some pledge, some previous effect of the sincerity of the Greeks, the answers of Barlaam were perspicuous and rational. "1. A general synod can alone consummate the union of the churches; nor can such a synod be held till the three Oriental patriarchs, and a great number of bishops, are enfranchised from the Mohammedan yoke. 2. The Greeks are alienated by a long series of oppression and injury: they must be reconciled by some act of brotherly love, some effectual succor, which may fortify the authority and arguments of the emperor and the friends of the union.

3. If some difference of faith or ceremonies should be found incurable, the Greeks, however, are the disciples of Christ; and the Turks are the common enemies of the Christian name. The Armenians, Cyprians, and Rhodians are equally attacked; and it will become the piety of the French princes to draw their swords in the general defense of religion. 4. Should the subjects of Andronicus be treated as the worst of schismatics, of heretics, of Pagans, a judicious policy may yet instruct the powers of the West to embrace a useful ally, to uphold a sinking empire, to guard the confines of Europe; and rather to join the Greeks against the Turks than to expect the union of the Turkish arms with the troops and treasures of captive Greece." The reasons, the offers, and the demands of Andronicus were eluded with cold and stately indifference. The kings of France and Naples declined the dangers and glory of a crusade; the pope refused to call a new synod to determine old articles of faith; and his regard for the obsolete claims of the Latin emperor and clergy engaged him to use an offensive superscription— "To the *moderator* of the Greeks, and the persons who style themselves the patriarchs of the Eastern churches." For such an embassy, a time and character less propitious could not easily have been found. Benedict the Twelfth was a dull peasant, perplexed with scruples and immersed in sloth and wine: his pride might enrich with a third crown the papal tiara, but he was alike unfit for the regal and the pastoral office.

After the decease of Andronicus, while the Greeks were distracted by intestine war, they could not presume to agitate a general union of the Christians. But as soon as Cantacuzene had subdued and pardoned his enemies, he was anxious to justify, or at least to extenuate, the introduction of the Turks into Europe, and the nuptials of his daughter with a Moslem prince. Two officers of state, with a Latin interpreter, were sent in his name to the Roman court [A.D. 1348], which was transplanted to Avignon, on the banks of the Rhone, during a period of seventy years: they represented the hard necessity which had urged him to embrace the alliance of the miscreants, and pronounced by his command the specious and edifying sounds of union and crusade. Pope Clement the Sixth, the successor of Benedict, received them with hospitality and honor, acknowledged the innocence of their sovereign, excused his distress, applauded his magnanimity, and displayed a clear knowledge of the state and revolutions of the Greek empire, which he had imbibed from the honest accounts of a Savoyard lady, an attendant of the empress Anne. If Clement was ill endowed with the virtues of a priest, he possessed, however, the spirit and magnificence of a prince, whose liberal hand distributed benefices and kingdoms with equal facility. Under his reign Avignon was the seat of pomp and pleasure: in his youth he had surpassed the licentiousness of a baron; and the palace, nay, the bed-chamber of the pope was adorned, or polluted, by the visits of his female favorites. The wars of France and England were adverse to the holy enterprise; but his vanity was amused by the splendid idea; and the Greek ambassadors returned with two Latin bishops, the ministers of the pontiff. On their arrival at Constantinople, the emperor and the nuncios admired each other's piety and eloquence; and their frequent conferences were filled with mutual praises and promises, by which both parties were amused and neither could be deceived. "I am delighted," said the devout Cantacuzene, "with the project of our holy war, which must redound to my personal glory, as well as to the public benefit of Christendom. My dominions will give a free passage to the armies of France: my troops, my galleys, my treasures shall be consecrated to the common cause; and happy would be my fate, could I deserve and obtain the crown of martyrdom. Words are insufficient to express the ardor with which I sigh for the reunion of the scattered members of Christ. If my death could avail, I would gladly present my sword and my neck: if the spiritual phoenix could arise from my ashes, I would erect the pile and kindle the flame with my own hands." Yet the Greek emperor presumed to observe that the articles of faith which divided the two churches had been introduced by the pride and precipitation of the Latins: he disclaimed the servile and arbitrary steps of the first Palaeologus; and firmly declared that he would never submit his conscience unless to the decrees of a free and universal synod. "The situation of the times," continued he, "will not allow the pope and myself to meet either at Rome or Constantinople; but some maritime city may be chosen on the verge of the two empires, to unite the bishops and to instruct the faithful of the East and West." The nuncios seemed content with the proposition; and Cantacuzene affects to deplore the failure of his hopes, which were soon overthrown by the death of Clement and the different temper of his successor. His own life was prolonged, but it was prolonged in a cloister; and except by his prayers, the humble monk was incapable of directing the counsels of his pupil or the state.

Yet of all the Byzantine princes, that pupil, John Palaeologus, was the best disposed to embrace, to believe, and to obey the shepherd of the West. His mother, Anne of Savoy, was baptized in the bosom of the Latin church: her marriage with Andronicus imposed a change of name, of apparel, and of worship, but her heart was still faithful to her country and religion: she had formed the infancy of her son, and she governed the emperor after his mind, or at least his stature, was enlarged to the size of man. In the first year of his deliverance and restoration, the Turks were still masters of the Hellespont; the son of Cantacuzene was in arms at Hadrianople; and Palaeologus could depend neither on himself nor on his people. By his mother's advice, and in the hope of foreign aid, he abjured the rights both of the church and state; and the act of slavery, subscribed in purple ink and sealed with the golden bull, was privately entrusted to an Italian agent [A.D. 1355]. The first article of the treaty is an oath of fidelity and obedience to Innocent the Sixth and his successors, the supreme pontiffs of the Roman and Catholic church. The emperor promises to entertain with due reverence their legates and nuncios; to assign a palace for their residence and a temple for their worship; and to deliver his second son Manuel as the hostage of his faith. For these condescensions he requires a prompt succor of fifteen galleys, with five hundred men at arms and a thousand archers, to serve against his Christian and Moslem enemies. Palaeologus engages to impose on his clergy and people the same spiritual yoke; but as the resistance of the Greeks might be justly foreseen, he adopts the two effectual methods of corruption and education. The legate was empowered to distribute the vacant benefices among the ecclesiastics who should subscribe the creed of the Vatican: three schools were instituted to instruct the youth of Constantinople in the language and doctrine of the Latins; and the name of Andronicus, the heir of the empire, was enrolled as the first student. Should he fail in the measures of persuasion or force, Palaeologus declares himself unworthy to reign; transfers to the pope all regal and paternal authority; and invests Innocent with full power to regulate the family, the government, and the marriage of his son and successor. But this treaty was neither executed nor published: the Roman galleys were as vain and imaginary as the submission of the Greeks; and it was only by the secrecy that their sovereign escaped the dishonor of this fruitless humiliation.

The tempest of the Turkish arms soon burst on his head; and after the loss of Hadrianople and Romania he was enclosed in his capital, the vassal of the haughty Amurath, with the miserable hope of being the last devoured by the savage. In this abject state, Palaeologus embraced the resolution of embarking for Venice and casting himself at the feet of the pope [A.D. 1369]: he was the first of the Byzantine princes who had ever visited the unknown regions of the West, yet in them alone he could seek consolation or relief; and with less violation of his dignity he might appear in the sacred college than at the Ottoman *Porte.* After a long absence, the Roman pontiffs were returning from Avignon to the banks of the Tiber: Urban the Fifth, of a mild and virtuous character, encouraged or allowed the pilgrimage of the Greek prince, and within the same year enjoyed the glory of receiving in the Vatican the two Imperial shadows who represented the majesty of Constantine and Charlemagne. In this suppliant visit, the emperor of Constantinople, whose vanity was lost in his distress, gave more than could be expected of empty sounds and formal submissions. A previous trial was imposed; and in the presence of four cardinals, he acknowledged, as a true Catholic, the supremacy of the pope and the double procession of the Holy Ghost. After this purification, he was introduced to a public audience in the church of St. Peter: Urban, in the midst of the cardinals, was seated on his throne; the Greek monarch, after three genuflections, devoutly kissed the feet, the hands, and at length the mouth of the holy father, who celebrated high mass in his presence, allowed him to lead the bridle of his mule, and treated him with a sumptuous banquet in the Vatican. The entertainment of Palaeologus was friendly and honorable; yet some difference was observed between the emperors of the East and West; nor could the former be entitled to the rare privilege of chanting the gospel in the rank of a deacon. In favor of his proselyte, Urban strove to rekindle the zeal of the French king and the other powers of the West; but he found them cold in the general cause, and active only in their domestic quarrels. The last hope of the emperor was in an English mercenary, John Hawkwood, or Acuto, who, with a band of adventurers, the white brotherhood, had ravaged Italy from the Alps to Calabria; sold his services to the hostile states; and incurred a just excommunication by shooting his arrows against the papal residence. A special license was granted to negotiate with the outlaw, but the forces, or the spirit, of Hawkwood were unequal to the enterprise: and it was for the advantage, perhaps, of Palaeologus to be disappointed of succor that must have been costly, that could not be effectual, and which might have been dangerous. The disconsolate Greek prepared for his return, but even his return was impeded by a most ignominious obstacle. On his arrival at Venice, he had borrowed large sums at exorbitant usury; but his coffers were empty, his creditors were impatient, and his person was detained as the best security for the payment. His eldest son, Andronicus, the regent of Constantinople, was repeatedly urged to exhaust every resource; and even by stripping the churches, to extricate his father from captivity and disgrace. But the unnatural youth was insensible of the disgrace, and secretly pleased with the captivity of the emperor: the state was poor, the clergy were obstinate; nor could some religious scruple be wanting to excuse the guilt of his indifference and delay. Such undutiful neglect was severely reproved by the piety of his brother Manuel, who instantly sold or mortgaged all that he possessed, embarked for Venice, relieved his father, and pledged his own freedom to be responsible for the debt. On his return to Constantinople [A.D. 1370], the parent and king distinguished his two sons with suitable rewards; but the faith and manners of the slothful Palaeologus had not been improved by his Roman pilgrimage; and his apostasy or conversion, devoid of any spiritual or temporal effects, was speedily forgotten by the Greeks and Latins.

Thirty years after the return of Palaeologus, his son and successor, Manuel, from a similar motive but on a larger scale, again visited the countries of the West [A.D. 1400–1402].

[*Manuel is likewise unsuccessful in securing Western military aid.*]

After his return, and the victory of Timour, Manuel reigned many years in prosperity and peace [A.D. 1402–1417]. As long as the sons of Bajazet solicited his friendship and spared his dominions, he was satisfied with the national religion; and his leisure was employed in composing twenty theological dialogues for its defense. The appearance of the Byzantine ambassadors at the council of Constance announces the restoration of the Turkish power, as well as of the Latin church: the conquest of the sultans, Mohammed and Amurath, reconciled the emperor to the Vatican; and the siege of Constantinople almost tempted him to acquiesce in the double procession of the Holy Ghost. When Martin the Fifth ascended without a rival the chair of St. Peter, a friendly intercourse of letters and embassies was revived between the East and West. Ambition on one side, and distress on the other, dictated the same decent language of charity and peace [A.D. 1417–1425]: the artful Greek expressed a desire of marrying his six sons to Italian princesses; and the Roman, not less artful, despatched the daughter of the marquis of Montferrat, with a company of noble virgins, to soften by their charms the obstinacy of the schismatics. Yet under this mask of zeal, a discerning eye will perceive that all was hollow and insincere in the court and church of Constantinople. According to the vicissitudes of danger and repose, the emperor advanced or retreated; alternately instructed and disavowed his ministers; and escaped from the importunate pressure by urging the duty of inquiry, the obligation of collecting the sense of his patriarchs and bishops, and the impossibility of convening them at a time when the Turkish arms were at the gates of his capital. From a review of the public transactions it will appear that the Greeks insisted on three successive measures, a succor, a council, and a final reunion, while the Latins eluded the second and only promised the first as a consequential and voluntary reward of the third. But we have an opportunity of unfolding the most secret intentions of Manuel, as he explained them in a private conversation without artifice or disguise. In his declining age, the emperor had associated John Palaeologus, the second of the name and the eldest of his sons, on whom he devolved the greatest part of the authority and weight of government. One day, in the presence only of the historian Phranza, his favorite chamberlain, he opened to his colleague and successor the true principle of his negotiations with the pope. "Our last resource," said Manuel, against the Turks, "is their fear of our union with the Latins, of the warlike nations of the West, who may arm for our relief and for their destruction. As often as you are threatened by the miscreants, present this danger before their eyes. Propose a council; consult on the means; but ever delay and avoid the convocation of an assembly, which cannot tend either to our spiritual or temporal emolument. The Latins are proud; the Greeks are obstinate; neither party will recede or retract; and the attempt of a perfect union will confirm the schism, alienate the churches, and leave us, without hope or defense, at the mercy of the Barbarians." Impatient of this salutary lesson, the royal youth arose from his seat and departed in silence; and the wise monarch (continued Phranza), casting his eyes on him, thus resumed his discourse: "My son deems himself a great and heroic prince; but, alas! our miserable age does not afford scope for heroism or greatness. His daring spirit might have suited the happier times of our ancestors; but the present state requires not an emperor, but a cautious steward of the last relics of our fortunes. Well do I remember the lofty expectations which he built on our alliance with Mustapha; and much do I fear that this rash courage will urge the ruin of our house, and that even religion may precipitate our downfall." Yet the experience and authority of Manuel preserved the peace and eluded the council; till, in the seventy-eighth year of his age and in the habit of a monk, he terminated his career, dividing his precious movables among his children and the poor, his physicians and his favorite servants. Of his six sons, Andronicus the Second was invested with the principality of Thessalonica, and died of a leprosy soon after the sale of that city to the Venetians and its final conquest by the Turks. Some fortunate incidents had restored Peloponnesus, or the Morea, to the empire; and in his more prosperous days, Manuel had fortified the narrow isthmus of six miles with a stone wall and one hundred and fifty-three towers. The wall was overthrown by the first blast of the Ottomans; the fertile peninsula might have been sufficient for the four younger brothers, Theodore and Constantine, Demetrius and Thomas; but they wasted in domestic contests the remains of their strength; and the least successful of the rivals were reduced to a life of dependence in the Byzantine palace.

The eldest of the sons of Manuel, John Palaeologus the Second, was acknowledged after his father's death as the sole emperor of the Greeks [A.D. 1425–1437]. He immediately proceeded to repudiate his wife and to contract a new marriage with the princess of Trebizond: beauty was in his eyes the first qualification of an empress; and the clergy had yielded to his firm assurance that unless he might be indulged in a divorce, he would retire to a cloister and leave the throne to his brother Constantine. The first, and in truth the only, victory of Palaeologus was over a Jew, whom, after a long and learned dispute, he converted to the Christian faith; and this momentous conquest is carefully recorded in the history of the times. But he soon resumed the design of uniting the East and West, and, regardless of his father's advice, listened, as it should seem with sincerity, to the proposal of meeting the pope in a general council beyond the Adriatic.

[*The Western church is itself divided (*A.D. *1377–1429). The bishops of Northern Europe attempt to assert their collective authority over the pope. The emperor of the East, John Palaeologus, who is anxious to heal the schism between East and West, negotiates with both Rome and the bishops of the North, but eventually accepts the invitation of Pope Eugenius IV. The Council of Greeks and Latins meets at Ferrara and Florence, October 8,* A.D. *1438–July 6,* A.D. *1439.*]

After the labor of nine months and the debates of twenty-five sessions, they attained the advantage and glory of the reunion of the Greeks. Four principal questions had been agitated between the two churches; 1. The use of unleavened bread in the communion of Christ's body. 2. The nature of purgatory. 3. The supremacy of the pope. And 4. The single or double procession of the Holy Ghost. The cause of either nation was managed by ten theological champions: the Latins were supported by the inexhaustible eloquence of Cardinal Julian; and Mark of Ephesus and Bessarion of Nice were the bold and able leaders of the Greek forces. We may bestow some praise on the progress of human reason by observing that the first of these questions was *now* treated as an immaterial rite which might innocently vary with the fashion of the age and country. With regard to the second, both parties were agreed in the belief of an intermediate state of purgation for the venial sins of the faithful; and whether their souls were purified by elemental fire was a doubtful point which in a few years might be conveniently settled on the spot by the disputants. The claims of supremacy appeared of a more weighty and substantial kind; yet by the Orientals the Roman bishop had ever been respected as the first of the five patriarchs; nor did they scruple to admit that his jurisdiction should be exercised agreeably to the holy canons; a vague allowance, which might be defined or eluded by occasional convenience. The procession of the Holy Ghost from the Father alone or from the Father and the Son was an article of faith which had sunk much deeper into the minds of men;

and in the sessions of Ferrara and Florence, the Latin addition of *fil-ioque* ["and the Son"] was subdivided into two questions, whether it were legal and whether it were orthodox. Perhaps it may not be necessary to boast on this subject of my own impartial indifference; but I must think that the Greeks were strongly supported by the prohibition of the council of Chalcedon against adding any article whatsoever to the creed of Nice, or rather of Constantinople. In earthly affairs, it is not easy to conceive how an assembly equal of legislators can bind their successors invested with powers equal to their own. But the dictates of inspiration must be true and unchangeable; nor should a private bishop or a provincial synod have presumed to innovate against the judgment of the Catholic church. On the substance of the doctrine, the controversy was equal and endless: reason is confounded by the procession of a deity: the gospel which lay on the altar was silent; the various texts of the fathers might be corrupted by fraud or entangled by sophistry; and the Greeks were ignorant of the characters and writings of the Latin saints. Of this at least we may be sure, that neither side could be convinced by the arguments of their opponents. Prejudice may be enlightened by reason, and a superficial glance may be rectified by a clear and more perfect view of an object adapted to our faculties. But the bishops and monks had been taught from their infancy to repeat a form of mysterious words: their national and personal honor depended on the repetition of the same sounds; and their narrow minds were hardened and inflamed by the acrimony of a public dispute.[†]

In the treaty between the two nations, several forms of consent were proposed such as might satisfy the Latins without dishonoring the Greeks; and they weighed the scruples of words and syllables till the theological balance trembled with a slight preponderance in favor of the Vatican. It was agreed (I must entreat the attention of the reader) that the Holy Ghost proceeds from the Father *and* the Son, as from one principle and one substance; that he proceeds *by* the Son, being of the same nature and substance; and that he proceeds from the Father *and* the Son, by one *spiration* and production. It is less difficult to understand the articles of the preliminary treaty: that the pope should defray all the expenses of the Greeks in their return home; that he should annually maintain two galleys and three hundred soldiers for the defense of Constantinople; that all the ships which transported pilgrims to Jerusalem should be obliged to touch at that port; that as often as they were required, the pope should furnish ten galleys for a year, or twenty for six months; and that he should powerfully solicit the princes of Europe if the emperor had occasion for land forces.

The same year, and almost the same day, were marked by the deposition of Eugenius [by the Northern bishops] at Basel [June 25, A.D. 1438]; and, at Florence, by his reunion of the Greeks and Latins [July 6, A.D. 1438]. In the former synod (which he styled indeed an assembly of demons) the pope was branded with the guilt of simony, perjury, tyranny, heresy, and schism; and declared to be incorrigible in his vices, unworthy of any title, and incapable of holding any ecclesiastical office. In the latter, he was revered as the true and holy vicar of Christ who, after a separation of six hundred years, had reconciled the Catholics of the East and West in one fold and under one shepherd. The act of union was subscribed by the pope, the emperor, and the principal members of both churches; even by those who, like Syropulus, had been deprived of the right of voting. Two copies might have sufficed for the East and West; but Eugenius was not satisfied unless four authentic and similar transcripts were signed and attested as the monuments of his victory. On a memorable day, the sixth of July, the successors of St. Peter and Constantine ascended their thrones; the two nations assembled in the cathedral of Florence; their representatives, Cardinal Julian and Bessarion, archbishop of Nice, appeared in the pulpit and, after reading in their respective tongues the act of union, they mutually embraced, in the name and the presence of their applauding brethren. The pope and his ministers then officiated according to the Roman liturgy; the creed was chanted with the addition of *filioque;* the acquiescence of the Greeks was poorly excused by their ignorance of the harmonious but inarticulate sounds; and the more scrupulous Latins refused any public celebration of the Byzantine rite. Yet the emperor and his clergy were not totally unmindful of national honor. The treaty was ratified by their consent: it was tacitly agreed that no innovation should be attempted in their creed or ceremonies: they spared and secretly respected the generous firmness of Mark of Ephesus; and on the decease of the patriarch, they refused to elect his successor, except in the cathedral of St. Sophia. In the distribution of public and private rewards, the liberal pontiff exceeded their hopes and his promises: the Greeks, with less pomp and pride, returned by the same road of Ferrara and Venice; and their reception at Constantinople was such as will be described in the following chapter [February 1, A.D. 1440]. The success of the first trial encouraged Eugenius to repeat the same edifying scenes; and the deputies of the Armenians, the Maronites, the Jacobites of Syria and Egypt, the Nestorians and the Aethiopians were successively introduced to kiss the feet of the Roman pontiff and to announce the obedience and the orthodoxy of the East. These Oriental embassies, unknown in the countries which they presumed to represent, diffused over the West the fame of Eugenius; and a clamor was artfully propagated against the remnant of a schism in Switzerland and Savoy, which alone impeded the harmony of the Christian world. The vigor of opposition was succeeded by the lassitude of despair: the council of Basel was silently dissolved; and Felix, renouncing the tiara, again withdrew to the devout or delicious hermitage of Ripaille. A general peace was secured by mutual acts of oblivion and indemnity [A.D. 1449]: all ideas of reformation subsided; the popes continued to exercise and abuse their ecclesiastical despotism; nor has Rome been since disturbed by the mischiefs of a contested election.

The journeys of three emperors were unavailing for their temporal, or perhaps their spiritual, salvation; but they were productive of a beneficial consequence—the revival of the Greek learning in Italy, from whence it was propagated to the last nations of the West and North. In their lowest servitude and depression, the subjects of the Byzantine throne were still possessed of a golden key that could unlock the treasures of antiquity; of a musical and prolific language that gives a soul to the objects of sense, and a body to the abstractions of philosophy.[†]

[T]he restoration of the Greek letters in Italy was prosecuted by a series of emigrants [A.D. 1400–1500], who were destitute of fortune and endowed with learning, or at least with language. From the terror or oppression of the Turkish arms, the natives of Thessalonica and Constantinople escaped to a land of freedom, curiosity, and wealth. The synod introduced into Florence the lights of the Greek church and the oracles of the Platonic philosophy.[†]

Italy was divided into many independent states; and at that time it was the ambition of princes and republics to vie with each other in the encouragement and reward of literature. The fame of Nicholas the Fifth has not been adequate to his merits [A.D. 1447–1455]. From a plebeian origin he raised himself by his virtue and learning: the character of the man prevailed over the interest of the pope; and he sharpened those weapons which were soon pointed against the Roman church. He had been the friend of the most eminent scholars of the age: he became their patron; and such was the humility of his manners that the change was scarcely discernible, either to them or to himself. If he pressed the acceptance of a liberal gift, it was not as the measure of desert but as the proof of benevolence; and when modest merit declined his bounty, "Accept it," would he say, with a consciousness of his own worth: "ye will not always have a Nicholas among you." The influence of the holy see pervaded Christendom; and he exerted that influence in the search not of benefices, but of books. From the ruins of the Byzantine libraries, from the darkest monasteries of Germany and Britain, he collected the dusty manuscripts of the writers of antiquity; and wherever the original could not be removed, a faithful copy was transcribed and transmitted for his use. The Vatican, the old repository for bulls and legends, for superstition and forgery, was daily replenished with more precious furniture; and such was the industry of Nicholas that in a reign of eight years he formed a library of five thousand volumes. To his munificence the Latin world was indebted for the versions of Xenophon, Diodorus, Polybius, Thucydides, Herodotus, and Appian; of Strabo's Geography, of the Iliad, of the most valuable works of Plato and Aristotle, of Ptolemy and Theophrastus, and of the fathers of the Greek church. The example of the Roman pontiff was preceded or imitated by a Florentine merchant, who governed the republic without arms and without a title. Cosmo of Medicis was the father of a line of princes, whose name and age are almost synonymous with the restoration of learning [circa A.D. 1428–1492]: his credit was ennobled into fame; his riches were dedicated to the service of mankind; he corresponded at once with Cairo and London: and a cargo of Indian spices and Greek books was often imported in the same vessel. The genius and education of his grandson Lorenzo rendered him not only a patron but a judge and candidate in the literary race. In his palace, distress was entitled to relief and merit to reward: his leisure hours were delightfully spent in the Platonic academy; he encouraged the emulation of Demetrius Chalcocondyles and Angelo Politian; and his active missionary Janus Lascaris returned from the East with a treasure of two hundred manuscripts, fourscore of which were as yet unknown in the libraries of Europe. The rest of Italy was animated by a similar spirit, and the progress of the nation repaid the liberality of their princes. The Latins held the exclusive property of their own literature; and these disciples of Greece were soon capable of transmitting and improving the lessons which they had imbibed. After a short succession of foreign teachers, the tide of emigration subsided; but the language of Constantinople was spread beyond the Alps, and the natives of France, Germany, and England imparted to their country the sacred fire which they had kindled in the schools of Florence and Rome. In the productions of the mind, as in those of the soil, the gifts of nature are excelled by industry and skill: the Greek authors, forgotten on the banks of the Ilissus, have been illustrated on those of the Elbe and the Thames: and Bessarion or Gaza might have envied the superior science of the Barbarians; the accuracy of Budaeus, the taste of Erasmus, the copiousness of Stephens, the erudition of Scaliger, the discernment of Reiske or of Bentley. On the side of the Latins, the discovery of printing was a casual advantage: but this useful art has been applied by Aldus and his innumerable successors to perpetuate and multiply the works of antiquity. A single manuscript imported from Greece is revived in ten thousand copies; and each copy is fairer than the original. In this form, Homer and Plato would peruse with more satisfaction their own writings; and their scholiasts must resign the prize to the labors of our Western editors.

Before the revival of classic literature, the Barbarians in Europe were immersed in ignorance; and their vulgar tongues were marked with the rudeness and poverty of their manners. The students of the more perfect idioms of Rome and Greece were introduced to a new world of light and science; to the society of the free and polished nations of antiquity; and to a familiar converse with those immortal men who spoke the sublime language of eloquence and reason. Such an intercourse must tend to refine the taste and to elevate the genius of the moderns; and yet, from the first experiments, it might appear that the study of the ancients had given fetters rather than wings to the human mind. However laudable, the spirit of imitation is of a servile cast; and the first disciples of the Greeks and Romans were a colony of strangers in the midst of their age and country. The minute and laborious diligence which explored the antiquities of remote times might have improved or adorned the present state of society; the critic and metaphysician were the slaves

Apse of the So-Called Hall of the Philosophers

anzi di una Sala appar-
ente al Castro Pretorio nel
Villa Adriana en Tivoli
Tribunale ornato di nicchie

HADRIAN'S VILLA, TIVOLI

of Aristotle; the poets, historians, and orators were proud to repeat the thoughts and words of the Augustan age: the works of nature were observed with the eyes of Pliny and Theophrastus; and some Pagan votaries professed a secret devotion to the gods of Homer and Plato. The Italians were oppressed by the strength and number of their ancient auxiliaries: the century after the deaths of Petrarch and Boccace was filled with a crowd of Latin imitators, who decently repose on our shelves; but in that era of learning it will not be easy to discern a real discovery of science, a work of invention or eloquence, in the popular language of the country. But as soon as it had been deeply saturated with the celestial dew, the soil was quickened into vegetation and life; the modern idioms were refined; the classics of Athens and Rome inspired a pure taste and a generous emulation; and in Italy, as afterwards in France and England, the pleasing reign of poetry and fiction was succeeded by the light of speculative and experimental philosophy. Genius may anticipate the season of maturity; but in the education of a people, as in that of an individual, memory must be exercised before the powers of reason and fancy can be expanded: nor may the artist hope to equal or surpass, till he has learned to imitate, the works of his predecessors.

CHAPTER LXVII

SCHISM OF THE GREEKS AND LATINS

*Schism of the Greeks and Latins. • Reign and character of
Amurath the Second. • Crusade of Ladislaus, king of Hungary. •
His defeat and death. • John Huniades. • Constantine Palaeologus,
last emperor of the East.*

The respective merits of Rome and Constantinople are compared and
celebrated by an eloquent Greek, the father of the Italian schools. The
view of the ancient capital, the seat of his ancestors, surpassed the
most sanguine expectations of Emanuel Chrysoloras; and he no longer
blamed the exclamation of an old sophist that Rome was the habitation
not of men, but of gods. Those gods, and those men, had long since
vanished; but to the eye of liberal enthusiasm, the majesty of ruin restored the image of her ancient prosperity. The monuments of the
consuls and Caesars, of the martyrs and apostles, engaged on all sides
the curiosity of the philosopher and the Christian; and he confessed
that in every age the arms and the religion of Rome were destined to
reign over the earth. While Chrysoloras admired the venerable beauties of the mother, he was not forgetful of his native country, her fairest
daughter, her Imperial colony; and the Byzantine patriot expatiates
with zeal and truth on the eternal advantages of nature and the more
transitory glories of art and dominion which adorned, or had adorned,
the city of Constantine. Yet the perfection of the copy still redounds
(as he modestly observes) to the honor of the original, and parents are
delighted to be renewed and even excelled by the superior merit of
their children.[†]

The last hope of the falling city and empire was placed in the harmony of the mother and daughter, in the maternal tenderness of Rome
and the filial obedience of Constantinople [A.D. 1440–1448]. In the
synod of Florence, the Greeks and Latins had embraced and subscribed and promised; but these signs of friendship were perfidious or
fruitless; and the baseless fabric of the union vanished like a dream.
The emperor and his prelates returned home in the Venetian galleys;
but as they touched at the Morea and the Isles of Corfu and Lesbos, the

subjects of the Latins complained that the pretended union would be an instrument of oppression. No sooner did they land on the Byzantine shore than they were saluted, or rather assailed, with a general murmur of zeal and discontent. During their absence, above two years, the capital had been deprived of its civil and ecclesiastical rulers; fanaticism fermented in anarchy; the most furious monks reigned over the conscience of women and bigots; and the hatred of the Latin name was the first principle of nature and religion. Before his departure for Italy, the emperor had flattered the city with the assurance of a prompt relief and a powerful succor; and the clergy, confident in their orthodoxy and science, had promised themselves and their flocks an easy victory over the blind shepherds of the West. The double disappointment exasperated the Greeks; the conscience of the subscribing prelates was awakened; the hour of temptation was past; and they had more to dread from the public resentment than they could hope from the favor of the emperor or the pope. Instead of justifying their conduct, they deplored their weakness, professed their contrition, and cast themselves on the mercy of God and of their brethren. To the reproachful question, what had been the event or the use of their Italian synod? they answered with sighs and tears, "Alas! we have made a new faith; we have exchanged piety for impiety; we have betrayed the immaculate sacrifice; and we are become *Azymites*." (The Azymites were those who celebrated the communion with unleavened bread; and I must retract or qualify the praise which I have bestowed on the growing philosophy of the times.) "Alas! we have been seduced by distress, by fraud, and by the hopes and fears of a transitory life. The hand that has signed the union should be cut off; and the tongue that has pronounced the Latin creed deserves to be torn from the root." The best proof of their repentance was an increase of zeal for the most trivial rites and the most incomprehensible doctrines; and an absolute separation from all, without excepting their prince, who preserved some regard for honor and consistency. After the decease of the patriarch Joseph, the archbishops of Heraclea and Trebizond had courage to refuse the vacant office; and Cardinal Bessarion preferred the warm and comfortable shelter of the Vatican. The choice of the emperor and his clergy was confined to Metrophanes of Cyzicus: he was consecrated in St. Sophia, but the temple was vacant. The cross-bearers abdicated their service; the infection spread from the city to the villages;

and Metrophanes discharged without effect some ecclesiastical thunders against a nation of schismatics. The eyes of the Greeks were directed to Mark of Ephesus, the champion of his country; and the sufferings of the holy confessor were repaid with a tribute of admiration and applause. His example and writings propagated the flame of religious discord; age and infirmity soon removed him from the world; but the gospel of Mark was not a law of forgiveness; and he requested with his dying breath that none of the adherents of Rome might attend his obsequies or pray for his soul.

The schism was not confined to the narrow limits of the Byzantine empire. Secure under the Mamaluke scepter, the three patriarchs of Alexandria, Antioch, and Jerusalem assembled a numerous synod; disowned their representatives at Ferrara and Florence; condemned the creed and council of the Latins; and threatened the emperor of Constantinople with the censures of the Eastern church. Of the sectaries of the Greek communion, the Russians were the most powerful, ignorant, and superstitious. Their primate, the cardinal Isidore, hastened from Florence to Moscow to reduce the independent nation under the Roman yoke. But the Russian bishops had been educated at Mount Athos; and the prince and people embraced the theology of their priests. They were scandalized by the title, the pomp, the Latin cross of the legate, the friend of those impious men who shaved their beards and performed the divine office with gloves on their hands and rings on their fingers: Isidore was condemned by a synod; his person was imprisoned in a monastery; and it was with extreme difficulty that the cardinal could escape from the hands of a fierce and fanatic people. The Russians refused a passage to the missionaries of Rome who aspired to convert the Pagans beyond the Tanais; and their refusal was justified by the maxim, that the guilt of idolatry is less damnable than that of schism. The errors of the Bohemians were excused by their abhorrence for the pope; and a deputation of the Greek clergy solicited the friendship of those sanguinary enthusiasts. While Eugenius triumphed in the union and orthodoxy of the Greeks, his party was contracted to the walls, or rather to the palace, of Constantinople. The zeal of Palaeologus had been excited by interest; it was soon cooled by opposition: an attempt to violate the national belief might endanger his life and crown; nor could the pious rebels be destitute of foreign and domestic aid. The sword of his brother Demetrius, who in Italy had maintained a prudent and popular silence, was half unsheathed in the cause of religion; and Amurath, the Turkish sultan, was displeased and alarmed by the seeming friendship of the Greeks and Latins.

"Sultan Murad, or Amurath, lived forty-nine and reigned thirty years, six months, and eight days [A.D. 1421–1451]. He was a just and valiant prince, of a great soul, patient of labors, learned, merciful, religious, charitable; a lover and encourager of the studious and of all who excelled in any art or science; a good emperor and a great general. No man obtained more or greater victories than Amurath; Belgrade alone withstood his attacks. Under his reign, the soldier was ever victorious, the citizen rich and secure. If he subdued any country, his first care was to build mosques and caravansaras, hospitals, and colleges. Every year he gave a thousand pieces of gold to the sons of the prophet and sent two thousand five hundred to the religious persons of Mecca, Medina, and Jerusalem." ... But the most striking feature in the life and character of Amurath is the double abdication of the Turkish throne [A.D. 1442–1444]; and were not his motives debased by an alloy of superstition, we must praise the royal philosopher who at the age of forty could discern the vanity of human greatness. Resigning the scepter to his son, he retired to the pleasant residence of Magnesia; but he retired to the society of saints and hermits. It was not till the fourth century of the Hegira that the religion of Mohammed had been corrupted by an institution so adverse to his genius; but in the age of the crusades, the various orders of Dervishes were multiplied by the example of the Christian, and even the Latin, monks. The lord of nations submitted to fast, and pray, and turn round in endless rotation with the fanatics, who mistook the giddiness of the head for the illumination of the spirit. But he was soon awakened from his dreams of enthusiasm by the Hungarian invasion; and his obedient son was the foremost to urge the public danger and the wishes of the people. Under the banner of their veteran leader, the Janizaries fought and conquered, but he withdrew from the field of Varna, again to pray, to fast, and to turn round with his Magnesian brethren. These pious occupations were again interrupted by the danger of the state. A victorious army disdained the inexperience of their youthful ruler: the city of Hadrianople was abandoned to rapine and slaughter; and the unanimous divan implored his presence to appease the tumult, and prevent the rebellion, of the Janizaries. At the well-known voice of their master, they trembled and obeyed; and the reluctant sultan was compelled to support his splendid servitude, till at the end of four years he was relieved by the angel of death. Age or disease, misfortune or caprice, have tempted several princes to descend from the throne; and they have had leisure to repent of their irretrievable step. But Amurath alone, in the full liberty of choice, after the trial of empire and solitude, has *repeated* his preference of a private life.

After the departure of his Greek brethren, Eugenius had not been unmindful of their temporal interest; and his tender regard for the Byzantine empire was animated by a just apprehension of the Turks, who approached and might soon invade the borders of Italy [A.D. 1443]. But the spirit of the crusades had expired; and the coldness of the Franks was not less unreasonable than their headlong passion. In the eleventh century, a fanatic monk could precipitate Europe on Asia for the recovery of the holy sepulchre; but in the fifteenth, the most pressing motives of religion and policy were insufficient to unite the Latins in the defense of Christendom. Germany was an inexhaustible storehouse of men and arms: but that complex and languid body required the impulse of a vigorous hand; and Frederic the Third was alike impotent in his personal character and his Imperial dignity. A long war had impaired the strength, without satiating the animosity, of France and England: but Philip, duke of Burgundy, was a vain and magnificent prince; and he enjoyed, without danger or expense, the adventurous piety of his subjects, who sailed in a gallant fleet from the coast of Flanders to the Hellespont. The maritime republics of Venice and Genoa were less remote from the scene of action; and their hostile fleets were associated under the standard of St. Peter. The kingdoms of Hungary and Poland, which covered as it were the interior pale of the Latin church, were the most nearly concerned to oppose the progress of the Turks. Arms were the patrimony of the Scythians and Sarmatians; and these nations might appear equal to the contest, could they point against the common foe those swords that were so wantonly drawn in bloody and domestic quarrels. But the same spirit was adverse to concord and obedience: a poor country and a limited monarch are incapable of maintaining a standing force; and the loose bodies of Polish and Hungarian horse were not armed with the sentiments and weapons which, on some occasions, have given irresistible weight to the French chivalry. Yet, on this side, the designs of the Roman pontiff and the eloquence of Cardinal Julian, his legate, were promoted by the circumstances of the times: by the union of the two crowns on the head of Ladislaus, a young and ambitious soldier; by the valor of a hero whose name, the name of John Huniades, was already popular among the Christians and formidable to the Turks. An endless treasure of pardons and indulgences was scattered by the legate; many private warriors of France and Germany enlisted under the holy banner; and the crusade derived some strength, or at least some reputation, from the new allies both of Europe and Asia.[†]

Of the Polish and Hungarian diets, a religious war was the unanimous cry; and Ladislaus, after passing the Danube, led an army of his confederate subjects as far as Sophia, the capital of the Bulgarian kingdom [A.D. 1443]. . . . The most solid proof, and the most salutary consequence, of victory was a deputation from the divan to solicit peace, to restore Servia, to ransom the prisoners, and to evacuate the Hungarian frontier. By this treaty, the rational objects of the war were obtained: the king, the despot, and Huniades himself, in the diet of Segedin, were satisfied with public and private emolument; a truce of ten years was concluded; and the followers of Jesus and Mohammed, who swore on the gospel and the Koran, attested the word of God as the guardian of truth and the avenger of perfidy. In the place of the gospel, the Turkish ministers had proposed to substitute the Eucharist, the real presence of the Catholic deity; but the Christians refused to profane their holy mysteries; and a superstitious conscience is less forcibly bound by the spiritual energy than by the outward and visible symbols of an oath.

During the whole transaction, the cardinal legate had observed a sullen silence, unwilling to approve and unable to oppose the consent of the king and people. But the diet was not dissolved before Julian was fortified by the welcome intelligence that Anatolia was invaded by the Caramanian and Thrace by the Greek emperor; that the fleets of Genoa, Venice, and Burgundy were masters of the Hellespont; and that the allies, informed of the victory and ignorant of the treaty of Ladislaus, impatiently waited for the return of his victorious army. "And is it thus," exclaimed the cardinal, "that you will desert their expectations and your own fortune? It is to them, to your God, and your fellow-Christians that you have pledged your faith; and that prior obligation annihilates a rash and sacrilegious oath to the enemies of

Christ. His vicar on earth is the Roman pontiff; without whose sanction you can neither promise nor perform. In his name I absolve your perjury and sanctify your arms: follow my footsteps in the paths of glory and salvation; and if still ye have scruples, devolve on my head the punishment and the sin." This mischievous casuistry was seconded by his respectable character, and the levity of popular assemblies: war was resolved on the same spot where peace had so lately been sworn; and in the execution of the treaty, the Turks were assaulted by the Christians; to whom, with some reason, they might apply the epithet of Infidels [A.D. 1444]. The falsehood of Ladislaus to his word and oath was palliated by the religion of the times: the most perfect, or at least the most popular, excuse would have been the success of his arms and the deliverance of the Eastern church. But the same treaty which should have bound his conscience had diminished his strength. On the proclamation of the peace, the French and German volunteers departed with indignant murmurs: the Poles were exhausted by distant warfare, and perhaps disgusted with foreign command; and their palatines accepted the first license and hastily retired to their provinces and castles. Even Hungary was divided by faction, or restrained by a laudable scruple; and the relics of the crusade that marched in the second expedition were reduced to an inadequate force of twenty thousand men.[†]

From Hadrianople, the sultan advanced by hasty marches at the head of sixty thousand men; and when the cardinal and Huniades had taken a nearer survey of the numbers and order of the Turks, these ardent warriors proposed the tardy and impracticable measure of a retreat. The king alone was resolved to conquer or die; and his resolution had almost been crowned with a glorious and salutary victory. . . . The Turkish wings were broken on the first onset: but the advantage was fatal; and the rash victors, in the heat of the pursuit, were carried away far from the annoyance of the enemy or the support of their friends. When Amurath beheld the flight of his squadrons, he despaired of his fortune and that of the empire: a veteran Janizary seized his horse's bridle; and he had magnanimity to pardon and reward the soldier who dared to perceive the terror and arrest the flight of his sovereign. A copy of the treaty, the monument of Christian perfidy, had been displayed in the front of battle; and it is said that the sultan in his distress, lifting his eyes and his hands to Heaven, implored the protection of the

God of truth; and called on the prophet Jesus himself to avenge the impious mockery of his name and religion. With inferior numbers and disordered ranks, the king of Hungary rushed forward in the confidence of victory, till his career was stopped by the impenetrable phalanx of the Janizaries. . . . Ten thousand Christians were slain in the disastrous battle of Warna [November 10, A.D. 1444]: the loss of the Turks, more considerable in numbers, bore a smaller proportion to their total strength; yet the philosophic sultan was not ashamed to confess that his ruin must be the consequence of a second and similar victory. At his command a column was erected on the spot where Ladislaus had fallen; but the modest inscription, instead of accusing the rashness, recorded the valor and bewailed the misfortune of the Hungarian youth.[†]

In the long career of the decline and fall of the Roman empire, I have reached at length the last reign of the princes of Constantinople, who so feebly sustained the name and majesty of the Caesars. On the decease of John Palaeologus . . . the royal family, by the death of Andronicus and the monastic profession of Isidore, was reduced to three princes, Constantine, Demetrius, and Thomas, the surviving sons of the emperor Manuel. Of these the first and the last were far distant in the Morea; but Demetrius, who possessed the domain of Selybria, was in the suburbs, at the head of a party: his ambition was not chilled by the public distress; and his conspiracy with the Turks and the schismatics had already disturbed the peace of his country. The funeral of the late emperor was accelerated with singular and even suspicious haste: the claim of Demetrius to the vacant throne was justified by a trite and flimsy sophism that he was born in the purple, the eldest son of his father's reign. But the empress-mother, the senate and soldiers, the clergy and people were unanimous in the cause of the lawful successor: and the despot Thomas, who, ignorant of the change, accidentally returned to the capital, asserted with becoming zeal the interest of his absent brother. An ambassador, the historian Phranza, was immediately despatched to the court of Hadrianople. Amurath received him with honor and dismissed him with gifts; but the gracious approbation of the Turkish sultan announced his supremacy and the approaching downfall of the Eastern empire. By the hands of two illustrious deputies, the Imperial crown was placed at Sparta on the head of Constantine. In the spring he sailed from the Morea, escaped the encounter of a

Turkish squadron, enjoyed the acclamations of his subjects, celebrated the festival of a new reign [November 1, A.D. 1448–May 29, A.D. 1453], and exhausted by his donatives the treasure, or rather the indigence, of the state. The emperor immediately resigned to his brothers the possession of the Morea; and the brittle friendship of the two princes, Demetrius and Thomas, was confirmed in their mother's presence by the frail security of oaths and embraces. His next occupation was the choice of a consort. A daughter of the doge of Venice had been proposed; but the Byzantine nobles objected the distance between an hereditary monarch and an elective magistrate; and in their subsequent distress, the chief of that powerful republic was not unmindful of the affront. Constantine afterwards hesitated between the royal families of Trebizond and Georgia; and the embassy of Phranza represents in his public and private life the last days of the Byzantine empire.

The *protovestiare,* or great chamberlain, Phranza sailed from Constantinople as the minister of a bridegroom; and the relics of wealth and luxury were applied to his pompous appearance. His numerous retinue consisted of nobles and guards, of physicians and monks: he was attended by a band of music; and the term of his costly embassy was protracted above two years [A.D. 1450–1452]. . . . [The] choice of Phranza was decided in favor of a Georgian princess; and the vanity of her father was dazzled by the glorious alliance. Instead of demanding, according to the primitive and national custom, a price for his daughter, he offered a portion of fifty-six thousand, with an annual pension of five thousand, ducats; and the services of the ambassador were repaid by an assurance that, as his son had been adopted in baptism by the emperor, the establishment of his daughter should be the peculiar care of the empress of Constantinople. On the return of Phranza, the treaty was ratified by the Greek monarch, who with his own hand impressed three vermilion crosses on the golden bull and assured the Georgian envoy that in the spring his galleys should conduct the bride to her Imperial palace. But Constantine embraced his faithful servant, not with the cold approbation of a sovereign but with the warm confidence of a friend who, after a long absence, is impatient to pour his secrets into the bosom of his friend. "Since the death of my mother and of Cantacuzene, who alone advised me without interest or passion, I am surrounded," said the emperor, "by men whom I can neither love nor trust nor esteem. You are not a stranger to Lucas Notaras, the great admiral; obstinately attached to his own sentiments, he declares, both in private and public, that his sentiments are the absolute measure of my thoughts and actions. The rest of the courtiers are swayed by their personal or factious views; and how can I consult the monks on questions of policy and marriage? I have yet much employment for your diligence and fidelity. In the spring you shall engage one of my brothers to solicit the succor of the Western powers; from the Morea you shall sail to Cyprus on a particular commission; and from thence proceed to Georgia to receive and conduct the future empress."—"Your commands," replied Phranza, "are irresistible; but deign, great sir," he added, with a serious smile, "to consider that if I am thus perpetually absent from my family, my wife may be tempted either to seek another husband, or to throw herself into a monastery." After laughing at his apprehensions, the emperor more gravely consoled him by the pleasing assurance that *this* should be his last service abroad, and that he destined for his son a wealthy and noble heiress; for himself, the important office of great logothete, or principal minister of state. The marriage was immediately stipulated: but the office, however incompatible with his own, had been usurped by the ambition of the admiral. Some delay was requisite to negotiate a consent and an equivalent; and the nomination of Phranza was half declared and half suppressed, lest it might be displeasing to an insolent and powerful favorite. The winter was spent in the preparations of his embassy; and Phranza had resolved that the youth his son should embrace this opportunity of foreign travel, and be left on the appearance of danger with his maternal kindred of the Morea. Such were the private and public designs which were interrupted by a Turkish war, and finally buried in the ruins of the empire.

CHAPTER LXVIII

REIGN OF MOHAMMED THE SECOND, EXTINCTION OF EASTERN EMPIRE

Reign and character of Mohammed the Second. • Siege, assault, and final conquest of Constantinople by the Turks. • Death of Constantine Palaeologus. • Servitude of the Greeks. • Extinction of the Roman empire in the East. • Consternation of Europe. • Conquests and death of Mohammed the Second.

The siege of Constantinople by the Turks attracts our first attention to the person and character of the great destroyer. Mohammed the Second [who reigned A.D. 1451–1481] was the son of the second Amurath; and though his mother has been decorated with the titles of Christian and princess, she is more probably confounded with the numerous concubines who peopled from every climate the harem of the sultan. His first education and sentiments were those of a devout Moslem; and as often as he conversed with an infidel, he purified his hands and face by the legal rites of ablution. Age and empire appear to have relaxed this narrow bigotry: his aspiring genius disdained to acknowledge a power above his own; and in his looser hours he presumed (it is said) to brand the prophet of Mecca as a robber and impostor. Yet the sultan persevered in a decent reverence for the doctrine and discipline of the Koran: his private indiscretion must have been sacred from the vulgar ear; and we should suspect the credulity of strangers and sectaries so prone to believe that a mind which is hardened against truth must be armed with superior contempt for absurdity and error. Under the tuition of the most skillful masters, Mohammed advanced with an early and rapid progress in the paths of knowledge; and besides his native tongue it is affirmed that he spoke or understood five languages, the Arabic, the Persian, the Chaldean or Hebrew, the Latin, and the Greek. The Persian might indeed contribute to his amusement, and the Arabic to his edification; and such studies are familiar to the Oriental youth. In the intercourse of the Greeks and Turks, a conqueror might wish to converse with the people over which he was ambitious

to reign: his own praises in Latin poetry or prose might find a passage
to the royal ear; but what use or merit could recommend to the statesman or the scholar the uncouth dialect of his Hebrew slaves? The history and geography of the world were familiar to his memory: the lives
of the heroes of the East, perhaps of the West, excited his emulation:
his skill in astrology is excused by the folly of the times, and supposes
some rudiments of mathematical science; and a profane taste for the
arts is betrayed in his liberal invitation and reward of the painters of
Italy. But the influence of religion and learning were employed without effect on his savage and licentious nature. I will not transcribe, nor
do I firmly believe, the stories of his fourteen pages whose bellies were
ripped open in search of a stolen melon; or of the beauteous slave
whose head he severed from her body to convince the Janizaries that
their master was not the votary of love. His sobriety is attested by the
silence of the Turkish annals, which accuse three, and three only, of
the Ottoman line of the vice of drunkenness. But it cannot be denied
that his passions were at once furious and inexorable; that in the palace
as in the field, a torrent of blood was spilt on the slightest provocation;
and that the noblest of the captive youth were often dishonored by his
unnatural lust. . . . [H]e studied the lessons, and soon surpassed the example, of his father; and the conquest of two empires, twelve kingdoms, and two hundred cities, a vain and flattering account, is ascribed
to his invincible sword. He was doubtless a soldier, and possibly a
general; Constantinople has sealed his glory; but if we compare the
means, the obstacles, and the achievements, Mohammed the Second
must blush to sustain a parallel with Alexander or Timour. Under his
command, the Ottoman forces were always more numerous than their
enemies; yet their progress was bounded by the Euphrates and the
Adriatic; and his arms were checked by Huniades and Scanderbeg, by
the Rhodian knights and by the Persian king.†

The Mohammedan, and more especially the Turkish casuists, have
pronounced that no promise can bind the faithful against the interest
and duty of their religion; and that the sultan may abrogate his own
treaties and those of his predecessors. The justice and magnanimity of
Amurath had scorned this immoral privilege; but his son, though the
proudest of men, could stoop from ambition to the basest arts of dissimulation and deceit. Peace was on his lips, while war was in his heart:
he incessantly sighed for the possession of Constantinople; and the

Greeks, by their own indiscretion, afforded the first pretense of the fatal rupture. Instead of laboring to be forgotten, their ambassadors pursued his camp to demand the payment, and even the increase, of their annual stipend: the divan was importuned by their complaints, and the vizier, a secret friend of the Christians, was constrained to deliver the sense of his brethren. "Ye foolish and miserable Romans," said Calil, "we know your devices, and ye are ignorant of your own danger! The scrupulous Amurath is no more; his throne is occupied by a young conqueror whom no laws can bind and no obstacles can resist: and if you escape from his hands, give praise to the divine clemency which yet delays the chastisement of your sins. Why do ye seek to affright us by vain and indirect menaces? Release the fugitive Orchan, crown him sultan of Romania; call the Hungarians from beyond the Danube; arm against us the nations of the West; and be assured that you will only provoke and precipitate your ruin." But if the fears of the ambassadors were alarmed by the stern language of the vizier, they were soothed by the courteous audience and friendly speeches of the Ottoman prince; and Mohammed assured them that on his return to Hadrianople he would redress the grievances, and consult the true interests, of the Greeks. No sooner had he repassed the Hellespont than he issued a mandate to suppress their pension and to expel their officers from the banks of the Strymon: in this measure he betrayed a hostile mind; and the second order announced, and in some degree commenced, the siege of Constantinople [A.D. 1451]. In the narrow pass of the Bosphorus, an Asiatic fortress had formerly been raised by his grandfather; in the opposite situation, on the European side, he resolved to erect a more formidable castle; and a thousand masons were commanded to assemble in the spring on a spot named Asomaton, about five miles from the Greek metropolis. Persuasion is the resource of the feeble, and the feeble can seldom persuade: the ambassadors of the emperor attempted without success to divert Mohammed from the execution of his design. They represented that his grandfather had solicited the permission of Manuel to build a castle on his own territories; but that this double fortification, which would command the strait, could only tend to violate the alliance of the nations; to intercept the Latins who traded in the Black Sea, and perhaps to annihilate the subsistence of the city. "I form the enterprise," replied the perfidious sultan, "against the city; but the empire of Constantinople is measured by her walls. Have you forgot the distress to which my father was reduced when you formed a league with the Hungarians; when they invaded our country by land, and the Hellespont was occupied by the French galleys? Amurath was compelled to force the passage of the Bosphorus; and your strength was not equal to your malevolence. I was then a child at Hadrianople; the Moslems trembled; and for a while, the *Gabours* insulted our disgrace. But when my father had triumphed in the field of Warna, he vowed to erect a fort on the western shore, and that vow it is my duty to accomplish. Have ye the right, have ye the power, to control my actions on my own ground? For that ground *is* my own: as far as the shores of the Bosphorus, Asia is inhabited by the Turks, and Europe is deserted by the Romans. Return and inform your king that the present Ottoman is far different from his predecessors; that *his* resolutions surpass *their* wishes; and that *he* performs more than *they* could resolve. Return in safety—but the next who delivers a similar message may expect to be flayed alive." After this declaration, Constantine, the first of the Greeks in spirit as in rank, had determined to unsheathe the sword and to resist the approach and establishment of the Turks on the Bosphorus. He was disarmed by the advice of his civil and ecclesiastical ministers, who recommended a system less generous, and even less prudent, than his own, to approve their patience and long-suffering, to brand the Ottoman with the name and guilt of an aggressor, and to depend on chance and time for their own safety and the destruction of a fort which could not long be maintained in the neighborhood of a great and populous city. Amidst hope and fear, the fears of the wise and the hopes of the credulous, the winter rolled away; the proper business of each man, and each hour, was postponed; and the Greeks shut their eyes against the impending danger, till the arrival of the spring and the sultan decided the assurance of their ruin.

Of a master who never forgives, the orders are seldom disobeyed. On the twenty-sixth of March, the appointed spot of Asomaton was covered with an active swarm of Turkish artificers; and the materials by sea and land were diligently transported from Europe and Asia. . . ! The Greek emperor beheld with terror the irresistible progress of the work; and vainly strove, by flattery and gifts, to assuage an implacable foe who sought, and secretly fomented, the slightest occasion of a quarrel. Such occasions must soon and inevitably be found. The ruins of stately churches, and even the marble columns which had been consecrated to Saint Michael the archangel, were employed without scruple by the profane and rapacious Moslems; and some Christians who presumed to oppose the removal received from their hands the crown of martyrdom. Constantine had solicited a Turkish guard to protect the fields and harvests of his subjects: the guard was fixed; but their first order was to allow free pasture to the mules and horses of the camp, and to defend their brethren if they should be molested by the natives. The retinue of an Ottoman chief had left their horses to pass the night among the ripe corn; the damage was felt; the insult was resented; and several of both nations were slain in a tumultuous conflict. Mohammed listened with joy to the complaint, and a detachment was commanded to exterminate the guilty village: the guilty had fled; but forty innocent and unsuspecting reapers were massacred by the soldiers [June A.D. 1452]. Till this provocation, Constantinople had been opened to the visits of commerce and curiosity: on the first alarm, the gates were shut; but the emperor, still anxious for peace, released on the third day his Turkish captives and expressed, in a last message, the firm resignation of a Christian and a soldier. "Since neither oaths, nor treaty, nor submission can secure peace, pursue," said he to Mohammed, "your impious warfare. My trust is in God alone; if it should please him to mollify your heart, I shall rejoice in the happy change; if he delivers the city into your hands, I submit without a murmur to his holy will. But until the Judge of the earth shall pronounce between us, it is my duty to live and die in the defense of my people." The sultan's answer was hostile and decisive: his fortifications were completed; and before his departure for Hadrianople, he stationed a vigilant Aga and four hundred Janizaries to levy a tribute on the ships of every nation that should pass within the reach of their cannon [September 1, A.D. 1452]. A Venetian vessel, refusing obedience to the new lords of the Bosphorus, was sunk with a single bullet [November 26, A.D. 1452]. The master and thirty sailors escaped in the boat; but they were dragged in chains to the *Porte:* the chief was impaled; his companions were beheaded; and the historian Ducas beheld at Demotica their bodies exposed to the wild beasts. The siege of Constantinople was deferred till the ensuing spring; but an Ottoman army marched into the Morea to divert the force of the brothers of Constantine. At this era of calamity, one of these princes, the despot Thomas, was blessed or afflicted with

the birth of a son [January 17, A.D. 1453]; "the last heir," says the plaintive Phranza, "of the last spark of the Roman empire."

The Greeks and the Turks passed an anxious and sleepless winter: the former were kept awake by their fears, the latter by their hopes;
both by the preparations of defense and attack; and the two emperors,
who had the most to lose or to gain, were the most deeply affected by
the national sentiment. In Mohammed, that sentiment was inflamed by
the ardor of his youth and temper: he amused his leisure with building
at Hadrianople the lofty palace of Jehan Numa (the watchtower of the
world); but his serious thoughts were irrevocably bent on the conquest
of the city of Caesar. At the dead of night, about the second watch, he
started from his bed and commanded the instant attendance of his
prime vizier. The message, the hour, the prince, and his own situation
alarmed the guilty conscience of Calil Basha; who had possessed the
confidence and advised the restoration of Amurath. On the accession
of the son, the vizier was confirmed in his office and the appearances
of favor; but the veteran statesman was not insensible that he trod on a
thin and slippery ice, which might break under his footsteps and
plunge him in the abyss. His friendship for the Christians, which might
be innocent under the late reign, had stigmatized him with the name
of Gabour Ortachi, or foster-brother of the infidels; and his avarice
entertained a venal and treasonable correspondence which was detected and punished after the conclusion of the war. On receiving
the royal mandate, he embraced, perhaps for the last time, his wife
and children; filled a cup with pieces of gold, hastened to the palace,
adored the sultan, and offered, according to the Oriental custom, the
slight tribute of his duty and gratitude. "It is not my wish," said Mohammed, "to resume my gifts, but rather to heap and multiply them on
thy head. In my turn, I ask a present far more valuable and important:
Constantinople." As soon as the vizier had recovered from his surprise,
"The same God," said he, "who has already given thee so large a portion of the Roman empire will not deny the remnant, and the capital.
His providence, and thy power, assure thy success; and myself, with
the rest of thy faithful slaves, will sacrifice our lives and fortunes."—
"Lala" (or preceptor), continued the sultan, "do you see this pillow?
All the night, in my agitation, I have pulled it on one side and the
other; I have risen from my bed, again have I lain down; yet sleep has

not visited these weary eyes. Beware of the gold and silver of the Romans: in arms we are superior; and with the aid of God and the prayers of the prophet, we shall speedily become masters of Constantinople." To sound the disposition of his soldiers, he often wandered through the streets alone and in disguise; and it was fatal to discover the sultan when he wished to escape from the vulgar eye. His hours were spent in delineating the plan of the hostile city; in debating with his generals and engineers on what spot he should erect his batteries; on which side he should assault the walls; where he should spring his mines; to what place he should apply his scaling-ladders: and the exercises of the day repeated and proved the lucubrations of the night.

Among the implements of destruction, he studied with peculiar care the recent and tremendous discovery of the Latins; and his artillery surpassed whatever had yet appeared in the world. A founder of cannon, a Dane or Hungarian who had been almost starved in the Greek service, deserted to the Moslems and was liberally entertained by the Turkish sultan. Mohammed was satisfied with the answer to his first question, which he eagerly pressed on the artist. "Am I able to cast a cannon capable of throwing a ball or stone of sufficient size to batter the walls of Constantinople? I am not ignorant of their strength; but were they more solid than those of Babylon, I could oppose an engine of superior power: the position and management of that engine must be left to your engineers." On this assurance, a foundry was established at Hadrianople: the metal was prepared; and at the end of three months, Urban produced a piece of brass ordnance of stupendous and almost incredible magnitude; a measure of twelve palms is assigned to the bore; and the stone bullet weighed above six hundred pounds. A vacant place before the new palace was chosen for the first experiment; but to prevent the sudden and mischievous effects of astonishment and fear, a proclamation was issued that the cannon would be discharged the ensuing day. The explosion was felt or heard in a circuit of a hundred furlongs: the ball, by the force of gunpowder, was driven above a mile; and on the spot where it fell, it buried itself a fathom deep in the ground. For the conveyance of this destructive engine, a frame or carriage of thirty wagons was linked together and drawn along by a team of sixty oxen: two hundred men on both sides were stationed to poise and support the rolling weight; two hundred and fifty workmen marched before to smooth the way and repair the bridges; and near two months were employed in a laborious journey of one hundred and fifty miles [February A.D. 1453].[†]

While Mohammed threatened the capital of the East, the Greek emperor implored with fervent prayers the assistance of earth and Heaven. But the invisible powers were deaf to his supplications; and Christendom beheld with indifference the fall of Constantinople, while she derived at least some promise of supply from the jealous and temporal policy of the sultan of Egypt. Some states were too weak, and others too remote; by some the danger was considered as imaginary, by others as inevitable: the Western princes were involved in their endless and domestic quarrels; and the Roman pontiff was exasperated by the falsehood or obstinacy of the Greeks. Instead of employing in their favor the arms and treasures of Italy, Nicholas the Fifth had foretold their approaching ruin; and his honor was engaged in the accomplishment of his prophecy. Perhaps he was softened by the last extremity of their distress; but his compassion was tardy; his efforts were faint and unavailing; and Constantinople had fallen before the squadrons of Genoa and Venice could sail from their harbors. Even the princes of the Morea and of the Greek islands affected a cold neutrality: the Genoese colony of Galata negotiated a private treaty; and the sultan indulged them in the delusive hope that by his clemency they might survive the ruin of the empire. A plebeian crowd and some Byzantine nobles basely withdrew from the danger of their country; and the avarice of the rich denied the emperor, and reserved for the Turks, the secret treasures which might have raised in their defense whole armies of mercenaries. The indigent and solitary prince prepared, however, to sustain his formidable adversary; but if his courage were equal to the peril, his strength was inadequate to the contest. In the beginning of the spring, the Turkish vanguard swept the towns and villages as far as the gates of Constantinople: submission was spared and protected; whatever presumed to resist was exterminated with fire and sword. The Greek places on the Black Sea, Mesembria, Acheloum, and Bizon, surrendered on the first summons; Selybria alone deserved the honors of a siege or blockade; and the bold inhabitants, while they were invested by land, launched their boats, pillaged the opposite coast of Cyzicus, and sold their captives in the public market. But on the approach of Mohammed himself all was silent and prostrate: he first halted at the distance of five miles; and from thence advancing in battle array, planted before the gates of St. Romanus the Imperial standard; and on the sixth day of April [A.D. 1453] formed the memorable siege of Constantinople.[†]

The primitive Romans would have drawn their swords in the resolution of death or conquest. The primitive Christians might have embraced each other and awaited in patience and charity the stroke of martyrdom. But the Greeks of Constantinople were animated only by the spirit of religion, and that spirit was productive only of animosity and discord. Before his death, the emperor John Palaeologus had renounced the unpopular measure of a union with the Latins; nor was the idea revived till the distress of his brother Constantine imposed a last trial of flattery and dissimulation. With the demand of temporal aid, his ambassadors were instructed to mingle the assurance of spiritual obedience: his neglect of the church was excused by the urgent cares of the state; and his orthodox wishes solicited the presence of a Roman legate. The Vatican had been too often deluded; yet the signs of repentance could not decently be overlooked; a legate was more easily granted than an army; and about six months before the final destruction, the cardinal Isidore of Russia appeared in that character with a retinue of priests and soldiers. The emperor saluted him as a friend and father; respectfully listened to his public and private sermons; and with the most obsequious of the clergy and laymen subscribed the act of union, as it had been ratified in the council of Florence. On the twelfth of December, the two nations, in the church of St. Sophia, joined in the communion of sacrifice and prayer; and the names of the two pontiffs were solemnly commemorated; the names of Nicholas the Fifth, the vicar of Christ, and of the patriarch Gregory, who had been driven into exile by a rebellious people.

But the dress and language of the Latin priest who officiated at the altar were an object of scandal; and it was observed with horror that he consecrated a cake or wafer of *unleavened* bread and poured cold water into the cup of the sacrament. A national historian acknowledges with a blush that none of his countrymen, not the emperor himself, were sincere in this occasional conformity. Their hasty and unconditional submission was palliated by a promise of future revisal; but the best or the worst of their excuses was the confession of their own perjury. When they were pressed by the reproaches of their honest brethren,

"Have patience," they whispered, "have patience till God shall have delivered the city from the great dragon who seeks to devour us. You shall then perceive whether we are truly reconciled with the Azymites." But patience is not the attribute of zeal; nor can the arts of a court be adapted to the freedom and violence of popular enthusiasm. From the dome of St. Sophia the inhabitants of either sex and of every degree rushed in crowds to the cell of the monk Gennadius, to consult the oracle of the church. The holy man was invisible; entranced, as it should seem, in deep meditation or divine rapture: but he had exposed on the door of his cell a speaking tablet; and they successively withdrew after reading those tremendous words: "O miserable Romans, why will ye abandon the truth? and why, instead of confiding in God, will ye put your trust in the Italians? In losing your faith you will lose your city. Have mercy on me, O Lord! I protest in thy presence that I am innocent of the crime. O miserable Romans, consider, pause, and repent. At the same moment that you renounce the religion of your fathers, by embracing impiety, you submit to a foreign servitude." According to the advice of Gennadius, the religious virgins, as pure as angels and as proud as demons, rejected the act of union, and abjured all communion with the present and future associates of the Latins; and their example was applauded and imitated by the greatest part of the clergy and people. From the monastery, the devout Greeks dispersed themselves in the taverns; drank confusion to the slaves of the pope; emptied their glasses in honor of the image of the holy Virgin; and besought her to defend against Mohammed the city which she had formerly saved from Chosroes and the Chagan. In the double intoxication of zeal and wine, they valiantly exclaimed, "What occasion have we for succor, or union, or Latins? Far from us be the worship of the Azymites!" During the winter that preceded the Turkish conquest, the nation was distracted by this epidemical frenzy; and the season of Lent, the approach of Easter, instead of breathing charity and love, served only to fortify the obstinacy and influence of the zealots. The confessors scrutinized and alarmed the conscience of their votaries, and a rigorous penance was imposed on those who had received the communion from a priest who had given an express or tacit consent to the union. His service at the altar propagated the infection to the mute and simple spectators of the ceremony: they forfeited, by the impure spectacle, the virtue of the sacerdotal character; nor was it lawful, even in danger of sudden death, to invoke the assistance of their prayers or absolution. No sooner had the church of St. Sophia been polluted by the Latin sacrifice, than it was deserted as a Jewish synagogue, or a heathen temple, by the clergy and people; and a vast and gloomy silence prevailed in that venerable dome, which had so often smoked with a cloud of incense, blazed with innumerable lights, and resounded with the voice of prayer and thanksgiving. The Latins were the most odious of heretics and infidels; and the first minister of the empire, the great duke, was heard to declare that he had rather behold in Constantinople the turban of Mohammed than the pope's tiara or a cardinal's hat. A sentiment so unworthy of Christians and patriots was familiar and fatal to the Greeks: the emperor was deprived of the affection and support of his subjects; and their native cowardice was sanctified by resignation to the divine decree, or the visionary hope of a miraculous deliverance.[†]

The nation was indeed pusillanimous and base; but the last Constantine deserves the name of a hero: his noble band of volunteers was inspired with Roman virtue; and the foreign auxiliaries supported the honor of the Western chivalry. The incessant volleys of lances and arrows were accompanied with the smoke, the sound, and the fire of their musketry and cannon. Their small arms discharged at the same time either five or even ten balls of lead, of the size of a walnut; and according to the closeness of the ranks and the force of the powder, several breastplates and bodies were transpierced by the same shot. But the Turkish approaches were soon sunk in trenches or covered with ruins. Each day added to the science of the Christians; but their inadequate stock of gunpowder was wasted in the operations of each day. Their ordnance was not powerful, either in size or number; and if they possessed some heavy cannon, they feared to plant them on the walls, lest the aged structure should be shaken and overthrown by the explosion. The same destructive secret had been revealed to the Moslems; by whom it was employed with the superior energy of zeal, riches, and despotism.[†]

After a siege of forty days, the fate of Constantinople could no longer be averted. The diminutive garrison was exhausted by a double attack: the fortifications, which had stood for ages against hostile violence, were dismantled on all sides by the Ottoman cannon: many breaches were opened; and near the gate of St. Romanus, four towers had been leveled with the ground. For the payment of his feeble and mutinous troops, Constantine was compelled to despoil the churches with the promise of a fourfold restitution; and his sacrilege offered a new reproach to the enemies of the union.†

During the siege of Constantinople, the words of peace and capitulation had been sometimes pronounced; and several embassies had passed between the camp and the city. The Greek emperor was humbled by adversity; and would have yielded to any terms compatible with religion and royalty. The Turkish sultan was desirous of sparing the blood of his soldiers; still more desirous of securing for his own use the Byzantine treasures: and he accomplished a sacred duty in presenting to the *Gabours* the choice of circumcision, of tribute, or of death. The avarice of Mohammed might have been satisfied with an annual sum of one hundred thousand ducats; but his ambition grasped the capital of the East: to the prince he offered a rich equivalent, to the people a free toleration or a safe departure: but after some fruitless treaty, he declared his resolution of finding either a throne or a grave under the walls of Constantinople. A sense of honor and the fear of universal reproach forbade Palaeologus to resign the city into the hands of the Ottomans; and he determined to abide the last extremities of war. Several days were employed by the sultan in the preparations of the assault; and a respite was granted by his favorite science of astrology, which had fixed on the twenty-ninth of May as the fortunate and fatal hour. On the evening of the twenty-seventh, he issued his final orders; assembled in his presence the military chiefs, and dispersed his heralds through the camp to proclaim the duty and the motives of the perilous enterprise. Fear is the first principle of a despotic government; and his menaces were expressed in the Oriental style, that the fugitives and deserters, had they the wings of a bird, should not escape from his inexorable justice. The greatest part of his bashaws and Janizaries were the offspring of Christian parents: but the glories of the Turkish name were perpetuated by successive adoption; and in the gradual change of individuals, the spirit of a legion, a regiment, or an *oda* is kept alive by imitation and discipline. In this holy warfare, the Moslems were exhorted to purify their minds with prayer, their bodies with seven ablutions; and to abstain from food till the close of the ensuing day. A crowd of dervishes visited the tents to instill the desire of martyrdom and the assurance of spending an immortal youth amidst the rivers and gardens of paradise, and in the embraces of the black-eyed virgins. Yet Mohammed principally trusted to the efficacy of temporal and visible rewards. A double pay was promised to the victorious troops: "The city and the buildings," said Mohammed, "are mine; but I resign to your valor the captives and the spoil, the treasures of gold and beauty; be rich and be happy. Many are the provinces of my empire: the intrepid soldier who first ascends the walls of Constantinople shall be rewarded with the government of the fairest and most wealthy; and my gratitude shall accumulate his honors and fortunes above the measure of his own hopes." Such various and potent motives diffused among the Turks a general ardor, regardless of life and impatient for action: the camp reechoed with the Moslem shouts of "God is God: there is but one God, and Mohammed is the apostle of God"; and the sea and land, from Galata to the seven towers, were illuminated by the blaze of their nocturnal fires.

Far different was the state of the Christians; who, with loud and impotent complaints, deplored the guilt or the punishment of their sins. The celestial image of the Virgin had been exposed in solemn procession; but their divine patroness was deaf to their entreaties: they accused the obstinacy of the emperor for refusing a timely surrender; anticipated the horrors of their fate; and sighed for the repose and security of Turkish servitude. The noblest of the Greeks and the bravest of the allies were summoned to the palace to prepare them, on the evening of the twenty-eighth, for the duties and dangers of the general assault. The last speech of Palaeologus was the funeral oration of the Roman empire: he promised, he conjured, and he vainly attempted to infuse the hope which was extinguished in his own mind. In this world all was comfortless and gloomy; and neither the gospel nor the church have proposed any conspicuous recompense to the heroes who fall in the service of their country. But the example of their prince and the confinement of a siege had armed these warriors with the courage of despair, and the pathetic scene is described by the feelings of the historian Phranza, who was himself present at this mournful assembly. They wept, they embraced; regardless of their families and fortunes, they devoted their lives; and each commander, departing to his station, maintained all night a vigilant and anxious watch on the rampart. The emperor and some faithful companions entered the dome of St. Sophia, which in a few hours was to be converted into a mosque; and devoutly received, with tears and prayers, the sacrament of the holy communion. He reposed some moments in the palace, which resounded with cries and lamentations; solicited the pardon of all whom he might have injured; and mounted on horseback to visit the guards and explore the motions of the enemy. The distress and fall of the last Constantine are more glorious than the long prosperity of the Byzantine Caesars.

In the confusion of darkness, an assailant may sometimes succeed; but in this great and general attack, the military judgment and astrological knowledge of Mohammed advised him to expect the morning, the memorable twenty-ninth of May, in the fourteen hundred and fifty-third year of the Christian era. . . . At daybreak, without the customary signal of the morning gun, the Turks assaulted the city by sea and land; and the similitude of a twined or twisted thread has been applied to the closeness and continuity of their line of attack. The foremost ranks consisted of the refuse of the host, a voluntary crowd who fought without order or command; of the feebleness of age or childhood, of peasants and vagrants, and of all who had joined the camp in the blind hope of plunder and martyrdom. The common impulse drove them onwards to the wall; the most audacious to climb were instantly precipitated; and not a dart, not a bullet of the Christians was idly wasted on the accumulated throng. But their strength and ammunition were exhausted in this laborious defense: the ditch was filled with the bodies of the slain; they supported the footsteps of their companions; and of this devoted vanguard the death was more serviceable than the life. Under their respective bashaws and sanjaks, the troops of Anatolia and Romania were successively led to the charge: their progress was various and doubtful; but after a conflict of two hours, the Greeks still maintained and improved their advantage; and the voice of the emperor was heard, encouraging his soldiers to achieve, by a last effort, the deliverance of their country. In that fatal moment, the Janizaries arose, fresh, vigorous, and invincible. The sultan himself, on horseback, with an iron mace in his hand, was the spectator and judge of their valor: he was surrounded by ten thousand of his domestic troops, whom he reserved for the decisive occasion; and the tide of battle was directed and impelled by his voice and eye. His numerous ministers of justice were posted behind the line, to urge, to restrain, and to punish; and if danger was in the front, shame and inevitable death were in the rear of the fugitives. The cries of fear and of pain were drowned in the martial music of drums, trumpets, and attaballs; and experience has proved that the mechanical operation of sounds, by quickening the circulation of the blood and spirits, will act on the human machine more forcibly than the eloquence of reason and honor. From the lines, the galleys, and the bridge, the Ottoman artillery thundered on all sides; and the camp and city, the Greeks and the Turks, were involved in a cloud of smoke which could only be dispelled by the final deliverance or destruction of the Roman empire. The single combats of the heroes of history or fable amuse our fancy and engage our affections: the skillful evolutions of war may inform the mind and improve a necessary though pernicious science. But in the uniform and odious pictures of a general assault, all is blood and horror and confusion, nor shall I strive, at the distance of three centuries and a thousand miles, to delineate a scene of which there could be no spectators, and of which the actors themselves were incapable of forming any just or adequate idea.[†]

[The Greeks] were overwhelmed by increasing multitudes. Amidst these multitudes, the emperor, who accomplished all the duties of a general and a soldier, was long seen and finally lost. The nobles who fought round his person sustained, till their last breath, the honorable names of Palaeologus and Cantacuzene: his mournful exclamation was heard, "Cannot there be found a Christian to cut off my head?" and his last fear was that of falling alive into the hands of the infidels. The prudent despair of Constantine cast away the purple: amidst the tumult he fell by an unknown hand, and his body was buried under a mountain of the slain. After his death, resistance and order were no more: the Greeks fled towards the city; and many were pressed and stifled in the narrow pass of the gate of St. Romanus. The victorious Turks rushed through the breaches of the inner wall; and as they advanced into the streets, they were soon joined by their brethren, who had forced the gate Phenar on the side of the harbor. In the first heat of the pursuit, about two thousand Christians were put to the sword; but avarice soon prevailed over cruelty; and the victors acknowledged that they should immediately have given quarter if the valor of the emperor and his chosen bands had not prepared them for a similar opposition in every part of the capital. It was thus, after a siege of fifty-three days, that

Constantinople, which had defied the power of Chosroes, the Chagan, and the caliphs, was irretrievably subdued by the arms of Mohammed the Second. Her empire only had been subverted by the Latins: her religion was trampled in the dust by the Moslem conquerors.

The tidings of misfortune fly with a rapid wing; yet such was the extent of Constantinople that the more distant quarters might prolong some moments the happy ignorance of their ruin. But in the general consternation, in the feelings of selfish or social anxiety, in the tumult and thunder of the assault, a sleepless night and morning must have elapsed; nor can I believe that many Grecian ladies were awakened by the Janizaries from a sound and tranquil slumber. On the assurance of the public calamity, the houses and convents were instantly deserted; and the trembling inhabitants flocked together in the streets like a herd of timid animals, as if accumulated weakness could be productive of strength, or in the vain hope that amid the crowd each individual might be safe and invisible. From every part of the capital, they flowed into the church of St. Sophia: in the space of an hour, the sanctuary, the choir, the nave, the upper and lower galleries were filled with the multitudes of fathers and husbands, of women and children, of priests, monks, and religious virgins: the doors were barred on the inside, and they sought protection from the sacred dome which they had so lately abhorred as a profane and polluted edifice. Their confidence was founded on the prophecy of an enthusiast or impostor that one day the Turks would enter Constantinople, and pursue the Romans as far as the column of Constantine in the square before St. Sophia: but that this would be the term of their calamities: that an angel would descend from Heaven with a sword in his hand and would deliver the empire, with that celestial weapon, to a poor man seated at the foot of the column. "Take this sword," would he say, "and avenge the people of the Lord." At these animating words, the Turks would instantly fly, and the victorious Romans would drive them from the West, and from all Anatolia as far as the frontiers of Persia. It is on this occasion that Ducas, with some fancy and much truth, upbraids the discord and obstinacy of the Greeks. "Had that angel appeared," exclaims the historian, "had he offered to exterminate your foes if you would consent to the union of the church, even then, in that fatal moment, you would have rejected your safety or have deceived your God."

While they expected the descent of the tardy angel, the doors were broken with axes; and as the Turks encountered no resistance, their bloodless hands were employed in selecting and securing the multitude of their prisoners. Youth, beauty, and the appearance of wealth attracted their choice; and the right of property was decided among themselves by a prior seizure, by personal strength, and by the authority of command. In the space of an hour, the male captives were bound with cords, the females with their veils and girdles. The senators were linked with their slaves; the prelates with the porters of the church; and young men of the plebeian class with noble maids whose faces had been invisible to the sun and their nearest kindred. In this common captivity, the ranks of society were confounded; the ties of nature were cut asunder; and the inexorable soldier was careless of the father's groans, the tears of the mother, and the lamentations of the children. The loudest in their wailings were the nuns, who were torn from the altar with naked bosoms, outstretched hands, and disheveled hair; and we should piously believe that few could be tempted to prefer the vigils of the harem to those of the monastery. Of these unfortunate Greeks, of these domestic animals, whole strings were rudely driven through the streets; and as the conquerors were eager to return for more prey, their trembling pace was quickened with menaces and blows. At the same hour, a similar rapine was exercised in all the churches and monasteries, in all the palaces and habitations of the capital; nor could any place, however sacred or sequestered, protect the persons or the property of the Greeks. Above sixty thousand of this devoted people were transported from the city to the camp and fleet; exchanged or sold according to the caprice or interest of their masters; and dispersed in remote servitude through the provinces of the Ottoman empire. Among these we may notice some remarkable characters. The historian Phranza, first chamberlain and principal secretary, was involved with his family in the common lot. After suffering four months the hardships of slavery, he recovered his freedom: in the ensuing winter he ventured to Hadrianople and ransomed his wife from the *mir bashi*, or master of the horse; but his two children, in the flower of youth and beauty, had been seized for the use of Mohammed himself. The daughter of Phranza died in the seraglio, perhaps a virgin: his son, in the fifteenth year of his age, preferred death to infamy, and was stabbed by the hand of the royal lover. A deed thus inhuman cannot surely be expiated by the taste and liberality with which he released a Grecian matron and her two daughters on receiving a Latin ode from Philelphus, who had chosen a wife in that noble family. The pride or cruelty of Mohammed would have been most sensibly gratified by the capture of a Roman legate; but the dexterity of Cardinal Isidore eluded the search, and he escaped from Galata in a plebeian habit. The chain and entrance of the outward harbor was still occupied by the Italian ships of merchandise and war. They had signalized their valor in the siege: they embraced the moment of retreat while the Turkish mariners were dissipated in the pillage of the city. When they hoisted sail, the beach was covered with a suppliant and lamentable crowd; but the means of transportation were scanty: the Venetians and Genoese selected their countrymen; and, notwithstanding the fairest promises of the sultan, the inhabitants of Galata evacuated their houses and embarked with their most precious effects.

In the fall and the sack of great cities, an historian is condemned to repeat the tale of uniform calamity: the same effects must be produced by the same passions; and when those passions may be indulged without control, small, alas! is the difference between civilized and savage man. Amidst the vague exclamations of bigotry and hatred, the Turks are not accused of a wanton or immoderate effusion of Christian blood: but according to their maxims (the maxims of antiquity), the lives of the vanquished were forfeited; and the legitimate reward of the conqueror was derived from the service, the sale, or the ransom of his captives of both sexes. The wealth of Constantinople had been granted by the sultan to his victorious troops; and the rapine of an hour is more productive than the industry of years. But as no regular division was attempted of the spoil, the respective shares were not determined by merit; and the rewards of valor were stolen away by the followers of the camp, who had declined the toil and danger of the battle. The narrative of their depredations could not afford either amusement or instruction: the total amount, in the last poverty of the empire, has been valued at four millions of ducats; and of this sum a small part was the property of the Venetians, the Genoese, the Florentines, and the merchants of Ancona. Of these foreigners, the stock was improved in quick and perpetual circulation: but the riches of the Greeks were displayed in the idle ostentation of palaces and wardrobes, or deeply buried in treasures of ingots and old coin, lest it should be demanded at their hands for the defense of their country. The profanation and plunder of the monasteries and churches excited the most tragic complaints. . . . The example of sacrilege was imitated, however, from the Latin conquerors of Constantinople; and the treatment which Christ, the Virgin, and the saints had sustained from the guilty Catholic might be inflicted by the zealous Moslem on the monuments of idolatry. Perhaps, instead of joining the public clamor, a philosopher will observe that in the decline of the arts the workmanship could not be more valuable than the work, and that a fresh supply of visions and miracles would speedily be renewed by the craft of the priests and the credulity of the people. He will more seriously deplore the loss of the Byzantine libraries, which were destroyed or scattered in the general confusion: one hundred and twenty thousand manuscripts are said to have disappeared; ten volumes might be purchased for a single ducat; and the same ignominious price, too high perhaps for a shelf of theology, included the whole works of Aristotle and Homer, the noblest productions of the science and literature of ancient Greece. We may reflect with pleasure that an inestimable portion of our classic treasures was safely deposited in Italy; and that the mechanics of a German town had invented an art which derides the havoc of time and barbarism.

From the first hour of the memorable twenty-ninth of May, disorder and rapine prevailed in Constantinople, till the eighth hour of the same day; when the sultan himself passed in triumph through the gate of St. Romanus. He was attended by his viziers, bashaws, and guards, each of whom (says a Byzantine historian) was robust as Hercules, dexterous as Apollo, and equal in battle to any ten of the race of ordinary mortals. The conqueror gazed with satisfaction and wonder on the strange, though splendid, appearance of the domes and palaces, so dissimilar from the style of Oriental architecture. In the hippodrome, or *atmeidan,* his eye was attracted by the twisted column of the three serpents; and as a trial of his strength, he shattered with his iron mace or battle-axe the under jaw of one of these monsters, which in the eyes of the Turks were the idols or talismans of the city. At the principal door of St. Sophia, he alighted from his horse and entered the dome; and such was his jealous regard for that monument of his glory that on observing a zealous Moslem in the act of breaking the marble pavement, he admonished him with his cimeter that if the spoil and captives were granted to the soldiers, the public and private buildings had been reserved for the prince. By his command the metropolis of the Eastern church was transformed into a mosque: the rich and portable instruments of superstition had been removed; the crosses were thrown down; and the walls, which were covered with images and mosaics, were washed and purified and restored to a state of naked simplicity. On the same day, or on the ensuing Friday, the *muezin,* or crier, ascended the most lofty turret and proclaimed the *ezan,* or public invitation in the name of God and his prophet; the *imam* preached; and Mohammed the Second performed the *namaz* of prayer and thanksgiving on the great altar where the Christian mysteries had so lately been celebrated before the last of the Caesars. From St. Sophia he proceeded to the august but desolate mansion of a hundred successors of the great Constantine, but which in a few hours had been stripped of the pomp of royalty. A melancholy reflection on the vicissitudes of human greatness forced itself on his mind; and he repeated an elegant distich of Persian poetry: "The spider has wove his web in the Imperial palace; and the owl hath sung her watch-song on the towers of Afrasiab."

Yet his mind was not satisfied, nor did the victory seem complete, till he was informed of the fate of Constantine; whether he had escaped, or been made prisoner, or had fallen in the battle. Two Janizaries claimed the honor and reward of his death: the body, under a heap of slain, was discovered by the golden eagles embroidered on his shoes; the Greeks acknowledged with tears the head of their late emperor; and after exposing the bloody trophy, Mohammed bestowed on his rival the honors of a decent funeral.[†]

Constantinople had been left naked and desolate, without a prince or a people. But she could not be despoiled of the incomparable situation which marks her for the metropolis of a great empire; and the genius of the place will ever triumph over the accidents of time and fortune. Boursa and Hadrianople, the ancient seats of the Ottomans, sunk into provincial towns; and Mohammed the Second established his own residence, and that of his successors, on the same commanding spot which had been chosen by Constantine.[†]

The importance of Constantinople was felt and magnified in its loss: the pontificate of Nicholas the Fifth, however peaceful and prosperous, was dishonored by the fall of the Eastern empire; and the grief and terror of the Latins revived, or seemed to revive, the old enthusiasm of the crusades. . . . Had every breast glowed with the same ardor; had the union of the Christians corresponded with their bravery; had every country, from Sweden to Naples, supplied a just proportion of cavalry and infantry, of men and money, it is indeed probable that Constantinople would have been delivered, and that the Turks might have been chased beyond the Hellespont or the Euphrates. But the secretary of the emperor, who composed every epistle and attended every meeting, Aeneas Sylvius, a statesman and orator, describes from his own experience the repugnant state and spirit of Christendom. "It is a body," says he, "without a head; a republic without laws or magistrates. The pope and the emperor may shine as lofty titles, as splendid images; but *they* are unable to command, and none are willing to obey: every state has a separate prince, and every prince has a separate interest. What eloquence could unite so many discordant and hostile powers under the same standard? Could they be assembled in arms, who would dare to assume the office of general? What order could be maintained?—what military discipline? Who would undertake to feed such an enormous multitude? Who would understand their various languages, or direct their stranger and incompatible manners? What mortal could reconcile the English with the French, Genoa with Arragon, the Germans with the natives of Hungary and Bohemia? If a small number enlisted in the holy war, they must be overthrown by the infidels; if many, by their own weight and confusion." Yet the same Aeneas, when he was raised to the papal throne under the name of Pius the Second, devoted his life to the prosecution of the Turkish war [A.D. 1459]. In the council of Mantua he excited some sparks of a false or feeble enthusiasm; but when the pontiff appeared at Ancona to embark in person with the troops, engagements vanished in excuses [A.D. 1464]; a precise day was adjourned to an indefinite term; and his effective army consisted of some German pilgrims, whom he was obliged to disband with indulgences and arms. Regardless of futurity, his successors and the powers of Italy were involved in the schemes of present and domestic ambition; and the distance or proximity of each object determined in their eyes its apparent magnitude. A more enlarged view of their interest would have taught them to maintain a defensive and naval war against the common enemy; and the support of [the] brave Albanians might have prevented the subsequent invasion of the kingdom of Naples. The siege and sack of Otranto by the Turks diffused a general consternation; and Pope Sixtus was preparing to fly beyond the Alps, when the storm was instantly dispelled by the death of Mohammed the Second, in the fifty-first year of his age [A.D. 1481]. His lofty genius aspired to the conquest of Italy: he was possessed of a strong city and a capacious harbor; and the same reign might have been decorated with the trophies of the NEW and the ANCIENT ROME.

CHAPTER LXIX

STATE OF ROME FROM THE TWELFTH CENTURY

State of Rome from the twelfth century. • Temporal dominion of the popes. • Seditions of the city. • The senators. • Pride of the Romans. • Their wars. • They are deprived of the election and presence of the popes, who retire to Avignon. • The Jubilee.[†]

In the first ages of the decline and fall of the Roman empire, our eye is invariably fixed on the royal city, which had given laws to the fairest portion of the globe. We contemplate her fortunes, at first with admiration, at length with pity, always with attention, and when that attention is diverted from the capital to the provinces, they are considered as so many branches which have been successively severed from the Imperial trunk. The foundation of a second Rome on the shores of the Bosphorus has compelled the historian to follow the successors of Constantine; and our curiosity has been tempted to visit the most remote countries of Europe and Asia to explore the causes and the authors of the long decay of the Byzantine monarchy. By the conquest of Justinian, we have been recalled to the banks of the Tiber, to the deliverance of the ancient metropolis; but that deliverance was a change, or perhaps an aggravation, of servitude. Rome had been already stripped of her trophies, her gods, and her Caesars; nor was the Gothic dominion more inglorious and oppressive than the tyranny of the Greeks. In the eighth century of the Christian era, a religious quarrel, the worship of images, provoked the Romans to assert their independence: their bishop became the temporal as well as the spiritual father of a free people; and of the Western empire, which was restored by Charlemagne, the title and image still decorate the singular constitution of modern Germany [that is, the Holy Roman Empire, which was finally extinguished by Napoleon in A.D. 1806]. The name of Rome must yet command our involuntary respect: the climate (whatsoever may be its influence) was no longer the same: the purity of blood had been contaminated through a thousand channels; but the venerable aspect of her ruins, and the memory of past greatness, rekindled a spark of the national character. The darkness of the middle ages exhibits some scenes not unworthy of our notice. Nor shall I dismiss the present work till I have reviewed the state and revolutions of the ROMAN CITY, which acquiesced under the absolute dominion of the popes about the same time that Constantinople was enslaved by the Turkish arms.

In the beginning of the twelfth century, the era of the first crusade, Rome was revered by the Latins as the metropolis of the world, as the throne of the pope and the emperor, who from the eternal city derived their title, their honors, and the right or exercise of temporal dominion. After so long an interruption, it may not be useless to repeat that the successors of Charlemagne and the Othos were chosen beyond the Rhine in a national diet; but that these princes were content with the humble names of kings of Germany and Italy, till they had passed the Alps and the Apennine to seek their Imperial crown [from the pope] on the banks of the Tiber. . . . The names of Caesar and Augustus, the laws of Constantine and Justinian, the example of Charlemagne and Otho, established the supreme dominion of the emperors: their title and image was engraved on the papal coins; and their jurisdiction was marked by the sword of justice, which they delivered to the praefect of the city. But every Roman prejudice was awakened by the name, the language, and the manners of a Barbarian lord. The Caesars of Saxony or Franconia were the chiefs of a feudal aristocracy; nor could they exercise the discipline of civil and military power which alone secures the obedience of a distant people impatient of servitude, though perhaps incapable of freedom. Once, and once only, in his life, each emperor, with an army of Teutonic vassals, descended from the Alps. I have described the peaceful order of his entry and coronation; but that order was commonly disturbed by the clamor and sedition of the Romans, who encountered their sovereign as a foreign invader: his departure was always speedy, and often shameful; and in the absence of a long reign, his authority was insulted and his name was forgotten. The progress of independence in Germany and Italy undermined the foundations of the Imperial sovereignty, and the triumph of the popes was the deliverance of Rome.

Of her two sovereigns, the emperor had precariously reigned by the right of conquest; but the authority of the pope was founded on the soft, though more solid, basis of opinion and habit. The removal of a foreign influence restored and endeared the shepherd to his flock. Instead of the arbitrary or venal nomination of a German court, the vicar of Christ was freely chosen by the college of cardinals, most of whom were either natives or inhabitants of the city. The applause of the magistrates and people confirmed his election, and the ecclesiastical power that was obeyed in Sweden and Britain had been ultimately derived from the suffrage of the Romans. The same suffrage gave a prince, as well as a pontiff, to the capital. It was universally believed that Constantine had invested the popes with the temporal dominion of Rome; and the boldest civilians, the most profane skeptics, were satisfied with disputing the right of the emperor and the validity of his gift. The truth of the fact, the authenticity of his donation, was deeply rooted in the ignorance and tradition of four centuries; and the fabulous origin was lost in the real and permanent effects. The name of *Dominus* or Lord was inscribed on the coin of the bishops: their title was acknowledged by acclamations and oaths of allegiance, and with the free, or reluctant, consent of the German Caesars, they had long exercised a supreme or subordinate jurisdiction over the city and patrimony of St. Peter. The reign of the popes, which gratified the prejudices, was not incompatible with the liberties, of Rome; and a more critical inquiry would have revealed a still nobler source of their power; the gratitude of a nation, whom they had rescued from the heresy and oppression of the Greek tyrant. In an age of superstition, it should seem that the union of the royal and sacerdotal characters would mutually fortify each other; and that the keys of Paradise would be the surest pledge of earthly obedience. The sanctity of the office might indeed be degraded by the personal vices of the man. But the scandals of the tenth century were obliterated by the austere and more dangerous virtues of Gregory the Seventh and his successors; and in the ambitious contests which they maintained for the rights of the church, their sufferings or their success must equally tend to increase the popular veneration. They sometimes wandered in poverty and exile, the victims of persecution; and the apostolic zeal with which they offered themselves to martyrdom must engage the favor and sympathy of every Catholic breast. And sometimes, thundering from the Vatican, they created, judged, and deposed the kings of the world; nor could the proudest Roman be disgraced by submitting to a priest whose feet were kissed and whose stirrup was held by the successors of Charlemagne. Even the temporal interest of the city should have protected in peace and honor the residence of the popes; from whence a vain and lazy people derived the greatest part of their subsistence and riches. The fixed revenue of the popes was probably impaired; many of the old patrimonial estates, both in Italy and the provinces, had been invaded by sacrilegious hands; nor could the loss be compensated by the claim, rather than the possession, of the more ample gifts of Pepin and his descendants. But the Vatican and Capitol were nourished by the incessant and increasing swarms of pilgrims and suppliants: the pale of Christianity was enlarged, and the pope and cardinals were overwhelmed by the judgment of ecclesiastical and secular causes. A new jurisprudence had established in the Latin church the right and practice of appeals; and from the North and West the bishops and abbots were invited or summoned to solicit, to complain, to accuse, or to justify before the threshold of the apostles.[†]

Such powerful motives should have firmly attached the voluntary and pious obedience of the Roman people to their spiritual and temporal father. But the operation of prejudice and interest is often disturbed by the sallies of ungovernable passion. The Indian who fells the tree that he may gather the fruit, and the Arab who plunders the caravans of commerce, are actuated by the same impulse of savage nature, which overlooks the future in the present and relinquishes for momentary rapine the long and secure possession of the most important blessings. And it was thus that the shrine of St. Peter was profaned by the thoughtless Romans, who pillaged the offerings and wounded the pilgrims without computing the number and value of similar visits which they prevented by their inhospitable sacrilege. Even the influence of superstition is fluctuating and precarious; and the slave whose reason is subdued will often be delivered by his avarice or pride. A credulous devotion for the fables and oracles of the priesthood most powerfully acts on the mind of a barbarian; yet such a mind is the least capable of preferring imagination to sense, of sacrificing to a distant motive, to an invisible, perhaps an ideal, object, the appetites and interests of the present world. In the vigor of health and youth, his practice will perpetually contradict his belief; till the pressure of age or sickness or calamity awakens his terrors and compels him to satisfy the double debt of piety and remorse. I have already observed that the modern times of religious indifference are the most favorable to the peace and security of the clergy. Under the reign of superstition, they had much to hope from the ignorance, and much to fear from the violence, of mankind. The wealth whose constant increase must have rendered them the sole proprietors of the earth was alternately bestowed by the repentant father and plundered by the rapacious son: their persons were adored or violated; and the same idol, by the hands of the same votaries, was placed on the altar or trampled in the dust. In the feudal system of Europe, arms were the title of distinction and the measure of allegiance; and amidst their tumult, the still voice of law and reason was seldom heard or obeyed. The turbulent Romans disdained the yoke and insulted the impotence of their bishop: nor would his education or character allow him to exercise, with decency or effect, the power of the sword. The motives of his election and the frailties of his life were exposed to their familiar observation; and proximity must diminish the reverence which his name and his decrees impressed on a barbarous world. This difference has not escaped the notice of our philosophic historian [David Hume]: "Though the name and authority of the court of Rome were so terrible in the remote countries of Europe, which were sunk in profound ignorance and were entirely unacquainted with its character and conduct, the pope was so little revered at home that his inveterate enemies surrounded the gates of Rome itself, and even controlled his government in that city; and the ambassadors, who from a distant extremity of Europe, carried to him the humble, or rather abject, submissions of the greatest potentate of the age found the utmost difficulty to make their way to him and to throw themselves at his feet."

Since the primitive times, the wealth of the popes was exposed to envy, their powers to opposition, and their persons to violence. But the long hostility of the mitre and the crown increased the numbers and inflamed the passions of their enemies. The deadly factions of the Guelphs and Ghibelines, so fatal to Italy, could never be embraced with truth or constancy by the Romans, the subjects and adversaries both of the bishop and emperor; but their support was solicited by both parties, and they alternately displayed in their banners the keys of St. Peter and the German eagle. Gregory the Seventh, who may be adored or detested as the founder of the papal monarchy, was driven from Rome and died in exile at Salerno. Six-and-thirty of his successors [A.D. 1086–1305], till their retreat to Avignon, maintained an un-equal contest with the Romans: their age and dignity were often violated; and the churches, in the solemn rites of religion, were polluted with sedition and murder. A repetition of such capricious brutality, without connection or design, would be tedious and disgusting; and I shall content myself with some events of the twelfth century, which represent the state of the popes and the city.... I cannot forget the sufferings of two pontiffs of [that] age, the second and third of the name of Lucius. The former, as he ascended in battle array to assault the Capitol, was struck on the temple by a stone, and expired in a few days [A.D. 1144]. The latter was severely wounded in the person of his servants [A.D. 1181–1185]. In a civil commotion, several of his priests had been made prisoners; and the inhuman Romans, reserving one as a guide for his brethren, put out their eyes, crowned them with ludicrous mitres, mounted them on asses with their faces towards the tail, and extorted an oath that in this wretched condition they should offer themselves as a lesson to the head of the church. Hope or fear, lassitude or remorse, the characters of the men and the circumstances of the times might sometimes obtain an interval of peace and obedience; and the pope was restored with joyful acclamations to the Lateran or Vatican, from whence he had been driven with threats and violence. But the root of mischief was deep and perennial; and a momentary calm was preceded and followed by such tempests as had almost sunk the bark of St. Peter. Rome continually presented the aspect of war and discord: the churches and palaces were fortified and assaulted by the factions and families; and after giving peace to Europe, Calistus the Second alone had resolution and power to prohibit the use of private arms in the metropolis [A.D. 1119–1124]. Among the nations who revered the apostolic throne, the tumults of Rome provoked a general indignation; and in a letter to his disciple Eugenius the Third, St. Bernard, with the sharpness of his wit and zeal, has stigmatized the vices of the rebellious people. "Who is ignorant," says the monk of Clairvaux, "of the vanity and arrogance of the Romans? a nation nursed in sedition, untractable, and scorning to obey, unless they are too feeble to resist. When they promise to serve, they aspire to reign; if they swear allegiance, they watch the opportunity of revolt; yet they vent their discontent in loud clamors if your doors or your counsels are shut against them. Dexterous in mischief, they have never learned the science of doing good. Odious to earth and Heaven, impious to God, seditious among themselves, jealous of their neighbors, inhuman to strangers, they love no one, by no one are they beloved; and while they wish to inspire fear, they live in base and continual apprehension. They will not submit; they know not how to govern; faithless to their superiors, intolerable to their equals, ungrateful to their benefactors, and alike impudent in their demands and their refusals. Lofty in promise, poor in execution; adulation and calumny, perfidy and treason, are the familiar arts of their policy." Surely this dark portrait is not colored by the pencil of Christian charity; yet the features, however harsh or ugly, express a lively resemblance of the Roman of the twelfth century.[†]

Under the reign of Hadrian, when the empire extended from the Euphrates to the Ocean, from Mount Atlas to the Grampian hills, a fanciful historian amused the Romans with the picture of their ancient wars. "There was a time," says Florus, "when Tibur and Praeneste, our summer retreats, were the objects of hostile vows in the Capitol, when we dreaded the shades of the Arician groves, when we could triumph without a blush over the nameless villages of the Sabines and Latins, and even Corioli could afford a title not unworthy of a victorious general." The pride of his contemporaries was gratified by the contrast of the past and the present: they would have been humbled by the prospect of futurity; by the prediction that after a thousand years Rome, despoiled of empire and contracted to her primeval limits, would renew the same hostilities, on the same ground which was then decorated with her villas and gardens. The adjacent territory on either side of the Tiber was always claimed, and sometimes possessed, as the patrimony of St. Peter; but the barons assumed a lawless independence, and the cities too faithfully copied the revolt and discord of the metropolis. In the twelfth and thirteenth centuries the Romans incessantly labored to reduce or destroy the contumacious vassals of the church and senate; and if their headstrong and selfish ambition was moderated by the pope, he often encouraged their zeal by the alliance of his spiritual arms. Their warfare was that of the first consuls and dictators, who were taken from the plough. They assembled in arms at the foot of the Capitol; sallied from the gates, plundered or burnt the harvests of their neighbors, engaged in tumultuary conflict, and returned home after an expedition of fifteen or twenty days. Their sieges were tedious and unskillful: in the use of victory, they indulged the meaner passions of jealousy and revenge; and instead of adopting the valor, they trampled on the misfortunes of their adversaries. The captives, in their shirts, with a rope round their necks, solicited their pardon: the fortifications and even the buildings of the rival cities were demolished, and the inhabitants were scattered in the adjacent villages. It was thus that the seats of the cardinal bishops, Porto, Ostia, Albanum, Tusculum, Præneste, and Tibur or Tivoli, were successively overthrown by the ferocious hostility of the Romans. Of these, Porto and Ostia, the two keys of the Tiber, are still vacant and desolate: the marshy and unwholesome banks are peopled with herds of buffaloes, and the river is lost to every purpose of navigation and trade. The hills, which afford a shady retirement from the autumnal heats, have again smiled with the blessings of peace; Frescati has arisen near the ruins of Tusculum; Tibur or Tivoli has resumed the honors of a city, and the meaner towns of Albano and Palestrina are decorated with the villas of the cardinals and princes of Rome.... Had the policy of the senate and the discipline of the legions been restored with the Capitol, the divided condition of Italy would have offered the fairest opportunity of a second conquest. But in arms the modern Romans were not *above*, and in arts they were far *below*, the common level of the neighboring republics. Nor was their warlike spirit of any long continuance; after some irregular sallies, they subsided in the national apathy, in the neglect of military institutions, and in the disgraceful and dangerous use of foreign mercenaries.

Ambition is a weed of quick and early vegetation in the vineyard of Christ. Under the first Christian princes, the chair of St. Peter was disputed by the votes, the venality, the violence of a popular election: the sanctuaries of Rome were polluted with blood; and from the third to the twelfth century, the church was distracted by the mischief of frequent schisms. As long as the final appeal was determined by the civil magistrate, these mischiefs were transient and local: the merits were tried by equity or favor; nor could the unsuccessful competitor long disturb the triumph of his rival. But after the emperors had been divested of their prerogatives, after a maxim had been established that the vicar of Christ is amenable to no earthly tribunal, each vacancy of the holy see might involve Christendom in controversy and war. The claims of the cardinals and inferior clergy, of the nobles and people, were vague and litigious: the freedom of choice was overruled by the tumults of a city that no longer owned or obeyed a superior. On the decease of a pope, two factions proceeded in different churches to a double election: the number and weight of votes, the priority of time, the merit of the candidates might balance each other: the most respectable of the clergy were divided; and the distant princes who bowed before the spiritual throne could not distinguish the spurious from the legitimate idol. The emperors were often the authors of the schism, from the political motive of opposing a friendly to a hostile pontiff; and each of the competitors was reduced to suffer the insults of his enemies, who were not awed by conscience, and to purchase the support of his adherents, who were instigated by avarice or ambition. A peaceful and perpetual succession was ascertained by Alexander the Third, who finally abolished the tumultuary votes of the clergy and people and defined the right of election in the sole college of cardinals. The three orders of bishops, priests, and deacons were assimilated to each other by this important privilege [A.D. 1179]; the parochial clergy of Rome obtained the first rank in the hierarchy: they were indifferently chosen among the nations of Christendom; and the possession of the richest benefices, of the most important bishoprics, was not incompatible with their title and office. The senators of the Catholic church, the coadjutors and legates of the supreme pontiff, were robed in purple, the symbol of martyrdom or royalty; they claimed a proud equality with kings; and their dignity was enhanced by the smallness of their number, which, till the reign of Leo the Tenth, seldom exceeded twenty or twenty-five persons. By this wise regulation, all doubt and scandal were removed, and the root of schism was so effectually destroyed that in a period of six hundred years a double choice has only once divided the unity of the sacred college. But as the concurrence of two thirds of the votes had been made necessary, the election was often delayed by the private interest and passions of the cardinals; and while they prolonged their independent reign, the Christian world was left destitute of a head. A vacancy of almost three years had preceded the elevation of George the Tenth, who resolved to prevent the future abuse; and his bull, after some opposition, has been consecrated in the code of the canon law [A.D. 1274]. Nine days are allowed for the obsequies of the deceased pope and the arrival of the absent cardinals; on the tenth, they are imprisoned, each with one domestic, in a common apartment or *conclave*, without any separation of walls or curtains: a small window is reserved for the introduction of necessaries; but the door is locked on both sides and guarded by the magistrates of the city, to seclude them from all correspondence with the world. If the election be not consummated in three days, the luxury of their table is contracted to a single dish at dinner and supper; and after the eighth day, they are reduced to a scanty allowance of bread, water, and wine. During the vacancy of the holy see, the cardinals are prohibited from touching the revenues or assuming, unless in some rare emergency, the government of the church: all agreements and promises among the electors are formally annulled; and their integrity is fortified by their solemn oath and the prayers of the Catholics. Some articles of inconvenient or superfluous rigor have been gradually relaxed, but the principle of confinement is vigorous and entire: they are still urged, by the personal motives of health and freedom, to accelerate the moment of their deliverance; and the improvement of ballot or secret votes has wrapped the struggles of the conclave in the silky veil of charity and politeness. By these institutions the Romans were excluded from the election of their prince and bishop; and in the fever of wild and precarious liberty, they seemed insensible of the loss of this inestimable privilege.[†]

Had the election been always held in the Vatican, the rights of the senate and people would not have been violated with impunity. But the Romans forgot, and were forgotten, in the absence of the successors of Gregory the Seventh, who did not keep as a divine precept their ordinary residence in the city and diocese. The care of that diocese was less important than the government of the universal church; nor could the popes delight in a city in which their authority was always opposed, and their person was often endangered. From the persecution of the emperors and the wars of Italy, they escaped beyond the Alps into the hospitable bosom of France.

[*The popes had not infrequently sought refuge in a variety of cities, but, after the death of Pope Boniface VIII (A.D. 1303) and the nine-month pontificate of Benedict XI, Clement V is elected (A.D. 1305). A more permanent transfer of residence ensues.*]

The cardinals of both parties were soon astonished by a summons to attend him beyond the Alps; from whence, as they soon discovered, they must never hope to return. He was engaged, by promise and affection, to prefer the residence of France; and after dragging his court through Poitou and Gascony, and devouring by his expense the cities and convents on the road, he finally reposed at Avignon [A.D. 1308], which flourished above seventy years the seat of the Roman pontiff and the metropolis of Christendom. . . . Under the shadow of a French monarchy, amidst an obedient people, the popes enjoyed an honorable and tranquil state, to which they long had been strangers: but Italy deplored their absence; and Rome, in solitude and poverty, might repent of the ungovernable freedom which had driven from the Vatican the successor of St. Peter. Her repentance was tardy and fruitless: after the death of the old members, the sacred college was filled with French cardinals, who beheld Rome and Italy with abhorrence and contempt, and perpetuated a series of national and even provincial popes, attached by the most indissoluble ties to their native country.

The progress of industry had produced and enriched the Italian republics: the era of their liberty is the most flourishing period of population and agriculture, of manufactures and commerce; and their mechanic labors were gradually refined into the arts of elegance and genius. But the position of Rome was less favorable, the territory less fruitful: the character of the inhabitants was debased by indolence and elated by pride; and they fondly conceived that the tribute of subjects must forever nourish the metropolis of the church and empire. This prejudice was encouraged in some degree by the resort of pilgrims to the shrines of the apostles; and the last legacy of the popes, the institution of the HOLY YEAR [A.D. 1300], was not less beneficial to the people than to the clergy. Since the loss of Palestine, the gift of plenary indulgences, which had been applied to the crusades, remained without an object; and the most valuable treasure of the church was sequestered above eight years from public circulation. A new channel was opened by the diligence of Boniface the Eighth, who reconciled the vices of ambition and avarice; and the pope had sufficient learning to recollect and revive the secular games which were celebrated in Rome at the conclusion of every century. To sound without danger the depth of popular credulity, a sermon was seasonably pronounced, a report was artfully scattered, some aged witnesses were produced; and on the first of January of the year thirteen hundred, the church of St. Peter was crowded with the faithful, who demanded the customary indulgence of the holy time. The pontiff, who watched and irritated their devout impatience, was soon persuaded by ancient testimony of the justice of their claim; and he proclaimed a plenary absolution to all Catholics who, in the course of that year and at every similar period, should respectfully visit the apostolic churches of St. Peter and St. Paul. The welcome sound was propagated through Christendom; and at first from the nearest provinces of Italy, and at length from the remote kingdoms of Hungary and Britain, the highways were thronged with a swarm of pilgrims who sought to expiate their sins in a journey, however costly or laborious, which was exempt from the perils of military service. All exceptions of rank or sex, of age or infirmity, were forgotten in the common transport; and in the streets and churches many persons were trampled to death by the eagerness of devotion. The calculation of their numbers could not be easy nor accurate; and they have probably been magnified by a dexterous clergy, well apprised of the contagion of example: yet we are assured by a judicious historian who assisted at the ceremony that Rome was never replenished with less than two hundred thousand strangers; and another spectator has fixed at two millions the total concourse of the year. A trifling oblation from each individual would accumulate a royal treasure; and two priests stood night and day, with rakes in their hands, to collect without counting the heaps of gold and silver that were poured on the altar of St. Paul. It was fortunately a season of peace and plenty; and if forage was scarce, if inns and lodgings were extravagantly dear, an inexhaustible supply of bread and wine, of meat and fish, was provided by the policy of Boniface and the venal hospitality of the Romans. From a city without trade or industry, all casual riches will speedily evaporate: but the avarice and envy of the next generation solicited Clement the Sixth to anticipate the distant period of the century. The gracious pontiff complied with their wishes; afforded Rome this poor consolation for his loss; and justified the change by the name and practice of the Mosaic Jubilee. His summons was obeyed; and the number, zeal, and liberality of the pilgrims did not yield to the primitive festival [A.D. 1350]. But they encountered the triple scourge of war, pestilence, and famine: many wives and virgins were violated in the castles of Italy; and many strangers were pillaged or murdered by the savage Romans, no longer moderated by the presence of their bishops. To the impatience of the popes we may ascribe the successive reduction to fifty, thirty-three, and twenty-five years; although the second of these terms is commensurate with the life of Christ. The profusion of indulgences, the revolt of the Protestants, and the decline of superstition have much diminished the value of the Jubilee; yet even the nineteenth and last festival was a year of pleasure and profit to the Romans; and a philosophic smile will not disturb the triumph of the priest or the happiness of the people.[†]

CHAPTER LXX

FINAL SETTLEMENT OF THE ECCLESIASTICAL STATE

Character and coronation of Petrarch. • Restoration of the freedom and government of Rome by the tribune Rienzi. • His virtues and vices, his expulsion and death. • Return of the popes from Avignon. • Great schism of the West. • Reunion of the Latin church. • Last struggles of Roman liberty. • Statutes of Rome. • Final settlement of the ecclesiastical state.

In the apprehension of modern times, Petrarch [A.D. 1304–1374] is the Italian songster of Laura and love. In the harmony of his Tuscan rhymes, Italy applauds, or rather adores, the father of her lyric poetry; and his verse, or at least his name, is repeated by the enthusiasm or affectation of amorous sensibility. Whatever may be the private taste of a stranger, his slight and superficial knowledge should humbly acquiesce in the judgment of a learned nation; yet I may hope or presume that the Italians do not compare the tedious uniformity of sonnets and elegies with the sublime compositions of their epic muse, the original wildness of Dante, the regular beauties of Tasso, and the boundless variety of the incomparable Ariosto. The merits of the lover I am still less qualified to appreciate: nor am I deeply interested in a metaphysical passion for a nymph so shadowy that her existence has been questioned; for a matron so prolific that she was delivered of eleven legitimate children while her amorous swain sighed and sung at the fountain of Vaucluse. But in the eyes of Petrarch and those of his graver contemporaries, his love was a sin, and Italian verse a frivolous amusement. His Latin works of philosophy, poetry, and eloquence established his serious reputation, which was soon diffused from Avignon over France and Italy: his friends and disciples were multiplied in every city; and if the ponderous volume of his writings be now abandoned to a long repose, our gratitude must applaud the man who by precept and example revived the spirit and study of the Augustan age. From his earliest youth, Petrarch aspired to the poetic crown. The academical honors of the three faculties had introduced a royal degree of master or doctor in the art of poetry; and the title of poet-laureate, which custom rather than vanity perpetuates in the English court, was first invented by the Caesars of Germany. In the musical games of antiquity, a prize was bestowed on the victor: the belief that Virgil and Horace had been crowned in the Capitol inflamed the emulation of a Latin bard; and the laurel was endeared to the lover by a verbal resemblance with the name of his mistress. The value of either object was enhanced by the difficulties of the pursuit; and if the virtue or prudence of Laura was inexorable, he enjoyed, and might boast of enjoying, the nymph of poetry. His vanity was not of the most delicate kind, since he applauds the success of his own *labors;* his name was popular; his friends were active; the open or secret opposition of envy and prejudice was surmounted by the dexterity of patient merit. In the thirty-sixth year of his age, he was solicited to accept the object of his wishes; and on the same day, in the solitude of Vaucluse, he received a similar and solemn invitation from the senate of Rome and the university of Paris. The learning of a theological school and the ignorance of a lawless city were alike unqualified to bestow the ideal though immortal wreath which genius may obtain from the free applause of the public and of posterity: but the candidate dismissed this troublesome reflection; and after some moments of complacency and suspense, preferred the summons of the metropolis of the world.

The ceremony of his coronation was performed in the Capitol, by his friend and patron the supreme magistrate of the republic [April 8, A.D. 1341]. Twelve patrician youths were arrayed in scarlet; six representatives of the most illustrious families, in green robes, with garlands of flowers, accompanied the procession; in the midst of the princes and nobles, the senator, count of Anguillara, a kinsman of the Colonna, assumed his throne; and at the voice of a herald Petrarch arose. After discoursing on a text of Virgil and thrice repeating his vows for the prosperity of Rome, he knelt before the throne and received from the senator a laurel crown, with a more precious declaration, "This is the reward of merit." The people shouted, "Long life to the Capitol and the poet!" A sonnet in praise of Rome was accepted as the effusion of genius and gratitude; and after the whole procession had visited the Vatican, the profane wreath was suspended before the shrine of St. Peter. In the act or diploma which was presented to Petrarch, the title and prerogatives of poet-laureate are revived in the Capitol, after the lapse of thirteen hundred years; and he receives the perpetual privilege of wearing, at his choice, a crown of laurel, ivy, or myrtle, of assuming the poetic habit, and of teaching, disputing, interpreting, and composing in all places whatsoever, and on all subjects of literature. The grant was ratified by the authority of the senate and people; and the character of citizen was the recompense of his affection for the Roman name. They did him honor, but they did him justice. In the familiar society of Cicero and Livy, he had imbibed the ideas of an ancient patriot; and his ardent fancy kindled every idea to a sentiment, and every sentiment to a passion. The aspect of the seven hills and their majestic ruins confirmed these lively impressions; and he loved a country by whose liberal spirit he had been crowned and adopted. The poverty and debasement of Rome excited the indignation and pity of her grateful son; he dissembled the faults of his fellow-citizens; applauded with partial fondness the last of their heroes and matrons; and in the remembrance of the past, in the hopes of the future, was pleased to forget the miseries of the present time.

[*The vicissitudes of Nicholas Rienzi Gabrini (1347–1354): a commoner, Rienzi briefly brings Rome's nobles to heel and attempts, under his "tribunate" (May 20–December 15, A.D. 1347), to restore the Roman republic. Rienzi falls, flees, is imprisoned, eventually returns, and is finally assassinated (September 8, A.D. 1354).*]

The first and most generous wish of Petrarch was the restoration of a free republic; but after the exile and death of his plebeian hero, he turned his eyes from the tribune to the king of the Romans. The Capitol was yet stained with the blood of Rienzi when Charles the Fourth descended from the Alps to obtain the Italian and Imperial crowns. In his passage through Milan he received the visit and repaid the flattery of the poet-laureate; accepted a medal of Augustus; and promised, without a smile, to imitate the founder of the Roman monarchy [A.D. 1355]. A false application of the name and maxims of antiquity was the source of the hopes and disappointments of Petrarch; yet he could not overlook the difference of times and characters; the immeasurable distance between the first Caesars and a Bohemian prince who by the favor of the clergy had been elected the titular head of the German aristocracy.

Instead of restoring to Rome her glory and her provinces, he had bound himself, by a secret treaty with the pope, to evacuate the city on the day of his coronation; and his shameful retreat was pursued by the reproaches of the patriot bard.

After the loss of liberty and empire, his third and more humble wish was to reconcile the shepherd with his flock; to recall the Roman bishop to his ancient and peculiar diocese. In the fervor of youth, with the authority of age, Petrarch addressed his exhortations to five successive popes, and his eloquence was always inspired by the enthusiasm of sentiment and the freedom of language. The son of a citizen of Florence invariably preferred the country of his birth to that of his education; and Italy, in his eyes, was the queen and garden of the world. Amidst her domestic factions, she was doubtless superior to France both in art and science, in wealth and politeness; but the difference could scarcely support the epithet of barbarous, which he promiscuously bestows on the countries beyond the Alps. Avignon, the mystic Babylon, the sink of vice and corruption, was the object of his hatred and contempt; but he forgets that her scandalous vices were not the growth of the soil, and that in every residence they would adhere to the power and luxury of the papal court. He confesses that the successor of St. Peter is the bishop of the universal church; yet it was not on the banks of the Rhone but of the Tiber that the apostle had fixed his everlasting throne; and while every city in the Christian world was blessed with a bishop, the metropolis alone was desolate and forlorn. Since the removal of the holy see, the sacred buildings of the Lateran and the Vatican, their altars and their saints, were left in a state of poverty and decay; and Rome was often painted under the image of a disconsolate matron, as if the wandering husband could be reclaimed by the homely portrait of the age and infirmities of his weeping spouse. But the cloud which hung over the seven hills would be dispelled by the presence of their lawful sovereign: eternal fame, the prosperity of Rome, and the peace of Italy would be the recompense of the pope who should dare to embrace this generous resolution. Of the five whom Petrarch exhorted, the three first, John the Twenty-second, Benedict the Twelfth, and Clement the Sixth, were importuned or amused by the boldness of the orator; but the memorable change which had been attempted by Urban the Fifth was finally accomplished by Gregory the Eleventh. The execution of their design was opposed by weighty and almost insuperable obstacles. A king of France, who has deserved the epithet of wise, was unwilling to release them from a local dependence: the cardinals, for the most part his subjects, were attached to the language, manners, and climate of Avignon; to their stately palaces; above all, to the wines of Burgundy. In their eyes, Italy was foreign or hostile; and they reluctantly embarked at Marseilles as if they had been sold or banished into the land of the Saracens. Urban the Fifth resided three years in the Vatican with safety and honor [A.D. 1367–1370]: his sanctity was protected by a guard of two thousand horse; and the king of Cyprus, the queen of Naples, and the emperors of the East and West devoutly saluted their common father in the chair of St. Peter. But the joy of Petrarch and the Italians was soon turned into grief and indignation. Some reasons of public or private moment, his own impatience or the prayers of the cardinals, recalled Urban to France; and the approaching election was saved from the tyrannic patriotism of the Romans. The powers of Heaven were interested in their cause: Bridget of Sweden, a saint and pilgrim, disapproved the return and foretold the death of Urban the Fifth: the migration of Gregory the Eleventh [January 17, A.D. 1377] was encouraged by St. Catharine of Sienna, the spouse of Christ and ambassadress of the Florentines; and the popes themselves, the great masters of human credulity, appear to have listened to these visionary females. Yet those celestial admonitions were supported by some arguments of temporal policy. The residents of Avignon had been invaded by hostile violence: at the head of thirty thousand robbers, a hero had extorted ransom and absolution from the vicar of Christ and the sacred college; and the maxim of the French warriors, to spare the people and plunder the church, was a new heresy of the most dangerous import. While the pope was driven from Avignon, he was strenuously invited to Rome. The senate and people acknowledged him as their lawful sovereign, and laid at his feet the keys of the gates, the bridges, and the fortresses; of the quarter at least beyond the Tiber. But this loyal offer was accompanied by a declaration that they could no longer suffer the scandal and calamity of his absence; and that his obstinacy would finally provoke them to revive and assert the primitive right of election. The abbot of Mount Cassin had been consulted whether he would accept the triple crown from the clergy and people:

"I am a citizen of Rome," replied that venerable ecclesiastic, "and my first law is the voice of my country."

If superstition will interpret an untimely death [March 27, A.D. 1378], if the merit of counsels be judged from the event, the heavens may seem to frown on a measure of such apparent season and propriety. Gregory the Eleventh did not survive above fourteen months his return to the Vatican; and his decease was followed by the great schism of the West, which distracted the Latin church above forty years. The sacred college was then composed of twenty-two cardinals: six of these had remained at Avignon; eleven Frenchmen, one Spaniard, and four Italians entered the conclave in the usual form. Their choice was not yet limited to the purple; and their unanimous votes acquiesced in the archbishop of Bari, a subject of Naples, conspicuous for his zeal and learning, who ascended the throne of St. Peter under the name of Urban the Sixth [April 9, A.D. 1378]. The epistle of the sacred college affirms his free and regular election, which had been inspired, as usual, by the Holy Ghost; he was adored, invested, and crowned with the customary rites; his temporal authority was obeyed at Rome and Avignon, and his ecclesiastical supremacy was acknowledged in the Latin world. During several weeks, the cardinals attended their new master with the fairest professions of attachment and loyalty; till the summer heats permitted a decent escape from the city. But as soon as they were united at Anagni and Fundi, in a place of security, they cast aside the mask, accused their own falsehood and hypocrisy, excommunicated the apostate and Antichrist of Rome, and proceeded to a new election of Robert of Geneva, Clement the Seventh, whom they announced to the nations as the true and rightful vicar of Christ [September 21, A.D. 1378]. Their first choice, an involuntary and illegal act, was annulled by fear of death and the menaces of the Romans; and their complaint is justified by the strong evidence of probability and fact. The twelve French cardinals, above two thirds of the votes, were masters of the election; and whatever might be their provincial jealousies, it cannot fairly be presumed that they would have sacrificed their right and interest to a foreign candidate, who would never restore them to their native country. In the various and often inconsistent narratives, the shades of popular violence are more darkly or faintly colored: but the licentiousness of the seditious Romans was inflamed by a sense of their privileges, and the danger of a second emigration. The conclave was intimidated by the shouts and encompassed by the arms of thirty thousand rebels; the bells of the Capitol and St. Peter's rang an alarm: "Death, or an Italian pope!" was the universal cry; the same threat was repeated by the twelve bannerets or chiefs of the quarters, in the form of charitable advice; some preparations were made for burning the obstinate cardinals; and had they chosen a Transalpine subject, it is probable that they would never have departed alive from the Vatican. The same constraint imposed the necessity of dissembling in the eyes of Rome and of the world; the pride and cruelty of Urban presented a more inevitable danger; and they soon discovered the features of the tyrant, who could walk in his garden and recite his breviary while he heard from an adjacent chamber six cardinals groaning on the rack. His inflexible zeal, which loudly censured their luxury and vice, would have attached them to the stations and duties of their parishes at Rome; and had he not fatally delayed a new promotion, the French cardinals would have been reduced to a helpless minority in the sacred college. For these reasons, and the hope of repassing the Alps, they rashly violated the peace and unity of the church; and the merits of their double choice are yet agitated in the Catholic schools. The vanity, rather than the interest, of the nation determined the court and clergy of France. The states of Savoy, Sicily, Cyprus, Arragon, Castille, Navarre, and Scotland were inclined by their example and authority to the obedience of Clement the Seventh, and after his decease of Benedict the Thirteenth. Rome and the principal states of Italy, Germany, Portugal, England, the Low Countries, and the kingdoms of the North adhered to the prior election of Urban the Sixth, who was succeeded by Boniface the Ninth, Innocent the Seventh, and Gregory the Twelfth.

From the banks of the Tiber and the Rhone, the hostile pontiffs encountered each other with the pen and the sword: the civil and ecclesiastical order of society was disturbed; and the Romans had their full share of the mischiefs of which they may be arraigned as the primary authors [A.D. 1378–1418].†

The Christian world was at length provoked by their obstinacy and fraud: [the rival popes] were deserted by their cardinals, who embraced each other as friends and colleagues; and their revolt was supported by a numerous assembly of prelates and ambassadors. With equal justice, the council of Pisa deposed the popes of Rome and Avignon [A.D. 1409]; the conclave was unanimous in the choice of Alexander the Fifth, and his vacant seat was soon filled by a similar election of John the Twenty-third, the most profligate of mankind. But instead of extinguishing the schism, the rashness of the French and Italians had given a third pretender to the chair of St. Peter. Such new claims of the synod and conclave were disputed; three kings, of Germany, Hungary, and Naples, adhered to the cause of Gregory the Twelfth; and Benedict the Thirteenth, himself a Spaniard, was acknowledged by the devotion and patriotism of that powerful nation. The rash proceedings of Pisa were corrected by the council of Constance [A.D. 1414–1418]; the emperor Sigismond acted a conspicuous part as the advocate or protector of the Catholic church; and the number and weight of civil and ecclesiastical members might seem to constitute the states-general of Europe. Of the three popes, John the Twenty-third was the first victim: he fled and was brought back a prisoner: the most scandalous charges were suppressed; the vicar of Christ was only accused of piracy, murder, rape, sodomy, and incest; and after subscribing his own condemnation, he expiated in prison the imprudence of trusting his person to a free city beyond the Alps. Gregory the Twelfth, whose obedience was reduced to the narrow precincts of Rimini, descended with more honor from the throne; and his ambassador convened the session in which he renounced the title and authority of lawful pope [A.D. 1415]. To vanquish the obstinacy of Benedict the Thirteenth or his adherents, the emperor in person undertook a journey from Constance to Perpignan. The kings of Castile, Arragon, Navarre, and Scotland obtained an equal and honorable treaty; with the concurrence of the Spaniards, Benedict was deposed by the council; but the harmless old man was left in a solitary castle to excommunicate twice each day the rebel kingdoms which had deserted his cause. After thus eradicating the remains of the schism, the synod of Constance proceeded with slow and cautious steps to elect the sovereign of Rome and the head of the church. On this momentous occasion, the college of twenty-three cardinals was fortified with thirty deputies; six of whom were chosen in each of the five great nations of Christendom—the Italian, the German, the French, the Spanish, and the English: the interference of strangers was softened by their generous preference of an Italian and a Roman; and the hereditary as well as personal merit of Otho Colonna recommended him to the conclave. Rome accepted with joy and obedience the noblest of her sons; the ecclesiastical state was defended by his powerful family; and the elevation of Martin the Fifth is the era of the restoration and establishment of the popes in the Vatican [A.D. 1417].[†]

The spiritual thunders of the Vatican depend on the force of opinion; and if that opinion be supplanted by reason or passion, the sound may idly waste itself in the air; and the helpless priest is exposed to the brutal violence of a noble or a plebeian adversary. But after their return from Avignon, the keys of St. Peter were guarded by the sword of St. Paul. Rome was commanded by an impregnable citadel: the use of cannon is a powerful engine against popular seditions: a regular force of cavalry and infantry was enlisted under the banners of the pope: his ample revenues supplied the resources of war: and, from the extent of his domain, he could bring down on a rebellious city an army of hostile neighbors and loyal subjects. Since the union of the duchies of Ferrara and Urbino, the ecclesiastical state extends from the Mediterranean to the Adriatic, and from the confines of Naples to the banks of the Po; and as early as the sixteenth century, the greater part of that spacious and fruitful country acknowledged the lawful claims and temporal sovereignty of the Roman pontiffs. Their claims were readily deduced from the genuine or fabulous donations of the darker ages: the successive steps of their final settlement would engage us too far in the transactions of Italy.... The French and Germans at length withdrew from the field of battle: Milan, Naples, Sicily, Sardinia, and the sea-coast of Tuscany were firmly possessed by the Spaniards; and it became their interest to maintain the peace and dependence of Italy, which continued almost without disturbance from the middle of the sixteenth to the opening of the eighteenth century. The Vatican was swayed and protected by the religious policy of the Catholic king [of Spain]: his prejudice and interest disposed him in every dispute to support the prince against the people; and instead of the encouragement, the aid, and the asylum which they obtained from the adjacent states, the friends of liberty or the enemies of law were enclosed on all sides within the iron circle of despotism. The long habits of obedience and education subdued the turbulent spirit of the nobles and commons of Rome. The barons forgot the arms and factions of their ancestors, and insensibly became the servants of luxury and government. Instead of maintaining a crowd of tenants and followers, the produce of their estates was consumed in the private expenses which multiply the pleasures and diminish the power of the lord. . . . In Rome the voice of freedom and discord is no longer heard; and instead of the foaming torrent, a smooth and stagnant lake reflects the image of idleness and servitude.

A Christian, a philosopher, and a patriot will be equally scandalized by the temporal kingdom of the clergy; and the local majesty of Rome, the remembrance of her consuls and triumphs, may seem to embitter the sense and aggravate the shame of her slavery. If we calmly weigh the merits and defects of the ecclesiastical government, it may be praised in its present state [i.e., A.D. 1787] as a mild, decent, and tranquil system, exempt from the dangers of a minority, the sallies of youth, the expenses of luxury, and the calamities of war. But these advantages are overbalanced by a frequent, perhaps a septennial, election of a sovereign who is seldom a native of the country; the reign of a *young* statesman of threescore, in the decline of his life and abilities, without hope to accomplish, and without children to inherit, the labors of his transitory reign. The successful candidate is drawn from the church, and even the convent; from the mode of education and life the most adverse to reason, humanity, and freedom. In the trammels of servile faith, he has learned to believe because it is absurd, to revere all that is contemptible, and to despise whatever might deserve the esteem of a rational being; to punish error as a crime, to reward mortification and celibacy as the first of virtues; to place the saints of the calendar above the heroes of Rome and the sages of Athens; and to consider the missal or the crucifix as more useful instruments than the plough or the loom. In the office of nuncio or the rank of cardinal, he may acquire some knowledge of the world, but the primitive stain will adhere to his mind and manners: from study and experience he may suspect the mystery of his profession; but the sacerdotal artist will imbibe some portion of the bigotry which he inculcates. The genius of Sixtus the Fifth burst from the gloom of a Franciscan cloister. In a reign of five years [A.D. 1585–1590], he exterminated the outlaws and banditti, abolished the *profane* sanctuaries of Rome, formed a naval and military force, restored and emulated the monuments of antiquity, and after a liberal use and large increase of the revenue, left five millions of crowns in the castle of St. Angelo. But his justice was sullied with cruelty, his activity was prompted by the ambition of conquest: after his decease the abuses revived; the treasure was dissipated; he entailed on posterity thirty-five new taxes and the venality of offices; and after his death, his statue was demolished by an ungrateful or an injured people. The wild and original character of Sixtus the Fifth stands alone in the series of the pontiffs; the maxims and effects of their temporal government may be collected from the positive and comparative view of the arts and philosophy, the agriculture and trade, the wealth and population, of the ecclesiastical state. For myself, it is my wish to depart in charity with all mankind, nor am I willing, in these last moments, to offend even the pope and clergy of Rome.

CHAPTER LXXI

PROSPECT OF THE RUINS OF ROME IN THE FIFTEENTH CENTURY

Prospect of the ruins of Rome in the fifteenth century. •
Four causes of decay and destruction. • Renovation of the city. •
Conclusion of the whole work.

In the last days of Pope Eugenius the Fourth [A.D. 1430], two of his servants, the learned Poggius and a friend, ascended the Capitoline hill; reposed themselves among the ruins of columns and temples; and viewed from that commanding spot the wide and various prospect of desolation. The place and the object gave ample scope for moralizing on the vicissitudes of fortune, which spares neither man nor the proudest of his works, which buries empires and cities in a common grave; and it was agreed that in proportion to her former greatness, the fall of Rome was the more awful and deplorable. "Her primeval state, such as she might appear in a remote age, when Evander entertained the stranger of Troy, has been delineated by the fancy of Virgil. This Tarpeian rock was then a savage and solitary thicket: in the time of the poet, it was crowned with the golden roofs of a temple; the temple is overthrown, the gold has been pillaged, the wheel of fortune has accomplished her revolution, and the sacred ground is again disfigured with thorns and brambles. The hill of the Capitol, on which we sit, was formerly the head of the Roman empire, the citadel of the earth, the terror of kings; illustrated by the footsteps of so many triumphs, enriched with the spoils and tributes of so many nations. This spectacle of the world, how is it fallen! how changed! how defaced! The path of victory is obliterated by vines, and the benches of the senators are concealed by a dunghill. Cast your eyes on the Palatine hill, and seek among the shapeless and enormous fragments the marble theater, the obelisks, the colossal statues, the porticos of Nero's palace: survey the other hills of the city, the vacant space is interrupted only by ruins and gardens. The forum of the Roman people, where they assembled to enact their laws and elect their magistrates, is now enclosed for the cultivation of pot-herbs, or thrown open for the reception of swine and buffaloes. The public and private edifices that were founded for eternity lie prostrate, naked, and broken, like the limbs of a mighty giant; and the ruin is the more visible from the stupendous relics that have survived the injuries of time and fortune."†

This melancholy picture was drawn above nine hundred years after the fall of the Western empire, and even of the Gothic kingdom of Italy. A long period of distress and anarchy, in which empire and arts and riches had migrated from the banks of the Tiber, was incapable of restoring or adorning the city; and as all that is human must retrograde if it does not advance, every successive age must have hastened the ruin of the works of antiquity. To measure the progress of decay, and to ascertain at each era the state of each edifice, would be an endless and a useless labor; and I shall content myself with two observations, which will introduce a short inquiry into the general causes and effects. 1. Two hundred years before the eloquent complaint of Poggius, an anonymous writer composed a description of Rome. His ignorance may repeat the same objects under strange and fabulous names. Yet this barbarous topographer had eyes and ears; he could observe the visible remains; he could listen to the tradition of the people; and he distinctly enumerates seven theaters, eleven baths, twelve arches, and eighteen palaces, of which many had disappeared before the time of Poggius. It is apparent that many stately monuments of antiquity survived till a late period, and that the principles of destruction acted with vigorous and increasing energy in the thirteenth and fourteenth centuries. 2. The same reflection must be applied to the three last ages; and we should vainly seek the Septizonium of Severus, which is celebrated by Petrarch and the antiquarians of the sixteenth century. While the Roman edifices were still entire, the first blows, however weighty and impetuous, were resisted by the solidity of the mass and the harmony of the parts; but the slightest touch would precipitate the fragments of arches and columns that already nodded to their fall.

After a diligent inquiry, I can discern four principal causes of the ruin of Rome, which continued to operate in a period of more than a thousand years. I. The injuries of time and nature. II. The hostile attacks of the Barbarians and Christians. III. The use and abuse of the materials. And IV. The domestic quarrels of the Romans.

I. The art of man is able to construct monuments far more permanent than the narrow span of his own existence; yet these monuments, like himself, are perishable and frail; and in the boundless annals of time, his life and his labors must equally be measured as a fleeting moment. Of a simple and solid edifice, it is not easy, however, to circumscribe the duration. As the wonders of ancient days, the pyramids attracted the curiosity of the ancients: a hundred generations, the leaves of autumn, have dropped into the grave; and after the fall of the Pharaohs and Ptolemies, the Caesars and caliphs, the same pyramids stand erect and unshaken above the floods of the Nile. A complex figure of various and minute parts is more accessible to injury and decay; and the silent lapse of time is often accelerated by hurricanes and earthquakes, by fires and inundations. The air and earth have doubtless been shaken, and the lofty turrets of Rome have tottered from their foundations; but the seven hills do not appear to be placed on the great cavities of the globe; nor has the city, in any age, been exposed to the convulsions of nature which, in the climate of Antioch, Lisbon, or Lima, have crumbled in a few moments the works of ages into dust.[†]

II. The crowd of writers of every nation who impute the destruction of the Roman monuments to the Goths and the Christians have neglected to inquire how far they were animated by a hostile principle, and how far they possessed the means and the leisure to satiate their enmity. In the preceding volumes of this History, I have described the triumph of barbarism and religion; and I can only resume, in a few words, their real or imaginary connection with the ruin of ancient Rome. Our fancy may create or adopt a pleasing romance that the Goths and Vandals sallied from Scandinavia, ardent to avenge the flight of Odin; to break the chains and to chastise the oppressors of mankind; that they wished to burn the records of classic literature, and to found their national architecture on the broken members of the Tuscan and Corinthian orders. But in simple truth, the Northern conquerors were neither sufficiently savage nor sufficiently refined to entertain such aspiring ideas of destruction and revenge. The shepherds of Scythia and Germany had been educated in the armies of the empire, whose discipline they acquired and whose weakness they invaded: with the familiar use of the Latin tongue, they had learned to reverence the name and titles of Rome; and though incapable of emulating, they were more inclined to admire than to abolish the arts and studies of a brighter period. In the transient possession of a rich and unresisting capital, the soldiers of Alaric and Genseric were stimulated by the passions of a victorious army; amidst the wanton indulgence of lust or cruelty, portable wealth was the object of their search; nor could they derive either pride or pleasure from the unprofitable reflection that they had battered to the ground the works of the consuls and Caesars. Their moments were indeed precious; the Goths evacuated Rome on the sixth, the Vandals on the fifteenth day: and, though it be far more difficult to build than to destroy, their hasty assault would have made a slight impression on the solid piles of antiquity. We may remember that both Alaric and Genseric affected to spare the buildings of the city; that they subsisted in strength and beauty under the auspicious government of Theodoric; and that the momentary resentment of Totila was disarmed by his own temper and the advice of his friends and enemies. From these innocent Barbarians, the reproach may be transferred to the Catholics of Rome. The statues, altars, and houses of the demons were an abomination in their eyes; and in the absolute command of the city, they might labor with zeal and perseverance to erase the idolatry of their ancestors. The demolition of the temples in the East affords to *them* an example of conduct, and to *us* an argument of belief; and it is probable that a portion of guilt or merit may be imputed with justice to the Roman proselytes. Yet their abhorrence was confined to the monuments of heathen superstition; and the civil structures that were dedicated to the business or pleasure of society might be preserved without injury or scandal. The change of religion was accomplished not by a popular tumult but by the decrees of the emperors, of the senate, and of time. Of the Christian hierarchy, the bishops of Rome were commonly the most prudent and least fanatic; nor can any positive charge be opposed to the meritorious act of saving or converting the majestic structure of the Pantheon.

III. The value of any object that supplies the wants or pleasures of mankind is compounded of its substance and its form, of the materials and the manufacture. Its price must depend on the number of persons by whom it may be acquired and used; on the extent of the market; and consequently on the ease or difficulty of remote exportation, according to the nature of the commodity, its local situation, and the temporary circumstances of the world. The Barbarian conquerors of Rome usurped in a moment the toil and treasure of successive ages; but except the luxuries of immediate consumption, they must view without desire all that could not be removed from the city in the Gothic wagons or the fleet of the Vandals. Gold and silver were the first objects of their avarice; as in every country, and in the smallest compass, they represent the most ample command of the industry and possessions of mankind. A vase or a statue of those precious metals might tempt the vanity of some Barbarian chief; but the grosser multitude, regardless of the form, was tenacious only of the substance; and the melted ingots might be readily divided and stamped into the current coin of the empire. The less active or less fortunate robbers were reduced to the baser plunder of brass, lead, iron, and copper: whatever had escaped the Goths and Vandals was pillaged by the Greek tyrants; and the emperor Constans, in his rapacious visit, stripped the bronze tiles from the roof of the Pantheon. The edifices of Rome might be considered as a vast and various mine; the first labor of extracting the materials was already performed; the metals were purified and cast; the marbles were hewn and polished; and after foreign and domestic rapine had been satiated, the remains of the city, could a purchaser have been found, were still venal. The monuments of antiquity had been left naked of their precious ornaments; but the Romans would demolish with their own hands the arches and walls if the hope of profit could surpass the cost of the labor and exportation. If Charlemagne had fixed in Italy the seat of the Western empire, his genius would have aspired to restore rather than to violate the works of the Caesars; but policy confined the French monarch to the forests of Germany; his taste could be gratified only by destruction; and the new palace of Aix la Chapelle was decorated with the marbles of Ravenna and Rome. Five hundred years after Charlemagne, a king of Sicily, Robert, the wisest and most liberal sovereign of the age, was supplied with the same materials by the easy navigation of the Tiber and the sea; and Petrarch sighs an indignant complaint that the ancient capital of the world should adorn from her own bowels the slothful luxury of Naples. But these examples of plunder or purchase were rare in the darker ages; and the Romans, alone and unenvied, might have applied to their private or public use the remaining structures of antiquity, if in their present form and situation they had not been useless in a great measure to the city and its inhabitants. The walls still described the old circumference, but the city had descended from the seven hills into the Campus Martius; and some of the noblest monuments which had braved the injuries of time were left in a desert, far remote from the habitations of mankind. The palaces of the senators were no longer adapted to the manners or fortunes of their indigent successors: the use of baths and porticos was forgotten: in the sixth century, the games of the theater, amphitheater, and circus had been interrupted: some temples were devoted to the prevailing worship; but the Christian churches preferred the holy figure of the cross; and fashion or reason had distributed after a peculiar model the cells and offices of the cloister. Under the ecclesiastical reign, the number of these pious foundations was enormously multiplied; and the city was crowded with forty monasteries of men, twenty of women, and sixty chapters and colleges of canons and priests, who aggravated instead of relieving the depopulation of the tenth century. But if the forms of ancient architecture were disregarded by a people insensible of their use and beauty, the plentiful materials were applied to every call of necessity or superstition; till the fairest columns of the Ionic and Corinthian orders, the richest marbles of Paros and Numidia, were degraded, perhaps, to the support of a convent or a stable. The daily havoc which is perpetrated by the Turks in the cities of Greece and Asia may afford a melancholy example; and in the gradual destruction of the monuments of Rome, Sixtus the Fifth may alone be excused for employing the stones of the Septizonium in the glorious edifice of St. Peter's. A fragment, a ruin, howsoever mangled or profaned, may be viewed with pleasure and regret; but the greater part of the marble was deprived of substance, as well as of place and proportion; it was burnt to lime for the purpose of cement. Since the arrival of Poggius, the temple of Concord and many capital structures had vanished from his eyes; and an epigram of the same age expresses a just and pious fear that the continuance of this practice would finally annihilate all the monuments of antiquity. The smallness of their numbers was the sole check on the demands and depredations of the Romans. The imagination of Petrarch might create the presence of a mighty people; and I hesitate to believe that even in the fourteenth century they could be reduced to a contemptible list of thirty-three thousand inhabitants. From that period to the reign of Leo the Tenth, if they multiplied to the amount of eighty-five thousand, the increase of citizens was in some degree pernicious to the ancient city.

IV. I have reserved for the last the most potent and forcible cause of destruction, the domestic hostilities of the Romans themselves. Under the dominion of the Greek and French emperors, the peace of the city was disturbed by accidental, though frequent, seditions: it is from the decline of the latter, from the beginning of the tenth century, that we may date the licentiousness of private war, which violated with impunity the laws of the Code and the gospel, without respecting the majesty of the absent sovereign, or the presence and person of the vicar of Christ. In a dark period of five hundred years, Rome was perpetually afflicted by . . . sanguinary quarrels . . . ; and if much has escaped the knowledge, and much is unworthy of the notice, of history, I have exposed in the two preceding chapters the causes and effects of the public disorders. At such a time, when every quarrel was decided by the sword, and none could trust their lives or properties to the impotence of law, the powerful citizens were armed for safety, or offense, against the domestic enemies whom they feared or hated. Except Venice alone, the same dangers and designs were common to all the free republics of Italy; and the nobles usurped the prerogative of fortifying their houses and erecting strong towers that were capable of resisting a sudden attack. The cities were filled with these hostile edifices; and the example of Lucca, which contained three hundred towers; her law, which confined their height to the measure of fourscore feet, may be extended with suitable latitude to the more opulent and populous states. The first step of the senator Brancaleone in the establishment of peace and justice was to demolish (as we have already seen) one hundred and forty of the towers of Rome; and in the last days of anarchy and discord, as late as the reign of Martin the Fifth, forty-four still stood in one of the thirteen or fourteen regions of the city. To this mischievous purpose the remains of antiquity were most readily adapted: the temples and arches afforded a broad and solid basis for the new structures of brick and stone; and we can name the modern turrets that were raised on the triumphal monuments of Julius Caesar, Titus, and the Antonines. With some slight alterations, a theater, an amphitheater, a mausoleum was transformed into a strong and spacious citadel. I need not repeat that the mole of Hadrian has assumed the title and form of the castle of St. Angelo; the Septizonium of Severus was capable of standing against a royal army; the sepulchre of Metella has sunk under its outworks; the theaters of Pompey and Marcellus were occupied by the Savelli and Ursini families; and the rough fortress has been gradually softened to the splendor and elegance of an Italian palace. Even the churches were encompassed with arms and bulwarks, and the military engines on the roof of St. Peter's were the terror of the Vatican and the scandal of the Christian world. Whatever is fortified will be attacked; and whatever is attacked may be destroyed. Could the Romans have wrested from the popes the castle of St. Angelo, they had resolved by a public decree to annihilate that monument of servitude. Every building of defense was exposed to a siege; and in every siege the arts and engines of destruction were laboriously employed. After the death of Nicholas the Fourth, Rome, without a sovereign or a senate, was abandoned six months to the fury of civil war. "The houses," says a cardinal and poet of the times, "were crushed by the weight and velocity of enormous stones; the walls were perforated by the strokes of the battering-ram; the towers were involved in fire and smoke; and the assailants were stimulated by rapine and revenge." The work was consummated by the tyranny of the laws; and the factions of Italy alternately exercised a blind and thoughtless vengeance on their adversaries, whose houses and castles they razed to the ground. In comparing the *days* of foreign with the *ages* of domestic hostility, we must pronounce that the latter have been far more ruinous to the city; and our opinion is confirmed by the evidence of Petrarch. "Behold," says the laureate, "the relics of Rome, the image of her pristine greatness! neither time nor the Barbarian can boast the merit of this stupendous destruction: it was perpetrated by her own citizens, by the most illustrious of her sons; and your ancestors (he writes to a noble Annabaldi) have done with the battering-ram what the Punic hero could not accomplish with the sword." The influence of the two last principles of decay must in some degree be multiplied by each other; since the houses and towers which were subverted by civil war required by a new and perpetual supply from the monuments of antiquity.[†]

But the clouds of barbarism were gradually dispelled; and the peaceful authority of Martin the Fifth and his successors restored the ornaments of the city as well as the order of the ecclesiastical state. The improvements of Rome since the fifteenth century have not been the spontaneous produce of freedom and industry.... The beauty and splendor of the modern city may be ascribed to the abuses of the government, to the influence of superstition. Each reign (the exceptions are rare) has been marked by the rapid elevation of a new family, en-riched by the childish pontiff at the expense of the church and country. The palaces of these fortunate nephews are the most costly monuments of elegance and servitude: the perfect arts of architecture, sculpture, and painting have been prostituted in their service; and their galleries and gardens are decorated with the most precious works of antiquity, which taste or vanity has prompted them to collect. The ecclesiastical revenues were more decently employed by the popes themselves in the pomp of the Catholic worship; but it is superfluous to enumerate their pious foundations of altars, chapels, and churches, since these lesser stars are eclipsed by the sun of the Vatican, by the dome of St. Peter, the most glorious structure that ever has been applied to the use of religion. The fame of Julius the Second, Leo the Tenth, and Sixtus the Fifth is accompanied by the superior merit of Bramante and Fontana, of Raphael and Michael-Angelo; and the same munificence which had been displayed in palaces and temples was directed with equal zeal to revive and emulate the labors of antiquity. Prostrate obelisks were raised from the ground and erected in the most con-spicuous places; of the eleven aqueducts of the Caesars and consuls, three were restored; the artificial rivers were conducted over a long se-ries of old or of new arches, to discharge into marble basins a flood of salubrious and refreshing waters: and the spectator, impatient to as-cend the steps of St. Peter's, is detained by a column of Egyptian gran-ite, which rises between two lofty and perpetual fountains to the height of one hundred and twenty feet. The map, the description, the monuments of ancient Rome have been elucidated by the diligence of the antiquarian and the student: and the footsteps of heroes, the relics not of superstition but of empire, are devoutly visited by a new race of pilgrims from the remote and once savage countries of the North.

FINAL CONCLUSION.

Of these pilgrims, and of every reader, the attention will be excited by an history of the decline and fall of the Roman empire; the greatest, perhaps, and most awful scene in the history of mankind. The various causes and progressive effects are connected with many of the events most interesting in human annals: the artful policy of the Caesars, who long maintained the name and image of a free republic; the disorders of military despotism; the rise, establishment, and sects of Christianity; the foundation of Constantinople; the division of the monarchy; the invasion and settlements of the Barbarians of Germany and Scythia; the institutions of the civil law; the character and religion of Mohammed; the temporal sovereignty of the popes; the restoration and decay of the Western empire of Charlemagne; the crusades of the Latins in the East; the conquests of the Saracens and Turks; the ruin of the Greek empire; the state and revolutions of Rome in the middle age. The historian may applaud the importance and variety of his subject; but while he is conscious of his own imperfections, he must often accuse the deficiency of his materials. It was among the ruins of the Capitol that I first conceived the idea of a work which has amused and exercised near twenty years of my life, and which, however inadequate to my own wishes, I finally delivered to the curiosity and candor of the public.

LAUSANNE, JUNE 27, 1787

TABLE OF ROMAN EMPERORS

JULIO-CLAUDIANS (31 B.C.–A.D. 68)

31 B.C.–A.D. 14	Augustus
14–37	Tiberius
37–41	Gaius (Caligula)
41–54	Claudius
54–68	Nero
68–69	Galba
69	Otho
69	Vitellius

FLAVIANS AND ANTONINES (69–192)

69–79	Vespasian
79–81	Titus
81–96	Domitian
96–98	Nerva
98–117	Trajan (97–98 with Nerva)
117–138	Hadrian
138–161	Antoninus Pius
161–180	Marcus Aurelius (161–169 with Lucius Verus)
180–192	Commodus

193	Pertinax
193	Didius Julianus

SEVERANS (193–235)

193–211	Septimius Severus
211–217	Aurelius Antoninus (Caracalla) (211–212 with Geta)
217–218	Macrinus
218–222	Elagabalus
222–235	Severus Alexander

235–238	Maximinus
238	Gordian I and Gordian II (in Africa)
238	Balbinus and Pupienus (in Italy)
238–244	Gordian III
244–249	Philip
249–251	Decius
251–253	Trebonianus Gallus
253	Aemilianus
253–260	Valerian
253–268	Gallienus (253–260 with Valerian)
268–270	Claudius II (Gothicus)
270	Quintillus
270–275	Aurelian

INDEPENDENT KINGDOMS WITHIN THE ROMAN EMPIRE (260–274)

	WEST		EAST
260–274	Empire in Gaul of Postumus, Victorinus, Tetricus	260–272	Palmyrene Empire of Odaenathus, Zenobia, Vaballathus

275–276	Tacitus
276	Florianus
276–282	Probus
282–283	Carus
283–284	Carinus and Numerian

TETRARCHY OF DIOCLETIAN (284–305) AND ITS AFTERMATH (305–324)

	WEST		EAST
286–305	Maximian as an *Augustus*	284–305	Diocletian as an *Augustus*
293–305	Constantius as a *Caesar*	293–305	Galerius as a *Caesar*
305–306	Constantius as an *Augustus*	305–311	Galerius as an *Augustus*
305–306	Severus as a *Caesar*	305–309	Maximinus as a *Caesar*
306–307	Severus as an *Augustus*	310–313	Maximinus as an *Augustus*
306–312	Maxentius (in Italy)	308–324	Licinius as an *Augustus*
306–307	Constantine as a *Caesar*		
307–324	Constantine as an *Augustus*		

REUNION OF THE ROMAN EMPIRE (324–337)

324–337   Constantine as sole emperor

THE SONS OF CONSTANTINE (337–361)

337–340   Constantine II
337–350   Constans
337–361   Constantius II

CO-REGENTS AND A USURPER (350–361)

350–353   Magnentius (usurper of Constans)
351–354   Gallus (colleague of Constantius II)
355–361   Julian (as colleague of Constantius II)

REUNION OF THE ROMAN EMPIRE (361–364)

361–363   Julian (as sole emperor)
363–364   Jovian

FINAL DIVISION OF THE ROMAN EMPIRE (364)

WEST		EAST	
	WEST		EAST
364–375	Valentinian	364–378	Valens
375–383	Gratian	378–395	Theodosius I
375–392	Valentinian II (Italy, Illyricum)		
383–388	Maximus (usurper)		
392–394	Eugenius (usurper)		
395–423	Honorius (395–408, Stilicho as regent)	395–408	Arcadius
421	Constantius III	408–450	Theodosius II
423–425	John (usurper)		
425–455	Valentinian III	450–457	Marcian
455	Petronius Maximus		
455–456	Avitus		
457–461	Majorian	457–474	Leo
461–465	Libius Severus		
467–472	Anthemius		
472	Olybrius		
473–474	Glycerius	474	Leo II
474–475	Nepos	474–475	Zeno
475–476	Romulus Augustulus	475–476	Basiliscus

EXTINCTION OF THE ROMAN EMPIRE IN THE WEST (476)

EASTERN EMPERORS (474–1453)

474–475	Zeno
475–476	Basiliscus
476–491	Zeno (again)
491–518	Anastasius I
518–527	Justin I
527–565	Justinian I the Great
565–578	Justin II
578–582	Tiberius II Constantinus
582–602	Maurice
602–610	Phocas
610–641	Heraclius

641	Constantine III and Heracleonas
641	Heracleonas
641–668	Constans II Pogonatus
668–685	Constantine IV
685–695	Justinian II Rhinotmetus
695–698	Leontius
698–705	Tiberius III
705–711	Justinian II (again)
711–713	Philippicus Bardanes
713–715	Anastasius II
716–717	Theodosius III
717–740	Leo III the Isaurian
741–775	Constantine V Copronymus
775–780	Leo IV the Khazar
780–797	Constantine VI
797–802	Irene
802–811	Nicephorus I
811	Stauracius
811–813	Michael I Rangabe
813–820	Leo V the Armenian
820–829	Michael II the Amorian
829–842	Theophilus
842–867	Michael III the Amorian
867–886	Basil I
886–912	Leo VI the Wise or the Philosopher
912–913	Alexander
913–959	Constantine VII Porphyrogenitus
920–944	Romanus I Lecapenus
959–963	Romanus II
963–969	Nicephorus II Phocas
969–976	John I Tzimisces
976–1025	Basil II Bulgaroctonus
1025–1028	Constantine VIII
1028–1034	Romanus III Argyrus
1034–1041	Michael IV the Paphlagonian
1041–1042	Michael V Calaphates
1042	Zoe and Theodora
1042–1055	Constantine IX Monomachus
1055–1056	Theodora (again)

1056–1057	Michael VI Stratioticus
1057–1059	Isaac I Comnenus
1059–1067	Constatine X Ducas
1068–1071	Romanus IV Diogenes
1071–1078	Michael VII Ducas (Parapinaces)
1078–1081	Nicephorus III Botaniates
1081–1118	Alexius I Comnenus
1118–1143	John II Comnenus
1143–1180	Manuel I Comnenus
1180–1183	Alexius II Comnenus
1183–1185	Andronicus I Comnenus
1185–1195	Isaac II Angelus
1195–1203	Alexius III Angelus
1203–1204	Isaac II (restored) with Alexius IV Angelus
1204	Alexius V Ducas Marzoufle

Loss of Constantinople (1204); Latin empire (1204–1261)

LASCARID DYNASTY IN NICEA (1204–1261)

1204–1222	Theodore I Lascaris
1222–1254	John III Ducas or Vatatzes
1254–1258	Theodore II Lascaris
1258–1261	John IV Lascaris

RECAPTURE OF CONSTANTINOPLE AND ESTABLISHMENT OF THE DYNASTY OF THE PALAEOLOGI (1259)

1259–1282	Michael VIII Palaeologus
1282–1328	Andronicus II Palaeologus
1328–1341	Andronicus III Palaeologus
1341–1391	John V Palaeologus
1347–1355	John VI Cantacuzenus
1376–1379	Andronicus IV Palaeologus
1390	John VII Palaeologus
1391–1425	Manuel II Palaeologus
1425–1448	John VIII Palaeologus
1449–1453	Constantine XI Palaeologus

A Note on the Illustrations

The artist GIOVANNI BATTISTA PIRANESI (1720–1778) was Gibbon's contemporary. His etchings of the ruins of ancient Rome as they stood in the eighteenth century, from which the illustrations in this volume are taken, were tremendously popular during his lifetime. While they are often embellished (Piranesi employed his artistic license freely), Piranesi's etchings provide a glimpse of the city as Gibbon himself must have encountered it.

A Note on the Type

The principal text of this Modern Library edition
was set in a digitized version of Janson, a typeface that
dates from about 1690 and was cut by Nicholas Kis,
a Hungarian working in Amsterdam. The original matrices have
survived and are held by the Stempel foundry in Germany.
Hermann Zapf redesigned some of the weights and sizes for
Stempel, basing his revisions on the original design.

MODERN LIBRARY IS ONLINE AT
WWW.MODERNLIBRARY.COM

MODERN LIBRARY ONLINE IS YOUR GUIDE TO CLASSIC LITERATURE ON THE WEB

THE MODERN LIBRARY E-NEWSLETTER

Our free e-mail newsletter is sent to subscribers, and features sample chapters, interviews with and essays by our authors, upcoming books, special promotions, announcements, and news.

To subscribe to the Modern Library e-newsletter, send a blank e-mail to: sub_modernlibrary@info.randomhouse.com or visit www.modernlibrary.com

THE MODERN LIBRARY WEBSITE

Check out the Modern Library website at
www.modernlibrary.com for:

- The Modern Library e-newsletter
- A list of our current and upcoming titles and series
- Reading Group Guides and exclusive author spotlights
- Special features with information on the classics and other paperback series
- Excerpts from new releases and other titles
- A list of our e-books and information on where to buy them
- The Modern Library Editorial Board's 100 Best Novels and 100 Best Nonfiction Books of the Twentieth Century written in the English language
- News and announcements

Questions? E-mail us at **modernlibrary@randomhouse.com**
For questions about examination or desk copies, please visit the Random House Academic Resources site at
www.randomhouse.com/academic